PRENTICE HALL
LITERATURE

WORLD MASTERPIECES

PEARSON

Prentice
Hall

Upper Saddle River, New Jersey
Needham, Massachusetts

ISBN 0-13-180235-6
2 3 4 5 6 7 8 9 10   08 07 06 05 04

Cover: *Charles Bridge and the Hradcany Castle in Prague,* 1935, Oskar Kokoschka, National Gallery, Prague, Czech Republic, ©2003 Artists Rights Society (ARS), New York / Pro Litteris, Zurich

ACKNOWLEDGMENTS

Grateful acknowledgment is made to the following for copyrighted material:

The American University in Cairo Press
"Half a Day," extract from "The Time and Place" by Naguib Mahfouz, first published in Arabic in 1962 as "Nisf Yawm, in al-fajn al Kadhib (The False Dawn)." Copyright © 1991 by The American University in Cairo Press. Reprinted by permission of The American University in Cairo Press.

The Asia Society and Dr. Nguyen Ngoc Bich
"Thoughts of Hanoi" by Nguyen Thi Vinh, from *A Thousand Years of Vietnamese Poetry,* edited by Nguyen Ngoc Bich. Copyright © 1962, 1967, 1968, 1969, 1970, 1971, 1974 by The Asia Society and Nguyen Ngoc Bich. Reprinted by permission.

Georges Borchardt, Inc.
"The Metamorphosis" by Franz Kafka, edited and translated by Stanley Corngold. Copyright © 1972 by Stanley Corngold. Reprinted by permission of Georges Borchardt, Inc.

The Citadel Press/Kensington Publishing Corp.
"The Lorelei" by Heinrich Heine, translated by Aaron Kramer, from *The Poetry of Heinrich Heine.* Copyright © 1969 by Citadel Press, Inc. All rights reserved. Reprinted by permission of Citadel Press/Kensington Publishing Corp. **www.kensingtonbooks.com**

(Continued on page R45, which is hereby considered an extension of this copyright page.)

PRENTICE HALL
LITERATURE

COPPER

BRONZE

SILVER

GOLD

PLATINUM

THE AMERICAN EXPERIENCE

THE BRITISH TRADITION

WORLD MASTERPIECES

Contributing Authors

The contributing authors guided the direction and philosophy of *Prentice Hall Literature: Timeless Voices, Timeless Themes.* Working with the development team, they helped to build the pedagogical integrity of the program and to ensure its relevance for today's teachers and students.

Kate Kinsella

Kate Kinsella, Ed.D., is a faculty member in the Department of Secondary Education at San Francisco State University. A specialist in second-language acquisition and adolescent reading and writing, she teaches coursework addressing language and literacy development across the secondary curricula. She has taught high-school ESL, and directed SFSU's *Intensive English Program* for first-generation bilingual college students. She maintains secondary classroom involvement by teaching an academic literacy class for second-language learners through the University's *Step to College* partnership program. A former Fulbright lecturer and perennial institute leader for TESOL, the California Reading Association, and the California League of Middle Schools, Dr. Kinsella provides professional development nationally, on topics ranging from learning-style enhancement to second-language reading. Her scholarship has been published in journals such as the *TESOL Journal,* the *CATESOL Journal,* and the *Social Studies Review.*

Kevin Feldman

Kevin Feldman, Ed.D., is the Director of Reading and Early Intervention with the Sonoma County Office of Education (SCOE). His career in education spans thirty-three years. As the Director of Reading and Early Intervention for SCOE, he develops, organizes, and monitors programs related to K–12 literacy and prevention of reading difficulties. He also serves as a Leadership Team Consultant to the California Reading and Literature Project and assists in the development and implementation of K–12 programs throughout California. Dr. Feldman earned his undergraduate degree in Psychology from Washington State University and has a Master's degree in Special Education, Learning Disabilities, and Instructional Design from U.C. Riverside. He earned his Ed.D. in Curriculum and Instruction from the University of San Francisco.

Colleen Shea Stump

Colleen Shea Stump, Ph.D., is a Special Education supervisor in the area of Resource and Inclusion for Seattle Public Schools. She served as a professor and chairperson for the Department of Special Education at San Francisco State University. She continues as a lead consultant in the area of collaboration for the California State Improvement Grant and travels the state of California providing professional development training in the areas of collaboration, content literacy instruction, and inclusive instruction. Dr. Stump earned her doctorate at the University of Washington, her M.A. in Special Education from the University of New Mexico, and her B.S. in Elementary Education from the University of Wisconsin–Eau Claire.

Joyce Armstrong Carroll

In her forty-two-year career, Joyce Armstrong Carroll, Ed.D., has taught on every grade level from primary to graduate school. In the past twenty years, she has trained teachers in the teaching of writing. A nationally known consultant, she has served as president of TCTE and on NCTE's Commission on Composition. More than fifty of her articles have appeared in journals such as *Curriculum Review, English Journal, Media & Methods, Southwest Philosophical Studies, English in Texas,* and the *Florida English Journal.* With Edward E. Wilson, Dr. Carroll co-authored *Acts of Teaching: How to Teach Writing* and co-edited *Poetry After Lunch: Poetry to Read Aloud.* She co-directs the New Jersey Writing Project in Texas.

Edward E. Wilson

A former editor of *English in Texas,* Edward E. Wilson has served as a high-school English teacher and a writing consultant in school districts nationwide. Wilson has served on both the Texas Teacher Professional Practices Commission and NCTE's Commission on Composition. Wilson's poetry appears in Paul Janeczko's anthology *The Music of What Happens.* With Dr. Carroll, he co-wrote *Acts of Teaching: How to Teach Writing* and co-edited *Poetry After Lunch: Poetry to Read Aloud.* Wilson co-directs the New Jersey Writing Project in Texas.

PROGRAM ADVISORS

The program advisors provided ongoing input throughout the development of *Prentice Hall Literature: Timeless Voices, Timeless Themes.* Their valuable insights ensure that the perspectives of teachers throughout the country are represented within this literature series.

Leslie Ballard
Teacher of English
South Vigo High School
Terre Haute, Indiana

Lee Bromberger
English Department Chairperson
Mukwonago High School
Mukwonago, Wisconsin

Denise Campbell
Student Achievement Resource
  Center
CCSD Literacy Content
  Coordinator
Centennial, Colorado

Holly Carr
Teacher of English
Central Crossing High School
Grove City, Ohio

Melody Chalmers
Teacher of English
E. E. Smith High School
Fayetteville, North Carolina

Karen Gibson, Ph.D.
Communication Arts Program
  Leader
Appleton Area School District
Appleton, Wisconsin

Gail Hacker
Teacher of English
North Charleston High School
North Charleston, South Carolina

Kim Hartman
English Department Chairperson
Franklin Heights High School
Columbus, Ohio

Helen Hudson, Ph.D.
Teacher of English
Crawfordsville High School
Crawfordsville, Indiana

Carrie Lichtenberg
Teacher of English
Highlands High School
Fort Thomas, Kentucky

Agathaniki Locklear
Teacher of English
Simon Kenton High School
Independence, Kentucky

John Ludy
Teacher of English
Fremont High School
Fremont, Indiana

Sherrie McDowell
English Department Chairperson
Central High School
Cheyenne, Wyoming

Nancy Monroe
Teacher of English
Bolton High School
Alexandria, Louisiana

Cathy Robbs
English Department Chairperson
Chattanooga Central High School
Harrison, Tennessee

Matthew Scanlon
Teacher of English
West Morris Central High School
Chester, New Jersey

John Scott
Teacher of English, Retired
Hampton High School
Hampton, Virginia

Helen Spaith
English Department Chair, Retired
Franklin Heights High School
Columbus, Ohio

Barbra Thompson
Teacher of English
Westover High School
Fayetteville, North Carolina

Sandra Van Belois
English Department Chairperson
Jack Britt High School
Fayetteville, North Carolina

Cheryl Wong-Lee
Teacher of English
Douglas Byrd High School
Fayetteville, North Carolina

Charles Youngs
Teacher of English
Bethel Park High School
Bethel Park, Pennsylvania

UNIT 1

Ancient Worlds (3000 B.C.–A.D. 1400)

SKILLS WORKSHOPS

SUGGESTIONS FOR SUSTAINED READING *from Penguin Group (USA)*

Related World Literature: Paul Roche, *The Bible's Greatest Stories*

Roger Lancelyn Green, *Tales of Ancient Egypt*

Related British Literature: Jeffrey Gantz, *Early Irish Myths and Sagas*

Related American Literature: Bernal Diaz del Castillo, *The Conquest of New Spain*

Other Suggestion: N. K. Sandars, *The Epic of Gilgamesh*

**For more information on these and other Penguin Group (USA) titles, see pages R1–R6.
You may want to consult your teacher before choosing one of these books.**

Indian Literature (c. 1400 B.C. – A.D. 500)

SUGGESTIONS FOR SUSTAINED READING *from Penguin Group (USA)*

Related World Literature:	R. K. Narayan, *A Tiger for Malgudi*
	Mohandas K. Gandhi, *The Penguin Gandhi Reader*
Related British Literature:	Rudyard Kipling, *Kim*
Related American Literature:	Martin Luther King, Jr., *Why We Can't Wait*
Other Suggestion:	R. K. Narayan, *The Ramayana*

For more information on these and other Penguin Group (USA) titles, see pages R1–R6.
You may want to consult your teacher before choosing one of these books.

UNIT 3

Chinese and Japanese Literature
(1000 B.C. – A.D. 1890)

Japanese Literature

SKILLS WORKSHOPS

SUGGESTIONS FOR SUSTAINED READING *from Penguin Group (USA)*

For more information on these and other Penguin Group (USA) titles, see pages R1–R6. You may want to consult your teacher before choosing one of these books.

UNIT
4

Ancient Greece and Rome
(c. 800 B.C. – A.D. 500)

Greek Literature

Introduction 312

Homer   from the **Iliad**

     from **Book 1: The Rage of Achilles** .... Epic Poem   326

     from **Book 6: Hector Returns to Troy** .... Epic Poem   336

     from **Book 22: The Death of Hector** .... Epic Poem   345

     from **Book 24: Achilles and Priam** .... Epic Poem   359

Comparing Literary Works

Sappho   **You Know the Place: Then** .... Poem   377

     He Is More Than a Hero .... Poem   378

Pindar   **Olympia 11** .... Poem   380

Thucydides   from **History of the Peloponnesian War:**
Pericles' Funeral Oration .... Nonfiction   386

Connections: *Literature Past and Present*

Abraham Lincoln   **The Gettysburg Address** .... United States .... Speech   398

Plato   from the **Apology** .... Philosophical Text   402

A Closer Look
Oedipus: The Myth 422

Sophocles   **Oedipus the King**

     Part I .... Drama   426

     Part II .... Drama   461

Reading Informational Materials: *Web Research Sources*
The Perseus Digital Library .... United States .... Web Site   486

Roman Literature

Virgil   from the **Aeneid**

     from **Book II: How They Took the City** .... Epic Poem   492

SKILLS WORKSHOPS

SUGGESTIONS FOR SUSTAINED READING *from Penguin Group (USA)*

For more information on these and other Penguin Group (USA) titles, see pages R1–R6.
You may want to consult your teacher before choosing one of these books.

UNIT 5 · The Middle Ages (A.D. 450–1300)

SUGGESTIONS FOR SUSTAINED READING *from Penguin Group (USA)*

**For more information on these and other Penguin Group (USA) titles, see pages R1–R6.
You may want to consult your teacher before choosing one of these books.**

UNIT 6

The Renaissance and Rationalism (1300–1800)

The Age of Rationalism

Romanticism and Realism (1800–1890)

A Closer Look

Reading Informational Materials: *Critical Reviews*

SKILLS WORKSHOPS

SUGGESTIONS FOR SUSTAINED READING *from Penguin Group (USA)*

Related World Literature:	Victor Hugo, *The Hunchback of Notre Dame*
	Nikolai Gogol, *Diary of a Madman and Other Stories*
Related British Literature:	Emily Brontë, *Wuthering Heights*
Related American Literature:	Edgar Allan Poe, *The Science Fiction of Edgar Allan Poe*
Other Suggestion:	Johann Wolfgang von Goethe, *Faust*

For more information on these and other Penguin Group (USA) titles, see pages R1–R6. You may want to consult your teacher before choosing one of these books.

The Modern World (1890–1945)

SKILLS WORKSHOPS

Writing About Literature: Compare and Contrast Literary Trends Across Cultures............ 1152
Writing Workshop: Exposition: Multimedia Report 1154
Listening and Speaking Workshop: Analyzing a Media Presentation 1158
Assessment Workshop: Writer's Point of View... 1159

SUGGESTIONS FOR SUSTAINED READING *from Penguin Group (USA)*

Related World Literature: Herman Hesse, *Siddhartha*
Edmond Rostand, *Cyrano de Bergerac*
Related British Literature: James Joyce, *A Portrait of the Artist as a Young Man*
Related American Literature: Willa Cather, *My Ántonia*
Other Suggestion: Franz Kafka, *The Transformation and Other Stories*

For more information on these and other Penguin Group (USA) titles, see pages R1–R6.
You may want to consult your teacher before choosing one of these books.

UNIT 9 — The Contemporary World (1946 – Present)

SUGGESTIONS FOR SUSTAINED READING *from Penguin Group (USA)*

Related World Literature:	Chinua Achebe, *Things Fall Apart*
	Alexander Solzhenitsyn, *One Day in the Life of Ivan Denisovich*
Related British Literature:	William Golding, *Lord of the Flies*
Related American Literature:	Julia Alvarez, *Something to Declare*
Other Suggestion:	Elie Wiesel, *Night*

For more information on these and other Penguin Group (USA) titles, see pages R1–R6. You may want to consult your teacher before choosing one of these books.

RESOURCES

COMPARING LITERARY WORKS

READING INFORMATIONAL MATERIALS

CONNECTIONS

A CLOSER LOOK

WRITING WORKSHOPS

LISTENING AND SPEAKING WORKSHOPS

ASSESSMENT WORKSHOPS

Walking Lion in Relief (detail), 605–562 B.C., Babylonian mosaic, Mesopotamia, The Metropolitan Museum of Art

> " *...then Anu and Bel called by name me, Hammurabi, the exalted prince, who feared God, to bring about the rule of righteousness in the land, to destroy the wicked and the evil-doers, so that the strong should not harm the weak...* "

— from The Code of Hammurabi

Timeline c. 3000 B.C.–A.D. 1400

3000 B.C.   2000 B.C.   1000 B.C.

Cultural and Historical Events

- **c. 3000 (Sumeria)** Sumerian civilization begins.
- **c. 2900 (Egypt)** The ruler Menes joins Upper Egypt and Lower Egypt.
  - **c. 2925–c. 2575 (Egypt)** This is the Early Dynastic Period.
  - **c. 2575–c. 2130 (Egypt)** This is the era called the Old Kingdom.
  - **c. 2500 (Egypt)** The pharaoh Khufu has the Great Pyramid built at Giza.
- **c. 2334–2279 (ancient Middle East)** King Sargon reigns in Mesopotamia. ▲

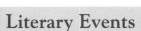

- **c. 2000 (Mesopotamia)** Amorites found the city of Babylon.
- **c. 2000 (Mesopotamia)** The Hebrew patriarch Abraham leaves the Sumerian city of Ur.
- **1938–c. 1600 (Egypt)** This is the era called the Middle Kingdom.
- **c. 1800 (Canaan)** Famine forces some Hebrews to migrate to Egypt, where they are enslaved.
- **c. 1792–1750 (Mesopotamia)** King Hammurabi reigns over Babylonian empire.
- **c. 1540–1075 (Egypt)** This is the era called the New Kingdom. ▶

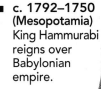

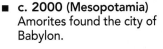

- **1000 (Mesopotamia)** A tribal group called the Parsa settles in what is now southern Iran; they become the Persians.
  - **c. 628–c. 551 (Persia)** Zoroaster, founder of Zoroastrianism, lives.
  - **500s (Persian Empire)** King Cyrus the Great of Persia establishes an empire.
  - **c. 330 (Persian Empire)** Alexander the Great conquers the Persian Empire. ▲

Literary Events

- **c. 2200–2100 (Mesopotamia)** Earliest written texts about King Gilgamesh appear. ▼

- **c. 1792–1750 (Mesopotamia)** The Code of Hammurabi, one of the world's first legal codes, is compiled.
- **c. 2000–1600 (Mesopotamia)** *The Epic of Gilgamesh* is written.
- **c. 1540–1075 (Egypt)** Love poetry of the New Kingdom is written.
- **c. 1200 (ancient Middle East)** This is the earliest date for the composition of biblical writings.

- **100 (ancient Middle East)** This is the latest date for the composition of biblical writings. ▼

Ancient Worlds

- **c. 570 (Arabia)** Muhammad, the founder of Islam, is born in Mecca.

- **c. 600s (West Africa)** Kingdom of Ghana begins to thrive.

- **c. 610 (Arabia)** Muhammad experiences his first revelation.

- **632 (Arabia)** Muhammad dies; Arabia is united as an Islamic nation.

- **636–637 (Iran)** Muslim Arabs begin to conquer Iran. ▶

- **1076 (West Africa)** Kingdom of Ghana ends.

- **1200s–1800s (West Africa)** Kingdom of Benin flourishes.

- **1300s (West Africa)** The Mali empire controls the gold trade.

- **1324 (West Africa)** The Muslim emperor of Mali, Mansa Musa, makes a religious pilgrimage to Mecca.

- **1400s (West Africa)** The Songhai kingdom emerges. ▲

- **c. 650 (Arabia)** A Muslim leader directs learned men to establish an official version of the Qur'an.

- **c. 850 (Persia)** A Persian storybook called *The Thousand Tales* is translated into Arabic and becomes known as *The Thousand and One Nights*.

- **c. 935–c. 1020 (Persia)** The Persian poet Firdawsi, author of the *Shah-nama* ("Epic of Kings"), lives.

- **c. 1207–1273 (Turkey)** Rumi, celebrated mystic and poet in the Persian language, lives.

- **1255 (West Africa)** This is the death date of Sundiata, founder of the Kingdom of Mali and protagonist of the epic that bears his name. ▼

Ancient Worlds

(c. 3000 B.C.–A.D. 1400)

Historical Background

Ancient Middle East: Origins About 5,000 years ago, several major civilizations developed in the fertile river valleys of southwest Asia. The region between the Tigris and Euphrates rivers, in modern Iraq, was one of these sites. Mesopotamia (mes′ ə pə tā′ mē ə), the Greek name for this region, means "the land between two rivers." (See the map on page 5.)

Even today, scholars disagree about the identity of the people or peoples who spoke and wrote Sumerian and who lived in ancient Sumer (sōō′ mər). In the succession of civilizations that arose in this region, however, theirs was the first, and it influenced the Babylonian and Assyrian civilizations that followed.

As the founders of Mesopotamian civilization, the Sumerians have many "firsts" to their credit: the region's earliest system of writing—cuneiform (kyōō nē′ ə fôrm′), or wedge-shaped, characters; a number system based on sixty that led to our 60-second minute, 60-minute hour, and 360-degree circle; the first wheeled vehicles; and the earliest city-states.

The Babylonians One of the greatest Mesopotamian kings was Sargon (reigned c. 2334–2279 B.C.). His new capital city of Agade, located near the site of Babylon, was north of Sumer—the northward shift of power in Mesopotamia became a trend. Agade contributed its name to the region where Sargon lived, Akkad (ak′ ad′), and to the language he spoke, Akkadian (ə kā′ dē ən). A Semitic language related to modern Hebrew and Arabic, Akkadian in its various forms became the tongue of the new northern centers of power, Babylon and Assur.

Those who spoke Semitic languages, the Semites, were nomadic peoples who had migrated to Mesopotamia from the Arabian peninsula. One such group, the Amorites, founded the village of Babylon on the Euphrates River (c. 2000 B.C.).

Not until the reign of Hammurabi (c. 1792–1750 B.C.), however, did Babylon come into its own as the capital of a great empire. (See the map on page 5.) Hammurabi's famous legal code was

▼ **Critical Viewing**
This clay tablet shows an ancient Babylonian map of the world. After comparing this map with the one on page 5, answer this question: What do you think some of the circles and lines on the ancient map represent? Explain. **[Speculate]**

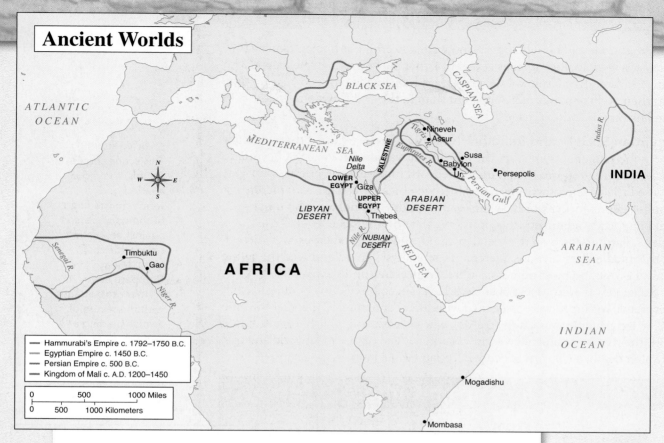

Ancient Worlds

ATLANTIC
OCEAN

BLACK SEA

CASPIAN SEA

MEDITERRANEAN SEA

Nineveh
Assur
Tigris R.
Susa
Euphrates R.
Babylon
Ur
Persian Gulf
Persepolis

Indus R.

INDIA

Nile
Delta

PALESTINE

LOWER
EGYPT
Giza

UPPER
EGYPT
Thebes

LIBYAN
DESERT

ARABIAN
DESERT

ARABIAN
SEA

Senegal R.

Timbuktu
Gao

Niger R.

AFRICA

Nile R.

NUBIAN
DESERT

RED SEA

INDIAN
OCEAN

— Hammurabi's Empire c. 1792–1750 B.C.
— Egyptian Empire c. 1450 B.C.
— Persian Empire c. 500 B.C.
— Kingdom of Mali c. A.D. 1200–1450

0   500   1000 Miles
0   500   1000 Kilometers

Mogadishu

Mombasa

an important step in the development of civilization. Engraved on a stone slab, this code contains 282 laws covering all aspects of daily life.

Ancient Egypt: "The gift of the Nile"   At the time that Sumerian civilization was developing along the Tigris and Euphrates rivers, Egyptian civilization arose along the banks of the Nile in northeastern Africa. The Greek historian Herodotus called Egypt "the gift of the Nile," and he was right. Every July the river would flood, replenishing farmland along its banks with moisture and rich silt. In addition to fertile land, the river provided a watery highway for travel and trade. It was also a source of fish. Without the river's life-giving bounty, Egypt would be as barren as the deserts that surround it.

At first, the villages along the Nile were divided into two countries: Upper Egypt in the south and Lower Egypt in the north. Around 2900 B.C., a ruler joined the two kingdoms to create a single realm. The history of the pharaohs (far′ ōz), or rulers, who then led Egypt for almost two thousand years can be divided into the following periods: Early Dynastic Period (c. 2925–c. 2575 B.C.), the Old Kingdom (c. 2575–c. 2130 B.C.), the Middle Kingdom (1938–c. 1600 B.C.), and the New Kingdom (c. 1540–1075 B.C.). In the periods between these eras, Egypt was prey to invasions and civil wars. By and large, however, the geographical barriers of desert and sea protected Egypt from its neighbors and made for a long-lived, stable, and conservative civilization.

▲ **Critical Viewing**
What does this map suggest about the relationship between rivers and civilizations? Explain.
[Read a Map]

Unlike the Mesopotamian kings, who were powerful but human figures, the pharaohs were looked upon as gods. (It is true, however, that the legendary King Gilgamesh of Uruk was viewed as part human and part god.) At no time was their godlike power more apparent than in the Old Kingdom. (See Art in the Historical Context, page 7.)

Egyptian Society and Religion Not only was the pyramid that housed a pharaoh's remains a symbol of the afterlife, it was also an image of Egyptian society. At the top was the pharaoh. Beneath him were the priests, who devised the system of writing called hieroglyphics (hī′ ər ō glif′ iks), pictures or symbols representing words, syllables, or sounds. The nobles, who usually held important administrative positions, were on the same level as the priests. Farther down on the social pyramid, and more numerous, were people of the middle class: artisans, merchants, and physicians who served the ruling class. Lowest and most numerous were the peasants and slaves.

Religion was a key aspect of ancient Egyptian culture. Many of the gods that Egyptians worshiped were associated with forces of nature. The god of the Nile River, for example, was Osiris (ō sī′ris), whose death and rebirth were linked with the river's rise and fall. Osiris was also the god of the underworld and of life after death, a concern of every Egyptian (see below).

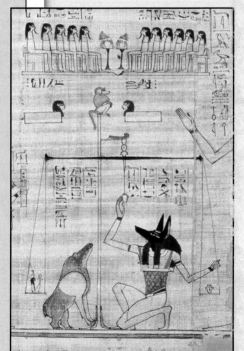

▼ **Critical Viewing**
This scene shows Anubis, the jackal-headed god, weighing the heart of the dead person against an image of the goddess of truth, Ma'at. Compare and contrast this image with the statue of Justice holding a scale that appears on many American courthouses. **[Compare and Contrast]**

Close-up on Culture

The Egyptian Book of the Dead

Ancient Egyptians believed that, after death, the soul journeyed in the underworld in search of eternal life. To prepare for the afterlife, they collected the numerous spells, confessions, and words of power known as the Egyptian Book of the Dead. This title refers not to a single volume but to many different texts. Written on long papyrus scrolls entombed with the deceased, these texts were like travel guides telling Egyptians what to do and say in the strange country of the hereafter.

The most dramatic moment of the underworld journey was the judgment of the dead by Osiris (ō sī′ ris). This god's story involved suffering, death, and resurrection, and he could grant eternal life to the deceased. First, however, the candidate's heart was weighed against a figure of Ma'at, goddess of law, truth, and justice. (See the picture.) Souls that failed this test of goodness were tortured and destroyed, while those who passed lived eternally.

Although everyone was judged, the afterlife continued the class divisions of Egyptian society. Pharaohs and wealthy bureaucrats were buried with a deluxe Book of the Dead, rendered by an expert scribe. Less-important Egyptians had to settle for a cut-rate edition. Presumably, the expensive text offered upper-class Egyptians a better chance for eternal life.

The famous burial practice of mummification was associated with the Book of the Dead. Egyptians used this method of embalming in the belief that preserving the body would ensure a satisfactory afterlife.

Art in the Historical Context

The Great Pyramid at Giza: The One and the Many

During the 4th dynasty (c. 2575–c. 2465 B.C.), the power of the pharaohs was at its height. A symbol of this power is still visible today at Giza, on the west bank of the Nile just south of Cairo. It is the Great Pyramid, built to house the remains of the pharaoh Khufu. Almost 500 feet tall and consisting of more than 2 million stones, this pyramid was meant to be Khufu's home forever—and, so far, forever has lasted about 4,500 years!

Seen from a distance, this structure seems to proclaim the power of one mighty ruler. Viewed more closely, however, it is a well-engineered assembly of many stone blocks (see the face of the pyramid in shadow). Thousands of sweating men dragged those blocks up ramps and then fit them together with stunning accuracy. These workers—either a special crew or farmers taking off during Nile floods—labored twenty years to build their pharaoh an eternal life.

▲ **Critical Viewing**
This picture shows the Great Pyramid. Are there any modern buildings or monuments that are comparable to the Great Pyramid in size or purpose? Explain. **[Connect]**

The Hebrews: People of the Covenant Not too long after the Amorites were founding the village of Babylon (c. 2000 B.C.), another Semitic group migrated westward from Mesopotamia to Palestine, or Canaan (kā´ nən), which corresponds to modern Israel and Lebanon. (In dating events, Jewish people normally use B.C.E., "Before the Common Era," rather than B.C., "Before Christ.") This group, the Hebrews, recorded their history in a sacred text that we now call the Bible. Unlike the Mesopotamians or Egyptians, the Hebrews believed in one God and the covenant, or solemn agreement, between God and the Hebrew people. This covenant provided that God would protect the Hebrews from their enemies as long as the Hebrews obeyed him.

Toward the beginning of the second millennium, famine forced some of the Hebrews to migrate from Canaan to Egypt. There, they were enslaved by the pharaohs. The Bible tells, however, that God inspired a leader called Moses to lead the Hebrews out of their captivity and back to Canaan (c. 1200s B.C.). Through Moses, God gave the Hebrews a set of laws called the Ten Commandments. In return for their obedience to these laws and their worship of him, the Hebrews believed, God granted them the land of Canaan.

The Kingdom of Israel For several hundred years, the Hebrews battled the Philistines and other peoples for control of this promised land. They finally conquered the region in about 1000 B.C. under the leadership of David. He became the ruler of the new Hebrew kingdom of Israel, and Solomon, his son, made Jerusalem into an impressive national capital. He erected a temple there that became the center of worship for the entire nation. After his death in the tenth century B.C., however, quarrels led to the division of the country into the northern kingdom of Israel and the southern kingdom of Judah.

In 721 B.C., Israel fell to the Assyrians. Not long after, in 587–586 B.C., Judah was conquered by the Babylonians, who destroyed the temple in Jerusalem and carried away many Hebrews to Babylon. At the end of the sixth century B.C., however, another turn of events led to the conquest of the Babylonians by the Persians. Cyrus, the Persian king, allowed the Hebrews to return to their homeland and rebuild the temple.

While ancient Israel never again achieved the power and independence it had enjoyed under David, the Hebrew contribution to Western culture has been great. (For more about this contribution, see pages 42 and 80–81.)

The Persian and Islamic Empires: Origins About 1000 B.C., a group of Aryan tribes arrived in the mountainous region that is now known as Iran. A tribal group called the Parsa settled in southern Iran. Gradually, this group became known as the Persians. Calling their language Persian and their region Persia, they emerged as a great power in the ancient Middle East.

The Persian Empire During the sixth century B.C., the Persian king Cyrus the Great established a vast and powerful empire. This Cyrus was the same king who conquered the Babylonian Empire and allowed the Hebrews to return to their homeland. By the time of his death, the Persian Empire stretched from the border of India to Asia Minor and from the edge of Egypt to the coasts of the Black Sea and the Caspian Sea. (See the map on page 5.) About 200 years later, this empire, weakened by its unsuccessful attempts to conquer Greece, fell to the forces of Alexander the Great.

Religion in Ancient Persia Although the Persian Empire was short-lived, its official state religion continued to thrive long after its downfall. Founded by a man whom the Greeks called Zoroaster (zō´ rō as´ tər) (c. 628 B.C.–c. 551), this religion taught that two gods—one good and one evil—battle each other and that the good god will prevail. Zoroastrianism remained dominant in Persia for over one thousand years. Then, it was replaced by Islam in the seventh century A.D.

Islam Muhammad, the founder of Islam, was born in about A.D. 570 in Mecca, a large town in what is today Saudi Arabia. At the time, Mecca was a city of extremes, where the rich lived in luxury and the poor lived in despair. Profoundly disturbed by these conditions, Muhammad frequently retreated to a mountain cave to meditate. At the age of forty, he had an experience during one of his retreats that dramatically changed his life. He believed that the angel Gabriel came to him and told him that he had been chosen to serve as God's prophet. Muhammad continued to receive such revelations throughout the rest of his life, and he recited them to his followers.

Although Muhammad taught people to recognize Allah (al´ ə) as the only God, he did not discount the principles of Judaism and Christianity. Instead,

▲ Critical Viewing
What does this picture of Cyrus the Great and his followers suggest about the nature of warfare in ancient Persia? Explain. **[Infer]**

he believed that he was the last in a long line of prophets, including Moses and all of the other prophets mentioned in the Bible.

The Spread of Islam Because Muhammad preached the importance of establishing a just and pious society on Earth, his message had great appeal among the poor in Arabian towns such as Mecca and Medina. These people converted to Islam in large numbers, enabling Muhammad to assemble an army and spread his message throughout the Arabian peninsula.

By the time of Muhammad's death in 632, all of Arabia had been united into an Islamic nation. Then, within a remarkably brief period, Arab armies established a massive Islamic empire that extended from Spain and North Africa to Central Asia.

Although they were deeply committed to the idea of converting people to Islam, Arab leaders did not force people to abandon their cultural traditions. Instead, the Arabs themselves embraced much of the heritage of their conquered peoples, even as these peoples were embracing elements of Arab culture. This blending of heritages resulted in the establishment of a vibrant and diverse Islamic civilization.

Africa: Kingdoms and Trading States From early times, people traded across a long route that stretched from the Middle East and North Africa to the savanna lands, or grasslands, of West Africa. Camel caravans crossed the Sahara, carrying valuable cargoes of gold or salt.

In time, trading empires arose in West Africa. Ghana flourished from the 600s to the 1200s A.D. By the 1300s, Mali controlled the gold trade. The Muslim emperor of Mali, Mansa Musa, won widespread fame when he made a religious pilgrimage to the Arabian city of Mecca in 1324. In the 1400s, a new empire, Songhai, arose in the savanna. Its great city of Timbuktu was a center of learning, attracting scholars from all over the Muslim world.

The kingdom of Benin, which flourished from the 1200s to the 1800s, arose in West African forests. Farther inland, the rulers of Great Zimbabwe (zim bä′ bwā), a city built of stone, controlled rich gold mines and established a trading empire. In East Africa, city-states such as Mogadishu (mō′ gä dē′ shoō), Kilwa, and Mombasa formed part of a prosperous trade route across the Indian Ocean.

▲ **Critical Viewing** Which details on these pages of the Qur'an indicate that it is a sacred book? Explain. [Infer]

Literature

Ancient Middle Eastern Literature: Babylonia
Babylonians had a reverent attitude toward Sumerian culture. Yet they were far more than slavish imitators. Reshaping a group of Sumerian tales about a legendary king, Babylonian scribes fashioned a brilliant work that we know today as *The Epic of Gilgamesh*.

Egyptian Literature Egyptian literature varied with the mood of the times. In the Old Kingdom, when the power of the pharaohs was unquestioned, literature was characterized by sacred hymns as cold and formal as the great pyramids themselves. As society became less rigidly structured in the Middle Kingdom, literature began to reflect personal feelings. The love poetry of the New Kingdom continued this trend.

Hebrew Scripture: The Bible Hebrew monotheism, or belief in a single God, served as a basis for two other world religions, Christianity and Islam. In addition, Hebrew law demonstrated a greater respect for human life than had

A Living Tradition

Ecclesiastes Becomes a Musical Hit
Ecclesiastes (e klē′ zē as′ tēz′), a book of the Bible dating from the third century B.C., furnished the lyrics for a 1960s rock hit. Earlier, the folk singer Pete Seeger had used words from Ecclesiastes to write the song "Turn! Turn! Turn!" Then, in the mid-1960s, Roger McGuinn of the Byrds did a rock version of the song that climbed to the top of the charts.

Here is what McGuinn said about this version: "It was a standard folk song by that time, but I played it, and it came out rock 'n' roll because that's what I was programmed to do like a computer. . . ." [from Johnny Rogan's *The Byrds: Timeless Flight Revisited: The Sequel* (Rogan House, 1998)]

The Greek word *Ecclesiastes*, meaning "member of an assembly," comes from the Hebrew *kohelet*, "someone who calls together an assembly—a preacher." Ecclesiastes, a book of wise sayings attributed to a "Preacher," stresses the "vanity" of ambition and the need to accept life's different seasons:

> . . . saith the Preacher . . . all is vanity. What profit hath a man of all his labor which he taketh under the sun? . . . To every thing there is a season, and a time to every purpose under the heaven: A time to be born and a time to die, a time to plant and a time to pluck up that which is planted. . . .

Seeger had used the section about different seasons, adding the refrain "Turn! Turn! Turn!" to suggest, perhaps, how Earth's turning brings different times and purposes. The song's final plea—"a time for peace, I swear it's not too late"—appealed to Vietnam War protesters in the United States.

previously existed in the ancient Near East. Also new was the Hebrews' deep concern with moral behavior.

All these qualities are evident in the Hebrew Bible, a series of books written during the period 1200 to 100 B.C. These books have deeply influenced Western morality and religious beliefs and, together with Greek thought, form the foundation of Western civilization.

Arabic and Persian Literature: Folk Tales In addition to appreciating poetry and prose of all kinds, Islamic Arabs enjoyed listening to fables and folk tales. Many anonymous collections of such stories exist, but the one entitled *The Thousand and One Nights* is by far the most famous.

Islamic Scripture: The Qur'an Shortly after Muhammad's death, the revelations he had received were arranged into a book called the Qur'an (kōō rän´), which became the sacred scripture of all Muslims. The central message of the Qur'an is that Allah is the single, unique God who is the creator and sustainer of all things: Allah means "the God" in Arabic. According to the Qur'an, all Muslims should submit their wills to Allah because he is not only their creator but also the one who will judge them at death. This duty is evident in the fact that *Islam* actually means "submission."

Persian Literature During the ninth and tenth centuries A.D., several poets attempted to write epic poems in Persian describing Persian history. The most famous of these poems, the *Shah-nama*, or "Epic of Kings," by Firdawsi (fir dou´ sē; also spelled Ferdowsi) is still considered a national treasure in Iran. Another Persian poetic form, the rubái—a poem in four-line stanzas—has been immortalized in the Western world through the translation of *The Rubáiyát*. This book is a collection of verse by the Persian scientist and poet Omar Khayyám (kī yäm´).

Many gifted Persian poets were Sufis (sōō´ fēz), members of an Islamic sect known as Sufism (sōō´ fiz´ əm). Sufis withdrew from society to live solitary lives of worship and piety in order to achieve a sense of oneness with Allah. Their attachment to Allah was similar to being in love and caused them to experience such feelings as intoxication, bliss, and pain. Sufi poets like Sa'di (sä´ dē) and Rumi (rü´ mē) wrote exquisite verses expressing their spiritual feelings in the language of love.

Africa: Oral Literature Africa has a rich heritage of oral literature. In traditional societies, the griot (grē´ ō), or storyteller, held a place of honor. The griot spoke the praises of the ruler, retold events from history, challenged listeners with riddles and proverbs, and recited poems and folk tales. *Sundiata* (sōōn dyä´ tä), by D. T. Niane, is named for the founder of the Kingdom of Mali and retells stories about him from the oral tradition.

▲ **Critical Viewing**
Which details on this page of the *Shah-nama* suggest that it is a book about kings? Why? [Infer]

Prepare to Read

from The Epic of Gilgamesh

The Gilgamesh Epic A long narrative poem named for a Sumerian king who lived between 2700 and 2500 B.C., the Gilgamesh epic describes an era about twenty-three times more distant from us than our own Revolutionary War. Its concerns, however, are timeless and universal: how to become known and respected, how to cope with the loss of a dear friend, and how to accept one's own inevitable death. It is also an action-packed story, featuring battles, gods and goddesses, heroes, tests of strength and wisdom, and arduous journeys.

How the Epic Endured Stories about King Gilgamesh were told and handed down by Sumerians for hundreds of years after his death. By the twenty-first century B.C., however, these tales existed in written form. When the Babylonians conquered the Sumerians soon afterward, they inherited the Sumerian cultural tradition. A Babylonian author, borrowing from some of these tales, created the start of the unified *Gilgamesh* epic that we have today. Other Babylonian writers modified the epic, adding the prologue and the flood story and emphasizing the friendship between Gilgamesh and Enkidu. Most important, these writers gave the narrative its central theme: the search for immortality. By the seventh century B.C., a written version was included in the library of the Assyrian king Ashurbanipal.

After the fall of Babylonia, the written epic was lost. The story survived only in folklore until archaeologists excavated Ashurbanipal's library in the mid-1880s. They discovered the poem on clay tablets in cuneiform, the wedge-shaped writing used by the Babylonians. Archaeologists were especially excited by the portion of the epic describing a great flood, an account remarkably similar to the story of Noah and the ark in the Bible.

The Story of "The Arrogant King" As the story begins, Gilgamesh is king of Uruk, an ancient Sumerian city. He is an arrogant king who is eager for fame. Periodically, the gods and goddesses intervene in his life to provide challenges, obstacles, and challenging tests of Gilgamesh's mettle. The goddess Aruru creates Enkidu to provide such a challenge to Gilgamesh. Enkidu begins his life as a wild man who lives on friendly terms with gazelles and other beasts. He confronts Gilgamesh just as the king is about to claim certain rights that anger the men of Uruk. Gilgamesh and Enkidu become engaged in a heated wrestling match, which Gilgamesh wins after a hard-fought battle with his opponent. In spite of the contentious start to their relationship, the two men become close friends.

A Name for Himself As he searches to make a name for himself, the king battles the giant Humbaba, the Bull of Heaven, as well as lions that he encounters along a great journey. Worried about his mortality, Gilgamesh goes in search of everlasting life. He seeks out Utnapishtim, the sole survivor of a great flood that had destroyed humanity centuries before. On his quest, Gilgamesh has many adventures. He passes through the mysterious Mount Mashu, guarded by Man-Scorpions, and crosses the waters of death with the ferryman, Urshanabi. Gilgamesh seeks immortality, but instead he learns that, for him, there is no permanence. Sometime later, Gilgamesh dies and is lamented by his people. Death, then, completes the cycle of life.

Preview

Connecting to the Literature

You may have tried to imagine what it would mean to live forever. The hero of *Gilgamesh* can think of nothing else. He is desperate to find the one man who has the secret to everlasting life.

Literary Analysis

Archetype: The Hero's Quest

An **archetype** is a basic plot, character, symbol, or idea that recurs in the literature of many cultures. One archetype is the **hero's quest,** a plot in which an extraordinary person goes on a difficult journey or mission. The hero may search for a person, place, or object of value; the answer to a problem or puzzling question; or some other kind of special knowledge.

In *Gilgamesh*, a heroic king searches for the secret of immortality. As you read, think about why Gilgamesh might want that knowledge.

Connecting Literary Elements

Part of telling a quest story is providing details about the extraordinary person at the center of the action. **Characterization** is the means by which characters are created and developed. Authors reveal characters' personalities through direct statements; through characters' actions, speech, and thoughts; or through descriptive details. Look for these methods of characterization in *Gilgamesh*.

Reading Strategy

Understanding the Cultural Context

Gilgamesh was a real Sumerian king, and learning about the culture in which he lived—and in which his story grew and changed—will illuminate this work. Follow these steps to help you **understand the cultural context:**

- Before you read, use the unit introduction on pages 2–11 to get an overview of Sumerian and Babylonian civilization.
- As you read the selection, look for details about the way people lived, worked, and believed. For example, notice the writing materials, the agriculture, and the powers of the gods.
- On a chart like the one shown, record details that provide clues to the culture that created this epic.

Detail
The gods gave Gilgamesh beauty and courage.

What It Suggests About the Culture
Gods provided physical and emotional qualities to humans.

Vocabulary Development

immolation (im′ ə lā′ shən) *n.* offering or killing made as a sacrifice (p. 16)

succor (suk′ ər) *n.* aid; relief (p. 16)

somber (säm′ bər) *adj.* dark; gloomy (p. 19)

incantation (in′ kan tā′ shən) *n.* chant (p. 20)

ecstasy (ek′ stə sē) *n.* great joy (p. 20)

teemed (tēmd) *v.* was full of; swarmed (p. 21)

babel (bab′ əl) *n.* confusion of voices or sounds (p. 21)

subsided (səb sīd′ ed) *v.* settled; lessened; died down (p. 23)

from *The Epic of Gilgamesh*

translated by N. K. Sandars

Background

Gilgamesh is a story shaped by centuries of story-tellers who lived in ancient Mesopotamia, a region between the Tigris and Euphrates rivers. Life in the desert region was simultaneously subject to poverty and plenty, opportunity and danger. Frequent floods enriched the soil, but they were also violent and unpredictable. The flat terrain left cities open to invaders. Ancient Near-Eastern religion reflected the insecurities of life in the region. For Mesopotamians, the underworld was a dreary, inhospitable place, and the quarreling, all-too-human gods had absolute control over human destiny.

The hero's quest is a theme found in the literature of many peoples. Usually, the hero must suffer a number of ordeals in the course of this search, yet this suffering leads to a special knowledge or understanding that could not otherwise have been gained. Gilgamesh's bravery, both during his journey and in battle, was legendary; such a role model may have been exceedingly necessary in a culture and time of tribal invasions. Nonetheless, accounts of this famous king—two thirds a god and one third a man—and his quest for everlasting life may have served as a lesson in accepting one's mortality for generations of listeners.

Critical Viewing ▶ In this statue of Gilgamesh holding a lion, which details reflect the legend that Gilgamesh was two thirds a god and one third a man? **[Explain]**

Prologue

I will proclaim to the world the deeds of Gilgamesh. This was the man to whom all things were known; this was the king who knew the countries of the world. He was wise, he saw mysteries and knew secret things, he brought us a tale of the days before the flood. He went on a long journey, was weary, worn-out with labor, returning he rested, he engraved on a stone the whole story.

When the gods created Gilgamesh they gave him a perfect body. Shamash the glorious sun endowed him with beauty, Adad the god of the storm endowed him with courage, the great gods made his beauty perfect, surpassing all others, terrifying like a great wild bull. Two thirds they made him god and one third man.

In Uruk he built walls, a great rampart, and the temple of blessed Eanna[1] for the god of the firmament Anu, and for Ishtar the goddess of love. Look at it still today: the outer wall where the cornice runs, it shines with the brilliance of copper; and the inner wall, it has no equal. Touch the threshold, it is ancient. Approach Eanna the dwelling of Ishtar, our lady of love and war, the like of which no latter-day king, no man alive can equal. Climb upon the wall of Uruk; walk along it, I say; regard the foundation terrace and examine the masonry: is it not burnt brick and good? The seven sages[2] laid the foundations.

The Battle With Humbaba

When the people of Uruk complain about Gilgamesh's arrogance, the goddess Aruru creates Enkidu to contend with the king and absorb his energies. At first, Enkidu lives like a wild animal and has no contact with other humans. Later, he enters Uruk, loses a wrestling match to Gilgamesh, and becomes his faithful friend. Then the two set off to destroy Humbaba, the giant who guards the cedar forest. As Gilgamesh prepares for battle, Enkidu expresses his fears.

---

1. **In Uruk . . . Eanna** Uruk was an important city in southern Babylonia, with temples to the gods Anu and Ishtar. Eanna was the temple site where these gods were worshiped.
2. **seven sages** legendary wise men who civilized Mesopotamia's seven oldest cities.

Literary Analysis
Archetype: The Hero's Quest What hints does the Prologue give about Gilgamesh's quest?

Reading Strategy
Understanding the Cultural Context What can you conclude about life in Gilgamesh's day from the importance placed on the rampart, or defensive wall, and other city walls?

✔**Reading Check**
Why does the goddess Aruru create Enkidu?

Then Enkidu, the faithful companion, pleaded, answering him, "O my lord, you do not know this monster and that is the reason you are not afraid. I who know him, I am terrified. His teeth are dragon's fangs, his countenance is like a lion, his charge is the rushing of the flood, with his look he crushes alike the trees of the forest and reeds in the swamp. O my lord, you may go on if you choose into this land, but I will go back to the city. I will tell the lady your mother all your glorious deeds till she shouts for joy: and then I will tell the death that followed till she weeps for bitterness." But Gilgamesh said, "Immolation and sacrifice are not yet for me, the boat of the dead[3] shall not go down, nor the three-ply cloth be cut for my shrouding. Not yet will my people be desolate, nor the pyre be lit in my house and my dwelling burnt on the fire. Today, give me your aid and you shall have mine: what then can go amiss with us two? All living creatures born of the flesh shall sit at last in the boat of the West, and when it sinks, when the boat of Magilum sinks, they are gone; but we shall go forward and fix our eyes on this monster. If your heart is fearful throw away fear; if there is terror in it throw away terror. Take your ax in your hand and attack. He who leaves the fight unfinished is not at peace."

Humbaba came out from his strong house of cedar. Then Enkidu called out, "O Gilgamesh, remember now your boasts in Uruk. Forward, attack, son of Uruk, there is nothing to fear." When he heard these words his courage rallied; he answered, "Make haste, close in, if the watchman is there do not let him escape to the woods where he will vanish. He has put on the first of his seven splendors but not yet the other six, let us trap him before he is armed." Like a raging wild bull he snuffed the ground; the watchman of the woods turned full of threatenings, he cried out. Humbaba came from his strong house of cedar. He nodded his head and shook it, menacing Gilgamesh; and on him he fastened his eye, the eye of death. Then Gilgamesh called to Shamash and his tears were flowing, "O glorious Shamash, I have followed the road you commanded but now if you send no succor how shall I escape?" Glorious Shamash heard his prayer and he summoned the great wind, the north wind, the whirlwind, the storm and the icy wind, the tempest and the scorching wind; they came like dragons, like a scorching fire, like a serpent that freezes the heart, a destroying flood and the lightning's fork. The eight winds rose up against Humbaba, they beat against his eyes; he was gripped, unable to go forward or back. Gilgamesh shouted, "By the life of Ninsun my mother and divine Lugulbanda my father, in the Country of the Living, in this Land I have discovered your dwelling; my weak arms and my small weapons I have brought to this Land against you, and now I will enter your house."

So he felled the first cedar and they cut the branches and laid them at the foot of the mountain. At the first stroke Humbaba blazed out, but still they advanced. They felled seven cedars and cut and bound the

---

3. **boat of the dead** ceremonial boat on which the dead were placed.

immolation (im´ ə lā´ shən) *n.* offering or killing made as a sacrifice

Literary Analysis
Archetype: The Hero's Quest and Characterization According to Gilgamesh, what character traits are required to battle a fierce enemy like Humbaba?

succor (suk´ ər) *n.* aid; relief

Literary Analysis
Archetype: The Hero's Quest and Characterization What do Gilgamesh's calls to Shamash—and Shamash's tremendous response—reveal about Gilgamesh's own powers and their limitations?

branches and laid them at the foot of the mountain, and seven times Humbaba loosed his glory on them. As the seventh blaze died out they reached his lair. He slapped his thigh in scorn. He approached like a noble wild bull roped on the mountain, a warrior whose elbows are bound together. The tears started to his eyes and he was pale, "Gilgamesh, let me speak. I have never known a mother, no, nor a father who reared me. I was born of the mountain, he reared me, and Enlil made me the keeper of this forest. Let me go free, Gilgamesh, and I will be your servant, you shall be my lord; all the trees of the forest that I tended on the mountain shall be yours. I will cut them down and build you a palace." He took him by the hand and led him to his house, so that the heart of Gilgamesh was moved with compassion. He swore by the heavenly life, by the earthly life, by the underworld itself: "O Enkidu, should not the snared bird return to its nest and the captive man return to his mother's arms?" Enkidu answered, "The strongest of men will fall to fate if he has no judgment. Namtar, the evil fate that knows no distinction between men, will devour him. If the snared bird returns to its nest, if the captive man returns to his mother's arms, then you my friend will never return to the city where the mother is waiting who gave you birth. He will bar the mountain road against you, and make the pathways impassable."

Humbaba said, "Enkidu, what you have spoken is evil: you, a hireling, dependent for your bread! In envy and for fear of a rival you have spoken

☑ Reading Check

Which god helps Gilgamesh in the battle against Humbaba?

evil words." Enkidu said, "Do not listen, Gilgamesh: this Humbaba must die. Kill Humbaba first and his servants after." But Gilgamesh said, "If we touch him the blaze and the glory of light will be put out in confusion, the glory and glamour will vanish, its rays will be quenched." Enkidu said to Gilgamesh, "Not so, my friend. First entrap the bird, and where shall the chicks run then? Afterwards we can search out the glory and the glamour, when the chicks run distracted through the grass."

Gilgamesh listened to the word of his companion, he took the ax in his hand, he drew the sword from his belt, and he struck Humbaba with a thrust of the sword to the neck, and Enkidu his comrade struck the second blow. At the third blow Humbaba fell. Then there followed confusion for this was the guardian of the forest whom they had felled to the ground. For as far as two leagues the cedars shivered when Enkidu felled the watcher of the forest, he at whose voice Hermon and Lebanon used to tremble. Now the mountains were moved and all the hills, for the guardian of the forest was killed. They attacked the cedars, the seven splendors of Humbaba were extinguished. So they pressed on into the forest bearing the sword of eight talents.[4] They uncovered the sacred dwellings of the Anunnaki[5] and while Gilgamesh felled the first of the trees of the forest Enkidu cleared their roots as far as the banks of Euphrates.[6] They set Humbaba before the gods, before Enlil; they kissed the ground and dropped the shroud and set the head before him. When he saw the head of Humbaba, Enlil raged at them. "Why did you do this thing? From henceforth may the fire be on your faces, may it eat the bread that you eat, may it drink where you drink." Then Enlil took again the blaze and the seven splendors that had been Humbaba's: he gave the first to the river, and he gave to the lion, to the stone of execration[7] to the mountain and to the dreaded daughter of the Queen of Hell.

O Gilgamesh, king and conqueror of the dreadful blaze; wild bull who plunders the mountain, who crosses the sea, glory to him, and from the brave the greater glory is Enki's![8]

*L*iterature
in context Cultural Connection

Ancient Gods and Goddesses

The Babylonians adopted much of the religion of the ancient Sumerians, including their gods and goddesses, though they often used different names for them. Listed below are some of the gods and goddesses mentioned in *Gilgamesh*:

- **Adad** (ā′ dad): god of storms and weather
- **Anunnaki** (ä nōō nä′ kē): Anu's sons, gods of the underworld
- **Anu** (ä′ nōō): father of gods; the god of the heavens
- **Aruru** (ä rōō′ rōō): goddess of creation
- **Ea** (ā′ ä), also called **Enki** (eŋ′ kē): god of waters and wisdom
- **Enlil** (en lil′): god of earth, wind, air, and agriculture
- **Irkalla** (ir kä′ lə), also called **Ereshkigal** (er esh kē′ gäl): queen of the underworld
- **Ishtar** (ish′ tär): goddess of love and war; patron goddess of the city of Uruk
- **Namtar** (näm′ tär): god of evil fate
- **Ninurta** (nə nʉr′ tə): god of war, wells, and irrigation
- **Samuqan** (säm′ ōō kän): god of cattle
- **Shamash** (shä′ mäsh): the sun god; also a lawgiver
- **Siduri** (sə dōō′rē): goddess of wine

---

4. **talents** large units of weight and money used in the ancient world.
5. **Anunnaki** gods of the underworld.
6. **Euphrates** (yōō frāt′ ēz) river flowing from eastern Turkey generally southeastward through Syria and Iraq.
7. **execration** (ek′ si krā′ shən) *n.* cursing, denunciation.
8. **Enki's** belonging to Enki, god of wisdom and one of the creators of human beings.

The Death of Enkidu

Gilgamesh rejects the advances of Ishtar, goddess of love. In revenge, she brings the mighty Bull of Heaven down to threaten Uruk. Gilgamesh and Enkidu kill the bull, but Enkidu dreams that the gods have decreed his death for helping to slaughter the bull and Humbaba. Enkidu is furious at his fate until Shamash, the sun god, allays some of his anger. Then Enkidu describes another dream about death.

As Enkidu slept alone in his sickness, in bitterness of spirit he poured out his heart to his friend. "It was I who cut down the cedar, I who leveled the forest, I who slew Humbaba and now see what has become of me. Listen, my friend, this is the dream I dreamed last night. The heavens roared, and earth rumbled back an answer; between them stood I before an awful being, the <u>somber</u>-faced man-bird; he had directed on me his purpose. His was a vampire face, his foot was a lion's foot, his hand was an eagle's talon. He fell on me and his claws were in my hair, he held me fast and I smothered; then he transformed me so that my arms became wings covered with feathers. He turned his stare towards me, and he led me away to the palace of Irkalla, the Queen of Darkness, to the house from which none who enters ever returns, down the road from which there is no coming back.

"There is the house whose people sit in darkness; dust is their food and clay their meat. They are clothed like birds with wings for covering, they see no light, they sit in darkness. I entered the house of dust and I saw the kings of the earth, their crowns put away for ever; rulers and princes, all those who once wore kingly crowns and ruled the world in the days of old. They who had stood in the place of the gods like Anu and Enlil, stood now like servants to fetch baked meats in the house of dust, to carry cooked meat and cold water from the water-skin. In the

somber (säm´ bər) *adj.* dark; gloomy

✔**Reading Check**

According to Enkidu, what actions resulted in dreams about his own death?

◀ **Critical Viewing**

Which details in this crown make it a worthy symbol for a king? **[Speculate]**

house of dust which I entered were high priests and acolytes[9] priests of the <u>incantation</u> and of <u>ecstasy</u>; there were servers of the temple, and there was Etana, that king of Kish whom the eagle carried to heaven in the days of old. I saw also Samuqan, god of cattle, and there was Ereshkigal the Queen of the Underworld; and Belit-Sheri squatted in front of her, she who is recorder of the gods and keeps the book of death. She held a tablet from which she read. She raised her head, she saw me and spoke: 'Who has brought this one here?' Then I awoke like a man drained of blood who wanders alone in a waste of rushes; like one whom the bailiff[10] has seized and his heart pounds with terror."

incantation (in´ kan tā´ shən) *n.* chant
ecstasy (ek´ stə sē) *n.* great joy

---

9. acolytes (ak´ ə līts´) *n.* attendants; faithful followers.
10. bailiff (bāl´ if) *n.* court officer; law officer.

Review and Assess

Thinking About the Selection

1. **Respond:** Is Gilgamesh the kind of hero that you admire? Why or why not?

2. **(a) Recall:** According to the Prologue, what combination of god and man is Gilgamesh? **(b) Analyze Cause and Effect:** How might this combination affect him as a leader?

3. **(a) Recall:** Why does the goddess Aruru create Enkidu? **(b) Infer:** Why do you think Enkidu and Gilgamesh eventually become good friends?

4. **(a) Recall:** Before the battle, what does Enkidu tell Gilgamesh about Humbaba? **(b) Interpret:** In his response, what attitude does Gilgamesh display toward death?

5. **(a) Recall:** What material has Humbaba used to build his house? **(b) Draw Conclusions:** What do the repeated references to cedar trees and Humbaba's offer of them in exchange for his life suggest about their value to this culture?

6. **(a) Summarize:** Summarize the battle with Humbaba, and identify Enkidu's role in it. **(b) Compare and Contrast:** What differences between Gilgamesh and Enkidu does the battle reveal?

7. **(a) Speculate:** What do you think will happen to Enkidu, and how do you think Gilgamesh will react? **(b) Support:** Which details led you to this conclusion?

8. **(a) Evaluate:** How effective is Gilgamesh as a leader? **(b) Apply:** In what way is he both like and unlike other strong leaders you have seen or read about?

from *The Epic of Gilgamesh*

Background

In the early sections of *Gilgamesh*, the goddess Aruru creates Enkidu to temper Gilgamesh's arrogance and his dynamic energies. Enkidu quickly becomes the king's valued companion. After many glorious battles, Enkidu dies, and Gilgamesh, greatly saddened by his death, goes on a quest for immortality. He seeks Utnapishtim and his family, the only humans who have defeated death. Will Utnapishtim explain how a human might achieve immortality? Will the king return to his people with the knowledge of everlasting life? Find the answers to these questions in "The Story of the Flood" and "The Return" from *Gilgamesh*.

The Story of the Flood

"You know the city Shurrupak, it stands on the banks of Euphrates? That city grew old and the gods that were in it were old. There was Anu, lord of the firmament, their father, and warrior Enlil their counselor, Ninurta the helper, and Ennugi watcher over canals; and with them also was Ea. In those days the world <u>teemed</u>, the people multiplied, the world bellowed like a wild bull, and the great god was aroused by the clamor. Enlil heard the clamor and he said to the gods in council, 'The uproar of mankind is intolerable and sleep is no longer possible by reason of the <u>babel</u>.' So the gods agreed to exterminate mankind. Enlil did this, but Ea because of his oath warned me in a dream. He whispered their words to my house of reeds, 'Reed-house, reed-house! Wall, O wall, harken reed-house, wall reflect: O man of Shurrupak, son of Ubara-Tutu; tear down your house and build a boat, abandon possessions and look for life, despise worldly goods and save your soul alive. Tear down your house, I say, and build a boat. These are the measurements of the barque as you shall build her: let her beam equal her length, let her deck be roofed like the vault that covers the abyss;[1] then take up into the boat the seed of all living creatures.'

"When I had understood I said to my lord, 'Behold, what you have commanded I will honor and perform, but how shall I answer the people, the city, the elders?' Then Ea opened his mouth and said to me, his

teemed (tēmd) *v.* was full of; swarmed

babel (bab´ əl) *n.* confusion of voices or sounds

---

1. **like … abyss** like the firmament, or heaven, that covers the depths.

☑ **Reading Check**

What arouses the ire and frustration of Enlil?

servant, 'Tell them this: I have learnt that Enlil is wrathful against me, I dare no longer walk in his land nor live in his city; I will go down to the Gulf[2] to dwell with Ea my lord. But on you he will rain down abundance, rare fish and shy wild-fowl, a rich harvest-tide. In the evening the rider of the storm will bring you wheat in torrents.'

"In the first light of dawn all my household gathered round me, the children brought pitch and the men whatever was necessary. On the fifth day I laid the keel and the ribs, then I made fast the planking. The ground-space was one acre, each side of the deck measured one hundred and twenty cubits[3] making a square. I built six decks below, seven in all, I divided them into nine sections with bulkheads between. I drove in wedges where needed, I saw to the punt-poles[4] and laid in supplies. The carriers brought oil in baskets, I poured pitch into the furnace and asphalt and oil; more oil was consumed in caulking[5] and more again the master of the boat took into his stores. I slaughtered bullocks for the people and every day I killed sheep. I gave the shipwrights wine to drink as though it were river water, raw wine and red wine and oil and white wine. There was feasting then as there is at the time of the New Year's festival; I myself anointed my head. On the seventh day the boat was complete.

"Then was the launching full of difficulty; there was shifting of ballast above and below till two thirds was submerged. I loaded into her all that I had of gold and of living things, my family, my kin, the beasts of the field both wild and tame, and all the craftsmen. I sent them on board, for the time that Shamash had ordained was already fulfilled when he said, 'In the evening, when the rider of the storm sends down the destroying rain, enter the boat and batten her down.' The time was fulfilled, the evening came, the rider of the storm sent down the rain. I looked out at the weather and it was terrible, so I too boarded the boat and

▼ **Critical Viewing**
Recitations of epics like *Gilgamesh* may have been accompanied by music from lyres like this one. In what ways would music contribute to such a reading? **[Hypothesize]**

2. **Gulf** the abyss, the great depths of the waters, where Ea, also called Enki, was supposed to dwell.
3. **cubits** (kyoo´ bitz) ancient units of linear measure, about 18–22 inches (originally, the distance from the elbow to the tip of the middle finger).
4. **punt-poles** poles that are pushed against the bottom of a shallow river or lake in order to propel a boat.
5. **caulking** (kôk´ iŋ) *v.* stopping up cracks or seams with a sealant.

battened her down. All was now complete, the battening and the caulking; so I handed the tiller to Puzur-Amurri the steersman, with the navigation and the care of the whole boat.

"With the first light of dawn a black cloud came from the horizon; it thundered within where Adad, lord of the storm, was riding. In front over hill and plain Shullat and Hanish, heralds of the storm, led on. Then the gods of the abyss rose up; Nergal pulled out the dams of the nether[6] waters, Ninurta the war-lord threw down the dykes, and the seven judges of hell, the Anunnaki, raised their torches, lighting the land with their livid flame. A stupor of despair went up to heaven when the god of the storm turned daylight to darkness, when he smashed the land like a cup. One whole day the tempest raged, gathering fury as it went, it poured over the people like the tides of battle; a man could not see his brother nor the people be seen from heaven. Even the gods were terrified at the flood, they fled to the highest heaven, the firmament of Anu; they crouched against the walls, cowering like curs. Then Ishtar the sweet-voiced Queen of Heaven cried out like a woman in travail: 'Alas the days of old are turned to dust because I commanded evil; why did I command this evil in the council of all the gods? I commanded wars to destroy the people, but are they not my people, for I brought them forth? Now like the spawn of fish they float in the ocean.' The great gods of heaven and of hell wept, they covered their mouths.

"For six days and six nights the winds blew, torrent and tempest and flood overwhelmed the world, tempest and flood raged together like warring hosts. When the seventh day dawned the storm from the south subsided, the sea grew calm, the flood was stilled; I looked at the face of the world and there was silence, all mankind was turned to clay. The surface of the sea stretched as flat as a roof-top; I opened a hatch and the light fell on my face. Then I bowed low, I sat down and I wept, the tears streamed down my face, for on every side was the waste of water. I looked for land in vain, but fourteen leagues[7] distant there appeared a mountain, and there the boat grounded; on the mountain of Nisir the boat held fast, she held fast and did not budge. One day she held, and a second day on the mountain of Nisir she held fast and did not budge. A third day, and a fourth day she held fast on the mountain and did not budge; a fifth day and a sixth day she held fast on the mountain. When the seventh day dawned I loosed a dove and let her go. She flew away, but finding no resting-place she returned. Then I loosed a swallow, and she flew away but finding no resting-place she returned. I loosed a raven, she saw that the waters had retreated, she ate, she flew around, she cawed, and she did not come back. Then I threw everything open to the four winds, I made a sacrifice and poured out a

---

6. **nether** (neth′ ər) *adj.* below the earth's surface; lower.
7. **leagues** units of linear measure, varying in different times and countries; in English-speaking countries, a league is usually about three miles.

Reading Strategy
Understanding the Cultural Context What does the reaction of the gods to the flood tell you about their powers?

subsided (səb sīd′ ed) *v.* settled; lessened; died down

**Reading Check**
How long does the storm last?

libation[8] on the mountain top. Seven and again seven cauldrons I set up on their stands, I heaped up wood and cane and cedar and myrtle. When the gods smelled the sweet savor, they gathered like flies over the sacrifice. Then, at last, Ishtar also came, she lifted her necklace with the jewels of heaven that once Anu had made to please her. 'O you gods here present, by the lapis lazuli[9] round my neck I shall remember these days as I remember the jewels of my throat: these last days I shall not forget. Let all the gods gather round the sacrifice, except Enlil. He shall not approach this offering, for without reflection he brought the flood; he consigned my people to destruction."

"When Enlil had come, when he saw the boat, he was wrath and swelled with anger at the gods, the host of heaven, 'Has any of these mortals escaped? Not one was to have survived the destruction.' Then the god of the wells and canals Ninurta opened his mouth and said to the warrior Enlil, 'Who is there of the gods that can devise without Ea? It is Ea alone who knows all things.' Then Ea opened his mouth and spoke to warrior Enlil, 'Wisest of gods, hero Enlil, how could you so senselessly bring down the flood?

> Lay upon the sinner his sin,
> Lay upon the transgressor his transgression,
> Punish him a little when he breaks loose,
> Do not drive him too hard or he perishes;
> Would that a lion had ravaged mankind
> Rather than the flood,
> Would that a wolf had ravaged mankind
> Rather than the flood,
> Would that famine had wasted the world
> Rather than the flood,
> Would that pestilence had wasted mankind
> Rather than the flood.

It was not I that revealed the secret of the gods; the wise man learned it in a dream. Now take your counsel what shall be done with him.'

"Then Enlil went up into the boat, he took me by the hand and my wife and made us enter the boat and kneel down on either side,

---

8. **libation** (lī bāʹ shən) *n.* liquid poured out as a sacrifice to a god.
9. **lapis lazuli** (lapʹ is lazʹ yoo lǐ) *n.* sky-blue semi-precious gemstone.

he standing between us. He touched our foreheads to bless us saying. 'In time past Utnapishtim was a mortal man; henceforth he and his wife shall live in the distance at the mouth of the rivers.' Thus it was that the gods took me and placed me here to live in the distance, at the mouth of the rivers."

☑ **Reading Check**

Why is Enlil enraged when he sees the boat?

◀ **Critical Viewing**
Which details from this mosaic accurately illustrate the end of the flood in *Gilgamesh*? **[Analyze]**

The Return

Utnapishtim said, "As for you, Gilgamesh, who will assemble the gods for your sake, so that you may find that life for which you are searching? But if you wish, come and put it to the test: only prevail against sleep for six days and seven nights." But while Gilgamesh sat there resting on his haunches, a mist of sleep like soft wool teased from the fleece drifted over him, and Utnapishtim said to his wife, "Look at him now, the strong man who would have everlasting life, even now the mists of sleep are drifting over him." His wife replied, "Touch the man to wake him, so that he may return to his own land in peace, going back through the gate by which he came." Utnapishtim said to his wife, "All men are deceivers, even you he will attempt to deceive; therefore bake loaves of bread, each day one loaf, and put it beside his head; and make a mark on the wall to number the days he has slept."

So she baked loaves of bread, each day one loaf, and put it beside his head, and she marked on the wall the days that he slept; and there came a day when the first loaf was hard, the second loaf was like leather, the third was soggy, the crust of the fourth had mold, the fifth was mildewed, the sixth was fresh, and the seventh was still on the embers. Then Utnapishtim touched him and he woke. Gilgamesh said to Utnapishtim the Faraway, "I hardly slept when you touched and roused me." But Utnapishtim said, "Count these loaves and learn how many days you slept, for your first is hard, your second like leather, your third is soggy, the crust of your fourth has mold, your fifth is mildewed, your sixth is fresh and your seventh was still over the glowing embers when I touched and woke you." Gilgamesh said, "What shall I do, O Utnapishtim, where shall I go? Already the thief in the night has hold of my limbs, death inhabits my room; wherever my foot rests, there I find death."

Then Utnapishtim spoke to Urshanabi the ferryman: "Woe to you Urshanabi, now and for ever more you have become hateful to this harborage; it is not for you, nor for you are the crossings of this sea. Go now, banished from the shore. But this man before whom you walked, bringing him here, whose body is covered with foulness and the grace of whose limbs has been spoiled by wild skins, take him to the washing-place. There he shall wash his long hair clean as snow in the water, he shall throw off his skins and let the sea carry them away, and the beauty of his body shall be shown, the fillet[10] on his forehead shall be renewed, and he shall be given clothes to cover his nakedness. Till he reaches his own city and his journey is accomplished, these clothes will show no sign of age, they will wear like a new garment." So Urshanabi took Gilgamesh and led him to the washing-place, he washed

Literary Analysis
Archetype: The Hero's Quest and Characterization What effect has Gilgamesh's quest had on him, in spite of his remarkable strength?

▼ **Critical Viewing**
In what ways is this serpent similar to the one Gilgamesh sees? **[Analyze]**

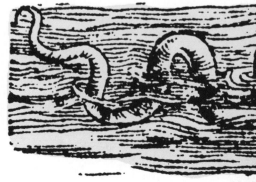

---

10. fillet (fil´ it) *n.* narrow band worn around the head to hold the hair in place.

his long hair as clean as snow in the water, he threw off his skins, which the sea carried away, and showed the beauty of his body. He renewed the fillet on his forehead, and to cover his nakedness gave him clothes which would show no sign of age, but would wear like a new garment till he reached his own city, and his journey was accomplished.

Then Gilgamesh and Urshanabi launched the boat onto the water and boarded it, and they made ready to sail away; but the wife of Utnapishtim the Faraway said to him, "Gilgamesh came here wearied out, he is worn out; what will you give him to carry him back to his own country?" So Utnapishtim spoke, and Gilgamesh took a pole and brought the boat in to the bank. "Gilgamesh, you came here a man wearied out, you have worn yourself out; what shall I give you to carry you back to your own country? Gilgamesh, I shall reveal a secret thing, it is a mystery of the gods that I am telling you. There is a plant that grows under the water, it has a prickle like a thorn, like a rose; it will wound your hands, but if you succeed in taking it, then your hands will hold that which restores his lost youth to a man."

When Gilgamesh heard this he opened the sluices so that a sweet-water current might carry him out to the deepest channel; he tied heavy stones to his feet and they dragged him down to the water-bed. There he saw the plant growing; although it pricked him he took it in his hands; then he cut the heavy stones from his feet, and the sea carried him and threw him onto the shore. Gilgamesh said to Urshanabi the ferryman, "Come here, and see this marvelous plant. By its virtue a man may win back all his former strength. I will take it to Uruk of the strong walls; there I will give it to the old men to eat. Its name shall be 'The Old Men Are Young Again'; and at last I shall eat it myself and have back all my lost youth." So Gilgamesh returned by the gate through which he had come, Gilgamesh and Urshanabi went together. They traveled their twenty leagues and then they broke their fast; after thirty leagues they stopped for the night.

Gilgamesh saw a well of cool water and he went down and bathed; but deep in the pool there was lying a serpent, and the serpent sensed

Literary Analysis
Archetype: The Hero's Quest How does the plant relate to Gilgamesh's quest?

✔**Reading Check**

What power does the plant possess?

the sweetness of the flower. It rose out of the water and snatched it away, and immediately it sloughed its skin and returned to the well. Then Gilgamesh sat down and wept, the tears ran down his face, and he took the hand of Urshanabi; "O Urshanabi, was it for this that I toiled with my hands, is it for this I have wrung out my heart's blood? For myself I have gained nothing; not I, but the beast of the earth has joy of it now. Already the stream has carried it twenty leagues back to the channels where I found it. I found a sign and now I have lost it. Let us leave the boat on the bank and go."

After twenty leagues they broke their fast, after thirty leagues they stopped for the night; in three days they had walked as much as a journey of a month and fifteen days. When the journey was accomplished they arrived at Uruk, the strong-walled city. Gilgamesh spoke to him, to Urshanabi the ferryman, "Urshanabi, climb up onto the wall of Uruk, inspect its foundation terrace, and examine well the brickwork; see if it is not of burnt bricks; and did not the seven wise men lay these foundations? One third of the whole is city, one third is garden, and one third is field, with the precinct of the goddess Ishtar. These parts and the precinct are all Uruk."

This too was the work of Gilgamesh, the king, who knew the countries of the world. He was wise, he saw mysteries and knew secret things, he brought us a tale of the days before the flood. He went a long journey, was weary, worn out with labor, and returning engraved on a stone the whole story.

Reading Strategy
Understanding the Cultural Context These last two paragraphs echo the first paragraphs of *Gilgamesh's* Prologue. How might Sumerian and Babylonian values be revealed in these repeated descriptions of the city and its king?

Review and Assess

Thinking About the Selection

1. **Respond:** Did the gods and goddesses in *Gilgamesh* behave in ways you expected? Explain.

2. **(a) Recall:** How does Gilgamesh come to hear the story of the flood? **(b) Make Inferences:** Relative to the other events in *Gilgamesh*, when did the flood happen? **(c) Draw Conclusions:** Why is Utnapishtim able to tell about it?

3. **(a) Recall:** Why do the gods decide to destroy humanity? **(b) Analyze Cause and Effect:** Why do they soon question the wisdom of their decision? **(c) Interpret:** What lessons might Gilgamesh draw from the gods' experiences?

4. **(a) Recall:** After telling the story of the flood, what mysterious gift does Utnapishtim direct Gilgamesh to find? **(b) Recall:** What happens to this gift? **(c) Interpret:** What lesson might Gilgamesh draw from this experience?

5. **Modify:** What changes would you make to *Gilgamesh* if you were adapting it into an adventure or science-fiction film for today's audiences? Explain.

Review and Assess

Literary Analysis

Archetype: The Hero's Quest

1. (a) How does *The Epic of Gilgamesh* fit the **archetype** of a **hero's quest**? (b) How does Gilgamesh respond to the difficult obstacles he encounters?

2. Would you say Gilgamesh's quest is a selfish or an altruistic one? Cite details to explain your opinion.

3. (a) What does the outcome of Gilgamesh's quest suggest about human limitations? (b) How might the tale he brings home to Uruk eventually grant Gilgamesh the immortality he seeks?

Connecting Literary Elements

4. List at least three examples of actions, speech, or thoughts that contribute to the **characterization** of Gilgamesh as a hero. Use a chart like the one shown to explain what each example reveals about Gilgamesh's personality, values, or talents.

Example of Indirect Characterization	What It Shows About Gilgamesh

5. (a) What part does Gilgamesh's nature—two thirds god, one third man—play in his behavior? (b) What part does his nature play in motivating his quest?

6. What drawbacks or limitations on Gilgamesh's powers and talents seem to exist?

Reading Strategy

Understanding Cultural Context

7. (a) Identify three qualities or beliefs in *Gilgamesh* that the Sumerians and Babylonians seemed to value. (b) For each one, cite supporting evidence in the selection that suggests this **cultural context.**

8. Identify three details that show that Sumerian or Babylonian society was highly organized. Consider such things as where people lived, what jobs they held, and their common beliefs.

Extend Understanding

9. **Cultural Connection:** What personal goals set by people today might be considered quests for immortality? Explain.

Quick Review

An **archetype** is a basic plot, character, symbol, or idea that recurs in the literature of many cultures. The **hero's quest** is an archetype in which an extraordinary person goes on a difficult journey to find something important.

Characterization is the means by which characters are developed. Authors may reveal characters' personalities directly, through statements and descriptions, or indirectly, through characters' actions, speech, and thoughts.

To **understand the cultural context,** look for details in ancient works about the way people lived and worked and what they believed.

 **Take It to the Net**
PHSchool.com

Take the interactive self-test online to check your understanding of this selection.

Integrate Language Skills

Vocabulary Development Lesson

Word Analysis: Latin Prefix *sub-*

Subsided contains the prefix *sub-*, which means "under," "lower," or "down." *Subsided*, therefore, means "died down," or "lessened." Use the prefix *sub-* with the roots below to form familiar words, and then define each one.

1. *-mar-* (sea)
2. *-merg-* (plunge)
3. *-terra-* (earth)
4. *-tract-* (pull)

Spelling Strategy

The *shun* sound is often spelled *-tion*. When a root word ends with the *s* or *d* sound, the suffix is spelled *-sion*: *tense* becomes *tension*; *extend* becomes *extension*. When the root ends in *-mit*, the suffix is spelled *-ssion*: *permit* becomes *permission*. Use these rules to add the correct form of the suffix to each word below.

1. transmit   2. pretend   3. destruct

Fluency: Words in Context

Complete each sentence below with the appropriate word from the list on page 13.

1. When afraid, Gilgamesh pleads to the gods for ___?___ .
2. The Sumerian high priestess was in charge of ___?___ and sacrifice.
3. When Enkidu died, the priestess chanted an ___?___ .
4. Residents of the Underworld seem ___?___ and submissive.
5. Gilgamesh would be in ___?___ if he could learn the secret of immortality.
6. Long before, when the world ___?___ with people, the gods caused a great flood.
7. They objected to the ___?___ of human voices.
8. Finally the violent storm ___?___ .

Grammar and Style Lesson

Commonly Confused Words: *in* and *into*

In *Gilgamesh*, the English translator correctly uses both *in* and *into*— two prepositions that are commonly confused. As the following examples from the epic *Gilgamesh* indicate, the preposition *in* refers to place or position, while *into* suggests motion.

Place or Position: "O Gilgamesh, remember now your boasts *in* Uruk."

Motion: "O my lord, you may go on if you choose *into* this land, but I will go back to the city."

Practice Choose the correct preposition to complete each sentence.

1. Gilgamesh was king (in, into) Uruk.
2. Humbaba retreated (in, into) his house of cedar.
3. (In, Into) the forest, it became dark.
4. The goddess spoke to Enkidu (in, into) a dream.
5. Gilgamesh went (in, into) the mysterious mountain of Manshu.

Writing Application Write four sentences about what might happen after Gilgamesh returns to Uruk. Use *in* in two of your sentences, and use *into* in the other two.

W̧ Prentice Hall Writing and Grammar Connection: Diamond Level, Chapter 25, Section 2

Writing Lesson

Comparison-and-Contrast Essay

Gilgamesh is a hero on a quest for the secret of immortality. Think about one modern-day hero—from books, movies, or TV—who is also on a quest of some kind. In an essay, compare and contrast Gilgamesh to this modern hero.

Prewriting   Brainstorm for similarities and differences between the two heroes. Consider the personality and talents of each hero, the goal of each quest, the obstacles that must be overcome, and his or her ultimate success or failure. Gather details in a chart like the one shown.

Model: Gathering Details

Points of Comparison	Gilgamesh	Modern-Day Hero

Drafting   Organize your essay by comparing the two heroes point by point or by detailing all the points about Gilgamesh before moving on to the modern hero. Include specific details to support each general point you make.

Revising   Check your draft against your prewriting chart to confirm that you have presented each point of comparison, discussing it in relation to each hero. Make sure that the details about each character are accurate.

*W*G *Prentice Hall Writing and Grammar Connection: Diamond Level, Chapter 9, Section 3*

Extension Activities

Research and Technology Find out more about the rediscovery of *Gilgamesh* in the nineteenth century. Use these questions to guide your research:

- Where and when was the discovery made?
- In what form was *Gilgamesh* preserved?
- What other poems or stories about Gilgamesh have survived?

Find information in reliable Internet sources, or consult the introductory material in a translation of *Gilgamesh*. Present your findings in a brief **research report.**

Listening and Speaking Hold a **press conference** in which the returning Gilgamesh answers questions about his quest. Review the selection to find the details Gilgamesh could report. Then, with several classmates, take on the roles of Gilgamesh, his advisers, and the reporters who ask questions. **[Group Activity]**

 **Take It to the Net**   PHSchool.com

Go online for an additional research activity using the Internet.

Prepare to Read

New Kingdom Love Lyrics

Egypt's New Kingdom (c.1540–1075 B.C.)

The period called the New Kingdom in Egypt was highly sophisticated, a time marked by the last great flowering of ancient Egyptian culture. It was a time of expansion abroad—the Egyptian empire reached to the Euphrates River—and increased opportunity at home. Women, in particular, enjoyed more rights and prestige than in most other ancient cultures. With a legal status equal to that of men, women could will property, initiate a lawsuit, and probably divorce a husband.

Indeed, a woman—Queen Hatshepsut—

ruled as the fifth pharaoh of the New Kingdom period. Her peaceful rule, which lasted for about twenty years, was marked by several extraordinary architectural projects, including her own temple in the Valley of the Kings. After her death, however, the young nephew whom she had shoved aside in order to assume the crown herself took his revenge by defacing her monuments. Among other famous figures of the New Kingdom is King Tutankhamen, the nine-year-old boy-king whose extravagant tomb in the Valley of the Kings was discovered nearly intact in 1922.

Literature in the New Kingdom Intellectual pursuits were highly valued during the New Kingdom period. The scribes who oversaw all aspects of the growing empire underwent long and arduous training to learn the period's hieroglyphic writing, in which pictures represent sounds and ideas. The poems that follow were originally written in hieratic, the cursive form of hieroglyphic writing that was adapted specifically for ink brushstrokes on stone or papyrus. Aside from love lyrics, other common literary forms of the period include hymns to the gods, autobiographical writings that illustrate a life well lived, "school texts" that provide composition exercises for scribes-in-training, and guides to the afterlife that were printed on papyrus and enclosed in tombs with the deceased.

The Goddess Ma'at The speaker in many of the New Kingdom love lyrics expresses a joy in the well-being of others, a selfless, generous impulse that Ma'at, the goddess of law, truth, and justice, may have represented for Egyptians of the New Kingdom. *Ma'at*, which no single English word can translate exactly, means "right," "just," "true," and "in order." These concepts became important as ancient Egyptians began to believe that good deeds, rather than status, guaranteed eternal life. In fact, Egyptian mythology held that when Osiris, god of the underworld, judged each person's life, he weighed the heart, or conscience, of the deceased against a figure of Ma'at. Those found to be true were sent to an afterlife of eternal happiness.

Pastoral Poetry for a Complex Time The poems that follow are pastoral poems. The term *pastoral* comes from the Latin word for shepherd—*pastor*—but pastoral poetry is not merely about shepherds and shepherdesses. Rather, a pastoral poem is one that deals with the pleasures of a simple rural life or that treats the longings and desires of simple people. It usually idealizes rural life, making it seem more innocent and pleasant than it really is.

Preview
Connecting to the Literature

Love in its fickle, true, and unrequited forms is a popular, universal theme. Today's songwriters mine this topic, but love is not a uniquely twenty-first century concern. Egyptian love poetry taps into the same wonders and heartaches that your favorite singers and poets describe today.

Literary Analysis
The Speaker in a Poem

In love poetry, the **speaker** is the voice of a poem, communicating his or her ideas and passionate feelings. Speakers can take many forms, both concrete and abstract. Details in the poetry can suggest the identity of the speaker as one of the following types:

- a fictional character or animal whose personality and situation the poet adopts
- an object or an abstract idea—such as a river or Time—for which the poet provides a voice

As you read each of these poems, use the details provided to determine the identity of the speaker and to interpret his or her unique personality.

Comparing Literary Works

In poetry, a speaker's feelings and attitudes are revealed through his or her **diction,** or word choice. As you compare and contrast the speakers in these four poems, consider what each speaker's diction—whether formal, informal, flowery, or detached—reveals about the speaker's situation and the strength of his or her feelings.

Reading Strategy
Inferring the Dramatic Context

A poem's details can help you **infer the dramatic context,** or the speaker's situation. Key adjectives, significant actions, vivid metaphors, and other details will help you uncover the speaker's story. As you read, use a diagram like the one shown to infer the dramatic situation in each poem.

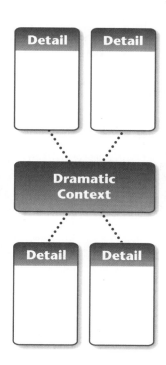

Vocabulary Development

flittering (flit′ ər iŋ) *adj.* flapping the wings rapidly; fluttering (p. 35)

well-being (wel bē′ iŋ) *n.* the state of being well; health, happiness, or prosperity (p. 36)

feigning (fān′ iŋ) *adj.* pretending (p. 37)

terminal (tʉr′ mə nəl) *adj.* fatal; ending in death (p. 37)

troop (tro͞op) *v.* to march in a group (p. 37)

laden (lād′ ′n) *adj.* weighed down (p. 38)

New Kingdom Love Lyrics

Background

The short love poems from Egypt's New Kingdom period survive on scrolls of the thick Egyptian paper known as papyrus and on smooth pieces of pottery called ostraca. Though the love these poems express is sometimes simple and naive and the speakers are both male and female, the sophisticated language suggests that the actual authors were professional poets. In each, the poet assumes a much simpler persona. Such poets would have no doubt been male, as only men were trained to read and write. The poems themselves may have been performed to music at one of the festive banquets depicted on many Egyptian tomb paintings.

The Voice of the Swallow, Flittering, Calls to Me

translated by John L. Foster

The voice of the swallow, <u>flittering</u>, calls to me:
       "Land's alight! Whither away?"
No, little bird, you cannot entice me,
       I follow you to the fields no more.

5 Like you in the dawn mist I rose,
       at sunrise discovered my lover abed
          (his voice is sweeter).
"Wake," I said, "or I fly with the swallow."
And my heart smiled back

10   when he, smiling, said:
"You shall not fly,
       nor shall I, bright bird.
          But hand in hand
We shall walk the Nileside pathways,

15   under cool of branches, hidden
          (only the swallows watching)—
Wide-eyed girl,
       I shall be with you in all glad places."

Can you match the notes of that song, little swallow?

20   I am first in his field of girls!
My heart, dear sister, sings in his hand—
       love never harmed a winged creature.

---

flittering (flit´ ər iŋ) *adj.* flapping the wings rapidly; fluttering

Literary Analysis
The Speaker in a Poem What do the first four lines suggest about the speaker's relationship to birds?

Reading Strategy
Inferring the Dramatic Context What feelings do the speaker and her beloved share?

◀ **Critical Viewing** Considering the details in this fresco, what elements of rural life do you expect to find in the New Kingdom love lyrics? **[Anticipate]**

Most Beautiful Youth Who Ever Happened

Translated by William Kelly Simpson

Most beautiful youth who ever happened,
I want to take your house as housekeeper;
we are arm in arm,
and love of you goes round and round.

5 I say to my heart within me in prayer:
if far away from me is my lover tonight,
then I am like someone already in the grave.
Are you not indeed <u>well-being</u> and life?

Joy has come to me through your well-being,
10 my heart seeks you out.

I Think I'll Go Home and Lie Very Still

translated by John L. Foster

I think I'll go home and lie very still,
    <u>feigning</u> <u>terminal</u> illness.
Then the neighbors will all <u>troop</u> over to stare,
    my love, perhaps, among them.
5 How she'll smile while the specialists
    snarl in their teeth!—

    she perfectly well knows what ails me.

feigning (fān´ iŋ) *adj.* pretending
terminal (tʉr´ mə nəl) *adj.* fatal; ending in death
troop (trōōp) *v.* to march in a group

Literary Analysis
The Speaker in a Poem
Judging from his actions, what sort of person does the speaker seem to be?

Literature in context   Humanities Connection

Pastoral Poetry

A pastoral poem presents rural or rustic life and the people who live it. Beginning in the third century B.C., Greek pastorals often consisted of a dialogue (or singing match) between two shepherds, a lament (or complaint) of a lovesick or forlorn lover, or an elegy for a dead friend. In subsequent centuries, the subject matter of pastoral poems has evolved, but many characteristics have remained relatively consistent. Most pastorals present country or rural life in a nostalgic or bittersweet manner, often greatly idealized. The speaker and audience of these poems tend to be somewhat sophisticated, although the language of the poems appears simplistic. Finally, images of rocky hills and woodlands abound in pastoral poetry, creating an escapist literature that allows readers to experience what they imagine to be the free and untroubled life of ordinary country folk. The love poems of the New Kingdom are some of the world's oldest surviving pastoral poetry.

The Voice of the Wild Goose

Translated by William Kelly Simpson

The voice of the wild goose,
caught by the bait, cries out.
Love of you holds me back,
and I can't loosen it at all.

5   I shall set aside my nets.
But what can I tell my mother
to whom I return every day
when I am <u>laden</u> with catch?

I did not set my traps today;
10   love of you has thus entrapped me.

Literary Analysis
The Speaker in a Poem
What job or activity do the details suggest that the speaker performs every day?

laden (lād 'n) *adj.* weighed down

Review and Assess

Thinking About the Selections

1. **Respond:** With which poem's speaker did you sympathize most? Why?

2. **(a) Recall:** In "The Voice of the Swallow," what choice does the speaker give her beloved? **(b) Connect:** How does her beloved respond to the choice he is given?

3. **(a) Summarize:** Describe the speaker's attitude toward her beloved in "Most Beautiful Youth Who Ever Happened." **(b) Draw Conclusions:** Would you say the speaker is selfish or unselfish in her love? Explain.

4. **(a) Recall:** What does the speaker plan to do in "I Think I'll Go Home and Lie Very Still"? **(b) Analyze Cause and Effect:** Why would his beloved smile at his actions?

5. **(a) Compare and Contrast:** In "The Voice of the Wild Goose," what does the speaker compare to her nets? **(b) Interpret:** What does this comparison show about her relationship with her beloved?

6. **Apply:** Which details in these poems suggest that women enjoyed respect and prestige in Egypt's New Kingdom? Explain.

Review and Assess

Literary Analysis

The Speaker in a Poem

1. Do you think the **speaker** in "I Think I'll Go Home and Lie Very Still" is most likely a teenager, a mature adult, or an elderly person? Explain your opinion.

2. (a) Which details in " The Voice of the Swallow" show that the speaker is familiar with birds? (b) What other poem in this grouping shows detailed familiarity with birds? Explain.

3. On a chart like the one shown, gather clues that reveal whether each poem's speaker is male or female—or whether the speaker's gender is unclear.

Poem	Clues	Gender

Comparing Literary Works

4. (a) Compare the **diction** in "The Voice of the Swallow" and "The Voice of the Wild Goose." (b) Cite examples of word choice in the poems that reveal each speaker's feelings. (c) How do the speakers' reactions to love differ in the two poems?

5. (a) Contrast the speakers' feelings and attitudes in "I Think I'll Go Home and Lie Very Still" and "Most Beautiful Youth Who Ever Happened." (b) In which of the two poems is the speaker's diction more flowery and romantic? Explain your answer.

Reading Strategy

Inferring the Dramatic Context

6. Sum up the **dramatic context** of "The Voice of the Swallow."

7. In "Most Beautiful Youth Who Ever Happened," what is the speaker's relationship to her beloved?

8. How important is it to infer the dramatic context in these poems? Explain.

Extend Understanding

9. **Humanities Link:** (a) Why do you think love has been such a timeless theme in poetry and music? (b) What other themes provide artists and writers with such inspiration?

Quick Review

The **speaker** is the voice assumed by the poet.

Diction, or word choice, refers to the words a writer or speaker chooses to communicate his or her ideas.

To **infer the dramatic context,** you must use details from the poem to make an educated guess about the situation of the speaker and others in the poem.

 **Take It to the Net**
PHSchool.com

Take the interactive self-test online to check your understanding of these selections.

Integrate Language Skills

Vocabulary Development Lesson

Word Analysis: Latin Root -term-

The Latin root -term- means "end." A terminal illness is one that ends in death. Use your knowledge of this root to answer the questions below.

1. When do you hand in a *term* paper?
2. How do you *terminate* a conversation?
3. What does an *exterminator* do to insects?
4. Where will you find a bus *terminal*?

Spelling Strategy

The word *feign* contains the long *a* sound spelled *ei*, followed by a silent *g*. The long *a* sound can also be spelled *ei* without the silent *g* or followed by both a silent *g* and a silent *h: vein, neigh*. Complete each word below.

1. wei__?__   2. rei__?__   3. ei__?__t

Concept Development: Synonyms

Rewrite each sentence below, replacing the word in italics with its synonym from the list on page 33.

1. The basket was *heavy* with apples and pears.
2. *Waving* in the breeze was an American flag.
3. With treatment, it need not be a *fatal* illness.
4. The doctor fretted over her patient's *health*.
5. When the bell rings, the whole class will *march* over here.
6. Though in fact extremely bored, he was *pretending* interest.

Grammar and Style Lesson

Compound Nouns

A **compound noun** is a noun that is made up of more than one word. The compound noun itself may be combined into a single word, hyphenated, or written as separate words.

Combined: house + keeper = housekeeper

Hyphenated: sister + in + law = sister-in-law

Separate: bald + eagle = bald eagle

Compound words are usually listed in dictionaries because they name something other than what the individual words suggest. The word *eardrum*, for example, names a specific object that is different from an ear or a drum.

Practice Identify the compound nouns in the following sentences.

1. Some of the speakers behave like characters in soap operas.
2. The young Egyptian nobleman in "I Think I'll Go Home" is childish.
3. One speaker visits her beloved at sunrise.
4. Another speaker takes a pathway to the river.
5. Is she really concerned for his well-being?

Writing Application Write a brief response to these poems. Include at least one single-word, one hyphenated, and one two-word compound noun.

Writing Lesson

Advice Column

An advice column provides readers with suggestions for solving problems or improving their lives. Suppose that one of the speakers in the four poems asked your advice about his or her love life. Write a letter to offer the speaker advice.

Prewriting Choose one of the poems and jot down clues to the dramatic context, such as the speaker's actions and attitude toward his or her situation. Then, identify what you think is the underlying problem. Use a chart like the one shown to organize your thoughts.

Model: Organizing Information

Clues to Dramatic Context	Underlying Problem	My Thoughts or Advice

Drafting Begin your advice column by rephrasing the situation in which the speaker finds himself or herself. Develop and support your advice based on what you know about the speaker's situation. Offer specific steps to resolve the speaker's problem.

Revising As you revise, look for a clear statement of the dramatic context presented in the poem and concrete support for your advice. Revise your diction to avoid sounding too harsh or too gentle.

W̶G̶ Prentice Hall Writing and Grammar Connection: Diamond Level, Chapter 7, Section 2

Extension Activities

Research and Technology Research to learn more about daily life in Egypt's New Kingdom. Focus on a cultural element such as one of these:

- poetry
- agriculture
- pastimes
- status of women
- music
- education

Use information from printed materials, reliable Internet sources, or museum exhibits. Present your findings in an **oral report** accompanied by visual aids.

Listening and Speaking With a group, role-play a **panel discussion** that might take place among the four poems' speakers. One student should act as moderator and lead a discussion focused on different aspects of love and overcoming obstacles on the path to love. **[Group Activity]**

 Take It to the Net PHSchool.com

Go online for an additional research activity using the Internet.

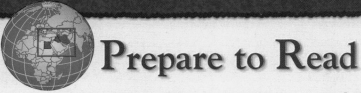

Prepare to Read

from the Bible: Genesis 1–3 (The Creation and the Fall) *and* Genesis 6–9 (The Story of the Flood)

The Hebrew Bible The most important example of Hebrew literature is the Hebrew Bible, known by Christians as the Old Testament. Translated into many languages, it has influenced three major religions: Judaism, Christianity, and Islam.

The word *Bible* comes from the Greek word *biblia,* meaning "a collection of writings." It is accurate to call the Bible a collection—even a library—rather than a single book. Like a library, it contains many types of books.

Traditionally, the books of the Hebrew Bible have been divided into three main sections. The Torah—from the Hebrew word *tora,* meaning "law"—consists of the first five books of the Bible (Genesis, Exodus, Leviticus, Numbers, and Deuteronomy). While the Torah is largely concerned with the law, it contains important narratives and an account of the world's creation. Another section, called Nevi'im, or Prophets, contains historical accounts, such as the Book of Samuel, and the writings of the prophets, those who summoned the Jews to the path of justice and faith in God. Still another section, called Ketuvim, or Writings, consists of a variety of works: poetry like the Psalms, short stories like the Book of Ruth, and religious dialogues like the Book of Job.

The Bible's Origins The Bible's authorship is a question that has intrigued people over the centuries. Many believe that the Bible is the word of God. Through the workings of divine inspiration, human beings wrote down God's message. It was once believed that Moses himself wrote the first five books of the Bible and that King David composed the Psalms. In the nineteenth century, however, some scholars began to theorize that differences in style and content suggest multiple sources for the Bible. Today, some experts infer that the oldest source for the Torah, for instance, dates back to the tenth century B.C. and the most recent dates to about the fifth century B.C.

A Book of Great Influence For Jews, the Bible was a "Written Temple," sustaining Jewish culture and beliefs when the actual Temple in Jerusalem was destroyed in 586 B.C. and again in A.D. 70. The Bible has also had major importance for Muslims and Christians, who, like Jews, worship a single God. In the sixteenth century, Martin Luther translated the Bible into German and stressed its importance for the individual believer, thereby inaugurating Protestantism. Still another famous translation of the Bible is the English version written by a committee of scholars for King James in 1611. The poetic phrasing and cadences of the King James version have influenced the prose and poetry of the English language for nearly four hundred years.

Themes of the Bible

Despite the diversity of the Bible, the text is unified by a few constant themes, or insights into life. These themes often address the power, goodness, and mercy of a single God; the covenant, or solemn agreement, into which God enters with the Hebrew people; the tendency of humans to stray from a right, or moral, path; and the forgiveness they can win from God. Such messages can be found in the various chapters of the Bible.

Within the Bible are numerous stories called *parables,* in which writers present themes that can be interpreted as life-lessons. Biblical parables teach lessons of deep personal strength in the face of overwhelming adversity; of the remarkable capacity of even the weak to survive the harshest of circumstances; and of the consequences of vices, such as greed and betrayal. Although such lessons are an integral part of parables in world literature, themes in the Bible are specifically rooted in the spirituality it presents.

Preview

Connecting to the Literature

Nearly everyone has a vision of paradise, or an ideal place. The Garden of Eden is one such paradise, described in the opening chapters of the Bible.

Literary Analysis

Archetypal Setting

An **archetypal setting** is a time, place, or landscape feature that has similar significance for different peoples and therefore connects to powerful, universal human experiences. One example is a paradise like the Bible's Garden of Eden. Common archetypal setting details include

- a universe of opposites
- a landscape that emerges from watery chaos
- a circle that symbolizes completion
- a great tree that connects the realms of heaven and earth

As you read, think about why the archetypal settings you encounter have been significant to so many cultures.

Connecting Literary Elements

To bring its archetypal settings to life, the writings of the Bible include **dialogue,** or conversation between characters. Dialogue can also

- reveal information about characters
- present events
- add variety to narratives
- arouse the reader's interest

As you read, consider how the dialogue reinforces the meanings of the archetypal settings.

Reading Strategy

Identifying Chronological Order

Chronological order is the order in which events happen in time. Transitional words and phrases like *first, later, on the next day,* or *after that* often help make the chronological order clear. Use a chart like the one shown to track events in Genesis 1–3.

Vocabulary Development

void (void) *n.* empty space; total emptiness (p. 44)

expanse (ek spans´) *n.* very large open area (p. 44)

shrewdest (shro͞od´ est) *adj.* most cunning or clever (p. 47)

duped (do͞opt) *v.* tricked; fooled (p. 48)

enmity (en´ mə tē) *n.* state of being enemies; antagonism; hostility (p. 48)

corrupt (kə rupt´) *adj.* spoiled by sin or dishonesty; rotten (p. 51)

covenant (kuv´ ə nənt) *n.* serious, binding agreement (p. 51)

comprised (kəm prīzd´) *v.* included; consisted of (p. 52)

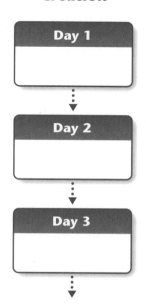

Chronological Order of the Creation

Day 1

Day 2

Day 3

Genesis 1-3
The Creation and the Fall

translated by THE JEWISH PUBLICATION SOCIETY

Background

The Jews of antiquity, the Hebrews, originated as a nomadic tribe in Iraq sometime around 2000 B.C. By 1600 B.C., they had arrived in the Promised Land of Canaan (now known as Israel and Lebanon). After migrating to Egypt to escape famine, the Hebrews suffered centuries of enslavement by the Egyptians and were ultimately liberated by Moses around 1200 B.C. By 1000 B.C., a monarchy was established by King David as a permanent institution in the city of Jerusalem. In subsequent ages, the Jews lost their established nation but reestablished one again in 1948, nearly 2000 years later. Resilient amid the upheavals of history, the Hebrews documented their nation's beginnings and other details of their history within the work now called the Bible. All of the English translations of the Bible presented here are from the Tanakh, the Jewish Publication Society edition translated from the original Hebrew.

CHAPTER 1

1   When God began to create heaven and earth—

2   the earth being unformed and <u>void</u>, with darkness over the surface of the deep and a wind from God sweeping over the water—

3   God said, "Let there be light"; and there was light.

4   God saw that the light was good, and God separated the light from the darkness.

5   God called the light Day, and the darkness He called Night. And there was evening and there was morning, a first day.

6   God said, "Let there be an <u>expanse</u> in the midst of the water, that it may separate water from water."

7   God made the expanse, and it separated the water which was below the expanse from the water which was above the expanse. And it was so.

8   God called the expanse Sky. And there was evening and there was morning, a second day.

9   God said, "Let the water below the sky be gathered into one area, that the dry land may appear." And it was so.

void (void) *n.* empty space; total emptiness

expanse (ek spans') *n.* very large open area

10   God called the dry land Earth, and the gathering of waters He called Seas. And God saw that this was good.

11   And God said, "Let the earth sprout vegetation: seed-bearing plants, fruit trees of every kind on earth that bear fruit with the seed in it." And it was so.

12   The earth brought forth vegetation: seed-bearing plants of every kind, and trees of every kind bearing fruit with the seed in it. And God saw that this was good.

13   And there was evening and there was morning, a third day.

14   God said, "Let there be lights in the expanse of the sky to separate day from night; they shall serve as signs for the set times—the days and the years;

15   and they shall serve as lights in the expanse of the sky to shine upon the earth." And it was so.

16   God made the two great lights, the greater light to dominate the day and the lesser light to dominate the night, and the stars.

17   And God set them in the expanse of the sky to shine upon the earth,

18   to dominate the day and the night, and to separate light from darkness. And God saw that this was good.

19   And there was evening and there was morning, a fourth day.

20   God said, "Let the waters bring forth swarms of living creatures, and birds that fly above the earth across the expanse of the sky."

21   God created the great sea monsters, and all the living creatures of every kind that creep, which the waters brought forth in swarms, and all the winged birds of every kind. And God saw that this was good.

22   God blessed them, saying, "Be fertile and increase, fill the waters in the seas, and let the birds increase on the earth."

23   And there was evening and there was morning, a fifth day.

24   God said, "Let the earth bring forth every kind of living creature: cattle, creeping things, and wild beasts of every kind." And it was so.

25   God made wild beasts of every kind and cattle of every kind, and all kinds of creeping things of the earth. And God saw that this was good.

26   And God said, "Let us make man in our image, after our likeness. They shall rule the fish of the sea, the birds of the sky, the cattle, the whole earth, and all the creeping things that creep on earth."

27   And God created man in His image, in the image of God He created him; male and female He created them.

28   God blessed them and God said to them, "Be fertile and increase, fill the earth and master it; and rule the fish of the sea, the birds of the sky, and all the living things that creep on earth."

29   God said, "See, I give you every seed-bearing plant that is upon all the earth, and every tree that has seed-bearing fruit; they shall be yours for food.

30   And to all the animals on land, to all the birds of the sky, and to everything that creeps on earth, in which there is the breath of life, [I give] all the green plants for food." And it was so.

31   And God saw all that He had made, and found it very good. And there was evening and there was morning, the sixth day.

Literary Analysis
Archetypal Setting What role do opposites play in the settings that God creates in the first four days?

Reading Strategy
Identifying Chronological Order In the description of each day, which sentence signals the end of one day and the start of another?

**Reading Check**

What does God create on the fourth day?

CHAPTER 2

1   The heaven and the earth were finished, and all their array.

2   On the seventh day God finished the work that He had been doing, and He ceased on the seventh day from all the work that He had done.

3   And God blessed the seventh day and declared it holy, because on it God ceased from all the work of creation that He had done.

4   Such is the story of heaven and earth when they were created. When the LORD God made earth and heaven—

5   when no shrub of the field was yet on earth and no grasses of the field had yet sprouted, because the LORD God had not sent rain upon the earth and there was no man to till the soil,

6   but a flow would well up from the ground and water the whole surface of the earth—

7   the LORD God formed man from the dust of the earth.[1] He blew into his nostrils the breath of life, and man became a living being.

8   The LORD God planted a garden in Eden, in the east, and placed there the man whom He had formed.

9   And from the ground the LORD God caused to grow every tree that was pleasing to the sight and good for food, with the tree of life in the middle of the garden, and the tree of knowledge of good and bad.

10   A river issues from Eden to water the garden, and it then divides and becomes four branches.

11   The name of the first is Pishon, the one that winds through the whole land of Havilah, where the gold is.

12   (The gold of that land is good; bdellium[2] is there, and lapis lazuli.)[3]

13   The name of the second river is Gihon, the one that winds through the whole land of Cush.

14   The name of the third river is Tigris, the one that flows east of Asshur. And the fourth river is the Euphrates.[4]

15   The LORD God took the man and placed him in the garden of Eden, to till it and tend it.

16   And the LORD God commanded the man, saying, "Of every tree of the garden you are free to eat;

17   but as for the tree of knowledge of good and bad, you must not eat of it; for as soon as you eat of it, you shall die."

18   The LORD God said, "It is not good for man to be alone; I will make a fitting helper for him."

19   And the LORD God formed out of the earth all the wild beasts and all the birds of the sky, and brought them to the man to see what

Literary Analysis
Archetypal Setting
Why do you think the Bible suggests a garden as the ideal setting for human beings?

▼ **Critical Viewing**
What moment from Genesis is depicted in the painting shown here? **[Analyze]**

---

1. **the Lord God . . . earth** The name Adam is said to come from the Hebrew word *'adhāmāh*, meaning "earth."

2. **bdellium** (del' ē əm) deep red gem.

3. **lapis lazuli** (lap' is laz' yoo lē) sky-blue semiprecious stone.

4. **Asshur . . . Euphrates** (yoo frāt' ēz) Asshur was the capital city of Assyria, an ancient empire in southwestern Asia; the Euphrates River flows from East Central Turkey southward through Syria and Iraq.

he would call them; and whatever the man called each living creature, that would be its name.

20   And the man gave names to all the cattle and to the birds of the sky and to all the wild beasts; but for Adam no fitting helper was found.

21   So the LORD God cast a deep sleep upon the man; and, while he slept, He took one of his ribs and closed up the flesh at that spot.

22   And the LORD God fashioned the rib that He had taken from the man into a woman; and He brought her to the man.

23   Then the man said,
"This one at last
Is bone of my bones
And flesh of my flesh.
This one shall be called Woman,
For from man was she taken."

24   Hence a man leaves his father and mother and clings to his wife, so that they become one flesh.

CHAPTER 3

The two of them were naked, the man and his wife, yet they felt no shame.

1   Now the serpent was the <u>shrewdest</u> of all the wild beasts that the LORD God had made. He said to the woman, "Did God really say: You shall not eat of any tree of the garden?"

2   The woman replied to the serpent, "We may eat of the fruit of the other trees of the garden.

3   It is only about fruit of the tree in the middle of the garden that God said: 'You shall not eat of it or touch it, lest you die.'"

4   And the serpent said to the woman, "You are not going to die,

5   but God knows that as soon as you eat of it your eyes will be opened and you will be like divine beings who know good and bad."

6   When the woman saw that the tree was good for eating and a delight to the eyes, and that the tree was desirable as a source of wisdom, she took of its fruit and ate. She also gave some to her husband, and he ate.

7   Then the eyes of both of them were opened and they perceived that they were naked; and they sewed together fig leaves and made themselves loincloths.

8   They heard the sound of the LORD God moving about in the garden at the breezy time of day; and the man and his wife hid from the LORD God among the trees of the garden.

9   The LORD God called out to the man and said to him, "Where are you?"

shrewdest (shrōōd′ est) *adj.* most cunning or clever

☑ **Reading Check**

From what tree does God forbid Adam to eat?

The Creation of Adam, Michelangelo, Scala

◀ **Critical Viewing**
Which details in this tapestry illustrate the intense emotions at the end of Genesis, Chapter 3? **[Interpret]**

10   He replied, "I heard the sound of You in the garden, and I was afraid because I was naked, so I hid."

11   Then He asked, "Who told you that you were naked? Did you eat of the tree from which I had forbidden you to eat?"

12   The man said, "The woman You put at my side—she gave me of the tree, and I ate."

13   And the LORD God said to the woman, "What is this you have done!" The woman replied, "The serpent <u>duped</u> me, and I ate."

14   Then the LORD God said to the serpent,
    "Because you did this,
    More cursed shall you be
    Than all cattle
    And all the wild beasts:
    On your belly shall you crawl
    And dirt shall you eat
    All the days of your life.

15   I will put <u>enmity</u>
    Between you and the woman,
    And between your offspring and hers;
    They shall strike at your head,
    And you shall strike at their heel."

16   And to the woman He said,
    "I will make most severe
    Your pangs in childbearing;
    In pain shall you bear children.
    Yet your urge shall be for your husband,
    And he shall rule over you."

17   To Adam He said, "Because you did as your wife said and ate of the tree about which I commanded you, 'You shall not eat of it,'
    Cursed be the ground because of you;

duped (do͞opt) *v.* tricked; fooled

enmity (en′ mə tē) *n.* state of being enemies; antagonism; hostility

By toil shall you eat of it
All the days of your life:

18 Thorns and thistles shall it sprout for you.
But your food shall be the grasses of the field;

19 By the sweat of your brow
Shall you get bread to eat,
Until you return to the ground—
For from it you were taken.
For dust you are,
And to dust you shall return."

20 The man named his wife Eve, because she was the mother of all the living.

21 And the LORD God made garments of skins for Adam and his wife, and clothed them.

22 And the LORD God said, "Now that the man has become like one of us, knowing good and bad, what if he should stretch out his hand and take also from the tree of life and eat, and live forever!"

23 So the LORD God banished him from the garden of Eden, to till the soil from which he was taken.

24 He drove the man out, and stationed east of the garden of Eden the cherubim and the fiery ever-turning sword, to guard the way to the tree of life.

Review and Assess

Thinking About the Selection

1. **Respond:** In what ways did you find this account of the Creation and the Fall interesting?

2. **(a) Recall:** What is the first thing God creates? **(b) Interpret:** What meanings does the first chapter of Genesis seem to give to light and darkness?

3. **(a) Recall:** What does God command human beings to do on the sixth day? **(b) Draw Conclusions:** Why is it significant that man is created in God's image?

4. **(a) Recall:** Find four places where God names things. **(b) Connect:** How does the act of naming seem related to the act of creation? **(c) Compare and Contrast:** What does Adam's naming of the animals reveal about him?

5. **(a) Interpret:** Explain two ways in which Adam and Eve change after they eat the forbidden fruit. **(b) Evaluate:** By the end of Chapter 3, are Adam and Eve more human than they were when they were first created? Explain.

6. **Apply:** What common problems of human existence does this section of Genesis help explain?

Genesis 6-9
The Story of the Flood

translated by
THE JEWISH PUBLICATION SOCIETY

Background

In Genesis 1–3, God creates the heavens, the earth, and Adam and Eve, who serve as the parents of humanity. Throughout the generations, God maintains a deep concern about humankind and their earthly doings. He establishes a covenant, or solemn agreement, with humans as a way to protect those who remain faithful and loyal to him. When he finds them threatening this sacred covenant, God appoints one man, Noah, to act as a mediator between God and his people. Will God exact a punishment on those who have violated his covenant? What purpose will Noah have in protecting not only the Hebrew people but also the viability of humanity? Find the answers to these questions in Genesis 6–9.

CHAPTER 6

1   When men began to increase on earth and daughters were born to them,

2   the divine beings saw how beautiful the daughters of men were and took wives from among those that pleased them.—

3   The Lord said, "My breath shall not abide in man forever, since he too is flesh; let the days allowed him be one hundred and twenty years."—

4   It was then, and later too, that the Nephilim appeared on earth—when the divine beings cohabited with the daughters of men, who bore them offspring. They were the heroes of old, the men of renown.

5   The Lord saw how great was man's wickedness on earth, and how every plan devised by his mind was nothing but evil all the time.

Reading Strategy
Identifying Chronological Order Which words in verse 4 help clarify the order of events?

6   And the Lord regretted that He had made man on earth, and His heart was saddened.

7   The Lord said, "I will blot out from the earth the men whom I created—men together with beasts, creeping things, and birds of the sky; for I regret that I made them."

8   But Noah found favor with the Lord.

9   This is the line of Noah.—Noah was a righteous man; he was blameless in his age; Noah walked with God.—

10   Noah begot three sons: Shem, Ham, and Japheth.

11   The earth became <u>corrupt</u> before God; the earth was filled with lawlessness.

corrupt (kə rupt′) *adj.* spoiled by sin or dishonesty; rotten

12   When God saw how corrupt the earth was, for all flesh had corrupted its ways on earth,

13   God said to Noah, "I have decided to put an end to all flesh, for the earth is filled with lawlessness because of them: I am about to destroy them with the earth.

14   Make yourself an ark of gopher wood; make it an ark with compartments, and cover it inside and out with pitch.

15   This is how you shall make it: the length of the ark shall be three hundred cubits,[1] its width fifty cubits, and its height thirty cubits.

16   Make an opening for daylight in the ark, and terminate it within a cubit of the top. Put the entrance to the ark in its side; make it with bottom, second, and third decks.

Literary Analysis
Archetypal Setting and Dialogue Which precise details in God's instructions help readers picture the ark?

17   "For My part, I am about to bring the Flood—waters upon the earth—to destroy all flesh under the sky in which there is breath of life; everything on earth shall perish.

18   But I will establish My <u>covenant</u> with you, and you shall enter the ark, with your sons, your wife, and your sons' wives.

covenant (kuv′ ə nənt) *n.* serious, binding agreement

19   And of all that lives, of all flesh, you shall take two of each into the ark to keep alive with you; they shall be male and female.

20   From birds of every kind, cattle of every kind, every kind of creeping thing on earth, two of each shall come to you to stay alive.

21   For your part, take of everything that is eaten and store it away, to serve as food for you and for them."

22   Noah did so; just as God commanded him, so he did.

CHAPTER 7

1   Then the Lord said to Noah, "Go into the ark, with all your household, for you alone have I found righteous before Me in this generation.

2   Of every clean animal you shall take seven pairs, males and their mates, and of every animal that is not clean, two, a male and its mate;

3   of the birds of the sky also, seven pairs, male and female, to keep seed alive upon all the earth.

✔**Reading Check**
What reason does God give for putting an end to all living things on earth?

---

1. **cubits** ancient units of linear measure, about 18–22 inches each.

4   For in seven days' time I will make it rain upon the earth, forty days and forty nights, and I will blot out from the earth all existence that I created."

5   And Noah did just as the Lord commanded him.

6   Noah was six hundred years old when the Flood came, waters upon the earth.

7   Noah, with his sons, his wife, and his sons' wives, went into the ark because of the waters of the Flood.

8   Of the clean animals, of the animals that are not clean, of the birds, and of everything that creeps on the ground,

9   two of each, male and female, came to Noah into the ark, as God had commanded Noah.

10   And on the seventh day the waters of the Flood came upon the earth.

11   In the six hundredth year of Noah's life, in the second month, on the seventeenth day of the month, on that day.

All the fountains of the great deep burst apart,
And the floodgates of the sky broke open.

12   (The rain fell on the earth forty days and forty nights.)

13   That same day Noah and Noah's sons, Shem, Ham, and Japheth, went into the ark, with Noah's wife and the three wives of his sons—

14   they and all beasts of every kind, all cattle of every kind, all creatures of every kind that creep on the earth, and all birds of every kind, every bird, every winged thing.

15   They came to Noah into the ark, two each of all flesh in which there was breath of life.

16   Thus they that entered <u>comprised</u> male and female of all flesh, and God had commanded him. And the Lord shut him in.

17   The Flood continued forty days on the earth, and the waters increased and raised the ark so that it rose above the earth.

18   The waters swelled and increased greatly upon the earth, and the ark drifted upon the waters.

19   When the waters had swelled much more upon the earth, all the highest mountains everywhere under the sky were covered.

20   Fifteen cubits higher did the waters swell, as the mountains were covered.

21   And all flesh that stirred on earth perished—birds, cattle, beasts, and all the things that swarmed upon the earth, and all man-kind.

22   All in whose nostrils was the merest breath of life, all that was on dry land, died.

23   All existence on earth was blotted out—man, cattle, creeping things, and birds of the sky; they were blotted out from the earth. Only Noah was left, and those with him in the ark.

Reading Strategy
Identifying Chronological Order Which precise details help readers pin-point when the Flood took place and when Noah entered the ark?

comprised (kəm prīzd´) v. included; consisted of

CHAPTER 8

And when the waters had swelled on the earth one hundred and fifty days,

1   God remembered Noah and all the beasts and all the cattle that were with him in the ark, and God caused a wind to blow across the earth, and the waters subsided.

2   The fountains of the deep and the floodgates of the sky were stopped up, and the rain from the sky was held back;

3   the waters then receded steadily from the earth. At the end of one hundred and fifty days the waters diminished,

4   so that in the seventh month, on the seventeenth day of the month, the ark came to rest on the mountains of Ararat.

5   The waters went on diminishing until the tenth month; in the tenth month, on the first of the month, the tops of the mountains became visible.

6   At the end of forty days, Noah opened the window of the ark that he had made

7   and sent out the raven; it went to and fro until the waters had dried up from the earth.

8   Then he sent out the dove to see whether the waters had decreased from the surface of the ground.

9   But the dove could not find a resting place for its foot, and returned to him to the ark, for there was water over all the earth. So putting out his hand, he took it into the ark with him.

10   He waited another seven days, and again sent out the dove from the ark.

11   The dove came back to him toward evening, and there in its bill was a plucked-off olive leaf! Then Noah knew that the waters had decreased on the earth.

12   He waited still another seven days and sent the dove forth; and it did not return to him any more.

13   In the six hundred and first year, in the first month, on the first of the month, the waters began to dry from the earth; and when Noah removed the covering of the ark, he saw that the surface of the ground was drying.

▲ Critical Viewing
Compare and contrast the details in this image to the events in Genesis, Chapter 8. **[Compare and Contrast]**

✔Reading Check
What causes the flood waters to subside?

14   And in the second month, on the twenty-seventh day of the month, the earth was dry.

15   God spoke to Noah, saying,

16   "Come out of the ark, together with your wife, your sons, and your sons' wives.

17   Bring out with you every living thing of all flesh that is with you: birds, animals, and everything that creeps on earth; and let them swarm on the earth and be fertile and increase on earth."

18   So Noah came out, together with his sons, his wife, and his sons' wives.

19   Every animal, every creeping thing, and every bird, everything that stirs on earth came out of the ark by families.

20   Then Noah built an altar to the LORD and, taking of every clean animal and of every clean bird, he offered burnt offerings on the altar.

21   The LORD smelled the pleasing odor, and the LORD said to Himself: "Never again will I doom the earth because of man, since the devisings of man's mind are evil from his youth; nor will I ever again destroy every living being, as I have done.

22   So long as the earth
           endures,
     Seedtime and harvest,
     Cold and heat,
     Summer and winter,
     Day and night
     Shall not cease."

Reading Strategy
Identifying Chronological Order In chronological order, list three significant events that occur at the end of the forty-day flood.

▼ **Critical Viewing**
Which details in the scene depicted here convey a sense of urgency? [Interpret]

Noah's Ark, Aaron Douglas, Fisk University Fine Art Galleries, Nashville, Tennessee

CHAPTER 9

1 God blessed Noah and his sons, and said to them, "Be fertile and increase, and fill the earth.

2 The fear and the dread of you shall be upon all the beasts of the earth and upon all the birds of the sky—everything with which the earth is astir—and upon all the fish of the sea; they are given into your hand.

3 Every creature that lives shall be yours to eat; as with the green grasses, I give you all these.

4 You must not, however, eat flesh with its life-blood in it.

5 But for your own life-blood I will require a reckoning: I will require it of every beast; of man, too, will I require a reckoning for human life, of every man for that of his fellow man!

6 Whoever sheds the blood of man,
By man shall his blood be shed;
For in His image.
Did God make man.

7 Be fertile, then, and increase; abound on the earth and increase on it."

8 And God said to Noah and to his sons with him,

9 "I now establish My covenant with you and your offspring to come,

10 and with every living thing that is with you—birds, cattle, and every wild beast as well—all that have come out of the ark, every living thing on earth.

11 I will maintain My covenant with you: never again shall all flesh be cut off by the waters of a flood, and never again shall there be a flood to destroy the earth."

12 God further said, "This is the sign that I set for the covenant between Me and you, and every living creature with you, for all ages to come.

13 I have set My bow in the clouds, and it shall serve as a sign of the covenant between Me and the earth.

14 When I bring clouds over the earth, and the bow appears in the clouds,

15 I will remember My covenant between Me and you and every creature among all flesh, so that the waters shall never again become a flood to destroy all flesh.

16 When the bow is in the clouds, I will see it and remember the everlasting covenant between God and all living creatures, all flesh that is on earth.

17 "That," God said to Noah, "shall be the sign of the covenant that I have established between Me and all flesh that is on earth."

18 The sons of Noah who came out of the ark were Shem, Ham, and Japheth—Ham being the father of Canaan.

19 These three were the sons of Noah, and from these the whole world branched out.

Literary Analysis
Archetypal Setting and Dialogue Where will God place a sign of His covenant?

✔**Reading Check**

What covenant does God establish with Noah and all living creatures?

20   Noah, the tiller of the soil, was the first to plant a vineyard.

21   He drank of the wine and became drunk, and he uncovered himself within his tent.

22   Ham, the father of Canaan, saw his father's nakedness and told his two brothers outside.

23   But Shem and Japheth took a cloth, placed it against both their backs and, walking backward, they covered their father's nakedness; their faces were turned the other way, so that they did not see their father's nakedness.

24   When Noah woke up from his wine and learned what his youngest son had done to him,

25   he said,
"Cursed be Canaan;
The lowest of slaves
Shall he be to his brothers."

26   And he said,
"Blessed be the LORD,
The God of Shem;
Let Canaan be a slave to them.

27   May God enlarge Japheth,
And let him dwell in the tents of Shem;
And let Canaan be a slave to them."

28   Noah lived after the Flood 350 years.

29   And all the days of Noah came to 950 years; then he died.

Review and Assess
Thinking About the Selection

1. **Respond:** Why do you think the story of Noah has such universal and timeless appeal?

2. **(a) Recall:** What reason does God give for destroying humanity? **(b) Compare and Contrast:** How is his reaction here both similar to and different from his earlier reaction to Adam and Eve?

3. **(a) Recall:** What covenant, or pact, does God make after the Flood? **(b) Analyze Cause and Effect:** How does Noah's behavior help prompt this covenant?

4. **(a) Compare and Contrast:** In what ways is Noah different from the rest of humanity in his day? **(b) Speculate:** In addition to Noah's virtues, what reason might God have for sparing Noah and his family?

5. **(a) Draw Conclusions:** What main moral lesson might readers draw from the story of the Flood? **(b) Support:** Cite details to support your conclusion.

6. **Synthesize:** What emotions do you think Noah and his family might have felt during the Flood? Why?

Review and Assess

Literary Analysis

Archetypal Setting

1. (a) Which details in these sections of the Bible reveal the **archetypal setting** of a universe consisting of opposites? (b) What other important opposites appear in the first three chapters of Genesis?

2. What evidence is there that the tree from which Eve eats an apple is an archetypal world-tree, or a link between the human and divine realms?

3. (a) Which adjectives would you use to describe the archetypal event of the Flood? (b) What does the setting of the Flood have in common with the setting of the Creation?

Connecting Literary Elements

4. (a) What is the first example of **dialogue** in Genesis 1? (b) How does this statement alter the archetypal setting? (c) What do you think this much-quoted statement has come to signify?

5. In the exchange between Eve and the serpent, how does the serpent demonstrate that he is a master of psychology?

6. (a) In a chart like the one shown, note the opposites that appear in the words God speaks in Genesis 8:22. (b) In general, what is God talking about in this section?

List of Opposites	

Reading Strategy

Identifying Chronological Order

7. (a) Make a list that **identifies in chronological order** what God does on each of the seven days of the Creation. (b) What significance does the seventh day continue to have for many people?

8. (a) During the Flood, how long does the rain last? (b) How long does the water swell? (c) In chronological order, explain how Noah uses birds to check on the flood waters.

Extend Understanding

9. **Science Connection:** What knowledge of the natural world is displayed in these chapters from Genesis?

Integrate Language Skills

Vocabulary Development Lesson

Word Analysis: Latin Prefix com-

The word *comprised* contains the Latin prefix *com-*, which means "with" or "together," and the root *-pris-*, which means "caught; held." *Comprised* means "included" or "consisted of." Define the following words.

1. compress
2. compare
3. combine
4. comprehend

Spelling Strategy

The *oy* sound is usually spelled *oi* or *oy*: *void, toy*. Complete each word below with the correct spelling of the *oy* sound.

1. t_?_l
2. b_?_hood
3. _?_ly
4. destr_?_ed
5. av_?_d
6. _?_ster
7. dec_?_
8. m_?_sture

Fluency: Sentence Completions

Fill in each blank below with the appropriate words from the vocabulary list on page 43.

Before the Creation, there was nothing but the black ___?___ of space. God set the sun, moon, and stars in the vast ___?___ of sky. Beneath the sky, Earth ___?___ land and water. Here Adam and Eve dwelled in the Garden of Eden until the serpent, who was the ___?___ of animals, ___?___ Eve into eating the forbidden fruit. Since then, there has been ___?___ and fear between serpents and human beings. When humanity became more ___?___, God destroyed everyone but Noah and his family in a great flood. With Noah, God made a pact, or ___?___, promising not to destroy the whole earth ever again.

Grammar and Style Lesson

Punctuation in Dialogue

In dialogue, a speaker's exact words are placed within opening (") and closing (") **quotation marks.** A period or a comma goes inside the closing quotation mark. A question mark or exclamation point goes inside only if it is the end punctuation of the quotation itself; otherwise, it goes outside.

God said, "Let there be light."

"You are not going to die," the serpent told Eve.

"Did you eat of the forbidden tree?" God asked.

Who said, "Let there be light"?

Practice Copy these sentences, adding the necessary quotation marks.

1. Be fertile and increase, God told the first human beings. Fill the earth and master it.
2. God asked Adam, Where are you?
3. Was it Adam who said, I was naked and so I hid from You?
4. After that God exclaimed, What is this you have done!
5. The serpent duped me, and I ate, Eve explained.

Writing Application Write a brief dialogue to show what Noah and his wife might have said during the Flood. Use correct punctuation.

*W*G *Prentice Hall Writing and Grammar Connection: Diamond Level: Chapter 27, Section 4*

Writing Lesson

Extended Definition

Suppose that you had to define the meaning of paradise to someone unfamiliar with this archetypal setting. Using the descriptions of Eden in Genesis 2–3, write an extended definition of paradise.

Prewriting	In a sentence, formulate a general definition of paradise, and then list more specific qualities based on the details in Genesis. For each detail, note the verse where you will gather support: *No death (see 3:19–23)* or *Humans can talk with animals (see 3:1–5)*.
Drafting	Begin with your general definition. Then, create an extended definition by explaining the qualities you listed and providing details from Genesis that illustrate each quality.
Revising	Review your draft, underlining each main quality you cite and placing a check mark beside each supporting detail. If there are not enough details, go back to the text to find additional examples.

Model: Revising to Add Examples

One important asset is the ready availability of food.

Eden is a paradise where life is easy.∧Adam need not

toil to survive, as he must after his exile.

> Additional details from the text strengthen the explanation.

WG Prentice Hall Writing and Grammar Connection: Diamond Level, Chapter 10, Section 3

Extension Activities

Listening and Speaking With a group, prepare and perform a **choral reading** from Genesis. Choose one of these sections:

- The Creation: Genesis 1 and Genesis 2:1–7
- The Fall: Genesis 2:8–24 and Genesis 3
- The Flood: Genesis 6–7
- After the Flood: Genesis 8–9

Decide whether any passages will be read by individuals. Discuss the appropriate tone and pace for the piece. Rehearse several times before performing for your classmates. **[Group Activity]**

Research and Technology Research and prepare a **written report** on flood stories as they appear in the literature or history of another culture. Use the Internet or your library's electronic sources to search for information. Be sure to identify the sources you use.

 **Take It to the Net** PHSchool.com

Go online for an additional research activity using the Internet.

CONNECTIONS
Literature Past and Present
The Beginning of the World

Explaining the emergence of the world from the chaos of nothingness has been a challenge for every civilization. Explanations vary from culture to culture, but there are remarkable elements of similarity. The Judeo-Christian tradition finds its explanation of creation in the account of the Hebrew Bible. In the excerpt from Genesis in this unit, God creates the heavens and the earth and populates the world with creatures, including man and woman. Later, as humans descend into wickedness, God destroys the evil in a great flood. The just Noah and his family, however, warned by God in time, save themselves and two of every species in an ark that they build—and survive to repopulate the earth.

The Maker, Modeler On the other side of the world, the Quiché Maya people call their God the Maker, Modeler, and their account of creation also includes a destruction by flood. "The Wooden People" describes a sort of rough draft of human beings—creatures made of wood who are not competent and do not speak. Overthrown and destroyed, they are left as a sign in a form that may surprise you.

Critical Viewing ▶
In what ways does this stone sculpture of a serpent's head suggest the power of ancient beliefs? [Interpret]

from *Popol Vuh*

The Wooden People

A QUICHÉ MAYAN MYTH

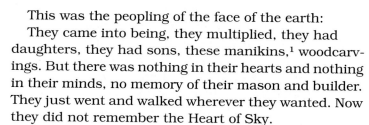

This was the peopling of the face of the earth:

They came into being, they multiplied, they had daughters, they had sons, these manikins,[1] woodcarvings. But there was nothing in their hearts and nothing in their minds, no memory of their mason and builder. They just went and walked wherever they wanted. Now they did not remember the Heart of Sky.

And so they fell, just an experiment and just a cutout for humankind. They were talking at first but their faces were dry. They were not yet developed in the legs and arms. They had no blood, no lymph. They had no sweat, no fat. Their complexions were dry, their faces were crusty. They flailed their legs and arms, their bodies were deformed.

And so they accomplished nothing before the Maker, Modeler who gave them birth, gave them heart. They became the first numerous people here on the face of the earth.

---

1. **manikin** (man´ i kin) *n.* little man; model.

✔ Reading Check

What was missing from the first people created?

▲ **Critical Viewing** How does this Mayan figure emerging from a water lily relate to the beings described in these paragraphs? [**Connect**]

Again there comes a humiliation, destruction, and demolition. The manikins, woodcarvings were killed when the Heart of Sky devised a flood for them. A great flood was made; it came down on the heads of the manikins, woodcarvings.

The man's body was carved from the wood of the coral tree by the Maker, Modeler. And as for the woman, the Maker, Modeler needed the pith[2] of reeds for the woman's body. They were not competent, nor did they speak before the builder and sculptor who made them and brought them forth, and so they were killed, done in by a flood:

There came a rain of resin from the sky.

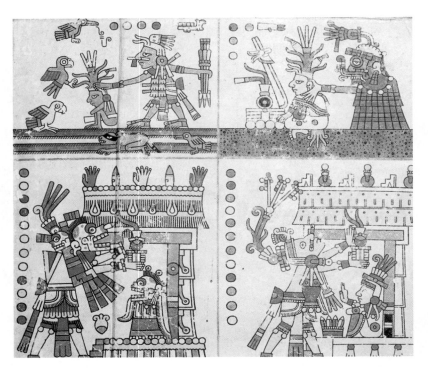

There came the one named Gouger of Faces: he gouged out their eyeballs.

There came Sudden Bloodletter: he snapped off their heads.

There came Crunching Jaguar: he ate their flesh.

There came Tearing Jaguar: he tore them open.

They were pounded down to the bones and tendons, smashed and pulverized even to the bones. Their faces were smashed because they were incompetent before their mother and their father, the Heart of Sky, named Hurricane. The earth was blackened because of this; the black rainstorm began, rain all day and rain all night. Into their houses came the animals, small and great. Their faces were crushed by things of wood and stone. Everything spoke: their water jars, their tortilla griddles, their plates, their cooking pots, their dogs, their grinding stones, each and every thing crushed their faces. Their dogs and turkeys told them:

"You caused us pain, you ate us, but now it is *you* whom *we* shall eat." And this is the grinding stone:

"We were undone because of you.

> Every day, every day,
> In the dark, in the dawn, forever,
> r-r-rip, r-r-rip,
> r-r-rub, r-r-rub,
> right in our faces, because of you.

This was the service we gave you at first, when you were still people, but today you will learn of our power. We shall pound and we shall grind your flesh," their grinding stones told them.

---

2. pith *n.* soft, spongy tissue in the center of certain plant stems.

And this is what their dogs said, when they spoke in their turn:

"Why is it you can't seem to give us our food? We just watch and you just keep us down, and you throw us around. You keep a stick ready when you eat, just so you can hit us. We don't talk, so we've received nothing from you. How could you not have known? You *did* know that we were wasting away there, behind you.

"So, this very day you will taste the teeth in our mouths. We shall eat you," their dogs told them, and their faces were crushed.

And then their tortilla griddles and cooking pots spoke to them in turn:

"Pain! That's all you've done for us. Our mouths are sooty, our faces are sooty. By setting us on the fire all the time, you burn us. Since *we* felt no pain, *you* try it. We shall burn you," all their cooking pots said, crushing their faces.

The stones, their hearthstones were shooting out, coming right out of the fire, going for their heads, causing them pain. Now they run for it, helter-skelter.

They want to climb up on the houses, but they fall as the houses collapse.

They want to climb the trees; they're thrown off by the trees.

They want to get inside caves, but the caves slam shut in their faces.

Such was the scattering of the human work, the human design. The people were ground down, overthrown. The mouths and faces of all of them were destroyed and crushed. And it used to be said that the monkeys in the forests today are a sign of this. They were left as a sign because wood alone was used for their flesh by the builder and sculptor.

So this is why monkeys look like people: they are a sign of a previous human work, human design—mere manikins, mere woodcarvings.

Connecting Literature Past and Present

1. (a) What is the reason for the flood in "The Wooden People"? (b) Why does God destroy by flood in Genesis? (c) Identify the elements that make these floods similar and those that make them different.

2. Compare the accounts of the creation of woman in Genesis and in "The Wooden People." (a) In what ways are the two accounts similar? (b) How are they different?

3. What do these creation stories suggest about the differences between Hebrew and Quiché Maya culture?

The Quiché Maya

The Quiché Maya, an Indian people living in Guatemala, come from a civilization that was politically and socially advanced in pre-Columbian times. *Popol Voh*, which is the record of the history and the mythology of the Quiché Maya, was originally written in hieroglyphics. After the Quiché Maya were conquered by the Spanish in 1524, the *Popol Voh* was written down in the Quiché language using the Latin alphabet. Dennis Tedlock, the award-winning translator of this excerpt from *Popol Voh*, is also a poet and a cultural anthropologist.

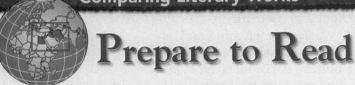

Prepare to Read

from the Bible: Book of Ruth ◆ Psalms 8, 19, 23, and 137

Book of Ruth (400s or 300s B.C.)

The Book of Ruth, in the part of the Hebrew Bible called the Writings, appeared in written form after the Jews returned from their exile in Babylon (597–538 B.C.).

Speaking for the Outsider Ruth, the central character, is not a Jew but displays exceptional loyalty toward her Jewish mother-in-law. The book's purpose, therefore, was to show the worth of an outsider at a time when the Jews, recalling their forced exile, were less willing to accept outsiders.

The Hebrew Short Story The Book of Ruth is also an excellent example of the Hebrew short story. Such a form was something new in the literature of the ancient Middle East. For the most part, such stories dispensed with the obvious magical and fairy-tale elements that characterized other Middle Eastern tales. As this story shows, they might also have had a serious purpose.

A Story That Speaks to Us The Book of Ruth still speaks to us today. Contemporary novelist Cynthia Ozick, for example, sees special meaning in it. In this brief story, she says, "death, loss, displacement, destitution" give rise to "mercy and redemption."

Book of Psalms (c. 900s – c. 400s B.C.)

Like the Book of Ruth, the Book of Psalms (sämz) is in the part of the Hebrew Bible called the Writings. The Book of Psalms, however, is not a short story but a collection of 150 religious poems that were set to music.

A Greek Name for Hebrew Poems The English word *psalms* comes from the Greek *psalmos*, meaning "a song accompanied by a plucked instrument." This Greek word, in turn, is the translation of the Hebrew terms for "song" and "praise." That is how Hebrew religious poems came to be called by an English word derived from Greek!

Many Authors, Different Moods The Hebrew psalms praised a single God, but they did not have a single author. The traditional belief was that King David (reigned c. 1000–962 B.C.) wrote them. In truth, however, the psalms were composed by many authors over a long period of time. They were included as part of religious ceremonies and expressed the different moods inspired by the relationship between God and the Hebrew people. These moods could vary from despair to joy.

Enduring Poems The psalms are among the most influential poems in the Western tradition. They have played a central role in both Christian and Jewish religious ceremonies. They have also influenced poets as diverse as John Milton, Walt Whitman, and Dylan Thomas.

Psalms and Bible Stories in the Oral Tradition

Before it was written down, the Book of Ruth was probably told orally. Just who told it—and where—is a matter for speculation. It may have been told in the small towns that dotted the countryside. Townsfolk might have gathered in the evening at the town spring or gate to hear the story of Ruth and her mother-in-law, Naomi.

The storytellers themselves may have been Levites, members of a Hebrew tribe whose role was to assist with religious ceremonies. An even more interesting possibility is that "wise women" told this tale. Such female storytellers are mentioned in a number of biblical narratives.

In contrast to the mysterious origins of the Book of Ruth, the background on the Psalms is clearer. The psalm is a literary form borrowed by the Jews from the peoples of Mesopotamia and Egypt. When the Jews borrowed this form, however, they made one crucial change. Their Middle Eastern neighbors used psalms to worship many gods, whereas the Jews used them to express emotions arising from their belief in a single God. Despite their differences, both groups of people used psalms as part of their respective religious services.

Preview
Connecting to the Literature
Living among people who view you as an outsider can both pose problems and offer opportunities. The heroine of the Book of Ruth finds herself in just such a situation.

Literary Analysis
Parallelism
Both the Book of Ruth and the Psalms use **parallelism**—a biblical style that involves stating an idea in the first half of a verse and then, using a similar grammatical structure, repeating, negating, completing, or otherwise elaborating on it in the second half.

- completion of an idea (Ruth 2:20): "[T]he man is related to us; he is one of our redeeming kinsmen."
- repetition with variations (Psalms 8:4): *what is man that You have been mindful of him, / mortal man that You have taken note of him …*

Parallelism creates balance, variation, and flowing rhythm in prose and poetry alike. Look for examples of this style as you read.

Comparing Literary Works
Parallelism—especially repetition with variation—can communicate a work's **theme,** or central idea. Ruth's repeated phrases suggest a theme of loyalty: "Wherever you go, I will go; wherever you lodge, I will lodge." In Psalm 23, parallelism underscores the central ideas of guidance and trust: "He leads me to water . . . He renews my life; He guides me. . . ." Look for such themes as you read these selections from the Bible.

Reading Strategy
Using Context Clues
Use context clues, or hints in the surrounding passage, to determine the meanings of unfamiliar words as you read. Common context clues are synonyms, antonyms, and examples that clarify a word's meaning. Use a chart like the one shown to find context clues as you read.

Vocabulary Development
glean (glēn) *v.* collect grain left by reapers (p. 68)

reapers (rē´ pərz) *n.* those who gather a crop by cutting (p. 68)

redeem (ri dēm´) *v.* buy back; fulfill a promise (p. 70)

avenger (ə venj´ ər) *n.* one who takes revenge (p. 73)

precepts (prē´ septs´) *n.* rules of conduct (p. 74)

lucid (lōō´ sid) *adj.* clear; apparent (p. 74)

steadfast (sted´ fast´) *adj.* firm; not changing (p. 74)

Passage

"Day to day makes utterance, night to night speaks out."

↓

Unfamiliar Word

utterance

↓

Context Clue

night to night speaks out

↓

Relation to Unfamiliar Word

synonym

↓

Conclusion

If *makes utterance* means *speaks out,* then *utterance* probably means "speech."

Book of Ruth

translated by **The Jewish Publication Society**

Background

The written version of the Book of Ruth dates from after the Babylonian exile (538 B.C.), but the story it tells is set around 1100 B.C. This era, called in the story "the days when the chieftains ruled," predates by about 100 years King David's reign over a united Israel. In fact, as the story establishes, David was Ruth's great-grandson.

Moab, Ruth's country, was a kingdom east of the Dead Sea. The story explains that Naomi's family fled there to escape a famine, and their reasons for doing so are easy to infer: Moab was near Bethlehem, Naomi's home, and the Moabites were closely linked with the Jews.

CHAPTER 1

1   In the days when the chieftains ruled, there was a famine in the land; and a man of Bethlehem in Judah, with his wife and two sons, went to reside in the country of Moab.[1]

2   The man's name was Elimelech, his wife's name was Naomi, and his two sons were named Mahlon and Chilion—Ephrathites of Bethlehem in Judah.[2]

3   Elimelech, Naomi's husband, died; and she was left with her two sons.

4   They married Moabite women, one named Orpah and the other Ruth, and they lived there about ten years.

5   Then those two—Mahlon and Chilion—also died; so the woman was left without her two sons and without her husband.

6   She started out with her daughters-in-law to return from the country of Moab; for in the country of Moab she had heard that the LORD had taken note of His people and given them food.

---

1. Moab (mō ab´) ancient kingdom east and south of the Dead Sea, and east of the Jordan River.
2. Judah Jewish kingdom in the southern part of Palestine.

7   Accompanied by her two daughters-in-law, she left the place where she had been living; and they set out on the road back to the land of Judah.

8   But Naomi said to her two daughters-in-law, "Turn back, each of you to her mother's house. May the LORD deal kindly with you, as you have dealt with the dead and with me!

9   May the LORD grant that each of you find security in the house of a husband!" And she kissed them farewell. They broke into weeping

10   and said to her, "No, we will return with you to your people."

11   But Naomi replied, "Turn back, my daughters! Why should you go with me? Have I any more sons in my body who might be husbands for you?

12   Turn back, my daughters, for I am too old to be married. Even if I thought there was hope for me, even if I were married tonight and I also bore sons,

13   should you wait for them to grow up? Should you on their account debar yourselves from marriage? Oh no, my daughters! My lot is far more bitter than yours, for the hand of the LORD has struck out against me."

14   They broke into weeping again, and Orpah kissed her mother-in-law farewell. But Ruth clung to her.

15   So she said, "See, your sister-in-law has returned to her people and her gods. Go follow your sister-in-law."

16   But Ruth replied, "Do not urge me to leave you, to turn back and not follow you. For wherever you go, I will go; wherever you lodge, I will lodge; your people shall be my people, and your God my God.

17   Where you die, I will die, and there I will be buried. Thus and more may the LORD do to me[3] if anything but death parts me from you."

18   When [Naomi] saw how determined she was to go with her, she ceased to argue with her;

19   and the two went on until they reached Bethlehem.

When they arrived in Bethlehem, the whole city buzzed with excitement over them. The women said, "Can this be Naomi?"

20   "Do not call me Naomi," she replied. "Call me Mara,[4] for Shaddai[5] has made my lot very bitter.

21   I went away full, and the LORD has brought me back empty. How can you call me Naomi, when the LORD has dealt harshly with me, when Shaddai[5] has brought misfortune upon me!"

22   Thus Naomi returned from the country of Moab; she returned with her daughter-in-law Ruth the Moabite. They arrived in Bethlehem at the beginning of the barley harvest.

Literary Analysis
Parallelism What is an example of parallelism in Ruth 1:16? Explain.

---

3. **do to me** punish me.
4. **Naomi . . . Mara** In Hebrew, Naomi means "my delight" and Mara means "bitter."
5. **Shaddai** usually, "the Almighty."

**Reading Check**

What tragedies befall Naomi and her family in the country of Moab?

CHAPTER 2

1   Now Naomi had a kinsman on her husband's side, a man of substance, of the family of Elimelech, whose name was Boaz.

2   Ruth the Moabite said to Naomi, "I would like to go to the fields and <u>glean</u> among the ears of grain, behind someone who may show me kindness." "Yes, daughter, go," she replied;

3   and off she went. She came and gleaned in a field, behind the <u>reapers</u>; and, as luck would have it, it was the piece of land belonging to Boaz, who was of Elimelech's family.

4   Presently Boaz arrived from Bethlehem. He greeted the reapers, "The LORD be with you" And they responded, "The LORD bless you!"

5   Boaz said to the servant who was in charge of the reapers, "Whose girl is that?"

6   The servant in charge of the reapers replied, "She is a Moabite girl who came back with Naomi from the country of Moab.

7   She said, 'Please let me glean and gather among the sheaves behind the reapers.' She has been on her feet ever since she came this morning. She has rested but little in the hut."

8   Boaz said to Ruth, "Listen to me, daughter. Don't go to glean in another field. Don't go elsewhere, but stay here close to my girls.

9   Keep your eyes on the field they are reaping, and follow them. I have ordered the men not to molest you. And when you are thirsty, go to the jars and drink some of [the water] that the men have drawn."

10   She prostrated herself with her face to the ground, and said to him, "Why are you so kind as to single me out, when I am a foreigner?"

11   Boaz said in reply, "I have been told of all that you did for your mother-in-law after the death of your husband, how you left your father and mother and the land of your birth and came to a people you had not known before.

12   May the LORD reward your deeds. May you have a full recompense from the LORD, the God of Israel, under whose wings you have sought refuge!"

13   She answered, "You are most kind, my lord, to comfort me and to speak gently to your maidservant—though I am not so much as one of your maidservants."

14   At mealtime, Boaz said to her, "Come over here and partake of the meal, and dip your morsel in the vinegar." So she sat down beside

▲ **Critical Viewing**
What verses from Chapter 2 might this painting illustrate? Why? **[Speculate]**

glean (glēn) *v.* collect grain left by reapers

reapers (rē′ pərz) *n.* those who gather a crop by cutting

Reading Strategy
Using Context Clues
Based on the context clues, what does *partake* mean?

the reapers. He handed her roasted grain, and she ate her fill and had some left over.

15   When she got up again to glean, Boaz gave orders to his workers, "You are not only to let her glean among the sheaves, without interference,

16   but you must also pull some [stalks] out of the heaps and leave them for her to glean, and not scold her."

17   She gleaned in the field until evening. Then she beat out what she had gleaned—it was about an *ephah*[6] of barley—

18   and carried it back with her to the town. When her mother-in-law saw what she had gleaned, and when she also took out and gave her what she had left over after eating her fill,

19   her mother-in-law asked her, "Where did you glean today? Where did you work? Blessed be he who took such generous notice of you!" So she told her mother-in-law whom she had worked with, saying, "The name of the man with whom I worked today is Boaz."

20   Naomi said to her daughter-in-law, "Blessed be he of the LORD, who has not failed in His kindness to the living or to the dead! For," Naomi explained to her daughter-in-law, "the man is related to us; he is one of our redeeming kinsmen."

21   Ruth the Moabite said, "He even told me, 'Stay close by my workers until all my harvest is finished.'"

22   And Naomi answered her daughter-in-law Ruth, "It is best, daughter, that you go out with his girls, and not be annoyed in some other field."

23   So she stayed close to the maidservants of Boaz, and gleaned until the barley harvest and the wheat harvest were finished. Then she stayed at home with her mother-in-law.

CHAPTER 3

1   Naomi, her mother-in-law, said to her, "Daughter, I must seek a home for you, where you may be happy.

2   Now there is our kinsman Boaz,[7] whose girls you were close to. He will be winnowing barley on the threshing floor tonight.

3   So bathe, anoint[8] yourself, dress up, and go down to the threshing floor. But do not disclose yourself to the man until he has finished eating and drinking.

4   When he lies down, note the place where he lies down, and go over and uncover his feet and lie down. He will tell you what you are to do."

5   She replied, "I will do everything you tell me."

6   She went down to the threshing floor and did just as her mother-in-law had instructed her.

---

6. **ephah** (ē′ fə) ancient Hebrew unit of dry measure, estimated at from one third of a bushel to a little over one bushel.

7. **our kinsman Boaz** According to Jewish law, the closest unmarried male relative of Ruth's deceased husband was obligated to marry her.

8. **anoint** (ə noint′) v. rub oil or ointment on.

Reading Strategy
Using Context Clues
Which context clues in verse 16 help define the word *sheaves* in verse 15?

Reading Check

What reasons does Boaz give for helping Ruth?

7   Boaz ate and drank, and in a cheerful mood went to lie down beside the grainpile. Then she went over stealthily and uncovered his feet and lay down.

8   In the middle of the night, the man gave a start and pulled back—there was a woman lying at his feet!

9   "Who are you?" he asked. And she replied, "I am your handmaid Ruth. Spread your robe over your handmaid, for you are a redeeming kinsman."

10   He exclaimed, "Be blessed of the LORD, daughter! Your latest deed of loyalty is greater than the first, in that you have not turned to younger men, whether poor or rich.

11   And now, daughter, have no fear. I will do in your behalf whatever you ask, for all the elders of my town know what a fine woman you are.

12   But while it is true I am a redeeming kinsman, there is another redeemer closer than I.

13   Stay for the night. Then in the morning, if he will act as a redeemer, good! let him redeem. But if he does not want to act as redeemer for you, I will do so myself, as the LORD lives! Lie down until morning."

14   So she lay at his feet until dawn. She rose before one person could distinguish another, for he thought, "Let it not be known that the woman came to the threshing floor."

15   And he said, "Hold out the shawl you are wearing." She held it while he measured out six measures of barley, and he put it on her back. When she got back to the town,

16   she came to her mother-in-law, who asked, "How is it with you, daughter?" She told her all that the man had done for her;

17   and she added, "He gave me these six measures of barley, saying to me, 'Do not go back to your mother-in-law empty-handed.'"

18   And Naomi said, "Stay here, daughter, till you learn how the matter turns out. For the man will not rest, but will settle the matter today."

CHAPTER 4

1   Meanwhile, Boaz had gone to the gate and sat down there. And now the redeemer whom Boaz had mentioned passed by. He called, "Come over and sit down here, So-and-so!" And he came over and sat down.

2   Then [Boaz] took ten elders of the town and said, "Be seated here"; and they sat down.

3   He said to the redeemer, "Naomi, now returned from the country of Moab, must sell the piece of land which belonged to our kinsman Elimelech.

4   I thought I should disclose the matter to you and say: Acquire it in the presence of those seated here and in the presence of the elders of my people. If you are willing to redeem it, redeem! But if you will not redeem, tell me, that I may know. For there is no one to redeem but you, and I come after you." "I am willing to redeem it," he replied.

Reading Strategy
Using Context Clues
Which context clues reveal the correct meaning of *start* in Ruth 3:8? Explain.

redeem (ri dēm´) *v.* buy back; fulfill a promise

5 Boaz continued, "When you acquire the property from Naomi and from Ruth the Moabite, you must also acquire the wife of the deceased, so as to perpetuate the name of the deceased upon his estate."

6 The redeemer replied, "Then I cannot redeem it for myself, lest I impair my own estate. You take over my right of redemption, for I am unable to exercise it."

7 Now this was formerly done in Israel in cases of redemption or exchange: to validate any transaction, one man would take off his sandal and hand it to the other. Such was the practice in Israel.

8 So when the redeemer said to Boaz, "Acquire for yourself," he drew off his sandal.

9 And Boaz said to the elders and to the rest of the people, "You are witnesses today that I am acquiring from Naomi all that belonged to Elimelech and all that belonged to Chilion and Mahlon.

10 I am also acquiring Ruth the Moabite, the wife of Mahlon, as my wife, so as to perpetuate the name of the deceased upon his estate, that the name of the deceased may not disappear from among his kinsmen and from the gate of his home town. You are witnesses today."

11 All the people at the gate and the elders answered, "We are. May the LORD make the woman who is coming into your house like Rachel and Leah,[9] both of whom built up the House of Israel! Prosper in Ephrathah and perpetuate your name in Bethlehem!

12 And may your house be like the house of Perez whom Tamar bore to Judah[10] — through the offspring which the LORD will give you by this young woman."

13 So Boaz married Ruth; she became his wife, and he cohabited with her. The LORD let her conceive, and she bore a son.

14 And the women said to Naomi, "Blessed be the LORD, who has not withheld a redeemer from you today! May his name be perpetuated in Israel!

15 He will renew your life and sustain your old age; for he is born of your daughter-in-law, who loves you and is better to you than seven sons."

16 Naomi took the child and held it to her bosom. She became its foster mother,

---

9. **Rachel . . . Leah** wives of Jacob, whose sons, along with those of their handmaids Bilhah and Zilpha, became the founders of the twelve tribes of Israel.
10. **Perez . . . Judah** Ruth, like Tamar, was a childless widow who conceived a son with her husband's kinsman.

Literature
in context Cultural Connection

Jewish Marriage Customs in Biblical Times

According to Jewish customs of Ruth's day, specific rules applied to her situation. As a widow without a son, she could expect her deceased husband's closest male relative to marry her. Also, the first son of the new marriage would be considered the deceased man's heir. This custom provided the widow with a man who could support her. It also gave the first husband an heir who could inherit family property and take on family obligations. One of those obligations would be saying mourning prayers for the first husband.

A document that spells out Jewish marriage customs in legal form is a ketubba (k' too´ bə), or Jewish marriage contract. The ketubba shown here is recent, but the use of such documents dates back to ancient times. One purpose of the ketubba is to safeguard a woman's right to property if her husband dies.

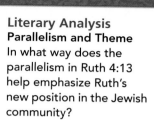

Literary Analysis
Parallelism and Theme
In what way does the parallelism in Ruth 4:13 help emphasize Ruth's new position in the Jewish community?

✔**Reading Check**

In what two ways does Boaz fulfill his obligations to his kinsman Elimelech?

17   and the women neighbors gave him a name, saying, "A son is born to Naomi!" They named him Obed; he was the father of Jesse, father of David.

18   This is the line of Perez: Perez begot Hezron,

19   Hezron begot Ram, Ram begot Amminadab,

20   Amminadab begot Nahshon, Nahshon begot Salmon,

21   Salmon begot Boaz, Boaz begot Obed,

22   Obed begot Jesse, and Jesse begot David.

Review and Assess

Thinking About the Selection

1. **Respond:** Do you think Ruth behaved heroically? Why or why not?

2. **(a) Recall:** What happens to Naomi's family during the time they live in Moab? **(b) Infer:** How do these events affect Naomi's attitude toward life?

3. **(a) Recall:** What decisions do Orpah and Ruth make about traveling to Judah with Naomi? **(b) Analyze Cause and Effect:** What motivates Ruth's decision?

4. **(a) Recall:** What reason does Boaz give for welcoming Ruth? **(b) Analyze Cause and Effect:** How might Boaz have learned about Ruth?

5. **(a) Recall:** In what way does Ruth respond to Naomi's instructions in Ruth 3:1–4? **(b) Infer:** What does Ruth's response reveal about her?

6. **(a) Recall:** What does Boaz do when he finds Ruth in his tent? **(b) Assess:** Is Boaz an honorable man? Why or why not?

7. **(a) Recall:** What status does Ruth achieve in Ruth 4:10–15? **(b) Connect:** How has her status changed from what it was in Ruth 1:5? **(c) Infer:** In what way does Naomi's action in Ruth 4:16 suggest that her attitude toward life has changed?

8. **Analyze:** What is significant about Ruth's relationship to David, one of Israel's greatest kings?

9. **Interpret:** In what way is God, who does not appear directly in the story, present throughout the story?

10. **Evaluate:** Does this story teach an effective lesson against prejudice? Why or why not?

The Psalms

translated by
The Jewish Publication Society

Background

The ancient Hebrew instrument that may have accompanied the Psalms was called a kinnor. It had from three to twelve strings, which a musician could pluck with his or her fingers or with a thin piece of metal or bone.

The "lyre" to which Psalm 137 refers is probably a kinnor. The bitterness in this Psalm, expressed as an unwillingness to play the lyre, arises from the time when the Jews were held captive in Babylon (597–538 B.C.).

PSALM 8

1 O LORD, our Lord, How majestic is Your name throughout the earth, You who have covered the heavens with Your splendor!

2 From the mouths of infants and sucklings
You have founded strength on account of Your foes, to put an end to enemy and <u>avenger</u>.

3 When I behold Your heavens, the work of Your fingers, the moon and stars that You set in place,

4 what is man that You have been mindful of him, mortal man that You have taken note of him,

5 that You have made him little less than divine, and adorned him with glory and majesty;

6 You have made him master over Your handiwork, laying the world at his feet,

7 sheep and oxen, all of them, and wild beasts, too;

8 the birds of the heavens, the fish of the sea, whatever travels the paths of the seas.

9 O LORD, our Lord, how majestic is Your name throughout the earth!

avenger (ə venj´ ər) *n.* one who takes revenge

Reading Strategy
Using Context Clues
Based on context clues in Psalm 8, what is the meaning of the word *handiwork*? Explain.

✔**Reading Check**

According to Psalm 8, what power has God granted to humans?

PSALM 19

1 The heavens declare the glory of God, the sky proclaims His handiwork.

2 Day to day makes utterance, night to night speaks out.

3 There is no utterance, there are no words, whose sound goes unheard.

4 Their voice carries throughout the earth, their words to the end of the world. He placed in them a tent for the sun,

5 who is like a groom coming forth from the chamber, like a hero, eager to run his course.

6 His rising-place is at one end of heaven, and his circuit reaches the other; nothing escapes his heat.

7 The teaching of the LORD is perfect, renewing life; the decrees of the LORD are enduring, making the simple wise;

8 The <u>precepts</u> of the LORD are just, rejoicing the heart; the instruction of the LORD is <u>lucid</u>, making the eyes light up.

9 The fear of the LORD is pure, abiding forever; the judgments of the LORD are true, righteous altogether,

10 more desirable than gold, than much fine gold;

11 sweeter than honey, than drippings of the comb. Your servant pays them heed; in obeying them there is much reward.

12 Who can be aware of errors? Clear me of unperceived guilt,

13 and from willful sins keep Your servant; let them not dominate me; then shall I be blameless and clear of grave offense.

14 May the words of my mouth and the prayer of my heart be acceptable to You, O LORD, my rock and my redeemer.

*   *   *

PSALM 23

1 The LORD is my shepherd; I lack nothing.

2 He makes me lie down in green pastures; He leads me to water in places of repose;

3 He renews my life; He guides me in right paths as befits His name.

4 Though I walk through a valley of deepest darkness; I fear no harm, for You are with me; Your rod and Your staff—they comfort me.

5 You spread a table for me in full view of my enemies; You anoint my head with oil;
my drink is abundant.

6 Only goodness and <u>steadfast</u> love shall pursue me all the days of my life, and I shall dwell in the house of the LORD for many long years.

David Composing the Psalms, from the Paris Psalter, 10th century, Photo Bibliothèque Nationale, Paris

▲ **Critical Viewing**   This illustration shows David composing psalms. What qualities of
the psalms do the details in the image suggest? **[Interpret]**

PSALM 137

1 By the rivers Babylon, there we sat, sat and wept, as we thought of Zion.

2 There on the poplars we hung up our lyres,

3 for our captors asked us there for songs, our tormentors, for amusement, "Sing us one of the songs of Zion."

4 How can we sing a song of the LORD on alien soil?

5 If I forget you, O Jerusalem, let my right hand wither;

6 let my tongue stick to my palate if I cease to think of you, if I do not keep Jerusalem in memory even at my happiest hour.

7 Remember, O LORD, against the Edomites[1] the day of Jerusalem's fall; how they cried, "Strip her, strip her to her very foundations!"

8 Fair Babylon, you predator, a blessing on him who repays you in kind what you have inflicted on us;

9 a blessing on him who seizes your babies and dashes them against the rocks!

---

1. **Edomites** (ē′ dəm ĭtz) the people of Edom, an ancient kingdom in southwest Asia, south of the Dead Sea and east of the Jordan River.

Review and Assess

Thinking About the Selections

1. **Respond:** Which of these psalms might you find most comforting in a time of crisis? Why?

2. **(a) Recall:** What does Psalm 8: 6–7 say about "mortal man"? **(b) Interpret:** According to Psalm 8, what role do human beings play in the universe?

3. **(a) Recall:** According to Psalm 19, what do the heavens declare and the sky proclaim? **(b) Interpret:** What achievement of God do verses 2–6 celebrate? **(c) Generalize:** What aspect of God do verses 7–15 praise?

4. **(a) Recall:** To what does the first line of Psalm 23 compare God? **(b) Infer:** Given this comparison, to what can the believer be compared? Explain. **(c) Analyze:** What do these comparisons convey about the relationship between God and human beings?

5. **(a) Connect:** In what way are verses 5–9 of Psalm 137 an answer to the command in verse 3? **(b) Analyze:** What is ironic or unexpected about this answer? **(c) Interpret:** In what way are verses 5–9 also an answer to the question in verse 4?

6. **Apply:** Why do you think songs or poetry—like Psalm 137—are especially valuable to people in exile or captivity? Explain.

Review and Assess

Literary Analysis

Parallelism

1. In a chart like the one shown, identify an example of each type of **parallelism** from the Book of Ruth or the Book of Psalms. Then, explain your choice.

Type of Parallelism	Example	Explanation
repetition with variation		
completion of an idea		
elaboration of an idea		

2. Is the effect of the parallelism in Psalm 19:1–4 mainly to repeat ideas with variation, to complete ideas, or to elaborate on them? Explain.
3. Psalms were composed to be sung. How might parallelism make it easier to perform them aloud?

Comparing Literary Works

4. Review the parallelism in Ruth 4:9–12. In what ways does this parallelism emphasize the **theme** of making an outsider part of the community?
5. (a) What theme do you think the speaker expresses in Psalm 8? (b) Which words or phrases support this theme?

Reading Strategy

Using Context Clues

6. (a) Using the context clues in Ruth 1:11–13, what does *lot* seem to mean? (b) Based on clues in this passage, what do you think *debar* means?
7. What word in these Psalms was unfamiliar to you? Explain how context clues helped you determine its meaning.
8. Which context clues in Psalm 137 might help readers define the meaning of the word *palate*? Explain.

Extend Understanding

9. **Music Link:** Which of these Psalms do you think would work best set to music? Explain.

Integrate Language Skills

Vocabulary Development Lesson

Word Analysis: Anglo-Saxon Root -stead-

The word *steadfast*, which appears in Psalm 23, contains the Anglo-Saxon root *-stead-*, meaning "place." *Steadfast* love is love that stays fixed in one place, or love that endures. Using the meaning of this word root, define each of the following words:

1. steady   2. instead   3. bedstead

Spelling Strategy

The sound of long *e* is often spelled *ea* or *ee*, as in *glean* or *redeeming*. It is sometimes spelled *e*, as in the first syllable of *precepts*.

Complete each word below with the correct spelling of the long *e* sound.

1. r_?_pers   3. ch_?_rful
2. _?_vening   4. c_?_sed

Fluency: True/False

Review the vocabulary list on page 65 and notice the way each word is used in the context of the selections. Then, use your knowledge of the italicized word's meaning to decide whether each statement below is true or false.

1. You can rely on a *steadfast* person.
2. When you *glean* information, you gather it bit by bit from one or more sources.
3. An upright citizen does not follow *precepts*.
4. A *lucid* argument will probably puzzle others.
5. An *avenger* might make sure that a criminal is caught and punished for his or her crimes.
6. *Reapers* work in early spring, turning the soil and planting seeds in the ground.
7. You *redeem* a mortgage when you pay it off.

Grammar and Style Lesson

Compound Predicates

The **predicate** is the part of the sentence that tells what the subject does or is. In a **compound predicate**—also called a **compound verb**—two or more verbs that have the same subject are joined by a conjunction such as *and*, *but*, or *or*.

> <u>She</u> *came* and *gleaned* in a field, . . .
>
> <u>Naomi's son</u> *had married* Ruth but then *died*.

Poets may use compound predicates to create effects similar to parallelism—repeating, varying, or contrasting actions and events through their choice of verbs joined in the predicate.

Practice Copy each sentence. Put a box around the subject, underline the verbs, and circle the conjunction that joins the compound predicate.

1. Naomi lost her husband but still had Ruth.
2. The two women returned to Bethlehem and worked on Boaz's lands.
3. Many people in the community did not like the outsider or at least took no interest in her.
4. Ruth came to Boaz's table, partook of the meal, and dipped her morsel in the vinegar.
5. Later she married Boaz and bore him a son.

Writing Application Write four sentences describing the community's reaction to Boaz's marriage. Use compound predicates in each sentence.

W̧G Prentice Hall Writing and Grammar Connection: Diamond Level, Chapter 18, Section 1

Writing Lesson

Response to a Biblical Narrative

As you read the Book of Ruth, you probably reacted to the words and decisions of the characters, the sequence of events, and the ideas that the story suggests. Write a response to this biblical narrative, focusing on any one of these elements.

Prewriting   Identify the element that affected you most strongly, and summarize your reaction to it. Then, find details in the work that you can focus on to help clarify and explain your response.

Drafting   Use the summary of your reaction to write a thesis statement. Support your thesis by discussing the ways in which your chosen element affected you at different points in the story. Include quotations from the story as well.

Model: Adding Quotations From the Selection

The language of the characters is simple but eloquent. In Ruth 1:21, Naomi expresses her unhappiness in a single sentence. ∧*"I went away full, and the LORD has brought me back empty," she says.*

> The added quotation shows the simplicity and eloquence of a character's language.

Revising   Make sure that you review the quotations and their verse numbers for accuracy. If your support seems weak, consider adding quotations.

 Prentice Hall Writing and Grammar Connection: Diamond Level, Chapter 14, Section 3

Extension Activities

Research and Technology   Research musical settings of the Psalms, and prepare a **multimedia report** on your findings. Include live or recorded music, written or oral explanations, and sheet music. Here are some sources to consider:

- library or other music collections
- local churches or choirs
- Web sites about religious music
- nonfiction books about religious music

Present your report to your classmates.

Listening and Speaking   Working with other students, develop an **improvised dialogue** to add to the Book of Ruth. Assign roles and decide which situations to enhance with added dialogue. Develop and rehearse your dialogue, then perform it for classmates. **[Group Activity]**

 **Take It to the Net**   PHSchool.com

Go online for an additional research activity using the Internet.

A Closer Look

The King James Version of the Bible

The King James Version of the Bible has flowed through the landscape of our language like a mighty river of prose and poetry.

Commissioned by King James I of England and completed in 1611, the English translation of the Bible known as the King James Version has influenced countless poems, novels, sermons, and speeches. A sacred book for Christians, it is revered by all lovers of our language as one of the greatest works to come from the English Renaissance.

"In the beginning . . ." So powerful is its influence that the description of the world's beginning in Chapter 1 of Genesis is, without rival, the sound of creation in English:

1 In the beginning God created the heaven and the earth.

2 And the earth was without form, and void; and darkness *was* upon the face of the deep. And the Spirit of God moved upon the face of the waters.

3 And God said, Let there be light: and there was light. . . .

Although it speaks so majestically of beginnings, however, the King James Version itself came rather late in the life of the Bible.

The Hebrew Bible was a collection of books written from 1200 to 100 B.C. (For the Jewish Publication Society translations of portions of the Bible, see pages 42–79.) Christians refer to this Bible as the Old Testament, and they refer to the smaller collection of books that they added to it as the New Testament. The King James Version is a translation into English of the Hebrew of the Old Testament and the Greek of the New Testament.

Protestantism and the Printing Press Yet the King James Version was not the first translation of the Bible into English. In the 1500s, the Christian movement called Protestantism emerged and began to place greater importance on the Bible as a source of religious authority. This new emphasis came shortly after Gutenberg's invention of movable type, which made possible the widespread distribution of the Bible for the first time. The combination of Protestantism and the modern printing press encouraged new translations of the Bible into English and other languages.

One influential English translation was that of William Tyndale, a Protestant chaplain and tutor whose act of translating the Bible from the Latin resulted in his being arrested for heresy and executed near Brussels, Belgium, in 1536. As England became more Protestant, however, Tyndale came to be viewed not as a heretic but as a hero. King James's translators closely followed the magnificent diction and rhythms of Tyndale's ground-breaking translation.

A Classic "created by a committee . . ." James I ascended to the English throne upon the death of Elizabeth I in 1603. The Bible project he approved a year later was ambitious. It involved the work of forty-seven scholars divided into six groups at three different locations. These teams used previous translations like Tyndale's, as well as texts in the original Hebrew and Greek. Also, they reviewed one another's work and did not hesitate to rewrite it. The result of their labors has been called "the only classic ever created by a committee."

A Sample of Riches The sample that follows comes from the New Testament Gospels, which record the words of Jesus, the founder of Christianity. His speeches contain memorable sayings and parables, brief stories that teach moral lessons.

In a famous passage from Chapter 6 of the Gospel According to St. Matthew, Jesus warns about the love of money and possessions (*mammon* is "money" and *raiment* is clothing):

24 No man can serve two masters: for either he will hate the one, and love the other; or else he will hold to the one, and despise the other. Ye cannot serve God and mammon.

25 Therefore I say unto you, Take no thought for your life, what ye shall eat, or what ye shall drink; nor yet for your body, what ye shall put on. Is not the life more than meat, and the body than raiment?

26 Behold the fowls of the air: for they sow not, neither do they reap, nor gather into barns; yet your heavenly Father feedeth them. Are ye not much better than they?

27 Which of you by taking thought can add one cubit unto his stature?

28 And why take ye thought for raiment? . . .

From Renaissance England to America Like Shakespeare's plays, written at about the same time, the King James Version of the Bible has enriched our language with many phrases—examples include "out of the mouths of babes" and "fat of the land." Its words, rhythms, and images have influenced not only English authors like John Milton and William Blake but also Americans like Walt Whitman and Abraham Lincoln. Scholar Bliss Perry says that Whitman found in the King James Version the "strong rolling music" he wanted in his own poetry. Lincoln used biblical quotations and cadences in great speeches like his Second Inaugural Address. In an important way, therefore, this Bible from the English Renaissance helped shape our own nation's literature and public life.

▲ **Critical Viewing**
What connection is there between the literary style of the King James Version and the style of the art on its title page? Explain. **[Connect]**

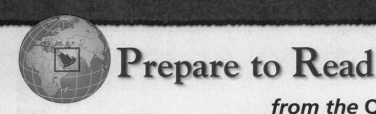

Prepare to Read

from the Qur'an

In the eyes of Muslims, the Qur'an (sometimes referred to as the Koran) is viewed as the most important scripture in the world, but not the only one. Muslims believe that Allah sent a series of heavenly books, or scriptures, to the world. These include the Torah (see pages 44–56), the Psalms (see pages 73–76) and the New Testament. The last of these heavenly books is the Qur'an, which Muslims believe to be the final revelation of Allah.

The Prophet Muhammad In the latter third of his life, revelations started coming to the prophet Muhammad as he meditated in a cave outside his hometown of Mecca, now in Saudi Arabia. Suddenly, the angel Gabriel came to him and commanded him to recite something. When Muhammad asked the angel what it was that he wanted him to recite, Gabriel said in Arabic, "Recite in the name of the Lord Who creates." This command was followed by the first of the revelations, and as a result it is the first line of the Qur'an. In fact, the name of the book may be taken from this line, because the word *Qur'an* means "recitation" in Arabic.

It is held that, from the age of forty, Muhammad continued to receive such revelations until his death approximately twenty years later. He repeated them to his followers, who either memorized them or wrote them down on bits of parchment, pieces of leather, or clay tablets. In the years after Muhammad's death, his followers organized the fragments into a book and named it the Qur'an. Copies of the Qur'an were sent to all major cities in the Islamic world, with orders that other unofficial versions should be destroyed, and the Qur'an was made the official scripture of the Islamic religion.

The Organization of the Qur'an The revelations of Muhammad are arranged in chapters called *Surahs*. There are 114 Surahs in the Qur'an, varying in length from three or four verses to well over 200. Each Surah's title is generally an unusual word or phrase appearing early in the Surah.

The earliest copies of the Qur'an were written in an imperfect Arabic script that included no vowels and used the same symbols for many different consonants. When Arabic script was reformed in the eighth century, the Qur'an was recopied in this script, and it has remained virtually unchanged to this day.

Revelations From God Although Muhammad uttered the words of the Qur'an, he is not considered its author; rather, he is viewed as the transmitter of Allah's message to humanity. Muslims believe that the Qur'an, word for word and syllable for syllable, is the exact message of Allah. Because this belief means that the words used in the Qur'an are Allah's words, and any translation loses some of its religious value, most Muslims feel that the Qur'an should be read in Arabic and that translations are only approximations of the real text. The vast majority of today's Muslims do not know Arabic and can only read the translations. However, all scholars of Islam use the original Arabic text for their studies.

Islam and the Five Pillars of Wisdom

The word *Islam* means "submission to the will of God" (who is called *Allah* in Arabic). Members of the Islamic faith are known as Muslims, and the Muslim creed states: "There is no god but Allah; Muhammad is his prophet." Muslims are expected to perform the following five acts of worship, known as the Five Pillars of Wisdom:

1. express one's faith by reciting the creed
2. pray five times each day (facing Mecca, the birthplace of the prophet Muhammad)
3. give alms, or charity, to the poor
4. fast from sunrise to sundown during the holy month of Ramadan, the ninth month of the Islamic calendar
5. make, in one's lifetime, at least one pilgrimage to Mecca; this trip is called a *hajj* or *hadj* in Arabic

Preview

Connecting to the Literature

Perhaps the world would be a kinder place if compassion and mercy filled more hearts. In the Qur'an, every Surah opens by calling on "God, the Compassionate, the Merciful."

Literary Analysis

Imagery

Imagery is language used to create word pictures by appealing to one or more of the five senses—sight, hearing, taste, smell, and touch. An **image** is a single instance of imagery: "hot dry wind," for example, or "cold wet rain." Imagery makes descriptions more vivid and abstract ideas more concrete.

As you read the selections from the Qur'an, track the images on a chart like the one shown.

Image	"straight path"
Selection	Exordium
Sense(s)	sight

Connecting Literary Elements

One form of imagery highlights contrasts and differences. **Antithesis** is the use of strongly contrasting language, images, or ideas. Antithesis can be expressed in various ways:

- two long contrasting pieces meant to be read together and balanced against each other
- shorter contrasts in words, phrases, clauses, or sentences that express their contrasting ideas in similar grammatical structures (parallelism): "By the light of day, and by the dark of night. . . ."

Notice how often the Qur'an employs antithesis to reinforce images and make them more memorable.

Reading Strategy

Setting a Purpose for Reading

When you **set a purpose for reading,** you decide beforehand why you are reading and what to focus on as you read. For example, if you read the Qur'an to learn more about Islamic culture, you may focus on its guidelines for human behavior. Identify your purpose before you begin to read and then read to achieve that goal.

Vocabulary Development

compassionate (kəm pash′ ən it) *adj.* feeling or showing sympathy or pity (p. 84)

incurred (in kurd′) *v.* brought about through one's own actions (p. 84)

affliction (ə flik′ shən) *n.* something that causes pain or distress (p. 85)

recompense (rek′ əm pens′) *n.* payment of what is owed; reward (p. 85)

abhor (ab hôr′) *v.* feel disgust for; hate (p. 86)

chide (chīd) *v.* scold (p. 86)

renown (ri noun′) *n.* fame (p. 86)

fervor (fur′ vər) *n.* strong or heated feeling; zeal (p. 86)

from the Qur'an

translated by
N. J. Dawood

Background

The fundamental message of all the Surahs of the Qur'an is that there is but one God who has created the world and everything in it. This God is all-powerful and all-knowing; just, loving, and merciful; the protector and sustainer of all life; and the final judge at death. As a result, the Qur'an says, it is the duty of all people to praise him, glorify him, and submit to him.

The Exordium

IN THE NAME OF GOD
THE COMPASSIONATE
THE MERCIFUL

Praise be to God, Lord of the Universe,
The Compassionate, the Merciful,
Sovereign of the Day of Judgment!
You alone we worship, and to You alone we turn for help.
Guide us to the straight path,
The path of those whom You have favored,
Not of those who have incurred Your wrath,
Nor of those who have gone astray.

compassionate (kəm pash´ ən it) *adj.* feeling or showing sympathy or pity

incurred (in kʉrd´) *v.* brought about through one's own actions

Night

In the Name of God, the Compassionate, the Merciful

By the night, when she lets fall her darkness, and by the radiant day! By Him that created the male and the female, your endeavors have varied ends!

For him that gives in charity and guards himself against evil and believes in goodness, We shall smooth the path of salvation; but for him that neither gives nor takes and disbelieves in goodness, We shall smooth the path of <u>affliction</u>. When he breathes his last, his riches will not avail him.

It is for Us to give guidance. Ours is the life to come, Ours the life of this world. I warn you, then, of the blazing Fire, in which none shall burn save the hardened sinner, who denies the Truth and pays no heed. But the good man who keeps himself pure by almsgiving shall keep away from it: and so shall he that does good works for the sake of the Most High only, seeking no <u>recompense</u>. Such men shall be content.

Literary Analysis
Imagery and Antithesis
What image contrasts with night in the first paragraph?

affliction (ə flik´ shən) *n.* something that causes pain or distress

recompense (rek´ əm pens´) *n.* payment of what is owed; reward

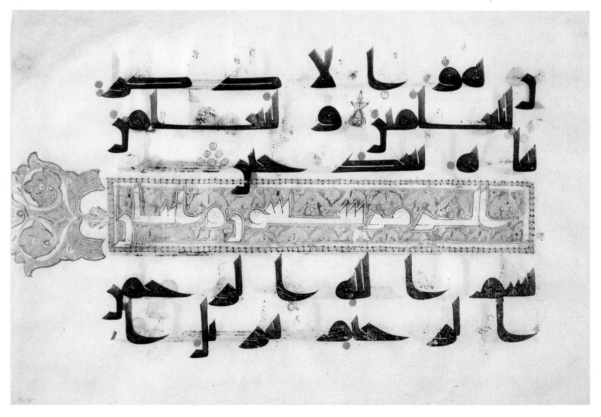

▲ **Critical Viewing** What effect does the artist achieve by using stylized lettering and graphics in this page from an illuminated Qur'an? **[Make a Judgment]**

Daylight

In the Name of God, the Compassionate, the Merciful

By the light of day, and by the dark of night, your Lord
has not forsaken you[1] nor does He <u>abhor</u> you.
    The life to come holds a richer prize for you than this
present life. You shall be gratified with what your Lord will give you.
    Did He not find you an orphan and give you shelter?
    Did He not find you in error and guide you?
    Did He not find you poor and enrich you?
    Therefore do not wrong the orphan, nor <u>chide</u> away the
beggar. But proclaim the goodness of your Lord.

Comfort

In the Name of God, the Compassionate, the Merciful

Have we not lifted up your heart and relieved you[2] of the
burden which weighed down your back?
    Have We not given you high <u>renown</u>?
    With every hardship there is ease. With every hardship
there is ease.
    When your prayers are ended resume your toil, and seek your
Lord with all <u>fervor</u>.

---

1. you here, Allah's prophet, Muhammad.
2. you here, Mecca, a city in Saudi Arabia and the birthplace of Muhammad.

abhor (ab hôr´) v. feel disgust for; hate

Literary Analysis
Imagery What image helps make the abstract idea of the afterlife more concrete?

chide (chīd) v. scold

renown (ri noun´) n. fame

fervor (fur´ vər) n. strong or heated feeling; zeal

Review and Assess

Thinking About the Selections

1. **Respond:** Which of these selections from the Qur'an did you find most interesting? Why?

2. **(a) Recall:** Whom does the Exordium address? **(b) Infer:** Who seems to be speaking? **(c) Interpret:** Why does the speaker wish to be guided?

3. **(a) Recall:** What kind of behavior does "Night" equate with goodness? **(b) Infer:** What drives someone to be a good person?

4. **(a) Recall:** According to "Daylight," what has the Lord *not* done? **(b) Compare and Contrast:** In what ways should human behavior reflect the Lord's behavior?

5. **(a) Recall:** What does "Comfort" say comes with every hardship? **(b) Evaluate:** In what ways does this Surah offer comfort?

6. **Apply:** "Night" describes the behavior of a good man. In what ways is this description applicable to good people today?

Review and Assess

Literary Analysis

Imagery

1. To which senses does the **imagery** in "Night" appeal? Cite examples of images to support your answer.
2. In "Daylight," what does the image of the orphan given shelter help express about God?
3. (a) What abstract idea does the imagery in "Comfort" help you perceive? (b) Which concrete aspects of the image help you perceive the abstract idea?

Connecting Literary Elements

4. Identify five examples of **antithesis** that help make the ideas and imagery in these selections clearer.
5. (a) Which two Surahs have titles that suggest an antithesis between them? (b) Does their content actually contrast? Explain by summarizing the main points of each one.

Reading Strategy

Setting a Purpose for Reading

6. Imagine that your **purpose for reading** is to learn about the Islamic view of Allah, or God. Reread the selections, and jot down five main characteristics of Allah. Record your examples in a chart like the one shown.

Selection	Characteristic of Allah

7. (a) If your purpose for reading is to learn about Islamic views of the afterlife, which of these Surahs contains information on which you might focus? (b) What does that information tell you about the afterlife?
8. Reread the selections with the purpose of learning more about Islamic values. What do you think are the three most important values of Islam?

Extend Understanding

9. **Social Studies Connection:** Based on these Surahs, what social practices would you expect to find in Islamic nations? Explain.

Quick Review

Imagery is the use of language that appeals to one or more of the five senses—sight, hearing, taste, smell, and touch. A single instance of imagery is called an **image.**

Antithesis is the use of strongly contrasting language, images, or ideas.

To **set a purpose for reading,** decide why you are reading and focus on the details that help you achieve that goal as you read.

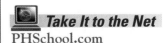 **Take It to the Net**
PHSchool.com

Take the interactive self-test online to check your understanding of these selections.

Integrate Language Skills

Vocabulary Development Lesson

Word Analysis: Latin Prefix *ab-*

The word *abhor* combines the Latin prefix *ab-*, meaning "away" or "from," with the root *-hor-*, meaning "shudder." To *abhor* is to shudder from something or find it disgusting. Match each numbered word below with its meaning.

1. abduct
2. abrupt

a. happening suddenly
b. kidnap

Spelling Strategy

If a verb ends in a single stressed vowel followed by a single consonant, you usually double the consonant before adding *-ed* or *-ing*: *incur* + *-ed* = *incurred*; *incur* + *-ing* = *incurring*. Do not double *w*, *x*, or *y*. Add *-ed* and *-ing* to the verbs below, making sure that they are spelled correctly.

1. sin   2. beg   3. abhor   4. favor

Concept Development: Synonyms

Choose the letter of the word that is closest in meaning to the first word.

1. incurred: (a) paid, (b) delivered, (c) caused
2. recompense: (a) repayment, (b) fullness, (c) whining
3. compassionate: (a) angry, (b) sympathetic, (c) emotional
4. fervor: (a) shine, (b) grief, (c) enthusiasm
5. affliction: (a) calamity, (b) vibration, (c) accent
6. renown: (a) wisdom, (b) celebrity, (c) perseverance
7. chide: (a) slice, (b) ignore, (c) reprimand
8. abhor: (a) distribute, (b) detest, (c) spend

Grammar and Style Lesson

Parallelism

Parallelism presents equal ideas in similar grammatical structures. Using parallelism often makes writing more rhythmic, powerful, and memorable.

> **Not Parallel:** He *created* the heavens, and the earth *was created* by Him.

> **Parallel Sentences:** He *created* the heavens, and He *created* the earth.

Practice Revise the italicized section in each sentence below so that parallel ideas are expressed in parallel grammatical structures.

1. In 622, Muhammad fled from Mecca and *Medina was the town in which he arrived.*

2. The Islamic calendar has twelve months per year, and *in a month there are about thirty days.*

3. During Ramadan, Muslims fast from sunrise to *when the sun goes down.*

4. The Qur'an stresses the value of work, prayer, and *being charitable.*

5. Just as Jews and Christians consider the Bible sacred, so *is the Qur'an considered sacred by Muslims.*

Writing Application Write four sentences about human behavior, giving advice or making observations. Use parallelism in each sentence.

*W*G *Prentice Hall Writing and Grammar Connection: Diamond Level, Chapter 20, Section 6*

Writing Lesson

Guidelines for Personal Behavior

After thinking about the Five Pillars of Wisdom and the passages you read from the Qur'an, create your own guidelines for personal behavior.

Prewriting   Jot down five or six human qualities that you think are important and the kinds of behavior you associate with each. Number each quality, using *1* for most important, *2* for next most important, and so on.

Drafting   For your guidelines, write a short paragraph identifying each quality and describing behavior that exemplifies or illustrates it. Organize your guidelines in order of importance, moving from least to most important or vice versa.

Revising   As you revise, focus on organization. Shift the positions of your guidelines, if necessary. Then, underline the clauses or sentences that introduce each guideline and make sure that they provide clear signals of your organization.

Model: Revising to Clarify Organization

Most important of all,

^Kindness is crucial to a worthy life. A worthy person is kind to his or her equals and especially to those who are weaker or less fortunate.

> The transitional phrase helps make the order of importance clear.

WG   *Prentice Hall Writing and Grammar Connection: Diamond Level, Chapter 11, Section 3*

Extension Activities

Listening and Speaking Prepare and give a brief **speech** on what compassion and mercy mean to you. Follow these guidelines:

- Define *compassion* and *mercy* and provide examples for each one.
- Draft an opening statement addressing the importance of compassion and mercy.
- As you speak, do not read your notes, but use them as a guide.

Practice your speech in front of a mirror or before friends or family. Then, present your speech to classmates.

Research and Technology In a small group, research the role that the Qur'an plays in Islamic life. Present your findings in a **magazine article** that includes copies of photos or paintings illustrating aspects of Islamic life. Assign some students to research the information and others to find the illustrations. Be sure to cite all sources.
[Group Activity]

 **Take It to the Net**   PHSchool.com

Go online for an additional research activity using the Internet.

Prepare to Read

from The Thousand and One Nights: The Fisherman and the Jinnee

About *The Thousand and One Nights*

The Thousand and One Nights is the most famous work of Arabic prose known to the Western world. Many of the stories, including those of Sindbad the Sailor, Ali Baba, and Aladdin, have become integral parts of Western literary and popular culture.

The Frame Story *The Thousand and One Nights* is actually a collection of unrelated tales pieced together into one long narrative. The connecting framework is the tale of King Shahriyar (depicted above), whose wife's betrayal has filled him with hatred for all women. Every night, motivated by vengeance and fear, he marries a different woman only to put her to death the following morning. Finally, a young woman named Scheherazade (shə her′ ə zäd′) devises a scheme to stop the bloodshed. She weds the king, and on the first night of their marriage, she tells him a spellbinding story. At daybreak, she has not yet finished. As the executioners await their orders, Scheherazade promises Shahriyar that she will finish the story that evening. Captivated by the tale, Shahriyar stays the order of execution. That night, Scheherazade finishes the first story but immediately starts another that is just as exciting as the first. In this way, she enthralls the king and prolongs her life for a thousand and one nights. By the time she has finished telling her final story, almost three years have passed. King Shahriyar, now in love with Scheherazade, decides not to kill her.

Varied Origins Most likely, King Shahriyar and Scheherazade never existed. Nor was there a single author who wrote all of *The Thousand and One Nights*. The book we know today is based on an ancient Persian work entitled the *Hazar Afsaneh (A Thousand Legends)*. When the book was translated into Arabic around the year A.D. 850 and renamed *The Thousand and One Nights*, it quickly became popular throughout the Arab world. People would gather around professional storytellers in marketplaces and shops to hear the fantastic tales retold. Over the years, storytellers embellished the original collection of tales with new stories they had invented or heard from other sources. They also changed the names of people and places as well as other details. Reshaped and enlarged by this battalion of anonymous storytellers, *The Thousand and One Nights* finally took the form with which modern readers are familiar. In 1704, Antoine Galland produced a French version of the book, its first major translation into a European language. An English version followed in 1708.

The Three Cultural Strands *The Thousand and One Nights* evolved over the course of centuries, incorporating three distinct cultural strands. The first strand is the original Persian book, which includes tales that many scholars believe originated in Persian folklore. The frame story of Princess Scheherazade is part of this strand. The second strand of tales is set in the Arabic city of Baghdad, which is now the capital of Iraq. These stories focus on the reign of King Harun ar-Rashid. Among the stories included in this strand are those of Sindbad and Aladdin. The final strand consists of many short, humorous tales that originated in the city of Cairo, which is now the capital of Egypt. All three strands are now woven together like a tapestry, containing stories within stories. Rich in characters, imagery, adventure, moral lessons, and humor, this collection of stories has inspired countless dramatizations, musical compositions, and other literary works.

Preview

Connecting to the Literature

For many people, the idea of finding a magical jinnee—also spelled genie or jinni—in a bottle is the stuff of pleasant daydreams. However, for the luckless fisherman in this story, the discovery soon leads to trouble.

Literary Analysis

Folk Tales

Folk tales are part of the oral tradition, the body of stories, poems, and songs that are passed down by word of mouth from generation to generation. Most folk tales include the following characteristics:

- a lesson about life
- magical or supernatural elements
- characters who possess one or two main traits
- a clear separation between good and evil

In addition, folk tales may share plot patterns and deceptively ordinary characters. As you read, look for these distinctive elements.

Connecting Literary Elements

Narrative structure refers to the way in which a work of fiction is organized. *The Thousand and One Nights* contains framed stories, or stories-within-a-story. That narrative structure occurs as characters in one story tell other stories. As you read, use a chart like the one shown to map the narrative structure of "The Fisherman and the Jinnee" and to identify similarities among the stories.

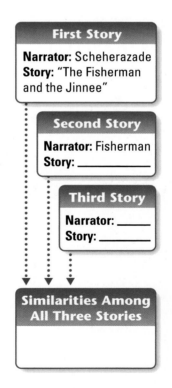

First Story

Narrator: Scheherazade
Story: "The Fisherman and the Jinnee"

Second Story

Narrator: Fisherman
Story: _____

Third Story

Narrator: _____
Story: _____

Similarities Among All Three Stories

Reading Strategy

Summarizing

A summary is a brief statement expressing the key details of a literary work. To **summarize**, identify the details that are essential to your understanding of a story. Then, organize those details into a concise statement. As you read, summarize to aid your understanding.

Vocabulary Development

inverted (in vʉrt′ id) *adj.* upside down (p. 93)

blasphemous (blas′ fə məs) *adj.* showing disrespect toward God or religious teachings (p. 94)

adjured (a joord′) *v.* ordered solemnly (p. 94)

indignantly (in dig′ nənt lē) *adv.* in a way showing righteous anger or scorn (p. 95)

resolutely (rez′ ə loot′ lē) *adv.* in a determined way; without hesitation (p. 95)

enraptured (en rap′ chərd) *adj.* completely delighted; spellbound (p. 97)

munificence (myoo nif′ ə səns) *n.* great generosity (p. 98)

ominous (äm′ ə nəs) *adj.* hinting at bad things to come (p. 98)

from The Thousand and One Nights

From The FISHERMAN and the JINNEE

translated by N. J. Dawood

Background

Most of the tales in *The Thousand and One Nights* are set in the Middle East, especially Egypt, Baghdad (now the capital of Iraq), and Persia (now Iran). In all of these areas, the dominant religion is Islam. "The Fisherman and the Jinnee" is typical of the tales that make up *The Thousand and One Nights*—two of the three interlocking stories presented here are set in Persia and all of them feature Muslim characters.

In Muslim folklore, a jinnee is a supernatural creature that can take human or animal form and exert powerful influences on human affairs. While many Westerners are familiar with the image of the all-powerful jinnee trapped in a bottle, the jinnee who makes his appearance in this story offers several surprises.

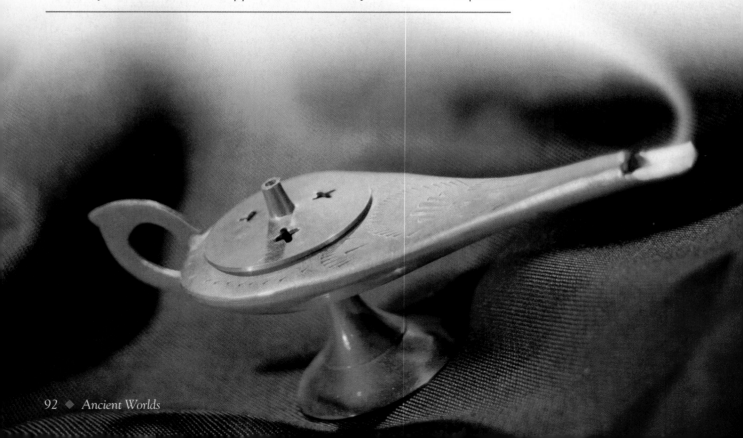

Once upon a time there was a poor fisherman who had a wife and three children to support.

He used to cast his net four times a day. It chanced that one day he went down to the sea at noon and, reaching the shore, set down his basket, rolled up his shirt-sleeves, and cast his net far out into the water. After he had waited for it to sink, he pulled on the cords with all his might; but the net was so heavy that he could not draw it in. So he tied the rope ends to a wooden stake on the beach and, putting off his clothes, dived into the water and set to work to bring it up. When he had carried it ashore, however, he found in it a dead donkey.

"By Allah,[1] this is a strange catch!" cried the fisherman, disgusted at the sight. After he had freed the net and wrung it out, he waded into the water and cast it again, invoking Allah's help. But when he tried to draw it in he found it even heavier than before. Thinking that he had caught some enormous fish, he fastened the ropes to the stake and, diving in again, brought up the net. This time he found a large earthen vessel filled with mud and sand.

Angrily the fisherman threw away the vessel, cleaned his net, and cast it for the third time. He waited patiently, and when he felt the net grow heavy he hauled it in, only to find it filled with bones and broken glass. In despair, he lifted his eyes to heaven and cried: "Allah knows that I cast my net only four times a day. I have already cast it for the third time and caught no fish at all. Surely He will not fail me again!"

With this the fisherman hurled his net far out into the sea, and waited for it to sink to the bottom. When at length he brought it to land he found in it a bottle made of yellow copper. The mouth was stopped with lead and bore the seal of our master Solomon son of David.[2] The fisherman rejoiced, and said: "I will sell this in the market of the coppersmiths. It must be worth ten pieces of gold." He shook the bottle and, finding it heavy, thought to himself: "I will first break the seal and find out what is inside."

The fisherman removed the lead with his knife and again shook the bottle; but scarcely had he done so, when there burst from it a great column of smoke which spread along the shore and rose so high that it almost touched the heavens. Taking shape, the smoke resolved itself into a jinnee of such prodigious[3] stature that his head reached the clouds, while his feet were planted on the sand. His head was a huge dome and his mouth as wide as a cavern, with teeth ragged like broken rocks. His legs towered like the masts of a ship, his nostrils were two <u>inverted</u> bowls, and his eyes, blazing like torches, made his aspect fierce and menacing.

The sight of this jinnee struck terror to the fisherman's heart; his limbs quivered, his teeth chattered together, and he stood rooted to the ground with parched tongue and staring eyes.

---

1. **Allah** (al´ ə) Muslim name for God.
2. **Solomon ... David** In the Old Testament, David and his son Solomon are both kings of Israel and are considered prophets by Muslims.
3. **prodigious** (prō dij´ əs) *n.* wonderful; amazing.

Literary Analysis
Folk Tales Which details in the first two paragraphs show that the fisherman is an ordinary person, perhaps less fortunate than most?

Literary Analysis
Folk Tales What supernatural element is introduced here?

inverted (in vʉrt´ id) *adj.* upside down

 **Reading Check**

What does the fisherman catch when he casts his net for the fourth time?

"There is no god but Allah and Solomon is His Prophet!" cried the jinnee. Then, addressing himself to the fisherman, he said: "I pray you, mighty Prophet, do not kill me! I swear never again to defy your will or violate your laws!"

"Blasphemous giant," cried the fisherman, "do you presume to call Solomon the Prophet of Allah? Solomon has been dead these eighteen hundred years, and we are now approaching the end of Time. But what is your history, pray, and how came you to be imprisoned in this bottle?"

On hearing these words the jinnee replied sarcastically: "Well, then; there is no god but Allah! Fisherman, I bring you good news."

"What news?" asked the old man.

"News of your death, horrible and prompt!" replied the jinnee.

"Then may heaven's wrath be upon you, ungrateful wretch!" cried the fisherman. "Why do you wish my death, and what have I done to deserve it? Have I not brought you up from the depths of the sea and released you from your imprisonment?"

But the jinnee answered: "Choose the manner of your death and the way that I shall kill you. Come, waste no time!"

"But what crime have I committed?" cried the fisherman.

"Listen to my story, and you shall know," replied the jinnee.

"Be brief, then, I pray you," said the fisherman, "for you have wrung my soul with terror."

"Know," began the giant, "that I am one of the rebel jinn who, together with Sakhr the Jinnee, mutinied against Solomon son of David. Solomon sent against me his Vizier,[4] Asaf ben Berakhya, who vanquished me despite my supernatural power and led me captive before his master. Invoking the name of Allah, Solomon adjured me to embrace his faith and pledge him absolute obedience. I refused, and he imprisoned me in this bottle, upon which he set a seal of lead bearing the Name of the Most High. Then he sent for several of his faithful jinn, who carried me away and cast me into the middle of the sea. In the ocean depths I vowed: 'I will bestow eternal riches on him who sets me free!' But a hundred years passed away and no one freed me. In the second hundred years of my imprisonment I said: 'For him who frees me I will open up the buried treasures of the earth!' And yet no one freed me. Whereupon I flew into a rage and swore: 'I will kill the man who sets me free, allowing him only to choose the manner of his death!' Now it was you who set me free; therefore prepare to die and choose the way that I shall kill you."

"O wretched luck, that it should have fallen to my lot to free you!" exclaimed the fisherman. "Spare me, mighty jinnee, and Allah will spare you; kill me, and so shall Allah destroy you!"

"You have freed me," repeated the jinnee. "Therefore you must die."

"Chief of the jinn," cried the fisherman, "will you thus requite[5] good with evil?"

4. **vizier** (vi zir´) high officer in the government; a minister.
5. **requite** (ri kwīt´) v. make return or repayment for.

blasphemous (blas´ fə məs) adj. showing disrespect toward God or religious teachings

adjured (a jōord´) v. ordered solemnly

Reading Strategy
Summarizing Summarize the story the jinnee tells about his past.

"Enough of this talk!" roared the jinnee. "Kill you I must."

At this point the fisherman thought to himself: "Though I am but a man and he is a jinnee, my cunning may yet overreach his malice." Then, turning to his adversary, he said: "Before you kill me, I beg you in the Name of the Most High engraved on Solomon's seal to answer me one question truthfully."

The jinnee trembled at the mention of the Name, and, when he had promised to answer truthfully, the fisherman asked: "How could this bottle, which is scarcely large enough to hold your hand or foot, ever contain your entire body?"

"Do you dare doubt that?" roared the jinnee <u>indignantly</u>.

"I will never believe it," replied the fisherman, "until I see you enter this bottle with my own eyes!"

Upon this the jinnee trembled from head to foot and dissolved into a column of smoke, which gradually wound itself into the bottle and disappeared inside. At once the fisherman snatched up the leaden stopper and thrust it into the mouth of the bottle. Then he called out to the jinnee: "Choose the manner of your death and the way that I shall kill you! By Allah, I will throw you back into the sea, and keep watch on this shore to warn all men of your treachery!"

Illustration from *Arabian Nights,* for the story "The Fisherman and the Genie," Edmund Dulac

When he heard the fisherman's words, the jinnee struggled desperately to escape from the bottle, but was prevented by the magic seal. He now altered his tone and, assuming a submissive air, assured the fisherman that he had been jesting with him and implored him to let him out. But the fisherman paid no heed to the jinnee's entreaties,[6] and <u>resolutely</u> carried the bottle down to the sea.

"What are you doing with me?" whimpered the jinnee helplessly.

"I am going to throw you back into the sea!" replied the fisherman. "You have lain in the depths eighteen hundred years, and there you shall remain till the Last Judgment![7] Did I not beg you to spare me so

---

6. **entreaties** (en trēt´ ēz) *n.* earnest requests.
7. **Last Judgment** the final judgment of humankind at the end of the world.

▲ **Critical Viewing**
Do you think the jinnee pictured is menacing or comical? Explain. **[Make a Judgment]**

indignantly (in dig´ nənt lē) *adv.* in a way showing righteous anger or scorn

resolutely (rez´ ə loot´ lē) *adv.* in a determined way; without hesitation

✔**Reading Check**

What name causes the jinnee to tremble?

that Allah might spare you? But you took no pity on me, and He has now delivered you into my hands."

"Let me out," cried the jinnee in despair, "and I will give you fabulous riches!"

"Perfidious[8] jinnee," retorted the fisherman, "you justly deserve the fate of the King in the tale of 'Yunan and the Doctor'.

"What tale is that?" asked the jinnee.

The Tale of King Yunan and Duban the Doctor

It is related (began the fisherman) that once upon a time there reigned in the land of Persia a rich and mighty king called Yunan. He commanded great armies and had a numerous retinue of followers and courtiers. But he was afflicted with a leprosy[9] which baffled his physicians and defied all cures.

One day a venerable[10] old doctor named Duban came to the King's capital. He had studied books written in Greek, Persian, Latin, Arabic, and Syriac, and was deeply versed in the wisdom of the ancients. He was master of many sciences, knew the properties of plants and herbs, and was above all skilled in astrology and medicine. When this physician heard of the leprosy with which Allah had plagued the King and of his doctors' vain endeavors to cure him, he put on his finest robes and betook himself to the royal palace. After he had kissed the ground before the King and called down blessings upon him, he told him who he was and said: "Great king, I have heard about the illness with which you are afflicted and have come to heal you. Yet will I give you no potion to drink, nor any ointment to rub upon your body."

The King was astonished at the doctor's words, and asked: "How will you do that? By Allah, if you cure me I will heap riches upon you and your children's children after you. Anything you wish for shall be yours and you shall be my companion and my friend."

Then the King gave him a robe of honor and other presents, and asked: "Is it really true that you can heal me without draft or ointment? When is it to be? What day, what hour?"

"Tomorrow, if the King wishes," he replied.

He took leave of the King, and hastening to the center of the town rented for himself a house, to which he carried his books, his drugs, and his other medicaments. Then he distilled balsams and elixirs,[11] and these he poured into a hollow polo-stick.

Next morning he went to the royal palace, and, kissing the ground before the King, requested him to ride to the field and play a game of

Themes in **World Literature**

Scheherazade and the West

From the time it was translated into French in 1704, *The Thousand and One Nights* has captured the imagination of many European writers. For example, William Wordsworth (1770–1850), father of English Romantic poetry, refers to the work in his long autobiographical poem *The Prelude*. Other European and American authors who were inspired by the book and who incorporated some of its ideas or imagery into their own works include Robert Louis Stevenson, Charles Dickens, Edgar Allan Poe, and Alfred, Lord Tennyson. In more recent times, numerous Hollywood filmmakers have adapted *The Thousand and One Nights* into successful movies, both live action and animated.

Reading Strategy
Summarizing Summarize the doctor's background and his actions up to this point in the tale.

---

8. **perfidious** (pər fid´ ē əs) *adj.* treacherous.
9. **leprosy** (lep´ rə sē) *n.* chronic infectious disease that attacks the skin, flesh, and nerves.
10. **venerable** (ven´ ər ə bəl) *adj.* worthy of respect by reason of age and dignity or character.
11. **balsams** (bôl´ səmz) **and elixirs** (i lik´ sərz) two potions with supposed healing powers.

polo with his friends. The King rode out with his viziers and his chamberlains,[12] and when he had entered the playing-field the doctor handed him the hollow club and said: "Take this and grasp it firmly. Strike the ball with all your might until the palm of your hand and the rest of your body begin to perspire. The cure will penetrate your palm and course through the veins and arteries of your body. When it has done its work, return to the palace, wash yourself, and go to sleep. Thus shall you be cured; and peace be with you."

The King took hold of the club and, gripping it firmly, struck the ball and galloped after it with the other players. Harder and harder he struck the ball as he dashed up and down the field, until his palm and all his body perspired. When the doctor saw that the cure had begun its work, he ordered the King to return to the palace. The slaves hastened to make ready the royal bath and prepare the linens and the towels. The King bathed, put on his night-clothes, and went to sleep.

Next morning the physician went to the palace. When he was admitted to the King's presence he kissed the ground before him and wished him peace. The King hastily rose to receive him; he threw his arms around his neck and seated him by his side.

For when the King had left the bath the previous evening, he looked upon his body and rejoiced to find no trace of the leprosy: his skin had become as pure as virgin silver.

The King regaled the physician sumptuously all day. He bestowed on him robes of honor and other gifts and, when evening came, gave him two thousand pieces of gold and mounted him on his own favorite horse. So <u>enraptured</u> was the King by the consummate skill of his doctor that he kept repeating to himself: "This wise physician has cured me without draft or ointment. By Allah, I will load him with honors and he shall henceforth be my companion and trusted friend." And that night the King lay down to sleep in perfect bliss, knowing that he was clean in body and rid at last of his disease.

Next morning, as soon as the King sat down upon his throne, with the officers of his court standing before him and his lieutenants and viziers seated on his right and left, he called for the physician, who went up to him and kissed the ground before him. The King rose and seated the doctor by his side. He feasted him all day, gave him a thousand pieces of gold and more robes of honor, and conversed with him till nightfall.

Now among the King's viziers there was a man of repellent aspect, an envious, black-souled villain, full of spite and cunning. When this Vizier saw that the King had made the physician his friend and lavished on him high dignities and favors, he became jealous and began to plot the doctor's downfall. Does not the proverb say: "All men envy, the strong openly, the weak in secret"?

---

12. **chamberlains** (chām´ bər linz) *n.* high officials in the king's court.

Literary Analysis
Folk Tales In what ways do the doctor's actions and instructions to the King seem magical or supernatural? Explain.

enraptured (en rap´ cherd) *adj.* completely delighted; spellbound

Literary Analysis
Folk Tales Which details in the description of the King's Vizier suggest the stark separation of good and evil that is common to folk tales? Explain.

Reading Check

What does the doctor pour into the hollow polo-stick?

from *The Fisherman and the Jinnee* ◆ 97

So, on the following day, when the King entered the council-chamber and was about to call for the physician, the Vizier kissed the ground before him and said: "My bounteous master, whose munificence extends to all men, my duty prompts me to forewarn you against an evil which threatens your life; nor would I be anything but a base-born wretch were I to conceal it from you."

Perturbed at these ominous words, the King ordered him to explain his meaning.

"Your majesty," resumed the Vizier, "there is an old proverb which says: 'He who does not weigh the consequences of his acts shall never prosper.' Now I have seen the King bestow favors and shower honors upon his enemy, on an assassin who cunningly seeks to destroy him. I fear for the King's safety."

"Who is this man whom you suppose to be my enemy?" asked the King, turning pale.

"If you are asleep, your majesty," replied the Vizier, "I beg you to awake. I speak of Duban, the doctor."

"He is my friend," replied the King angrily, "dearer to me than all my courtiers; for he has cured me of my leprosy, an evil which my physicians had failed to remove. Surely there is no other physician like him in the whole world, from East to West. How can you say these monstrous things of him? From this day I will appoint him my personal physician, and give him every month a thousand pieces of gold. Were I to bestow on him the half of my kingdom, it would be but a small reward for his service. Your counsel, my Vizier, is the prompting of jealousy and envy. Would you have me kill my benefactor and repent of my rashness, as King Sindbad repented after he had killed his falcon?"

The Tale of King Sindbad and the Falcon

Once upon a time (went on King Yunan) there was a Persian King who was a great lover of riding and hunting. He had a falcon which he himself had trained with loving care and which never left his side for a moment; for even at night-time he carried it perched upon his fist, and when he went hunting took it with him. Hanging from the bird's neck was a little bowl of gold from which it drank. One day the King ordered his men to make ready for a hunting expedition and, taking with him his falcon, rode out with his courtiers. At length they came to a valley where they laid the hunting nets. Presently a gazelle fell into the snare, and the King said: "I will kill the man who lets her escape!"

They drew the nets closer and closer round the beast. On seeing the King the gazelle stood on her haunches and raised her forelegs to her head as if she wished to salute him. But as he bent forward to lay hold of her she leapt over his head and fled across the field. Looking round, the King saw his courtiers winking at one another.

"Why are they winking?" he asked his Vizier.

"Perhaps because you let the beast escape," ventured the other, smiling.

munificence (myoo nif′ ə səns) *n.* great generosity

ominous (äm′ ə nəs) *adj.* hinting at bad things to come

Literary Analysis
Folk Tales What motivates the King to tell the story of Sindbad and the falcon?

"On my life," cried the King, "I will chase this gazelle and bring her back!"

At once he galloped off in pursuit of the fleeing animal, and when he had caught up with her, his falcon swooped upon the gazelle, blinding her with his beak, and the King struck her down with a blow of his sword. Then dismounting he flayed the animal and hung the carcass on his saddle-bow.

It was a hot day and the King, who by this time had become faint with thirst, went to search for water. Presently, however, he saw a huge tree, down the trunk of which water was trickling in great drops. He took the little bowl from the falcon's neck and, filling it with this water, placed it before the bird. But the falcon knocked the bowl with its beak and toppled it over. The king once again filled the bowl and placed it before the falcon, but the bird knocked it over a second time. Upon this the King became very angry, and, filling the bowl a third time, set it down before his horse. But the falcon sprang forward and knocked it over with its wings.

"Allah curse you for a bird of ill omen!" cried the King. "You have prevented yourself from drinking and the horse also."

So saying, he struck the falcon with his sword and cut off both its wings. But the bird lifted its head as if to say: "Look into the tree!" The King raised his eyes and saw in the tree an enormous serpent spitting its venom down the trunk.

The King was deeply grieved at what he had done, and, mounting his horse, hurried back to the palace. He threw his kill to the cook, and no sooner had he sat down, with the falcon still perched on his fist, than the bird gave a convulsive gasp and dropped down dead.

The King was stricken with sorrow and remorse for having so rashly killed the bird which had saved his life.

When the Vizier heard the tale of King Yunan, he said: "I assure your majesty that my counsel is prompted by no other motive than my devotion to you and my concern for your safety. I beg leave to warn you that, if you put your trust in this physician, it is certain that he will destroy you. Has he not cured you by a device held in the hand? And might he not cause your death by another such device?"

"You have spoken wisely, my faithful Vizier," replied the King. "Indeed, it is quite probable that this physician has come to my court

▲ **Critical Viewing**
Which details in this image illustrate moments from "The Fisherman and the Jinnee"? [**Analyze**]

Reading Strategy
Summarizing Which are the most important events and details in the tale of King Sindbad and the falcon? Explain.

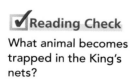

✔**Reading Check**
What animal becomes trapped in the King's nets?

from *The Fisherman and the Jinnee* ◆ 99

as a spy to destroy me. And since he cured my illness by a thing held in the hand, he might as cunningly poison me with the scent of a perfume. What should I do, my Vizier?"

"Send for him at once," replied the other, "and when he comes, strike off his head. Only thus shall you be secure from his perfidy."

Thereupon the King sent for the doctor, who hastened to the palace with a joyful heart, not knowing what lay in store for him.

"Do you know why I have sent for you?" asked the King.

"Allah alone knows the unspoken thoughts of men," replied the physician.

"I have brought you here to kill you," said the King.

The physician was thunderstruck at these words, and cried: "But why should you wish to kill me? What crime have I committed?"

"It has come to my knowledge," replied the King, "that you are a spy sent here to cause my death. But you shall be the first to die."

Then he called out to the executioner, saying: "Strike off the head of this traitor!"

"Spare me, and Allah will spare you!" cried the unfortunate doctor. "Kill me, and so shall Allah kill you!"

But the King gave no heed to his entreaties. "Never will I have peace again," he cried, "until I see you dead. For if you cured me by a thing held in the hand, you will doubtless kill me by the scent of a perfume, or by some other foul device."

"Is it thus that you repay me?" asked the doctor. "Will you thus requite good with evil?"

But the King said: "You must die; nothing can now save you."

When he saw that the King was determined to put him to death, the physician wept, and bitterly repented the service he had done him. Then the executioner came forward, blindfolded the doctor and, drawing his sword, held it in readiness for the King's signal. But the doctor continued to wail, crying: "Spare me, and Allah will spare you! Kill me, and so shall Allah kill you!"

Moved by the old man's lamentations, one of the courtiers interceded for him with the King, saying: "Spare the life of this man, I pray you. He has committed no crime against you, but rather has he cured you of an illness which your physicians have failed to remedy."

"If I spare this doctor," replied the King, "he will use his devilish art to kill me. Therefore he must die."

Again the doctor cried: "Spare me, and Allah will spare you! Kill me, and so shall Allah kill you!" But when at last he saw that the King was fixed in his resolve, he said: "Your majesty, if you needs must kill me, I

Literary Analysis
Folk Tales In what ways do the Vizier's words and the doctor's response emphasize the separation of good and evil?

beg you to grant me a day's delay, so that I may go to my house and wind up my affairs. I wish to say farewell to my family and my neighbors, and instruct them to arrange for my burial. I must also give away my books of medicine, of which there is one, a work of unparalleled virtue, which I would offer to you as a parting gift, that you may preserve it among the treasures of your kingdom."

"What may this book be?" asked the King.

"It holds secrets and devices without number, the least of them being this: that if, after you have struck off my head, you turn over three leaves of this book and read the first three lines upon the left-hand page, my severed head will speak and answer any questions you may ask it."

The King was astonished to hear this, and at once ordered his guards to escort the physician to his house. That day the doctor put his affairs in order, and next morning returned to the King's palace. There had already assembled the viziers, the chamberlains, the nabobs,[13] and all the chief officers of the realm, so that with their colored robes the court seemed like a garden full of flowers.

The doctor bowed low before the King; in one hand he held an ancient book, and in the other a little bowl filled with a strange powder. Then he sat down and said: "Bring me a platter!" A platter was instantly brought in, and the doctor sprinkled the powder on it, smoothing it over with his fingers. After that he handed the book to the King and said: "Take this book and set it down before you. When my head has been cut off, place it upon the powder to stanch the bleeding. Then open the book."

The King ordered the executioner to behead the physician. He did so.

---

13. **nabobs** (nā bäbz) *n.* very rich or important people; aristocrats.

Literary Analysis
Folk Tales and Narrative Structure In what ways do the doctor's words echo those of the fisherman in the first story?

✔**Reading Check**
What favor does the doctor ask the King to grant before the execution takes place?

◀ **Critical Viewing**
What might the facial expressions and the general energy of these caricatures convey about life as a palace servant for the kings in these tales? **[Hypothesize]**

from The Fisherman and the Jinnee ◆ *101*

Then the King opened the book, and, finding the pages stuck together, put his finger to his mouth and turned over the first leaf. After much difficulty he turned over the second and the third, moistening his finger with his spittle at every page, and tried to read. But he could find no writing there.

"There is nothing written in this book," cried the King.

"Go on turning," replied the severed head.

The King had not turned six pages when poison (for the leaves of the book had been treated with venom) began to work in his body. He fell backward in an agony of pain, crying: "Poisoned! Poisoned!" and in a few moments breathed his last.

"Now, treacherous jinnee," continued the fisherman, "had the King spared the physician, he in turn would have been spared by Allah. But he refused, and Allah brought about the King's destruction. And as for you, if you had been willing to spare me, Allah would have been merciful to you, and I would have spared your life. But you sought to kill me; therefore I will throw you back into the sea and leave you to perish in this bottle!". . .

Review and Assess

Thinking About the Selection

1. **Respond:** Did you enjoy the tales-within-tales format? Why or why not?

2. **(a) Recall:** What question does the fisherman ask the jinnee "in the name of the Most High"? **(b) Analyze Cause and Effect:** How does the jinnee respond? **(c) Analyze:** Which character trait in the jinnee allows the fisherman to defeat him? Explain.

3. **(a) Recall:** How does King Yunan react when the Vizier first denounces Duban the Doctor? **(b) Interpret:** Why does he change his mind? **(c) Generalize:** What does Yunan's willingness to believe the Vizier suggest about his character? Explain.

4. **(a) Recall:** In the story of King Sindbad and the falcon, how does the falcon save the King's life? **(b) Analyze Cause and Effect:** Why is the King later stricken with sorrow and remorse? **(c) Interpret:** What does this story suggest about the dangers of unrestrained anger?

5. **Apply:** The evil Vizier tells King Yunan, "He who does not weigh the consequences of his acts shall never prosper." In what ways might this statement apply to the jinnee, King Yunan, and King Sindbad? Explain.

6. **Take a Position:** Are stories such as these an effective vehicle for teaching moral lessons? Why or why not?

Review and Assess

Literary Analysis

Folk Tales

1. Identify the magical or supernatural element in each of these interlocking **folk tales.**
2. Use a chart like the one shown to identify the main personality traits of the fisherman, the jinnee, King Yunan, Duban the Doctor, the Vizier, the falcon, and King Sindbad. Note the details that support your answers.

Character	Main Personality Trait	Supporting Details

3. (a) Which characters are seemingly weak or powerless? Explain. (b) Which seemingly powerless characters use cunning or trickery to achieve their goals? Explain.
4. Are any of these characters purely good or purely evil? Explain.

Connecting Literary Elements

5. (a) Describe the **narrative structure** of "The Fisherman and the Jinnee" by explaining who narrates each interlocking tale. (b) What motivates each narrator to tell each story?
6. (a) In what ways are the tales connected by theme or message? (b) How does the ending of the tale of King Sindbad and the falcon differ from the endings of the other two stories?

Reading Strategy

Summarizing

7. (a) Which main events and key details would you include in a **summary** of the main story about the fisherman and the jinnee? Explain. (b) Write a summary of that story.
8. In what ways might the use of summaries help a reader who is struggling with the narrative structure of interlocking stories? Explain.

Extend Understanding

9. **History Connection:** What do these tales reveal about the daily life and culture of the medieval Muslim world? Explain your response, citing examples.

Integrate Language Skills

Vocabulary Development Lesson

Word Analysis: Latin Root -vert-

The Latin root -vert- means "turn." *Inverted* means "turned upside down." Using your understanding of the root -vert-, write a brief definition of the italicized word in each of the following sentences.

1. We can *convert* this old theater into a store.
2. If the new system does not work, we will *revert* to the old one.
3. The plane was *diverted* to another airport.

Spelling Strategy

The *f* sound is sometimes spelled *ph*, as in *blasphemous*. More often, it is spelled *f* or *ff*: *fish, staff*. Rewrite the following sentence, correcting the misspelled words in italics:

The *fysician* was *bafled* by the *ffisherman's afliction*.

Concept Development: Synonyms

Select the letter of the word that is closest in meaning to the first word.

1. inverted: (a) reversed, (b) wicked, (c) shy
2. blasphemous: (a) loud, (b) unwise, (c) sinful
3. adjured: (a) disliked, (b) commanded, (c) healed
4. indignantly: (a) angrily, (b) noisily, (c) slyly
5. resolutely: (a) weakly, (b) helpfully, (c) stubbornly
6. enraptured: (a) puzzled, (b) repressed, (c) charmed
7. munificence: (a) poverty, (b) violence, (c) generosity
8. ominous: (a) shining, (b) threatening, (c) open

Grammar and Style Lesson

Action and Linking Verbs

Action verbs, such as *saw, thought,* and *went,* express physical or mental action. **Linking verbs,** such as *was, felt,* and *became,* express a state of being. Linking verbs are followed by a noun or pronoun that renames the subject or by an adjective that describes it.

Some linking verbs can also function as action verbs. If you can replace the verb with a form of *be*—such as *is, are, was,* or *were*—and still express a similar meaning, the verb is a linking verb.

Action: The fisherman *looked* in the bottle. We *tasted* the food.

Linking: The jinnee *looked* monstrous. (was) The food *tasted* good. (was)

Practice Identify the verb in each sentence below as an action verb or a linking verb.

1. The bottle appeared heavy.
2. The fisherman broke the seal.
3. Once outside, the jinnee seemed like a powerful giant.
4. The fisherman felt enormous fear.
5. The fisherman tricked the jinnee in the end.

Writing Application Write four sentences about a character in "The Fisherman and the Jinnee." Use at least two action verbs and two linking verbs in your writing.

$\mathcal{W}_G$ Prentice Hall Writing and Grammar Connection: Diamond Level, Chapter 17, Section 2

Writing Lesson

Critique of a Work

The interlocking stories that make up "The Fisherman and the Jinnee" have been told and retold for centuries. Write a brief critique that attempts to account for the enduring popularity of these tales.

Prewriting   Reread "The Fisherman and the Jinnee," noting details that could appeal to readers of different cultures in different times. Then, list those details that you think give the stories universal appeal.

Drafting   Begin your critique with a statement about the enduring appeal of "The Fisherman and the Jinnee." Then, provide examples to support that statement. Dedicate one paragraph to each story.

Revising   As you review your draft, study the cause-and-effect relationships you have proposed. Add transitions like *therefore* and *as a result* to make your reasoning clear.

Model: Revising to Show Cause and Effect

The fisherman is a poor man with little power or

As a result,

influence. ^ Everyday people hearing or reading his

story can identify with him.

> Transitional terms like *as a result* help clarify cause-and-effect relationships.

Prentice Hall Writing and Grammar Connection: Diamond Level, Chapter 9, Section 4

Extension Activities

Research and Technology   Conduct research to find out more about jinnees and their role in Persian and Middle Eastern folklore. Use a variety of sources such as the following:

- encyclopedias
- handbooks of literature or folklore
- reliable Internet Web sites with information on Persian or Arabic literature

Present your findings in a written **report**.

Listening and Speaking   Listen to Nikolai Rimsky-Korsakov's orchestral work *Scheherazade*, a musical interpretation of *The Thousand and One Nights*. Then, hold a **panel discussion** to determine how well the music captures the mood of *The Thousand and One Nights*, based on the tales you have read from it. Present your findings to your class. [**Group Activity**]

 **Take It to the Net**   PHSchool.com

Go online for an additional research activity using the Internet.

Prepare to Read

from The Rubáiyát ◆ *from the* Gulistan ◆ *from the* Masnavi

Omar Khayyám (1048–1131)

A Persian poet, scientist, and mathematician, Omar Khayyám (ō´ mär kī yäm´) is probably the best-known Islamic poet in the West, where his poems, called rubáiyát, have been read and appreciated for centuries.

Khayyám was born in Persia (now Iran) in the city of Nishapur (nē´ shä p o o r), a major center of art and learning in the Middle Ages. He quickly earned a reputation as a mathematician and as a scholar of philosophy, history, law, and astrology. Despite his accomplishments in all these fields, he wrote very little, focusing mostly on scholarly writings about mathematics.

Khayyám's Poetry In recent times, Omar Khayyám's reputation as a poet has eclipsed his scientific fame. A collection of poetry called *The Rubáiyát* is attributed to him, although it is now known that Khayyám did not write the majority of the poems in the collection. Over the years, many poems written by other authors have been added to *The Rubáiyát* and ascribed to Khayyám. The question of authorship, however, is of little concern to Omar Khayyám's admirers, who read and enjoy *The Rubáiyát* to this day.

Sa'di (c.1213–1291)

Sa'di (sä´ dē) is revered for his wit, learning, and elegant style of writing. Persian-speaking people of all ages still read his works for enjoyment and ethical guidance in their lives.

Born in the Persian city of Shiraz, Sa'di, whose real name was Muslihuddin (m o o s lə h o o dēn´), adopted the pseudonym Sa'di to show his appreciation for his royal patron, a local ruler named Sa'd bin Zangi (säd´ bēn zän gē´). After devoting the first three decades of his life to his education, Sa'di spent approximately thirty years traveling and composing poetry. Then, he spent another three decades in religious seclusion, devoting much of his time and energy to revising his poems. During the last ten years of his life, Sa'di focused on teaching the ways of the mystic and taking care of the needy. Among his major works is a collection of fables entitled the *Gulistan*, or "Rose Garden." Its speculations on life and proper behavior are so accessible to Westerners that it has been repeatedly translated since 1787.

Rumi (1207–1273)

Rumi (rü´ mē) was born in the central Asian city of Balkh—now part of Afghanistan—but lived most of his life in Anatolia, which is now Turkey. When Rumi's father died in 1231, Rumi assumed his father's position as a teacher of religion, quickly developing into a famous Sufi master with a large circle of disciples. Rumi himself was the founder of the Sufi order known as "Whirling Dervishes," whose hypnotic dancing was the means to spiritual enlightenment. Muslims from all over the world now follow the teachings presented in his verse and even reenact the whirling dance that Rumi used as part of his mystical exercises.

The *Masnavi* Rumi is regarded as not only one of the finest Persian mystical poets but also one of the finest poets the world has ever seen. His most famous work is the *Masnavi*, a long poem written at the suggestion of one of his students and intended to provide guidance for his disciples and for future generations. The *Masnavi* has stood through time as one of the most important Sufi works ever written, and it has been translated into many languages and analyzed by countless religious and literary scholars.

Preview

Connecting to the Literature

Fairy tales, fables with animal characters, and other stories often try to guide readers toward proper and humane behavior. Consider what such stories have in common with the selections you are about to read.

Literary Analysis

Didactic Literature

Didactic literature teaches lessons on ethics, or principles regarding right and wrong conduct, and it often reflects the values of the society that produces it. This literature usually presents specific situations or details from which a more general lesson, or **moral,** may be drawn. Look for the moral within each of these didactic works.

Comparing Literary Works

To better teach its lessons, didactic literature uses literary tools such as the following:

- **Aphorisms**—short, pointed statements expressing a truth about human experience.

- **Personification**—a technique that gives human qualities to non-human things.

- **Metaphor**—a figure of speech in which one thing is spoken of as though it were something else.

Although these devices appear in all of the selections you are about to read, each selection uses them in different ways. As you read, look for these tools of didactic literature and compare the differing ways each one is used.

Reading Strategy

Breaking Down Long Sentences

Analyze meaning by **breaking down long sentences** and considering what they say, one section at a time. Separate a sentence's key parts (the *who* and the *what*) from the difficult language to get to the main idea. Use a diagram like the one shown to analyze long sentences.

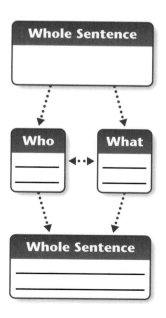

Vocabulary Development

repentance (ri pen´ təns) *n.* sorrow for wrongdoing; remorse (p. 108)

pomp (pämp) *n.* ceremonial splendor; magnificence (p. 109)

myriads (mir´ ē ədz) *n.* great numbers of persons or things (p. 111)

piety (pī´ ə tē) *n.* devotion to religious duties or practices (p. 111)

beneficent (bə nef´ ə sənt) *adj.* charitable (p. 112)

extortions (eks tôr´ shənz) *n.* acts of obtaining money or something else through threats, violence, or misuse of authority (p. 114)

wiles (wīlz) *n.* sly tricks (p. 117)

assertions (ə sur´ shənz) *n.* declarations or claims (p. 117)

from The Rubáiyát

Omar Khayyám *translated by* Edward FitzGerald

Background

In the eleventh century, Seljuk Turks took over the Persian Empire, imposing authoritarian government and strict religious practices on the population. Many believe that Omar Khayyám wrote his poems as a quiet protest against Seljuk rule. The poems, unpublished in his lifetime, offer an alternative philosophy that stresses enjoying life in the here and now. This philosophy is often expressed as *carpe diem*, Latin for "seize the day."

I

Wake! For the Sun, who scatter'd into flight
The Stars before him from the Field of Night,
   Drives Night along with them from Heav'n, and strikes
The Sultán's Turret[1] with a Shaft of Light.

VII

Come, fill the Cup, and in the fire of Spring
Your Winter-garment of <u>Repentance</u> fling:
   The Bird of Time has but a little way
To flutter—and the Bird is on the Wing.

VIII

Whether at Naishápúr or Babylon,[2]
Whether the Cup with sweet or bitter run,
   The Wine of Life keeps oozing drop by drop,
The Leaves of Life keep falling one by one.

Literary Analysis
Didactic Literature Which lines or phrases in poem VII might serve as a moral in a didactic story?

repentance (ri pen´ təns) *n.* sorrow for wrongdoing; remorse

---

1. **turret** (tʉr´ it) *n.* small tower projecting from a large building.
2. **Naishápúr** (nā shä pōōr´) **... Babylon** (bab´ ə lən) Naishápúr, also known as Neyshabur, is a city in northeastern Iran. It was one of the foremost cities of the Persian Empire and was the birthplace of Omar Khayyám. Babylon, an ancient city that was famous for its wealth, luxury, and wickedness, was the capital of the Babylonian Empire, which flourished from 2100 to 689 B.C.

XII

A Book of Verses underneath the Bough,
A Jug of Wine, a Loaf of Bread—and Thou
   Beside me singing in the Wilderness—
Oh, Wilderness were Paradise enow![3]

XIII

Some for the Glories of This World; and some
Sigh for the Prophet's Paradise to come;
   Ah, take the Cash, and let the Credit go,
Nor heed the rumble of a distant Drum!

XVI

The Worldly Hope men set their Hearts upon
Turns Ashes—or it prospers; and anon,[4]
   Like Snow upon the Desert's dusty Face,
Lighting a little hour or two—is gone.

XVII

Think, in this batter'd Caravanserai[5]
Whose Portals are alternate Night and Day,
   How Sultán after Sultán with his <u>Pomp</u>
Abode[6] his destined Hour, and went his way.

XXVII

Myself when young did eagerly frequent
Doctor and Saint, and heard great argument
   About it and about: but evermore
Came out by the same door where in I went.

XXVIII

With them the seed of Wisdom did I sow,
And with mine own hand wrought to make it grow;
   And this was all the Harvest that I reap'd—
"I came like Water, and like Wind I go."

XLVII

When You and I behind the Veil are past,
Oh, but the long, long while the World shall last,
   Which of our Coming and Departure heeds
As the Sea's self should heed a pebble-cast.

---

3. **enow** (i nou´) *adj.* enough.
4. **anon** (ə nän´) *adv.* immediately; at once.
5. **caravanserai** (kar´ ə van´ sə rī) *n.* inn with a large central court.
6. **abode** (ə bōd´) *v.* awaited.

Rubáiyát of Omar Khayyám, Edmund Dulac

▲ Critical Viewing

In what ways does the setting in this illustration capture the imaginary quality in Khayyám's poetry? **[Analyze]**

pomp (pämp) *n.* ceremonial splendor; magnificence

Literary Analysis
Didactic Literature and Metaphor For what condition is "behind the Veil" a metaphor?

☑ Reading Check

In poem XXVIII, what seeds did the speaker sow?

Rubáiyát of Omar Khayyám, Edmund Dulac

XLVIII

A Moment's Halt—a momentary taste
Of BEING from the Well amid the Waste—
    And Lo!—the phantom Caravan has reach'd
The NOTHING it set out from—Oh, make haste!

▲ Critical Viewing
Which of Khayyám's poems
does this scene best illustrate? Explain. [Interpret]

LXIV

Strange, is it not? that of the <u>myriads</u> who
Before us pass'd the door of Darkness through,
    Not one returns to tell us of the Road,
Which to discover we must travel too.

LXXI

The Moving Finger writes; and, having writ,
Moves on: nor all your <u>Piety</u> nor Wit
    Shall lure it back to cancel half a Line,
Nor all your Tears wash out a Word of it.

XCIX

Ah, Love! could you and I with Him conspire
To grasp this sorry Scheme of Things entire,
    Would not we shatter it to bits—and then
Remold it nearer to the Heart's Desire!

myriads (mir´ ē ədz) *n.* great numbers of persons or things

piety (pī´ ə tē) *n.* devotion to religious duties or practices

Review and Assess

Thinking About the Selection

1. **Respond:** Which images did you find especially vivid and powerful? Why?

2. **(a) Recall:** In line 3 of poem VIII, what image describes life? **(b) Infer:** What does the imagery in the next line suggest life is like? **(c) Connect:** What do the images in both lines stress about life? Explain.

3. **(a) Recall:** According to poem XII, what four things does the speaker need to enjoy paradise? **(b) Infer:** Who might "Thou" be? **(c) Make a Judgment:** Do you think the speaker requires a great deal to be happy? Explain.

4. **(a) Recall:** What two possibilities does poem XVI offer regarding human hopes? **(b) Relate:** How does the description of the Sultan in poem XVII relate to one of these two possibilities? **(c) Speculate:** What does the speaker suggest about the lives of both the least and greatest of people?

5. **(a) Evaluate:** What do you think of the speaker's view of life and how to spend it? **(b) Criticize:** Do you find inconsistencies in his ideas? Explain.

6. **Relate:** In what ways is *carpe diem* still a relevant philosophy today?

from the Gulistan

Sa'di *translated by* Edward Rehatsek

Background

Sa'di was a mystic, or dervish, in the Islamic sect of Sufism, which stresses the importance of freeing oneself from material desires and living a simple life of prayer and meditation. Like many Sufi mystics, Sa'di often used literature to convey his moral convictions. His *Gulistan* is comprised of fables—such as "The Manners of Kings"— that offer moral guidance through simple, didactic stories sprinkled with poems and aphorisms. The following sections from "The Manners of Kings" offer moral guidance to rulers.

from The Manners of Kings

1

I heard a padshah[1] giving orders to kill a prisoner. The helpless fellow began to insult the king on that occasion of despair, with the tongue he had, and to use foul expressions according to the saying:

> Who washes his hands of life
> Says whatever he has in his heart.

When a man is in despair his tongue becomes long and he is like a vanquished cat assailing a dog.

> In time of need, when flight is no more possible,
> The hand grasps the point of the sharp sword.

When the king asked what he was saying, a good-natured vizier[2] replied: "My lord, he says: *Those who bridle their anger and forgive men; for Allah loveth the <u>beneficent</u>.*"[3]

The king, moved with pity, forbore taking his life, but another vizier, the antagonist of the former, said: "Men of our rank ought to speak nothing but the truth in the presence of padshahs. This fellow has insulted the king and spoken unbecomingly." The king, being

beneficent (bə nef´ ə sənt) *adj.* charitable

---

1. **padshah** (päd´ shä) king.
2. **vizier** (vi zir´) high officer in the government; a minister.
3. **Those who bridle . . . beneficent** passage from the Qur'an. The beneficent are those who are kind and charitable.

displeased with these words, said: "That lie was more acceptable to me than this truth thou hast uttered because the former proceeded from a conciliatory disposition and the latter from malignity;[4] and wise men have said: 'A falsehood resulting in conciliation is better than a truth producing trouble.'"

> He whom the shah follows in what he says,
> It is a pity if he speaks anything but what is good.

The following inscription was upon the portico of the hall of Feridun:[5]

> O brother, the world remains with no one,
> Bind the heart to the Creator, it is enough.

---

4. **malignity** (mə lig´ nə tē) *n.* persistent or intense ill will or desire to do harm to others.
5. **Feridun** (fer ə dön´) legendary Persian king whose life is recorded in Firdawsi's *Shah-nama*. Feridun's three sons all died as a result of their dispute concerning who should succeed their father.

Literary Analysis
Didactic Literature and Aphorisms Which of the aphorisms in section 1 seem to guide the good-natured vizier's behavior? Explain.

✔**Reading Check**
What decision does the king make regarding the desperate prisoner?

◀ **Critical Viewing** Which details in this portrait suggest that this grand vizier is a respected member of society? **[Interpret]**

Rely not upon possessions and this world
Because it has cherished many like thee and slain them.
When the pure soul is about to depart,
What boots it if one dies on a throne or on the ground?

6

It is narrated that one of the kings of Persia had stretched forth his tyrannical hand to the possessions of his subjects and had begun to oppress them so violently that in consequence of his fraudulent <u>extortions</u> they dispersed in the world and chose exile on account of the affliction entailed by his violence. When the population had diminished, the prosperity of the country suffered, the treasury remained empty and on every side enemies committed violence.

> Who desires succor in the day of calamity,
> Say to him: "Be generous in times of prosperity."
> The slave with a ring in his ear, if not cherished will depart.
> Be kind because then a stranger will become thy slave.

One day the *Shah-namah* was read in his assembly, the subject being the ruin of the dominion of Zohak[6] and the reign of Feridun. The vizier asked the king how it came to pass that Feridun, who possessed neither treasure nor land nor a retinue, established himself upon the throne. He replied: "As thou hast heard, the population enthusiastically gathered around him and supported him so that he attained royalty." The vizier said: "As the gathering around of the population is the cause of royalty, then why dispersest thou the population? Perhaps thou hast no desire for royalty?"

> It is best to cherish the army as thy life
> Because a sultan reigns by means of his troops.

The king asked: "What is the reason for the gathering around of the troops and the population?" He replied: "A padshah must practice justice that they may gather around him and clemency that they may dwell in safety under the shadow of his government; but thou possessest neither of these qualities."

> A tyrannic man cannot be a sultan
> As a wolf cannot be a shepherd.
> A padshah who establishes oppression
> Destroys the basis of the wall of his own reign.

The king, displeased with the advice of his censorious vizier, sent him to prison. Shortly afterward the sons of the king's uncle rose in rebellion, desirous of recovering the kingdom of their father. The population, which had been reduced to the last extremity by the king's oppression and scattered, now assembled around them and supported them, till he lost control of the government and they took possession of it.

---

6. Zohak (zä´ hāk) legendary and tyrannical Persian king who was dethroned by Feridun.

extortions (eks tôr´ shənz) *n.* acts of obtaining money or something else through threats, violence, or misuse of authority

Literary Analysis
Didactic Literature What lesson does the vizier attempt to teach the king?

Reading Strategy
Breaking Down Long Sentences Break down the last sentence of this paragraph to determine the order of events within the sentence.

A padshah who allows his subjects to be oppressed
Will in his day of calamity become a violent foe.
Be at peace with subjects and sit safe from attacks of foes
Because his subjects are the army of a just shahanshah.[7]

▼ **Critical Viewing**
Which of the men pictured is a visiting ambassador, and which is a sultan? Which details helped you determine your answer? [Speculate]

7

A padshah was in the same boat with a Persian slave who had never before been at sea and experienced the inconvenience of a vessel. He began to cry and to tremble to such a degree that he could not be pacified by kindness, so that at last the king became displeased as the matter could not be remedied. In that boat there happened to be a philosopher, who said: "With thy permission I shall quiet him." The padshah replied: "It will be a great favor." The philosopher ordered the slave to be thrown into the water so that he swallowed some of it, whereon he was caught and pulled by his hair to the boat, to the stern of which he clung with both his hands. Then he sat down

in a corner and became quiet. This appeared strange to the king who knew not what wisdom there was in the proceeding and asked for it. The philosopher replied: "Before he had tasted the calamity of being drowned, he knew not the safety of the boat; thus also a man does not appreciate the value of immunity from a misfortune until it has befallen him."

O thou full man, barley-bread pleases thee not.
She is my sweetheart who appears ugly to thee.
To the huris[8] of paradise purgatory seems hell.
Ask the denizens[9] of hell. To them purgatory is paradise.

There is a difference between him whose friend is in his arms
And him whose eyes of expectation are upon the door.

Literary Analysis
Didactic Literature and Aphorisms What modern aphorism might be a good substitute for the philosopher's words?

Reading Check

In story 6, what punishment is given to the vizier who displeases his king?

---

7. **shahanshah** (shä´ hän shä) emperor or King of kings, usually referred to as a *shah*.
8. **huris** (hoo͞´ rēs) dark-eyed women who, in Islamic legend, live with the blessed in paradise.
9. **denizens** (den´ i zənz) *n*. Inhabitants or occupants.

I was sitting in a vessel with a company of great men when a boat which contained two brothers happened to sink near us. One of the great men promised a hundred dinars[10] to a sailor if he could save them both. Whilst however the sailor was pulling out one, the other perished. I said: "He had no longer to live and therefore delay took place in rescuing him." The sailor smiled and replied: "What thou hast said is certain. Moreover, I preferred to save this one because, when I once happened to lag behind in the desert, he seated me on his camel, whereas I had received a whipping by the hands of the other. When I was a boy I recited: *He, who doth right, doth it to his own soul and he, who doth evil, doth against the same.*"[11]

> As long as thou canst, scratch the interior[12] of no one
> Because there are thorns on this road.
> Be helpful in the affairs of a dervish[13]
> Because thou also hast affairs.

---

10. **dinars** (di närz´) *n.* gold coins used in a number of Islamic countries.
11. **He, who doth right . . . the same** passage from the Qur'an.
12. **scratch the interior** injure the feelings.
13. **dervish** (dʉr´ vish) Muslim dedicated to a life of poverty and chastity.

Review and Assess

Thinking About the Selection

1. **Respond:** Which of the lessons from the *Gulistan* would you share with a friend? Why?

2. **(a) Recall:** In story 1, what kinds of comments does the prisoner direct toward the king? **(b) Analyze Cause and Effect:** Why does the vizier lie on the prisoner's behalf?

3. **(a) Recall:** In story 6, why does the economy of the kingdom fail? **(b) Draw Conclusions:** What do the details of the fable reveal about the effectiveness of the king's rule? **(c) Hypothesize:** What do you think history will remember about this king? Explain.

4. **(a) Recall:** To whom does the padshah, or king, turn for help in story 7? **(b) Infer:** What do his actions reveal about the kind of ruler the padshah is?

5. **(a) Interpret:** What does the incident in story 35 suggest about the effect of individual human choice? **(b) Speculate:** In what way might this story be relevant to kings or rulers, even though none appear in it?

6. **Evaluate:** In what ways do you think the fables in "The Manner of Kings" might be relevant to leaders today?

from the MASNAVI

Rumi   *translated by* E. H. Whinfield

Concourse of the Birds, c. 1600, Habib Allah, The Metropolitan Museum of Art

Background

Like Sa'di, Rumi was a dervish in the Islamic sect of Sufism, and he is regarded as one of the finest poets in the world. His most important work, the *Masnavi,* is a verse composition of some 30,000 couplets, or two-line groupings. Often called the Qur'an of the Persian language, the *Masnavi* combines Sufi teachings with stories of advice like "The Counsels of the Bird."

THE COUNSELS OF THE BIRD

A man captured a bird by <u>wiles</u> and snares;
The bird said to him, "O noble sir,
In your time you have eaten many oxen and sheep,
And likewise sacrificed many camels;
You have never become satisfied with their meat,
So you will not be satisfied with my flesh.
Let me go, that I may give you three counsels,
Whenever you will see whether I am wise or foolish.
The first of my counsels shall be given on your wrist,
The second on your well-plastered roof,
And the third I will give you from the top of a tree.
On hearing all three you will deem yourself happy.
As regards the counsel on your wrist, 'tis this,
'Believe not foolish <u>assertions</u> of anyone!'"
When he had spoken this counsel on his wrist, he flew
Up to the top of the roof, entirely free.
Then he said, "Do not grieve for what is past;
When a thing is done, vex not yourself about it."
He continued, "Hidden inside this body of mine

wiles (wīlz) *n.* sly tricks

Reading Strategy
Breaking Down Long Sentences Break down the second sentence to identify one reason the bird gives for deserving freedom from the man.

assertions (ə sʉr shənz) *n.* declarations or claims

✓**Reading Check**

What will the bird give his captor if the man sets the bird free?

Is a precious pearl, ten drachms[1] in weight.
That jewel of right belonged to you,
Wealth for yourself and prosperity for your children.
You have lost it, as it was not fated you should get it,
That pearl whose like can nowhere be found."
Thereupon the man, like a woman in her travail,[2]
Gave vent to lamentations and weeping.
The bird said to him, "Did I not counsel you, saying,
'Beware of grieving over what is past and gone'?
When 'tis past and gone, why sorrow for it?
Either you understood not my counsel or are deaf.
The first counsel I gave you was this, namely,
'Be not misguided enough to believe foolish assertions.'
O fool, altogether I do not weigh three drachms,
How can a pearl of ten drachms be within me?"
The man recovered himself and said, "Well then,
Tell me now your third good counsel!"
The bird replied, "You have made a fine use of the others,
That I should waste my third counsel upon you!
To give counsel to a sleepy ignoramus
Is to sow seeds upon salt land.
Torn garments of folly and ignorance cannot be patched.
O counselors, waste not the seed of counsel on them!"

---

1. **drachms** (dramz) *n.* ancient Greek unit of weight approximately equal to the weight of a silver coin of the same name.
2. **travail** (trə vāl´) *n.* pains of childbirth.

Review and Assess

Thinking About the Selection

1. **Respond:** If you were the bird, what additional counsel would you give the man? Why?

2. **(a) Recall:** From what location does the bird give his second counsel? **(b) Analyze Cause and Effect:** Why does he go to that location?

3. **(a) Recall:** What are the first two counsels? **(b) Analyze:** In what ways does the man go against each of them?

4. **(a) Recall:** What choice does the bird make regarding the third counsel? **(b) Analyze:** What reason does the bird give for his choice? **(c) Draw Conclusions:** Who is the "sleepy ignoramus" to which the bird refers at the end of his counsel?

5. **Criticize:** In what way does the bird's counsel encourage a culture of distrust?

6. **Apply:** In what way is the counsel of the bird important in today's material world?

Review and Assess

Literary Analysis

Didactic Literature

1. In what ways does *The Rubáiyát* qualify as **didactic literature**?
2. (a) What behavior does Sa'di encourage in the four sections from "The Manners of Kings"? (b) Why might these behaviors be particularly important for kings?
3. State in your own words the moral of "The Counsels of the Bird."

Comparing Literary Works

4. (a) Which three **metaphors** represent life in poem VIII of *The Rubáiyát*? (b) What single metaphor represents wisdom in "The Counsels of the Bird"? (c) Which use of metaphor do you think is more effective? Explain.
5. (a) On a chart like the one shown, list two **aphorisms** from each selection. (b) In the circles, list those qualities the aphorisms share and identify ways in which they differ.

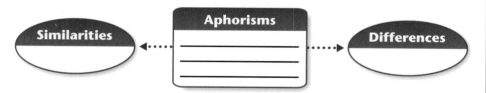

6. (a) In "The Counsels of the Bird," how does the use of a bird instead of a person make the verse more appealing? (b) In what way is the use of **personification** different in *The Rubáiyát*? (c) Why do you think didactic stories often use personification?

Reading Strategy

Breaking Down Long Sentences

7. **Break down the long sentence** in poem I of *The Rubáiyát*. (a) Who performs the main action? (b) What action is performed?
8. (a) In section 7 of "The Manner of Kings," what actions finally calm the distraught slave? (b) In what way does breaking down a long sentence help you determine this answer?

Extend Understanding

9. **Cultural Connection:** Based on the selections, what can you conclude about the relationship, centuries ago, between a good padshah and his vizier?

Integrate Language Skills

Vocabulary Development Lesson

Word Analysis: Latin Root *-tort-*

The word *extortions* contains the Latin root *-tort-*, which means "twist." *Extortions* are acts that wring money or valuables from others through threats, violence, or the misuse of power. Explain how the words below reflect the meaning of the root *-tort-*.

1. contortion   2. distort   3. tortuous

Spelling Strategy

Nouns ending in *ance* usually end in *ant* in their adjective forms: *repentance* becomes *repentant*. Nouns ending in *ence* usually end in *ent* in their adjective forms.

1. Write the noun form of *magnificent*.
2. Write the adjective form of *defiance*.
3. Write the noun form of *competent*.
4. Write the adjective form of *repugnance*.

Fluency: Sentence Completions

Review the vocabulary list on page 107. Then, fill in each blank below with an appropriate word from that list.

1. You seem very sure, but can you prove these __?__?
2. For the celebration, the queen appeared in all her __?__.
3. __?__ of stars shine in the nighttime sky.
4. The fox used its __?__ to sneak into the hen house.
5. Because she was rich, she could afford to be __?__.
6. He was a holy man praised for his __?__.
7. After doing wrong, she said a prayer as an act of __?__.
8. The criminal used threats and violence to back up his __?__.

Grammar and Style Lesson

Interjections

An **interjection** is a word that expresses emotion and functions independently of a sentence. Interjections express sentiments such as happiness, fear, anger, frustration, and surprise. Use a comma to punctuate an interjection that expresses mild emotion, and use an exclamation point for interjections expressing strong emotions.

Examples:

Lo! The phantom caravan has returned.

Oh, make haste!

Ah, my Love!

Practice Correctly punctuate the interjections in each item below. Add capital letters and end punctuation where necessary.

1. Hey I finally got my copy of *The Rubáiyát* hurray.
2. Oh I just read it.
3. Well did you like it? Huh.
4. Wow it was really good.
5. The *Masnavi* still has not arrived alas.

Writing Application Write four sentences about the lessons in one of the selections. Include correctly punctuated interjections with each sentence.

WG Prentice Hall Writing and Grammar Connection: Diamond Level, Chapter 17, Section 4

Writing Lesson

Fable

Both "The Manners of Kings" and "The Counsels of the Bird" qualify as fables, simple didactic stories in which each character usually has just one flaw or virtue. Often the characters are animals that behave like people. Write a fable aimed at a modern-day leader or role model.

Prewriting   Consider the issues modern-day leaders or role models face, and choose a lesson to address that issue. Then, brainstorm for the plot of a simple story. Finally, list each character, animal or human, and indicate a chief flaw or virtue next to each one.

Drafting   Use your lists to guide you in writing your fable. Include dialogue to make the events livelier. Make sure that you have a strong conclusion that states the moral clearly, either through a character or within the narrative.

Model: Drafting a Strong Conclusion

In the next election, the greedy politician was finally voted from office. And so he learned that his desire for money had cost him the trust of the community.

> A strong conclusion transforms the moral of didactic literature into a simple lesson that all readers can understand.

Revising   Reread your draft, making sure that the characters are clearly drawn and that the events of the story lead to the moral. Check that the moral is a message your readers can relate to their own lives.

*W*G *Prentice Hall Writing and Grammar Connection: Diamond Level, Chapter 5, Section 2*

Extension Activities

Research and Technology Write a brief **research report** on Sufism and whirling dervishes, including the order that Rumi founded. Sources for your report might include some of the following:

- print or online reference works on Sufism and Rumi
- Internet Web sites about Sufism or Rumi
- interviews with people who practice Sufism
- nonfiction books on Sufism or Rumi

Include a list of your sources in your finished work.

Listening and Speaking In a small group, listen to a brief selection from a contemporary English-language recording of Rumi's works. Then, hold a **group discussion** to share your responses to the recording. **[Group Activity]**

 **Take It to the Net** PHSchool.com

Go online for an additional research activity using the Internet.

Prepare to Read

African Proverbs ◆ *from* Sundiata

African Proverbs and *Sundiata*

Much of West Africa's rich history is not found on paper. Instead, the history is preserved in the elaborate recountings of the oral historians known as *griots* (grē´ ōz). Griots serve as a kind of living library for their communities. As a combined historian, storyteller, and teacher, a griot travels from village to village, retelling ancestral histories and legends. Griots think of themselves as the memory of their people, and many African ethnic groups rely on the memories of their griots to preserve a record of the past.

The Power of Proverbs

Embedded within the stories of the griots are many proverbs, or concise sayings, that reveal a truth about human experience. Proverbs play an important role in cultures with a strong oral tradition. They are the distillation of the culture's common wisdom. Because proverbs often use fresh or surprising metaphors, they can communicate a complicated idea in a clear, artful, and often diplomatic way. In many African cultures, these sayings have been used for centuries to teach children, settle arguments, and offer advice. Furthermore, using them deftly is often seen as a sign of the speaker's eloquence and intellect. (A collection of proverbs from several African ethnic groups appears on pp. 124–125).

Sundiata, An Unlikely Hero

A griot tale that combines the instructive role of proverbs with an entertaining story is the epic of *Sundiata*. In the thirteenth century, Sundiata was a legendary hero-king who ruled a region that included most of

what is now the West African republic of Mali. Initially, Sundiata seems an unlikely hero, one who might be considered an "underdog" today. As the story progresses, however, Sundiata's early childhood struggles lead to later dramatic successes in battle.

For those looking for factual accuracy, it is difficult to tell how much of the original story of Sundiata has been preserved. Over the centuries, Sundiata's story has become so embellished that it is perhaps just as much fiction as fact. Because the epic is told to instruct and entertain, individual griots have adapted the tale to emphasize particular lessons or details. Sundiata's story, in particular, was often told to warriors before battle to spur them to greater feats than they thought possible. Like other oral tales told by griots, *Sundiata* recounts the positive or negative results of its hero's actions in order to instruct listeners in appropriate behavior.

From Griot's Story to the Printed Page

Folklorist D. T. Niane wrote *Sundiata: An Epic of Old Mali* in his Malinke language after listening to the stories told by Mamadou Kouyate (mä´ mä dōō kōō ya´ te), a griot of the Keita clan. Niane's work was then translated into English and other languages, enabling the griot's wisdom to reach the farthest corners of the globe. In fact, Niane's own ancestors were griots, and his documentation of ancient oral histories is a direct continuation of their work. In addition to *Sundiata*, he has collected and retold many other legends of Mali.

Preview

Connecting to the Literature

If someone has ever made fun of you—even over something trivial—you know that the temptation to strike back can be very strong. Sundiata finds a noble way to stop ridicule and, in the process, becomes a hero.

Literary Analysis

Epic Conflict

An **epic** is a narrative or narrative poem that focuses on the deeds of heroes. At its heart is an **epic conflict,** a challenge in which the hero struggles against an obstacle or a series of obstacles and usually emerges triumphant. The obstacles may include the following:

- menacing enemies
- natural dangers
- moral dilemmas
- problems with society
- difficulties with fate
- challenging decisions

As you read *Sundiata*, notice the conflict that drives the epic's action.

Comparing Literary Works

While epic poems are among the longest literary genres, proverbs are among the shortest. **Proverbs** are sayings that offer cultural wisdom and practical truths about life. Both literary forms express key cultural values by offering suggestions about living correctly. As you read the African proverbs presented here, consider the ways in which the details apply to human experiences. Then, look for the proverbs contained within *Sundiata*. Notice the way these proverbs flavor the epic and direct the characters' actions. Then, consider the view of African culture that both selections provide.

Reading Strategy

Rereading for Clarification

Rereading passages can often help clarify characters' identities, the relationships among characters, the sequence of events, and even puzzling language. Sometimes, earlier passages provide the key to understanding information that seems confusing or unclear. Use a diagram like the one shown to clarify difficult passages that you encounter.

Vocabulary Development

fathom (fath´ əm) *v.* probe the depths of; understand (p. 127)

taciturn (tas´ ə tʉrn) *adj.* not given to talking (p. 127)

malicious (mə lish´ əs) *adj.* intending harm; spiteful (p. 128)

infirmity (in fʉr´ mə tē) *n.* weakness; illness (p. 129)

innuendo (in´ yo͞o en´ dō) *n.* indirect remark or gesture that hints at something bad; sly suggestion (p. 129)

diabolical (dī ə bäl´ ik əl) *adj.* devilish; wicked (p. 129)

estranged (ə strānjd´) *adj.* isolated and unfriendly; alienated (p. 129)

Passage

With the help of Sassouma Bérété's intrigues, Dankaran Touman was proclaimed king.

Reread Earlier Passage

Dankaran Touman, the son of Sassouma Bérété, was now a fine youth.

Clarification

Dankaran Touman is Sassouma Bérété's son.

African Proverbs

Background

Proverbs, or wise sayings, are an important part of the folk literature of many African peoples. Though they may appear to be the shortest of all literary forms, proverbs and the wisdom they convey can be found in lengthy epic works such as *Sundiata*. The proverbs presented here reflect the cultures of seven different tribes, representing nations from all parts of the African continent.

Uganda: The Baganda

A small deed out of friendship is worth more than a great service that is forced.
One who loves you, warns you.
The one who has not made the journey calls it an easy one.
Where there are no dogs, the wild cats move about freely.
Words are easy, but friendship is difficult.

Liberia: The Jabo

One who cannot pick up an ant and wants to pick up an elephant will someday see his folly.
The butterfly that flies among the thorns will tear its wings.
A man's ways are good in his own eyes.
Daring talk is not strength.
Children are the wisdom of the nation.
The one who listens is the one who understands.

South Africa: The Zulu

Do not speak of a rhinoceros if there is no tree nearby.
The one offended never forgets; it is the offender who forgets.
It never dawns in the same way.
Look as you fell a tree.
Eyes do not see all.
You cannot chase two gazelles.
What has happened before happens again.
No dew ever competed with the sun.
There is no foot which does not stumble.

Reading Strategy
Rereading for Clarification Reread the Zulu proverb about trees. Based on the context, what does the word *fell* seem to mean here?

Ghana: The Ashanti

Rain beats a leopard's skin, but it does not wash out the spots.
If you are in hiding, don't light a fire.
One falsehood spoils a thousand truths.
No one tests the depth of a river with both feet.

Nigeria: The Yoruba

The day on which one starts out is not the time to start one's
  preparations.
He who is being carried does not realize how far the town is.
Time destroys all things.
Little is better than nothing.

Tanzania and Kenya: The Masai

The hyena said, "It is not only that I have luck, but my leg is strong."
Baboons do not go far from the place of their birth.
We begin by being foolish and we become wise by experience.
The zebra cannot do away with his stripes.
Do not repair another man's fence until you have seen to your own.
It is better to be poor and live long than rich and die young.
Do not say the first thing that comes to your mind.

Review and Assess

Thinking About the Selections

1. **Respond:** Which of the proverbs did you find the most thought-provoking or relevant to today's world? Why?

2. **(a) Recall:** What does a Baganda proverb say about a person who has not made the journey? **(b) Infer:** Does the proverb imply that the journey is actually easy? Explain. **(c) Generalize:** What does the proverb say about human experience in general?

3. **(a) Recall:** What does a Jabo proverb say about daring talk? **(b) Compare and Contrast:** What is similar about the messages in that proverb and the proverb about lifting ants and elephants? **(c) Connect:** Describe a situation in which one of these proverbs might apply.

4. **(a) Recall:** What does a Masai proverb say about baboons? **(b) Interpret:** What lesson do you think this proverb teaches?

5. **(a) Compare and Contrast:** Give examples of sayings you know that have messages similar to those in some of these African proverbs, explaining what these proverbs have in common. **(b) Generalize:** Why do you think proverbs like these can transcend their culture? Explain.

FROM SUNDIATA:
An Epic of Old Mali

D. T. Niane

Background

Nearly one thousand years ago, the region of West Africa that included what is now Ghana and Mali was caught up in turmoil as rival kings fought for control of the profitable salt and gold trade. In the Keita clan of the Mandingo, there arose a heroic leader named Mari, or Sogolon, Djata, who united his people, fought off their rivals, and ushered in a glorious period of peace and prosperity. (In the rapidly spoken Mandingo language, "Sogolon Djata" became "Sundiata.") In this epic, Sogolon Djata's battle for strength echoes the Mandingos' struggle for survival.

CHARACTERS IN *SUNDIATA*

BALLA FASSÉKÉ (bä´ lä fä sä´ kā): Griot and counselor of Sundiata.

BOUKARI (bōō kä´ rē): Son of the king and Namandjé, one of his wives; also called Manding (män´ diŋ) Boukari.

DANKARAN TOUMAN (dän´ kä rän tōō män): Son of the king and his first wife, Sassouma, who is also called Sassouma Bérété.

DJAKMAROU (jä mä´ rōō): Daughter of the king and Sogolon; sister of Sundiata and Kolonkan.

FARAKOUROU (fä rä kōō´ rōō): Master of the forges.

GNANKOUMAN DOUA (nän kōō´ män dōō´ ə): The king's griot; also called simply Doua.

KOLONKAN (kō lōn´ kən): Sundiata's elder sister.

NAMANDJÉ (nä män´ jā): One of the king's wives.

NARE MAGHAN (nä´ rä mäg´ hän): Sundiata's father.

NOUNFAÏRI (nōōn´ fä ē´ rē): Soothsayer and smith; father of Farakourou.

SASSOUMA BÉRÉTÉ (sä sōō´ mä bä rä´ tā): The king's first wife.

SOGOLON (sô gô lōn´): Sundiata's mother; also called Sogolon Kedjou (ked´ jōō).

SUNDIATA (sōōn dyä´ tä): Legendary king of Mali; referred to as Djata (dyä´ tä) and Sogolon Djata, which means son of Sogolon. Also called Mari (mä´ rē) Djata.

Childhood

God has his mysteries which none can <u>fathom</u>. You, perhaps, will be a king. You can do nothing about it. You, on the other hand, will be unlucky, but you can do nothing about that either. Each man finds his way already marked out for him and he can change nothing of it.

Sogolon's son had a slow and difficult childhood. At the age of three he still crawled along on all-fours while children of the same age were already walking. He had nothing of the great beauty of his father Naré Maghan. He had a head so big that he seemed unable to support it; he also had large eyes which would open wide whenever anyone entered his mother's house. He was <u>taciturn</u> and used to spend the whole day just sitting in the middle of the house. Whenever his mother went out he would crawl on all-fours to rummage about in the calabashes[1] in search of food, for he was very greedy.

---

1. **calabashes** (kal′ ə bash′ iz) *n.* dried, hollow shells of gourds, used as bowls.

fathom (fath′ əm) *v.* probe the depths of; understand

taciturn (tas′ ə turn) *adj.* not given to talking

☑ **Reading Check**

What effect does Sogolon's son's illness have on his childhood?

▲ **Critical Viewing** In many cultures, storytellers narrate tales about their community's history. Which details in this tapestry suggest such an activity? **[Interpret]**

<u>Malicious</u> tongues began to blab. What three-year-old has not yet taken his first steps? What three-year-old is not the despair of his parents through his whims and shifts of mood? What three-year-old is not the joy of his circle through his backwardness in talking? Sogolon Djata (for it was thus that they called him, prefixing his mother's name to his), Sogolon Djata, then, was very different from others of his own age. He spoke little and his severe face never relaxed into a smile. You would have thought that he was already thinking, and what amused children of his age bored him. Often Sogolon would make some of them come to him to keep him company. These children were already walking and she hoped that Djata, seeing his companions walking, would be tempted to do likewise. But nothing came of it. Besides, Sogolon Djata would brain the poor little things with his already strong arms and none of them would come near him any more.

malicious (mə lish´ əs) *adj.* intending harm; spiteful

▲ **Critical Viewing** In what ways might this image represent the hope Sogolon held for her son? **[Speculate]**

The king's first wife was the first to rejoice at Sogolon Djata's <u>infirmity</u>. Her own son, Dankaran Touman, was already eleven. He was a fine and lively boy, who spent the day running about the village with those of his own age. He had even begun his initiation in the bush.[2] The king had had a bow made for him and he used to go behind the town to practice archery with his companions. Sassouma was quite happy and snapped her fingers at Sogolon, whose child was still crawling on the ground. Whenever the latter happened to pass by her house, she would say, "Come, my son, walk, jump, leap about. The jinn[3] didn't promise you anything out of the ordinary, but I prefer a son who walks on his two legs to a lion that crawls on the ground." She spoke thus whenever Sogolon went by her door. The <u>innuendo</u> would go straight home and then she would burst into laughter, that <u>diabolical</u> laughter which a jealous woman knows how to use so well.

Her son's infirmity weighed heavily upon Sogolon Kedjou; she had resorted to all her talent as a sorceress to give strength to her son's legs, but the rarest herbs had been useless. The king himself lost hope.

How impatient man is! Naré Maghan became imperceptibly <u>estranged</u> but Gnankouman Doua never ceased reminding him of the hunter's words. Sogolon became pregnant again. The king hoped for a son, but it was a daughter called Kolonkan. She resembled her mother and had nothing of her father's beauty. The disheartened king debarred Sogolon from his house and she lived in semi-disgrace for a while. Naré Maghan married the daughter of one of his allies, the king of the Kamaras. She was called Namandjé and her beauty was legendary. A year later she brought a boy into the world. When the king consulted soothsayers[4] on the destiny of this son he received the reply that Namandjé's child would be the right hand of some mighty king. The king gave the newly-born the name of Boukari. He was to be called Manding Boukari or Manding Bory later on.

Naré Maghan was very perplexed. Could it be that the stiff-jointed son of Sogolon was the one the hunter soothsayer had foretold?

"The Almighty has his mysteries," Gnankouman Doua would say and, taking up the hunter's words, added, "The silk cotton tree emerges from a tiny seed."

One day Naré Maghan came along to the house of Nounfaïri, the blacksmith seer of Niani. He was an old, blind man. He received the king in the anteroom which served as his workshop. To the king's question he replied, "When the seed germinates growth is not always easy; great trees grow slowly but they plunge their roots deep into the ground."

---

2. **initiation in the bush** education in tribal lore given to twelve-year-old West African boys so they can become full members of the tribe.
3. **jinn** (jin) *n.* supernatural beings that influence human affairs; their promise was that the son of Sogolon would make Mali a great empire.
4. **soothsayers** (sooth′ sā ərz) *n.* people who can foretell the future.

infirmity (in fur′ mə tē) *n.* weakness; illness

innuendo (in′ yoo en′ dō) *n.* indirect remark or gesture that hints at something bad; sly suggestion

diabolical (dī ə bäl′ ik əl) *adj.* devilish; wicked

estranged (e strānjd′) *adj.* isolated and unfriendly; alienated

Literary Analysis
Epic Conflict and Proverbs What does the proverb about the silk cotton tree suggest will be the outcome of Mari Djata's childhood conflict?

Reading Check
What special talent does Sogolon use to try to heal her son?

"But has the seed really germinated?" said the king.

"Of course," replied the blind seer. "Only the growth is not as quick as you would like it; how impatient man is."

This interview and Doua's confidence gave the king some assurance. To the great displeasure of Sassouma Bérété the king restored Sogolon to favor and soon another daughter was born to her. She was given the name of Djamarou.

However, all Niani talked of nothing else but the stiff-legged son of Sogolon. He was now seven and he still crawled to get about. In spite of all the king's affection, Sogolon was in despair. Naré Maghan aged and he felt his time coming to an end. Dankaran Touman, the son of Sassouma Bérété, was now a fine youth.

One day Naré Maghan made Mari Djata come to him and he spoke to the child as one speaks to an adult. "Mari Djata, I am growing old and soon I shall be no more among you, but before death takes me off I am going to give you the present each king gives his successor. In Mali every prince has his own griot. Doua's father was my father's griot, Doua is mine and the son of Doua, Balla Fasséké here, will be your griot. Be inseparable friends from this day forward. From his mouth you will hear the history of your ancestors, you will learn the art of governing Mali according to the principles which our ancestors have bequeathed to us. I have served my term and done my duty too. I have done everything which a king of Mali ought to do. I am handing an enlarged kingdom over to you and I leave you sure allies. May your destiny be accomplished, but never forget that Niani is your capital and Mali the cradle of your ancestors."

The child, as if he had understood the whole meaning of the king's words, beckoned Balla Fasséké to approach. He made room for him on the hide he was sitting on and then said, "Balla, you will be my griot."

"Yes, son of Sogolon, if it pleases God," replied Balla Fasséké.

The king and Doua exchanged glances that radiated confidence.

The Lion's Awakening

A short while after this interview between Naré Maghan and his son the king died. Sogolon's son was no more than seven years old. The council of elders met in the king's palace. It was no use Doua's defending the king's will which reserved the throne for Mari Djata, for the council took no account of Naré Maghan's wish. With the help of Sassouma Bérété's intrigues, Dankaran Touman was proclaimed king and a regency council was formed in which the queen mother was all-powerful. A short time after, Doua died.

As men have short memories, Sogolon's son was spoken of with nothing but irony and scorn. People had seen one-eyed kings, one-armed kings, and lame kings, but a stiff-legged king had never been heard tell of. No matter how great the destiny promised for Mari Djata might be, the throne could not be given to someone who had no power in his legs; if the jinn loved him, let them begin by giving him the use of

Reading Strategy
Rereading for Clarification Reread to clarify the way in which lineage plays a part in being a griot.

Critical Viewing ▶
A mature baobab's trunk can measure 30 feet in diameter. In what ways might the baobab, like the one pictured, represent Sogolon Djata? [Infer]

Literary Analysis
Epic Conflict Which three events succeed in shifting more power to Mari Djata's enemies? Explain.

his legs. Such were the remarks that Sogolon heard every day. The queen mother, Sassouma Bérété, was the source of all this gossip.

Having become all-powerful, Sassouma Bérété persecuted Sogolon because the late Naré Maghan had preferred her. She banished Sogolon and her son to a back yard of the palace. Mari Djata's mother now occupied an old hut which had served as a lumber-room of Sassouma's.

The wicked queen mother allowed free passage to all those inquisitive people who wanted to see the child that still crawled at the age of seven. Nearly all the inhabitants of Niani filed into the palace and the poor Sogolon wept to see herself thus given over to public ridicule. Mari Djata took on a ferocious look in front of the crowd of sightseers. Sogolon found a little consolation only in the love of her eldest daughter, Kolonkan. She was four and she could walk. She seemed to understand all her mother's miseries and already she helped her with the housework. Sometimes, when Sogolon was attending to the chores, it was she who stayed beside her sister Djamarou, quite small as yet.

Sogolon Kedjou and her children lived on the queen mother's leftovers, but she kept a little garden in the open ground behind the village. It was there that she passed her brightest moments looking after her onions and gnougous.[5] One day she happened to be short of condiments and went to the queen mother to beg a little baobab leaf.[6]

"Look you," said the malicious Sassouma, "I have a calabash full. Help yourself, you poor woman. As for me, my son knew how to walk at seven and it was he who went and picked these baobab leaves. Take them then, since your son is unequal to mine." Then she laughed derisively with that fierce laughter which cuts through your flesh and penetrates right to the bone.

---

5. **gnougous** (nōō′ gōōz) *n.* root vegetables.
6. **baobab** (bā′ ō bab′) **leaf** *n.* The baobab is a thick-trunked tree; its leaves are used to flavor foods.

Literary Analysis
Epic Conflict In what way is the young Mari Djata in conflict with his own society?

Reading Check
How old is Sogolon Djata when Dankaran Touman is pronounced king?

Sogolon Kedjou was dumbfounded. She had never imagined that hate could be so strong in a human being. With a lump in her throat she left Sassouma's. Outside her hut Mari Djata, sitting on his useless legs, was blandly eating out of a calabash. Unable to contain herself any longer, Sogolon burst into sobs and seizing a piece of wood, hit her son.

"Oh son of misfortune, will you never walk? Through your fault I have just suffered the greatest affront of my life! What have I done, God, for you to punish me in this way?"

Mari Djata seized the piece of wood and, looking at his mother, said, "Mother, what's the matter?"

"Shut up, nothing can ever wash me clean of this insult."

"But what then?"

"Sassouma has just humiliated me over a matter of a baobab leaf. At your age her own son could walk and used to bring his mother baobab leaves."

"Cheer up, Mother, cheer up."

"No. It's too much. I can't."

"Very well then, I am going to walk today," said Mari Djata. "Go and tell my father's smiths to make me the heaviest possible iron rod. Mother, do you want just the leaves of the baobab or would you rather I brought you the whole tree?"

"Ah, my son, to wipe out this insult I want the tree and its roots at my feet outside my hut."

Balla Fasséké, who was present, ran to the master smith, Farakou-rou, to order an iron rod.

Sogolon had sat down in front of her hut. She was weeping softly and holding her head between her two hands. Mari Djata went calmly back to his calabash of rice and began eating again as if nothing had happened. From time to time he looked up discreetly at his mother, who was murmuring in a low voice, "I want the whole tree, in front of my hut, the whole tree."

All of a sudden a voice burst into laughter behind the hut. It was the wicked Sassouma telling one of her serving women about the scene of humiliation and she was laughing loudly so that Sogolon could hear. Sogolon fled into the hut and hid her face under the blankets so as not to have before her eyes this heedless boy, who was more preoccupied with eating than with anything else. With her head buried in the bed-clothes Sogolon wept and her body shook violently. Her daughter, Sogolon Djamarou, had come and sat down beside her and she said, "Mother, Mother, don't cry. Why are you crying?"

Mari Djata had finished eating and, dragging himself along on his legs, he came and sat under the wall of the hut for the sun was scorching. What was he thinking about? He alone knew.

The royal forges were situated outside the walls and over a hundred smiths worked there. The bows, spears, arrows and shields of Niani's warriors came from there. When Balla Fasséké came to order the iron rod, Farakourou said to him, "The great day has arrived then?"

Literary Analysis
Epic Conflict In what way does this event contribute to the epic conflict?

Reading Strategy
Rereading for Clarification Reread to find out who Balla Fasséké is. Where do you locate information about Noun-faïri's connection to Mari Djata?

"Yes. Today is a day like any other, but it will see what no other day has seen."

The master of the forges, Farakourou, was the son of the old Nounfaïri, and he was a soothsayer like his father. In his workshops there was an enormous iron bar wrought by his father, Nounfaïri. Everybody wondered what this bar was destined to be used for. Farakourou called six of his apprentices and told them to carry the iron bar to Sogolon's house.

When the smiths put the gigantic iron bar down in front of the hut the noise was so frightening that Sogolon, who was lying down, jumped up with a start. Then Balla Fasséké, son of Gnankouman Doua, spoke.

"Here is the great day, Mari Djata. I am speaking to you, Maghan, son of Sogolon. The waters of the Niger can efface the stain from the body, but they cannot wipe out an insult. Arise, young lion, roar, and may the bush know that from henceforth it has a master."

The apprentice smiths were still there, Sogolon had come out, and everyone was watching Mari Djata. He crept on all-fours and came to the iron bar. Supporting himself on his knees and one hand, with the other hand he picked up the iron bar without any effort and stood it up vertically. Now he was resting on nothing but his knees and held the bar with both his hands. A deathly silence had gripped all those present. Sogolon Djata closed his eyes, held tight, the muscles in his arms tensed. With a violent jerk he threw his weight on to it and his knees left the ground. Sogolon Kedjou was all eyes and watched her son's legs which were trembling as though from an electric shock. Djata was sweating and the sweat ran from his brow. In a great effort he straightened up and was on his feet at one go—but the great bar of iron was twisted and had taken the form of a bow!

Then Balla Fasséké sang out the "Hymn to the Bow," striking up with his powerful voice:

> "Take your bow, Simbon,
> Take your bow and let us go.
> Take your bow, Sogolon Djata."

When Sogolon saw her son standing she stood dumb for a moment, then suddenly she sang these words of thanks to God, who had given her son the use of his legs:

> "Oh day, what a beautiful day,
> Oh day, day of joy;
> Allah[7] Almighty, you never created a finer day.
> So my son is going to walk!"

---

7. **Allah** (al′ ə) Muslim name for God.

Themes in World Literature

The Trials of an Epic Hero

The literature of vastly different times and cultures portrays epic heroes who face great struggles or conflicts. Such heroes always display superhuman bravery, strength, or perseverance during their struggles, and their success often affects the fate of others—a tribe, a nation, or even all of humankind. In the Sumerian epic *Gilgamesh* (page 14), for example, the hero struggles to defeat evil Humbaba and find the secret of eternal life. In the ancient Greek epic the *Odyssey*, Odysseus struggles against many perils on his long journey home from the Trojan War. In the early English epic *Beowulf*, Beowulf struggles against three monsters that threaten his community as well as his own weakness in old age. In his struggle for respect and recognition, Sundiata is part of a great tradition in world literature.

Literary Analysis
Epic Conflict Why might the iron bar take the shape of a bow?

Reading Check

What does Farakourou use to help Sogolon Djata stand?

Standing in the position of a soldier at ease, Sogolon Djata, supported by his enormous rod, was sweating great beads of sweat. Balla Fasséké's song had alerted the whole palace and people came running from all over to see what had happened, and each stood bewildered before Sogolon's son. The queen mother had rushed there and when she saw Mari Djata standing up she trembled from head to foot. After recovering his breath Sogolon's son dropped the bar and the crowd stood to one side. His first steps were those of a giant. Balla Fasséké fell into step and pointing his finger at Djata, he cried:

> "Room, room, make room!
> The lion has walked;
> Hide antelopes,
> Get out of his way."

Behind Niani there was a young baobab tree and it was there that the children of the town came to pick leaves for their mothers. With all his might the son of Sogolon tore up the tree and put it on his shoulders and went back to his mother. He threw the tree in front of the hut and said, "Mother, here are some baobab leaves for you. From henceforth it will be outside your hut that the women of Niani will come to stock up."

Review and Assess

Thinking About the Selection

1. **Respond:** How did you feel about Mari Djata's feat at the end of the selection? Why?

2. **(a) Recall:** Up that point, how did most of the community treat Mari Djata? **(b) Infer:** Why was he treated that way? **(c) Generalize:** What does this treatment show about human nature?

3. **(a) Analyze Cause and Effect:** How do the soothsayers' predictions affect the king's view of Mari Djata? **(b) Infer:** After the king dies, why do you think his wishes for Mari Djata are not followed?

4. **(a) Recall:** What happens that causes Sogolon to want her son to bring her baobab leaves? **(b) Infer:** How has pressure from Sassouma Bérété and the rest of the community affected Sogolon?

5. **(a) Summarize:** What does Mari Djata do to get the baobab leaves and bring them to his mother? **(b) Speculate:** How do you think the community reacted to this act?

6. **(a) Connect:** Based on the Background on page 126 and the soothsayer's predictions, what rank will Mari Djata eventually achieve in his community? **(b) Draw Conclusions:** Considering Mari Djata's past infirmity, what lesson might readers draw from this outcome?

7. **Apply:** What does the selection show about customs and traditions in Old Mali? Explain.

Review and Assess

Literary Analysis

Epic Conflict

1. Think about the **epic conflict** that Mari Djata faces in this part of *Sundiata*. (a) In what sense is it a conflict with nature? (b) In what sense is it a conflict with society? (c) In what sense is it an internal conflict that takes place within Mari Djata himself?

2. What role do Sassouma Bérété and Sogolon play in Mari Djata's childhood conflict? Explain.

3. (a) How could the Zulu proverb about feet that do not stumble apply to Mari Djata and his conflict? (b) How does the Jabo proverb about lifting ants and elephants contrast with or contradict Mari Djata's experiences?

Comparing Literary Works

4. On a chart like the one below, list and explain at least two of the **proverbs** that appear in *Sundiata*. Also, indicate how they apply to Mari Djata and his situation.

Proverb	General Meaning	How It Applies

5. Choose three African proverbs about nature that you find the most thought-provoking or perceptive. Explain how the lessons they draw from nature apply to human experience.

Reading Strategy

Rereading for Clarification

6. The first paragraph of "The Lion's Awakening" reveals that the king's will reserved the throne for Mari Djata. **Reread** the first two paragraphs of that section. Which details explain why the king left Mari Djata the throne?

7. (a) In the final paragraph of *Sundiata*, why does Mari Djata tear out the whole baobab tree? (b) Identify the passages that helped you answer this question.

Extend Understanding

8. **Science Link:** What do *Sundiata* and the African proverbs suggest about the traditional African knowledge of nature? Explain.

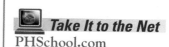

Integrate Language Skills

Vocabulary Development Lesson

Word Analysis: Latin Root -firm-

The word *infirmity* contains the prefix *in-*, meaning "not," and the Latin root *-firm-*, meaning "strengthen" or "strong." Sundiata's *infirmity* is "a condition that is not strong" or "a weakness; an illness." Explain how the meaning of *-firm-* figures into the meanings of these words.

   1. confirm   **2.** infirmary   **3.** affirm

Spelling Strategy

Many adjectives end in the suffix *-ious: malicious, previous*. Sometimes, after an *n* or a *t*, this suffix is spelled *eous: instantaneous, righteous*. Complete each word below with the correct spelling of the suffix. Check your answers in a dictionary.

   1. delic_?_ous   **3.** env_?_ous
   2. court_?_ous   **4.** beaut_?_ous

Fluency: True/False

Use the meanings of the italicized words to decide whether each statement below is true or false. Be prepared to explain your responses.

1. You can rely on the kindness of a *malicious* person.
2. A *taciturn* person talks a lot.
3. A chronic illness can be an *infirmity*.
4. An *innuendo* hints at something instead of saying it directly.
5. A *diabolical* smile is sweet and innocent.
6. A couple who become *estranged* probably will stop dating.
7. A mystery is something most people find hard to *fathom*.

Grammar and Style Lesson

Sentence Variety

Many sentences begin with a subject and a verb, but **sentence variety** keeps writing interesting. Writers can add variety by using different sentence beginnings:

Adverb: *Now* he was resting on nothing but his own two feet.

Prepositional Phrase: *With a lump in her throat,* she left Sassouma's.

Participial Phrase: *Having become all-powerful,* Sassouma Bérété persecuted Sogolon.

Subordinate Clause: *When the seed germinates,* growth is not always easy.

Practice Revise the following sentences using the sentence beginnings suggested in parentheses. Add new words wherever necessary.

1. The stiff-legged boy still crawled although he was now seven. (*subordinate clause*)
2. Sogolon tried to heal her son using potions and herbs. (*adverb*)
3. The queen mother was very wicked and cruel. (*prepositional phrase*)
4. Sogolon wept with her head buried in the bedclothes. (*participial phrase*)
5. The young prince slowly straightened up and stood on his feet. (*prepositional phrase*)

Writing Application Write a paragraph predicting what will happen to Mari Djata. Use at least three different sentence beginnings in your writing.

 Prentice Hall Writing and Grammar Connection: Diamond Level, Chapter 5, Section 4

Writing Lesson

Storytelling Notes

Although the griots of Old Mali presented epics from memory, a modern story-teller might want to work from a good set of notes. Create notes in outline form for a retelling of a story you know.

Prewriting   On a chart like the one shown, list the characters and events in your story, and jot down details you think should be included to make the retelling clear and interesting.

Model: Gathering Details

Character	Character Details

Event	Event Details

Drafting   Drawing on the details in your chart, create a set of notes in outline form. Under important headings such as *background*, *conflict*, *complications*, *climax*, and *resolution*, jot down phrases that will prompt your memory during your performance.

Revising   Review your notes and make sure that you have included enough information for a good retelling. Add any background detail or action that makes your story complete.

W̶G̶ Prentice Hall Writing and Grammar Connection: Diamond Level, Chapter 7, Section 2

Extension Activities

Listening and Speaking Practice and perform an **oral retelling** of the selection from *Sundiata*. Follow these guidelines:

- Take notes on the details that are important to include in your retelling.
- Use your notes as you practice. Work on achieving the right tone of voice for each character.
- Practice before performing. Do not read your notes; use them as a guide.

Retell the story to classmates. Afterward, invite feedback from your listeners.

Research and Technology Working in a group, create a **booklet of proverbs** from around the world. Students who gather the proverbs might consult books of quotations, proverbs, and folk literature. Other students should work on the editing and organization of the booklet, as well as its production, including typing, printing, binding, and illustrating it. **[Group Activity]**

 **Take It to the Net** PHSchool.com

Go online for an additional research activity using the Internet.

READING INFORMATIONAL MATERIALS

Brochures

About Brochures

A **brochure** is a pamphlet that combines information and advertising to highlight an attraction or a place of interest. Brochures usually contain some of the following elements:

- Historical background
- Details about the attraction
- Images that highlight the attraction
- Map to guide visitors
- Hours of operation
- Ticket and contact information

A brochure may also contain a persuasive message financed by a sponsor or company. As you read this brochure about an exhibit on ancient Egyptian civilization at the Museum of Science in Boston, note which of these elements it contains.

Reading Strategy

Adjusting Your Reading Rate

Brochures often include more information than you want or need. To find the specific information that you want, **adjust your reading rate.** Using the techniques of skimming and scanning will help you locate information quickly and efficiently. The chart shown gives instructions for skimming and scanning.

	Obtaining Information Quickly
To Skim	• Read quickly across a page, without reading word for word. • Stop at headlines, italics, and other text features if the words are related to what you want to know.
To Scan	• Run your eyes across and down the page. • Scan headlines, bold type, italics, and other text features to locate information quickly.

As you read this brochure about the exhibit on ancient Egyptian civilization, adjust your reading rate by skimming and scanning the material to learn as much as you can about the exhibit.

THE QUEST for IMMORTALITY
Treasures of Ancient Egypt

Confronting the mystery of death is a fundamental human endeavor. The ancient Egyptians believed they could ensure their continued existence after death, and they devoted tremendous energy and resources to achieving this goal. The pursuit of immortality was the central feature of a complex, evolving set of beliefs that characterized Egyptian civilization throughout its first 3,000 years of history.

Photographs of these artifacts from the exhibit provide a preview for readers.

For modern archaeologists, Egyptian tombs are treasure houses—not of objects, but of evidence. It is through examination and excavation of tombs and their furnishings that archaeologists have begun to understand the remarkably complex religion of ancient Egypt. This exhibition explores Egyptians' quest for immortality from the Old Kingdom (2686–2125 BCE*) through the Late Period (664–332 BCE). It also

*Before Common Era

tells the story of archaeologists' 200-year quest to understand the thought and practices of an accomplished and intricate culture.

The Afterlife

The boat is a recurring image in Egyptian funerary art. It is a reminder of Egypt's reliance on the Nile River, the country's life giver and major artery. For the Egyptians, the Nile was the center of the world. It was also a metaphor for the soul's journey through the netherworld: sailing in a solar boat, the sun god Re travels through the hours of night to be reborn with each dawn. In imitation of the gods, pharaohs hoped to secure their own immortality. While some rituals seemed to have been reserved exclusively for the pharaohs, the quest was shared by all Egyptians. Scribes and maids, mayors and generals all sought to deny the impermanence of the body. Through the material remains of their endeavors, their names and histories live again—immortality of a sort.

This cover image of a sphinx attracts readers' interest and gives the brochure visual appeal.

This page of the brochure provides historical background information.

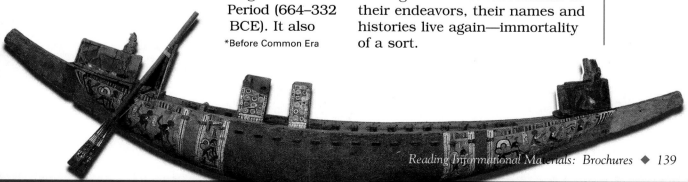

Exhibition Map

Burial Chamber of Thutmose III

Red Wing, Level 2

↓ ↑

The New Kingdom

Mummification

Video Theater

The Gods

Reconstructing the Past

Hieroglyphics

The Afterlife

Exit
Audio Tour Drop-Off

Audio Tour Pick-Up

Entrance

Elevator

Restrooms (Down)

Access to Exhibition

Atrium

Quest Exhibition Store

Red Wing, Level 1

Museum of Science
It's Alive!

Museum of Science • Science Park • Boston MA 02114-1099
617-723-2500 • 617-589-0417 (TTY) • www.mos.org

277M11/02

The map helps visitors navigate their way through the exhibit.

EXHIBITION INFORMATION

EXHIBITION AMENITIES
- Audio tour provided by Antenna Audio.
- Exhibition store featuring Egypt-inspired gifts and merchandise, including the beautifully illustrated catalog.
- Science Street Café on Thursday and Friday evenings, offering cocktails, gourmet appetizers, and special desserts, 6–10 p.m.

EXHIBITION HOURS
The Quest for Immortality gallery will be open during regular Exhibit Halls hours, plus special extended hours on Thursday evening, just for adults. Timed ticket entry.
- **Saturday–Wednesday: 9 a.m.–5 p.m.**
- **Thursday–Friday: 9 a.m.–9 p.m.**

TICKETING INFORMATION AND RESERVATIONS
Full-price admission to *The Quest for Immortality* includes a separate ticket for general admission to the Exhibit Halls that may be used on the same day or on another day within six months.

Individual & Group
Reserve by Phone
(daily 9 a.m.–5 p.m.)
617-723-2500
617-589-0417 (TTY)

Event Options
Reserve by Phone
(Mon.–Fri. 9 a.m.–5 p.m.)
617-589-0125
617-589-0417 (TTY)

Individual tickets may also be reserved online at www.mos.org/quest

WWW.MOS.ORG/QUEST
Find out more about ancient Egypt, explore a 3-D mummy, or learn how to play the ancient game of senet. This site also offers the latest information about *The Quest for Immortality* exhibition and related Museum attractions, tickets, events, lectures, hotel packages, special offers, shopping, visiting tips, and directions.

MUSEUM MEMBERSHIP
Becoming a member is the best way to receive priority treatment for *The Quest for Immortality* and enjoy the Museum all year long. Hold on to your Exhibit Halls ticket vouchers—we will apply a portion of your ticket price toward the cost of any membership level.
For details, visit the Membership Booth or contact us at 617-589-0180, membership@mos.org.

UNITED EXHIBITS GROUP

The Quest for Immortality is organized by the United Exhibits Group™, Denmark, and the National Gallery of Art, Washington, in association with the Supreme Council of Antiquities, Cairo.

Check Your Comprehension

1. What was the ancient Egyptian belief about life after death?
2. In Egyptian funerary art, what does the boat represent?
3. Using the map, identify the first three parts of the exhibit that visitors will see as they enter.
4. Identify three exhibition amenities that the museum provides.

Applying the Reading Strategy

Adjusting Your Reading Rate

5. (a) By skimming this brochure, what did you learn about the museum's Web site? (b) What text feature alerted you to stop skimming and begin reading word for word?
6. Identify three specific things you learned by scanning the headlines.

Activity

Designing a Brochure

Design a brochure for an event in your school or an attraction in your town. Use a local newspaper, your library, or the Internet to find information about the event. You might also consult the group or school official who is sponsoring it. Use note cards like the one shown to organize details for your brochure. Then, using headlines, text, graphics, maps, or lists, organize your brochure to promote the event and interest readers. Share your completed brochure with classmates.

> **Event: *town carnival***
>
> Date: Time:
> Location: Cost:
> Other details:
>
> Why this carnival is fun for all ages:
> - *Adult and kiddie rides*
> - *Children's zoo with pony rides*
> - *Games of skill and chance*
> - *International food pavilions*
> - *Music and entertainment every night*

Comparing Informational Materials

Brochures and Press Releases

In addition to brochures, publicity departments of organizations produce press releases and send them to news outlets, where writers can use them as reference materials.

1. Press releases are written for reporters and editors. Contrast this audience with the general public, the audience of a brochure.
2. Indicate whether you would expect to find each element listed below in a press release, a brochure, or both. Explain your answers.
   - pricing
   - maps
   - date, time, and address
   - attractive photographs and art
   - long quotations from experts
   - publicity contact information
   - parking information
   - detailed descriptions of events

Writing About Literature

Analyze Literary Periods

In the ancient world, life was short and often brutal, dependent on ill-understood and unpredictable natural forces and events. Much of the literature of ancient times was morally instructive, providing a pattern for life in a chaotic world. The Bible, for example, transmitted the core religious values of Judaism and Christianity, just as the Qur'an transmitted the values of Islam.

Examine the literary works in this unit to discover the values expressed in them. Note especially the values that seem most universal. Then, write an essay that describes some of these shared values, using specific examples from the literature to support your ideas. Consult the box at the right for details of this assignment.

Prewriting

Review the selections. List the values that the writers of the selections express directly or indirectly. You may use the following questions as a guide:

- What is the theme of the selection?
- How do the actions and statements of the main character express and amplify the theme?
- What societal values does that theme reflect?
- Which other selections reflect similar values?

Review at least five of the selections. Take notes using a chart similar to the one below. Then, review your chart and select two or more works that express common values.

Model: Listing to Find Values

Selection	Value	Example	Page #
The Epic of Gilgamesh	bravery	"If your heart is fearful throw away fear . . ."	16

Gather examples. Return to the works that you have selected and, using your chart, gather additional examples reflecting the values they share. In addition to direct statements about right and wrong in the works, consider what characters' actions, motives, and fates may imply.

Write a working thesis. After you have gathered examples, write a working thesis. Introduce the values you will discuss and explain the way in which they are central to the selections.

Assignment: Shared Values in the Literature of the Ancient World

Write an analytical essay that explores the shared values expressed in two or more of the excerpts from the literature of the ancient world that you have read in this unit.

Criteria:

- Include a thesis statement drawn from your analysis of the literature.
- Support your thesis with detailed analyses of at least two of the selections.
- Cite several examples from each work you explore.
- Approximate length: 1,500 words

Read to Write

As you reread the texts, pay special attention to the main characters' actions and speech. What values do these words and deeds demonstrate?

Drafting

Organize logically. A logical organization makes your ideas clear to readers. After you introduce your thesis, you may want to write a paragraph for each value you discuss and include examples from each of the selections. If the paragraphs seem too long using this method of organization, you may decide to write a separate paragraph for each selection.

Model: Use a Logical Organization

I Value 1
> Selection 1
> Selection 2
> Selection 3

II Value 2
> Selection 1
> Selection 2
> Selection 3

Provide examples. Illustrate the values you cite with specific examples from the selections, such as direct value statements by the author or a character or values you infer from the behavior of the characters and the twists and turns of the plot.

Revising and Editing

Review content: Check the validity of your connections. Make sure that the examples you have chosen clearly and unambiguously illustrate the values you are discussing. Add transition sentences as necessary to make those connections clear.

Review style: Rephrase for clarity. Reword sentences to make your intended meaning as clear as possible.

Original: Psalm 8 expresses the belief that humans are close to God. So are angels, but the Psalm expresses the belief that humans are better than other animals.

Revised: Psalm 8 expresses the belief that humans are close to God. In their position as God's favorites—just a little lower than the angels—humans rule over the rest of creation.

Publishing and Presenting

Write and present a summary. Gather with classmates who wrote about some of the same selections you did. Compare your group's reactions to the literature. Summarize the discussion in writing, and share your summary with the rest of the class.

W͟G Writing and Grammar Connection: Diamond Level, Chapter 14

Write to Learn
As you write your first draft, you may notice that some examples you have chosen do not adequately support the values you are discussing. Be flexible and willing to reexamine the literature to choose other examples or to revise your thesis.

Write to Explain
Remember that your reader may not be as familiar with the selections as you are. Provide enough context so that the examples you cite make sense and support your thesis persuasively.

Writing WORKSHOP

Narration: Autobiographical Narrative

An **autobiographical narrative** is a work in which the writer describes an experience from his or her life. In this workshop, you will write an autobiographical narrative about an incident that was in some way significant to you.

Assignment Criteria Your autobiographical narrative should have the following characteristics:

- Well-established characters, including the writer as the main character
- An organized sequence of events with a significance that is clearly communicated
- Action that incorporates shifts in time and mood
- Conflict or tension between characters or between a character and another force
- Insights that the writer has gained from the experience

To preview the criteria on which your autobiographical narrative may be assessed, see the Rubric on page 147.

Prewriting

Choose a topic. Select an event or incident that was significant for you in some way: For example, choose an event that taught you an important lesson or a new way of looking at life. If a significant incident doesn't immediately spring to mind, complete one of these **sentence starters**:

I really learned what being responsible means the time I _____.

A day that turned out just the opposite from what I expected was ___.

Families suddenly become very important when _____.

Make setting and characters vivid. To enliven your narrative, work to make your list of details as concrete and specific as possible. Sensory images can convey the sights, sounds, and smells of scenes. Details recording characters' acts, movements, thoughts, words, and gestures add depth and realism.

Pace out the action. When you are happy with your details, create a chart like the one shown here. Approximate how much space and emphasis you will need for elements like background, the event itself, and an explanation of its importance, or use the percentages in the chart. Group the details into the part of the story where you want to tell about them; then roughly plot out your narrative to ensure balanced coverage.

Story Element	Proportion of Total
introduction (characters, setting, background)	10%
the incident itself (conflict, development, resolution)	80%
significance of incident	10%

Student Model

Before you begin drafting, read this student model and review the characteristics of an effective autobiographical narrative.

Sarah Beck
Harrison, TN

My Underground Experience

A few years ago, when I was fourteen, I got stuck in a hole that my cousin and I dug. It was the middle of summer in beautiful Mancelona, Michigan. Woodpeckers were yammering away, the dogs were chasing chipmunks, and my cousin and I were out exploring thirty-two acres of woods.

> Sarah provides specific details that establish the time and place of the incident she is describing.

Ashley and I had come upon a fox den, not uncommon in the area. Somehow, we got it into our heads to build an "underground house" of our own, in a clearing near the house. For a good half-hour or more we dug, every now and then testing its depth. First it was up to our knees, then our waists, and finally our chests. I was a bit jealous that Ashley could crawl in backward and pull her knees up to her chest and then get out again.

I crawled in and tried to pull my knees up, but I could not. I crawled in again, this time with my knees already up, and I slid right in. I then attempted to crawl back out, to no avail. I tried moving my knees to inch out, but I was stuck. I tried pushing on the side of the hill, but still nothing happened.

> Sarah creates a clear sequence relating how she became stuck.

"Ash, help me. Get me out!" I yelled, half-angrily. She grabbed my wrists and began to pull her hardest, while I tried to make myself smaller. I was still stuck fast. I yelled for her to get my mom, fast.

One minute, then two, passed. Ashley reappeared with Mom walking slowly behind, carrying a wooden spoon and a shovel. When Mom saw my predicament, she started to laugh. "I should have brought the camera."

"I would burn the picture!" I sobbed. "Just get me out of here."

> Sarah adds dialogue to capture both the humor and frustration of the moment.

Mom tried to pull me out. One knee almost slid out, but my left leg was still stuck. It felt as though my joints would pop. My grandmother volunteered to get our neighbor, Dan, who lived almost a quarter mile away. Mom grabbed the shovel and told me to cover my head while she used it. It was then that I realized that I was sliding farther into the hole.

Mom began shoveling out a ramp for my knees. Just as I was finally pulled out, Dan walked up. The first words out of his mouth were, "Sarah, this is the stupidest thing I've ever seen you do." He had known me for a long time. I tried standing up but fell right back down. I had little circulation in my legs for more than thirty minutes. Grandmother and Mom helped me get to the porch until I could stand.

Mom told me to thank Dan for coming anyway, so I wobbled over to give him my thanks. "Thank goodness you didn't go in head first," he replied. His eyes said, "You're welcome." Mom then told me to fill in the hole. I did this very well. For a while, I was in pain and afraid to go to sleep. What did I learn? Never dig a hole and climb in after.

> Sarah concludes her narrative with a terse statement of what she has learned.

Drafting

Establish the background and characters. Use the opening paragraph of your narrative to establish the setting (time and place) of the story and to begin to show its importance to events. Introduce yourself and significant characters as they were at that time. Use especially vivid or telling details that will make characters memorable to the reader.

Follow your pacing plan. Using the pacing plan you developed earlier, tell your story from start to finish. Introduce the conflict early on, and relate events that show its development and resolution. Remember to make the overall significance of the incident clear.

Add interest through plot enhancements. To make your story more interesting, consider adding one or more of the following:

- **Foreshadowing**—Give a hint early in the story of what is to come.
- **Flashback**—Go back in time to relate an incident that has a bearing on your story.
- **Interior monologue**—Re-create the thoughts that occurred to you while events were taking place.

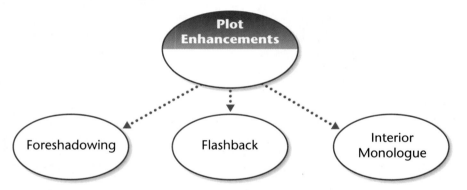

Revising

Revise to add dialogue. Reread your draft, and highlight any points in the narrative at which the addition of dialogue could help better establish characters. Look especially for passages in which emotion is most intense. Use a separate piece of paper to create precise, succinct dialogue, and then add the dialogue to your narrative.

Model: Revising to Add Dialogue

When Mom saw my predicament, she started to

. "I should have brought the camera."

laugh, ~~and wished she'd had a camera.~~

"I would burn the picture!" I sobbed.

Write to Explain

The use of dialogue makes the passage more vivid and interesting to read.

Revise for unnecessary tense changes. Though your narrative may move back and forth in time, check to make sure that you have not changed tenses unnecessarily. Look, for example, for passages in which you have moved from past to present within the same sentence for no reason.

Example: It *was* an hour after closing time, and I *am* still waiting.

Corrected: It *was* an hour after closing time, and I *was* still waiting.

Compare the model and the nonmodel. Note the changes in tense and decide why they were made.

Nonmodel	Model
I crawl in and try to pull my knees up, but I could not.	I crawled in and tried to pull my knees up, but I could not.

Publishing and Presenting

Consider the following activities to share your writing with classmates or a wider audience.

Make an oral presentation. Rehearse reading your story aloud. Mark up a copy of it, underlining words to be emphasized and starring points at which you will change your tone of voice or reading rate to create drama. Use these notations as you read your narrative to your class.

Create an illustrated anthology. Combine your narrative with those of several classmates into a single binder. Illustrate each narrative with photographs or artwork that captures the mood of the written work.

$\mathcal{W}_G$ *Writing and Grammar Connection: Diamond Level, Chapter 4*

Rubric for Self-Assessment

Evaluate your autobiographical narrative using the following criteria and rating scale:

Criteria	Rating Scale Not very				Very
How well do descriptions and dialogue establish the characters?	1	2	3	4	5
How effectively organized is the sequence of events?	1	2	3	4	5
How well does the action convey shifts in time and mood?	1	2	3	4	5
How well-paced is the action?	1	2	3	4	5
How clearly does the narrative communicate the significance of the incident for you and the insights it gave you?	1	2	3	4	5

Listening and Speaking WORKSHOP

Delivering a Speech

Whether you are comparing translations of *The Epic of Gilgamesh*, recounting an anecdote from your childhood, or persuading your peers to get involved in a political campaign, giving a speech can be an effective way to share your ideas. Whatever the topic or goal, follow these strategies to **organize and deliver an effective speech**.

Organizing Content

Take time to develop and organize the content of your speech.

Focus on purpose. Ask yourself what your goal is in giving the speech—whether to persuade, to entertain, or to inform. Formulate your purpose clearly and in detail. Keep this all-important purpose in mind as you organize the structure and content of your speech.

I. Need for a Student Cafeteria Committee
A. Purpose
B. Needs
C. Examples from other schools

II. Benefits of a Cafeteria Committee
A. Advantages for students
B. Advantages for cafeteria management
C. Possible complications

III. Establishing the Committee
A. Election of members
B. Responsibilities
C. Coordinating with cafeteria management

Consider your audience. Be aware of the background and interests of your audience as you develop your speech. A speech about the future of computers, for example, would be very different for a general audience from a speech on the same topic for an audience of computer programmers. The overall tone, the level and type of details, and the examples you choose will vary depending on the audience. If you are discussing a topic that may be intimidating, consider beginning with an anecdote or a joke.

Craft the speech. Organize your speech. Use an informal outline, perhaps by writing your main ideas on numbered index cards. Rewrite until you are satisfied that your speech is engaging and clear.

Giving the Speech

Effective speakers know what they want to say and how to say it.

- Rehearse aloud and listen to your words; revise awkward language. Become familiar with any visual aids that you plan to use.
- Memorize the main ideas of your speech. Refer as little as possible to your notes so that you can make eye contact with your audience.
- Make sure that your listeners can hear you, and don't race through your speech. If you think you may be talking too fast, you probably are.

Activity:
Prepare and Deliver a Speech Prepare, rehearse, and deliver a three-minute speech on a topic and for a purpose and an audience of your choice. Ask your classmates for feedback to improve your performance.

Assessment WORKSHOP

Conventions of Grammar and Language Usage

On the writing sections of some tests, you may be required to show your knowledge of the conventions of Standard Written English. Use the following strategies to help you answer test questions about punctuation, grammar, usage, and sentence structure:

- You can often identify errors in a sentence by quietly reading the sentence aloud. Mistakes that you might not notice when you read a sentence silently will often sound wrong when you hear them.

- Be alert to common mistakes, such as confusing *its* and *it's* or *who* and *whom*. Make sure that verbs agree with their subjects. Watch for unclear antecedents for pronouns.

- Learn to recognize structural errors, such as run-on sentences, sentence fragments, and misplaced modifiers.

Test-Taking Strategies

- When you are looking for errors in a passage, remember that there may be more than one error in each item.
- Choose the answer that corrects *all* the errors in an item.

Sample Test Item

Directions: Read the sentence, and then choose the letter of the best answer to the question.

The Romans adopted many of the Greek gods, they changed the names.

1. Which of the following choices is the best revision of the underlined words?

   A gods. They changed the names.

   B gods, but they changed the names.

   C gods, and they changed the names.

   D correct as is

Answer and Explanation

The best answer is *B* because it corrects the run-on sentence and meaningfully connects the two independent clauses. Answer *D* is incorrect; the original sentence is a run-on. Answers *A* and *C* correct the run-on problem but fail to relate the two ideas appropriately.

▶ Practice

Directions: Read the passage, and then choose the letter of the best answer to the question.

(1) Like giants, pygmies, and griffins, centaurs were monsters of Greek myth. (2) A centaur was a man from head through torso, and a horse in the lower part of his body. (3) Because the Greeks admired horses, they assigned centaurs many admirable traits, and unlike the other monsters in Greek myth, centaurs were often admitted to the company of humans. (4) When Chiron, the wisest of the centaurs, died, Zeus placed him in the constellation Sagittarius.

1. Which sentence contains an error in punctuation?

   A 1

   B 2

   C 3

   D 4

Assessment Workshop ◆ 149

UNIT 2

Indian Literature

Krishna's Magic Flute, Unknown artist, Kangra Valley. c. 18th–19th century. New York Public Library, Astor, Lenox and Tilden Foundations.

> **In the English-speaking world the strongest Indian influence was felt in America, where Emerson, Thoreau and other New England writers avidly studied much Indian religious literature in translation, and exerted immense influence on their contemporaries and successors, notably Walt Whitman.**
>
> — A. L. Basham,
> from *The Wonder That Was India*

Timeline c. 1400 B.C.–A.D. 500

Indian Events

- **1400** Indus Valley civilization had ended by this date.

- **1400** The Aryan migration began about 1,000 years earlier.

- **c. 1000** A compilation of the Vedic hymns is made. ▼

- **c. 700** This is the final date for the composition of the *Brahmanas*, texts that discuss religious rituals.

- **c. 600s** This is the earliest possible period for the founding of Jainism. ▼

- **c. 500s** This is the earliest possible period for the founding of Buddhism. ▶

- **400s** Panini describes and standardizes Sanskrit in an important grammar text.

- **327** Alexander the Great invades India.

- **c. 321–185** This is the period during which the Maurya emperors ruled much of India.

- **c. 300** This is the earliest possible date for the composition of the *Ramayana*.

- **c. 272** The Maurya emperor Asoka comes to power and rules for almost 40 years.

Buddha Standing, bronze, first ha of 7th century, The Metropolitan Museum of Art

World Events

- **1353–1336 (Egypt)** Akhenaton reigns and establishes the monotheistic worship of the sun-god Aton. ▶

- **c. 1150 (Mexico)** Olmecs, first major culture in Americas, are active.

- **1000–800 (Greece)** Tribes evolve into city-states.

- **mid-900s (Israel)** King Solomon reigns over a united country.

- **800s or 700s (Greece)** The legendary poet Homer composes the *Iliad* and the *Odyssey*. ▶

- **mid-600s (Italy)** Most of the major Etruscan towns have been established.

- **509 (Rome)** The Roman republic is founded.

- **c. 500 (China)** The *Shih Ching* ("Classic of Poetry"), classic anthology of psalms and folk songs, is compiled.

- **c. 495 (Greece)** The great Athenian statesman Pericles is born.

- **492–449 (Greece)** Greeks triumph in a series of wars fought against the Persian Empire.

- **479 (China)** The philosopher Confucius dies.

Indian and World Events

- **100 B.C.** This is the earliest possible date for the composition of the *Panchatantra*.
- **100–0 B.C.** The *Bhagavad-Gita* ("Divine Song") is composed; it is part of the *Mahabharata*.

- **100–0 B.C.** Early Indian sculpture decorates the gateways of the Buddhist relic mound called the Great Stupa.
- **100–0 B.C.** Work on the Ajanta caves begins; construction continues through the seventh century A.D. ▲

- **27 B.C. (Rome)** The Roman Empire is established.
- **c. A.D. 30 (ancient Palestine)** Jesus Christ is crucified.
- **A.D. 43–85 (Britain)** Romans conquer Britain.
- **A.D. 70 (ancient Palestine)** The temple at Jerusalem is destroyed, ending the sacrificial rituals called for in the Old Testament.
- **A.D. 75–100 (Roman Empire)** The four Gospels, which describe the life of Jesus Christ, are written; they become a significant part of the New Testament.

- **early 300s–late 500s** The Gupta dynasty rules an empire that includes northern sections of western and central India.
- **late 300s–early 400s** The Hindu author of an astronomical handbook tabulates the sine function.
- **c. 400** The Pillar of Delhi, a solid metal column 23 feet tall and weighing more than 6 tons, is constructed.
- **c. 400** The final compilation of the *Mahabharata* is made. ▼
- **400s and 500s** Using the concept of zero, Indian mathematicians develop the decimal system.

- **220 (China)** Warlords overthrow the last Han emperor; Han dynasty helped establish basis for Chinese culture.
- **250 (Mexico and Central America)** Rise of Mayan civilization begins; classic period lasts until about 900.
- **c. 300 (Africa)** Ghana emerges as a state. ▶
- **c. 320 (Rome)** From this time, Christianity is supported by the Roman Empire.
- **395 (Rome)** The Roman Empire divides into Eastern and Western empires.
- **476 (Rome)** The Western Roman Empire falls.

Indian Literature

(C. 1400 B.C.–A.D. 500)

Historical Background

The modern nation of India has existed since 1947. Through most of history, though, the term *India* has been used to describe the entire sub-continent that is also called South Asia. Surrounded by oceans and by the forbidding Himalayan Mountains, India remained isolated for long periods of its history. This isolation was broken periodically by invasions. Often, however, invading peoples became cut off from their original homelands and then were gradually absorbed into the Indian population.

The Indus Valley, Aryans, and Dravidians Some early settlers developed an impressive civilization in the northwest, where modern Pakistan and western India are located. This culture—the Indus Valley civilization, named for the river that runs through the region—was urban and highly sophisticated. The Indus Valley civilization mysteriously ended around 1500 B.C. At about the same time, people who called themselves Aryans (arʹ ē ənz)—from the word *arya*, meaning "noble"—migrated into India from the north and west. The Aryans brought with them the hymns of the *Rig Veda*, which expressed their religious ideas.

Point/Counterpoint

Was There an Aryan Invasion of India?
Two scholars express opposing points of view.

Yes! About 2000 B.C. the great steppeland which stretches from Poland to Central Asia was inhabited by semi-nomadic barbarians, who were tall, comparatively fair, and mostly long-headed. They had tamed the horse, which they harnessed to light chariots. . . . In the early part of the 2nd millennium, . . . [t]hey migrated in bands westwards, southwards and eastwards, conquering local populations, and intermarrying with them to form a ruling class.
—from *The Wonder That Was India,* by A. L. Basham

No! The concept of invading hordes of Aryans conquering northern India around 1500 B.C. arose in the nineteenth century for a variety of reasons. . . .

Although . . . there was little supporting evidence, the reason this theory became popular was that it . . . reinforced the racial attitudes popular in the nine-teenth century so that the highly regarded Vedas [collections of hymns] could be assigned to a time before the Aryans in India mixed with the indigenous races.
—from *"The Aryans and Ancient Indian History,"* by Subhash Kak

---

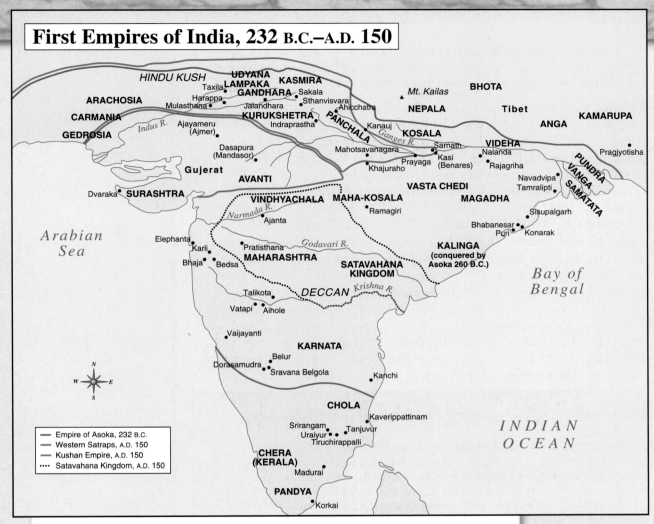

First Empires of India, 232 B.C.–A.D. 150

HINDU KUSH
UDYANA
KASMIRA
Taxila
LAMPAKA
BHOTA
ARACHOSIA
GANDHARA
Sakala
Mt. Kailas
Harappa
Sthanvisvara
NEPALA
Tibet
KAMARUPA
Mulasthana
Jalandhara
Ahicchatra
ANGA
CARMANIA
KURUKSHETRA
PANCHALA
Kanauj
KOSALA
Indus R.
Ajayameru
Indraprastha
Ganges R.
Sarnath
VIDEHA
GEDROSIA
(Ajmer)
Mahotsavanagara
Nalanda
Pragjyotisha
Dasapura
Prayaga
Kasi
Rajagriha
PUNDRA
(Mandasor)
Khajuraho
(Benares)
Navadvipa
VANGA
Gujerat
AVANTI
Tamralipti
SAMATATA
Dvaraka
SURASHTRA
VINDHYACHALA
MAHA-KOSALA
VASTA CHEDI
MAGADHA
Sisupalgarh
Narmada R.
Ramagiri
Bhabanesar
Ajanta
Godavari R.
Puri
Konarak
Arabian
Elephanta
Karli
Pratisthana
KALINGA
Sea
Bhaja
Bedsa
MAHARASHTRA
SATAVAHANA
(conquered by
Asoka 260 B.C.)
Bay of
KINGDOM
Bengal
Talikota
DECCAN
Krishna R.
Vatapi
Aihole
Vaijayanti
KARNATA
INDIAN
Belur
OCEAN
Dorasamudra
Sravana Belgola
Kanchi
CHOLA
Kaverippattinam
Srirangam
Tanjuvur
Uraiyur
Tiruchirappalli
CHERA
(KERALA)
Madurai
PANDYA
Korkai

— Empire of Asoka, 232 B.C.
— Western Satraps, A.D. 150
— Kushan Empire, A.D. 150
••• Satavahana Kingdom, A.D. 150

Another cultural group, the Dravidians (drə vid′ ē ənz), inhabited southern India in ancient times. We do not know much about the earliest history of these dark-skinned, small-framed people, but we do know that they developed a thriving culture sometime during the first millennium B.C.

A Political Checkerboard The map of India's political history is a checkerboard of continually changing boundaries between kingdoms that do battle, absorb one another, and then split into new divisions. There were many empires in India's history (see the map above). Perhaps the greatest was that carved out by Candragupta Maurya (chän drə gōōp′ tə mä oor yə), ruled by his son Bindusāra and expanded by his grandson Asoka. Much later, in the sixteenth century A.D., the Moguls (mō′ gulz), Islamic rulers who were descendants of Genghis Khan, established a great empire in north India.

The subcontinent, however, was never united under any single political administration until the British succeeded in making India a colony. While the British did leave a significant mark on the region, we must also remember

▲ **Critical Viewing** Asoka (ə sō′ kə), who reigned in the third century B.C., was one of India's greatest kings and embraced the compassionate teachings of Buddhism. What evidence from this map supports A. L. Basham's assertion that after Asoka, "the political . . . unity of India was lost for nearly two thousand years"? Explain. [Read a Map]

that their rule of nearly the entire subcontinent lasted for a relatively short period, from the early 1800s to 1947. For most of its history, India has been a collection of kingdoms with ever-changing boundaries.

Religious Thought Indian creativity is especially evident in the field of religion. The subcontinent was the birthplace of many important faiths: Hinduism (hin´ dōō´ iz əm), the dominant religion of India; Buddhism (bood´ iz´ əm), which had been virtually extinct in India but has been reestablished and has spread throughout Asia; Jainism (jīn´ iz´ əm); and Sikhism (sēk´ iz əm). India has also added its own flavor to religions like Christianity and Islam.

The mixture of three early cultures—Indus Valley, Dravidian, and Aryan—contributed to India's Hindu civilization. The word *Hindu* comes from *sindhu*, a word in the ancient Indian language Sanskrit (san´ skrit´) that means "river" or "the Indus River." This word refers to both a religion and a social system. The Hindu religion recognizes many gods, but central to its belief is a final reality known as *brahman* (brä´ mən). Not only is *brahman* the foundation of all things, but it is present in every living being as its essential identity, or *atman* (ät´ mən). Hindu society was rigidly divided into groups, or castes, each of which had its own special duties. These castes were, in order of importance, learned people and priests (Brahmans); warriors; farmers and merchants;

Close-up on Culture

Religion in India: The Body Is an Old Shirt

The following images are part of the kaleidoscope of Indian religious practices: gigantic bonfires consuming effigies of ten-headed demons; sacred texts that are chanted without interruption for a month at a time; naked ascetics smeared with ashes from sacred fires; and monks absorbed in silent meditation.

As the richness of these images suggests, few places on Earth have devoted more creative energy to religious expression than has India. The best-known religious belief to come out of India—one shared by Hindus, Jains, and Buddhists—is the notion that the soul is repeatedly reborn into this world. As the body is cast off like an old shirt, the soul can go to heaven for a period of time or it can be reborn in a human body, an animal, or even an insect.

Whether a soul is reborn in better circumstances depends on a person's deeds, the totality of which is known as karma (kär´ mə). A good and virtuous person, with good karma, will be reborn as a higher-ranking person; for example, an honorable merchant may become a warrior. However, the texts record unpleasant punishments for those with bad karma. A person who steals grain, for instance, will be reborn as a rat.

Indian religions tend to view this life as a place of impermanence and inevitable disappointment. Continual rebirth, therefore, can result only in continual suffering. The way to avoid such suffering is to escape from the process of death and rebirth.

▲ **Critical Viewing**
Do these pictures of the wall of a Hindu temple (left) and the Taj Mahal (right) suggest the Hindu belief in many gods and the Islamic belief in one God? Why or why not? [**Compare and Contrast**]

serfs; and finally, menials who, because of their "low" occupations, were considered "untouchable" by members of other castes.

A revealing fact about Indian religious life is that no Indian language has an exact counterpart for the English word *religion*. The explanation for this is that Indians do not divide life into "religious" and "secular" spheres. Instead, religious concerns pervade all aspects of thought in Hindu India.

Religions Other Than Hinduism Jainism (7th–5th century B.C.) and Buddhism (6th–4th century B.C.) arose in protest against certain Hindu beliefs and complex rituals of sacrifice. Jains—a name that derives from the Sanskrit for "saint," *jina*—renounced earthly pleasures and devoted themselves to protecting all forms of life.

Buddhism was founded by Siddhartha Gautama (sid där′ tə gout′ ə mə), an Indian prince. When he left the palace grounds and learned about suffering and death for the first time, he was so affected by this experience that he renounced luxury and became a wandering religious man. After years of fasting and intense study, he achieved *nirvana* (nir vä′ nə). This Sanskrit word refers to a state of being in which the desire for earthly things has been quenched and the soul therefore need not be reborn. Gautama was given the name Buddha, Sanskrit for "enlightened one," to honor his achievement.

The Sikh religion developed in northern India about two thousand years after the origins of Buddhism and Jainism. Like these two religions, Sikhism rejected the caste system and rituals of Hinduism; however, the Sikhs' belief in a single god set them apart.

Seagoing Arab traders brought the Muslim religion to western India in the eighth century. Later, Muslim armies invaded India from the north and established the Mogul empire. Under the Mogul emperors (1526–1857), Islamic and Indian traditions mingled to produce a distinctive style of art and architecture. The most famous example of this style is the Taj Mahal, built by a Muslim emperor after the death of his favorite wife.

Mathematics Some of India's cultural achievements are so much a part of our everyday lives that they have lost their identity as Indian discoveries. Among these is our number system. The numerals that we use come from India; they are called Arabic numerals because Arab traders brought them from India to Europe. In addition, ancient Indian mathematicians are responsible for the invention of the zero and the decimal notation that this discovery made possible.

A Link Between Religion and Mathematics Scholars speculate that philosophical and religious ideas may have led Indian mathematicians to invent the zero and develop other advanced concepts. For example, in the religious writings of Hindus and Jains, time and space were regarded as limitless. It is not surprising, therefore, that mathematicians familiar with these beliefs would study the problems of defining infinite numbers and distinguishing between various types of infinity. Similarly, the Buddhist belief in nirvana and philosophical ideas about emptiness and the void may have prompted mathematicians to develop the concept of zero.

Technology and Medicine Indians also excelled in metalworking. A monument that testifies to their skill is the Iron Pillar of Delhi, a solid metal column that measures more than 23 feet tall and weighs more than 6 tons. It was erected c. A.D. 400 by the ruler Kumāra Gupta I in honor of his father.

Medicine was another field in which Indians distinguished themselves. Ancient Indian physicians were able to set broken bones, knew the importance of keeping wounds clean, and developed plastic surgery long before it was practiced in Europe.

Painting, Sculpture, and Architecture Indian painters and sculptors were patronized by kings and wealthy merchants. As artists traveled from kingdom to kingdom to show their work, they spread the inventions and secrets of their craft. For the most part, they depicted religious themes. However, their work also reveals the daily life, dress, and pastimes of ancient India, so it is a valuable record for us today.

Among the most notable achievements of Indian art are the frescoes, or wall paintings, in caves near the village of Ajanta in western India. These caves were created by Buddhist monks during the period from the first century B.C. to the seventh century A.D. The vibrant and colorful paintings on their walls depict Buddhist themes. (See Timeline, page 153.)

The artificial caves at Ajanta and elsewhere in western India are also great architectural achievements. Their interiors were designed to imitate the brightly colored halls in which Buddhist monks gathered during the rainy season to recite texts and debate religious questions. Some of the cave temples are also Hindu or Jain. The Hindu cave-temple Kailasa at Ellora was carved downward from a basaltic hillside. It is about 164 feet long, 108 feet wide, and 100 feet high.

Zero, 1980–1996, Robert Indiana, Morgan Art Foundation Limited

▲ **Critical Viewing**
The contemporary artist Robert Indiana created this sculpture of the numeral zero. Why do you think the concept of zero, first developed by Indian mathematicians, continues to fascinate artists and thinkers? **[Speculate]**

Literature

The Sacredness of Language The universal concern with religious values in Hindu life explains the lack of a clear separation between religion and literature. In fact, language itself—the sound of words—was regarded as sacred. An example of this belief is the practice of repeating the word *om* (ōm) during Hindu prayers. The repetition of this word is a religious act, a means of saying "yes" to the universe. While all language was considered sacred, the ancient Indian language Sanskrit was considered to be the perfect language. It ceased being a spoken language many hundreds of years ago, but all of the selections in this unit were written in Sanskrit. (Today, we recognize that Sanskrit is related to other ancient Indo-European languages like Latin and Greek.)

Because they believed that language was holy, Indians speculated a great deal about its power to convey ideas and emotions. This speculation led to a greater understanding about how language works. The Sanskrit grammars written by Panini in the sixth century B.C. are still admired by modern linguists.

Ancient Hymns and Epics The earliest surviving record of Indian religious thought, and the basis of Hinduism, is the collection of hymns known as the *Rig Veda* (rig´ vā´ də). These hymns do not set forth religious ideas in a systematic manner. Their homage to the gods of nature, however, sets a tone of devotion and piety that carries down to the present day.

These ancient hymns accompanied elaborate sacrifices to the gods, some of which lasted as long as a year! The writings that were developed to describe the details of these sacrifices had a profound effect on the way that Hindus thought. This influence is apparent, for example, in the structure of India's longest epic poem, the *Mahabharata* (mə hä´ bä´ rə tə), which means "Great Epic of the Bharata Dynasty." Just as a sacrificial ritual was divided into many small parts, the *Mahabharata* was divided into many small episodes told by different narrators.

Still another ancient epic is the *Ramayana* (rä mä´yə nə), which means "Romance of Rama." The hero, Rama, is one of the forms of the Hindu god Vishnu, and the high point of the epic is the battle between Rama and the evil demon Ravana (rə vä´ nə). An army of monkeys led by the monkey-general Hanuman (hän´ o͞o män´) assists Rama in this battle.

Rama and Lakshman Confer with the Animal Armies, from the *Adventures of Rama*, Courtesy of the Freer Gallery of Art, Smithsonian Institution, Washington, D.C.

▲ **Critical Thinking** This picture illustrates a scene from the *Ramayana*. Which details suggest that the *Ramayana* is a fantastic—not realistic—tale? Explain. **[Infer]**

Epics and Storytelling Both the *Mahabharata* and the *Ramayana* are extremely popular in India and in Southeast Asia. People dramatize events from these poems in colorful pageants, dance performances, and puppet shows. Also, storytellers recount the tales of epic heroes in villages across India. The modern writer R. K. Narayan, for example, describes the typical village storyteller, who knows "by heart all the . . . 100,000 stanzas of the *Mahabharata,*" beginning an evening session:

> . . . the storyteller will dress himself for the part by smearing sacred ash on his forehead and wrapping himself in a green shawl, while his helpers set up a framed picture of some god on a pedestal in the veranda, decorate it with jasmine garlands, and light incense to it. After these preparations, when the storyteller enters to seat himself in front of the lamps, he looks imperious and in complete control of the situation. He begins the session with a prayer, prolonging it until the others join and the valleys echo with the chants, drowning the cry of jackals."

The Importance of Memory As the recitation of the storyteller suggests, Indians placed great importance on memory, more so perhaps than did other ancient cultures. The traditional way of studying a subject in India was to memorize—completely and perfectly—the *entire* text and then to hear the teacher explain it. In the case of a sacred text like the *Rig Veda*, every syllable, every accent, every pause in the recitation had to be correct; otherwise, when these hymns were recited during a sacrifice, their power would be lost.

Students of the *Rig Veda* were first taught to memorize all 1,028 hymns in the normal way. One hymn, for example, begins, "I pray to the God of Fire, the household priest. . . ." After memorizing this hymn, each student would be assigned another way to memorize it—for example, "I pray I to pray the to God the of God Fire of the Fire household the priest household. . . ." This second version of the hymn was purposely nonsensical so that the student's act of memory would not be dependent on meaning. These incredible feats of memory took years, of course, and they seem utterly impossible to us. Yet it was just such dedication that preserved the hymns unchanged from 1500 B.C. to the present.

Texts were also written down in ancient India, but Hindus believed that trusting to the written medium involved too great a risk. A written copy could be lost or damaged. Strange as it may seem to us, a person's memory was regarded as a far safer means of preserving a text.

▲ **Critical Thinking** This photograph shows an Indian dancer performing a peacock dance. Compare and contrast the colors, gestures, and mood of the dancer with those of the characters in the *Ramayana* illustration, page 159. **[Compare and Contrast]**

The Evolution of Sanskrit Literature Ancient Indians had no literary genres like the novel or the short story. Except for poetry and drama, most Sanskrit texts imitated the *Rig Veda* in attempting to convey general and timeless truths. Even the myths that tell the story of the god Krishna— another form of Vishnu, one of the three most important Indian deities— deal with abstract principles. The same is true of the animal fables of the *Panchatantra* (pun´ chə tun´ trə). They use vivid language and are disarmingly naïve, but their purpose is to enable people to fulfill their *dharma* (dur´ mə), or unique obligations in life.

Indian poetry and drama did not come into their own until centuries after the *Rig Veda* was compiled. The greatest Indian poet was Kalidasa (see below). His plays and epic poems set the standards for those two genres.

The Continuing Influence of Indian Literature The selections in this unit come from the earliest products of India's literary tradition. Despite the fact that some of these works are 3,500 years old, however, their influence continues to be felt in modern times. They inspired the American authors Emerson and Thoreau, the Indian writer Rabindranath Tagore (see page 1140), and the Indian leader who pioneered the methods of nonviolent protest, Mohandas K. Gandhi.

A Writer's Voice

Kalidasa, The Sanskrit Shakespeare

Kalidasa (kä´ lē dä´ sä), who is as important in Indian literature as Shakespeare is in English literature, wrote verse dramas, love lyrics, and verse epics. His birth and death dates are unknown, but the sophistication of his work leads many scholars to link him with the sparkling court of Candragupta II (reigned c. A.D. 380–c. 415). As a court poet, Kalidasa wrote in Sanskrit, the ancient Indian tongue that by his day had become a literary rather than a spoken language.

One of his dramas, *Vikramorvasiya* ("Urvashi Won by Valor"), tells about a king's love for the goddess Urvashi. In this excerpt from the drama (translated by John Brough), the jealous goddess has fled to the forest and the grief-crazed king is searching for her:

> . . . The woods are desolate, who will tell me of my beloved?
> There, on top of that massive rock which breathes out steam after the rain-storm,
>
>   A peacock perches,
>   While east-wind gusts ruff every tail-fan feather,
>   And stretches
>   His shriek-filled throat, eyeing the rain-cloud weather.
>
>   [*He goes up to it.*] I can at least ask.
>
>   In this wild woodland, bird of lovely blue,
>   Saw you my wife whose love is true?
>   How could your white-flecked eyes have failed to mark
>   A face so fair, slant-eyes so dark?

Prepare to Read

from the Rig Veda

About the *Rig Veda*

The earliest surviving record of Indian religious thought, and the basis of Hinduism, is the sacred text known as the *Rig Veda*. Compiled around 1400 B.C., the *Rig Veda* is a collection of 1,028 hymns composed by different authors at different times. These hymns do not set forth religious ideas in a systematic manner. However, their homage to the gods of nature sets a tone of devotion and piety that carries down to the present day.

The Authors of the *Rig Veda*

The identity of the hymns' authors remains a mystery. We know only that they were part of the Indo-European race that gradually migrated into the Indian subcontinent from central Europe via what are now Iran and Afghanistan. These Indo-Europeans, who also migrated throughout Europe, referred to themselves as Aryans, a name that in Sanskrit means "noble" and that distinguished the migrants from the native peoples. Traces of the word *Aryan* can still be found in the names of countries like *Ireland* and *Iran*.

Wherever they traveled, Indo-Europeans naturally took their language with them. Over a long period of time, modern languages as diverse as English, Greek, French, Polish, Bengali, and Albanian evolved from Indo-European. (Most dictionaries and encyclopedias have a chart of Indo-European languages.) Sanskrit, the language of the *Rig Veda*, is one of the oldest Indo-European tongues.

The Religion of the *Rig Veda*

The poets of the *Rig Veda* were awed by the forces of nature. In many hymns, they portray natural phenomena—the sun, the moon, rain, night, wind, storms—as godlike beings. The authors praise these gods for their power and beauty and for the benefits they bring to humankind.

Because the hymns were composed at different times, they indicate different stages of religious thought. There is, however, a general interest in prosperity and comfort. The gods are invoked for protection and sustenance. Unlike later Hindu writings, the hymns place little emphasis on doing good for its own sake. They reflect the concerns of an agricultural people who needed rain for their crops, protection from storms, and a feeling of security in the night. Hymns that appear later in the *Rig Veda* diverge from this pattern by speculating about the purpose and creation of the universe.

Sacrifice and the *Rig Veda*

The *Rig Veda* describes a world in which the forces of nature are both benevolent and threatening. Rain, which is necessary for crops, can also bring catastrophe if it comes at the wrong time. The hymns were therefore recited at sacrificial offerings intended to win the favor of the gods and to ward off natural disturbances and chaos.

The earliest Vedic poets sought to please the gods through offerings of food and drink. They thought that such gifts would incline the forces of nature to perform beneficially for humans. The idea gradually evolved, however, that sacrifice is not only helpful to the gods, since it provides them with sustenance and praise, but is actually necessary for them. Eventually, the notion emerged that sacrifice *controls* the gods and the order of the universe. This belief gave the priests, who supervised the sacrifice, enormous power and influence.

The ancient practice of Vedic sacrifice is slowly dying out in modern India and is being replaced by other religious rituals based on the *Rig Veda*.

Preview

Connecting to the Literature

The *Rig Veda* offers clues to an ancient civilization yet also reflects time-less concerns. Like the speaker in the hymn "Night," we too have night-time fears, despite all our modern protections. Also, like the speaker in "Creation Hymn," we wonder about the origin of the universe.

Literary Analysis

Vedic Hymn

A hymn is a poem or song of praise. **Vedic hymns** emphasize the importance of gods and nature in Indian life and ponder timeless questions, such as the origin of the universe. These hymns were originally meant to be chanted, and they were passed down through the ages by word of mouth before they were written. While reading, look for devices that reflect this oral tradition, such as the repetition of words or of grammatical structure.

Comparing Literary Works

"Creation Hymn" and "Night" both involve mysteries of nature, but they approach their uncertainties from different angles. "Night" uses concrete language and familiar terms to make the unknown easier to comprehend. For example, the speaker uses **personification,** a description of something non-human as if it were human, to make the night seem less foreboding. The speaker also addresses the night directly, as in the following passage:

> As you came near to us today, we turned homeward to rest,
> as birds go to their home in a tree.

"Creation Hymn," in contrast, confronts the unknown on an abstract level. The hymn speaks of concepts such as existence and immortality and leaves many questions purposely unanswered.

As you read these hymns, think about the ways in which "Night" tries to remove nature's mystery while "Creation Hymn" embraces it.

Reading Strategy

Paraphrasing

Poets use concise language, compressing a wealth of meaning into just a few words. To unpack this meaning, pause occasionally as you read, and **paraphrase** the hymns, restating in your own words what each line says. Use a chart like the one shown to paraphrase passages from the hymns.

Vocabulary Development

immortality (im′ môr tal′ i tē) *n.* quality or state of being exempt from death; unending existence (p. 165)

distinguishing (di stiŋ′ gwish iŋ) *adj.* serving to mark as separate or different (p. 165)

stems (stemz) *v.* stops or dams up (as a river) (p. 166)

palpable (pal′ pə bəl) *adj.* able to be touched, felt, or handled (p. 166)

Poet's Words

The goddess Night has drawn near, looking about on many sides with her eyes. She has put on all her glories.

Paraphrase

It is dusk. The stars have begun to come out.

from the
Rig Veda

translated by
Wendy Doniger O'Flaherty

Creation Hymn

1 There was neither non-existence nor existence then; there was neither the realm of space nor the sky which is beyond. What stirred? Where? In whose protection? Was there water, bottomlessly deep?

2 There was neither death nor <u>immortality</u> then. There was no <u>distinguishing</u> sign of night nor of day. That one breathed, windless, by its own impulse. Other than that there was nothing beyond.

3 Darkness was hidden by darkness in the beginning; with no distinguishing sign, all this was water. The life force that was covered with emptiness, that one arose through the power of heat.

4 Desire came upon that one in the beginning; that was the first seed of mind. Poets seeking in their heart with wisdom found the bond of existence in non-existence.

5 Their cord was extended across. Was there below? Was there above? There were seed-placers; there were powers. There was impulse beneath; there was giving-forth above.

6 Who really knows? Who will here proclaim it? Whence was it produced? Whence is this creation? The gods came afterwards, with the creation of this universe. Who then knows whence it has arisen?

7 Whence this creation has arisen—perhaps it formed itself, or perhaps it did not—the one who looks down on it, in the highest heaven, only he knows—or perhaps he does not know.

immortality (im´môr tal´ i tē) *n.* quality or state of being exempt from death; unending existence

distinguishing (di stin´gwish in) *adj.* serving to mark as separate or different

✔**Reading Check**

According to the speaker, why wouldn't the gods know how the universe was created?

Night

1 The goddess Night has drawn near, looking about on many sides with her eyes. She has put on all her glories.

2 The immortal goddess has filled the wide space, the depths and the heights. She <u>stems</u> the tide of darkness with her light.

3 The goddess has drawn near, pushing aside her sister the twilight. Darkness, too, will give way.

4 As you came near to us today, we turned homeward to rest, as birds go to their home in a tree.

5 People who live in villages have gone home to rest, and animals with feet, and animals with wings, even the ever-searching hawks.

6 Ward off the she-wolf and the wolf; ward off the thief. O night full of waves, be easy for us to cross over.

7 Darkness—<u>palpable</u>, black, and painted—has come upon me. O Dawn, banish it like a debt.

8 I have driven this hymn to you as the herdsman drives cows. Choose and accept it, O Night, daughter of the sky, like a song of praise to a conqueror.

Review and Assess

Thinking About the Selections

1. **Respond:** To which of the hymns did you relate more, "Creation Hymn" or "Night"? Explain.

2. **(a) Recall:** How is the world described in the first two lines of "Creation Hymn"? **(b) Infer:** Why does the hymn say what was *not* rather than what was?

3. **(a) Recall:** Identify two specific questions the poet wants answered in "Creation Hymn." **(b) Infer:** Why can't the gods answer these questions? **(c) Deduce:** What does the gods' inability to answer suggest about the questions themselves?

4. **(a) Recall:** In "Night," what does the speaker ask the goddess Night to do? **(b) Analyze:** How might this request help the speaker and audience of this hymn feel safer in the darkness?

5. **Evaluate:** How successful are these hymns at expressing their central ideas? Explain.

Review and Assess

Literary Analysis

Vedic Hymn

1. Complete a chart like the one shown to identify two devices in the opening verses of "Creation Hymn" that suggest the oral tradition of **Vedic hymns**.

Device	Examples

2. (a) What eternal question does "Creation Hymn" explore? (b) What conclusion, if any, does the hymn reach with regard to this question?
3. Explain how the hymn "Night" reflects the Vedic sense of awe and respect for the forces of nature.

Comparing Literary Works

4. Why do you think "Creation Hymn" avoids using concrete language, such as **personification**, in questioning the origin of the universe?
5. (a) Which three natural phenomena are personified in "Night"? (b) In what way does personification support the hymn's purpose?
6. Why do you think the speaker of "Night" refers to the night using the concrete terms "tide of darkness" and "night full of waves"?

Reading Strategy

Paraphrasing

7. Reread the seventh verse of "Creation Hymn" and provide a **paraphrase** of that verse.
8. The fifth verse of "Night" is made up of one long sentence. Paraphrase this verse by breaking it down into several sentences.

Extend Understanding

9. **Science Connection:** According to "Creation Hymn," water existed before anything else. Many Native American creation myths also assert that water was the first element to exist. Why do you think many different peoples have imagined that the world began with water?

Quick Review

A **Vedic hymn** is an ancient Indian religious poem originally intended as a chant. Vedic hymns reflect a sense of awe toward nature.

Personification is the description of something nonhuman as if it were human.

When you **paraphrase,** you restate something in your own words.

 **Take It to the Net**
PHSchool.com

Take the interactive self-test online to check your understanding of these selections.

Integrate Language Skills

Vocabulary Development Lesson

Word Analysis: Latin Prefix *im-* / *in-*

The Latin prefix *im-* / *in-* means "not." The word *impossible* means "not possible." Consider the meaning of the prefix *im-* / *in-* as you choose the word from the following list that best completes each sentence below.

informal	immobile	infinite
impure	imperfection	inflexible

1. There are no limits to what you can achieve; the possibilities are ___.
2. The diamond was flawless, without a single ___.
3. Do not dress up for this event; it's ___.
4. Smoke from the factory made the air ___.
5. We tried to convince him to change his mind, but his will was ___.
6. The doctor said that the broken arm could heal only if it remained ___.

Concept Development: Synonyms

Match each vocabulary word on the left with its synonym, or word with a similar meaning, on the right.

1. distinguishing
2. immortality
3. palpable
4. stems

a. touchable
b. stops
c. differentiating
d. deathlessness

Spelling Strategy

When you add a prefix to a word, keep all the letters of the original word. For example, *im-* + *mortality* = *immortality*. Add the prefix *im-* / *in-* to each word listed below to create a new word.

1. numerable
2. modest
3. mature
4. adequate

Grammar and Style Lesson

Concrete and Abstract Nouns

A **noun** is the name of a person, place, or thing. A **concrete noun** names something that you can physically see, touch, hear, or smell. An **abstract noun** names something that is nonphysical, or that you cannot readily perceive through any of your five senses.

Concrete: eyes, tree, wolf

Abstract: existence, desire, wisdom

Practice Copy each item, circling all *concrete* nouns and underlining all *abstract* nouns.

1. What stirred? Where? In whose protection?
2. Was there water, bottomlessly deep?
3. There was neither death nor immortality then.
4. I have driven this hymn to you as the herdsman drives cows.
5. The rising sun brings warmth and hope to those who fear darkness.

Writing Application Write five sentences about some aspect of nature that inspires a sense of awe in you. For example, you might describe a thunderstorm or sunset. Underline at least three nouns in your writing, and indicate whether each one is concrete or abstract.

WG Prentice Hall Writing and Grammar Connection: Diamond Level, Chapter 17, Section 1

Writing Lesson

Comparison-and-Contrast Essay

"Creation Hymn" and "Night" both express awe about nature, but they differ in their treatment of the subject. In a **comparison-and-contrast** essay, examine the similarities and differences in how these hymns approach natural mysteries.

Prewriting   Review the hymns to consider how each one attempts to comprehend the workings of nature. Use a Venn diagram, like the one shown, to identify points to compare and contrast. Then, gather details and passages that support the points you have noted.

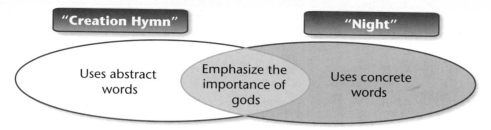

"Creation Hymn" — Uses abstract words

Emphasize the importance of gods

"Night" — Uses concrete words

Drafting   Decide how to organize your essay. One possibility is to discuss each point in turn, using examples from both hymns. You could also discuss all aspects of one hymn first and then all aspects of the second hymn. Cite passages and details from the hymns to support your points.

Revising   Review your work to be sure that you have supported your main points. You might also ask the following questions and revise accordingly: *Have I organized points logically? Have I used transitions to show comparisons?*

W̲G̲ *Prentice Hall Writing and Grammar Connection: Diamond Level, Chapter 9, Section 3*

Extension Activities

Listening and Speaking With a small group, give an **oral interpretation** of one of the hymns. To prepare, consider these questions:

- What is the mood of the hymn?
- What ideas are being expressed?
- Which words and phrases best capture these elements?

Have each member of the group practice reading a verse aloud. Then, perform your reading for the class. **[Group Activity]**

Research and Technology The *Rig Veda* reflects religious ideas of the Aryans, a people who migrated to India around 1400 B.C. Research the Aryans using library resources, such as encyclopedias and other print materials. Then, create a **culture spreadsheet** summarizing the information you find.

 **Take It to the Net** PHSchool.com

Go online for an additional research activity using the Internet.

from the *Rig Veda* ◆ 169

The Upanishads: Teaching Philosophy

Questions about life that concern us today fascinated Indian philosophers thousands of years ago.

Indian philosophers pursued the answers to questions about the meaning of life in texts called the Upanishads (o͞o pan´ i shadz´), which were written by many different authors from 1000 to 600 B.C.

The Upanishads: "to sit nearby" *Upanishad* in the ancient Indian language Sanskrit means "to sit nearby," in the sense of sitting near a teacher and learning from him. In accordance with this meaning, the Upanishads often present complicated subjects, such as the nature of reality, in dialogues between teachers and students.

The Upanishads are the final stage in the development of the sacred books called the Vedas (vā´ dez). (For more on the Vedas, see page 162.) The teaching in the Upanishads is therefore called *vedanta* (vi dän´ tə), which means the conclusion of the Vedas. Unlike the Vedas, however, the Upanishads tend to diminish the importance of individual gods. The authors of the Vedas express the wishes and fears of an agricultural people by appealing for protection to the gods of storm and other natural forces. By contrast, the Upanishads pursue philosophical questions about the meaning of life.

Brahman, "the Absolute" The abstract questions considered in the Upanishads lead to its central concept, the idea of Brahman (brä´ mən). This term, which is difficult to translate, has been rendered in English as "the one, universal Soul," "the Self-existent," and "the Absolute."

You may wonder why translators did not simply express this notion as "God." The answer is that Brahman is neither a god nor an object of worship. As the reality that underlies all appearances, Brahman is something that one "knows." It is the subject of meditation, a kind of prayerlike thought that focuses the mind on what is most real.

Peeling the Onion: "not this, not that" Because Brahman is such a difficult concept to grasp, it can best be defined by stating what it is *not*. This process is similar to peeling away the layers of an onion. When everything that is mere appearance has been stripped away, the remaining core will be Brahman. In the Upanishads, this type of negative description of Brahman is called "not this, not that."

The Mystery of Brahman: from the Taittiriya Upanishad The boxed excerpt from the Taittiriya Upanishad illustrates how these sacred books stress the importance of prayer and use dialogue and the "not this, not that" method to arrive at truth.

Secret and Dangerous Books In ancient India, scholars who searched the Upanishads for answers to life's questions were engaged in a secret, even dangerous, activity. It was dangerous because these books, which focused on Brahman rather than the Hindu gods, might be considered antireligious. Yet this once-secret literature went on to influence many great thinkers, including Ralph Waldo Emerson in nineteenth-century America.

The Mystery of Brahman *translated by* Juan Mascaró

Once Bhrigu Varuni went to his father Varuna and said: "Father, explain to me the mystery of Brahman."

Then his father spoke to him of the food of the earth, of the breath of life, of the one who sees, of the one who hears, of the mind that knows, and of the one who speaks. And he further said to him: "Seek to know him from whom all beings have come, by whom they all live, and unto whom these all return. He is Brahman."

So Bhrigu went and practiced *tapas*, spiritual prayer. Then he thought that Brahman was the food of the earth: for from earth all beings have come, by food of the earth they all live, and unto the earth they all return.

After this he went again to his father Varuna and said: "Father, explain further to me the mystery of Brahman." To him his father answered: "Seek to know Brahman by *tapas*, by prayer, because Brahman is prayer."

So Bhrigu went and practiced *tapas*, spiritual prayer. Then he thought that Brahman was life: for from life all beings have come, by life they all live, and unto life they all return.

After this he went again to his father Varuna and said: "Father, explain further to me the mystery of Brahman." To him his father answered: "Seek to know Brahman by *tapas*, by prayer, because Brahman is prayer."

So Bhrigu went and practiced *tapas*, spiritual prayer. Then he thought that Brahman was mind: for from mind all beings have come, by mind they all live, and unto mind they all return.

After this he went again to his father Varuna and said: "Father, explain further to me the mystery of Brahman." To him his father answered: "Seek to know Brahman by *tapas*, by prayer, because Brahman is prayer."

So Bhrigu went and practiced *tapas*, spiritual prayer. Then he thought that Brahman was reason: for from reason all beings have come, by reason they all live, and unto reason they all return.

He went again to his father, asked the same question, and received the same answer.

So Bhrigu went and practiced *tapas*, spiritual prayer. And then he *saw* that Brahman is joy: for FROM JOY ALL BEINGS HAVE COME, BY JOY THEY ALL LIVE, AND UNTO JOY THEY ALL RETURN.

This was the vision of Bhrigu Varuni which came from the Highest: and he who sees this vision lives in the Highest.

▲ **Critical Viewing**
How does this drawing reflect Bhrigu Varuni's attempt in "The Mystery of Brahman" to arrive at ultimate reality? Explain.
[Connect]

Prepare to Read

from the Mahabharata ◆ *from the* Bhagavad-Gita ◆ *from the* Ramayana

About the *Mahabharata*

The *Mahabharata* (mə hä ́ bä ́ rə tə) is the world's longest epic. Although it was compiled sometime between 200 B.C. and A.D. 200, Indian storytellers who have memorized it still entertain and instruct their village audiences with recitations from this epic poem.

The myths and tales of the *Mahabharata* are woven into the fabric of its main story: the account of a fight over the rights to a kingdom. Two branches of a family, the Pandavas and the Kauravas, are involved in this dispute.

Many of these myths and tales concern the Indian concept of **dharma** (där ́ mə), the unique obligations that each person must fulfill in order to maintain harmony in the universe. The stories reflect the belief that unrighteous behavior leads one astray, while righteous behavior will eventually be rewarded.

About the *Bhagavad-Gita*

The *Bhagavad-Gita* (bug ́ ə vəd gē ́ tä), which means "Song of the Lord," has been one of the most important texts in the Hindu tradition. It has been translated more often and into more languages than any other Sanskrit text, and many Hindu religious teachers have written commentaries on it. This ancient Sanskrit book has also played a role in modern politics. During the struggle for his country's independence, the Indian leader Mohandas Gandhi turned to the *Gita* for inspiration almost daily.

Although it can be read as a self-contained book, the *Bhagavad-Gita* is actually a small part in the middle of the *Mahabharata*. As in the

Mahabharata, the main story in the *Bhagavad-Gita* is the conflict between the Pandavas and the Kauravas.

About the *Ramayana*

Written by the poet Valmiki, the great Indian epic the *Ramayana* (rä mä ́ yə nə) consists of 24,000 couplets, parts of which date from 300 B.C. The *Ramayana* tells the story of Prince Rama. It is divided into seven sections, or *kandas*, each focusing on a different period of Rama's life. The purpose of the *Ramayana* is to spread the teaching of the Vedas, the sacred texts of Hinduism, in an entertaining and easy-to-understand manner through stories that focus on themes of duty and morality. Like the *Bhagavad-Gita*, the *Ramayana* teaches the ideal way to live and reinforces the theory that good prevails over evil.

The main villain in the *Ramayana* is Ravana, an evil giant with ten heads and twenty arms. Ravana believed himself to be immortal because no god had the power to slay him. When Ravana began to persecute both gods and men, the Indian god Vishnu took the form of a man in order to conquer Ravana and put an end to his destruction. Vishnu's mortal form was Rama. Rama, who grew up to be brave and honorable, was the favorite son of King Dasharatha (dä sä rä ́ tä), who upon retiring decided to make Rama king. However, just as Rama was about to assume the throne, Dasharatha was tricked into banishing him for 14 years. The *Ramayana* chronicles Rama's efforts during his exile to fulfill his dharma (his unique duties in life) by killing Ravana and reclaiming the throne.

Preview

Connecting to the Literature

Mythical heroes from all times and cultures—from King Arthur to Luke Skywalker—possess certain traits in common. Notice how the heroes in these selections display such characteristics as bravery, loyalty, and integrity.

Literary Analysis

The Indian Epic

An **Indian epic** is a long narrative—often a poem—about the deeds and adventures of an Indian hero. It usually tells a story that bears great religious significance and can include elements of myth, legend, and history. In the *Mahabharata,* the *Bhagavad-Gita,* and the *Ramayana,* the actions of the heroes reflect the values of Hinduism and Indian society. As you read each selection, note the personal qualities and actions of its epic hero.

Comparing Literary Works

An **epic hero** is the central figure of an epic, possessing such qualities as

- courage
- loyalty
- great physical strength

This larger-than-life hero usually faces some challenge in which he must prove his heroic qualities and achieve something of great value to his society. Use a chart like the one shown to compare the qualities of the epic heroes in these selections.

Epic Hero	Heroic Traits
Sibi	
Arjuna	
Rama	

Reading Strategy

Inferring Beliefs of the Period

By paying close attention to the ideas expressed in these selections, you can **infer beliefs of the period** in which they were written. For example, Sri Krisha's discussion of the Atman in the *Bhagavad-Gita* reveals the ancient Indian belief in an eternal soul. As you read, look for words and actions that reflect the values and beliefs of ancient India.

Vocabulary Development

mitigated (mit´ ə gāt´ id) *v.* moderated; eased (p. 174)

caricature (kar´ i kə chər) *n.* likeness or imitation that is so distorted or inferior as to seem ridiculous (p. 175)

scruples (skroo̅´ pəlz) *n.* feelings of doubt over what is ethical (p. 182)

pervades (pər vādz´) *v.* spreads throughout (p. 183)

manifested (man´ ə fest´ id) *v.* proved or revealed (p. 185)

dispel (di spel´) *v.* cause to vanish (p. 191)

invoked (in vōkt´) *v.* called on for help (p. 197)

pristine (pris´ tēn´) *adj.* unspoiled; uncorrupted (p. 197)

FROM THE
MAHABHARATA

retold by R. K. Narayan

Background

The *Mahabharata* has been handed down orally from generation to generation, and its stories are still told today. Indian writer and translator R. K. Narayan describes the typical village storyteller beginning an evening session: ". . . the storyteller will dress himself for the part by smearing sacred ash on his forehead and wrapping himself in a green shawl, while his helpers set up a framed picture of some god on a pedestal in the veranda, decorate it with jasmine garlands, and light incense to it. . . . He begins the session with a prayer, prolonging it until the others join and the valleys echo with the chants, drowning the cry of jackals."

SIBI

There is a half-moon in the sky today which will disappear shortly after midnight, said the storyteller. I'll select a tale which will end before the moon sets, so that you may all go home when there is still a little light.

The tale concerns a king and two birds. The king was Sibi, who had just performed a holy sacrifice on the banks of the Jumna.[1] The guests were resting in the tree shade after partaking of a feast. The air was charged with the scent of flowers and incense. Sibi went round to make sure that everyone was comfortable. A cool breeze blew from the south, patches of clouds <u>mitigated</u> the severity of the sun in the blue sky, the embers of the holy fire subsided into a soft glow under the ash.

The king, satisfied that all his guests were happy, dismissed his attendants and proceeded to his own corner of the camp to rest under a canopy. He had closed his eyes, half in sleep and half in prayer, when he felt a gust of air hitting him in the face and some object suddenly dropping on his lap. He awoke and noticed a dove, white and soft,

mitigated (mit´ ə gāt´ id) *v.* moderated; eased

Literary Analysis
The Indian Epic What values does the king's behavior toward his guests reflect?

---

1. **Jumna** (jum´ nə) river in northern India, flowing from the Himalayas southwest into the Ganges.

nestling in his lap. Its feathers were ruffled in terror and its eyes were shut. It looked so limp that he thought it was dead, but then he noticed a slight flutter of breath. He sat still in order not to frighten away the bird, and looked about for a servant.

Just then a hawk whirled down in pursuit, and perched itself on a low branch of the tree beside the canopy. The hawk exclaimed, "Ah, at last! What a game of hide and seek!"

"What do you want?" asked the king.

"I am addressing myself to that creature on your lap! Never been so much tricked in my life! If every mouthful of food has to be got after such a trial, a nice outlook indeed for the so-called king of birds! As one king to another, let me tell you, the dove nestling in your lap is mine. Throw it back to me."

The king thought over the statement of the hawk and said, "I am indeed honored by a visit from the king of birds, although I had thought till now that the eagle was the king!"

"I am a hawk, not a kite.[2] Know you that the hawk belongs to the kingly race while the kite is a mere <u>caricature</u> of our family, pursuing a career of deception by seeming no bigger than its victim and then attacking it. How often one mistakes a kite for a dove!"

Sibi wanted to divert the attention of the hawk from the subject of the dove and so said, "The kite also goes out of sight when it flies, so don't be offended if we land-bound creatures imagine that the kite floats in the same heaven as the hawk."

The hawk sharpened his beak on the tree-trunk and lifted one leg to display his talons and said, "I'm sorry to see the mistakes you human beings make. The kite no doubt flies—but not beyond the back of the lowest cloud. And you think that it sports in the heavens itself! The only common element between us is that we both have pointed, curved beaks, that's all; but the kite has a taste for helpless little creatures such as mice and sparrows —creatures which we would not care to notice."

The king realized that the subject was once more drifting towards food and diverted the hawk's attention again by saying, "The general notion is that the eagle is the king of birds."

The hawk chuckled cynically. "Ignorant mankind! How the eagle came to be so much respected, I shall never understand; what is there to commend the eagle? Its wingspread? You people are too easily carried away by appearances! Do you know that the hawk can fly just as high as the eagle? And yet you have no regard for us!"

Sibi said, "You can't blame us, we take things as they seem from here! I now know better."

The hawk looked pleased at this concession and said, "Have you ever seen a mountain eagle walk on the ground? Is there anything more

caricature (kar´ i kə chər) *n.* likeness or imitation that is so distorted or inferior as to seem ridiculous

---

2. **kite** any of various birds, including the hawk, that prey on insects, reptiles, and small mammals. The hawk is haughtily distinguishing himself from his smaller, less significant relatives.

Reading Check

From what is the king trying to divert the hawk's attention?

grotesque? Don't you agree that the first requirement for kingliness would be grace of movement? Only we hawks have it."

"True, true," said the king. "When I move from my bed to the bathroom, even if alone at night, I catch myself strutting along as in a parade, I suppose!" The king laughed, to entertain the hawk; he thought it might please the bird to be treated as a fellow king. The hawk looked pleased, and the king hoped that it would take itself off after these pleasantries.

The dove slightly stirred on his lap, and he hastened to draw over it his silk scarf. The hawk noticed this and bluntly said, "King, what is the use of your covering the dove? I will not forget that my food, which I have earned by honest chase, is there, unfairly held by you."

The king said, "This bird has come to me for asylum; it is my duty to protect it."

"I may brave your sword and swoop on my prey, and if I die in the attempt the spirits of my ancestors will bless me. We have known no fear for one thousand generations, what should we fear when the back of our prime ancestor serves as the vehicle of the great god Vishnu?"[3]

Reading Strategy
Inferring Beliefs of the Period What does the king's statement reveal about ancient Indian beliefs concerning animals?

---

3. **Vishnu** (vish´ n$\overline{oo}$) Hindu god known as the Preserver because he became a human being on nine separate occasions to save humanity from destruction.

Vishnu and Lakshmi Riding on Garuda, Ann & Bury Peerless Picture Library

▲ **Critical Viewing** This image depicts Garuda, half-man and half-eagle, carrying the god Vishnu and Vishnu's wife. What does the image suggest about the claim that the hawk, not the eagle, is the king of birds? **[Analyze]**

Again the king was on the point of correcting him, that it was a golden eagle that Vishnu rode, not a hawk, but he checked himself.

The bird emphasized his own status again. "You who are reputed to be wise, O king, don't confuse me with the carrion[4] birds wheeling over your head. I know where I stand," said the bird, preening its feathers.

The king felt it was time to say something agreeable himself, secretly worrying that he was reaching the limits of his wit. The dove nestled within the silk scarf. There was an uneasy pause while the king dreaded what might be coming next.

The hawk suddenly said, "All the world speaks of you as one who has the finest discrimination between right and wrong. And so you have a serious responsibility at this moment. You must not do anything that goes contrary to your reputation. Remember, I am in the agonies of hunger, and you refuse me my legitimate diet. By your act you cause me suffering, you injure me every second that you keep your hold on that parcel of meat. You have attained immeasurable spiritual merit by your deeds of perfection; now this single selfish act of yours will drain away all your merit and you will probably go to hell."

"O infinitely wise bird, does it seem to you that I am holding this dove out of selfishness so that I may eat it myself?"

"I am not so simple-minded," said the bird haughtily. "By selfish I meant that you were thinking of your own feelings, totally ignoring my viewpoint."

"When I recollect the terror in its eye as it fell on my lap, I feel nothing ever matters except affording it protection."

"O prince among princes, food is life, out of food all things exist and stir. Between life and death stands what? Food! I am faint with hunger. If you deny me my food any longer I may die. In a cranny of yonder rock my wife has hatched four eggs, the little ones are guarded by their mother, and all of them await my return home. If I die here of hunger, they will keep peeping out for my return home until they perish of the same hunger. And the sin of ending six lives will be on you. O maharaja,[5] consider well whether you want to save one doubtful life, which is probably half gone already, or six lives. Let not the performance of what seems to you a rightful act conflict with bigger issues. You know all this, king, but choose to ignore the issues. And all this talking only fatigues me and takes me nearer to death. So please spare me further argument."

Sibi said, "I notice that you are an extraordinary bird. You talk wisely, knowledgeably; there is nothing that you do not know. Your mind journeys with ease at subtle heights of thought. But, bird, tell me, how is it that you fail to notice the sheer duty I owe a creature that cries for protection? As a king is it not my duty?"

"I am only asking for food; food is to life what oil is to a lamp."

---

4. **carrion** (karʹ ē ən) *adj.* feeding on the dead.
5. **maharaja** (mä hə räʹ jə) prince ruling over one of the native states in India; here, king.

Literary Analysis
The Indian Epic and the Epic Hero In what ways do the hawk's words reinforce Sibi's heroic status?

Literary Analysis
The Indian Epic What ancient Indian values does Sibi express in this paragraph?

Reading Check
What does the hawk say will happen if Sibi does not give him the dove?

"Very well. You see all these people lying around, they have all rested after a feast in which nothing was lacking to satisfy the sixfold demands of the palate. Tell me what you want, and I will spread a feast before you in no time."

"King, the nature of food differs with different creatures. What you call a feast seems to me just so much trash. We observe from our heights all the activity that goes on in your royal kitchen and ever wonder why you take all that trouble with spice, salt, and fire to ruin the taste of God-given stuff. King, I do not want to speak at length. I am famished and I feel my eyes dimming. Have consideration for me too."

"If it is flesh you want, I will ask them to get it for you."

The hawk gave an ironical laugh at this. "See where all this leads you! How are you going to get flesh without killing something else? When you interfere with what God has ordained, you complicate everything."

"What is God's plan, actually? Please enlighten me."

"The dove is intended for me; God has no other purpose in creating it and letting it multiply so profusely. Are you not aware of the ancient saying that hawks eat doves?"

The king thought it over and said, "If you spare this dove, I'll guarantee you food every day in my palace all your life."

"I have already told you, my lord, that your food is inedible. Your assurance of daily feeding does not appeal to me. I hunt for food when I want it. I do not see why I should bother about tomorrow. Hoarding for generations ahead is a human failing, a practice unknown to us. I repeat the ancient saying that hawks eat doves."

The king brooded over the words of the hawk for a moment. "Ask for anything, except this little bird on my lap. I won't give it up, whichever way you may argue."

The hawk tilted its head, rolled its eyes, and said, "So be it. I will ask for the next best thing. I want warm flesh, with warm blood dripping, equal in weight to the dove. We are used to eating only fresh meat, we are not carrion birds, let me remind you. You will have to cut it out of your own body, as I know you will not choose to kill another creature for it."

The king brooded over this. "Yes, but I must consider which part of my body will yield the flesh you want without destroying my life. Give me a little time. Bear your hunger for a moment." And he added, "A ruler has no liberty to die. Many depend on him."

"In the same way as my family," said the hawk.

The king beckoned to an attendant. "Bring a pair of weighing scales."

The attendant was nonplussed. "Your Majesty, how can we find one here, in this remote place?"

The king repeated, "I want a pair of scales for accurate weighing."

"May I send a messenger to fetch one from the city?"

"How long will he take?" asked the king.

The courtier made a swift reckoning and declared, "If he rides a galloping horse, he should be back tomorrow at dawn."

Literary Analysis
The Indian Epic and the Epic Hero What personal quality does Sibi demonstrate by claiming not to know God's plan?

Reading Strategy
Inferring Beliefs of the Period In explaining why he must stay alive, what belief does Sibi reveal regarding a ruler's responsibilities?

The king looked at the hawk, who already seemed to droop. He did not want to hear again about his family on the mountain. It was also time to clear up all this situation and feed the refugee on his lap. He said to the courtier, "Construct a balance immediately with whatever is available here. I'll give you ten minutes!"

"Whoever fails will have his head cut off, I suppose?" sneered the hawk. "That would be truly kinglike, but let me tell you straight away that I am not interested in a cut-off head."

"You shall have my flesh and nothing less," said the king.

They bustled about. By now the whole camp was astir, watching this incredible duel between the king and the hawk. They managed to dangle a beam from the branch of a tree. Suspended from either end was a plate from the kitchen; a pointer, also improvised, marked the dead center of the beam.

The king looked at the hawk and said, "This is the best we can manage."

"I understand. A little fluctuation should not matter in the least. Only I do not want you to lose more flesh than is necessary to balance the dove."

The king did not let the bird finish his sentence, but rose, bearing the dove in his hand. He walked up to the crude scales in order to test them. He addressed the hawk, "Will you step nearer?"

"I can watch quite well from here. Also I can trust you."

The king placed the dove on the right-hand side of the scale pan, which immediately went down, making the king wonder how a little bird which had lain so lightly on his lap could weigh down the balance in this manner.

He wasted no further time in speculation. He sat on the ground, stretched out his leg, and after a brief prayer, incised his thigh with a sharp knife. The courtiers and guests assembled groaned at the sight of the blood. The king gritted his teeth and tore out a handful of flesh and dropped it on the scale.

The pan became bloodstained but the pointer did not move. Someone cursed the dove, "It has the weight of an abandoned corpse. It looks dead, see if it is dead."

Another added, "Just pick it up and fling it to that hawk and be done with it, the miserable creature."

The king was too faint to talk; he gestured to them to stop commenting. He had now only the skin on his right thigh. Still the scales were

A Hawk, Indian Mughal, 18th century miniature, Victoria and Albert Museum

▲ **Critical Viewing**
Does the hawk in this painting convey a mood that is similar to that of the hawk in the story? Explain. **[Compare and Contrast]**

✓**Reading Check**
What does the hawk agree to take in place of the dove?

from the *Mahabharata* ◆ 179

unbalanced. The king went on to scoop the flesh from his other leg; the pointer was still down.

People averted their eyes from the gory spectacle. The hawk watched him critically.

"O hawk, take all that meat and begone!" they said.

"I have been promised the exact equal weight of the dove," insisted the hawk, at which all those assembled cursed the hawk and drew their swords. The king was faint with pain now, but mustered the last ounce of his strength to command his followers to keep away.

He beckoned to his chief minister to come nearer. "One has no right to end one's life, but this is unforeseen. Even if this means hell to me, I have to face it," he said. Everyone looked at the dove with distaste. "My brother shall be the regent[6] till the prince comes of age."

With this he struggled onto his feet and stepped on the flesh-filled pan. At once the other pan went up and equalized.

The hawk now flitted nearer and said, "This is more than a mouthful for me and my family. How am I to carry you to the mountain?"

---

6. **regent** (rē´ jənt) *n.* person appointed to rule when the king is too young to rule himself.

▲ **Critical Viewing**   In this depiction of Sibi's sacrifice, how does Sibi appear to have been affected by the experience? **[Infer]**

The king mumbled feebly, "I did not think of that problem," and added, "You wouldn't have been able to lift the dove either! So bring your family here."

The hawk flapped its wings and rose in the air and swooped down as if to peck at the king's flesh. People shut their eyes, unable to bear the spectacle. But presently they heard divine instruments filling the skies with music. The hawk was gone, but in its place they found Indra,[7] the god with the dazzling crown, armed with the diamond spear, seizing Sibi's hand and helping him down off the weighing scales. A flame rose where the dove had lain, and from the heart of it emerged the God of Fire.

They said, "O king, we put you to a severe test. We challenged your integrity; and we happily accept defeat. You are indeed blessed, and as long as human beings recollect your tale, they will partake of the spiritual merit that you have yourself acquired"—and vanished. The king recovered his energy in a moment, while the pieces of flesh in the scale pan turned to fragrant flowers.

---

7. **Indra** (in´ drə) chief god of the early Hindu religion, often depicted wielding a thunderbolt.

Review and Assess

Thinking About the Selection

1. **Respond:** Do you think that Sibi was foolish to keep his promise to the dove regardless of the consequences? Why or why not?

2. **(a) Recall:** Explain the duties of Sibi and the hawk.
   (b) Analyze: How do their duties conflict?

3. **(a) Recall:** How does Sibi first attempt to resolve his conflict with the hawk? **(b) Infer:** What does this strategy reveal about his attitude toward the painful sacrifice he later undertakes?

4. **(a) Recall:** What arrangement finally satisfies the hawk's demand for food?
   (b) Analyze: Why do you think the king agrees to this plan?

5. **(a) Recall:** What happens after Sibi steps onto the scale?
   (b) Interpret: What is the meaning of this event?

6. **(a) Interpret:** What values do Sibi's actions demonstrate?
   (b) Infer: What do these values suggest about the purpose of this story?

7. **Apply:** How does the importance that ancient Indians placed on keeping one's word compare with attitudes toward honesty and duty in the modern world? Explain.

from the
Bhagavad-Gita
translated by Swami Prabhavananda and Christopher Isherwood

Background

Arjuna (är´ jōō nə), a Pandava, has chosen his brother-in-law, Krishna (krish´ nə), as his charioteer and trusted advisor for the coming battle with the Kauravas. At this early point in the story, Arjuna knows only that Krishna is a special person. He does not yet realize that Krishna is a god. As the poem begins, Arjuna faces a dilemma: He knows it is wrong to kill his cousins and uncles who are on the opposing side, but he also knows that it is his duty to fight. In the first chapter of the *Gita*, he refuses to take part in the battle; dropping his bow, he asks Krishna for advice. The great warrior Arjuna appears here in Chapter 2, weeping with frustration and confusion.

One of the main themes of the *Bhagavad-Gita* is the concept of **nonattached work,** the performance of one's duty without concern for the results. This idea is tied to both the structure of Indian society and the Indian belief in reincarnation. Indian society was rigidly divided into social classes, or **castes** (kasts), each of which had its own special duties. In this selection, narrated by a character named Sanjaya, Krishna reminds Arjuna that as a member of the warrior caste, he is obligated to fight. He reminds him that the Atman, or soul, is eternal; it can be reborn into countless bodies.

The Yoga of Knowledge

SANJAYA: Then his eyes filled with tears, and his heart grieved and was bewildered with pity. And Sri Krishna spoke to him, saying:

SRI KRISHNA: Arjuna, is this hour of battle the time for <u>scruples</u> and fancies? Are they worthy of you, who seek enlightenment? Any brave man who merely hopes for fame or heaven would despise them.

What is this weakness? It is beneath you. Is it for nothing men call you the foe-consumer? Shake off this cowardice, Arjuna. Stand up.

scruples (skrōō´ pəlz) n. feelings of doubt over what is ethical

ARJUNA: Bhisma and Drona are noble and ancient, worthy of the deepest reverence. How can I greet them with arrows, in battle? If I kill them, how can I ever enjoy my wealth, or any other pleasure? It will be cursed with blood-guilt. I would much rather spare them, and eat the bread of a beggar.

Which will be worse, to win this war, or to lose it? I scarcely know. Even the sons of Dhritarashtra stand in the enemy ranks. If we kill them, none of us will wish to live.

Is this real compassion that I feel, or only a delusion? My mind gropes about in darkness. I cannot see where my duty lies. Krishna, I beg you, tell me frankly and clearly what I ought to do. I am your disciple. I put myself into your hands. Show me the way.

> Not this world's kingdom,
> Supreme, unchallenged,
> No, nor the throne
> Of the gods in heaven,
> Could ease this sorrow
> That numbs my senses!

SANJAYA: When Arjuna, the foe-consuming, the never-slothful, had spoken thus to Govinda, ruler of the senses, he added: "I will not fight," and was silent.

Then to him who thus sorrowed between the two armies, the ruler of the senses spoke, smiling:

SRI KRISHNA: Your words are wise, Arjuna, but your sorrow is for nothing. The truly wise mourn neither for the living nor for the dead.

There was never a time when I did not exist, nor you, nor any of these kings. Nor is there any future in which we shall cease to be.

Just as the dweller in this body passes through childhood, youth and old age, so at death he merely passes into another kind of body. The wise are not deceived by that.

Feelings of heat and cold, pleasure and pain, are caused by the contact of the senses with their objects. They come and they go, never lasting long. You must accept them.

A serene spirit accepts pleasure and pain with an even mind, and is unmoved by either. He alone is worthy of immortality.

That which is non-existent can never come into being, and that which is can never cease to be. Those who have known the inmost Reality know also the nature of *is* and *is not*.

That Reality which <u>pervades</u> the universe is indestructible. No one has power to change the Changeless.

Bodies are said to die, but That which possesses the body is eternal. It cannot be limited, or destroyed. Therefore you must fight.

> Some say this Atman[1]
> Is slain, and others

---

1. Atman (ät´ mən) universal soul; source of all individual souls.

Literary Analysis
The Indian Epic What ancient Indian values does Arjuna express in this passage?

pervades (pər vādz´) *v.* spreads throughout

**Reading Check**

According to Sri Krishna, how should one accept both pleasure and pain?

Call It the slayer:
They know nothing.
How can It slay
Or who shall slay It?

Know this Atman
Unborn, undying,
Never ceasing,
Never beginning,
Deathless, birthless,
Unchanging for ever.
How can It die
The death of the body?

Knowing It birthless,
Knowing It deathless,
Knowing It endless,
For ever unchanging,
Dream not you do
The deed of the killer,
Dream not the power
Is yours to command it.

Worn-out garments
Are shed by the body:
Worn-out bodies
Are shed by the dweller
Within the body.
New bodies are donned
By the dweller, like garments.

Reading Strategy
Inferring Beliefs of the Period In what way does this passage reflect ancient Indian beliefs about the spirit?

▼ **Critical Viewing**
What does this painting suggest about the danger Arjuna would face going into battle? **[Infer]**

Arjuna and Krishna in the Chariot, Between the Two Armies, Illustration from *Bhagavad-Gita*

Not wounded by weapons,
Not burned by fire,
Not dried by the wind,
Not wetted by water:
Such is the Atman,
Not dried, not wetted,
Not burned, not wounded,
Innermost element,
Everywhere, always,
Being of beings,
Changeless, eternal,
For ever and ever.

This Atman cannot be <u>manifested</u> to the senses, or thought about by the mind. It is not subject to modification. Since you know this, you should not grieve.

But if you should suppose this Atman to be subject to constant birth and death, even then you ought not to be sorry.

Death is certain for the born. Rebirth is certain for the dead. You should not grieve for what is unavoidable.

Before birth, beings are not manifest to our human senses. In the interim between birth and death, they are manifest. At death they return to the unmanifest again. What is there in all this to grieve over?

There are some who have actually looked upon the Atman, and understood It, in all Its wonder. Others can only speak of It as wonderful beyond their understanding. Others know of Its wonder by hearsay. And there are others who are told about It and do not understand a word.

He Who dwells within all living bodies remains for ever indestructible. Therefore, you should never mourn for any one.

Even if you consider this from the standpoint of your own caste-duty, you ought not to hesitate; for, to a warrior, there is nothing nobler than a righteous war. Happy are the warriors to whom a battle such as this comes: it opens a door to heaven.

But if you refuse to fight this righteous war, you will be turning aside from your duty. You will be a sinner, and disgraced. People will speak ill of you throughout the ages. To a man who values his honor, that is surely worse than death. The warrior-chiefs will believe it was fear that drove you from the battle; you will be despised by those who have admired you so long. Your enemies, also, will slander your courage. They will use the words which should never be spoken. What could be harder to bear than that?

Die, and you win heaven. Conquer, and you enjoy the earth. Stand up now, son of Kunti, and resolve to fight. Realize that pleasure and pain, gain and loss, victory and defeat, are all one and the same: then go into battle. Do this and you cannot commit any sin.

I have explained to you the true nature of the Atman. Now listen to the method of Karma Yoga.[2] If you can understand and follow it, you

---

2. **Karma Yoga** the path of selfless, God-dedicated action.

manifested (man´ ə fest´ id) v. proved or revealed

Reading Strategy
Inferring Beliefs of the Period What do Krishna's words regarding Arjuna's duty reveal about the importance of dharma in ancient India?

**Reading Check**

According to Sri Krishna, how will others view Arjuna if he does not fight?

will be able to break the chains of desire which bind you to your actions.

In this yoga, even the abortive attempt is not wasted. Nor can it produce a contrary result. Even a little practice of this yoga will save you from the terrible wheel of rebirth and death.

In this yoga, the will is directed singly toward one ideal. When a man lacks this discrimination, his will wanders in all directions, after innumerable aims. Those who lack discrimination may quote the letter of the scripture, but they are really denying its inner truth. They are full of worldly desires, and hungry for the rewards of heaven. They use beautiful figures of speech. They teach elaborate rituals which are supposed to obtain pleasure and power for those who perform them. But, actually, they understand nothing except the law of Karma,[3] that chains men to rebirth.

Those whose discrimination is stolen away by such talk grow deeply attached to pleasure and power. And so they are unable to develop that concentration of the will which leads a man to absorption in God.

The Vedas[4] teach us about the three gunas[5] and their functions. You, Arjuna, must overcome the three gunas. You must be free from the pairs of opposites.[6] Poise your mind in tranquillity. Take care neither to acquire nor to hoard. Be established in the consciousness of the Atman, always.

When the whole country is flooded, the reservoir becomes superfluous. So, to the illumined seer, the Vedas are all superfluous.

You have the right to work, but for the work's sake only. You have no right to the fruits of work. Desire for the fruits of work must never be your motive in working. Never give way to laziness, either.

Perform every action with your heart fixed on the Supreme Lord. Renounce attachment to the fruits. Be even-tempered in success and failure; for it is this evenness of temper which is meant by yoga.

Work done with anxiety about results is far inferior to work done without such anxiety, in the calm of self-surrender. Seek refuge in the knowledge of Brahman.[7] They who work selfishly for results are miserable.

In the calm of self-surrender you can free yourself from the bondage of virtue and vice during this very life. Devote yourself, therefore, to reaching union with Brahman. To unite the heart with Brahman and then to act: that is the secret of non-attached work. In the calm of self-surrender, the seers renounce the fruits of their actions, and so reach enlightenment. Then they are free from the bondage of rebirth, and pass to that state which is beyond all evil.

Literary Analysis
The Indian Epic and the Epic Hero What does Krishna's statement about "the fruits of work" reveal about the Indian idea of heroism?

---

3. **the law of Karma** Hindus believe that everyone is reborn many times and that one's actions in each life determine one's fate in future lives.
4. **Vedas** sacred books of the Hindus.
5. **the three gunas** (gঞon′ez) qualities of nature: passion, dullness or inertia, and goodness or purity.
6. **opposites** The world that seems real is composed of illusory opposites like heat and cold.
7. **Brahman** the oversoul of which each individual's Atman is a part.

When your intellect has cleared itself of its delusions, you will become indifferent to the results of all action, present or future. At present, your intellect is bewildered by conflicting interpretations of the scriptures. When it can rest, steady and undistracted, in contemplation of the Atman, then you will reach union with the Atman.

ARJUNA: Krishna, how can one identify a man who is firmly established and absorbed in Brahman? In what manner does an illumined soul speak? How does he sit? How does he walk?

SRI KRISHNA:
He knows bliss in the Atman
And wants nothing else.
Cravings torment the heart:
He renounces cravings.
I call him illumined.

Not shaken by adversity,
Not hankering after happiness:
Free from fear, free from anger,
Free from the things of desire.
I call him a seer, and illumined.
The bonds of his flesh are broken.
He is lucky, and does not rejoice:
He is unlucky, and does not weep.
I call him illumined.

The tortoise can draw in his legs:
The seer can draw in his senses.
I call him illumined.

The abstinent[8] run away from what they desire
But carry their desires with them:
When a man enters Reality,
He leaves his desires behind him.

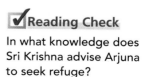

▲ **Critical Viewing**
In what way does this painting suggest the kind of serenity that Sri Krishna describes? **[Interpret]**

✔**Reading Check**
In what knowledge does Sri Krishna advise Arjuna to seek refuge?

---

8. The abstinent (ab′ stə nənt) those who voluntarily do without food, drink, or other pleasures.

Even a mind that knows the path
Can be dragged from the path:
The senses are so unruly.
But he controls the senses
And recollects the mind
And fixes it on me.
I call him illumined.

Thinking about sense-objects
Will attach you to sense-objects;
Grow attached, and you become addicted;
Thwart your addiction, it turns to anger;
Be angry, and you confuse your mind;
Confuse your mind, you forget the lesson of experience;
Forget experience, you lose discrimination;
Lose discrimination, and you miss life's only purpose.

When he has no lust, no hatred,
A man walks safely among the things of lust and hatred.
To obey the Atman
Is his peaceful joy:
Sorrow melts
Into that clear peace:
His quiet mind
Is soon established in peace.

The uncontrolled mind
Does not guess that the Atman is present:
How can it meditate?[9]
Without meditation, where is peace?
Without peace, where is happiness?

The wind turns a ship
From its course upon the waters:
The wandering winds of the senses
Cast man's mind adrift
And turn his better judgment from its course.
When a man can still the senses
I call him illumined.
The recollected mind is awake
In the knowledge of the Atman
Which is dark night to the ignorant:
The ignorant are awake in their sense-life
Which they think is daylight:
To the seer it is darkness.

Reading Strategy
Inferring Beliefs of the Period What ancient Indian ideas about materialism does this paragraph reveal?

Literary Analysis
The Indian Epic What Indian values does this verse convey?

---

9. meditate (med′ ə tāt′) *v.* to think deeply and continuously.

Water flows continually into the ocean
But the ocean is never disturbed:
Desire flows into the mind of the seer
But he is never disturbed.
The seer knows peace:
The man who stirs up his own lusts
Can never know peace.
He knows peace who has forgotten desire.
He lives without craving:
Free from ego, free from pride.

This is the state of enlightenment in Brahman:
A man does not fall back from it
Into delusion.
Even at the moment of death
He is alive in that enlightenment:
Brahman and he are one.

Review and Assess

Thinking About the Selection

1. **Respond:** Do you agree with Sri Krishna's advice to Arjuna? Why or why not?

2. **(a) Recall:** When Arjuna is distraught at the beginning of the selection, whom does he ask for advice? **(b) Analyze Causes and Effects:** What is the cause of his confusion?

3. **(a) Recall:** What does Krishna explain to Arjuna about the Atman? **(b) Infer:** Why might that knowledge comfort Arjuna?

4. **(a) Recall:** What action does Krishna advise Arjuna to take? **(b) Analyze:** Does Arjuna have a choice? Why or why not?

5. **(a) Recall:** In what manner does Krishna advise Arjuna to fight? **(b) Deduce:** What will Arjuna ultimately gain from acting this way?

6. **(a) Analyze:** What do Krishna's statements about the Atman suggest about the relationship between knowledge and action? **(b) Draw Conclusions:** Is one element in this relationship more important than the other? Explain.

7. **(a) Deduce:** What three Hindu beliefs does the dialogue between Krishna and Arjuna promote? **(b) Connect:** How do these concepts relate to each other?

8. **Apply:** What advice might Krishna give to people in modern society who believe that wealth is the measure of success?

FROM THE

RAMAYANA

retold by R. K. Narayan

Background

As an adult, Rama is about to inherit the throne from his father when evil plots result in his banishment from the kingdom. For fourteen years, he wanders in exile with his wife, Sita, and his brother, Lakshmana. During this time, Sita is kidnapped by the evil giant Ravana, whose name means "He who makes the universe scream." Rama sets out to rescue Sita with the help of Hanuman, the monkey god, and a huge battle ensues. This selection opens as the battle is reaching its climax.

Rama and Ravana in Battle

Every moment, news came to Ravana of fresh disasters in his camp. One by one, most of his commanders were lost. No one who went forth with battle cries was heard of again. Cries and shouts and the wailings of the widows of warriors came over the chants and songs of triumph that his courtiers arranged to keep up at a loud pitch in his assembly hall. Ravana became restless and abruptly left the hall and went up on a tower, from which he could obtain a full view of the city. He surveyed the scene below but could not stand it. One who had spent a lifetime in destruction, now found the gory spectacle intolerable. Groans and wailings reached his ears with deadly clarity; and he noticed how the monkey hordes[1] reveled in their bloody handiwork. This was too much for him. He felt a terrific rage rising within him, mixed with some admiration for Rama's valor. He told himself, "The time has come for me to act by myself again."

He hurried down the steps of the tower, returned to his chamber, and prepared himself for the battle. He had a ritual bath and performed special prayers to gain the benediction of Shiva;[2] donned his battle dress, matchless armor, armlets, and crowns. He had on a protective armor for every inch of his body. He girt his sword-belt and attached to his body his accouterments[3] for protection and decoration.

When he emerged from his chamber, his heroic appearance was breathtaking. He summoned his chariot, which could be drawn by

---

1. **monkey hordes** Rama's army, the result of his alliance with Sugriva, the monkey king.
2. **Shiva** (shē´ və) Hindu god of destruction and reproduction.
3. **accouterments** (ə kōōt´ ər mənts) *n.* soldier's equipment, other than clothes and weapons.

horses or move on its own if the horses were hurt or killed. People stood aside when he came out of the palace and entered his chariot. "This is my resolve," he said to himself: "Either that woman Sita, or my wife Mandodari, will soon have cause to cry and roll in the dust in grief. Surely, before this day is done, one of them will be a widow."

The gods in heaven noticed Ravana's determined move and felt that Rama would need all the support they could muster. They requested Indra[4] to send down his special chariot for Rama's use. When the chariot appeared at his camp, Rama was deeply impressed with the magnitude and brilliance of the vehicle. "How has this come to be here?" he asked.

"Sir," the charioteer answered, "my name is Matali. I have the honor of being the charioteer of Indra. Brahma, the four-faced god and the creator of the Universe, and Shiva, whose power has emboldened Ravana now to challenge you, have commanded me to bring it here for your use. It can fly swifter than air over all obstacles, over any mountain, sea, or sky, and will help you to emerge victorious in this battle."

Rama reflected aloud, "It may be that the rakshasas[5] have created this illusion for me. It may be a trap. I don't know how to view it." Whereupon Matali spoke convincingly to <u>dispel</u> the doubt in Rama's mind. Rama, still hesitant, though partially convinced, looked at Hanuman[6] and Lakshmana[7] and asked, "What do you think of it?" Both answered, "We feel no doubt that this chariot is Indra's; it is not an illusory creation."

Rama fastened his sword, slung two quivers full of rare arrows over his shoulders, and climbed into the chariot.

The beat of war drums, the challenging cries of soldiers, the trumpets, and the rolling chariots speeding along to confront each other, created a deafening mixture of noise. While Ravana had instructed his charioteer to speed ahead, Rama very gently ordered his chariot driver, "Ravana is in a rage; let him perform all the antics he desires and exhaust himself. Until then be calm; we don't have to hurry forward. Move slowly and calmly, and you must strictly follow my instructions; I will tell you when to drive faster."

Ravana's assistant and one of his staunchest supporters, Mahodara—the giant among giants in his physical appearance—begged Ravana, "Let me not be a mere spectator when you confront Rama. Let me have the honor of grappling with him. Permit me to attack Rama."

"Rama is my sole concern," Ravana replied. "If you wish to engage yourself in a fight, you may fight his brother Lakshmana."

Noticing Mahodara's purpose, Rama steered his chariot across his path in order to prevent Mahodara from reaching Lakshmana.

Literary Analysis
The Indian Epic How do the gods help Rama as he is about to face Ravana?

dispel (di spel′) v. cause to vanish

---

4. **Indra** (in′ drə) Hindu god of rain and thunder; chief god in early Hinduism.
5. **rakshasas** (räk′ shə səz) demons that can change form at will.
6. **Hanuman** (hun′ o͞o män′) leader of Rama's army of monkeys.
7. **Lakshmana** (läk shmä′ nə) Rama's half-brother and loyal companion.

Reading Check
For whom do Hanuman and the monkeys fight in the battle?

Whereupon Mahodara ordered his chariot driver, "Now dash straight ahead, directly into Rama's chariot."

The charioteer, more practical-minded, advised him, "I would not go near Rama. Let us keep away." But Mahodara, obstinate and intoxicated with war fever, made straight for Rama. He wanted to have the honor of a direct encounter with Rama himself in spite of Ravana's advice; and for this honor he paid a heavy price, as it was a moment's work for Rama to destroy him, and leave him lifeless and shapeless on the field. Noticing this, Ravana's anger mounted further. He commanded his driver, "You will not slacken now. Go." Many ominous signs were seen now—his bowstrings suddenly snapped; the mountains shook; thunders rumbled in the skies; tears flowed from the horses' eyes; elephants with decorated foreheads moved along dejectedly. Ravana, noticing them, hesitated only for a second, saying, "I don't care. This mere mortal Rama is of no account, and these omens do not concern me at all." Meanwhile, Rama paused for a moment to consider his next step; and suddenly turned towards the armies supporting Ravana, which stretched away to the horizon, and destroyed them. He felt that this might be one way of saving Ravana. With his armies gone, it was possible that Ravana might have a change of heart. But it had only the effect of spurring Ravana on; he plunged forward and kept coming nearer Rama and his own doom.

Rama's army cleared and made way for Ravana's chariot, unable to stand the force of his approach. Ravana blew his conch[8] and its shrill challenge reverberated through space. Following it another conch, called "Panchajanya," which belonged to Mahavishnu (Rama's original form before his present incarnation), sounded of its own accord in answer to the challenge, agitating the universe with its vibrations. And then Matali picked up another conch, which was Indra's, and blew it. This was the signal indicating the commencement of the actual battle. Presently Ravana sent a shower of arrows on Rama; and Rama's followers, unable to bear the sight of his body being studded with arrows, averted their heads. Then the chariot horses of Ravana and Rama glared at each other in hostility, and the flags topping the chariots—Ravana's ensign of the Veena[9] and Rama's with the whole universe on it—clashed, and one heard the stringing and twanging of bow-strings on both sides, overpowering in volume all other sound. Then followed a shower of arrows from Rama's own bow. Ravana stood gazing at the chariot sent by Indra and swore, "These gods, instead of supporting me, have gone to the support of this petty human being. I will teach them a lesson. He is not fit to be killed with my arrows but I shall seize him and his chariot together and fling them into high heaven and dash them to destruction." Despite his oath, he still strung his bow and sent a shower of arrows at Rama, raining in thousands, but they were all invariably shattered and neutralized by the arrows from Rama's bow, which met arrow for arrow. Ultimately

Literary Analysis
The Indian Epic and the Epic Hero What heroic trait does Rama demonstrate with the strategy he employs in this passage?

---

8. **conch** (käŋk) *n.* large shell that can be used as a trumpet.
9. **Veena** (vē′ nä′) *n.* stringed musical instrument.

Ravana, instead of using one bow, used ten with his twenty arms, multiplying his attack tenfold; but Rama stood unhurt.

Ravana suddenly realized that he should change his tactics and ordered his charioteer to fly the chariot up in the skies. From there he attacked and destroyed a great many of the monkey army supporting Rama. Rama ordered Matali, "Go up in the air. Our young soldiers are being attacked from the sky. Follow Ravana, and don't slacken."

There followed an aerial pursuit at dizzying speed across the dome of the sky and rim of the earth. Ravana's arrows came down like rain; he was bent upon destroying everything in the world. But Rama's arrows diverted, broke, or neutralized Ravana's. Terror-stricken, the gods watched this pursuit. Presently Ravana's arrows struck Rama's horses and pierced the heart of Matali himself. The charioteer fell. Rama paused for a while in grief, undecided as to his next step. Then he recovered and resumed his offensive. At that moment the divine eagle Garuda was seen perched on Rama's flag-post, and the gods who were watching felt that this could be an auspicious sign.

▲ **Critical Viewing**
Which details in this depiction of Hanuman suggest that he is an ally of the hero and not an evil character? **[Infer]**

After circling the globe several times, the dueling chariots returned, and the fight continued over Lanka.[10] It was impossible to be very clear about the location of the battleground as the fight occured here, there, and everywhere. Rama's arrows pierced Ravana's armor and made him wince. Ravana was so insensible to pain and impervious to attack that for him to wince was a good sign, and the gods hoped that this was a turn for the better. But at this moment, Ravana suddenly changed his tactics. Instead of merely shooting his arrows, which were powerful in themselves, he also invoked several supernatural forces to create strange effects: He was an adept in the use of various asthras[11] which could be made dynamic with special incantations. At this point, the

---

10. **Lanka** (läṇ´ kə) Ravana's kingdom.
11. **asthras** (äs´ trəz) *n.* weapons with supernatural powers.

☑**Reading Check**

Why does Ravana order his charioteer to fly the chariot up in the skies?

from the *Ramayana* ◆ 193

fight became one of attack with supernatural powers, and parrying of such an attack with other supernatural powers.

Ravana realized that the mere aiming of shafts with ten or twenty of his arms would be of no avail because the mortal whom he had so contemptuously thought of destroying with a slight effort was proving formidable, and his arrows were beginning to pierce and cause pain. Among the asthras sent by Ravana was one called "Danda," a special gift from Shiva, capable of pursuing and pulverizing its target. When it came flaming along, the gods were struck with fear. But Rama's arrow neutralized it.

Now Ravana said to himself, "These are all petty weapons. I should really get down to proper business." And he invoked the one called "Maya"—a weapon which created illusions and confused the enemy.

With proper incantations and worship, he sent off this weapon and it created an illusion of reviving all the armies and its leaders—Kumbakarna and Indrajit and the others—and bringing them back to the battlefield. Presently Rama found all those who, he thought, were no more, coming on with battle cries and surrounding him. Every man in the enemy's army was again up in arms. They seemed to fall on Rama with victorious cries. This was very confusing and Rama asked Matali, whom he had by now revived, "What is happening now? How are all these coming back? They were dead." Matali explained, "In your original identity you are the creator of illusions in this universe. Please know that Ravana has created phantoms to confuse you. If you make up your mind, you can dispel them immediately." Matali's explanation was a great help. Rama at once invoked a weapon called "Gnana"—which means "wisdom" or "perception." This was a very rare weapon, and he sent it forth. And all the terrifying armies who seemed to have come on in such a great mass suddenly evaporated into thin air.

Ravana then shot an asthra called "Thama," whose nature was to create total darkness in all the worlds. The arrows came with heads exposing frightening eyes and fangs, and fiery tongues. End to end the earth was enveloped in total darkness and the whole of creation was paralyzed. This asthra also created a deluge of rain on one side, a rain of stones on the other, a hailstorm showering down intermittently, and a tornado sweeping the earth. Ravana was sure that this would arrest Rama's enterprise. But Rama was able to meet it with what was named "Shivasthra." He understood the nature of the phenomenon and the cause of it and chose the appropriate asthra for counteracting it.

Literature
in context   Religion Connection

Hindu Gods

Hindus worship thousands of gods. Each god is part of a single supreme force called Brahman, which only a few sages can truly understand. The three main gods of Hinduism are *Brahma*, the creator of the world; *Vishnu*, the preserver, who restores moral order; and *Shiva*, the destroyer, who regularly destroys the world in order to re-create it. Rama, the epic hero, is believed to be an incarnation of Vishnu, who combines qualities of both a man and a god.

Statue of Shiva

Literary Analysis
The Indian Epic Explain how Rama's and Ravana's use of asthras reinforces their roles in this epic.

Ravana now shot off what he considered his deadliest weapon—a trident endowed with extraordinary destructive power, once gifted to Ravana by the gods. When it started on its journey there was real panic all round. It came on flaming toward Rama, its speed or course unaffected by the arrows he flung at it.

When Rama noticed his arrows falling down ineffectively while the trident sailed towards him, for a moment he lost heart. When it came quite near, he uttered a certain mantra[12] from the depth of his being and while he was breathing out that incantation, an esoteric syllable in perfect timing, the trident collapsed. Ravana, who had been so certain of vanquishing Rama with his trident, was astonished to see it fall down within an inch of him, and for a minute wondered if his adversary might not after all be a divine being although he looked like a mortal. Ravana thought to himself, "This is, perhaps, the highest God. Who could he be? Not Shiva, for Shiva is my supporter; he could not be Brahma, who is four faced; could not be Vishnu, because of my immunity from the weapons of the whole trinity. Perhaps this man is the primordial being, the cause behind the whole universe. But whoever he may be, I will not stop my fight until I defeat and crush him or at least take him prisoner."

With this resolve, Ravana next sent a weapon which issued forth monstrous serpents vomiting fire and venom, with enormous fangs and red eyes. They came darting in from all directions.

Rama now selected an asthra called "Garuda" (which meant "eagle"). Very soon thousands of eagles were aloft, and they picked off the serpents with their claws and beaks and destroyed them. Seeing this also fail, Ravana's anger was roused to a mad pitch and he blindly emptied a quiverful of arrows in Rama's direction. Rama's arrows met them half way and turned them round so that they went back and their sharp points embedded themselves in Ravana's own chest.

Ravana was weakening in spirit. He realized that he was at the end of his resources. All his learning and equipment in weaponry were of no avail and he had practically come to

Rama and Lakshmana shooting arrows at the demon Ravana, © Victoria and Albert Museum

☑ **Reading Check**

How does Rama fend off Ravana's deadliest weapon, the trident?

---

12. **mantra** (män´ trə) *n.* hymn or portion of text that is chanted or spoken as a prayer or incantation.

the end of his special gifts of destruction. While he was going down thus, Rama's own spirit was soaring up. The combatants were now near enough to grapple with each other and Rama realized that this was the best moment to cut off Ravana's heads.[13] He sent a crescent-shaped arrow which sliced off one of Ravana's heads and flung it far into the sea, and this process continued; but every time a head was cut off, Ravana had the benediction of having another one grown in its place. Rama's crescent-shaped weapon was continuously busy as Ravana's heads kept cropping up. Rama lopped off his arms but they grew again and every lopped-off arm hit Matali and the chariot and tried to cause destruction by itself, and the tongue in a new head wagged, uttered challenges, and cursed Rama. On the cast-off heads of Ravana devils and minor demons, who had all along been in terror of Ravana and had obeyed and pleased him, executed a dance of death and feasted on the flesh.

Ravana was now desperate. Rama's arrows embedded themselves in a hundred places on his body and weakened him. Presently he collapsed in a faint on the floor of his chariot. Noticing his state, his charioteer pulled back and drew the chariot aside. Matali whispered to Rama, "This is the time to finish off that demon. He is in a faint. Go on. Go on."

▼ **Critical Viewing**
In what way is this depiction of Ravana appropriate for this story? **[Connect]**

---

13. **Ravana's heads** Ravana is usually depicted as having ten heads and twenty arms.

But Rama put away his bow and said, "It is not fair warfare to attack a man who is in a faint. I will wait. Let him recover," and waited.

When Ravana revived, he was angry with his charioteer for withdrawing, and took out his sword, crying, "You have disgraced me. Those who look on will think I have retreated." But his charioteer explained how Rama suspended the fight and forebore to attack when he was in a faint. Somehow, Ravana appreciated his explanation and patted his back and resumed his attacks. Having exhausted his special weapons, in desperation Ravana began to throw on Rama all sorts of things such as staves, cast-iron balls, heavy rocks, and oddments he could lay hands on. None of them touched Rama, but glanced off and fell ineffectually. Rama went on shooting his arrows. There seemed to be no end of this struggle in sight.

Now Rama had to pause to consider what final measure he should take to bring this campaign to an end. After much thought, he decided to use "Brahmasthra," a weapon specially designed by the Creator Brahma on a former occasion, when he had to provide one for Shiva to destroy Tripura, the old monster who assumed the forms of flying mountains and settled down on habitations and cities, seeking to destroy the world. The Brahmasthra was a special gift to be used only when all other means had failed. Now Rama, with prayers and worship, <u>invoked</u> its fullest power and sent it in Ravana's direction, aiming at his heart rather than his head; Ravana being vulnerable at heart. While he had prayed for indestructibility of his several heads and arms, he had forgotten to strengthen his heart, where the Brahmasthra entered and ended his career.

Rama watched him fall headlong from his chariot face down onto the earth, and that was the end of the great campaign. Now one noticed Ravana's face aglow with a new quality. Rama's arrows had burnt off the layers of dross, the anger, conceit, cruelty, lust, and egotism which had encrusted his real self, and now his personality came through in its <u>pristine</u> form—of one who was devout and capable of tremendous attainments. His constant meditation on Rama, although as an adversary, now seemed to bear fruit, as his face shone with serenity and peace. Rama noticed it from his chariot above and commanded Matali, "Set me down on the ground." When the chariot descended and came to rest on its wheels, Rama got down and commanded Matali, "I am grateful for your services to me. You may now take the chariot back to Indra."

Surrounded by his brother Lakshmana and Hanuman and all his other war chiefs, Rama approached Ravana's body, and stood gazing on it. He noted his crowns and jewelry scattered piecemeal on the ground. The decorations and the extraordinary workmanship of the armor on his chest were blood-covered. Rama sighed as if to say, "What might he not have achieved but for the evil stirring within him!"

At this moment, as they readjusted Ravana's blood-stained body, Rama noticed to his great shock a scar on Ravana's back and said with a smile, "Perhaps this is not an episode of glory for me as I seem

Literary Analysis
The Indian Epic and the Epic Hero What heroic qualities does Rama display through his actions when Ravana is in a faint?

invoked (in vōkt´) v. called on for help

pristine (pris´ tēn´) adj. unspoiled; uncorrupted

✓**Reading Check**
Which weapon finally brings the battle to an end?

to have killed an enemy who was turning his back and retreating. Perhaps I was wrong in shooting the Brahmasthra into him." He looked so concerned at this supposed lapse on his part that Vibishana, Ravana's brother, came forward to explain. "What you have achieved is unique. I say so although it meant the death of my brother."

"But I have attacked a man who had turned his back," Rama said. "See that scar."

Vibishana explained, "It is an old scar. In ancient days, when he paraded his strength around the globe, once he tried to attack the divine elephants that guard the four directions. When he tried to catch them, he was gored in the back by one of the tuskers and that is the scar you see now; it is not a fresh one though fresh blood is flowing on it."

Rama accepted the explanation. "Honor him and cherish his memory so that his spirit may go to heaven, where he has his place. And now I will leave you to attend to his funeral arrangements, befitting his grandeur."

Review and Assess

Thinking About the Selection

1. **Respond:** What did you most admire about Rama? What did you most admire about Ravana?

2. **(a) Recall:** What does Ravana resolve as he prepares to go into battle? **(b) Infer:** What does this resolution reveal about his character?

3. **(a) Recall:** What does Indra send to Rama before Rama goes into battle? **(b) Infer:** Why do you think the gods want to help Rama win?

4. **(a) Compare and Contrast:** How does Rama's approach to the battle differ from Ravana's? **(b) Infer:** What do their actions reveal about their characters?

5. **(a) Infer:** What message is revealed by Rama's defeat of Ravana? **(b) Draw Conclusions:** What does this message suggest about the ancient Indian attitude toward justice? **(c) Speculate:** What effect might the message of this story have had on ancient Indian society?

6. **(a) Connect:** How does Rama compare with modern superheroes, such as Superman? **(b) Take a Position:** Who would you say is the more heroic figure—Rama or Superman? Explain your answer.

Review and Assess

Literary Analysis

Indian Epic

1. (a) What purpose do **Indian epics** serve in Indian culture? (b) What message do "Sibi," "The Yoga of Knowledge," and "Rama and Ravana in Battle" each attempt to convey?
2. (a) In the *Mahabharata*, what values does Sibi represent? (b) What details of his character or actions support your answer?
3. Identify an ancient Indian religious idea that is conveyed by "The Yoga of Knowledge."

Comparing Literary Works

4. Explain how the heroic traits of each **epic hero** are demonstrated in these selections.
5. What message can be inferred from the gods' willingness to assist the hero in each of these epics?
6. (a) What challenge must each hero face and overcome in order to fulfill his sacred duty? (b) Who do you think has the most difficult challenge? Explain.

Reading Strategy

Inferring Beliefs of the Period

7. Use a chart like the one shown to **infer beliefs** of ancient Indian culture. Provide a detail from each of the epics, and explain what it suggests about ancient Indian beliefs.

Epic	Detail	Belief It Suggests

8. Which of these selections reinforces most strongly the ancient Indian belief in nonattached work? Explain.

Extend Understanding

9. **Social Studies Connection:** Which modern leaders have made major sacrifices for their people? Explain.

Integrate Language Skills

Vocabulary Development Lesson

Word Analysis: Latin Root -voc- / -vok-

The Latin root -voc-/-vok- means "speak" or "say." It derives from the Latin word *vox*, meaning "voice." For example, notice how the root -vok- influences the meaning of the word *invoke*. Explain how each of the following words is related to "speaking" or "saying." If necessary, use a dictionary to check word origins.

1. vocal   **2.** provoke   **3.** vociferous

Spelling Strategy

The *chur* sound is spelled *ture* at the ends of words with Latin origins, like *caricature* and *miniature*. For each of the following verbs, write its noun form ending in *ture*.

1. depart   **2.** legislate   **3.** forfeit

Concept Development: Synonyms and Antonyms

Review each of the following items, and indicate whether the paired words are synonyms—words with similar meanings—or antonyms—words with opposite meanings.

1. mitigated, lessened
2. caricature, mockery
3. scruples, doubts
4. pervades, vacates
5. manifested, concealed
6. dispel, disperse
7. invoked, summoned
8. pristine, tarnished

Grammar and Style Lesson

Participles as Adjectives

A **participle** is a verb form that can be used as an adjective. Participles usually end in *-ing* or *-ed*. A participle used as an adjective answers the question *What kind?* or *Which one?* about the noun or pronoun it modifies.

Examples: The <u>bewildered</u> warrior sought advice from his friend. (modifies *warrior*)

After circling the globe several times, the <u>dueling</u> chariots returned. (modifies *chariots*)

Practice Identify the participle in each item that follows, as well as the noun or pronoun each participle modifies.

1. It has the weight of an abandoned corpse.
2. In the hawk's place, they found Indra, the god with the dazzling crown.
3. In what manner does an illumined soul speak?
4. The recollected mind is awake / In the knowledge of the Atman.
5. The gods in heaven noticed Ravana's determined move.

Writing Application Write a paragraph on the importance of performing one's duties. Use at least three participles as adjectives in your writing.

W̧G Prentice Hall Writing and Grammar Connection: Diamond Level, Chapter 19, Section 2

Writing Lesson

Editorial

These selections explore ancient Indian ideas such as *dharma* and nonattachment. Consider which of these ideas might be beneficial when applied to a modern issue. Write an editorial to argue your point of view persuasively.

Prewriting Choose a topic that is important to you and that can be discussed in a brief paper. Then, make notes to clarify how ancient Hindu wisdom could address this problem.

Drafting Begin with an introduction that outlines your point of view. Then, construct a persuasive argument, and support it with examples. Use engaging language to convey your idea's appeal.

Revising Reread your editorial, and evaluate its language for connotations— the ideas and feelings associated with words. Make sure that you have chosen words that convey the meaning you intend.

Model: Revise for Connotations of Words

People would not be motivated by worldly success and

                                   corruption

rewlards but by the sincere desire to do good. The ~~crime~~

     taxpayers   *dollars*

that robs ~~citizens~~ of their hard-earned ~~money~~ would

disappear, and in its place . . .

> Precise language helps support the main points of an editorial.

Prentice Hall Writing and Grammar Connection: Diamond Level, Chapter 7, Section 7

Extension Activities

Listening and Speaking Work in a group to write and "broadcast" a **TV news report** on the battle between Rama and Ravana. Remember to answer these questions:

- *Who?*
- *What?*
- *Where?*
- *When?*
- *Why?*
- *How?*

You might consider having one student act as anchor, while others give live reports. Rehearse until you are ready to deliver your news report to the class. **[Group Activity]**

Research and Technology The ideas of *dharma* and nonattached work had a profound influence on Dr. Martin Luther King, Jr. Use the Internet and other resources to prepare an **oral presentation** on the influence of these ideas on Dr. King and the civil rights movement in the United States.

 **Take It to the Net** PHSchool.com

Go online for an additional research activity using the Internet.

Prepare to Read

from the Panchatantra

About the *Panchatantra*

The *Panchatantra* (pun´ chə tun´ trə), which simply means "a treatise in five chapters," is a collection of Indian animal fables that was intended to teach Indian princes how to govern a kingdom. These entertaining stories give advice related to political matters and to interpersonal relationships in general.

For example, a fable called "The Jackal Who Killed No Elephants" taught princes the importance of knowing themselves and others. This fable tells about a baby jackal that is brought up in a family of lions. Everything goes well until, one day, the jackal's two lion cub brothers want to attack an elephant. The jackal dissuades them. Later, in the family circle, the lion cubs tease the jackal about his cowardice, and he becomes furious. The mother lion calms him down, but when he insists on his courage, she gives him this humorous warning:

> Handsome you are, and valorous;
> You have a scholar's brain:
> But in your family, my boy,
> No elephants are slain.

Taking the hint in good grace, the jackal departs before his brothers grow up, realize he is not a lion, and turn on him.

The moral of the fable is that one must appreciate human limitations and capacities—in oneself and in others. Just as jackals and lions have different strengths and weaknesses, so do human beings. Fables like this one typically convey their moral in a graceful and entertaining verse. By memorizing the verse quoted above, a young prince would have quick access to this fable's important lesson.

Animal Stories: A Long Tradition The use of animal stories to teach moral lessons is familiar to many people in the West because of Aesop's fables from ancient Greece. However, such instructive stories are also an ancient tradition in India: They are found in both the *Rig Veda* and the Upanishads. Buddhists, too, used these kinds of animal fables to depict previous lives of the Buddha and to teach the principles of compassion and mercy, which are so important to the Buddhist tradition.

An Ancient and Influential Book It is uncertain exactly when the *Panchatantra* was written, but scholars estimate that it was sometime between 200 B.C. and A.D. 500. What is known, however, is that the *Panchatantra* has had a wide-ranging influence. In the sixth century A.D., for example, it was translated into Pahlavi, a language of ancient Iran. There are old Syrian and Arabic versions of the fables, as well.

An Unknown Author Little is known about the author of these instructive tales. The collection is attributed to a man named Vishnusharman, who was charged with the responsibility of instructing the sons of a king named Amarashakti. The author's name indicates that he was a Brahman and a devotee of the god Vishnu. However, no record of his life has survived.

From the fables themselves, one can infer that the author was an artist of considerable accomplishment. The tales are woven together ingeniously, and they combine prose with poetry in a way that is fluid and natural. Realizing that poetry is easier to remember than prose, the author includes instructive verses designed to help students recall key points. The fact that the *Panchatantra* is still read today attests to the timeless wisdom of these fables and the narrative skill of their author.

Preview

Connecting to the Literature

Many self-help titles teach such skills as how to dress or how to succeed in business. The *Panchatantra* is an ancient Indian equivalent of these books. This story from the *Panchatantra* teaches a lesson about the interaction between a king and his subjects.

Literary Analysis

Indian Fable

An **Indian fable** is a brief, simple tale that teaches a lesson about conduct in Indian culture. These fables often feature animal characters who behave like humans. Events in the fable point to a lesson called a **moral.** The moral may be stated directly or merely implied.

Use an organizer like the one shown to help you determine the moral that this fable from the *Panchatantra* teaches.

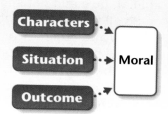

Connecting Literary Elements

The rabbit in this fable is an example of a type of character well known in folklore, the **trickster.** This character uses wit to overcome the greater strength of others. In African folklore, for instance, the spider Anansi often deceives larger animals like the leopard.

In this fable from the *Panchatantra*, the rabbit expresses the credo of all tricksters—"brains over brawn"—in a small poem:

> In what can wisdom not prevail?
> In what can resolution fail?
> What cannot flattery subdue?
> What cannot enterprise put through?

Notice how the rabbit's success highlights the weaknesses of the lion.

Reading Strategy

Reread for Clarification

To avoid misunderstanding a literature selection, **reread to clarify** any parts that you find unclear or confusing. For example, you might want to review details of the setting or of a key event. Also, remember to review footnotes for important information.

Vocabulary Development

obsequiously (əb sē′ kwē əs lē) *adj.* in a manner that shows too great a willingness to serve (p. 204)

rank (raŋk) *adj.* foul; odorous (p. 204)

elixir (ē liks′ ir) *n.* magical potion that cures all ailments (p. 204)

accrue (ə krōō′) *v.* come to as an advantage or a right (p. 205)

tardily (tär′ də lē) *adv.* late (p. 206)

reprobate (rep′ rə bāt′) *n.* scoundrel (p. 206)

extirpate (ek′ stər pāt′) *v.* exterminate; destroy or remove completely (p. 206)

skulks (skulks) *v.* lurks in a cowardly way (p. 207)

from the Panchatantra

translated by Arthur W. Ryder

Numskull and the Rabbit

In a part of a forest was a lion drunk with pride, and his name was Numskull. He slaughtered the animals without ceasing. If he saw an animal, he could not spare him.

So all the natives of the forest—deer, boars, buffaloes, wild oxen, rabbits, and others—came together, and with woe-begone countenances,[1] bowed heads, and knees clinging to the ground, they undertook to beseech <u>obsequiously</u> the king of beasts: "Have done, O King, with this merciless, meaningless slaughter of all creatures. It is hostile to happiness in the other world. For the Scripture says:

> A thousand future lives
> > Will pass in wretchedness
> For sins a fool commits
> > His present life to bless.

Again:

> What wisdom in a deed
> > That brings dishonor fell,
> That causes loss of trust,
> > That paves the way to hell?

And yet again:

> The ungrateful body, frail
> > And <u>rank</u> with filth within,
> Is such that only fools
> > For its sake sink in sin.

"Consider these facts, and cease, we pray, to slaughter our generations. For if the master will remain at home, we will of our own motion send him each day for his daily food one animal of the forest. In this way neither the royal sustenance nor our families will be cut short. In this way let the king's duty be performed. For the proverb says:

> The king who tastes his kingdom like
> > <u>Elixir</u>, bit by bit,
> Who does not overtax its life,
> > Will fully relish it.

---

1. **countenances** (kɒun´ tə nən səz) *n.* faces.

obsequiously (əb sē´ kwē əs lē) *adv.* in a manner that shows too great a willingness to serve

Literary Analysis
Fable Identify elements of a fable in the opening paragraphs of the story.

rank (raŋk) *adj.* foul; odorous

elixir (ē liks´ ir) *n.* magical potion that cures all ailments

The king who madly butchers men,
    Their lives as little reckoned
As lives of goats, has one square meal,
    But never has a second.

A king desiring profit, guards
    His world from evil chance;
With gifts and honors waters it
    As florists water plants.

Guard subjects like a cow, nor ask
    For milk each passing hour:
A vine must first be sprinkled, then
    It ripens fruit and flower.

The monarch-lamp from subjects draws
    Tax-oil to keep it bright:
Has any ever noticed kings
    That shone by inner light?

A seedling is a tender thing,
    And yet, if not neglected,
It comes in time to bearing fruit:
    So subjects well protected.

Their subjects form the only source
    From which <u>accrue</u> to kings
Their gold, grain, gems, and varied drinks,
    And many other things.

The kings who serve the common weal,
    Luxuriantly sprout;
The common loss is kingly loss,
    Without a shade of doubt."

▼ **Critical Viewing**
Does the lion in this painting convey the image of "king of the jungle"? Explain. **[Make a Judgment]**

A Lion at Rest, The Metropolitan Museum of Art

accrue (ə krōō´) *v.* come to as an advantage or a right

After listening to this address, Numskull said: "Well, gentlemen, you are quite convincing. But if an animal does not come to me every day as I sit here, I promise you I will eat you all." To this they assented with much relief, and fearlessly roamed the wood. Each day at noon one of them appeared as his dinner, each species taking its turn and providing an individual grown old, or religious, or grief-smitten, or fearful of the loss of son or wife.

One day a rabbit's turn came, it being rabbit-day. And when all the thronging animals had given him directions, he reflected: "How is it possible to kill this lion—curse him! Yet after all,

☑**Reading Check**

What are the animals trying to convince Numskull to do?

In what can wisdom not prevail?
In what can resolution fail?
What cannot flattery subdue?
What cannot enterprise put through?

I can kill even a lion."

So he went very slowly, planning to arrive <u>tardily</u>, and meditating with troubled spirit on a means of killing him. Late in the day he came into the presence of the lion, whose throat was pinched by hunger in consequence of the delay, and who angrily thought as he licked his chops: "Aha! I must kill all the animals the first thing in the morning."

While he was thinking, the rabbit slowly drew near, bowed low, and stood before him. But when the lion saw that he was tardy and too small at that for a meal, his soul flamed with wrath, and he taunted the rabbit, saying: "You <u>reprobate</u>! First, you are too small for a meal. Second, you are tardy. Because of this wickedness I am going to kill you, and tomorrow morning I shall <u>extirpate</u> every species of animal."

Then the rabbit bowed low and said with deference: "Master, the wickedness is not mine, nor the other animals'. Pray hear the cause of it." And the lion answered: "Well, tell it quick, before you are between my fangs."

"Master," said the rabbit, "all the animals recognized today that the rabbits' turn had come, and because I was quite small, they dispatched me with five other rabbits. But in mid-journey there issued from a great hole in the ground a lion who said: 'Where are *you* bound? Pray to your favorite god.' Then I said: 'We are traveling as the dinner of lion Numskull, our master, according to agreement.' 'Is that so?' said he. 'This forest belongs to me. So all the animals, without exception, must deal with me—according to agreement. This Numskull is a sneak thief. Call him out and bring him here at once. Then whichever of us proves stronger, shall be king and shall eat all these animals.' At his command, master, I have come to you. This is the cause of my tardiness. For the rest, my master is the sole judge."

After listening to this, Numskull said: "Well, well, my good fellow, show me that sneak thief of a lion, and be quick about it. I cannot find peace of mind until I have vented on him my anger against the animals. He should have remembered the saying:

> Land and friends and gold at most
>   Have been won when battles cease;
> If but one of these should fail,
>   Do not think of breaking peace.
>
> Where no great reward is won,
>   Where defeat is nearly sure,
> Never stir a quarrel, but
>   Find it wiser to endure."

Literary Analysis
Fable and the Trickster
How does the choice of a rabbit as the trickster emphasize the importance of cleverness over strength?

tardily (tär′ də lē) *adv.* late

reprobate (rep′ rə bāt′) *n.* scoundrel

extirpate (ek′ stər pāt) *v.* exterminate; destroy or remove completely

Literary Analysis
Fable What human flaws does Numskull show in this passage?

"Quite so, master," said the rabbit. "Warriors fight for their country when they are insulted. But this fellow <u>skulks</u> in a fortress. You know he came out of a fortress when he held us up. And an enemy in a fortress is hard to handle. As the saying goes:

> A single royal fortress adds
> 　　More military force
> Than do a thousand elephants,
> 　　A hundred thousand horse.
>
> A single archer from a wall
> 　　A hundred foes forfends;
> And so the military art
> 　　A fortress recommends.
>
> God Indra used the wit and skill
> 　　Of gods in days of old,
> When Devil Gold-mat plagued the world,
> 　　To build a fortress-hold.
>
> And he decreed that any king
> 　　Who built a fortress sound,
> Should conquer foemen. This is why
> 　　Such fortresses abound."

When he heard this, Numskull said: "My good fellow, show me that thief. Even if he is hiding in a fortress, I will kill him. For the proverb says:

> The strongest man who fails to crush
> 　　At birth, disease or foe,
> Will later be destroyed by that
> 　　Which he permits to grow.

And again:

> The man who reckons well his power,
> 　　Nor pride nor vigor lacks,
> May single-handed smite his foes
> 　　Like Rama-with-the-ax.[2]

"Very true," said the rabbit. "But after all it was a mighty lion that I saw. So the master should not set out without realizing the enemy's capacity. As the saying runs:

---

2. **Rama-with-the-ax** the sixth incarnation of the Hindu god Vishnu. He became angry with the warrior caste and killed them all with his ax. (Rama of the *Ramayana* was the seventh incarnation of Vishnu.)

skulks (skulks) v. lurks in a cowardly way

✔**Reading Check**
What does Numskull plan to do to the other lion described by the rabbit?

A warrior failing to compare
    Two hosts, in mad desire
For battle, plunges like a moth
    Headforemost into fire.

And again:

The weak who challenge mighty foes
    A battle to abide,
Like elephants with broken tusks,
    Return with drooping pride."

But Numskull said: "What business is it of yours? Show him to me, even in his fortress." "Very well," said the rabbit. "Follow me, master." And he led the way to a well, where he said to the lion: "Master, who can endure your majesty? The moment he saw you, that thief crawled clear into his hole. Come, I will show him to you." "Be quick about it, my good fellow," said Numskull.

So the rabbit showed him the well. And the lion, being a dreadful fool, saw his own reflection in the water, and gave voice to a great roar. Then from the well issued a roar twice as loud, because of the echo. This the lion heard, decided that his rival was very powerful, hurled himself down, and met his death. Thereupon the rabbit cheerfully carried the glad news to all the animals, received their compliments, and lived there contentedly in the forest.

Review and Assess

Thinking About the Selection

1. **Respond:** Do you agree with the rabbit's solution to the problem? Why or why not?

2. **(a) Recall:** What moral and political reasons do the animals give Numskull for stopping the slaughter? **(b) Deduce:** To what instinct are the animals hoping to appeal?

3. **(a) Recall:** How does the lion respond to the animals' plea? **(b) Analyze:** What does his response reveal about his character?

4. **(a) Recall:** What explanation does the rabbit give for his tardiness? **(b) Infer:** How does the rabbit expect Numskull to react to this information?

5. **(a) Infer:** What prevents the lion from recognizing his own reflection when he looks into the well? **(b) Draw Conclusions:** What does the rabbit's trick suggest about who is the lion's greatest enemy?

6. **Apply:** What moral or morals do you think this fable teaches?

Review and Assess

Literary Analysis

Indian Fable

1. (a) What does this **Indian fable** suggest about the qualities that ancient Indians admired in their rulers? (b) Which details in the fable reflect those values?
2. Which actions of the characters support the fable's **moral**(s)?
3. In what ways might this fable be instructive to princes or other political leaders?

Connecting Literary Elements

4. Which of the rabbit's behaviors identify him as the fable's **trickster**?
5. (a) What human weaknesses does Numskull display over the course of the story? (b) What human strengths does the rabbit display?
6. Why does the rabbit use the image of another fierce lion to trick Numskull?
7. Would you say that the rabbit is a virtuous character? Explain.

Reading Strategy

Reread for Clarification

8. Complete a chart like this one to show how the character traits of Numskull and the rabbit are revealed. First, identify a trait of one of the characters. Then, **reread** to identify the earliest details in the story that **clarify** that information.

Character	Character Traits	Clarifying Details
Numskull		
Rabbit		

9. If a reader does not know whether the rabbit is lying when he tells Numskull about the other lion, what earlier passage would clarify this point?

Extend Understanding

10. **Social Studies Connection:** Do you think that political cartoons and comic strips perform the same function in our society as the *Panchatantra* did in ancient India? Explain.

Integrate Language Skills

Vocabulary Development Lesson

Word Analysis: Latin Prefix *ex-*

The Latin prefix *ex-* means "out," as in *extend*, which means "to stretch out." Consider how the prefix *ex-* influences the meaning of the words in the left column, and then match each word with its definition on the right.

1. extract   a. leave out
2. exclude   b. speak out strongly
3. exclaim   c. pull or draw out

Spelling Strategy

When a word ends in *y* preceded by a consonant, change the *y* to *i* before adding most suffixes. For example, *happy* + *-ness* = *happiness*. Combine each word below with its suffix.

1. duty +*-ful*   2. copy + *-er*   3. easy + *-ly*

Concept Development: Antonyms

Review the vocabulary words on page 203. Then, complete the following activity by matching each vocabulary word on the left with its antonym, or a word with the opposite meaning, on the right.

1. obsequiously   a. gentleman
2. rank   b. toxin
3. elixir   c. swaggers
4. accrue   d. restore
5. tardily   e. arrogantly
6. reprobate   f. dissipate
7. extirpate   g. punctually
8. skulks   h. fragrant

Grammar and Style Lesson

Adjective Clauses

An **adjective clause** is a subordinate clause that modifies a noun or a pronoun. The clause usually begins with a relative pronoun—such as *that*, *which*, *who*, *whom*, or *whose*—that acts as a subject, and it always includes a verb.

> The king who tastes his kingdom like Elixir . . . will fully relish it. (modifies *king*)

Practice Identify the adjective clause in each sentence that follows, and name the noun or pronoun that the clause modifies.

1. The king who madly butchers men . . . has one square meal, but never has a second.

2. Numskull claimed to be king of the forest, which included all the animals.

3. The rabbit came into the presence of the lion, whose throat was pinched by hunger.

4. The rabbit was the only animal in the forest who refused to surrender to the lion.

5. It was ingenuity that saved the rabbit's life.

Writing Application Write a one-paragraph plot summary of "Numskull and the Rabbit." Use at least three adjective clauses in your summary, and indicate the noun or pronoun that each clause modifies.

WG ***Prentice Hall Writing and Grammar Connection: Diamond Level, Chapter 19, Section 3***

Writing Lesson

Animal Fable

Basing your work on what you have learned about fables, write a brief fable of your own, using animal characters to teach a lesson about human behavior. Close your fable with a moral that flows logically from the events in the narrative.

Prewriting List sayings that offer rules or observations about human behavior, and choose one of them to be the moral of your fable. Jot down ideas for animal characters and a plot related to your moral. Then, narrow and organize those ideas into a rough outline of the story you will tell.

Drafting Write a fable based on your rough outline. Keep your moral in mind as you write, and choose details that help point to it.

Revising Share your draft with classmates, inviting them to use the questions below as a checklist. Consider their responses as you revise your work.

Fable Checklist for Peer Review
☐ Are my characters related to the qualities treated in my moral? For example, if my moral is about greed, is at least one of my characters greedy?
☐ Does the outcome of my fable illustrate my moral? For example, if my moral says that greed is bad, does the greedy behavior in my fable lead to an unhappy outcome?
☐ If the moral is stated within my fable, is the statement brief and clear?

Prentice Hall Writing and Grammar Connection: Diamond Level, Chapter 5, Section 2

Extension Activities

Listening and Speaking Prepare a **retelling** of "Numskull and the Rabbit." Imagine that you are Vishnusharman telling the fable to the sons of the king, and use these tips to guide your retelling:

- Speak expressively, using tones appropriate for each character.
- Vary the pace and intensity of your speaking according to the action in the story.
- Speak clearly so that your audience understands you.

Perform your retelling for an audience of younger students.

Research and Technology Work with a small group of classmates to prepare a **multimedia report** on the role of the trickster in folklore. For example, you might prepare a slide show pairing images of tricksters from different cultures with excerpts from corresponding fables. [**Group Activity**]

 **Take It to the Net** PHSchool.com

Go online for an additional research activity using the Internet.

The fable of "Numskull and the Rabbit" in this unit comes from the *Panchatantra*, an ancient Indian "how-to" book for young princes. Like fables from other cultures and time periods, it uses animal characters to teach universal lessons about life. While offering entertainment and amusement, it provides insights into human weaknesses and strengths.

Because fables tell amusing tales about animals, they have a real advantage as moral teaching. Readers can enjoy them as funny stories on one level while, on another level, absorbing the moral lesson effortlessly and connecting it to their own lives.

A Twentieth-Century Fable "Numskull and the Rabbit" was written thousands of years ago—sometime between 200 B.C. and A.D. 500—but it has much in common with this twentieth-century fable by James Thurber, "The Tiger Who Would Be King." Both fables use animal characters with human characteristics and have simple plots with humorous twists at the end. They both also contain devastating and dramatic conflicts, and each teaches a timeless lesson.

The Tiger Who Would Be King

James Thurber

One morning the tiger woke up in the jungle and told his mate that he was king of beasts.

"Leo, the lion, is king of beasts," she said.

"We need a change," said the tiger. "The creatures are crying for a change."

The tigress listened but she could hear no crying, except that of her cubs.

"I'll be king of beasts by the time the moon rises," said the tiger. "It will be a yellow moon with black stripes, in my honor."

"Oh, sure," said the tigress as she went to look after her young, one of whom, a male, very like his father, had got an imaginary thorn in his paw.

The tiger prowled through the jungle till he came to the lion's den. "Come out," he roared, "and greet the king of beasts! The king is dead, long live the king!"

Inside the den, the lioness woke her mate. "The king is here to see you," she said.

"What king?" he inquired, sleepily.

"The king of beasts," she said.

"I am the king of beasts," roared Leo, and he charged out of the den to defend his crown against the pretender.

It was a terrible fight, and it lasted until the setting of the sun. All the animals of the jungle joined in, some taking the side of the tiger and others the side of the lion. Every creature from the aardvark to the zebra took part in the struggle to overthrow the lion or to <u>repulse</u> the tiger, and some did not know which they were fighting for, and some fought for both, and some fought whoever was nearest, and some fought for the sake of fighting.

"What are we fighting for?" someone asked the aardvark.

"The old order," said the aardvark.

"What are we dying for?" someone asked the zebra.

"The new order," said the zebra.

When the moon rose, fevered and gibbous,[1] it shone upon a jungle in which nothing stirred except a macaw[2] and a cockatoo,[3] screaming in horror. All the beasts were dead except the tiger, and his days were numbered and his time was ticking away. He was monarch of all he surveyed, but it didn't seem to mean anything.

MORAL: You can't very well be king of beasts if there aren't any.

---

1. **gibbous** (gib′ əs) *adj.* more than half but less than completely illuminated.
2. **macaw** (mə kô′) *n.* large parrot of Central or South America with bright colors and a harsh voice.
3. **cockatoo** (käk′ ə too′) *n.* crested parrot with white plumage tinged with yellow or pink.

Connecting Literature Past and Present

1. (a) In what ways is the tiger in "The Tiger Who Would Be King" like the lion in "Numskull and the Rabbit"? (b) In what ways are the two characters different?
2. Which fable is more relevant to today's world? Explain.

repulse (ri puls′) *v.* drive back; repel, as an attack

James Thurber

(1894–1961)
James Thurber left college to become a clerk in the U.S. State Department, but he soon left this serious position to pursue his love of laughter through writing and cartooning. Much of his early work appeared in *The New Yorker* magazine. When failing eyesight forced him to give up drawing, Thurber kept making people laugh with his writing. Many of his funny stories, like "The Tiger Who Would Be King," have a serious message behind the humor.

Atlases and Maps

About Atlases and Maps

An **atlas** is a book of maps showing physical information about the world, such as cities, mountains, rivers, and roads. Some atlases also include facts and statistics about the places depicted. The pages from the modern Dorling Kindersley atlas shown here include the following additional information:

- Climate
- People and Society
- Government
- Economy

The general purpose of a **map** is to present geographical information in a convenient graphic form. To use a map effectively, you should be familiar with the following components of most maps:

- A *legend* or *key* defines the symbols used on the map.
- A *scale* shows the ratio between distances on the map and actual distances on Earth.
- A *compass rose* shows cardinal directions (north, south, east, and west).

Reading Strategy

Locating Information Using Atlases and Maps

Atlases and maps provide a variety of information, some as text and some as visual images. To **locate the information** you need, follow these steps:

1. Decide what category of information you need. Keep in mind that an atlas or a map will provide statistics and basic facts rather than detailed background.
2. Use the heads on the atlas pages, the colors of the map, or the legend or scale to locate the category of information.

Use a graphic organizer like the one shown to record the kind of information that you can find on the pages of the Dorling Kindersley atlas. One example is given.

Location of Information in an Atlas

Category	Location	Information
Population	Fact File box	953 million

INDIA

Separated from the rest of Asia by the Himalayan mountain range, India forms a subcontinent. It is the world's second most populous country.

> Clearly marked sections of the atlas entry provide important information.

GEOGRAPHY

Three main regions: Himalayan mountains; northern plain between Himalayas and Vindhya Mountains; southern Deccan plateau. The Ghats are smaller mountain ranges on the east and west coasts.

CLIMATE

Varies greatly according to latitude, altitude, and season. Most of India has three seasons: hot, wet, and cool. In summer, the north is usually hotter than the south, with temperatures often over 104°F (40°C).

PEOPLE AND SOCIETY

Cultural and religious pressures encourage large families. Today, nationwide awareness campaigns aim to promote the idea of smaller families. Most Indians are Hindu. Each Hindu is born into one of thousands of castes and subcasts, which determine their future status and occupation. Middle class enjoys a very comfortable lifestyle, but at least 30% of Indians live in extreme poverty. In Bombay alone, over 100,000 people live on the streets.

THE ECONOMY

Undergoing radical changes from protectionist mixed economy to free market. Increasing foreign investment. New high-tech industries. Principal exports are clothing, jewelry, gems, and engineering products.

◆ *INSIGHT India's national animal, the tiger, was chosen by the Mohenjo-Daro civilization as its emblem, 4,000 years ago*

FACT FILE
OFFICIAL NAME: Republic of India
DATE OF FORMATION: 1947 / 1961
CAPITAL: New Delhi
POPULATION: 953 million
TOTAL AREA: 1,269,338 sq miles (3,287,590 sq km)
DENSITY: 751 people per sq mile

LANGUAGES: Hindi, English, other
RELIGIONS: Hindu 83%, Muslim 11%, Christian 2%, Sikh 2%, other 2%
ETHNIC MIX: Indo-Aryan 72%, Dravidian 25%, Mongoloid and other 3%
GOVERNMENT: Multiparty republic
CURRENCY: Rupee = 100 paisa

> Essential information about India is set off in a separate box.

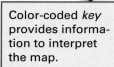

Color-coded *key* provides information to interpret the map.

The map gives an overview of geographical information about the country.

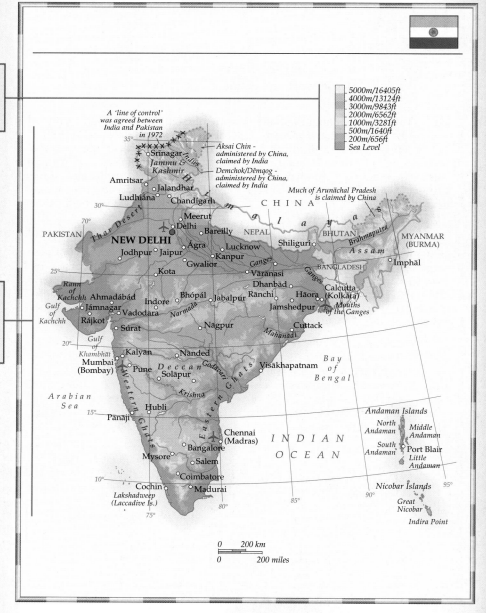

5000m/16405ft
4000m/13124ft
3000m/9843ft
2000m/6562ft
1000m/3281ft
500m/1640ft
200m/656ft
Sea Level

A 'line of control' was agreed between India and Pakistan in 1972

Aksai Chin - administered by China, claimed by India

Demchok/Dêmqog - administered by China, claimed by India

Much of Arunāchal Pradesh is claimed by China

Srīnagar

Jammu & Kashmir

CHINA

Amritsar
Jalandhar
Ludhiāna
Chandīgarh

Meerut
Delhi
Bareilly
NEPAL
Shiliguri
BHUTAN
MYANMAR (BURMA)

PAKISTAN
Thar Desert
NEW DELHI
Jodhpur Jaipur
Āgra
Lucknow
Kanpur
Ganges
Assam
Brahmaputra
Imphāl

Kota
Gwalior
Varānasi
Dhanbād
Ranchi
Hāora
Calcutta (Kolkata)
BANGLADESH

Rann of Kachchh
Ahmadābád
Indore
Bhópāl
Jabalpur
Jamshedpur
Mouths of the Ganges

Gulf of Kachchh
Jámnagar
Vadodara
Narmada
Nagpur
Cuttack

Rājkot
Súrat

Gulf of Khambhát
Kalyan
Nánded
Mahanadi

Mumbai (Bombay)
Pune
Deccan
Godāvari
Solāpur
Visākhapatnam
Bay of Bengal

Arabian Sea
Western Ghats
Krishna
Eastern Ghats

Hubli
Panaji
Chennai (Madras)
INDIAN OCEAN

Andaman Islands
North Andaman
Middle Andaman
South Andaman
Port Blair
Little Andaman

Mysore
Bangalore
Salem

Cochin
Coimbatore
Madurai

Lakshadweep (Laccadive Is.)

Nicobar Islands

Great Nicobar
Indira Point

0   200 km
0   200 miles

Check Your Comprehension

1. What are the three main regions of India?
2. What currency is used in India?
3. Why is the color of the area around the city of Imphāl a different color from the surrounding area on the map?

Applying the Reading Strategy

Locating Information Using Atlases and Maps

4. (a) What is the approximate elevation of the city of Bangalore?
   (b) How did you locate this information?
5. (a) Why is *New Delhi* printed in bold capital letters on the map?
   (b) Where else in the atlas entry is New Delhi mentioned?
6. How would you determine the total area of India?

Activity

Understanding Atlas Entries

Help your classmates assess how well they understand the atlas entry about India. Write several questions based on information on the map and in the text. Challenge your classmates to answer using the atlas entry.

Comparing Informational Materials

Atlases and Guidebooks

An atlas entry is one place to locate information about India. However, if you were visiting India as a tourist, you would probably use a guidebook instead of an atlas to learn about the country.

1. Find a recent tourist guidebook for India or for any other country. Choose one section that you find interesting and helpful. Summarize the information for classmates, and indicate how you located it.

2. Complete a chart like the one shown to note key differences between an atlas and a guidebook.

Contrasting Sources

	Tourist Guidebook	Atlas Entry
Maps		
Articles		

3. Using the information in your chart, explain how the purpose of informational materials determines their content.

Writing About Literature

Analyze Literary Themes

The core texts of ancient Indian literature in this unit—the *Rig Veda*, the Upanishads, and the *Mahabharata*—explore the basic questions of religion: How did this world come to be? How can we lead righteous lives? What happens after we die? The answers are perhaps uniquely Indian. They develop from a perception of a deep difference between the tumultuous world of the senses and the unchanging, unified truth that manifests in that world.

To explore this theme in greater depth, write an essay that analyzes its treatment in the works. Refer to the box at right for details.

Prewriting

Review selections. Review the selections in this unit, taking notes on the theme of appearance versus reality in each. To guide your review, ask yourself the following questions:

- Does the work present the world as divided into distinct, individual beings, or does it present a different idea?
- What attitudes do characters in the selection take toward their own passions or self-interests?
- What truths are contrasted with passion or self-interest?

Use your notes to fill out a chart like the one shown.

Assignment: Appearance Versus Reality

Write an analytical essay exploring the contrast that the works in this unit present between the world of appearances or of individual existence and an underlying universal truth.

Criteria:

- Include a thesis statement that defines the theme and explains the specific contrasts through which this theme is expressed in two or three of the selections.
- Support your analysis of the theme with examples from the selections.
- Discuss the likenesses and differences between the treatments of the theme in the selections.
- Approximate length: 1,500 words

Model: Charting to Analyze Theme

Selection	Underlying Reality/ Universal Principle	Appearance/ Desire
"Creation Hymn"	In the beginning, all is "water," indistinct.	"Desire" creates differences; individual things emerge.
"Sibi"	Sibi must fulfill his dharma.	Sibi should protect his own life.

Choose selections. Review your chart, and choose the two or three selections that suggest rich ideas on the theme of appearance versus reality. To help you make your choice, look for contrasts as well as similarities.

Focus your analysis. Write a sentence or two defining which aspects of your chosen works express the theme—whether the theme appears in the philosophical statements of a character or in the transformation that characters undergo. When you begin drafting, keep your focus in mind.

Read to Write

As you reread the texts, note both significant statements by characters and their actions and transformations. Both are likely to convey the theme.

Drafting

Organize your ideas. Decide how best to organize your ideas before you begin to write your essay. Use one of the following strategies:

- **Organize by work.** Discuss each work in turn, analyzing its use of the theme. Then, sum up the similarities and differences.

- **Discuss how and then why.** Compare the means that each work uses to present the theme, and then sum up the conclusions or questions suggested by each work's presentation of the theme.

Revising and Editing

Review content: Check for sufficient support. Circle each main point in your draft, and then draw an arrow to the quotation, paraphrase, or reference to the text that supports the point. If you do not find such a supporting reference, consider adding one or deleting the point.

Model: Revising for Support

"Creation Hymn" expresses the theme of appearance versus reality by contrasting the world before creation with the world we live in. *The poet writes, "Darkness was hidden by darkness in the beginning: with no distinguishing sign, all this was water," suggesting that the world at creation was formless, without distinctions among individual things.*

Review style: Replace pronouns that have unclear antecedents. Reread your essay. Make sure that each pronoun has a single, clear antecedent (the noun or noun phrase that names the thing to which the pronoun refers).

Vague Antecedent:	Many epics, such as the *Mahabharata*, were written by several poets. That is why *they* include such a variety of voices.
Clarification:	Many epics, such as the *Mahabharata*, were written by several poets. That is why *these epics* include such a variety of voices.

Publishing and Presenting

Present a theme map. Create a map or other graphic representation of the ideas in your essay. Your map should be large enough to display to a group. Then, "walk" classmates through your map, explaining each point.

W̶G Writing and Grammar Connection: Diamond Level, Chapter 14

Write to Learn

As you analyze some of the questions ancient Indian literature poses, you may begin to relate these questions to your own life and to other works you have read.

Write to Explain

As you draft, put yourself in the reader's place. Spell out each step in your analysis. The reader can see only what is on the paper, not what is in your mind.

Writing WORKSHOP

Narration: Reflective Essay

A **reflective essay** is a work in which a writer explores personal experiences or events in order to reflect on their broader meaning. In this workshop, you will write a reflective essay about experiences that have shaped your understanding of yourself or the world.

Assignment Criteria Your reflective essay should feature the following elements:

- A statement of a belief or an insight that you have gained from experience
- A narrative account of the events that led to the belief or insight
- A balance between the narration of incidents and statements of general ideas
- An organization that shows clear connections between insights and events
- A consistent and appropriate tone

To preview the criteria on which your reflective essay may be assessed, see the Rubric on page 223.

Prewriting

Choose a topic. To write a strong reflective essay, you must uncover a theme, or central meaning, in an experience or series of experiences that you have had. To find the right topic, use **freewriting,** writing down whatever comes to mind as you respond to one of these prompts:

- Jot down important experiences in your life, and then write for ten minutes on what each one has meant to you.
- Jot down beliefs that you hold strongly, and then write for ten minutes, tracing the experiences you associate with each.

Review your freewriting notes, and identify significant connections between the events and any themes, insights, or beliefs. Formulate a topic based on these connections.

Compile your ideas. Once you have a good idea of your topic, use a chart like the one shown to gather and focus your ideas on the topic. Draw on your chart as you begin to draft, referring to it for examples and insights.

General Belief: People use words in deceptive and damaging ways.	
Incident	**What It Showed**
Watching Lila talk her way onto the team	People talk to be accepted by others.
Listening to Sam convince Mrs. Day that he was really smart	People talk to impress others.
What happened when I tried tricks like these with Evie	Insincerity can destroy friendships.

Student Model

Before you begin your first draft, read this student model and review the characteristics of a powerful reflective composition.

Akar Bharadvaj
Monroe, Louisiana

The Sound of My Name

When I was a young child, my parents encouraged me not to give up my Indian heritage for the strange American culture of blue jeans and rock music. For the first five years of my life, I was familiar with no Americans save the mailman and the garbage man. I simply stayed at home, learning Gujarati and a little bit of English. When I first went out in public life, I encountered problems.

On my first day of preschool, I was scared by the number of Americans around me. All these white faces were Johnnys, Rosies, and Matthews—not a single Varendra or Vikram in the entire bunch. When I told my classmates my name was Akar, they all looked at me strangely. They had lived their entire five years never having to make the *aardh* sound; their small tongues had slowly molded into an American shape. As a result, my classmates called me "Aye-KAR" or "Acre" or "Acorn" or "Achy-Breaky." They could never get it right.

In the midst of my confusion, someone called me "A-Car." I liked the way that sounded, and I had a brilliant idea. I simply met people halfway by calling myself "Uh-Car." The simplified name could be pronounced easily. Everyone knew what a car was; they just had to get used to the idea that this was a person, not a thing. Even allowing for some inevitable corny "A Boat, A Truck, A . . ." jokes, it was the perfect idea.

My father hated the idea. "Why must you change yourself to help the Americans? Anyone can pronounce anything perfectly, unless he doesn't try," he said in his strongly accented English.

The battle over the sounding of my name was the first symbol I recognized of the rift that existed between my Indian heritage and the American culture in which I will spend my future. Even today, my conservative Indian parents still want me to live by the customs they observed as children. And so I live in a home where I am "AH-Kahr." Yet by day, I am "Uh-Car." My mask is that of a left-brained devout Hindu vegetarian who studies hard and does well in mathematics and science. My face is that of an American teenager who wears blue jeans and listens to the music of his era. My parents cannot fathom my preferences for bread over chapati, guitars over sitars, or American action movies over tedious Bollywood films. They see my brown Indian skin, not the quick American spirit yearning to be set free.

The sound of my name is a trigger. When I hear "Uh-Car," I am myself, an American with Indian parents. When I hear "AH-Kahr," I don the mask of the Indian boy my father was. The sounds tell me who I must be. As I look to the future, I wonder whether my face will not outgrow and so crack the mask.

> Akar is the main character of his reflective essay.

> Specific examples contribute interest and authenticity to Akar's essay.

> Akar's description of his father's accented English adds humor to the essay.

> Akar develops incidents about the sound of his name into a generalization about his two cultural identities.

> Still poised between his two identities, Akar ends his reflective essay with a speculation.

Drafting

Write a strong opening. A reflective essay invites readers into your private world, where they can look at the discoveries that have made you *you*. Set the scene in your opening paragraph: Re-create the spirit of these discoveries—whether of wonder, regret, or conviction. Briefly indicate the changes in your viewpoint or the events that you will discuss, and give a general idea of your reactions.

Follow a logical organization. A well-organized reflective essay weaves together specific incidents and the insights or lessons you draw from them. As you draft, organize your narration of incidents and your discussion of general points in a logical way. The outline shown here is one effective way to organize.

Establish a tone. Your essay will be stronger if you establish and maintain a recognizable, consistent tone. A serious, straightforward tone may be suitable. If your examples are amusing, however, consider adding witty remarks throughout to establish a humorous tone. An ironic tone is a good choice if your examples show that things don't always work out as intended.

Organize Your Essay

- Introduce your belief.
- Narrate an incident from your life.
- Make generalizations about the incident.
- Narrate other, related incidents.
- Generalize about each incident.
- Summarize. Reiterate your belief.

Revising

Revise to balance narration with commentary. In your essay, maintain a balance between the incidents you narrate and your general ideas about them.

1. Circle any sections that offer general insights.

2. Have a partner read these sections and place a check mark next to any that do not clearly illuminate a specific incident or that seem to stray from the point.

3. Consider your partner's notes, and rewrite as necessary. Cut unnecessary points, or replace them with details that help clarify your point.

Model: Revising for Balance

in his strongly accented English.

My father hated the idea. "Why must you change yourself to help the Americans? Anyone can pronounce anything perfectly, unless he doesn't try," he said. Yet it is a known fact that if your language does not include a given sound, you will have trouble pronouncing foreign words using that sound. Besides, my father himself tends to pronounce English *v*'s as *w*'s.

Akar deleted the circled general sentences, which strayed from his point. He rewrote one humorous detail as a brief phrase.

Revise to strengthen connections. Review passages in which you move from the narration of an event to a generalization. Where necessary, rewrite to spell out connections between incidents and insights, adding appropriate linking sentences and transitional phrases, such as *afterward, I realized that* and *these events showed me that.*

Compare the model and the nonmodel. Notice how connections have been clarified in the model.

Nonmodel	Model
They had lived their entire five years never having to make the *aardh* sound; their small tongues had slowly molded into an American shape. My classmates called me "Aye-KAR" or "Acre" or "Acorn" or "Achy-Breaky."	They had lived their entire five years never having to make the *aardh* sound; their small tongues had slowly molded into an American shape. As a result, my classmates called me "Aye-KAR" or "Acre" or "Acorn" or "Achy-Breaky."

Publishing and Presenting

Consider the following activities to share your writing.

Read to a discussion group. Share your reflective essay by reading it to a small group of classmates. After each member of the group has read his or her essay, discuss the various insights offered, looking for common themes or divergent insights.

Make a formal oral presentation. Use your reflective essay as the basis of a formal oral presentation to your class. As you speak, "tell" incidents or events, rather than reading them verbatim.

WG Writing and Grammar Connection: Diamond Level, Chapter 4

Rubric for Self-Assessment

Evaluate your reflective essay using the following criteria and rating scale:

Criteria	Rating Scale				
	Not very				Very
How well does the essay convey the general belief on which it is based?	1	2	3	4	5
How effectively organized is the essay?	1	2	3	4	5
How well does the essay balance incidents and generalizations?	1	2	3	4	5
How clearly are connections between incidents and generalizations established?	1	2	3	4	5
How well is tone established through word choice?	1	2	3	4	5

Listening and Speaking WORKSHOP

Interviewing Techniques

Obtaining a job requires going on an interview with an employer. Your best chances of obtaining a job will come if you apply specific skills for **interviewing**. Follow the strategies below to prepare for and participate in job interviews. To help you practice, complete the Activity that follows.

Preparing for an Interview

Preparing properly is the first step in a successful job interview. Follow these steps before an interview:

- **Research the job and the company.** Find out all you can in advance about the company and the job for which you will interview. Speak to friends, neighbors, and family members who may know the company. Also, consult library and Internet sources.

- **Prepare questions and talking points.** As you do your research, jot down any questions about the company that come to mind. At the same time, take notes on how your experiences, skills, and ambitions could fit in with the work done by the company.

Participating in an Interview

Make sure that you present yourself at your best for a job interview, dressing suitably and grooming yourself properly. During the interview, sit up straight and meet the interviewer's look without shyness or fear. Keep these interviewing tips in mind:

- **Speak clearly.** Use Standard English and speak at a comfortable volume, avoiding "space fillers" such as *like*, *umm*, and *well*. Do not use slang or jargon.

- **Relax and listen.** By staying relaxed, you ensure that you are listening carefully to what the interviewer is saying. Make sure that you understand each question, requesting a clarification if you do not.

- **Take the time you need to respond.** Organize your thoughts before you answer a question. If you have more than one point to make, mentally count off points as you respond. Avoid repeating yourself, and stay on the subject of the question.

- **Draw on your prepared questions and talking points.** Ask informed questions about the company and the position, drawing on the research you have conducted. At appropriate points in the discussion, explain which special skills or interests qualify you for the job.

Feedback Form for an Interview

Rating System
+ = Excellent   ✓ = Average   — = Weak

Preparation
Knowledge of company _____
Knowledge of job requirements _____
List of questions _____

Interview
Appropriate language _____
Demonstration of knowledge of company _____
Ability to highlight skills _____

Post-Interview
Which of my questions about the company were answered?
What will I write in a follow-up letter?
What will I do differently in my next interview?

Activity: Role-Play an Interview Working with a partner, select a job and take turns role-playing an interview for it. Use a Feedback Form like the one shown to evaluate each other's interviews.

Assessment WORKSHOP

Cause-and-Effect Relationships

In the reading sections of some tests, you may be required to recognize the cause-and-effect relationships described or implied in a passage and to make predictions based on these relationships. Use the following strategies to answer such test questions:

- Recognize cause-and-effect relationships by first asking, *What happened?* (effect) and then asking, *Why did it happen?* (cause).

- Remember that a single cause can have many effects, and a single effect can have many causes.

- Remember that an event can be both an effect and a cause. For example, hitting a home run is an *effect* of a sure swing. At the same time, it may be the *cause* of the team's winning the game.

Sample Test Item

Directions: Read the passage, and then answer the question.

What really happens to kids who play lots of video games—particularly violent video games? No one can say for sure. But seeing violent images regularly makes players more comfortable with such images. Does an increased comfort level lead to an increase in violent behavior? All the evidence is anecdotal. Long-term studies have yet to prove a connection between violence and video games.

1. According to the passage, what is one effect violent video games have on those who play them?

 A poor grades in school

 B better hand-eye coordination

 C violent behavior

 D comfort with violent imagery

Answer and Explanation

The correct answer is **D**. Answers **A** and **B** are plausible, but they are not mentioned in the passage. Answer **C** is a possible effect, but the passage states that the link between violent imagery and violent behavior has not been proved.

▶ Practice

Directions: Read the passage, and then answer the question.

What sort of community does the traditional Amish way of life foster, and what are its strengths and weaknesses? Amish people who follow a traditional way of life strive to be as removed from the rest of the world as possible. To keep their communities cohesive, they adhere to strict codes of moral behavior with little tolerance for differences. The people conform, work hard, and seldom pursue formal higher education. As a result, Amish people enjoy stable, productive lives, sure of their place in the world because of their clear, and clearly valuable, roles in the community.

1. Which of the following does the passage give as an effect of the cohesiveness of Amish communities?

 A strict moral codes

 B conformism

 C stable lives

 D lack of tolerance for differences

UNIT 3

Chinese and Japanese Literature

冨嶽三十六景 神奈川沖 浪裏

The Great Wave of Kanagawa, from 36 Views of Mount Fuji, Katsusika Hokusai, Private Collection

**"The Four Seasons go on
for ever and ever:
In all Nature
nothing stops to rest
Even for a moment . . ."**

— Po Chü-i, from "Illness"

**"And so,
young though he was,
fleeting beauty took its
hold upon his thoughts . . ."**

—Lady Murasaki Shikibu,
from *The Tale of Genji*

Timeline 1000 B.C.–A.D. 1890

Chinese and Japanese Events

- **1000 B.C. (China)** The Shang dynasty fell about 100 years earlier.

- **551 (China)** Confucius is born. ▼

- **c. 500s (China)** *The Book of Songs* is compiled.

- **256/255 B.C. (China)** The Chou dynasty is overthrown.

- **221–206 (China)** The Ch'in dynasty reigns. ▼

- **206 (China)** The Han dynasty takes power.

- **200 (Japan)** By this date, the Japanese cultivate irrigated rice.

- **c. 100s A.D. (China)** Buddhism begins to take hold.

- **220 (China)** The Han dynasty is deposed.

- **300s (Japan)** The Yamato emerge as the most powerful clan, opening the way to Chinese cultural influences.

- **365–427 (China)** T'ao Ch'ien, one of China's greatest poets, lives.

World Events

- **c. 1000 B.C. (India)** The Vedic hymns are compiled.

- **1000–800 (Greece)** Tribes evolve into city-states.

- **mid-900s (Israel)** King Solomon reigns over a united country.

- **800s or 700s (Greece)** Homer composes the *Iliad* and the *Odyssey*.

- **600s (India)** Hindu sages flourish in India, recording their thoughts in the Upanishads.

- **400s (Greece)** Sophocles writes *Oedipus the King.*

- **431–404 B.C. (Greece)** Sparta defeats Athens in the Peloponnesian War.

- **330 (Persian Empire)** An inscription recognizes Alexander the Great as lord of the Persian Empire.

- **320 (India)** Chandragupta begins the Maurya dynasty.

- **c. 300 (southern Mexico/ Central America)** The Mayas begin to build elaborate cities. ▼

- **392 (Roman empire)** Christianity becomes the official religion of the empire.

Chinese, Japanese, and World Events

A.D. 500   A.D. 1000   A.D. 1500   A.D. 1890

- **618–907 (China)** The T'ang dynasty rules.
- **early 700s (Japan)** The first works of Japanese prose appear.
- **762 (China)** The great T'ang poet Li Po dies.
- **770 (China)** The great T'ang poet Tu Fu dies.
- **794 (Japan)** A new imperial capital is built at Heian (Kyoto). ◀
  - **700s (Japan)** "Collection of Ten Thousand Leaves," an early poetry anthology, appears.
    - **960 (China)** The Sung dynasty begins.

- **c. 1000 (Japan)** Lady Murasaki Shikibu writes *The Tale of Genji*.
- **1192 (Japan)** Yoritomo founds the shogunate, a system of rule that continues for 700 years.
- **1279 (China)** The Sung dynasty ends.
- **1279–1368 (China)** The Yuan dynasty, founded by Mongols, rules all of China.
- **1300s (Japan)** First Nō dramas emerge.
- **1368 (China)** The Ming dynasty reestablishes Chinese rule.

- **1639 (Japan)** The Tokugawas close Japan to the rest of the world.
- **1644 (China)** The Ming dynasty is overthrown by armies from Manchuria.
- **1763–1828 (Japan)** The haiku poet Kobayashi Issa lives.
- **1842 (China)** China is forced to sign treaties with Western nations.
- **1853 (Japan)** Commander Perry opens Japan to the world. ▲

- **527 (Turkey)** Justinian begins to rule the Byzantine empire.
- **500s (Western Europe)** German tribes like the Franks dominate the region.
- **600s (Africa)** Islam spreads to North Africa.
- **622 (Arabian Peninsula)** Muhammad journeys from Mecca to Yathrib, an event that marks the rise of Islam.
- **711 (Spain)** Muslims enter Spain.
- **800 (France)** King Charlemagne is crowned emperor by the pope.

- **c. 1100 (France)** The *Song of Roland* is composed.
- **1215 (England)** King John signs the Magna Carta, limiting royal power.
- **1321 (Italy)** Dante completes *The Divine Comedy*.
- **1492 (Americas)** Christopher Columbus reaches the New World. ▶

- **1503–1506 (Italy)** Leonardo da Vinci paints the *Mona Lisa*.
- **1508–1512 (Italy)** Michelangelo paints the Sistine Chapel ceiling.
  - **1517 (Germany)** The Reformation begins as Martin Luther posts his Ninety-Five Theses.
  - **1558–1603 (England)** Queen Elizabeth I reigns.

Chinese and Japanese Literature

(1000 B.C.–A.D. 1890)

Historical Background

China: A Long Line of Dynasties Chinese civilization, which has endured for about 3,500 years, is the world's oldest surviving civilization. It began in the Yellow River basin in northern China when the people who lived there established permanent farming villages. By 1600 B.C., they had developed a complex social and economic system. At about this time, an elite group of kings established authority over northern China and founded the Shang dynasty, the first in a long series of Chinese dynasties.

The Mandate of Heaven The Chinese came to believe that heaven granted each dynastic ruler a mandate, or right to rule. In return for good government, the people owed the ruler complete obedience. If the ruler failed to maintain order, however, the people had the right to rebel. Following are some highlights from China's dynastic history.

Close-up on Culture

Confucianism, Taoism, and Buddhism in Chinese Culture

Chinese culture has been dominated by three schools of thought—Confucianism, Taoism, and Buddhism (bood´ iz´ əm). Through the centuries, elements of all these schools have influenced the way in which Chinese people live.

Confucianism, the official Chinese state doctrine for over two thousand years, is more of a social philosophy than a religion. Founded by Confucius (kən fyoo´ shəs) (551–479 B.C.), it is primarily concerned with the moral nature of social relationships. It emphasizes the need to respect and obey people in authority, such as heads of households and government officials.

By contrast, Taoism, founded by the legendary Lao Tzu (Lao Zi) (lou´ dzu´), is more concerned with the relation of humanity to the larger world of nature. In the classical Taoist view, human beings are perceived as being merely one of the many manifestations of nature, on an equal level with all other creatures. Taoism teaches that people should withdraw from society and strive to live a simple life.

The third school of thought, Buddhism, began to take hold in China in the second century A.D. during the period of disunity that followed the decline of the Han dynasty. Because Buddhism taught that life on Earth is filled with suffering and is characterized by illusion, it was appealing during a chaotic era.

The Chou Dynasty (1122–256/255 B.C.) The Shang dynasty was overthrown by a Central Asian people known as the Chou (Zhou), who established the longest of all the Chinese dynasties. Despite political turmoil, the final centuries of the Chou dynasty saw major advances in Chinese philosophy with the founding of Taoism (dou´ iz´ əm) and Confucianism (kən fyoo´ shən iz´ əm) (see page 230).

The Ch'in Dynasty (221–206 B.C.) By 221 B.C., the feudal state of Ch'in (Qin) had succeeded in unifying China. The Ch'in dynasty was overthrown within fifteen years. Yet it managed to build a system of roads, establish an administrative system that lasted for 2,000 years, and patch together defensive walls on the northern border to form the Great Wall of China. Eventually this wall would stretch for about 4,500 miles!

The Han Dynasty (206 B.C.–A.D. 220) The next dynasty, the Han, produced one of the most glorious eras in Chinese history. During this period, China established trade with Europe and western Asia. One significant effect of increased foreign contacts was the introduction of the Buddhist religion from India (see page 230).

The T'ang Dynasty (618–907) The T'ang (Tang) dynasty is regarded as the Golden Age of Chinese civilization. T'ang rulers created an empire that extended from the Pacific Ocean to the borders of Persia and India, and they established the world's most effective system of government. Major technological advances of the time included the invention of gunpowder and block printing.

The Sung Dynasty (960–1279) Reacting against Buddhist influence, Sung (Song) philosophers created a new school of thought called Neo-Confucianism—a school that would dominate Chinese intellectual life for the next thousand years. Neo-Confucianists unconsciously borrowed from Buddhism, however, in seeking enlightenment through a combination of meditation and moral action.

The Yüan Dynasty (1206–1368) During the late twelfth and early thirteenth centuries, northern China was overrun by Mongol invaders led by Genghis Khan (gen´ gis kän´). He established the Yüan (Yuan) dynasty, the first foreign dynasty in China's history. The Sung dynasty, however, ruled in southern China until 1279. One of the many traders to visit China during this period was the Venetian Marco Polo.

The Ming Dynasty (1368–1644) Chinese rule was reestablished with the foundation of the Ming dynasty. Because of lingering resentment from the Mongol conquest, the Ming emperors tried to avoid foreign influence.

The Ch'ing Dynasty (1644–1911/1912) Armies from Manchuria conquered China and established a second foreign dynasty, the Ch'ing (Qing). The country prospered during the early years of the Ch'ing dynasty. Yet unrest ultimately toppled this dynasty and put an end to imperial rule.

▲ **Critical Viewing** The first Ch'in emperor began the Great Wall in the third century B.C., but it was worked on throughout Chinese history. What do you think it reveals about Chinese civilization? Explain. **[Infer]**

Traditional Chinese Government By the time the Ch'ing dynasty was overthrown, imperial rule had lasted in China for thousands of years. Throughout most of this period, the Chinese government was organized into a pyramid-shaped hierarchy. At the top of this hierarchy was an all-powerful emperor, and beneath him were numerous officials.

China and the West While China pursued isolation, Europe expanded. In 1793, the Ch'ing emperor refused Britain's request for trading rights, calling the British "barbarians." In 1842, however, China was forced to sign treaties with Westerners when British "barbarians" on warships destroyed the outdated Chinese fleet. By 1900, European powers and Japan had carved China into spheres of influence for themselves.

Japan: Beginnings of Civilization Little is known about the first inhabitants of the Japanese islands, who arrived there several thousand years ago. By 200 B.C., however, the Japanese people had begun to practice farming, using irrigation to cultivate rice. At the same time, a steady flow of immigrants began to arrive from Korea and other regions of continental Asia. This influx of people lasted for centuries and gradually led to the emergence of a distinct Japanese culture.

Yet the nation was not politically unified. Japanese society was divided into tribal organizations called *uji*, or clans, which were dominated by aristocrats and also included warriors and spiritual leaders. Because the islands' mountainous terrain forced settlements in scattered coastal plains or in narrow valleys divided by sharply rising slopes, the clans were able to remain relatively independent.

The Yamato Clan and Chinese Influence During the fourth century A.D., the Yamato emerged as the nation's most powerful clan. Forging a relationship with the Chinese, the Yamato brought many Chinese beliefs to Japanese society, including those associated with Buddhism and Confucianism. The Japanese copied Chinese architectural and artistic forms and clothing styles, and they adapted the Chinese system of writing to the Japanese language. Yamato leaders also reformed the Japanese political structure by using the Chinese system of central imperial rule as a model.

The Heian Age The central government retained its authority for only a brief period. In 794, a new imperial capital was built at Heian (hā' än'), which is now Kyoto (kē' ōt' ō). There, courtiers lived a refined life devoted to elaborate ceremonies and festivals, but the emperor's power began to diminish. The real political authority had slipped into the hands of the powerful, aristocratic Fujiwara family.

Meanwhile, ambitious aristocrats who were not part of the Fujiwara family settled in the countryside, beyond the reach of the central government. There, they established huge estates and assembled bands of warriors, hoping to challenge the authority of the Fujiwaras.

▼ **Critical Viewing** Which qualities of this fan-shaped sutra, or section of Buddhist scripture, suggest that it belongs to the Heian Age? Explain. **[Connect]**

Feudal Japan As rural lords grew more powerful, Japan became a feudal society that was similar in some ways to that of Western Europe. Feudal Japan was dominated by the *samurai* (sam´ ə rī) class, which included lords, or *daimyo*, and their *samurai* soldiers. Each *samurai* carried a pair of swords and followed a code of conduct that emphasized bravery, loyalty, and honor.

In 1185, the *daimyo* Minamoto Yoritomo became the most powerful figure in Japan. Later, he accepted the title of *shogun* (shō´ gun´), or chief general. Other shoguns who followed him, however, had trouble unifying the country, and Japan experienced feudal warfare for centuries.

Japan Shuts Out the World In the 1600s, the Tokugawa shoguns created a peaceful, orderly society; strengthened the central government; and built a new capital at Edo (Tokyo). The Tokugawas, however, felt threatened by the arrival of European traders and missionaries. Finally, in 1639, they closed Japan to the world.

Perry Opens the Door In 1853, a United States fleet under Commander Perry arrived in Edo (Tokyo) Bay, intent on ending Japanese isolation. Japanese leaders, realizing that their weapons were no match for American cannon, granted limited trading rights to Americans. Before long, the United States and other Western nations won additional rights.

Fourteen years after Perry's visit, the Tokugawa shogunate ended. The new emperor called his reign Meiji (mā´ jē´), or "enlightened rule." During the Meiji restoration, many Japanese studied western ways, and by 1900, Japan had become a modern industrial nation.

Japanese Religious Traditions Two major religious faiths, Shintoism (shin´ tō iz´ əm) and Buddhism, were important in Japanese society. By the 500s A.D., the practice of nature worship became known as *Shintoism*, "the way of the gods," to distinguish it from Buddhism. Central to Shintoism was the belief that elements of nature were inhabited by spirits called *kami*. For this reason, a waterfall, a gnarled tree, or a full moon could inspire reverence.

Though popular, Buddhism did not compete with Shintoism. Instead, the Japanese embraced both religions. They looked to Buddhism, which emphasized life's impermanence, to overcome the sorrows of earthly existence. Military aristocrats favored a form of Buddhism known as Zen. In contrast to other Buddhist sects, Zen rejects the notion that salvation is attained outside of life. Instead, Zen emphasizes the attainment of tranquillity and insight through mental and physical discipline. Both the rituals of the tea ceremony and the rigors of samurai training reflect Zen values.

▲ **Critical Viewing** How is this *samurai* warrior similar to and different from a medieval European knight? [**Compare and Contrast**]

Literature

China: Philosophy Along with poetry, the most highly valued Chinese literary works are philosophical texts. Of these books, the most notable are *The Analects* of Confucius and the *Tao Te Ching* of Lao Tzu—the principal works of Confucianism and Taoism respectively (see page 230).

Chinese Poetry As is suggested by the content of civil-service examinations, poetry has always held an especially important place in Chinese culture. Even after the current Communist regime came into power in the mid-twentieth century, poetry continued to be highly valued. In fact, Mao Tse-tung (Mao Zedong; 1893–1976), the leader of the Communist Revolution, was himself a gifted poet.

The oldest collection of Chinese poetry is *The Book of Songs*, or the *Shih Ching*. Compiled around the sixth century B.C., this collection consists of 305 poems, many of which were originally folk songs, focusing on such themes as farming, love, and war. Throughout Chinese history, *The Book of Songs* has retained an honored status in Chinese society, and students have been expected to memorize it.

Despite the importance of *The Book of Songs*, most great Chinese poetry was written after the fall of the Han dynasty. At about the same time that the Han collapsed, poets began writing beautiful, emotive verses using a fairly rigid poetic form known as the *shih* (shə). One of the first masters of the *shih* form, T'ao Ch'ien (Tao Qian) (dou' chē' en), is still ranked as one of the finest Chinese poets.

The *shih* form was raised to its greatest heights, however, by the poets of the T'ang dynasty. Among the many talented poets of this period, Li Po (Li Bo) (lē' bō') and Tu Fu (Du Fu) (dōō' fōō') are highly regarded. Many of Li Po's verses are best described as romantic, imaginative, or playful. Tu Fu, on the other hand, is known for his superb craftsmanship and his command of the language.

Chinese poetry continued to flourish in later ages, and new poetic forms, such as the lyrical *tz'u* form, emerged. Yet the T'ang era, with its many fine poets, has come to be universally acknowledged as the golden age of Chinese poetry.

▼ **Critical Viewing** What does this picture of the Chinese poet Li Po suggest about the source of inspiration for his poetry? Explain. **[Infer]**

The Poet Li Po Admiring a Waterfall, Hokusai, Honolulu Academy of Arts

A Living Tradition

Bertolt Brecht and Chinese Drama

The German playwright Bertolt Brecht (ber´ tôlt brekt´) (1898–1956) was one of the most innovative dramatists of the modern age. Rejecting the traditional Western approach to theater, he established a new type of drama known as "epic theater." In doing so, he was heavily influenced by traditional Chinese theater.

A fervent political activist, Brecht used his plays to convey political and social messages. He felt that audiences would not grasp his messages, however, if they became emotionally involved in the stage action. As a result, his epic theater employs techniques to distance the audience from the characters and action.

Many of Brecht's distancing techniques reflect the influence of traditional Chinese theater. As in Chinese dramas, the actors in Brecht's plays express an awareness that they are being watched and at times address the audience directly. In addition, rather than submerging themselves in the emotions of their characters, the actors merely demonstrate these emotions. An actor might demonstrate fear by simply rubbing white makeup on his or her face.

Another similarity between Brecht's plays and the Chinese theater is the exaggerated, highly stylized manner in which the actors move. Still another similarity is that both types of drama generally blend dialogue with singing and dancing, performed to the accompaniment of musicians who sit in full view.

Two of Brecht's plays that most clearly exhibit the influence of Chinese theater are *The Good Woman of Setzuan* (1943) and *The Caucasian Chalk Circle* (1948). The first is set in China, and the second was inspired by a thirteenth-century Chinese play.

Chinese Drama and Fiction For the most part, the Chinese have always regarded drama and fiction as inferior to poetry. Despite this fact, however, the Chinese have produced a number of notable dramas and works of fiction.

The golden age of Chinese drama occurred during the Yuan dynasty. By this time, the Chinese already had a longstanding tradition of dramatic entertainments involving singing and dancing. Like these earlier spectacles, the plays produced during the Yuan dynasty combined singing and dancing with dialogue, but they differed from their predecessors in that they had a consistent plot. Among the most famous plays written during this period are *The Romance of the Western Chamber* by Wang Shih-fu (Wang Shi-fu) and *Injustice Suffered by Tou-o* by Kuan Han-ch'ing (Guan Han-qing).

Although the Chinese had a rich oral tradition that included countless legends and folk tales, Chinese fiction did not come into its own until the Ming and Ch'ing dynasties. The most famous Chinese novel, *Dream of the Red Chamber* by Ts'ao Chan (Cao Zhan), was written in the eighteenth century. A long, complicated work filled with penetrating psychological insights, this novel chronicles the decline of a prominent aristocratic family.

Japan: Poetry Poetry is one of the oldest and most popular means of expression and communication in Japanese culture. Although poetry had already existed for centuries as part of an oral tradition, the first anthology of Japanese poetry, the *Man'yoshu*, or "Collection of Ten Thousand Leaves," did not appear until the eighth century. Containing more than four thousand poems, the anthology includes works by poets from a wide range of social classes. The anthology makes it clear that poetry was an integral part of daily life in ancient Japanese society.

Poetry Contests In the centuries that followed, Japanese emperors and their courts became increasingly interested in and supportive of the efforts of poets. The court held regular poetry contests and published a series of poetry anthologies that included the best poems of the time.

Nearly all the poems in these anthologies were written in tanka form, consisting of five lines of five, seven, five, seven, and seven syllables. In previous centuries, the choka, consisting of an unlimited number of alternating lines of five and seven syllables, had rivaled the tanka in popularity. However, as the court began playing an active role in establishing poetic standards, an increasing emphasis was placed on brevity, and the choka form was almost completely abandoned.

A Writer's Voice

The Humanity of Kakinomoto Hitomaro

Little is known about the life of poet Kakinomoto Hitomaro (kä´ kē´ nä´ mō´ tō´ hē´ tō´ mä´ rō´), who lived during the late seventh and early eighth centuries A.D. Yet from his poetry we can infer that he was extremely dignified, genuine, and perceptive.

Hitomaro served as the court poet for three Japanese emperors and wrote a number of poems extolling the causes of the rulers he served. In other poems, he relates his personal experiences, both triumphs and tragedies, in a style that enables readers to share those experiences. For example, in "I Loved Her Like the Leaves" (translated by Geoffrey Bownas), he expresses deep sorrow for the death of his wife:

> . . . To the wide fields where the heat haze shimmers,
> Hidden in a white cloud,
> White as white mulberry scarf,
> She soared like the morning bird
> 5 Hidden from our world like the setting sun.
> The child she left as token
> Whimpers, begs for food; but always
> Finding nothing that I might give,
> Like birds that gather rice-heads in their beaks,
> 10 I pick him up and clasp him in my arms. . . .

The Haiku During the age of Japanese feudalism, groups of poets worked together to write chains of interlocking tanka, known as renga. Each tanka within a renga was divided into verses of seventeen and fourteen syllables, composed by different poets.

Eventually, the opening verse of a renga, known as the hokku, developed into a distinct literary form, consisting of three lines of five, seven, and five syllables. The haiku (hī kōō′), the name by which this verse form came to be known, soon became more popular than the tanka.

Three famous haiku masters were Matsuo Bashō (ma′ tzōō′ ō ba′ shō′), Yosa Buson (yō′ sä′ bōō′ sän′), and Kobayashi Issa (kō′ bä′ yä′ shē′ ē′ sä′).

Japanese Prose Appearing early in the eighth century, the first works of Japanese prose, the *Kojiki*, or "Record of Ancient Matters," and *Nihon shoki*, or "Chronicles of Japan," focused on Japanese history.

Among the court ladies who vividly captured the lives of the Heian aristocracy in prose were Murasaki Shikibu (mōō′ rä sä′ kē shē′ kē bōō′) and Sei Shōnagon (sā′ shō′ nä′ gōn′). Aside from Lady Murasaki Shikibu's novel *The Tale of Genji*, the most famous early Japanese prose work may be *The Tale of the Heike*. Written by an unknown author during the thirteenth century, this work presents a striking portrait of war-torn Japan during the early stages of the age of feudalism. Another important work of prose produced during the age of feudalism is *Essays in Idleness*, a loosely organized collection of insights, reflections, and observations written by a Buddhist priest named Kenko.

Japanese Drama Nō plays, the earliest surviving form of Japanese drama, emerged during the fourteenth century. In some respects, the Nō theater is like the drama of ancient Greece: The plays are performed on an almost-bare stage by a small but elaborately costumed cast of actors wearing masks; the actors are accompanied by a chorus; and the plays are written either in verse or in highly poetic prose. Yet the dramas themselves are decidedly Japanese, reflecting many Shinto and Buddhist beliefs.

▲ **Critical Viewing** This illustration comes from an edition of *The Tale of Genji*, the great Japanese novel by Lady Murasaki Shikibu. Judging by this picture, what would you expect to find in the novel? Why? **[Speculate]**

Prepare to Read

from the Tao Te Ching ◆ *from* The Analects

Lao Tzu (c. sixth century B.C.)

Lao Tzu (lou´ dzu´), which means "Old Master" or "Ancient One," is the name given to the author of a book called the *Tao Te Ching*, one of the two basic texts of Taoist philosophy.

The Legend of Lao Tzu No one knows exactly who the "Old Master" was or when he lived, though it seems most likely that he lived during the sixth century B.C. According to legend, he remained in his mother's womb for sixty-two years before birth and emerged as a white-haired old man. He then served as Keeper of the Archives in the ancient Chinese kingdom of Chou. Unhappy with the political situation of his day, he mounted a black ox and headed for a western pass, hoping to leave the chaos in China. As he approached the pass, the gatekeeper recognized him as a sage and refused to let him through unless he wrote down some words of wisdom. Lao Tzu proceeded to write the 5,000-word *Tao Te Ching* and was allowed to depart through the pass. Some say he was 160 years old when he departed, while others put his age at 200.

The Philosophy of Lao Tzu *Tao Te Ching* is translated into English as *The Way and Its Power*. In writing this book, Lao Tzu had two primary concerns: understanding the way of the universe and using that understanding for self-preservation. He was not interested in how to win fame, glory, honor, or wealth, but rather in how to survive. Some of the passages of the *Tao Te Ching* seem to be addressed to a ruler, advising how to ensure the survival of a kingdom in a time of political upheaval. Others are addressed to anyone who wishes to understand the fundamental principles of existence and to use them to preserve himself or herself in a chaotic world.

Confucius (551–479 B.C.)

The ideas of Confucius (kən fyōō´ shəs) have shaped the pattern of Chinese life for over two thousand years, yet the details of Confucius's life remain a mystery. No writings from his own hand are known to exist. *The Analects*, or collected sayings of Confucius, were compiled long after his death by disciples of his disciples.

A Transmitter of Truth Confucius was a scholar from the state of Lu, now part of the Shantung province in northeast China. Confucius wished to be an adviser to kings but never achieved that goal. Instead, he made his living by wandering from place to place instructing any young men who appeared to have talent for learning. He considered himself to be a transmitter of ancient truths and believed that the values of the ancient golden age were generally ignored by his generation. In his opinion, his generation cared more about appearances than about the soul.

In all of his teachings, Confucius emphasized the importance of moral conduct. He believed that people in positions of authority, such as political officials, should maintain high standards for themselves, even when out of office.

A Teacher of Tradition Confucius lived at a time when corruption and civil strife raged in China. He taught that by following tradition and authority with the proper spirit of reverence, the country's moral health could be restored.

The words of one who warned of the decline of tradition became a tradition in their own right. Starting in the second century B.C., under the Han emperors, Confucianism became an official state doctrine and its study was required of all who served in government.

Preview

Connecting to the Literature

Have you ever heard the expression "Sometimes, less is more"? Often, the best way to say something is also the simplest way. The *Tao Te Ching* and *The Analects* both illustrate this principle, conveying profound ideas in short, simple statements.

Literary Analysis

Aphorisms

Aphorisms, sometimes called maxims or proverbs, are short statements expressing general truths or principles. Here are two famous aphorisms:

- "A penny saved is a penny earned." (Benjamin Franklin)
- "Look before you leap." (John Heywood)

The *Tao Te Ching* and *The Analects* are collections of philosophical aphorisms that express universal truths about life. They are not fully reasoned explanations; instead, these selections provide a hint of truth to get readers thinking and leave them to draw conclusions.

Comparing Literary Works

Lao Tzu and Confucius both embrace the idea of a Tao, a "way" that refers to the force that controls the universe. Confucius speaks of this "way" as a "moral force" with which people should align their behavior, but Lao Tzu teaches that the Tao is a natural order with which people should not interfere. As you read, notice the examples each philosopher uses to illustrate and support his essential ideas.

Reading Strategy

Questioning Causes and Effects

These selections offer lessons by showing causes and effects. For example, Lao Tzu says, "Not to honor men of worth will keep the people from contention." However, Lao Tzu does not explain why this statement is true. When you **question causes and effects,** you can fully understand the author's message. Use a chart like the one shown to analyze cause-and-effect relationships and to identify the principles they demonstrate.

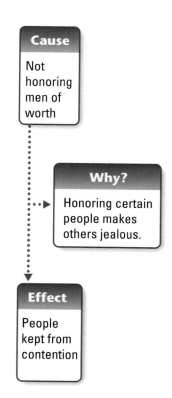

Cause

Not honoring men of worth

Why?

Honoring certain people makes others jealous.

Effect

People kept from contention

Vocabulary Development

manifestations (man´ ə fes tā´ shənz) *n.* material forms (p. 240)

contention (kən ten´ shən) *n.* disputing; quarreling (p. 240)

calamity (kə lam´ ə tē) *n.* deep trouble (p. 241)

submissive (sub mis´ iv) *adj.* yielding; giving in without resistance (p. 241)

homage (häm´ ij) *n.* act of reverence and respect (p. 243)

chastisements (chas´ tiz mənts) *n.* punishments (p. 243)

ritual (rich´ o͞o əl) *n.* observance of prescribed rules (p. 243)

bias (bī´ əs) *n.* prejudice; partiality (p. 243)

from the Tao Te Ching

Lao Tzu   translated by D. C. Lau

Background

Early Taoists and Confucianists both believed the Tao was the force that controlled the universe. However, as these selections demonstrate, Taoists differed from Confucianists in that they did not ascribe human moral qualities to the Tao. They considered it as being beyond the scope of human concerns, but they believed that people could see its workings by observing nature.

I

The way that can be spoken of
Is not the constant way;
The name that can be named
Is not the constant name,
5　The nameless was the beginning of heaven and earth;
The named was the mother of the myriad creatures.
Hence always rid yourself of desires in order to observe its secrets;
But always allow yourself to have desires in order to observe its
　　<u>manifestations</u>.
These two are the same
10　But diverge in name as they issue forth.
Being the same they are called mysteries,
Mystery upon mystery—
The gateway of the manifold secrets.

manifestations (man´ ə fes tā´ shənz) *n.* material forms

III

Not to honor men of worth will keep the people from <u>contention</u>; not to value goods which are hard to come by will keep them from theft; not to display what is desirable will keep them from being unsettled of mind.

Therefore in governing the people, the sage empties their minds but fills their bellies, weakens their wills but strengthens their bones. He always keeps them innocent of knowledge and free from desire, and ensures that the clever never dare to act.

Do that which consists in taking no action, and order will prevail.

contention (kən ten´ shən) *n.* disputing; quarreling

Reading Strategy
Questioning Causes and Effects What causes the clever not to act, and what is the effect of this inaction?

IX

Rather than fill it to the brim by keeping it upright
Better to have stopped in time;[1]
Hammer it to a point
And the sharpness cannot be preserved for ever;

5 There may be gold and jade to fill a hall
But there is none who can keep them.
To be overbearing when one has wealth and position
Is to bring <u>calamity</u> upon oneself.
To retire when the task is accomplished

10 Is the way of heaven.

XLIII

The most <u>submissive</u> thing in the world can ride roughshod over the hardest in the world—that which is without substance entering that which has no crevices.

That is why I know the benefit of resorting to no action. The teaching that uses no words, the benefit of resorting to no action, these are beyond the understanding of all but a very few in the world.

---

1. **Rather than . . . in time** These lines refer to a container that stands in position when empty but overturns when full.

▲ **Critical Viewing**
Which elements in this painting support the ideas expressed in the *Tao Te Ching*? **[Connect]**

calamity (kə lam´ ə tē) *n.* deep trouble

submissive (sub mis´ iv) *adj.* yielding; giving in without resistance

☑**Reading Check**
What does Lao Tzu say is "the way of heaven"?

from The Analects

CONFUCIUS
translated by Arthur Waley

Background

Confucius lived in a chaotic period in Chinese history. Responding to such upheaval in society, he taught the value and importance of tradition and social order. Unlike Taoism, which advocates submission and taking no action, Confucianism focuses on moral behavior, duty, and education.

Confucianism deals with all types of social units, from the most basic (the family) to the largest (the state). In the Confucian system, social relations are based on a system of subordination, with younger family members subordinate to older members and subjects subordinate to government officials. However, all must be governed by the concept of *ren*, or benevolence.

In addition to obeying those of superior status, people are expected to conduct themselves in a virtuous manner. Confucianists believe that Heaven is the supreme moral authority that dictates an ethical code by which all people, including rulers, must live. People in positions of authority are expected to serve as models of virtue for their subordinates.

▲ Critical Viewing
What Confucian ideas are reflected in the fact that the people are de-emphasized in this painting? **[Apply]**

The Master[1] said, To learn and at due times to repeat what one has learnt, is that not after all[2] a pleasure? That friends should come to one from afar, is this not after all delightful? To remain unsoured even though one's merits are unrecognized by others, is that not after all what is expected of a gentleman?

---

1. **The Master** Confucius.
2. **after all** even though one does not hold public office.

The Master said, A young man's duty is to behave well to his parents at home and to his elders abroad, to be cautious in giving promises and punctual in keeping them, to have kindly feelings towards everyone, but seek the intimacy of the Good. If, when all that is done, he has any energy to spare, then let him study the polite arts.[3]

The Master said, (the good man) does not grieve that other people do not recognize his merits. His only anxiety is lest he should fail to recognize theirs.

The Master said, He who rules by moral force is like the pole-star,[4] which remains in its place while all the lesser stars do <u>homage</u> to it.

The Master said, If out of three hundred *Songs*[5] I had to take one phrase to cover all my teaching, I would say, "Let there be no evil in your thoughts."

The Master said, Govern the people by regulations, keep order among them by <u>chastisements</u>, and they will flee from you, and lose all self-respect. Govern them by moral force, keep order among them by <u>ritual</u> and they will keep their self-respect and come to you of their own accord.

Mêng Wu Po[6] asked about the treatment of parents. The Master said, Behave in such a way that your father and mother have no anxiety about you, except concerning your health.

The Master said, A gentleman can see a question from all sides without <u>bias</u>. The small man is biased and can see a question only from one side.

The Master said, Yu,[7] shall I teach you what knowledge is? When you know a thing, to recognize that you know it, and when you do not know a thing, to recognize that you do not know it. That is knowledge.

The Master said, High office filled by men of narrow views, ritual performed without reverence, the forms of mourning observed without grief—these are things I cannot bear to see!

The Master said, In the presence of a good man, think all the time how you may learn to equal him. In the presence of a bad man, turn your gaze within!

The Master said, In old days a man kept a hold on his words, fearing the disgrace that would ensue should he himself fail to keep pace with them.

homage (häm´ ij) *n.* act of reverence and respect

chastisements (chas´ tiz mənts) *n.* punishments

ritual (rich´o͞o əl) *n.* observance of prescribed rules

bias (bī´əs) *n.* prejudice; partiality

---

3. **the polite arts** such activities as reciting from *The Book of Songs*, practicing archery, and learning proper behavior.
4. **pole-star** Polaris, the North Star.
5. **three hundred *Songs*** poems in *The Book of Songs*.
6. **Mêng Wu Po** (muŋ wo͞o bō) the son of one of Confucius's disciples.
7. **Yu** (yo͞o) Tzu-lu, one of Confucius's disciples.

**Reading Check**

What is a young man's duty, according to Confucius?

The Master said, A gentleman covets the reputation of being slow in word but prompt in deed.

The Master said, In old days men studied for the sake of self-improvement; nowadays men study in order to impress other people.

The Master said, A gentleman is ashamed to let his words outrun his deeds.

The Master said, He who will not worry about what is far off will soon find something worse than worry close at hand.

The Master said, To demand much from oneself and little from others is the way (for a ruler) to banish discontent.

Review and Assess

Thinking About the Selections

1. **Respond:** Do you agree with Lao Tzu's basic philosophy that the way to achieve happiness is to take no action? Explain your answer.

2. **(a) Recall:** In section I of the *Tao Te Ching*, what advice does Lao Tzu give with regard to desires? **(b) Connect:** In what way does this advice relate to his overall philosophy of the natural order?

3. **(a) Analyze:** What three images does Lao Tzu present in the first six lines of section IX? **(b) Interpret:** In what way do these images illustrate Lao Tzu's message about wealth in the last four lines of the section? **(c) Connect:** Explain how this message relates to Lao Tzu's earlier statements about desires.

4. **(a) Recall:** What advice does Confucius give regarding promises? **(b) Infer:** Why is this principle important to Confucius and to his philosophy?

5. **(a) Recall:** To what does Confucius compare a leader who rules by "moral force"? **(b) Interpret:** Based on this comparison, describe Confucius's belief about the power of "moral force."

6. **(a) Recall:** According to Confucius, how should one's words relate to one's deeds? **(b) Connect:** In what way does this advice support Confucius's earlier statements about promises?

7. **(a) Speculate:** How do you think Confucius would view the concept of democracy? **(b) Apply:** Do you think Confucius's ideas can be applied to a democratic society? Explain.

Review and Assess

Literary Analysis

Aphorisms

1. (a) In the **aphorism** that concludes section IX of the *Tao Te Ching*, what does Lao Tzu say that one should do when a task is accomplished? (b) What kind of behavior does he mean to discourage?
2. Explain how the aphorism form supports Lao Tzu's philosophy of the Tao, as expressed in the *Tao Te Ching*.
3. In what way is Confucius's use of aphorisms in *The Analects* consistent with his belief that a gentleman "is ashamed to let his words outrun his deeds"?

Comparing Literary Works

4. (a) In what way do Lao Tzu and Confucius differ on the subject of education? (b) Explain how this contrast reflects each philosopher's essential ideas.
5. (a) Use a Venn diagram like the one shown to compare and contrast the two philosophies of government presented by Lao Tzu and Confucius. (b) Do you find these two philosophers to be in disagreement with each other? Why or why not?

Reading Strategy

Questioning Causes and Effects

6. (a) According to Lao Tzu, what is the effect of being "overbearing when one has wealth and position"? (b) How might Lao Tzu explain this **cause-and-effect** relationship?
7. (a) What does Confucius say will happen to a person "who will not worry about what is far off"? (b) Do you think this is a valid cause-and-effect relationship? Why or why not?

Extend Understanding

8. **Social Studies Connection:** Compare the philosophies of Taoism and Confucianism with the principle of nonviolent protest, demonstrated by marches, sit-ins, and boycotts. What does this approach share with both Taoism and Confucianism?

Integrate Language Skills

Vocabulary Development Lesson

Word Analysis: Latin Suffix -ment

When added to a verb, the Latin suffix -ment forms a noun. Adding -ment to the verb *chastise*, which means "to punish," forms the noun *chastisement*, "an act of punishing." Change the following verbs to nouns by adding the suffix -ment. Then, use each new word in a sentence.

   1. achieve   2. agree   3. fulfill

Spelling Strategy

When you add a suffix that begins with a consonant to a word ending in *e*, do not drop the *e*: *chastise + -ment = chastisement*. Combine each of these words with its suffix to form a new word.

   1. appease + -ment   3. advance + -ment
   2. immediate + -ly   4. grace + -ful

Concept Development: Analogies

Study the relationship presented in each first pair. Then, complete each analogy with a vocabulary word from the list on page 239 to make a word pair expressing the same relationship.

1. active : passive :: aggressive : _____
2. improvisation : spontaneous :: _____ : planned
3. narrowness : broadness :: _____ : open-mindedness
4. peace : calm :: war : _____
5. respect : irreverence :: _____ : ridicule
6. admirer : praises :: accuser : _____
7. plans : actions :: abstractions : _____
8. health : wellness :: disaster : _____

Grammar and Style Lesson

Infinitives and Infinitive Phrases

An **infinitive** is the base form of a verb, usually preceded by *to*. It can be used as a noun, an adjective, or an adverb. An **infinitive phrase** is an infinitive with modifiers or complements, words that complete the meaning of the verb, all acting together as one part of speech. In each example below, the infinitive or infinitive phrase is underlined.

> **As a noun:** Lao Tzu's advice in the *Tao Te Ching* is <u>to take no action</u>.
>
> **As an adverb:** This advice may be difficult <u>to understand</u>.
>
> **As an adjective:** One must have a willingness <u>to consider new ideas</u>.

Practice Identify each infinitive or infinitive phrase below and indicate whether it is acting as a noun, an adjective, or an adverb.

1. To demand much from oneself and little from others is the way . . . to banish discontent.
2. To be overbearing when one has wealth and position / Is to bring calamity upon oneself.
3. To retire when the task is accomplished / Is the way of heaven.
4. . . . nowadays men study in order to impress other people.
5. To learn and at due times to repeat what one has learnt, is that not after all a pleasure?

Writing Application Write three aphorisms of your own, using at least one infinitive or infinitive phrase in each.

𝒲𝒢 *Prentice Hall Writing and Grammar Connection: Diamond Level, Chapter 19, Section 2*

Writing Lesson

Critical Comparison

The *Tao Te Ching* and *The Analects* offer differing philosophies on how people should live. Yet, there are many ideas that the two works share. In an essay, compare and evaluate the validity of the main ideas in these two selections.

Prewriting Create a two-column chart, labeling one column *Tao Te Ching* and the other *The Analects*. Review the selections, using the chart to note key ideas and identify similarities and differences among them.

Drafting Choose an organization before you begin drafting. In a subject-by-subject organization, address all the points for the *Tao Te Ching* first, then address *The Analects*. In a point-by-point organization, move between the selections as you discuss each point of comparison.

Revising Reread your essay to be sure that you have shown connections between ideas when making comparisons. Consider adding transitional words and phrases to clarify relationships between points.

Model: Revising to Show Connections Between Ideas

Lao Tzu believed that order comes about when

In contrast,

individuals take no action. ∧ Confucius taught that

people must take action to create order.

> Transitional phrases like *In contrast* strengthen the connection between two points.

W₍G₎ *Prentice Hall Writing and Grammar Connection: Diamond Level, Chapter 9, Section 4*

Extension Activities

Listening and Speaking With a group, hold a **philosophical debate** on Taoism and Confucianism. One team should argue for Taoism; the other, for Confucianism. Each team should prepare to answer these questions:

- What are the strengths of each philosophy?
- What are the weaknesses of each?
- Which philosophy is more applicable in today's world?

Present the debate to an audience of classmates. **[Group Activity]**

Research and Technology The teachings of Confucius influenced Chinese government from the days of ancient emperors to the era of Mao Zedong. Using print and electronic sources, make a **research presentation** explaining that influence. Include visual aids with your presentation.

 **Take It to the Net** PHSchool.com

Go online for an additional research activity using the Internet.

CONNECTIONS
Literature Past and Present
Voices of Wisdom

Today, advice columns, self-help books, and motivational speakers recommending specific behaviors are found everywhere. Centuries ago, however, Confucius and Lao Tzu were masters of aphorisms, or short statements that express universal truths about life. *The Analects,* a summary of the doctrines of Confucius, provides guidelines to his code of conduct, and the *Tao Te Ching* by Lao Tzu helps readers remember the basic principles of existence in a chaotic world.

Later, in eighteenth-century America, a group of revolutionaries founded an entirely new nation. In the process, they worked diligently to define the culture of that nation and to determine the characteristics of a good citizen. One of the revolutionaries' most eminent statesmen, Benjamin Franklin, was influential in building the new culture, asserting in *Poor Richard's Almanack* and other writings the importance of hard work, discipline, and appropriate behavior.

Proverbs to Live By Franklin adapted traditional proverbs and folk sayings into aphorisms of his own. Believing that clarity and brevity are two of the most important characteristics of good prose, Franklin rewrote many proverbs to create short, witty sayings that teach a lesson. Franklin's aphorisms, like those of Confucius and Lao Tzu, reflect his culture's views of the world. As memorable bits of wisdom that have survived for centuries, the words of Confucius, Lao Tzu, and Benjamin Franklin represent unchanging truths about human nature.

Poor Richard, 1733.

AN

Almanack

For the Year of Chrift

1733,

Being the Firft after LEAP YEAR:

	And makes fince the Creation	Years
By the Account of the Eaftern *Greeks*		7241
By the Latin Church, when ☉ ent. ♈		6932
By the Computation of *W. W.*		5742
By the *Roman* Chronology		5682
By the *Jewifh* Rabbies		5494

Wherein is contained

The Lunations, Eclipfes, Judgment of the Weather, Spring Tides, Planets Motions & mutual Afpects, Sun and Moon's Rifing and Setting, Length of Days, Time of High Water, Fairs, Courts, and obfervable Days.

Fitted to the Latitude of Forty Degrees, and a Meridian of Five Hours Weft from *London,* but may without fenfible Error, ferve all the adjacent Places, even from *Newfoundland* to *South-Carolina.*

By *RICHARD SAUNDERS,* Philom.

PHILADELPHIA:

Printed and fold by *B. FRANKLIN,* at the New Printing-Office near the Market.

▲ **Critical Viewing** The abbreviation "Philom.," short for *philomath,* follows Franklin's pseudonym, Richard Saunders. Can you guess the meaning of the word *philomath*? **[Speculate]**

from *Poor Richard's Almanack*

BENJAMIN FRANKLIN

- Fools make feasts, and wise men eat them.
- Be slow in choosing a friend, slower in changing.
- Keep thy shop, and thy shop will keep thee.
- Early to bed, early to rise, makes a man healthy, wealthy, and wise.
- Three may keep a secret if two of them are dead.
- God helps them that help themselves.
- The rotten apple spoils his companions.
- An open foe may prove a curse; but a pretended friend is worse.
- Have you somewhat to do tomorrow, do it today.
- A true friend is the best possession.
- A small leak will sink a great ship.
- No gains without pains.
- 'Tis easier to prevent bad habits than to break them.
- Well done is better than well said.
- Dost thou love life? Then do not squander time; for that's the stuff life is made of.
- Write injuries in dust, benefits in marble.
- A slip of the foot you may soon recover, but a slip of the tongue you may never get over.
- If your head is wax, don't walk in the sun.
- A good example is the best sermon.
- Hunger is the best pickle.
- Genius without education is like silver in the mine.
- For want of a nail the shoe is lost; for want of a shoe the horse is lost; for want of a horse the rider is lost.
- Haste makes waste.
- The doors of wisdom are never shut.
- Love your neighbor; yet don't pull down your hedge.
- He that lives upon hope will die fasting.

squander (skwän´ dər) *v.* spend or use wastefully

fasting (fast´ iŋ) *v.* eating very little or nothing

Benjamin Franklin

(1706–1790)

Benjamin Franklin, a renowned statesman during the early years of the United States, worked as a printer from his youth until his retirement at age forty-two. After moving from Boston to Philadelphia at seventeen, Franklin began publishing *Poor Richard's Almanack,* an annual publication containing information, observations, and advice that was very popular with readers. When he retired, Franklin devoted himself to science. In spite of his many scientific achievements, Franklin is best remembered for his career in politics. He played an important role in drafting the Declaration of Independence and the United States Constitution, and in his later years, he served as America's ambassador, first to England and then to France.

Connecting Literature Past and Present

1. Which of Benjamin Franklin's aphorisms is your favorite? Why?
2. What beliefs about human nature do you think Benjamin Franklin shares with Confucius and Lao Tzu? Explain.
3. Do you agree that there are certain truths about human nature that do not change from century to century or from culture to culture? Explain.

Prepare to Read

Chinese Poetry

The Book of Songs (c. sixth century B.C.)

The Book of Songs, also known as *The Book of Odes*, is an anthology of 305 ancient Chinese poems. According to tradition, Confucius (see p. 238) chose the poems to be included. It is doubtful that Confucius actually selected the poems, but he did know them well and recommended their study.

Because of the book's honored status and its association with Confucius, traditional Chinese interpreters of the poems have stressed their political and social importance. These interpreters have sometimes gone to great lengths to find hidden meanings in what appear to be simple love songs. In recent years, however, scholars have begun to interpret the ancient songs more literally, appreciating them for their simplicity and directness and using them as a window into the lives of the early Chinese people.

T'ao Ch'ien (A.D. 365–427)

T'ao Ch'ien (dou′ chē′ en′) was born into a family of prominent but impoverished government officials. As an adult, T'ao Ch'ien himself began a career in government service, but he found it difficult to behave in the subservient manner required of lower-ranking officials. When he was about thirty-five, he resigned from office and retired to a farm on the outskirts of a rural village.

In his later years, T'ao Ch'ien devoted most of his energy to writing poetry. Inspired by the serenity of his life in the countryside, T'ao Ch'ien wrote many poems about the simple beauty of the landscapes surrounding farms and villages. In addition to showing his love for nature, T'ao Ch'ien's poetry reveals his passion for some of his favorite activities—farming, spending time with his family, and writing poetry.

Li Po (701–762)

Along with Tu Fu, Li Po (lē′ bō′) is considered one of the supreme masters of Chinese poetry. The details of Li Po's early life are not clear, but he probably grew up in southwestern China, in the region that is now Szechuan province.

During his mid-twenties, he moved to eastern China, and throughout the remainder of his life he moved from place to place.

Li Po is known for his free-spirited, graceful, and lyrical style. His poetry frequently conveys a love of freedom and a sense of harmony with nature. These qualities, along with Li Po's vivid imagery and timeless insights, have earned his poems a secure place among China's finest works of literature.

Tu Fu (712–770)

Tu Fu (dōō′ fōō′) is regarded as the supreme craftsman of Chinese *shih* (shi) poetry. In all of his poetry—poems dealing with social issues and those that focus on his personal experiences—Tu Fu shows a command of language and a mastery of the *shih* form. As a result, his poems are admired as much for their form as for their content.

Early in Tu Fu's career, China was relatively peaceful and prosperous, but later the poet witnessed a major rebellion, the destruction of the capital city, and an invasion by tribes from the northwest. In his poems, Tu Fu gives some of the most vivid accounts of war and destruction in all of Chinese literature. He also harshly criticizes the nobility's extravagance in the face of extreme poverty among the common people.

Preview

Connecting to the Literature

If you have ever reflected on life, love, or nature, then you already have something in common with the poets whose work follows. Look for universal themes in these poems, and compare the poets' reflections with your own.

Literary Analysis

Chinese Poetic Forms

You may be familiar with certain European forms of poetry, such as the sonnet, but Chinese literature has its own poetic forms.

- *Shih* **poems** are poems that, in the original Chinese, have an even number of lines, each with the same number of words. Old-style *shih* poems, like those of T'ao Ch'ien, can be of any length. The new style, the one used by Tu Fu, has strict rules about length and form.

- **Songs** are poems that were originally set to music and have strong, regular rhythms. Songs may also include **refrains**—words or phrases repeated at regular intervals. "Indeed I am afraid" is a refrain in "I Beg of You, Chung Tzu." If one or two words within a refrain are varied in successive stanzas, this technique is called **incremental variation.**

- **Ballads** are songs that tell stories. "The River-Merchant's Wife: A Letter" is an example of a ballad.

As you read these poems, notice the ways in which their forms are both similar to and different from poems that you have read from other cultures.

Comparing Literary Works

Each speaker in these poems has a unique **tone,** or attitude, toward his or her subject or audience. Tone is revealed by the speaker's diction, or word choice. It can be described using words like *friendly, distant, serious,* or *playful.* Use a chart like the one shown to identify key words and phrases from each poem and to compare the tones of the varied speakers in these poems.

Reading Strategy

Responding

When you **respond** to a poem, you reflect on the poet's message and how that message relates to your own life. As you read these selections, take time to respond to them. Note the emotions you feel and the images each work prompts in your imagination.

Vocabulary Development

bashful (bash′ fəl) *adj.* shy (p. 258)

eddies (ed′ ēz) *n.* waters moving in circles against the main current (p. 258)

scurry (skʉr′ ē) *v.* to run hastily; to scamper (p. 261)

pathos (pā′ thäs′) *n.* quality in something that evokes sorrow or compassion (p. 261)

imperceptibly (im′ pər sep′ tə blē) *adv.* without being noticed (p. 261)

Poem
"Addressed Humorously to Tu Fu"
Representative Diction
"You must have been suffering from poetry again."
Speaker's Tone
playful, ironic

from

The Book of Songs

translated by
Arthur Waley

Background

The poems in *The Book of Songs* come from many different regions of China. Most of them were originally folk songs describing people's daily activities, such as farming, fishing, or gathering herbs. Others focus on love or courtship. The book also contains a group of poems written by courtiers in praise of kings, describing banquets and court ceremonies.

All of the songs were originally set to music. Some, especially the songs of the court, may have been accompanied by dancing and by musical instruments, such as bells and drums. The tunes are long lost, but the songs' powerful rhythms are preserved in their four-beat lines.

I Beg of You, Chung Tzu

I beg of you, Chung Tzu,
Do not climb into our homestead,
Do not break the willows we have planted.
Not that I mind about the willows,
5 But I am afraid of my father and mother.
Chung Tzu I dearly love;
But of what my father and mother say
Indeed I am afraid.

I beg of you, Chung Tzu,
10 Do not climb over our wall,
Do not break the mulberry trees we have planted.
Not that I mind about the mulberry trees,
But I am afraid of my brothers.
Chung Tzu I dearly love;
15 But of what my brothers say
Indeed I am afraid.

I beg of you, Chung Tzu,
Do not climb into our garden,
Do not break the hardwood we have planted.
20 Not that I mind about the hardwood,
But I am afraid of what people will say.
Chung Tzu I dearly love;
But of all that people will say
Indeed I am afraid.

Literary Analysis
Chinese Poetic Forms
Find two refrains in this stanza that identify the poem as a song.

Reading Strategy
Responding What is your response to the speaker's fears? Explain.

Thick Grow the Rush Leaves

Thick grow the rush leaves;
Their white dew turns to frost.
He whom I love
Must be somewhere along this stream.
5   I went up the river to look for him,
But the way was difficult and long.
I went down the stream to look for him,
And there in mid-water
Sure enough, it's he!

10   Close grow the rush leaves,
Their white dew not yet dry.
He whom I love
Is at the water's side.
Up stream I sought him;
15   But the way was difficult and steep.
Down stream I sought him,
And away in mid-water
There on a ledge, that's he!

Very fresh are the rush leaves;
20   The white dew still falls.
He whom I love
Is at the water's edge.
Up stream I followed him;
But the way was hard and long.
25   Down stream I followed him,
And away in mid-water
There on the shoals is he!

▲ **Critical Viewing**
Judging from this painting, why might it be difficult to search for someone on a river, as the speaker does in "Thick Grow the Rush Leaves"? Explain.
[Apply]

Review and Assess

Thinking About the Selections

1. **(a) Recall:** In "I Beg of You, Chung Tzu," what are the speaker's fears? **(b) Analyze:** What conflicting feelings does she have?

2. **(a) Recall:** In "Thick Grow the Rush Leaves," what words describe the rush leaves and their growth? **(b) Interpret:** In what way might the rush leaves be symbolic of the speaker's feelings?

3. **(a) Compare:** In terms of their subjects, how are these two poems similar? **(b) Contrast:** What makes them different?

FORM, SHADOW, SPIRIT

T'ao Ch'ien   translated by David Hinton

Background

T'ao Ch'ien was among the finest "old style" *shih* poets. In classical Chinese, each line of a *shih* poem has the same number of syllables, words, and characters. Classical Chinese is not written with letters; instead, characters stand for words. For example, the character 木 means "tree" or "wood." T'ao Ch'ien's simple, direct style is easy to enjoy in translation, but his carefully formed structure, unfortunately, is not preserved.

Rich or poor, wise or foolish, people are all busy clinging jealously to their lives. And it's such delusion. So, I've presented as clearly as I could the sorrows of Form and Shadow. Then, to dispel those sorrows, Spirit explains occurrence coming naturally of itself. Anyone who's interested in such things will see what I mean.

1 Form Addresses Shadow

Heaven and earth last. They'll never end.
Mountains and rivers know no seasons,

and there's a timeless law plants and trees
follow: frost then dew, vigor then ruin.

5 They call us earth's most divine and wise
things, but we alone are never as we are

again. One moment we appear in this world,
and the next, we vanish, never to return.

And who notices one person less? Family?
10 Friends? They only remember when some

everyday little thing you've left behind
pushes grief up to their eyes in tears.

I'm no immortal. I can't just soar away
beyond change. There's no doubt about it,

15 death's death. Once you see that, you'll
see that turning down drinks is for fools.

Reading Strategy
Responding How does your response to the argument made in lines 7–15 compare with Form's conclusion in lines 15–16?

◀ **Critical Viewing**
In what way does this painting suggest the time-lessness of nature that Form describes?
[Connect]

2 Shadow Replies

Who can speak of immortality when simply
staying alive makes such sad fools of us?

We long for those peaks of the immortals,
20 but they're far-off, and roads trail away

early. Coming and going together, we've
always shared the same joys and sorrows.

Resting in shade, we may seem unrelated,
but living out in the sun, we never part.

25 This togetherness isn't forever, though.
Soon, we'll smother in darkness. The body

can't last, and all memory of us also ends.
It sears the five feelings. But in our

good works, we bequeath our love through
30 generations. How can you spare any effort?

Though it may be true wine dispels sorrow,
how can such trifles ever compare to this?

Reading Strategy
Responding Do you think Shadow's argument is more valid than Form's? Why or why not?

✓ **Reading Check**

To whom or to what does Shadow reply?

3 Spirit Answers

The Great Potter[1] never hands out favors.
These ten thousand things thrive each

35 of themselves alone. If humans rank with
heaven and earth, isn't it because of me?

And though we're different sorts of things
entirely, we've been inseparable since

birth, together through better and worse,
40 and I've always told you what I thought.

The Three Emperors[2] were the wisest of men,
but where are they now? And loving his

eight-hundred-year life, old P'eng-tsu[3]
wanted to stay on here, but he too set out.

45 Young and old die the same death. When it
comes, the difference between sage and fool

vanishes. Drinking every day may help you
forget, but won't it bring an early grave?

And though good works may bring lasting
50 joy, who will sing your praise? Listen—

it's never-ending analysis that wounds us.
Why not circle away in the seasons, adrift

on the Great Transformation, riding its vast
swells without fear or delight? Once your

55 time comes to an end, you end: not another
moment lost to all those lonely worries.

Literary Analysis
Chinese Poetic Forms In what way does this poem, even in translation, follow the *shih* form?

---

1. **The Great Potter** the force that gives things their form, sometimes translated as *God.*
2. **The Three Emperors** three mythical rulers of ancient times.
3. **P'eng-tsu** the archetypal Chinese aged man.

I BUILT MY HOUSE NEAR WHERE OTHERS DWELL

T'ao Ch'ien
translated by William Acker

I built my house near where others dwell,
And yet there is no clamor of carriages and
   horses.
You ask of me "How can this be so?"
"When the heart is far the place of itself is distant."
5 I pluck chrysanthemums under the eastern hedge,
And gaze afar towards the southern mountains.
The mountain air is fine at evening of the day
And flying birds return together homewards.
Within these things there is a hint of Truth,
10 But when I start to tell it, I cannot find the words.

▲ **Critical Viewing**
What qualities does the setting of this painting share with the setting of this poem? **[Connect]**

Review and Assess

Thinking About the Selections

1. **Respond:** Do you agree that "When the heart is far the place of itself is distant"? Why or why not?

2. **(a) Recall:** In lines 1–8 of "Form, Shadow, Spirit," what key difference does Form identify between humans and mountains, rivers, plants, and trees? **(b) Connect:** In what way does this contrast support Form's conclusion in lines 15–16?

3. **(a) Infer:** What attitude toward nature does the speaker reveal in lines 5–8 of "I Built My House Near Where Others Dwell"?
   (b) Connect: What lines in "Form, Shadow, Spirit" reflect a similar attitude toward nature?

4. **Take a Position:** Considering the ideas he expresses in these poems, how do you think T'ao Ch'ien would respond to living in a modern industrial city? Explain.

THE RIVER-MERCHANT'S WIFE:
A Letter

LI PO *translated by* EZRA POUND

Background

Li Po and Tu Fu first met in 744 and formed a lasting friendship. The two poets greatly admired each other's work but were very different people. Li Po was known to be free-spirited, while Tu Fu was more serious-minded. The poetry of Li Po and Tu Fu reflects the differences in their personalities. In "Addressed Humorously to Tu Fu," Li Po teases his somber young friend, who seems to be "suffering from poetry again."

While my hair was still cut straight across my forehead
I played about the front gate, pulling flowers.
You came by on bamboo stilts, playing horse,
You walked about my seat, playing with blue plums.
5 And we went on living in the village of Chōkan:[1]
Two small people, without dislike or suspicion.

At fourteen I married My Lord you.
I never laughed, being <u>bashful</u>.
Lowering my head, I looked at the wall.
10 Called to, a thousand times, I never looked back.

At fifteen I stopped scowling,
I desired my dust to be mingled with yours
Forever and forever and forever.
Why should I climb the look out?

At sixteen you departed,
You went into far Ku-tō-en,[2] by the river of swirling <u>eddies</u>,
And you have been gone five months.

Reading Strategy
Responding What memories or feelings about the past do these lines evoke in you?

bashful (bash´ fəl) *adj.* shy

Literary Analysis
Chinese Poetic Forms In what way does the first line of each stanza help to tell the story of this ballad?

eddies (ed´ ēz) *n.* waters moving in circles against the main current

---

1. **Chōkan** (chō´ kän´) Japanese name for Ch'ang-kan (chäŋ´ gän), a village in eastern China.
2. **Ku-tō-en** (ko͞o´ tō´ yen´) Japanese name for Ch'ü-t'ang-yen (cho͞o´ taŋ´ yen´), the shoals at the mouth of the dangerous Yangtze (yäŋk´ sē) Gorges, in the upper reaches of the Yangtze River.

The monkeys make sorrowful noise overhead.
You dragged your feet when you went out.
20 By the gate now, the moss is grown, the different mosses,
Too deep to clear them away!
The leaves fall early this autumn, in wind.
The paired butterflies are already yellow with August
Over the grass in the West garden;
25 They hurt me. I grow older.
If you are coming down through the narrows of the river Kiang,[3]
Please let me know beforehand,
And I will come out to meet you
                  As far as Chō-fū-Sa.[4]

---

3. **the river Kiang** (kyaŋ) the Yangtze River.
4. **Chō-fū-Sa** (chō´ fōō´ sä´) Japanese name for Chang-feng Sha (chaŋ´ fuŋ´ shä´), a village on the Yangtze River, about 200 miles upstream from Chōkan.

☑ **Reading Check**

How old was the speaker when her husband went away?

◀ **Critical Viewing**

Why might an image like this one make the poem's speaker fearful about her husband's safety?
[Connect]

Addressed Humorously to Tu Fu

Li Po translated by Shigeyoshi Obata

Here! is this you on top of Fan-ko Mountain,
Wearing a huge hat in the noonday sun?
How thin, how wretchedly thin, you have grown!
You must have been suffering from poetry again.

Review and Assess

Thinking About the Selections

1. **Respond:** Based on his poem "Addressed Humorously to Tu Fu,"
   do you think Li Po is a good friend to Tu Fu? Why or why not?

2. **(a) Recall:** In "The River-Merchant's Wife: A Letter," how does
   the speaker describe her behavior when she first married her husband? **(b) Infer:** How did the speaker feel about her marriage at
   first? **(c) Analyze:** How does her attitude change over time?

3. **(a) Recall:** How does the speaker of "The River-Merchant's
   Wife: A Letter" describe the butterflies she sees? **(b) Interpret:**
   Why do you think the butterflies "hurt" the speaker?

4. **(a) Recall:** In "Addressed Humorously to Tu Fu," how does the
   speaker describe Tu Fu's appearance? **(b) Infer:** What does the
   manner in which the speaker addresses Tu Fu suggest about their
   relationship?

5. **(a) Recall:** In "Addressed Humorously to Tu Fu," what does the
   speaker conclude about Tu Fu's condition? **(b) Interpret:** What
   do you think the speaker means by this comment?

6. **Speculate:** How do you think Tu Fu would have responded to
   "Addressed Humorously to Tu Fu"?

Jade Flower Palace

Tu Fu *translated by Kenneth Rexroth*

Background

Tu Fu was a master of the "new style" *shih* form. New style *shih* poetry has very strict rules that dictate the number of lines, the number of words per line, and the rhyme scheme. Even within these restrictions, Tu Fu established his own style.

Unfortunately, Tu Fu's stylistic achievements cannot be appreciated in translation. In the original Chinese, new style *shih* poems have a blocklike structure; each line is made up of the same number of one-syllable characters. For example, Tu Fu's "Sent to Li Po as a Gift" is four lines long and each line has seven characters. The translation on page 262 has eleven lines of varying lengths.

The stream swirls. The wind moans in
The pines. Gray rats <u>scurry</u> over
Broken tiles. What prince, long ago,
Built this palace, standing in
5   Ruins beside the cliffs? There are
Green ghost fires in the black rooms.
The shattered pavements are all
Washed away. Ten thousand organ
Pipes whistle and roar. The storm
10 Scatters the red autumn leaves.
His dancing girls are yellow dust.
Their painted cheeks have crumbled
Away. His gold chariots
And courtiers are gone. Only
15 A stone horse is left of his
Glory. I sit on the grass and
Start a poem, but the <u>pathos</u> of
It overcomes me. The future
Slips <u>imperceptibly</u> away.
20 Who can say what the years will bring?

scurry (skʉr´ ē) *v.* to run hastily; to scamper

pathos (pā´ thäs´) *n.* quality in something that evokes sorrow or compassion

imperceptibly (im´ pər sep´ tə blē) *adv.* without being noticed

☑ **Reading Check**

What feeling overcomes the speaker of "Jade Flower Palace"?

Sent to *Li Po* as a Gift

Tu Fu

translated by
Florence Ayscough and Amy Lowell

Autumn comes,
We meet each other.
You still whirl about as a thistledown in the wind.
Your Elixir of Immortality[1] is not yet perfected
5   And, remembering Ko Hung,[2] you are ashamed.
You drink a great deal,
You sing wild songs,
Your days pass in emptiness.
Your nature is a spreading fire,
10   It is swift and strenuous.
But what does all this bravery amount to?

Literary Analysis
Chinese Poetic Forms and Tone How would you describe the speaker's tone in lines 6–8?

---

1. **Elixir** (ē liks´ir) **of Immortality** hypothetical substance, sought by alchemists in the Middle Ages, believed to prolong life indefinitely.
2. **Ko Hung** (kō´ hơn) Chinese philosopher and alchemist who tried to create an Elixir of Immortality.

Review and Assess

Thinking About the Selections

1. **Respond:** What feelings does seeing the ruins of a building like the one in "Jade Flower Palace" evoke in you?

2. **(a) Recall:** In "Jade Flower Palace," what remains of the long-gone prince's "glory"? **(b) Connect:** In what way does this image contrast with the speaker's description of what used to be in the palace? **(c) Draw Conclusions:** What point do you think the speaker is making through this contrast?

3. **(a) Recall:** What does the speaker of "Sent to Li Po as a Gift" say about Li Po's "nature"? **(b) Interpret:** What do you think the speaker means by this comparison?

4. **(a) Analyze:** Why do you think Tu Fu considers "Sent to Li Po as a Gift" to be a gift? **(b) Make a Judgment:** Do you think the speaker is criticizing Li Po or simply teasing him? Explain your answer.

Review and Assess

Literary Analysis

Chinese Poetic Forms

1. (a) Identify a **refrain** in the **song** "I Beg of You, Chung Tzu."
   (b) Identify a refrain with **incremental variation** in "Thick Grow the Rush Leaves." (c) Explain the effect of refrains in each poem.

2. (a) What feature of "The River-Merchant's Wife: A Letter" indicates that it is a **ballad**? (b) In what way does each of the poem's four stanzas reveal a part of the ballad's subject?

3. In what way do the structures of these translations of "Form, Shadow, Spirit" and "I Built My House Near Where Others Dwell" reflect the original Chinese structure of these *shih* poems?

Comparing Literary Works

4. (a) How would you describe the speaker's **tone** in "Thick Grow the Rush Leaves"? (b) What words and phrases reveal the speaker's tone?

5. What do the contrasting tones of "Addressed Humorously to Tu Fu" and "Sent to Li Po as a Gift" suggest about each poet?

Reading Strategy

Responding

6. Which of these poems evoked your strongest emotional **response**?

7. (a) Using a chart like the one shown, note your response to each stanza of "The River-Merchant's Wife: A Letter," as well as to the poem as a whole, by jotting down words and phrases that describe the feelings evoked by the poem. (b) Did your response to the poem change between the beginning and the end of the poem? Explain.

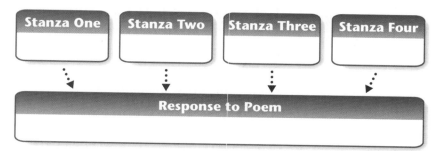

Extend Understanding

8. **Philosophy Connection:** Which of these poems most reflects the Taoist idea that one should submit oneself to the way of the universe and not interfere with the natural order? Explain.

Integrate Language Skills

Vocabulary Development Lesson

Word Analysis: Greek root -path-

Pathos is a Greek word whose root, *-path-*, means "feeling" or "suffering." The word *pathos* refers to the quality in something experienced or observed that arouses feelings of pity or sympathy. However, the root *-path-* appears in other words that are related in different ways to feeling or suffering. The root *-path-* can also mean "disease."

Use your understanding of this word root to match each word on the left with its definition on the right.

1. pathetic	a. to share the feelings of another
2. apathy	b. the study of disease
3. pathogen	c. disease-causing agent
4. pathology	d. evoking compassion, as for suffering; pitiful
5. sympathize	e. lack of feeling or concern

Fluency: Sentence Completion

Choose the vocabulary word from the list on page 251 that best completes each sentence below.

1. He moved slowly, almost ____.
2. We saw a chipmunk ___ across the trail.
3. The kitten was ____ around people.
4. The ____ of her story brought us to tears.
5. Leaves swirled in the ____ of the stream.

Spelling Strategy

Adjectives with endings that sound like *full* and that name a quality, like *bashful*, end with one *l*, not two. For each quality described below, provide the appropriate word that ends with the *full* sound.

1. full of hope
2. showing respect
3. having force
4. evoking pity

Grammar and Style Lesson

Prepositional Phrases

A preposition shows the relationship between a noun or pronoun—called the object of the preposition—and another word in the sentence. A **prepositional phrase** is a group of words that includes a preposition and a noun or pronoun. Prepositional phrases never include the subject or verb of the sentence.

> OP (relates to *climb*)
> Do not climb <u>into our homestead</u>.
>
> OP (relates to *went*)
> I went <u>down the stream</u>.
>
> OP (relates to *is*)
> He . . . is <u>at the water's edge</u>.

Practice For each item below, identify the prepositional phrase, the object of the preposition, and the word to which the object is related.

1. I beg of you, Chung Tzu . . .
2. Lowering my head, I looked at the wall.
3. Gray rats scurry over broken tiles.
4. I sit on the grass and start a poem.
5. Your days pass in emptiness.

Writing Application Using "Jade Flower Palace" as inspiration, write a short poem reflecting on the ruins of an old building. Your poem should have at least four lines, each containing at least one prepositional phrase.

 Prentice Hall Writing and Grammar Connection: Diamond Level, Chapter 17, Section 4

Writing Lesson

Response to Criticism

The critic Herbert A. Giles wrote, "Brevity is indeed the soul of a Chinese poem, which is valued not so much for what it says as for what it suggests." In an essay, use evidence from the Chinese poems you have read to support or refute Giles's statement.

Prewriting   In each poem, note passages that clearly "say" or express something, as well as passages in which an idea is merely suggested or implied. Then, decide whether you agree or disagree with Giles's thesis.

Drafting   As you draft, use examples from the poems to support your position. Quote passages that demonstrate that the effect of a poem is the result of either what is expressed or what is implied.

Model: Using Quotations as Evidence

Chinese poems suggest, rather than express, their themes. For example, T'ao Ch'ien conveys a sense of harmony with nature through small details: "The mountain air is fine at evening of the day / And flying birds return together homewards."

> Quotations provide concrete examples that strengthen an argument.

Revising   Reread your essay to be sure that all of the quotations are needed to support your argument. If you have more than two quotations per paragraph, eliminate all but the strongest examples.

W̶G̶ Prentice Hall Writing and Grammar Connection: Diamond Level, Chapter 13, Section 3

Extension Activities

Research and Technology Li Po and Tu Fu lived during the T'ang Dynasty, which lasted from c. 600 to c. 900. This was widely seen as the Golden Age of China. With a group, make a **poster** illustrating the structure of T'ang society.

- Use print and electronic resources to research the different classes in T'ang society, including the role played by poets.
- Organize the information and design graphics to illustrate facts and statistics.

Present your poster in class. [**Group Activity**]

Listening and Speaking Prepare and present an **oral report** on the life and times of T'ao Ch'ien, Li Po, or Tu Fu. Choose a poet and research his life, as well as the historical period in which he lived. In your report, explain how the poet's life and times affected his poetry.

 **Take It to the Net**   PHSchool.com

Go online for an additional research activity using the Internet.

Prepare to Read

Tanka ◆ Haiku

Ki Tsurayuki (c. 868–964)

The chief aid of Emperor Daigo (dī gō´), Ki Tsurayuki (kē´ tsoor´ ī oo´ kē´) was one of the leading poets, critics, and diarists of his time. Tsurayuki deserves much of the credit for assembling the *Kokinshu* (kō´ kēn´ shoo´), an anthology of over eleven hundred poems of the Heian (hā´ än´) Age. In addition, his *Tosa Diary* helped to establish the Japanese tradition of the literary diary. This tradition includes some of Japan's finest works of literature, one of the most famous being Sei Shōnagon's *Pillow Book.*

Ono Komachi (833–857)

A great beauty with a strong personality, Ono Komachi (ō´ nō´ kō´ mä´ chē´) was an early tanka (tän´ kə) poet whose poems are characterized by their passion and energy. Few details of Ono Komachi's life are known. However, there are a vast number of legends about her, and these legends serve as the basis for a well-known series of plays.

Priest Jakuren (1139?–1202)

Jakuren (jä´ koo´ ren´) was a Buddhist priest and prominent tanka poet whose poems are filled with beautiful yet melancholic imagery. After entering the priesthood at the age of twenty-three, Jakuren spent much of his time traveling the Japanese countryside, writing poetry and seeking spiritual fulfillment. In addition to contributing poems to the *Senzishu* (sen´ zē´ shoo´), a court anthology, he produced *Jakuren Hoshi Shu* (hō´ shē´ shoo´), a personal collection of poetry.

Matsuo Bashō (1644–1694)

Generally regarded as the greatest Japanese haiku poet, Matsuo Bashō (mä´ tzoo´ ō´ bä´ shō´) began studying and writing poetry at an early age. As an adult, he became a Zen Buddhist and lived the life of a hermit, supporting himself by teaching and judging poetry contests. When he traveled, he did so with only the barest essentials and relied on the hospitality of temples and fellow poets. Bashō's poems reflect the natural beauty he observed in his travels, as well as the simplicity encouraged by his faith.

Yosa Buson (1716–1784)

Although Yosa Buson (yō´ sä´ boo´ sän´) is widely regarded as the second-greatest Japanese haiku poet, little is known about him. It is known that, in addition to being a celebrated poet, he was one of the finest painters of his time. In both his paintings and his poetry, Buson presents a romantic view of the Japanese landscape that captures the wonder and mystery of nature.

Kobayashi Issa (1763–1828)

Although his talent was not widely recognized until after his death, Kobayashi Issa (kō´ bä´ yä´ shē´ ē´ sä´) is now considered to be on the same poetic level as Bashō and Buson. Born into poverty, Issa wrote haiku that reflect an appreciation for the hardships faced by the common people. His poems capture the essence of daily life in Japan and convey his compassion for the less fortunate.

Preview

Connecting to the Literature

Have you ever had an experience that seemed unimportant on the surface but had great emotional impact? These very short poems each capture a single, simple image or moment, yet each one has great depth of meaning.

Literary Analysis

Japanese Poetic Forms

The **tanka** is the most prevalent verse form in traditional Japanese literature. In the original Japanese, each short poem consists of five lines of five, seven, five, seven, and seven syllables. Most tanka include at least one **caesura** (si zyoor´ ə), or pause, often indicated by punctuation in English translations. Tanka usually tell a brief story or express a single thought or insight, often about love or nature.

A **haiku** consists of three lines of five, seven, and five syllables in the original Japanese. Haiku typically focus on some aspect of nature and often include a *kigo,* or seasonal word such as "snow" or "cherry blossom," that indicates the time of year being described. Most haiku present a comparison or contrast of two images, actions, or states of being, as in this poem by Bashō:

> Summer grasses—
>
> All that remains
>
> Of soldiers' visions.

As you read each of these simple poems, consider what deeper meaning the poet might be suggesting.

Comparing Literary Works

Tanka and haiku poets convey a great deal of meaning in a small number of words by using vivid **imagery,** language that appeals to the senses. For example, "summer grasses" appeals to the senses of sight, touch, and smell by evoking the sight of a green field, the feeling of warm air, and the smell of fragrant grass. As you read, note the different senses to which these poems' nature imagery appeals.

Reading Strategy

Picturing Imagery

A tanka or haiku often presents two images that imply a contrast. To fully appreciate this contrast, try to **picture** the imagery. Use your memory and imagination to see, feel, hear, smell, or taste what the poet describes. In a chart like the one shown, list associations that help you see pairs of images, and then note the contrast implied by each pair.

Vocabulary Development

veiled (vāld) *v.* covered (p. 270)

bland (bland) *adj.* mild (p. 272)

serenity (sə ren´ ə tē) *n.* peace; tranquillity (p. 272)

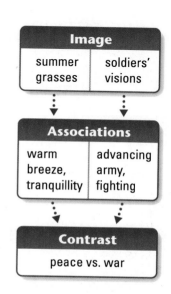

Image	
summer grasses	soldiers' visions

↓ ↓

Associations	
warm breeze, tranquillity	advancing army, fighting

↓ ↓

Contrast
peace vs. war

Tanka

Background

When tanka are translated into English, the translator often must alter the syllabic structure of the poem and, in some cases, also change the number of lines. Therefore, when reading a tanka in translation, it is more important to focus on the imagery used and the emotions evoked than on the poem's form.

Ki Tsurayuki *translated by Geoffrey Bownas*

When I went to visit
The girl I love so much,
That winter night
The river blew so cold
That the plovers[1] were crying.

1. **plovers** (pluv´ ərz) *n.* wading shorebirds with short tails; long, pointed wings; and short, stout beaks.

Reading Strategy
Picturing Imagery What feelings and associations do the words *winter night* call to mind?

◀ **Critical Viewing**
How does this winter scene compare with the one described in Ki Tsurayuki's tanka? Explain. **[Compare and Contrast]**

Ono Komachi translated by Geoffrey Bownas

Was it that I went to sleep
Thinking of him,
That he came in my dreams?
Had I known it a dream
I should not have wakened.

Literary Analysis
Japanese Lyric Forms
Where does the caesura occur in this tanka?

Priest Jakuren translated by Geoffrey Bownas

One cannot ask loneliness
How or where it starts.
On the cypress-mountain,[2]
Autumn evening.

---

2. **cypress-mountain** Cypress trees are cone-bearing evergreen trees, native to North America, Europe, and Asia.

Review and Assess

Thinking About the Selections

1. **Respond:** To which of these tanka could you relate most? Explain your answer.

2. **(a) Recall:** What is the setting of Tsurayuki's tanka? **(b) Infer:** What does the speaker's willingness to face that setting suggest about the depth of his love? **(c) Interpret:** What does the setting suggest about the outcome of his visit?

3. **(a) Recall:** What question does the speaker of Ono Komachi's tanka ask? **(b) Infer:** What do her question and her response to that question suggest about her feelings toward the man in her dreams?

4. **Make a Judgment:** Do you think a poem is more effective when it suggests a feeling or when it describes the feeling in detail? Explain.

Haiku

Matsuo Bashō
translated by Harold G. Henderson

Background

The haiku evolved from a form of collaborative poetry known as *renga*. At festive poetry contests during the Middle Ages, groups of writers would gather to create interlocking groups of renga verses, which consisted of seventeen and fourteen syllables. The results were judged by a poetry master. Listeners who attended the contests developed a love for this simple yet profound poetic form. Eventually, the *hokku*, the opening verse of a renga, developed into a distinct literary form known as haiku.

The sun's way:
hollyhocks turn toward it
through all the rain of May.

Clouds come from time to time—
and bring to men a chance to rest
from looking at the moon.

The cuckoo—
Its call stretching
Over the water.

Seven sights were <u>veiled</u>
In mist—then I heard
Mii Temple's bell.[1]

Summer grasses—
All that remains
Of soldiers' visions.

Literary Analysis
Japanese Poetic Forms
What is the *kigo* in the third line of this haiku?

veiled (vāld) *v.* covered

◀ **Critical Viewing**
Which characteristics of haiku are also evident in this painting? **[Connect]**

1. **Mii** (mē′ ē′) **Temple's bell** The bell at Mii Temple is known for its extremely beautiful sound. The temple is located near Otsu, a city in southern Japan.

Haiku

Yosa Buson

translated by Geoffrey Bownas

Spring rain:
Telling a tale as they go,
Straw cape, umbrella.

Spring rain:
In our sedan
Your soft whispers.

Spring rain:
A man lives here—
Smoke through the wall.

Spring rain:
Soaking on the roof
A child's rag ball.

▲ **Critical Viewing**
Which of the four haiku by
Yosa Buson would you
choose to accompany this
painting? Why? **[Connect]**

Haiku

Kobayashi Issa

translated by
Geoffrey Bownas

Beautiful, seen through holes
Made in a paper screen:
The Milky Way.

Far-off mountain peaks
Reflected in its eyes:
The dragonfly.

A world of dew:
Yet within the dewdrops—
Quarrels.

With bland serenity
Gazing at the far hills:
A tiny frog.

Literary Analysis
Japanese Poetic Forms
What two images are being contrasted in this haiku?

bland (bland) *adj.* mild

serenity (sə ren´ə tē) *n.* peace; tranquillity

Review and Assess

Thinking About the Selections

1. **Respond:** Which haiku created the strongest mental images for you? Why?

2. **(a) Recall:** In "Clouds come from time to time," with what is the image of clouds contrasted? **(b) Interpret:** What does this contrast suggest about humanity's relationship with nature?

3. **(a) Compare and Contrast:** In what ways are these haiku similar to and different from traditional Western nature poems that you have read? **(b) Evaluate:** What do you think a traditional Western poet could learn from haiku poems?

Review and Assess

Literary Analysis

Japanese Poetic Forms

1. (a) What brief story is told in the **tanka** by Ki Tsurayuki? (b) How would you describe the emotion conveyed by this poem?
2. (a) Where does the **caesura** occur in the tanka by Priest Jakuren? (b) What effect does this pause create?
3. (a) What contrasting images are presented in the **haiku** "Seven sights were veiled"? (b) What is the effect of this contrast?
4. (a) Identify the *kigo* in the haiku "Summer grasses—." (b) In what way does this *kigo* help create a contrast between the first and third lines of the poem?

Comparing Literary Works

5. (a) Identify the nature **imagery** in the tanka by Priest Jakuren. (b) To what sense or senses does this imagery appeal?
6. (a) Use a Venn diagram like the one shown to compare and contrast the nature imagery in the tanka by Ki Tsurayuki and the Bashō haiku "The sun's way." (b) In what way do these poems present two different views of nature?

Reading Strategy

Picturing Imagery

7. (a) Which words help you **picture the imagery** in the four haiku by Yosa Buson? (b) What other images do you associate with these words or phrases that help you see the images in the poem?
8. (a) Which haiku or tanka created the strongest mental picture for you? (b) Identify the words or phrases in the poem that created this effect.

Extend Understanding

9. **Humanities Connection:** The process by which renga poetry is created has been compared to the artistic collaboration seen in jazz music. To what kind of music or visual art form or style would you compare tanka and haiku? Give examples to support your answer.

Integrate Language Skills

Vocabulary Development Lesson

Connotations and Denotations

A word's **denotation** is its direct, literal meaning. For example, the denotation of *spring* is "the season that follows winter." The **connotations** of a word are the ideas associated with it. *Spring's* connotations include warmth and rebirth.

Writers and translators have connotations in mind when they choose words. For example, one might use the word *gazing* instead of *looking* in order to imply "looking thoughtfully," rather than simply "directing one's eyes." Connotations are especially important in tanka and haiku. Because these poems contain so few words, each word must convey a great deal of meaning.

For each of the following words, provide another word that has the same denotation but different connotations.

1. loneliness   2. evening   3. tale

Concept Development: Analogies

Complete the following analogies using the words from the vocabulary list on page 267.

1. jagged : smooth :: harsh : _____
2. uncovered : exposed :: _____ : concealed
3. volcano : turmoil :: flower : _____

Spelling Strategy

The suffixes *-ity* and *-ety* are both used to form nouns from adjectives. The suffix *-ity* is more common, but the suffix *-ety* is used for a few adjectives that end in *e* or *i*: *safe/safety; various/variety*. Add the correct suffix, *-ity* or *-ety*, to each of the following roots.

1. electric-   3. intens-
2. propri-   4. activ-

Grammar and Style Lesson

Participial Phrases

Participles are forms of verbs that can act as adjectives. Participles usually end in *-ing* or *-ed*. A **participial phrase** is a participle that is modified by an adverb or adverb phrase or accompanied by a complement. The entire participial phrase functions as an adjective. Participles and participial phrases answer the question *Which one?* or *What kind?* and can either precede or follow the words they modify.

Participle: <u>exciting</u> news

Participial Phrase: The runners, <u>exhausted from the race</u>, rested on the grass. (modifies *runners*)

Practice Identify the participles and participial phrases in these items. Indicate which word or words each one modifies.

1. Was it that I went to sleep / Thinking of him,
2. Its call stretching / Over the water.
3. Soaking on the roof / A child's rag ball.
4. Far-off mountain peaks / Reflected in its eyes:
5. Telling a tale as they go, / Straw cape, umbrella.

Writing Application Write three haiku of your own. In each one, use at least one participial phrase to convey the same sort of concise imagery found in the haiku and tanka you have read.

Writing Lesson

Short Story

In just a few short lines, a tanka or haiku can provide a glimpse into an entire world. Yet, there is more that could be said about that world. Write a short story that expands on the scene described in one of the tanka or haiku you have read.

Prewriting   Choose a poem on which to base your story. Also, decide what kind of tone you would like your story to have. For example, it can be happy or sad, humorous or serious.

Drafting   Begin your story by describing the characters and setting. Then, describe an incident that introduces an element of conflict—a struggle between opposing forces. This conflict should build to a climax, or high point of tension, before being resolved.

Revising   Reread your draft to be sure that you have used words that create the right tone. If you find words that do not suit the tone you intended, replace them with more appropriate ones.

Model: Choosing Words to Create Tone

      carefree   *sprang from*

The frog looked ~~apathetic~~ as he ~~abandoned~~ his lily

                    cool

pad. He swam through the ~~cold~~ water to the shore

of the pond.

> Words with positive associations create a cheerful tone.

Prentice Hall Writing and Grammar Connection: Diamond Level, Chapter 6, Section 4

Extension Activities

Listening and Speaking With a small group of classmates, hold a **poetry reading.** Consult poetry anthologies to find more haiku. Then, have each member of the group read at least four favorite haiku. Consider enhancing the reading in the following ways:

- Select and play appropriate music to accompany each poem.
- Make a backdrop with seasonal colors.

Rehearse your reading as a group, and then perform it for the class. **[Group Activity]**

Research and Technology Research Japan's weather, landscape, and seasons, and present a **climate report.** Be sure to note aspects of the landscape and climate that are reflected in the haiku you have read, such as hollyhocks and spring rain. Include photographs of Japanese landscapes and graphics to explain climate data in your report.

 **Take It to the Net**   PHSchool.com

Go online for an additional research activity using the Internet.

Prepare to Read

from The Pillow Book

Sei Shōnagon
(c. tenth century A.D.)

Sei Shōnagon (sā´ shō´ nä´ gōn´) is responsible for providing us with a detailed portrait of upper-class life in Japan during the Heian (hā´ än´) Age, which lasted from 794 to 1185 A.D. Her *Pillow Book*, a collection of personal notes written during her ten years of court service, is filled with character sketches, descriptions, anecdotes, lists, and witty insights. A precursor of the Japanese literary form *zuihitsu*, or "occasional writings," *The Pillow Book* is widely recognized as one of the finest works of Japanese prose.

A Complex Figure Sei Shōnagon was the daughter of a provincial official who was also a noted scholar and poet. She was a lady-in-waiting for the Empress Sadako (sā´ dä´ kō´) during the last decade of the tenth century, and she may have been married briefly to a government official. Aside from what *The Pillow Book* reveals about her years of court service, however, little is known about Sei Shōnagon. In fact, her life following her court service remains a mystery.

Although few details are known about Sei Shōnagon's life, *The Pillow Book* offers a wealth of insights into her personality. The 185 sections of the book reveal her to be an intelligent, observant, and quick-witted woman. While she had a tremendous amount of admiration for the imperial family, she seems to have had little respect for the lower social orders. Sei Shōnagon's scorn for the less fortunate, her judgmental nature, her competitive attitude toward men, and her lack of restraint have angered some scholars and critics—even some of her contemporaries. The great Japanese novelist Murasaki Shikibu (mōō´ rä´ sä´ kē´ shē´ kē´ bōō´) wrote, "Sei Shōnagon has the most

extraordinary air of self-satisfaction. . . . Someone who makes such an effort to be different from others is bound to fall in people's esteem, and I can only think that her future will be a hard one. She is a gifted woman, to be sure. Yet, if one gives free rein to one's emotions even under the most inappropriate circumstances, if one has to sample each interesting thing that comes along, people are bound to regard one as frivolous. And how can things turn out well for such a woman?" However, it should be remembered that these two women were not only contemporaries—they were rivals, as well.

An Uncontested Classic Despite the criticism Sei Shōnagon has received, it is impossible to deny the literary and historical value of her book. Filled with vivid and evocative language, *The Pillow Book* is clearly the work of an extremely gifted writer. When evaluating Japanese works of prose, many critics rank *The Pillow Book* above Murasaki Shikibu's *The Tale of Genji*, which is widely regarded as the greatest Japanese novel. Among these critics is Arthur Waley, who wrote, "As a writer [Sei Shōnagon] is incomparably the best poet of her time, a fact which is apparent only in her prose. . . . Passages such as that about the stormy lake or the few lines about crossing a moonlit river show a beauty of phrasing that Murasaki, a much more deliberate writer, certainly never surpassed."

The Language of Literature One might wonder how it is possible that two of the most important writers of the Heian court were women. During this time, boys at court were trained to write in Chinese, much as monks in medieval Europe were trained to write in Latin. Girls, on the other hand, were taught to write in low Japanese because Chinese was considered to be beyond their ability. This discrimination backfired, however, because more people were able to read low Japanese than Chinese. As a result, works written by women were widely read, and their place in Japanese literary history was assured.

Preview

Connecting to the Literature

If you have ever kept a diary, you probably know that it is easier to write openly and honestly when your only audience is yourself. This kind of free expression can be found in *The Pillow Book*, which Sei Shōnagon says she wrote "entirely for my own amusement."

Literary Analysis

Journal

A **journal** is a day-by-day account of the writer's thoughts and experiences. By reading a journal from the past, one can gain a unique perspective on the culture and the historical period in which the journal was written. A journal can also reveal a great deal about its author's personality, as this example from *The Pillow Book* shows:

> ". . . it strikes me as a strange and moving scene; when people talk to me about it, I start crying myself."

As you read Sei Shōnagon's observations and reflections, look for details that reveal information about the author's personality and her life in the Heian court.

Connecting Literary Elements

In *The Pillow Book*, many of the author's observations take the form of **anecdotes,** short accounts of amusing or interesting events. Anecdotes can be told purely for entertainment, but they are often used to illustrate a point or to share insight that the author gained from an experience. Use a chart like the one shown to note the insights Sei Shōnagon offers in her anecdotes.

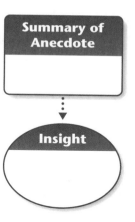

Reading Strategy

Relating to Your Own Experiences

Sei Shōnagon lived and wrote centuries ago, yet you may find that you share some of the feelings she expresses. For example, just as finding an old letter arouses a fond memory of the past for the author, finding an old photograph may arouse fond memories for you. **Relating to your own experiences** will increase your understanding and enjoyment of Sei Shōnagon's observations. As you read, note similarities between your own feelings and experiences and those that the author describes.

Vocabulary Development

earnest (ur′ nist) *adj.* serious; not joking (p. 279)

chastised (chas′ tīzd) *v.* punished (p. 279)

loathsome (lō*th*′ səm) *adj.* detestable (p. 280)

indefinitely (in def′ ə nit lē) *adv.* without a specified limit (p. 281)

from The Pillow Book

Sei Shōnagon *translated by* Ivan Morris

Background

During Sei Shōnagon's time, Japan was dominated by the powerful Fujiwara family. The leader of the family was the true ruler of Japan; the emperor was merely a figurehead. In addition, other members of the family usurped the power of officials in the various national and provincial offices. As a result, many of the people referred to by title in *The Pillow Book* had few official responsibilities.

Despite the essentially ceremonial nature of the positions, members of the Japanese aristocracy placed a great deal of importance on obtaining a government post. The offices were closely tied to social rank; holders of rank were often given land or servants and were entitled to a variety of privileges, including exemption from military service.

In Spring It Is the Dawn

In spring it is the dawn that is most beautiful. As the light creeps over the hills, their outlines are dyed a faint red and wisps of purplish cloud trail over them.

In summer the nights. Not only when the moon shines, but on dark nights too, as the fireflies flit to and fro, and even when it rains, how beautiful it is!

In autumn the evenings, when the glittering sun sinks close to the edge of the hills and the crows fly back to their nests in threes and fours and twos; more charming still is a file of wild geese, like specks in the distant sky. When the sun has set, one's heart is moved by the sound of the wind and the hum of the insects.

In winter the early mornings. It is beautiful indeed when snow has fallen during the night, but splendid too when the ground is white with frost; or even when there is no snow or frost, but it is simply very cold and the attendants hurry from room to room stirring up the fires and bringing charcoal, how well this fits the season's mood! But as noon approaches and the cold wears off, no one bothers to keep the braziers[1] alight, and soon nothing remains but piles of white ashes.

Literary Analysis
Journal What do these observations reveal about the author's personality?

---

1. **braziers** (brā′ zhərz) *n.* metal pans or bowls used to hold burning coals or charcoal.

The Cat Who Lived in the Palace

The cat who lived in the Palace had been awarded the headdress of nobility and was called Lady Myōbu. She was a very pretty cat, and His Majesty saw to it that she was treated with the greatest care.

One day she wandered on to the veranda, and Lady Uma, the nurse in charge of her, called out, "Oh, you naughty thing! Please come inside at once." But the cat paid no attention and went on basking sleepily in the sun. Intending to give her a scare, the nurse called for the dog, Okinamaro.

"Okinamaro, where are you?" she cried. "Come here and bite Lady Myōbu!" The foolish Okinamaro, believing that the nurse was in <u>earnest</u>, rushed at the cat, who, startled and terrified, ran behind the blind in the Imperial Dining Room, where the Emperor happened to be sitting. Greatly surprised, His Majesty picked up the cat and held her in his arms. He summoned his gentlemen-in-waiting. When Tadataka, the Chamberlain,[2] appeared, His Majesty ordered that Okinamaro be <u>chastised</u> and banished to Dog Island. The attendants all started to chase the dog amid great confusion. His Majesty also reproached Lady Uma. "We shall have to find a new nurse for our cat," he told her. "I no longer feel I can count on you to look after her." Lady Uma bowed; thereafter she no longer appeared in the Emperor's presence.

The Imperial Guards quickly succeeded in catching Okinamaro and drove him out of the Palace grounds. Poor dog! He used to swagger about so happily. Recently, on the third day of the Third Month,[3] when the Controller First Secretary paraded him through the Palace grounds, Okinamaro was adorned with garlands of willow leaves, peach blossoms on his head, and cherry blossoms round his body. How could the dog have imagined that this would be his fate? We all felt sorry for him. "When Her Majesty was having her meals," recalled one of the ladies-in-waiting, "Okinamaro always used to be in attendance and sit opposite us. How I miss him!"

It was about noon, a few days after Okinamaro's banishment, that we heard a dog howling fearfully. How could any dog possibly cry so long? All the other dogs rushed out in excitement to see what was happening. Meanwhile a woman who served as a cleaner in the Palace latrines[4] ran up to us. "It's terrible," she said. "Two of the Chamberlains are flogging a dog. They'll surely kill him. He's being punished for

▲ **Critical Viewing**
How does this painting compare with your mental image of Sei Shōnagon writing *The Pillow Book*? Explain. **[Compare and Contrast]**

earnest (ur´ nist) *adj.* serious; not joking

chastised (chas´ tīzd´) *v.* punished

---

2. **Chamberlain** (chām´ bər lin) *n.* high official in the emperor's court.
3. **the third day of the Third Month** the day of the Jōmi Festival, an event during which the dogs in the palace were often decorated with flowers.
4. **latrines** (lə trēnz´) *n.* lavatories.

Reading Check

Why does the Emperor banish Okinamaro?

having come back after he was banished. It's Tadataka and Sanefusa who are beating him." Obviously the victim was Okinamaro. I was absolutely wretched and sent a servant to ask the men to stop; but just then the howling finally ceased. "He's dead," one of the servants informed me. "They've thrown his body outside the gate."

That evening, while we were sitting in the Palace bemoaning Okinamaro's fate, a wretched-looking dog walked in; he was trembling all over, and his body was fearfully swollen.

"Oh dear," said one of the ladies-in-waiting. "Can this be Okinamaro? We haven't seen any other dog like him recently, have we?"

We called to him by name, but the dog did not respond. Some of us insisted that it was Okinamaro, others that it was not. "Please send for Lady Ukon,"[5] said the Empress, hearing our discussion. "She will certainly be able to tell." We immediately went to Ukon's room and told her she was wanted on an urgent matter.

"Is this Okinamaro?" the Empress asked her, pointing to the dog.

"Well," said Ukon, "it certainly looks like him, but I cannot believe that this <u>loathsome</u> creature is really our Okinamaro. When I called Okinamaro, he always used to come to me, wagging his tail. But this dog does not react at all. No, it cannot be the same one. And besides, wasn't Okinamaro beaten to death and his body thrown away? How could any dog be alive after being flogged by two strong men?" Hearing this, Her Majesty was very unhappy.

When it got dark, we gave the dog something to eat; but he refused it, and we finally decided that this could not be Okinamaro.

On the following morning I went to attend the Empress while her hair was being dressed and she was performing her ablutions.[6] I was holding up the mirror for her when the dog we had seen on the previous evening slunk into the room and crouched next to one of the pillars. "Poor Okinamaro!" I said. "He had such a dreadful beating yesterday. How sad to think he is dead! I wonder what body he has been born into this time. Oh, how he must have suffered!"

At that moment the dog lying by the pillar started to shake and tremble, and shed a flood of tears. It was astounding. So this really was Okinamaro! On the previous night it was to avoid betraying himself that he had refused to answer to his name. We were immensely moved and pleased. "Well, well, Okinamaro!" I said, putting down the mirror. The dog stretched himself flat on the floor and yelped loudly, so that the Empress beamed with delight. All the ladies gathered round, and Her Majesty summoned Lady Ukon. When the Empress explained what had happened, everyone talked and laughed with great excitement.

The news reached His Majesty, and he too came to the Empress's room. "It's amazing," he said with a smile. "To think that even a dog

loathsome (lōth′ səm) adj. detestable

---

5. **Lady Ukon** (oō′ kôn′) one of the ladies in the Palace Attendants' Office, a bureau of female officials who waited on the emperor.
6. **ablutions** (ab loō′ shənz) n. washings of the body.

has such deep feelings!" When the Emperor's ladies-in-waiting heard the story, they too came along in a great crowd. "Okinamaro!" we called, and this time the dog rose and limped about the room with his swollen face. "He must have a meal prepared for him," I said. "Yes," said the Empress, laughing happily, "now that Okinamaro has finally told us who he is."

The Chamberlain, Tadataka, was informed, and he hurried along from the Table Room. "Is it really true?" he asked. "Please let me see for myself." I sent a maid to him with the following reply: "Alas, I am afraid that this is not the same dog after all." "Well," answered Tadataka, "whatever you say, I shall sooner or later have occasion to see the animal. You won't be able to hide him from me <u>indefinitely</u>."

Before long, Okinamaro was granted an Imperial pardon and returned to his former happy state. Yet even now, when I remember how he whimpered and trembled in response to our sympathy, it strikes me as a strange and moving scene; when people talk to me about it, I start crying myself.

Literary Analysis
Journal and Anecdote
What insight does the Emperor express in this paragraph?

indefinitely (in def´ə nit lē) *adv.* without a specified limit

☑**Reading Check**

What does Okinamaro do that reveals his identity when everyone believes he has died?

Things That Arouse a Fond Memory of the Past

Reading Strategy
Relating to Your Own Experiences Identify a time when an object reminded you of an experience in your past.

Dried hollyhock. The objects used during the Display of Dolls. To find a piece of deep violet or grape-colored material that has been pressed between the pages of a notebook.

It is a rainy day and one is feeling bored. To pass the time, one starts looking through some old papers. And then one comes across the letters of a man one used to love.

Last year's paper fan. A night with a clear moon.

I Remember a Clear Morning

I remember a clear morning in the Ninth Month when it had been raining all night. Despite the bright sun, dew was still dripping from the chrysanthemums in the garden. On the bamboo fences and the criss-cross hedges I saw tatters of spider webs; and where the threads were broken the raindrops hung on them like strings of white pearls. I was greatly moved and delighted.

As it became sunnier, the dew gradually vanished from the clover and the other plants where it had lain so heavily; the branches began to stir, then suddenly sprang up of their own accord. Later I described to people how beautiful it all was. What most impressed me was that they were not at all impressed.

Review and Assess

Thinking About the Selection

1. **Respond:** Do you agree with the author about springtime dawn? Why or why not?

2. **(a) Recall:** In "In Spring It Is the Dawn," what time of day does Sei Shōnagon say she finds most beautiful during autumn?
   (b) Generalize: What does Sei Shōnagon's description of this time of day reveal about her sense of detail?

3. **(a) Recall:** What items does Sei Shōnagon list in "Things That Arouse a Fond Memory of the Past"? **(b) Interpret:** Why do you think she avoids sharing the fond memories that these items evoke?

4. **Evaluate:** Do you think Sei Shōnagon succeeds in conveying what is amusing or interesting about what she observes? Why or why not?

5. **(a) Generalize:** Based on the events described in "The Cat Who Lived in the Palace," how would you describe the life of the upper class in Japan during the Heian Age? **(b) Criticize:** Do you think the anecdote shows the Japanese nobility to be responsible, effective leaders? Explain.

Review and Assess

Literary Analysis

Journal

1. In the final paragraph of the **journal** entry "In Spring It Is the Dawn," what detail of day-to-day court life does Sei Shōnagon describe?

2. In "The Cat Who Lived in the Palace," what does the cat's name suggest about certain animals' status in the emperor's court during Sei Shōnagon's time?

3. Which aspects of her personality does Sei Shōnagon reveal in her journal entry "Things That Arouse a Fond Memory of the Past"? Explain.

Connecting Literary Elements

4. What would you identify as the main insight or point of interest in the **anecdote** "The Cat Who Lived in the Palace"? Explain.

5. (a) What impresses Sei Shōnagon the most about the scene she describes in "I Remember a Clear Morning"? (b) Summarize the insight she gains from other people's reactions to her description of the scene.

Reading Strategy

Relating to Your Own Experiences

6. Use a chart like the one shown to note the relationships you can find between Sei Shōnagon's observations in *The Pillow Book* and your own experiences.

Writer's Experience	My Experience	How They Relate

7. Which of Sei Shōnagon's experiences or reflections could you most easily relate to your own? Why?

Extend Understanding

8. **Cultural Connection:** Which of Sei Shōnagon's reflections seem to have universal meaning? Which ones seem to apply only to Sei Shōnagon's own life and times? Explain.

Quick Review

A **journal** is a day-by-day account of one's thoughts and experiences.

An **anecdote** is a short account of an amusing or interesting event.

To **relate to your own experiences,** look for similarities between your own feelings and experiences and those described by the author.

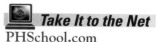 **Take It to the Net**
PHSchool.com

Take the interactive self-test online to check your understanding of this selection.

Integrate Language Skills

Vocabulary Development Lesson

Word Analysis: Latin Prefix *in-*

The Latin prefix *in-* usually means "not," as in *indefinitely*, which can be defined as "not definitely." Use this knowledge to define the following words:

1. incomplete
2. indistinct
3. insignificant
4. intolerable

Spelling Strategy

The negative prefix *in-* is spelled differently depending on the letter it precedes. It becomes

- *im-* before *m*, as in *immortal*, and before *b* or *p*, as in *improper*.
- *il-* before *l*, as in *illegal*.
- *ir-* before *r*, as in *irrelevant*.

Add the correct prefix to each word below to create a word with the opposite meaning.

1. logical   2. responsible   3. modest

Fluency: Words in Context

Review the vocabulary list on page 277 and consider the context in which each word is used in *The Pillow Book*. Then, choose the word from the vocabulary list that best completes each sentence below.

1. Due to a shortage of funds, the concert organizers have decided to postpone the event ___?___ .
2. The coach ___?___ the team and made them run extra laps.
3. Tim is a very ___?___ person who seldom makes jokes.
4. Many people who love cats find dogs to be ___?___ .

Grammar and Style Lesson

Noun Clauses

A **noun clause** is a subordinate clause that acts as a noun. It can be used as a subject, a predicate nominative, a direct object, an indirect object, or the object of a preposition. Noun clauses are commonly introduced by words such as *that, which, where, what, who, whatever, whoever,* and *why.*

Subject: *What most impressed me* was that . . .

Predicate Nominative: That is *what I heard.*

Direct Object: We finally decided *that this could not be Okinamaro.*

Object of a Preposition: No one was impressed by *what I described.*

Practice Identify the noun clause in each item and explain the clause's function.

1. How could the dog have imagined that this would be his fate?
2. The saddest part is that he was innocent.
3. What amazed us was his reaction.
4. We couldn't stop talking about what we saw.
5. People did not believe what we were saying.

Writing Application In a paragraph, describe an experience of finding something beautiful that others did not. Use at least three noun clauses in your writing.

Prentice Hall Writing and Grammar Connection: Diamond Level, Chapter 19, Section 3

Writing Lesson

Journal Entry

"The Cat Who Lived in the Palace" tells the story of Okinamaro from the perspective of Sei Shōnagon. Using the author's account as inspiration, write a journal entry describing the same events from the perspective of the Empress.

Prewriting   Decide on an appropriate "voice" in which to write the Empress's journal entry. Review "The Cat Who Lived in the Palace" and gather details that reveal the Empress's personality.

Model: Using a Cluster Diagram to Gather Details

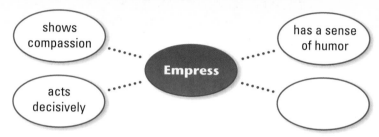

Drafting   Refer to your notes about the Empress's personality and begin to draft your journal entry. As you write, consider how the Empress might have reacted to the events Sei Shōnagon describes.

Revising   Reread your journal entry to be sure that the voice you developed is consistent with the character of the Empress in "The Cat Who Lived in the Palace." Revise or delete sentences that do not suit the Empress's personality.

W͟G Prentice Hall Writing and Grammar Connection: Diamond Level, Chapter 5, Section 4

Extension Activities

Research and Technology Conduct a poll among your classmates to determine some of the things that evoke fond memories for them. Then, create a **graphic presentation of poll results** to illustrate your findings. You might represent the most popular responses in one of the following forms:

- bar graph
- pie chart
- illustrated table

Display your graphic presentation and explain the results of the poll to the class.

Listening and Speaking With a group of classmates, research and prepare an **oral report** on Japanese court life during the Heian Age. Each member of the group should focus on a specific aspect of court life, such as the roles of officials or how people dressed. Present your report to the class. **[Group Activity]**

 **Take It to the Net** PHSchool.com

Go online for an additional research activity using the Internet.

A Closer Look

Women Writers in Japan

Despite restrictions on their freedom of expression, women were pioneers in the creation of Japan's native literature.

During Japan's Nara period (710–784) and Heian Age (794–1185), most women were not allowed to speak or write Chinese, the language of scholars and serious literature. Paradoxically, the strictures that kept women from learning Chinese left them free to write in Japanese, the spoken language that had, at that time, no clear literary form. In so doing, they became pioneers in the creation of Japan's distinctive literature, especially diaries, poetry, and romances. Included here are just a few of the women writers who created the foundations of Japanese literature.

Poet: Lady Otomo *Manyoshu*, which means *Collection of 10,000 Leaves*, is an anthology of Japanese poetry that was compiled sometime after 760. The volume contains more than 4,500 poems, one third of which were written by women. A number of the poems in the volume are by Lady Otomo, who stands at the beginning of a long line of talented Japanese women. She wrote about nature, the small details of daily life, her daughters, and the promises and pains of love:

> You come no more, who came so often,
> Nor yet arrives a messenger with your letter.
> There is—alas!—nothing I can do.
> Though I sorrow the black night through
> And all day till the red sun sinks,
> It avails me nothing. Though I pine,
> I know not how to soothe my heart's pain.

—from "Love's Complaint" by Lady Otomo

Other women writers also produced fine collections of poetry. For instance, Lady Dabu, a member of the imperial court of the late 1100s, wrote *The Poetic Memoirs of Lady Dabu*, which includes the following poem:

> Caught in the last rays
> Of the setting sun, the treetops
> Darken in the chilling rain:
> So too my heart is dimmed
> And clouded over in its misery.

The Celebrated Beauty of the Teahouse, Kagiya, at Kasamori Shrine, Suzuki Harunobu, 18th century, The Metropolitan Museum of Art

Novelist: Lady Murasaki Shikibu Many scholars consider Lady Murasaki Shikibu's novel *The Tale of Genji* to be the single greatest work of Japanese literature. Extremely long and complex, the book is filled with profound insights and beautiful prose. Note the intimacy and precision in this description of the emperor's reaction to the death of a loved one:

> But when he thought of the lost lady's
> Voice and form, he could find neither in
> The beauty of flowers nor in the song of
> Birds any fit comparison. Continually he
> Pined that fate should not have allowed
> Them to fulfill the vow which morning and
> Evening was ever talked of between them
> —the vow that their lives should be as the
> twin birds that share a wing, the twin trees
> that share a bough. The rustling of the
> wind, the chirping of an insect would cast
> him into the deepest melancholy . . .

Like the works of Homer, Milton, Dante, and Shakespeare in the Western literary tradition, *The Tale of Genji* has provided a rich source of characters and themes that have been reworked by Japanese writers for nearly a thousand years. It is a seminal work—one that has defined Japan's national identity.

Women Writers and Diaries Lady Murasaki Shikibu, like most notable Japanese women writers, was a member of the imperial court. In addition to writing *The Tale of Genji,* Murasaki produced a diary that offers vivid insights into the realities of court life during the Heian Age.

Throughout the Heian Age, diaries like Lady Murasaki's allowed women of the court to express their most intimate thoughts. Despite their highly personal nature, many of these diaries exhibit a level of literary sophistication that has earned them a place among the great works of Japanese literature.

Brilliant Stylist: Sei Shōnagon Another woman of the Heian court, Sei Shōnagon, wrote a book of prose that is neither a diary nor a work of fiction: *The Pillow Book* is a loosely organized collection of about 320 separate pieces that include reminiscences, character sketches, opinions, descriptions, anecdotes, witty insights, and lists. Many scholars celebrate Sei Shōnagon's pure gift with language, seeing in her work some of the finest examples of the clarity and precision of classical Japanese. Some regard *The Pillow Book* as an even greater work than *The Tale of Genji* due to its variety, extraordinary language, and wit.

Today, the voices of these and other pioneering Japanese women writers still speak to the modern reader across the gulf of a thousand years. They show that even when it is restricted or confined, the human need for self-expression will find a way to free itself. These women writers changed Japanese culture and gave the gifts of their voices to all the cultures of the world.

Prepare to Read

Zen Parables

About Zen Buddhism

In a famous saying of Zen Buddhism, a monk is asked to discard everything. "But I have nothing!" the monk exclaims, to which his master responds, "Discard that too!" This puzzling exchange illustrates the basic outlook of Zen Buddhism. Falling somewhere between religion and philosophy, Zen Buddhism seeks to leap over everyday logic and reach enlightenment through intuition.

From China to Japan Zen is a branch of Buddhism that arose in sixth-century China, where Buddhist ideas intermingled with the Taoist philosophy of Lao Tzu. From China, Zen Buddhism traveled to Japan, where it continued to evolve and to flourish, eventually spreading to Korea and Vietnam, as well.

Defining Zen Buddhism Stressing neither worship nor scripture nor good deeds, as other religions do, Zen instead focuses on a sudden breakthrough to enlightenment, which is achieved through meditation, or deep thought. In fact, the word *Zen* comes from the Chinese *ch'an*, which means "meditation." According to Zen teachings, every human being has the potential to achieve this state. Qualities of the enlightened state include mental tranquillity, spontaneity, and fearlessness.

Zen Buddhism does not have the same kind of communal worship found in other religions. Instead, it emphasizes individual enlightenment passed down personally from master to student. The master cannot teach enlightenment; rather, the master must prompt the student on his or her own personal journey.

Zen Training The path to enlightenment varies with different Zen sects. The Rinzai sect, for

Large Enso, hanging scroll, Torei Enji, Gitter-Yelen Art Center

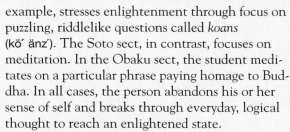

example, stresses enlightenment through focus on puzzling, riddlelike questions called *koans* (kō´ änz´). The Soto sect, in contrast, focuses on meditation. In the Obaku sect, the student meditates on a particular phrase paying homage to Buddha. In all cases, the person abandons his or her sense of self and breaks through everyday, logical thought to reach an enlightened state.

Enlightenment may also be achieved by self-disciplined focus on a ritualized everyday activity, like chopping wood, or on one of the Zen arts—archery, for example, or swordsmanship. Tutored by a master, the Zen student practices over and over until one day enlightenment comes with complete spontaneity, fusing the mind, body, and spirit so that performer and activity are one.

Impact of Zen Swordsmanship and the Zen qualities of mental tranquillity, spontaneity, self-discipline, and fearlessness proved particularly valuable to samurai warriors of medieval Japan, who were among those who practiced Zen. Japanese painting also began to reflect Zen influence, as pen-and-ink drawing is another of the ritualized Zen arts. Indeed, by the sixteenth century, Zen influenced almost all aspects of Japanese culture.

Zen Today Zen Buddhism continues to be an influential school of thought. People often study it along with the martial arts. Many businesspeople find it helps them to focus and relax. Books like *Zen in the Art of Archery* have exposed Western readers to Zen teachings and have become bestsellers. Zen thinking is even evident in the *Star Wars* films, which feature an order of knights—the Jedi (je´ dī´)— whose beliefs, conduct, and societal role bear striking similarities to those of the samurai warriors of feudal Japan.

Preview
Connecting to the Literature
Some stories entertain, while others teach a lesson. Zen parables do both and more: They allow readers to contemplate a subject that, according to Zen masters, will help them achieve enlightenment.

Literary Analysis
Zen Parables
A **parable** is a short story that teaches a moral or spiritual lesson. **Zen parables** teach the principles of Zen Buddhism. They do so by inspiring contemplation rather than by expressing a clear moral. As you read each of these enlightening tales, notice the absence of a statement summarizing the parable's lesson.

Comparing Literary Works
Zen parables often are based on a **paradox**—a statement or situation that seems contradictory but actually presents a truth. For example, "The more things change, the more they stay the same" is a paradoxical statement. Some Zen parables contain paradoxical statements, but others present situations that are paradoxical because they contradict logic or expectation, as in this exchange:

> "If I become your devoted servant, how long might it be [before I am a master swordsman]?"
> "Oh, maybe ten years," Banzo relented.
> ". . . If I studied far more intensively, how long would it take me?"
> "Oh, maybe thirty years," said Banzo.

As you read each parable, note whether it presents ideas that contradict each other or ideas that contradict your expectations.

Reading Strategy
Interpreting Paradox
To **interpret** the paradox in a Zen parable, identify the contradiction—the statements, images, or ideas that do not logically go together. Then, draw a conclusion about what point the contradiction forces you to consider. Use a chart like the one shown to help you interpret these stories' paradoxes.

Vocabulary Development
sustained (sə stānd´) *v.* maintained; supported (p. 290)

epidemic (ep´ ə dem´ ik) *n.* rapidly and widely spreading disease (p. 291)

mediocre (mē´ dē ō´ kər) *adj.* not good enough; inferior (p. 291)

anticipate (an tis´ ə pāt´) *v.* expect (p. 291)

rebuked (ri byo͞okt´) *v.* scolded sharply (p. 292)

Situation

man facing certain doom pauses to enjoy a strawberry

↓

Contradiction

gravity of situation vs. enjoyment of food

↓

Point to Consider

When worrying won't help, why not enjoy?

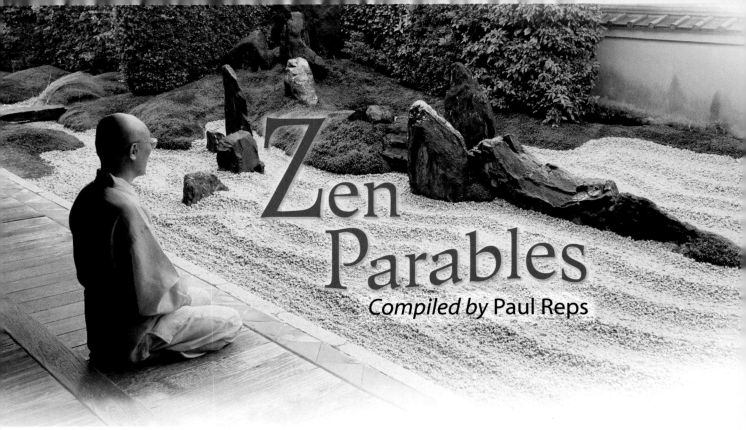

Zen Parables

Compiled by Paul Reps

Background

"A Parable" begins with a reference to the Buddha. *Buddha* means "Enlightened One" and refers to Siddhartha Gautama (sid där´ tə goʊt´ ə mə) (563?–483? B.C.), the Hindu prince who founded Buddhism. Although Gautama is considered *the* Buddha, the term *buddha* can also refer to any Buddhist who has attained full *prajna* (pruj´ nyə), or enlightenment.

A Parable

Buddha told a parable in a sutra:[1]

A man traveling across a field encountered a tiger. He fled, the tiger after him. Coming to a precipice, he caught hold of the root of a wild vine and swung himself down over the edge. The tiger sniffed at him from above. Trembling, the man looked down to where, far below, another tiger was waiting to eat him. Only the vine <u>sustained</u> him.

Two mice, one white and one black, little by little started to gnaw away the vine. The man saw a luscious strawberry near him. Grasping the vine with one hand, he plucked the strawberry with the other. How sweet it tasted!

sustained (sə stānd´) *v.* maintained; supported

---

1. **sutra** (soo´ trə) Buddhist scriptural narrative.

Publishing the Sutras

Tetsugen, a devotee of Zen in Japan, decided to publish the sutras, which at that time were available only in Chinese. The books were to be printed with wood blocks in an edition of seven thousand copies, a tremendous undertaking.

Tetsugen began by traveling and collecting donations for this purpose. A few sympathizers would give him a hundred pieces of gold, but most of the time he received only small coins. He thanked each donor with equal gratitude. After ten years Tetsugen had enough money to begin his task.

It happened that at that time the Uji River[2] overflowed. Famine followed. Tetsugen took the funds he had collected for the books and spent them to save others from starvation. Then he began again his work of collecting.

Several years afterwards an <u>epidemic</u> spread over the country. Tetsugen again gave away what he had collected, to help his people.

For a third time he started his work, and after twenty years his wish was fulfilled. The printing blocks which produced the first edition of sutras can be seen today in the Obaku monastery in Kyoto.

The Japanese tell their children that Tetsugen made three sets of sutras, and that the first two invisible sets surpass even the last.

The Taste of Banzo's Sword

Matajuro Yagyu was the son of a famous swordsman. His father, believing that his son's work was too <u>mediocre</u> to <u>anticipate</u> mastership, disowned him.

So Matajuro went to Mount Futara and there found the famous swordsman Banzo. But Banzo confirmed the father's judgment. "You wish to learn swordsmanship under my guidance?" asked Banzo. "You cannot fulfill the requirements."

"But if I work hard, how many years will it take me to become a master?" persisted the youth.

"The rest of your life," replied Banzo.

"I cannot wait that long," explained Matajuro. "I am willing to pass through any hardship if only you will teach me. If I become your devoted servant, how long might it be?"

"Oh, maybe ten years," Banzo relented.

"My father is getting old, and soon I must take care of him," continued Matajuro. "If I work far more intensively, how long would it take me?"

"Oh, maybe thirty years," said Banzo.

"Why is that?" asked Matajuro. "First you say ten and now thirty years. I will undergo any hardship to master this art in the shortest time!"

---

2. **Uji** (o͞o′ jē) **River** river near the city of Kyoto (kyō′ tō) in central Japan.

epidemic (ep′ ə dem′ ik) *n.* rapidly and widely spreading disease

mediocre (mē′ dē ō′ kər) *adj.* not good enough; inferior

anticipate (an tis′ ə pāt′) *v.* expect

*T*hemes in World Literature

Parables and Paradox

Religions around the world use parables to teach lessons. One famous Christian parable is "The Parable of the Prodigal Son." In this story, a young man leaves home and squanders his inheritance. He returns home in disgrace and tells his father that he is no longer worthy of being called his son. Instead of punishing his son, the father calls for a celebration. The parable is meant to teach forgiveness.

Like many parables, "The Parable of the Prodigal Son" is based on a paradox. One might have expected that the father would punish his son, but he does the opposite—he rewards him. By presenting this paradox, the parable suggests a contrast between a natural behavior and the correct behavior—between wrong and right. If the parable succeeds in teaching its lesson, then the reader will know what to do when presented with a similar choice.

Reading Check

Why has Matajuro's father disowned him?

"Well," said Banzo, "in that case you will have to remain with me for seventy years. A man in such a hurry as you are to get results seldom learns quickly."

"Very well," declared the youth, understanding at last that he was being <u>rebuked</u> for impatience, "I agree."

Matajuro was told never to speak of fencing and never to touch a sword. He cooked for his master, washed the dishes, made his bed, cleaned the yard, cared for the garden, all without a word of swordsmanship.

Three years passed. Still Matajuro labored on. Thinking of his future, he was sad. He had not even begun to learn the art to which he had devoted his life.

But one day Banzo crept up behind him and gave him a terrific blow with a wooden sword.

The following day, when Matajuro was cooking rice, Banzo again sprang upon him unexpectedly.

After that, day and night, Matajuro had to defend himself from unexpected thrusts. Not a moment passed in any day that he did not have to think of the taste of Banzo's sword.

He learned so rapidly he brought smiles to the face of his master. Matajuro became the greatest swordsman in the land.

rebuked (ri byŌŌkt´) *v.* scolded sharply

Literary Analysis
Zen Parables What Zen principles does the master seem to be teaching Matajuro?

Review and Assess

Thinking About the Selections

1. **Respond:** Of the lessons these Zen parables teach, which one is most applicable to your own life? Explain.

2. **(a) Recall:** In what situation does the man in "A Parable" find himself? **(b) Analyze:** Given his situation, why is it surprising when he decides to enjoy a strawberry?

3. **(a) Recall:** In "Publishing the Sutras," what happens the first two times Tetsugen attempts to publish the sutras?
   (b) Interpret: What do you think the Japanese mean when they tell their children that "the first two invisible sets surpass even the last"?

4. **(a) Recall:** In "The Taste of Banzo's Sword," why is Matajuro so eager to learn swordsmanship from Banzo?
   (b) Recall: How does Banzo train Matajuro?
   (c) Draw Conclusions: Why do you think Banzo's instruction is so successful?

5. **Make a Judgment:** Do you agree with the methods that Banzo uses to train Matajuro in "The Taste of Banzo's Sword"? Why or why not?

Review and Assess

Literary Analysis

Zen Parables

1. (a) What lesson or outlook on life is illustrated in "A Parable"? (b) In what way does this **Zen parable** reflect Zen beliefs about the qualities of an enlightened mind?

2. In one or two sentences, state the moral of the story in "Publishing the Sutras."

3. (a) What principles of Zen philosophy are illustrated by "The Taste of Banzo's Sword"? (b) Do you think the lessons of this parable are more or less apparent than those of the other two? Explain.

Comparing Literary Works

4. (a) What is the **paradox** of the last sentence in "Publishing the Sutras"? (b) In what way does this paradox help convey the parable's lesson?

5. (a) Use a chart like the one shown to indicate whether "A Parable" and "Publishing the Sutras" make their points by presenting paradoxical statements or paradoxical situations. (b) Which parable do you think uses paradox more effectively to convey its message?

Parable	Paradox	Statement or Situation
"A Parable"		
"Publishing the Sutras"		

Reading Strategy

Interpreting Paradox

6. (a) Identify a pair of contradictory statements, images, or ideas in "The Taste of Banzo's Sword" that represent a paradox. (b) Explain why these statements, images, or ideas do not logically go together. (c) What point does this paradox force you to consider?

Extend Understanding

7. **Cultural Connection:** (a) Based on "The Taste of Banzo's Sword," how would you describe the relationship between teacher and student in feudal Japan? (b) How does this relationship compare to the teacher/student relationship in modern America? Explain.

Quick Review

Zen parables are short stories that teach the principles of Zen Buddhism.

A **paradox** is a statement or situation that seems contradictory but actually presents a truth.

To **interpret** a paradox, identify the contradiction, then draw a conclusion about the point the paradox forces you to consider.

 **Take It to the Net**
PHSchool.com

Take the interactive self-test online to check your understanding of these selections.

Integrate Language Skills

Vocabulary Development Lesson

Word Analysis: Latin Prefix *ante-/anti-*

The Latin prefix *anti-*, as in *anticipate*, is a variant of the prefix *ante-*, which means "before" or "preceding in time." It should not be confused with the Greek prefix *anti-*, which appears in words like *antipathy* and *anticlimactic* and which means "opposed to."

Using your understanding of the Latin prefix *ante-/anti-*, match each of the following words on the left with its definition on the right.

1. antebellum	**a.** early history, before the Middle Ages
2. antiquity	**b.** before the war
3. antecedent	**c.** earlier form
4. antetype	**d.** something prior to another

Concept Development: Synonyms or Antonyms?

Decide whether the words in each pair below are antonyms (*opposites*) or synonyms (*similar*).

1. sustained, released
2. epidemic, plague
3. mediocre, superior
4. anticipate, foresee
5. rebuked, praised

Spelling Strategy

When adding a prefix like *ante-* or *post-* to a word part that is a proper adjective, also add a hyphen: *post-Confucian*. Otherwise, a hyphen is usually not needed. Add the prefix *ante-* to each word root below, including a hyphen if needed.

1. date   2. chamber   3. Roman

Grammar and Style Lesson

Adverb Clauses

Subordinate clauses contain subjects and verbs but do not express a complete idea. An **adverb clause** is a subordinate clause that modifies a verb, an adjective, or an adverb. Adverb clauses explain *how*, *where*, *when*, *why*, *to what extent*, or *under what circumstances*.

> **Under What Circumstances:**
>
> I am willing to pass through any hardship *if only you will teach me*. (modifies *willing*)

Practice Identify the adverb clause and the word it modifies in each of the following items.

1. If I work hard, how long will it take me?
2. I will learn as quickly as I need to learn.
3. Banzo taught slowly so that Matajuro would learn to be patient.
4. The following day, when Matajuro was cooking rice, Banzo again sprang upon him unexpectedly.
5. Banzo kept attacking Matajuro when he did not expect it.

Writing Application Write a short parable of your own with a lesson that can be applied to everyday life. Use at least three adverb clauses in your writing.

WG *Prentice Hall Writing and Grammar Connection: Diamond Level, Chapter 19, Section 3*

Writing Lesson

Annotated Bibliography

These parables are just a few of the writings relating to Zen Buddhism that are available. Compile an annotated bibliography—a bibliography with descriptions and evaluations of sources—on Zen practice and ideas.

Prewriting   Use print materials and the Internet to develop your bibliography. Consult style guides to determine a style for citing the sources you find—for example, MLA style.

Drafting   Prepare your bibliography, writing annotations that show why each source is unique and valuable. Each annotation should be only a few sentences long.

Revising   Review your bibliography to make sure that you have cited each source according to the style you have chosen. Correct any omissions or inconsistencies you find.

Model: Citing Sources Using MLA Style

"Zen." *Britannica Student Encyclopedia.* 2003.

16 Apr. 2003

Encyclopædia Britannica Online.

<http://search.eb.com/ebi/article?eu=298026>

> MLA style includes the date that the Web site was accessed.

𝒲G *Prentice Hall Writing and Grammar Connection: Diamond Level, Chapter 13, Section 5*

Extension Activities

Research and Technology   Research and present a **multimedia report** that shows the influence of Zen thought on Japanese architecture and landscaping. You might use the following media in your presentation:

- music
- photographs
- models of buildings or gardens

Rehearse your presentation to make sure that it flows smoothly. When you are ready, share your report with the class.

Listening and Speaking   With several classmates, hold a **panel discussion** on the application of Zen ideas and practices in such fields as business and professional sports. Consider this question: *Are these applications valid, or do they distort the message of Zen?* Hold your panel discussion in class. **[Group Activity]**

 Take It to the Net   PHSchool.com

Go online for an additional research activity using the Internet.

READING INFORMATIONAL MATERIALS

Reference Materials

About Reference Materials

When you need to find information about a certain topic, learn how to do something, or check the spelling of a word, you might use a reference book. **Reference materials** are sources of information on specific topics. They are available in libraries and media centers, in both print and electronic form. Here are examples of common reference materials:

- A **dictionary** lists word pronunciations, origins, and definitions.
- A **thesaurus** contains synonyms and antonyms.
- An **encyclopedia** provides comprehensive information on all branches of knowledge, including history, science, and literature.
- An **almanac** contains information about such topics as weather forecasts; astronomical data; and statistics about people, places, and events.
- A **how-to book** gives practical and detailed instruction on making or doing something.

Reading Strategy

Following Directions

Whether you are taking a test or assembling a tent, your ability to **follow directions** is an important life skill. Directions may contain simple or complex instructions, but you must follow them carefully to ensure success. The chart shown provides helpful tips for following directions.

Tips for Following Directions
1. Read the directions thoroughly before beginning the task.
2. As you work through the task, do not skip any steps.
3. Study diagrams or illustrations.
4. Consider whether your finished product is what you expected it to be.
5. If there are problems with your product, review the directions and diagrams to determine where you went wrong. Make adjustments as necessary.

The reference material you are about to read gives information about the Japanese art of origami. As you read the directions for making a paper dove, notice the text elements, such as illustrations and headings, that make the instruction clear.

The Origins Of Origami

Steve and Megumi Biddle

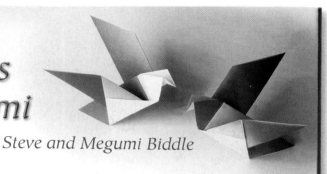

The development of paper folding in the West can be traced back to a company of Japanese jugglers who visited Europe in the 1860s, at the time when the Japanese were beginning to make contact with other cultures. The jugglers brought with them the method for folding the "flapping bird." Soon directions for this and other folds were appearing in various European publications. Magicians, including Harry Houdini, were especially interested in paper folding, attesting to the association between origami and magic, which continues today.

Paper folding, of course, had begun long before—in fact nearly two thousand years before, with the invention of paper in China in 105 A.D. Paper documents were usually rolled and their ends tied. There is a long tradition in China of folding paper into decorative shapes that are tossed onto coffins as symbols of objects for the departed to take with them into the next world.

For more than five hundred years, the Chinese kept the paper-making process a secret.

Then in the eighth century, Chinese invaders captured in Arabia were forced to reveal the technique. Eventually the process reached southern Europe.

Documents show that the Spanish symbol of paper folding, the *pajarita*, or "little bird," existed in the seventeenth century. Elsewhere in Europe, the art of paper folding was echoed in decorative napkin folds. At a banquet given by the sixteenth-century pope Gregory XIII, the setting included a table "decorated with wonderfully folded napkins." And the English diarist Samuel Pepys wrote in March 1668, "Thence home and there find one laying napkins against tomorrow in figures of all sorts."

The Japanese tradition of folding paper is a long and continuous one. It probably began in the sixth century, when a Buddhist priest brought paper-making methods to Japan from China by way of Korea. At that time, paper was a rare and precious commodity, and a formal kind of paper folding developed for use in both religious and secular life. There is perhaps another reason for the

> Like many paragraphs in reference materials, this one provides historical information.

> The illustration helps readers understand the information about paper folding.

importance of paper in Japanese life. The Japanese word *kami* can mean "paper" as well as "God," even though they are written differently. This has given rise to the belief that paper is sacred. It has long been associated with the Shinto religion and the folding of human figures (*hitogata*) that are blessed by God.

During Japan's Edo period (1600–1868), a time of development in the arts, paper became inexpensive enough to be used by everyone, and origami became a form of entertainment. Japanese woodblock prints from this period show origami models, people folding paper, and origami in kimono patterns.

In the 1890s, the Japanese government introduced a widespread system of preschool education, and origami was introduced as a tool for bringing minds and hands into coordination. It is still taught to young children today.

This paragraph provides more recent information to complement the historical facts.

Since the 1950s, interest in origami has proliferated in the United States and Great Britain as well as Japan, resulting in a variety of books and articles on the subject and in the founding of many origami societies worldwide.

Despite its popularity, for many years origami generated only a dozen or so noteworthy creations, such as the flapping bird and jumping frog. Today, however, it seems there is no shape that cannot be folded. And it can be tremendously exciting to see a flat piece of paper become transformed into a three-dimensional object. Learning how to fold new models is thrilling: Enjoy the one you encounter on the next page.

Helpful Tips

- Before you start, make sure your paper is the correct shape.

- Fold on a smooth, flat surface, such as a table or a book. Make your folds neat and accurate.

- Press your folds into place by running your thumbnail along them. Do not panic if your first few attempts at folding are not very successful. With practice you will come to understand the ways a piece of paper behaves when it is folded.

- Look at each diagram carefully, read the instructions, then look ahead to the next diagram to see what shape should be created when you have completed the step you are working on.

- Above all, if a fold or whole model does not work out, do not give up hope. Go through all the illustrations one by one, checking that you have read the instructions correctly and have not missed an important word or overlooked a symbol. If you are still unable to complete the model, put it to one side and come back to it another day with a fresh mind.

This section provides helpful tips that will make the project easier.

Dove Hato

A passage from the eighth-century chronicle the *Kojiki* describes the mournful sound of the dove like this:

Hasa no yama no hato no shitanaki ni nauku.

I weep with the murmuring sound of doves crying at Mount Hasa.

Making an Origami Dove

Try changing the angle of the head and wings each time you fold this model to see how many different doves you can create. Use a square piece of paper, white side up.

1. Begin with a diaper fold. Fold and unfold it in half from side to side.

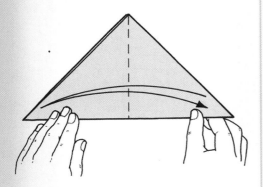

2. Valley fold the top points down two thirds of the way as shown.

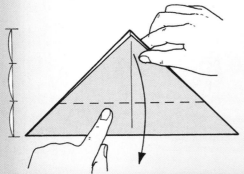

3. Valley fold the front flap of paper up as shown.

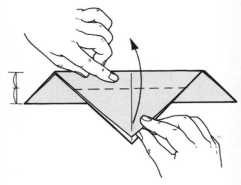

4. To make the wings, valley fold the paper in half from right to left.

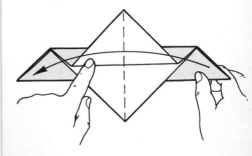

Step-by-step directions guide the process and make it easier to complete the activity.

Illustrations provide visual assistance to help clarify the directions.

5. Now inside reverse fold the top point. This is what you do:

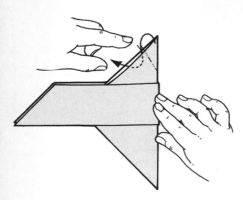

7. Valley fold the front wing over as shown. Repeat behind.

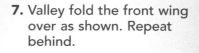
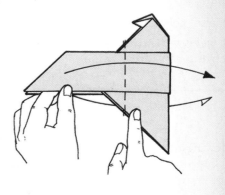

6. Place your thumb into the point's groove and, with your forefinger on top, pull the point down inside itself. To make the head and beak, press the paper flat.

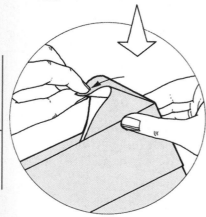

8. Open out the wings slightly.

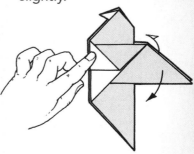

9. To complete the dove, turn the paper around.

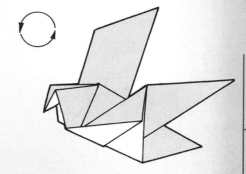

The illustrations clarify the directions by using arrows and showing exactly what your hands should do.

The final illustration shows what the finished product should look like.

Check Your Comprehension

1. Who introduced paper folding to Western civilization?
2. Where and when did the process of paper folding first begin?
3. In what innovative way did the Europeans use the art of paper folding?

Applying the Reading Strategy

Following Directions

4. Identify two elements the authors add to the text to make it easier to follow the directions.
5. In what way are the illustrations useful?

Activity

Writing Directions

Write step-by-step directions for going from your classroom to the cafeteria. Draw a diagram to clarify the steps. Include details along the route:

- Specific hallways
- Left or right turns
- Up and down staircases
- Landmarks, such as offices

When you have finished, give your directions to a classmate to follow. Ask your classmate to offer suggestions to make your directions clearer.

Comparing Informational Materials

Instructions and Recipes

Find a recipe and compare the directions with the instructions for making a paper dove. Using a chart like the one shown, record the similarities and differences in the instructions. Compare the following elements:

- Text features, such as headlines and bold type
- Diagrams or photographs
- Bulleted or numbered lists

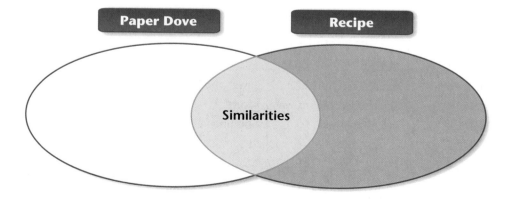

Paper Dove   Recipe

Similarities

Writing About Literature

Analyze Literary Trends

Taoism, Confucianism, and Buddhism are three of the world's major systems of belief. In this unit, you can find texts teaching basic insights of each: the *Tao Te Ching* for Taoism, *The Analects* for Confucianism, and Zen parables for Zen, a Japanese school of Buddhism. You can also find literary texts showing the influence of each system of belief. For instance, the Confucian tradition in China, in which poetry was a part of civic life, might help you understand an exchange of poems between friends. To trace the literary impact of one of these schools, complete the assignment outlined in the box at the right.

Prewriting

Identify core themes. Select the teachings of one of the three schools of thought—the *Tao Te Ching* for Taoism, *The Analects* for Confucianism, or the Zen parables for Buddhism. As you review these teachings, take notes on passages that explore the following themes:

- Confucianism: the power of a virtuous character; the importance of social relations, such as family duty, friendship, and leadership

- Taoism: the harmony of nature; nature's mysterious, inexpressible essence; the virtue of quiet contemplation

- Buddhism: the illusions and suffering caused by reason and desire; the virtue of quiet contemplation; the concept of nothingness

Choose a literary work. To find a literary work influenced by your chosen school of thought, review the Unit Introduction, pages 228–237, and the biographies accompanying the selections. Reread the works of writers who lived in the right time and place to have been influenced by the school. Complete a chart similar to the one shown, and select a work based on the connections you uncover.

Assignment: The Influence of Confucianism, Taoism, or Buddhism

Write an analytical essay that first analyzes a core Taoist, Confucian, or Buddhist belief in a philosophical work in this unit and then shows the impact of that belief on another work in this unit.

Criteria:

- Include a thesis statement that explains the impact of a Taoist, Confucian, or Buddhist belief on a specific literary work.

- Show how this belief is presented in the *Tao Te Ching*, *The Analects*, or the Zen parables.

- Support your thesis with a detailed analysis of your selected literary work, showing the influence of the belief.

- Approximate length: 1,500 words

Read to Write

As you reread texts, note any emphasis on social and family relationships (Confucianism), nature (Taoism), or the illusions created by desire (Zen).

Model: Listing to Trace Beliefs		
Selection	**Plausible Connection**	**Theme/ Evidence**
T'ao Chien, "I Built My House Near Where Others Dwell"	T'ao Chien wrote in China when Taoism was well established.	Power and harmony in nature: "The mountain air is fine at evening of the day. . . ."

Review the work. Once you have chosen a work, reread it, taking notes on passages that reflect the influence of your selected school of thought.

Drafting

Organize using an outline. Use an outline similar to the one below to organize your thoughts logically. Don't lock yourself rigidly into your outline, though. If you gain new insights as you write, insert additional information where it makes sense.

Model: Create an Informal Outline

I Introduction: Zen Buddhist idea that care creates illusions influences Bashō's haiku.

II Buddhist Idea of Illusion: Parable of the man trapped between two tigers—rather than worrying about what has not yet happened (illusion), he enjoys a strawberry

III Bashō's Relationship to Buddhism: Bashō became a Zen Buddhist later in his life.

IV Examples: "Clouds Come From Time to Time": moon might symbolize hopes, dreams—clouds interrupt the illusion; moon might symbolize truth—clouds of illusion interfere

V Conclusion: Bashō's haiku, like Zen parables, can create a moment of sudden illumination through contrast.

Frame your ideas. Write an engaging introduction to your essay. Consider beginning with a telling detail, a quotation, or an anecdote. Conclude your paper by summing up or extending your argument.

Revising and Editing

Review content: Check the relevance of details. Review your essay paragraph by paragraph to evaluate the connection between each main idea and the supporting details. Delete any details, no matter how interesting, that don't support the points you are making in a paragraph.

Review style: Revise to eliminate wordiness. Reread your paper, underlining any words that do not add to or clarify your meaning. Replace any unclear expressions with precise phrases.

Publishing and Presenting

Present an oral summary. Give a brief oral summary of the main points in your paper to your class. Then, encourage your classmates to ask questions to clarify their understanding of your summary.

*W*G *Writing and Grammar Connection: Diamond Level, Chapter 13*

Write to Learn
As you write your first draft, strive to be as specific as possible. Make sure that you include examples to support any global statements you make.

Write to Explain
Make sure that paraphrases and quotations in your paper illuminate the points you are trying to make. Be as specific as possible in making each connection clear to readers.

Writing WORKSHOP

Persuasion: Persuasive Essay

In a **persuasive essay,** a writer presents a case for or against some viewpoint. In this workshop, you will write an essay persuading your audience to accept your viewpoint and to take action on an issue.

Assignment Criteria Your persuasive essay should have the following elements:

- A focus on a controversial issue that is important to you
- A clear statement of your views and the action you suppport
- Clearly organized support suited to the intended audience
- Effective rhetorical devices such as charged language, vivid images, and dramatic analogies

To preview the criteria on which your essay may be assessed, see the Rubric on page 307.

Prewriting

Choose a topic. Select a topic that meets these three criteria:

- It must be an issue with more than one side.
- It should be one about which you have a strong opinion.
- It must be one that can be supported with arguments.

Read and listen to news media to learn more about current local and national controversies. Choose an issue on which you can take a clear, supportable position.

> **Weak:** I dislike having to wait for parking at the mall.
>
> **Better:** The growth of a "mall society" has led to standardization of styles, less personal attention to customers, and many inconveniences.

Consider your audience.
Present arguments tailored to your audience. If your audience is the school board, for example, you will probably use arguments different from those you would use with students.

Gather evidence. Conduct research on the arguments for and against your position.

A World of Small Stores Is Better Than a World of Malls

Evidence For	Evidence Against
• Service: Personal relations between owners and customers lead to better service.	• Service: Transactions at malls often move quickly.
• Convenience: Malls lead to large traffic jams.	• Convenience: Malls make it easy to shop in a variety of stores.
• Community: Owners participate in community affairs.	• Community: Malls give teenagers a place to hang out.

Student Model

Before you begin drafting, read this student model and review the characteristics of an effective persuasive essay.

Maggie Korn
Hawthorne, NY

Proverbs: Believe Them or Not

A proverb is a short, pithy saying in widespread use that expresses a basic truth. However, what if these "basic truths" aren't always truthful? I have made an unpleasant discovery about the saying "An apple a day keeps the doctor away." As a result, I believe that proverbs should never be applied uncritically to personal experience.

In her introduction, Maggie clearly states her position, based on a personal experience.

When I was five, I took the "apple advice" quite literally because I hated doctor visits. However, daily apples did not save me from going to the doctor when I developed a bad cold. By sixteen, I was less gullible. I understood the apple proverb to mean that if you ate healthy foods, you would enjoy good health. Despite my healthy diet, I was diagnosed with a hereditary illness, ironically one that affects my digestive tract: Crohn's Disease. No matter how many apples I devoured, or how many hamburgers I declined, I would still have to live with my illness. This bitter taste of reality has made me think twice about old proverbs.

Maggie explains the experience that caused her to revise her opinion about proverbs.

Some proverbs are terribly lame truisms: "Nothing ventured, nothing gained," "Something is better than nothing," and my personal favorite, "There are only twenty-four hours in a day." These are so obvious that they are not worth remembering, much less heeding.

This paragraph begins a series of progressively more significant points in support of Maggie's opinion.

Sometimes proverbs are contradictory. "Haste makes waste," for example, can easily be contradicted by another proverb: "He who hesitates is lost." Another saying, "A stitch in time saves nine" also emphasizes the importance of taking immediate action. Everyone can recall an emergency in which it was vitally important to "make haste" to resolve a medical problem, to fix a leak, or to avoid an accident.

Some proverbs make generalizations that have painful exceptions. My unhappy experience with "apples" is one example, and, because of that, I would be very careful about assuming that "Barking dogs seldom bite." It takes only one biting, barking dog to leave a scar. Forgive me if I *don't* assume that "Lightning never strikes twice in the same place."

My point is not that proverbs are useless. I believe that they do offer suggestions that may help you cope with life. However, proverbs should always be measured against your own common sense, your own experience, your own particular situation. Follow the advice of an older and wiser me—and take your proverbs with a "grain of salt." After all, an apple a day simply keeps the orchards in business!

Maggie's concession that proverbs have some usefulness adds credibility to her conclusion.

Maggie clinches her argument with a humorous reference.

Drafting

State your position up front. For greatest effectiveness, state your view on the issue in the first paragraph. Present it in a clearly worded thesis statement. You can build up to the statement by opening with dramatic facts.

Organize to emphasize the strongest support. Make your case by presenting your arguments in favor of it. Acknowledge good arguments on the other side of the issue, but then show why your position is better. The organization shown here is one way to make your case forcefully.

The Body of a Persuasive Essay

- Start with your second-best argument.
- State and then argue against an opposing view.
- Organize the rest of your argument to lead up to your conclusion.
- Present your strongest argument last.

Use effective arguing techniques. Consider using appeals of the following kinds in the course of making your points:

- **Logical appeals:** claims, for example, that if a certain event occurs, something else will inevitably follow.
- **Ethical appeals:** claims that it is morally right that a certain event occur.
- **Emotional appeals:** claims that readers will be happy, proud, or angry if a certain event occurs.

End with a call for action. Make the closing paragraph of your essay a clear call for action—a statement of what you want done.

Revising

Revise to strengthen language. Strengthen your case by improving the way you state ideas. Review your draft, following these steps:

1. For each passage, jot down a sentence summarizing your point on a self-sticking note. Place the note next to the passage.
2. For each note, underline any charged words, vivid images, or dramatic analogies you have used in the passage to support your point.
3. If you find few or none of these forms of support in a passage, jot down additional ideas for support on a new note next to the passage.
4. Incorporate your best ideas into your draft.

Model: Revising to Strengthen Language

biting, barking dog to leave a scar.

I would be very careful about assuming that "Barking dogs seldom bite." It takes only one ~~bad dog to change the rule.~~

"Scar" creates a vivid image that drives home Maggie's point, while "biting, barking" are punchy modifiers used to make the point memorably.

Revise for parallel structure. Review your draft for concepts that are related or contrasting. Consider expressing them in parallel form—that is, phrasing the ideas using the same grammatical structure.

Not parallel: . . . a place *crammed* with people, *lit* with glaring lights, and *that offers* the same brands you can find in the mall down the highway.

Parallel: . . . a place *crammed* with people, *lit* with glaring lights, and *offering* the same brands you can find in the mall down the highway.

Compare these items. Why is the model more effective?

Nonmodel	Model
Everyone can recall an emergency in which it was vitally important to "make haste" to resolve a medical problem. Leaking pipes can't wait. And what about trying to avoid an accident?	Everyone can recall an emergency in which it was vitally important to "make haste" to resolve a medical problem, to fix a leak, or to avoid an accident.

Publishing and Presenting

Present your essay orally. Use your essay as the basis of an oral presentation to your class. Rehearse reading it so that you can determine the best way to make your points. For example, you might change the pitch of your voice or use gestures for emphasis.

Publish in a print medium. If your topic relates to your school, submit your essay to your school newspaper. If your essay could appeal to a larger audience, you might submit it to an opinion column in a local newspaper.

WG *Writing and Grammar Connection: Diamond Level, Chapter 7*

Rubric for Self-Assessment

Use the following criteria and rating scale to evaluate your persuasive essay:

Criteria	Rating Scale				
	Not very				Very
How clearly is your position stated?	1	2	3	4	5
How well organized is the support for your position?	1	2	3	4	5
How effective are your arguments?	1	2	3	4	5
How appropriate are your arguments and examples to your audience?	1	2	3	4	5
How strong are the language, images, and analogies you have used?	1	2	3	4	5

Listening and Speaking WORKSHOP

Delivering a Persuasive Argument

A **persuasive argument** delivered in a speech is meant to convince an audience to believe something or to take a specific course of action. A good persuasive argument uses clear, logical reasoning and effective emotional appeals. (For a review of the characteristics of persuasive writing, see the Writing Workshop on pages 304–307.) Follow these strategies to deliver an effective persuasive argument.

Plan the Content

To begin, choose a debatable topic for your presentation—that is, one on which reasonable people disagree.

Research supporting material. Gather facts and statistics, examples, expert opinions, and other evidence that supports your position. Select the strongest facts and figures, and present them in your speech.

Use rhetorical techniques. To catch your audience's imagination, strengthen your argument with rhetorical devices, including the following:

- **Dramatic questions:** Consider posing your key issue in the form of a stirring question. (For example, "How long before parents, worried by aging swing sets, forbid their kids to play in the park?")
- **Analogies:** By comparing an abstract idea to a simple, familiar relationship, an analogy makes even a complicated idea easy to grasp. (For example, "Developing a new ball field without repairing the playground is like spending your money on a great haircut while walking around in torn-up shoes.")

Focus on Delivery

Use these techniques to make your speech engaging:

- **Vary your pace and tone of voice.** Slow down to stress key statements, and speed up to convey emotion. Raising and lowering your voice can be a very effective way to build drama.
- **Be aware of body language.** Relax! Avoid a stiff, wooden posture. Gesturing occasionally for emphasis and taking a few steps from time to time will help you communicate with your audience effectively.

(Activity:)
Presentation and Feedback Prepare a persuasive speech on a controversial issue. Have a partner use the Feedback Form shown above to evaluate your presentation. Use the evaluation to improve your speech. Then, deliver it to your class.

Feedback Form for a Persuasive Argument

Rating System
+ = Excellent   ✓ = Average   − = Weak

Content
Uses supporting evidence effectively _____
Anticipates opposing arguments _____

Uses rhetorical techniques to strengthen argument _____

Which techniques? _____
_____

Delivery
Varies pace and tone _____
Gestures effectively _____
Makes eye contact _____

Other comments on delivery: _____
_____

Assessment WORKSHOP

Sequential Order

In the reading sections of some tests, you may be required to answer questions on the order of events in a passage. Use the following strategies to help you answer such questions:

- Distinguish the order of the statements (what is *stated* first) from the order of events (what *happens* first).
- To help clarify sequential order, determine the logical relation between causes and effects.
- Take note of words signaling sequence, such as *first, next, then, after that, last,* and *finally.*

Test-Taking Strategy

As you read a test passage, number the events in order, indicating which one happened first, which next, and which last.

Sample Test Item

Directions: Read the passage, and then choose the letter of the best answer to the question.

Thanks for offering to give my dog, Juno, a bath, but it won't be easy! First, gather the supplies—bucket, shampoo, and old towels—and put them outside beside the hose. Change into a bathing suit. Try not to let Juno notice that anything unusual is happening, or she will disappear. Then, put on her collar and leash and lead her outside. Stand on her leash, and use the hose to wet her down. Ignore her barks and shivering. Next, apply plenty of shampoo and massage the shampoo into her fur. After that, rinse thoroughly. Be sure to remove all the shampoo. Finally, dry her with the towels.

1. What should you do right before you wet down the dog?

   A shampoo her

   B gather the supplies

   C stand on the leash

   D towel her off

Answer and Explanation

The correct answer is *C*. *A*, *B*, and *D* are incorrect: One does not do these things immediately before wetting down the dog.

Practice

Directions: Read the passage, and then choose the letter of the best answer to the question.

Confucius was an influential thinker who led an eventful life. During his difficult childhood, it is said, he began to wonder why there was so much pain in the world. As Confucius grew older, he decided the answer to this question lay in respect for *li*, or rituals and rules of courtesy. Confucius began to share his views, and he gradually attracted followers from various kingdoms of China. Eventually, he became an official of the Kingdom of Lu. In this post, he applied his ideas of *li* and of virtue to politics and diplomacy. Confucius, however, fell victim to the power struggles that swirled around the king of Lu. Confucius resigned, and he and some followers traveled through various kingdoms of China looking for a great king to serve.

1. When did Confucius wander through various kingdoms of China looking for a king to serve?

   A before he gained followers

   B when he was an official of Lu

   C before developing his idea of *li*

   D after he resigned as an official of Lu

" *Wonders are many,
and none is more
wonderful than man.* **"**
— Sophocles, from *Antigone*

Timeline c. 800 B.C.–A.D. 500

Ancient Greek and Roman Events

- **700s (Greece)** It was likely during this period that the polis, or city-state, emerged.
- **700s (Greece)** Probable era of the life of Homer, author of the *Iliad* and the *Odyssey*.
- **776 (Greece)** The first Olympic games are held. ▼
- **753 (Rome)** The city of Rome is founded.

- **525/524 (Greece)** The tragic dramatist Aeschylus is born.
- **509 (Rome)** Rome becomes a republic.
- **early 400s (Greece)** Athens and Sparta are the most powerful city-states.
- **c. 496 (Greece)** The tragic dramatist Sophocles is born.
- **495–429 (Greece)** Pericles, Athenian statesman, lives.
- **490–479 (Greece)** Greco-Persian Wars are fought.
- **c. 470–399 (Greece)** The philosopher Socrates lives.
- **447 (Greece)** Ordered by Pericles, work begins on the Parthenon, a great temple of Athena in Athens. ▲
- **431–404 (Greece)** Athens is defeated by Sparta in the Peloponnesian War.

- **275 (Rome)** Rome is dominant in Italy, having defeated all other groups.
- **264–146 (Rome)** Rome fights three Punic Wars with Carthage.
- **70–19 (Rome)** Virgil, author of the *Aeneid*, lives.
- **65–8 (Rome)** The poet Horace lives.
- **63 (Rome)** Augustus, first Roman emperor, is born.

World Events

- **721 (ancient Israel)** The Assyrians conquer the northern kingdom of Israel.
- **c. 700 (India)** This is the final date for the composition of the *Brahmanas*, texts that discuss religious rituals.
- **c. 628–c. 551 (Persia)** Zoroaster, founder of Zoroastrianism, lives. ▶

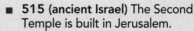

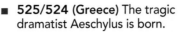

- **515 (ancient Israel)** The Second Temple is built in Jerusalem.
- **400s (India)** Panini standardizes Sanskrit in an important grammar text.
- **c. 330 (Persian Empire)** Alexander the Great conquers the Persian Empire.

- **256/255 (China)** The Chou dynasty is overthrown.
- **221–206 (China)** The Ch'in dynasty reigns.
- **206 (China)** The Han dynasty takes power. ▶
- **200 (Japan)** By this date, the Japanese cultivate irrigated rice.
- **100–0 (India)** Work on the Ajanta caves begins; construction continues through the 7th century A.D.

Ancient Greek, Roman, and World Events

- **A.D. 8 (Rome)** The emperor Augustus banishes the poet Ovid to Tomis, near the Black Sea.
- **14 (Rome)** Augustus, the first Roman Emperor, dies.
- **30 (Roman Empire)** Jesus of Nazareth is crucified.
- **56–120 (Rome)** The historian Tacitus lives.
- **70–72 (Rome)** Construction of the Colosseum, a giant stadium for gladiatorial combats, begins. ▼

- **c. 376 (Roman Empire)** The fierce tribe known as the Huns reaches the frontier of the empire. ▶
- **379–395 (Roman Empire)** Under the emperor Theodosius I, Christianity becomes essential to Roman citizenship.
- **391 (Roman Empire)** The emperor Theodosius I ends all visits to the Oracle at Delphi.
- **410 (Rome)** Rome is sacked by the Visigoths, a Germanic tribe.
- **476 (Roman Empire)** The Western Roman Empire falls.

- **c. A.D. 100s (China)** Buddhism begins to take hold. ▼
- **c. 200 (Mexico/Central America)** Mayan villages have developed into cities.

- **300s (Japan)** The Yamato emerge as the most powerful clan, opening the way to Chinese cultural influences.
- **365–427 (China)** T'ao Ch'ien, one of China's greatest poets, lives.
- **late 300s to early 400s (India)** The Hindu author of an astronomical handbook tabulates the sine function.
- **c. 400 (India)** The Pillar of Delhi, a solid metal column over 23 feet tall and weighing more than 6 tons, is constructed.
- **c. 400 (India)** The final compilation of the *Mahabharata* is made.
- **476–750 (France)** Merovingian kings rule the Franks.

Ancient Greece and Rome

(c. 800 B.C.–A.D. 500)

Historical Background

Ancient Greece: The Minoans The brilliant Minoan (mi nō´ ən) culture, named after the mythical king Minos (mī´ näs´), thrived on the island of Crete from about 3000 to 1100 B.C. The Minoans were sophisticated palace dwellers accustomed to comfort, luxury, and beauty. By about 1600 B.C., Minoan civilization was influencing the entire Greek world through trade and colonization.

Mycenean Civilization Minoan influence gave rise to the Mycenaean (mī sə nē´ ən) palace culture on the Greek mainland. The Mycenaeans' empire flourished in Greece from about 1600 B.C. to 1200 B.C. In about 1250 B.C., the Mycenaeans defeated the city of Troy in Asia Minor in a legendary struggle known as the Trojan War, but they made no other important conquests. By 1100 B.C., their network of imperial palaces had disappeared.

The Dark Age and After Because no written evidence survives, we call the approximately 300-year period after the collapse of Mycenaean civilization the Dark Age. During this era, a relatively primitive group called the Dorians invaded Greece.

Somewhat later, in the eighth century B.C., the Greeks established major colonies throughout Sicily and southern Italy. Greek traders voyaged and settled throughout the Mediterranean. This commerce brought the Greeks in contact with the Phoenicians (fi nish´ ənz), a trading people who lived in what is now Lebanon and Syria. The Greeks adapted the Phoenicians' written signs to create the first true alphabet, one that became the basis for our own. The use of this new alphabet explains why there is evidence of literacy everywhere in Greece by 750 B.C.

Literacy, new currents in art and intellectual history, colonization, and the creation of the polis (pō´ lis), or city-state, all resulted from thriving trade. City-states were small, independent cities that functioned as nations. It is no surprise that Greece, with its rugged mainland terrain and many islands, was not politically unified. True, the many different city-states had a common heritage, but differences in dialect, customs, and government fostered rivalries and prompted conflicts among these mini-nations.

The Greco-Persian Wars By the beginning of the fifth century B.C., Athens and Sparta had emerged as the two most powerful city-states. Together, they resisted the Persian invasions of Europe during the period 490–479 B.C. Success in defeating the Persians, however, was largely due to victories won by the Athenians at the Battle of Marathon and the naval Battle of Salamis.

Growth of Roman Power to 44 B.C.

The Athenian Empire, c. 450 B.C.

MACEDONIA

Thermopylae
Marathon
Salamis • Athens
PELOPONNESUS
Sparta

PERSIAN EMPIRE

Aegean Sea

CRETE

Mediterranean Sea

0   200 Miles
0   200 Kilometers

North Sea

BRITAIN

ATLANTIC OCEAN

Rhine R.

Danube R.

GAUL

ALPS

PYRENEES MTS.

Rhône R.

Po R.

Rubicon R.

Tiber R.

SPAIN

Rome

New Carthage

SICILY

Carthage

Zama

NUMIDIA

AFRICA

Mediterranean Sea

Cyrene

Byzantium

ASIA MINOR

Athens

CRETE

Black Sea

Euphrates R.

Antioch
SYRIA
CYPRUS
Damascus

Alexandria

EGYPT

Nile R.

Legend:
- ⧄ Areas settled by Greeks
- Athenian Empire, c. 450 B.C.
- Roman Empire, c. 44 B.C.

0   250   500 Miles
0   250   500 Kilometers

Pericles and the Golden Age of Athens Athens' role in the war against Persia led to the rise of the Athenian Empire. At home, Athenian democracy was experiencing a golden age under the statesman Pericles (per´ i klēz´). He fostered the highest ideals of citizen participation and channeled the city's prosperity into impressive new public architecture and art. Abroad, his hawkish foreign policy fostered the growth of an empire but also caused resentment among other city-states. (See the map above.)

One of Athens' greatest rivals was Sparta, a totalitarian society in which individuals were subordinate to the state. Spartan discipline contributed to the superiority of its army, and the army allowed Sparta to control most of the city-states in Peloponnesus (pel´ ə pə nē´ səs), a peninsula forming the southern part of the Greek mainland.

The Peloponnesian War Gradually, Greece became polarized between Athens and Sparta. These two city-states fought each other in a long conflict called the Peloponnesian War (431–404 B.C.), which Sparta won.

Alexander the Great After the defeat of Athens, however, Macedonia—not Sparta—emerged as a power. Macedonia was a kingdom in the northeastern part of the Greek peninsula. It was ruled by King Philip, whose son Alexander (356–323 B.C.) became known as "the Great" due to his military skills. Alexander's armies marched south and east, spreading Greek language and culture throughout what is today Egypt, Turkey, Iraq, Iran (Persia), and part of India.

▲ **Critical Viewing**
The Romans greatly admired Greek culture. What does this map suggest about the role of the Roman Empire in spreading Greek thought and beliefs? Explain. [**Read a Map**]

Close-up on Culture

The Delphic Oracle

The ancient Greeks regarded the city of Delphi (del′ fi), perched dramatically on the slope of Mount Parnassus, as the "navel," or center of the world. This was the place where Apollo (ə päl′ ō), the Greek god of music, poetry, prophecy, and medicine, spoke to humans through the mouth of his priestess, the Oracle.

Delegations would come from throughout the known world to question the Oracle, especially about the outcome of wars or other political situations. They hoped that Apollo would answer human uncertainties with his divine knowledge. Private individuals also attended the monthly sessions of the Oracle, in the hope of solving life's small but urgent dilemmas: Should I marry? Is this a good time to travel? Should I move to a new city?

The Oracle, an elderly woman, followed a strict ritual in order to give Apollo's answers to these questions. She bathed, drank from sacred waters, descended to the basement of Apollo's temple, climbed onto a sacred stool, and chewed the leaves of a plant, the laurel, associated with Apollo. Entering into a trance, she would answer questions with words that the god inspired her to speak. Priests would write down these words in verse that sounded like riddles.

▲ **Critical Viewing**
Which qualities of Apollo, as he is portrayed in this famous statue, suggest that he is a god? Explain. **[Infer]**

Greek Religion: The Gods As personifications of war, plague, or earthquake, the Greek gods were formidable. Yet because they had human qualities and foibles, they were approachable and even comic. The Greeks perceived their relationship to the gods as one of mutually advantageous exchange. They often held religious festivals in honor of the gods, hoping that the gods would reward them. The most famous example of such a festival is the Olympic Games, first held in 776 B.C. in honor of Zeus (zyo͞os), the king of the gods. (For more on Greek and Roman gods, see page 317).

Rome: Earliest History Until Rome emerged as a power in the fourth century B.C., Italy was dominated by the Etruscans in the north and the Greeks in the south. Both these cultures enjoyed a level of civilization Rome would not achieve for centuries. Nevertheless, a distinct culture was emerging in the region of west-central Italy called Latium, a culture that would come to be known as "Roman."

The Rise of Rome Surrounded by Etruscan and Greek powers, early Latin settlements joined in self-defense. The strongest city in this group was Rome, which gave its name to the region's culture. Tradition assigns Rome's founding to 753 B.C. At first, Rome was ruled by kings, advised by a council of elders. Offices were held by members of the ruling class. In 509 B.C., however, Rome became a republic.

By 275 B.C., Rome had defeated all other Italian groups, as well as the Etruscans and the Greeks. African and Asian countries recognized Rome as a world power.

The Punic Wars In the Punic Wars (264–146 B.C.), Rome battled with Carthage, a prosperous city-state in North Africa. Rome's victories in each of these three conflicts mark key dates in its history. The initial victory, in 241 B.C., ushered in the first flowering of Roman literature and art. The second victory, in 201 B.C., signaled a turning point in Roman foreign policy. Rome went on to wage aggressive rather than defensive wars, conquering Macedonia and what is now Spain and Portugal. The third victory against Carthage, in 146 B.C., allowed Rome to seize its former trading rival as a province.

Civil Wars By the late second century B.C., Roman society was divided between a conservative, slave-owning senatorial aristocracy and more liberal senatorial aristocrats. Meanwhile, poorer citizens often rioted, and groups of slaves sometimes staged revolts. Attempts at reform did not take hold, and Rome experienced a series of bitter conflicts. During the period 49–45 B.C., Gaius Julius Caesar seized power. His brief dictatorship lasted until March 15, 44 B.C., when he was assassinated by a group of senators headed by Brutus and Cassius.

In the power struggles that followed, Caesar's grandnephew Octavius emerged victorious. Elected consul and given special emergency powers, Octavius was named *imperator*, the word from which we derive "emperor." He began using the name Augustus.

The Birth of the Empire Augustus' reign, the beginning of the Roman Empire, is marked by a flowering of literature and architecture. Although he ruled as an emperor, he declared that he was restoring the old republic. Also, he instituted religious and legal reforms that were meant to promote old-fashioned virtues. Augustus ruled skillfully for more than forty years. Many of his immediate successors, however, were cruel and inept, and the general quality of Roman emperors was uneven.

The Fall of the Empire As time went on, the empire came under stress both at home and abroad, with its very size making it vulnerable on its frontiers. The size of the empire also led to a split between the eastern and western parts. Eventually, these two parts came to be ruled by different emperors.

The eastern Roman Empire survived longer than did the western, which ended in A.D. 476 when Germanic tribes overran it and replaced it with a multitude of kingdoms.

A selection of Greek and Roman Gods

God or Goddess		Powers and Relationships
Greek	Zeus	■ King of the gods
Roman	Jupiter	■ Husband of Hera; father of Ares, Athena, and Hephaestus, the black-smith god; brother of Poseidon and Hades
Greek	Poseidon	■ God of the sea
Roman	Neptune	■ Brother of Zeus
Greek	Hades	■ God of the underworld
Roman	Pluto	■ Brother of Zeus
Greek	Hera	■ Queen of the gods
Roman	Juno	■ Wife of Zeus; mother of Ares and Hephaestus
Greek	Athena	■ Goddess of war, crafts, and wisdom
Roman	Minerva	■ Daughter of Zeus; sprang from his forehead
Greek	Aphrodite	■ Goddess of love
Roman	Venus	■ Born from the foam of the sea; wife of Hephaestus and lover of Ares
Greek	Ares	■ God of war
Roman	Mars	■ Son of Zeus and Hera

Religion: Rome Versus Greece Unlike the Greeks, the Romans were obsessed with correct ritual, and they had a practice, unknown to the Greeks, of beginning a public religious ceremony all over again if any detail went wrong. Also, Romans viewed fate as a command to be obeyed, while Greeks thought of it as an allotment, like a plot of land given to a person for cultivation.

Native Gods and Greek Influences The Romans were polytheistic, believing in many gods, and their native deities reveal the Romans' concern with home, cattle, and agriculture. The worship of the family *genius*, or ancestor of the clan, and the obedience owed a living father led Romans to view themselves as dutiful sons of a father-like emperor.

Through contact with Greek religion, literature, and art, the Romans came to see their own gods as corresponding to those of the Greeks. (For more on Greek and Roman gods, see the chart on page 317).

Christianity Christianity began under the Roman Empire as a first century A.D. movement within Judaism. Believing in the divinity of Jesus of Nazareth (c. 6–4 B.C.–A.D. 30), Christians soon developed a faith distinct from Judaism and were frequently persecuted by the Romans. Yet Christianity strengthened as the empire declined. Finally, the emperor Theodosius I (reigned A.D. 379–395) made belief in Christianity essential to Roman citizenship.

▼ **Critical Viewing**
In this picture taken at the Lincoln Memorial, which details reveal the influence of the classical world on Washington, D.C.? Why? **[Connect]**

A Living Tradition

Washington, D.C., and the Classical World

Benjamin Latrobe, the architect who oversaw the building of the Capitol in Washington, D.C., spoke of "the days of Greece. . . in the woods of America." Like many other late-eighteenth-century Americans, Latrobe hoped that the nation's new capital city would reflect the spirit of the ancient Greek and Roman republics.

This goal was not surprising, considering that America's founders were believers in the Enlightenment, an intellectual movement that praised reason and looked to the classical world for examples of reason in action—in science, law, and architecture.

Thomas Jefferson, one of the greatest Founding Fathers, was a friend of Latrobe's and a distinguished architect in his own right. Together, these two men pioneered the Federal style of architecture, which was based on ancient Roman models.

Today, visitors to the nation's capital can appreciate this new Athens or Rome on the Potomac. Surveyed by the African American mathematician Benjamin Banneker and planned by architect Pierre-Charles L'Enfant, the city consists of wide avenues that radiate diagonally from circles, interspersed with parks and squares for monuments. Imposing marble buildings with classical columns proclaim the nation's allegiance to reason and classical civilization.

Literature

Greek Literature: The Epic From the Dark Age of Greece came oral epic poetry that served as the raw material for Homer's sophisticated epics, the *Iliad* and the *Odyssey*. These two works deal, respectively, with the Greek conquest of Troy and the wanderings of the hero Odysseus (ō dis′ ē əs) after the Trojan War. The Homeric epics convey such values of ancient Greek culture as physical bravery, skill, honor, reverence for the gods, and intelligence.

Lyric Poetry Of all the genres of Greek literature, lyric poetry loses the most in translation. Specifically, it loses its musical quality—*lyric* originally meant "sung to the lyre." Nevertheless, Greek lyric poets like Sappho influenced the Roman poets and still influence today's writers.

Philosophy In the fifth century B.C., the philosopher Socrates (säk′ rə tēz′) developed a method of uncovering truth by asking probing questions. Socrates' most famous follower was Plato (plāt′ ō), who recorded the dialogues that show his master practicing the Socratic method. Plato's vision of a realm of changeless, perfect forms that are imperfectly reflected in this world attracted some of the finest minds of later generations. (See Music in the Historical Context on page 320). Aristotle, Plato's most famous student, pioneered in developing logic, zoology, psychology, and many other arts and sciences. His work was a dominant force in Western culture for almost 2,000 years and still influences philosophy.

The Romans admired Greek philosophy and helped make it the basis for Western thought. In fact, some scholars have half-humorously referred to the Western philosophical tradition as a 2500-year disagreement between Plato and Aristotle!

Tragedy Greek drama developed in connection with religious rituals and reached its peak in fifth-century Athens. Tragedies, which chronicled the downfall of a noble person, raised difficult questions about justice, evil, and the reasons for human suffering. In keeping with its religious origin, tragedy provided an emotional rather than a philosophical resolution for the questions it raised.

As a means of making the audience feel purged or cleansed, Greek tragedy aroused in them the powerful emotions of pity for the tragic hero and awe at his or her fate.

▼ **Critical Viewing** The sorceress Circe both helps and hinders the hero Odysseus in the *Odyssey*. What can you tell about her from this picture? Explain. **[Infer]**

Circe Meanwhile Had Gone Her Ways . . . , 1924, From the *Odyssey* by Homer, William Russell Flint, Collection of the New York Public Library; Astor, Lenox and Tilden Foundations

In order of birth, the three greatest Greek tragedians are Aeschylus (es´ ki ləs); Sophocles (säf´ ə klēz´), who wrote *Oedipus the King*; and Euripides (yoo rip´ ə dēz). Although the surviving Greek tragedies are among the best works of world literature, we have available only a small percentage of the dramas these men actually wrote.

History Two great historians of the fifth century B.C., like playwrights and philosophers, saw themselves as teachers: Herodotus (hə räd´ ə təs), who wrote on the Persian Wars, and Thucydides (thoo sid´ i dēz´), who wrote about the Peloponnesian War between Athens and Sparta.

Roman Literature: Epic and Drama Until Rome defeated Carthage in 241 B.C. and emerged as a world power, educated Romans still conducted foreign policy and read literature in Greek. After winning their victory, Romans began to create a national literature. One product of this era was the historical epic, a form that the first-century B.C. poet Virgil perfected in the *Aeneid* (ē nē´ id). This long narrative poem describes the fall of Troy and the founding of Rome by the legendary Trojan hero Aeneas.

Music in the Historical Context

Ancient Greek Modes, or the Morality of Music

When rock-and-roll exploded onto the scene in the 1950s, some people claimed it was immoral and should be banned. They argued that the "wild" rhythms of rock would encourage wild behavior. A similar debate about the morality of music took place more than 2000 years ago in ancient Greece. This debate, however, focused on Greek musical scales, called modes, rather than on rhythms.

Scales and modes are sets of notes that are separated by definite intervals. Each Greek mode had seven notes. Also, the names of the modes were associated with groups and regions. The Dorian mode, for instance, was linked with the Dorians, a tribe that had conquered part of mainland Greece. The Lydian mode was linked with Lydia, a western kingdom in ancient Asia Minor.

These regions and the modes named for them had definite meanings for the Greeks. The Dorian mode, linked with a warlike area, was regarded as strong and manly. Songs composed in this mode were suitable for inspiring soldiers. By contrast, songs in the Lydian mode—named for Lydia, viewed as a corrupt place—were suitable for feasts.

In Book III of the *Republic* (c. 360 B.C.), the Greek philosopher Plato joined the debate about music. He warned against the influence of the Lydian mode, which seems to have been the rock music of its time. Plato banned these songs from his ideal republic because they made men "soft" and encouraged "drinking." He favored the Dorian mode, which was "warlike" and sounded "the note or accent which a brave man utters in the hour of danger. . . ."

If he were living today, what would Plato say about heavy metal, grunge, or rap?

▲ **Critical Viewing**
This ancient fresco, or wall painting, comes from a Roman villa in Pompeii, Italy. What does it suggest about the type of painting that upper-class Romans preferred? Explain. [Infer]

Drama also flourished after 241 B.C., with the state funding elaborate productions of tragedy and comedy. Two masters of Roman comedy from that time were Plautus (plôt' əs) and Terence. Both these writers have influenced Western drama.

As drama gave way to the epic, two long works stand out in addition to Virgil's. Both are anti-epics, however, in the sense that they do not promote heroic values. The *Metamorphoses* by Ovid (äv' id) contains a series of mythical stories involving changes of shape (*metamorphosis* means "transformation"). This poem angered the Emperor Augustus, who saw it as a sly attack on established religion and rulers. Later, Petronius (pi trō' nē əs) Arbiter wrote the *Satyricon*, perhaps the first novel to describe the adventures of a wandering, mischievous hero.

History and Biography In works of history and biography, Romans examined major events and sought to find in great men's lives the causes of these events. The historian Tacitus (tas' i təs), who lived from A.D. 56 to c. 120, was keenly analytical and included in his work examples of public oration as well as the biographies of public figures.

Lyric Poetry Lyric poetry for the Romans was an essentially derivative form, although the greatest poets transformed their models. For instance, Catullus (kə tul' əs) and Horace, poets of the first century B.C., imitated Greek forms but created poems essentially Roman in their point of view.

Philosophy As philosophers, the Romans were masterful imitators rather than original thinkers. The major philosophical work in Latin literature is a poem by Lucretius (loo krē' shəs) entitled *On the Nature of Things*. In this work, he uses the atomic theory of Greek thinkers to present a world in which everything results from the random combination of particles rather than the actions of the gods. He urges a way of life that promotes freedom from violent emotion and irrational behavior.

Prepare to Read

from the Iliad

Homer (c. eighth century B.C.)

The ancient Greeks ascribed the *Iliad* and the *Odyssey,* their two oldest, monumental epic poems, to Homer, whom they called simply "The Poet." Nothing certain is known about Homer's life. His name, which means "hostage," gives no clue to his origins, since small wars and raids between neighboring towns were frequent in ancient Greece, and prisoners were routinely held for ransom or sold into slavery. Homer is commonly referred to as the "Ionian bard," or poet; more than likely, he came from Ionia in the eastern Mediterranean, where Eastern and Western cultures met and new intellectual currents were born. In support of that theory, the *Iliad* contains several accurate descriptions of the Ionian landscape and its natural features, whereas Homer's grasp of the geography of mainland Greece seems less authoritative.

A Sightless Visionary Legend has it that Homer was blind. This legend may have some basis in fact; if he lived to be an old man, he may simply have become blind. However, the idea of Homer's blindness may have arisen because of its symbolic implications. The Greeks contrasted inner vision with physical vision, as in the case of the blind seer Teiresias and of Oedipus himself, who becomes blind in *Oedipus the King.* Also, Homer's image—the blind bard singing the myths of his people—is a striking symbol for the beginning of Western literature.

Heroes and Legends Although it is not known for certain when Homer lived, the *Iliad* was almost certainly composed late in the eighth century B.C. Historically, however, both the *Iliad* and the *Odyssey* take place in a long-past heroic age known as the Late Bronze Age. One might wonder how Homer was able to depict an era five hundred years before his time. The answer is that Homer did not create the plot or characters of the epics he is credited with writing; rather, he inherited the stories of those epics. Generations of Greeks had preserved orally the subject matter of the *Iliad* and the *Odyssey*—the story of the Trojan War and the heroic mythology that pervades both poems. As a result, Homer is the ultimate spokesman of a long and rich tradition of oral poetry developed over centuries.

From generation to generation, ancient Greek poets transmitted tales of warriors' heroic deeds. Many of the stories were about those who fought in the war against Troy (twelfth or thirteenth century B.C.). A bard might choose to sing about the exploits of a particular war hero, at Troy or elsewhere, about his homecoming, and about his ancestors or his descendants. In the world of Homer's audience, the landed warrior aristocracy claimed descent from the heroes of legend and ultimately from the gods. For such a society, the legends about heroes formed a kind of tribal, and later national, family history.

A Culture's Identity The *Iliad* was, in fact, considered history; children in the fifth century B.C. memorized large sections of the poem and practiced the ethical codes that Homer presents. Athenians even claimed the Homeric gods and heroes as founders or champions of Athens and its people. Homer's epics also had a tremendous influence on later generations of Greek writers. Greek lyric poets, dramatists, and philosophers considered themselves Homer's heirs, drawing on his work either to imitate it or to argue with it. As Greek culture spread through the eastern Mediterranean and west to Italy, Homer's epics formed a common text for a large part of the Western world.

The Epic Form

Just as the oral tradition supplied Homer with a vast body of legend, it also provided him with the form and structure in which to express the legend. Although Homer was free to choose and shape the elements of the story according to his own vision, his language, meter, and style were formulaic. Over time, bards had developed a common fund of expressions, phrases, and descriptions that fit the rhythms of the epic verse line. These conventions became the building blocks of the epic genre.

The Invocation In Medias Res Homer begins the *Iliad* powerfully by stating the epic's theme and invoking one of the Muses. The Muses are nine goddesses in Greek mythology who were believed to preside over all forms of art and science. The poet calls on the Muse to inspire him with the material he needs to tell his story. This type of opening is one of the defining features of a Homeric epic.

Homer observes another epic convention by beginning the story *in medias res*, which is Latin for "in the middle of things." Reading a Greek epic from the beginning is like tuning in to a story already in progress, in that many of the story's events have already taken place. Information about those events is revealed later in the poem through flashbacks and other narrative devices. Homer could begin his poems *in medias res* because the general outline of the plot and the main characters were already familiar to his audience. The *Iliad*, like other epics, is a small fragment of a large body of legendary material that formed the cultural and historical heritage of its society.

Homeric Epithets The particular demands of composing and listening to oral poetry gave rise to the use of stock descriptive words or phrases, such as "brilliant Achilles" or "Hector breaker of horses." These epithets, often compound adjectives like "blazing-eyed Athena," allowed the poet to describe an object or a character quickly and economically, in terms his audience would recognize. Homeric epithets and other formulaic language may have helped the poet shape his story and compose while reciting, and the repetition of familiar expressions also would have helped the audience follow the narrative.

How the War Began

The *Iliad* recounts only part of a long series of events in the Trojan War, which was fought, according to legend, because of a quarrel among gods and the resulting incidents of betrayal among mortals. How did the war start? King Peleus and the sea-goddess Thetis were the parents of Achilles, hero of the Iliad. When Peleus and Thetis were married, all the gods were invited except Eris, the goddess of discord. Angry at being excluded, Eris tossed a golden apple among the guests; on it was inscribed "for the fairest one." Hera, Athena, and Aphrodite each claimed the prize. They chose the Trojan prince Paris, a handsome and unworldly man, to decide which goddess was the fairest. Each goddess offered him a bribe, and Paris chose Aphrodite's: She promised to give him the most beautiful woman alive, Helen, who was already married to Menelaus, king of Sparta.

Paris violated the sacred bond of hospitality when he went to Menelaus' court as a guest and abducted the host's wife. Menelaus sought the help of his brother Agamemnon, king of Mycenae and the most powerful ruler of his time. Together with other kings, they mounted an expedition against Troy, to reclaim Helen and to sack a city famed for its opulence. The war lasted for ten years until Troy was finally taken.

Out of a vast body of material that his audience knew, Homer chose to focus on a period of less than two months in the tenth year of the war. Homer did not concentrate on the war as such, but on the Greek warrior Achilles and the consequences of his rage.

Preview

Connecting to the Literature

When you read the epics of Homer, you take part in a cultural tradition that spans more than two thousand years. Generations of writers, from Shakespeare to Sting, have been inspired by and have alluded to Homer. The warriors in the *Iliad* are from a distant time and culture, yet many of their basic concerns will be familiar to you.

Literary Analysis

Theme

The **theme** of a literary work is its central idea, concern, or message. Long works, such as novels and epics, often contain more than one major theme. For example, the theme stated at the beginning of the *Iliad* is "the rage of Peleus' son Achilles" and its consequences, but the poem also contains profound insights about war and peace, honor, duty, compassion, and life and death. Among the means Homer uses to reveal these themes are the following:

- characters' statements and actions
- events in the plot
- images and their associations

As you read, note the ideas and insights that the poem conveys.

Connecting Literary Elements

The *Iliad*'s opening statement of theme is also its first instance of **fore-shadowing,** the use of clues to suggest future events in a literary work. This technique creates suspense by building the audience's anticipation. For exam-ple, the *Iliad*'s opening lines leave the reader wondering why Achilles is enraged and what consequences might follow. Look for other examples of fore-shadowing as you read, and consider what effect the poet is trying to create.

Reading Strategy

Analyze Confusing Sentences

Homer wove lines dense with images and other details. To **analyze confusing sentences,** consider one section at a time. Look at a complex sen-tence, and separate its essential parts (the *who* and *what*) from the difficult language until you get to the main idea. As you read, use a chart like the one shown to help you analyze and interpret the meaning of difficult sentences.

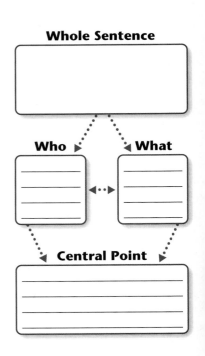

Vocabulary Development

incensed (in senst′) *adj.* very angry; enraged (p. 326)

plunder (plun′ dər) *v.* rob by force in warfare (p. 326)

sacrosanct (sak′ rō saŋkt′) *adj.* very holy; sacred (p. 327)

brazen (brā′ zən) *adj.* literally, of brass; shamelessly bold (p. 334)

harrowed (har′ ōd) *v.* distressed; tor-mented (p. 334)

bereft (bē reft′) *adj.* deprived or robbed (p. 337)

from the
ILIAD
Homer
translated by Robert Fagles

CHARACTERS

THE GREEKS
(Also called Achaeans, Danaans, and Argives)

ACHILLES (ə kil´ ēz): Son of Peleus, a mortal king, and the sea-goddess Thetis. The best warrior among the Achaeans; leader of the Myrmidons. Other names: Pelides, Aeacides.

AGAMEMNON (ag´ ə mem´ nän): King of Mycenae; husband of Clytemnestra; brother of Menelaus. Leader of the Greek expeditionary force. Other name: Atrides.

AJAX (ā´ jaks): The strongest warrior on the Greek side after Achilles.

HELEN (hel´ ən): Wife of Menelaus, king of Sparta.

CLYTEMNESTRA (klī´ təm nes´ trə): Wife of Agamemnon, sister of Helen.

MENELAUS (men´ ə lā´ əs): King of Sparta and the surrounding area (Lacedaemon). Son of Atreus, brother of Agamemnon, husband of Helen.

NESTOR (nes´ tər): King of Pylos, belonging to an older generation than the other Greek warriors. He serves as a wise old counselor.

ODYSSEUS (ō dis´ yōos´): King of Ithaca. The smoothest talker and wiliest thinker among the Greeks; a favorite of the goddess Athena.

PATROCLUS (pə träk´ ləs): Son of Menoetius, a companion and henchman to Achilles.

PELEUS (pēl´ yōos): Father of Achilles; husband of the goddess Thetis.

THE TROJANS
(Also called Dardanians and Phrygians)

ANDROMACHE (an dräm´ ə kē): Wife of Hector.

ASTYANAX (ə stī´ ə naks): Infant son of Hector and Andromache. Other name: Scamandrius.

BRISEIS (brī sē´ is): A Trojan captive girl, named after her father Briseus, given as a prize to Achilles.

CHRYSEIS (krī sē´ is): The daughter of Chryses, priest of Apollo. A captive girl given to Agamemnon as his prize.

HECTOR (hek´ tər): Son of Priam; leader of the Trojans and their greatest fighter.

PARIS (par´ is): Son of Priam.

PRIAM (prī´ əm): King of Troy; husband of Hecuba, father of Hector and Paris.

IMMORTALS

APHRODITE (af´ rō dī´ tē): Goddess of love, beauty; protects Helen and Paris and favors the Trojans. Other name: Lady of Cyprus.

APOLLO (ə päl´ ō): The archer god; a god of light and of healing. Apollo not only heals, he visits pestilence on men. He favors and protects the Trojans. Other names: Phoebus, Smintheus.

ARES (a´ rēz): God of war; favors the Trojans.

ATHENA (ə thē´ nə): Daughter of Zeus only (she has no mother). She emerged from her father's head fully armed and is associated with victory in war and clever thinking and speaking. She protects the Greeks. Other names: Pallas and Tritogenia.

HADES (hā´ dēz): Ruler of the dead and the underworld; brother of Zeus.

HERA (her´ ə): Sister and wife of Zeus; favors the Greeks.

HERMES (hʉr´ mēz´): Messenger god; son of Zeus.

THETIS (thet´ is): Sea goddess; wife of the mortal Peleus and mother of Achilles.

ZEUS (zōōs): The most powerful of the gods, known as "father of men and gods."

Background

   At the time of the Trojan War, Greece was not a unified nation. The Greek campaign against the Trojans was led by a loose group of independent tribal lords, or kings, who commanded their own soldiers. Leaders like Achilles and Agamemnon did not owe each other unconditional allegiance.

> Rage—Goddess, sing[1] the rage of Peleus' son Achilles,
> murderous, doomed, that cost the Achaeans[2] countless losses,
> hurling down to the House of Death so many sturdy souls,
> great fighters' souls, but made their bodies carrion,
> 5 feasts for the dogs and birds,
> and the will of Zeus was moving toward its end.
> Begin, Muse, when the two first broke and clashed,
> Agamemnon lord of men and brilliant Achilles.
>
>   What god drove them to fight with such a fury?
> 10 Apollo the son of Zeus and Leto. <u>Incensed</u> at the king
> he swept a fatal plague through the army—men were dying
> and all because Agamemnon spurned Apollo's priest.
> Yes, Chryses approached the Achaeans' fast ships
> to win his daughter back, bringing a priceless ransom
> 15 and bearing high in hand, wound on a golden staff,
> the wreaths of the god, the distant deadly Archer.
> He begged the whole Achaean army but most of all
> the two supreme commanders, Atreus' two sons,
> "Agamemnon, Menelaus—all Argives geared for war!
> 20 May the gods who hold the halls of Olympus[3] give you
> Priam's city[4] to <u>plunder</u>, then safe passage home.

Literary Analysis
Theme In these opening lines, what does the poet single out as his major theme?

incensed (in senst´) *adj.* very angry; enraged

plunder (plun´ dər) *v.* rob by force in warfare

---

1. **Goddess, sing** conventional epic opening whereby the narrator invites a goddess called a Muse to inspire in him the epic's story.
2. **Achaeans** (ə kē´ ənz) tribal name for the Greeks.
3. **Olympus** (ō lim´ pəs) mountain in Greece between Thessaly and Macedonia; mythological home of the gods.
4. **Priam's city** Troy.

Just set my daughter free, my dear one . . . here,
accept these gifts, this ransom. Honor the god
who strikes from worlds away—the son of Zeus, Apollo!"

25   And all ranks of Achaeans cried out their assent:
"Respect the priest, accept the shining ransom!"
But it brought no joy to the heart of Agamemnon.
The king dismissed the priest with a brutal order
ringing in his ears: "Never again, old man,
30 let me catch sight of you by the hollow ships!
Not loitering now, not slinking back tomorrow.
The staff and the wreaths of god will never save you then.
The girl—I won't give up the girl. Long before that,
old age will overtake her in *my* house, in Argos,[5]
35 far from her fatherland, slaving back and forth
at the loom, forced to share my bed!

                                    Now go,
don't tempt my wrath—and you may depart alive."

        The old man was terrified. He obeyed the order,
turning, trailing away in silence down the shore
40 where the battle lines of breakers crash and drag.
And moving off to a safe distance, over and over
the old priest prayed to the son of sleek-haired Leto,
lord Apollo, "Hear me, Apollo! God of the silver bow
who strides the walls of Chryse and Cilla <u>sacrosanct</u>—
45 lord in power of Tenedos[6]—Smintheus,[7] god of the
        plague!
If I ever roofed a shrine to please your heart,
ever burned the long rich bones of bulls and goats
on your holy altar, now, now bring my prayer to pass.
Pay the Danaans back—your arrows for my tears!"

50   His prayer went up and Phoebus Apollo heard him.
Down he strode from Olympus' peaks, storming at
        heart
with his bow and hooded quiver slung across his
        shoulders.
The arrows clanged at his back as the god quaked
        with rage,
the god himself on the march and down he came like
        night.
55 Over against the ships he dropped to a knee, let fly a
        shaft

---

sacrosanct (sak´ rō saŋkt´)
adj. very holy; sacred

▼ Critical Viewing
What are the advantages
and disadvantages of
armor like that worn by
Achilles, who is depicted
here? **[Analyze]**

---

5. **Argos** (är´ gäs´) city in the northwest of Peloponnese.
6. **Tenedos** (ten´ ə däs) island off the coast of Troad, the name given to the country of the Trojans.
7. **Smintheus** (smin´ thyo͞os) another name for Apollo; Smintheus means "rat/mouse god," an appropriate name for him as the god of plague.

☑ Reading Check
What does the priest
Chryses ask the Achaeans
to do?

and a terrifying clash rang out from the great silver bow.
First he went for the mules and circling dogs but then,
launching a piercing shaft at the men themselves,
he cut them down in droves—
60 and the corpse-fires burned on, night and day, no end in sight.

    Nine days the arrows of god swept through the army.
On the tenth Achilles called all ranks to muster—
the impulse seized him, sent by white-armed Hera
grieving to see Achaean fighters drop and die.
65 Once they'd gathered, crowding the meeting grounds,
the swift runner Achilles rose and spoke among them:
"Son of Atreus, now we are beaten back, I fear,
the long campaign is lost. So home we sail . . .
if we can escape our death—if war and plague
70 are joining forces now to crush the Argives.
But wait: let us question a holy man,
a prophet, even a man skilled with dreams—
dreams as well can come our way from Zeus—
come, someone to tell us why Apollo rages so,
75 whether he blames us for a vow we failed, or sacrifice.
If only the god would share the smoky savor of lambs

▼ **Critical Viewing**
Which details in this painting indicate that Achilles (left) is a soldier and Agamemnon (right) is a king? **[Infer]**

and full-grown goats, Apollo might be willing, still,
somehow, to save us from this plague."

                                                     So he proposed
and down he sat again as Calchas rose among them,

80   Thestor's son, the clearest by far of all the seers
who scan the flight of birds.[8] He knew all things that are,
all things that are past and all that are to come,
the seer who had led the Argive ships to Troy
with the second sight that god Apollo gave him.

85   For the armies' good the seer began to speak:

"Achilles, dear to Zeus . . .
you order me to explain Apollo's anger,
the distant deadly Archer? I will tell it all.
But strike a pact with me, swear you will defend me

90   with all your heart, with words and strength of hand.
For there is a man I will enrage—I see it now—
a powerful man who lords it over all the Argives,
one the Achaeans must obey . . . A mighty king,
raging against an inferior, is too strong.

95   Even if he can swallow down his wrath today,
still he will nurse the burning in his chest
until, sooner or later, he sends it bursting forth.
Consider it closely, Achilles. Will you save me?"

       And the matchless runner reassured him: "Courage!

100   Out with it now, Calchas. Reveal the will of god,
whatever you may know. And I swear by Apollo
dear to Zeus, the power you pray to, Calchas,
when you reveal god's will to the Argives—no one,
not while I am alive and see the light on earth, no one

105   will lay his heavy hands on you by the hollow ships.
None among all the armies. Not even if you mean
Agamemnon here who now claims to be, by far,
the best of the Achaeans."

                         The seer took heart
and this time he spoke out, bravely: "Beware—

110   he casts no blame for a vow we failed, a sacrifice.
The god's enraged because Agamemnon spurned his priest,
he refused to free his daughter, he refused the ransom.
That's why the Archer sends us pains and he will send us more
and never drive this shameful destruction from the Argives,

115   not till we give back the girl with sparkling eyes
to her loving father—no price, no ransom paid—
and carry a sacred hundred bulls to Chryse town.
Then we can calm the god, and only then appease him."

---

8. seers . . . birds people who read omens that are believed to be carried by certain birds.

Literary Analysis
Theme and Foreshadowing To whom do you think Calchas is referring when he speaks of the "wrath" of a "mighty king"? How do you know?

Reading Strategy
Analyze Confusing Sentences What is the central point of what Achilles says to Calchas in these lines?

**Reading Check**
According to Calchas, why is Apollo enraged?

So he declared and sat down. But among them rose
120 the fighting son of Atreus, lord of the far-flung kingdoms,
Agamemnon—furious, his dark heart filled to the brim,
blazing with anger now, his eyes like searing fire.
With a sudden, killing look he wheeled on Calchas first:
"Seer of misery! Never a word that works to my advantage!
125 Always misery warms your heart, your prophecies—
never a word of profit said or brought to pass.
Now, again, you divine[9] god's will for the armies,
bruit it about, as fact, why the deadly Archer
multiplies our pains: because I, I refused
130 that glittering price for the young girl Chryseis.
Indeed, I prefer *her* by far, the girl herself,
I want her mine in my own house! I rank her higher
than Clytemnestra, my wedded wife—she's nothing less
in build or breeding, in mind or works of hand.
135 But I am willing to give her back, even so,
if that is best for all. What I really want
is to keep my people safe, not see them dying.
But fetch me another prize, and straight off too,
else I alone of the Argives go without my honor.
140 That would be a disgrace. You are all witness,
look—*my* prize is snatched away!"
                                        But the swift runner
Achilles answered him at once, "Just how, Agamemnon,
great field marshal . . . most grasping man alive,
how can the generous Argives give you prizes now?
145 I know of no troves of treasure, piled, lying idle,
anywhere. Whatever we dragged from towns we plundered,
all's been portioned out. But collect it, call it back
from the rank and file? *That* would be the disgrace.
So return the girl to the god, at least for now.
150 We Achaeans will pay you back, three, four times over,
if Zeus will grant us the gift, somehow, someday,
to raze Troy's massive ramparts to the ground."

     But King Agamemnon countered, "Not so quickly,
brave as you are, godlike Achilles—trying to cheat *me*.
155 Oh no, you won't get past me, take me in that way!
What do you want? To cling to your own prize
while I sit calmly by—empty-handed here?
Is that why you order me to give her back?
No—if our generous Argives *will* give me a prize,
160 a match for my desires, equal to what I've lost,
well and good. But if they give me nothing
I will take a prize myself—your own, or Ajax'

---

9. divine (də vīn´) *v.* conjecture; guess.

Literary Analysis
Theme What does Agamemnon's insistence on having a prize imply about the values of Homeric warriors?

or Odysseus' prize—I'll commandeer her myself
and let that man I go to visit choke with rage!

165   Enough. We'll deal with all this later, in due time.
Now come, we haul a black ship down to the bright sea,
gather a decent number of oarsmen along her locks
and put aboard a sacrifice, and Chryseis herself,
in all her beauty . . . we embark her too.

170   Let one of the leading captains take command.
Ajax, Idomeneus, trusty Odysseus or you, Achilles,
you—the most violent man alive—so you can perform
the rites for us and calm the god yourself."

                                      A dark glance
and the headstrong runner answered him in kind: "Shameless—

175   armored in shamelessness—always shrewd with greed!
How could any Argive soldier obey your orders,
freely and gladly do your sailing for you
or fight your enemies, full force? Not I, no.
It wasn't Trojan spearmen who brought me here to
        fight.

180   The Trojans never did *me* damage, not in the least,
they never stole my cattle or my horses, never
in Phthia[10] where the rich soil breeds strong men
did they lay waste my crops. How could they?
Look at the endless miles that lie between us . . .

185   shadowy mountain ranges, seas that surge and thunder.
No, you colossal, shameless—we all followed you,
to please you, to fight for you, to win your honor
back from the Trojans—Menelaus and you, you dog-face!
What do *you* care? Nothing. You don't look right or left.

190   And now you threaten to strip me of my prize in person—
the one I fought for long and hard, and sons of Achaea
handed her to me.

                      My honors never equal yours,
whenever we sack some wealthy Trojan stronghold—
my arms bear the brunt of the raw, savage fighting,

195   true, but when it comes to dividing up the plunder
the lion's share is yours, and back I go to my ships,
clutching some scrap, some pittance that I love,
when I have fought to exhaustion.

                                      No more now—
back I go to Phthia. Better that way by far,

200   to journey home in the beaked ships of war.
I have no mind to linger here disgraced,
brimming your cup and piling up your plunder."

      But the lord of men Agamemnon shot back,

▲ Critical Viewing
This mask, thought to be
one of Agamemnon, is
made of solid gold. What
does this fact suggest
about Agamemnon's sta-
tus in society? [Infer]

✔ Reading Check
Why does Achilles
threaten to leave the
battle?

---

10. **Phthia** (fthi´ ə) Achilles' home in northern Greece.

Minerva restrains Achilles from killing Agamemnon, Giambattista Tiepolo, Scala

▲ **Critical Viewing** This painting depicts Athena restraining Achilles from attacking Agamemnon. Based on the painting, what do you think would have happened if Athena had not intervened? **[Speculate]**

"*Desert*, by all means—if the spirit drives you home!
205 I will never beg you to stay, not on *my* account.
Never—others will take my side and do me honor,
Zeus above all, whose wisdom rules the world.
You—I hate you most of all the warlords
loved by the gods. Always dear to your heart,
210 strife, yes, and battles, the bloody grind of war.
What if you are a great soldier? That's just a gift of god.
Go home with your ships and comrades, lord it over
          your Myrmidons![11]
You *are* nothing to me—you and your overweening anger!
But let this be my warning on your way:
215 since Apollo insists on taking my Chryseis,
I'll send her back in my own ships with *my* crew.
But I, I will be there in person at your tents
to take Briseis in all her beauty, your own prize—
so you can learn just how much greater I am than you
220 and the next man up may shrink from matching words with me,
from hoping to rival Agamemnon strength for strength!"

      He broke off and anguish gripped Achilles.
The heart in his rugged chest was pounding, torn . . .
Should he draw the long sharp sword at his hip,
225 thrust through the ranks and kill Agamemnon now?—
or check his rage and beat his fury down?
As his racing spirit veered back and forth,
just as he drew his huge blade from its sheath,
down from the vaulting heavens swept Athena,
230 the white-armed goddess Hera sped her down:
Hera loved both men and cared for both alike.
Rearing behind him Pallas seized his fiery hair—
only Achilles saw her, none of the other fighters—
struck with wonder he spun around, he knew her at once,
235 Pallas Athena! the terrible blazing of those eyes,
and his winged words went flying: "Why, why now?
Child of Zeus with the shield of thunder, why come now?
To witness the outrage Agamemnon just committed?
I tell you this, and so help me it's the truth—
240 he'll soon pay for his arrogance with his life!"

      Her gray eyes clear, the goddess Athena answered,
"Down from the skies I come to check your rage
if only you will yield.
The white-armed goddess Hera sped me down:
245 she loves you both, she cares for you both alike.
Stop this fighting, now. Don't lay hand to sword.
Lash him with threats of the price that he will face.

---

11. **Myrmidons** (mur´ mə dänz´) Achilles' warriors from his home in northern Greece.

Reading Check

Whom does Agamemnon claim as his prize in place of Chryseis?

And I tell you this—and I *know* it is the truth—
one day glittering gifts will lie before you,
250   three times over to pay for all his outrage.
Hold back now. Obey us both."

                                    So she urged
and the swift runner complied at once: "I must—
when the two of you hand down commands, Goddess,
a man submits though his heart breaks with fury.
255   Better for him by far. If a man obeys the gods
they're quick to hear his prayers."

                                    And with that
Achilles stayed his burly hand on the silver hilt
and slid the huge blade back in its sheath.
He would not fight the orders of Athena.
260   Soaring home to Olympus, she rejoined the
          gods
aloft in the halls of Zeus whose shield is
          thunder.

      But Achilles rounded on Agamemnon
          once again,
lashing out at him, not relaxing his anger for a
          moment:
"Staggering drunk, with your dog's eyes, your fawn's heart!
265   Never once did you arm with the troops and go to battle
or risk an ambush packed with Achaea's picked men—
you lack the courage, you can see death coming.
Safer by far, you find, to foray all through camp,
commandeering the prize of any man who speaks against you.
270   King who devours his people! Worthless husks, the men you rule—
if not, Atrides,[12] this outrage would have been your last.
I tell you this, and I swear a mighty oath upon it . . .
by this, this scepter, look,
that never again will put forth crown and branches,
275   now it's left its stump on the mountain ridge forever,
nor will it sprout new green again, now the <u>brazen</u> ax
has stripped its bark and leaves, and now the sons of Achaea
pass it back and forth as they hand their judgments down,
upholding the honored customs whenever Zeus commands—
280   This scepter will be the mighty force behind my oath:
someday, I swear, a yearning for Achilles will strike
Achaea's sons and all your armies! But then, Atrides,
<u>harrowed</u> as you will be, *nothing* you do can save you—
not when your hordes of fighters drop and die,
285   cut down by the hands of man-killing Hector! Then—
then you will tear your heart out, desperate, raging
that you disgraced the best of the Achaeans!"

▲ **Critical Viewing**
Do you think that this
stone carving of Achilles
conveys the hero's "god-
like" qualities? Why or
why not? **[Evalulate]**

brazen (brā´ zən) *adj.* literally, of brass; shamelessly
bold

harrowed (har´ ōd) *v.* distressed; tormented

---

12. Atrides (ə trī´ dəz) literally, son of Atreus; another name for Agamemnon.

Nestor, one of the wisest Greek commanders and counselors, advises Agamemnon and Achilles to concede to each other; both men refuse. To appease the gods and spare the Achaeans further annihilation, Agamemnon orders Odysseus to return Chryseis. As compensation for his lost war prize, Agamemnon abducts Achilles' Briseis. Dishonored, Achilles swears that never again will he join the Achaeans in fighting against the Trojans. He convinces Thetis to persuade Zeus to help the Trojans defeat the Achaeans.

But he raged on, grimly camped by his fast fleet,
the royal son of Peleus, the swift runner Achilles,
290 Now he no longer haunted the meeting grounds
where men win glory, now he no longer went to war
but day after day he ground his heart out, waiting there,
yearning, always yearning for battle cries and combat.

But now as the twelfth dawn after this shone clear
295 the gods who live forever marched home to Olympus,
all in a long cortege, and Zeus led them on.
And Thetis did not forget her son's appeals.
She broke from a cresting wave at first light
and soaring up to the broad sky and Mount Olympus,
300 found the son of Cronus gazing down on the world,
peaks apart from the other gods and seated high
on the topmost crown of rugged ridged Olympus.
And crouching down at his feet,
quickly grasping his knees with her left hand,
305 her right hand holding him underneath the chin,
she prayed to the lord god Zeus, the son of Cronus:
"Zeus, Father Zeus! If I ever served you well
among the deathless gods with a word or action,
bring this prayer to pass: honor my son Achilles!—
310 doomed to the shortest life of any man on earth.
And now the lord of men Agamemnon has disgraced him,
seizes and keeps his prize, tears her away himself. But you—
exalt him, Olympian Zeus: your urgings rule the world!
Come, grant the Trojans victory after victory
315 till the Achaean armies pay my dear son back,
building higher the honor he deserves!"

Literary Analysis
Theme In what way does this passage reinforce the theme stated at the opening of the *Iliad*?

✔**Reading Check**

Whose help does Thetis seek on behalf of her son, Achilles?

HECTOR RETURNS TO TROY

At Thetis' request, Zeus intervenes to help the Trojans defeat the Achaeans. Bitter fighting resumes, causing massive casualties on both sides. Although the Achaeans suffer a disadvantage from Achilles' absence, they manage to subdue the Trojans. Under the leadership of Diomedes, the Achaeans drive the Trojans back into temporary retreat behind the city gates. Realizing the gravity of the Trojan cause, Hector and his men go to Priam's palace to urge the gods to take pity on Troy. Hector also tries to persuade his brother Paris, who caused the war by abducting Helen, to fight. Finally, Hector goes in search of his wife, Andromache.

A flash of his helmet

and off he strode and quickly reached his sturdy,
well-built house. But white-armed Andromache—
Hector could not find her in the halls.
5   She and the boy and a servant finely gowned
were standing watch on the tower, sobbing, grieving.
When Hector saw no sign of his loyal wife inside
he went to the doorway, stopped and asked the servants,
"Come, please, tell me the truth now, women.
10   Where's Andromache gone? To my sisters' house?
To my brothers' wives with their long flowing robes?
Or Athena's shrine where the noble Trojan women
gather to win the great grim goddess over?"

A busy, willing servant answered quickly,
15   "Hector, seeing you want to know the truth,
she hasn't gone to your sisters, brothers' wives
or Athena's shrine where the noble Trojan women
gather to win the great grim goddess over.
Up to the huge gate-tower of Troy she's gone
20   because she heard our men are so hard-pressed,
the Achaean fighters coming on in so much force.
She sped to the wall in panic, like a madwoman—
the nurse went with her, carrying your child."

                    At that, Hector spun and rushed from his house,
25   back by the same way down the wide, well-paved streets
        throughout the city until he reached the Scaean Gates,[1]
        the last point he would pass to gain the field of battle.
        There his warm, generous wife came running up to meet him,
        Andromache the daughter of gallant-hearted Eetion[2]
30   who had lived below Mount Placos[3] rich with timber,
        in Thebe below the peaks, and ruled Cilicia's people.[4]
        His daughter had married Hector helmed in bronze.
        She joined him now, and following in her steps
        a servant holding the boy against her breast,
35   in the first flush of life, only a baby,
        Hector's son, the darling of his eyes
        and radiant as a star . . .
        Hector would always call the boy Scamandrius,
        townsmen called him Astyanax, Lord of the City,
40   since Hector was the lone defense of Troy.
        The great man of war breaking into a broad smile,
        his gaze fixed on his son, in silence. Andromache,
        pressing close beside him and weeping freely now,
        clung to his hand, urged him, called him: "Reckless one,
45   my Hector—your own fiery courage will destroy you!
        Have you no pity for *him*, our helpless son? Or me,
        and the destiny that weighs me down, your widow,
        now so soon? Yes, soon they will kill you off,
        all the Achaean forces massed for assault, and then,
50   <u>bereft</u> of you, better for me to sink beneath the earth.
        What other warmth, what comfort's left for me,
        once you have met your doom? Nothing but torment!
        I have lost my father. Mother's gone as well.
        Father . . . the brilliant Achilles laid him low
55   when he stormed Cilicia's city filled with people,
        Thebe with her towering gates. He killed Eetion,
        not that he stripped his gear—he'd some respect at least—
        for he burned his corpse in all his blazoned bronze,
        then heaped a grave-mound high above the ashes
60   and nymphs[5] of the mountain planted elms around it,
        daughters of Zeus whose shield is storm and thunder.
        And the seven brothers I had within our halls . . .
        all in the same day went down to the House of Death,
        the great godlike runner Achilles butchered them all,
65   tending their shambling oxen, shining flocks.

---

1. **Scaean** (sē´ ən) **Gates** northwest gates of Troy.
2. **Eetion** (ē ē´ tē än´) king of Thebe, a city near Troy.
3. **Mount Placos** (pla´ käs) mountain dominating Thebe.
4. **Cilicia's** (sə li´ shəz) **people** people of a region in southeast Asia Minor.
5. **nymphs** (nimfs) goddesses of nature.

Reading Strategy
Analyze Confusing Sentences Which details in lines 28–31 are not essential to the central point of the sentence?

bereft (bē reft´) *adj.* deprived or robbed

Reading Check

Who does Andromache say killed her father, Eetion?

And mother,

who ruled under the timberline of woody Placos once—
he no sooner haled her here with his other plunder
than he took a priceless ransom, set her free
and home she went to her father's royal halls
70 where Artemis,[6] showering arrows, shot her down.
You, Hector—you are my father now, my noble mother,
a brother too, and you are my husband, young and warm
      and strong!
Pity me, please! Take your stand on the rampart here,
before you orphan your son and make your wife a widow.
75 Draw your armies up where the wild fig tree stands,
there, where the city lies most open to assault,
the walls lower, easily overrun. Three times
they have tried that point, hoping to storm Troy,
their best fighters led by the Great and Little Ajax,[7]
80 famous Idomeneus,[8] Atreus' sons, valiant Diomedes.[9]
Perhaps a skilled prophet revealed the spot—
or their own fury whips them on to attack."

    And tall Hector nodded, his helmet flashing:
"All this weighs on my mind too, dear woman.
85 But I would die of shame to face the men of Troy
and the Trojan women trailing their long robes
if I would shrink from battle now, a coward.
Nor does the spirit urge me on that way.
I've learned it all too well. To stand up bravely,
90 always to fight in the front ranks of Trojan soldiers,
winning my father great glory, glory for myself.
For in my heart and soul I also know this well:
the day will come when sacred Troy must die,
Priam must die and all his people with him,
95 Priam who hurls the strong ash spear . . .

Even so,

it is less the pain of the Trojans still to come
that weighs me down, not even of Hecuba[10] herself
or King Priam, or the thought that my own brothers
in all their numbers, all their gallant courage,
100 may tumble in the dust, crushed by enemies—
That is nothing, nothing beside your agony
when some brazen Argive hales you off in tears,
wrenching away your day of light and freedom!

---

6. **Artemis** (är′ tə mis) goddess of the hunt and of the moon; daughter of Zeus and Leto; sister of Apollo.
7. **Great and Little Ajax** Ajax of Salamis, son of Telamon, and Ajax of Locris, son of Oileus.
8. **Idomeneus** (ī dä′ men yōōs) commander of the Achaean forces from Crete; son of Deucalion.
9. **Diomedes** (dī′ ə mē′ dēz) son of Tydeus, king of Argos.
10. **Hecuba** (hek′ yōō bə) queen of Troy; wife of Priam; mother of Hector.

Literary Analysis
Theme and Foreshadowing What do Andromache's comments in this passage suggest about the fate of Hector, his family, and the city of Troy?

Critical Viewing ▶
How well do you think this painting captures the mood of Hector's farewell to his family? Explain. **[Evaluate]**

Then far off in the land of Argos you must live,
105 laboring at a loom, at another woman's beck and call,
fetching water at some spring, Messeis or Hyperia,[11]
resisting it all the way—
the rough yoke of necessity at your neck.
And a man may say, who sees you streaming tears,
110 'There is the wife of Hector, the bravest fighter
they could field, those stallion-breaking Trojans,
long ago when the men fought for Troy.' So he will say

---

11. **Messeis** (me sē′ is) . . . **Hyperia** (hip′ ə rī′ ə) locations of springs in Greece.

☑Reading Check

What does Andromache think will happen to Hector if he goes into battle?

Hector Taking Leave of Andromache, Angelica Kauffmann, Tate Gallery, London

and the fresh grief will swell your heart once more,
widowed, robbed of the one man strong enough
115   to fight off your day of slavery.
                                          No, no,
let the earth come piling over my dead body
before I hear your cries, I hear you dragged away!"

    In the same breath, shining Hector reached down
for his son—but the boy recoiled,
120   cringing against his nurse's full breast,
screaming out at the sight of his own father,
terrified by the flashing bronze, the horsehair crest,
the great ridge of the helmet nodding, bristling terror—
so it struck his eyes. And his loving father laughed,
125   his mother laughed as well, and glorious Hector,
quickly lifting the helmet from his head,
set it down on the ground, fiery in the sunlight,
and raising his son he kissed him, tossed him in his arms,
lifting a prayer to Zeus and the other deathless gods:
130   "Zeus, all you immortals! Grant this boy, my son,
may be like me, first in glory among the Trojans,
strong and brave like me, and rule all Troy in power
and one day let them say, 'He is a better man than his father!'—
when he comes home from battle bearing the bloody gear
135   of the mortal enemy he has killed in war—
a joy to his mother's heart."
                                          So Hector prayed
and placed his son in the arms of his loving wife.
Andromache pressed the child to her scented breast,
smiling through her tears. Her husband noticed,
140   and filled with pity now, Hector stroked her gently,
trying to reassure her, repeating her name: "Andromache,
dear one, why so desperate? Why so much grief for me?
No man will hurl me down to Death, against my fate.
And fate? No one alive has ever escaped it,
145   neither brave man nor coward, I tell you—
it's born with us the day that we are born.
So please go home and tend to your own tasks,
the distaff and the loom, and keep the women
working hard as well. As for the fighting,
150   men will see to that, all who were born in Troy
but I most of all."

    *Andromache goes home, where she and her handmaidens
    mourn Hector in anticipation of his death. Paris takes arms and
    joins Hector in driving the Achaeans out of Troy. Hector and the
    Trojans campaign vigorously until they completely drive the*

Literary Analysis
Theme What outlook on
life and death does Hector
express in this passage?

Achaeans off the battlefield back to their ships. To prevent the Achaeans from sailing away, the Trojans light watchfires and camp on the plain overnight, ready to attack in the morning. The demoralized Achaean army feels handicapped by Achilles' absence. To persuade their most valuable fighter to reconsider and join the battle, Agamemnon sends Ajax and Odysseus on an embassy to Achilles.

In his speech to Achilles, Odysseus reminds him of his father's advice. Peleus had told Achilles that the Argives would hold him in higher honor if he did not let the anger of his proud heart get the best of him. Odysseus adds that if Achilles gives up his anger and joins the Achaeans in battle, Agamemnon has promised to give Achilles numerous war prizes, including the prize he stole: Briseis. Finally, Odysseus pleads with Achilles to fight, if not in acceptance of Agamemnon's offer, at least for the afflicted Achaeans who will honor Achilles as a god. Agamemnon's offer serves only to drive Achilles deeper into his pride. Hurt, dishonored, and, above all, angry, he refuses to help the Greeks defeat Hector and the Trojans. Odysseus and Ajax return to Agamemnon with the news of their unsuccessful embassy.

Odysseus' Mission to Achilles, Cleophrades Painter, Staatliche Antikensammlungen und Glyptothek, Munich

▲ **Critical Viewing**
This urn depicts Ajax's and Odysseus' embassy to Achilles. Why do you think the ancient Greeks depicted scenes from the *Iliad* in various art forms? **[Infer]**

Review and Assess

Thinking About the Selection

1. **Respond:** With whom would you side in the argument between Achilles and Agamemnon in Book 1? Why?

2. **(a) Recall:** As the *Iliad* begins, what problem confronts the Greeks? **(b) Infer:** Why is the problem of such importance to the soldiers and their campaign?

3. **(a) Recall:** Why does Agamemnon claim Briseis as his prize? **(b) Analyze Causes and Effects:** How does this action relate to Achilles' decision to withdraw from battle?

4. **(a) Recall:** In Book 6, what prediction does Hector make about Troy's destiny? **(b) Compare and Contrast:** In light of this prediction, compare and contrast the poem's portrayals of Achilles and Hector as heroes so far.

5. **(a) Generalize:** What does the concept of honor seem to mean in the Homeric world? Explain. **(b) Take a Position:** Do you agree with this notion of honor? Why or why not?

Review and Assess

Literary Analysis

Theme

1. What **theme** does the quarrel between Agamemnon and Achilles reveal regarding the nature of honor and status in Homeric society?

2. (a) What conflicting feelings does Achilles experience as a result of his decision to withdraw from battle? (b) What theme of the poem does this dilemma help convey?

3. (a) Using a chart like the one shown, compare and contrast Hector's outlook on war, duty, and heroism with that of Achilles.

	Achilles' Outlook	Hector's Outlook
War		
Duty		
Heroism		

(b) What themes are highlighted by the similarities or differences in the two characters' outlooks on each of these subjects?

Connecting Literary Elements

4. In her speech to Zeus in Book 1, what fact about Achilles' destiny does his mother Thetis **foreshadow**?

5. Considering that Homer's audience knew the Greeks would ultimately defeat the Trojans, what effect do you think the foreshadowing in Book 6 is meant to have? Explain.

Reading Strategy

Analyze Confusing Sentences

6. Are the words *"dreams as well can come our way from Zeus"* essential to the main idea of the sentence beginning on line 71 of Book 1? Why or why not?

7. Identify the main idea of the sentence that begins on line 298 of Book 1 by rewriting it to include only essential information.

Extend Understanding

8. **Cultural Connection:** Do the characters in the *Iliad* place greater value on prizes and material possessions than do people in contemporary American society? Explain your answer.

Integrate Language Skills

Vocabulary Development Lesson

Word Analysis: Latin Root -sacr-

The word *sacrosanct* contains the Latin root *-sacr-*, which means "sacred or holy." Add the root *-sacr-* to the following word parts. Then, write a brief definition of each word.

1. -ed   2. -ilege   3. -ifice

Spelling Strategy

In American English, words ending in the sound *ens* are usually spelled with *ence*, as in *reverence*. However, there are some that end with *ense*, such as *incense*. Complete each word below with the correct spelling of the *ens* sound.

1. nons-   2. pres-   3. int-

Grammar and Style Lesson

Compound Adjectives

An adjective modifies or clarifies the meaning of a noun or pronoun. A **compound adjective** is an adjective made up of two or more words. Most are hyphenated; others are combined into one word.

Hyphenated: *well-built* house
full-grown goats

Combined: *godlike* Achilles
topmost crown

Practice Use the italicized words to form compound adjectives in the following sentences.

1. The old priest prayed to the son of *sleek haired* Leto, lord Apollo.

Concept Development: Synonyms

Select the letter of the word that is closest in meaning to the first word.

1. incensed: (a) eager, (b) angry, (c) anxious
2. plunder: (a) flatter, (b) rebuild, (c) ransack
3. sacrosanct: (a) abundant, (b) empty, (c) respected
4. harrowed: (a) troubled, (b) relieved, (c) denounced
5. bereft: (a) joyful, (b) deprived, (c) humbled
6. brazen: (a) impudent, (b) ashamed, (c) mournful

2. Among them rose Agamemnon, lord of the *far flung* kingdoms.
3. The *head strong* runner answered him in kind.
4. Andromache was the daughter of *gallant hearted* Eetion.
5. She was *heart broken* when Hector went off to battle.

Writing Application In a paragraph, describe what you think will happen when Hector enters the battle. Use four compound adjectives in your writing: two with hyphens and two without.

WG *Prentice Hall Writing and Grammar Connection: Diamond Level, Chapter 17, Section 3*

Extension Activities

Writing Take an event from your daily life and write an **everyday epic** version of it. Use Homeric techniques to make your characters and events seem larger than life.

Research and Technology With classmates, create a **multimedia map** of the region in which the *Iliad* takes place. Include pictures, recordings, and references to the poem. **[Group Activity]**

Prepare to Read

from the Iliad, Books 22 and 24

Literary Analysis

Imagery

Imagery is the descriptive language that writers use to re-create sensory experiences. It is what helps you see, hear, feel, smell, and taste what is being described. Imagery can enrich a passage by making it more vivid, by setting a tone, by suggesting emotions, or by guiding a reader's reactions. In the *Iliad*, certain recurring images also help establish and reinforce the poem's themes. As you read, use a chart like the one shown to link patterns of images with the poem's central ideas.

Connecting Literary Elements

Among the most vivid images in the *Iliad* are those in Homer's **epic similes.** An epic simile, also called a Homeric or an extended simile, is a lengthy comparison of two dissimilar things introduced by the word *like* or *as*. Unlike a simple simile, which involves a single, distinct image, an epic simile is longer and more elaborate. It might recall an entire place or story.

Notice how this description of Hector heightens the suspense of his battle with Achilles:

> . . . like a soaring eagle
> launching down from the dark clouds to earth
> to snatch some helpless lamb or trembling hare.
> So Hector swooped now, swinging his whetted sword

Look for other epic similes as you read, and consider how they enrich the story.

Reading Strategy

Picture the Action

To keep track of the fast-paced action and fully appreciate Homer's verse, pause occasionally to **picture the action.** Use the details and descriptions to help you form a mental image of what you are reading. These mental pictures will help the poem come alive.

Vocabulary Development

implore (im plôr´) *v.* beg (p. 346)

marshals (mär´ shəlz) *v.* arranges in order; commands (p. 348)

whetted (wet´ id) *adj.* sharpened (p. 351)

brandished (bran´ disht) *v.* waved or shook in a threatening manner (p. 351)

stinted (stint´ id) *v.* limited to a certain quantity (p. 361)

lustrous (lus´ trəs) *adj.* shining (p. 365)

gaunt (gônt) *adj.* thin and bony; haggard (p. 366)

illustrious (i lus´ trē əs) *adj.* distinguished; famous (p. 370)

Review and Anticipate

As Book 1 opens, the Greek army besieging Troy is stricken by a plague, sent by the god Apollo to punish Agamemnon's refusal to ransom a captive girl, Chryseis. Agamemnon reluctantly returns the girl to her father, but he replaces her with another female captive, Briseis, who is Achilles' prize. The two warriors quarrel, and Achilles withdraws from the battle in protest.

The tide of battle then turns in favor of Hector and the Trojans. Achilles refuses Agamemnon's offer of compensation for returning to battle, and the Greeks suffer heavy losses. Achilles finally agrees to allow his friend Patroclus to fight wearing Achilles' armor. Patroclus manages to drive the Trojans back to the city walls, but Apollo intervenes, allowing Hector to slay Patroclus and strip the body of its armor. Almost mad with grief, Achilles re-enters the battle wearing new armor made for him by the god Hephaestus. The confrontation in Book 22 between Achilles and Hector, so long delayed, is the dramatic climax of the epic.

Clad in his divine armor, Achilles re-enters the war to avenge Patroclus' death. He kills every Trojan in his path. During Achilles' combat with Hector's half-brother Agenor, Apollo assumes Agenor's shape and diverts Achilles from Troy, allowing the Trojan troops to take refuge in the city. Priam and Hecuba try unsuccessfully to convince Hector to stay within the walls, safe from Achilles.

    So they wept, the two of them crying out
to their dear son, both pleading time and again
but they could not shake the fixed resolve of Hector.
No, he waited Achilles, coming on, gigantic in power.
5 As a snake in the hills, guarding his hole, awaits a man—
bloated with poison, deadly hatred seething inside him,
glances flashing fire as he coils round his lair . . .
so Hector, nursing his quenchless fury, gave no ground,
leaning his burnished shield against a jutting wall,
10 but harried still, he probed his own brave heart:
"No way out. If I slip inside the gates and walls,
Polydamas[1] will be first to heap disgrace on me—

Literary Analysis
Imagery What emotions does the image in these lines convey?

---

1. **Polydamas** (pǝ lid′ ǝ mǝs) Trojan commander who frequently opposed Hector's recklessness.

he was the one who urged me to lead our Trojans
back to Ilium just last night, the disastrous night

15 Achilles rose in arms like a god. But did I give way?
Not at all. And how much better it would have been!
Now my army's ruined, thanks to my own reckless pride,
I would die of shame to face the men of Troy
and the Trojan women trailing their long robes . . .

20 Someone less of a man than I will say, 'Our Hector—
staking all on his own strength, he destroyed his army!'
So they will mutter. So now, better by far for me
to stand up to Achilles, kill him, come home alive
or die at his hands in glory out before the walls.

25 But wait—what if I put down my studded shield
and heavy helmet, prop my spear on the rampart
and go forth, just as I am, to meet Achilles,
noble Prince Achilles . . .
why, I could promise to give back Helen, yes,

30 and all her treasures with her, all those riches
Paris once hauled home to Troy in the hollow ships—
and they were the cause of all our endless fighting—
Yes, yes, return it all to the sons of Atreus now
to haul away, and then, at the same time, divide

35 the rest with all the Argives, all the city holds,
and then I'd take an oath for the Trojan royal council
that we will hide nothing! Share and share alike the hoards
our handsome citadel stores within its depths and—
Why debate, my friend? Why thrash things out?

40 I must not go and <u>implore</u> him. He'll show no mercy,
no respect for me, my rights—he'll cut me down
straight off—stripped of defenses like a woman
once I have loosed the armor off my body.
No way to parley with that man—not now—

45 not from behind some oak or rock to whisper,
like a boy and a young girl, lovers' secrets
a boy and girl might whisper to each other . . .
Better to clash in battle, now, at once—
see which fighter Zeus awards the glory!"

                                          So he wavered,

50 waiting there, but Achilles was closing on him now
like the god of war, the fighter's helmet flashing,
over his right shoulder shaking the Pelian[2] ash spear,
that terror, and the bronze around his body flared
like a raging fire or the rising, blazing sun.

55 Hector looked up, saw him, started to tremble,
nerve gone, he could hold his ground no longer,

implore (im plôr′) *v.* beg

---

2. Pelian (pēl′ ē ən) of Achilles' spear, which was made on Pelion, a mountain in Magnesia.

he left the gates behind and away he fled in fear—
and Achilles went for him, fast, sure of his speed
as the wild mountain hawk, the quickest thing on wings,
60 launching smoothly, swooping down on a cringing dove
and the dove flits out from under, the hawk screaming
over the quarry, plunging over and over, his fury
driving him down to beak and tear his kill—
so Achilles flew at him, breakneck on in fury
65 with Hector fleeing along the walls of Troy,
fast as his legs would go. On and on they raced,
passing the lookout point, passing the wild fig tree
tossed by the wind, always out from under the ramparts
down the wagon trail they careered until they reached
70 the clear running springs where whirling Scamander
rises up from its double wellsprings bubbling strong—
and one runs hot and the steam goes up around it,
drifting thick as if fire burned at its core
but the other even in summer gushes cold
75 as hail or freezing snow or water chilled to ice . . .
And here, close to the springs, lie washing-pools
scooped out in the hollow rocks and broad and smooth
where the wives of Troy and all their lovely daughters
would wash their glistening robes in the old days,
80 the days of peace before the sons of Achaea came . . .
Past these they raced, one escaping, one in pursuit
and the one who fled was great but the one pursuing
greater, even greater—their pace mounting in speed
since both men strove, not for a sacrificial beast
85 or oxhide trophy, prizes runners fight for, no,
they raced for the life of Hector breaker of horses.
Like powerful stallions sweeping round the post for trophies,
galloping full stretch with some fine prize at stake,
a tripod, say, or woman offered up at funeral games
90 for some brave hero fallen—so the two of them
whirled three times around the city of Priam,
sprinting at top speed while all the gods gazed down,
and the father of men and gods broke forth among them now:
"Unbearable—a man I love, hunted round his own city walls
95 and right before my eyes. My heart grieves for Hector.
Hector who burned so many oxen in my honor, rich cuts,
now on the rugged crests of Ida,[3] now on Ilium's heights.
But now, look, brilliant Achilles courses him round
the city of Priam in all his savage, lethal speed.
100 Come, you immortals, think this through. Decide.
Either we pluck the man from death and save his life

Literary Analysis
Imagery and Epic Simile
What does this epic simile suggest about the character of Achilles?

Reading Strategy
Picture the Action In what way does the image of Trojan women at the washing-pools enrich the battle scene?

✓**Reading Check**
Why does Hector rule out the idea of approaching Achilles peacefully?

---

3. **Ida** (īd´ ə) central mountain and range of Troad; favored seat of Zeus.

from the *Iliad*, Book 22: *The Death of Hector* ◆ 347

or strike him down at last, here at Achilles' hands—
for all his fighting heart."
                    But immortal Athena,
her gray eyes wide, protested strongly: "Father!
105 Lord of the lightning, king of the black cloud,
what are you saying? A man, a mere mortal,
his doom sealed long ago? You'd set him free
from all the pains of death?
                    Do as you please—
but none of the deathless gods will ever praise you."

110 And Zeus who <u>marshals</u> the thunderheads replied,
"Courage, Athena, third-born of the gods, dear child.
Nothing I said was meant in earnest, trust me,
I mean you all the good will in the world. Go.
Do as your own impulse bids you. Hold back no more."

115 So he launched Athena already poised for action—
down the goddess swept from Olympus' craggy peaks.

    And swift Achilles kept on coursing Hector, nonstop
as a hound in the mountains starts a fawn from its lair,
hunting him down the gorges, down the narrow glens
120 and the fawn goes to ground, hiding deep in brush
but the hound comes racing fast, nosing him out
until he lands his kill. So Hector could never throw
Achilles off his trail, the swift racer Achilles—
time and again he'd make a dash for the Dardan Gates,
125 trying to rush beneath the rock-built ramparts, hoping
men on the heights might save him, somehow, raining spears
but time and again Achilles would intercept him quickly,
heading him off, forcing him out across the plain
and always sprinting along the city side himself—
130 endless as in a dream . . .
when a man can't catch another fleeing on ahead
and he can never escape nor his rival overtake him—
so the one could never run the other down in his speed
nor the other spring away. And how could Hector have fled
135 the fates of death so long? How unless one last time,
one final time Apollo had swept in close beside him,
driving strength in his legs and knees to race the wind?
And brilliant Achilles shook his head at the armies,
never letting them hurl their sharp spears at Hector—
140 someone might snatch the glory, Achilles come in second.
But once they reached the springs for the fourth time,
then Father Zeus held out his sacred golden scales:
in them he placed two fates of death that lays men low—

▲ Critical Viewing
How does this sculpture
of Apollo compare with
the way the god is pre-
sented in the *Iliad*?
[Compare and Contrast]

marshals (mär´ shəlz)
v. arranges in order;
commands

one for Achilles, one for Hector breaker of horses—
145 and gripping the beam mid-haft the Father raised it high
and down went Hector's day of doom, dragging him down
to the strong House of Death—and god Apollo left him.
Athena rushed to Achilles, her bright eyes gleaming,
standing shoulder-to-shoulder, winging orders now:
150 "At last our hopes run high, my brilliant Achilles—
Father Zeus must love you—
we'll sweep great glory back to Achaea's fleet,
we'll kill this Hector, mad as he is for battle!
No way for him to escape us now, no longer—
155 not even if Phoebus the distant deadly Archer
goes through torments, pleading for Hector's life,
groveling over and over before our storming Father Zeus.
But you, you hold your ground and catch your breath
while I run Hector down and persuade the man
160 to fight you face-to-face."

                            So Athena commanded
and he obeyed, rejoicing at heart—Achilles stopped,
leaning against his ashen spearshaft barbed in bronze.
And Athena left him there, caught up with Hector at once,
and taking the build and vibrant voice of Deiphobus[4]
165 stood shoulder-to-shoulder with him, winging orders:
"Dear brother, how brutally swift Achilles hunts you—
coursing you round the city of Priam in all his lethal speed!
Come, let us stand our ground together—beat him back."

    "Deiphobus!"—Hector, his helmet flashing, called out to her—
170 "dearest of all my brothers, all these warring years,
of all the sons that Priam and Hecuba produced!
Now I'm determined to praise you all the more,
you who dared—seeing me in these straits—
to venture out from the walls, all for *my* sake,
175 while the others stay inside and cling to safety."

    The goddess answered quickly, her eyes blazing,
"True, dear brother—how your father and mother both
implored me, time and again, clutching my knees,
and the comrades round me begging me to stay!
180 Such was the fear that broke them, man for man,
but the heart within me broke with grief for you.
Now headlong on and fight! No letup, no lance spared!
So now, now we'll *see* if Achilles kills us both
and hauls our bloody armor back to the beaked ships
185 or *he* goes down in pain beneath your spear."

---

4. Deiphobus (dē ĭ´ fə bəs) son of Priam; powerful Trojan warrior.

Reading Strategy
Picture the Action What does the image of Zeus with his scales suggest about the role of the gods in the lives of mortals?

✔**Reading Check**

In whose form does Athena appear to Hector?

Athena luring him on with all her immortal cunning—
and now, at last, as the two came closing for the kill
it was tall Hector, helmet flashing, who led off:
"No more running from you in fear, Achilles!
190   Not as before. Three times I fled around
the great city of Priam—I lacked courage then
to stand your onslaught. Now my spirit stirs me
to meet you face-to-face. Now kill or be killed!
Come, we'll swear to the gods, the highest witnesses—
195   the gods will oversee our binding pacts. I swear
I will never mutilate you—merciless as you are—
if Zeus allows me to last it out and tear your life away.
But once I've stripped your glorious armor, Achilles,
I will give your body back to your loyal comrades.
200   Swear you'll do the same."

                                    A swift dark glance
and the headstrong runner answered, "Hector, stop!
You unforgivable, you . . . don't talk to me of pacts.
There are no binding oaths between men and lions—
wolves and lambs can enjoy no meeting of the minds—
205   they are all bent on hating each other to the death.
So with you and me. No love between us. No truce
till one or the other falls and gluts with blood
Ares who hacks at men behind his rawhide shield.
Come, call up whatever courage you can muster.
210   Life or death—now prove yourself a spearman,
a daring man of war! No more escape for you—
Athena will kill you with my spear in just a moment.
Now you'll pay at a stroke for all my comrades' grief,
all you killed in the fury of your spear!"

                                         With that,
215   shaft poised, he hurled and his spear's long shadow flew
but seeing it coming glorious Hector ducked away,
crouching down, watching the bronze tip fly past
and stab the earth—but Athena snatched it up
and passed it back to Achilles
220   and Hector the gallant captain never saw her.
He sounded out a challenge to Peleus' princely son:
"You missed, look—the great godlike Achilles!
So you knew nothing at all from Zeus about my death—
and yet how sure you were! All bluff, cunning with words,
225   that's all you are—trying to make me fear you,
lose my nerve, forget my fighting strength.
Well, you'll never plant your lance in my back
as I flee *you* in fear—plunge it through my chest
as I come charging in, if a god gives you the chance!
230   But now it's for you to dodge *my* brazen spear—
I wish you'd bury it in your body to the hilt.

Literary Analysis
Imagery What theme is reinforced by the recurring image of a helmet flashing?

How much lighter the war would be for Trojans then
if you, their greatest scourge, were dead and gone!"

Shaft poised, he hurled and his spear's long shadow
flew
235 and it struck Achilles' shield—a dead-center hit—
but off and away it glanced and Hector seethed,
his hurtling spear, his whole arm's power poured
in a wasted shot. He stood there, cast down . . .
he had no spear in reserve. So Hector shouted out
240 to Deiphobus bearing his white shield—with a ringing
shout he called for a heavy lance—
                              but the man was nowhere near him,
vanished—
                  yes and Hector knew the truth in his heart
and the fighter cried aloud, "My time has come!
At last the gods have called me down to death.
245 I thought he was at my side, the hero Deiphobus—
he's safe inside the walls, Athena's tricked me blind.
And now death, grim death is looming up beside me,
no longer far away. No way to escape it now. This,
this was their pleasure after all, sealed long ago—
250 Zeus and the son of Zeus, the distant deadly Archer—
though often before now they rushed to my defense.
So now I meet my doom. Well let me die—
but not without struggle, not without glory, no,
in some great clash of arms that even men to come
will hear of down the years!"
255   And on that resolve
he drew the whetted sword that hung at his side,
tempered, massive, and gathering all his force
he swooped like a soaring eagle
launching down from the dark clouds to earth
260 to snatch some helpless lamb or trembling hare.
So Hector swooped now, swinging his whetted sword
and Achilles charged too, bursting with rage, barbaric,
guarding his chest with the well-wrought blazoned
    shield,
head tossing his gleaming helmet, four horns strong
265 and the golden plumes shook that the god of fire
drove in bristling thick along its ridge.
Bright as that star amid the stars in the night sky,
star of the evening, brightest star that rides the heavens,
so fire flared from the sharp point of the spear Achilles
270 brandished high in his right hand, bent on Hector's death,
scanning his splendid body—where to pierce it best?
The rest of his flesh seemed all encased in armor,
burnished, brazen—*Achilles*' armor that Hector stripped

Themes in World Literature

Homer and the Epic Tradition

For centuries, Homer's *Iliad* and *Odyssey* had an unparalleled influence on Greek culture and education. As very young children, the Greeks memorized the epics, and Homer's language shaped their words and the ways they thought.

In later ages, when epics were written rather than recited, the *Iliad* and *Odyssey* still served as models. Thus, the Roman poet Virgil loosely modeled the first six books of his *Aeneid* on the *Odyssey* and the last six books on the *Iliad*. Virgil was a literate poet, but he retained many of the epic conventions of oral poetry, including an invocation of the Muse, lengthy speeches, and Homeric similes. Virgil fashioned a uniquely Roman national epic, but at the same time he upheld the tradition of Homeric language and style.

During the Middle Ages, Homer and Virgil served as inspiration for Dante Alighieri in the *Divine Comedy*. Homer also profoundly influenced the English epic tradition, notably in John Milton's *Paradise Lost* and in Alexander Pope's satirical mock-epic poems, *The Rape of the Lock* and *The Dunciad*.

whetted (wet´ id) *adj.*
sharpened

brandished (bran´ disht) *v.*
waved or shook in a
threatening manner

☑ **Reading Check**

Whom does Athena support in the battle between Achilles and Hector?

from strong Patroclus when he killed him—true,
275 but one spot lay exposed,
where collarbones lift the neckbone off the shoulders,
the open throat, where the end of life comes quickest—*there*
as Hector charged in fury brilliant Achilles drove his spear
and the point went stabbing clean through the tender neck
280 but the heavy bronze weapon failed to slash the windpipe—
Hector could still gasp out some words, some last reply . . .
he crashed in the dust—

godlike Achilles gloried over him:
"Hector—surely you thought when you stripped Patroclus' armor
that you, you would be safe! Never a fear of me—
285 far from the fighting as I was—you fool!
Left behind there, down by the beaked ships
his great avenger waited, a greater man by far—
that man was I, and I smashed your strength! And you—
the dogs and birds will maul you, shame your corpse
290 while Achaeans bury my dear friend in glory!"

Struggling for breath, Hector, his helmet flashing,
said, "I beg you, beg you by your life, your parents—
don't let the dogs devour me by the Argive ships!
Wait, take the princely ransom of bronze and gold,
295 the gifts my father and noble mother will give you—
but give my body to friends to carry home again,
so Trojan men and Trojan women can do me honor
with fitting rites of fire once I am dead."

Staring grimly, the proud runner Achilles answered,
300 "Beg no more, you fawning dog—begging me by my parents!
Would to god my rage, my fury would drive me now
to hack your flesh away and eat you raw—
such agonies you have caused me! Ransom?
No man alive could keep the dog-packs off you,
305 not if they haul in ten, twenty times that ransom
and pile it here before me and promise fortunes more—
no, not even if Dardan Priam should offer to weigh out
your bulk in gold! Not even then will your noble mother
lay you on your deathbed, mourn the son she bore . . .
310 The dogs and birds will rend you—blood and bone!"

At the point of death, Hector, his helmet flashing,
said, "I know you well—I see my fate before me.
Never a chance that I could win you over . . .
Iron inside your chest, that heart of yours.
315 But now beware, or my curse will draw god's wrath
upon your head, that day when Paris and lord Apollo—

Reading Strategy
Picture the Action In
what way does the image
presented in these lines
illustrate the extent of
Achilles' rage?

for all your fighting heart—destroy you at the Scaean Gates!"

Death cut him short. The end closed in around him.
Flying free of his limbs
320 his soul went winging down to the House of Death,
wailing his fate, leaving his manhood far behind,
his young and supple strength. But brilliant Achilles
taunted Hector's body, dead as he was, "Die, die!
For my own death, I'll meet it freely—whenever Zeus
325 and the other deathless gods would like to bring it on!"

With that he wrenched his bronze spear from the corpse,
laid it aside and ripped the bloody armor off the back.
And the other sons of Achaea, running up around him,
crowded closer, all of them gazing wonder-struck
330 at the build and marvelous, lithe beauty of Hector.
And not a man came forward who did not stab his body,
glancing toward a comrade, laughing: "Ah, look here—
how much softer he is to handle now, this Hector,
than when he gutted our ships with roaring fire!"

335 Standing over him, so they'd gloat and stab his body.
But once he had stripped the corpse the proud runner Achilles
took his stand in the midst of all the Argive troops

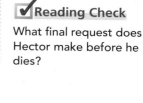

✓ Reading Check

What final request does
Hector make before he
dies?

Achilles defeating Hector, Peter Paul Rubens, Musée des Beaux-Arts, Giraudon

◄ Critical Viewing

Do you think this depic-
tion of Hector's death is
consistent with Homer's
description of it? Why or
why not? **[Evaluate]**

and urged them on with a flight of winging orders:
"Friends—lords of the Argives, O my captains!
340 Now that the gods have let me kill this man
who caused us agonies, loss on crushing loss—
more than the rest of all their men combined—
come, let us ring their walls in armor, test them,
see what recourse the Trojans still may have in mind.
345 Will they abandon the city heights with this man fallen?
Or brace for a last, dying stand though Hector's gone?
But wait—what am I saying? Why this deep debate?
Down by the ships a body lies unwept, unburied—
Patroclus . . . I will never forget him,
350 not as long as I'm still among the living
and my springing knees will lift and drive me on.
Though the dead forget their dead in the House of Death,
I will remember, even there, my dear companion.
                                                    Now,
come, you sons of Achaea, raise a song of triumph!
355 Down to the ships we march and bear this corpse on high—
we have won ourselves great glory. We have brought
magnificent Hector down, that man the Trojans

▼ **Critical Viewing**
This painting depicts
Achilles and the Greeks
with the body of Patro-
clus. What details indicate
the figure of Achilles?
[Analyze]

glorified in their city like a god!"

                         So he triumphed
and now he was bent on outrage, on shaming noble Hector.
360   Piercing the tendons, ankle to heel behind both feet,
he knotted straps of rawhide through them both,
lashed them to his chariot, left the head to drag
and mounting the car, hoisting the famous arms aboard,
he whipped his team to a run and breakneck on they flew,
365   holding nothing back. And a thick cloud of dust rose up
from the man they dragged, his dark hair swirling round
that head so handsome once, all tumbled low in the dust—
since Zeus had given him over to his enemies now
to be defiled in the land of his own fathers.

370   So his whole head was dragged down in the dust.
And now his mother began to tear her hair . . .
she flung her shining veil to the ground and raised
a high, shattering scream, looking down at her son.
Pitifully his loving father groaned and round the king
375   his people cried with grief and wailing seized the city—
for all the world as if all Troy were torched and smoldering
down from the looming brows of the citadel to her roots.
Priam's people could hardly hold the old man back,
frantic, mad to go rushing out the Dardan Gates.
380   He begged them all, groveling in the filth,
crying out to them, calling each man by name,
"Let go, my friends! Much as you care for me,
let me hurry out of the city, make my way,
all on my own, to Achaea's waiting ships!
385   I must implore that terrible, violent man . . .
Perhaps—who knows?—he may respect my age,
may pity an old man. He has a father too,
as old as I am—Peleus sired him once,
Peleus reared him to be the scourge of Troy
390   but most of all to me—he made my life a hell.
So many sons he slaughtered, just coming into bloom . . .
but grieving for all the rest, one breaks my heart the most
and stabbing grief for him will take me down to Death—
my Hector—would to god he had perished in my arms!
395   Then his mother who bore him—oh so doomed,
she and I could glut ourselves with grief."

        So the voice of the king rang out in tears,
the citizens wailed in answer, and noble Hecuba
led the wives of Troy in a throbbing chant of sorrow:
400   "O my child—my desolation! How can I go on living?
What agonies must I suffer now, now *you* are dead and gone?

Literary Analysis
Imagery To which senses does the imagery in lines 371–373 appeal?

**Reading Check**

What do Achilles and the Greeks do with the body of Hector?

You were my pride throughout the city night and day—
a blessing to us all, the men and women of Troy:
throughout the city they saluted you like a god.
405 You, you were their greatest glory while you lived—
now death and fate have seized you, dragged you down!"

Her voice rang out in tears, but the wife of Hector
had not heard a thing. No messenger brought the truth
of how her husband made his stand outside the gates.
410 She was weaving at her loom, deep in the high halls,
working flowered braiding into a dark red folding robe.
And she called her well-kempt women through the house
to set a large three-legged cauldron over the fire
so Hector could have his steaming hot bath
415 when he came home from battle—poor woman,
she never dreamed how far he was from bathing,
struck down at Achilles' hands by blazing-eyed Athena.
But she heard the groans and wails of grief from the rampart now
and her body shook, her shuttle dropped to the ground,
420 she called out to her lovely waiting women, "Quickly—
two of you follow me—I must see what's happened.
That cry—that was Hector's honored mother I heard!
My heart's pounding, leaping up in my throat,
the knees beneath me paralyzed—Oh I know it . . .
425 something terrible's coming down on Priam's children.
Pray god the news will never reach my ears!
Yes but I dread it so—what if great Achilles
has cut my Hector off from the city, daring Hector,
and driven him out across the plain, and all alone?—
430 He may have put an end to that fatal headstrong pride
that always seized my Hector—never hanging back
with the main force of men, always charging ahead,
giving ground to no man in his fury!"
So she cried,
dashing out of the royal halls like a madwoman,
435 her heart racing hard, her women close behind her.
But once she reached the tower where soldiers massed
she stopped on the rampart, looked down and saw it all—
saw him dragged before the city, stallions galloping,
dragging Hector back to Achaea's beaked warships—
440 ruthless work. The world went black as night
before her eyes, she fainted, falling backward,
gasping away her life breath . . .
She flung to the winds her glittering headdress,
the cap and the coronet, braided band and veil,
445 all the regalia golden Aphrodite gave her once,
the day that Hector, helmet aflash in sunlight,
led her home to Troy from her father's house

Literary Analysis
Imagery What theme is reinforced by the recurring image of voices ringing out in tears?

Literary Analysis
Imagery What word pictures in this passage show the state of Andromache's emotions?

with countless wedding gifts to win her heart.
But crowding round her now her husband's sisters
450 and brothers' wives supported her in their midst,
and she, terrified, stunned to the point of death,
struggling for breath now and coming back to life,
burst out in grief among the Trojan women: "O Hector—
I am destroyed! Both born to the same fate after all!
455 You, you at Troy in the halls of King Priam—
I at Thebes, under the timberline of Placos,
Eetion's house . . . He raised me as a child,
that man of doom, his daughter just as doomed—
would to god he'd never fathered *me*!

Now you go down

Reading Check

How does Andromache react to the sight of Hector's dead body?

◀ Critical Viewing

How well do you think this depiction of Andromache and Astyanax captures Andromache's feelings for her son? [Evaluate]

460 to the House of Death, the dark depths of the earth,
and leave me here to waste away in grief, a widow
lost in the royal halls—and the boy only a baby,
the son we bore together, you and I so doomed.
Hector, what help are you to him, now you are dead?—

465 what help is he to you? Think, even if he escapes
the wrenching horrors of war against the Argives,
pain and labor will plague him all his days to come.
Strangers will mark his lands off, stealing his estates.
The day that orphans a youngster cuts him off from friends.

470 And he hangs his head low, humiliated in every way . . .
his cheeks stained with tears, and pressed by hunger
the boy goes up to his father's old companions,
tugging at one man's cloak, another's tunic,
and some will pity him, true,

475 and one will give him a little cup to drink,
enough to wet his lips, not quench his thirst.
But then some bully with both his parents living
beats him from the banquet, fists and abuses flying:
'You, get out—you've got no father feasting with us here!'

480 And the boy, sobbing, trails home to his widowed mother . . .
Astyanax!

And years ago, propped on his father's knee,
he would only eat the marrow, the richest cuts of lamb,
and when sleep came on him and he had quit his play,
cradled warm in his nurse's arms he'd drowse off,

485 snug in a soft bed, his heart brimmed with joy.
Now what suffering, now he's lost his father—
Astyanax!

The Lord of the City, so the Trojans called him,
because it was you, Hector, you and you alone
who shielded the gates and the long walls of Troy.

491 But now by the beaked ships, far from your parents,
glistening worms will wriggle through your flesh,
once the dogs have had their fill of your naked corpse—
though we have such stores of clothing laid up in the halls,
fine things, a joy to the eye, the work of women's hands.

496 Now, by god, I'll burn them all, blazing to the skies!
No use to you now, they'll never shroud your body—
but they will be your glory
burned by the Trojan men and women in your honor!"

Her voice rang out in tears and the women wailed in answer.

Achilles and the Greeks perform Patroclus' funeral rites. Following the funeral, they hold a feast. The next morning, in honor of Patroclus, the Greeks hold funeral games—chariot races, discus throwing, boxing, and wrestling.

The games were over now. The gathered armies scattered,
each man to his fast ship, and fighters turned their minds
to thoughts of food and the sweet warm grip of sleep.
But Achilles kept on grieving for his friend,
5   the memory burning on . . .
and all-subduing sleep could not take him,
not now, he turned and twisted, side to side,
he longed for Patroclus' manhood, his gallant heart—
What rough campaigns they'd fought to an end together,
10   what hardships they had suffered, cleaving their way
through wars of men and pounding waves at sea.
The memories flooded over him, live tears flowing,
and now he'd lie on his side, now flat on his back,
now facedown again. At last he'd leap to his feet,
15   wander in anguish, aimless along the surf, and dawn on dawn
flaming over the sea and shore would find him pacing.
Then he'd yoke his racing team to the chariot-harness,
lash the corpse of Hector behind the car for dragging
and haul him three times round the dead Patroclus' tomb,
20   and then he'd rest again in his tents and leave the body
sprawled facedown in the dust. But Apollo pitied Hector—
dead man though he was—and warded all corruption off
from Hector's corpse and round him, head to foot,
the great god wrapped the golden shield of storm
25   so his skin would never rip as Achilles dragged him on.

And so he kept on raging, shaming noble Hector,
but the gods in bliss looked down and pitied Priam's son.

"Achilles," detail from the fresco "Thetis consoling Achilles," Giovanni Battista Tiepolo, Scala

▲ **Critical Viewing**
What does this depiction of Achilles suggest about the way he is feeling at this point in the story? **[Infer]**

✔**Reading Check**
Which god pities Hector and prevents his body from being damaged?

They kept on urging the sharp-eyed giant-killer Hermes
to go and steal the body, a plan that pleased them all
30 but not Hera, Poseidon or the girl with blazing eyes.[1]
They clung to their deathless hate of sacred Troy,
Priam and Priam's people, just as they had at first
when Paris in all his madness launched the war.
He offended Athena and Hera—both goddesses.
35 When they came to his shepherd's fold he favored Love
who dangled before his eyes the lust that loosed disaster.
But now, at the twelfth dawn since Hector's death,
lord Apollo rose and addressed the immortal powers:
"Hard-hearted you are, you gods, you live for cruelty!
40 Did Hector never burn in your honor thighs of oxen
and flawless, full-grown goats? Now you cannot
bring yourselves to save him—even his corpse—
so his wife can see him, his mother and his child,
his father Priam and Priam's people: how they'd rush
45 to burn his body on the pyre and give him royal rites!
But murderous Achilles—you gods, you *choose* to help
        Achilles.
That man without a shred of decency in his heart . . .
his temper can never bend and change—like some lion
going his own barbaric way, giving in to his power,
50 his brute force and wild pride, as down he swoops
on the flocks of men to seize his savage feast.
Achilles has lost all pity! No shame in the man,
shame that does great harm or drives men on to good.
No doubt some mortal has suffered a dearer loss than this,
55 a brother born in the same womb, or even a son . . .
he grieves, he weeps, but then his tears are through.
The Fates have given mortals hearts that can endure.
But this Achilles—first he slaughters Hector,
he rips away the noble prince's life
60 then lashes him to his chariot, drags him round
his beloved comrade's tomb. But why, I ask you?
What good will it do him? What honor will he gain?
Let that man beware, or great and glorious as he is,
we mighty gods will wheel on him in anger—look,
65 he outrages the senseless clay in all his fury!"

        But white-armed Hera flared at him in anger:
"Yes, there'd be some merit even in what *you* say,
lord of the silver bow—if all you gods, in fact,
would set Achilles and Hector high in equal honor.
70 But Hector is mortal. He sucked a woman's breast.[2]

---

1. **the girl with blazing eyes** Athena.
2. **sucked a woman's breast** was breast-fed as an infant by a mortal woman, not a goddess.

Honor in Ancient Greece
    Honor was a fundamental part of the ancient Greek code of ethics. It was understood that a warrior fought for honor and that a glorious reputation would outlive him. The tangible expression of honor consisted of the prizes distributed to a warrior according to his rank, valor, and achievement. Thus, a warrior's share of prizes was a visible symbol of his merit and status. This is why, in the *Iliad*, Achilles and Agamemnon feel so shamed when they must forfeit their prizes and why such importance is placed on the treatment of fallen soldiers' bodies. Ultimately, a hero's honor depended on how the world saw him, not on how he saw himself.

Achilles sprang from a goddess—one I reared myself:
I brought her up and gave her in marriage to a man,
to Peleus, dearest to all your hearts, you gods.
All you gods, you shared in the wedding rites,
75 and so did you, Apollo—there you sat at the feast
and struck your lyre. What company you keep now,
these wretched Trojans. You—forever faithless!"

    But Zeus who marshals the storm clouds warned his queen,
"Now, Hera, don't fly into such a rage at fellow gods.
80 These two can never attain the same degree of honor.
Still, the immortals loved Prince Hector dearly,
best of all the mortals born in Troy . . .
so *I* loved him, at least:
he never <u>stinted</u> with gifts to please my heart.
85 Never once did my altar lack its share of victims,
winecups tipped and the deep smoky savor. These,
these are the gifts we claim—they are our rights.
But as for stealing courageous Hector's body,
we must abandon the idea—not a chance in the world
90 behind Achilles' back. For Thetis is always there,
his mother always hovering near him night and day.
Now, would one of you gods call Thetis to my presence?—
so I can declare to her my solemn, sound decree:
Achilles must receive a ransom from King Priam,
95 Achilles must give Hector's body back."

stinted (stint' id) *v.* limited
to a certain quantity

Literary Analysis
Imagery To what senses
does Zeus' description of
sacrifice appeal?

    *On Olympus, Zeus orders Thetis to tell Achilles to return Hector's
body to Priam. Then Zeus commands Iris to tell Priam to ransom
his son by bringing gifts to Achilles. Concerned for Priam's safety,
Zeus tells Hermes to guide Priam through the hollow Achaean
ships. Hermes assures Priam that the gods preserved Hector's
body from defilement even while Achilles dragged the corpse for
nine days.*

                                    With that urging
Hermes went his way to the steep heights of Olympus.
But Priam swung down to earth from the battle-car
and leaving Idaeus[3] there to rein in mules and team,
100 the old king went straight up to the lodge
where Achilles dear to Zeus would always sit.
Priam found the warrior there inside . . .
many captains sitting some way off, but two,
veteran Automedon and the fine fighter Alcimus
105 were busy serving him. He had just finished dinner,

---

3. Idaeus (ī dē' əs) herald of Priam.

✔Reading Check
What decree does Zeus
make regarding Hector's
body?

eating, drinking, and the table still stood near.
The majestic king of Troy slipped past the rest
and kneeling down beside Achilles, clasped his knees
and kissed his hands, those terrible, man-killing hands
110   that had slaughtered Priam's many sons in battle.
Awesome—as when the grip of madness seizes one
who murders a man in his own fatherland and flees
abroad to foreign shores, to a wealthy, noble host,
and a sense of marvel runs through all who see him—
115   so Achilles marveled, beholding majestic Priam.
His men marveled too, trading startled glances.
But Priam prayed his heart out to Achilles:
"Remember your own father, great godlike Achilles—
as old as *I* am, past the threshold of deadly old age!
120   No doubt the countrymen round about him plague him now,
with no one there to defend him, beat away disaster.
No one—but at least he hears you're still alive
and his old heart rejoices, hopes rising, day by day,
to see his beloved son come sailing home from Troy.
125   But I—dear god, my life so cursed by fate . . .
I fathered hero sons in the wide realm of Troy
and now not a single one is left, I tell you.
Fifty sons I had when the sons of Achaea came,
nineteen born to me from a single mother's womb
130   and the rest by other women in the palace. Many,
most of them violent Ares cut the knees from under.
But one, one was left me, to guard my walls, my people—
the one you killed the other day, defending his fatherland,
my Hector! It's all for him I've come to the ships now,
135   to win him back from you—I bring a priceless ransom.
Revere the gods, Achilles! Pity me in my own right,
remember your own father! I deserve more pity . . .
I have endured what no one on earth has ever done before—
I put to my lips the hands of the man who killed my son."

140   Those words stirred within Achilles a deep desire
to grieve for his own father. Taking the old man's hand
he gently moved him back. And overpowered by memory
both men gave way to grief. Priam wept freely
for man-killing Hector, throbbing, crouching
145   before Achilles' feet as Achilles wept himself,
now for his father, now for Patroclus once again,
and their sobbing rose and fell throughout the house.
Then, when brilliant Achilles had had his fill of tears
and the longing for it had left his mind and body,
150   he rose from his seat, raised the old man by the hand
and filled with pity now for his gray head and gray beard,
he spoke out winging words, flying straight to the heart:

Literary Analysis
Imagery and Epic Simile
Why do you think Homer
describes Achilles' reac-
tion to Priam the way that
he does in lines 111–115?

Critical Viewing ▶
This painting depicts
Priam begging Achilles to
return Hector's body to
Troy. How might seeing
their king in this position
have affected the
Trojans? [Speculate]

"Poor man, how much you've borne—pain to break the spirit!
What daring brought you down to the ships, all alone,
155　to face the glance of the man who killed your sons,
so many fine brave boys? You have a heart of iron.
Come, please, sit down on this chair here . . .
Let us put our griefs to rest in our own hearts,
rake them up no more, raw as we are with mourning.
160　What good's to be won from tears that chill the spirit?
So the immortals spun our lives that we, we wretched men
live on to bear such torments—the gods live free of sorrows.
There are two great jars that stand on the floor of Zeus's halls
and hold his gifts, our miseries one, the other blessings.
165　When Zeus who loves the lightning mixes gifts for a man,
now he meets with misfortune, now good times in turn.
When Zeus dispenses gifts from the jar of sorrows only,
he makes a man an outcast—brutal, ravenous hunger
drives him down the face of the shining earth,
170　stalking far and wide, cursed by gods and men.
So with my father, Peleus. What glittering gifts
the gods rained down from the day that he was born!
He excelled all men in wealth and pride of place,
he lorded the Myrmidons, and mortal that he was,
175　they gave the man an immortal goddess for a wife.

✔Reading Check

How does Achilles react
when Priam reminds
Achilles of his father?

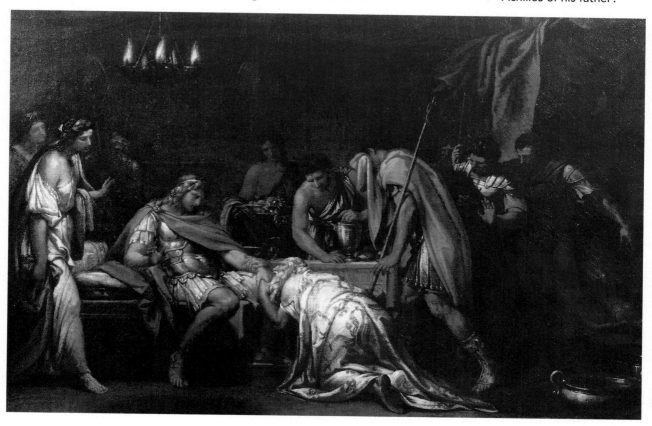

Yes, but even on him the Father piled hardships,
no powerful race of princes born in his royal halls,
only a single son he fathered, doomed at birth,
cut off in the spring of life—

180   and I, I give the man no care as he grows old
since here I sit in Troy, far from my fatherland,
a grief to you, a grief to all your children . . .
And you too, old man, we hear you prospered once:
as far as Lesbos, Macar's kingdom, bounds to
       seaward,

185   Phrygia east and upland, the Hellespont
       vast and north—
that entire realm, they say, you lorded over
       once,
you excelled all men, old king, in sons and
       wealth.
But then the gods of heaven brought this agony on
       you—
ceaseless battles round your walls, your armies
       slaughtered.

190   You must bear up now. Enough of endless tears,
the pain that breaks the spirit.
Grief for your son will do no good at all.
You will never bring him back to life—
sooner you must suffer something worse."

195   But the old and noble Priam protested strongly:
"Don't make me sit on a chair, Achilles, Prince,
not while Hector lies uncared-for in your camp!
Give him back to me, now, no more delay—
I must see my son with my own eyes.

200   Accept the ransom I bring you, a king's ransom!
Enjoy it, all of it—return to your own native land,
safe and sound . . . since now you've spared my life."

      A dark glance—and the headstrong runner answered,
"No more, old man, don't tempt my wrath, not now!

205   My own mind's made up to give you back your son.
A messenger brought me word from Zeus—my mother,
Thetis who bore me, the Old Man of the Sea's daughter.
And what's more, I can see through you, Priam—
no hiding the fact from me: one of the gods

210   has led you down to Achaea's fast ships.
No man alive, not even a rugged young fighter,
would dare to venture into our camp. Never—
how could he slip past the sentries unchallenged?
Or shoot back the bold of my gates with so much ease?

215   So don't anger me now. Don't stir my raging heart still more.

▼ **Critical Viewing**
How does this depiction
of Priam's plea for Hec-
tor's body compare with
the way that you envision
this scene? Explain.
[Compare and Contrast]

Reading Strategy
Picture the Action How
do you think Priam might
stand or gesture as he
speaks these lines to
Achilles?

Or under my own roof I may not spare your life, old man—
suppliant that you are—may break the laws of Zeus!"

The old man was terrified. He obeyed the order.
But Achilles bounded out of doors like a lion—
220 not alone but flanked by his two aides-in-arms,
veteran Automedon and Alcimus, steady comrades,
Achilles' favorites next to the dead Patroclus.
They loosed from harness the horses and the mules,
they led the herald in, the old king's crier,
225 and sat him down on a bench. From the polished wagon
they lifted the priceless ransom brought for Hector's corpse
but they left behind two capes and a finely-woven shirt
to shroud the body well when Priam bore him home.
Then Achilles called the serving-women out:
230 "Bathe and anoint the body—
bear it aside first. Priam must not see his son."
He feared that, overwhelmed by the sight of Hector,
wild with grief, Priam might let his anger flare
and Achilles might fly into fresh rage himself,
235 cut the old man down and break the laws of Zeus.
So when the maids had bathed and anointed the body
sleek with olive oil and wrapped it round and round
in a braided battle-shirt and handsome battle-cape,
then Achilles lifted Hector up in his own arms
240 and laid him down on a bier, and comrades helped him
raise the bier and body onto the sturdy wagon . . .
Then with a groan he called his dear friend by name:
"Feel no anger at me, Patroclus, if you learn—
even there in the House of Death—I let his father
245 have Prince Hector back. He gave me worthy ransom
and you shall have your share from me, as always,
your fitting, lordly share."

So he vowed
and brilliant Achilles strode back to his shelter,
sat down on the well-carved chair that he had left,
250 at the far wall of the room, leaned toward Priam
and firmly spoke the words the king had come to hear:
"Your son is now set free, old man, as you requested.
Hector lies in state. With the first light of day
you will see for yourself as you convey him home.
255 Now, at last, let us turn our thoughts to supper.
Even Niobe⁴ with her <u>lustrous</u> hair remembered food,
though she saw a dozen children killed in her own halls,
six daughters and six sons in the pride and prime of youth.
True, lord Apollo killed the sons with his silver bow

---

4. **Niobe** (nī´ ə bē).

Literary Analysis
Imagery What theme is supported by the comparison of Achilles to a lion?

Reading Strategy
Picture the Action Which details in lines 236–238 help you form a mental image of Hector's dead body?

lustrous (lus´ trəs) *adj.* shining

Reading Check

How does Achilles respond to Priam's request for the return of Hector's body?

260 and Artemis showering arrows killed the daughters.
Both gods were enraged at Niobe. Time and again
she placed herself on a par with their own mother,
Leto in her immortal beauty—how she insulted Leto:
'All you have borne is two, but I have borne so many!'
265 So, two as they were, they slaughtered all her children.
Nine days they lay in their blood, no one to bury them—
Cronus' son had turned the people into stone . . .
then on the tenth the gods of heaven interred them.
And Niobe, <u>gaunt</u>, worn to the bone with weeping,
270 turned her thoughts to food. And now, somewhere,
lost on the crags, on the lonely mountain slopes,
on Sipylus[5] where, they say, the nymphs who live forever,
dancing along the Achelous River[6] run to beds of rest—
there, struck into stone, Niobe still broods
275 on the spate of griefs the gods poured out to her.

    So come—we too, old king, must think of food.
Later you can mourn your beloved son once more,
when you bear him home to Troy, and you'll weep many tears."

    Never pausing, the swift runner sprang to his feet
280 and slaughtered a white sheep as comrades moved in
to skin the carcass quickly, dress the quarters well.
Expertly they cut the meat in pieces, pierced them with spits,
roasted them to a turn and pulled them off the fire.
Automedon brought the bread, set it out on the board
285 in ample wicker baskets. Achilles served the meat.
They reached out for the good things that lay at hand
and when they had put aside desire for food and drink,
Priam the son of Dardanus gazed at Achilles, marveling
now at the man's beauty, his magnificent build—
290 face-to-face he seemed a deathless god . . .
and Achilles gazed and marveled at Dardan Priam,
beholding his noble looks, listening to his words.
But once they'd had their fill of gazing at each other,
the old majestic Priam broke the silence first:
295 "Put me to bed quickly, Achilles, Prince.
Time to rest, to enjoy the sweet relief of sleep.
Not once have my eyes closed shut beneath my lids
from the day my son went down beneath your hands . . .
day and night I groan, brooding over the countless griefs,
300 groveling in the dung that fills my walled-in court.
But now, at long last, I have tasted food again
and let some glistening wine go down my throat.
Before this hour I had tasted nothing."

gaunt (gônt) *adj.* thin and bony; haggard

Literary Analysis
Imagery What images in these lines recall earlier scenes in the *Iliad*?

---

5. **Sipylus** (sip´ i ləs) mountain in Asia Minor.
6. **Achelous River** (ak´ ə lō´ əs) river near Sipylus in Asia Minor, east of Troy.

Achilles calls a twelve-day truce while the Trojans
perform Hector's funeral rites. Cassandra watches as her father
Priam approaches Troy in his chariot. She sees her brother Hec-
tor's body drawn by the mules on a litter.

She [Cassandra] screamed and her scream rang out through all
      Troy:
305 "Come, look down, you men of Troy, you Trojan women!
Behold Hector now—if you ever once rejoiced
to see him striding home, home alive from battle!
He was the greatest joy of Troy and all our people!"

Her cries plunged Troy into uncontrollable grief
310 and not a man or woman was left inside the walls.
They streamed out at the gates to meet Priam
bringing in the body of the dead. Hector—
his loving wife and noble mother were first
to fling themselves on the wagon rolling on,
315 the first to tear their hair, embrace his head
and a wailing throng of people milled around them.
And now, all day long till the setting sun went down
they would have wept for Hector there before the gates
if the old man, steering the car, had not commanded,
320 "Let me through with the mules! Soon, in a moment,
you can have your fill of tears—once I've brought him home."

So he called and the crowds fell back on either side,
making way for the wagon. Once they had borne him
into the famous halls, they laid his body down
325 on his large carved bed and set beside him singers
to lead off the laments, and their voices rose in grief—
they lifted the dirge high as the women wailed in answer.
And white-armed Andromache led their songs of sorrow,
cradling the head of Hector, man-killing Hector
330 gently in her arms: "O my husband . . .
cut off from life so young! You leave me a widow,
lost in the royal halls—and the boy only a baby,
the son we bore together, you and I so doomed.
I cannot think he will ever come to manhood.
335 Long before *that* the city will be sacked,
plundered top to bottom! Because you are dead,
her great guardian, you who always defended Troy,
who kept her loyal wives and helpless children safe,
all who will soon be carried off in the hollow ships
340 and I with them—
               And you, my child, will follow me
to labor, somewhere, at harsh, degrading work,
slaving under some heartless master's eye—that,

Reading Check

What does Andromache believe will happen to Troy now that Hector is dead?

or some Achaean marauder will seize you by the arm
and hurl you headlong down from the ramparts—horrible death—
345 enraged at *you* because Hector once cut down his brother,
his father or his son, yes, hundreds of armed Achaeans
gnawed the dust of the world, crushed by Hector's hands!
Your father, remember, was no man of mercy . . .
not in the horror of battle, and that is why
350 the whole city of Troy mourns you now, my Hector—
you've brought your parents accursed tears and grief
but to me most of all you've left the horror, the heartbreak!
For you never died in bed and stretched your arms to me
or said some last word from the heart I can remember,
355 always, weeping for you through all my nights and days!"

Her voice rang out in tears and the women wailed in answer
and Hecuba led them now in a throbbing chant of sorrow:
"Hector, dearest to me by far of all my sons . . .
and dear to the gods while we still shared this life—
360 and they cared about you still, I see, even after death.
Many the sons I had whom the swift runner Achilles
caught and shipped on the barren salt sea as slaves
to Samos, to Imbros, to Lemnos[7] shrouded deep in mist!
But you, once he slashed away your life with his brazen spear
365 he dragged you time and again around his comrade's tomb,
Patroclus whom you killed—not that he brought Patroclus
back to life by that. But I have you with me now . . .
fresh as the morning dew you lie in the royal halls
like one whom Apollo, lord of the silver bow,
370 has approached and shot to death with gentle shafts."

Her voice rang out in tears and an endless wail rose up
and Helen, the third in turn, led their songs of sorrow:
"Hector! Dearest to me of all my husband's brothers—
my husband, Paris, magnificent as a god . . .
375 he was the one who brought me here to Troy—
Oh how I wish I'd died before that day!
But this, now, is the twentieth year for me
since I sailed here and forsook my own native land,
yet never once did I hear from *you* a taunt, an insult.
380 But if someone else in the royal halls would curse me,
one of your brothers or sisters or brothers' wives
trailing their long robes, even your own mother—
not your father, always kind as my own father—
why, you'd restrain them with words, Hector,
385 you'd win them to my side . . .
you with your gentle temper, all your gentle words.

---

7. **Samos** (sam′ äs) . . . **Imbros** (im′ bräs) . . . **Lemnos** (lem′ näs) islands in the Aegean Sea.

Literary Analysis
Imagery Which details in this passage stress the violence and cruelty of war and its consequences?

Literary Analysis
Imagery To which sense does the imagery in lines 356 and 357 appeal most?

Andromache mourning Hector, Jacques Louis David, photo by Peter Willi

And so in the same breath I mourn for you and me,
my doom-struck, harrowed heart! Now there is no one left
in the wide realm of Troy, no friend to treat me kindly—
390   all the countrymen cringe from me in loathing!"

      Her voice rang out in tears and vast throngs wailed
and old King Priam rose and gave his people orders:
"Now, you men of Troy, haul timber into the city!
Have no fear of an Argive ambush packed with danger—
395   Achilles vowed, when he sent me home from the black ships,
not to do us harm till the twelfth dawn arrives."

      At his command they harnessed oxen and mules to wagons,
they assembled before the city walls with all good speed
and for nine days hauled in a boundless store of timber.
400   But when the tenth Dawn brought light to the mortal world

▲ **Critical Viewing**

Which details in this painting illustrate Andromache's grief over her husband's death and her concern for her child? [**Analyze**]

☑ **Reading Check**

Why does Andromache think that the Achaeans will be especially enraged at Astyanax?

they carried gallant Hector forth, weeping tears,
and they placed his corpse aloft the pyre's crest,
flung a torch and set it all aflame.

                              At last,
when young Dawn with her rose-red fingers shone once more,
405   the people massed around <u>illustrious</u> Hector's pyre . . .
And once they'd gathered, crowding the meeting grounds,
they first put out the fires with glistening wine,
wherever the flames still burned in all their fury.
Then they collected the white bones of Hector—
410   all his brothers, his friends-in-arms, mourning,
and warm tears came streaming down their cheeks.
They placed the bones they found in a golden chest,
shrouding them round and round in soft purple cloths.
They quickly lowered the chest in a deep, hollow grave
415   and over it piled a cope of huge stones closely set,
then hastily heaped a barrow, posted lookouts all around
for fear the Achaean combat troops would launch their attack
before the time agreed. And once they'd heaped the mound
they turned back home to Troy, and gathering once again
420   they shared a splendid funeral feast in Hector's honor,
held in the house of Priam, king by will of Zeus.

    And so the Trojans buried Hector breaker of horses.

illustrious (i lus´ trē əs) *adj.*
distinguished; famous

Review and Assess

Thinking About the Selection

1. **Respond:** Describe your reaction to Achilles' treatment of Hector after Hector's death.

2. **(a) Recall:** In Book 22, lines 11–49, what three courses of action does Hector consider? **(b) Recall:** What does Hector decide to do? **(c) Analyze:** In what way is this decision consistent with his character?

3. **(a) Recall:** After he has been fatally wounded, for what does Hector plead with Achilles? **(b) Analyze:** What does Achilles' response to Hector's dying wish suggest about him?

4. **(a) Infer:** In Book 24, what change does Homer portray in Achilles? **(b) Draw Conclusions:** What message do you think Homer meant to convey through this change?

5. **Evaluate:** Do you think that Achilles behaves heroically in the *Iliad?* Why or why not?

Review and Assess

Literary Analysis

Imagery

1. What theme or themes in the *Iliad* are reinforced by the recurring **imagery** of cutting?
2. (a) In line 3 of Book 24, to what senses does the imagery of "the sweet warm grip of sleep" appeal? (b) What is the effect of the contrast between this image and the description of Achilles in the following lines?
3. Two of the most striking images in Book 24 are those of Priam kissing the "man-killing hands" of Achilles and Achilles gazing in admiration at "majestic Priam." What message might Homer be trying to convey with these two images and with the ransoming scene as a whole?

Connecting Literary Elements

4. What is the effect of the **epic simile** in lines 5–8 of Book 22?
5. In what way does the epic simile in lines 267–270 of Book 22 convey the importance of that moment in the narrative?
6. (a) Complete a chart like the one shown to compare and contrast the epic simile describing Achilles in Book 22, lines 59–64, with the one describing Hector in lines 258–261. (b) In what way do the similarities and differences between these two similes reflect the qualities of each warrior?

Reading Strategy

Picture the Action

7. (a) Identify three details that help you **picture the action** in the battle between Hector and Achilles. (b) Explain why you think these details make such a strong impression.
8. Of which character in Book 22 or 24 do you have the clearest mental picture? Explain your answer.

Extend Understanding

9. **Social Studies Connection:** What can Homer's *Iliad* tell readers about war that a history textbook might not?

Quick Review

Imagery is language that appeals to the senses.

An **epic simile** is a lengthy comparison of two dissimilar things using the word *like* or *as*.

To **picture the action** in a literary work, use details from the text to see the events in your mind.

 **Take It to the Net**
PHSchool.com

Take the interactive self-test online to check your understanding of this selection.

Integrate Language Skills

Vocabulary Development Lesson

Word Analysis: Latin Root -lustr-

The words *lustrous* and *illustrious* both contain the Latin root -*lustr*-, which means "light" or "shine." Use your understanding of this root to write a brief definition of the words below. Use a dictionary to check your work.

1. luster   2. lackluster   3. illustrate

Spelling Strategy

When you use the suffix -*ous* to form an adjective, you may have to alter the ending of the base word. For example, the adjective *lustrous* comes from the noun *luster*. Use the suffix -*ous* to form an adjective from the following nouns.

1. glory   2. number   3. volume

Concept Development: Synonym or Antonym?

Review the vocabulary words on page 344. Then, indicate whether the word pairs below are synonyms—words with the same meaning—or antonyms—words with opposite meanings.

1. implore, plead
2. whetted, blunted
3. brandished, wielded
4. marshals, manages
5. stinted, limited
6. lustrous, dull
7. gaunt, robust
8. illustrious, eminent

Grammar and Style Lesson

Commas With Quotations

Use a comma after short introductory expressions that precede direct quotations. Do not use a comma when you are only quoting a word, phrase, or fragment of a complete sentence.

Direct quotations:

. . . the fighter cried aloud, "My time has come!"

But Zeus who marshals the storm clouds warned his queen, "Now, Hera, don't fly into such a rage at fellow gods. . . ."

Partial quotations:

Homer refers to Achilles as "the swift runner."

The epithet "white-armed" is often used for the goddess Hera in the *Iliad*.

Practice Revise each sentence below as necessary for the correct use of commas. If a sentence requires no revision, write *Correct*.

1. Hector begs Achilles "Don't let the dogs devour me by the Argive ships!"
2. The phrase, "breaker of horses" is used to describe Hector.
3. Achilles replies, "Beg no more."
4. Before he dies, Hector predicts "But now beware, or my curse will draw god's wrath upon your head."
5. In a striking image, Homer speaks of "young Dawn with her rose-red fingers."

Writing Application Write a paragraph summarizing the action in Book 24. Include at least two direct quotations and one partial quotation in your writing.

WG *Prentice Hall Writing and Grammar Connection: Diamond Level, Chapter 27, Section 4*

Writing Lesson

Editorial

Newspaper columnists often write persuasive editorials condemning or defending the conduct of prominent figures in society. Imagine that you are a columnist during the Trojan War. Write an editorial persuading your audience that Achilles does or does not conduct himself appropriately in the *Iliad*.

Prewriting   Review the *Iliad* and decide whether or not you think Achilles' actions and statements are honorable. Then, find quotations and examples that support your point of view.

Drafting   Begin your editorial by briefly describing what you think is appropriate behavior for a warrior in the time of the *Iliad*. Then, give a point-by-point explanation to show why Achilles meets or fails to meet that standard. Support your points with quotations and examples that portray Achilles either positively or negatively.

Revising   Review your draft, circling vague or general words and phrases. Replace these words and phrases with forceful, persuasive language.

Model: Revising for Persuasive Language

Achilles calls himself "the best of the Achaeans," but

brutal and arrogant

it is clear that this ~~headstrong~~ soldier fights only for

himself.

> A specific description using strong words adds persuasive force.

Prentice Hall Writing and Grammar Connection: Diamond Level, Chapter 8, Section 4

Extension Activities

Listening and Speaking With a group of classmates, write and perform the narration for a **movie preview** of a film version of "The Death of Hector." Consider using the following features to enhance your preview:

- excerpts of dialogue from the poem
- background music
- sound effects

Rehearse and perform your preview for the class. **[Group Activity]**

Research and Technology Using library and Internet resources, explore the efforts of archaeologists over the past 150 years to identify and excavate the historical city of Troy. Prepare and present an **oral report** to summarize your findings.

 **Take It to the Net**   PHSchool.com

Go online for an additional research activity using the Internet.

Prepare to Read

You Know the Place: Then ◆
He Is More Than a Hero ◆ Olympia 11

Sappho
(c. 630 B.C.–c. 570 B.C.)

Late in the seventh century B.C., the fame of earlier lyric poets was eclipsed by Sappho (saf´ ō) of Lesbos, one of the most prolific ancient lyricists. Sappho wrote nearly five hundred poems, only a small fraction of which remain, intact or in fragments. In most of her surviving poems, she addresses various girls of Lesbos, a group of female companions. Some critics believe that Sappho was the priestess of a *thiasos* (*th*ī´ ə sōs), an organized group of women who worshipped Aphrodite. Recent scholars, however, maintain that the circle of girls evident in her poetry were students, or apprentices, who studied poetry and the lyre with Sappho.

Praise and Disapproval Sappho's poetry was admired in antiquity; Plato praised her, and the Roman poets Catullus, Horace, and Ovid alluded to her in their work. In fact, at least six Greek comedies parodied her on the late Greek comic stage. Those plays are now lost, but from them sprang a number of legends about Sappho that were the source of disapproval and, later, hatred of her and her work. For example, according to legend, she was short, dark, and ugly; she was a prostitute; and she committed suicide by throwing herself off a cliff after the ferryman Phaon did not return her love. Although these legends are now discredited, they led the Bishop of Constantinople to order all copies of Sappho's work burned early in the Middle Ages. As a result of the bishop's order and a general loss of classical manuscripts during the Middle Ages, no collection of Sappho's poetry survived the Medieval period.

Rebirth in the Renaissance Interest in Sappho revived during the Renaissance, when scholars used lines quoted by other Greek and Latin writers to reconstruct Sappho's work. Then, in 1879, an incredible discovery in an ancient Egyptian trash site uncovered additional poems by Sappho. Later archaeological digs in the 1890s brought to light shredded papyrus scrolls of Sappho's poetry; these scrolls had been used to wrap mummies and to stuff crocodiles.

Pindar
(522 B.C.–440 B.C.)

Little information is available about the life of Pindar (pin´ dər), but it is known that he wrote in a century full of intellectual and political ferment. Although Pindar was born in Thebes, which stood outside the intellectual movements of the time, as a youth he spent a great deal of time away from his provincial birthplace. He may have studied music and poetry in Athens, the intellectual hub of classical Greece.

Odes for Athletes In his twenties, Pindar was commissioned by a great aristocratic family to write an ode in honor of their son's victory in the Olympic double footrace. Eventually, Pindar was commissioned to write for many athletic victors. He was sought after by powerful monarchs and nobles, and he spent time at the courts of the wealthy Sicilian tyrants. Like Sappho, the great fame he achieved in his lifetime lasted through antiquity. The Roman poet Horace, for example, considered Pindar to be a poet of unrivaled eloquence and originality.

Preview

Connecting to the Literature

Both Sappho and Pindar invite their readers into a unique poetic universe. As you read each poem, identify the characteristics of this new cosmos and compare it with the world you know.

Literary Analysis

Lyric Poetry

Lyric poetry expresses the observations and feelings of a single speaker. Lyric poems were originally sung to the accompaniment of a stringed instrument called a lyre. Unlike narrative poems that tell stories, lyric poems focus on producing a single effect. In these lines from "He Is More Than a Hero," for example, the speaker emphasizes the powerful reaction she has to her hero:

> hearing only my own ears
> drumming, I drip with sweat;
> trembling shakes my body

As you read each poem, use a chart like the one shown to record the words and phrases that contribute to a single unifying effect.

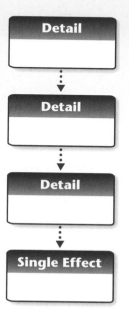

Comparing Literary Works

The poems of Sappho and Pindar share the musical quality of lyric poems, but each poem's **form**—its organization and structure—creates a different poetic impression or emotional effect on the reader. Sappho's poems take the form of simple lyrics that are highly personal. In contrast, Pindar's poem, reflecting its purpose to honor winning athletes, uses a more complex and public form known as the **ode.** As you read, consider the ways in which your reaction is affected by each poem's form.

Reading Strategy

Responding to Imagery

Lyric poems nearly always use images of the senses—taste, touch, sight, hearing, and smell—to convey ideas and emotions. To **respond to imagery,**

- Identify the sensory word pictures in the poem.
- Take time to consider how these images relate to your own life.

As you read, connect your own experiences to the images and ideas that Sappho and Pindar present.

Vocabulary Development

sleek (slēk) *adj.* smooth; glossy (p. 377)

murmur (mur´ mər) *n.* low, indistinct, continuous sound (p. 378)

tenuous (ten´ yo͞o əs) *adj.* slender or fine, as a fiber (p. 379)

suffuses (sə fyo͞o´ zəz) *v.* overspreads; fills with a glow (p. 379)

endeavor (en dev´ ər) *n.* earnest attempt at achievement (p. 380)

accordance (ə kôrd´ 'ns) *n.* agreement; harmony (p. 380)

Poetry of Sappho

You Know the Place: Then

Sappho

translated by Mary Barnard

Background

Sappho wrote her poems for a group of female students who came to the famed poetess to learn the graceful arts of music, dance, and poetry. The school's patron deity was Aphrodite, the goddess of love. Ancient Greeks believed that under Aphrodite's influence the world thrived, flowered, and blossomed. In her poems, Sappho often calls on Aphrodite, who is called "Queen" and "Cyprian" in "You Know the Place: Then," to serve as an ally in love's turmoil.

You know the place: then

Leave Crete and come to us
waiting where the grove is
pleasantest, by precincts

5   sacred to you; incense
smokes on the altar, cold
streams murmur through the

apple branches, a young
rose thicket shades the ground
10   and quivering leaves pour

down deep sleep; in meadows
where horses have grown <u>sleek</u>
among spring flowers, dill

scents the air. Queen! Cyprian!
15   fill our gold cups with love
stirred into clear nectar

sleek (slēk) *adj.* smooth, glossy

Literary Analysis
Lyric Poetry What kind of musical accompaniment do you think would suit the final lines of this lyric? Explain.

HE IS MORE THAN A HERO

Sappho

Comparing Translations

Presented here are two translations of the same poem by Sappho, illustrating some of the choices that translators make when translating poetry. Beyond technical choices, such as whether or not to preserve the poem's original meter, a translator must also decide how—and how much—to interpret the poet's words. What translators do is attempt to re-create for readers the experience of reading a poem in its original language. However, as these two translations of "He Is More Than a Hero" demonstrate, the resulting translation is influenced greatly by the translator's own experience with the text.

translated by Mary Barnard

He is more than a hero

He is a god in my eyes—
the man who is allowed
to sit beside you—he

5 who listens intimately
to the sweet <u>murmur</u> of
your voice, the enticing

laughter that makes my own
heart beat fast. If I meet
10 you suddenly, I can't

speak—my tongue is broken;
a thin flame runs under
my skin; seeing nothing,

hearing only my own ears
15 drumming, I drip with sweat;
trembling shakes my body

and I turn paler than
dry grass. At such times
death isn't far from me

murmur (mur´ mər) *n.* low, indistinct, continuous sound

Reading Strategy
Responding to Imagery
To what emotions do these sensory images appeal?

translated by Richmond Lattimore

Like the very gods in my sight is he who
sits where he can look in your eyes, who listens
close to you, to hear the soft voice, its sweetness
    murmur in love and

5 laughter, all for him. But it breaks my spirit;
underneath my breast all the heart is shaken.
Let me only glance where you are, the voice dies,
    I can say nothing,

but my lips are stricken to silence, under-
10 neath my skin the <u>tenuous</u> flame <u>suffuses</u>;
nothing shows in front of my eyes, my ears are
    muted in thunder.

And the sweat breaks running upon me, fever
shakes my body, paler I turn than grass is;
15 I can feel that I have been changed, I feel that
    death has come near me.

tenuous (ten´ yōo əs) *adj.*
slender or fine, as a fiber

suffuses (sə fyōoz´ əz) *v.*
overspreads; fills with a
glow

Review and Assess

Thinking About the Selections

1. **Respond:** Which images in these two poems were most appealing to you? Why?

2. **(a) Recall:** What two requests does the speaker of "You Know the Place: Then" make of Aphrodite? **(b) Infer:** What does the speaker expect from Aphrodite?

3. **(a) Recall:** To what senses do the images in lines 9–18 of the Barnard translation of "He Is More Than a Hero" appeal? **(b) Interpret:** What is the overall effect of these images?

4. **(a) Recall:** At the end of "He Is More Than a Hero," what does the speaker say is close to her? **(b) Interpret:** What emotion does this figurative reference evoke?

5. In "He Is More Than a Hero," the speaker's emotions cloud her ability to think clearly. **(a) Apply:** What other emotions, such as fear, can cause emotions to interfere with reason? **(b) Generalize:** What can people do in these situations?

Olympia 11

Pindar

translated by Richmond Lattimore

There is a time when men need most favoring
gales; there is a time for water from the sky,
the rainy children of cloud.
But if by <u>endeavor</u> a man win fairly, soft-spoken songs
5   are given, to be a beginning of men's
speech to come and a trusty pledge for great achievements.

Abundant is such praise laid up for Olympian
winners. My lips have good will
to marshal these words; yet only
10   by God's grace does a man blossom in <u>accordance</u> with his
        mind's wisdom.
Son of Archestratos,[1] know
that for the sake, Agesidamos,[2] of your boxing

I shall enchant in strain of song a glory upon
your olive wreath of gold
15   and bespeak the race of the West Wind Lokrians.[3]
There acclaim him; I warrant you,
Muses, you will visit no gathering cold to strangers
nor lost to lovely things
but deep to the heart in wisdom, and spearmen also. No
        thing, neither hot-colored fox
20   nor loud lion, may change the nature born in his blood.

endeavor (en dev´ ər) *n.* earnest attempt at achievement

accordance (ə kôrd´ 'ns) *n.* agreement; harmony

---

1. **Archestratos** (ärk ə strā´ tōs) father of Agesidamos.
2. **Agesidamos** (ə ges´ i dä´ mōs) victor in the boys' boxing competition in 476 B.C.
3. **West Wind Lokrians** (lō krē´ ənz) Lokris was a city on the Gulf of Corinth in Greece; "West Wind Lokrians" were Greek-speaking people from the colony of Lokris in southern Italy.

Review and Assess

Thinking About the Selection

1. **(a) Recall:** In the first stanza, what two natural forces does the speaker mention? **(b) Analyze:** Why do you think the speaker begins with these references to nature?

2. **(a) Recall:** According to lines 4–7, what is the function of "soft-spoken songs"? **(b) Infer:** To what "great achievements" do you think the speaker refers in line 7?

3. **(a) Evaluate:** In your opinion, is this poem an effective way to praise an athletic hero? Why or why not?

Review and Assess

Literary Analysis

Lyric Poetry

1. (a) Identify the observations and feelings of the speaker in the **lyric poem** "You Know the Place: Then." (b) What single, overall effect does the poem achieve?

2. In ancient Greece, lyrics were composed to be sung to musical accompaniment. In what ways might such music have reinforced the imagery and the overall effect in "He Is More Than a Hero"?

3. Which characteristics of lyric poetry are found in "Olympia 11"?

Comparing Literary Works

4. (a) Compare and contrast the **forms** of the lyrics of Sappho and Pindar. (b) How does each poem's form contribute to its effect?

5. In what ways might you describe Sappho's poems as "private" and Pindar's as "public"?

Reading Strategy

Responding to Imagery

6. (a) Use a chart like the one shown to list the images that are used to describe the precincts of Aphrodite in Crete in "You Know the Place: Then."

Images for Aphrodite in Crete			
Image	**Image**	**Image**	**Image**

(b) What is your **response** to these images?

7. Describe a contemporary experience or event that relates to the images of a "strain of song" and an "olive wreath of gold" in lines 13–14 of "Olympia 11."

Extend Understanding

8. **Cultural Connection:** Pindar's odes celebrate the Olympic athletes of ancient Greece. In what ways are athletes honored in American culture?

Integrate Language Skills

Vocabulary Development Lesson

Word Analysis: Echoic Words

Echoic is the term that dictionaries use to give the etymology, or origin and history, of words whose sound suggests their meaning. These words are called echoic because they echo, or imitate, the sounds that they name.

Murmur is an example of an echoic word. Pronounce *murmur* slowly and softly. Notice that the sound of the word suggests its meaning: a low, indistinct, continuous sound.

Pronounce each of the following words, paying close attention to the sound that each word seems to imitate. Then, use the sound of each word to write a brief definition.

1. buzz
2. thump
3. pop
4. chatter
5. crunch
6. hiss
7. drizzle
8. squawk

Concept Development: Synonyms

Select the letter of the word that is closest in meaning to the first word in each item below.

1. sleek: (a) sly, (b) glossy, (c) candid
2. murmur: (a) hum, (b) crash, (c) melody
3. tenuous: (a) tentative, (b) resigned, (c) slender
4. suffuses: (a) fills, (b) drains, (c) empties
5. endeavor: (a) failure, (b) attempt, (c) defeat
6. accordance: (a) insult, (b) harmony, (c) deprivation

Spelling Strategy

In nouns, the ending *-er* is more common than *-or*. Many nouns ending in *-or* name a quality or role. For each word root below, use *-er* or *-or* to add the proper suffix.

1. cand___   2. hum___   3. conduct___

Grammar and Style Lesson

Direct Address

When the speaker in a poem talks directly to someone or something, the form of speech is called **direct address.** Nouns or pronouns of direct address may be followed either by a comma or by an exclamation mark, depending on the degree of emotion in the sentence.

Comma: *Son of Archestratos,* know that for the sake, *Agesidamos,* of your boxing . . .

Exclamation Mark: *Queen! Cyprian!* fill our gold cups with love . . .

Practice In each sentence below, insert a comma or an exclamation mark, as appropriate.

1. Sappho I call upon you as the tenth muse.
2. O moon You far outshine the stars.
3. Agesidamos future ages will remember your victory.
4. Aphrodite Hear my prayer, I beg you.
5. You who sit nearby remember these songs.

Writing Application Write a paragraph in which you address either Sappho or Pindar and give your reactions to a poem you have read and enjoyed. In your paragraph, use two examples of direct address.

W_G *Prentice Hall Writing and Grammar Connection: Diamond Level, Chapter 27, Section 2*

Writing Lesson

Comparative Analysis of Translations

Translators of poems work hard to preserve the poem's original meaning and structure within the limits of a different language. Because translators' interpretations vary, translations sometimes differ dramatically. Write an analysis in which you compare and contrast the translations by Mary Barnard and Richmond Lattimore of Sappho's "He Is More Than a Hero."

Prewriting   Read each version of the poem carefully. Note specific differences in words, phrases, and emphasis. Use a chart like the one shown to organize your observations.

Model: Comparing and Contrasting Translations

Barnard	Lattimore
Uses metaphor in line 2: "He is a god in my eyes"	Uses simile in line 1: "Like the very gods . . . is he"

Drafting   As you draft, choose an effective organization. Either discuss your observations point by point, or discuss your observations about one translation fully and then move on to the next.

Revising   Ask a partner to read your draft and help you identify any weak or vague comparisons or contrasts. Replace these points with specific examples.

 Prentice Hall Writing and Grammar Connection: Diamond Level, Chapter 9, Section 3

Extension Activities

Listening and Speaking Memorize one of Sappho's poems. Then, rehearse a **recitation** of the poem. Use the following tips to enhance your interpretation:

- Adjust the pitch of your voice to echo the poem's tone.
- Change your rate of speaking to reflect the message of the poem.

Present your recitation to an audience of classmates or friends.

Research and Technology With a partner, use library and Internet resources to research the history of the lyre. Then, collect illustrations and notes on other stringed instruments from various cultures. Present your findings in an **illustrated report.** [Group Activity]

 Take It to the Net   PHSchool.com

Go online for an additional research activity using the Internet.

Prepare to Read

Pericles' Funeral Oration *from* History of the Peloponnesian War

Thucydides
(460 B.C.–404 B.C.)

The Athenian Thucydides (thoo sid´ i dēz´) is known as the greatest historian in antiquity and one of the most influential historians ever. No certain information about his life exists beyond what he reveals about himself in the course of his writing. However, his objective, scientific approach to history laid the foundation for modern historical methods.

Military Failure Thucydides was an important military magistrate in the Peloponnesian War, the long and bloody conflict between Athens and Sparta that ended with the fall of the Athenian empire. He appointed himself historian of the Peloponnesian War at its outset, and he called it the "greatest war of all." During his command of a fleet based at Thasos, he failed to protect the crucial Athenian colony of Amphipolis from a surprise Spartan attack. He went to trial for his military failure and was exiled for twenty years until the war ended.

Historical Success Exile provided Thucydides with the opportunity to observe the war from a distance. He took notes of events as they occurred, researched extensively, and recorded firsthand accounts of events told to him by Athenians and Spartans. Using the information he gathered, he wrote his historical masterpiece, the *History of the Peloponnesian War*.

In the first stages of his work, Thucydides took notes on events in which he participated or that he observed from a distance. Then, he rewrote and arranged his notes into a consecutive narrative. Finally, he elaborated the narrative so that it would not read as a mere chronicle of events. Unfortunately, he died before he could complete the *History*; it stops abruptly six years before the end of the war, though all the speeches are very polished. Thucydides is believed to have died suddenly in 404 B.C., shortly after Athens' defeat.

A Lasting Legacy Thucydides believed that history could be understood in terms of human behavior. Consequently, he presented character studies of leading Athenian and Spartan statesmen, in which he examined the human mind in wartime. Through the speeches included in the *History*, he articulated the motives and ambitions of both armies impartially. He aimed to teach people so that they would avoid making the same mistakes he witnessed in this war.

With a passion for truth, Thucydides refused to "accept all stories of ancient times in an uncritical way," and he adhered to rigorous standards of accuracy. Achieving accuracy was, by his own admission, difficult when he had to reconstruct speeches. Because he used speeches to paint a kind of moral portrait, he may have given himself freedom in shaping the speeches while maintaining their basic truth. In his words:

> I have found it difficult to remember the precise words used in the speeches which I listened to myself and my various informants have experienced the same difficulty; so my method has been, while keeping as closely as possible to the general sense of the words that were actually used, to make the speakers say what, in my opinion, was called for by each situation.

To what extent Thucydides relied on his opinion in reconstructing Pericles' funeral oration is uncertain, but he was a great admirer of Pericles, and he probably heard Pericles deliver the annual speech honoring the Athenian war dead in the winter of 430 B.C.

Preview

Connecting to the Literature

War always causes great loss of life, even for the winning side. In this speech, Pericles offers comfort to families of slain Athenian soldiers and inspires them to deal with their grief in positive ways.

Literary Analysis

Speech

A **speech** is an oral presentation on an important issue. The speaker determines the content of the speech by considering the speech's *purpose*, the *occasion* for which it is being given, and the *audience* to whom it is addressed.

Speeches often include rhetorical techniques such as *restatement* (repeating an idea in different words) and *parallelism* (repeating grammatical structures).

Connecting Literary Elements

One form of speech is an **oration,** a formal address intended to inspire listeners and incite them to action. Orators deliver an impassioned appeal to the audience's religious, moral, or patriotic values. Classical orations like Pericles' have seven identifiable parts:

- an *opening*, intended to capture the audience's attention
- a *narration*, or recital of facts
- an *exposition*, or definition, of issues to be addressed
- a *proposition* to clarify the issues and state the speaker's purpose
- a *confirmation* to address arguments for and against the proposition
- a *confutation*, or refutation, to disprove opposing arguments
- a *conclusion*, or epilogue, to summarize arguments and stir listeners

Notice how Pericles develops his oration using these techniques.

Reading Strategy

Recognizing Cultural Attitudes

Pericles' speech reveals the values and attitudes of Athenian society. For example, when he says that "the greatest glory of a woman is to be least talked about by men, whether they are praising you or criticizing you," he reveals women's inferior status in that society. Complete a chart like this one, listing and explaining passages that reveal Athenians' **cultural attitudes.**

Passage	Attitude It Reveals

Vocabulary Development

incredulous (in krej´ oo ləs) *adj.* disbelieving; doubtful; skeptical (p. 387)

manifold (man´ ə fōld´) *adj.* many; various (p. 391)

tangible (tan´ jə bəl) *adj.* definite; objective (p. 391)

consummation (kän´ sə mā´ shən) *n.* state of supreme perfection, skillfulness, and expertise (p. 391)

culmination (kul´ mə nā´ shən) *n.* highest point or climax (p. 392)

commiserate (kə miz´ ər āt´) *v.* share grief or sorrow (p. 393)

PERICLES' FUNERAL ORATION

from HISTORY OF THE PELOPONNESIAN WAR
Thucydides

translated by Rex Warner

Background

Pericles, a great statesman of ancient Greece, tried to unite his country under the leadership of his own city, Athens. He also promoted democracy in Athens. During his rule, which is sometimes called the Golden Age of Greece, many magnificent buildings, including the Parthenon, were built. Pericles was one of Athens' ten generals, or *strategoi* (strat´ ə goi), during the Peloponnesian War and is considered the greatest Athenian politician in the early days of that war. In isolation, his speech is a glowing account of Athens and of Athenian democracy, but it is not a complete picture of Athens as an imperial power. In fact, later in the war, Pericles was the target of angry criticism for his aggressive, expansionist policies.

In the same winter the Athenians, following their annual custom, gave a public funeral for those who had been the first to die in the war. These funerals are held in the following way: two days before the ceremony the bones of the fallen are brought and put in a tent which has been erected, and people make whatever offerings they wish to their own dead. Then there is a funeral procession in which coffins of cypress wood are carried on wagons. There is one coffin for each tribe, which contains the bones of members of that tribe. One empty bier is decorated and carried in the procession: this is for the missing, whose bodies could not be recovered. Everyone who wishes to, both citizens and foreigners, can join in the procession, and the women who are related to the dead are there to make their laments at the tomb. The bones are laid in the public burial-place, which is in the most beautiful quarter outside the city walls. Here the Athenians always bury those who have fallen in war. The only exception is those who died at Marathon,[1] who, because their achievement was considered absolutely outstanding, were buried on the battlefield itself.

When the bones have been laid in the earth, a man chosen by the city for his intellectual gifts and for his general reputation makes an appropriate speech in praise of the dead, and after the speech all depart. This is the procedure at these burials, and all through the war, when the time came to do so, the Athenians followed this ancient custom. Now, at the burial of those who were the first to fall in the war Pericles, the son of Xanthippus,[2] was chosen to make the speech. When the moment arrived, he came forward from the tomb and, standing on a high platform, so that he might be heard by as many people as possible in the crowd, he spoke as follows:

"Many of those who have spoken here in the past have praised the institution of this speech at the close of our ceremony. It seemed to them a mark of honor to our soldiers who have fallen in war that a speech should be made over them. I do not agree. These men have shown themselves valiant in action, and it would be enough, I think, for their glories to be proclaimed in action, as you have just seen it done at this funeral organized by the state. Our belief in the courage and manliness of so many should not be hazarded on the goodness or badness of one man's speech. Then it is not easy to speak with a proper sense of balance, when a man's listeners find it difficult to believe in the truth of what one is saying. The man who knows the facts and loves the dead may well think that an oration tells less than what he knows and what he would like to hear: others who do not know so much may feel envy for the dead, and think the orator over-praises them, when he speaks of exploits that are beyond their own capacities. Praise of other people is tolerable only up to a certain point, the point where one still believes that one could do oneself some of the things one is hearing about. Once you get beyond this point, you will find people becoming jealous and <u>incredulous</u>. However, the fact is that this institution was set up and approved by our forefathers, and it is my duty to follow the tradition and do my best to meet the wishes and the expectations of every one of you.

"I shall begin by speaking about our ancestors, since it is only right and proper on such an occasion to pay them the honor of

Literary Analysis
Speech According to Thucydides, what is the purpose of Pericles' speech?

Literary Analysis
Speech and Oration Why might Pericles open his oration by questioning the tradition of funeral orations?

incredulous (in krej´ oo ləs) *adj.* disbelieving; doubtful; skeptical

Reading Check

Why does Pericles object to the tradition of a funeral oration for fallen Athenian soldiers?

---

1. **Marathon** (mar´ ə thän´) ancient Greek village near Athens where the Athenians defeated the Persians in 490 B.C.
2. **Xanthippus** (zan´ thi pəs) victorious Athenian general in the war against Persia, and a member of one of the most illustrious noble families of Athens.

recalling what they did. In this land of ours there have always been the same people living from generation to generation up till now, and they, by their courage and their virtues, have handed it on to us, a free country. They certainly deserve our praise. Even more so do our fathers deserve it. For to the inheritance they had received they added all the empire we have now, and it was not without blood and toil that they handed it down to us of the present generation. And then we ourselves, assembled here today, who are mostly in the prime of life, have, in most directions, added to the power of our empire and have organized our State in such a way that it is perfectly well able to look after itself both in peace and in war.

"I have no wish to make a long speech on subjects familiar to you all: so I shall say nothing about the warlike deeds by which we acquired our power or the battles in which we or our fathers gallantly resisted our enemies, Greek or foreign. What I want to do is, in the first place, to discuss the spirit in which we faced our trials and also our constitution and the way of life which has made us great. After that I shall speak in praise of the dead, believing that this kind of speech is not inappropriate to the present occasion, and that this whole assembly, of citizens and foreigners, may listen to it with advantage.

"Let me say that our system of government does not copy the institutions of our neighbors. It is more the case of our being a model to others, than of our imitating anyone else. Our constitution is called a democracy because power is in the hands not of a minority but of the whole people. When it is a question of settling private disputes, everyone is equal before the law; when it is a question of putting one person before another in positions of public responsibility, what counts is not membership of a particular class, but the actual ability which the man possesses. No one, so long as he has it in him to be of service to the state, is kept in political obscurity because of poverty. And, just as our political life is free and open, so is our day-to-day life in our relations with each other. We do not get into a state with our next-door neighbor if he enjoys himself in his own way, nor do we give him the kind of black looks which, though they do no real harm, still do hurt people's feelings. We are free and tolerant in our private lives; but in public affairs we keep to the law. This is because it commands our deep respect.

"We give our obedience to those whom we put in positions of authority, and we obey the laws themselves, especially those which are for the protection of the oppressed, and those unwritten laws which it is an acknowledged shame to break.

"And here is another point. When our work is over, we are in a position to enjoy all kinds of recreation for our spirits. There are various kinds of contests and sacrifices regularly throughout the year; in our own homes we find a beauty and a good taste

Literary Analysis
Speech and Oration
Which of the seven parts of a classical oration is Pericles using in this paragraph?

Reading Strategy
Recognizing Cultural Attitudes What do Pericles' comments on public and private life show about the Athenian attitude toward tolerance of people's differences?

which delight us every day and which drive away our cares. Then the greatness of our city brings it about that all the good things from all over the world flow in to us, so that to us it seems just as natural to enjoy foreign goods as our own local products.

"Then there is a great difference between us and our opponents, in our attitude towards military security. Here are some examples: Our city is open to the world, and we have no periodical deportations[3] in order to prevent people observing or finding out secrets which might be of military advantage to the enemy. This is because we rely, not on secret weapons, but on our own real courage and loyalty. There is a difference, too, in our educational systems. The Spartans, from their earliest boyhood, are submitted to the most laborious training in courage; we pass our lives without all these restrictions, and yet are just as ready to face the same dangers as they are. Here is a proof of this: When the Spartans invade our land, they do not come by themselves, but bring all their allies with them; whereas we, when we launch an attack abroad, do the job by ourselves, and, though fighting on foreign soil, do not often fail to defeat opponents who are fighting

---

3. **deportations** (dē′ pôr tā′ shənz) *n.* orders that force people to leave the country.

▲ **Critical Viewing**
What does the painting on this urn suggest about Athenians' attitude toward education? **[Infer]**

☑**Reading Check**
Name one way in which Pericles considers Athens superior to Sparta.

Pericles' Funeral Oration ◆ 389

for their own hearths and homes. As a matter of fact none of our enemies has ever yet been confronted with our total strength, because we have to divide our attention between our navy and the many missions on which our troops are sent on land. Yet, if our enemies engage a detachment[4] of our forces and defeat it, they give themselves credit for having thrown back our entire army; or, if they lose, they claim that they were beaten by us in full strength. There are certain advantages, I think, in our way of meeting danger voluntarily, with an easy mind, instead of with a laborious training, with natural rather than with state-induced courage. We do not have to spend our time practicing to meet sufferings which are still in the future; and when they are actually upon us we show ourselves just as brave as these others who are always in strict training. This is one point in which, I think, our city deserves to be admired. There are also others:

"Our love of what is beautiful does not lead to extravagance; our love of the things of the mind does not make us soft. We regard wealth as something to be properly used, rather than as something to boast about. As for poverty, no one need be ashamed to admit it: the real shame is in not taking practical measures to escape from it. Here each individual is interested not only in his own affairs but in the affairs of the state as well: even those who are mostly occupied with their own business are extremely well-informed on general politics—this is a peculiarity of ours: we do not say that a man who takes no interest in politics is a man who minds his own business; we say that he has no business here at all. We Athenians, in our own persons, take our decisions on policy or submit them to proper discussions: for we do not think that there is an incompatibility between words and deeds; the worst thing is to rush into action before the consequences have been properly debated. And this is another point where we differ from other people. We are capable at the same time of taking risks and of estimating them beforehand. Others are brave out of ignorance; and, when they stop to think, they begin to fear. But the man who can most truly be accounted brave is he who best knows the meaning of what is sweet in life and of what is terrible, and then goes out undeterred to meet what is to come.

"Again, in questions of general good feeling there is a great contrast between us and most other people. We make friends by doing good to others, not by receiving good from them. This makes our friendship all the more reliable, since we want to keep alive the gratitude of those who are in our debt by showing continued goodwill to them: whereas the feelings of one who owes us something lack the same enthusiasm, since he knows that, when he repays our kindness, it will be more like paying back a debt than giving something spontaneously. We are unique in this.

Reading Strategy
Recognizing Cultural Attitudes Explain the Athenian attitude toward individual responsibility and duty.

Reading Strategy
Recognizing Cultural Attitudes What do these lines about goodwill suggest about the Athenian attitude toward generosity?

---

4. **engage a detachment** enter into conflict with troops.

When we do kindnesses to others, we do not do them out of any calculations of profit or loss: we do them without afterthought, relying on our free liberality. Taking everything together then, I declare that our city is an education to Greece, and I declare that in my opinion each single one of our citizens, in all the <u>manifold</u> aspects of life, is able to show himself the rightful lord and owner of his own person, and do this, moreover, with exceptional grace and exceptional versatility. And to show that this is no empty boasting for the present occasion, but real <u>tangible</u> fact, you have only to consider the power which our city possesses and which has been won by those very qualities which I have mentioned. Athens, alone of the states we know, comes to her testing time in a greatness that surpasses what was imagined of her. In her case, and in her case alone, no invading enemy is ashamed at being defeated, and no subject can complain of being governed by people unfit for their responsibilities. Mighty indeed are the marks and monuments of our empire which we have left. Future ages will wonder at us, as the present age wonders at us now. We do not need the praises of a Homer, or of anyone else whose words may delight us for the moment, but whose estimation of facts will fall short of what is really true. For our adventurous spirit has forced an entry into every sea and into every land; and everywhere we have left behind us everlasting memorials of good done to our friends or suffering inflicted on our enemies.

"This, then, is the kind of city for which these men, who could not bear the thought of losing her, nobly fought and nobly died. It is only natural that every one of us who survive them should be willing to undergo hardships in her service. And it was for this reason that I have spoken at such length about our city, because I wanted to make it clear that for us there is more at stake than there is for others who lack our advantages; also I wanted my words of praise for the dead to be set in the bright light of evidence. And now the most important of these words has been spoken. I have sung the praises of our city; but it was the courage and gallantry of these men, and of people like them, which made her splendid. Nor would you find it true in the case of many of the Greeks, as it is true of them, that no words can do more than justice to their deeds.

"To me it seems that the <u>consummation</u> which has overtaken these men shows us the meaning of manliness in its first revelation and in its final proof. Some of them, no doubt, had their faults; but what we ought to remember first is their gallant conduct against the enemy in defense of their native land. They have blotted out evil with good, and done more service to the commonwealth than they ever did harm in their private lives. No one of these men weakened because he wanted to go on enjoying his wealth: no one put off the awful day in the hope that he might live to escape his poverty and grow rich. More to be desired than

manifold (man´ ə fōld´) *adj.* many; various

tangible (tan´ jə bəl) *adj.* definite; objective

consummation (kän´ sə mā´ shən) *n.* state of supreme perfection, skillfulness, and expertise

✔**Reading Check**

Why has Pericles spoken at such length about Athens?

such things, they chose to check the enemy's pride. This, to them, was a risk most glorious, and they accepted it, willing to strike down the enemy and relinquish everything else. As for success or failure, they left that in the doubtful hands of Hope, and when the reality of battle was before their faces, they put their trust in their own selves. In the fighting, they thought it more honorable to stand their ground and suffer death than to give in and save their lives. So they fled from the reproaches of men, abiding with life and limb the brunt of battle; and, in a small moment of time, the climax of their lives, a <u>culmination</u> of glory, not of fear, were swept away from us.

"So and such they were, these men—worthy of their city. We who remain behind may hope to be spared their fate, but must resolve to keep the same daring spirit against the foe. It is not simply a question of estimating the advantages in theory. I could tell you a long story (and you know it as well as I do) about what is to be gained by beating the enemy back. What I would prefer is that you should fix your eyes every day on the greatness of Athens as she really is, and should fall in love with her. When you realize her greatness, then reflect that what made her great was men with a spirit of adventure, men who knew their duty, men who were ashamed to fall below a certain standard. If they ever failed in an enterprise, they made up their minds that at any rate the city should not find their courage lacking to her, and they gave to her the best contribution that they could. They gave her their lives, to her and to all of us, and for their own selves they won praises that never grow old, the most splendid of sepulchers[5]—not the sepulcher in which their bodies are laid, but where their glory remains eternal in men's minds, always there on the right occasion to stir others to speech or to action. For famous men have the whole earth as their memorial: it is not only the inscriptions on their graves in their own country that mark them out; no, in foreign lands also, not in any visible form but in people's hearts, their memory abides and grows. It is for you to try to be like them. Make up your minds that happiness depends on being free, and freedom depends on being courageous. Let there be no relaxation in face of the perils of the war. The people who have most excuse for despising death are not the wretched and unfortunate, who have no hope of doing well for themselves, but those who run the risk of a complete reversal in their lives, and who would feel the difference most intensely, if things went wrong for them. Any intelligent man would find a humiliation caused by his own slackness more painful to bear than death, when

Themes in World Literature

History as Literature

Just as a great deal of history can be found in literature, many historical works can be read as literature. Thucydides' *History of the Peloponnesian War* is part of a long tradition of works that are informative enough to be read for historical purposes but compelling enough to be read for pure entertainment. Another example of this type of work is the *Annals* (c. 117) of Tacitus, which details the excesses of the Roman emperors who succeeded Augustus Caesar. *A Journal of the Plague Year* (1722), by Daniel Defoe, gives a fictional narrator's first-person account of the outbreak of bubonic plague in the 1660s. More than two centuries later, Mark Bowden's *Black Hawk Down* gives a gripping account of an American military mission gone awry. Published in 1999, Bowden's book was hailed by historians and literary critics alike, proving that the tradition of history as literature is alive in modern times.

culmination (kul′ mə nā′ shən) *n.* highest point or climax

---

5. **sepulchers** (sep′ əl kərz) *n.* graves.

death comes to him unperceived, in battle, and in the confidence of his patriotism.

"For these reasons I shall not <u>commiserate</u> with those parents of the dead, who are present here. Instead I shall try to comfort them. They are well aware that they have grown up in a world where there are many changes and chances. But this is good fortune—for men to end their lives with honor, as these have done, and for you honorably to lament them: their life was set to a measure where death and happiness went hand in hand. I know that it is difficult to convince you of this. When you see other people happy you will often be reminded of what used to make you happy too. One does not feel sad at not having some good thing which is outside one's experience: real grief is felt at the loss of something which one is used to. All the same, those of you who are of the right age must bear up and take comfort in the thought of having more children. In your own homes these new children will prevent you from brooding over those who are no more, and they will be a help to the city, too, both in filling the empty places, and in assuring her security. For it is impossible for a man to put forward fair and honest views about our affairs if he has not, like everyone else, children whose lives may be at stake. As for those of you who are now too old to have children, I would ask you to count as gain the greater part of your life, in which you have been happy, and remember that what remains is not long, and let your hearts be lifted up at the thought of the fair fame of the dead. One's sense of honor is the only thing that does not grow old, and the last pleasure, when one is worn out with age, is not, as the poet said, making money, but having the respect of one's fellow men.

"As for those of you here who are sons or brothers of the dead, I can see a hard struggle in front of you. Everyone always speaks well of the dead, and, even if you rise to the greatest heights of heroism, it will be a hard thing for you to get the reputation of having come near, let alone equaled, their standard. When one is alive, one is always liable to the jealousy of one's competitors, but when one is out of the way, the honor one receives is sincere and unchallenged.

"Perhaps I should say a word or two on the duties of women to those among you who are now widowed. I can say all I have to say in a short word of advice. Your great glory is not to be inferior to what God has made you, and the greatest glory of a woman is to be least talked about by men, whether they are praising you or criticizing you. I have now, as the law demanded, said what I had

commiserate (kə miz´ ər āt´) *v.* share grief or sorrow

▼ **Critical Viewing**
What does this painting suggest about how war was viewed in ancient Greece? [Infer]

☑ **Reading Check**
Why does Pericles encourage the parents of fallen soldiers to have more children?

to say. For the time being our offerings to the dead have been made, and for the future their children will be supported at the public expense by the city, until they come of age. This is the crown and prize which she offers, both to the dead and to their children, for the ordeals which they have faced. Where the rewards of valor are the greatest, there you will find also the best and bravest spirits among the people. And now, when you have mourned for your dear ones, you must depart."

Review and Assess

Thinking About the Selection

1. **Respond:** What do you admire most about Athenian society as described by Pericles in his funeral oration? What do you admire least?

2. **(a) Recall:** According to Pericles, how does the Athenian system of government compare to that of its neighbors?
   (b) Deduce: What emotions is Pericles trying to arouse in his listeners by making this comparison?

3. **(a) Recall:** What does Pericles say about the educational systems of Sparta and Athens with regard to courage?
   (b) Infer: What is Pericles suggesting about the nature of Athenians?

4. **(a) Recall:** What is Pericles' attitude toward a man who has no interest in politics? **(b) Infer:** What does this suggest about the Athenians' commitment to the principles of democracy?

5. **(a) Recall:** In honoring the war dead, Pericles says that their deaths accomplished two things. What are these two things?
   (b) Analyze Causes and Effects: Explain what each accomplishment has meant to the soldiers and to Athens.

6. **(a) Recall:** On what do happiness and freedom depend, according to Pericles? **(b) Interpret:** What values seem to be most important to Pericles?

7. **(a) Recall:** What comfort does Pericles offer to the parents of the dead? **(b) Draw Conclusions:** What does this tell you about the Athenian attitude toward honor?

8. **Apply:** Think about speeches you have heard given by political figures and community leaders, or even a pep talk given by a good coach. Then, give an example of how one of these speakers used elements of oration in his or her speech.

Review and Assess

Literary Analysis

Speech

1. Complete a chart like this one to analyze the techniques Pericles uses in his **speech.**

	Example	Effect
Restatement		
Parallelism		

2. (a) Give one example of how Pericles appeals to his audience's sense of morality. (b) Why might this kind of appeal be particularly effective?

3. In your opinion, what is Pericles' most successful appeal to his audience's patriotism? Explain.

Connecting Literary Elements

4. (a) What is Pericles' proposition in this **oration**? (b) Where does he state his proposition most clearly?

5. List the arguments that Pericles presents in support of his proposition.

6. Explain how Pericles uses the example of the Spartans to address opposing viewpoints.

7. What is inspiring about the concluding paragraph of Pericles' oration?

Reading Strategy

Recognizing Cultural Attitudes

8. Explain the Athenian **cultural attitudes** toward wealth and poverty that are revealed in this selection.

9. Pericles says that a man achieves a position of public responsibility based on his actual ability, not on his social class. What does this say about the Athenian attitude toward the individual?

Extend Understanding

10. **Social Studies Connection:** In a time of mourning, crisis, or emergency, what effect can a speech like Pericles' have on those who hear it? Explain.

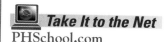

Integrate Language Skills

Vocabulary Development Lesson

Word Analysis: Latin Root -cred-

The word *incredulous* derives from the root -*cred*-, which comes from the Latin word *credere*, meaning "to believe." With the prefix *in*-, meaning "not," *incredulous* means "not believing." Use your understanding of the meaning of the root -*cred*- to choose the word from this list that best completes each sentence:

a. incredible   **b.** discredit   **c.** credence

1. The fact that he was a Spartan tended to ___?___ him in Athens.

2. The general put great ___?___ in the accuracy of the report.

3. The ___?___ bravery of the soldier made him a hero.

Grammar and Style Lesson

Colons

A **colon** is a punctuation mark (:) used before an extended quotation, an explanation, an example, or a series, and after the salutation in a formal letter.

These funerals are held in the following way: two days before the ceremony . . .

Practice Copy each item on a separate sheet of paper, inserting a colon where needed.

1. Pericles spoke as follows "Many of those who have spoken here in the past have praised the institution of this speech. . . ."

2. Here are some examples Our city is open to the world, and we have no periodical deportations. . . .

Concept Development: Antonyms

Match each vocabulary word on the left with its antonym, or opposite, on the right.

1. commiserate   **a.** beginning
2. consummation   **b.** believing
3. culmination   **c.** few
4. incredulous   **d.** abstract
5. manifold   **e.** incompleteness
6. tangible   **f.** rejoice

Spelling Strategy

When adding the suffix -*tion* to a verb that ends in -*te*, first drop these letters. For example, *culminate* + -*tion* = *culmination*. For each of the following words, write its noun form ending in -*tion*.

1. commiserate   2. consummate   3. fascinate

3. This is a peculiarity of ours We do not say that a man who takes no interest in politics is a man who minds his own business. . . .

4. Several orators of the twentieth century come to mind Winston Churchill, Franklin D. Roosevelt, and Martin Luther King.

5. Dear Sir or Madam
   It has come to my attention that there is a problem. . . .

Writing Application Write an example of each use of the colon: before an extended quotation, an explanation, an example, or a series, and after the salutation in a formal letter.

Writing Lesson

Essay About Leadership

In his funeral oration, Pericles demonstrates why he is considered to have been the greatest Athenian statesman. Using details from his speech, write an essay in which you discuss qualities of leadership.

Prewriting   Review the speech to identify qualities of leadership. Then, organize them into an outline of your essay.

Drafting   Begin with an introduction in which you define leadership and discuss why it is important in wartime. Refer to Pericles' speech as you develop your essay, using examples of how Pericles demonstrates leadership.

Model: Using Quotations to Support Main Points

Realizing the importance of leadership even in mourning, Pericles offers comfort to the families of the fallen. "But this is a good fortune—for men to end their lives with honor, as these have done . . . ," he says, lightening the burden of the survivors.

> Examples from the work help support the main points of an essay.

Revising   Review your paper, making sure you have supported your main points. Consider color-coding to identify supporting details. Use a different color to highlight details that answer each of these questions: *Who? What? When? Where? Why?* If you find you have not included information that answers each question, revise your draft.

WG Prentice Hall Writing and Grammar Connection: Diamond Level, Chapter 13, Section 3

Extension Activities

Listening and Speaking With a small group, present an **oral interpretation** of Pericles' oration. Take turns interpreting paragraphs, keeping in mind the following questions:

- What is Pericles saying?
- To what Athenian values is Pericles trying to appeal?

As you prepare your presentation, make sure that your interpretation suits the mood of the occasion. [**Group Activity**]

Research and Technology Pericles claims that everyone is equal under Athenian law. Evaluate the truth of this claim through research, including use of the Internet. Present your findings in the form of a **rights chart.** Your chart might include these headings: *men, women, slaves, boys, girls.* It also might include a list of rights and privileges, such as voting, owning property, and marrying.

 **Take It to the Net**   PHSchool.com

Go online for an additional research activity using the Internet.

CONNECTIONS
Literature Past and Present

Honoring the Dead

The battle of Gettysburg, Pennsylvania, fought in July 1863, was an important Union victory and marked a turning point in the Civil War in the United States. More than 50,000 Union and Confederate soldiers were killed or wounded in the battle. On November 19, 1863, while the war still raged, a military cemetery on the Gettysburg battlefield was dedicated. Unsure of President Lincoln's availability, the dedication organizers slated him as a secondary speaker, asking him to make only "a few appropriate remarks." In his brief address, Lincoln wanted to lead the 15,000 citizens attending the dedication through an emotional rite of passage. He also needed to gain continuing support for a bloody conflict that was far from over.

Timeless Praise for Fallen Soldiers Like Pericles in his Funeral Oration, Lincoln maintains in his address that a speech cannot really honor the soldiers who have died. Their brave actions have already brought them honor, and those actions will be remembered long after the speeches have ended. Centuries separate ancient Greece from nineteenth-century America, but Pericles and Lincoln speak with similar eloquence about their honored dead and the ideals for which they died. Though Lincoln's speech is much briefer than Pericles' oration—just 272 words—its reaffirmation of the democratic principles at the heart of American government is comparable to Pericles' pride in the democratic government of Athens.

◀ **Critical Viewing**
What mood does the facial expression of this statue—the centerpiece of the Lincoln Memorial in Washington, D.C.—convey? **[Analyze]**

The Gettysburg Address

Abraham Lincoln

Four score and seven years ago our fathers brought forth on this continent a new nation, conceived in Liberty, and dedicated to the proposition that all men are created equal.

Now we are engaged in a great civil war, testing whether that nation, or any nation so conceived and so dedicated, can long endure. We are met on a great battle-field of that war. We have come to dedicate a portion of that field, as a final resting place for those who here gave their lives that that nation might live. It is altogether fitting and proper that we should do this.

But, in a larger sense, we can not dedicate—we can not <u>consecrate</u>—we can not <u>hallow</u>—this ground. The brave men, living and dead, who struggled here, have consecrated it, far above our poor power to add or detract. The world will little note, nor long remember what we say here, but it can never forget what they did here. It is for us the living, rather, to be dedicated here to the unfinished work which they who fought here have thus far so nobly advanced. It is rather for us to be here dedicated to the great task remaining before us—that from these honored dead we take increased devotion to that cause for which they gave the last full measure of devotion—that we here highly resolve that these dead shall not have died in vain—that this nation, under God, shall have a new birth of freedom—and that government of the people, by the people, for the people, shall not perish from the earth.

consecrate (kän′ si krāt′) *v.* cause to be revered or honored

hallow (hal′ ō) *v.* make holy or sacred

Abraham Lincoln

(1809–1865)

Abraham Lincoln served in the Illinois state legislature and the United States Congress, where he earned a reputation as a champion of emancipation. He ran for the United States Senate in 1858. Lincoln lost the election, but his heated debates with Stephen Douglas brought him national recognition and helped him win the presidency in 1860.

Shortly after his election, the Civil War erupted. Throughout the war, Lincoln showed great strength and courage. He also demonstrated his gift for oratory, working diligently and thoughtfully to prepare effective messages. Lincoln was assassinated in 1865 while attending the theater with his wife.

Connecting Literature Past and Present

1. (a) Which speech is longer: Lincoln's address or Pericles' oration? (b) How does the length of a speech affect audience reaction?
2. How does the setting of a speech affect the way it is prepared and the way it is heard by an audience?
3. From each speech, give three examples of powerful language.
4. Which of these two speeches do you think would have been more interesting to hear? Explain.

Prepare to Read

from the Apology

Plato (429 B.C.–347 B.C.)

Plato is considered the most influential thinker in the history of Western culture. So revered was Plato in his day and throughout history that his written work has survived practically undamaged and more completely than that of any other ancient Greek writer. Originally named Aristocles (ə ris´ tə klēz´), he took the nickname Plato, meaning "broad-shouldered." He was born during the Golden Age of Athens to a prominent family active in Athenian politics. Belonging to an aristocratic and influential family groomed him to be a political leader like Pericles, but the political corruption he observed in his youth led Plato to withdraw from political activity. However, his life changed and gained direction when he met the philosopher Socrates (säk´ rə tēz´): He turned his attention to philosophy, the love of wisdom.

The Influence of Socrates Although the Athens of Plato's youth was experiencing a period of cultural flowering, it was also engaged in a devastating war with Sparta. This war ended with Athens' defeat in 404 B.C. After the war, a repressive government called the Thirty Tyrants ruled Athens for a year until democracy was restored. At the same time, self-proclaimed thinkers called Sophists (from *sophia*, or wisdom) went about teaching Athenian youths the art of rhetoric, the ability to use language effectively and persuasively. Sophist teaching came to be considered empty, however, because it had little grounding in morals or values.

In the midst of this intellectual ferment, the philosopher Socrates wandered the streets, shabbily dressed and unbathed, questioning people about their ideas and values. He believed that the unexamined life was not worth living, and so he questioned daily the meaning of virtue, the value of knowledge, and the importance of truth. He compared himself to a gadfly because he knew he was an annoying presence, pressing others to think more clearly about their values and ideals. In Socrates' view, a consistently thorough examination of beliefs was the path to wisdom and goodness. Plato was one of a group of young men who collected about Socrates, drawn to his magnetic personality. In fact, Plato is responsible for nearly all the information we have about Socrates.

The Dialogues Plato revealed his philosophy in the form of dialogues. Similar to works of drama, Plato's dialogues feature Socrates as a character engaging in philosophical discourse with various other characters. These dialogues constitute a portrait of Socrates: a representation of his interests, his methods, and his self-appointed mission to teach by questioning. Plato portrays Socrates as unwavering in his fidelity to the philosophic life.

The Academy After Socrates' death, Plato withdrew from Athens to travel in Italy, Cyrene, Sicily, and Egypt. Upon his return to Athens, he founded the Academy, the first European university and institution of pure research. Plato spent the next twenty years of his life directing the Academy, lecturing, and discussing philosophical and mathematical questions with members of the school.

Preview

Connecting to the Literature

At some time, most of us have had to defend or explain our actions. In this excerpt from the *Apology*, Socrates defends his philosophy in court. The stakes are high—if he fails to persuade the authorities that his ideas are not criminal, he could be sentenced to death.

Literary Analysis

Monologue

A **monologue** is a long and revealing speech by one character. In this monologue from the *Apology*, Socrates explains and defends his philosophy and his life's mission, the pursuit of knowledge. This excerpt reveals Socrates' commitment to his beliefs:

> . . . a man who is good for anything ought not to calculate the chance of living or dying; he ought only to consider whether in doing anything he is doing right or wrong. . . .

As you read, look for other statements that reveal Socrates' character and philosophy.

Connecting Literary Elements

Socrates often makes his points through **analogy,** an extended comparison of relationships. An analogy shows how the relationship between one pair of things is like the relationship between another pair. Notice how Socrates compares himself to a gadfly and uses other comparisons to clarify his arguments.

Reading Strategy

Challenging the Text

When reading a work that presents an argument, do not simply accept ideas—challenge them. To **challenge a text,** critically evaluate its assertions and reasoning. Compare the evidence and arguments with your own knowledge and experience or with other reading. Then, decide whether you agree or disagree with the ideas. Use a chart like the one shown to record your thinking.

Vocabulary Development

eloquence (el´ ə kwəns) *n.* fluent, persuasive speech (p. 402)

affidavit (af ə dā´ vit) *n.* legal document containing sworn testimony (p. 404)

lamented (lə ment´ id) *v.* felt deep sorrow for (p. 406)

avenged (ə venjd´) *v.* took revenge on behalf of (p. 408)

exhorting (eg zôrt´ iŋ) *v.* urging (p. 409)

impudence (im´ pyoo dəns) *n.* rashness; boldness (p. 410)

indictment (in dīt´ mənt) *n.* formal accusation (p. 410)

piety (pī´ ə tē) *n.* respect for the gods (p. 412)

Socrates' Argument

A man who is good for anything ought not to calculate the chance of living or dying.

↓

Arguments From the Text

↓

Your Experiences

↓

Agree or Disagree?

from the

APOLOGY

Plato

translated by Benjamin Jowett

Background

Socrates was critical of local politicians and their ways of governing, and he advocated a moral code that was independent of religious dictates—one that would not change with the changing governments. In 399 B.C., prominent Athenians brought Socrates to trial for atheism (belief that no gods exist) and for corrupting Athenian youth. The *Apology* is Plato's account of what happened at Socrates' trial. In this excerpt, Socrates presents his defense.

How you, O Athenians, have been affected by my accusers, I cannot tell; but I know that they almost made me forget who I was—so persuasively did they speak; and yet they have hardly uttered a word of truth. But of the many falsehoods told by them, there was one which quite amazed me;—I mean when they said that you should be upon your guard and not allow yourselves to be deceived by the force of my eloquence. To say this, when they were certain to be detected as soon as I opened my lips and proved myself to be anything but a great speaker, did indeed appear to me most shameless—unless by the force of eloquence they mean the force of truth; for if such is their meaning, I admit that I am eloquent. But in how different a way from theirs! Well, as I was saying, they have scarcely spoken the truth at all; but from me you shall hear the whole truth: not, however, delivered after their manner in a set oration duly ornamented with words and phrases. No, by heaven! but I shall use the words and arguments which occur to me at the moment; for I am confident in the justice of my cause: at my time of life I ought not to be appearing before you, O men of Athens, in the character of a juvenile orator—let no one expect it of me. And I must beg of you to grant me a favor:—If I defend myself in my accustomed manner, and you hear me using the words which

eloquence (el´ ə kwəns) *n.* fluent, persuasive speech

I have been in the habit of using in the agora,[1] at the tables of the money-changers, or anywhere else, I would ask you not to be surprised, and not to interrupt me on this account. For I am more than seventy years of age, and appearing now for the first time in a court of law, I am quite a stranger to the language of the place; and therefore I would have you regard me as if I were really a stranger, whom you would excuse if he spoke in his native tongue, and after the fashion of his country:—Am I making an unfair request of you? Never mind the manner, which may or may not be good; but think only of the truth of my words, and give heed to that: let the speaker speak truly and the judge decide justly.

Well, then, I must make my defense, and endeavor to clear away in a short time, a slander which has lasted a long time. May I succeed, if to succeed be for my good and yours, or likely to avail me in my cause! The task is not an easy one; I quite understand the nature of it. And so leaving the event with God, in obedience to the law I will now make my defense.

---

1. agora (ag´ ə rə) *n.* ancient Greek marketplace.

▲ **Critical Viewing**
Based on this depiction, how would you describe ancient Athens? [**Analyze**]

Literary Analysis
Monologue What attitudes does Socrates reveal in this paragraph?

☑ **Reading Check**
According to Socrates' accusers, why should Athenians be on guard while Socrates speaks?

I will begin at the beginning, and ask what is the accusation which has given rise to the slander of me, and in fact has encouraged Meletus to prefer[2] this charge against me. Well, what do the slanderers say? They shall be my prosecutors, and I will sum up their words in an <u>affidavit</u>: "Socrates is an evildoer, and a curious person, who searches into things under the earth and in heaven, and he makes the worse appear the better cause; and he teaches the aforesaid doctrines to others." Such is the nature of the accusation: it is just what you have yourselves seen in the comedy of Aristophanes,[3] who has introduced a man whom he calls Socrates, going about and saying that he walks in air, and talking a deal of nonsense concerning matters of which I do not pretend to know either much or little— not that I mean to speak disparagingly[4] of any one who is a student of natural philosophy. I should be very sorry if Meletus could bring so grave a charge against me. But the simple truth is, O Athenians, that I have nothing to do with physical speculations. Very many of those here present are witnesses to the truth of this, and to them I appeal. Speak then, you who have heard me, and tell your neighbors whether any of you have ever known me hold forth in few words or in many upon such matters. . . . You hear their answer. And from what they say of this part of the charge you will be able to judge of the truth of the rest.

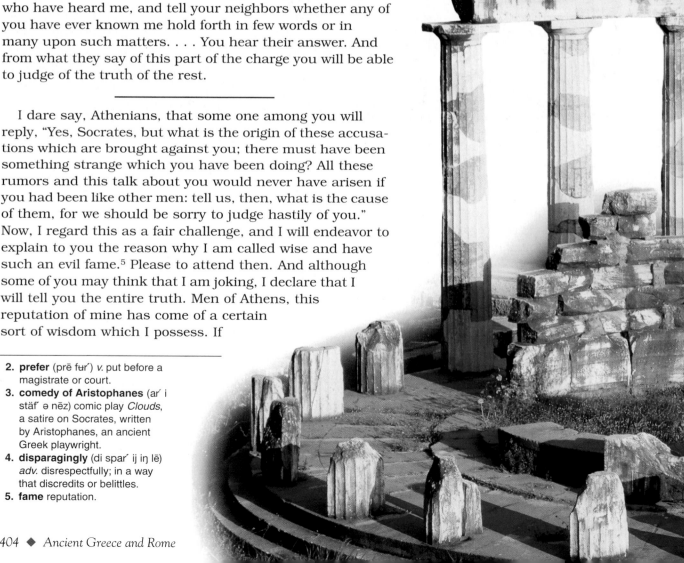

affidavit (af´ ə dā´ vit) n. legal document containing sworn testimony

———————

I dare say, Athenians, that some one among you will reply, "Yes, Socrates, but what is the origin of these accusations which are brought against you; there must have been something strange which you have been doing? All these rumors and this talk about you would never have arisen if you had been like other men: tell us, then, what is the cause of them, for we should be sorry to judge hastily of you." Now, I regard this as a fair challenge, and I will endeavor to explain to you the reason why I am called wise and have such an evil fame.[5] Please to attend then. And although some of you may think that I am joking, I declare that I will tell you the entire truth. Men of Athens, this reputation of mine has come of a certain sort of wisdom which I possess. If

———————

2. **prefer** (prē fur´) v. put before a magistrate or court.
3. **comedy of Aristophanes** (ar´ i stäf´ ə nēz) comic play *Clouds*, a satire on Socrates, written by Aristophanes, an ancient Greek playwright.
4. **disparagingly** (di spar´ ij iŋ lē) *adv.* disrespectfully; in a way that discredits or belittles.
5. **fame** reputation.

you ask me what kind of wisdom, I reply, wisdom such as may perhaps be attained by man, for to that extent I am inclined to believe that I am wise; whereas the persons of whom I was speaking have a superhuman wisdom, which I may fail to describe, because I have it not myself; and he who says that I have, speaks falsely, and is taking away my character. And here, O men of Athens, I must beg you not to interrupt me, even if I seem to say something extravagant. For the word which I will speak is not mine. I will refer you to a witness who is worthy of credit; that witness shall be the god of Delphi[6]—he will tell you about my wisdom, if I have any, and of what sort it is. You must have known Chaerephon; he was early a friend of mine, and also a friend of yours, for he shared in the recent exile of the people, and returned with you. Well, Chaerephon, as you know, was very impetuous in all his doings, and he went to Delphi and boldly asked the oracle to tell him whether—as I was saying, I must beg you not to interrupt—he asked the oracle to tell him whether any one was wiser than I was, and the Pythian prophetess answered, that there was no man wiser. Chaerephon is dead himself; but his brother, who is in court, will confirm the truth of what I am saying.

Why do I mention this? Because I am going to explain to you why I have such an evil name. When I heard the answer, I said to myself, What can the god mean? and what is the interpretation of his riddle? for I know that I have no wisdom, small or great. What then can he mean when he says that I am the wisest of men? And yet he is a god, and cannot lie; that would be against his nature. After long consideration, I thought of a method of trying the question. I reflected that if I could only find a man wiser than myself, then I might go to the god with a refutation[7] in my hand. I should say to him, "Here is a man who is wiser than I am; but you said that I was the wisest." Accordingly I went to one who had the reputation of wisdom, and observed him—his name I need not mention; he was a politician whom I selected for examination—and the result was as follows: When I began to talk with him, I could not help thinking that he was not

---

6. **god of Delphi** (del´ fī) Apollo.
7. **refutation** (ref´ yə tā´ shən) *n.* something that proves an argument false or wrong.

Reading Strategy
Challenging the Text Do you agree with the strategy that Socrates uses to refute the god's claim that Socrates is the wisest of all men? Why or why not?

✔**Reading Check**
What did Chaerephon ask the oracle at Delphi? What was the oracle's answer?

◀ **Critical Viewing**
How might temples like the one shown have inspired respect for the gods of ancient Greece? [Speculate]

really wise, although he was thought wise by many, and still wiser by himself; and thereupon I tried to explain to him that he thought himself wise, but was not really wise; and the consequence was that he hated me, and his enmity[8] was shared by several who were present and heard me. So I left him, saying to myself, as I went away: Well, although I do not suppose that either of us knows anything really beautiful and good, I am better off than he is,—for he knows nothing, and thinks that he knows; I neither know nor think that I know. In this latter particular, then, I seem to have slightly the advantage of him. Then I went to another who had still higher pretensions to wisdom, and my conclusion was exactly the same. Whereupon I made another enemy of him, and of many others besides him.

Then I went to one man after another, being not unconscious of the enmity which I provoked, and I <u>lamented</u> and feared this: but necessity was laid upon me,—the word of God, I thought, ought to be considered first. And I said to myself, Go I must to all who appear to know, and find out the meaning of the oracle. And I swear to you, Athenians, by the dog I swear!—for I must tell you the truth—the result of my mission was just this: I found that the men most in repute[9] were all but the most foolish; and that others less esteemed were really wiser and better. I will tell you the tale of my wanderings and of the "Herculean" labors,[10] as I may call them, which I endured only to find at last the oracle irrefutable. After the politicians, I went to the poets; tragic, dithyrambic,[11] and all sorts. And there, I said to myself, you will be instantly detected; now you will find out that you are more ignorant than they are. Accordingly I took them some of the most elaborate passages in their own writings, and asked what was the meaning of them—thinking that they would teach me something. Will you believe me? I am almost ashamed to confess the truth, but I must say that there is hardly a person present who would not have talked better about their poetry than they did themselves. Then I knew that not by wisdom do poets write poetry, but by a sort of genius and inspiration; they are like diviners[12] or soothsayers[13] who also say many fine things, but do not understand the meaning of them. The poets appeared to me to be much in the same case; and I further observed that upon the strength of their poetry they believed themselves to be the wisest of men in other things in which they were not wise. So I departed, conceiving myself to be superior to them for the same reason that I was superior to the politicians.

lamented (lə ment′ id) *v.* felt deep sorrow for

Reading Strategy
Challenging the Text Do you agree with Socrates' assertion that poets write with "a sort of genius and inspiration"? Explain.

Literary Analysis
Monologue According to what he reveals in this passage, what is Socrates' mission in life?

---

8. **enmity** (en′ mə tē) *n.* bitter attitude; hostility.
9. **in repute** (ri pyo͞ot′) here, regarded as being wise.
10. **Herculean** (hər kyo͞o′ lē ən) **labors** In a fit of madness, the hero Hercules killed his children. The Delphic oracle told him to perform twelve labors as punishment. Through these twelve feats of strength and courage, Hercules won immortality.
11. **dithyrambic** (dith′ ə ram′ bik) *adj.* in the style of impassioned, choric hymns that honor Dionysus, the god of wine.
12. **diviners** (də vīn′ ərz) *n.* people who interpret divine omens.
13. **soothsayers** (so͞oth′ sā′ ərz) *n.* people who foretell the future.

At last I went to the artisans. I was conscious that I knew nothing at all, as I may say, and I was sure that they knew many fine things; and here I was not mistaken, for they did know many things of which I was ignorant, and in this they certainly were wiser than I was. But I observed that even the good artisans fell into the same error as the poets;—because they were good workmen they thought that they also knew all sorts of high matters, and this defect in them overshadowed their wisdom: and therefore I asked myself on behalf of the oracle, whether I would like to be as I was, neither having their knowledge nor their ignorance, or like them in both; and I made answer to myself and to the oracle that I was better off as I was.

This inquisition[14] has led to my having many enemies of the worst and most dangerous kind, and has given occasion also to many calumnies.[15] And I am called wise, for my hearers always imagine that I myself possess the wisdom which I find wanting in others: but the truth is, O men of Athens, that God only is wise; and by his answer he intends to show that the wisdom of men is worth little or nothing; he is not speaking of Socrates, he is only using my name by way of illustration, as if he said, He, O men, is the wisest, who, like Socrates, knows that his wisdom is in truth worth nothing. And so I go about the world obedient to the god, and search and make enquiry into the wisdom of any one, whether citizen or stranger, who appears to be wise; and if he is not wise, then in vindication[16] of the oracle I show him that he is not wise; and my occupation quite absorbs me, and I have no time to give either to any public matter of interest or to any concern of my own, but I am in utter poverty by reason of my devotion to the god.

There is another thing:—young men of the richer classes, who have not much to do, come about me of their own accord; they like to hear the pretenders examined, and they often imitate me, and proceed to examine others; there are plenty of persons, as they quickly discover, who think that they know something, but really know little or nothing; and then those who are examined by them instead of being angry with themselves are angry with me: This confounded Socrates, they say; this villainous misleader of youth!—and then if somebody asks them, Why, what evil does he practice or teach? they do not know, and cannot tell; but in order that they may not appear to be at a loss, they repeat the ready-made charges which are used against all philosophers about teaching things up in the clouds and under the earth, and having no gods, and making the worse

---

14. **inquisition** (in′ kwə zish′ ən) *n.* severe and intensive questioning.
15. **calumnies** (kal′ əm nēz) *n.* false, malicious statements meant to slander.
16. **vindication** (vin′ də kā′ shən) *n.* defense.

Literature
in context Humanities Connection

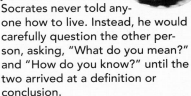

The Socratic Method

The Socratic method is a question-and-answer technique of philosophical dialogue that is used to arrive at a definition of some abstract idea, such as justice or virtue. Socrates never told anyone how to live. Instead, he would carefully question the other person, asking, "What do you mean?" and "How do you know?" until the two arrived at a definition or conclusion.

Socrates would begin his inquiry with a hypothesis that seemed to be true, then question the consequences that resulted from it. For example, if justice means keeping promises and paying debts, what are some consequences of universally applying that principle of justice? If the consequences are true and consistent, then the hypothesis would be confirmed.

The Socratic method of establishing a working hypothesis and then testing it became central to Western thought and to science, in particular. It remains the foundation of the scientific method today.

✔Reading Check

Why is Socrates in "utter poverty"?

appear the better cause; for they do not like to confess that their pretense of knowledge has been detected—which is the truth; and as they are numerous and ambitious and energetic, and are drawn up in battle array and have persuasive tongues, they have filled your ears with their loud and inveterate[17] calumnies.

––––––––––

Some one will say: And are you not ashamed, Socrates, of a course of life which is likely to bring you to an untimely end? To him I may fairly answer: There you are mistaken: a man who is good for anything ought not to calculate the chance of living or dying; he ought only to consider whether in doing anything he is doing right or wrong—acting the part of a good man or of a bad. Whereas, upon your view, the heroes who fell at Troy were not good for much, and the son of Thetis[18] above all, who altogether despised danger in comparison with disgrace; and when he was so eager to slay Hector, his goddess mother said to him, that if he <u>avenged</u> his companion Patroclus, and slew Hector, he would die himself—"Fate," she said, in these or the like words, "waits for you next after Hector"; he, receiving this warning, utterly despised danger and death, and instead of fearing them, feared rather to live in dishonor, and not to avenge his friend. "Let me die forthwith," he replies, "and be avenged of my enemy, rather than abide here by the beaked ships, a laughing stock and a burden of the earth." Had Achilles any thought of death and danger? For wherever a man's place is, whether the place which he has chosen or that in which he has been placed by a commander, there he ought to remain in the hour of danger; he should not think of death or of anything but of disgrace. And this, O men of Athens, is a true saying.

Strange, indeed, would be my conduct, O men of Athens, if I, who, when I was ordered by the generals whom you chose to command me at Potidaea and Amphipolis and Delium,[19] remained where they placed me, like any other man, facing death—if now, when, as I conceive and imagine, God orders me to fulfil the philosopher's mission of searching into myself and other men, I were to desert my post through fear of death, or any other fear; that would indeed be strange, and I might justly be arraigned in court for denying the existence of the gods, if I disobeyed the oracle because I was afraid of death, fancying that I was wise when I was not wise. For the fear of death is indeed the pretense of wisdom, and not real wisdom, being a pretense of knowing the unknown; and no one knows whether death, which men in their fear apprehend to be the greatest evil, may not be the greatest good. Is not this ignorance of a disgraceful sort, the ignorance which is the conceit that a man knows what he does not know?

avenged (ə venjd´) v. took revenge on behalf of

Literary Analysis
Monologue and Analogy
What point does Socrates make by comparing his duty as a philosopher to his duty as a soldier?

––––––––––

17. **inveterate** (in vet´ ər it) *adj.* firmly established over time; deep rooted.
18. **son of Thetis** Achilles, epic hero of the *Iliad*.
19. **Potidaea** (pä ti dē´ ə) **and Amphipolis** (am fi´ pə lis) **and Delium** (dē´ lē əm) three of the battles in which Socrates fought in the Peloponnesian War.

And in this respect only I believe myself to differ from men in general, and may perhaps claim to be wiser than they are:—that whereas I know but little of the world below, I do not suppose that I know: but I do know that injustice and disobedience to a better, whether God or man, is evil and dishonorable, and I will never fear or avoid a possible good rather than a certain evil. And therefore if you let me go now, and are not convinced by Anytus, who said that since I had been prosecuted I must be put to death; (or if not that I ought never to have been prosecuted at all); and that if I escape now, your sons will all be utterly ruined by listening to my words—if you say to me, Socrates, this time we will not mind Anytus, and you shall be let off, but upon one condition, that you are not to enquire and speculate in this way any more, and that if you are caught doing so again you shall die;—if this was the condition on which you let me go, I should reply: Men of Athens, I honor and love you; but I shall obey God rather than you, and while I have life and strength I shall never cease from the practice and teaching of philosophy, <u>exhorting</u> any one whom I meet and saying to him after my manner: You, my friend,— a citizen of the great and mighty and wise city of Athens,—are you not ashamed of heaping up the greatest amount of money and honor and reputation, and caring so little about wisdom and truth and the greatest improvement of the soul, which you never regard or heed at all? And if the person with whom I am arguing, says: Yes, but I do care; then I do not leave him or let him go at once; but I proceed to interrogate and examine and cross-examine him, and if I think that he has no virtue in him, but only says that he has, I reproach him with undervaluing the greater, and overvaluing the less. And I shall repeat the same words to every one whom I meet, young and old, citizen and alien, but especially to the citizens, inasmuch as they are my brethren. For know that this is the command of God; and I believe that no greater good has ever happened in the State than my service to the God. For I do nothing but go about persuading you all, old and young alike, not to take thought for your persons or your properties, but first and chiefly to care about the greatest improvement of the soul. I tell you that virtue is not given by money, but that from virtue comes money and every other good of man, public as well as private. This is my teaching, and if this is the doctrine which corrupts the youth, I am a mischievous person. But if any one says that this is not my teaching, he is speaking an untruth. Wherefore, O men of Athens, I say to you do as Anytus bids or not as Anytus bids, and either acquit me or not; but whichever you do, understand that I shall never alter my ways, not even if I have to die many times.

Men of Athens, do not interrupt, but hear me; there was an understanding between us that you should hear me to the end: I have something more to say, at which you may be inclined to cry out; but I believe that to hear me will be good for you, and therefore I beg that you will not cry out. I would have you know, that if you kill such an one as I am, you will injure yourselves more than you will injure me.

exhorting (eg zôrt´ iŋ) *v.* urging

Reading Check

According to Socrates, what should be the primary concern of all Athenians?

Nothing will injure me, not Meletus nor yet Anytus—they cannot, for a bad man is not permitted to injure a better than himself. I do not deny that Anytus may, perhaps, kill him, or drive him into exile, or deprive him of civil rights; and he may imagine, and others may imagine, that he is inflicting a great injury upon him: but there I do not agree. For the evil of doing as he is doing—the evil of unjustly taking away the life of another—is greater far.

And now, Athenians, I am not going to argue for my own sake, as you may think, but for yours, that you may not sin against the God by condemning me, who am his gift to you. For if you kill me you will not easily find a successor to me, who, if I may use such a ludicrous[20] figure of speech, am a sort of gadfly,[21] given to the State by God; and the State is a great and noble steed[22] who is tardy in his motions owing to his very size, and requires to be stirred into life. I am that gadfly which God has attached to the State, and all day long and in all places am always fastening upon you, arousing and persuading and reproaching you. You will not easily find another like me, and therefore I would advise you to spare me. I dare say that you may feel out of temper (like a person who is suddenly awakened from sleep), and you think that you might easily strike me dead as Anytus advises, and then you would sleep on for the remainder of your lives, unless God in his care of you sent you another gadfly. When I say that I am given to you by God, the proof of my mission is this:—if I had been like other men, I should not have neglected all my own concerns or patiently seen the neglect of them during all these years, and have been doing yours, coming to you individually like a father or elder brother, exhorting you to regard virtue; such conduct, I say, would be unlike human nature. If I had gained anything, or if my exhortations had been paid, there would have been some sense in my doing so; but now, as you will perceive, not even the <u>impudence</u> of my accusers dares to say that I have ever exacted or sought pay of any one; of that they have no witness. And I have a sufficient witness to the truth of what I say— my poverty.

Some one may wonder why I go about in private giving advice and busying myself with the concerns of others, but do not venture to come forward in public and advise the State. I will tell you why. You have heard me speak at sundry[23] times and in diverse places of an oracle or sign which comes to me, and is the divinity which Meletus ridicules in the <u>indictment</u>. This sign, which is a kind of voice, first began to come to me when I was a child; it always

impudence (im´ pyoo dəns) *n.* rashness; boldness

indictment (in dīt´ mənt) *n.* formal accusation

▼ **Critical Viewing**
What does this statue suggest about the true nature of justice? **[Infer]**

---

20. ludicrous (loo´ di krəs) *adj.* absurd; ridiculous.
21. gadfly (gad´ flī) *n.* horsefly.
22. steed (stēd) *n.* horse.
23. sundry (sun´ drē) *adj.* various.

forbids but never commands me to do anything which I am going to do. This is what deters me from being a politician. And rightly, as I think. For I am certain, O men of Athens, that if I had engaged in politics, I should have perished long ago, and done no good either to you or to myself. And do not be offended at my telling you the truth: for the truth is, that no man who goes to war with you or any other multitude, honestly striving against the many lawless and unrighteous deeds which are done in a State, will save his life: he who will fight for the right, if he would live even for a brief space, must have a private station and not a public one.

Now, do you really imagine that I could have survived all these years, if I had led a public life, supposing that like a good man I had always maintained the right and had made justice, as I ought, the first thing? No, indeed, men of Athens, neither I nor any other man. But I have been always the same in all my actions, public as well as private, and never have I yielded any base compliance[24] to those who are slanderously termed my disciples, or to any other. Not that I have any regular disciples. But if any one likes to come and hear me while I am pursuing my mission, whether he be young or old, he is not excluded. Nor do I converse only with those who pay; but any one, whether he be rich or poor, may ask and answer me and listen to my words; and whether he turns out to be a bad man or a good one, neither result can be justly imputed[25] to me; for I never taught or professed to teach him anything. And if any one says that he has ever learned or heard anything from me in private which all the world has not heard, let me tell you that he is lying.

Well, Athenians, this and the like of this is all the defense which I have to offer. Yet a word more. Perhaps there may be some one who is offended at me, when he calls to mind how he himself on a similar, or even a less serious occasion, prayed and entreated the judges with many tears, and how he produced his children in court, which was a moving spectacle, together with a host of relations and friends; whereas I, who am probably in danger of my life, will do none of these things. The contrast may occur to his mind, and he may be set against me, and vote in anger because he is displeased at me on this account. Now, if there be such a person among you,—mind, I do not say that there is,—to him I may fairly reply: My friend, I am a man, and like other men, a creature of flesh and blood, and not "of wood or stone," as Homer says; and I have a family, yes, and sons, O Athenians, three in

Reading Strategy
Challenging the Text Do you think Socrates is right in saying that anyone who is a public figure cannot also be a just person before all else? Explain.

---

24. **yielded any base compliance** given in to unjustified demands out of self-interest or cowardice.
25. **imputed** (im pyo͞ot′ id) v. attributed to; charged to.

☑**Reading Check**

Why has Socrates stayed out of politics?

number, one almost a man, and two others who are still young; and yet I will not bring any of them hither in order to petition you for an acquittal. And why not? Not from any self-assertion or want of respect for you. Whether I am or am not afraid of death is another question, of which I will not now speak. But, having regard to public opinion, I feel that such conduct would be discreditable to myself, and to you, and to the whole State. One who has reached my years, and who has a name for wisdom, ought not to demean himself. Whether this opinion of me be deserved or not, at any rate the world has decided that Socrates is in some way superior to other men. And if those among you who are said to be superior in wisdom and courage, and any other virtue, demean themselves in this way, how shameful is their conduct! I have seen men of reputation, when they have been condemned, behaving in the strangest manner: they seemed to fancy that they were going to suffer something dreadful if they died, and that they could be immortal if you only allowed them to live; and I think that such are a dishonor to the State, and that any stranger coming in would have said of them that the most eminent men of Athens, to whom the Athenians themselves give honor and command, are no better than women. And I say that these things ought not to be done by those of us who have a reputation; and if they are done, you ought not to permit them; you ought rather to show that you are far more disposed to condemn the man who gets up a doleful[26] scene and makes the city ridiculous, than him who holds his peace.

But, setting aside the question of public opinion, there seems to be something wrong in asking a favor of a judge, and thus procuring[27] an acquittal, instead of informing and convincing him. For his duty is, not to make a present of justice, but to give judgment; and he has sworn that he will judge according to the laws, and not according to his own good pleasure; and we ought not to encourage you, nor should should you allow yourselves to be encouraged, in this habit of perjury[28]—there can be no <u>piety</u> in that. Do not then require me to do what I consider dishonorable and impious and wrong, especially now, when I am being tried for impiety on the indictment of Meletus. For if, O men of Athens, by force of persuasion and entreaty I could overpower your oaths, then I should be teaching you to believe that there are no gods, and in defending should simply convict myself of the charge of not believing in them. But that is not so—far otherwise. For I do believe that there are gods, and in a sense higher than that in which any of my accusers believe in them. And to you and to God I commit my cause, to be determined by you as is best for you and me.

There are many reasons why I am not grieved, O men of Athens, at the vote of condemnation. I expected it, and am only surprised that the votes are so nearly equal; for I had thought that the majority

---

26. **doleful** (dōl′ fəl) *adj.* mournful; melancholy.
27. **procuring** (prō kyoor′ iŋ) *v.* securing; obtaining.
28. **perjury** (pʉr′ jə rē) *n.* act of lying while under lawful oath.

against me would have been far larger; but now, had thirty votes gone over to the other side, I should have been acquitted. And I may say, I think, that I have escaped Meletus. I may say more; for without the assistance of Anytus and Lycon, any one may see that he would not have had a fifth part of the votes, as the law requires, in which case he would have incurred a fine of a thousand drachmae.

And so he proposes death as the penalty. And what shall I propose on my part, O men of Athens? Clearly that which is my due. And what is my due? What returns shall be made to the man who has never had the wit to be idle during his whole life; but has been careless of what the many care for—wealth, and family interests, and military offices, and speaking in the assembly, and magistracies, and plots, and parties. Reflecting that I was really too honest a man to be a politician and live, I did not go where I could do no good to you or to myself; but where I could do the greatest good privately to every one of you, thither I went, and sought to persuade every man among you that he must look to himself, and seek virtue and wisdom before he looks to his private interests, and look to the State before he looks to the interests of the State; and that this should be the order which he observes in all his actions. What shall be done to such an one? Doubtless some good thing, O men of Athens, if he has his reward; and the good should be of a kind suitable to him. What would be a reward suitable to a poor man who is your benefactor, and who desires leisure that he may instruct you? There can be no reward so fitting as maintenance in the Prytaneum,[29] O men of Athens, a reward which he deserves far more than the citizen who has won the prize at Olympia in the horse or chariot race, whether the chariots were drawn by two horses or by many. For I am in want, and he has enough; and he only gives you the appearance of happiness, and I give you the reality. And if I am to estimate the penalty fairly, I should say that maintenance in the Prytaneum is the just return.

Perhaps you think that I am braving you in what I am saying now, as in what I said before about the tears and prayers. But this is not so. I speak rather because I am convinced that I never intentionally wronged any one, although I cannot convince you—the time has been too short; if there were a law at Athens as there is in other cities, that a capital cause should not be decided in one day, then I believe that I should have convinced you. But I cannot in a moment refute great slanders; and, as I am convinced that I never wronged another, I will assuredly not wrong myself. I will not say of myself that I deserve any

▲ **Critical Viewing**
Based on this depiction of the Academy, in what way does Plato seem to be continuing the work of Socrates? **[Analyze]**

✔️**Reading Check**

What penalty does Meletus propose for Socrates?

---

29. **Prytaneum** (pri tā′ nē əm) place in which the Prytanes, representatives of the city, entertained distinguished visitors and winners of athletic contests at Olympia.

evil, or propose any penalty. Why should I? Because I am afraid of the penalty of death which Meletus proposes? When I do not know whether death is a good or an evil, why should I propose a penalty which would certainly be an evil? Shall I say imprisonment? And why should I live in prison, and be the slave of the magistrate of the year—of the Eleven?[30] Or shall the penalty be a fine, and imprisonment until the fine is paid? There is the same objection. I should have to lie in prison, for money I have none, and cannot pay. And if I say exile (and this may possibly be the penalty which you will affix), I must indeed be blinded by the love of life, if I am so irrational as to expect that when you, who are my own citizens, cannot endure my discourses[31] and words, and have found them so grievous and odious[32] that you will have no more of them, others are likely to endure me. No, indeed, men of Athens, that is not very likely. And what a life should I lead, at my age, wandering from city to city, ever changing my place of exile, and always being driven out! For I am quite sure that wherever I go, there, as here, the young men will flock to me; and if I drive them away, their elders will drive me out at their request; and if I let them come, their fathers and friends will drive me out for their sakes.

Some one will say: Yes, Socrates, but cannot you hold your tongue, and then you may go into a foreign city, and no one will interfere with you? Now, I have great difficulty in making you understand my answer to this. For if I tell you that to do as you say would be a disobedience to the God, and therefore that I cannot hold my tongue, you will not believe that I am serious; and if I say again that daily to discourse about virtue, and of those other things about which you hear me examining myself and others, is the greatest good of man, and that the unexamined life is not worth living, you are still less likely to believe me. Yet I say what is true, although a thing of which it is hard for me to persuade you. Also, I have never been accustomed to think that I deserve to suffer any harm. Had I money I might have estimated the offense at what I was able to pay, and not have been much the worse. But I have none, and therefore I must ask you to proportion the fine to my means. Well, perhaps I could afford a mina,[33] and therefore I propose that penalty: Plato, Crito, Critobulus, and Apollodorus, my friends here, bid me say thirty minae, and they will be the sureties.[34] Let thirty minae be the penalty; for which sum they will be ample security to you.

Critical Viewing ▶

How would you describe the mood of Socrates' followers in this painting? [Interpret]

Not much time will be gained, O Athenians, in return for the evil name which you will get from the detractors[35] of the city, who will

---

30. **the Eleven** committee in charge of prisons and public executions.
31. **discourses** (dis´ kôrs´ iz) *n.* communications of ideas.
32. **odious** (ō´ dē əs) *adj.* disgusting; offensive.
33. **mina** (mī´ nə) very small sum of money.
34. **sureties** (shŏŏr´ ə tēz) *n.* people who take responsibility for another person's debts.
35. **detractors** (dē trakt´ ərz) *n.* here, people who belittle.

say that you killed Socrates, a wise man; for they will call me wise, even although I am not wise, when they want to reproach you. If you had waited a little while, your desire would have been fulfilled in the course of nature. For I am far advanced in years, as you may perceive, and not far from death. I am speaking now not to all of you, but only to those who have condemned me to death. And I have another thing to say to them: You think that I was convicted because I had no words of the sort which would have procured my acquittal—I mean, if I had thought fit to leave nothing undone or unsaid. Not so; the deficiency which led to my conviction was not of words—certainly not. But I had not the boldness or impudence or inclination to address you as you would have liked me to do, weeping and wailing and lamenting, and saying and doing many things which you have been accustomed to hear from others, and which, as I maintain, are unworthy of me. I thought at the time that I ought not to do anything common or mean when in danger: nor do I now repent of the style of my defense; I would rather die having spoken after my manner, than speak in your manner and live. For neither in war nor yet at law ought I or any man to use every way of escaping death. Often in battle there can be no doubt that if a man will throw away his arms, and fall on his knees before his pursuers, he may escape death; and in other dangers there are other ways of escaping death, if a man is willing to say and do anything. The difficulty, my friends, is not to avoid death, but to avoid unrighteousness; for that runs faster than death. I am old and move slowly, and the slower runner has overtaken me, and my accusers are keen and quick, and the faster runner, who is unrighteousness, has overtaken them. And now I depart

Reading Strategy
Challenging the Text Does Socrates truly believe that he is not wise, or is his humility false? Explain.

Literary Analysis
Monologue What does Socrates reveal in his statement, "I would rather die having spoken after my manner, than speak in your manner and live"?

✔Reading Check

Why does Socrates reject the idea of exile as his penalty?

The Death of Socrates, 1787, Jacques-Louis David, The Metropolitan Museum of Art, New York

from the *Apology* ◆ 415

hence condemned by you to suffer the penalty of death,—they too go their ways condemned by the truth to suffer the penalty of villainy and wrong; and I must abide by my award—let them abide by theirs. I suppose that these things may be regarded as fated,—and I think that they are well.

And now, O men who have condemned me, I would fain prophesy to you; for I am about to die, and in the hour of death men are gifted with prophetic power. And I prophesy to you who are my murderers, that immediately after my departure punishment far heavier than you have inflicted on me will surely await you. Me you have killed because you wanted to escape the accuser, and not to give an account of your lives. But that will not be as you suppose: far otherwise. For I say that there will be more accusers of you than there are now; accusers whom hitherto I have restrained: and as they are younger they will be more inconsiderate with you, and you will be more offended at them. If you think that by killing men you can prevent some one from censuring your evil lives, you are mistaken; that is not a way of escape which is either possible or honorable; the easiest and the noblest way is not to be disabling others, but to be improving yourselves. This is the prophecy which I utter before my departure to the judges who have condemned me.

Friends, who would have acquitted me, I would like also to talk with you about the thing which has come to pass, while the magistrates are busy, and before I go to the place at which I must die. Stay then a little, for we may as well talk with one another while there is time. You are my friends, and I should like to show you the meaning of this event which has happened to me. O my judges—for you I may truly call judges—I should like to tell you of a wonderful circumstance. Hitherto the divine faculty of which the internal oracle is the source has constantly been in the habit of opposing me even about trifles, if I was going to make a slip or error in any matter; and now as you see there has come upon me that which may be thought, and is generally believed to be, the last and worst evil. But the oracle made no sign of opposition, either when I was leaving my house in the morning, or when I was on my way to the court, or while I was speaking, at anything which I was going to say; and yet I have often been stopped in the middle of a speech, but now in nothing I either said or did touching the matter in hand has the oracle opposed me. What do I take to be the explanation of this silence? I will tell you. It is an intimation[36] that what has happened to me is a good, and that those of us who think that death is an evil are

Themes in World Literature

Courtroom Drama

Some of the most dramatic and memorable moments in literature and film have taken place in the courtroom. Often the stakes are high, as in the *Apology*, when the accused's life hangs in the balance. Sometimes it is the deliberation of the judges or the jury that provides the drama.

In the film *Twelve Angry Men* (1957), for example, a young man is accused of murder and stands to lose his life if convicted. The jury is ready to convict until a lone juror persuades the others to re-examine the evidence. His persistence in calling for reasonable deliberation eventually leads to the young man's acquittal.

Startling revelations and climactic cross-examinations help make courtroom dramas among the most suspenseful and entertaining works in all of literature. From Harper Lee's novel *To Kill a Mockingbird* (1960) to Aaron Sorkin's play *A Few Good Men* (1989), literary works set in a courtroom have a way of keeping the audience on the edge of their seats, waiting eagerly to find out whether justice will be served.

---

36. intimation (in´ tə mā´shən) *n.* indirect suggestion.

in error. For the customary sign would surely have opposed me had I been going to evil and not to good.

Let us reflect in another way, and we shall see that there is great reason to hope that death is a good; for one of two things—either death is a state of nothingness and utter unconsciousness, or, as men say, there is a change and migration of the soul from this world to another. Now, if you suppose that there is no consciousness, but a sleep like the sleep of him who is undisturbed even by dreams, death will be an unspeakable gain. For if a person were to select the night in which his sleep was undisturbed even by dreams, and were to compare with this the other days and nights of his life, and then were to tell us how many days and nights he had passed in the course of his life better and more pleasantly than this one, I think that any man, I will not say a private man, but even the great king will not find many such days or nights, when compared with the others. Now, if death be of such a nature, I say that to die is gain, for eternity is then only a single night. But if death is the journey to another place, and there, as men say, all the dead abide, what good, O my friends and judges, can be greater than this? If, indeed, when the pilgrim arrives in the world below, he is delivered from the professors of justice in this world, and finds the true judges who are said to give judgment there, Minos and Rhadamanthus and Aeacus and Triptolemus,[37] and other sons of God who were righteous in their own life, that pilgrimage will be worth making. What would not a man give if he might converse with Orpheus and Musaeus and Hesiod[38] and Homer? Nay, if this be true, let me die again and again. I myself, too, shall have a wonderful interest in there meeting and conversing with Palamedes,[39] and Ajax[40] the son of Telamon, and any other ancient hero who has suffered death through an unjust judgment; and there will be no small pleasure, as I think, in comparing my own sufferings with theirs. Above all, I shall then be able to continue my search into true and false knowledge; as in this world, so also in the next; and I shall find out who is wise, and who pretends to be wise, and is not. What would not a man give, O judges, to be able to examine the leader of the great Trojan expedition, or Odysseus or Sisyphus,[41] or numberless others, men and women too! What infinite delight would there be in conversing with them and asking them questions! In another world they do not put a man to death for asking questions: assuredly not. For

Reading Strategy
Challenging the Text
What assumptions about dreams does Socrates make in this argument? Do you agree with this idea?

---

37. **Minos** (min′ ōs) **and Rhadamanthus** (rad′ ə man′ thəs) **and Aeacus** (ē a′ kəs) **and Triptolemus** (trip′ tä′ lə məs) models of just judges in life and after death.
38. **Orpheus** (ôr′ fē əs) **and Musaeus** (my$\overline{oo}$ zā′ əs) **and Hesiod** (hē′ sē əd) poets and religious teachers.
39. **Palamedes** (pal′ə mē′ dēz) one of the Greek chieftains at Troy who was unjustly executed for treason.
40. **Ajax** (ā′ jaks) Greek warrior who committed suicide after Achilles′ arms were given to Odysseus as the bravest Greek warrior.
41. **Sisyphus** (sis′ ə fəs) in Greek mythology, a king of Corinth, famous for his cunning.

✓**Reading Check**

What does Socrates honor about Palamedes, Ajax, and other ancient heroes?

besides being happier than we are, they will be immortal, if what is said is true.

Wherefore, O judges, be of good cheer about death, and know of a certainty, that no evil can happen to a good man, either in life or after death. He and his are not neglected by the gods; nor has my own approaching end happened by mere chance. But I see clearly that the time had arrived when it was better for me to die and be released from trouble; wherefore the oracle gave no sign. For which reason, also, I am not angry with my condemners, or with my accusers; they have done me no harm, although they did not mean to do me any good; and for this I may gently blame them.

Still, I have a favor to ask of them. When my sons are grown up, I would ask you, O my friends, to punish them; and I would have you trouble them, as I have troubled you, if they seem to care about riches, or anything, more than about virtue; or if they pretend to be something when they are really nothing,—then reprove[42] them, as I have reproved you, for not caring about that for which they ought to care, and thinking that they are something when they are really nothing. And if you do this, both I and my sons will have received justice at your hands.

The hour of departure has arrived, and we go our ways—I to die, and you to live. Which is better God only knows.

---

42. reprove (ri prōōv′) *v.* express disapproval of.

Review and Assess

Thinking About the Selection

1. **Respond:** Imagine yourself as a juror at Socrates' trial. Would his speech have moved you? Explain.

2. **(a) Recall:** According to Socrates, why does he go about questioning people to see whether they are wise? **(b) Deduce:** Why does his questioning make so many people his enemies?

3. **(a) Recall:** What does Socrates call "the pretense of wisdom"? **(b) Interpret:** In what respect does Socrates consider himself wiser than the people he questions? **(c) Define:** What kind of person does Socrates claim is wisest?

4. **(a) Recall:** Why does Socrates refuse to compromise and stop teaching? **(b) Evaluate:** Considering that Socrates' refusal to compromise will cost him his life, do you believe he has made the right choice? Explain.

5. **(a) Speculate:** Do you agree with Socrates that "the unexamined life is not worth living"? Why or why not?

Review and Assess

Literary Analysis

Monologue

1. In the opening remarks of his **monologue,** Socrates portrays himself as a simple old man who is not very eloquent. Why might Socrates portray himself in this way?
2. Socrates frequently mentions the gods. Why might he do this?
3. In addressing the court, Socrates frequently asks questions and then answers them. How might this technique affect his audience?
4. Use a chart like the one shown to analyze the character of Socrates as revealed in his monologue. Choose three statements made by Socrates, and explain what each one reveals about his character.

Statement	What It Reveals
1.	1.
2.	2.
3.	3.

Connecting Literary Elements

5. At one point, Socrates compares himself to Achilles, the hero of the *Iliad*. How might this **analogy** affect Socrates' audience?
6. What point does Socrates make by describing himself as a gadfly?
7. What does Socrates mean when he compares Athenians to people "suddenly awakened from sleep"?

Reading Strategy

Challenging the Text

8. (a) **Challenge** Socrates' claim that "the men most in repute were all but the most foolish." How does he support this assertion? (b) Is his evidence convincing? Why or why not?
9. (a) Do you agree with Socrates' assertion that "he who will fight for the right . . . must have a private station and not a public one"? (b) What evidence from your experience or readings supports your opinion?

Extend Understanding

10. **Cultural Connection:** (a) What failures of the State and of politicians does Socrates seem to be criticizing in this text? (b) Would Socrates be critical of today's states and politicians? Explain.

Quick Review

A **monologue** is a long and revealing speech by one character.

An **analogy** is an extended comparison of relationships.

To **challenge the text,** critically evaluate the author's assertions and reasoning.

 **Take It to the Net**
PHSchool.com

Take the interactive self-test online to check your understanding of this selection.

Integrate Language Skills

Vocabulary Development Lesson

Word Analysis: Legal Terminology

Socrates uses the words *affidavit* and *indictment*. These are examples of legal terminology, or words that pertain to the law and to legal proceedings.

Socrates also uses the following legal terms. Use each word in a sentence.

1. prosecutors
2. arraigned
3. acquittal

Spelling Strategy

Nouns ending in *-ence* usually end in *-ent* in their adjective form and in *-ently* in their adverb form. For example, *eloquence* becomes *eloquent* and *eloquently*.

Write the adjective and adverb forms of each of the following words:

1. impudence
2. prudence
3. magnificence
4. benevolence

Fluency: Sentence Completion

Review the vocabulary list on page 401. Then, select the vocabulary word that best completes each of the following sentences.

1. Socrates wandered the streets, questioning people and ___?___ them to examine their lives.
2. He was charged with atheism, so he demonstrated his ___?___ in court.
3. The charges were listed in the ___?___ .
4. The ___?___ was signed by the witnesses.
5. Despite the ___?___ of his speech, he failed to persuade the judges.
6. His ___?___ angered the judges.
7. His tearful followers ___?___ his death.
8. His death may be ___?___ by angry gods.

Grammar and Style Lesson

Transitions and Transitional Phrases

Transitions are words that show chronological, spatial, comparison and contrast, cause and effect, and order of importance relationships among ideas. Groups of words that function in this way are called **transitional phrases.**

Chronological: *At last* I went to the artisans.
Spatial: *Outside the courtroom,* people speculated about the verdict.
Comparison and contrast: . . . *whereas* I, who am probably in danger. . .
Cause and effect: *Accordingly,* I went to one. . .
Order of importance: *Above all,* I shall. . .

Practice Identify the transitional word or phrase in each item below. Then, indicate the kind of relationship it reveals.

1. They have done me no harm, although they did not mean to do me any good.
2. Then I went to another who had still higher pretensions to wisdom.
3. After the politicians, I went to the poets.
4. Whereupon I made another enemy.
5. Still, I have a favor to ask them.

Writing Application Write a paragraph describing the occasion of Socrates' speech. Use at least three transitions in your writing.

WG Prentice Hall Writing and Grammar Connection: Diamond Level, Chapter 9, Section 4

Writing Lesson

Account of a Remarkable Person

Plato found Socrates to be a remarkable person. Review the excerpt from the *Apology*, and determine which character traits Plato admired most in Socrates. Use Plato's writing as a springboard for your own essay. Think about the character traits of a remarkable person whom you know, and write an essay describing that person.

Prewriting   Use a chart like the one shown to record details about what makes Socrates remarkable. Then, complete the chart with details about what makes the person you know remarkable.

Socrates	A Remarkable Person I Know

Drafting   Plato wrote the *Apology* as a dramatic re-creation of Socrates' trial, using Socrates' own words to reveal the philosopher's character and beliefs. As you draft your essay, include your own reactions and the actual words of your subject to reveal his or her character.

Revising   Show your essay to classmates to see whether your subject's remarkable qualities are clear. Then, revise your writing, adding quotations and precise details to convey your subject's character.

W͏G Prentice Hall Writing and Grammar Connection: Diamond Level, Chapter 6, Section 2

Extension Activities

Listening and Speaking With a partner, develop and role-play an **interview** with someone who witnessed or was involved in the trial of Socrates. Use the following strategies to capture the drama of the courtroom scene:

- Develop questions and answers that describe the crowd at the trial.

- Have the interviewee directly quote some of Socrates' statements.

- Have the interviewee describe the mood of the courtroom when the verdict is announced.

Present your interview for the class. Following the presentation, allow time for a question-and-answer period. [**Group Activity**]

Research and Technology Use library resources and the Internet to gather information on the justice system in ancient Athens. Write a **research report** describing the system, focusing on what behaviors were considered criminal, how a person was brought to trial, who were the judges, and what types of punishments were handed out. Share your research report with the class.

 **Take It to the Net**   PHSchool.com

Go online for an additional research activity using the Internet.

A Closer Look

Oedipus: The Myth

The oracle presents a horrifying prophecy: The son of Laius and Jocasta will kill his father and marry his mother.

Laius and Jocasta's son, Oedipus, tries desperately to avoid fulfilling the oracle's prophecy, but he cannot escape it. Sophocles' play *Oedipus the King* dramatizes the tragic results. Written in the early years of the Peloponnesian War (431–404 B.C.), *Oedipus the King* begins as Thebes is suffering from a devastating plague and the city's political leadership is being seriously challenged.

The Origin of the Oedipus Myth Cadmus, a prince of Phoenicia, founded the city of Thebes. The god Apollo's oracle at Delphi told Cadmus to follow a cow and build a city where the cow stopped to rest. Before building the city, Cadmus had to kill a dragon that was guarding the water supply. This dragon, unfortunately, was Apollo's favorite. As punishment, Apollo's oracle put a curse on Cadmus' descendants. According to the oracle's curse, at some point in the family history, a king and queen of Thebes would produce a son who would kill his father and marry his mother.

Therefore, when King Laius of Thebes and his wife, Jocasta, had a son, Laius had a rivet driven between the baby's ankles and instructed a servant to leave him on Mt. Cithaeron to die from exposure to the elements. Instead, the servant pitied the infant and, without revealing his identity, gave him to a shepherd. The shepherd gave the child to Merope, wife of Polybus, king of Corinth. Merope and Polybus named the child Oedipus (swollen foot) for the wounds in his feet.

The Oracle's Prophecy As a young man, Oedipus was taunted for not being the true son of King Polybus. Deeply troubled, Oedipus consulted the oracle of Apollo at Delphi about the accusation. The priestess, Pythia, drove him away from Apollo's shrine before he could ask his question, declaring that Oedipus would kill his father and marry his mother. Oedipus, horrified at the prophecy, fled Corinth, the home of his supposed parents, in an attempt to avoid fulfilling the prophecy.

Not far from Delphi, Oedipus met a man in a chariot whose charioteer demanded that Oedipus move aside. Oedipus refused, but the charioteer drove his horses forward anyway. As the chariot passed Oedipus, a wheel grazed his foot and someone inside the chariot struck him on the head with a goad. Enraged, Oedipus killed the rider and the charioteer and continued on his way.

The Riddle of the Sphinx Eventually, Oedipus found his way to Thebes, where the city was in turmoil. A monster called the Sphinx was terrorizing the Thebans. According to various tales, the Sphinx had the head of a woman, the body of a lion, the tail of a serpent, and wings. The monster destroyed the Theban fields and killed many of its citizens, refusing to depart unless someone answered her riddle. Before eating her victims, the Sphinx would ask them: "What is it that goes on four legs in the morning, two at midday, and three in the evening?" Until someone answered her riddle, the torment would continue.

A nearby king, Damasistratus, had reported to the Thebans that their king, Laius, had been killed on his way to Delphi, but the frightened and preoccupied Thebans had no time to seek the murderer. Their priority was to find someone who could solve the riddle and save Thebes from the Sphinx. Jocasta's brother Creon offered the hand of his sister Jocasta, Laius' widow, and a share in the kingdom to any man who could answer the Sphinx's riddle correctly.

The Riddle's Answer Oedipus visited the Sphinx to give her the correct answer: "Man, who crawls in infancy, walks upright in his prime, and leans on a cane in old age." The Sphinx flung herself to her death, and Thebes welcomed Oedipus as its new king. Oedipus married Jocasta, Laius' widow.

Oedipus had ruled for almost two decades, leading the city in prosperity and fathering four children. Thebes was visited with a plague that killed animals, children, and crops. Oedipus vowed to rid the city of the plague. The oracle told him that the plague was caused by the fact that Laius' murderer was living in Thebes unpunished for his crime. As a responsible and dedicated leader, Oedipus immediately began an investigation to locate the murderer and relieve Thebes of the plague. At this point in the Oedipus story, Sophocles begins his play *Oedipus the King*.

▲ **Critical Viewing**
In what way does this image of the Sphinx reinforce the frightening mystery of her riddle? **[Interpret]**

Prepare to Read

Oedipus the King

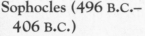

Sophocles (496 B.C.– 406 B.C.)

Sophocles' (säf´ ə klēz´) life corresponded with the splendid rise and tragic fall of fifth-century Athens. At 16, he was one of the young men chosen by the city to perform a choral ode, dancing and singing in a public celebration of the Athenian naval victory over the Persians at Salamis. In 442 B.C., he was one of the treasurers of the imperial league, which was organized to resist Persia. With Pericles, Sophocles served as one of the generals in the war against the island of Samos, which later tried to secede from the Athenian league. In 413 B.C., he was also appointed to a special government committee when the Athenian expedition to Sicily failed. He died in 406 B.C., two years before Athens surrendered to Sparta in the Peloponnesian War.

Winning Playwright Sophocles' life also coincided with the rise and fall of the Golden Age of Greek tragedy. His career as a dramatist began in 468 B.C. when he entered the Dionysia (dī´ ə nē´ sē ə), the annual theatrical competition dedicated to the god Dionysus (dī´ ə nī´ səs). Competing against the established and brilliant playwright Aeschylus (es´ ki ləs), Sophocles won first prize. Over the next 62 years, he wrote more than 120 plays, 24 of which won first prize; those that did not come in first placed second.

Enriching the Drama Greek plays had their origins in religious festivals honoring the god Dionysus. At first, a chorus narrated stories of the god's life in song. The choral leader would occasionally step forward to recite part of the story alone. Eventually, the recitation grew longer and involved a second speaker. Sophocles increased the number of singers in the chorus and introduced a third speaking part. The addition of a third actor allowed for more dramatically complex dialogue than that of the earlier Aeschylean plays.

Sophocles also introduced technical innovations to Greek tragedy. Originally, Greek drama was presented in an open-air theater with few sets or props. Sophocles expanded the use of stage machinery and sets. For instance, he was the first to use a crane that lowered actors "miraculously" onto the stage. These miraculous appearances were reserved for gods, who might appear at the end of a play to wrap up loose ends in the plot. The Romans called this device *deus ex machina* (dā´əs eks mak´ē nə)—literally "god from a machine." It came to signify a contrived ending, an unexpected last-minute reprieve, the intervention of a supernatural force in the nick of time.

Faithfulness to Human Experience In addition to his technical innovations, Sophocles is known for his fidelity to universal human experience. In his plays, the world order consists of human beings, nature, and the inscrutable forces of the gods and fate. Sophocles suggests that while gods can predetermine or influence human action, they do not necessarily define one's character. People are responsible for finding out who they are and where they belong; they must then take moral responsibility for their lives.

Only seven of Sophocles' plays have survived intact. These were carefully reconstructed in 303 B.C. by Athenians concerned with preserving this crucial part of their literary heritage. The extant plays are *Ajax, The Women of Trachis, Antigone, Oedipus the King, Electra, Philoctetes,* and finally, *Oedipus at Colonus. Oedipus the King* has often been considered not only the masterpiece among Sophocles' creations but the most important and influential drama ever written.

Preview

Connecting to the Literature

We often envision brave people as those who overcome a fear of death or injury to succeed in physical conflict. However, there are other ways of being brave. In this play, a bold king risks everything in his pursuit of a terrible truth. In doing so, he provides an unforgettable example of courage.

Literary Analysis

Tragedy

A **tragedy** is a work of dramatic literature that shows the downfall of a person, usually of high birth or noble status. Often, the *protagonist*, or main character, is a brilliant leader who has gained the love and respect of his or her subjects. In most tragedies, the protagonist initiates a series of events that lead to his or her own destruction.

Tragedies explore powerful emotions, such as love, hate, revenge, and loyalty. Aristotle wrote that tragedy triggers two main emotions in the audience—pity and fear. We pity the protagonist's suffering while we also fear for him or her and for ourselves.

Connecting Literary Elements

The **tragic hero** is the main character of a tragedy. Traditionally, the tragic hero possesses a fault or weakness in character that causes the hero's downfall. This weakness is called a **tragic flaw.** As you read, pay attention to details in Oedipus' actions and statements that suggest heroic qualities or a possible flaw. Use a chart like the one shown at right to organize your observations about his character.

Heroic Qualities	Actions
	Statements
"Flawed" Qualities	Actions
	Statements

Reading Strategy

Reading Drama

When you **read drama**, try to picture a live performance. Note stage directions, which are usually set in italics to provide information about characters' thoughts, attitudes, and behavior. As you read, try to picture how characters look, sound, move, and relate to one another.

Vocabulary Development

blight (blīt) *n.* destructive disease (p. 428)

pestilence (pes´ tə lens) *n.* plague (p. 428)

induced (in doost´) *v.* persuaded; caused (p. 432)

dispatch (di spach´) *v.* kill (p. 432)

invoke (in vōk´) *v.* summon; cause to appear (p. 435)

prophecy (präf´ ə sē) *n.* prediction of the future (p. 438)

countenance (koun´ tə nəns) *n.* the look on a person's face (p. 442)

malignant (mə lig´ nənt) *adj.* very harmful (p. 455)

OEDIPUS THE KING

Sophocles
translated by David Grene

Background

In the fifth century B.C., when Greek drama was at its height, plays were performed in Athens at annual festivals honoring Dionysus, the god of wine. The performances were staged in an outdoor theater, which held thousands of spectators. There were no curtains or lighting; scenery and props were minimal. Actors wore outsized masks appropriate to the characters they played. Although violent events were often central to plots, no violence occurred on stage. Such events took place offstage and were reported in dialogue.

Ancient Greek plays follow this consistent format:

- A prologue presents background and describes the conflict.
- Then, the chorus, or group of dancers, enters and sings a *parodos*, (par´ ə däs), or opening song.
- Choral songs, called odes, separate scenes. The odes are divided into alternating parts called strophe (strō´ fē) and antistrophe (an tis´ trə fē).

Greek tragedies took their plots from well-known myths and legends. For example, the audience in the fifth century B.C. would have known that the story of Oedipus involved a ruler who fulfilled a terrible destiny by killing his father and marrying his mother.

CHARACTERS

OEDIPUS, King of Thebes
JOCASTA, His Wife
CREON, His Brother-in-Law
TEIRESIAS, an Old Blind Prophet
A PRIEST

FIRST MESSENGER
SECOND MESSENGER
A HERDSMAN
A CHORUS OF OLD MEN OF THEBES

Part I

Scene: *In front of the palace of Oedipus at Thebes. To the right of the stage near the altar stands the* PRIEST *with a crowd of children.* OEDIPUS *emerges from the central door.*

> **OEDIPUS:** Children, young sons and daughters of old Cadmus,[1]
> why do you sit here with your suppliant crowns?[2]
> The town is heavy with a mingled burden
> of sounds and smells, of groans and hymns and incense;
> 5 I did not think it fit that I should hear
> of this from messengers but came myself,—
> I Oedipus whom all men call the Great.
>
> [*He turns to the* PRIEST.]
>
> You're old and they are young; come, speak for them.
> What do you fear or want, that you sit here
> 10 suppliant? Indeed I'm willing to give all
> that you may need; I would be very hard
> should I not pity suppliants like these.
>
> **PRIEST:** O ruler of my country, Oedipus,
> you see our company around the altar;
> 15 you see our ages; some of us, like these,
> who cannot yet fly far, and some of us
> heavy with age; these children are the chosen
> among the young, and I the priest of Zeus.
> Within the market place sit others crowned
> 20 with suppliant garlands,[3] at the double shrine
> of Pallas[4] and the temple where Ismenus
> gives oracles by fire.[5] King, you yourself
> have seen our city reeling like a wreck

---

1. **Cadmus** (kad′ məs) *n.* mythical founder and first king of Thebes, a city in central Greece where the play takes place.
2. **suppliant** (sup′ lē ənt) **crowns** wreaths worn by people who ask favors of the gods.
3. **suppliant garlands** branches wound in wool, which were placed on the altar and left there until the suppliant's request was granted.
4. **double shrine of Pallas** the two temples of Athena.
5. **temple where Ismenus gives oracles by fire** Temple of Apollo, located by Ismenus, the Theban river, where the priests studied patterns in the ashes of sacrificial victims to foretell the future.

Reading Strategy
Reading Drama
According to the stage directions and dialogue, whom does Oedipus address when he first appears?

Reading Strategy
Reading Drama As Oedipus turns to address the Priest, how might his tone of voice change?

**Reading Check**

Where does the opening scene take place?

already; it can scarcely lift its prow
25　out of the depths, out of the bloody surf.
A <u>blight</u> is on the fruitful plants of the earth,
A blight is on the cattle in the fields,
a blight is on our women that no children
are born to them; a God that carries fire,
30　a deadly <u>pestilence</u>, is on our town,
strikes us and spares not, and the house of Cadmus
is emptied of its people while black Death
grows rich in groaning and in lamentation.[6]
We have not come as suppliants to this altar
35　because we thought of you as of a God,
but rather judging you the first of men
in all the chances of this life and when
we mortals have to do with more than man.
You came and by your coming saved our city,
40　freed us from tribute which we paid of old
to the Sphinx,[7] cruel singer. This you did
in virtue of no knowledge we could give you,
in virtue of no teaching; it was God
that aided you, men say, and you are held
45　with God's assistance to have saved our lives.
Now Oedipus, Greatest in all men's eyes,
here falling at your feet we all entreat you,
find us some strength for rescue.
Perhaps you'll hear a wise word from some God,
50　perhaps you will learn something from a man

blight (blīt) *n.* destructive disease

pestilence (pes´ tə lens) *n.* plague

Literary Analysis
Tragedy What major conflict or problem does the first scene introduce?

---

6. **lamentation** (lam´ ən tā´ shən) *n.* expression of deep sorrow.
7. **Sphinx** (sfinks) winged female monster at Thebes that ate men who could not answer her riddle: "What is it that walks on four legs at dawn, two legs at midday, and three legs in the evening, and has only one voice; when it walks on most feet, it is weakest?" Creon, appointed ruler of Thebes, offered the kingdom and the hand of his sister Jocasta to anyone who could answer the riddle. Oedipus saved Thebes by answering correctly, "Man, who crawls in infancy, walks upright in his prime, and leans on a cane in old age." Outraged, the Sphinx destroyed herself, and Oedipus became King of Thebes.

(for I have seen that for the skilled of practice
the outcome of their counsels live the most).
Noblest of men, go, and raise up our city,
go,—and give heed. For now this land of ours
55 calls you its savior since you saved it once.
So, let us never speak about your reign
as of a time when first our feet were set
secure on high, but later fell to ruin.
Raise up our city, save it and raise it up.
60 Once you have brought us luck with happy omen;
be no less now in fortune.
If you will rule this land, as now you rule it,
better to rule it full of men than empty.
For neither tower nor ship is anything
65 when empty, and none live in it together.

OEDIPUS: I pity you, children. You have come full of longing,
but I have known the story before you told it
only too well. I know you are all sick,
yet there is not one of you, sick though you are,
70 that is as sick as I myself.
Your several sorrows each have single scope
and touch but one of you. My spirit groans
for city and myself and you at once.
You have not roused me like a man from sleep;
75 know that I have given many tears to this,
gone many ways wandering in thought,
but as I thought I found only one remedy
and that I took. I sent Menoeceus' son
Creon, Jocasta's brother, to Apollo,
80 to his Pythian temple,[8]
that he might learn there by what act or word
I could save this city. As I count the days,

▲ **Critical Viewing**
What does this image of Oedipus and the Sphinx suggest about Oedipus' attitude toward the Sphinx and her riddle? **[Interpret]**

✔ **Reading Check**
What great service did Oedipus provide the city when he first arrived in Thebes?

---

8. **Pythian** (pith′ ē ən) **temple** shrine of Apollo at Delphi, below Mount Parnassus in central Greece.

it vexes me what ails him; he is gone
far longer than he needed for the journey.
85 But when he comes, then, may I prove a villain,
if I shall not do all the God commands.

PRIEST: Thanks for your gracious words. Your servants here
signal that Creon is this moment coming.

OEDIPUS: His face is bright. O holy Lord Apollo,
90 grant that his news too may be bright for us
and bring us safety.

PRIEST: It is happy news,
I think, for else his head would not be crowned
with sprigs of fruitful laurel.[9]

OEDIPUS: We will know soon,
he's within hail. Lord Creon, my good brother,
95 what is the word you bring us from the God?

[CREON *enters.*]

CREON: A good word,—for things hard to bear themselves
if in the final issue all is well
I count complete good fortune.

OEDIPUS: What do you mean?
What you have said so far
100 leaves me uncertain whether to trust or fear.

---

9. **sprigs of fruitful laurel** Laurel symbolized triumph; a crown of
laurel signified good news.

CREON: If you will hear my news before these others
I am ready to speak, or else to go within.

OEDIPUS: Speak it to all;
the grief I bear, I bear it more for these
105 than for my own heart.

CREON: I will tell you, then,
what I heard from the God.
King Phoebus[10] in plain words commanded us
to drive out a pollution from our land,
pollution grown ingrained within the land;
110 drive it out, said the God, not cherish it,
till it's past cure.

OEDIPUS: What is the rite
of purification? How shall it be done?

CREON: By banishing a man, or expiation[11]
of blood by blood, since it is murder guilt
115 which holds our city in this destroying storm.

OEDIPUS: Who is this man whose fate the God pronounces?

CREON: My Lord, before you piloted the state
we had a king called Laius.

OEDIPUS: I know of him by hearsay. I have not seen him.

120 **CREON:** The God commanded clearly: let some one
punish with force this dead man's murderers.

OEDIPUS: Where are they in the world? Where would a trace
of this old crime be found? It would be hard
to guess where.

CREON: The clue is in this land;
125 that which is sought is found;
the unheeded thing escapes:
so said the God.

OEDIPUS: Was it at home,
or in the country that death came upon him,
or in another country travelling?

130 **CREON:** He went, he said himself, upon an embassy,[12]
but never returned when he set out from home.

OEDIPUS: Was there no messenger, no fellow traveller
who knew what happened? Such a one might tell
something of use.

---

10. **King Phoebus** (fē′ bəs) Apollo, god of the sun.
11. **expiation** (eks′ pē ā shən) *n.* the act of making amends for wrongdoing.
12. **embassy** (em′ be sē) *n.* important mission or errand.

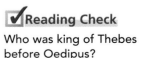

Reading Check

Who was king of Thebes before Oedipus?

135 **CREON:** They were all killed save one. He fled in terror
and he could tell us nothing in clear terms
of what he knew, nothing, but one thing only.

OEDIPUS: What was it?
If we could even find a slim beginning
140 in which to hope, we might discover much.

CREON: This man said that the robbers they encountered
were many and the hands that did the murder
were many; it was no man's single power.

OEDIPUS: How could a robber dare a deed like this
145 were he not helped with money from the city,
money and treachery?

CREON: That indeed was thought.
But Laius was dead and in our trouble
there was none to help.

OEDIPUS: What trouble was so great to hinder you
150 inquiring out the murder of your king?

CREON: The riddling Sphinx <u>induced</u> us to neglect
mysterious crimes and rather seek solution
of troubles at our feet.

OEDIPUS: I will bring this to light again. King Phoebus
155 fittingly took this care about the dead,
and you too fittingly.
And justly you will see in me an ally,
a champion of my country and the God.
For when I drive pollution from the land
160 I will not serve a distant friend's advantage,
but act in my own interest. Whoever
he was that killed the king may readily
wish to <u>dispatch</u> me with his murderous hand;
so helping the dead king I help myself.

165 Come, children, take your suppliant boughs and go;
up from the altars now. Call the assembly
and let it meet upon the understanding
that I'll do everything. God will decide
whether we prosper or remain in sorrow.

170 **PRIEST:** Rise, children—it was this we came to seek,
which of himself the king now offers us.
May Phoebus who gave us the oracle
come to our rescue and stay the plague.

[*Exit all but the* CHORUS.]

induced (in dōōst´) *v.*
persuaded; caused

Literary Analysis
Tragedy and Tragic Hero
According to the emotions Oedipus expresses toward both his subjects and himself, what kind of leader does he seem to be? Explain.

dispatch (di spach´) *v.* kill

CHORUS:

Strophe

What is the sweet spoken word of God from the
175   shrine of Pytho[13] rich in gold
that has come to glorious Thebes?
I am stretched on the rack of doubt, and terror and
         trembling hold
my heart, O Delian Healer,[14] and I worship full of fears
for what doom you will bring to pass, new or renewed
180   in the revolving years.
Speak to me, immortal voice,
child of golden Hope.

Antistrophe

First I call on you, Athene, deathless daughter of Zeus,
and Artemis, Earth Upholder,
185   who sits in the midst of the market place in the throne
         which men call Fame,
and Phoebus, the Far Shooter, three averters of Fate,[15]
come to us now, if ever before, when ruin rushed upon
         the state,
you drove destruction's flame away
out of our land.

Strophe

190   Our sorrows defy number;
all the ship's timbers are rotten;
taking of thought is no spear for the driving away of
         the plague.
There are no growing children in this famous land;
there are no women bearing the pangs of childbirth.
195   You may see them one with another,
         like birds swift on the wing,
quicker than fire unmastered,
speeding away to the coast of the
         Western God.[16]

Antistrophe

In the unnumbered deaths
of its people the city dies;
those children that are born lie
         dead on the naked earth

in context Humanities Connection

The Greek Chorus and Players

In ancient Greek tragedies, the role of the chorus was central to the production and important to the meaning of the play. The chorus consisted of 12 or 15 dancers called *choreuts,* who were young men about to enter the military. The chorus danced as it sang, moving from right to left during the strophe (strō′ fē), then left to right during the anti-strophe (an tis′ trə fē).

Originally, the plays included only one actor in addition to the chorus. Thespis, from whom we derive the English word *thespian,* or actor, is said to have been the first actor. The great dramatist Aeschylus (es′ ki ləs) is said to have introduced the second actor, and Sophocles the third.

In most dramas, actors played several different parts each. Their costumes consisted of long, flowing garments and expressive, wide-mouthed masks, which they would change as they changed characters. The actors' shoes also featured a high wooden sole called a *cothurnus* (kō thur′ nəs) to make the individual look taller and more impressive and to heighten visibility in the vast theater.

---

13. **Pytho** (pī′ thō) *n.* another name for Delphi, location of Apollo's oracular shrine. Delphi was the principal religious center for all ancient Greeks.
14. **Delian Healer** Born on the island of Delos, Apollo's title was "healer"; he caused and averted plagues.
15. **three averters of Fate** The chorus is praying to three gods—Athene, Artemis, and Apollo—as a triple shield against death.
16. **Western God** Since the sun sets in the west, this is the god of night, or Death.

Reading Check

What happened to King Laius?

200 unpitied, spreading contagion of death; and gray-haired mothers and wives
everywhere stand at the altar's edge, suppliant, moaning;
the hymn to the healing God[17] rings out but with it the wailing voices are blended.
205 From these our sufferings grant us, O golden Daughter of Zeus,[18]
glad-faced deliverance.

   Strophe
There is no clash of brazen[19] shields but our fight is with the War God,[20]
a War God ringed with the cries of men, a savage God who burns
210   us;
grant that he turn in racing course backwards out of our country's bounds
to the great palace of Amphitrite[21] or where the waves of the Thracian sea
deny the stranger safe anchorage.
215 Whatsoever escapes the night
at last the light of day revisits;
so smite the War God, Father Zeus,
beneath your thunderbolt,
for you are the Lord of the lightning, the lightning that
220   carries fire.

   Antistrophe
And your unconquered arrow shafts, winged by the golden corded bow,
Lycean King,[22] I beg to be at our side for help;
and the gleaming torches of Artemis with which she scours the Lycean hills,
and I call on the God with the turban of gold,[23] who gave his
225   name to this country of ours,
the Bacchic God with the wind flushed face,[24]
Evian One,[25] who travel
with the Maenad company,[26]
combat the God that burns us

Reading Strategy
Reading Drama What kinds of gestures might the chorus perform during this strophe? Why?

---

17. **healing God** Apollo.
18. **golden Daughter of Zeus** Athena.
19. **brazen** (brā´ zən) *adj.* of brass or like brass in color
20. **War God** Ares.
21. **Amphitrite** (am´ fi trīt´ ē) sea goddess who was the wife of Poseidon, god of the sea.
22. **Lycean** (lī sē´ ən) **King** Apollo, whose title *Lykios* means "god of light."
23. **God with the turban of gold** Dionysus, god of wine, who was born of Zeus and a woman of Thebes, the first Greek city to honor him. He wears an oriental turban because he has come from the East.
24. **Bacchic** (bak´ ik) **God with the wind-flushed face** refers to Dionysus, who had a youthful, rosy complexion; Bacchus means "riotous god."
25. **Evian One** Dionysus, called Evios because his followers address him with the ritual cry "evoi."
26. **Maenad company** female followers of Dionysus.

with your torch of pine;
for the God that is our enemy is a God unhonored among the
230   Gods.

[OEDIPUS *returns.*]

OEDIPUS: For what you ask me—if you will hear my words,
and hearing welcome them and fight the plague,
you will find strength and lightening of your load.

Hark to me; what I say to you, I say
235   as one that is a stranger to the story
as stranger to the deed. For I would not
be far upon the track if I alone
were tracing it without a clue. But now,
since after all was finished, I became
240   a citizen among you, citizens—
now I proclaim to all the men of Thebes:
who so among you knows the murderer
by whose hand Laius, son of Labdacus,
died—I command him to tell everything
245   to me,—yes, though he fears himself to take the blame
on his own head; for bitter punishment
he shall have none, but leave this land unharmed.
Or if he knows the murderer, another,
a foreigner, still let him speak the truth.
250   For I will pay him and be grateful, too.
But if you shall keep silence, if perhaps
some one of you, to shield a guilty friend,
or for his own sake shall reject my words—
hear what I shall do then:
255   I forbid that man, whoever he be, my land,
my land where I hold sovereignty[27] and throne;
and I forbid any to welcome him
or cry him greeting or make him a sharer
in sacrifice or offering to the Gods,
260   or give him water for his hands to wash.
I command all to drive him from their homes,
since he is our pollution, as the oracle
of Pytho's God[28] proclaimed him now to me.
So I stand forth a champion of the God
265   and of the man who died.
Upon the murderer I <u>invoke</u> this curse—
whether he is one man and all unknown,
or one of many—may he wear out his life
in misery to miserable doom!
270   If with my knowledge he lives at my hearth

---

27. **sovereignty** (säv′ rən tē) *n.* supreme authority.
28. **Pytho's God** Apollo.

Literary Analysis
Tragedy In lines
234–236, what aspects
of his life story does
Oedipus' description
of himself emphasize?

invoke (in vōk′) *v.* summon;
cause to appear

Reading Check

With which god is the
chorus most distressed?

I pray that I myself may feel my curse.
On you I lay my charge to fulfill all this
for me, for the God, and for this land of ours
destroyed and blighted, by the God forsaken.

275 Even were this no matter of God's ordinance
it would not fit you so to leave it lie,
unpurified, since a good man is dead
and one that was a king. Search it out.
Since I am now the holder of his office,
280 and have his bed and wife that once was his,
and had his line not been unfortunate
we would have common children—(fortune leaped
upon his head)—because of all these things,
I fight in his defense as for my father,
285 and I shall try all means to take the murderer
of Laius the son of Labdacus
the son of Polydorus and before him
of Cadmus and before him of Agenor.
Those who do not obey me, may the Gods
290 grant no crops springing from the ground they plow
nor children to their women! May a fate
like this, or one still worse than this consume them!
For you whom these words please, the other Thebans,
may Justice as your ally and all the Gods
295 live with you, blessing you now and for ever!

CHORUS: As you have held me to my oath, I speak:
I neither killed the king nor can declare
the killer; but since Phoebus set the quest
it is his part to tell who the man is.

300 **OEDIPUS:** Right; but to put compulsion[29] on the Gods
against their will—no man can do that.

CHORUS: May I then say what I think second best?

OEDIPUS: If there's a third best, too, spare not to tell it.

CHORUS: I know that what the Lord Teiresias
305 sees, is most often what the Lord Apollo
sees. If you should inquire of this from him
you might find out most clearly.

OEDIPUS: Even in this my actions have not been sluggard.[30]
On Creon's word I have sent two messengers
310 and why the prophet is not here already
I have been wondering.

---

29. compulsion (kəm pul´ shən) *n.* driving force; coercion.
30. sluggard (slug´ ərd) *adj.* lazy or idle.

Literary Analysis
Tragedy and Tragic Hero
How does Oedipus' decision to seek out the murderer of Laius add to his stature as a hero?

Critical Viewing ▶
What emotions do these actors playing Oedipus (standing) and Teiresias (kneeling) convey? [Interpret]

436 ◆ *Ancient Greece and Rome*

CHORUS: His skill apart
  there is besides only an old faint story.

OEDIPUS: What is it?
  I look at every story.

CHORUS: It was said
  that he was killed by certain wayfarers.

315 **OEDIPUS:** I heard that, too, but no one saw the killer.

CHORUS: Yet if he has a share of fear at all,
  his courage will not stand firm, hearing your curse.

OEDIPUS: The man who in the doing did not shrink
  will fear no word.

CHORUS: Here comes his prosecutor:
320   led by your men the godly prophet comes
  in whom alone of mankind truth is native.

                    [*Enter* TEIRESIAS, *led by a little boy.*]

OEDIPUS: Teiresias, you are versed in everything,
  things teachable and things not to be spoken,
  things of the heaven and earth-creeping things.
325   You have no eyes but in your mind you know
  with what a plague our city is afflicted.
  My lord, in you alone we find a champion,

☑ **Reading Check**

Why has Oedipus sum-
moned Lord Teiresias?

in you alone one that can rescue us.
Perhaps you have not heard the messengers,
330   but Phoebus sent in answer to our sending
an oracle declaring that our freedom
from this disease would only come when we
should learn the names of those who killed King Laius,
and kill them or expel from our country.
335   Do not begrudge us oracles from birds,
or any other way of <u>prophecy</u>
within your skill; save yourself and the city,
save me; redeem the debt of our pollution
that lies on us because of this dead man.
340   We are in your hands; pains are most nobly taken
to help another when you have means and power.

TEIRESIAS: Alas, how terrible is wisdom when
it brings no profit to the man that's wise!
This I knew well, but had forgotten it,
345   else I would not have come here

OEDIPUS: What is this?
How sad you are now you have come!

TEIRESIAS: Let me
go home, It will be easiest for us both
to bear our several destinies to the end
if you will follow my advice.

OEDIPUS: You'd rob us
350   of this your gift of prophecy? You talk
as one who had no care for law nor love
for Thebes who reared you.

TEIRESIAS: Yes, but I see that even your own words
miss the mark; therefore I must fear for mine.

355 OEDIPUS: For God's sake if you know of anything,
do not turn from us; all of us kneel to you,
all of us here, your suppliants.

TEIRESIAS: All of you here know nothing. I will not
bring to the light of day my troubles, mine—
rather than call them yours.

360 OEDIPUS: What do you mean?
You know of something but refuse to speak.
Would you betray us and destroy the city?

TEIRESIAS: I will not bring this pain upon us both,
neither on you nor on myself. Why is it
365   you question me and waste your labor? I
will tell you nothing.

Reading Strategy
Reading Drama How
might the actor playing
Oedipus vary his tone of
voice in this dialogue with
Teiresias? Explain.

438 ◆ *Ancient Greece and Rome*

OEDIPUS: You would provoke a stone! Tell us, you villain,
tell us, and do not stand there quietly
unmoved and balking[31] at the issue.

370 **TEIRESIAS:** You blame my temper but you do not see
your own that lives within you; it is me
you chide.[32]

OEDIPUS: Who would not feel his temper rise
at words like these with which you shame our city?

375 **TEIRESIAS:** Of themselves things will come, although I
hide them
and breathe no word of them.

OEDIPUS: Since they will come
tell them to me.

TEIRESIAS: I will say nothing further.
Against this answer let your temper rage
as wildly as you will.

380 **OEDIPUS:** Indeed I am
so angry I shall not hold back a jot
of what I think. For I would have you know
I think you were complotter[33] of the deed
and doer of the deed save in so far

385 as for the actual killing. Had you had eyes
I would have said alone you murdered him.

TEIRESIAS: Yes? Then I warn you faithfully to keep
the letter of your proclamation and
from this day forth to speak no word of greeting

390 to these nor me; you are the land's pollution.

OEDIPUS: How shamelessly you started up this taunt!
How do you think you will escape?

TEIRESIAS: I have.
I have escaped; the truth is what I cherish

395 and that's my strength.

OEDIPUS: And who has taught you truth?
Not your profession surely!

TEIRESIAS: You have taught me,
for you have made me speak against my will.

400 **OEDIPUS:** Speak what? Tell me again that I may learn it better.

TEIRESIAS: Did you not understand before or would you
provoke me into speaking?

---

31. **balking** (bôk´ iŋ) *v.* obstinately refusing to act.
32. **chide** (chīd) *v.* scold.
33. **complotter** (käm plät´ ər) *n.* person who plots against another person.

The Delphic Oracle

The Greeks called Delphi the "navel," or center, of the world. It was the place to which Greeks and foreigners alike traveled from all over the Mediterranean area to seek advice from the god Apollo.

The oracle at Delphi was a shrine to Apollo where the god, speaking through his priestess, would answer questions from mortals. Rulers who wanted to know whether they should go to war, or when and where they should found a colony, consulted the Oracle. No one would consider amending the constitution or establishing a new religious festival without advice from Delphi.

Sometimes Apollo gave straightforward answers. Often, however, the answers were ambiguous riddles that had to be solved with care and subtlety. Apollo knew all and always spoke the truth, but human beings could misinterpret his responses. For example, when King Croesus of Lydia, fabled for his wealth, asked whether he should invade Persia, the Oracle responded, "If you do, you will destroy a great kingdom." The king took this as a green light and invaded Persia as he had planned. Against everyone's expectations, he was defeated. Too late he realized that the "great kingdom" he had destroyed was his own.

Reading Check

Why is Oedipus angry
with Teiresias?

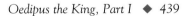

OEDIPUS: I did not grasp it,
not so to call it known. Say it again.

TEIRESIAS: I say you are the murderer of the king
405 whose murderer you seek.

OEDIPUS: Not twice you shall
say calumnies[34] like this and stay unpunished.

TEIRESIAS: Shall I say more to tempt your anger more?

OEDIPUS: As much as you desire; it will be said
in vain.

410 **TEIRESIAS:** I say that with those you love best
you live in foulest shame unconsciously
and do not see where you are in calamity.[35]

OEDIPUS: Do you imagine you can always talk
like this, and live to laugh at it hereafter?

415 **TEIRESIAS:** Yes, if the truth has anything of strength.

OEDIPUS: It has, but not for you; it has no strength
for you because you are blind in mind and ears
as well as in your eyes.

TEIRESIAS: You are a poor wretch
420 to taunt me with the very insults which
every one soon will heap upon yourself.

OEDIPUS: Your life is one long night so that you cannot
hurt me or any other who sees the light.

TEIRESIAS: It is not fate that I should be your ruin,
Apollo is enough; it is his care
425 to work this out.

OEDIPUS: Was this your own design
or Creon's?

TEIRESIAS: Creon is no hurt to you,
but you are to yourself.

OEDIPUS: Wealth, sovereignty and skill outmatching skill
for the contrivance[36] of an envied life!
430 Great store of jealousy fill your treasury chests,
if my friend Creon, friend from the first and loyal,
thus secretly attacks me, secretly
desires to drive me out and secretly
suborns[37] this juggling, trick devising quack,
435 this wily beggar who has only eyes

Reading Strategy
Reading Drama How do you think the actor playing Oedipus should speak lines 428–436? Explain.

---

34. calumnies (kalʹ əm nēz)) *n.* false and malicious statements; slander.
35. calamity (kə lamʹ ə tē) *n.* extreme misfortune that leads to disaster.
36. contrivance (kən trīʹ vəns) *n.* act of devising or scheming.
37. suborns (sə bôrnzʹ) *v.* instigates a person to commit perjury.

for his own gains, but blindness in his skill.
For, tell me, where have you seen clear, Teiresias,
with your prophetic eyes? When the dark singer,
the sphinx, was in your country, did you speak
440 word of deliverance to its citizens?
And yet the riddle's answer was not the province
of a chance comer. It was a prophet's task
and plainly you had no such gift of prophecy
from birds nor otherwise from any God
445 to glean a word of knowledge. But I came,
Oedipus, who knew nothing, and I stopped her.
I solved the riddle by my wit alone.
Mine was no knowledge got from birds. And now
you would expel me,
450 because you think that you will find a place
by Creon's throne. I think you will be sorry,
both you and your accomplice, for your plot
to drive me out. And did I not regard you
as an old man, some suffering would have taught you
455 that what was in your heart was treason.

    CHORUS: We look at this man's words and yours, my king,
and we find both have spoken them in anger.
We need no angry words but only thought
how we may best hit the God's meaning for us.

460 **TEIRESIAS:** If you are king, at least I have the right
no less to speak in my defense against you.
Of that much I am master. I am no slave
of yours, but Loxias', and so I shall not
enroll myself with Creon for my patron.
465 Since you have taunted me with being blind,
here is my word for you.
You have your eyes but see not where you are
in sin, nor where you live, nor whom you live with.
Do you know who your parents are? Unknowing
470 you are an enemy to kith and kin
in death, beneath the earth, and in this life.
A deadly footed, double striking curse,
from father and mother both, shall drive you forth
out of this land, with darkness on your eyes,
475 that now have such straight vision. Shall there be
a place will not be harbor to your cries,[38]
a corner of Cithaeron[39] will not ring
in echo to your cries, soon, soon,—
when you shall learn the secret of your marriage,

38. **Shall . . . . cries** Is there any place that won't be full of your cries?
39. **Cithaeron** (si´ ther än) *n.* mountain near Thebes on which Oedipus was abandoned as an infant.

Reading Strategy
Reading Drama What change in the actor's posture or gestures should accompany lines 437–440?

▼ **Critical Viewing**
Does this image of a sphinx suggest a creature that is a "cruel singer"? Why or why not? [Evaluate]

Literary Analysis
Tragedy What emotions might Teiresias' speech, which emphasizes a curse and Oedipus' "blindness," have evoked in the Athenian audience? Explain

✔**Reading Check**
According to Teiresias, who is the murderer whom Oedipus seeks?

480 which steered you to a haven in this house,—
     haven no haven, after lucky voyage?
     And of the multitude of other evils
     establishing a grim equality
     between you and your children, you know nothing.
485 So, muddy with contempt my words and Creon's!
     Misery shall grind no man as it will you.

OEDIPUS: Is it endurable that I should hear
     such words from him? Go and a curse go with you!
     Quick, home with you! Out of my house at once!

490 **TEIRESIAS:** I would not have come either had you not called me.

OEDIPUS: I did not know then you would talk like a fool—
     or it would have been long before I called you.

TEIRESIAS: I am a fool then, as it seems to you—
     but to the parents who have bred you, wise.

495 **OEDIPUS:** What parents? Stop! Who are they of all the world?

TEIRESIAS: This day will show your birth and will destroy you.

OEDIPUS: How needlessly your riddles darken everything.

TEIRESIAS: But it's in riddle answering you are strongest.

OEDIPUS: Yes. Taunt me where you will find me great.

500 **TEIRESIAS:** It is this very luck that has destroyed you.

OEDIPUS: I do not care, if it has saved this city.

TEIRESIAS: Well, I will go. Come, boy, lead me away.

OEDIPUS: Yes, lead him off. So long as you are here,
     you'll be a stumbling block and a vexation;
505 once gone, you will not trouble me again.

TEIRESIAS: I have said
     what I came here to say not fearing your
     <u>countenance</u>; there is no way you can hurt me.
     I tell you, king, this man, this murderer
     (whom you have long declared you are in search of,
510 indicting him in threatening proclamation
     as murderer of Laius)—he is here.
     In name he is a stranger among citizens
     but soon he will be shown to be a citizen
     true native Theban, and he'll have no joy
515 of the discovery: blindness for sight
     and beggary for riches his exchange,
     he shall go journeying to a foreign country
     tapping his way before him with a stick.
     He shall be proved father and brother both
520 to his own children in his house; to her
     that gave him birth, a son and husband both;
     a fellow sower in his father's bed

countenance (koun´ tə nəns)
n. the look on a person's face

▼ **Critical Viewing**
In what ways do the expressions of the masks in this image of the chorus reflect varied responses to the play's events? [**Analyze**]

with that same father that he murdered.
Go within, reckon that out, and if you find me
525   mistaken, say I have no skill in prophecy.

[*Exit separately* TEIRESIAS *and* OEDIPUS.]

CHORUS:

Strophe
Who is the man proclaimed
by Delphi's prophetic rock
as the bloody handed murderer,
the doer of deeds that none dare name?
530   Now is the time for him to run
with a stronger foot
than Pegasus[40]
for the child of Zeus leaps in arms upon him
with fire and the lightning bolt,
535   and terribly close on his heels
are the Fates that never miss.

Antistrophe
Lately from snowy Parnassus
clearly the voice flashed forth,
bidding each Theban track him down,
540   the unknown murderer.

✔ **Reading Check**

How does Oedipus react
to the information that
Teiresias gives him?

---

40. Pegasus (peg´ ə səs) mythical winged horse.

In the savage forests he lurks and in
the caverns like
the mountain bull.
He is sad and lonely, and lonely his feet
545   that carry him far from the navel of earth;[41]
but its prophecies, ever living,
flutter around his head.

    Strophe
The augur[42] has spread confusion,
terrible confusion;
550   I do not approve what was said
nor can I deny it.
I do not know what to say;
I am in a flutter of foreboding;
I never heard in the present
555   nor past of a quarrel between
the sons of Labdacus and Polybus,
that I might bring as proof
in attacking the popular fame
of Oedipus, seeking
560   to take vengeance for undiscovered
death in the line of Labdacus.

    Antistrophe
Truly Zeus and Apollo are wise
and in human things all knowing;
but amongst men there is no
565   distinct judgment, between the prophet
and me—which of us is right.
One man may pass another in wisdom
but I would never agree
with those that find fault with the king
570   till I should see the word
proved right beyond doubt. For once
in visible form the Sphinx
came on him and all of us
saw his wisdom and in that test
575   he saved the city. So he will not be condemned by my mind.

                                  [*Enter* CREON.]

CREON: Citizens, I have come because I heard
deadly words spread about me, that the king
accuses me. I cannot take that from him.
If he believes that in these present troubles
580   he has been wronged by me in word or deed

---

41. navel of earth fissure, or crack, on Mount Parnassus from which mysterious vapors arose
to inspire Pythia, priestess of the Oracle of Apollo at Delphi.

42. augur (ô´ gər) *n.* fortuneteller or prophet; refers here to Teiresias.

Reading Strategy
Reading Drama
Considering the content
and tone of this passage,
how should the actor
playing Creon make his
entrance?

I do not want to live on with the burden
of such a scandal on me. The report
injures me doubly and most vitally—
for I'll be called a traitor to my city
585 and traitor also to my friends and you.

CHORUS: Perhaps it was a sudden gust of anger
that forced that insult from him, and no judgment.

CREON: But did he say that it was in compliance
with schemes of mine that the seer told him lies?

590 **CHORUS:** Yes, he said that, but why, I do not know.

CREON: Were his eyes straight in his head? Was his mind right
when he accused me in this fashion?

CHORUS: I do not know; I have no eyes to see
what princes do. Here comes the king himself.

[*Enter* OEDIPUS.]

595 **OEDIPUS:** You, sir, how is it you come here? Have you so much
brazen-faced daring that you venture in
my house although you are proved manifestly[43]
the murderer of that man, and though you tried,
openly, highway robbery of my crown?
600 For God's sake, tell me what you saw in me,
what cowardice or what stupidity,
that made you lay a plot like this against me?
Did you imagine I should not observe
the crafty scheme that stole upon me or
605 seeing it, take no means to counter it?
Was it not stupid of you to make the attempt,
to try to hunt down royal power without
the people at your back or friends? For only
with the people at your back or money can
610 the hunt end in the capture of a crown.

CREON: Do you know what you're doing? Will you listen
to words to answer yours, and then pass judgment?

OEDIPUS: You're quick to speak, but I am slow to grasp you,
for I have found you dangerous,—and my foe.

615 **CREON:** First of all hear what I shall say to that.

OEDIPUS: At least don't tell me that you are not guilty.

CREON: If you think obstinacy[44] without wisdom
a valuable possession, you are wrong.

OEDIPUS: And you are wrong if you believe that one,

---

43. **proved manifestly** (man′ə fest lē) clearly proved with evidence.
44. **obstinacy** (äb′ stə nə sē) *n.* stubbornness; state of being unyielding to reason. Creon
means that Oedipus cannot see—or refuses to see—the facts.

Literary Analysis
**Tragedy, Tragic Hero,
and Tragic Flaw** Up to this
point in the play, in what
ways does Oedipus seem
heroic and in what ways
does he seem flawed?
Explain.

Reading Check
Why does Creon return?

620 a criminal, will not be punished only
because he is my kinsman.

CREON: This is but just—
but tell me, then, of what offense I'm guilty?

OEDIPUS: Did you or did you not urge me to send
to this prophetic mumbler?

CREON: I did indeed,
625 and I shall stand by what I told you.

OEDIPUS: How long ago is it since Laius. . . .

CREON: What about Laius? I don't understand.

OEDIPUS: Vanished—died—was murdered?

CREON: It is long,
a long, long time to reckon.

OEDIPUS: Was this prophet
630 in the profession then?

CREON: He was, and honored
as highly as he is today.

OEDIPUS: At that time did he say a word about me?

CREON: Never, at least when I was near him.

OEDIPUS: You never made a search for the dead man?

635 **CREON:** We searched, indeed, but never learned of anything.

OEDIPUS: Why did our wise old friend not say this then?

CREON: I don't know; and when I know nothing, I
usually hold my tongue.

OEDIPUS: You know this much,
and can declare this much if you are loyal.

640 **CREON:** What is it? If I know, I'll not deny it.

OEDIPUS: That he would not have said that I killed Laius
had he not met you first.

CREON: You know yourself
whether he said this, but I demand that I
should hear as much from you as you from me.

645 **OEDIPUS:** Then hear,—I'll not be proved a murderer.

CREON: Well, then. You're married to my sister.

OEDIPUS: Yes,
that I am not disposed to deny.

CREON: You rule
this country giving her an equal share
in the government?

Literary Analysis
Tragedy and Tragic Flaw
What flaw in Oedipus' character is suggested by his choosing to accuse Creon?

OEDIPUS: Yes, everything she wants
650 she has from me.

CREON: And I, as thirdsman to you,
am rated as the equal of you two?

OEDIPUS: Yes, and it's there you've proved yourself false friend.

CREON: Not if you will reflect on it as I do.
655 Consider, first, if you think any one
would choose to rule and fear rather than rule
and sleep untroubled by a fear if power
were equal in both cases. I, at least,
I was not born with such a frantic yearning
660 to be a king—but to do what kings do.
And so it is with every one who has learned
wisdom and self-control. As it stands now,
the prizes are all mine—and without fear.
But if I were the king myself, I must
665 do much that went against the grain.
How should despotic[45] rule seem sweeter to me
than painless power and an assured authority?
I am not so besotted[46] yet that I
want other honors than those that come with profit.
670 Now every man's my pleasure; every man greets me;
now those who are your suitors fawn on me,—
success for them depends upon my favor.
Why should I let all this go to win that?
My mind would not be traitor if it's wise;
675 I am no treason lover, of my nature,
nor would I ever dare to join a plot.
Prove what I say. Go to the oracle
at Pytho and inquire about the answers,
if they are as I told you. For the rest,
680 if you discover I laid any plot
together with the seer, kill me, I say,
not only by your vote but by my own.
But do not charge me on obscure opinion
without some proof to back it. It's not just
685 lightly to count your knaves as honest men,
nor honest men as knaves. To throw away
an honest friend is, as it were, to throw
your life away, which a man loves the best.
In time you will know all with certainty;
690 time is the only test of honest men,
one day is space enough to know a rogue.

Reading Strategy
Reading Drama How do you think the actor playing Oedipus should react as Creon is making this speech?

---

45. **despotic** (des pät′ ik) *adj.* absolute; unlimited; tyrannical.
46. **besotted** (bē sät′ əd) *v.* stupefied; foolish.

☑**Reading Check**

What does Oedipus accuse Creon of doing?

CHORUS: His words are wise, king, if one fears to fall.
Those who are quick of temper are not safe.

OEDIPUS: When he that plots against me secretly
695   moves quickly, I must quickly counterplot.
If I wait taking no decisive measure
his business will be done, and mine be spoiled.

CREON: What do you want to do then? Banish me?

OEDIPUS: No, certainly; kill you, not banish you.

700   **CREON:** I do not think that you've your wits about you.

OEDIPUS: For my own interests, yes.

CREON: But for mine, too,
you should think equally.

OEDIPUS: You are a rogue.

CREON: Suppose you do not understand?

OEDIPUS: But yet
705   I must be ruler.

CREON: Not if you rule badly.

OEDIPUS: O, city, city!

CREON: I too have some share
in the city; it is not yours alone.

CHORUS: Stop, my lords! Here—and in the nick of time
710   I see Jocasta coming from the house;
with her help lay the quarrel that now stirs you.

[*Enter* JOCASTA.]

JOCASTA: For shame! Why have you raised this foolish squabbling
brawl? Are you not ashamed to air your private
griefs when the country's sick? Go in, you, Oedipus,
715   and you, too, Creon, into the house. Don't magnify
your nothing troubles.

CREON: Sister, Oedipus,
your husband, thinks he has the right to do
terrible wrongs—he has but to choose between
720   two terrors: banishing or killing me.

OEDIPUS: He's right, Jocasta; for I find him plotting
with knavish[47] tricks against my person.

CREON: That God may never bless me! May I die
accursed, if I have been guilty of
725   one tittle[48] of the charge you bring against me!

Reading Strategy
Reading Drama From
their words in lines
692–693, as well as in
lines 709–711, what do
you think the chorus
wants Oedipus to do?

---

47. knavish (nāv´ ish) *adj.* deceitful.
48. tittle (tit´ 'l) *n.* very small particle.

JOCASTA: I beg you, Oedipus, trust him in this,
spare him for the sake of this his oath to God,
for my sake, and the sake of those who stand here.

CHORUS: Be gracious, be merciful,
we beg of you.

730 **OEDIPUS:** In what would you have me yield?

CHORUS: He has been no silly child in the past.
He is strong in his oath now.
Spare him.

OEDIPUS: Do you know what you ask?

735 **CHORUS:** Yes.

OEDIPUS: Tell me then.

CHORUS: He has been your friend before all men's eyes; do not cast
him away dishonored on an obscure conjecture.

OEDIPUS: I would have you know that this request of yours
740 really requests my death or banishment.

CHORUS: May the Sun God,[49] king of Gods, forbid! May I die
without God's blessing, without friends' help, if I had any such
thought. But my spirit is broken by my unhappiness for my
745 wasting country; and this would but add troubles
amongst ourselves to the other troubles.

OEDIPUS: Well, let him go then—if I must die ten times for it,
or be sent out dishonored into exile.
It is your lips that prayed for him I pitied,
750 not his; wherever he is, I shall hate him.

CREON: I see you sulk in yielding and you're dangerous
when you are out of temper; natures like yours
are justly heaviest for themselves to bear.

OEDIPUS: Leave me alone! Take yourself off, I tell you.

755 **CREON:** I'll go, you have not known me, but they have,
and they have known my innocence.

[*Exit.*]

CHORUS: Won't you take him inside, lady?

JOCASTA: Yes, when I've found out what was the matter.

CHORUS: There was some misconceived suspicion of a story, and
760 on the other side the sting of injustice.

JOCASTA: So, on both sides?

CHORUS: Yes.

JOCASTA: What was the story?

---

49. **Sun God** Apollo.

Literary Analysis
Tragedy Is Oedipus' interpretation of his own situation justified? Why or why not?

✔**Reading Check**
How does Oedipus want to punish Creon?

CHORUS: I think it best, in the interests of the country, to leave it
765   where it ended.

OEDIPUS: You see where you have ended, straight of judgment
although you are, by softening my anger.

CHORUS: Sir, I have said before and I say again—be sure that I
would have been proved a madman, bankrupt in sane council, if I
770   should put you away, you who steered the country I love safely
when she was crazed with troubles. God grant that now, too, you
may prove a fortunate guide for us.

JOCASTA: Tell me, my lord, I beg of you, what was it
775   that roused your anger so?

OEDIPUS: Yes, I will tell you.
I honor you more than I honor them.
It was Creon and the plots he laid against me.

JOCASTA: Tell me—if you can clearly tell the quarrel—

OEDIPUS: Creon says
780   that I'm the murderer of Laius.

JOCASTA: Of his own knowledge or on information?

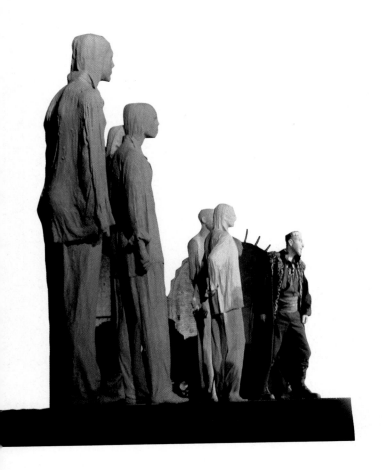

◀ **Critical Viewing**

In what ways does this
photograph suggest that
the tragic hero is unique,
while the chorus—here
shown as sculptures—
speaks for a community?
[Analyze]

OEDIPUS: He sent this rascal prophet to me, since
he keeps his own mouth clean of any guilt.

JOCASTA: Do not concern yourself about this matter;
785 listen to me and learn that human beings
have no part in the craft of prophecy.
Of that I'll show you a short proof.
There was an oracle once that came to Laius,—
I will not say that it was Phoebus' own,
790 but it was from his servants—and it told him
that it was fate that he should die a victim
at the hands of his own son, a son to be born
of Laius and me. But, see now, he,
the king, was killed by foreign highway robbers
795 at a place where three roads meet—so goes the story;
and for the son—before three days were out
after his birth King Laius pierced his ankles
and by the hands of others cast him forth
upon a pathless hillside. So Apollo
800 failed to fulfill his oracle to the son,
that he should kill his father, and to Laius
also proved false in that the thing he feared,
death at his son's hands, never came to pass.
So clear in this case were the oracles,
805 so clear and false. Give them no heed, I say;
what God discovers need of, easily
he shows to us himself.

OEDIPUS: O dear Jocasta,
as I hear this from you, there comes upon me
810 a wandering of the soul—I could run mad.

JOCASTA: What trouble is it, that you turn again
and speak like this?

OEDIPUS: I thought I heard you say
that Laius was killed at a crossroads.

JOCASTA: Yes, that was how the story went and still
that word goes round.

OEDIPUS: Where is this place, Jocasta,
where he was murdered?

JOCASTA: Phocis is the country
815 and the road splits there, one of two roads from Delphi,
another comes from Daulia.

OEDIPUS: How long ago is this?

JOCASTA: The news came to the city just before
you became king and all men's eyes looked to you.
820 What is it, Oedipus, that's in your mind?

Reading Strategy
Reading Drama From Oedipus' comment in lines 808–810, how do you think he should react during Jocasta's long speech in lines 784–807?

**Reading Check**

According to Jocasta, what did the oracle say would happen to Laius?

OEDIPUS: What have you designed, O Zeus, to do with me?

JOCASTA: What is the thought that troubles your heart?

OEDIPUS: Don't ask me yet—tell me of Laius—
How did he look? How old or young was he?

825 **JOCASTA:** He was a tall man and his hair was grizzled
already—nearly white—and in his form
not unlike you.

OEDIPUS: O God, I think I have
called curses on myself in ignorance.

JOCASTA: What do you mean? I am terrified
when I look at you.

OEDIPUS: I have a deadly fear
that the old seer had eyes. You'll show me more
830 if you can tell me one more thing.

JOCASTA: I will.
I'm frightened,—but if I can understand,
I'll tell you all you ask.

OEDIPUS: How was his company?
Had he few with him when he went this journey,
835 or many servants, as would suit a prince?

JOCASTA: In all there were but five, and among them
a herald;[50] and one carriage for the king.

OEDIPUS: It's plain—it's plain—who was it told you this?

JOCASTA: The only servant that escaped safe home.

840 **OEDIPUS:** Is he at home now?

JOCASTA: No, when he came home again
and saw you king and Laius was dead,
he came to me and touched my hand and begged
that I should send him to the fields to be
845 my shepherd and so he might see the city
as far off as he might. So I
sent him away. He was an honest man,
as slaves go, and was worthy of far more
than what he asked of me.

850 **OEDIPUS:** O, how I wish that he could come back quickly!

JOCASTA: He can. Why is your heart so set on this?

OEDIPUS: O dear Jocasta, I am full of fears
that I have spoken far too much; and therefore
I wish to see this shepherd.

855 **JOCASTA:** He will come;

---

50. herald (her´ əld) *n.* person who makes proclamations and carries messages.

452 ◆ *Ancient Greece and Rome*

but, Oedipus, I think I'm worthy too
to know what it is that disquiets you.

OEDIPUS: It shall not be kept from you, since my mind
has gone so far with its forebodings. Whom
860   should I confide in rather than you, who is there
of more importance to me who have passed
through such a fortune?
Polybus was my father, king of Corinth,[51]
and Merope, the Dorian,[52] my mother.
865   I was held greatest of the citizens
in Corinth till a curious chance befell me
as I shall tell you—curious, indeed,
but hardly worth the store I set upon it.
There was a dinner and at it a man,
870   a drunken man, accused me in his drink
of being bastard. I was furious

---

51. **Corinth** (kōr′ inth) city at the western end of the isthmus (Greece) that joins the Peloponnesus to Boeotia.
52. **Dorian** (dôr′ ē ən) *n.* one of the main branches of the Hellenes; the Dorians invaded the Peloponnesus.

Literary Analysis
Tragedy How does Oedipus' story about growing up in Corinth relate to Jocasta's description of Laius' murder?

✔**Reading Check**

What does the servant ask of Jocasta when he sees that Laius is dead and Oedipus is king?

*L*iterature
in context   History Connection

The Theater of Dionysus at Athens

The great dramatic festivals of fifth-century Athens were staged in the Theater of Dionysus, an immense, semicircular, open-air theater set on the slope of the Acropolis (ə kräp′ ə lis). The theater held seventeen thousand spectators, who sat on long benches. The front row contained stone chairs with backs, which were reserved for priests and government officials. The performance area included a level circular area called the orchestra, or "dancing space." Beyond the orchestra stood the altar of the god Dionysus, and beyond that, the stage where the actors performed. Although scholars once believed that the masks the actors wore functioned like bullhorns, making their voices audible to the thousands of spectators, scholars now think that the theater was simply a perfect acoustical space in which even the smallest whisper could easily be heard.

but held my temper under for that day.
Next day I went and taxed[53] my parents with it;
they took the insult very ill from him,
875   the drunken fellow who had uttered it.
So I was comforted for their part, but
still this thing rankled[54] always, for the story
crept about widely. And I went at last
to Pytho, though my parents did not know.
880   But Phoebus sent me home again unhonored
in what I came to learn, but he foretold
other and desperate horrors to befall me,
that I was fated to lie with my mother,
and show to daylight an accursed breed
885   which men would not endure, and I was doomed
to be murderer of the father that begot me.
When I heard this I fled, and in the days
that followed I would measure from the stars
the whereabouts of Corinth—yes, I fled
890   to somewhere where I should not see fulfilled
the infamies[55] told in that dreadful oracle.
And as I journeyed I came to the place
where, as you say, this king met with his death.
Jocasta, I will tell you the whole truth.
895   When I was near the branching of the crossroads,
going on foot, I was encountered by
a herald and a carriage with a man in it,
just as you tell me. He that led the way
and the old man himself wanted to thrust me
900   out of the road by force. I became angry
and struck the coachman who was pushing me.
When the old man saw this he watched his moment,
and as I passed he struck me from his carriage,
full on the head with his two pointed goad.[56]
905   But he was paid in full and presently
my stick had struck him backwards from the car
and he rolled out of it. And then I killed them
all. If it happened there was any tie
of kinship twixt this man and Laius,
910   who is then now more miserable than I,
what man on earth so hated by the Gods,
since neither citizen nor foreigner
may welcome me at home or even greet me,

---

53. taxed (takst) *v.* imposed a burden on; put a strain on.
54. rankled (raŋˊ keld) *v.* caused to have long-lasting anger and resentment.
55. infamies (inˊ fə mēz) *n.* items of notorious disgrace and dishonor.
56. goad (gōd) *n.* sharp, pointed stick used to drive animals.

but drive me out of doors? And it is I,
915 I and no other have so cursed myself.
And I pollute the bed of him I killed
by the hands that killed him. Was I not born evil?
Am I not utterly unclean? I had to fly
and in my banishment not even see
920 my kindred nor set foot in my own country,
or otherwise my fate was to be yoked
in marriage with my mother and kill my father,
Polybus who begot me and had reared me.
Would not one rightly judge and say that on me
925 these things were sent by some <u>malignant</u> God?
O no, no, no—O holy majesty
of God on high, may I not see that day!
May I be gone out of men's sight before
I see the deadly taint of this disaster
come upon me.

930 **CHORUS:** Sir, we too fear these things. But until you see this man
face to face and hear his story, hope.

OEDIPUS: Yes, I have just this much of hope—to wait until the
herdsman comes.

JOCASTA: And when he comes, what do you want with him?

935 **OEDIPUS:** I'll tell you; if I find that his story is the same as yours, I
at least will be clear of this guilt.

JOCASTA: Why what so particularly did you learn from my story?

OEDIPUS: You said that he spoke of highway *robbers*
who killed Laius. Now if he uses the same num-
940 ber, it was not I who killed him. One man cannot
be the same as many. But if he speaks of a man
travelling alone, then clearly the burden of the
guilt inclines toward me.

JOCASTA: Be sure, at least, that this was how he
945 told the story. He cannot unsay it now, for every
one in the city heard it—not I alone. But, Oedipus, even if he diverges from what he said then,
he shall never prove that the murder of Laius
squares rightly with the prophecy—for Loxias
950 declared that the king should be killed by his own
son. And that poor creature did not kill him
surely,—for he died himself first. So as far as
prophecy goes, henceforward I shall not look to
the right hand or the left.

955 **OEDIPUS:** Right. But yet, send some one for the peasant to bring
him here; do not neglect it.

malignant (mə lig′ nənt)
adj. very harmful

Literary Analysis
Tragedy On what details
in the tale of Laius' murder
does Oedipus base his
hope that he is innocent?

☑**Reading Check**
What did Oedipus do to
avoid fulfilling the horrors
he was told awaited him?

JOCASTA: I will send quickly. Now let me go indoors. I will do nothing except what pleases you.

[*Exit.*]

CHORUS:

Strophe
960 May destiny ever find me
pious in word and deed
prescribed by the laws that live on high:
laws begotten in the clear air of heaven,
whose only father is Olympus;
no mortal nature brought them to birth,
965 no forgetfulness shall lull them to sleep;
for God is great in them and grows not old.

Antistrophe
Insolence[57] breeds the tyrant, insolence
if it is glutted with a surfeit,[58] unseasonable, unprofitable,
climbs to the roof-top and plunges
970 sheer down to the ruin that must be,
and there its feet are no service.
But I pray that the God may never
abolish the eager ambition that profits the state.
For I shall never cease to hold the God as our protector.

Strophe
975 If a man walks with haughtiness
of hand or word and gives no heed
to Justice and the shrines of Gods
despises—may an evil doom
980 smite him for his ill-starred pride of heart!—
if he reaps gains without justice
and will not hold from impiety
and his fingers itch for untouchable things.
985 When such things are done, what man shall contrive
to shield his soul from the shafts of the God?
When such deeds are held in honor,
why should I honor the Gods in the dance?

Antistrophe
No longer to the holy place,
to the navel of earth I'll go
to worship, nor to Abae
990 nor to Olympia,
unless the oracles are proved to fit,
for all men's hands to point at.

Literary Analysis
Tragedy How do you think this ode may have affected the audience? Explain.

---

57. insolence (in´ sə ləns) *n.* arrogance; bold disrespectfulness.
58. surfeit (sur´ fit) *n.* excessive supply.

O Zeus, if you are rightly called
the sovereign lord, all-mastering,
995   let this not escape you nor your ever-living power!
The oracles concerning Laius
are old and dim and men regard them not.
Apollo is nowhere clear in honor; God's service perishes.

Review and Assess

Thinking About the Selection

1. **Respond:** What do you think is Oedipus' most admirable character trait? What is his worst character trait?

2. **(a) Recall:** As the play opens, what disaster has struck Thebes? **(b) Infer:** In the opening scene, what does Oedipus' response to this disaster suggest about him as a ruler?

3. **(a) Recall:** What are Oedipus' two main reasons for seeking out Laius' murderer? **(b) Analyze Cause and Effect:** How does Oedipus' curse on the murderer foreshadow, or hint at, a tragic outcome for the drama?

4. **(a) Recall:** What physical ailment afflicts Teiresias? **(b) Classify:** Which details in Teiresias' speech in lines 460–486 refer to darkness, vision, and insight? **(c) Compare and Contrast:** Compare and contrast Oedipus and Teiresias in terms of blindness and insight at the end of Part I.

5. **(a) Recall:** Of what does Oedipus accuse Creon in the scene beginning at line 576? **(b) Assess:** How convincing is Creon's argument about his own motives in lines 654–691? Explain.

6. **(a) Recall:** In lines 784–807, what reasons does Jocasta give for not having faith in prophecy? **(b) Compare and Contrast:** At this point in the play, what do both Jocasta and Oedipus seem to believe about their abilities to control their own destinies? Explain.

7. **(a) Analyze:** What role does the chorus play in clarifying both the events and characters' emotions in the play? **(b) Analyze:** In what ways does the chorus heighten the dramatic tension?

8. **(a) Interpret:** In lines 705–708—the scene between Oedipus and Creon—what insights does Sophocles provide about the rights of the ruler and of the ruled? **(b) Evaluate:** In what ways are these ideas applicable to contemporary American life? Explain.

Review and Assess

Literary Analysis

Tragedy

1. The leading figure in a **tragedy** is usually a person of high birth or noble status who also possesses outstanding personal traits. In what ways does Oedipus meet these requirements?

2. On the basis of what you have learned in Part I, which of Oedipus' choices have determined his destiny? Explain.

3. In Greek tragedies, the chorus often comments on universal issues raised by the action. Use a chart like the one shown to cite at least two specific examples of such choral commentary.

Action or Event ····▸ **Issue/ Question** ····▸ **Choral Commentary**

Connecting Literary Elements

4. Trace the motif, or idea, of the search for knowledge in Part I by noting three moments in which Oedipus persists in a quest for knowledge.

5. (a) How does the chorus try to modify Oedipus' insistence on acquiring knowledge? (b) How does Oedipus respond? (c) How does his response affect your view of him as a **tragic hero?**

6. (a) What negative traits do you see in Oedipus? (b) Might any of these be considered a **tragic flaw?** Explain.

Reading Strategy

Reading Drama

7. As you **read drama,** stage directions supply key information. List three details that appear in the stage directions in Part I. Then, write a brief comment on the significance of each detail.

8. Note two examples of dialogue in Part I that provide hints about a character's body language or tone of voice. Explain your choices.

Extend Understanding

9. **Social Studies Connection:** (a) Identify at least three qualities a leader needs in a time of crisis. (b) In your view, does Oedipus possess each of these qualities?

Quick Review

A **tragedy** is a work of literature—usually a play—that portrays the downfall of a noble or outstanding person.

The main character in a tragedy is the **tragic hero** who possesses a **tragic flaw** in his or her character that leads to his or her downfall.

To **read drama,** use the stage directions and other clues in the text to picture a live performance.

Take It to the Net
PHschool.com

Take the interactive test online to check your understanding of this selection.

Integrate Language Skills

Vocabulary Development Lesson

Word Analysis: Prefix *pro-*

The prefix *pro-*, as in *prophecy*, means "before in place or time" or "forward." Add the prefix *pro-* to the word roots below. Then, write a definition of each word.

1. -ceed
2. -gnosis
3. -logue

Spelling Strategy

In words like *malignant*, the *g* and *n* have separate sounds. Sometimes, however, *gn* stands for only the *n* sound, as in *sign*. Finish spelling the words below; then, pronounce each word.

1. bring into line: al____
2. standing water: sta__ant

Grammar and Style Lesson

Participial Phrases

A participle is a form of a verb that can act as an adjective. A **participial phrase** consists of a participle and its complements and modifiers.

Present Participle: King, you yourself have seen our city <u>reeling like a wreck</u> . . . (modifies *city*)

Past Participle: Within the marketplace sit others <u>crowned with suppliant garlands</u> . . . (modifies *others*)

Concept Development: Synonyms

Select the letter of the word that is closest in meaning to each numbered vocabulary word.

1. blight: (a) glow, (b) disease, (c) harvest
2. pestilence: (a) plague, (b) heat, (c) omen
3. prophecy: (a) event, (b) death, (c) prediction
4. dispatch: (a) respond, (b) kill, (c) resent
5. invoke: (a) warn, (b) offer, (c) summon
6. induced: (a) caused, (b) stopped, (c) held
7. countenance: (a) joy, (b) expression, (c) exit
8. malignant: (a) harmful, (b) dull, (c) edgy

Practice Identify each participial phrase, and explain the word it modifies.

1. Standing before the people, Oedipus curses.
2. They speak of waves crashing on the shore.
3. Teiresias, seeing deeply, refuses to answer.
4. Disturbed by his anger, the chorus urges calm.
5. Jocasta recalls a prophecy delivered by Apollo's servant.

Writing Application Write a paragraph describing an event that you recently witnessed. Include at least three participial phrases.

*W*ᴳ *Prentice Hall Writing and Grammar Connection: Diamond Level, Chapter 19, Section 2*

Extension Activities

Writing Write a **news article** about the events in the play so far. Include details to address the 5 *w*'s: Who? What? When? Where? Why?

Listening and Speaking Present a **dramatic reading** of a speech from Part I. Include music that complements the mood of the speech.

Prepare to Read

Literary Analysis

Irony

Irony is the result of a pointed contrast between appearances or expectations and reality. In literature, there are three main types of irony:

- **Verbal irony** is the use of words to suggest the opposite of their usual meaning.
- **Situational irony** occurs when the outcome of an action or situation directly contradicts expectations.
- **Dramatic irony** occurs when readers or audience members are aware of truths that the characters themselves do not perceive.

This play provides one of literature's best examples of dramatic irony. As you read Part II, notice the contrast between what Oedipus believes to be true and what the reader or viewing audience knows to be true.

Connecting Literary Elements

An outstanding example of **dramatic irony** occurs when the Corinthian Messenger tells Jocasta that Oedipus' father, believed to be Polybus, is dead. The audience knows that Oedipus' father is actually Laius, whom Oedipus killed on his way to Thebes. Sophocles reveals the painful truths to Oedipus only gradually. That gradual revelation builds **suspense**—a feeling of tension or uncertainty—as Oedipus relentlessly pursues the knowledge that will ultimately cause his downfall. As you read, notice the ways in which Oedipus' pursuit of the truth adds to the mounting suspense.

Reading Strategy

Questioning the Characters' Motives

Like people in real life, characters in literature are not always what they seem. To gain additional insight as you read, **question the characters' motives**—their reasons for behaving as they do. Ask whether characters are motivated by fear, greed, guilt, love, loyalty, revenge, or another emotion or desire. As you read, use a chart like the one shown at right to examine the motives of the characters in Part II of the play.

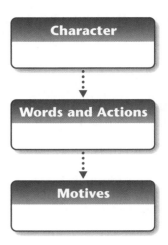

Vocabulary Development

fettered (fet′ ərd) *adj.* shackled; chained (p. 465)

beneficent (bə nef′ ə sənt) *adj.* kind; helpful (p. 467)

consonant (kän′ sə nənt) *adj.* in harmony or agreement (p. 467)

gratify (grat′ i fī) *v.* please (p. 469)

infamous (in′ fə məs) *adj.* disgraceful (p. 474)

reverence (rev′ rəns) *v.* show great respect (p. 478)

Review and Anticipate

In Part I of *Oedipus the King*, the people of Thebes beg Oedipus to save them from a disastrous plague. When Creon, the brother of Queen Jocasta, reports that the Delphic Oracle demands the punishment of King Laius' killer, Oedipus commits himself to solving the crime. He becomes enraged with the prophet, Teiresias, who tells Oedipus that he himself is the murderer. Teiresias adds that Oedipus will suffer a terrible destiny, blinded and outcast from society. Is Oedipus truly the murderer of King Laius? Will he suffer the terrible fate Teiresias has prophesied? Find the answers to these questions in Part II.

[*Enter* JOCASTA, *carrying garlands.*]

JOCASTA: Princes of the land, I have had the thought to go
1000   to the Gods' temples, bringing in my hand
garlands and gifts of incense, as you see.
For Oedipus excites himself too much
at every sort of trouble, not conjecturing,[1]
like a man of sense, what will be from what was,
1005   but he is always at the speaker's mercy,
when he speaks terrors. I can do no good
by my advice, and so I came as suppliant
to you, Lycaean Apollo, who are nearest.
These are the symbols of my prayer and this
1010   my prayer: grant us escape free of the curse.
Now when we look to him we are all afraid;
he's pilot of our ship and he is frightened.

[*Enter* MESSENGER.]

MESSENGER: Might I learn from you, sirs, where is
the house of Oedipus? Or best of all, if you
1015   know, where is the king himself?

Reading Strategy
Questioning the Characters' Motives
Which aspects of Oedipus' behavior have motivated Jocasta to visit the gods' temples?

☑**Reading Check**

To which god does Jocasta direct her prayers?

---

1. **conjecturing** (kən jek′ chər iŋ) *v.* inferring or predicting from incomplete evidence.

CHORUS: This is his house and he is within doors.
This lady is his wife and mother of his children.

MESSENGER: God bless you, lady, and God bless your household!
God bless Oedipus' noble wife!

1020 **JOCASTA:** God bless you, sir, for your kind greeting! What do you
want of us that you have come here? What have you to tell us?

MESSENGER: Good news, lady. Good for your house and for your
husband.

1025 **JOCASTA:** What is your news? Who sent you to us?

MESSENGER: I come from Corinth and the news I bring will give
you pleasure. Perhaps a little pain too.

JOCASTA: What is this news of double meaning?

MESSENGER: The people of the Isthmus will choose Oedipus to be
1030 their king. That is the rumor there.

JOCASTA: But isn't their king still old Polybus?

MESSENGER: No. He is in his grave. Death has got him.

JOCASTA: Is that the truth? Is Oedipus' father dead?

MESSENGER: May I die myself if it be otherwise!

1035 **JOCASTA** [*to a* SERVANT]: Be quick and run to the King with the
news! O oracles of the Gods, where are you now? It was from
this man Oedipus fled, lest he should be his murderer! And
now he is dead, in the course of nature, and not killed by
Oedipus.

[*Enter* OEDIPUS.]

Literary Analysis
Irony In what ways is
Jocasta's change of heart
toward the oracles an
example of situational
irony?

1040 **OEDIPUS:** Dearest Jocasta, why have you sent for me?

JOCASTA: Listen to this man and when you hear reflect what is the outcome of the holy oracles of the Gods.

OEDIPUS: Who is he? What is his message for me?

JOCASTA: He is from Corinth and he tells us that
1045 your father Polybus is dead and gone.

OEDIPUS: What's this you say, sir? Tell me yourself.

MESSENGER: Since this is the first matter you want clearly told: Polybus has gone down to death. You may be sure of it.

1050 **OEDIPUS:** By treachery or sickness?

MESSENGER: A small thing will put old bodies asleep.

OEDIPUS: So he died of sickness, it seems,—poor old man!

MESSENGER: Yes, and of age—the long years he had measured.

OEDIPUS: Ha! Ha! O dear Jocasta, why should one
1055 look to the Pythian hearth?² Why should one look
to the birds screaming overhead? They prophesied
that I should kill my father! But he's dead,
and hidden deep in earth, and I stand here
who never laid a hand on spear against him,—
1060 unless perhaps he died of longing for me,
and thus I am his murderer. But they,
the oracles, as they stand—he's taken them
away with him, they're dead as he himself is,
and worthless.

JOCASTA: That I told you before now.

1065 **OEDIPUS:** You did, but I was misled by my fear.

JOCASTA: Then lay no more of them to heart, not one.

OEDIPUS: But surely I must fear my mother's bed?

JOCASTA: Why should man fear since chance is all in all
for him, and he can clearly foreknow nothing?
1070 Best to live lightly, as one can, unthinkingly.
As to your mother's marriage bed,—don't fear it.
Before this, in dreams too, as well as oracles,
many a man has lain with his own mother.
But he to whom such things are nothing bears
his life most easily.

1075 **OEDIPUS:** All that you say would be said perfectly
if she were dead; but since she lives I must
still fear, although you talk so well, Jocasta:

JOCASTA: Still in your father's death there's light of comfort?

---

2. **Pythian hearth** (piʹ thē ən härth) *n.* the Delphic oracle that prophesied Oedipus' crime.

Literary Analysis
Irony In what ways is Jocasta and Oedipus' discussion about the Messenger's news an example of dramatic irony?

Reading Check

What news does the Messenger bring from Corinth?

OEDIPUS: Great light of comfort; but I fear the living.

1080 **MESSENGER:** Who is the woman that makes you afraid?

OEDIPUS: Merope, old man, Polybus' wife.

MESSENGER: What about her frightens the queen and you?

OEDIPUS: A terrible oracle, stranger, from the Gods.

MESSENGER: Can it be told? Or does the sacred law
1085   forbid another to have knowledge of it?

OEDIPUS: O no! Once on a time Loxias said
    that I should lie with my own mother and
    take on my hands the blood of my own father.
    And so for these long years I've lived away
1090   from Corinth; it has been to my great happiness;
    but yet it's sweet to see the face of parents.

MESSENGER: This was the fear which drove you out of Corinth?

OEDIPUS: Old man, I did not wish to kill my father.

MESSENGER: Why should I not free you from this fear, sir,
1095   since I have come to you in all goodwill?

OEDIPUS: You would not find me thankless if you did.

MESSENGER: Why, it was just for this I brought the news,—
    to earn your thanks when you had come safe home.

OEDIPUS: No, I will never come near my parents.

MESSENGER: Son,
1100   it's very plain you don't know what you're doing.

OEDIPUS: What do you mean, old man? For God's sake, tell me.

MESSENGER: If your homecoming is checked by fears like these.

OEDIPUS: Yes, I'm afraid that Phoebus may prove right.

MESSENGER: The murder and the incest?

OEDIPUS: Yes, old man;
1105   that is my constant terror.

MESSENGER: Do you know
    that all your fears are empty?

OEDIPUS: How is that,
    if they are father and mother and I their son?

1110 **MESSENGER:** Because Polybus was no kin to you in blood.

OEDIPUS: What, was not Polybus my father?

MESSENGER: No more than I but just so much.

OEDIPUS: How can
    my father be my father as much as one
    that's nothing to me?

▼ **Critical Viewing**
Compare and contrast the emotions displayed by the actress playing Jocasta (below) and the actor playing Oedipus (facing page). **[Compare and Contrast]**

Reading Strategy
Questioning the Characters' Motives Characterize the Messenger's demeanor since his first appearance. What might the Messenger seek from Oedipus in exchange for his "good news"?

MESSENGER: Neither he nor I
  begat you.

OEDIPUS: Why then did he call me son?

1115 **MESSENGER:** A gift he took you from these hands of mine.

OEDIPUS: Did he love so much what he took from another's hand?

MESSENGER: His childlessness before persuaded him.

OEDIPUS: Was I a child you bought or found when I
  was given to him?

MESSENGER: On Cithaeron's slopes
  in the twisting thickets you were found.

OEDIPUS: And why
1120   were you a traveler in those parts?

MESSENGER: I was
  in charge of mountain flocks.

OEDIPUS: You were a shepherd?
  A hireling vagrant?³

MESSENGER: Yes, but at least at that time
  the man that saved your life, son.

1125 **OEDIPUS:** What ailed me when you took me in your arms?

MESSENGER: In that your ankles should be witnesses.

OEDIPUS: Why do you speak of that old pain?

MESSENGER: I loosed you;
  the tendons of your feet were pierced and <u>fettered</u>,—

1130 **OEDIPUS:** My swaddling clothes⁴ brought me a rare disgrace.

MESSENGER: So that from this you're called your present name.⁵

OEDIPUS: Was this my father's doing or my mother's?
  For God's sake, tell me.

MESSENGER: I don't know, but he
1135   who gave you to me has more knowledge than I.

OEDIPUS: You yourself did not find me then? You took me
  from someone else?

MESSENGER: Yes, from another shepherd.

1140 **OEDIPUS:** Who was he? Do you know him well enough
  to tell?

MESSENGER: He was called Laius' man.

---

3. **hireling vagrant** (hīr´ liŋ vā grənt) person who wanders from place to place and works at
   odd jobs.
4. **swaddling** (swäd´ liŋ) **clothes** long, narrow bands of cloth wrapped around infants in
   ancient times.
5. **your present name** "Oedipus" means "swollen foot."

Literary Analysis
**Dramatic Irony and
Suspense** In what ways
does the audience's
knowledge about
Oedipus' infancy create
dramatic irony and add to
the suspense?

fettered (fet´ ərd) *adj.*
shackled or chained

✓**Reading Check**
Where was the infant
Oedipus found?

OEDIPUS: You mean the king who reigned here in the old days?

MESSENGER: Yes, he was that man's shepherd.

OEDIPUS: Is he alive
   still, so that I could see him?

MESSENGER: You who live here
1145 would know that best.

OEDIPUS: Do any of you here
   know of this shepherd whom he speaks about
   in town or in the fields? Tell me. It's time
   that this was found out once for all.

1150 **CHORUS:** I think he is none other than the peasant
   whom you have sought to see already; but
   Jocasta here can tell us best of that.

OEDIPUS: Jocasta, do you know about this man
   whom we have sent for? Is he the man he mentions?

1155 **JOCASTA:** Why ask of whom he spoke? Don't give it heed;
   nor try to keep in mind what has been said.
   It will be wasted labor.

OEDIPUS: With such clues
   I could not fail to bring my birth to light.

JOCASTA: I beg you—do not hunt this out—I beg you,
1160 if you have any care for your own life.
   What I am suffering is enough.

OEDIPUS: Keep up
   your heart, Jocasta. Though I'm proved a slave,
   thrice slave, and though my mother is thrice slave,
   you'll not be shown to be of lowly lineage.

JOCASTA: O be persuaded by me, I entreat you;
1165 do not do this.

OEDIPUS: I will not be persuaded to let be
   the chance of finding out the whole thing clearly.

JOCASTA: It is because I wish you well that I
   give you this counsel—and it's the best counsel.

OEDIPUS: Then the best counsel vexes me, and has
1170 for some while since.

JOCASTA: O Oedipus, God help you!
   God keep you from the knowledge of who you are!

OEDIPUS: Here, some one, go and fetch the shepherd for me;
   and let her find her joy in her rich family!

1175 **JOCASTA:** O Oedipus, unhappy Oedipus!
   that is all I can call you, and the last thing
   that I shall ever call you.

                                                                       [Exit.]

▲ **Critical Viewing**
What emotions does each actor's posture and facial expression convey? Explain. **[Interpret]**

Reading Strategy
Questioning the Characters' Motives Why does Jocasta suddenly discourage Oedipus from pursuing information about his birth?

CHORUS: Why has the queen gone, Oedipus, in wild
grief rushing from us? I am afraid that trouble
1180 will break out of this silence.

OEDIPUS: Break out what will! I at least shall be
willing to see my ancestry, though humble.
Perhaps she is ashamed of my low birth,
for she has all a woman's high-flown pride.
1185 But I account myself a child of Fortune,[6]
<u>beneficent</u> Fortune, and I shall not be
dishonored. She's the mother from whom I spring;
the months, my brothers, marked me, now as small,
and now again as mighty. Such is my breeding,
1190 and I shall never prove so false to it,
as not to find the secret of my birth.

CHORUS:

Strophe
If I am a prophet and wise of heart
you shall not fail, Cithaeron,
by the limitless sky, you shall not!—
1195 to know at tomorrow's full moon
that Oedipus honors you,
as native to him and mother and nurse at once;
and that you are honored in dancing by us, as finding favor in
    sight of our king.
1200 Apollo, to whom we cry, find these things pleasing!

Antistrophe
Who was it bore you, child? One of
the long-lived nymphs[7] who lay with Pan[8]—
the father who treads the hills?
Or was she a bride of Loxias, your mother? The grassy slopes
1205 are all of them dear to him. Or perhaps Cyllene's king[9]
or the Bacchants' God that lives on the tops
of the hills received you a gift from some
one of the Helicon Nymphs, with whom he mostly plays?

[*Enter an* OLD MAN, *led by* OEDIPUS' SERVANTS.]

OEDIPUS: If some one like myself who never met him
1210 may make a guess,—I think this is the herdsman,
whom we were seeking. His old age is <u>consonant</u>

---

6. **child of Fortune** Since Fortune, or good luck, saved him from death, Oedipus refuses to
feel shame at being illegitimate or of humble origins.
7. **nymphs** (nimfs) *n.* minor female divinities with youthful, beautiful, and amorous qualities;
"nymph" means young woman.
8. **Pan** Arcadian shepherd god who lived in the mountains, danced and sang with the
nymphs, and played his pipes.
9. **Cyllene's king** Hermes, the messenger god.

beneficent (bə nef´ ə sənt)
adj. kind, helpful

Literary Analysis
**Dramatic Irony and
Suspense** How do the
speculations of the chorus
both create dramatic irony
and increase suspense?

consonant (kän´ sə nənt) *adj.*
in harmony or agreement

Reading Check

What knowledge does
Jocasta pray Oedipus will
not learn?

Oedipus the King, Part II ◆ 467

with the other. And besides, the men who bring him
I recognize as my own servants. You
perhaps may better me in knowledge since
1215 you've seen the man before.

    CHORUS: You can be sure
I recognize him. For if Laius
had ever an honest shepherd, this was he.

    OEDIPUS: You, sir, from Corinth, I must ask you first,
1220 is this the man you spoke of?

    MESSENGER: This is he
before your eyes.

    OEDIPUS: Old man, look here at me
and tell me what I ask you. Were you ever
a servant of King Laius?

1225 **HERDSMAN:**   I was,—
no slave he bought but reared in his own house.

    OEDIPUS: What did you do as work? How did you live?

    HERDSMAN: Most of my life was spent among the flocks.

    OEDIPUS: In what part of the country did you live?

1230 **HERDSMAN:** Cithaeron and the places near to it.

    OEDIPUS: And somewhere there perhaps you knew this man?

    HERDSMAN: What was his occupation? Who?

    OEDIPUS: This man here,
have you had any dealings with him?

1235 **HERDSMAN:**   No—
not such that I can quickly call to mind.

Reading Strategy
Questioning the Characters' Motives
What does Oedipus hope to learn from the Herdsman?

MESSENGER: That is no wonder, master. But I'll
make him remember what he does not know. For
I know, that he well knows the country of
1240 Cithaeron, how he with two flocks, I with one
kept company for three years—each year half a
year—from spring till autumn time and then
when winter came I drove my flocks to our fold
home again and he to Laius' steadings. Well—am
1245 I right or not in what I said we did?

HERDSMAN: You're right—although it's a long time ago.

MESSENGER: Do you remember giving me a child
to bring up as my foster child?

HERDSMAN: What's this?
Why do you ask this question?

MESSENGER: Look old man,
1250 here he is—here's the man who was that child!

HERDSMAN: Death take you! Won't you hold your tongue?

OEDIPUS: No, no,
do not find fault with him, old man. Your words
are more at fault than his.

HERDSMAN: O best of masters,
1255 how do I give offense?

OEDIPUS: When you refuse
to speak about the child of whom he asks you.

HERDSMAN: He speaks out of his ignorance, without meaning.

OEDIPUS: If you'll not talk to <u>gratify</u> me, you
will talk with pain to urge you.

HERDSMAN: O please, sir,
1260 don't hurt an old man, sir.

OEDIPUS [*to the* SERVANTS]:   Here, one of you,
twist his hands behind him.

HERDSMAN: Why, God help me, why?
What do you want to know?

OEDIPUS: You gave a child
to him,—the child he asked you of?

HERDSMAN: I did.
I wish I'd died the day I did.

OEDIPUS: You will
1265 unless you tell me truly.

HERDSMAN: And I'll die
far worse if I should tell you.

gratify (grat′ i fī) *v.* please

Literary Analysis
Situational Irony Does
Oedipus' sudden anger
and threatening behavior
surprise you? Explain?

**Reading Check**

How does Oedipus try to
make the Herdsman talk?

OEDIPUS: This fellow
　　is bent on more delays, as it would seem.

HERDSMAN: O no, no! I have told you that I gave it.

OEDIPUS: Where did you get this child from? Was
1270　it your own or did you get it from another?

HERDSMAN: Not
　　my own at all; I had it from some one.

OEDIPUS: One of these citizens? or from what house?

HERDSMAN: O master, please—I beg you, master, please
　　don't ask me more.

OEDIPUS: You're a dead man if I
1275　ask you again.

HERDSMAN: It was one of the children
　　of Laius.

OEDIPUS: A slave? Or born in wedlock?

HERDSMAN: O God, I am on the brink of frightful speech.

OEDIPUS: And I of frightful hearing. But I must hear.

1280 **HERDSMAN:** The child was called his child; but she within,
　　your wife would tell you best how all this was.

OEDIPUS: *She* gave it to you?

HERDSMAN: Yes, she did, my lord.

OEDIPUS: To do what with it?

1285 **HERDSMAN:**   Make away with it.

OEDIPUS: She was so hard—its mother?

HERDSMAN: Aye, through fear
　　of evil oracles.

OEDIPUS: Which?

HERDSMAN: They said that he
　　should kill his parents.

OEDIPUS: How was it that you
1290　gave it away to this old man?

HERDSMAN: O master,
　　I pitied it, and thought that I could send it
　　off to another country and this man
　　was from another country. But he saved it
1295　for the most terrible troubles. If you are
　　the man he says you are, you're bred to misery.

OEDIPUS: O, O, O, they will all come,
　　all come out clearly! Light of the sun, let me
　　look upon you no more after today!
1300　I who first saw the light bred of a match

Reading Strategy
Questioning the Characters' Motives Why does the Herdsman beg Oedipus to allow him to be silent?

Literary Analysis
Irony In what ways does the Herdsman's pity for the infant Oedipus present an example of situational irony?

accursed, and accursed in my living
with them I lived with, cursed in my killing.

[*Exit all but the* CHORUS.]

CHORUS:

    Strophe
O generations of men, how I
count you as equal with those who live
not at all!
1305   What man, what man on earth wins more
of happiness than a seeming
and after that turning away?
Oedipus, you are my pattern of this,
Oedipus, you and your fate!
1310   Luckless Oedipus, whom of all men
I envy not at all.

    Antistrophe
In as much as he shot his bolt
beyond the others and won the prize
of happiness complete—
1315   O Zeus—and killed and reduced to nought
the hooked taloned maid of the riddling speech,[10]
standing a tower against death for my land:
hence he was called my king and hence
was honored the highest of all
1320   honors; and hence he ruled
in the great city of Thebes.

    Strophe
But now whose tale is more miserable?
Who is there lives with a savager fate?
Whose troubles so reverse his life as his?

1325   O Oedipus, the famous prince
for whom a great haven
the same both as father and son
sufficed for generation,
how, O how, have the furrows plowed
1330   by your father endured to bear you, poor wretch,
and hold their peace so long?

    Antistrophe
Time who sees all has found you out
against your will; judges your marriage accursed,
begetter and begot at one in it.

1335   O child of Laius,

---

10. **hooked taloned maid of the riddling speech** the Sphinx; talons are claws.

▲ **Critical Viewing**
Which details in this image
of Oedipus and the chorus
might evoke both pity and
fear in the audience?
Explain. **[Analyze]**

would I had never seen you.
I weep for you and cry
a dirge of lamentation.

To speak directly, I drew my breath
1340   from you at the first and so now I lull
my mouth to sleep with your name.

[*Enter a* SECOND MESSENGER.]

SECOND MESSENGER: O Princes always honored by our country,
what deeds you'll hear of and what horrors see,
what grief you'll feel, if you as true born Thebans
1345   care for the house of Labdacus's sons.

Phasis nor Ister[11] cannot purge[12] this house,
I think, with all their streams, such things
it hides, such evils shortly will bring forth
into the light, whether they will or not;
1350 and troubles hurt the most
when they prove self-inflicted.

CHORUS: What we had known before did not fall short
of bitter groaning's worth; what's more to tell?

SECOND MESSENGER: Shortest to hear and tell—our
1355 glorious queen Jocasta's dead.

---

11. Phasis (fā′ sis) **... Ister** (is′ tər) rivers that flow to the Black Sea.
12. purge (purj) v. cleanse of guilt or sin.

☑ **Reading Check**

What news about
Jocasta does the
Second Messenger
report?

CHORUS: Unhappy woman! How?

SECOND MESSENGER: By her own hand. The worst of what was done
   you cannot know. You did not see the sight.
   Yet in so far as I remember it
1360   you'll hear the end of our unlucky queen.
   When she came raging into the house she went
   straight to her marriage bed, tearing her hair
   with both her hands, and crying upon Laius
   long dead—Do you remember, Laius,
1365   that night long past which bred a child for us
   to send you to your death and leave
   a mother making children with her son?
   And then she groaned and cursed the bed in which
   she brought forth husband by her husband, children
1370   by her own child, an <u>infamous</u> double bond.
   How after that she died I do not know,—
   for Oedipus distracted us from seeing.
   He burst upon us shouting and we looked
   to him as he paced frantically around,
1375   begging us always: Give me a sword, I say,
   to find this wife no wife, this mother's womb,
   this field of double sowing whence I sprang
   and where I sowed my children! As he raved
   some god showed him the way—none of us there.
1380   Bellowing terribly and led by some
   invisible guide he rushed on the two doors,—
   wrenching the hollow bolts out of their sockets,
   he charged inside. There, there, we saw his wife
   hanging, the twisted rope around her neck.
1385   When he saw her, he cried out fearfully
   and cut the dangling noose. Then, as she lay,
   poor woman, on the ground, what happened after,
   was terrible to see. He tore the brooches—
   the gold chased brooches fastening her robe—
1390   away from her and lifting them up high
   dashed them on his own eyeballs, shrieking out
   such things as: they will never see the crime
   I have committed or had done upon me!
   Dark eyes, now in the days to come look on
1395   forbidden faces, do not recognize
   those whom you long for—with such imprecations[13]
   he struck his eyes again and yet again
   with the brooches. And the bleeding eyeballs gushed
   and stained his beard—no sluggish oozing drops
1400   but a black rain and bloody hail poured down.

infamous (in´ fə məs) *adj.*
disgraceful

Reading Strategy
Questioning the Characters' Motives What do
you think motivates Oedipus to ask for a sword in
line 1375? How might that
motivation change in lines
1383–1385?

---

13. imprecations (im´ pri kā´ shənz) *n.* acts of cursing and invoking evil.

So it has broken—and not on one head
but troubles mixed for husband and for wife.
The fortune of the days gone by was true
good fortune—but today groans and destruction
and death and shame—of all ills can be named
1405   not one is missing.

    CHORUS: Is he now in any ease from pain?

    SECOND MESSENGER: He shouts
for some one to unbar the doors and show him
to all the men of Thebes, his father's killer,
1410   his mother's—no I cannot say the word,
it is unholy—for he'll cast himself,
out of the land, he says, and not remain
to bring a curse upon his house, the curse
he called upon it in his proclamation. But
1415   he wants for strength, aye, and some one to guide him;
his sickness is too great to bear. You, too,
will be shown that. The bolts are opening.
Soon you will see a sight to waken pity
even in the horror of it.

                                  [*Enter the blinded* OEDIPUS.]

1420 **CHORUS:** This is a terrible sight for men to see!
I never found a worse!
Poor wretch, what madness came upon you!
What evil spirit leaped upon your life
to your ill-luck—a leap beyond man's strength!
1425   Indeed I pity you, but I cannot
look at you, though there's much I want to ask
and much to learn and much to see.
I shudder at the sight of you.

    OEDIPUS: O, O,
1430   where am I going? Where is my voice
borne on the wind to and fro?
Spirit, how far have you sprung?

    CHORUS: To a terrible place whereof men's ears
may not hear, nor their eyes behold it.

1435 **OEDIPUS:** Darkness!
Horror of darkness enfolding, resistless, unspeakable
visitant sped by an ill wind in haste!
madness and stabbing pain and memory
of evil deeds I have done!

1440 **CHORUS:** In such misfortunes it's no wonder
if double weighs the burden of your grief.

    OEDIPUS: My friend,

Literary Analysis
Irony What is ironic about the chorus's finding the sight of Oedipus too painful to bear?

Reading Check
What injury does Oedipus inflict upon himself?

you are the only one steadfast, the only one that attends on me;
you still stay nursing the blind man.

1445   Your care is not unnoticed. I can know
your voice, although this darkness is my world.

   CHORUS: Doer of dreadful deeds, how did you dare
so far to do despite to your own eyes?
What spirit urged you to it?

1450 **OEDIPUS:** It was Apollo, friends, Apollo,
that brought this bitter bitterness, my sorrows to completion.
But the hand that struck me
was none but my own.
Why should I see
1455   whose vision showed me nothing sweet to see?

   CHORUS: These things are as you say.

   OEDIPUS: What can I see to love?
What greeting can touch my ears with joy?
1460   Take me away, and haste—to a place out of the way!
Take me away, my friends, the greatly miserable,
the most accursed, whom God too hates
above all men on earth!

   CHORUS: Unhappy in your mind and your misfortune,
would I had never known you!

1465 **OEDIPUS:** Curse on the man who took
the cruel bonds from off my legs, as I lay in the field.
He stole me from death and saved me,
no kindly service.
Had I died then
I would not be so burdensome to friends.

1470 **CHORUS:** I, too, could have wished it had been so.

   OEDIPUS: Then I would not have come
to kill my father and marry my mother infamously.
Now I am godless and child of impurity,
begetter in the same seed that created my wretched self.
1475   If there is any ill worse than ill,
that is the lot of Oedipus.

   CHORUS: I cannot say your remedy was good;
you would be better dead than blind and living.

   OEDIPUS: What I have done here was best
1480   done—don't tell me
otherwise, do not give me further counsel.
I do not know with what eyes I could look
upon my father when I die and go
under the earth, nor yet my wretched mother—
1485   those two to whom I have done things deserving

worse punishment than hanging. Would the sight
of children, bred as mine are, gladden me?
No, not these eyes, never. And my city,
its towers and sacred places of the Gods,
1490 of these I robbed my miserable self
when I commanded all to drive *him* out,
the criminal since proved by God impure
and of the race of Laius.
To this guilt I bore witness against myself—
1495 with what eyes shall I look upon my people?
No. If there were a means to choke the fountain
of hearing I would not have stayed my hand
from locking up my miserable carcass,[14]
seeing and hearing nothing; it is sweet
1500 to keep our thoughts out of the range of hurt.

Cithaeron, why did you receive me? why
having received me did you not kill me straight?
And so I had not shown to men my birth.

O Polybus and Corinth and the house,
1505 the old house that I used to call my father's—
what fairness you were nurse to, and what foulness
festered beneath! Now I am found to be
a sinner and a son of sinners. Crossroads,
and hidden glade, oak and the narrow way
1510 at the crossroads, that drank my father's blood
offered you by my hands, do you remember
still what I did as you looked on, and what
I did when I came here? O marriage, marriage!
you bred me and again when you had bred
1515 bred children of your child and showed to men
brides, wives and mothers and the foulest deeds
that can be in this world of ours.

Come—it's unfit to say what is unfit
to do.—I beg of you in God's name hide me
1520 somewhere outside your country, yes, or kill me,
or throw me into the sea, to be forever
out of your sight. Approach and deign to touch me
for all my wretchedness, and do not fear.
No man but I can bear my evil doom.

1525 **CHORUS:** Here Creon comes in fit time to perform
or give advice in what you ask of us.
Creon is left sole ruler in your stead.

OEDIPUS: Creon! Creon! What shall I say to him?
How can I justly hope that he will trust me?

---

14. carcass (kär´ kəs) *n.* dead body of an animal; here, scornful reference to Oedipus' own body.

Reading Strategy
Questioning the Characters' Motives What do you think motivates Oedipus to condemn his past actions—fear, shame, anger, or some other emotion? Explain.

✔**Reading Check**

Why does Oedipus curse the man who saved him when he was an infant?

In what is past I have been proved towards him
1530   an utter liar.

[*Enter* CREON.]

CREON: Oedipus, I've come
not so that I might laugh at you nor taunt you
with evil of the past. But if you still
are without shame before the face of men
1535   <u>reverence</u> at least the flame that gives all life,
our Lord the Sun, and do not show unveiled
to him pollution such that neither land
nor holy rain nor light of day can welcome.

[*To a* SERVANT.]

Be quick and take him in. It is most decent
that only kin should see and hear the troubles
1540   of kin.

OEDIPUS: I beg you, since you've torn me from
my dreadful expectations and have come
in a most noble spirit to a man
that has used you vilely[15]—do a thing for me.
1545   I shall speak for your own good, not for my own.

CREON: What do you need that you would ask of me?

OEDIPUS: Drive me from here with all the speed you can
to where I may not hear a human voice.

─────────────────────────────────────

15. vilely (vīlʹ lē) *adv.* wickedly.

Literary Analysis
Irony In what ways is
Oedipus' changed posi-
tion with respect to Creon
an example of situational
irony?

reverence (revʹ rəns) *v.* show
great respect

▼ Critical Viewing
What does this image of
Oedipus and the chorus
suggest about their rela-
tionship? Explain.
[Interpret]

CREON: Be sure, I would have done this had not I
1550 wished first of all to learn from the God the course
of action I should follow.

OEDIPUS: But his word
has been quite clear to let the parricide,[16]
the sinner, die.

CREON: Yes, that indeed was said.
But in the present need we had best discover
1555 what we should do.

OEDIPUS: And will you ask about
a man so wretched?

CREON: Now even you will trust
the God.

OEDIPUS: So. I command you—and will beseech you—
to her that lies inside that house give burial
1560 as you would have it; she is yours and rightly
you will perform the rites for her. For me—
never let this my father's city have me
living a dweller in it. Leave me live

---

16. **parricide** (par´ ə sīd) *n.* one who murders one's father.

Reading Check

What information does Creon want to learn from the God?

in the mountains where Cithaeron is, that's called
1565 *my* mountain, which my mother and my father
while they were living would have made my tomb.
So I may die by their decree who sought
indeed to kill me. Yet I know this much:
no sickness and no other thing will kill me.
1570 I would not have been saved from death if not
for some strange evil fate. Well, let my fate
go where it will.
                                    Creon, you need not care
about my sons; they're men and so wherever
they are, they will not lack a livelihood.
1575 But my two girls—so sad and pitiful—
whose table never stood apart from mine,
and everything I touched they always shared—
O Creon, have a thought for them! And most
I wish that you might suffer me to touch them
1580 and sorrow with them.

          [*Enter* ANTIGONE *and* ISMENE, OEDIPUS' *two daughters.*]

O my lord! O true noble Creon! Can I
really be touching them, as when I saw?
What shall I say?
Yes, I can hear them sobbing—my two darlings!
and Creon has had pity and has sent me
1585 what I loved most?
Am I right?

  CREON: You're right: it was I gave you this
because I knew from old days how you loved them
as I see now.

1590 **OEDIPUS:**   God bless you for it, Creon,
and may God guard you better on your road
than he did me!
                              O children,
where are you? Come here, come to my hands,
a brother's hands which turned your father's eyes,
1595 those bright eyes you knew once, to what you see,
a father seeing nothing, knowing nothing,
begetting you from his own source of life.
I weep for you—I cannot see your faces—
I weep when I think of the bitterness
1600 there will be in your lives, how you must live
before the world. At what assemblages
of citizens will you make one? to what
gay company will you go and not come home
in tears instead of sharing in the holiday?
1605 And when you're ripe for marriage, who will he be,

Reading Strategy
Questioning the Characters' Motives What is Creon's motivation for bringing Antigone and Ismene to their father?

the man who'll risk to take such infamy
as shall cling to my children, to bring hurt
on them and those that marry with them? What
curse is not there? "Your father killed his father

1610   and sowed the seed where he had sprung himself
and begot you out of the womb that held him."
These insults you will hear. Then who will marry you?
No one, my children; clearly you are doomed
to waste away in barrenness unmarried.

1615   Son of Menoeceus,[17] since you are all the father
left these two girls, and we, their parents, both
are dead to them—do not allow them wander
like beggars, poor and husbandless.
They are of your own blood.

1620   And do not make them equal with myself
in wretchedness; for you can see them now
so young, so utterly alone, save for you only.
Touch my hand, noble Creon, and say yes.
If you were older, children, and were wiser,

1625   there's much advice I'd give you. But as it is,
let this be what you pray: give me a life
wherever there is opportunity
to live, and better life than was my father's.

CREON: Your tears have had enough of scope; now go within the
1630   house.

OEDIPUS: I must obey, though bitter of heart.

CREON: In season, all is good.

OEDIPUS: Do you know on what conditions I obey?

CREON: You tell me them,
1635   and I shall know them when I hear.

OEDIPUS: That you shall send me out
to live away from Thebes.

CREON: That gift you must ask of the God.

OEDIPUS: But I'm now hated by the Gods.

1640 **CREON:**   So quickly you'll obtain your prayer.

OEDIPUS: You consent then?

CREON: What I do not mean, I do not use to say.

OEDIPUS: Now lead me away from here.

CREON: Let go the children, then, and come.

1645 **OEDIPUS:** Do not take them from me.

---

17. **Son of Menoeceus** (mə nē′ sē əs) Creon.

Reading Strategy
Questioning the Characters' Motives What effect might Oedipus expect his statements to his daughters about their future to have on Creon?

Reading Check

What plea for his daughters does Oedipus make to Creon?

CREON: Do not seek to be master in everything,
for the things you mastered did not follow you throughout your life.

[As CREON and OEDIPUS go out.]

CHORUS: You that live in my ancestral Thebes, behold this
Oedipus,—
him who knew the famous riddles and was a man most masterful;
1650 not a citizen who did not look with envy on his lot—
see him now and see the breakers of misfortune swallow him!
Look upon that last day always. Count no mortal happy till
he has passed the final limit of his life secure from pain.

Review and Assess

Thinking About the Selection

1. **Respond:** At the end of the play, do you sympathize with Oedipus or blame him? Explain.

2. **(a) Recall:** What is the literal meaning of Oedipus' name? **(b) Assess:** What clue to Oedipus' identity does his name contain?

3. **(a) Recall:** What is Oedipus' reaction to Jocasta's abrupt exit at line 1177? **(b) Analyze:** Why do you think Oedipus continues his investigation despite Jocasta's strong objections? **(c) Extend:** What might the playwright be saying about the importance of "knowing thyself"?

4. **(a) Recall:** Whom or what does the chorus address in the strophe beginning at line 1192? **(b) Interpret:** What hope does the chorus express here?

5. **(a) Recall:** What facts does Oedipus establish by questioning the Herdsman? **(b) Draw Conclusions:** Why might this scene be considered the climax, or high point, of the tragedy?

6. **(a) Recall:** What events does the Second Messenger report? **(b) Relate:** Does this speech achieve the goal of dramatic tragedy? That is, does it evoke both pity and fear in you? Explain.

7. **(a) Recall:** What does Oedipus want Creon to do at the end of the play? **(b) Analyze:** Why does Oedipus insist that he is better off blind and living than dead? **(c) Make a Judgment:** At the play's end, do you think Oedipus is ennobled by suffering? Explain.

Review and Assess

Literary Analysis

Irony

1. At line 1042, Jocasta refers to "the holy oracles of the Gods." Given the context, what is **verbally ironic** about her words?

2. The Messenger attempts to cheer Oedipus when he reveals that Polybus and Merope were not the king's true parents. How do the Messenger's efforts result in a wrenching **situational irony?**

3. Oedipus misinterprets the reasons for Jocasta's departure at lines 1183–1184. (a) Use a chart like the one shown to examine elements of irony in his interpretation of her motives. (b) What does Oedipus' response to Jocasta's flight suggest about his character?

Oedipus' Conclusions	┈▶	Ironic Elements

Connecting Literary Elements

4. What information about Oedipus' past underlies the **dramatic irony** in the scene involving Oedipus, Jocasta, and the Messenger from Corinth?

5. Why is Oedipus' description of himself as a "child of Fortune" (line 1185) dramatically ironic?

6. Sophocles reveals the truth of Oedipus' identity slowly, thus postponing the crisis, or climax, of the play. In what ways does this strategy add both to the play's dramatic irony and to its **suspense?**

Reading Strategy

Questioning the Characters' Motives

7. (a) Compare and contrast the attitudes of the Corinthian Messenger and the Herdsman toward the information they possess. (b) What contrasting **motives** are attributed to each?

8. Oedipus tries desperately to avoid his fate and at the same time learn his identity. How are both goals connected?

Extend Understanding

9. **Humanities Connection:** Chance plays a major role in the Oedipus story. In what other works of literature or film is chance important?

Integrate Language Skills

Vocabulary Development Lesson

Word Analysis: Latin Prefix *con-*

The Latin prefix *con-* means "with" or "together." If something is *consonant* with something else, it "sounds with" it; the two are harmonious. Add the prefix *con-* to the word roots below. Then, define each word and explain how the prefix contributes to its meaning.

1. -cert
2. -duct
3. -versation
4. -temporary
5. -solation
6. -gratulate

Spelling Strategy

You can form adjectives from some nouns by adding the suffix *-ous*. Sometimes, however, you will need to make a spelling change when adding this suffix. For example, *zeal* becomes *zealous*; *space* becomes *spacious*; *beauty* becomes *beauteous*. Use the suffix *-ous* to form an adjective from the following nouns.

1. treason
2. grace
3. bounty

Concept Development: Antonyms

Select the letter of the word most nearly opposite in meaning to each vocabulary word.

1. fettered: (a) loosened, (b) used, (c) hot, (d) angry
2. beneficent: (a) productive, (b) geneous, (c) malignant, (d) polished
3. consonant: (a) loud, (b) joyful, (c) agreeing, (d) inconsistent
4. gratify: (a) please, (b) annoy, (c) resist, (d) steal
5. infamous: (a) notorious, (b) respectable, (c) glorious, (d) vivid
6. reverence: (a) insult, (b) respect, (c) grant, (d) report

Grammar and Style Lesson

Gerunds and Gerund Phrases

A **gerund** is a verb form ending in *-ing* that can act as a noun. Like nouns, gerunds function in sentences as subjects, direct objects, predicate nominatives, and objects of prepositions. A **gerund phrase** consists of a gerund and its complements and modifiers.

Direct Object:
Do you remember <u>giving me a child</u> . . . ?

Object of Preposition:
—O God, I am on the brink of frightful speech.
—And I of frightful <u>hearing</u>. But I must hear.

Practice Identify each gerund or gerund phrase, and tell how it is used in the sentence.

1. Questioning is one of Oedipus' skills.
2. Jocasta doesn't believe in respecting the oracles.
3. Oedipus is cursed in living and killing.
4. The Messenger describes the blinding.
5. According to the chorus, counting any man happy until he is dead is a mistake.

Writing Application Write a paragraph in which you describe working at a hobby or playing a sport. Include at least three gerunds.

Writing Lesson

Character Study

Some critics believe that Oedipus caused his own destruction through poor choices and character flaws. Others believe that his wrongdoing was involuntary and his suffering out of all proportion to the responsibility he truly bears. Write an essay in which you make your own judgment of Oedipus' character and guilt.

Prewriting   Reread the play, noting passages that describe or demonstrate Oedipus' reactions, statements, and decisions. Interpret these details, and write a statement, or working thesis, about his character.

Drafting   State your thesis in the introduction, and plan one main supporting idea for each paragraph. Organize the details from your notes into paragraphs.

Model: Organizing Details into Paragraphs

Main idea: One of Oedipus' worst flaws is his temper.
Supporting details:

- his anger at Laius
- his suspicion of Creon
- his anger at Teiresias
- his threats against the Herdsman

> To be supported effectively, each main idea is defended by at least two specific examples from the text.

Revising   Review your essay, making sure that your opinion is well supported by the text. Underline main ideas and place marks next to supporting details. Identify opportunities to further elaborate with specific examples or accurate quotations from the play.

WG Prentice Hall Writing and Grammar Connection: Diamond Level, Chapter 14, Section 2

Extension Activities

Listening and Speaking Conduct a **mock trial** of Oedipus. Use these tips to prepare:

- Organize the personnel needed for a trial— a defense team, a prosecution team, a jury, witnesses, and the defendant.
- Have each side discuss its best strategies for winning. Keep in mind that each side must anticipate the opposing team's arguments.

As you conduct the trial, use accurate quotations from the play as evidence. **[Group Activity]**

Research and Technology Write an **illustrated report** on ancient Greek theaters. Use Internet and library resources to locate information for your report. Explore topics such as location, size, acoustics, masks, and costumes. When you have finished, share your report with the class.

 **Take It to the Net** PHSchool.com

Go online for an additional research activity using the Internet.

READING INFORMATIONAL MATERIALS

Web Research Sources

About Web Research Sources

Web sites—sets of linked Web pages (screens) assembled by an individual or group and accessible via the Internet—offer a tremendous diversity of information, making the Web an attractive research tool. **Web research sources** include any Web site dedicated to providing information on a given topic for researchers. [See the Internet Resource Handbook on pages R26 and R27 for details about searching the Web.]

Unfortunately, not all "information" on the Web is of equal value. Furthermore, the information may be packaged in a misleading way. To make the best use of this great research tool, you need to read critically.

Reading Strategy

Analyzing the Usefulness and Credibility of Web Sources

Once you find a Web site, you must **analyze the usefulness and credibility** of the source before using it for your research. A useful site is easy to understand and easy to navigate, and a credible site provides trustworthy, current information. Analyze and evaluate the site, basing your judgment on the factors listed in the chart shown.

A Useful Web Site . . .	A Credible Web Site . . .
• contains vocabulary and details appropriate to your research needs and to your intended audience	• presents thorough coverage of a subject
• includes interesting and easy-to-follow graphics	• may be peer-reviewed: many sites are sponsored by academic institutions or endorsed by subject-matter specialists
• offers a clear site map	• includes a bibliography or identifies the source of its information
• features a search engine within the site itself	• is updated periodically

As you review The Perseus Digital Library Olympics Exhibit on the following pages, note factors affecting the usefulness and credibility of the site.

A home page such as this one is the "front door" of a Web site. A good home page identifies the sponsoring organization, provides an overview of the information on the site, and offers a search feature to help users look for specific information. Because the Perseus site houses several different kinds of information, it offers this "secondary home page" for its Olympics Exhibit. From this page, you can tour the original site of the Olympic Games and then navigate to information about ancient Greek Olympic athletes and sports and a discussion of contrasts between the original games and those held today.

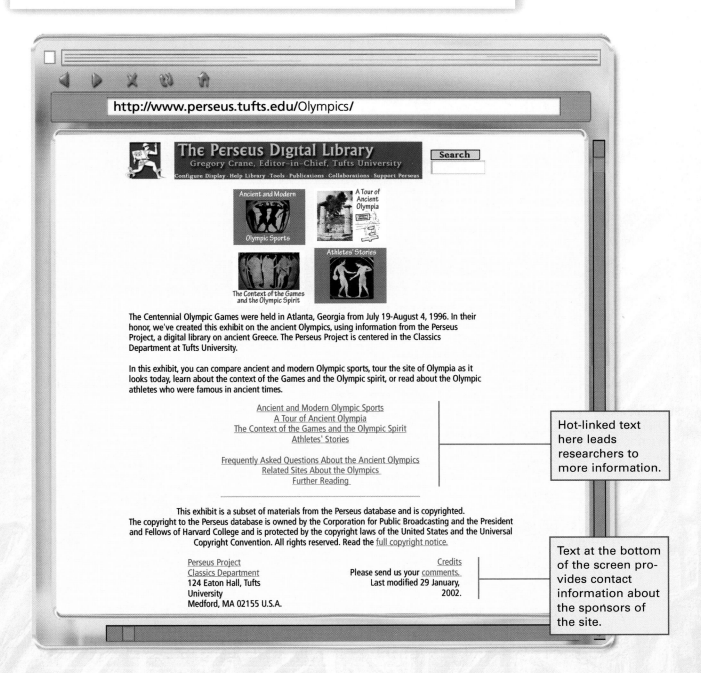

Hot-linked text here leads researchers to more information.

Text at the bottom of the screen provides contact information about the sponsors of the site.

Credits

Content reviewers
Prof. Gregory Crane, Tufts University
Prof. Tom Martin, College of the Holy Cross
Dr. Suzanne Bonefas, Associated Colleges of the South

Web site coordinator and interface designer
Maria Daniels

Research and writing
Lisa Cerrato, Maria Daniels, Krista Woodbridge

Site tour text and video
Prof. Frederick Hemans

Programming
David A. Smith

This web site on the Ancient Olympics was created by the staff of the Perseus Project, a digital library on ancient Greece. Much of this web site's content is excerpted from resources in the Perseus library.

The Perseus Project's editor-in-chief is Professor Gregory Crane of the Tufts University Classics Department. The Project is wholly funded by grants and support from the Annenberg/CPB Project, the National Science Foundation, Apple Computer, the National Endowment for the Arts, the National Endowment for the Humanities, the Packard Humanities Institute, the Getty Grant Program, Xerox Corporation, Boston University, Harvard University, and the Fund to Improve Post-Secondary Education. Perseus is a non-profit enterprise based in the Classics Department, Tufts University.

This exhibit is a subset of materials from the Perseus Project database and is copyrighted. Please send us your comments.

Credits online allow users to confirm the validity of the posted material.

The Context of the Games and the Olympic Spirit

Today, the Olympic Games are the world's largest pageant of athletic skill and competitive spirit. They are also displays of nationalism, commerce and politics. These two opposing elements of the Olympics are not a modern invention. The conflict between the Olympic movement's high ideals and the commercialism or political acts which accompany the Games has been noted since ancient times.

Sotades at the ninety-ninth Festival was victorious in the long race and proclaimed a Cretan, as in fact he was. But at the next Festival he made himself an Ephesian, being bribed to do so by the Ephesian people. For this act he was banished by the Cretans. Pausanias, *Description of Greece*, 6.18.6

The ancient Olympic Games, part of a major religious festival honoring Zeus, the chief Greek god, were the biggest event in their world. They were the scene of political rivalries between people from different parts of the Greek world, and the site of controversies, boasts, public announcements and humiliations. In this section you can explore the context of the Olympics and read stories about the participants and spectators who came to Olympia from all over the Greek world.

To read more about these topics, see Further Resources.

- The Greek city-states and the religious festival
- Excellence and the competitive spirit
- The Olympic truce
- The ancient athlete: amateur or professional?
- Did politics ever affect the ancient Games?
- Spectators at the Games
- Cultural achievements and the Games

map of some cities which sent competitors to the Olympics in the 5th century B.C.

This exhibit is a subset of materials from the Perseus Project database and is copyrighted. Please send us your comments.

Icons in the margin of most pages serve as links and allow for easy navigation among pages.

Check Your Comprehension

1. Which button on The Perseus Digital Library Olympics Exhibit home page will provide more information about the place where the original games were held?

2. With what university is this Web site associated?

3. What information is provided on the map shown on "The Context of the Games and the Olympic Spirit" page?

Applying the Reading Strategy

Analyzing the Usefulness and Credibility of Web Sources

1. Using the information on page 488, complete a chart like the one shown below, for The Perseus Digital Library Olympics Web site.

2. (a) Identify three details on these Web pages that provide evidence about the credibility of information on this site. (b) For each detail you cite, draw a conclusion about the credibility of this site.

> **Analyzing Usefulness and Credibility of a Web Research Source**
>
> Subject: _____
>
> Usefulness: _____
>
> Credibility: _____
>
> **My Overall Ranking of Site:**
>
> | 1 | 2 | 3 | 4 | 5 |
> |---|---|---|---|---|
> | (least useful/credible) | | | (most useful/credible) | |

Activity

Locating and Analyzing Online Sources

Search the Web for three sites suitable for each of the following purposes:
- writing a brief presentation on the Olympic Games, for sixth graders
- writing a research paper on ancient Greek sports

For each site, prepare a written analysis that evaluates the site's usefulness and credibility for each research purpose identified above. Be sure to explain your reasoning.

Comparing Informational Materials

Comparing Print and Online Sources

Locate a book on the ancient Greek Olympic Games. Write an evaluation comparing it as a source to a Web site on the same subject. Focus your comparison on each item's usefulness and credibility. In your evaluation, consider the credentials of the authors of each source, the amount and depth of information provided by each, and the organization of material in each.

Prepare to Read

from the *Aeneid*

Virgil (70–19 B.C.)

Publius Vergilius Maro (pub´ lē əs vʉr jil´ ē əs ma´ rō), unquestionably the greatest Roman poet, was born near Mantua in what was then the province of Gaul. Virgil's childhood experiences on his family's farm marked his outlook in a profound and permanent way. Throughout his life, he would remain a person who was sensitive to nature and acutely aware of the beauty and wisdom of the natural world.

A Country Boy When Virgil was eleven years old, Julius Caesar came to govern Gaul. His arrival opened Virgil's eyes to a world different from his father's farm in a culturally isolated town. Virgil traveled to study in various cities, including Rome. It was there that he took courses in rhetoric, the construction and delivery of speeches. Rhetoric was an essential part of instruction for young Romans being trained for public affairs. Although Virgil was trained as a lawyer, he never pursued a legal career.

Virgil felt the effects of the ongoing Roman civil war directly. When Mark Antony, a factional leader, needed to reward his soldiers with land grants in 41 B.C., he confiscated many farms, including Virgil's. During this time, Virgil withdrew from the turmoil of the capital. He retreated to Naples and there began the study of Epicureanism, a Greek philosophy that emphasizes simple pleasures and serenity of mind.

Soon afterward, Octavian, who would eventually become the emperor Caesar Augustus, recognized the poet's genius and gave Virgil back his land. Understandably, Virgil felt deep and enduring gratitude to Octavian all his life. Virgil became the official poet of the empire. He was welcome at the emperor's court, but his heart remained in the countryside. Augustus had given Virgil an estate in the south of Italy, and the shy, delicate poet spent as much time there as he could.

Early Writing Virgil's early works were poetry collections called *Eclogues* and *Georgics*. Throughout these pastoral poems, Virgil idealizes the return to peace made possible by Caesar Augustus after a long civil war. One of the poems, the fourth *Eclogue*, had profound significance among later Christians. Written around 40 B.C., the poem speaks of a divine child whose birth would bring about peace and a return to the Golden Age. Many Christians believed Virgil had predicted the birth of Jesus, and so they considered the poet an honorary Christian and a prophet.

A National Epic When Caesar Augustus became the first emperor of Rome in 27 B.C., his new empire had no national epic. The Greeks had the *Iliad* and the *Odyssey*, venerated by Greeks and Romans alike, but Roman culture had produced nothing comparable. There were a number of impressive works of prose, theater, and even poetry by Roman writers. However, there was no national epic for Roman citizens, whose patriotism might be aroused by a mythic account of their origins.

Virgil undertook to remedy that deficiency. He spent the last eleven years of his life working on the *Aeneid* (ē nē´ id), Rome's national epic and the greatest single work of Latin literature. He wrote many drafts, revising and polishing his verse "like a she-bear licking her cubs into shape," as he put it. When he fell ill after a hard voyage and died, Virgil left instructions to destroy the manuscript he thought imperfect. Naturally, and luckily, Augustus intervened and saved the masterpiece.

Virgil's epic tells a story of adventure and bravery, with a beauty of language and style rarely equaled in world literature. During the Middle Ages and the Renaissance, Europeans considered the *Aeneid* to be the greatest literary work of all time—the ideal every writer dreamed of equaling, though none ever did.

Preview

Connecting to the Literature

Ancient Romans viewed Aeneas, the hero of the *Aeneid*, in much the same way that Americans view George Washington. Aeneas was considered the father of Rome and the embodiment of its ideals.

Literary Analysis

National Epic

An epic is a long narrative—often a poem—about the adventures of gods or of a hero. A **national epic** tells a story about the founding or development of a nation or culture. Virgil's goal in writing the *Aeneid* was to give Rome a national epic that would equal Homer's *Iliad* and *Odyssey* in literary greatness and prove that Rome was as great a civilization as Greece. As you read, note details that would make Romans proud of their culture and their origins.

Connecting Literary Elements

An **epic hero** is the central figure of an epic. The hero of a national epic usually serves as a model for an entire culture. These characters are admired not just for their strength or skill in battle but for their integrity and beliefs. Ancient Roman values included the following:

- devotion to duty
- compassion and mercy for opponents in battle
- honesty and fairness

Note the ways in which Aeneas embodies and promotes these values in recounting the fall of Troy.

Reading Strategy

Applying Background Information

When reading certain literary works, you must **apply background information** to fully understand them. Virgil makes frequent reference to characters and events in Homer's *Iliad*. Therefore, information about that work is useful when reading the *Aeneid*. Review the selections from the *Iliad* (p. 325). Then, use a chart like the one shown to apply that background information to Virgil's epic.

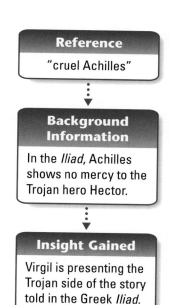

Reference

"cruel Achilles"

↓

Background Information

In the *Iliad*, Achilles shows no mercy to the Trojan hero Hector.

↓

Insight Gained

Virgil is presenting the Trojan side of the story told in the Greek *Iliad*.

Vocabulary Development

notions (nō′ shənz) *n.* ideas (p. 494)

perjured (pur′ jərd) *adj.* purposely false (p. 496)

guile (gīl) *n.* trickery (p. 497)

tumult (too′ mult) *n.* commotion; confusion (p. 498)

unfettered (un fet′ ərd) *adj.* unrestrained (p. 499)

blaspheming (blas fēm′ iŋ) *adj.* irreverent (p. 499)

desecrating (des′ i krāt′ iŋ) *v.* treating as not sacred (p. 500)

portents (pôr′ tents′) *n.* signs that suggest what is about to occur (p. 500)

from the Aeneid

Book II: How They Took the City

Virgil *translated by* Robert Fitzgerald

Aeneas and Dido, Pierre Narcisse Guérin, The Louvre, Paris, Scala

▲ **Critical Viewing** As Aeneas speaks in this painting, what effect does he appear to have on his listeners? **[Infer]**

Background

Virgil opens the *Aeneid* with an invocation of the Muse, a goddess who presides over the arts. He calls on her to remind him why Aeneas, an exiled hero who survived the destruction of his native Troy by the Greeks, had to suffer so much before he could found Rome. The reason is that Juno (Hera, in Greek mythology), the queen of heaven, persecutes the Trojan hero. Juno is still angry that Aeneas' cousin Paris judged her to be less fair than Aeneas' mother, the goddess Venus (Aphrodite, in Greek mythology).

As the *Aeneid* begins, Aeneas is at sea, about to land safely in Italy, but Juno creates a storm that wrecks the hero's fleet. Aeneas is tossed about and lands on the African coast near Carthage, a city being built by Queen Dido. The Queen holds a banquet in the Trojans' honor. Disguised as Aeneas' son, the god Cupid attends the banquet and causes Dido to fall in love with Aeneas. To prolong his stay, Dido asks Aeneas to recount the fall of Troy and his subsequent wanderings, which he does as Book II begins.

The room fell silent, and all eyes were on him,
As Father Aeneas from his high couch began:

"Sorrow too deep to tell, your majesty,
You order me to feel and tell once more:
5 How the Danaans[1] leveled in the dust
The splendor of our mourned-forever kingdom—
Heartbreaking things I saw with my own eyes
And was myself a part of. Who could tell them,
Even a Myrmidon[2] or Dolopian[3]
10 Or ruffian of Ulysses,[4] without tears?
Now, too, the night is well along, with dewfall
Out of heaven, and setting stars weigh down
Our heads toward sleep. But if so great desire
Moves you to hear the tale of our disasters,
15 Briefly recalled, the final throes[5] of Troy,[6]
However I may shudder at the memory
And shrink again in grief, let me begin.

Knowing their strength broken in warfare, turned
Back by the fates, and years—so many years—
20 Already slipped away, the Danaan captains
By the divine handicraft of Pallas built
A horse of timber, tall as a hill,
And sheathed its ribs with planking of cut pine.
This they gave out to be an offering

Reading Strategy
Applying Background Information Use background information to explain why Aeneas is given the title "Father" here.

---

1. **Danaans** (dā´ nā ənz) tribal name for the Greeks.
2. **Myrmidon** (mʉr´ mə dän) Phthian warrior who fought under Achilles.
3. **Dolopian** (də lō´ pē ən) person from Thessaly, a Greek ally.
4. **Ulysses** (yoo lis´ ēz´) Roman name for Odysseus, a Greek warrior.
5. **throes** (thrōz) *n.* acts of struggling.
6. **Troy** (troi) city in Asia Minor, home of the Trojans.

✔**Reading Check**

What event does Aeneas begin to recount?

For a safe return by sea, and the word went round.
But on the sly they shut inside a company
Chosen from their picked soldiery by lot,
Crowding the vaulted caverns in the dark—
The horse's belly—with men fully armed.

30 Offshore there's a long island, Tenedos,[7]
Famous and rich while Priam's kingdom[8] lasted,
A treacherous anchorage now, and nothing more.
They crossed to this and hid their ships behind it
On the bare shore beyond. We thought they'd gone,
35 Sailing home to Mycenae[9] before the wind,
So Teucer's[10] town is freed of her long anguish,
Gates thrown wide! And out we go in joy
To see the Dorian[11] campsites, all deserted,
The beach they left behind. Here the Dolopians
40 Pitched their tents, here cruel Achilles lodged,
There lay the ships, and there, formed up in ranks,
They came inland to fight us. Of our men
One group stood marveling, gaping up to see
The dire gift of the cold unbedded goddess,
The sheer mass of the horse.
45   Thymoetes[12] shouts
It should be hauled inside the walls and moored
High on the citadel[13]—whether by treason
Or just because Troy's fate went that way now.
Capys[14] opposed him; so did the wiser heads:
50 'Into the sea with it,' they said, 'or burn it,
Build up a bonfire under it,
This trick of the Greeks, a gift no one can trust,
Or cut it open, search the hollow belly!'

Contrary <u>notions</u> pulled the crowd apart.
55 Next thing we knew, in front of everyone,
Laocoön[15] with a great company
Came furiously running from the Height,[16]
And still far off cried out: 'O my poor people,
Men of Troy, what madness has come over you?

Critical Viewing ▶
Do you think this depiction
of the wooden horse is
consistent with the way
Virgil describes it? Why
or why not? **[Make a
Judgment]**

notions (nō´ shənz) *n.* ideas

---

7. **Tenedos** (ten´ ə dōs) island off the coast of Troy.
8. **Priam's kingdom** Troy.
9. **Mycenae** (mi sē´ nē) Greek city ruled by Agamemnon, a principal character in the *Iliad*.
10. **Teucer's** (tōō´ sərz) **town** Troy; Teucer, from Crete, was the original king of Troy.
11. **Dorian** (dôr´ ē ən) Greek.
12. **Thymoetes** (thī mē´ tēz) a Trojan leader.
13. **citadel** (sit´ ə del) *n.* safe, fortified place of defense in a city.
14. **Capys** (kā´ pis) a Trojan leader.
15. **Laocoön** (lā äk´ ə wän´) Trojan priest of the god Neptune.
16. **the Height** the Acropolis.

60 Can you believe the enemy truly gone?
A gift from the Danaans, and no ruse?[17]
Is that Ulysses' way, as you have known him?
Achaeans[18] must be hiding in this timber,
Or it was built to butt against our walls,
65 Peer over them into our houses, pelt
The city from the sky. Some crookedness
Is in this thing. Have no faith in the horse!
Whatever it is, even when Greeks bring gifts
I fear them, gifts and all.'
                                        He broke off then
70 And rifled his big spear with all his might
Against the horse's flank, the curve of belly.
It stuck there trembling, and the rounded hull
Reverberated[19] groaning at the blow.
If the gods' will had not been sinister,
75 If our own minds had not been crazed,
He would have made us foul that Argive[20] den
With bloody steel, and Troy would stand today—
O citadel of Priam,[21] towering still!

---

17. **ruse** (rō͞oz) *n.* trick.
18. **Achaeans** (ə kē′ ənz) Greeks.
19. **reverberated** (ri vʉr′ bə rāt′ id) *v.* echoed repeatedly.
20. **Argive** (är′ gīv) Greek.
21. **Priam** (prī′ əm) King of Troy.

Reading Check

What disagreement is taking place among the Trojans?

But now look: hillmen, shepherds of Dardania,[22]

80 Raising a shout, dragged in before the king
An unknown fellow with hands tied behind—
This all as he himself had planned,
Volunteering, letting them come across him,
So he could open Troy to the Achaeans.

85 Sure of himself this man was, braced for it
Either way, to work his trick or die.
From every quarter Trojans run to see him,
Ring the prisoner round, and make a game
Of jeering at him. Be instructed now

90 In Greek deceptive arts: one barefaced deed
Can tell you of them all.
As the man stood there, shaken and defenseless,
Looking around at ranks of Phrygians,[23]
'Oh god,' he said, 'what land on earth, what seas

95 Can take me in? What's left me in the end,
Outcast that I am from the Danaans,
Now the Dardanians will have my blood?'

The whimpering speech brought us up short; we felt
A twinge for him. Let him speak up, we said,

100 Tell us where he was born, what news he brought,
What he could hope for as a prisoner.
Taking his time, slow to discard his fright,
He said:
            'I'll tell you the whole truth, my lord,
No matter what may come of it. Argive

105 I am by birth, and will not say I'm not.
That first of all: Fortune has made a derelict
Of Sinon,[24] but the witch
Won't make an empty liar of him, too.
Report of Palamedes[25] may have reached you,

110 Scion of Belus' line,[26] a famous man
Who gave commands against the war. For this,
On a trumped-up charge, on <u>perjured</u> testimony,
The Greeks put him to death—but now they mourn him,
Now he has lost the light. Being kin to him,

115 In my first years I joined him as companion,
Sent by my poor old father on this campaign,
And while he held high rank and influence

---

22. **Dardania** (där dā´ nē ə) generalized name for Troy and its surrounding area.
23. **Phrygians** (fri´ jē ənz) Trojans.
24. **Sinon** (sī´ nän)
25. **Palamedes** (pal´ ə mē´ dēz) Greek warrior who advised Agamemnon to abandon the war against Troy; he was brought down by Ulysses, who forged proof that Palamedes cooperated with the enemy in the Trojan war.
26. **Scion of Belus'** (bel´ əs) **line** descendant of Belus, king of Egypt and father of Dido, queen of Carthage.

Literary Analysis
National Epic and Epic Hero What Roman value does Aeneas demonstrate in these lines?

perjured (pʉr´ jərd) *adj.* purposely false

In royal councils, we did well, with honor.
Then by the <u>guile</u> and envy of Ulysses—
120   Nothing unheard of there!—he left this world,
And I lived on, but under a cloud, in sorrow,
Raging for my blameless friend's downfall.
Demented, too, I could not hold my peace
But said if I had luck, if I won through
125   Again to Argos,[27] I'd avenge him there.
And I roused hatred with my talk; I fell
Afoul now of that man. From that time on,
Day in, day out, Ulysses
Found new ways to bait and terrify me,
130   Putting out shady rumors among the troops,
Looking for weapons he could use against me.
He could not rest till Calchas served his turn—
But why go on? The tale's unwelcome, useless,
If Achaeans are all one,
135   And it's enough I'm called Achaean, then
Exact the punishment, long overdue;
The Ithacan[28] desires it; the Atridae[29]
Would pay well for it.'
                  Burning with curiosity,
We questioned him, called on him to explain—
140   Unable to conceive such a performance,
The art of the Pelasgian.[30] He went on,
Atremble, as though he feared us:
                  'Many times
The Danaans wished to organize retreat,
To leave Troy and the long war, tired out.
145   If only they had done it! Heavy weather
At sea closed down on them, or a fresh gale
From the Southwest would keep them from embarking,
Most of all after this figure here,
This horse they put together with maple beams,
150   Reached its full height. Then wind and thunderstorms
Rumbled in heaven. So in our quandary[31]
We sent Eurypylus[32] to Phoebus' oracle,[33]
And he brought back this grim reply:

'Blood and a virgin slain
155   You gave to appease the winds, for your first voyage

Literature
in context History Connection

The Reign of Augustus

In 27 B.C., Augustus, great-nephew of and heir to Julius Caesar, quashed all opposition and took power in Rome, putting an end to more than a hundred years of civil war. Many who had experienced the violence and terror of the late Republic welcomed the prospect of peace. Augustus marked the beginning of his reign by funding an ambitious building program and supporting poets and artists.

Augustus ruled as "first citizen" rather than as emperor, out of deference to the traditional Roman distrust of kings. Yet there was no doubt that his power was absolute. Peace, prosperity, and a long reign solidified his authority and legitimacy, and the Romans would never again return to a republican system of government.

guile (gīl) *n.* trickery

---

27. **Argos** (är´ gōs) home city of Agamemnon and Menelaus; a generalized name for Greece.
28. **Ithacan** (ith´ ə kən) Ulysses, who comes from Ithaca in western Greece.
29. **Atridae** (ə trī´ dē) Agamemnon and Menelaus, the two sons of Atreus.
30. **Pelasgian** (pə laz´ jē ən) *n.* early inhabitant of Greece.
31. **quandary** (kwän´ də rē) *n.* state of uncertainty.
32. **Eurypylus** (yoo rip´ ə ləs) Greek.
33. **Phoebus' oracle** oracle of Apollo at Delphi.

Reading Check

With which Greek soldier does Sinon say he is in conflict?

The Wooden Horse of Troy, Master of the Aeneid Series, Louvre, Paris

◀ **Critical Viewing**
Which details in this depiction of the fall of Troy reveal that the painting is not meant to be historically accurate? [**Analyze**]

Troyward, O Danaans. Blood again
And Argive blood, one life, wins your return.'

When this got round among the soldiers, gloom
Came over them, and a cold chill that ran
160   To the very marrow. Who had death in store?
Whom did Apollo call for? Now the man
Of Ithaca haled Calchas out among us
In <u>tumult</u>, calling on the seer to tell
The true will of the gods. Ah, there were many
165   Able to divine the crookedness
And cruelty afoot for me, but they
Looked on in silence. For ten days the seer
Kept still, kept under cover, would not speak
Of anyone, or name a man for death,
170   Till driven to it at last by Ulysses' cries—
By prearrangement—he broke silence, barely
Enough to designate me for the altar.
Every last man agreed. The torments each
Had feared for himself, now shifted to another,
175   All could endure. And the infamous day came,
The ritual, the salted meal, the fillets[34] . . .

tumult (tōō′ mult′) *n.* commotion; confusion

---

34. fillets (fil′ its) *n.* woolen bands worn by sacrificial victims.

I broke free, I confess it, broke my chains,
Hid myself all night in a muddy marsh,
Concealed by reeds, waiting for them to sail
If they were going to.

180   Now no hope is left me
Of seeing my home country ever again,
My sweet children, my father, missed for years.
Perhaps the army will demand they pay
For my escape, my crime here, and their death,
185 Poor things, will be my punishment. Ah, sir,
I beg you by the gods above, the powers
In whom truth lives, and by what faith remains
Uncontaminated to men, take pity
On pain so great and so unmerited!'

190 For tears we gave him life, and pity, too.
Priam himself ordered the gyves[35] removed
And the tight chain between. In kindness then
He said to him:
               'Whoever you may be,
The Greeks are gone; forget them from now on;
195 You shall be ours. And answer me these questions:
Who put this huge thing up, this horse?
Who designed it? What do they want with it?
Is it religious or a means of war?'

These were his questions. Then the captive, trained
200 In trickery, in the stagecraft of Achaea,
Lifted his hands <u>unfettered</u> to the stars.
'Eternal fires of heaven,' he began,
'Powers inviolable, I swear by thee,
As by the altars and <u>blaspheming</u> swords
205 I got away from, and the gods' white bands[36]
I wore as one chosen for sacrifice,
This is justice, I am justified
In dropping all allegiance to the Greeks—
As I had cause to hate them; I may bring
210 Into the open what they would keep dark.
No laws of my own country bind me now.
Only be sure you keep your promises
And keep faith, Troy, as you are kept from harm
If what I say proves true, if what I give
215 Is great and valuable.

unfettered (un fet´ ərd) *adj.* unrestrained

blaspheming (blas fēm´ iŋ) *adj.* irreverent

---

35. **gyves** (gīvz) *n.* fetters or shackles used to restrain.
36. **gods' white bands** fillets.

☑**Reading Check**

Why does Sinon say he deserted the Greeks?

                    The whole hope
Of the Danaans, and their confidence
In the war they started, rested all along
In help from Pallas. Then the night came
When Diomedes and that criminal,
220   Ulysses, dared to raid her holy shrine.
They killed the guards on the high citadel
And ripped away the statue, the Palladium,[37]
<u>Desecrating</u> with bloody hands the virginal
Chaplets[38] of the goddess. After that,
225   Danaan hopes waned and were undermined,
Ebbing away, their strength in battle broken,
The goddess now against them. This she made
Evident to them all with signs and <u>portents</u>.
Just as they set her statue up in camp,
230   The eyes, cast upward, glowed with crackling flames,

Reading Strategy
Applying Background Information Explain how knowing Athena's role in the *Iliad* adds to your understanding of this passage.

desecrating (des´ i krāt´ iŋ) *v.* treating as not sacred

portents (pôr´ tents´) *n.* signs that suggest what is about to occur

---

37. **Palladium** (pə lā´ dē əm) statue of Pallas Athena at her shrine in Troy. According to the oracle, Troy could not be captured as long as the Palladium remained in place.
38. **chaplets** (chap´ lits) *n.* fillets; garlands.

And salty sweat ran down the body. Then—
I say it in awe—three times, up from the ground,
The apparition of the goddess rose
In a lightning flash, with shield and spear atremble.
235   Calchas divined at once that the sea crossing
Must be attempted in retreat—that Pergamum[39]
Cannot be torn apart by Argive swords
Unless at Argos first they get new omens,
Carrying homeward the divine power
240   Brought overseas in ships. Now they are gone
Before the wind to the fatherland, Mycenae,
Gone to enlist new troops and gods. They'll cross
The water again and be here, unforeseen.
So Calchas read the portents. Warned by him,
245   They set this figure up in reparation
For the Palladium stolen, to appease
The offended power and expiate[40] the crime.
Enormous, though, he made them build the thing
With timber braces, towering to the sky,

---

39. Pergamum (pʉr′ gə məm) *n.* the citadel of Troy.
40. expiate (eks′ pē āt′) *v.* atone for; make amends for.

☑**Reading Check**
According to Sinon, why did the Greeks build the wooden horse?

◀ **Critical Viewing**
How do you think Trojan citizens would have reacted to a horse like this one being brought inside their city's walls? [Speculate]

250   Too big for the gates, not to be hauled inside
     And give the people back their ancient guardian.
     If any hand here violates this gift
     To great Minerva, then extinction waits,
     Not for one only—would god it were so—
255   But for the realm of Priam and all Phrygians.
     If this proud offering, drawn by your hands,
     Should mount into your city, then so far
     As the walls of Pelops'[41] town the tide of Asia
     Surges in war: that doom awaits our children.'

260   This fraud of Sinon, his accomplished lying,
     Won us over; a tall tale and fake tears
     Had captured us, whom neither Diomedes
     Nor Larisaean Achilles[42] overpowered,
     Nor ten long years, nor all their thousand ships.

Despite warnings that Greeks are hiding in the horse, the Trojans bring it inside the walls of Troy. During the night, the Greeks emerge from the horse, ready for combat. Aeneas is also ready. In fierce spirit, he and his men fight against desperate odds. Toward daybreak, Aeneas finds a crowd of refugees gathered for exile, waiting for him to lead them to safety. He does so, with characteristic courage.

41. **Pelops'** (pel´ əps) **town** Argos. Pelops was an early king of Mycenae and an ancestor of Menelaus and Agamemnon.
42. **Larisaean Achilles** (lə ris´ ē ən ə kil´ ēz) Achilles, the foremost Greek warrior, was so called after Larissa, a town in his homeland of Thessaly.

Review and Assess

Thinking About the Selection

1. **Respond:** If you were a Trojan listening to Sinon's lying tale, do you think you would have sympathized with him? Why or why not?

2. **(a) Recall:** Who recounts the story of Troy's fall, and where? **(b) Interpret:** In what way do this perspective and setting color the narrative?

3. **(a) Recall:** According to Sinon, why did the Danaans leave him behind? **(b) Infer:** In what way does his explanation help him gain the Trojans' trust?

4. **(a) Recall:** Why did the Danaans build the wooden horse, according to Sinon's story? **(b) Analyze:** To what Trojan feelings might Sinon be trying to appeal with this story?

5. **Make a Judgment:** Do you think the Trojans' compassion is what allows Sinon to trick them, or do you think the Trojans were really blinded by pride? Explain.

Review and Assess

Literary Elements

National Epic

1. (a) Who is Aeneas' mother? (b) Why might this fact have been a source of pride for ancient Romans reading their **national epic**?
2. Why do you think Virgil repeatedly portrays the Greeks in the *Aeneid* as ruthless liars?
3. In what way do the last five lines of this selection allow Romans to remain proud of their origins despite the Trojans' defeat?

Connecting Literary Elements

4. The **epic hero** Aeneas recounts the fall of Troy even though it grieves him to do so. What Roman value does he demonstrate by agreeing to tell the story?
5. Which qualities of Aeneas and the Trojans might Romans have admired even though those qualities bring about Troy's downfall?
6. (a) Based on what the *Aeneid* reveals or suggests about each character, compare and contrast Aeneas with Ulysses (Odysseus), the epic hero of Homer's *Odyssey*. Use a Venn diagram like the one shown.

(b) By contrasting the two heroes in the way that he does, what do you think Virgil suggests about the difference between Roman and Greek culture?

Reading Strategy

Applying Background Information

7. Knowing that Ulysses' (Odysseus') reputation in Homer's epics is that of a cunning and resourceful warrior, what do you think Laocoön means in the following lines?

> A gift from the Danaans, and no ruse?
> Is that Ulysses' way, as you have known him?

Extend Understanding

8. **Psychology Connection:** Sometimes a talent or strength can also be a weakness. In what way does the story of Troy's fall support this paradox, or seeming contradiction?

Integrate Language Skills

Vocabulary Development Lesson

Word Analysis: Latin Root -jur-

The word root -jur- comes from the Latin word *jurare*, meaning "to swear an oath." For example, the word *perjury* (lying while under oath) literally means a statement that runs "through" or "against" an oath. The root -jur- is also related to the Latin words *jus* and *juris*, which mean "law."

Using the meaning of -jur-, write a brief definition of each of the following words.

   1. jury   **2.** jurisdiction   **3.** abjure

Spelling Strategy

The letters *ui* in English can represent several different sounds, including *ī* (guile), *i* (biscuit), *o͞o* (fruit), and *wi* (languish). Indicate the sound that the letters *ui* make in each of these words.

   1. suitable   **2.** liquid   **3.** disguise

Concept Development: Analogies

For each of the following items, study the relationship presented in the first word pair. Then, complete the analogies by using the vocabulary words on p. 491 to build word pairs expressing the same relationship.

   1. forged : signature :: ___?___ : testimony
   2. riot : order :: ___?___ : calm
   3. memories : past :: ___?___ : future
   4. honesty : integrity :: ___?___ : treachery
   5. actions : concrete :: ___?___ : abstract
   6. fleeting : temporary :: ___?___ : disrespectful
   7. confined : released :: restrained : ___?___
   8. polishing : lustrous :: ___?___ : unholy

Grammar and Style Lesson

Sentence Beginnings: Adverb Phrases

One way in which writers create sentence variety and interest is by beginning a sentence with an **adverb phrase.** An adverb phrase is a group of words acting together to modify a verb, an adjective, or an adverb by pointing out *where, when, in what way,* or *to what extent.*

Examples:	From that time on, / Day in, day out, Ulysses / Found new ways . . . (modifies *Found*, tells when)
	Inside the wooden horse, the Greeks stood poised to attack. (modifies *stood*, tells where)

Practice Rewrite each of these sentences so that it begins with an adverb phrase.

   1. Aeneas told his story at Dido's request.
   2. The Greeks laid siege to Troy for ten long years.
   3. Sinon wove his deceptive tale with expert skill.
   4. The Greeks emerged in the dead of night.
   5. Sinon could be considered a hero in the eyes of the Greeks.

Writing Application Write a dialogue in which the Trojans debate what to do with the wooden horse. Begin at least two sentences with adverb phrases.

WG Prentice Hall Writing and Grammar Connection: Diamond Level, Chapter 5, Section 4

Writing Lesson

Analysis of Storytelling Technique

In the *Aeneid*, Virgil interweaves Aeneas' account of the fall of Troy with long speeches by Sinon. Thus, Virgil, Aeneas, and Sinon can all be considered tellers of this story. Write an analysis of Virgil's storytelling technique, explaining how it supports the overall purpose of his epic: to glorify the origins of Rome and Roman culture.

Prewriting Review the selection, noting passages in which your perceptions of characters and events are influenced by the way in which they are presented. For example, consider how your impressions of Sinon are colored by the comments Aeneas interjects about him.

Drafting Organize and draft your essay, citing passages that demonstrate how Virgil's narrative technique helps portray the Trojans positively.

Revising As you review your work, make sure that you have clearly linked your ideas. Add transitions such as *therefore*, *furthermore*, and *in contrast* to clarify connections between ideas.

Model: Clarifying Connections With Transitions

Sinon tells a convincing story that appeals to his

Therefore,

listeners' emotions. Readers can understand how

he was able to deceive the Trojans.

> Words like *therefore* strengthen the connections between ideas.

Prentice Hall Writing and Grammar Connection: Diamond Level, Chapter 9, Section 4

Extension Activities

Listening and Speaking Write a **persuasive speech** in which you argue that the Trojans should not let the horse inside the city gates. Consider using the following to strengthen your speech:

- arguments from the speech of Laocoön (lines 58–69)
- references to some of the less credible assertions of Sinon

Rehearse and deliver your speech before an audience of classmates.

Research and Technology With a group of classmates, research the complete story of the *Aeneid*. Then, create an illustrated **travelogue** showing the wanderings of Aeneas on his journey from Troy to Italy. Include pictures of the places he visited. **[Group Activity]**

 **Take It to the Net** PHSchool.com

Go online for an additional research activity using the Internet.

from the *Aeneid* ◆ 505

Prepare to Read

Poetry of Catullus and Horace

Catullus
(c. 84–c. 54 B.C.)

Gaius Valerius Catullus (gā´ əs va ler´ ē əs kə tul´ əs) was born in Verona, Italy, to a prosperous and well-connected family. As a prominent local citizen, his father played host to the provincial governor Julius Caesar, who remained a family friend. Catullus came to Rome in his early twenties armed with introductions to the best families. Witty, wealthy, and well educated, the gifted young poet was always welcome among members of the upper class.

A Tormented Lover The most glamorous social circle in Rome was presided over by Clodia (Pulcher) Metelli. Descended from an old noble family and married to a powerful man, she combined status and wealth with chic beauty. Clodia immediately captivated Catullus, who wrote dazzling, passionate love lyrics to her. With a powerful immediacy that still grips readers today, his poems convey his mixed feelings—his ecstatic happiness, his depression, and his bitterness at still loving a woman who has betrayed and manipulated him.

A Lyric Legacy Catullus did not spend all his time loving and languishing over Clodia. He established himself as an accomplished and "learned" (to use his own term) poet whose polished verses rivaled those of his Greek predecessors, including Sappho. Catullus died sometime in his early thirties, but his fame lives on in his poetry. His love lyrics in particular have inspired successors and imitators for thousands of years, including the English poets Edmund Spenser, Ben Jonson, Robert Herrick, John Keats, and Alfred, Lord Tennyson.

Horace
(65–8 B.C.)

Horace was the finest lyric poet of ancient Rome. He enjoyed praise and success during his own lifetime, and his work was so frequently read by later generations that he became their principal interpreter of Roman culture. His widely quoted phrases *carpe diem* ("seize the day") and *dulce et decorum est pro patria mori* ("it is sweet and proper to die for the fatherland") sum up two of the dominant—and conflicting—attitudes of his era. Horace was a member of the generation that followed Cicero and Catullus—the generation that survived the civil wars and lived on to witness the unification of the Roman Empire under Caesar Augustus.

A Public Poet Horace's first three books of *Odes* appeared in 23 B.C., when the poet was 42 years old. Unlike the odes of the Greek writer Pindar, Horace's odes are relatively brief, using repeating stanza forms and usually taking an informal tone. They illustrate a shift occurring in the culture of his day. Some recall the themes of Catullus, urging a friend to enjoy the pleasures of the moment. However, the emotional extremes of Catullus—the extreme joy and the bitter pain—are gone, replaced by a more even temperament.

There are other poems that are very different from those of Catullus and his school, such as the first six odes of Book III, which describe traditional Roman ideals. They echo the efforts of Caesar Augustus to restore a way of life that wealth and power were eroding and to revive in Romans the virtues of their ancestors.

Preview

Connecting to the Literature

If you tune in to any pop music radio station, it probably will not be long before you hear a song about a troubled romance. Even though the poems in this grouping were written more than two thousand years ago, some of them similarly explore the bittersweet nature of love.

Literary Analysis

Tone

The **tone** of a poem is the speaker's attitude toward his or her subject or audience. A speaker's tone can be described as formal or informal, friendly or distant, personal or objective. Poets create tone through their choice of words, images, and details.

As you read these poems by Catullus and Horace, use a chart like the one shown to record how specific words and details affect the tone of each poem.

Comparing Literary Works

The tone of the speaker in Catullus' lyrics is very different from the speaker's tone in Horace's "Carpe Diem." This difference is due in large part to each poet's **diction,** or choice and arrangement of words. Horace's diction is complex and ornate. He uses sophisticated sentence structure and vocabulary. Catullus, on the other hand, uses simple, direct diction that appeals to the emotions, rather than the intellect, of the reader.

Note the way in which diction contributes to the tone and overall effect of each of these poems.

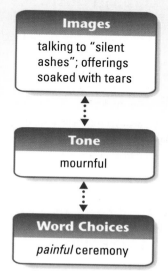

Reading Strategy

Analyzing Imagery

When you read poetry, **analyze imagery**—language that appeals to the senses—to clarify the deeper meaning that the author is conveying. For example, notice how in these lines Catullus uses the visual image of "wind and swift water" to convey the fleeting nature of words of love:

> . . . what a woman says to a hungry lover
> You might as well scribble in wind and swift water.

As you read each of the poems in this grouping, note the ideas and emotions associated with the images presented. Then, consider the larger insight that each image offers.

Vocabulary Development

consult (kən sult´) v. seek advice from (p. 510)

protracted (prō trakt´ id) adj. extended; drawn out (p. 510)

Poetry of
Catullus *translated by* Carl Sesar

Background

Funeral rites for prominent Romans were elaborate. Before being buried or cremated, the deceased was laid out fully dressed and mourned for a few days. Then, the person's relatives carried the body in a formal procession to the place of burial or cremation. Actors wore masks representing the dead person's deceased kinsmen, while professional mourners and musicians sang and played a funeral dirge. In "I Crossed Many Lands and a Lot of Ocean," the speaker refers directly to some of these funeral customs.

I Crossed Many Lands and a Lot of Ocean

I crossed many lands and a lot of ocean
to get to this painful ceremony, my brother,
so I could finally give you gifts for the dead,
and waste time talking to some silent ashes
5   being that you're not here yourself with me.
Fate did wrong, my brother, to tear us apart.
But I bring you these offerings now anyway,
after the old custom our parents taught us.
Take them, soaked with your brother's tears,
10 and forever more, my brother, goodbye.

Reading Strategy
Analyzing Imagery What insight about funeral ceremonies does the image in line 4 suggest?

I Hate Her and I Love Her

I hate her and I love her. Don't ask me why.
It's the way I feel, that's all, and it hurts.

My Woman Says There's Nobody She'd Rather Marry

My woman says there's nobody she'd rather marry
than me, not even Jupiter himself if he asked her.
She says, but what a woman says to a hungry lover
you might as well scribble in wind and swift water.

Literary Analysis
Tone What kind of tone
does the word *scribble*
help create?

Review and Assess

Thinking About the Selections

1. **Respond:** Which of these poems evokes your strongest sympathy for the speaker? Explain your answer.

2. **(a) Recall:** How many times does the word *says* appear in the poem "My Woman Says . . ."? **(b) Interpret:** What idea does the speaker seem to be emphasizing with these repetitions?

3. **(a) Recall:** In "I Crossed Many Lands . . . ," why does the speaker say he has brought offerings for his dead brother? **(b) Infer:** What seems to be the speaker's attitude toward the funeral ceremony?

4. **Apply:** Do you think Catullus' observations about love are still relevant in today's world? Why or why not?

CARPE DIEM

Horace *translated by* Thomas Hawkins

Background

The title of Horace's poem "Carpe Diem" has become proverbial. Literally, the phrase means "seize the day." Figuratively, it expresses a principle: "Enjoy life fully while you can."

Strive not, Leuconoe, to know what end
The gods above to me or thee will send:
Nor with astrologers <u>consult</u> at all,
That thou mayst better know what can befall;
5 Whether thou liv'st more winters, or thy last
Be this, which Tyrrhen waves 'gainst rocks do cast.
Be wise! Drink free, and in so short a space
Do not <u>protracted</u> hopes of life embrace:
Whilst we are talking, envious time doth slide;
10 This day's thine own; the next may be denied.

consult (kən sult′) *v.* seek advice from

protracted (prō trakt′ id) *adj.* extended; drawn out

Review and Assess

Thinking About the Selection

1. **Respond:** Do you agree with the philosophy that the speaker expresses in "Carpe Diem"? Why or why not?

2. **(a) Recall:** In the first two lines of the poem, what does the speaker urge his friend *not* to do? **(b) Analyze:** In what way does this warning foreshadow the poem's major theme?

3. **(a) Recall:** What advice does the speaker give Leuconoe in lines 7 and 8? **(b) Analyze:** In what way do these lines both echo and extend lines 1 and 2?

4. **Speculate:** How do you think Leuconoe might have responded to the advice that the speaker gives in "Carpe Diem"? Explain your answer.

Review and Assess

Literary Analysis

Tone

1. (a) How would you describe the speaker's **tone** in "My Woman Says . . ."? (b) What words and images convey this tone?
2. What strong image, or use of sensory language, in the second line of "I Hate Her and I Love Her" reveals the speaker's tone?
3. In line 2 of "I Crossed Many Lands . . .," what phrase establishes a mournful tone for the poem as a whole?
4. In what ways does the speaker's tone in "Carpe Diem" differ from the tone of the speaker in the three poems by Catullus?

Comparing Literary Works

5. Which words in "My Woman Says . . ." illustrate the poet's use of informal or colloquial **diction**?
6. (a) Compare and contrast Catullus' diction in "I Hate Her and I Love Her" with Horace's diction in "Carpe Diem." (b) In what way does each poem's diction help convey the tone of its speaker?

Reading Strategy

Analyzing Imagery

7. (a) Use a chart like the one shown to **analyze** the images of a "hungry" lover and words scribbled "in wind and swift water" in Catullus' "My Woman Says . . . ."

(b) What contrast do these images help create between the first two lines of the poem and the last two? (c) In what way does this contrast convey the poem's central insight? Explain.
8. In "I Crossed Many Lands . . .," what image in the final two lines sums up the speaker's grief for his dead brother?

Extend Understanding

9. **Media Connection:** What might an advertising agency do to promote the message of "Carpe Diem"? Give examples of the kinds of advertisements that could be run in various media.

Quick Review

The **tone** of a poem is the speaker's attitude toward his or her subject or audience.

Diction is a writer's choice and arrangement of words.

To **analyze images,** determine how sensory details relate to larger ideas.

Take It to the Net
PHSchool.com

Take the interactive self-test online to check your understanding of these selections.

Integrate Language Skills

Vocabulary Development Lesson

Word Analysis: Latin Root -tract-

The Latin root -tract- means "to draw or pull." For example, the word *protracted* literally means "drawn or pulled forward."

Use your understanding of the Latin root -tract- to match each word on the left with its definition on the right.

1. extract   a. draw or pull together
2. retract   b. draw or pull toward itself
3. contract   c. draw or pull apart or away
4. distract   d. vehicle used for drawing or pulling
5. attract   e. draw or pull out
6. tractor   f. draw or pull back

Concept Development: Synonyms

Select the letter of the word that is closest in meaning to each numbered word.

1. consult: (a) praise, (b) ask, (c) reject
2. protracted: (a) performed, (b) examined, (c) extended

Spelling Strategy

The suffixes -ant and -ent are used to form nouns with endings that sound like the one in *consultant*. There is no rule that governs which ending should be used in these formations. Therefore, you should refer to a dictionary if you are unsure of how to spell this sound at the end of a noun.

Form a noun by adding the correct ending, -ant or -ent, to each of the following words.

1. account   2. reside   3. descend

Grammar and Style Lesson

Inverted Word Order

In English, the word order in most sentences is subject-verb-complement (s/v/c). However, writers sometimes use **inverted,** or reversed, word order. Poets often use inverted word order for the sake of rhythm, meter, or rhyme. Writers of both poetry and prose use inverted word order to emphasize a certain part of a sentence, to create interest and suspense, or simply to add sentence variety.

Normal word order: Those who heed this advice are happy. (s/v/c)

Inverted word order: Happy are those who heed this advice. (c/v/s)

Practice Rewrite each of the following sentences in normal subject-verb-complement word order.

1. No relief from this bitter winter comes.
2. The traveler never from those shores returns.
3. Like the snows of winter, time slowly melts away.
4. Do not seek the gods' plans to learn.
5. Do not protracted hopes of life embrace.

Writing Application Using inverted word order in at least three sentences, write a paragraph in which you offer advice to a younger student.

 Prentice Hall Writing and Grammar Connection: Diamond Level, Chapter 20, Section 3

Writing Lesson

Comparison-and-Contrast Essay

These poems by Catullus and Horace present two strikingly different kinds of speakers. Write an essay in which you compare and contrast the speakers in Catullus' poems with the speaker in Horace's "Carpe Diem," discussing the effect of each one's distinct voice.

Prewriting   Reread each poem and make notes about the personality and attitude of the speaker. Also, note how the tone of each speaker influences the poem's central message or insight.

Drafting   Begin your draft by introducing the speakers and briefly summarizing the poems. Then, state your main ideas about how the speakers of the poems are alike and how they are different. As you draft, discuss how each speaker's voice contributes to the poem's overall effect.

Revising   Review your essay to make sure you have expressed your points with conviction. Identify any weak or unclear passages and strengthen them with more precise modifiers.

Model: Revising for a Stronger Statement

and lighthearted

The speaker in Horace's poem may seem casual at

cautionary

first, but as the poem unfolds his words take on a

, almost urgent,

serious tone.

> Precise modifiers create a stronger argument.

W̶G̶ Prentice Hall Writing and Grammar Connection: Diamond Level, Chapter 14, Section 4

Extension Activities

Listening and Speaking   With a group of classmates, hold a **panel discussion** to explore the validity of the *carpe diem* attitude. Panelists should address the following questions:

- How practical is it to apply the *carpe diem* philosophy to everyday life?
- Does the *carpe diem* philosophy encourage irresponsible behavior?

Present the discussion in class, inviting questions from classmates. **[Group Activity]**

Research and Technology   Using library and Internet resources, compile an **annotated list** of love lyrics from the past and present. For each lyric, provide a brief summary, comment, or evaluation. Be sure to include some contemporary songs about love.

 **Take It to the Net**   PHSchool.com

Go online for an additional research activity using the Internet.

Prepare to Read

The Story of Daedalus and Icarus

Ovid (43 B.C.–A.D. 17)

Publius Ovidius Naso (pub´ lē əs ä vid´ ē əs nā´ sō), known as Ovid (äv´ id), was born in Sulmo, a small village about ninety miles east of Rome, in the year after Julius Caesar's assassination. Ovid's father wanted him to go into public life, so he sent Ovid to Rome to be educated. After completing his studies in Rome, Ovid went on a long tour of the major cities of the ancient world in Greece, Asia Minor, and Sicily. On his return, Ovid dutifully joined the legal profession and became a judge. However, Ovid preferred to be a poet. His father discouraged him from writing poetry, reminding him that Homer died poor, but Ovid pursued his goal.

Poetry and Politics Ovid was only twelve when Octavian defeated Antony and effectively established himself as the absolute ruler of Rome. Therefore, the Rome that Ovid knew was untroubled by the civil wars that had haunted the work of earlier writers. Perhaps as a reaction to this more secure, carefree society, Ovid's poetry usually speaks of pleasure, and especially love. His first work was the *Amores* (c. 20 B.C.), a series of love lyrics addressed to an imaginary woman named Corinna. He followed this work with the *Heroides*, a collection of fifteen fictional verse letters from famous women of the past to the men they loved. He then went on to a more theoretical study in three books called *Ars amatoria* (The Art of Love), which appeared around 9 B.C.

Unfortunately for Ovid, he was producing provocative literature at a time when Octavian, now the emperor Caesar Augustus, was seeking to improve Roman life through a series of laws that punished adultery and other kinds of immoral conduct. The poet soon turned to less controversial subjects that would not be seen as disrespectful to the new emperor and his vision of an ideal Roman state.

Ovid's Masterpiece The *Metamorphoses* (Transformations) stands as Ovid's greatest literary achievement. A poem of nearly 12,000 lines, it tells a series of stories beginning with the creation of the world and ending with the death of Julius Caesar. Among these stories is "The Story of Daedalus and Icarus," a famous myth about a boy who flies too close to the sun. Others include the well-known myths of King Midas, Echo and Narcissus, Hercules, and Orpheus. In each story, someone or something undergoes a change. The stories are linked by clever transitions, so that the entire work reads as one long, uninterrupted tale. In addition to its literary value, the *Metamorphoses* also has historical value because it documents some of the most famous myths of ancient Mediterranean culture.

The *Metamorphoses* is divided into fifteen books and is written in the same meter as Virgil's *Aeneid*. Ovid knew that he was writing in the shadow of Virgil's great epic, and he met this challenge by producing a lighthearted and entertaining poem that seems to mock the very serious *Aeneid*.

Banishment Shortly after Ovid completed the *Metamorphoses* in A.D. 8, Caesar Augustus banished him to Tomis, a remote village on the Black Sea. The reasons for the poet's exile are not entirely clear, but the emperor might have felt that Ovid endangered public morals.

Banishment to a half-civilized place at the far edge of the empire was a severe punishment for this worldly poet. Although he kept his property and continued to write, he was never allowed to return to Rome.

Preview

Connecting to the Literature

World literature is filled with tales that teach the dangers of excessive ambition. In this famous story, a boy ignores his father's warnings and meets a tragic end.

Literary Analysis

Narrative Poetry

A **narrative poem** is a poem that tells a story. Narrative poems are distinct from lyric poems, in which the main purpose is to express the thoughts or feelings of the speaker. Ballads are one type of narrative poetry; epic poems like Virgil's *Aeneid* are another.

In the *Metamorphoses*, Ovid uses the epic form. Unlike Virgil, however, Ovid does not tell the story of an important historical event or a famous hero. Instead, he weaves together entertaining tales about gods, demigods, and mortals. As you read "The Story of Daedalus and Icarus" from the *Metamorphoses*, notice how Ovid makes use of both narrative and poetic techniques.

Connecting Literary Elements

A **myth** is a fictional tale that arises out of a culture's oral tradition and usually involves supernatural characters or events. In addition to providing entertainment, myths often teach the values and ideals of a culture or attempt to explain such unknowns as the following:

- causes of natural phenomena, such as the origins of earthly life
- origins of place names
- reasons for certain customs

Consider what lesson "The Story of Daedalus and Icarus" might be meant to teach and what questions it might answer.

Reading Strategy

Anticipating Events

As you read this story, you will probably find yourself **anticipating events**—looking forward to what happens next. More emotional than the logical process of predicting, anticipating events leads you to connect with characters as you watch their lives unfold. As you read "The Story of Daedalus and Icarus," use a chart like the one shown to note clues that cause you to anticipate later events in the story.

Vocabulary Development

dominion (də min′ yən) *n.* kingdom; area of rule (p. 517)

sequence (sē′ kwəns) *n.* order; succession (p. 517)

poised (poizd) *adj.* balanced and steady, as though suspended (p. 517)

from the *Metamorphoses*

The Story of
Daedalus and Icarus

Ovid *translated by* Rolphe Humphries

Background

"The Story of Daedalus and Icarus" is just one of a series of myths in the *Metamorphoses* involving artists or craftspeople. In most of these myths, Ovid associates skill and ingenuity with pride, danger, and risk. Daedalus' very name means "cunning craftsman." As you read "The Story of Daedalus and Icarus," you will recognize the theme of danger, loss, or grief associated with artistic or technological achievement.

The myth begins with Daedalus and his son Icarus in exile on the island of Crete, where King Minos rules. Daedalus has been exiled from Athens for the murder of his nephew Perdix, who had shown signs of surpassing his uncle in artistic ability.

◀ **Critical Viewing**
What emotions does this sculpture convey? **[Analyze]**

Homesick for homeland, Daedalus hated Crete
And his long exile there, but the sea held him.
"Though Minos blocks escape by land or water,"
Daedalus said, "surely the sky is open,
5 And that's the way we'll go. Minos' <u>dominion</u>
Does not include the air." He turned his thinking
Toward unknown arts, changing the laws of nature.
He laid out feathers in order, first the smallest,
A little larger next it, and so continued,
10 The way that pan-pipes[1] rise in gradual <u>sequence</u>.
He fastened them with twine and wax, at middle,
At bottom, so, and bent them, gently curving,
So that they looked like wings of birds, most surely.
And Icarus, his son, stood by and watched him,
15 Not knowing he was dealing with his downfall,
Stood by and watched, and raised his shiny face
To let a feather, light as down,[2] fall on it,
Or stuck his thumb into the yellow wax,
Fooling around, the way a boy will, always,
20 Whenever a father tries to get some work done.
Still, it was done at last, and the father hovered,
<u>Poised</u>, in the moving air, and taught his son:
"I warn you, Icarus, fly a middle course:
Don't go too low, or water will weigh the wings down;
25 Don't go too high, or the sun's fire will burn them.
Keep to the middle way. And one more thing,
No fancy steering by star or constellation,
Follow my lead!" That was the flying lesson,
And now to fit the wings to the boy's shoulders.
30 Between the work and warning the father found
His cheeks were wet with tears, and his hands trembled.
He kissed his son (*Good-bye*, if he had known it),
Rose on his wings, flew on ahead, as fearful
As any bird launching the little nestlings[3]
35 Out of high nest into thin air. *Keep on,*
Keep on, he signals, *follow me!* He guides him
In flight—O fatal art!—and the wings move
And the father looks back to see the son's wings moving.
Far off, far down, some fisherman is watching
40 As the rod dips and trembles over the water,
Some shepherd rests his weight upon his crook,[4]

dominion (də min′ yən) *n.*
kingdom; area of rule

sequence (sē′ kwəns) *n.*
order; succession

poised (poizd) *adj.* balanced
and steady, as though
suspended

Reading Strategy
Anticipating Events Based
on the clues in these lines,
what do you anticipate will
happen later in the poem?

---

1. **pan-pipes** musical instrument consisting of a series of tubes of varying lengths bound
   together and played by blowing across the open upper ends.
2. **down** soft, fluffy feathers, like those of a young bird.
3. **nestlings** young birds that have not yet left the nest.
4. **crook** shepherd's staff, with a hook at one end.

Reading Check

Why does Daedalus
construct wings for himself
and Icarus?

Some ploughman on the handles of the ploughshare,[5]
And all look up, in absolute amazement,
At those air-borne above. They must be gods!
45   They were over Samos, Juno's sacred island,
Delos and Paros toward the left, Lebinthus
Visible to the right, and another island,
Calymne,[6] rich in honey. And the boy
Thought *This is wonderful!* and left his father,
50   Soared higher, higher, drawn to the vast heaven,
Nearer the sun, and the wax that held the wings
Melted in that fierce heat, and the bare arms
Beat up and down in air, and lacking oarage[7]
Took hold of nothing. *Father!* he cried, and *Father!*
55   Until the blue sea hushed him, the dark water
Men call the Icarian now. And Daedalus,
Father no more, called "Icarus, where are you!
Where are you, Icarus? Tell me where to find you!"
And saw the wings on the waves, and cursed his talents,
60   Buried the body in a tomb, and the land
Was named for Icarus.[8]

---

5. **ploughshare** cutting blade of a plow.
6. **Samos** (sā′ mäs)...**Delos** (dē′ läs)...**Paros** (per′ äs′)...**Lebinthus** (lə bin′ thəs)...
Calymne (kə lim′ nē) islands in the Aegean Sea, between mainland Greece and Asia
Minor.
7. **oarage** something functioning as oars with which to row.
8. **the land was named for Icarus** a reference to the island now called Icaria.

Review and Assess

Thinking About the Selection

1. **Respond:** Do you think Icarus deserved his fate? Explain.
2. **(a) Recall:** In lines 14–20, what does Icarus do as he watches his father prepare the wings? **(b) Infer:** Why do you think Ovid includes these details?
3. **(a) Recall:** What warning does Daedalus give his son as the two prepare to take off? **(b) Apply:** In what way might this advice apply to life in general?
4. **(a) Recall:** What does Icarus do to cause his demise? **(b) Evaluate:** In your opinion, is his motivation for taking this action believable?
5. **Make a Judgment:** Do you think Daedalus takes proper responsibility for what happened to Icarus? Explain your answer.

Review and Assess

Literary Analysis

Narrative Poetry

1. (a) What conflict sets the plot of this **narrative poem** in motion? (b) How does Daedalus plan to resolve this conflict?
2. (a) To what does Ovid compare Daedalus and Icarus when they first take flight? (b) How does this comparison enrich the story?
3. What does Ovid do to make his narrative interesting and suspenseful even for readers who are familiar with the story? Explain.

Connecting Literary Elements

4. (a) Which details in this **myth** would you point to as supernatural? (b) Which details are realistic? (c) Why do you think Ovid includes both supernatural and realistic elements? Explain.
5. (a) Using a chart like the one shown, show how certain details in "The Story of Daedalus and Icarus" teach lessons or convey values.

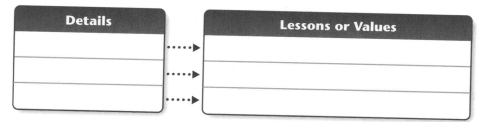

Details		Lessons or Values
	····▶	
	····▶	
	····▶	

   (b) What would you say is the main lesson of the story?
6. What do you think "The Story of Daedalus and Icarus" suggests about the uses of art and technology? Explain your answer with examples from the story.

Reading Strategy

Anticipating Events

7. At what point in the story can readers first **anticipate** that Daedalus' plan might lead to disaster? Cite specific lines.
8. What do you think Daedalus' life will be like after the point at which the narrative ends? Explain.

Extend Understanding

9. **Psychology Connection:** Psychologists sometimes refer to an "Icarus complex." Based on "The Story of Daedalus and Icarus," what do you think this term means?

Integrate Language Skills

Vocabulary Development Lesson

Word Analysis: Latin Root -domin-

The word *dominion* contains the Latin root -*domin*-, which means "rule" or "master." Thus, *dominion* means "region or area of rule." Applying the meaning of the root -*domin*-, use each of the following words in a sentence.

1. dominance
2. dominate
3. domineering
4. predominantly

Spelling Strategy

Words ending in a silent *e* usually drop the *e* before adding suffixes that start with vowels. For example, *poise* + -*ed* = *poised*. Combine each of the following words with its suffix.

1. like + -*able*
2. aspire + -*ing*
3. synthesize + -*ed*
4. judge + -*ment*

Grammar and Style Lesson

Appositives and Appositive Phrases

An **appositive** is a noun or pronoun placed next to another noun or pronoun to provide more information about it. When an appositive is accompanied by its own modifiers, it forms an **appositive phrase.**

If an appositive can be omitted from a sentence without altering its basic meaning, it must be set off by commas. If the appositive is essential to the meaning of a sentence, commas are not used. Appositive phrases are always set off by commas or dashes.

> **Nonessential:** Ovid, a Roman poet, wrote the *Metamorphoses*.
>
> **Essential:** The Roman poet Ovid wrote the *Metamorphoses*.

Fluency: True or False

Review the vocabulary words on page 515. Then, indicate whether each of the following statements is true or false. Explain the reason for each of your answers.

1. An emperor or a king is someone who might hold *dominion* over an entire nation or region.
2. The pages of a book are usually numbered in no particular *sequence*.
3. Fish generally appear more *poised* when they are out of water than when they are swimming.

Practice Rewrite each sentence below, incorporating the information given as an appositive. Add words as necessary.

1. Daedalus devised an escape plan. (*clever artisan*)
2. He fitted Icarus with wings. (*his son*)
3. The boy ignored his father's advice. (*novice at flying*)
4. Daedalus and Icarus flew over Samos. (*Juno's sacred island*)
5. Daedalus lamented his son's death. (*father no more*)

Writing Application Write a paragraph about a journey that you or someone you know has taken recently. Use at least three appositives or appositive phrases in your writing.

W͟G Prentice Hall Writing and Grammar Connection: Diamond Level, Chapter 19, Section 1

Writing Lesson

Script for the Multimedia Presentation of a Story

In his story, Ovid conjures up vivid scenes and dialogue. Plan a multimedia presentation of "The Story of Daedalus and Icarus." Prepare a script describing the audiovisual aids that will bring out the imagery and emotion of the work.

Prewriting Reread the selection, making a list of photographs, artwork, music, video clips, and sound effects that could highlight the poem's images and emotional dynamics.

Drafting Draft your script, clearly showing the line-by-line relationship between the text and the sounds and images you will use.

Revising Make sure that the format of your script is clear and easy to follow. Adjust the script to achieve the clearest, strongest arrangement of multimedia elements.

Model: Following Script Format

SPEAKER: . . . surely the sky is open,
   [VISUAL: video slide of sky with sea gulls soaring]
And that's the way we'll go. Minos' dominion
Does not include the air.
   [VISUAL: slide dissolves into picture of Daedalus]
   [AUDIO: fade in music with brass instrument
   playing a melody that conveys a sense of hope]

> Bracketed directions convey the timing of audiovisual effects with the reading of the poem.

Prentice Hall Writing and Grammar Connection: Diamond Level, Chapter 28, Section 3

Extension Activities

Listening and Speaking As a news anchor, present a **videotaped news report** on the fall of Icarus. Interview Daedalus, as well as the other witnesses to the tragedy: the fisherman, the shepherd, and the ploughman.

- In a group, assign roles and rehearse.
- Create pacing by timing segments.
- Use lighting or staging to direct audience attention from one speaker to the next.

Videotape your broadcast, and then play it for the class. [**Group Activity**]

Research and Technology Using a historical atlas, draw a **map of the Roman Empire** in Ovid's time. On your map, trace the route that Ovid might have taken from Rome to his place of exile—on the site of present-day Constanta in Romania.

 **Take It to the Net** PHSchool.com

Go online for an additional research activity using the Internet.

Tacitus (A.D. 56–c. 120)

The worldview and the works of the Roman historian Publius Cornelius Tacitus (pub´ lē əs kôr nēl´ yəs tas´ ət əs) were shaped by the tumultuous era in which he lived. Nearly one hundred years before his birth, a long period of civil strife had brought an end to the Roman republic. In 27 B.C., Octavian, the grand-nephew and adopted son of Julius Caesar, had seized power as emperor, given himself the name "Augustus"—from a Latin word meaning "to increase"—and launched the Roman Empire.

Rubber-Stamp Senators The rule of Augustus was marked by a loss of liberty for his subjects. Senators merely rubber-stamped his decisions, and his displeasure could mean—as it did for the poet Ovid—perpetual exile, with no legal right of appeal. Nonetheless, Augustus was an able and sane leader, and under him the empire enjoyed relative peace and prosperity.

His immediate successors, however, form a parade of irresponsible, capricious individuals who managed the state poorly. Understandably, many Romans longed for the days when a dutiful citizen could play a role in governing the state.

A Survivor Tacitus not only survived the sometimes brief and always repressive reigns of more than half a dozen emperors but even managed to enjoy a successful public career as a brilliant trial lawyer and judge. He seems to have been able to do that by keeping his political views to himself and spending some of the most tumultuous years away from Rome, in a government office overseas.

When the vicious emperor Domitian died in A.D. 96 and was succeeded by more reasonable rulers, Tacitus returned to Rome. He then enjoyed a distinguished public career, first in Rome and later

in Asia. He was also finally able to turn his pen against the depraved rule of the emperors who immediately followed Augustus.

Influencing Future Opinion Through his incisive *Annals*, Tacitus has helped shape the world's opinion of Augustus' first four successors, particularly Nero, who is rumored to have sung while Rome burned. To be Nero's relative or close friend often marked one for an untimely death. It was his persecution of vulnerable groups like the early Christians, however, that earned him a lasting reputation for savagery.

The Dangers of Dynasty Tacitus' purpose in writing the *Annals* was to show how the four emperors who followed Augustus reduced Romans' freedoms. Rome's greatest historian did not object to strong leadership. He was distressed, however, by the way in which domination of the government by a single family, or dynasty, could deny power to men of ability.

Tacitus had planned to write about good emperors like Nerva and Trajan, and perhaps about Augustus as well, but the historian died before he could fulfill this goal. Perhaps he could not bring himself to turn his keen analytical gaze on good government for fear of having to recognize its imperfections.

Tacitus Today It is a tribute to Tacitus that after almost 2,000 years, historians still read his works to understand the beginnings of the Roman Empire. Yet they study his writings with a critical eye, knowing that he is not a completely objective observer. All readers, however, can appreciate the style of this ancient historian and his ability to portray vivid personalities and stirring events. You will see evidence of these talents in "The Burning of Rome."

Preview

Connecting to the Literature

You have probably seen news stories about disasters like fires, earthquakes, and floods. This selection tells about one of the greatest disasters of the ancient world: the fire that devastated Rome in A.D. 64.

Literary Analysis

Annals

Annals are histories that present a year-by-year account of events—the word *annus* is Latin for "year." In the *Annals*, for example, Tacitus records important events of the first century of the Roman Empire. Yet he also includes these elements:

- narratives of events or incidents
- vivid descriptions
- explanations of causes and effects

As you read, look for ways in which Tacitus uses narratives, descriptions, and explanations of causes and effects to go beyond a mere listing of events.

Connecting Literary Elements

Tacitus uses several types of **descriptive detail** to enhance his account—details that appeal to the senses, give a precise fact, or name something specific. One precise fact, for example, is the selling price of corn. This detail and others make the *Annals* more vivid and believable. Look for descriptive details as you read.

Reading Strategy

Recognize Author's Bias

If you **recognize the author's bias,** or point of view on details and events, you will be able to understand why he or she stresses certain facts or makes certain statements. Clues to bias include phrases or assertions with negative or positive associations. For example, in Tacitus' descriptions of Nero, words like *brutality* and suggestions of ambition and cruelty reflect the historian's negative opinion of the emperor. To uncover this bias, use a chart like the one shown.

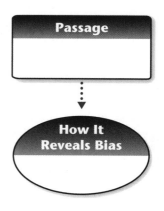

Vocabulary Development

conflagration (kän´ flə grā´ shən) *n.* large, destructive fire (p. 524)

unhampered (un ham´ pərd) *adv.* freely; without interference (p. 525)

destitute (des´ tə to͞ot´) *adj.* extremely poor (p. 526)

antiquity (an tik´ wə tē) *n.* early period of history (p. 526)

precipitous (prē sip´ ə təs) *adj.* steep like a precipice; sheer (p. 527)

demarcation (dē´ mär kā´ shən) *n.* boundary (p. 527)

munificence (myo͞o nif´ ə səns) *n.* great generosity (p. 529)

from the Annals

Tacitus *translated by* **Michael Grant**

Background

Nero became emperor of Rome—and potentially the most powerful person in the world—when he was just sixteen years old. The scheming of his mother, Agrippina, had cleared the way to the throne for him. As emperor, Nero at first enacted wise measures. Soon, however, he had both his mother and his wife put to death. He combined cruelty with artistic pretensions, shocking Romans by acting the parts of low-ranking characters on stage. By the time the great fire broke out ten years into his reign, Nero was so hated that many thought he had started the fire just to rebuild Rome as a monument to himself. Tacitus reports this popular belief in the *Annals*, but modern historians doubt the truth of this rumor.

The fire, which broke out in July, spread rapidly because summer winds fanned it and many Roman buildings were made of wood. A new, more splendid Rome of marble and stone was born from the ruins of this disaster.

from *The Burning of Rome*

Now started the most terrible and destructive fire which Rome had ever experienced. It began in the Circus,[1] where it adjoins the Palatine and Caelian hills.[2]

Breaking out in shops selling inflammable goods, and fanned by the wind, the <u>conflagration</u> instantly grew and swept the whole length of the Circus. There were no walled mansions or temples, or any other

conflagration (kän´ flə grā´ shən) *n.* large, destructive fire

Critical Viewing ▶
Which senses does this depiction of the burning of Rome engage, other than the sense of sight? Explain. [**Analyze**]

---

1. **Circus** (sur´ kəs) In ancient Rome, games and chariot races were held in the Circus, an oval arena surrounded by tiers of seats.
2. **Palatine** (pal´ ə tīn) **and Caelian** (kē´ lē ən) **hills** locations of Nero's imperial palaces.

obstructions, which could arrest it. First, the fire swept violently over the level spaces. Then it climbed the hills—but returned to ravage the lower ground again. It outstripped every counter-measure. The ancient city's narrow winding streets and irregular blocks encouraged its progress.

Terrified, shrieking women, helpless old and young, people intent on their own safety, people unselfishly supporting invalids or waiting for them, fugitives and lingerers alike—all heightened the confusion. When people looked back, menacing flames sprang up before them or out-flanked them. When they escaped to a neighboring quarter, the fire fol-lowed—even districts believed remote proved to be involved. Finally, with no idea where or what to flee, they crowded on to the country roads, or lay in the fields. Some who had lost everything—even their food for the day—could have escaped, but preferred to die. So did oth-ers, who had failed to rescue their loved ones. Nobody dared fight the flames. Attempts to do so were prevented by menacing gangs. Torches, too, were openly thrown in, by men crying that they acted under orders. Perhaps they had received orders. Or they may just have wanted to plunder <u>unhampered</u>.

unhampered (un ham´ pərd) *adv.* freely; without inter-ference

☑**Reading Check**

According to Tacitus, where did the fire begin?

The Burning of Rome, Hubert Robert, Giraudon

Nero was at Antium.[3] He only returned to the city when the fire was approaching the mansion he had built to link the Gardens of Maecenas to the Palatine. The flames could not be prevented from overwhelming the whole of the Palatine, including his palace. Nevertheless, for the relief of the homeless, fugitive masses he threw open the Field of Mars, including Agrippa's public buildings, and even his own Gardens. Nero also constructed emergency accommodation for the <u>destitute</u> multitude. Food was brought from Ostia[4] and neighboring towns, and the price of corn was cut to less than one quarter sesterce[5] a pound. Yet these measures, for all their popular character, earned no gratitude. For a rumor had spread that, while the city was burning, Nero had gone on his private stage and, comparing modern calamities with ancient, had sung of the destruction of Troy.

By the sixth day enormous demolitions had confronted the raging flames with bare ground and open sky, and the fire was finally stamped out at the foot of the Esquiline Hill. But before panic had subsided, or hope revived, flames broke out again in the more open regions of the city. Here there were fewer casualties; but the destruction of temples and pleasure arcades was even worse. This new conflagration caused additional ill-feeling because it started on Tigellinus' estate[6] in the Aemilian district. For people believed that Nero was ambitious to found a new city to be called after himself.

Of Rome's fourteen districts only four remained intact. Three were leveled to the ground. The other seven were reduced to a few scorched and mangled ruins. To count the mansions, blocks, and temples destroyed would be difficult. They included shrines of remote <u>antiquity</u>, such as Servius Tullius' temple of the Moon, the Great Altar and holy place dedicated by Evander to Hercules, the temple vowed by Romulus to Jupiter the Stayer, Numa's sacred residence, and Vesta's shrine containing Rome's household gods. Among the losses, too, were the precious spoils of countless victories, Greek artistic masterpieces, and authentic records of old Roman genius. All the splendor of the rebuilt city did not prevent the older generation from remembering these irreplaceable objects. It was noted that the fire had started on July 19th, the day on which the Senonian Gauls[7] had captured and burnt the city. Others elaborately calculated that the two fires were separated by the same number of years, months, and days.[8]

But Nero profited by his country's ruin to build a new palace. Its wonders were not so much customary and commonplace luxuries like gold and jewels, but lawns and lakes and faked rusticity—woods here,

▲ **Critical Viewing**
What impression of Nero do you think this sculpture is meant to convey? **[Infer]**

destitute (des´ tə tōōt´) *adj.* extremely poor

antiquity (an tik´ wə tə) *n.* early period of history

---

3. **Antium** (an´ tē əm) town in central Italy where Nero was born.
4. **Ostia** (äs´ tē ə) Roman port at the mouth of the Tiber River.
5. **sesterce** (ses´ tərs) Roman coin, equal in value to two and a half cents.
6. **Tigellinus' estate** (ti´ jə li´ nəs) land belonging to Tigellinus, second to Nero in power.
7. **Senonian Gauls** (sə nō´ nē ən gôlz) barbarians from Gaul, an ancient region in western Europe; they burned Rome in 390 B.C.
8. **the same number of years, months, and days** 418 years, 418 months, and 418 days.

open spaces and views there. With their cunning, impudent[9] artificialities, Nero's architects and engineers, Severus and Celer, did not balk at effects which Nature herself had ruled out as impossible.

They also fooled away an emperor's riches. For they promised to dig a navigable canal from Lake Avernus to the Tiber estuary,[10] over the stony shore and mountain barriers. The only water to feed the canal was in the Pontine marshes. Elsewhere, all was <u>precipitous</u> or waterless. Moreover, even if a passage could have been forced, the labor would have been unendurable and unjustified. But Nero was eager to perform the incredible; so he attempted to excavate the hills adjoining Lake Avernus. Traces of his frustrated hopes are visible today.

In parts of Rome unfilled by Nero's palace, construction was not—as after the burning by the Gauls—without plan or <u>demarcation</u>. Street-fronts were of regulated alignment, streets were broad, and houses built round courtyards. Their height was restricted, and their frontages protected by colonnades. Nero undertook to erect these at his own expense, and also to clear debris from building-sites before transferring them to their owners. He announced bonuses, in proportion to rank and resources, for the completion of houses and blocks before a given date. Rubbish was to be dumped in the Ostian marshes by corn-ships returning down the Tiber.

A fixed proportion of every building had to be massive, untimbered stone from Gabii[11] or Alba[12] (these stones being fireproof). Furthermore, guards were to ensure a more abundant and extensive public water-supply, hitherto diminished by irregular private enterprise. Householders were obliged to keep fire-fighting apparatus in an accessible place; and semi-detached houses were forbidden— they must have their own walls. These measures were welcomed for their practicality, and they beautified the new city. Some, however,

Literature
in context Science Connection

Roman Engineering

Tacitus refers to an expensive scheme "to dig a navigable canal." In this case, Tacitus is sarcastic, but Roman architects and engineers accomplished amazing feats, including the rebuilding of Rome after the fire. For example, they built about 50,000 miles of roads, some of which are still in use today. These carefully layered roads had a slight downward curve at the edges to facilitate drainage. Engineers also built many miles of aqueducts, "conduits for carrying water," to supply Rome and other cities. These aqueducts brought water from miles away and sometimes crossed over valleys on great stone arches.

Roman aqueduct

---

9. **impudent** (im´ pyo͞o dənt) *adj.* shamelessly bold and disrespectful.
10. **Tiber estuary** (tī´ bər es´ tyo͞o er ē) the wide mouth of the Tiber, a river in central Italy that flows south through Rome.
11. **Gabii** (gā´ bē ī´) ancient Roman town where Romulus, legendary founder of Rome, was reared. Gabii supposedly resisted a siege and was an important city until it was overshadowed by Rome.
12. **Alba** (äl´ bə) Alba Longa, a powerful ancient Roman city; legendary birthplace of Romulus and Remus.

precipitous (prē sip´ ə təs) *adj.* steep like a precipice; sheer

demarcation (dē´ mär kā´ shən) *n.* boundary

**Reading Check**

In what way did Nero profit from the fire, according to Tacitus?

believed that the old town's configuration had been healthier, since its narrow streets and high houses had provided protection against the burning sun, whereas now the shadowless open spaces radiated a fiercer heat.

So much for human precautions. Next came attempts to appease heaven. After consultation of the Sibylline books,[13] prayers were addressed to Vulcan, Ceres, and Proserpina. Juno, too, was propitiated.[14] Women who had been married were responsible for the rites—first on the Capitol, then at the nearest sea-board, where water was taken to sprinkle her temple and statue. Women with husbands living also celebrated ritual banquets and vigils.

---

13. **Sibylline** (sib′ ə lin) **books** books of prophecies by Sibyl, Apollo's priestess at Cumae, a city in southwest Italy near Naples.
14. **propitiated** (prō pish′ ē āt′ id) v. appeased.

▼ **Critical Viewing**
Compare and contrast this artist's rendering of Rome with Tacitus' description of the city. **[Compare and Contrast]**

But neither human resources, nor imperial <u>munificence</u>, nor appeasement of the gods, eliminated sinister suspicions that the fire had been instigated. To suppress this rumor, Nero fabricated scapegoats—and punished with every refinement the notoriously depraved Christians (as they were popularly called). Their originator, Christ, had been executed in Tiberius' reign[15] by the governor of Judaea,[16] Pontius Pilatus. But in spite of this temporary setback the deadly superstition had broken out afresh, not only in Judaea (where the mischief had started) but even in Rome. All degraded and shameful practices collect and flourish in the capital.

First, Nero had self-acknowledged Christians arrested. Then, on their information, large numbers of others were condemned—not so much for incendiarism[17] as for their anti-social tendencies. Their deaths were made farcical. Dressed in wild animals' skins, they were torn to pieces by dogs, or crucified, or made into torches to be ignited after dark as substitutes for daylight. Nero provided his Gardens for the spectacle, and exhibited displays in the Circus, at which he mingled with the crowd—or stood in a chariot, dressed as a charioteer. Despite their guilt as Christians, and the ruthless punishment it deserved, the victims were pitied. For it was felt that they were being sacrificed to one man's brutality rather than to the national interest.

Meanwhile Italy was ransacked for funds, and the provinces were ruined—unprivileged and privileged communities alike. Even the gods were included in the looting. Temples at Rome were robbed, and emptied of the gold dedicated for the triumphs and vows, the ambitions and fears, of generations of Romans. Plunder from Asia and Greece included not only offerings but actual statues of the gods. Two agents were sent to these provinces. One, Acratus, was an ex-slave, capable of any depravity. The other, Secundus Carrinas, professed Greek culture, but no virtue from it percolated to his heart.

Seneca,[18] rumor went, sought to avoid the odium of this sacrilege by asking leave to retire to a distant country retreat, and then—permission being refused—feigning a muscular complaint and keeping to his bedroom. According to some accounts one of his former slaves, Cleonicus by name, acting on Nero's orders intended to poison Seneca but he escaped—either because the man confessed or because Seneca's own fears caused him to live very simply on plain fruit, quenching his thirst with running water.

At this juncture there was an attempted break-out by gladiators at Praeneste.[19] Their army guards overpowered them. But the Roman public, as always terrified (or fascinated) by revolution, were already talking of ancient calamities such as the rising of Spartacus.[20] Soon

---

15. **Tiberius'** (tī bir´ ē əs) **reign** Tiberius was emperor of Rome A.D. 14–37.
16. **Judaea** (jōō dē´ ə) ancient region of South Palestine.
17. **incendiarism** (in sen´ dē ə riz´ əm) *n.* willful destruction of property by fire.
18. **Seneca** (sen´ ə kə) philosopher and minister of Nero.
19. **Praeneste** (prī nest´) town in central Italy.
20. **Spartacus** (spärt´ ə kəs) ancient Thracian slave and gladiator who led a slave revolt.

munificence (myoō nif´ ə səns) *n.* great generosity

Literary Analysis
Annals According to Tacitus, what chain of causes and effects links the fire to the persecution of Christians?

Reading Strategy
Recognizing Author's Bias How does the implied contrast of Seneca's actions with Nero's reveal Tacitus' bias against Nero?

✔**Reading Check**
According to Tacitus, what group of people were Nero's "fabricated scapegoats"?

afterwards a naval disaster occurred. This was not on active service; never had there been such profound peace. But Nero had ordered the fleet to return to Campania by a fixed date regardless of weather. So, despite heavy seas the steersmen started from Formiae. But when they tried to round Cape Misenum a south-westerly gale drove them ashore near Cumae and destroyed numerous warships and smaller craft.

As the year ended omens of impending misfortune were widely rumored—unprecedentedly frequent lightning; a comet (atoned for by Nero, as usual, by aristocratic blood); two-headed offspring of men and beasts, thrown into the streets or discovered among the offerings to those deities to whom pregnant victims are sacrificed. Near Placentia a calf was born beside the road with its head fastened to one of its legs. Soothsayers deduced that a new head was being prepared for the world—but that it would be neither powerful nor secret since it had been deformed in the womb and given birth by the roadside.

Review and Assess

Thinking About the Selection

1. **Respond:** Based on this account, what is your reaction to the emperor Nero? Why?

2. **(a) Recall:** In what part of Rome did the fire first break out? **(b) Analyze:** In what way did the city's layout encourage the fire's progress?

3. **(a) Recall:** What are two ways in which Nero tried to help people during the fire? **(b) Interpret:** What does the people's reaction to Nero's help suggest about his reputation as their leader? Explain.

4. **(a) Recall:** What are three regulations that were part of Nero's plan to rebuild the city? **(b) Evaluate:** Do these regulations make sense? Why or why not?

5. **(a) Recall:** Why did Nero turn against the Christians? **(b) Interpret:** Why do you think people felt the Christians "were being sacrificed to one man's brutality rather than to the national interest"?

6. **(a) Recall:** What are two "omens" that Tacitus mentions in the final paragraph? **(b) Connect:** What is the relationship between these omens and the account of the fire?

7. **Evaluate:** What are two details in this account that a modern historian might praise and two details that he or she might criticize? Explain.

Review and Assess

Literary Analysis

Annals

1. On the right side of a chart like the one shown, give an example from the selection for each element of an **annal** listed on the left.

Elements of an Annal	Examples From the Annals of Tacitus
review of a year's important events	
explanation of cause-effect relationships	
vivid descriptions	

2. Do the *Annals* follow a chronological sequence? Why or why not?
3. To what extent does Tacitus report verified facts and to what extent does he report rumors? Explain.
4. (a) What are three sources that a modern annals writer could use? (b) Explain the type of information available from each.

Connecting Literary Elements

5. Give an example of each type of **descriptive detail** in the *Annals*: precise fact, specific name, and detail that appeals to the senses.
6. What does each type of detail add to the account of the year's events?

Reading Strategy

Recognizing Author's Bias

7. You can **recognize the author's bias** by analyzing both positive and negative statements about Nero. (a) Which type of statement tends to come at the end of a paragraph? (b) What is the effect of this pattern of placement?
8. What are two examples in which Tacitus, rather than criticizing Nero directly, allows the voice of public opinion to criticize him?
9. What are two phrases that reveal Tacitus' attitude toward Christianity? Explain.

Extend Understanding

10. **Media Connection:** Do you think that today's newspaper or television reporters ever reveal a bias as Tacitus does? Why or why not?

Integrate Language Skills

Vocabulary Development Lesson

Word Analysis: Latin Suffix *-tion*

The Latin suffix *-tion* forms nouns that indicate the action, state, or quality of something. The word *conflagration*, for example, means "the act of burning"—the Latin *conflagare* means "to burn."

Use your understanding of the suffix *-tion* to define each of the following words. If necessary, check the definition of the root in a dictionary. Then, use each word in an original sentence.

1. conflagration
2. demarcation
3. medication
4. definition
5. alteration
6. attrition

Concept Development: Synonyms

Identify the letter of the word or phrase that is closest in meaning to each numbered word below.

1. conflagration   a. steep
2. unhampered   b. generosity
3. destitute   c. early era
4. antiquity   d. large fire
5. precipitous   e. boundary
6. demarcation   f. very poor
7. munificence   g. not impeded

Spelling Strategy

The suffix *-ity* is more common than *-ety*, which often follows the letter *i*. Complete each word below with the correct suffix.

1. calam___   2. lev___   3. vari___

Grammar and Style Lesson

Commonly Confused Words: *less* and *fewer*

Use the word *less* with qualities or amounts that cannot be counted. It modifies a singular noun and answers the question "How much?"

It takes *less* time to start a conflagration than it does to extinguish it.

Use the word *fewer* with objects that can be counted. It modifies a plural noun and answers the question "How many?"

Here there were *fewer* casualties; but the destruction of temples and pleasure arcades was even worse.

Practice In your notebook, complete each sentence below by inserting *fewer* or *less*.

1. Does this selection contain ___?___ details than you expected?
2. Tacitus had ___?___ admiration for the empire than for the republic.
3. No ___?___ than ten of Rome's fourteen districts were destroyed by the fire.
4. The fire caused ___?___ damage on the seventh day than on the fifth.
5. There was ___?___ wealth in the provinces after Nero's agents visited them.

Writing Application Write a paragraph to describe Rome's building laws after the fire. Use the words *less* and *fewer* at least once each.

WG Prentice Hall Writing and Grammar Connection: Diamond Level, Chapter 25, Section 2

Writing Lesson

Eyewitness Narrative Essay

People enjoy reading reports of events by those who witnessed them. Such eyewitness accounts often contain vivid details and convey the excitement of firsthand impressions. Using the *Annals* as a model, write an eyewitness narrative essay about an event that you have witnessed.

Prewriting After choosing an exciting event that you have witnessed, freewrite to gather details about it. Review what you have written. Next, arrange your details in chronological order.

Drafting Begin with an introduction that creates the proper mood and provides necessary background information. Then, tell what happened in chronological order, including descriptive details that appeal to the senses.

Revising Reread your draft. Add transitions where necessary—words like *then*, *next*, *first*, *before*, *during*, *while*, and *after*—to clarify the sequence of events.

Model: Adding Transitions to Clarify the Sequence of Events

First,
Coach Donaldson welcomed everyone to the pep

Then,
rally. As each player's name was called, the player

stood up to the accompaniment of the band.

> Time transitions clarify the sequence of events.

WG Prentice Hall Writing and Grammar Connection: Diamond Level, Chapter 9, Section 4

Extension Activities

Listening and Speaking With a small group, develop a **skit,** or brief dramatic scene, in which a group of Romans gossip about the fire. Consider these tips:

- Include historical details from the *Annals*.
- Have characters express the concerns of their social class and occupation.
- In rehearsals, allow actors to improvise, and include improvised dialogue in the script.

Present your skit to the class. **[Group Activity]**

Research and Technology Use library and Internet resources to create an **illustrated timeline of Roman history** during the first century A.D. Include a portrait of each emperor and illustrations for each major event, like the fire of A.D. 64.

 **Take It to the Net** PHSchool.com

Go online for an additional research activity using the Internet.

Writing About Literature

Analyze Literary Themes

The ancient Greek writers whose works appear in this unit speak to the modern era across great expanses of time, revealing not only their individual points of view but also the values that drove their culture. One such value was the importance of citizenship—the idea that the individual owes certain obligations to the community. Use the assignment outlined in the yellow box to analyze the concept of citizenship as the ancient Greeks saw it.

Prewriting

Review the material. Review each selection in the unit, gathering details relevant to the theme of citizenship. These questions can help you identify useful information:

- Which qualities does the author praise in his fellow citizens?
- How does the author see his fellow citizens in comparison with people in the rest of the world?
- How does the author describe what he or another citizen has done for the good of society?
- How does the author criticize citizens who do not live up to their obligations?

As you review the material, note any especially clear or compelling passages that you may want to use as quotations in your essay.

Find a focus. Use a chart like the one below to organize the details you have gathered. As you work, note both similarities and differences in the authors' positions.

Assignment:
The Citizen and Society

Write an analytical essay that explores the ancient Greek perspective on citizenship as it is expressed in the works in this unit.

Criteria:
- Include an explanation of each writer's position on the theme of citizenship.
- Include a thesis statement that states your main idea.
- Support your ideas with examples from the selections.
- Approximate length: 1,500 words

Read to Write

As you reread the selections, note direct statements, but also draw inferences—make informed guesses—about each author's position on the topic.

Model: Charting to Find a Focus

Title	Point #1	Point #2	Point #3
Pericles' Funeral Oration	Obey the laws and those in authority.	Show courage and loyalty in times of war.	Get involved in affairs of the state.

Identify beliefs about citizenship that these writers share and that may express a typical Greek point of view. Write a sentence expressing this idea. This sentence will be the focus of your essay—your working thesis statement. Remember that you can modify your thesis as you draft and revise.

Drafting

Write an outline. Prepare an outline like the one shown below to plan the logical progression of your ideas and to identify the best placement of supporting details.

> **Model: Constructing an Outline**
>
> **Thesis:** Greek culture valued citizens who worked selflessly for the good of their community.
>
> I. Socrates is a citizen who devotes himself to the public good.
>
>   A.   Socrates refuses to accept money.
>
>   B.   Socrates will not stop his work, even though it means he will be executed.
>
> II. In *Oedipus the King,* Sophocles shows that the king's personal welfare is less important than the common good.

Write a memorable conclusion. The most effective essays end with a strong, memorable paragraph. For this assignment, end by presenting a final thought that ties your analysis together. For example, you might make a statement that emphasizes the relevance of ancient Greek values and ideas to the modern world.

Revising and Editing

Review content: Revise to support ideas with details. Ensure that each point you make about the theme of citizenship is supported with details from at least one of the selections. Underline main ideas in your essay, and make sure that each one is supported. Add more proof as needed.

Review style: Revise to improve word choice. Be sure that you know the meanings of all the words you have used and that you have used the words accurately. Note whether you have repeated certain words, such as *citizenship* or *theme*, too often. Your essay will be more effective if you carefully edit to avoid such word-choice problems.

Publishing and Presenting

Hold a panel discussion. Begin by having each participant present a summary version of his or her essay on the Greek concept of citizenship. After each student has spoken, hold a panel discussion on the relevance of Greek ideas about citizenship to today's world. One student should act as the moderator and call for questions from the audience.

Write to Learn

As you write, you may change your mind or discover a surprising idea. Allow for such changes in opinion; recognize that the writing process can give you a new perspective on a topic.

Write to Explain

You need clear, specific details from the selections—including quotations, where appropriate—to support your points. Vague references will not get the job done.

Prentice Hall Writing and Grammar Connection: Diamond Level, Chapter 9

Writing WORKSHOP

Exposition: Problem-and-Solution Essay

A **problem-and-solution essay** identifies and explains a problem and then offers one or more solutions. In this workshop, you will plan, draft, and revise a problem-and-solution essay.

Assignment Criteria Your problem-and-solution essay should feature the following elements:

- A clear statement of a problem and its significance
- A presentation and an evaluation of one or more solutions to the problem
- Precise details and relevant examples
- A logical and effective organization
- An effective ending

To preview the criteria on which your problem-and-solution essay may be assessed, refer to the Rubric on page 539.

Prewriting

Choose a topic. Write your problem-and-solution essay about a consumer, community, or social issue that interests you. To find a topic, **scan a newspaper** and highlight news stories that intrigue you. Then, list the topics you highlighted. Review your list to select the most interesting problem for which you can provide a solution.

Topic List

Problem	Ideas
car accidents at dangerous intersection	Yes
inequities in campaign spending	No
injuries during soccer games	Yes
too little time to write college applications	Yes

Analyze your audience. As you write your problem-and-solution essay, keep a specific audience in mind: readers who can implement your solutions. Ask yourself these questions to tailor your essay to your audience:

- Who is my audience?
- What does my audience already know about my topic?
- What information do I need to provide?
- How can I convince my audience that this problem is important?

Brainstorm for solutions. List all the possible solutions to the problem that you can possibly generate. To develop more solutions, exchange ideas with a fellow student, friend, or family member who is familiar with the problem. Then, rank the solutions in order from least to most viable. Eliminate solutions that seem unworkable or unconvincing.

Student Model

Before you begin writing, read this student model and review the characteristics of an effective problem-and-solution essay.

Andrew Hutchinson
Redwood City, California

Too Little Time, Too Many College Applications

The process of applying to college is extremely time consuming. If you are like most students, you are already busy with clubs, sports, volunteer work, or a job, plus you have to study, walk the dog, set the table, keep up with certain TV shows, and talk online with your friends. You seem to have hardly any time at all, and the mere thought of these applications can make you feel "stressed out." In fact, a study by Reuters [http://www.intelihealth.com, 27 Oct. 1999] reports that one third of American teens feel stressed out on a daily basis. The competition to get into college is one major reason for this. However, there are steps you can take to make this process less time-consuming and stressful.

If you feel overwhelmed, take one step at a time. Mary Pilat of Purdue University notes that if you set reasonable goals, you will have less stress [http://www .ces.purdue.edu/Living_on_Less/Pubs/FF-37.html]. To set reasonable goals, break the application process down into small steps, as follows:

Step 1: Get copies of the applications. Forms are usually available online, or you can call the colleges and have them send you copies. Estimated time: 30 minutes.

Step 2: Read the forms and make a list of special information they require. Estimated time: 45 minutes.

Step 3: Gather missing information. You may need to provide names, addresses, years of participation, etc. Estimated time: 30 minutes.

Step 4: Fill out the forms. Estimated time: 2 hours

If the thought of writing the essay causes you to panic, do it in stages. The essay is usually the most time-consuming task. To do it well, you need a solid block of thinking time, but you can do that in steps, too. First, determine the kind of essay the college wants and then think about it during free minutes. Make some notes and let the ideas grow. Then, set aside an hour on one day to write a draft and an hour on another day to revise it.

If you are always too busy, find hidden pockets of time. If you rearrange your priorities, you can open up spaces of time for working on your application. For instance, instead of spending a full hour chatting online, spend a half hour. Watch less TV. Use a spare hour on the weekend just for your applications.

By planning ahead, taking one step at a time, and finding ways to make time, you will reduce the stress and hassle of filling out your college applications. You might find that time management is a better way of organizing everything in your life. What are you waiting for? The clock is ticking!

Andrew clearly appeals to his audience—students who are feeling pinched for time.

Andrew supports his claim that the problem is widespread.

This logical point-by-point form of organization, with main points emphasized by subheads, is effective in a problem-and-solution essay.

Andrew provides information, such as estimated times, to make his solutions both clear and useful.

Andrew uses his conclusion to summarize his main points and to end on an upbeat note.

Drafting

Choose an organization. To help readers understand the problem you have tackled and the solutions you provide, you need to present information in a clear, organized manner. Review the following forms of organization, and decide which will be the most effective for the problem you have chosen.

- **Point-by-Point:** Using this organizational strategy, a writer breaks the main problem down into an array of smaller problems and then addresses each one, point by point, offering small-scale solutions.

- **Block:** The writer lays out the problem as a whole and then proposes a comprehensive solution.

Provide evidence. Support all statements with precise details, examples, facts, statistics, and other documentation that will persuade your audience of the legitimacy of the problem and the soundness of your solution. Use a chart like the one shown to guide your selection of evidence.

Include an effective ending. Make sure your essay has a strong ending. You may want to restate the problem and solution, or you may conclude with a statement about the urgency of the problem. A final anecdote can also be a strong, memorable way to end an essay.

Collect Types of Evidence

Type of Evidence	
Fact	Applications are available online.
Statistics	One third of American teens feel "stressed out" every day.
Anecdote	I face this challenge myself.
Expert Testimony	Mary Pilat's points about handling stress

Revising

Revise to strengthen support. Look in your essay for ideas with which critics might disagree, and answer their likely objections. A few common objections are listed below, along with strategies you might use to respond to them. Use these strategies to guide your revision.

- **Why should I care?** Include information to demonstrate how the problem affects your audience.

- **Why should I help?** Persuade readers that their participation is crucial to solving the problem.

- **The solution is too difficult.** Convince readers that the solution is not as difficult as it may seem.

Model: Strengthen Your Support

In fact, a study by Reuters [http://www.intelihealth.com, 27 Oct.1999] reports that one third of American teens feel stressed out on a daily basis.

You seem to have hardly any time at all, and the mere thought of these applications can make you feel "stressed out."

Andrew added documented evidence to support his point.

Revise for word choice. Review your draft as if you were a member of your intended audience. Circle terms or ideas that you need to define or vocabulary words that seem inappropriate for your readers. For example, in the following passage, the word *hybridization* is defined for a general audience.

Without definition: The plants feature a genetic *hybridization* that modifies their color.

With definition: The plants feature a genetic *hybridization*, or blending, that modifies their color.

Compare the model and the nonmodel. Why is the model more effective?

Nonmodel	Model
If you are like most students, you are already really busy.	If you are like most students, you are already busy with clubs, sports, volunteer work, or a job, plus you have to study, walk the dog, set the table, keep up with certain TV shows, and talk online with your friends.

Publishing and Presenting

Consider the following activity to share your writing with classmates or a wider audience.

Deliver an oral presentation. Read your problem-and-solution essay aloud to your class. When you have finished, invite comments and questions. Determine whether or not your classmates are convinced that your solution is the best way to address the problem.

 Prentice Hall Writing and Grammar Connection: Diamond Level, Chapter 11

Rubric for Self-Assessment

Use the following criteria and rating scale to evaluate your problem-and-solution essay:

Criteria	Rating Scale				
	Not very				Very
How clearly stated is the problem and its importance?	1	2	3	4	5
Have I clearly defined and used language suited to the intended audience?	1	2	3	4	5
How effective are the facts, details, examples, and statistics in illustrating the problem and suggesting a solution?	1	2	3	4	5
Is the organization logical and consistent?	1	2	3	4	5
Is the conclusion effective?	1	2	3	4	5

Listening and Speaking WORKSHOP

Listening to Speeches

Imagine being in the audience when the orations you read in this unit were delivered. To fully appreciate them, you would need to do more than just sit there; you would need to listen effectively. Effective listening involves two parts—preparation and analysis.

Prepare to Listen

To prepare to listen to a speech, use the following guidelines:

- **Identify cultural context.** In addition to expressing an individual's point of view, speeches also express a cultural context—the values, traditions, beliefs, and assumptions of the culture that produced them. To get the most out of a presentation from another culture, determine its cultural context. If you understand the underlying values and beliefs, you will be able to listen more effectively.

- **Connect to personal knowledge and experience.** Your own life experience and knowledge are great resources for effective listening. To prepare to listen to a speech, learn what topics it will cover and think about your own knowledge of and experience with those subjects.

Analyze What You Have Heard

After you listen to a speech, follow these steps to analyze the information and attitudes conveyed:

- Summarize the main ideas, and identify supporting details.
- Note key facts that you found persuasive.
- Note statements that reveal the speaker's values.
- Note any words that were especially effective.
- Note visual aids that were used and whether or not they were effective.
- Decide whether you agree with the speech as a whole, in part, or not at all.
- Ask additional questions to gain further understanding.

Activity: Analyzing an Oration In small groups, deliver and analyze orations from the unit. One member of the group should rehearse and present one of the orations. The others should prepare to listen and then analyze the presentation. Use the Feedback Form shown above to focus your preparation and analysis.

Feedback Form for Listening to Speeches

Preparation:
What is the cultural context of the speech? _____
What is the subject of the speech? _____
What personal knowledge do you have of the subject? _____

Analysis:
Note the main idea: _____
Note three supporting details or points:
    1. Persuasive facts: _____
    2. Speaker's values: _____
    3. Effective words: _____
What visual aids, if any, are being used? _____

Response:
1. What were the most persuasive elements of the speech? _____
2. If visual aids were used, were they effective? _____
3. Do you agree or disagree with the speaker? _____ Why? _____

Assessment WORKSHOP

Inferences and Generalizations

In the reading sections of some tests, you are often required to read a passage of fiction and draw inferences and make generalizations about the plot, setting, characters, and mood. The following strategies will help you answer such test questions:

- Remember that to infer is to read between the lines, recognizing the implied message of a passage.
- Look in the passage for clues about the characters, setting, plot, and mood.
- Identify significant word choices, patterns of events, and other clues that can help you understand the writer's implied message.

Test-Taking Strategies

- Before answering questions, review the passage and highlight the main points.
- Look for descriptive details to help you make inferences about character, setting, plot, and mood.

Sample Test Item

Directions: Read the passage, and then answer the question that follows.

Penelope tried to scoot out the front door, but it closed too quickly. It was spring, and that meant it was time to chase squirrels and roll in puddles of sunshine. She had spent most of the winter in the house where she was warm and coddled, but fresh air and the thrill of the hunt beckoned now. She wound herself around Jenna's ankles and glanced at the door, but her efforts prompted no response.

1. In this passage, Penelope can best be described as

   A a stubborn child.

   B a frightened squirrel.

   C an impatient cat.

   D an eager student.

Answer and Explanation

The correct answer is *C*. Penelope's desire to chase squirrels, her reference to the "thrill of the hunt," and her ability to wind around Jenna's ankles suggest the behavior of a cat. The clues in the passage do not suggest a child, a squirrel, or a student, so the remaining answers are incorrect.

▷ Practice

Directions: Read the passage, and then answer the questions that follow.

If his parents had their way, David would buy the most sensible car on the lot. But he had other ideas in mind. He was done driving the family car. He wanted something new, something splashy that would make heads turn. He was a working man now, and it was high time he owned his own car. When David saw the metallic blue sports model in the corner of the lot, he knew he had found the perfect set of wheels.

1. Which of the following inferences about the family car does the passage support?

   A It is sporty and fast.

   B It is conservative and slow.

   C It was very expensive.

   D It is a metallic blue.

2. Which of the following most accurately describes David?

   A headstrong

   B cautious

   C lucky

   D hesitant

The Middle Ages

The Lady and the Unicorn

**"*Where there is
peace and meditation,
there is neither
anxiety nor doubt.*"**

— St. Francis of Assisi,
from *The Counsels of St. Francis*

Timeline A.D. 450–1300

European Events

- **476** The Western Roman Empire ceases to exist.
- **476–750** Merovingian kings rule the Franks.
- **511** Merovingian King Clovis dies; he was the first important Catholic king.
- **597** Roman cleric Saint Augustine converts English King Ethelbert to Christianity.
- **700** This is the earliest possible date for the composition of the English epic *Beowulf*. ◄

- **711** The Moors invade Spain.
- **732** Charles Martel defeats the Moors at the Battle of Tours.
- **778** Charlemagne crosses the Pyrenees to fight the Moors in Spain.
- **800** Charlemagne is crowned Holy Roman Emperor by Pope Leo III.
- **mid-800s** Latin books are written using the style called Carolingian minuscule.
- **800s** Vikings begin to raid and settle in Europe. ▼

World Events

- **400s and 500s (India)** Using the concept of zero, mathematicians develop decimals.
- **c. 400 (Middle East)** Jews compile religious teachings called the Palestinian Talmud.
- **500s (India)** The game of chess is invented.
- **618–907 (China)** The T'ang dynasty rules.
- **622 (Middle East)** Muhammad journeys from Mecca to Yathrib, an event that marks the rise of Islam.
- **600s (Africa)** Islam spreads to North Africa.
- **c. 600s (Tibet)** Buddhism begins to take hold.

- **early 700s (Japan)** The first works of Japanese prose appear.
- **700s (Japan)** "Collection of Ten Thousand Leaves," an early poetry anthology, appears.
- **762–763 (Middle East)** Baghdad is founded as the new capital of the Abassid dynasty.
- **794 (Japan)** A new imperial capital is built at Heian (Kyoto).
- **800 (New Zealand)** This is the earliest known date for habitations of the Polynesian people known as the Maori. ►
- **813–833 (Middle East)** Science and scholarship thrive during Ma'mun's reign (Abassid dynasty).
- **c. 850 (Africa)** The trading empire of Kanem-Bornu is founded.

European and World Events

- **900s** The game of chess is introduced into Europe. ▼

- **1000s** Serious efforts begin to drive the Moors from Spain.

- **1043–1099** Rodrigo Díaz de Vivar, Spain's national hero, lives and battles the Moors.

- **1066** William the Conqueror successfully invades England.

- **1095** Pope Urban II urges a crusade to retake the Holy Land from Muslims.

- **1099** Crusaders retake Jerusalem from Muslims.

- **1100s** Use of windmills starts to spread.

- **1100s** Society experiences a rebirth; the Gothic style develops.

- **1122–1204** Eleanor of Aquitane, the most influential woman of her time, lives.

- **1215** King John of England signs the Magna Carta, limiting royal power. ▲

- **mid-1200s** Eyeglasses are in use.

- **1300** Universities exist in a number of European cities.

- **early 1300s** Dante, exiled from Florence, writes the *Divine Comedy*.

- **1300s** Paper mills exist in Europe.

- **c. 900 (Mexico/Central America)** Classic period of Mayan culture ends.

- **c. 1000 (Japan)** Lady Murasaki Shikibu writes *The Tale of Genji*.

- **c. 1020 (Persia)** The poet Firdawsi, author of the *Book of Kings*, dies.

- **1048–1131 (Persia)** Omar Khayyam—poet, mathematician, and astronomer—lives.

- **1100 (Africa)** The city of Timbuktu is founded in West Africa.

- **c. 1100s (Mexico/Central America)** The Aztecs first appear.

- **1187 (Middle East)** Jerusalem is again under Islamic control. ▼

The Middle Ages

(A.D. 450–1300)

Historical Background

From the Fall of Rome to the Renaissance Scholars usually refer to the historical period between approximately A.D. 450 and 1300 as the Middle Ages—but why is this considered a "middle" period? The Middle Ages may be seen as a historical filling, sandwiched between the Latin civilization of the Roman Empire and the later rediscovery of the classical civilizations of Greece and Rome in the Renaissance.

The dates of the Middle Ages are somewhat arbitrary. The fifth century, a period marked by the rapid decay of those institutions that held the Roman Empire together, is the beginning of this period: Rome was sacked by the Visigoths, a Germanic tribe, in 410 and the western part of the empire ceased to exist in 476. The end of the Middle Ages, however, is more complex an issue. The Renaissance began in the south of Europe. In Italy, the early fourteenth century brought the rediscovery of classical forms in art and architecture, together with the production of new editions of classical literature. In northern Europe, however, such innovations did not occur until the end of the fifteenth century.

A New European Structure In the third century A.D., Rome was master of most of Europe. The empire extended from England in the north to Africa in the south and from Portugal in the west to Syria in the east. Ultimately, this territory was far too large to administer, both politically and militarily. The Roman Empire was then divided into two distinct empires, with the emperor of the West ruling from Rome and the emperor of the East ruling from Constantinople (now Istanbul, Turkey).

For some time, the northern frontiers of the empire had been experiencing pressure from several Germanic tribes. The northern border, however, had generally remained secure. Then, a population explosion among these tribes triggered a need for expansion. This need for more territory, coupled with the tribes' warlike disposition, provoked what is sometimes called the "barbarian invasions." In reality, the incursion of the Germanic tribes into Roman territory more accurately resembled a mass migration sometimes marked by hostilities. Germanic historians, sensitive about using the word "invasion," called this period in history the *Volkerwanderung*—the wandering of the peoples.

▼ **Critical Viewing**
What does this statue of a Roman soldier suggest about the values of the Roman Empire? Explain. **[Infer]**

Close-up on Culture

The Code of Chivalry

Superheroes who defend the weak are today's knights, following the code of chivalry first developed in the Middle Ages.

The chivalric code evolved slowly out of the feudal system. Under this system, the king granted land to his lords, or vassals, so that they could afford to maintain mounted troops. Each lord, therefore, had a group of loyal knights ready to serve him in battle at a moment's notice.

Knights were experienced horsemen. They were also experienced in the use and repair of elaborate metal armor and of weapons such as lances, long wooden shafts tipped with iron or steel; maces, heavy clublike weapons with metal spikes at the end; and double-edged broadswords, about three feet long but weighing only a few pounds.

Equally important as these weapons, however, was the code of chivalry that dictated their use. A knight's loyalty to his lord was crucial, as was the obligation to defend those weaker than himself, especially women. Knights also offered their services to the greater glory of God. The Crusades, campaigns to retake Jerusalem and the Holy Land from Muslims, were opportunities for knights to fight for their most powerful lord, God himself.

The code of chivalry was impossibly idealistic. Yet the view of the perfect knight offered by medieval literature softened a brutal feudal system based on warlike qualities. Eventually, however, knights became less effective in warfare. In various fourteenth-century battles, French knights were like tin cans on horseback, easy targets for English archers with longbows.

Nevertheless, the code of chivalry has survived its armored adherents. It is still practiced by Batman and Spiderman, and it lives every time a man treats a woman with courtesy and respect.

▲ Critical Viewing
This weapon is a spiked mace. What does it indicate about the importance of armor to a knight? Why? **[Infer]**

The Germanic Contribution Hardly a portion of the old Western Roman Empire was left untouched by the various Germanic tribes: Lombards, Visigoths, and Ostrogoths settled in Italy; Visigoths, in southern France and Spain; Franks, in northern France; Angles and Saxons, in England. The presence of these peoples radically changed the political structure of what had been, until then, a unified empire. As these tribes began to dominate the land in which they settled, they established individual kingdoms, ending Roman rule once and for all.

The Birth of Feudalism These tribes also helped shape the feudal system that spread through medieval Europe. The act of vassalage, in which one lord swears allegiance to another in exchange for privileges or "feuds," originated in tribal organization. The concepts of kingship, knighthood, and chivalry all emerged from these Germanic peoples. (See Close-up on Culture, above.) After settling in the empire, Germanic tribes were quickly converted to Christianity, which had become the empire's official religion during the fourth century A.D. Because of this religious conversion, their political institutions were also Christianized. With their adoption of Roman religion, they also adopted Latin, the official language of the Western Church, as their language. Many linguists believe that the Romance languages descended from Latin—such as French, Spanish, Portuguese, Italian, and Romanian—owe their modern differences to the various Germanic tribes that learned Latin in an imperfect manner. Many words of Germanic origin, especially those relating to warfare and feudalism, still exist in these languages.

Feudalism and Peasants The feudal system did not involve only lords and knights. It also spelled out the duties of poor farmers known as peasants. They lived on a lord's manor—a village and its surrounding fields—and owed service to the lord in exchange for protection. Usually, they were not free to leave the land. They contributed to the manor by raising sheep and cattle and growing grain and vegetables. Their self-sufficient community often included a mill, a blacksmith shop, and a church.

The Moors Threaten Europe In A.D. 711, the Muslims, or Moors, inspired by their successful subjugation of the Middle East and North Africa, swept into Spain and quickly conquered all but a few mountain strongholds. The Muslim advance into Europe's heartland was not stopped until A.D. 732, when Charles Martel (mär tel´), "the Hammer," defeated the Moors at the Battle of Tours, in central France. The struggle between Christianity and Islam became one of the most important conflicts in medieval Europe.

A New Stability: The Reemergence of Learning On December 25, A.D. 800, Charles I, King of the Franks, also known as Charles the Great or Charlemagne (shär´ lə mān´), was crowned Holy Roman Emperor by Pope Leo III. (For the size of this empire four hundred years later, see the map on page 549.) This event represents the complete integration of the Germanic peoples into the mainstream of European society. In addition, the use of a title and an office linked to the traditions of the ancient Roman Empire was an attempt at creating a new unified political order. This action revealed a need and willingness to revive some kind of historical continuity, and there is little doubt that at this time Europe needed all the unity it could muster.

A Crusade Having contained the Islamic threat in Europe, the Christian rulers of Europe turned their eyes to the Holy Land. This Middle Eastern region, located in what is now Jordan and Israel, was at that time a Muslim stronghold. Its sacred associations, however, made it "holy" for Jews and Christians as well. In 1095, Pope Urban II preached a sermon in Clermont, France, urging European knights to participate in a crusade that would win back the Holy Land.

▼ **Critical Viewing** These images from an illuminated manuscript show scenes from the life of Charlemagne. The upper picture, for example, shows him being crowned. Which details in this scene suggest a close association between religious and political power? Explain. **[Interpret]**

Europe in the 13th Century

NORWAY
Oslo
Upsala
SWEDEN
ESTHONIA
TERRITORY OF NOVGOROD
KAMA BULGARIA
SCOTLAND
Perth
North Sea
Baltic Sea
Mordvins
IRELAND
Dublin
WALES
ENGLAND
London
DENMARK
Roskilde
LITHUANIA
Prussians
RUSSIA
ATLANTIC OCEAN
Rhine R.
Gnesen
POLAND
HOLY ROMAN EMPIRE
Danube R.
Cumans or Polovtsi
Paris
FRANCE
Stuhlweissenburg
HUNGARY
Venice
NAVARRE
LEON
Coimbra
CASTILLE
Toledo
ARAGON
PORTUGAL
CORSICA
Rome
REP. OF RAGUSA
SERBIA
BULGARIA
Tirnovo
PR. OF TMUTARAKAN
Black Sea
SARDINIA
KINGDOM OF THE TWO SICILIES
Palermo
DESPOTATE OF EPIRUS
LATIN EMPIRE
Constantinople
EMPIRE OF NICAEA
KINGDOM OF RUM
Athens
DOMINIONS OF THE ALMOHADES
LESSER ARMENIA
CRETE
KINGDOM OF CYPRUS
Mediterranean Sea

0   125   250 Miles
0   250   500 Kilometers

A Powerful Sermon

Urban's sermon was perhaps one of the most effective orations in history. The pope even claimed that he was not ready for the intense fervor generated by his discourse. Nevertheless, one year later, the first crusade was launched. This army, under the leadership of several powerful lords, initially met with great success. They regained Jerusalem in 1099, but the Arabs reorganized and began to exploit the internal discord of the crusaders. Several crusades were subsequently undertaken. Their success was minimal because the European lords were more interested in protecting and expanding their own domains than in pursuing any international cooperative venture. By 1187, Jerusalem was once again under Islamic control.

Stirrings of Nationalism

With nationalism beginning to take hold in Europe, there arose a natural antagonism between the single most important international office, the Catholic Church, and the various kingdoms. This conflict of interest between the papacy and the secular order reshaped the political landscape of Europe. One of the most famous victims of this controversy was the great Italian poet Dante (dän´ tā). Exiled from his native Florence in 1302 for opposing papal meddling in Florentine politics, he expressed his aversion to the worldly pursuits of the papacy as a recurring theme in the *Inferno*, the first part of his epic poem, the *Divine Comedy*.

▲ **Critical Viewing**
In thirteenth-century Europe, what was the status of present-day Spain, Germany, and Italy? Explain. **[Read a Map]**

Art in the Historical Context

The Gothic Cathedral

Consider the relationship between the lowly bean and the soaring Gothic cathedral. The growing of beans, which provided better food for people of all social levels, was part of a twelfth-century renaissance in which towns thrived, trade increased, and travel conditions improved. The development of the Gothic style of architecture was the spiritual expression of this social rebirth.

The Gothic style was also an expression of the brilliance of stonemasons. These artisans discovered how to use flying buttresses (supports on the outer walls) to build tall cathedrals whose walls were thin enough to accommodate stained-glass windows. These architectural innovations give us our most vivid images of the Middle Ages: stone towers that seem to fly toward heaven and windows that make a multicolored heaven of sunlight.

▲ **Critical Viewing** Which details in these pictures of Notre Dame Cathedral, Paris, reveal two major elements of the Gothic style? Explain. **[Connect]**

The Impact of the Crusades Despite their limited military success, the crusades had a tremendous impact on medieval civilization. As crusaders returned from the Middle East, they brought back with them new spices, textiles, and other products. A demand for these new and exotic items inspired commerce. This trading created a new merchant class in the Italian city-states of Genoa, Florence, and Venice, and new markets sprang up elsewhere as well. Small towns in Europe were quickly transformed into large trading centers. By the effective end of the crusades in the late thirteenth century, the merchant class was becoming increasingly important in many parts of Europe.

As the medieval city grew, so did the new centers of learning. By 1300, universities existed in a number of important European cities. The University of Paris was the most eminent center of theology and philosophy in the Western world, and the University of Bologna in Italy was the most important center for the study of law.

Transformation of Medieval Life Despite disease and poverty during this time, new capital generated by commerce stimulated the quest for learning and the rediscovery of classical literature. In addition, explorers searching for better trade routes would soon expand European knowledge of the world. Europe was entering the period of rebirth that we now call the Renaissance.

Literature

Literature in Native Languages As previously mentioned, Latin became the language of religion, scholarship, and government. It was no longer understood by common people, who spoke German or one of the Romance languages that were evolving from Latin, such as Italian, French, and Spanish. These languages were known as the vernacular, or "the native language of a place."

This new linguistic situation affected the way culture was passed on. Two cultures existed side by side: a high culture based on Latin and a popular culture based on vernacular languages. The history of medieval literature is the story of how the various national literatures emerged in native languages while Latin became increasingly specialized.

Reforms in Latin As vernacular literatures were emerging, however, Latin underwent important reforms that ensured the more accurate transmission of texts. Under Charlemagne's patronage, monks created a new writing style called the Carolingian minuscule. This style, featuring a neater script penmanship and distinct breaks between words, made documents much easier to read. In addition, new Latin grammars helped to standardize the language by eliminating elements introduced from the vernacular.

A New Kind of Vernacular Epic While monks in monasteries were refining Latin and copying out libraries of books, the oral tradition was thriving in the rough-and-tumble world. Germanic storytellers, for example, developed a new kind of epic, or long narrative heroic poem. Epic poetry existed in classical Latin, but these Latin poems, such as Virgil's *Aeneid*, were extremely refined and literary. The Germanic epics existed in oral form centuries before they were written down. Their verse form is irregular, and they were meant to be performed to stimulate a warrior's courage before battle. The most famous Germanic epic is the *Nibelungenlied* ("Song of the Nibelungs"), which an unknown author composed from earlier tales sometime around 1200.

▲ **Critical Viewing**
This fifteenth-century Holy Book provides some idea of what a medieval illuminated manuscript looked like. Compare and contrast the relationship between words and pictures in such a manuscript and in a modern illustrated book. **[Compare and Contrast]**

Epic Heroes for Different Nationalities The Spanish *Song of My Cid* and the French *Song of Roland*, although written in medieval Spanish and medieval French, respectively, are also descendants of this ancient Germanic tradition. These two epics describe conflicts between Christians and Moors.

The Moors had invaded Spain and Portugal in the early 700s. Charlemagne took part in early efforts to expel the Moors. In 778, he crossed the Pyrenees into Spain to accomplish this goal. The *Song of Roland*, dating from around 1100, relates the tragedy that befell Charlemagne's nephew, Roland, during this campaign.

In the eleventh century, Christians in Spain launched a new campaign against the Moors. Eventually, several independent Christian kingdoms emerged. *Song of My Cid*, written in the mid-1100s, tells the story of Spain's national hero, Rodrigo Díaz de Vivar (1043–1099), who helped spearhead the expansion of these Christian kingdoms.

Icelandic Sagas Meanwhile, from the ninth through the eleventh centuries, conflicts also occurred between Europeans and Viking raiders from Scandinavia. These Vikings, or Norsemen, settled in England and in northern France, where they became known as Normans. Under William the Conqueror, a Norman army conquered England in 1066.

Vikings also settled in Iceland. There, in the late 1100s, they carried their restless, adventurous spirit into literature, producing works like *Njáls saga* and *Egils saga*. These tales draw upon oral traditions and fictionalize historical events.

Troubadour Poetry In the second half of the eleventh century, a group of poets began writing verse in Provençal (prō′ vän säl′), a Romance language spoken in the south of France. These troubadours—from *trobar*, meaning "to find or invent"—were associated with the courts of certain powerful lords and invented new ways to sing about love. As a result, the theme of their poetry became known as courtly love. The rules of courtly love required a troubadour to praise in poetry a distant, unattainable lady, usually someone else's wife.

Courtly Love and the Status of Women
This type of poetry, which helped foster enlightened attitudes toward women, took Europe by storm. Poets followed courtly love traditions, writing in their own native languages rather than in Latin. Among those who helped popularize the new poetry was Eleanor of Aquitane (c. 1122–1204). As queen of France and England, successively, she was the most influential woman of her time.

Chrétien de Troyes (krā tyän də trwä′), writing at the court of France's Marie de Champagne in the twelfth century, created a new poetic form, the courtly romance. This

▼ **Critical Viewing**
Troubadours played music and composed poetry. What does this picture of medieval troubadours reveal about the kinds of instruments they played? Explain. [Infer]

François Villon, Outlaw Poet

Today, gangsta rappers stir up controversy with lyrics about their outlaw lives. Yet medieval French poet François Villon (*frän* swä´ vē yōn´) (1431–c. 1463) beat rappers like Dr. Dre to the punch. Villon, who came from a poor family, ran with the roughest crowds in Paris. Although he studied at the Sorbonne, a college that taught religion, he was involved in brawling and thievery. He even killed a priest but was pardoned due to extenuating circumstances.

Villon wrote his poem "Ballade" at a time when he thought he would be hanged. In the poem, he speaks as a dead man and asks forgiveness of those who view his body. Villon's actual death, however, remains mysterious. Instead of being executed, he was exiled from Paris. At this point, he vanishes from history and enters legend as an outlaw poet.

from "Ballade" by François Villon, translated by Galway Kinnell

Brother humans who live on after us
Don't let your hearts harden against us
For if you have pity on wretches like us
More likely God will show mercy to you
5 You see us five, six, hanging here
As for the flesh we loved too well
A while ago it was eaten and has rotted away
And we the bones turn to ashes and dust
Let no one make us the butt of jokes
10 But pray God that he absolve us all. . . .

▲ **Critical Viewing**
Do any details in this picture of François Villon suggest that he was an outlaw poet? Why or why not? **[Interpret]**

form combined the elements of courtly love with the longer narrative form of the romance. Many of his works, like *Perceval*, recount adventures associated with the legendary King Arthur of Britain.

Dante Makes a Fateful Choice As medieval society evolved and education became more available with the growth of the universities, popular and Latin culture at times intersected. These traditions combined in the greatest poem of medieval times, Dante's *Divine Comedy*, written in the early 1300s. This epic, which expresses a Christian vision of the world, is based in part on Latin culture. Dante's guide for his imaginary trip through Hell, for example, is the great Roman poet Virgil. At the same time, Dante chose to write his poem in Italian rather than in Latin. His choice gave added prestige to the vernacular and caused other writers to use it as well.

The Dark Side Starting in the 1100s, European towns began to increase rapidly in size. Although this urbanization was part of a social rebirth, it had its dark side as well. Impoverished city-dwellers, menaced by crime and disease, had a hard time surviving. Especially threatening was the plague, a highly contagious disease carried from rats to humans by fleas. The dark side of medieval life found expression in the work of Parisian poet François Villon (see above).

Prepare to Read

from the Song of Roland ◆ *from* The Nibelungenlied

About the *Song of Roland*

Some scholars believe that French literature begins with the *Chanson de Roland* (shän sōn´ də rō län´), or *Song of Roland*. This poem about a great warrior is by far the best known of all medieval epics. Despite its popularity, scholars cannot determine exactly when it was written or who wrote it. The manuscript at Oxford University, England, dates from the decades after A.D. 1100 and is written in the Norman dialect of Old French. The original poem, however, is much older.

Tales of a Great King The

Song of Roland treats one of the great themes of medieval heroic literature: the deeds surrounding Charlemagne (shär´ lə mān´) and his court. Charlemagne, or Charles the Great, was king of the Franks from 768 to 814 and emperor of the Holy Roman Empire from 800 to 814. Because Charlemagne ruled France about 300 years before the *Song of Roland* was composed, there is a great distance between the poem and the events it narrates.

The poem transforms a rather minor historical event. In 778, Charlemagne intervened in a dispute in Spain between two rival Moorish rulers. The Moors were Muslims from northwest Africa who invaded Spain in the eighth century. While returning to France through the Pyrenees (pir´ ə nēz´), Charlemagne's rear guard, led by his nephew Roland, was attacked in the valley of Roncesvalles (rän´ sə valz´) by a band of Basques (bäsks). To a man, the rear guard perished.

Fiction Not Fact The author of the *Song of Roland*

takes considerable poetic license with the historical facts. Most significantly, the Basques become

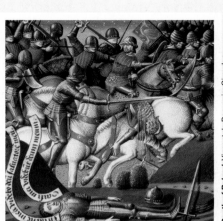

Death of Roland, Vincent de Beauvais, Giraudon

Moors, a more contemporary and meaningful foe for a twelfth-century audience. Charlemagne, thirty-six years old at the time of the massacre at Roncesvalles, is transformed into a miraculous two-hundred-year-old figure. Because Roland is the victim of a treacherous betrayal, his demise is narrated far more dramatically than history could ever have witnessed.

About *The Nibelungenlied*

Composed more than 800 years ago by a now-unknown author, *The Nibelungenlied* (nē´ bə loon´ ən lēt´) is one of the great works of German literature. The name means "song of the Nibelungs," a term that is sometimes used in the poem as another name for Burgundians.

Love and Deception *The Nibelungenlied* is a trag-

edy in two parts. The first part describes the life and death of Siegfried, who falls in love with the lovely Burgundian princess Kriemhild. The second part of the tragedy features the vengeance of Kriemhild after Siegfried's murder.

A Window Into History Scholars believe that

elements of the story reflect historical facts. For example, the destruction of the Burgundians was inspired by the overthrow of the Burgundian kingdom by the Huns in A.D. 437. Likewise, the story of Brunhild and Siegfried may have been inspired by actual events that took place among the Franks around A.D. 600.

With its potent combination of romance, power, betrayal, and violence, *The Nibelungenlied* has survived the ages and inspired numerous adaptations and dramatizations, including Richard Wagner's famous four-part opera, *The Ring of the Nibelung* (1874).

Preview

Connecting to the Literature

Hollywood movies portray action heroes as infallible. While Roland and Siegfried, the champions in these stories, are prototypes of the modern action hero, they show that being heroic does not mean being perfect.

Literary Analysis

Medieval Epic

Medieval epics originated in the great halls of the Germanic tribes and focused on ideas, such as loyalty and valor, that bound societies together. In addition, medieval epics

- defined and expressed the character of a people.
- were based on historical events but prized adventure more than accuracy.
- were performed long before they were written down.

The early Germanic epics dealt with conflicts between traditional beliefs and the tribes' newfound Christianity. However, as the tribes migrated southward, epics were altered to address a different threat—the religion of Islam. With Muslims settled in Spain and southern France, Christendom felt menaced. As you read, identify the values these stories express.

Comparing Literary Works

The **epic hero** is a person of extraordinary abilities who represents a culture's highest values. In most epics, the hero also possesses a **heroic flaw**—a defect of character that may lead to suffering or even death. As you read, compare the ways in which both Roland and Siegfried exemplify the highest values of their cultures, and identify the flaw in each that leads to his demise.

Reading Strategy

Recognizing Feudal Values

Feudalism was the economic, political, and social system of medieval Europe. Under the feudal system, serfs worked the land, which was held by vassals, who took oaths of loyalty to their lords. The society emphasized the warrior virtues of military prowess, loyalty, and honor. As you read, use a chart like the one shown to identify **feudal values.**

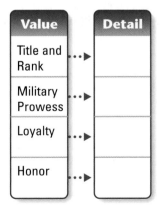

Value	Detail
Title and Rank	
Military Prowess	
Loyalty	
Honor	

Vocabulary Development

vassal (vas´ əl) *n.* person who holds land under the feudal system, pledging loyalty to an overlord (p. 558)

prowess (prou´ is) *n.* ability (p. 558)

exulting (eg zult´ iŋ) *v.* rejoicing (p. 558)

unrestrained (un ri strānd´) *v.* not checked or controlled (p. 567)

malice (mal´ is) *n.* ill will; spite (p. 567)

sinister (sin´ is tər) *adj.* wicked; threatening harm (p. 567)

intrepid (in trep´ id) *adj.* brave; fearless (p. 568)

thwarted (thwôrt´ əd) *v.* hindered; frustrated (p. 569)

from the Song of Roland

translated by Frederick Goldin

Background

After seven years of war between the French Christians and the Spanish Muslims, or Saracens, a single Muslim stronghold remains—the city of Saragossa, which is ruled by King Marsile. Certain of his own defeat, Marsile sends a message to King Charlemagne saying that he will convert to Christianity and become Charlemagne's vassal if the French will leave Spain. (Once Charlemagne is gone, however, Marsile intends to break his promises.) Roland, Charlemagne's greatest knight, suggests that his stepfather, Ganelon, serve as the emissary to Marsile to discuss the offer. Ganelon perceives this nomination for the perilous mission as a thinly veiled attempt at his murder. He accepts the mission but then plots with Marsile to defeat the French by ambushing Charlemagne's rear guard, which Ganelon knows will be led by Roland.

Ganelon returns to Charlemagne with assurances of Marsile's good faith, and they organize the departure from Spain. As Ganelon promised, Roland is chosen to lead the rear guard, which also includes the Twelve Peers—Charlemagne's most beloved vassals—the Archbishop Turin, and Oliver, Roland's best friend. All told, the French rear guard constitutes a force of 20,000 men, but at the pass of Roncesvalles, the rear guard meets a Saracen force numbering in the hundreds of thousands. Oliver begs Roland to blow his horn, the Olifant, to call back Charlemagne's main army, but Roland refuses, saying,

> "I'd be a fool to do it.
> I would lose my good name all through sweet France.
> I will strike now, I'll strike with Durendal,
> the blade will be bloody to the gold from striking!
> These pagan traitors came to these passes doomed!
> I promise you, they are marked men, they'll die."

This excerpt begins as Roland, Oliver, and the rest of the French rear guard face the massive Saracen army.

Critical Viewing ▶
Do you think this medieval illustration of Roland's battle glorifies war? Why or why not? **[Make a Judgment]**

110

The battle is fearful and full of grief.
Oliver and Roland strike like good men,
the Archbishop, more than a thousand blows,
and the Twelve Peers do not hang back, they strike!
the French fight side by side, all as one man.
The pagans die by hundreds, by thousands:
whoever does not flee finds no refuge from death,
like it or not, there he ends all his days.
And there the men of France lose their greatest arms;
they will not see their fathers, their kin again,
or Charlemagne, who looks for them in the passes.
Tremendous torment now comes forth in France,
a mighty whirlwind, tempests of wind and thunder,
rains and hailstones, great and immeasurable,
bolts of lightning hurtling and hurtling down:
it is, in truth, a trembling of the earth.
From Saint Michael-in-Peril to the Saints,
from Besançon to the port of Wissant,[1]
there is no house whose veil of walls does not crumble.
A great darkness at noon falls on the land,
there is no light but when the heavens crack.
No man sees this who is not terrified,

---

1. **Saint Michael-in-Peril . . . Saints . . . Besançon** (bə zän sōń) **. . . Wissant** (wə sän´) four points marking out tenth-century France.

Literary Analysis
Medieval Epic In what ways does this description of the battle suggest both the tribal origins of this epic and the values of military prowess?

✔**Reading Check**

What is the nature of the battle at Roncesvalles?

Battle of Roncevaux and the Death of Roland, Giraudon

from the *Song of Roland* ◆ 557

and many say: "The Last Day! Judgment Day!
The end! The end of the world is upon us!"
They do not know, they do not speak the truth:
it is the worldwide grief for the death of Roland.

130

And Roland says: "We are in a rough battle.
I'll sound the olifant,[2] Charles will hear it."
Said Oliver: "No good vassal would do it.
When I urged it, friend, you did not think it right.
If Charles were here, we'd come out with no losses.
Those men down there—no blame can fall on them."
Oliver said: "Now by this beard of mine,
If I can see my noble sister, Aude,[3]
once more, you will never lie in her arms!" AOI.[4]

131

And Roland said: "Why are you angry at me?"
Oliver answers: "Companion, it is your doing.
I will tell you what makes a vassal good:
        it is judgment, it is never madness;
restraint is worth more than the raw nerve of a fool.
Frenchmen are dead because of your wildness.
And what service will Charles ever have from us?
If you had trusted me, my lord would be here,
we would have fought this battle through to the end,
Marsilion would be dead, or our prisoner.
Roland, your prowess—had we never seen it!
        And now, dear friend, we've seen the last of it.
No more aid from us now for Charlemagne,
a man without equal till Judgment Day,
you will die here, and your death will shame France.
We kept faith, you and I, we were companions;
        and everything we were will end today.
We part before evening, and it will be hard." AOI.

132

Turpin the Archbishop hears their bitter words,
digs hard into his horse with golden spurs
and rides to them; begins to set them right:
"You, Lord Roland, and you, Lord Oliver,
I beg you in God's name do not quarrel.
To sound the horn could not help us now, true,
but still it is far better that you do it:
let the King come, he can avenge us then—
these men of Spain must not go home exulting!

---

2. **olifant** Roland's horn, the name of which derives from the word "elephant" because it was carved from a tusk.
3. **Aude** (ôd) Roland's intended bride.
4. **AOI**: These three mysterious letters appear at certain points throughout the text, 180 times in all. No one has ever adequately explained them.

Literary Analysis
Medieval Epic and Epic Heroes The poet associates the death of Roland with the chaos of the end of the world. What does this suggest about the importance of Roland, the epic hero?

vassal (vas′ əl) *n.* person who holds land under the feudal system, pledging loyalty to an overlord

prowess (prou′ is) *n.* ability

Reading Strategy
Recognizing Feudal Values What lesson about being a good vassal does Oliver point out to Roland?

exulting (eg zult′ iŋ) *v.* rejoicing

Our French will come, they'll get down on their feet,
and find us here—we'll be dead, cut to pieces.
They will lift us into coffins on the backs of mules,
and weep for us, in rage and pain and grief,
and bury us in the courts of churches;
and we will not be eaten by wolves or pigs or dogs."
Roland replies, "Lord, you have spoken well." AOI.

133

Roland has put the olifant to his mouth,
he sets it well, sounds it with all his strength.
The hills are high, and that voice ranges far,
they heard it echo thirty great leagues away.
King Charles heard it, and all his faithful men.
And the King says: "Our men are in a battle."
And Ganelon disputed him and said:
"Had someone else said that, I'd call him liar!" AOI.

134

And now the mighty effort of Roland the Count:
he sounds his olifant; his pain is great,
and from his mouth the bright blood comes leaping out,
and the temple bursts in his forehead.
That horn, in Roland's hands, has a mighty voice:
King Charles hears it drawing through the passes.
Naimon heard it, the Franks listen to it.
And the King said: "I hear Count Roland's horn;
he'd never sound it unless he had a battle."
Says Ganelon: "Now no more talk of battles!
You are old now, your hair is white as snow,
the things you say make you sound like a child.
You know Roland and that wild pride of his—
what a wonder God has suffered it so long!
Remember? he took Noples without your command:
the Saracens rode out, to break the siege;
they fought with him, the great vassal Roland.
Afterward he used the streams to wash the blood
from the meadows: so that nothing would show.
He blasts his horn all day to catch a rabbit,
he's strutting now before his peers and bragging—
who under heaven would dare meet him on the field?
So now: ride on! Why do you keep on stopping?
The Land of Fathers lies far ahead of us." AOI.

135

The blood leaping from Count Roland's mouth,
the temple broken with effort in his forehead,
he sounds his horn in great travail and pain.
King Charles heard it, and his French listen hard.
And the King said: "That horn has a long breath!"

✔ **Reading Check**

Why is Oliver mad at
Roland?

Naimon answers: "It is a baron's breath.
There is a battle there, I know there is.
He betrayed him! and now asks you to fail him!
Put on your armor! Lord, shout your battle cry,
and save the noble barons of your house!
You hear Roland's call. He is in trouble."

136

The Emperor commanded the horns to sound,
the French dismount, and they put on their armor:
their hauberks, their helmets, their gold-dressed swords,
their handsome shields; and take up their great lances,
the gonfalons of white and red and blue.
The barons of that host mount their war horses
and spur them hard the whole length of the pass;

Reading Strategy
**Recognizing Feudal
Values** What is the funda-
mental feudal value that
Ganelon has violated?

◀ **Critical Viewing**
Which details in this image
help portray Roland as a
heroic figure? **[Analyze]**

and every man of them says to the other:
"If only we find Roland before he's killed,
we'll stand with him, and then we'll do some fighting!"
What does it matter what they say? They are too late.

138

High are the hills, and tenebrous,[5] and vast, AOI.
the valleys deep, the raging waters swift;
to the rear, to the front, the trumpets sound:
they answer the lone voice of the olifant.
The Emperor rides on, rides on in fury,
the men of France in grief and indignation.
There is no man who does not weep and wail,
and they pray God: protect the life of Roland
till they come, one great host, into the field
and fight at Roland's side like true men all.
What does it matter what they pray? It does no good.
They are too late, they cannot come in time. AOI.

156

Roland the Count fights well and with great skill,
but he is hot, his body soaked with sweat;
has a great wound in his head, and much pain,
his temple broken because he blew the horn.
But he must know whether King Charles will come;
draws out the olifant, sounds it, so feebly.
The Emperor drew to a halt, listened.
"Seigneurs," he said, "it goes badly for us—
My nephew Roland falls from our ranks today.
I hear it in the horn's voice: he hasn't long.
Let every man who wants to be with Roland
ride fast! Sound trumpets! Every trumpet in this host!"
Sixty thousand, on these words, sound, so high
the mountains sound, and the valleys resound.
The pagans hear: it is no joke to them;
cry to each other: "We're getting Charles on us!"

160

Say the pagans: "We were all born unlucky!
The evil day that dawned for us today!
We have lost our lords and peers, and now comes Charles—
that Charlemagne!—with his great host. Those trumpets!
that shrill sound on us—the trumpets of the French!
And the loud roar of that Munjoie! This Roland
is a wild man, he is too great a fighter—
What man of flesh and blood can ever hope
to bring him down? Let us cast at him, and leave him there."

---
5. tenebrous (ten´ ə brəs) *adj.* dark; gloomy.

Literary Analysis
Medieval Epic Which details in stanzas 136 and 138 suggest that this poem was originally performed before live audiences?

Literary Analysis
Medieval Epic and Heroic Flaw In what ways does the description of Roland as a "wild man" have elements of truth? Explain.

Reading Check

What truth about Roland's situation does Charlemagne hear in the "horn's voice"?

And so they did: arrows, wigars, darts,
lances and spears, javelots dressed with feathers;
struck Roland's shield, pierced it, broke it to pieces,
ripped his hauberk, shattered its rings of mail,
but never touched his body, never his flesh.
They wounded Veillantif in thirty places,
struck him dead, from afar, under the Count.
The pagans flee, they leave the field to him.
Roland the Count stood alone, on his feet.[6] AOI.

161

The pagans flee, in bitterness and rage,
strain every nerve running headlong toward Spain,
and Count Roland has no way to chase them,
he has lost Veillantif, his battle horse;
he has no choice, left alone there on foot.
He went to the aid of Archbishop Turpin,
unlaced the gold-dressed helmet, raised it from his head,
lifted away his bright, light coat of mail,
cut his under tunic into some lengths,
stilled his great wounds with thrusting on the strips;
then held him in his arms, against his chest,
and laid him down, gently, on the green grass;
and softly now Roland entreated him:
"My noble lord, I beg you, give me leave:
our companions, whom we have loved so dearly,
are all dead now, we must not abandon them.
I want to look for them, know them once more,
and set them in ranks, side by side, before you."
Said the Archbishop: "Go then, go and come back.
The field is ours, thanks be to God, yours and mine."

168

Now Roland feels that death is very near.
His brain comes spilling out through his two ears;
prays to God for his peers: let them be called;
and for himself, to the angel Gabriel;
took the olifant: there must be no reproach!
took Durendal his sword in his other hand,
and farther than a crossbow's farthest shot
he walks toward Spain, into a fallow land,[7]
and climbs a hill: there beneath two fine trees
stand four great blocks of stone, all are of marble;
and he fell back, to earth, on the green grass,
has fainted there, for death is very near.

---

6. **The pagans flee . . . feet** This respite, granted to Roland and Turpin after the pagans
have fled and before these heroes die, is a sign of the two men's blessedness.

7. **fallow land** land plowed but not seeded for one or more growing seasons.

169

High are the hills, and high,
    high are the trees;
there stand four blocks of
    stone, gleaming of marble.
Count Roland falls fainting on
    the green grass,
and is watched, all this time, by
    a Saracen:
who has feigned death and lies
    now with the others,
has smeared blood on his face
    and on his body;
and quickly now gets to his feet
    and runs—
a handsome man, strong,
    brave, and so crazed with
    pride
that he does something mad
    and dies for it:
laid hands on Roland, and on
    the arms of Roland,
and cried: "Conquered!
    Charles's nephew conquered!
I'll carry this sword home to Arabia!"
As he draws it, the Count begins to come round.

Death of Roland, Vincent de Beauvais, Giraudon

▲ **Critical Viewing**

Which details from the
epic appear in this
medieval illustration
of the death of Roland?
[Connect]

Literary Analysis
Medieval Epic What quality of the medieval epic is
suggested by Roland's
words, "you aren't one of
ours"?

170

Now Roland feels: *someone taking his sword!*
opened his eyes, and had one word for him:
"I don't know you, you aren't one of ours";
grasps that olifant that he will never lose,
strikes on the helm beset with gems in gold,
shatters the steel, and the head, and the bones,
sent his two eyes flying out of his head,
dumped him over stretched out at his feet dead;
and said: "You nobody! how could you dare
lay hands on me—rightly or wrongly: how?
Who'll hear of this and not call you a fool?
Ah! the bell-mouth of the olifant is smashed,
the crystal and the gold fallen away."

171

Now Roland the Count feels: his sight is gone;
gets on his feet, draws on his final strength,
the color on his face lost now for good.
Before him stands a rock; and on that dark rock
in rage and bitterness he strikes ten blows:
the steel blade grates, it will not break, it stands unmarked.

☑ **Reading Check**

What object does a
Saracen try to take from
Roland?

"Ah!" said the Count, "Blessed Mary, your help!
Ah Durendal, good sword, your unlucky day,
for I am lost and cannot keep you in my care.
The battles I have won, fighting with you,
the mighty lands that holding you I conquered,
that Charles rules now, our King, whose beard is white!
Now you fall to another: it must not be
    a man who'd run before another man!
For a long while a good vassal held you:
there'll never be the like in France's holy land."

173

Roland the Count strikes down on a dark rock,
and the rock breaks, breaks more than I can tell,
and the blade grates, but Durendal will not break,
the sword leaped up, rebounded toward the sky.
The Count, when he sees that sword will not be broken,
softly, in his own presence, speaks the lament:
"Ah Durendal, beautiful, and most sacred,
the holy relics in this golden pommel!
Saint Peter's tooth and blood of Saint Basile,
a lock of hair of my lord Saint Denis,
and a fragment of blessed Mary's robe:[8]
your power must not fall to the pagans,
you must be served by Christian warriors.
May no coward ever come to hold you!
It was with you I conquered those great lands
that Charles has in his keeping, whose beard is white,
the Emperor's lands, that make him rich and strong."

174

Now Roland feels: death coming over him,
death descending from his temples to his heart.
He came running underneath a pine tree
and there stretched out, face down, on the green grass,
lays beneath him his sword and the olifant.
He turned his head toward the Saracen hosts,
and this is why: with all his heart he wants
King Charles the Great and all his men to say,
he died, that noble Count, a conqueror;
makes confession, beats his breast often, so feebly,
offers his glove, for all his sins, to God. AOI.

176

Count Roland lay stretched out beneath a pine;
he turned his face toward the land of Spain,
began to remember many things now:

Reading Strategy
**Recognizing Feudal
Values** In what ways does
Roland's concern for his
sword demonstrate the
feudal value of military
prowess?

---

8. **Saint Peter's tooth . . . Mary's robe** Such relics—remains of holy men and women—
    were thought to have miraculous power.

how many lands, brave man, he had conquered;
and he remembered: sweet France, the men of his line,
remembered Charles, his lord, who fostered him:
cannot keep, remembering, from weeping, sighing;
but would not be unmindful of himself:
he confesses his sins, prays God for mercy:
"Loyal Father, you who never failed us,
who resurrected Saint Lazarus from the dead,
and saved your servant Daniel from the lions:[9]
now save the soul of me from every peril
for the sins I committed while I still lived."
Then he held out his right glove to his Lord:[10]
Saint Gabriel took the glove from his hand.
He held his head bowed down upon his arm,
he is gone, his two hands joined, to his end.
Then God sent him his angel Cherubin
and Saint Michael, angel of the sea's Peril;
and with these two there came Saint Gabriel:
they bear Count Roland's soul to Paradise.

---

9. **Saint Lazarus . . . Daniel from the lions** reference to two famous miracles described in the Bible (John 11:1–44 and Daniel 6:16–23, respectively).
10. **he held out . . . to his Lord** ritual act of resignation to a feudal lord.

Reading Strategy
Recognizing Feudal Values Which feudal values does Roland express in his final thoughts? Explain.

Review and Assess

Thinking About the Selection

1. **Respond:** If you could speak to Roland as he heads into battle, what advice would you give him?

2. **(a) Recall:** In the second line of stanza 130, what does Roland say he will now do? **(b) Analyze Cause and Effect:** Why does he decide to take this action?

3. **(a) Recall:** According to Oliver, what makes one a good vassal? **(b) Interpret:** According to Oliver, why would Roland not be considered a good vassal?

4. **(a) Recall:** In stanza 171, as he tries to destroy his sword, how does Roland describe himself? **(b) Interpret:** How does Roland seem to feel about the service he has rendered to Charlemagne? **(c) Analyze:** In what ways does this stanza suggest that Roland is undergoing an internal struggle about his own life and identity?

5. **Analyze:** What truth about himself, if any, do you think Roland faces as he lies dying? Explain your answer.

6. **Evaluate:** Would Roland be considered a hero in today's world? Explain your answer.

from *The Nibelungenlied*

How Siegfried Was Slain

translated by A. T. Hatto

Background

Brave prince Siegfried has proven gifts as a warrior and hero. He has captured a treasure, a fabled sword, and a cloak of invisibility. He has slain a dragon and bathed in its blood, thus becoming almost invincible—just one small spot between his shoulder blades remains vulnerable to attack.

Siegfried has heard of Princess Kriemhild's great beauty and has journeyed to the city of Worms, the capital of Burgundy, to woo her. He enters into the service of her brother, King Gunther. After leading the Burgundian forces in battle, he becomes Gunther's trusted vassal and friend. Using his cloak of invisibility, he also helps Gunther win the hand of Brunhild, a powerful warrior queen. However, Kriemhild reveals the deception, and Brunhild vows revenge. With Hagen, her loyal servant, and Gunther, who appears to have forgotten both his friendship and his debt to Siegfried, Brunhild plots to kill the hero. Kriemhild then makes a terrible mistake by revealing the location of Siegfried's vulnerable spot.

This excerpt describes Siegfried's death, the pivotal point of the epic.

The Hunt, Paolo Uccello

The fearless warriors Gunther and Hagen treacherously proclaimed a hunt in the forest where they wished to chase the boar, the bear, and the bison—and what could be more daring? Siegfried rode with their party in magnificent style. They took all manner of food with them; and it was while drinking from a cool stream that the hero was to lose his life at the instigation of Brunhild, King Gunther's queen.

Bold Siegfried went to Kriemhild while his and his companions' hunting-gear was being loaded on to the sumpters in readiness to cross the Rhine,[1] and she could not have been more afflicted. "God grant that I may see you well again, my lady," he said, kissing his dear wife, "and that your eyes may see me too. Pass the time pleasantly with your relations who are so kind to you, since I cannot stay with you at home."

Kriemhild thought of what she had told Hagen, but she dared not mention it and began to lament that she had ever been born. "I dreamt last night—and an ill-omened dream it was—" said lord Siegfried's noble queen, weeping with <u>unrestrained</u> passion, "that two boars chased you over the heath and the flowers were dyed with blood! How can I help weeping so? I stand in great dread of some attempt against your life.—What if we have offended any men who have the power to vent their <u>malice</u> on us? Stay away, my lord, I urge you."

"I shall return in a few days time, my darling. I know of no people here who bear me any hatred. Your kinsmen without exception wish me well, nor have I deserved otherwise of them."

"It is not so, lord Siegfried. I fear you will come to grief. Last night I had a <u>sinister</u> dream of how two mountains fell upon you and hid you

---

1. **sumpters . . . Rhine** Sumpters are pack horses; the Rhine River flows from eastern Switzerland north through Germany, then west through the Netherlands into the North Sea.

Reading Strategy
Recognizing Feudal Values Which details in this description of the planned hunt reflect the feudal values of bravery, skill with weaponry, and pageantry, or theatrical display? Explain.

unrestrained (un ri strānd′) *adj.* not checked or controlled

malice (mal′ is) *n.* ill will; spite

sinister (sin′ is tər) *adj.* wicked; threatening harm

☑ **Reading Check**

What event have Gunther and Hagen organized?

◀ **Critical Viewing**

Based on this image of a medieval hunt, why might such an event spark rivalry or jealousy among the participants? **[Deduce]**

from my sight! I shall suffer cruelly if you go away and leave me." But he clasped the noble woman in his arms and after kissing and caressing her fair person very tenderly, took his leave and went forthwith. Alas, she was never to see him alive again.

They rode away deep into the forest in pursuit of their sport. Gunther and his men were accompanied by numbers of brave knights, but Gernot and Giselher stayed at home. Ahead of the hunt many horses had crossed the Rhine laden with their bread, wine, meat, fish, and various other provisions such as a King of Gunther's wealth is bound to have with him.

The proud and <u>intrepid</u> hunters were told to set up their lodges on a spacious isle in the river on which they were to hunt, at the skirt of the greenwood over towards the spot where the game would have to break cover. Siegfried, too, had arrived there, and this was reported to the King. Thereupon the sportsmen everywhere manned their relays.[2]

"Who is going to guide us through the forest to our quarry, brave warriors?" asked mighty Siegfried.

"Shall we split up before we start hunting here?" asked Hagen. "Then my lords and I could tell who are the best hunters on this foray into the woods. Let us share the huntsmen and hounds between us and each take the direction he likes—and then all honor to him that hunts best!" At this, the hunters quickly dispersed.

"I do not need any hounds." said lord Siegfried, "except for one tracker so well fleshed that he recognizes the tracks which the game leave through the wood: then we shall not fail to find our quarry."

An old huntsman took a good sleuth-hound and quickly led the lord to where there was game in abundance. The party chased everything that was roused from its lair, as good hunting-men still do today. Bold Siegfried of the Netherlands killed every beast that his hound started, for his hunter was so swift that nothing could elude him. Thus, versatile as he was, Siegfried outshone all the others in that hunt.

The very first kill was when he brought down a strong young tusker,[3] after which he soon chanced on an enormous lion. When his hound had roused it he laid a keen arrow to his bow and shot it so that it dropped in its tracks at the third bound. Siegfried's fellow-huntsmen acclaimed him for this shot. Next, in swift succession, he killed a wisent, an elk, four mighty aurochs,[4] and a fierce and monstrous buck—so well mounted was he that nothing, be it hart or hind, could evade him. His hound then came upon a great boar, and, as this turned to flee, the champion hunter at once blocked his path, bringing him to bay; and when in a trice the beast sprang at the hero in a fury,

intrepid (in trep´ id) *adj.* brave; fearless

Literary Analysis
Medieval Epic and Epic Heroes What does Siegfried's comment reveal about his character?

---

2. **relays** fresh horses brought in to relieve tired ones.
3. **tusker** (tusk´ ər) wild boar.
4. **wisent** (vē´ zənt) . . . **aurochs** (ô´ räks´) European bison and wild oxen.

Siegfried slew him with his sword, a feat no other hunter could have performed with such ease. After the felling of this boar, the tracker was returned to his leash and Siegfried's splendid bag was made known to the Burgundians.

"If it is not asking too much, lord Siegfried," said his companions of the chase, "do leave some of the game alive for us. You are emptying the hills and woods for us today." At this the brave knight had to smile.

There now arose a great shouting of men and clamor of hounds on all sides, and the tumult grew so great that the hills and the forest re-echoed with it—the huntsmen had unleashed no fewer than four and twenty packs! Thus, many beasts had to lose their lives there, since each of these hunters was hoping to bring it about that *he* should be given the high honors of the chase. But when mighty Siegfried appeared beside the camp fire there was no chance of that.

Reading Strategy
Recognizing Feudal Values Which feudal ideals are reflected in each huntsman's desire to win "the high honors of the chase"?

The hunt was over, yet not entirely so. Those who wished to go to the fire brought the hides of innumerable beasts, and game in plenty— what loads of it they carried back to the kitchen to the royal retainers! And now the noble King had it announced to those fine hunters that he wished to take his repast, and there was one great blast of the horn to tell them that he was back in camp.

At this, one of Siegfried's huntsmen said: "Sir, I have heard a horn-blast telling us to return to our lodges.—I shall answer it." There was much blowing to summon the companions.

"Let us quit the forest, too," said lord Siegfried. His mount carried him at an even pace, and the others hastened away with him but with the noise of their going they started a savage bear, a very fierce beast. "I shall give our party some good entertainment," he said over his shoulder. "Loose the hound, for I can see a bear which will have to come back to our lodges with us. It will not be able to save itself unless it runs very fast." The hound was unleashed, and the bear made off at speed. Siegfried meant to ride it down but soon found that his way was blocked and his intention <u>thwarted</u>, while the mighty beast fancied it would escape from its pursuer. But the proud knight leapt from his horse and started to chase it on foot, and the animal, quite off its guard, failed to elude him. And so he quickly caught and bound it, without having wounded it at all—nor could the beast use either claws or teeth on the man. Siegfried tied it to his saddle, mounted his horse, and in his high-spirited fashion led it to the camp fire in order to amuse the good knights.

And in what magnificent style Siegfried rode! He bore a great spear, stout of shaft and broad of head; his handsome sword reached down to his spurs; and the fine horn which this lord carried was of the reddest gold. Nor have I ever heard tell of a better hunting outfit: he wore a sur-coat of costly black silk and a splendid hat of sable,[5] and you should

thwarted (thwôrt′ əd) *v.* hindered; frustrated

---

5. **surcoat ... sable** (sā′ bəl) A surcoat is a loose, short cloak worn over armor, and sable is the costly fur of the marten.

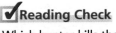

☑**Reading Check**

Which hunter kills the most game?

have seen the gorgeous silken tassels on his quiver, which was covered in panther-skin for the sake of its fragrant odor![6] He also bore a bow so strong that apart from Siegfried any who wished to span it would have had to use a rack. His hunting suit was all of otter-skin, varied throughout its length with furs of other kinds from whose shining hair clasps of gold gleamed out on either side of this daring lord of the hunt. The handsome sword that he wore was Balmung, a weapon so keen and with such excellent edges that it never failed to bite when swung against a helmet. No wonder this splendid hunter was proud and gay. And (since I am bound to tell you all) know that his quiver was full of good arrows with gold mountings and heads a span[7] in width, so that any beast they pierced must inevitably soon die.

Thus the noble knight rode along, the very image of a hunting man. Gunther's attendants saw him coming and ran to meet him to take his horse—tied to whose saddle he led a mighty bear! On dismounting, he loosed the bonds from its muzzle and paws, whereupon all the hounds that saw it instantly gave tongue. The beast made for the forest and the people were seized with panic. Affrighted by the tumult, the bear strayed into the kitchen—and how the cooks scuttled from their fire at its approach! Many cauldrons were sent flying and many fires were

---

6. **panther-skin . . . odor** The odor of panther skin was supposed to lure other animals and therefore help with the hunt.
7. **span** nine inches.

Siegfried's Death, Staatsbibliothek Preussischer Kulturbesitz, Berlin

Literary Analysis
Medieval Epic In what ways does the long description of Siegfried's appearance reflect the origins of the medieval epic in the oral tradition?

◀ **Critical Viewing**
What does this illustration from the Hundeshagen Codex, the only surviving Nibelungen manuscript with illustrations, add to your understanding of the epic? **[Interpret]**

scattered, while heaps of good food lay among the ashes. Lord and retainers leapt from their seats, the bear became infuriated, and the King ordered all the hounds on their leashes to be loosed—and if all had ended well they would have had a jolly day! Bows and spears were no longer left idle, for the brave ones ran towards the bear, yet there were so many hounds in the way that none dared shoot. With the whole mountain thundering with people's cries the bear took to flight before the hounds and none could keep up with it but Siegfried, who ran it down and then dispatched it with his sword. The bear was later carried to the camp fire, and all who had witnessed this feat declared that Siegfried was a very powerful man.

The proud companions were then summoned to table. There were a great many seated in that meadow. Piles of sumptuous dishes were set before the noble huntsmen, but the butlers who were to pour their wine were very slow to appear. Yet knights could not be better cared for than they and if only no treachery had been lurking in their minds those warriors would have been above reproach.

"Seeing that we are being treated to such a variety of dishes from the kitchen," said lord Siegfried, "I fail to understand why the butlers bring us no wine. Unless we hunters are better looked after, I'll not be a companion of the hunt. I thought I had deserved better attention."

"We shall be very glad to make amends to you for our present lack," answered the perfidious[8] King from his table. "This is Hagen's fault—he wants us to die of thirst."

"My very dear lord," replied Hagen of Troneck, "I thought the day's hunting would be away in the Spessart and so I sent the wine there. If we go without drink today I shall take good care that it does not happen again."

"Damn those fellows!" said lord Siegfried. "It was arranged that they were to bring along seven panniers of spiced wine and mead[9] for me. Since that proved impossible, we should have been placed nearer the Rhine."

"You brave and noble knights," said Hagen of Troneck, "I know a cool spring nearby—do not be offended!—let us go there."—A proposal which (as it turned out) was to bring many knights into jeopardy.

Siegfried was tormented by thirst and ordered the board to be removed all the sooner in his eagerness to go to that spring at the foot of the hills. And now the knights put their treacherous plot into execution.

Word was given for the game which Siegfried had killed to be conveyed back to Worms on wagons, and all who saw it gave him great credit for it.

Hagan of Troneck broke his faith with Siegfried most grievously, for as they were leaving to go to the spreading lime-tree he said: "I have often been told that no one can keep up with Lady Kriemhild's lord when he cares to show his speed. I wish he would show it us now."

---

8. **perfidious** (pər fid´ ē əs) *adj.* treacherous.
9. **panniers** (pan´ yərz) . . . **mead** (mēd) Panniers are pairs of large baskets that straddle the backs of pack animals; mead is an alcoholic liquor made of fermented honey and water.

Literary Analysis
Medieval Epic and Epic Heroes In what ways does this episode with the bear add to Siegfried's mystique?

Reading Check

Why is Siegfried unhappy at the meal following the hunt?

from *The Nibelungenlied* ◆ 571

"You can easily put it to the test by racing me to the brook," replied gallant Siegfried of the Netherlands. "Then those who see it shall declare the winner."

"I accept your challenge," said Hagen.

"Then I will lie down in the grass at your feet, as a handicap," replied brave Siegfried, much to Gunther's satisfaction. "And I will tell you what more I shall do. I will carry all my equipment with me, my spear and my shield and all my hunting clothes." And he quickly strapped on his quiver and sword. The two men took off their outer clothing and stood there in their white vests. Then they ran through the clover like a pair of wild panthers. Siegfried appeared first at the brook.

Gunther's magnificent guest who excelled so many men in all things quickly unstrapped his sword, took off his quiver, and after leaning his great spear against a branch of the lime, stood beside the rushing brook. Then he laid down his shield near the flowing water, and although he was very thirsty he most courteously refrained from drinking until the King had drunk. Gunther thanked him very ill for this.

The stream was cool, sweet, and clear. Gunther stooped to its running waters and after drinking stood up and stepped aside. Siegfried in turn would have liked to do the same, but he paid for his good manners. For now Hagen carried Siegfried's sword and bow beyond his reach, ran back for the spear, and searched for the sign on the brave man's tunic.[10] Then, as Siegfried bent over the brook and drank, Hagen hurled the spear at the cross, so that the hero's heart's blood leapt from the wound and splashed against Hagen's clothes. No warrior will ever do a darker deed. Leaving the spear fixed in Siegfried's heart, he fled in wild desperation, as he had never fled before from any man.

When lord Siegfried felt the great wound, maddened with rage he bounded back from the stream with the long shaft jutting from his heart. He was hoping to find either his bow or his sword, and, had he succeeded in doing so, Hagen would have had his pay. But finding no sword, the gravely wounded man had nothing but his shield. Snatching this from the bank he ran at Hagen, and King Gunther's vassal was unable to elude him. Siegfried was wounded to death, yet he struck so powerfully that he sent many precious stones whirling from the shield as it smashed to pieces. Gunther's noble guest would dearly have loved to avenge himself. Hagen fell reeling under the weight of the blow and the riverside echoed loudly. Had Siegfried had his sword in his hand it would have been the end of Hagen, so enraged was the wounded man, as indeed he had good cause to be.

The hero's face had lost its color and he was no longer able to stand. His strength had ebbed away, for in the field of his bright countenance he now displayed Death's token. Soon many fair ladies would be weeping for him.

Literary Analysis
Medieval Epic and Epic Heroes What does Siegfried fail to realize about the effects his unrivaled abilities are having on the other knights?

Reading Strategy
Recognizing Feudal Values How does Siegfried's treatment of Gunther exemplify the ideal relationship between a vassal and his king?

Critical Viewing ▶
In this painting depicting Siegfried's funeral, how does the artist's portrayal of the characters compare to the images you had formed in your mind? **[Compare and Contrast]**

---

10. **sign . . . tunic** Siegfried is invulnerable except for a spot beween his shoulder blades. Earlier, Hagen had tricked Kriemhild into sewing a cross-shaped patch on Siegfried's tunic to indicate the exact location of the spot.

The lady Kriemhild's lord fell among the flowers, where you could see the blood surging from his wound. Then—and he had cause—he rebuked those who had plotted his foul murder. "You vile cowards," he said as he lay dying. "What good has my service done me now that you have slain me? I was always loyal to you, but now I have paid for it. Alas, you have wronged your kinsmen so that all who are born in days to come will be dishonored by your deed. You have cooled your anger on me beyond all measure. You will be held in contempt and stand apart from all good warriors."

The knights all ran to where he lay wounded to death. It was a sad day for many of them. Those who were at all loyal-hearted mourned for him, and this, as a gay and valiant knight, he had well deserved.

The King of Burgundy too lamented Siegfried's death.

"There is no need for the doer of the deed to weep when the damage is done," said the dying man. "He should be held up to scorn. It would have been better left undone."

"I do not know what you are grieving for," said Hagen fiercely. "All our cares and sorrows are over and done with. We shall not find many who will dare oppose us now. I am glad I have put an end to his supremacy."

"You may well exult," said Siegfried. "But had I known your murderous bent I should easily have guarded my life from you. I am sorry for none so much as my wife, the lady Kriemhild. May God have mercy on me for ever having got a son who in years to come will suffer the

Reading Strategy
Recognizing Feudal Values What feudal values does Siegfried's condemnation of his murderers express?

✔**Reading Check**
What happens to Siegfried as he drinks from the brook?

The Burial of Siegfried, Richard Jack, City of New York Art Gallery

reproach that his kinsmen were murderers. If I had the strength I would have good reason to complain. But if you feel at all inclined to do a loyal deed for anyone, noble King," continued the mortally wounded man, "let me commend my dear sweetheart to your mercy. Let her profit from being your sister. By the virtue of all princes, stand by her loyally! No lady was ever more greatly wronged through her dear friend. As to my father and his vassals, they will have long to wait for me."

The flowers everywhere were drenched with blood. Siegfried was at grips with Death, yet not for long, since Death's sword ever was too sharp. And now the warrior who had been so brave and gay could speak no more.

When those lords saw that the hero was dead they laid him on a shield that shone red with gold, and they plotted ways and means of concealing the fact that Hagen had done the deed. "A disaster has befallen us," many of them said. "You must all hush it up and declare with one voice that Siegfried rode off hunting alone and was killed by robbers as he was passing through the forest."

"I shall take him home," said Hagen of Troneck. "It is all one to me if the woman who made Brunhild so unhappy should come to know of it. It will trouble me very little, however much she weeps."

Review and Assess

Thinking About the Selection

1. **Respond:** Did you find the death of Siegfried noble and uplifting or tragic and depressing? Explain your answer.

2. **(a) Recall:** Before the hunt, what does Kriemhild dream?
(b) Interpret: What does Kriemhild fear her dream may represent? **(c) Analyze:** In what ways do Siegfried's and Kriemhild's responses to her dream reveal differences in their characters?

3. **(a) Recall:** What three weapons does Siegfried take to the hunt?
(b) Analyze: What other details convey the sense that Siegfried is "the very image of a hunting man"?

4. **(a) Classify:** Identify three moments in which Siegfried bests the other knights in a physical challenge. **(b) Interpret:** What is Siegfried's attitude toward the other knights? **(c) Make a Judgment:** Do you think Siegfried's character contributes to his death? Explain your answer.

5. **Take a Position:** At the end of the excerpt, Hagen says, "All our cares are over and done with," while others say, "A disaster has befallen us." Which opinion do you think is accurate? Explain your answer.

Review and Assess

Literary Analysis

Medieval Epic

1. **Medieval epics** favored adventure over factual accuracy. (a) How might this emphasis have aided a storyteller? (b) How might this emphasis have affected a people's sense of its own history?

2. Which elements in the following passage suggest that the *Song of Roland* was first performed as an entertainment for live audiences?

   > The French dismount, and they put on their armor: / their hauberks, their helmets, their gold-dressed swords, / their handsome shields; and take up their great lances, / the gonfalons of white and red and blue . . .

3. (a) In what ways do you think these stories might have inspired their audiences? (b) In what ways might these stories have been viewed as cautionary tales? Explain.

Comparing Literary Works

4. Use a chart like the one shown to identify details that reveal specific elements of each **epic hero's** character.

Hero	Appearance	Abilities and Skills	Others' Opinions of Him	Opinion of Himself
Roland				
Siegfried				

5. (a) Identify three examples of Siegfried's thoughtlessness about other people. (b) What is Siegfried's **heroic flaw**?

6. (a) Why does Roland not call for help? (b) What is his heroic flaw?

Reading Strategy

Recognizing Feudal Values

7. Loyalty was one of the most esteemed **feudal values,** and betrayal was one of the most serious violations. Does Roland betray Charlemagne by his actions? Explain.

8. (a) In what ways does Siegfried express respect for Gunther? (b) In what ways does Roland express respect for Charlemagne?

Extend Understanding

9. **Social Studies Connection:** Which elements of these epic works provide insight into the conditions of life during the Middle Ages?

Quick Review

Medieval epics are long works that were originally performed in dramatic theatricals to present the exploits of larger-than-life heroes.

The **epic hero** is a person of extraordinary abilities who embodies a people's core beliefs and values.

A **heroic flaw** is a character defect that may lead to the failure, suffering, or death of the hero.

To **recognize feudal values** as you read, identify those details of a literary work that reveal the values underlying the economic, political, and social system of medieval Europe.

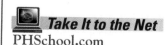 **Take It to the Net**
PHSchool.com

Take the interactive self-test online to check your understanding of these selections.

Integrate Language Skills

Vocabulary Development Lesson

Word Analysis: Latin Prefix *mal-*

The prefix *mal-*, which means "bad," derives from the Latin word *malus*, which means "evil." Thus, *malice* means "ill will." Fill in each blank below with the word that best completes each sentence.

a. malady   **b.** malfunction   **c.** malpractice

1. The doctor was sued for _____.
2. The patient recovered from her _____.
3. The engine started to _____.

Spelling Strategy

When words that derive from French end in the *is* sound, they are often spelled with the letter combination *ice*, as in *malice*. Use the clues below to finish the spelling of each word.

1. a cuplike vessel   chal_____
2. building   edif_____
3. trainee   apprent_____

Fluency: Words in Context

Review the vocabulary list on page 555, and notice the way the words are used in the context of the selection. Then, fill in the blanks in the paragraph below with the best word from the vocabulary list.

vassal	malice
prowess	thwarted
exulting	sinister
unrestrained	intrepid

When the knights gathered at the tournament, the young ___?___ displayed his strength and ___?___. He left the field ___?___ in his victory. He had proved he was fearless and ___?___, and his celebration was ___?___. However, his ___?___ enemy, who wanted attention for himself, saw his own plans ___?___. He looked at the young knight with ___?___.

Grammar and Style Lesson

Interrupting Phrases and Clauses

Writers sometimes interrupt sentences with phrases and clauses that express strong feeling. When such interrupters break into the middle of a sentence, they are often set off with dashes. When they end a sentence, they are often preceded by a dash. **Interrupting phrases and clauses** may imitate speech, provide explanations, or suggest an intense, irrepressible feeling.

> Roland, your prowess—had we never seen it!
>
> Charles—that Charlemagne!—with his great host.

Practice Correctly punctuate the following items.

1. I read the *Song of Roland* what a great work
2. *The Nibelungenlied* the medieval epic reminds me of *The Lord of the Rings*
3. The death of Roland someday you must read it is a powerful scene
4. Roland's friend Oliver I just recalled his name tries to give him advice
5. Monday what an amazing day it was I felt like Roland at Roncesvalles

Writing Application Write a paragraph about heroes. Use at least two interrupting phrases or clauses.

W̶G̶ Prentice Hall Writing and Grammar Connection: Diamond Level, Chapter 27, Section 5

Writing Lesson

Persuasive Essay on Values

Roland and Siegfried demonstrate many virtues, including courage and strength. However, when it comes to prudence, they are somewhat less gifted. Using the stories of Roland and Siegfried as evidence, write an essay defining the virtues of courage and prudence and determining whether one is more important than the other.

Prewriting   Use a chart to examine details from the stories that demonstrate either courage or prudence. Under "Conclusions Drawn," describe what each detail reveals about the value of that virtue.

Model: Charting to Analyze Details

Selection	Detail	Virtue Shown	Conclusions Drawn
Song of Roland	Roland refuses to blow his horn.	courage	Courage can erase prudence; a virtue can be destructive.
Nibelungenlied			

Drafting   Decide on a structure for your essay. For example, you might discuss all your observations about courage and then all your observations about prudence, or you might list all your ideas about Roland and then all your ideas about Siegfried.

Revising   Reread your essay, making sure you have presented your ideas persuasively by organizing them clearly and including strong support from the text. Add quotations or other details as needed.

WG *Prentice Hall Writing and Grammar Connection: Diamond Level, Chapter 7, Section 2*

Extension Activities

Listening and Speaking In a small group, conduct a **press conference** in which Charlemagne describes the events at Roncevalles. Have one student play Charlemagne, while the others act as reporters. Use these tips to prepare:

- Reporters should prepare at least two questions in advance.
- Follow-up questions should be allowed after Charlemagne's responses.

You may also create a map as a visual aid for use during the press conference. **[Group Activity]**

Research and Technology Use electronic and print resources to create an **informative poster** about medieval dress. Consider organizing the material according to occupation or social status. Alternatively, present outfits worn for various occasions or times of day. Clearly identify the different styles and purposes of dress in your poster.

 Take It to the Net PHSchool.com

Go online for an additional research activity using the Internet.

READING INFORMATIONAL MATERIALS

Interviews

About Interviews

An **interview** is a record of an exchange between two or more people for the purpose of obtaining specific information about a person, a topic, or an event. Interviews may be formal, with the interview and the questions planned in advance, or informal and occurring spontaneously, as in a news report. An interview can also provide an expert opinion or a first-hand account—an eyewitness recollection or a description of an event. Sometimes, an interview previews the release of a movie, a book, or even a comic book, as does the interview from the online magazine *ComicFan* that you are about to read.

Interviews are published in print and online newspapers and magazines or broadcast on television and radio shows. Most print interviews include these elements:

- Italic or boldface type, formatting, color, or other design elements to distinguish between the words of the interviewer and those of the interviewee
- A limited scope, with questions that focus on a particular subject or time period
- Introductory and closing material providing background information about the topic of the interview or the person being interviewed

Reading Strategy

Analyzing Purpose

Interviews are held for many reasons, such as to entertain, inform, inspire, or persuade readers, listeners, or viewers. **Analyzing the purpose** of a print interview will help you understand why it took place.

Start by examining the language the writer has chosen, including words, details, and events. Look for specific information that points to a particular purpose.

As you read the *ComicFan* interview, use a chart like the one shown to list the details that help you determine the interview's purpose.

Detail	Detail	Purpose

from ComicFan

INTERVIEW WITH SHANE L. AMAYA,
Writer of the comic *Roland: Days of Wrath*

Slated for release in July [1999], Shane L. Amaya's *Roland: Days of Wrath* has all the ingredients to be a hit. Recently chosen worthy of the Small Press Snapshot and Certified Cool mentions in May's Previews catalog, *Roland: Days of Wrath* promises beautiful art and an epic storyline. We recently caught up with the busy writer for a little one-on-one.

ComicFan: I understand that *Roland: Days of Wrath* is your first published work. Do you see this series as a springboard to other projects or have you committed yourself to this project for the long run?

Shane: The Roland comic is my first self-published work. My artists and I see this comic as our debut—as a way of getting our foot in the industry door. I hope to continue to self-publish and write comics after Roland: I am already thinking about two new projects for next year; I know my artists, Gabriel Ba and Fabio Moon, have stories to tell as well. Since our collaboration on the Roland comic has gone so well, we will definitely work together again, and sooner rather than later.

ComicFan: Now for those not familiar with your upcoming comic *Roland: Days of Wrath*. How would you describe the story and characters?

Shane: The Roland comic is based on the early medieval French war epic the *Song of Roland*. It was probably written late in the 11th century but the action is set in a glorified past—Charlemagne's 8th century Holy Roman Empire. It is the story of Roland's sacrifice, his stepfather's betrayal, and Charlemagne's eternal embattlement. The story is incredibly powerful and the language—having been refined orally for over three hundred years—is strong and beautiful. The characters are all warriors, feudal lords, kings and vassals. They are cut sharply: Roland is brave and Oliver is wise; they boast and betray; they weep and roar with anger—and these men fight, with all the strength in their hearts, and kill and die on the battlefield.

ComicFan: So what do you think fuels your passion for comic books? Is there a particular aspect?

Shane: Comic books tell more powerful, more emotionally evocative and more stimulating stories than any other medium. Comics are capable of the best storytelling art and literature can offer: they feature the best of two infinitely productive universes—the imagination literature excites coupled with the emotion art evokes. There is no medium more potent than comics, more intelligent, or more interactive. Reading a comic is not a passive experience: it requires work, it demands your imagination at the same time it feeds your eyes and heart with visual inspirations.

This is the aspect of comics that I love the most: its ability to express, relate, share and encourage the creativity of two art forms in one unique—and amazing—medium.

The interviewer's questions focus carefully on the particular subject of the interview.

ComicFan: I know you've done a lot of research into the historical aspects of the *Song of Roland,* which your comic is based on. What do you find so captivating about the *Song of Roland*?

Shane: The Middle Ages are an incredibly fascinating, important and—despite popular belief—creatively astounding period. I love the medieval imagination; medieval imagination has, I think, influenced the modern world in profound, unshakeable ways. The *Song of Roland* captivates me in more ways than I can say here: but for one, it is an amazing example of medieval ingenuity. How does Charlemagne's actual, historical and shameful defeat become a poem that, throughout time, transforms this skirmish into a story of apocalyptic struggle and Christ-like sacrifice; of battlefields packed with hundreds of thousands of warriors; of Anti-Gods and Judas figures; and where the stakes are no higher than the fate of the entire universe?!

ComicFan: Which writers do you think have had the most influence on you?

Shane: The works I enjoy reading most of all are those created by countless, anonymous authors. These include ancient epics and sagas, much of medieval literature, folk tales and other oral narratives. I enjoy medieval literature especially for the way it is created: through the hands and voices of many, . . . through marginalia and glosses upon glosses, and because of the way it is constantly interpreted, translated—and forever changing. To a medieval mind, authorship is wholly unimportant: it is only the story that matters, and still more important than the story is the way that it is well told. . . .

ComicFan: What do you think you enjoy more, the creating of Roland or the reading of it?

Shane: I never get tired of reading either the *Song of Roland* or my comic! Though the process of creation is a lot of fun, there's nothing like seeing the finished product.

ComicFan: Finally, what can readers expect to see in the coming issues of *Roland: Days of Wrath*?

Shane: The Roland comic is a moving and poignant story of war and vengeance, fraternity and betrayal, faith and wisdom. Readers can expect a beautifully drawn and colored mini-series that will take them into a vivid medieval world of tenuous politics and treacherous pagan citadels; they will witness justice, bloody vengeance, epic battle-storm and battlefields choked with dying warriors; readers will know the depths of Charlemagne's terrible grief, and the heart of one of the world's greatest heroes!

ComicFan: Thanks again for your time, Shane, and good luck with your great comic! You've got what looks like a hit on your hands, keep it up.

Roland: Days of Wrath from Terra Major debuts in July [1999] at comic-book shops everywhere.

The closing paragraph provides information about the availability of the comic book discussed in the interview.

Check Your Comprehension

1. On which work of literature is Amaya's comic book based?
2. Summarize Amaya's description of his story and his characters.
3. What inspires Amaya to write comic books?

Applying the Reading Strategy
Analyzing Purpose

4. Identify one detail indicating that the purpose of the interview is to entertain and one detail indicating that the purpose is to inform.
5. An interview can advance a person's career. In what way might the interview of Shane L. Amaya support that purpose? Explain.
6. What would you say is the overall purpose of this interview? Explain.

Activity
Conducting an Interview

Interview a classmate about one of his or her accomplishments. The chart shown gives helpful tips on conducting an interview.

Tips on Conducting an Interview
1. Contact the person to set up a day and time for the interview.
2. Write your questions in advance.
3. Gather the material you will need, such as a note pad, pens or pencils, and a tape recorder.
4. While interviewing, listen carefully to the interviewee's responses. A response to one question might give you an idea for another question.
5. Take thorough notes during your interview.

Then, write up your interview. Include a description of the interviewee and a summary of the accomplishment. Use text features to distinguish your questions from your interviewee's responses.

Comparing Informational Materials
Print and Television Interviews

View a television interview show, and compare it with the interview you read from *ComicFan*. As you watch, note the ways in which the television interview is similar to the written interview and the ways it is different. Note also the benefits—if any—in seeing the interview on television, and list any disadvantages. Share your findings with classmates.

Prepare to Read

from Perceval ◆ The Lay of the Werewolf

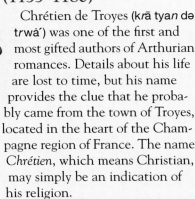

Chrétien de Troyes (1135–1180)

Chrétien de Troyes (krā´ tyan də trwä´) was one of the first and most gifted authors of Arthurian romances. Details about his life are lost to time, but his name provides the clue that he probably came from the town of Troyes, located in the heart of the Champagne region of France. The name *Chrétien*, which means Christian, may simply be an indication of his religion.

An Educated Courtier Most of what scholars know about Chrétien's life is based on an analysis of his work. Clearly, he was well educated. His work reflects knowledge of Latin as well as the cultures of Provence, a region in southern France, and Bretagne (Brittany), a region in northwest France. He wrote in the vernacular—the language of common people—and was inspired by a French translation of Geoffrey of Monmouth's *Historia Regum Britanniae*, which introduced the British legends of King Arthur to continental Europe.

The Grail Tale Chrétien's *Perceval* is the earliest known version of the Grail legend, which describes the quest for the Holy Grail, the cup from which Jesus drank at the Last Supper. According to medieval legend, both this cup and the lance that pierced Jesus' side during the Crucifixion were hidden in a magical castle. Sometime in the late Middle Ages, the Grail legend was woven into the tales of King Arthur and his knights. The knights sought to find this mystical object, which would then enable Arthur to found a new holy kingdom. Only a knight of absolute purity would be able to find the Grail. In *Perceval*, Chrétien created a knight virtuous enough to see the Grail but not quite pure enough to obtain it.

Chrétien died before completing this story; nevertheless, it remains one of the most enduring tales to emerge from the Middle Ages.

Marie de France (c. 1155–1190)

Little is known about the life of Marie de France, one of the finest storytellers of the Middle Ages. Yet her works, which were read by Boccaccio and Chaucer, were crucial to the development of the short story. Scholars know that she lived in the French-speaking English court of the late twelfth century, about one hundred years after the Norman Conquest. She was well educated, a member of the nobility, and possibly an abbess. Her name suggests that she came from France.

Magical Worlds Marie's work combines elements of the classical, Christian, and Celtic traditions. For example, in *Saint Patrick's Purgatory*, which she translated from the Latin, the hero travels to another land, where he learns the secrets of the Christian faith. The theme of a voyage to another world, usually the magical world of the dead, is typical of Celtic mythology. In Marie's work, however, the magical journey reinforces Christian morality.

Radical Ideas Marie's most original works, the *lais* (lā), explore the conflict between passionate love and marital duty. The *lais* are short stories, written in verse, that combine folkloric elements of magic with the newly popular concept of courtly love. Initially, the idea of courtly love involved the hopeless adoration of an unobtainable woman by a young man of inferior social standing. Marie revised this perception to achieve a more realistic view of human relationships. For Marie, a man and a woman should choose each other because of a genuine affinity. In an era when most marriages were based on political or economic interests, this idea was a radical departure from the norm. Through her work, Marie helped lay the foundations for modern ideas about love and marriage.

Preview

Connecting to the Literature

You have probably had dreams in which odd things happen. You may fly over rooftops or find yourself in a strange situation that nevertheless seems familiar. The adventures in these selections echo such dreamlike images.

Literary Analysis

Archetypes

Archetypes are details, plot patterns, character types, or themes that appear in the literature of many different cultures. Chrétien de Troyes' tale contains the archetype of the quest, while Marie de France's story contains the archetype of disguised identity.

- *The quest:* A quest is the pursuit of someone or something of great importance. While on a quest, a hero journeys great distances, defeats evil, demonstrates valor, and grows in wisdom and maturity.

- *Disguised identity:* Characters use disguises, transformations, and tricks to hide their true identities.

As you read these selections, notice the ways in which they follow archetypal patterns.

Comparing Literary Works

Archetypes almost always have a deeper, symbolic significance. A **symbol** is a person, a place, an animal, or an object that has its own meaning but also suggests a larger meaning. For example, a rose might symbolize love. In many medieval tales, the entire story centers on a symbol. In *Perceval*, the grail is not merely a golden cup but an object symbolizing the story's most important ideas. As you read these selections, compare the ways in which symbols express each tale's central meaning.

Reading Strategy

Interpreting Symbols

To **interpret a symbol** and better appreciate archetypal narratives, examine the details associated with characters, places, objects, or events, and consider them in the context of the story. For example, when Perceval nears the edge of a cliff, the cliff might symbolize the danger of his quest. As you read these selections, use a chart like the one shown to interpret symbols.

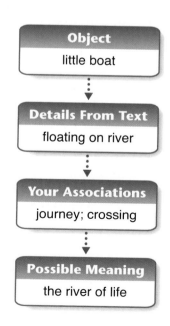

Object
little boat

⬇

Details From Text
floating on river

⬇

Your Associations
journey; crossing

⬇

Possible Meaning
the river of life

Vocabulary Development

sovereign (säv´ rən) *adj.* chief; superior; highest (p. 584)

navigated (nav´ i gāt´ əd) *v.* piloted; steered (a boat) (p. 585)

elated (ē lāt´ əd) *adj.* extremely happy; joyful (p. 587)

serene (sə rēn´) *adj.* clear; calm; peaceful (p. 591)

nimble (nim´ bəl) *adj.* able to move quickly and lightly; agile (p. 593)

esteemed (e stēmd´) *v.* valued; respected (p. 596)

importunity (im´ pôr tōōn´ i tē) *n.* persistence (p. 598)

abases (ə bās´ əz) *v.* lowers; brings down (p. 599)

from *Perceval*
The Grail

Chrétien de Troyes   *translated by Ruth Harwood Cline*

Background

Perceval is a young man whose mother raised him in isolation after losing her husband and two other sons to chivalric combat. One day, Perceval meets a group of knights, who so impress him that he decides to become a knight himself. He journeys to King Arthur's court, proves his valor, and is accepted. As part of his training for knighthood, Perceval learns never to ask questions and never to speak until spoken to first. Once his training is complete, Perceval sets out on a quest for the Grail, or holy cup. This excerpt begins just before Perceval stumbles upon a mysterious castle, that of the ailing Fisher King.

The youth began his journey from
the castle, and the daytime whole
he did not meet one living soul:
no creature from the wide earth's span,

5   no Christian woman, Christian man
who could direct him on his way.
The young man did not cease to pray
the <u>sovereign</u> father, God, Our Lord,
if He were willing, to accord

10 that he would find his mother still
alive and well. He reached a hill
and saw a river at its base.
So rapid was the current's pace,
so deep the water, that he dared

15 not enter it, and he declared,
"Oh God Almighty! It would seem,
if I could get across this stream,
I'd find my mother, if she's living."
He rode the bank with some misgiving

20 and reached a cliff, but at that place
the water met the cliff's sheer face
and kept the youth from going through.

Literary Analysis
Archetypes In what ways does the absence of any other people emphasize the danger and uncertainty of Perceval's quest?

sovereign (säv´ rən) *adj.* chief; superior; highest

Reading Strategy
Interpreting Symbols Which details in the description of the river suggest its possible symbolic meaning? Explain.

A little boat came into view;
it headed down the river, floating
25 and carrying two men out boating.
The young knight halted there and waited.
He watched the way they <u>navigated</u>
and thought that they would pass the place
he waited by the cliff's sheer face.
30 They stayed in mid-stream, where they stopped
and took the anchor, which they dropped.
The man afore,[1] a fisher, took
a fish to bait his line and hook;
in size the little fish he chose
35 was larger than a minnow grows.
The knight, completely at a loss,
not knowing how to get across,
first greeted them, then asked the pair,
"Please, gentlemen, nearby is there
40 a bridge to reach the other side?"
To which the fisherman replied,
"No, brother, for besides this boat,
the one in which we are afloat,
which can't bear five men's weight as charge,
45 there is no other boat as large
for twenty miles each way and more,
and you can't cross on horseback, for
there is no ferry, bridge, nor ford."
"Tell me," he answered, "by Our Lord,
50 where I may find a place to stay."
The fisherman said, "I should say
you'll need a roof tonight and more,
so I will lodge you at my door.
First find the place this rock is breached
55 and ride uphill, until you've reached
the summit of the cliff," he said.
"Between the wood and river bed
you'll see, down in the valley wide,
the manor house where I reside."
60 The knight rode up the cliff until
he reached the summit of the hill.
He looked around him from that stand
but saw no more than sky and land.
He cried, "What have I come to see?
65 Stupidity and trickery!
May God dishonor and disgrace
the man who sent me to this place!
He had the long way round in mind,

---

1. **afore** (ə fôr´) before.

from *Perceval* ◆ 585

navigated (nav´ i gāt´ əd) *v.*
piloted; steered (a boat)

Literary Analysis
Archetypes At this stage
of the quest, is the challenge the knight faces
physical, emotional, or
intellectual? Explain.

Reading Strategy
Interpreting Symbols
Which details in this
exchange suggest that the
fisherman might be more
than he seems to be?

✔**Reading Check**
Whom does Perceval
meet at the river?

Parsifal Sees the Grail's Castle, Martin Weigan

▲ **Critical Viewing** Which details in this painting of Perceval suggest that the castle has magical or supernatural qualities? **[Analyze]**

when he told me that I would find
a manor when I reached the peak.
Oh, fisherman, why did you speak?
For if you said it out of spite,
you tricked me badly!" He caught sight
of a tower starting to appear
down in a valley he was near,
and as the tower came into view,
if people were to search, he knew,
as far as Beirut,[2] they would not
find any finer tower or spot.
The tower was dark gray stone, and square,
and flanked by lesser towers, a pair.
Before the tower the hall was laid;
before the hall was the arcade.[3]
On toward the tower the young man rode
in haste and called the man who showed
the way to him a worthy guide.
No longer saying he had lied,
he praised the fisherman, <u>elated</u>
to find his lodgings as he stated.
The youth went toward the gate and found
the drawbridge lowered to the ground.
He rode across the drawbridge span.
Four squires awaited the young man.
Two squires came up to help him doff
his arms and took his armor off.
The third squire led his horse away
to give him fodder, oats, and hay.
The fourth brought a silk cloak, new-made,
and led him to the hall's arcade,
which was so fine, you may be sure
you'd not find, even if you were
to search as far as Limoges,[4] one
as splendid in comparison.
The young man paused in the arcade,
until the castle's master made
two squires escort him to the hall.
The young man entered with them all
and found the hall was square inside:
it was as long as it was wide;
and in the center of its span
he saw a handsome nobleman
with grayed hair, sitting on a bed.

70
75
80
85
90
95
100
105
110

Literary Analysis
Archetypes What lesson should Perceval learn from accusing, and then praising, the fisherman?

elated (ē lāt′ əd) *adj.*
extremely happy; joyful

---

2. **Beirut** (bā rōōt′) capital of Lebanon and a seaport on the Mediterranean.
3. **arcade** (är kād′) passage with an arched roof, or any covered passageway.
4. **Limoges** (lē mōzh′) city in west central France.

Reading Check

What appears "down in a valley" as Perceval watches?

The nobleman wore on his head
a mulberry-black sable cap
115 and wore a dark silk robe and wrap.
He leaned back in his weakened state
and let his elbow take his weight.
Between four columns, burning bright,
a fire of dry logs cast its light.
120 In order to enjoy its heat,
four hundred men could find a seat
around the outsized fire, and not
one man would take a chilly spot.
The solid fireplace columns could
125 support the massive chimney hood,
which was of bronze, built high and wide.
The squires, one squire on either side,
appeared before their lord foremost
and brought the youth before his host.
130 He saw the young man, whom he greeted.
"My friend," the nobleman entreated,
"don't think me rude not to arise;
I hope that you will realize
that I cannot do so with ease."
135 "Don't even mention it, sir, please,
I do not mind," replied the boy,
"may Heaven give me health and joy."
The lord rose higher on the bed,
as best he could, with pain, and said,
140 "My friend, come nearer, do not be
embarrassed or disturbed by me,
for I command you to come near.
Come to my side and sit down here."
The nobleman began to say,
145 "From where, sir, did you come today?"
He said, "This morning, sir, I came
from Belrepeire, for that's its name."
"So help me God," the lord replied,
"you must have had a long day's ride:
150 to start before the light of morn
before the watchman blew his horn."
"Sir, I assure you, by that time
the morning bells had rung for prime,"[5]
the young man made the observation.
155 While they were still in conversation,
a squire entered through the door
and carried in a sword he wore
hung from his neck and which thereto

Themes in World Literature

Quest Narratives

The quest archetype is central to literature because it is central to the imagination. The journey, which is motivated by the pursuit of love or glory, filled with peril, stalled by monsters, aided by friends, and completed in a joyous homecoming, mirrors the path of life. Many of literature's most compelling narratives—including Jason's search for the Golden Fleece, Don Quixote's struggle against imaginary monsters, Frodo's passage into the heart of evil, and even Indiana Jones's pursuit of ancient treasures—are quest tales. The quest is the archetypal pattern that people follow in order to become the heroes of their own lives.

---

5. prime first hour of daylight, usually 6 A.M.

he gave the rich man, who withdrew
160 the sword halfway and checked the blade
to see where it was forged and made,
which had been written on the sword.
The blade was wrought, observed the lord,
of such fine steel, it would not break
165 save with its bearer's life at stake
on one occasion, one alone,
a peril that was only known
to him who forged and tempered it.
The squire said, "Sir, if you permit,
170 your lovely blonde niece sent this gift,
and you will never see or lift
a sword that's lighter for its strength,
considering its breadth and length.
Please give the sword to whom you choose,
175 but if it goes to one who'll use
the sword that he is given well,
you'll greatly please the demoiselle.
The forger of the sword you see
has never made more swords than three,
180 and he is going to die before
he ever forges any more.
No sword will be quite like this sword."
Immediately the noble lord
bestowed it on the newcomer,
185 who realized that its hangings were
a treasure and of worth untold.
The pommel[6] of the sword was gold,
the best Arabian or Grecian;
the sheath's embroidery gold Venetian.
190 Upon the youth the castle's lord
bestowed the richly mounted sword
and said to him, "This sword, dear brother,
was destined for you and none other.
I wish it to be yours henceforth.
195 Gird on the sword and draw it forth."
He thanked the lord, and then the knight
made sure the belt was not too tight,
and girded on the sword, and took
the bare blade out for a brief look.
200 Then in the sheath it was replaced:
it looked well hanging at his waist
and even better in his fist.
It seemed as if it would assist

▲ **Critical Viewing**
The bottom band of this illustrated manuscript shows Perceval and others nearing the Castle of the Grail. Is the mood of this scene similar to or different from the mood created by the poem? **[Compare and Contrast]**

☑ **Reading Check**
What gift does the nobleman give to Perceval?

---

6. pommel (pum´ el) *n.* knob on the end of the hilt of a sword or dagger.

the youth in any time of need
205 to do a brave and knightly deed.
Beside the brightly burning fire
the youth turned round and saw a squire,
who had his armor in his care,
among the squires standing there.
210 He told this squire to hold the sword
and took his seat beside the lord,
who honored him as best he might.
The candles cast as bright a light
as could be found in any manor.
215 They chatted in a casual manner.
Out of a room a squire came, clasping
a lance of purest white: while grasping
the center of the lance, the squire
walked through the hall between the fire
220 and two men sitting on the bed.
All saw him bear, with measured tread,
the pure white lance. From its white tip
a drop of crimson blood would drip
and run along the white shaft and
225 drip down upon the squire's hand,
and then another drop would flow.
The knight who came not long ago
beheld this marvel, but preferred
not to inquire why it occurred,
230 for he recalled the admonition
the lord made part of his tuition,[7]
since he had taken pains to stress
the dangers of loquaciousness.[8]
The young man thought his questions might
235 make people think him impolite,
and that's why he did not inquire.
Two more squires entered, and each squire
held candelabra, wrought of fine
pure gold with niello work design.[9]
240 The squires with candelabra fair
were an extremely handsome pair.
At least ten lighted candles blazed
in every holder that they raised.
The squires were followed by a maiden
245 who bore a grail, with both hands laden.

The Damsel of Sanct Grael, 1857, Dante Gabriel Rossetti, Tate Gallery, London

▲ **Critical Viewing**
Which details in the poet's description of the grail and the maiden have been included in this painting, and which have been changed or omitted? Explain. **[Distinguish]**

---

7. **the admonition . . . tuition** the warning that the lord made part of his teaching.
8. **loquaciousness** (lō kwā′ shəs nis) *n.* talkativeness.
9. **niello** (nē el′ ō) **work design** deep black inlaid work used to decorate metal.

The bearer was of noble mien,[10]
well dressed, and lovely, and <u>serene,</u>
and when she entered with the grail,
the candles suddenly grew pale,
250   the grail cast such a brilliant light,
as stars grow dimmer in the night
when sun or moonrise makes them fade.
A maiden after her conveyed
a silver platter past the bed.
255   The grail, which had been borne ahead,
was made of purest, finest gold
and set with gems; a manifold
display of jewels of every kind,
the costliest that one could find
260   in any place on land or sea,
the rarest jewels there could be,
let not the slightest doubt be cast.
The jewels in the grail surpassed
all other gems in radiance.
265   They went the same way as the lance:
they passed before the lord's bedside
to another room and went inside.
The young man saw the maids' procession
and did not dare to ask a question
270   about the grail or whom they served;
the wise lord's warning he observed,
for he had taken it to heart.
I fear he was not very smart;
I have heard warnings people give:
275   that one can be too talkative,
but also one can be too still.
But whether it was good or ill,
I do not know, he did not ask.
The squires who were assigned the task
280   of bringing in the water and
the cloths obeyed the lord's command.
The men who usually were assigned
performed these tasks before they dined.
They washed their hands in water, warmed,
285   and then two squires, so I'm informed,
brought in the ivory tabletop,
made of one piece: they had to stop
and hold it for a while before

---

10. **grail** (grāl) . . . **mien** (mēn) The Grail is the legendary cup or platter used by Jesus at the Last Supper and by Joseph of Arimathea to collect drops of Jesus' blood at the Crucifixion. **Mien** signifies "appearance."

serene (sə rēn´) *adj.* clear; calm; peaceful

Literary Analysis
Archetypes and Symbols
What might the radiant light of the grail symbolize?

Literary Analysis
Archetypes Quests often include tests—some difficult, some easy. How would you characterize Perceval's test? Explain.

**Reading Check**
What two extraordinary objects does Perceval observe as they are paraded around the hall?

the lord and youth, until two more
290 squires entered, each one with a trestle.[11]
The trestles had two very special,
rare properties, which they contained
since they were built, and which remained
in them forever: they were wrought
295 of ebony, a wood that's thought
to have two virtues: it will not
ignite and burn and will not rot;
these dangers cause no harm nor loss.
They laid the tabletop across
300 the trestles, and the cloth above.
What shall I say? To tell you of
the cloth is far beyond my scope.
No legate, cardinal, or pope
has eaten from a whiter one.
305 The first course was of venison,
a peppered haunch, cooked in its fat,
accompanied by a clear wine that
was served in golden cups, a pleasant,
delicious drink. While they were present
310 a squire carved up the venison.
He set the peppered haunch upon
a silver platter, carved the meat,
and served the slices they would eat
by placing them on hunks of bread.
315 Again the grail passed by the bed,
and still the youth remained reserved
about the grail and whom they served.
he did not ask, because he had
been told so kindly it was bad
320 to talk too much, and he had taken
these words to heart. He was mistaken;
though he remembered, he was still
much longer than was suitable.
At every course, and in plain sight,
325 the grail was carried past the knight,
who did not ask whom they were serving,
although he wished to know, observing
in silence that he ought to learn
about it prior to his return.
330 So he would ask: before he spoke
he'd wait until the morning broke,
and he would ask a squire to tell,
once he had told the lord farewell

Literary Analysis
Archetypes and Symbols
In what ways does the
long description of the
meal add to the air of
mystery surrounding the
nobleman?

---

11. trestle (tres´ əl) *n.* frame consisting of a horizontal beam fastened to two pairs of
v-shaped supports.

and all the others in his train.
335 He put the matter off again
and turned his thoughts toward drink
    and food.
They brought, and in no stingy mood,
the foods and different types of wine,
which were delicious, rich and fine.
340 The squires were able to provide
the lord and young knight at his side
with every course a count, king, queen,
and emperor eat by routine.
At dinner's end, the two men stayed
345 awake and talked, while squires made
the beds and brought them fruit: they ate
the rarest fruits: the nutmeg, date,
fig, clove, and pomegranate red.
With Alexandrian gingerbread,
350 electuaries[12] at the end,
restoratives, a tonic blend,
and pliris archonticum
for settling his stomachum.
Then various liqueurs were poured
355 for them to sample afterward:
straight piment, which did not contain
sweet honey or a single grain
of pepper, wine of mulberries,
clear syrups, other delicacies.
360 The youth's astonishment persisted;
he did not know such things existed.
"Now, my dear friend," the great lord said,
"the time has come to go to bed.
I'll seek my room—don't think it queer—
365 and you will have your bed out here
and may lie down at any hour.
I do not have the slightest power
over my body anymore
and must be carried to my door."
370 Four <u>nimble</u> servants, strongly set,
came in and seized the coverlet
by its four corners (it was spread
beneath the lord, who lay in bed)
and carried him away to rest.
375 The others helped the youthful guest.
As he required, and when he chose,
they took his clothing off, and hose,

Perceval at Amfortas, wall painting from the "Parsifal saga," Ferdinand Piloty, the Younger

▲ **Critical Viewing**
Is this painting a faithful rendering of the grail scene as described by the poet? Explain. **[Evaluate]**

nimble (nim′ bəl) *adj.* able to move quickly and lightly; agile

✔**Reading Check**

What question about the lord of the castle does Perceval fail to ask?

---

12. electuaries (ē lek′ chōō er′ ēz) medicines made by mixing drugs with honey or syrup to form a paste. Pliris archonticum, mentioned two lines later, is such a medicine.

and put him in a bed with white,
smooth linen sheets; he slept all night
380   at peace until the morning broke.
But when the youthful knight awoke,
he was the last to rise and found
that there was no one else around.
Exasperated and alone,
385   he had to get up on his own.
He made the best of it, arose,
and awkwardly drew on his hose
without a bit of help or aid.
He saw his armor had been laid
390   at night against the dais' head
a little distance from his bed.
When he had armed himself at last,
he walked around the great hall past
the rooms and knocked at every door
395   which opened wide the night before,
but it was useless: juxtaposed,[13]
the doors were tightly locked and closed.
He shouted, called, and knocked outside,
but no one opened or replied.
400   At last the young man ceased to call,
walked to the doorway of the hall,
which opened up, and passed through there,
and went on down the castle stair.
His horse was saddled in advance.
405   The young man saw his shield and lance
were leaned against the castle wall
upon the side that faced the hall.
He mounted, searched the castle whole,
but did not find one living soul,
410   one servant, or one squire around.
He hurried toward the gate and found
the men had let the drawbridge down,
so that the knight could leave the town
at any hour he wished to go.
415   His hosts had dropped the drawbridge so
the youth could cross it undeterred.
The squires were sent, the youth inferred,
out to the wood, where they were set
to checking every trap and net.
420   The drawbridge lay across the stream.
He would not wait and formed a scheme
of searching through the woods as well
to see if anyone could tell

Reading Strategy
Interpreting Symbols
What does the complete absence of people suggest about Perceval's experience of the night before?

---

13. juxtaposed (juks′ tə pōzd′) *adj.* placed side by side or close together.

about the lance, why it was bleeding,
425　about the grail, whom they were feeding,
and where they carried it in state.
The youth rode through the castle gate
and out upon the drawbridge plank.
Before he reached the other bank,
430　the young man started realizing
the forefeet of his horse were rising.
His horse made one great leap indeed.
Had he not jumped well, man and steed
would have been hurt. His rider swerved
435　to see what happened and observed
the drawbridge had been lifted high.
He shouted, hearing no reply,
"Whoever raised the bridge," said he,
"where are you? Come and talk to me!
440　Say something to me; come in view.
There's something I would ask of you,
some things I wanted to inquire,
some information I desire."
His words were wasted, vain and fond;
445　no one was willing to respond.

Review and Assess

Thinking About the Selection

1. **Respond:** Which aspect of Perceval's adventure do you find most interesting? Explain.

2. **(a) Recall:** What invitation does the fisherman extend to Perceval? **(b) Analyze:** Do you think the fisherman and the Fisher King are the same person? Explain.

3. **(a) Recall:** What is the Fisher King's physical condition? **(b) Analyze:** What do you think might be causing his condition? Support your answer.

4. **(a) Interpret:** When Perceval sees the lance and the Grail, what fateful decision does he make? **(b) Analyze Causes and Effects:** Why do you think he makes this decision?

5. **(a) Speculate:** In what ways, if any, do you think Perceval will grow as a result of this adventure? **(b) Support:** Which details in the excerpt support your position? Explain.

6. **Evaluate:** What do you think the story of Perceval suggests about the pros and cons of innocence? Explain.

The Lay of the Werewolf

Marie de France
translated by **Eugene Mason**

Background

The ancient Greeks wrote that people could be transformed into wolves, remain in that form for years, and then return to their human form. Medieval intellectuals were ready to dismiss werewolves as mere hallucinations, but the common people believed these creatures truly existed. For medieval villagers, such creatures were either demons or men being punished for horrible sins. However, in this story, Marie de France questions the assumption that the beast is evil or sinful. Instead, the werewolf displays a deep, sensitive humanity, while human beings show themselves to be the real beasts.

Amongst the tales I tell you once again, I would not forget the Lay of the Werewolf. Such beasts as he are known in every land. Bisclavaret he is named in Brittany; whilst the Norman[1] calls him Garwal.

It is a certain thing, and within the knowledge of all, that many a christened man has suffered this change, and ran wild in woods, as a Werewolf. The Werewolf is a fearsome beast. He lurks within the thick forest, mad and horrible to see. All the evil that he may, he does. He goeth to and fro, about the solitary place, seeking man, in order to devour him. Hearken, now, to the adventure of the Werewolf, that I have to tell.

In Brittany there dwelt a baron who was marvelously <u>esteemed</u> of all his fellows. He was a stout knight, and a comely, and a man of office and repute. Right private was he to the mind of his lord, and dear to the counsel of his neighbors. This baron was wedded to a very worthy dame, right fair to see, and sweet of semblance. All his love was set on her, and all her love was given again to him. One only grief had this

Literary Analysis
Archetypes and Symbols
Based on this description, which human emotions do werewolves seem to embody?

esteemed (e stēmd´) *v.* valued; respected

---

1. **Brittany** (brit´ ´n ē) . . . **Norman** Brittany is a region of northwestern France, adjacent to Normandy.

lady. For three whole days in every week her lord was absent from her side. She knew not where he went, nor on what errand. Neither did any of his house know the business which called him forth.

On a day when this lord was come again to his house, altogether joyous and content, the lady took him to task, right sweetly, in this fashion,

"Husband," said she, "and fair, sweet friend, I have a certain thing to pray of you. Right willing would I receive this gift, but I fear to anger you in the asking. It is better for me to have an empty hand, than to gain hard words."

When the lord heard this matter, he took the lady in his arms, very tenderly, and kissed her.

"Wife," he answered, "ask what you will. What would you have, for it is yours already?"

▼ **Critical Viewing**

Compare and contrast the portrayal of the werewolf in this fifteenth-century woodcut with the description of werewolves in the story. **[Compare and Contrast]**

"By my faith," said the lady, "soon shall I be whole. Husband, right long and wearisome are the days that you spend away from your home. I rise from my bed in the morning, sick at heart, I know not why. So fearful am I, lest you do aught to your loss, that I may not find any comfort. Very quickly shall I die for reason of my dread. Tell me now, where you go, and on what business! How may the knowledge of one who loves so closely, bring you to harm?"

"Wife," made answer the lord, "nothing but evil can come if I tell you this secret. For the mercy of God do not require it of me. If you but knew, you would withdraw yourself from my love, and I should be lost indeed."

Werewolf Attacking a Man, German woodcut, 15th century

When the lady heard this, she was persuaded that her baron sought to put her by with jesting words. Therefore she prayed and required him the more urgently, with tender looks and speech, till he was overborne, and told her all the story, hiding naught.

"Wife, I become Bisclavaret. I enter in the forest, and live on prey and roots, within the thickest of the wood."

After she had learned his secret, she prayed and entreated the more as to whether he ran in his raiment, or went spoiled of vesture.

"Wife," said he, "I go naked as a beast."

"Tell me, for hope of grace, what you do with your clothing?"

"Fair wife, that will I never. If I should lose my raiment, or even be marked as I quit my vesture, then a Werewolf I must go for all the days of my life. Never again should I become man, save in that hour my clothing were given back to me. For this reason never will I show my lair."

"Husband," replied the lady to him, "I love you better than all the world. The less cause have you for doubting my faith, or hiding any

✔**Reading Check**

What happens to the baron for three days of every week?

◀ **Critical Viewing**
Would the forest portrayed in this painting offer Bisclavaret the kind of secrecy he seeks? Why or why not? [Interpret]

tittle from me. What savor is here of friendship? How have I made forfeit of your love; for what sin do you mistrust my honor? Open now your heart, and tell what is good to be known."

So at the end, outwearied and overborne by her <u>importunity</u>, he could no longer refrain, but told her all.

"Wife," said he, "within this wood, a little from the path, there is a hidden way, and at the end thereof an ancient chapel, where oftentimes I have bewailed my lot. Near by is a great hollow stone, concealed by a bush, and there is the secret place where I hide my raiment, till I would return to my own home."

On hearing this marvel the lady became sanguine[2] of visage, because of her exceeding fear. She dared no longer to lie at his side, and turned over in her mind, this way and that, how best she could get her from him. Now there was a certain knight of those parts, who, for a great while, had sought and required this lady for her love. This knight had spent long years in her service, but little enough had he got thereby, not even fair words, or a promise. To him the dame wrote a letter, and meeting, made her purpose plain.

"Fair friend," said she, "be happy. That which you have coveted so long a time, I will grant without delay. Never again will I deny your suit. My heart, and all I have to give, are yours, so take me now as love and dame."

Literary Analysis
Archetypes How does the wife manipulate her husband into revealing the entirety of his secret?

importunity (im′ pôr tōōn′ i tē) *n.* persistence

---

2. **sanguine** (saŋ′ gwin) *adj.* reddish; ruddy.

Right sweetly the knight thanked her for her grace, and pledged her faith and fealty. When she had confirmed him by an oath, then she told him all this business of her lord—why he went, and what he became, and of his ravening[3] within the wood. So she showed him of the chapel, and of the hollow stone, and of how to spoil the Werewolf of his vesture. Thus, by the kiss of his wife, was Bisclavaret betrayed. Often enough had he ravished his prey in desolate places, but from this journey he never returned. His kinsfolk and acquaintance came together to ask of his tidings, when this absence was noised abroad. Many a man, on many a day, searched the woodland, but none might find him, nor learn where Bisclavaret was gone.

The lady was wedded to the knight who had cherished her for so long a space. More than a year had passed since Bisclavaret disappeared. Then it chanced that the King would hunt in that self-same wood where the Werewolf lurked. When the hounds were unleashed they ran this way and that, and swiftly came upon his scent. At the view the huntsman winded on his horn, and the whole pack were at his heels. They followed him from morn to eve, till he was torn and bleeding, and was all adread lest they should pull him down. Now the King was very close to the quarry, and when Bisclavaret looked upon his master, he ran to him for pity and for grace. He took the stirrup within his paws, and fawned upon the prince's foot. The King was very fearful at this sight, but presently he called his courtiers to his aid.

"Lords," cried he, "hasten hither, and see this marvelous thing. Here is a beast who has the sense of man. He <u>abases</u> himself before his foe, and cries for mercy, although he cannot speak. Beat off the hounds, and let no man do him harm. We will hunt no more today, but return to our own place, with the wonderful quarry we have taken."

The King turned him about, and rode to his hall, Bisclavaret following at his side. Very near to his master the Werewolf went, like any dog, and had no care to seek again the wood. When the King had brought him safely to his own castle, he rejoiced greatly, for the beast was fair and strong, no mightier had any man seen. Much pride had the King in his marvelous beast. He held him so dear, that he bade all those who wished for his love, to cross the Wolf in naught, neither to strike him with a rod, but ever to see that he was richly fed and kenneled warm. This commandment the Court observed willingly. So all the day the Wolf sported with the lords, and at night he lay within

---

3. **ravening** (rav´ ən iŋ) *n.* greedy searching for prey.

*L*iterature
in context History Connection

Wolves in the Middle Ages

During the Middle Ages, the natural world was far more threatening than it is today. Dense forest covered most of Europe. Residents of tiny villages only a few miles apart often spoke different languages and never encountered each other, so forbidding was the forest that lay between them.

Wolves embodied the threat posed by the natural world. Wolves wandered the forest, sometimes venturing into villages to snatch up small livestock. The terror people felt for wolves is captured in familiar fairy tales, such as the story of Little Red Riding Hood.

As frightening as wolves were, human beings could be worse. Children occasionally disappeared from their homes, possibly carried off by wolves but more likely abandoned by parents who could not afford to feed them. Only vagabonds and thieves ventured into the forest, and they were more terrifying than the wolves. The brutality of life in the Middle Ages sometimes diminished the distance between human and animal behavior—a harsh fact of life reflected in literature like Marie de France's tale.

abases (ə bās´ əz) *v.* lowers; brings down

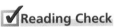Reading Check

Who betrayed Bisclavaret?

the chamber of the King. There was not a man who did not make much of the beast, so frank was he and debonair.[4] None had reason to do him wrong, for ever was he about his master, and for his part did evil to none. Every day were these two companions together, and all perceived that the King loved him as his friend.

Hearken now to that which chanced.

The King held a high Court, and bade his great vassals and barons, and all the lords of his venery[5] to the feast. Never was there a goodlier feast, nor one set forth with sweeter show and pomp. Amongst those who were bidden, came that same knight who had the wife of Bisclavaret for dame. He came to the castle, richly gowned, with a fair company, but little he deemed whom he would find so near. Bisclavaret marked his foe the moment he stood within the hall. He ran towards him, and seized him with his fangs, in the King's very presence, and to the view of all. Doubtless he would have done him much mischief, had not the King called and chidden him, and threatened him with a rod. Once, and twice, again, the Wolf set upon the knight in the very light of day. All men marveled at his malice, for sweet and serviceable was the beast, and to that hour had shown hatred of none. With one consent the household deemed that this deed was done with full reason, and that the Wolf had suffered at the knight's hand some bitter wrong. Right wary of his foe was the knight until the feast had ended, and all the barons had taken farewell of their lord, and departed, each to his own house. With these, amongst the very first, went that lord whom Bisclavaret so fiercely had assailed. Small was the wonder that he was glad to go.

No long while after this adventure it came to pass that the courteous King would hunt in that forest where Bisclavaret was found. With the prince came his wolf, and a fair company. Now at nightfall the King abode

4. **debonair** (deb´ ə ner´) *adj.* pleasant, charming, and friendly.
5. **venery** (ven´ ər ē) the act or practice of hunting game.

Reading Strategy
Interpreting Symbols
Why do you think the author emphasizes the marvel of the beast's good conduct?

▼ **Critical Viewing**
In what ways does this painting of a festive gathering of medieval nobility emphasize the qualities shown by the king and his court in this story? **[Analyze]**

within a certain lodge of that country, and this was known of that dame who before was the wife of Bisclavaret. In the morning the lady clothed her in her most dainty apparel, and hastened to the lodge, since she desired to speak with the King, and to offer him a rich present. When the lady entered in the chamber, neither man nor leash might restrain the fury of the Wolf. He became as a mad dog in his hatred and malice. Breaking from his bonds he sprang at the lady's face, and bit the nose from her visage. From every side men ran to the succor of the dame. They beat off the wolf from his prey, and for a little would have cut him in pieces with their swords. But a certain wise counselor said to the King,

"Sire, hearken now to me. This beast is always with you, and there is not one of us all who has not known him for long. He goes in and out amongst us, nor has molested any man, neither done wrong or felony to any, save only to this dame, one only time as we have seen. He has done evil to this lady, and to that knight, who is now the husband of the dame. Sire, she was once the wife of that lord who was so close and private to your heart, but who went, and none might find where he had gone. Now, therefore, put the dame in a sure place, and question her straitly, so that she may tell—if perchance she knows thereof—for what reason this Beast holds her in such mortal hate. For many a strange deed has chanced, as well we know, in this marvelous land of Brittany."

The King listened to these words, and deemed the counsel good. He laid hands upon the knight, and put the dame in surety in another place. He caused them to be questioned right straitly, so that their torment was very grievous. At the end, partly because of her distress, and partly by reason of her exceeding fear, the lady's lips were loosed, and she told her tale. She showed them of the betrayal of her lord, and how his raiment was stolen from the hollow stone. Since then she knew not where he went, nor what had befallen him, for he had never come again to his own land. Only, in her heart, well she deemed and was persuaded, that Bisclavaret was he.

Straightway the King demanded the vesture of his baron, whether this were to the wish of the lady, or whether it were against her wish. When the raiment was brought him, he caused it to be spread before Bisclavaret, but the Wolf made as though he had not seen. Then that cunning and crafty counselor took the King apart, that he might give him a fresh rede.[6]

---

6. **rede** (rēd) counsel; advice.

▲ **Critical Viewing**
Do you think contemporary viewers would have found this seventeenth-century engraving of a werewolf frightening? Explain. **[Speculate]**

☑**Reading Check**
How does Bisclavaret react to his ex-wife and her new husband?

"Sire," said he, "you do not wisely, nor well, to set this raiment before Bisclavaret, in the sight of all. In shame and much tribulation must he lay aside the beast, and again become man. Carry your wolf within your most secret chamber, and put his vestment therein. Then close the door upon him, and leave him alone for a space. So we shall see presently whether the ravening beast may indeed return to human shape."

The King carried the Wolf to his chamber, and shut the doors upon him fast. He delayed for a brief while, and taking two lords of his fellow-ship with him, came again to the room. Entering therein, all three, softly together, they found the knight sleeping in the King's bed, like a little child. The King ran swiftly to the bed and taking his friend in his arms, embraced and kissed him fondly, above a hundred times. When man's speech returned once more, he told him of his adventure. Then the King restored to his friend the fief that was stolen from him, and gave such rich gifts, moreover, as I cannot tell. As for the wife who had betrayed Bisclavaret, he bade her avoid his country, and chased her from the realm. So she went forth, she and her second lord together, to seek a more abiding city, and were no more seen.

The adventure that you have heard is no vain fable. Verily and indeed it chanced as I have said. The Lay of the Werewolf, truly, was written that it should ever be borne in mind.

Review and Assess

Thinking About the Selection

1. **Respond:** If you were the wife in this story, how would you feel about your husband's secret? Explain.

2. **(a) Recall:** What is the wife's "one grief"? **(b) Infer:** What does she do to address this grief? **(c) Interpret:** What does her pursuit of her husband's secret suggest about her character?

3. **(a) Recall:** To whom does the wife turn for help? **(b) Distinguish:** With what telling words does the narrator describe the nature of the wife's betrayal? **(c) Analyze:** Why do the wife's actions constitute a particularly terrible form of treachery?

4. **(a) Interpret:** At the beginning of the story, how does the narrator describe the wife's appearance? **(b) Analyze:** In what ways does the injury inflicted by Bisclavaret upon his ex-wife reveal her true nature?

5. **(a) Infer:** What happens to the wife and her new husband at the end of the tale? **(b) Compare and Contrast:** In what ways is their fate both similar to and different from the harm they inflicted on Bisclavaret?

6. **Evaluate:** On the surface, this tale seems to have a happy ending. Does it? Explain.

Review and Assess

Literary Analysis

Archetypes

1. Use a chart like the one shown to examine the ways in which the story of Perceval exemplifies the **archetype** of the **quest.**

Elements of the Quest Archetype		
Characters	**Young hero:** Perceval	**Wise teacher:**
Goals	**Valuable object:**	**Restoration of kingdom/rescue:**
Obstacles	**Natural:**	**Supernatural:**
Magical Objects	**Devices:**	**Weapons:**

2. (a) In "The Lay of the Werewolf," in what ways is the archetype of **disguised identity** present in a physical sense? (b) How is it present in an emotional sense?

Comparing Literary Works

3. (a) In *Perceval*, which object serves as the story's main **symbol**? Explain. (b) In "The Lay of the Werewolf," which character serves as the central symbol? Explain.

4. (a) Which characters in each story fail to understand the meaning of the main symbol? Explain. (b) How does this lack of understanding affect their actions?

Reading Strategy

Interpreting Symbols

5. Jesus has been referred to as a fisher of men. Does this information affect your **interpretation** of the Fisher King as a symbol?

6. (a) Near the end of the story, what advice does the counselor give the king regarding Bisclavaret's clothing? (b) In what ways does his advice add to your understanding of the werewolf as a symbol?

Extend Understanding

7. **Cultural Connection:** What object or idea might be called the "holy grail" of contemporary American culture? Explain.

Integrate Language Skills

Vocabulary Development Lesson

Word Analysis: Latin Root -naviga-

The root -naviga- means "to steer a ship." Words from sailing are also used when speaking of air travel or driving. Fill in each blank below with a word that contains the root -naviga-.

1. The ___?___ changed the route.
2. The river was ___?___ by the barges.
3. If you give me the map, I'll ___?___.

Spelling Strategy

The *ay* sound can be spelled *ei*, as in *neighbor*, but never *ie*. Use the clues on the left to finish the spelling of each word below.

1. measure: w___gh
2. temporary: trans___nt
3. short-lived: br___f

Concept Development: Synonyms

Select the letter of each word or phrase below that is closest in meaning to the first word.

1. navigated: (a) reached an agreement, (b) became sick, (c) steered a boat
2. sovereign: (a) highest, (b) lowest, (c) wealthiest
3. elated: (a) late, (b) raised, (c) joyful
4. serene: (a) proud, (b) pretty, (c) calm
5. nimble: (a) cloudy, (b) careless, (c) agile
6. abases: (a) lowers, (b) raises, (c) establishes
7. esteemed: (a) heated, (b) valued, (c) ignored
8. importunity: (a) chance, (b) laziness, (c) persistence

Grammar and Style Lesson

Compound-Complex Sentences

A clause is a group of words with a subject and a verb. An independent clause can stand alone as a sentence; a subordinate clause cannot. A **compound-complex sentence** contains two independent clauses and one subordinate clause.

Example:

SUBORDINATE CLAUSE | INDEPENDENT CLAUSE

If you but knew, | you would

INDEPENDENT CLAUSE

withdraw yourself from my love,

INDEPENDENT CLAUSE

and I should be lost indeed.

Practice Identify the independent and dependent clauses in each item below.

1. Nearby is a hollow stone, concealed by a bush, and there is the place where I hide my clothes.

2. He told the squire to hold the sword and took his seat beside the lord, who honored him as best he might.

3. The King was close to the quarry, and when Bisclavaret looked upon his master, he ran to him.

4. The young man saw the maid's procession, but he did not ask a question about the grail or whom they served.

5. When he was ready, he walked around the great hall and he knocked at every door.

Writing Application Write a paragraph about the kinds of stories that you like. Use at least two compound-complex sentences.

WG Prentice Hall Writing and Grammar Connection: Diamond Level, Chapter 13, Section 4

Writing Lesson

Modern Symbolic Tale

Write either a tale of a quest or a tale of disguised identity set in the modern world. For a quest story, select an object or a person to serve as both the goal of the quest and the story's main symbol. For a story of disguised identity, feature a disguise that also has symbolic value.

Prewriting Write an outline of the plot. If your story is a quest, specify the hero's skills, weapons, obstacles, and goal. If your story involves a transformation of identity, specify the physical, emotional, and moral traits of both identities.

Drafting Using your plot outline, write a rough draft. Include sensory details, descriptions, and dialogue to make each scene vivid and believable.

Revising As you review your draft, pay attention to the descriptions of the symbolic object or person. Consider adding details to enrich the meaning.

Model: Revising to Enrich Symbolic Meaning

Mark had turned into a human DVD player. *a walking cinema.* He spoke only in movie dialogue, and he found himself sounding like all the characters of every movie he had ever seen. *He even made sound effects. Worst of all, he kept "playing back" the same movies, over and over.*

> Vivid and precise details enrich the meaning of a symbol.

Prentice Hall Writing and Grammar Connection: Diamond Level, Chapter 5, Section 4

Extension Activities

Listening and Speaking Present a **panel discussion** on the topic of symbolism in *Perceval* and "The Lay of the Werewolf." Use these tips to prepare:

- Include four to six panelists and a moderator.
- Ask each panelist to prepare an opening statement.
- Ask the moderator to develop questions to encourage discussion.

End the discussion with several critical comments on which all panelists agree. **[Group Activity]**

Research and Technology Using both print and electronic sources, create a **research presentation** on the historical foundations of the Arthurian legends. Illustrate the information with maps, artworks, and photographs.

 **Take It to the Net** PHSchool.com

Go online for an additional research activity using the Internet.

Sir Galahad

Alfred, Lord Tennyson

At some point during their lives, most people will likely take a long journey, work hard to reach a goal, make a series of difficult decisions, or even face personal danger. In the literature of the Middle Ages, all these elements are combined in long poems like *Perceval*, in which a young knight sets out to find the Holy Grail, the legendary cup from which Christ drank at the Last Supper.

A Failed Search The excerpt from Chrétien de Troyes's poem *Perceval* in this unit (p. 584) recounts Perceval's failure to find the Grail. In spite of the purity of his heart and his stature as one of the bravest knights in the court of King Arthur, Perceval has much to learn about his own weaknesses and the need to ask for help from others. Until he learns those lessons, the Grail remains elusive.

The Grail legend and the other tales of the famous knights of King Arthur's Round Table had such a hold on the imagination of poets and readers that one of nineteenth-century England's most renowned poets, Alfred, Lord Tennyson, used them in several of his poems, including "Sir Galahad." Like Perceval, Galahad sets out with a pure heart on a mystical quest—but neither knight ever finds the Holy Grail. Over centuries and across cultures, the magical cup has become a symbol for all unfulfilled desires and unattainable goals.

My good blade carves the casques[1] of men,
　My tough lance thrusteth sure,
My strength is as the strength of ten,
　Because my heart is pure.
5　The shattering trumpet shrilleth high,
　The hard brands shiver on the steel,
The splinter'd spear-shafts crack and fly,
　The horse and rider reel:
They reel, they roll in clanging lists,
10　And when the tide of combat stands,
Perfume and flowers fall in showers,
　That lightly rain from ladies' hands.

How sweet are looks that ladies bend
　On whom their favours fall!
15　From them I battle till the end,
　To save from shame and thrall:[2]
But all my heart is drawn above,
　My knees are bow'd in crypt and shrine:
I never felt the kiss of love,
20　Nor maiden's hand in mine.
More bounteous aspects on me beam,
　Me mightier transports move and thrill;
So keep I fair thro' faith and prayer
　A virgin heart in work and will.

25　When down the stormy crescent goes,
　A light before me swims,
Between dark stems the forest glows,
　I hear a noise of hymns:
Then by some secret shrine I ride;
30　I hear a voice but none are there;
The stalls are void, the doors are wide,
　The tapers burning fair.
Fair gleams the snowy altar-cloth,
　The silver vessels sparkle clean,
35　The shrill bell rings, the censer[3] swings,
　And solemn chaunts[4] resound between.

Sometime on lonely mountain-meres
　I find a magic bark;
I leap on board: no helmsman steers:
40　I float till all is dark.
A gentle sound, an awful light!

▲ **Critical Viewing**

Does this painting of Sir Galahad match your mental picture of the knight? Why or why not? **[Analyze]**

---

1. **casques** (kasks) *n.* helmets.
2. **thrall** (thrôl) *n.* slavery.
3. **censer** (sen´ sər) *n.* container in which incense is burned during religious rites.
4. **chaunts** (chänts) *n.* chants.

Three angels bear the holy Grail:
With folded feet, in stoles of white,
   On sleeping wings they sail.
45   Ah, blessed vision! blood of God!
   My spirit beats her mortal bars,
As down dark tides the glory slides,
   And star-like mingles with the stars.

When on my goodly charger borne
50   Thro' dreaming towns I go,
The cock crows ere the Christmas morn,
   The streets are dumb with snow.
The tempest crackles on the leads,
   And, ringing, springs from brand and mail;[5]
55   But o'er the dark a glory spreads,

---

5. **brand and mail** sword and armor.

◀ **Critical Viewing**

In what ways is the mood created by the colors and light of this painting similar to the mood of this poem? [Compare]

And gilds the driving hail.
I leave the plain, I climb the height;
  No branchy thicket shelter yields;
But blessed forms in whistling storms
60 Fly o'er waste fens[6] and windy fields.

A maiden knight—to me is given
  Such hope, I know not fear;
I yearn to breathe the airs of heaven
  That often meet me here.
65 I muse on joy that will not cease,
  Pure spaces clothed in living beams,
Pure lilies of eternal peace,
  Whose odours haunt my dreams;
And, stricken by an angel's hand,
70 This mortal armour that I wear,
This weight and size, this heart and eyes,
  Are touch'd, are turn'd to finest air.

The clouds are broken in the sky,
  And thro' the mountain-walls
75 A rolling organ-harmony
  Swells up, and shakes and falls.
Then move the trees, the copses nod,
  Wings flutter, voices hover clear:
"O just and faithful knight of God!
80 Ride on! the prize is near!"
So pass I hostel, hall, and grange;
  By bridge and ford, by park and pale,
All-arm'd I ride, whate'er betide,
  Until I find the holy Grail.

---

6. **fens** swamps or bogs.

Connecting Literature Past and Present

1. (a) In what ways are Perceval and Sir Galahad similar? (b) How are these two characters different?
2. Which of these two characters do you find more interesting or sympathetic? Explain.
3. Which details in each poem express a universal human desire for adventure?

Alfred, Lord Tennyson

(1809–1892)

Tennyson was born in the rural town of Somersby in Lincolnshire, England, the fourth of twelve children. His father, a clergyman, had a large library and supervised Tennyson's early education. At Cambridge University, Tennyson met Arthur Henry Hallam, who became his closest friend and encouraged him to publish his poems. When Hallam died suddenly in 1833, Tennyson was devastated, but his grief inspired one of his greatest works, *In Memoriam, A.H.H.* The royalties from this poem enabled Tennyson and his wife to buy a farm on the Isle of Wight, where they raised two children. Tennyson continued to write poetry into his eighties.

Prepare to Read

from the Divine Comedy: Inferno

Dante Alighieri (1265–1321)

Dante Alighieri (dän´ tā al əg yer´ ē), whose visions of Hell have haunted readers for centuries, is widely considered one of the greatest poets of Western civilization. T. S. Eliot wrote, "Dante and Shakespeare divide the modern world between them. There is no third."

Political Chaos Dante was born into a poor but noble family in Florence, Italy. At the time, Italy was not a unified country but a collection of independent city-states. These city-states were marked by fierce political turbulence and power struggles between ruling families. The states were constantly at war with each other while they simultaneously battled civil unrest within their own borders.

Painful Exile As a member of the nobility, Dante became an elected official. Along with six other officials, he ran Florence's government. However, in 1300, a street accident led to a skirmish, which escalated into a full-blown civil war. Dante's political party and all its representatives were overthrown. In 1302, Dante was officially exiled from his beloved city, never to return. His experience of exile would later play an important role in his writing.

Writing in Italian Scholars believe that Dante studied law and rhetoric at the University of Bologna, one of Europe's most prestigious institutions of higher learning. Bologna also boasted a great poetic tradition, and it was there that Dante discovered a school of writers who sought to free poetry from the limitations imposed by the church and government. At the time, most writers wrote in Latin, the language of scholars. Dante believed that poets should write in the language of the people—in his case, Italian. In 1304, he published *De Vulgari Eloquentia*, in which he argued for the use of the common tongue in works of literature. He wrote many lyric poems in Italian; however, it was with his *Divine Comedy* that he created the crowning achievement of medieval literature.

Principle of the Trinity Completed shortly before his death, the *Commedia*, which later gained the honorific title *Divina*, documents the physical and spiritual journey of a man who is also named Dante. Dante used the number three, which represents the Christian concept of the trinity, as an organizing principle for the *Divine Comedy*. Consisting of 100 cantos, the poem is divided into three parts—the *Inferno*, the *Purgatorio*, and the *Paradiso*. Each part contains thirty-three cantos; there is also an introductory first canto for the *Inferno*, the only one that takes place on Earth. Within each canto, the verse form is *terza rima*, a stanza of three lines. In addition, Dante's journey takes three days, beginning on Good Friday and ending on Easter Sunday.

The Love of His Life Guiding Dante on his pilgrimage is his beloved Beatrice, whose name means "she who blesses." It is believed that Dante modeled his literary Beatrice on the real-life Beatrice Portinari. Although evidence suggests that Dante saw the real Beatrice only twice in his life—first when he was nine years old and then again nine years later—she became for Dante the force that led him out of his despair. She was first the subject of his love poetry; later, she became both the object of his religious quest and a symbol of spiritual purity. Beatrice, the guiding presence in Dante's life and in his poem, is literally and symbolically his link between heaven and Earth.

In 1321, shortly after completing *Paradiso*, Dante died in the city of Ravenna in northern Italy.

Preview

Connecting to the Literature

Imagine a movie that begins with a lone man lost in a dark forest. Suddenly, a leopard and a lion leap from the shadows, baring their fangs. The man runs, only to come face to face with a vicious wolf. This selection opens with just such a scene and contains all the drama of a Hollywood film.

Literary Analysis

Allegory

An **allegory** is a literary work with two levels of meaning—the literal and the symbolic. In an allegory, every detail, character, and plot point has an equivalent symbolic meaning. For example, an allegory in which a rowboat floating down a river symbolizes the journey of life might have these symbolic equivalents:

- rowboat = person
- water = flow of time
- two oars = hard work and persistence
- rudder = love or guidance

The *Divine Comedy* is a complex allegory in which a literal journey symbolizes a man's struggle for redemption. As you read, try to identify the allegorical meanings of the places and characters Dante encounters.

Connecting Literary Elements

Imagery is the use of language that appeals to one or more of the five senses and creates mental pictures for the reader. Dante uses imagery to make the allegorical world of his poem seem tangible and real, helping the reader *feel* the ideas. As you read, notice language that appeals to the senses and creates powerful word pictures in your mind.

Reading Strategy

Interpreting Imagery

To **interpret an image,** identify which of the five senses it involves. Then, classify the physical experience the image creates by the sight, sound, taste, smell, or sense of touch it evokes. Finally, define the emotion or idea the image conveys. As you read, use a chart like the one shown to interpret imagery.

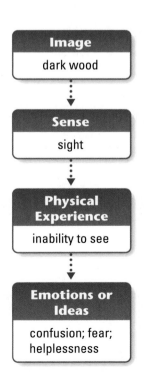

Image
dark wood

Sense
sight

Physical Experience
inability to see

Emotions or Ideas
confusion; fear; helplessness

Vocabulary Development

flounders (floun′ dərz) *v.* struggles to move (p. 614)

tremulous (trem′ yōō ləs) *adj.* quivering; shaking (p. 616)

zeal (zēl) *n.* ardor; fervor (p. 616)

putrid (pyōō′ trid) *adj.* rotten; stinking (p. 619)

despicable (dəs′ pi kə bəl) *adj.* deserving to be despised; contemptible (p. 621)

lamentation (lam′ ən tā′ shən) *n.* weeping; wailing (p. 621)

scorn (skôrn) *v.* reject (p. 621)

reprimand (rep′ rə mand′) *v.* chastise; blame (p. 622)

from the

Inferno

Dante Alighieri

translated by John Ciardi

Background

The *Divine Comedy* is composed of three sections—the *Inferno*, the *Purgatorio*, and the *Paradiso*. In the *Inferno*, the poet Virgil has been sent by Beatrice to lead Dante through Hell. Hell, a series of downward spiraling circles, is organized according to the gravity of the sin being punished. The lowest circle is reserved for traitors and Lucifer himself, the ultimate betrayer.

In Canto I of the *Inferno*, Dante first awakens to his plight and meets his guide. In Canto III, Virgil leads Dante through the Gate and into Hell itself.

Canto I

THE DARK WOOD OF ERROR

Midway in his allotted threescore years and ten, Dante comes to himself with a start and realizes that he has strayed from the True Way into the Dark Wood of Error (Worldliness). As soon as he has realized his loss, Dante lifts his eyes and sees the first light of the sunrise (the Sun is the Symbol of Divine Illumination) lighting the shoulders of a little hill (The Mount of Joy). It is the Easter Season, the time of resurrection, and the sun is in its equinoctial rebirth.[1] This juxtaposition of joyous symbols fills Dante with hope and he sets out at once to climb directly up the Mount of Joy, but almost immediately his way is blocked by the Three Beasts of Worldliness: *The Leopard of Malice and Fraud, The Lion of Violence and Ambition,* and *The She-Wolf of Incontinence.*[2] These beasts, and especially the She-Wolf, drive him back despairing into the darkness of error. But just as all seems lost, a figure appears to him. It is the shade of *Virgil,*[3] Dante's symbol of *Human Reason.*

Virgil explains that he has been sent to lead Dante from error. There can, however, be no direct ascent past the beasts: the man who would escape them must go a longer and harder way. First he must descend through Hell (The Recognition of Sin), then he must ascend through Purgatory (The Renunciation of Sin), and only then may he reach the pinnacle of joy and come to the Light of God. Virgil offers to guide Dante, but only as far as Human Reason can go. Another guide (*Beatrice,* symbol of *Divine Love*) must take over for the final ascent, for Human Reason is self-limited. Dante submits himself joyously to Virgil's guidance and they move off.

> Midway in our life's journey,[4] I went astray
>   from the straight road and woke to find myself
>   alone in a dark wood. How shall I say

---

1. **equinoctial** (ē′ kwi näk′ shəl) **rebirth** After the vernal equinox, which occurs about March 21, days become longer than nights.
2. **incontinence** (in kän′ tə nəns) *n.* lack of self-restraint.
3. **Virgil** (vʉr′ jəl) great Roman poet (70–19 B.C.).
4. **Midway in our life's journey** The biblical life span is threescore years and ten—seventy years. The action opens in Dante's thirty-fifth year, i.e., A.D. 1300.

◀ **Critical Viewing** Which elements in this engraving portray Dante's "dark wood of error" as an ominous, threatening place? [**Analyze**]

Literary Analysis
Allegory Which details in the opening lines immediately suggest the allegorical nature of the poem? Explain.

✔**Reading Check**
At what time of year does Dante's tale take place?

what wood that was! I never saw so drear,
5   so rank, so arduous⁵ a wilderness!
    Its very memory gives a shape to fear.

Death could scarce be more bitter than that place!
    But since it came to good, I will recount
    all that I found revealed there by God's grace.

10 How I came to it I cannot rightly say,
    so drugged and loose with sleep had I become
    when I first wandered there from the True Way.

But at the far end of that valley of evil
    whose maze had sapped my very heart with fear
15   I found myself before a little hill

and lifted up my eyes. Its shoulders glowed
    already with the sweet rays of that planet⁶
    whose virtue leads men straight on every road,

and the shining strengthened me against the fright
20   whose agony had wracked the lake of my heart
    through all the terrors of that piteous night.

Just as a swimmer, who with his last breath
    <u>flounders</u> ashore from perilous seas, might turn
    to memorize the wide water of his death—

25 so did I turn, my soul still fugitive
    from death's surviving image, to stare down
    that pass that none had ever left alive.

And there I lay to rest from my heart's race
    till calm and breath returned to me. Then rose
30   and pushed up that dead slope at such a pace

each footfall rose above the last. And lo!
    almost at the beginning of the rise
    I faced a spotted Leopard,⁷ all tremor and flow

flounders (floun′ dərz) *v.*
struggles to move

▲ **Critical Viewing**
Do you think these illustrations of the leopard (this page), the lion, and the wolf (facing page) emphasize each animal's realistic appearance or its symbolic meaning? Explain.
[Make a Judgment]

---

5. **so rank, so arduous** (är′ jōō əs) so overgrown, so difficult to cross.
6. **that planet** the sun. Medieval astronomers considered the sun a planet. In the *Divine Comedy*, the sun is also symbolic of God.
7. **a spotted Leopard** The three beasts that Dante encounters are taken from the Bible, Jeremiah 5:6. While numerous interpretations have been advanced for them, many scholars agree that they foreshadow the three divisions of Hell (incontinence, violence, and fraud), which Virgil explains at length in Canto XI, 16–111.

and gaudy pelt. And it would not pass, but stood
     so blocking my every turn that time and again
35   I was on the verge of turning back to the wood.

This fell at the first widening of the dawn
     as the sun climbing Aries with those stars
     that rode with him to light the new creation.[8]

40 Thus the holy hour and the sweet season
     of commemoration did much to arm my fear
     of that bright murderous beast with their good omen.

Yet not so much but what I shook with dread
     at sight of a great Lion that broke upon me
45   raging with hunger, its enormous head

held high as if to strike a mortal terror
     into the very air. And down his track,
     a She-Wolf drove upon me, a starved horror

ravening and wasted beyond all belief.
50   She seemed a rack for avarice,[9] gaunt and craving.
     Oh many the souls she has brought to endless grief!

She brought such heaviness upon my spirit
     at sight of her savagery and desperation,
     I died from every hope of that high summit.

55 And like a miser—eager in acquisition
     but desperate in self-reproach when Fortune's wheel
     turns to the hour of his loss—all tears and attrition[10]

I wavered back; and still the beast pursued,
     forcing herself against me bit by bit
60   till I slid back into the sunless wood.

Literary Analysis
Allegory In what ways is Dante's reaction to the beasts more realistic than heroic? Explain.

---

8. **Aries . . . new creation** The medieval tradition held that the sun was in the zodiacal sign of Aries at the time of the Creation. The significance of the astronomical and religious conjunction is an important part of Dante's intended allegory. It is just before dawn of Good Friday A.D. 1300 when he awakens in the Dark Wood. Thus, his new life begins under Aries, the sign of creation, at dawn (rebirth) and in the Easter Season (which commemorates the resurrection of Jesus). Moreover, the moon is full and the sun is in the equinox, conditions that did not fall together on any Friday of 1300. Dante is poetically constructing the perfect Easter as a symbol of his new awakening.
9. **a rack for avarice** an instrument of torture for greed.
10. **attrition** (ə trish´ ən) *n.* weakening; wearing away.

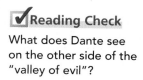

Reading Check

What does Dante see on the other side of the "valley of evil"?

And as I fell to my soul's ruin, a presence
    gathered before me on the discolored air,
    the figure of one who seemed hoarse from long silence.

At sight of him in that friendless waste I cried:
65   "Have pity on me, whatever thing you are,
    whether shade or living man." And it replied:

"Not man, though man I once was, and my blood
    was Lombard, both my parents Mantuan.[11]
    I was born, though late, *sub Julio,*[12] and bred

70   in Rome under Augustus in the noon
    of the false and lying gods.[13] I was a poet
    and sang of old Anchises' noble son

who came to Rome after the burning of Troy.[14]
    But you—why do *you* return to these distresses
75   instead of climbing that shining Mount of Joy

which is the seat and first cause of man's bliss?"
    "And are you then that Virgil and that fountain
    of purest speech?" My voice grew <u>tremulous</u>:

"Glory and light of poets! now may that <u>zeal</u>
80   and love's apprenticeship that I poured out
    on your heroic verses serve me well!

For you are my true master and first author,
    the sole maker from whom I drew the breath
    of that sweet style whose measures have
    brought me honor.

85 See there, immortal sage, the beast I flee.
    For my soul's salvation, I beg you, guard me from her,
    for she has struck a mortal tremor through me."

▼ Critical Viewing
In this fifteenth-century illustration of Canto I, what do you think Virgil, in red, is telling Dante? **[Connect]**

tremulous (trem´ yoo ləs) *adj.* quivering; shaking

zeal (zēl) *n.* ardor; fervor

11. **Lombard . . . Mantuan** Lombardy is a region of northern Italy; Mantua, the birthplace of Virgil, is a city in that region.
12. *sub Julio* in the reign of Julius Caesar. It would be more accurate to say that he was born during the lifetime of Caesar (102?–44 B.C.). Augustus did not begin his rule as dictator until long after Virgil's birth, which occurred in 70 B.C.
13. **under Augustus . . . gods** Augustus, the grandnephew of Julius Caesar, was the emperor of Rome from 27 B.C. to A.D.14. The "lying gods" are the gods of classical mythology.
14. **and sang . . . Troy** Virgil's epic poem, the *Aeneid*, describes the destruction of Troy by the Greeks and the founding of Roman civilization by the Trojan Aeneas, son of Anchises (an kī´ sēz).

And he replied, seeing my soul in tears:
    "He must go by another way who would escape
90   this wilderness, for that mad beast that fleers[15]

before you there, suffers no man to pass.
    She tracks down all, kills all, and knows no glut,
    but, feeding, she grows hungrier than she was.

She mates with any beast, and will mate with more
95   before the Greyhound comes to hunt her down.
    He will not feed on lands nor loot, but honor

and love and wisdom will make straight his way.
    He will rise between Feltro and Feltro,[16] and in him
    shall be the resurrection and new day

100   of that sad Italy for which Nisus died,
    and Turnus, and Euryalus, and the maid Camilla.[17]
    He shall hunt her through every nation of sick pride

till she is driven back forever to Hell
    whence Envy first released her on the world.
105   Therefore, for your own good, I think it well

you follow me and I will be your guide
    and lead you forth through an eternal place.
    There you shall see the ancient spirits tried

in endless pain, and hear their lamentation
110   as each bemoans the second death[18] of souls.
    Next you shall see upon a burning mountain[19]

souls in fire and yet content in fire,
    knowing that whensoever it may be
    they yet will mount into the blessed choir.

Literary Analysis
Allegory Based on Virgil's comments, do you think the She-Wolf symbolizes Dante's social, political, religious, or moral concerns? Explain.

---

15. **fleers** (flirz) laughs scornfully.
16. **the Greyhound . . . Feltro and Feltro** The Greyhound almost certainly refers to Can Grande della Scala (1290–1329), a great Italian leader born in Verona, which lies between the towns of Feltre and Montefeltro.
17. **Nisus . . . Camilla** All were killed in the war between the Trojans and the Latians when, according to legend, Aeneas led the survivors of Troy into Italy. Nisus and Euryalus (*Aeneid* IX) were Trojan comrades-in-arms who died together. Camilla (*Aeneid* XI) was the daughter of the Latian king and one of the warrior women. She was killed in a horse charge against the Trojans after displaying great gallantry. Turnus (*Aeneid* XII) was killed by Aeneas in a duel.
18. **the second death** damnation.
19. **a burning mountain** Mountain of Purgatory.

✔**Reading Check**
What assistance does Virgil offer Dante?

115   To which, if it is still your wish to climb,
        a worthier spirit[20] shall be sent to guide you.
        With her shall I leave you, for the King of Time,

    who reigns on high, forbids me to come there[21]
        since, living, I rebelled against his law.
120   He rules the waters and the land and air

    and there holds court, his city and his throne.
        Oh blessed are they he chooses!" And I to him:
        "Poet, by that God to you unknown,

    lead me this way. Beyond this present ill
125   and worse to dread, lead me to Peter's gate[22]
        and be my guide through the sad halls of Hell."

    And he then: "Follow." And he moved ahead
    in silence, and I followed where he led.

---

20. **a worthier spirit** Beatrice.
21. **forbids me to come there** In Dante's theology, salvation is achieved only through Christ. Virgil lived and died before the establishment of Christ's teachings in Rome and therefore cannot enter Heaven.
22. **Peter's gate** the gate of Purgatory. The gate is guarded by an angel with a gleaming sword. The angel is Peter's vicar and is entrusted with the two great keys.

Literary Analysis
Allegory At the end of Canto I, Dante lays out the structure of his entire poem. In what ways does this help the reader grasp the allegory?

Review and Assess

Thinking About the Selection

1. **Respond:** Which part of Dante's experience in the Dark Wood did you find most frightening? Explain.

2. **(a) Recall:** Which three beasts block Dante's path?
   (b) Interpret: What emotion or idea does each beast represent?
   (c) Analyze: Why is each beast an appropriate choice for the emotion or idea it represents?

3. **(a) Recall:** Who rescues Dante? **(b) Infer:** What does the author's choice of rescuer and guide reveal about Dante's values?

4. **(a) Interpret:** Identify at least two lines in Canto I that reveal strong emotion in Dante. **(b) Analyze:** Based on his thoughts, emotions, and actions thus far, how would you describe Dante's character?
   (c) Speculate: Based on your understanding of his character, how do you think Dante will respond to the sights and sounds of Hell? Explain.

5. **Evaluate:** Does Dante the character seem like a real man on a real journey, or does the whole situation presented in Canto I seem like a fantasy? Explain.

Canto III

THE VESTIBULE OF HELL   *The Opportunists*

The Poets pass the Gate of Hell and are immediately assailed by cries of anguish.
Dante sees the first of the souls in torment. They are *The Opportunists*, those souls
who in life were neither for good nor evil but only for themselves. Mixed with them
are those outcasts who took no sides in the Rebellion of the Angels.[1] They are neither in Hell nor out of it. Eternally unclassified, they race round and round pursuing a wavering banner that runs forever before them through the dirty air; and as
they run they are pursued by swarms of wasps and hornets, who sting them and
produce a constant flow of blood and <u>putrid</u> matter which trickles down the bodies
of the sinners and is feasted upon by loathsome worms and maggots who coat
the ground.

putrid (pyoo′ trid) *adj.*
rotten; stinking

The law of Dante's Hell is the law
of symbolic retribution. As they
sinned so are they punished. They
took no sides, therefore they are
given no place. As they pursued the
ever-shifting illusion of their own
advantage, changing their courses with
every changing wind, so they pursue
eternally an elusive, ever-shifting banner.
As their sin was a darkness, so they move
in darkness.
As their own guilty conscience pursued
them, so they are pursued by swarms
of wasps and hornets. And as their
actions were a moral filth, so they run
eternally through the filth of worms and
maggots which they
themselves feed.

▼ **Critical Viewing**
Which details in this
illustration of Dante
help convey the fear
and horror he is ex-
periencing? Explain.
[Interpret]

Dante recognizes several, among them *Pope
Celestine V*,[2] but without delaying to speak to any
of these souls, the Poets move on to *Acheron*,[3] the
first of the rivers of Hell. Here the newly arrived souls
of the damned gather and wait for monstrous *Charon*[4]
to ferry them over to punishment. Charon recognizes
Dante as a living man and angrily refuses him passage. Virgil forces Charon to serve them, but Dante
swoons with terror, and does not reawaken until
he is on the other side.

> I AM THE WAY INTO THE CITY OF WOE.
>
> I AM THE WAY TO A FORSAKEN PEOPLE.
>
> I AM THE WAY INTO ETERNAL SORROW.

---

1. **Rebellion of the Angels** In Christian tradition, Satan and other angels who rebelled
   against God were cast out of heaven; see the Bible, Revelation 12:7–9.
2. **Pope Celestine V** He lived from 1215 to 1296.
3. **Acheron** (ak′ ər än′)
4. **Charon** (ker′ ən)

☑ **Reading Check**

What is the law of Dante's
Hell?

SACRED JUSTICE MOVED MY ARCHITECT.

5   I WAS RAISED HERE BY DIVINE OMNIPOTENCE,
    PRIMORDIAL[5] LOVE AND ULTIMATE INTELLECT.

    ONLY THOSE ELEMENTS TIME CANNOT WEAR[6]
    WERE MADE BEFORE ME, AND BEYOND TIME I STAND.[7]
    ABANDON ALL HOPE YE WHO ENTER HERE.

10   These mysteries I read cut into stone
        above a gate. And turning I said: "Master,
        what is the meaning of this harsh inscription?"

    And he then as initiate to novice:[8]
        "Here must you put by all division of spirit
15   and gather your soul against all cowardice.

    This is the place I told you to expect.
        Here you shall pass among the fallen people,
        souls who have lost the good of intellect."

    So saying, he put forth his hand to me,
20   and with a gentle and encouraging smile
        he led me through the gate of mystery.

    Here sighs and cries and wails coiled and recoiled
        on the starless air, spilling my soul to tears.
        A confusion of tongues and monstrous accents toiled

25   in pain and anger. Voices hoarse and shrill
        and sounds of blows, all intermingled, raised
        tumult and pandemonium[9] that still

    whirls on the air forever dirty with it
        as if a whirlwind sucked at sand. And I,
30   holding my head in horror, cried: "Sweet Spirit,

    what souls are these who run through this black haze?"
        And he to me: "These are the nearly soulless
        whose lives concluded neither blame nor praise.

Literary Analysis
Allegory In what ways does Dante's use of a gate, an object familiar to all medieval people, make his allegory seem all the more real?

Literary Analysis
Allegory and Imagery Why do you think the imagery at this point in the poem appeals almost solely to the sense of hearing?

---

5. **primordial** (prī mȏr′ dē əl) *adj.* existing from the beginning.
6. **only . . . wear** The Angels, the Empyrean (the highest heaven), and the First Matter are the elements time cannot wear, for they will last forever. Human beings, being mortal, are not eternal. The Gate of Hell, therefore, was created before people.
7. **and . . . stand** So odious is sin to God that there can be no end to its just punishment.
8. **as initiate to novice** as one who knows to one who does not.
9. **pandemonium** (pan′ də mō′ nē əm) word coined by English poet John Milton (1608–1674) to identify the demons' capital in hell; now describes any place or scene of noise, wild disorder, and confusion.

They are mixed here with that <u>despicable</u> corps
    of angels who were neither God nor Satan,
35   but only for themselves. The High Creator

scourged[10] them from Heaven for its perfect beauty,
    and Hell will not receive them since the wicked
    might feel some glory over them." And I:

40 "Master, what gnaws at them so hideously
    their <u>lamentation</u> stuns the very air?"
    "They have no hope of death," he answered me,

"and in their blind and unattaining state
    their miserable lives have sunk so low
45   that they must envy every other fate.

No word of them survives their living season.
    Mercy and Justice deny them even a name.
    Let us not speak of them: look, and pass on."

I saw a banner there upon the mist.
50   Circling and circling, it seemed to <u>scorn</u> all pause.
    So it ran on, and still behind it pressed

a never-ending rout of souls in pain.
    I had not thought death had undone so many
    as passed before me in that mournful train.

55 And some I knew among them; last of all
    I recognized the shadow of that soul
    who, in his cowardice, made the Great Denial.[11]

At once I understood for certain: these
    were of that retrograde[12] and faithless crew
60   hateful to God and to His enemies.

These wretches never born and never dead
    ran naked in a swarm of wasps and hornets
    that goaded them the more the more they fled,

despicable (des´ pi kə bel)
adj. deserving to be
despised; contemptible

lamentation (lam´ ən tā´ shen)
n. weeping; wailing

scorn (skôrn) *v.* reject

---

10. scourged (skʉrj´d) *v.* whipped.
11. who, in . . . Denial This is almost certainly intended to be Celestine V, who became pope
in 1294. He was a man of saintly virtue, but he allowed himself to be convinced by a priest
named Benedetto that his soul was in danger since no man could live in the world without
being damned. In fear for his soul, he withdrew from all worldly affairs and renounced the
papacy. Benedetto promptly assumed the mantle himself and became Boniface VIII, a
pope who became for Dante a symbol of all the worst corruptions of the church.
12. retrograde (re´ trə grād´) *adj.* moving backward.

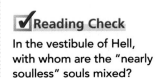

Reading Check

In the vestibule of Hell,
with whom are the "nearly
soulless" souls mixed?

and made their faces stream with bloody gouts
65   of pus and tears that dribbled to their feet
        to be swallowed there by loathsome worms and maggots.

Then looking onward I made out a throng
        assembled on the beach of a wide river,
        whereupon I turned to him: "Master, I long

70 to know what souls these are, and what strange usage
        makes them as eager to cross as they seem to be
        in this infected light." At which the Sage:

"All this shall be made known to you when we stand
        on the joyless beach of Acheron." And I
75   cast down my eyes, sensing a <u>reprimand</u>

in what he said, and so walked at his side
        in silence and ashamed until we came
        through the dead cavern to that sunless tide.

There, steering toward us in an ancient ferry
80   came an old man[13] with a white bush of hair,
        bellowing: "Woe to you depraved souls! Bury

here and forever all hope of Paradise:
        I come to lead you to the other shore,
        into eternal dark, into fire and ice.

85 And you who are living yet, I say begone
        from these who are dead." But when he saw me stand
        against his violence he began again:

"By other windings[14] and by other steerage
        shall you cross to that other shore. Not here! Not here!
90   A lighter craft than mine must give you passage."

And my Guide to him: "Charon, bite back your spleen:
        this has been willed where what is willed must be,
        and is not yours to ask what it may mean."[15]

Literary Analysis
Allegory Judging from
this character, in what
ways has the mythology of
ancient Greece and Rome
provided Dante with
source material for his
allegory?

---

13. an old man Charon, the ferryman who transports dead souls across the Acheron in all classical mythology.
14. By other windings Charon recognizes Dante not only as a living man but as a soul in grace and knows, therefore, that the Infernal Ferry was not intended for him. He is probably referring to the fact that souls destined for Purgatory and Heaven assemble not at his ferry point but on the banks of the Tiber (a river that runs through Rome), from which they are transported by an Angel.
15. Charon . . . mean Virgil tells Charon to suppress his bad temper because God has ordained that Dante shall make this journey. Charon has no right to question God's orders.

The steersman of that marsh of ruined souls,
95 who wore a wheel of flame around each eye,
  stifled the rage that shook his woolly jowls.

But those unmanned and naked spirits there
  turned pale with fear and their teeth began to chatter
  at sound of his crude bellow. In despair

100 they blasphemed God, their parents, their time on earth,
  the race of Adam, and the day and the hour
  and the place and the seed and the womb that gave
   them birth.

But all together they drew to that grim shore
  where all must come who lose the fear of God.
105 Weeping and cursing they come for evermore,

and demon Charon with eyes like burning coals
  herds them in, and with a whistling oar
  flails on the stragglers to his wake[16] of souls.

As leaves in autumn loosen and stream down
110 until the branch stands bare above its tatters
  spread on the rustling ground, so one by one

the evil seed of Adam in its Fall[17]
  cast themselves, at his signal, from the shore
  and streamed away like birds who hear their call.

115 So they are gone over that shadowy water,
  and always before they reach the other shore
  a new noise stirs on this, and new throngs gather.

"My son," the courteous Master said to me,
  "all who die in the shadow of God's wrath
120 converge to this from every clime and country.

And all pass over eagerly, for here
  Divine Justice transforms and spurs them so
  their dread turns wish: they yearn for what they fear.[18]

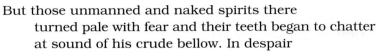

Themes in World Literature

The Vulgar Tongue

 By composing the *Divine Comedy* in Italian, Dante implicitly rejected the use of Latin, the literary language of his day, in favor of the "vulgar" tongue. A vulgar tongue is the language spoken by the *vulgus*, the common people. In many cultures, centuries passed before the language spoken by ordinary people was accepted as a medium for the composition of literature. For example, in Japan, works written in Japanese were considered less significant than works written in Chinese until well into the twentieth century.

 Works composed in "vulgar" tongues are more accessible to more people. As the common tongue becomes the dominant literary language, literature takes an increasingly important place in the life of a society. Literary works better express the real lives of the people; in turn, literature exerts a greater influence on the culture itself.

---

16. **wake** *n.* a watch over a corpse before burial, with a pun on waking up.
17. **Fall** This word has at least three different meanings: the season of fall, the fall of all humans with the sin of Adam and Eve, and the fall of individual sinners.
18. **they yearn . . . fear** Hell (allegorically, Sin) is what the souls of the damned really wish for. Hell is their actual and deliberate choice, for divine grace is denied to none who wish for it in their hearts.

 **Reading Check**

What hope does Charon tell the dead souls they must abandon?

◀ **Critical Viewing**
In this fifteenth-century illumination of Dante and Virgil crossing the river into Hell, how do Dante's posture and attitude compare and contrast with those of both Virgil and the ferryman? [**Compare and Contrast**]

No soul in Grace comes ever to this crossing;
125   therefore if Charon rages at your presence
             you will understand the reason for his cursing."

When he had spoken, all the twilight country
          shook so violently, the terror of it
          bathes me with sweat even in memory:

Reading Strategy
Interpreting Imagery
To which senses do the images in this passage appeal?

130   the tear-soaked ground gave out a sigh of wind
        that spewed itself in flame on a red sky,
        and all my shattered senses left me. Blind,

like one whom sleep comes over in a swoon,[19]
I stumbled into darkness and went down.

---

19. swoon the act of fainting. This device (repeated at the end of Canto V) serves a double purpose. The first is technical: Dante uses it to cover a transition. We are never told how he crossed Acheron, for that would involve certain narrative matters he can better deal with when he crosses Styx (stiks), another river of the underworld, in Canto VII. The second purpose is to provide a point of departure for a theme that is carried through the entire descent: Dante's emotional reaction to Hell. These two swoons early in the descent show him most susceptible to the grief about him. As he descends, pity leaves him, and he even goes so far as to add to the torments of one sinner.

Review and Assess

Thinking About the Selection

1. **Respond:** Do you think that the Opportunists deserve the punishment Dante envisioned for them? Why or why not?

2. **(a) Recall:** According to the inscription on the Gate of Hell, which feeling must be abandoned by all who enter? **(b) Analyze Causes and Effects:** What effect do you think Dante intends this passage to have on the reader? Explain.

3. **(a) Recall:** Which creatures torment the Opportunists? **(b) Analyze:** In what ways do these small but fierce creatures suggest Dante's attitude toward the sins of the Opportunists? Explain.

4. **(a) Recall:** As they prepare to cross the river Acheron into Hell itself, what physical reactions do the spirits have? **(b) Interpret:** Judging from their outbursts, what emotional reactions do they experience? **(c) Infer:** What is the greatest spiritual torment of Hell? Explain.

5. **Analyze:** Why do you think Dante dwells on the physical torments of Hell?

6. **(a) Draw Conclusions:** What message does this Canto provide about those who will not or cannot make a commitment to God? Explain. **(b) Synthesize:** What image might be appropriate to appear on the banner pursued by the Opportunists? Explain your answer.

Review and Assess

Literary Analysis

Allegory

1. Who or what do you think Dante the character represents in this **allegory**?
2. Use a chart like the one shown to explore the allegorical meanings of other elements in Cantos I and III.

Detail	Literal Meaning	Allegorical Meanings
straight road		
dark wood		
leopard		
wasps and hornets		

3. Dante chose the poet Virgil rather than a philosopher, such as Socrates or Aristotle, to be his symbol of human reason. What does this choice suggest about the intellectual qualities he admires most?
4. (a) In Canto I, what prediction does Virgil make about the She-Wolf and the Greyhound? (b) How does this prediction reveal Dante's intention to explore both spiritual matters and earthly concerns in this allegory?

Connecting Literary Elements

5. How does Dante's **imagery** in Canto I contribute to the poem's verisimilitude—its sense of reality or truth?
6. Does the image of souls as falling leaves merely convey a sense of great numbers, or does it contribute to the sense of despair in Canto III? Explain.

Reading Strategy

Interpreting Imagery

7. (a) Begin to **interpret imagery** by listing images of light in Canto I. (b) What do you think light represents to Dante? Explain.
8. (a) Identify the senses to which the images in the last three stanzas of Canto III appeal. (b) Why do you think Dante swoons at this point?

Extend Understanding

9. **Cultural Connection:** Dante is a national hero for the Italians. Which writers, if any, play a similar role for Americans? Explain.

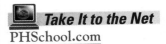

Integrate Language Skills

Vocabulary Development Lesson

Word Analysis: Latin Root -trem-

The word *tremulous*, which means "trembling, as with fear," is based on the Latin root *-trem-*, meaning "tremble." Match each of the following words with its definition.

1. tremble
2. tremor
3. tremolo

a. musical vibration
b. vibration
c. shiver; vibrate

Spelling Strategy

The *us* sound at the end of a word is often spelled *ous* when it represents the suffix *-ous*, meaning "full of " (*tremulous* = "full of trembling"). Write a word ending in the *us* sound that meets each definition below.

1. full of fame
2. full of caution

Fluency: Sentence Completion

Review the vocabulary list on page 611, and notice the way the words are used in the context of the selection. Then, complete each sentence below with the appropriate words.

1. They looked down with __?__ on the __?__ criminals.
2. "Please do not __?__ me," the driver says to the policeman in a __?__ voice.
3. The __?__ smell of rotting food dampened the __?__ of the diners.
4. She hears the cries and __?__ and sees the poor soul who __?__ in the waves.

Grammar and Style Lesson

Present Perfect Verb Tense

The **present perfect tense** shows either a single action or repeated actions that were completed at an indefinite time before the present.

Single action . . . this <u>has been willed</u>
Repeated action . . . that sweet style whose measures <u>have brought</u> me honor . . .

Practice Identify the example of the present perfect tense in each item, and state whether it describes a single or a repeated action.

1. For centuries, Dante has been considered the greatest Italian writer.
2. Have you read his *Divine Comedy*?
3. Do you know someone who has read it?
4. The *Inferno* has become my favorite.
5. The *Divine Comedy* is the most complex allegory we have studied.

Writing Application Write a paragraph about an amazing sight that you have seen. Include at least three examples of the present perfect tense.

W͠G *Prentice Hall Writing and Grammar Connection: Diamond Level, Chapter 21, Section 2*

Extension Activities

Listening and Speaking Dante's crisis occurred "midway" through his life. With a small group, create a **presentation** on changing images of middle age. [Group Activity]

Writing Write a **new version** of this part of the journey from Virgil's point of view.

Prepare to Read

Inferno, Cantos V and XXXIV

Literary Analysis

Characterization

Characterization is the art of revealing character. There are two main types of characterization:

- In *direct characterization*, a writer simply tells the reader what a character is like.
- In *indirect characterization*, a writer suggests what a character is like by showing what the character says and does, what other characters say about him or her, or how other characters behave toward him or her.

As you read, notice the techniques Dante uses to paint vivid portraits of his characters.

Connecting Literary Elements

An **allusion** is a reference within a literary work to something outside the work. Allusions are a kind of literary shorthand because they quickly add layers of meaning. For example, when Francesca alludes to the story of Lancelot, she associates her misadventure with the well-known romance of the tragic knight. Pay attention to Dante's use of allusions, and identify the layers of meaning they add to his tale.

Reading Strategy

Distinguishing Between the Speaker and the Poet

The *Inferno* uses the first-person point of view—the reader sees events through the speaker's eyes. Yet, the Dante who relates this tale is simply a literary character created by the poet. Along with Virgil, Francesca, and other characters, Dante the poet uses Dante the character to express his ideas. As you read, use a chart like the one shown to **distinguish between the speaker and the poet.**

Vocabulary Development

grotesque (grō tesk´) *adj.* strangely distorted (p. 630)

degree (di grē´) *n.* step; stage; level (p. 630)

anguish (aŋ´ gwish) *n.* great suffering; agony (p. 631)

tempest (tem´ pist) *n.* storm (p. 633)

perilous (per´ ə ləs) *adj.* dangerous (p. 635)

awe (ô) *n.* feelings of reverence, fear, and wonder (p. 639)

writhes (rīthz) *v.* twists and turns the body, as in agony (p. 640)

nimble (nim´ bəl) *adj.* able to move quickly and lightly; agile (p. 641)

Speaker

Dante the character

Statement

Francesca's suffering "melts me to tears."

Poet's Judgment

He has written Francesca into Hell, suggesting a lack of sympathy.

Poet's Purpose

to show that Dante the character needs to outgrow his sympathy for sinners

Review and Anticipate

In Canto III, Dante and Virgil paused at Hell's outer edge, where they witnessed the torments suffered by the Opportunists. As they prepared to cross the river Acheron into the first circle of Hell, Dante was so overcome by terror he fell into a swoon.

In Canto V, Dante and Virgil will enter the second circle of Hell, where they will observe the carnal sinners.

Then, in Canto XXXIV, Dante and his guide will enter the ninth and lowest circle of Hell, the lair of Satan himself. How do you think Dante will react when he witnesses the horrors ahead? Read to find out.

Canto V

CIRCLE TWO   *The Carnal*

The Poets leave Limbo and enter the *Second Circle*. Here begin the torments of Hell proper, and here, blocking the way, sits *Minos*,[1] the dread and semi-bestial judge of the damned who assigns to each soul its eternal torment. He orders the Poets back; but Virgil silences him as he earlier silenced Charon, and the Poets move on.

They find themselves on a dark ledge swept by a great whirlwind, which spins within it the souls of the *Carnal*, those who betrayed reason to their appetites. Their sin was to abandon themselves to the tempest of their passions: so they are swept forever in the tempest of Hell, forever denied the light of reason and of God. Virgil identifies many among them.[2] *Semiramis* is there, and *Dido, Cleopatra, Helen, Achilles, Paris*, and *Tristan*. Dante sees *Paolo* and *Francesca* swept together, and in the name of love he calls to them to tell their sad story. They pause from their eternal flight to come to him, and Francesca tells their history while Paolo weeps at her side. Dante is so stricken by compassion at their tragic tale that he swoons once again.

> So we went down to the second ledge alone;
> a smaller circle[3] of so much greater pain
> the voice of the damned rose in a bestial moan.

---

1. **Minos** (mī´ näs´) Like all the monsters Dante assigns to the various offices of Hell, Minos is drawn from classical mythology. He was the son of Europa and of Zeus, who descended to her in the form of a bull. Minos became a mythological king of Crete, so famous for his wisdom and justice that after death his soul was made judge of the dead. In the *Aeneid*, Virgil presents him fulfilling the same office at Aeneas' descent to the underworld. Dante, however, transforms him into an irate and hideous monster with a tail.
2. **many among them** The names that follow are those of famous lovers from legend and history: Semiramis (si mir´ ə mis); Dido (dī´ dō); Cleopatra (klē´ ō pa´ trə); Achilles (ə kil´ ēz´); Tristan (tris´ tən); Paolo (pä´ ô lô); Francesca (frän ches´ kä).
3. **a smaller circle** The pit of Hell tapers like a funnel. The circles of ledges accordingly grow smaller as they descend.

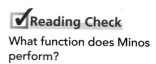

Reading Check

What function does Minos perform?

Minos, the infernal judge, sitting at the entrance to the second circle of hell, waiting to pass sentence on the souls brought before him, Gustave Doré

◀ **Critical Viewing**
In this illustration of Minos sitting in judgment, how do the relative sizes of the figures emphasize the drama of the scene? **[Interpret]**

There Minos sits, grinning, <u>grotesque</u>, and hale.[4]
5   He examines each lost soul as it arrives
      and delivers his verdict with his coiling tail.

That is to say, when the ill-fated soul
      appears before him it confesses all,[5]
      and that grim sorter of the dark and foul

10   decides which place in Hell shall be its end,
      then wraps his twitching tail about himself
      one coil for each <u>degree</u> it must descend.

The soul descends and others take its place:
      each crowds in its turn to judgment, each confesses,
15   each hears its doom and falls away through space.

"O you who come into this camp of woe,"
      cried Minos when he saw me turn away
      without awaiting his judgment, "watch where you go

once you have entered here, and to whom you turn!
20   Do not be misled by that wide and easy passage!"
      And my Guide to him: "That is not your concern;

Literary Analysis
Characterization Dante uses three adjectives to directly characterize Minos. Which adjective do you find surprising? Explain.

grotesque (grō tesk´) *adj.* strangely distorted

degree (di grē´) *n.* step; stage; level

---

4. **hale** (hāl) *adj.* healthy.
5. **it confesses all** Just as the souls appeared eager to cross Acheron, so they are eager to confess even while they are filled with dread. Dante is once again making the point that sinners elect their Hell by an act of their own will.

it is his fate to enter every door.
    This has been willed where what is willed must be,
    and is not yours to question. Say no more."

25 Now the choir of <u>anguish</u>, like a wound,
    strikes through the tortured air. Now I have come
    to Hell's full lamentation, sound beyond sound.

I came to a place stripped bare of every light
    and roaring on the naked dark like seas
30   wracked by a war of winds. Their hellish flight

of storm and counterstorm through time foregone,
    sweeps the souls of the damned before its charge.
    Whirling and battering it drives them on,

and when they pass the ruined gap of Hell[6]
35   through which we had come, their shrieks begin anew.
    There they blaspheme the power of God eternal.

And this, I learned, was the never ending flight
    of those who sinned in the flesh, the carnal and lusty
    who betrayed reason to their appetite.

40 As the wings of wintering starlings bear them on
    in their great wheeling flights, just so the blast
    wherries[7] these evil souls through time foregone.

Here, there, up, down, they whirl and, whirling, strain
    with never a hope of hope to comfort them,
45   not of release, but even of less pain.

As cranes go over sounding their harsh cry,
    leaving the long streak of their flight in air,
    so come these spirits, wailing as they fly.

And watching their shadows lashed by wind, I cried:
50   "Master, what souls are these the very air
    lashes with its black whips from side to side?"

"The first of these whose history you would know,"
    he answered me, "was Empress of many tongues.[8]
    Mad sensuality corrupted her so

---

6. **the ruined gap of Hell** At the time of the Harrowing of Hell—the supposed descent of
   Christ into Limbo to rescue and bring to Heaven his "ancestors" from the Hebrew Bible—
   a great earthquake shook the underworld, shattering rocks and cliffs.
7. **wherries** (hwer´ ēz) v. transports.
8. **Empress of many tongues** Semiramis, a legendary queen of Assyria.

anguish (aŋ´ gwish) *n.* great
suffering; agony

Reading Strategy
**Distinguishing Between
the Speaker and the Poet**
Which images does Dante
the poet use to convey
the physical experience of
Dante the character?

Literary Analysis
Characterization In lines
38–39, what does Dante's
definition of carnal sin
reveal about his values?

Reading Check

What force whirls and
batters the souls of the
damned?

that to hide the guilt of her debauchery
   she licensed all depravity alike,
   and lust and law were one in her decree.

She is Semiramis of whom the tale is told
   how she married Ninus and succeeded him
60   to the throne of that wide land the Sultans hold.

▼ Critical Viewing
In what ways does this map
of Dante's Hell help you
better understand the
poem? [Connect]

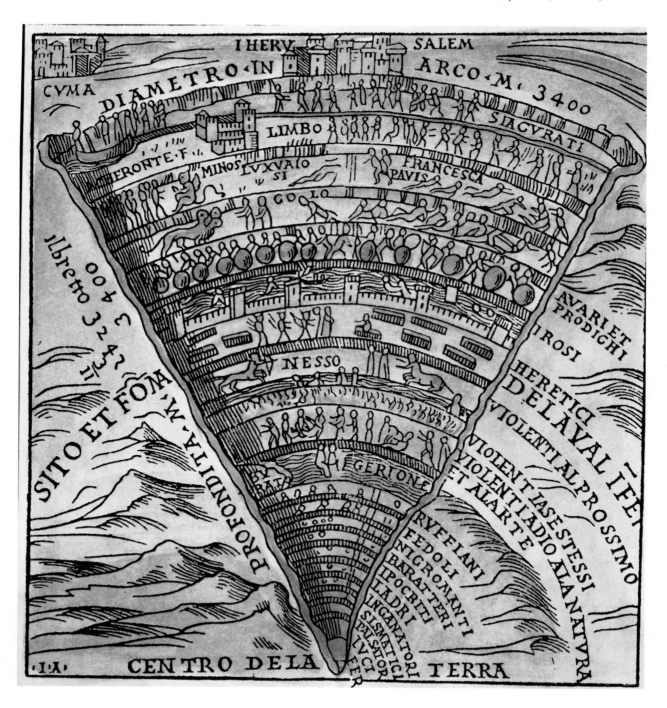

The other is Dido;[9] faithless to the ashes
    of Sichaeus, she killed herself for love.
    The next whom the eternal <u>tempest</u> lashes

        is sense-drugged Cleopatra. See Helen[10] there,
65   from whom such ill arose. And great Achilles,[11]
    who fought at last with love in the house of prayer.

And Paris. And Tristan."[12] As they whirled above
    he pointed out more than a thousand shades
    of those torn from the mortal life by love.

70 I stood there while my Teacher one by one
    named the great knights and ladies of dim time;
    and I was swept by pity and confusion.

At last I spoke: "Poet, I should be glad
    to speak a word with those two swept together[13]
75   so lightly on the wind and still so sad."

And he to me: "Watch them. When next they pass,
    call to them in the name of love that drives
    and damns them here. In that name they will pause."

Thus, as soon as the wind in its wild course
80   brought them around, I called: "O wearied souls!
    if none forbid it, pause and speak to us."

As mating doves that love calls to their nest
    glide through the air with motionless raised wings,
    borne by the sweet desire that fills each breast—

Literary Analysis
Characterization and Allusion In what ways do these allusions to both historical and legendary figures add to the sense of reality in Dante's tale? Explain.

tempest (tem´ pist) *n.* storm

Literary Analysis
Characterization How does the poet's use of the word "swept" enrich his characterization of Dante's character?

---

9. **Dido** Queen and founder of Carthage, an ancient kingdom in northern Africa. She had vowed to remain faithful to her husband, Sichaeus (sə kē´ əs), but she fell in love with Aeneas.
10. **Cleopatra . . . Helen** Cleopatra was a queen of Egypt (51–49; 48–30 B.C.) and the mistress of the powerful Romans Julius Caesar and Mark Antony. Helen was the beautiful wife of the King of Sparta. According to legend, the Trojan War was started when she was forcibly taken away to Troy by Paris, a son of the Trojan king Priam.
11. **Achilles** greatest warrior on the Greek side during the Trojan War; placed in this company because of his passion for Polyxena (pō lik´ sə nə), the daughter of Priam. For love of her, he agreed to desert the Greeks and to join the Trojans, but when he went to the temple for the wedding (according to the legend Dante has followed), he was killed by Paris.
12. **Tristan** knight sent to Ireland by King Mark of Cornwall to bring back the princess Isolde (i sōl´ də) to be the king's bride. Isolde and Tristan fell in love and tragically died together.
13. **those two swept together** Paolo and Francesca. In 1275, Giovanni Malatesta (jō vä´ nē mä´ lä tes´ tä) of Rimini made a political marriage with Francesca, daughter of Guido da Polenta (gwē´ dō dä pō len´ tä) of Ravenna. Francesca came to Rimini and fell in love with Giovanni's younger brother Paolo. Paolo had married in 1269 and had had two daughters by 1275, but his affair with Francesca continued for many years. Sometime between 1283 and 1286, Giovanni surprised and killed them in Francesca's bedroom.

Reading Check

According to Virgil, what tore the souls in this circle of Hell from their mortal lives?

85   Just so those spirits turned on the torn sky
          from the band where Dido whirls across the air;
          such was the power of pity in my cry.

      "O living creature, gracious, kind, and good,
          going this pilgrimage through the sick night,
90   visiting us who stained the earth with blood,

      were the King of Time our friend, we would pray His peace
          on you who have pitied us. As long as the wind
          will let us pause, ask of us what you please.

      The town where I was born lies by the shore
95   where the Po[14] descends into its ocean rest
          with its attendant streams in one long murmur.

      Love, which in gentlest hearts will soonest bloom
          seized my lover with passion for that sweet body
          from which I was torn unshriven[15] to my doom.

100 Love, which permits no loved one not to love,
          took me so strongly with delight in him
          that we are one in Hell, as we were above.[16]

      Love led us to one death. In the depths of Hell
          Caïna waits for him[17] who took our lives."
105   This was the piteous tale they stopped to tell.

      And when I had heard those world-offended lovers
          I bowed my head. At last the Poet spoke:
          "What painful thoughts are these your lowered brow covers?"

      When at length I answered, I began: "Alas!
110   What sweetest thoughts, what green and young desire
          led these two lovers to this sorry pass."

      Then turning to those spirits once again,
          I said: "Francesca, what you suffer here
          melts me to tears of pity and of pain.

Literary Analysis
Characterization What
does the repetition of
the word "Love" at the
beginning of these three
stanzas add to Francesca's
characterization?

---

14. **Po** (pō) river in northern Italy.
15. **unshriven** unconfessed and so with her sin unforgiven.
16. **that we . . . above** Dante frequently expresses the principle that the souls of the damned
    are locked so blindly into their own guilt that none can feel sympathy for another. The
    temptation of many readers is to interpret this line romantically. The more Dantean inter-
    pretation, however, is that Paolo and Francesca add to each other's anguish as mutual
    reminders of their sin.
17. **Caïna . . . him** Giovanni Malatesta was still alive at the time this was written. According to
    Dante, his fate is already decided, however, and upon his death, his soul will fall to Caïna,
    the first ring of the last circle (Canto XXXII), where lie those who performed acts of treach-
    ery against their kin.

115   But tell me: in the time of your sweet sighs
            by what appearances found love the way
            to lure you to his <u>perilous</u> paradise?"

        And she: "The double grief of a lost bliss
            is to recall its happy hour in pain.
120   Your Guide and Teacher knows the truth of this.

        But if there is indeed a soul in Hell
            to ask of the beginning of our love
            out of his pity, I will weep and tell:

        On a day for dalliance we read the rhyme
125   of Lancelot,[18] how love had mastered him.
            We were alone with innocence and dim time.[19]

        Pause after pause that high old story drew
            our eyes together while we blushed and paled;
            but it was one soft passage overthrew

---

18. the rhyme of Lancelot The story of Lancelot exists in many forms. The details Dante uses are from an Old French version.

19. dim time the olden time depicted in the Lancelot story. This phrase was added by the translator; the original reads, "We were alone, suspecting nothing."

▲ **Critical Viewing**
This three-part illustration shows Paolo and Francesca in life, Virgil and Dante, and Paolo and Francesca in Hell. Do you think the artist shares Dante's sympathy for the doomed pair? Explain. **[Take a Position]**

perilous (per′ ə ləs) *adj.* dangerous

☑ **Reading Check**
With which condemned soul does Dante speak?

130   our caution and our hearts. For when we read
        how her fond smile was kissed by such a lover,
        he who is one with me alive and dead

    breathed on my lips the tremor of his kiss.
        That book, and he who wrote it, was a pander.[20]
135   That day we read no further." As she said this,

    the other spirit, who stood by her, wept
        so piteously, I felt my senses reel
        and faint away with anguish. I was swept

    by such a swoon as death is, and I fell,
140   as a corpse might fall, to the dead floor of Hell.

---

20. **That book . . . pander** *Galeotto,* the Italian word for "pander," is also the Italian rendering of the name of Gallehault, who, in the French Romance Dante refers to here, urged Lancelot and Guinevere on to love. A pander is a go-between in a love affair.

Review and Assess

Thinking About the Selection

1. **Respond:** Do you share Dante's sympathy for Paolo and Francesca? Why or why not?

2. **(a) Recall:** What punishment do the lustful suffer? **(b) Analyze:** In what ways does this punishment match their sins? Explain.

3. **(a) Recall:** In line 39, what does Dante say the sinners relinquished in favor of "appetite"? **(b) Classify:** In lines 55 through 67, note words and phrases that liken sensual indulgence to madness. **(c) Evaluate:** What kind of love does Dante condemn in this Canto? Explain.

4. **(a) Recall:** In line 72, what two emotions does Dante experience in reaction to the sight of the carnal sinners? **(b) Interpret:** Why does Dante feel each of these emotions? Support your answer with details from the text.

5. **(a) Recall:** According to Francesca, what motivates her descent into sin? **(b) Infer:** What does Dante suggest about the effects of certain kinds of literature? **(c) Take a Stand:** Do you agree with Dante's assessment?

Literary Analysis
Characterization and Allusion How is the *Divine Comedy*, in its message and purpose, quite different from the Arthurian romance Francesca describes?

Canto XXXIV

NINTH CIRCLE: COCYTUS[1]   *Compound Fraud*

ROUND FOUR: JUDECCA   *The Treacherous to Their Masters*

THE CENTER   *Satan*

"On march the banners of the King,"[2] Virgil begins as the Poets face the last depth. He is quoting a medieval hymn, and to it he adds the distortion and perversion of all that lies about him. "On march the banners of the King—of Hell." And there before them, in an infernal parody of Godhead, they see Satan in the distance, his great wings beating like a windmill. It is their beating that is the source of the icy wind of Cocytus, the exhalation of all evil.

All about him in the ice are strewn the sinners of the last round, *Judecca*, named for Judas Iscariot.[3] These are the *Treacherous to Their Masters*. They lie completely sealed in the ice, twisted and distorted into every conceivable posture. It is impossible to speak to them, and the Poets move on to observe Satan.

He is fixed into the ice at the center to which flow all the rivers of guilt; and as he beats his great wings as if to escape, their icy wind only freezes him more surely into the polluted ice. In a grotesque parody of the Trinity, he has three faces, each a different color, and in each mouth he clamps a sinner whom he rips eternally with his teeth. *Judas Iscariot* is in the central mouth: *Brutus* and *Cassius*[4] in the mouths on either side.

Having seen all, the Poets now climb through the center, grappling hand over hand down the hairy flank of Satan himself—a last supremely symbolic action— and at last, when they have passed the center of all gravity, they emerge from Hell. A long climb from the earth's center to the Mount of Purgatory awaits them, and they push on without rest, ascending along the sides of the river Lethe, till they emerge once more to see the stars of Heaven, just before dawn on Easter Sunday.

> "On march the banners of the King of Hell,"
>> my Master said. "Toward us. Look straight ahead:
>> can you make him out at the core of the frozen shell?"

> Like a whirling windmill seen afar at twilight,
> 5   or when a mist has risen from the ground—
>> just such an engine rose upon my sight

> stirring up such a wild and bitter wind
>> I cowered for shelter at my Master's back,
>> there being no other windbreak I could find.

> I stood now where the souls of the last class
> 10   (with fear my verses tell it) were covered wholly;
>> they shone below the ice like straws in glass.

---

1. **Cocytus** (kō sīt´ əs) Greek: "river of wailing."
2. **On . . . King** This hymn was written in the sixth century by Venantius Fortunatus, Bishop of Poitiers. The original celebrates the Holy Cross and part of the service for Good Friday, to be sung at the moment of uncovering the cross.
3. **Judas Iscariot** (is ker´ ē ət) disciple who betrayed Jesus; see the Bible, Matthew 26:14, 48.
4. **Brutus and Cassius** They took part in a plot to assassinate Julius Caesar.

Reading Check

What is the source of the icy wind of Cocytus?

Some lie stretched out; others are fixed in place
    upright, some on their heads, some on their soles;
    another, like a bow, bends foot to face.

15 When we had gone so far across the ice
    that it pleased my Guide to show me the foul creature[5]
    which once had worn the grace of Paradise,

he made me stop, and, stepping aside, he said:
    "Now see the face of Dis![6] This is the place
20   where you must arm your soul against all dread."

▲ **Critical Viewing**
Which figure in this illustration is Dante, and which is Virgil? Explain how you know. **[Distinguish]**

---

5. **the foul creature** Satan.
6. **Dis** (dis) in Greek mythology, the god of the lower world or the lower world itself. Here, it stands for Satan.

Do not ask, Reader, how my blood ran cold
    and my voice choked up with fear. I cannot write it:
    this is a terror that cannot be told.

I did not die, and yet I lost life's breath:
25   imagine for yourself what I became,
    deprived at once of both my life and death.

The Emperor of the Universe of Pain
    jutted his upper chest above the ice;
    and I am closer in size to the great mountain

30 the Titans[7] make around the central pit,
    than they to his arms. Now, starting from this part,
    imagine the whole that corresponds to it!

If he was once as beautiful as now
    he is hideous, and still turned on his Maker,
35   well may he be the source of every woe!

With what a sense of <u>awe</u> I saw his head
    towering above me! for it had three faces:[8]
    one was in front, and it was fiery red;

the other two, as weirdly wonderful,
40   merged with it from the middle of each shoulder
    to the point where all converged at the top of the skull;

the right was something between white and bile;
    the left was about the color one observes
    on those who live along the banks of the Nile.

45 Under each head two wings rose terribly,
    their span proportioned to so gross a bird:
    I never saw such sails upon the sea.

They were not feathers—their texture and their form
    were like a bat's wings—and he beat them so
50   that three winds blew from him in one great storm:

it is these winds that freeze all Cocytus.
    He wept from his six eyes, and down three chins
    the tears ran mixed with bloody froth and pus.[9]

Reading Strategy
Distinguishing Between the Speaker and the Poet
In what ways does Dante the character's direct address to the reader intensify both the drama and the sense of reality of this scene? Explain.

Literary Analysis
Characterization and Allusion Why is an allusion to the Titans an appropriate detail in Satan's characterization? Explain.

awe (ô) *n.* feelings of reverence, fear, and wonder

---

7. **Titans** giant deities who were overthrown by Zeus and the Olympian gods of Greece.
8. **three faces** There are many interpretations of these three faces. The common theme in all of them is that the faces are a perversion of the qualities of the Trinity.
9. **bloody froth and pus** the gore of the sinners he chews, which is mixed with his saliva.

Reading Check
In what substance are the souls of the damned trapped?

from the *Inferno: Canto XXXIV* ◆ 639

Judecca - Lucifer, Inferno XXXIV, 1862, Gustave Doré

In every mouth he worked a broken sinner
55   between his rake-like teeth. Thus he kept three
        in eternal pain at his eternal dinner.

For the one in front the biting seemed to play
        no part at all compared to the ripping: at times
        the whole skin of his back was flayed away.

60 "That soul that suffers most," explained my Guide,
        "is Judas Iscariot, he who kicks his legs
        on the fiery chin and has his head inside.

Of the other two, who have their heads thrust forward,
        the one who dangles down from the black face
65   is Brutus: note how he <u>writhes</u> without a word.

▲ **Critical Viewing**
How does the artist's depiction of Lucifer in this engraving compare and contrast with Dante's description? Explain. **[Compare and Contrast]**

writhes (rῑthz) v. twists and turns the body, as in agony

And there, with the huge and sinewy arms, is the soul,
    of Cassius,—But the night is coming on[10]
    and we must go, for we have seen the whole."

Then, as he bade, I clasped his neck, and he,
70   watching for a moment when the wings
    were opened wide, reached over dexterously[11]

and seized the shaggy coat of the king demon;
    then grappling matted hair and frozen crusts
    from one tuft to another, clambered down.

75 When we had reached the joint where the great thigh
    merges into the swelling of the haunch,
    my Guide and Master, straining terribly,

turned his head to where his feet had been
    and began to grip the hair as if he were climbing;[12]
80   so that I thought we moved toward Hell again.

"Hold fast!" my Guide said, and his breath came shrill
    with labor and exhaustion. "There is no way
    but by such stairs to rise above such evil."

At last he climbed out through an opening
85   in the central rock, and he seated me on the rim;
    then joined me with a <u>nimble</u> backward spring.

I looked up, thinking to see Lucifer
    as I had left him, and I saw instead
    his legs projecting high into the air.

90 Now let all those whose dull minds are still vexed
    by failure to understand what point it was
    I had passed through, judge if I was perplexed.

"Get up. Up on your feet," my Master said.
    "The sun already mounts to middle tierce,[13]
95   and a long road and hard climbing lie ahead."

Reading Strategy
Distinguishing Between the Speaker and the Poet
What spiritual and emotional change does the poet express through a physical description? Explain.

nimble (nim′ bəl) *adj.* able to move quickly and lightly; agile

---

10. the night is coming on It is now Saturday evening.
11. dexterously *adv.* skillfully.
12. as if he were climbing They have passed the center of gravity and so must turn around and start climbing.
13. middle tierce According to the church's division of the day for prayer, tierce is the period from about six to nine A.M. Middle tierce, therefore, is seven-thirty. In going through the center point, Dante and Virgil have gone from night to day. They have moved ahead twelve hours.

Reading Check

What torture do Judas Iscariot, Brutus, and Cassius suffer?

It was no hall of state we had found there,
    but a natural animal pit hollowed from rock
    with a broken floor and a close and sunless air.

"Before I tear myself from the Abyss,"
100   I said when I had risen, "O my Master,
    explain to me my error in all this:

where is the ice? and Lucifer—how has he
    been turned from top to bottom: and how can the sun
    have gone from night to day so suddenly?"

105 And he to me: "You imagine you are still
    on the other side of the center where I grasped
    the shaggy flank of the Great Worm of Evil

which bores through the world—you *were* while
    I climbed down,
    but when I turned myself about, you passed
110   the point to which all gravities are drawn.

You are under the other hemisphere where you stand;
    the sky above us is the half opposed
    to that which canopies the great dry land.

Under the midpoint of that other sky
115   the Man[14] who was born sinless and who lived
    beyond all blemish, came to suffer and die.

You have your feet upon a little sphere
    which forms the other face of the Judecca.
    There it is evening when it is morning here.

120 And this gross Fiend and Image of all Evil
    who made a stairway for us with his hide
    is pinched and prisoned in the ice-pack still.

On this side he plunged down from heaven's height,
    and the land that spread here once hid in the sea
125   and fled North to our hemisphere for fright;[15]

Themes in World Literature

Literary Views of the Underworld

Although the *Divine Comedy* is probably the most famous literary excursion into the afterlife, there are many others. The Sumerian-Babylonian epic of *Gilgamesh* contains a vivid description of an underworld in which people sit in darkness and eat dust and clay. In Homer's *Odyssey*, Odysseus visits the Greek underworld, where he converses with the shades of mortals. In Plato's *Apology*, Socrates is optimistic about the afterlife, saying that death may be a state of nothingness, a kind of sleep, or a journey to a place where he will meet all who have gone before him. John Milton's *Paradise Lost* and Goethe's *Faust* present images of Heaven and Hell in which goodness on Earth is rewarded and excessive pride and egoism are punished. However, Dante's version of Hell, with its clear structure, sharp physical descriptions, and fully realized characters, remains perhaps the most detailed and vividly imagined of all the literary underworlds.

---

14. **the Man** Jesus, who suffered and died in Jerusalem, which was thought to be the middle of the Earth.
15. **fled North . . . for fright** Dante believed that the Northern Hemisphere was mostly land and the Southern Hemisphere, mostly water. Here, he explains the reason for this state of affairs.

Poets emerge from Hell, Inferno XXXIV, 139, Gustave Doré

And it may be that moved by that same fear,
    the one peak[16] that still rises on this side
    fled upward leaving this great cavern[17] here."

Down there, beginning at the further bound
130   of Beelzebub's[18] dim tomb, there is a space
    not known by sight, but only by the sound

---

16. **the one peak** the Mount of Purgatory.
17. **this great cavern** the natural animal pit of line 98. It is also "Beelzebub's dim tomb," line 130.
18. **Beelzebub's** (bē el′ zə bubz′) Beelzebub, which in Hebrew means "god of flies," was another name for Satan.

✔**Reading Check**

What "stairway" did Virgil take to climb out of Hell?

of a little stream[19] descending through the hollow
    it has eroded from the massive stone
    in its endlessly entwining lazy flow."

135   My Guide and I crossed over and began
    to mount that little known and lightless road
    to ascend into the shining world again.

He first, I second, without thought of rest
    we climbed the dark until we reached the point
140   where a round opening brought in sight the blest

and beauteous shining of the Heavenly cars.
And we walked out once more beneath the Stars.[20]

---

19. a little stream Lethe (lē′ thē); in classical mythology, the river of forgetfulness, from which
souls drank before being born. In Dante's symbolism, it flows down from Purgatory, where
it has washed away the memory of sin from the souls who are undergoing purification.
That memory it delivers to Hell, which draws all sin to itself.

20. Stars As part of his total symbolism, Dante ends each of the three divisions of the *Divine
Comedy* with this word. Every conclusion of the upward soul is toward the stars, symbols
of hope and virtue. It is just before dawn of Easter Sunday that the Poets emerge—a
further symbolism.

Review and Assess

Thinking About the Selection

1. **Respond:** Which aspect of the ninth circle of Hell do you find
   most horrible? Why?

2. **(a) Recall:** In lines 22–23, what does Dante say he cannot write
   or describe? **(b) Interpret:** How does he succeed nevertheless in
   communicating his experience?

3. **(a) Recall:** Who are the three figures in Satan's mouth?
   (b) Infer: What sin do all three have in common? **(c) Analyze:**
   Why do you think Dante chooses to situate the punishment for
   such sin in a frozen lake?

4. **(a) Recall:** In line 65, which aspect of Brutus' suffering does Virgil emphasize? **(b) Generalize:** Why might language be denied to
   the inhabitants of the ninth circle of Hell?

5. **(a) Evaluate:** In what ways do you think Dante the character's
   feelings about the lost inhabitants of Hell have changed since the
   beginning of the *Inferno*? **(b) Analyze:** What message about tolerance for sin might Dante the poet be expressing through his
   character's emotional evolution?

6. **Hypothesize:** If you were to undertake a journey such as Dante's,
   whom would you choose as your guide? Explain your answer.

Review and Assess

Literary Analysis

Characterization

1. Which words and phrases in Francesca's first statements to Dante provide **direct characterization** of Dante the character?
2. Use a chart like the one shown to analyze the **indirect characterization** of Dante in the *Inferno*.

Method of Characterization	Example	Trait Revealed
Dante's Actions	He questions Francesca.	curiosity; sympathy
Dante's Words	"I cowered for shelter."	
Other Characters' Behavior Toward Dante	Virgil carries him.	

3. (a) Cite two statements another character makes about Virgil. (b) In what ways do each of these statements add to your understanding of Virgil's character?

Connecting Literary Elements

4. In Canto V, Francesca mentions "him who took our lives." (a) To whom is she referring with this **allusion**? (b) How does this allusion increase the realism of the *Inferno*?
5. At the beginning of Canto XXXIV, Virgil cites a line from a hymn. (a) How does Virgil change the line? (b) How does this allusion add to the reader's understanding of Hell as a world of distortions?

Reading Strategy

Distinguishing Between the Speaker and the Poet

6. At key transitional points in the story, Dante, **the speaker** of the poem, loses consciousness. In what ways does this solve literary problems for Dante **the poet**?
7. In lines 105–135 of Canto XXXIV, Dante the poet has Virgil explain where the two travelers are standing. (a) Why does Dante the character need this explanation? (b) Why does the reader need it?

Extend Understanding

8. **Psychology Connection:** At the banks of the river Acheron, Charon tells the souls to "Bury / here and forever all hope of Paradise." Is hope necessary for happiness? Explain your answer.

Quick Review

Characterization is the art of revealing character. Writers use both **direct** and **indirect** characterization to reveal the personalities of their characters.

An **allusion** is a reference within a literary work to a well-known person, place, event, story, work of literature, or work of art.

To **distinguish between the speaker and the poet** as you read, make a distinction between the speaker's feelings and reactions and the overall meaning and purpose of a poem.

 **Take It to the Net**
PHSchool.com

Take the interactive self-test online to check your understanding of this selection.

Integrate Language Skills

Vocabulary Development Lesson

Words Related to *Awe*

Some words formed with the word *awe* have either positive or negative meanings, depending upon their context. *Awful*, for example, can mean either "bad" or "awe-inspiring." Define each of the following words, and determine which of them, if any, possess both positive and negative meanings.

1. awesome
2. awestruck
3. overawed
4. awfully

Spelling Strategy

For most words ending in *e*, make no change when adding a suffix beginning with a consonant (*care* + *-ful* = *careful*). Add the indicated suffix to each word below.

1. love + *-ly*
2. grace + *-ful*
3. complete + *-ly*
4. whole + *-some*

Grammar and Style Lesson

Past Perfect Verb Tense

The **past perfect verb tense** expresses actions that were completed before a specific moment in the past. Use the past perfect tense to show a connection between two past actions or conditions.

> **Past Actions:** And when I <u>had heard</u> those world-offended lovers I bowed my head.

> **Past Condition:** He <u>had been</u> beautiful until he turned on his Maker.

Practice Identify examples of the past perfect tense in each item below, and explain whether they connect past actions or past conditions.

1. We had finished reading the *Inferno* before we went on to the *Purgatorio*.

Concept Development: Synonyms

Review the vocabulary list on page 628. Then, complete the activity below by matching each of the words in the left column with the correct synonym in the right column.

1.	grotesque	a.	dangerous
2.	degree	b.	storm
3.	anguish	c.	reverence
4.	tempest	d.	agony
5.	perilous	e.	twists
6.	awe	f.	level
7.	writhes	g.	agile
8.	nimble	h.	distorted

2. We were able to compare translations because our teacher had brought three different ones to class.
3. Previously, Martina had favored the Sayers translation.
4. Before we read it in English, I had translated some of the Italian text myself.
5. I had never thought I would love medieval literature until I read Dante.

Writing Application Write a dialogue in which two people discuss the *Inferno*. Use at least three examples of the past perfect tense.

W̶G *Prentice Hall Writing and Grammar Connection: Diamond Level, Chapter 21, Section 2*

Writing Lesson

Response to Criticism

Dorothy Sayers, one of Dante's finest translators, wrote that Dante's depiction of Francesca balances good and evil with "a deadly accuracy." Sayers notes, "All the good is there; . . . but also all the evil; the easy yielding, the inability to say No, the intense self-pity." Write an essay in which you respond to Sayers's criticism.

Prewriting   Brainstorm for responses to Sayers's statement by writing freely about these questions: Are good and evil balanced in Francesca? Does she yield easily? Is she self-pitying or merely human? Then, reread Canto V, gathering details to support your opinions.

Drafting   Quote Sayers's statement in your introduction. Then, assert your own opinion of Francesca. In your body paragraphs, elaborate on your opinion, using evidence from the poem. When you use quotations from the text, tie each one directly to the point you are making.

Model: Elaborating Using Supporting Quotations

Sayers pinpoints Dante's portrayal of Francesca as a sinner who feels sorry for herself. She has not accepted her guilt and wallows in "intense self-pity." This is shown in line 100 when Francesca blames her downfall on "Love, which permits no loved one not to love." She is saying she is a victim.

> Quotations from the text are most effective when directly connected to the writer's point.

Revising   Review your essay, making sure that you have supported each point with quotations, examples, or reasons.

WG *Prentice Hall Writing and Grammar Connection: Diamond Level, Chapter 14, Section 3*

Extension Activities

Listening and Speaking Develop and present a **movie proposal** for a screen adaptation of the *Inferno.* Use these tips to prepare:

- Reread the poem, taking notes about the setting, characters, and plot.
- Identify opportunities for special effects.
- Summarize the plot, emphasizing the thrills, drama, and adventure of the tale.

Deliver your pitch to classmates as they play the role of the producers you seek to convince.

Research and Technology With a small group, use print and electronic sources to research Dante's politics and the real-life characters who appear in the *Inferno.* Then, create a **biographical analysis chart** that reveals the connections between Dante's political and literary lives. **[Group Activity]**

 Take It to the Net PHSchool.com

Go online for an additional research activity using the Internet.

A Closer Look

The Art of Translation

The words, expressions, and attitudes of one language do not always match those of another language; translation is a far more complex task than one might think.

When Dante started the *Divine Comedy*, did he write these lines?

> *Midway in our life's journey, I went astray*
> *from the straight road and woke to find myself*
> *alone in a dark wood.*

Or, did he write these lines?

> *Halfway along the road we have to go,*
> *I found myself obscured in a great forest,*
> *Bewildered, and I knew I had lost the way.*

Then again, perhaps he started out with these words:

> *Midway this way of life we're bound upon,*
> *I woke to find myself in a dark wood,*
> *Where the right road was wholly lost and gone.*

Actually, Dante began his masterpiece with these lines:

> *Nel mezzo del cammin di nostra vita*
> *mi ritrovai per una selva oscura,*
> *che la diritta via era smarrita.*

For those of us who are not well versed in medieval Italian, translators are essential to our understanding of Dante. The three English versions shown above—John Ciardi's lucid and dynamic verse, C. H. Sisson's elegant blank verse, and Dorothy Sayers's rhymed lines—are just a few of the many attempts to make Dante's personal adventure and his medieval worldview clear to modern readers.

A translation is an interpretation of a work of literature. When we read Dante, the translator of his work serves as our own personal Virgil—our guide and interpreter. Whether the text is Dante's *Commedia* or a brand-new masterpiece of world literature, a great translator conveys both the meaning and the musical sense of the original.

▲ **Critical Viewing**
Which details in this painting of Dante explaining the *Divine Comedy* suggest that the poet is trying to educate or teach people? **[Analyze]**

The Levels of Meaning A translator must be conscious of several levels of meaning—the literal, the idiomatic, and the symbolic.

- **Literal:** A literal translation is a word-for-word rendition of the words of an original text. Usually, these word-for-word translations are stiff and awkward; they do not fully capture the meaning or music of the original. For example, in Spanish, the word for "sky" and the word for "heaven" are the same—*cielo*. A word-for-word translation might indicate both English meanings.
- **Idiomatic:** Each culture's day-to-day experiences create distinct ways of looking at everyday objects and events. These distinctions result in idiomatic meanings—the unique ways in which a language expresses the characteristics of a culture. A translator must be aware of idiomatic meanings in both languages.
- **Symbolic:** Symbolic meanings involve the figures of speech, images, and ideas that an author may use to convey an artistic or a philosophical vision. For example, Dante's word *via* may be translated literally as "road"—an ordinary path in the woods. However, a translator may also try to suggest the symbolic meaning of Dante's faith in the road to Heaven.

Capturing the Music Every language has its unique sound, its particular beauties, and its quirks. Translation requires the skills of a writer who can make the work sing in the *new* language. Word choice and syntax, rhythm and meter, sentence structure and variety, assonance and consonance, onomatopoeia, and tone contribute to the impression that the translated work captures the original.

Translation is an art of sacrifices, and every Dante translation is a good example of necessary compromises. Some translators favor meaning and accuracy over music and style. Others blur meaning for poetic effect. Some translators turn the poem into prose; others would never dream of doing so. Still others simply want to make a vital, readable modern English poem.

Each age needs its own Dante. Today, we can still admire the formal translation written by Henry Wadsworth Longfellow in the nineteenth century:

> *Midway upon the journey of our life*
> *I found myself within a forest dark,*
> *For the straightforward pathway had been lost.*

Nevertheless, we seem to respond more intensely to the voices of our own time. Here is the compressed but fluid version of former United States poet laureate Robert Pinsky:

> *Midway on our life's journey, I found myself*
> *In dark woods, the right road lost.*

As the centuries have passed, one of the continuing lessons of the *Commedia*, whether Dante intended it or not, is that every age needs not only great writers but also great translators.

You, *too*, can be a translator!

The second tercet of the *Inferno*, shown below, is an emotional outburst. Write your own version of these lines. As you write, experiment with prose and poetry, rhyme and no rhyme. Decide whether you want your version to be dramatic, emotional, formal, or informal, as well as how you can make it meaningful for contemporary readers.

Original

Ahi quanto a dir qual era è cosa dura / esta selva selvaggia e aspra e forte / che nel pensier rinova la paura!

Literal Translation

"Ah, how hard it is to tell what that wood was, / wild, rugged, harsh; the very thought of it / renews the fear!" (Charles S. Singleton)

Writing About Literature

Evaluate Literary Themes

One of the most characteristic themes of the literature of the Middle Ages is the quest, or search. In a world filled with mysterious forces, characters embark on quests with goals such as the discovery of the Holy Grail or proof of true love. Heroes test their courage as they go beyond the apparent objects of their quests to discover insights about God, love, and loyalty. Far from being the inert, inactive era that people had long considered it to be, the medieval period was one of political, social, and religious change. Perhaps this is why the theme of the quest for meaning in an unstable world held such allure for writers of this period.

To evaluate the theme of the quest in medieval literature, complete the assignment described in the box at right.

Prewriting

Review the selections. Identify the selections in which a quest is a dominant theme. Then, describe the object of the quest. To narrow the focus of your essay, ask yourself questions such as the following:

- How do plot and characterization reveal the quest theme?
- In what ways does the quest theme reveal the values and concerns of writers of the Middle Ages?
- Does the quest make the story interesting, even gripping, or does it lead to a predictable or undramatic story?
- As it appears in the selection, does the quest-theme shed light on life or people in general? Or is its relevance limited to the Middle Ages?

Find a focus for your essay by jotting down notes in a format similar to the example below.

Assignment: The Quest in Medieval Literature

Write an analytical essay that evaluates the theme of the quest in the literature of the Middle Ages, as revealed in the selections in this unit.

Criteria:

- Include a thesis statement that evaluates the theme of the quest in the Middle Ages.
- Evaluate this theme in each of the works you discuss by answering these questions: Does the theme create narrative interest? Does it have relevance for modern readers?
- Support your evaluations with detailed analyses of this theme in at least two of the selections.
- Approximate length: 1,500 words

Read to Write

As you reread the texts, ask yourself what the main character desires more than anything else. That desire prompts the character's search, or quest.

Model: Identifying Evidence of the Quest Theme

Selection	Object of Quest	Details	Quotes
"The Grail" from *Perceval*	Holy Grail; true faith	Perceval prays to God; help of fisherman	"'There's something I would ask of you, / some things I wanted to inquire, / some information I desire.'"

Choose selections. Reread your notes, and choose two selections that illuminate the theme of the quest or that might make an interesting thematic contrast.

Drafting

Use a logical order. Follow an organization that makes sense. For instance, you might discuss one point of evaluation for both selections, and then move to the next point.

Present clear evaluations. For each selection you discuss, show how the quest theme adds to or detracts from the story's excitement. For instance, you might argue that the mysteries surrounding the quest in *Perceval* add interest. Also, discuss whether the quest theme has relevance for modern readers. For instance, you might argue that Dante's thirst for answers about life reflects a desire that everyone feels.

Provide specific support. For each evaluation you give, quote specific passages in support. It is not enough to say that *Perceval* is "slow-moving." To support such an evaluation, you must first quote a relevant passage and then explain why it slows the story down.

Revising and Editing

Review content: Check the accuracy of details. Your responsibility to readers includes absolute accuracy of content. Check the examples you used in your paper to make sure they are accurate. Make sure that quotations are complete and accurately spelled and punctuated.

Review style: Vary sentence length. One way to make your writing livelier and more interesting is to vary the length of your sentences. Short sentences add emphasis. Longer sentences flow smoothly. Read your paper aloud and split or combine sentences as needed.

> ### Model: Revising to Vary Sentence Length
>
> *As for most ordinary people of the Middle Ages,* the character
> ∧Faith in God animates∧Perceval's life and his journey. ~~In this way, Perceval as a character is like most people in the Middle Ages.~~ In ordinary speech, Perceval constantly refers to God. He says such phrases as "Oh God Almighty! It would seem, I'd find my mother, if she's living."

Publishing and Presenting

Oral presentation. Choose one of the works you analyzed in your essay, and read an excerpt to your classmates. Then, explain how the excerpt illuminates an aspect of the theme of the quest.

Writing and Grammar Connection: Diamond Level, Chapter 14

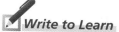
Write to Learn
Do not force the examples you have chosen to fit your thesis statement. Be willing to choose other examples or to revise your thesis statement if necessary.

Write to Explain
Make sure that the arguments you make and the conclusions you draw are clear. Remember, readers can follow only what is on paper, not what is in your mind.

Writing WORKSHOP

Research: Research Paper

A **research paper** is an in-depth examination of a topic in which the writer puts forth a thesis, or main point, and supports it with information drawn from several outside sources. In this workshop, you will write a research paper that presents your findings on a topic of interest to you.

Assignment Criteria Your research paper should have the following characteristics:

- A clear thesis statement that presents a key point about the topic
- Factual information from a variety of sources
- A comparison of information, including a consideration of the reliability of the sources
- A consistent and effective organization
- A correctly formatted works-cited list

To preview the criteria on which your research paper may be assessed, see the Rubric on page 657.

Prewriting

Choose a topic. A successful topic for this report will be one that is of interest to you. It will also be focused enough to be adequately discussed in a paper of several pages. Finally, it will be one for which a variety of sources are available. **Create a web** like this one to examine the possibilities, and select from them.

Identify your purpose. Write a question that further focuses the topic you've chosen. While your question must be narrow enough to be manageable, it must still have enough breadth to allow you to find sufficient resource material.

> **Sample Question:**
> Why does the film *Schindler's List* have historical value?

Do the research. Use a library for secondary sources such as books and encyclopedias. Use the Internet for secondary sources, such as newspapers and magazines, and for many primary sources, such as letters and interviews. List and briefly summarize all sources.

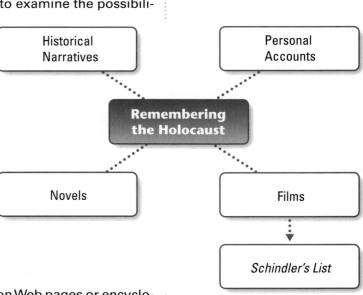

Historical Narratives

Personal Accounts

Remembering the Holocaust

Novels

Films

Schindler's List

Choose varied documents. Do not rely solely on Web pages or encyclopedias for research. Instead, consult a variety of sources, including books, periodicals, and documentaries. Use a minimum of five credible sources.

Student Model

Before you begin drafting, read this student model and review the characteristics of an effective research paper.

Marcus Martin
Chilhowie, VA

"He Who Saves a Single Life Saves the World Entire"

Sixty years ago, the world experienced one of the darkest periods in human history—the Holocaust. Fifty years later, director Steven Spielberg achieved the goal of creating a biographical drama set during the Holocaust by making *Schindler's List*. Although the film is a Hollywood production about a horrific tragedy, *Schindler's List* manages to attain a true historical value because of Spielberg's realistic filming techniques, accuracy of setting, and honesty of characterization.

> Marcus identifies his thesis in his opening paragraph.

Winner of Best Film at the 1993 Academy Awards, *Schindler's List* tells the story of Oskar Schindler, a German entrepreneur who "saw his chance" during World War II and opened a factory employing Jews "at starvation wages" (Ebert). After defrauding the Nazis for months with a factory that never produced anything of use to the German army, Schindler became a hero. Outfoxing the evil prison commandant Amon Goeth and other Nazis through the creation of a list of "necessary" Jewish workers, Schindler and Jewish accountant Itzhak Stern were able to protect and save more than 1,100 workers ("Behind the Scenes").

> Next, Marcus provides general background on his subject.

Schindler's remarkable story first came to world attention through the publication of Thomas Keneally's book *Schindler's List* in 1982. Steven Spielberg immediately saw the movie potential in a book that "faithfully recounts episodes from the lives of its characters . . . Poldek Pfefferberg really did escape a roundup by convincing Goeth he had been detailed to collect strewn suitcases; and, just as the book records, Oskar Schindler did play for the life of Goeth's maid Helen Hirsch in a single game of blackjack" ("Behind the Scenes"). According to Spielberg, he had been wanting to document the story of Schindler for public record for over ten years: "No one can do anything to fix the past – that's already happened, . . . But a picture like this can impact on us, delivering a mandate about what must never happen again" ("Behind the Scenes"). Spielberg's goal in creating the film was for viewers to "see the Holocaust in a vivid and terrible way," and to give the victims of the Holocaust a voice that they had been robbed of for so long (Ebert).

> Marcus provides a detailed explanation of Spielberg's motives for making the film.

Spielberg was able to accomplish his goal of not merely making a movie but also creating a timeless record of history through specific film-making choices. Spielberg explained that he filmed in black and white because most news film and photographs of the Holocaust are in black and white and that his vision of the Holocaust had "largely been stark black-and-white images" ("Behind the Scenes"). Shooting forty percent of the film with hand-held cameras also added

> Marcus now addresses his first major point.

to the realistic feel of the film. Through both of these filming techniques, Spielberg was able to achieve an effect more like a historical documentary than a Hollywood movie. "The black-and-white and hand-held camera gives the film a sort of *cinéma vérité,* documentary feel. It embodied the truth we were trying to explore and communicate[d] what happened. It made it seem real, somehow" ("Behind the Scenes").

In addition to using special filming techniques, Spielberg was attentive to historical accuracy in choosing the movie's locations and sets. A nationally diverse crew began filming on March 1, 1993, in Krakow, one of the few Polish cities to survive World War II. "One of the great historical cities of the world," Krakow offered streets and buildings that gave the movie an authentic setting ("Behind the Scenes"). Actual locations that were part of Schindler's life, such as his old factory and apartment, were used for filming as much as possible. After meeting resistance to shooting inside Auschwitz/Birkenau, Spielberg was able to film a scene of prisoners entering Auschwitz by shooting outside the camp's actual guardhouse (Royal). Because the forced-labor camp Plaszow was no longer intact, Spielberg had a replica of the camp constructed next to the site of the original camp. Using plans from the old camp, the production company built thirty-four barracks, seven watchtowers, and a replica of the villa that Goeth occupied during his rule of the camp. The company also "recreated the road into the camp that was paved with Jewish tombstones" ("Behind the Scenes"). The feeling of authenticity in the film comes from the fact that it was shot where events actually happened (Royal).

Spielberg was also realistic in his presentation of Schindler's character and behavior of Schindler throughout the movie. Instead of depicting Schindler as a noble hero, the film shows him as vice-driven and self-indulgent. He is portrayed as a man who only wanted to maintain his own lavish lifestyle, yet he is shown as having a caring side as well (*Schindler's List*). Most accounts of the real-life Schindler resemble the character in the movie (Ebert). However, some critics argue that Spielberg did not go far enough in exploring Schindler's true motivation for saving the Jews. Those closest to him would say that greed was his chief motivation, but Schindler himself said there was simply no choice but to do what he could: "I felt that the Jews were being destroyed. I had to help them; there was no choice" (Roberts 91). However, Ruth Kander, a German who knew Schindler personally, has maintained that he cared only about his own good (Roberts 89–90). Whatever Schindler's motivation, it is a question that Spielberg does not probe deeply.

> Points here are presented in the same sequence as Marcus presented them in his thesis statement.

> Sources are cited throughout the paper. At the end, Marcus identifies sources on his Works-Cited list properly, following MLA style.

Is *Schindler's List* an accurate account of a tragic period of time, or is it just another of Spielberg's box-office hits? Through the use of black-and-white film and hand-held cameras, the accurate re-creation of settings, and the honest portrayal of Schindler, Spielberg was able to create a timeless film of historical value. Just as Schindler touched hundreds of lives with his actions, the cinematic retelling of his efforts continues to touch lives today.

Perhaps the true effect of Schindler and the film is best shown in the scene in which Schindler parts from the people he saved. An inmate at Brinnlitz volunteered his gold dental bridgework to be made into a ring for Schindler when the Jews were liberated. Inside the ring was inscribed a verse from the book of Jewish law, the Talmud, which read, "He who saves a single life saves the world entire" (*Schindler's List*).

Works Cited

Ebert, Roger. "Schindler's List." *Chicago Sun Times*. 15 Dec 1993. 17 Mar. 2003 <www.suntimes.com/ebert/ebert_reviews/1993/12/894536.html>

Leventhal, Robert S. "Romancing the Holocaust, or Hollywood and Horror: Steven Spielberg's *Schindler's List*." 1995. The Institute for Advanced Technology in the Humanities, University of Virginia. 17 Mar. 2003 <http://www.iath.virginia.edu/holocaust/schinlist.html>

Roberts, Jack. *The Importance of Oskar Schindler*. San Diego, CA: Lucent Books, 1996.

Royal, Susan. "*Schindler's List*: An Interview With Steven Spielberg." *Inside Film Magazine Online*. 6 Dec. 1999. 17 Mar. 2003 <http://insidefilm.com/spielberg.htm>

Schindler's List. Dir. Steven Spielberg. Perf. Ralph Fiennes, Ben Kingsley, and Liam Neeson. Universal, 1993.

"*Schindler's List*: Behind the Scenes." *PBS Online*. 17 Mar. 2003 <http://www.pbs.org/holocaust/schindler/behindthescenes.html>

Thompson, Bruce, ed. *Oskar Schindler*. San Diego, CA: Greenhaven Press, 2002.

Marcus clearly states his conclusions.

The report ends with a powerful quotation.

Marcus provides a complete, detailed, and properly formatted list of all the works he has cited in his report.

Marcus follows MLA style in documenting his primary sources.

Drafting

Create a thesis statement. A good thesis statement expresses a position that can be supported by research. Review your notes to create a thesis statement that will control and direct the content of your paper. Present it in your introductory paragraph.

Establish your organizational plan. Decide whether you will present conclusions about your information at the start or build toward them throughout the paper. Use one of the plans shown here.

Effective Organizations	
Introduction	**Introduction**
present thesis statement explain/give background for topic DRAW CONCLUSION	present thesis statement explain/give background for topic
Body	**Body**
PROVE CONCLUSION present/analyze/compare sources	present/analyze/compare sources LEAD TO CONCLUSION
Closing	**Closing**
summarize	DRAW CONCLUSION

Use information well. Don't string quotations together without interpretation. Directly state or clearly indicate the significance of each quotation you provide and the conclusions that you draw from it.

Analyze your sources. When discussing different versions of or opinions about an event, describe your sources. Explain why you think they differ by analyzing the writers' values, commitments, circumstances, and motives.

Prepare to document your information. As you draft, underline information or quotations that you will need to document. At the end of each underlined sentence, indicate in parentheses the author's last name. Later, go back and set up citations according to a standard format, such as MLA style.

Revising

Revise to give proper credit. Commonly known facts need not be credited within the body of the paper, but for lesser-known facts, quotations, and writers' opinions, you should identify your sources.

1. Have a partner read your draft and star any passages for which the source of the information should be cited.
2. Supply additional citations where needed.
3. Reread your draft. Combine and condense information as necessary to avoid excessive or repetitious references.

Revise to establish validity and reliability of sources. In addition to identifying sources, you also need to establish their credibility. Add information identifying any special qualifications a source may have. If a source is potentially biased, briefly explain the reasons readers may have for suspecting bias. Then, clearly state your evaluation of the trustworthiness of the source.

Compare the model and the nonmodel. Ask yourself: Why is the model more credible?

Nonmodel	Model
According to Ruth Kander, however, Schindler cared only about his own welfare.	However, Ruth Kander, *who knew Schindler personally,* has maintained that he cared only about his own welfare.

Publishing and Presenting

Create a works-cited list. Your paper is ready for presentation only when you've concluded it with a works-cited list, an alphabetical list of all the sources mentioned in the paper. Follow the style that your teacher prefers in making this list. (See pages R30–R31 for more information.)

Submit your paper to a magazine. Select a magazine that publishes student writing or that focuses on the subject area of your paper. Submit your paper for possible publication.

Present your report orally. Use your report as the basis of an oral presentation to the class. Give your classmates a handout outlining key points in your paper and listing the resources you've consulted.

 Writing and Grammar Connection: Diamond Level, Chapter 13

Rubric for Self-Assessment

Evaluate your research paper using the following criteria and rating scale:

Criteria	Rating Scale				
	Not very				Very
How clear and accurately focused is the thesis statement?	1	2	3	4	5
How strong and varied are the source materials?	1	2	3	4	5
How effectively are source materials analyzed and compared?	1	2	3	4	5
How consistent and effective is the organization?	1	2	3	4	5
How complete and accurate are the citations and works-cited list?	1	2	3	4	5

Listening and Speaking WORKSHOP

Analyzing the Impact of Media

The influence of the media on the democratic process is a topic of current and vigorous debate. As a future voter, you need to develop critical listening and viewing skills in order to **analyze the impact of media** on the public. The strategies described below will help you understand some aspects of media influence.

Analyze Explicit Influence

News commentators and various "experts" seek to affect the political process with direct statements of opinion. Familiarize yourself with the most common opinion forums.

- **Identify editorials.** Be aware that any printed or televised feature billed as an "editorial" or as "commentary" will present a persuasive case for one side of an issue. In addition, news shows may host discussions in which the participants express opinions. Learn to recognize such segments by listening for words such as *views, thoughts*, or *comments* as participants are introduced.

- **Recognize opinion forums.** Debate forums in which journalists express opposing views offer you an opportunity to hear several opinions. Note, however, that each speaker is using persuasive techniques to influence you to share his or her views.

Analyze Implicit Influence

Media makers also exert indirect influence on public opinion. Learn to identify these forms of indirect influence:

- **Reporting priorities** Media makers exert influence through the stories they choose to report and the sequence in which they present the stories. For example, the lead story on a television news show usually attracts the largest audience—and so may distract public attention from stories run later in the show. Consider whether the choice of lead story reflects a true sense of priorities.

- **Images of leaders** When the media show politicians or CEOs appearing strong, the media transmit a positive message. If these people look tired or distracted, the media telegraph a lack of confidence. Consider the influence such images may have on public perceptions of leaders.

- **Shaping attitudes** As journalists conduct interviews, the questions they ask determine the information readers or viewers receive. Consider whether an interviewer's questions will uncover a complete picture or whether they fail to probe important issues.

Activity: View and Analyze For at least one week, analyze the coverage of an important news story. Use the chart shown to analyze the coverage of the story each day.

News Story: _____
Dates Followed: _____

Program 1: _____

Format: Editorial / News Hour / Opinion Forum / Other _____

Placement: Main Story / Lead Story / Close / Other _____

Issues Addressed _____

Key Phrases Used _____

Images Used _____

Direct Influence? Y/N
Views stated _____
Support offered _____

Indirect Influence? Y/N
Views implied _____
Ways in which views are implied: _____
  Loaded language _____
  Provocative images _____
  Story placement _____
  Choice of questions _____

Assessment WORKSHOP

Comparing and Contrasting

In the reading sections of some tests, you may be required to make comparisons and contrasts within a passage or between passages. The following strategies can help you do this:

- Identify similarities and differences in the passage(s).
- Summarize likenesses and differences in a few words.

Test-Taking Strategy

If topics, themes, and other elements are similar, identify contrasting details.

Sample Test Item

Directions: Read the passages, and then answer the question.

Passage A: The chivalrous ideal of courtly love grew from the poems of Ovid and the songs of the troubadours. Courtly love, which thrived mostly in England and France during the Middle Ages, required that a man fall in love with a highborn but unavailable woman.

Passage B: In contemporary society, songs, stories, and poems celebrate the concept of ideal love. Two people meet, fall in love, marry, and their love grows ever stronger. The fact that many contemporary people marry later in life may testify to the difficulty of attaining this ideal.

1. What main topic is addressed by both passages?
   - **A** the strength of marriage
   - **B** stories and poems of love
   - **C** contemporary society
   - **D** ideals of love

Answer and Explanation

The correct answer is **D**. Marriage and contemporary society are each mentioned in only one passage, so answers **A** and **C** are incorrect. Stories of love are not the main topic of either passage, so answer **B** is incorrect.

▶ Practice

Directions: Read the passages, and then answer the questions.

Passage A: Is that small amphibian you see resting on a lily pad a frog or a toad? Take a good look at its skin. Frogs have smooth, wet skin. Look inside the amphibian's mouth. Frogs have tiny teeth in their upper and lower jaws. They also have long hind legs, so they can jump quite a distance. Frogs lay eggs in clumps.

Passage B: It's easy to distinguish toads from frogs. If you spy a small disgruntled amphibian with warty, dry skin, it can only be a toad. Toads have stubby back legs—they can't jump; they hop. Can you look in the animal's mouth? Toads have no teeth at all. Toads lay their eggs in long strings.

1. What is the most obvious difference between frogs and toads?
   - **A** their eggs
   - **B** their teeth
   - **C** their skin
   - **D** none of the above

2. In what way are they identical?
   - **A** They are green.
   - **B** They are amphibians.
   - **C** They like to jump.
   - **D** They have stubby legs.

The Renaissance and Rationalism

The School of Athens, Raphael. Scala.

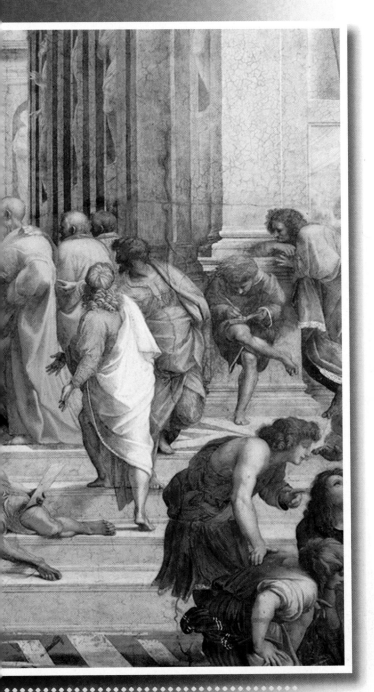

66 *Of course
Sacred Scripture is
the basic authority
in everything; yet I
sometimes run across
ancient sayings
or pagan writings—
even the poets'—so purely
and reverently expressed,
and so inspired, that
I can't help believing
their authors' hearts
were moved by
some divine power.* **99**

— from "The Godly Feast,"
by Erasmus

Timeline c. 1300–1800

1300   1400   1500

European Events

- **early 1300s** The Renaissance begins in Italy.
- **1304–1374** Petrarch, great Italian poet and Humanist, lives. ◄
- **1313–1375** Boccaccio, great Italian author and Humanist, lives.
- **1300s** Gunpowder is introduced into Europe.
- **1347–1351** The Black Death ravages Europe, killing about 25 million people.

- **1425** The artist Masaccio is the first to use perspective in a fresco.
- **1450s** Gutenberg uses his invention of movable type to print the Bible.
- **1452** Leonardo da Vinci, great Italian Renaissance artist and inventor, is born. ▼

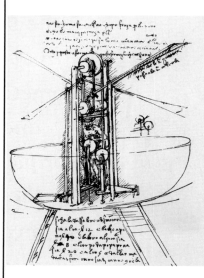

- **1516** Christian Humanist Erasmus publishes his annotations of the Greek New Testament.
- **1519** Magellan begins his voyage around the world.
- **1524–1585** Pierre de Ronsard, French poet, lives.
- **1527** Niccolò Machiavelli, author of *The Prince*, dies.
- **1543** Polish astronomer Nicolaus Copernicus declares in print that Earth circles the sun.
- **1546** Martin Luther, founder of the Protestant Reformation, dies.
- **c. 1550** Approximate date for the end of the Renaissance in Italy.

World Events

- **1300s (Japan)** First Nō dramas emerge.
- **1300s (West Africa)** The Mali empire controls the gold trade.
- **1324 (West Africa)** The Muslim emperor of Mali, Mansa Musa, makes a religious pilgrimage to Mecca.
- **1328–1341 (Russia)** Moscow emerges as an important city.

- **1431 (Southeast Asia)** Angkor, capital of Cambodia, is abandoned after being pillaged. ►
- **1453 (Turkey)** Ottoman Turks conquer Constantinople.
- **1462–1505 (Russia)** During the reign of Ivan III, Moscow extends its power.

- **1513 (China)** The Portuguese arrive at Macau, a peninsula and islands off China's coast.
- **1513 (America)** Ponce de Léon lands in Florida and claims it for Spain.
- **1517 (Middle East)** Ottoman Turks conquer Syria and Egypt.
- **1519–1521 (Mexico)** ▲ Cortés conquers the Aztec empire.

European and World Events

- **1605** Cervantes publishes the first part of *Don Quixote*.

- **1608–1674** English poet John Milton lives.

- **1609** Galileo improves the telescope and begins observing the solar system with telescopes that magnify up to 20x.

- **1610** Galileo observes four moons orbiting around Jupiter. ▼

- **1625** The Renaissance in England ends.

- **1657** Pascal begins writing his *Pensées*.

- **1660** The Royal Society, a group formed to promote science, is founded in London, England.

- **1664–1666** There is an outbreak of plague in London, England.

- **1687** Sir Isaac Newton publishes a book describing the laws of gravity and motion.

- **1613 (Russia)** The Time of Troubles, a fifteen-year period of political crisis, ends.

Night of August 4, 1789, or "Patriotic Delirium," Bibliothèque Nationale, Paris, Giraudon

- **1702** First daily English newspaper appears.

- **early 1700s** Addison and Steele publish periodicals.

- **1744** English poet Alexander Pope dies.

- **1765** James Watt helps launch the Industrial Revolution by improving the steam engine.

- **1772** Diderot completes the *Encyclopedia*, a major achievement of the Enlightenment.

- **1778** Voltaire, author of *Candide*, dies.

- **1787–1799** The French Revolution is fought. ▲

- **1799** Napoleon Bonaparte assumes control in France.

- **1703 (Russia)** Czar Peter the Great begins the construction of St. Petersburg. ▼

- **1776–1781 (America)** The colonies defeat Great Britain in the American Revolution.

- **1639 (Japan)** The Tokugawas close Japan to the rest of the world. ◀

- **1644 (China)** The Ming dynasty is overthrown by armies from Manchuria.

- **1644–1694 (Japan)** Haiku poet Matsuo Bashō lives.

- **1669 (Greece)** The Ottoman empire seizes Crete.

The Renaissance and Rationalism

(c. 1300–1800)

Historical Background

The Renaissance in Western Europe The Renaissance, which means "rebirth," is a period that saw many changes and innovations. Among them were the rediscovery of classical art and literature; the exploration of regions of the globe that were previously unknown in Europe; the discovery that Earth revolves around the sun; and an upsurge in trade and invention. This rebirth, which lasted in Italy from the early 1300s until 1550, gradually extended its influence northward. In England, it lasted from 1485 to 1625.

Status and Insecurity The Renaissance was a period during which rank and status mattered a great deal. For every social class, however, this era was a time of insecurity. The Black Death (see page 666) devastated Europe in the late 1340s, toward the beginning of the Italian Renaissance.

Point/Counterpoint

Was the Renaissance a Rebirth of Consciousness?

Did the Renaissance mark a complete rebirth of human consciousness? Two scholars—writing about a hundred years apart—disagree on this question.

Yes! In the Middle Ages both sides of human consciousness—that which was turned within as that which was turned without—lay dreaming or half awake beneath a common veil. The veil was woven of faith, illusion, and childish prepossession, through which the world and history were seen clad in strange hues. Man was conscious of himself only as a member of a race, people, party, family, or corporation—only through some general category. In Italy this veil first melted into air . . . man became a spiritual *individual*, . . .

—**Jacob Burckhardt, from**
***The Civilization of the
Renaissance in Italy* (1860)**

No! Certainly the hundred years before and after 1450 were enormously fertile in innovation. But the great discoveries and historical mutations of the age were not confined to Italy; while even in Italy continuity and tradition mark the age as deeply as change and innovation. The history of discovery and novelty must be balanced by the equally interesting and important story of the survival and adaptation of traditional institutions, social distinctions, professional disciplines, and modes of thought.

—**Eugene F. Rice, Jr., from**
***The Columbia History
of the World* (1972)**

In addition to sickness, other disasters contributed to the insecurity of the times. With the exception of castles and churches, most buildings were built of wood, and fire in cities was a constant hazard.

Kings Up, Nobles Down Against this backdrop of general insecurity, the power of kings tended to increase during the Renaissance. This centralization of power helped create the nations that are familiar to us today. Meanwhile, the great nobility were losing their importance. Their mighty castles, for instance, were threatened by the introduction of gunpowder into Europe in the 1300s. Castle walls became vulnerable to cannon shot, and even well-armored knights could be toppled by a well-placed bullet.

Humanism: Out of the "Dark" Ages The most important cultural movement of the Renaissance was Humanism, which advocated a return to classical studies and ideals. This movement began in fourteenth-century Italy, where the first Humanists were the famous writers Petrarch (pē′ trärk′) and Boccaccio (bō kä′ chô). For the first time in about a thousand years, the intellectual life of Western Europe was directly influenced by the works of classical writers known before only through inaccurate summaries or quotations. The Humanists viewed the classics as sources of moral and practical wisdom. Humanist ideals also influenced Italian Renaissance artists like Michelangelo (mī′ kel an′ jə lō′) and Leonardo da Vinci (də vin′ chē), who followed classical artists in portraying the beauty of the human form.

According to the Humanists, the Middle Ages were "dark" because the Germanic tribes that had invaded Rome, the Goths, had destroyed classical civilization. Humanists believed that with the rediscovery of classical learning, these "dark" times had given way to an age of "enlightenment." Today, scholars no longer accept this belief, which might be called the Humanist Myth, without qualifications. (See Point/Counterpoint on page 664.)

Humanism started in Italy, yet as it moved northward it changed somewhat in character. The enthusiasm for classical antiquity remained, but it was influenced by a Christian fervor. This slightly different movement, called Christian Humanism, tended to look back to early Christian as well as classical sources. Unlike medieval thinkers, Christian Humanists stressed the importance of the active life. They also ridiculed the performing of mechanical acts in the place of inner worship. In this way, Christian Humanism prepared for the more radical protests of the Reformation.

Mona Lisa, Leonardo da Vinci, Louvre, Dep. des Peintures, Paris, France

▲ **Critical Viewing** The *Mona Lisa* by Leonardo da Vinci is one of the most famous paintings of all time. Many critics and viewers have remarked on the "mystery" of the subject's smile. What, if anything, do you think is mysterious about her expression? Explain. **[Interpret]**

The Reformation: From Debate to Bloodshed In the early 1500s, an obscure German professor of theology, Martin Luther, protested against the corruption of the church. His key ideas—that salvation depends on one's faith, rather than one's actions, and that the priesthood and church ritual are less important than the truths of the Bible—launched the movement called the Reformation. This movement gave birth to new Protestant denominations, whose name comes from the term *to protest*. Protestants dominated in Switzerland, northern Germany, parts of France, and eventually in England and Scotland. The Catholic Church, on the other hand, was strong in Spain, Italy, most of France, and southern Germany. Religious debates soon escalated into war, and in France the civil conflict led to years of bloodshed.

The Globe Explored, the Earth Displaced Not only were religious truths being questioned, but the face of the globe was changing with each new voyage of discovery. (See the map on page 667.) In 1492, for instance, Columbus sailed to the West Indies; and in 1519, Magellan began a voyage around the world.

    The image of the universe itself was changing. According to older views, Earth was the center of the universe. The astronomer Copernicus (1473–1543), however, argued that Earth revolved around the sun.

▼ **Critical Viewing**
This image is a detail from a picture depicting the effects of the Great Plague of London in 1665. What do the gestures of the skeleton indicate about the outbreak of the plague? Why? **[Infer]**

Close-up on History

The Black Death

    Between 1347 and 1351, a disease people called the Black Death, and which we know as the plague, ravaged Europe. It killed about one fourth of the population, perhaps 25 million people. Those afflicted with the disease developed fever and other symptoms, either swellings that turned into black spots or infected lungs together with weakness and loss of memory. Few recovered.

    The plague was usually spread by fleas that lived on rodents— the rats that in fourteenth-century Europe were everywhere in the overcrowded and dirty cities and in the countryside as well. When a rat died, its fleas often migrated to a nearby person. To people of the time, however, it seemed a terrible mystery why some were spared and some perished.

    Faced with this horrible and mysterious disease, people looked for someone to blame. Usually, outsiders of some kind—Arabs, lepers, or Jews—were chosen as scapegoats. Massacres of these groups only added to the sum of suffering.

    Among the longer-lasting effects of the plague were a decrease in farmed land, an increase in wages for surviving workers, and—in northern Europe—a new obsession with death. Thomas Nashe, writing about a later outbreak of plague in England, expressed such a mood in his poem "Litany in Time of Plague": "Physic [the doctor] himself must fade, / all things to end are made."

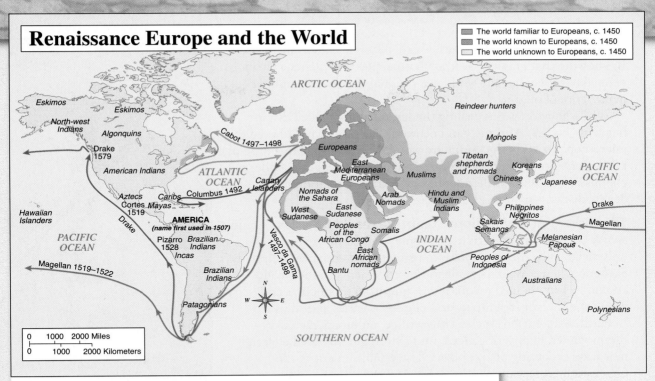

Renaissance Europe and the World

Legend:
- The world familiar to Europeans, c. 1450
- The world known to Europeans, c. 1450
- The world unknown to Europeans, c. 1450

ARCTIC OCEAN

Eskimos
Eskimos
North-west Indians
Algonquins
Cabot 1497–1498
Reindeer hunters
Drake 1579
Mongols
American Indians
ATLANTIC OCEAN
Europeans
East Mediterranean Europeans
Muslims
Tibetan shepherds and nomads
Koreans
Chinese
Japanese
PACIFIC OCEAN
Canary Islanders
Columbus 1492
Nomads of the Sahara
Arab Nomads
Hindu and Muslim Indians
Aztecs Cortes 1519
Caribs Mayas
West Sudanese
East Sudanese
Philippines Negritos
Drake
Hawaiian Islanders
AMERICA (name first used in 1507)
Sakais Semangs
Magellan
PACIFIC OCEAN
Drake
Pizarro 1528 Incas
Brazilian Indians
Vasco da Gama 1497–1498
Peoples of the African Congo
Somalis
INDIAN OCEAN
Melanesian Papous
East African nomads
Peoples of Indonesia
Magellan 1519–1522
Brazilian Indians
Bantu
Australians
Patagonians
Polynesians
SOUTHERN OCEAN

0 1000 2000 Miles
0 1000 2000 Kilometers

The Age of Rationalism: From Lore to Law

The Renaissance ushered in the Age of Rationalism, or the Enlightenment, an era that spanned the seventeenth and eighteenth centuries. During this time, reason was accepted as the greatest authority in art, thought, and politics. Philosophers challenged folk wisdom, attempting to replace traditional lore with formal laws based on the analysis of natural phenomena.

Rationalism and Nature: Mud Baths and Artful Foliage

The application of reason to natural phenomena coincided with a renewed focus on nature throughout society. Notable painters, such as the French artist Jean-Antoine Watteau (wä tō´), for example, captured the beauty of outdoor scenes. In addition, people who could afford to do so made pilgrimages to spas and hot springs. There, nature could exert its healing influence as sufferers bathed in the waters and coated their limbs with medicinal mud. Nature could also delight the eye in formal gardens, whose symmetrical rows of plants showed that even foliage followed reason's laws.

The new interest in nature included human nature as well. The English Enlightenment philosopher John Locke described the human mind as a blank slate on which impressions are recorded. By denying the existence of prenatal, and therefore unlearned, ideas, Locke placed a stronger emphasis on experience and the satisfaction of natural curiosity.

Rationalism and Science: Falling Apples and Orbiting Planets

In science, the delights of curiosity led to intellectual triumphs. Sir Isaac Newton, the greatest scientist of the age, discovered the laws of motion, the

▲ **Critical Viewing** Compare and contrast the world familiar or known to Europeans in 1450 with the world unknown to them. **[Read a Map]**

law of gravitation, and the mathematical system called calculus. By showing that gravity governed both apples and planets, Newton seemed to prove that the world was rational and that the mind could make sense of matter.

While Newton was revealing the laws that controlled distant heavenly bodies, Antonie van Leeuwenhoek (lā´ vən hōōk´) used the microscope to study the miniature worlds that swarmed in a drop of rainwater. Also, Robert Boyle earned a reputation as the "father of chemistry," and Edward Jenner discovered a vaccination for the deadly disease smallpox.

The Industrial Revolution: Steam Flexes Its Muscles Across a wide span of human activities, people were employing reason not only to advance theory but also to regulate and enhance their daily existence. James Watt's significant improvements to the steam engine in 1765 helped revolutionize industrial production and paved the way for steam-powered railroad engines and ships.

Further, inventions such as the syringe, air pump, mercury thermometer, mainspring clock, and cotton gin provided effective new ways of solving old problems. The establishment of the Greenwich Observatory in England (1675) led to the systematic use of astronomy for such practical purposes as navigation and timekeeping.

Rationalism and Politics: Experiment and Explosion Like a chemistry experiment, the application of reason to political discontent led to an explosion called revolution. John Locke declared that government was a contract between ruler and ruled and that all people had natural rights to life, liberty, and property. These two "rational" ideas undermined the notion that kings had a divine right to rule. In America, these ideas added to the dissatisfaction of colonists with British repression, a dissatisfaction that erupted into the American Revolution (1776–1781). After the colonists won, the ideas of Locke and other Enlightenment thinkers influenced the framers of the American Constitution.

The French Revolution (1787–1799) was also inspired by Enlightenment ideas, especially those of Jean-Jacques Rousseau (zhän zhäk rōō sō´). This philosopher wrote in *The Social Contract* (1762), "Man was born free, but he is everywhere in chains." In France, however, sharper differences between the rich and the poor made the conflict more of a war between classes than the American Revolution had been. The result was a Reign of Terror in the early 1790s during which the king and many aristocrats were executed. By 1799, the revolution yielded to the dictatorial rule of Napoleon Bonaparte.

These two "experiments" in revolution indicated two different ways in which the Age of Rationalism would influence politics in the following centuries: on the one hand, the "reasonableness" of democratic institutions; on the other, the use of "reason" to justify revolt or even repression.

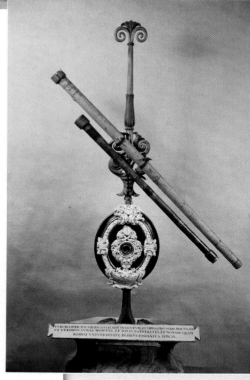

▲ **Critical Viewing**
This telescope belonged to Galileo, the Italian Renaissance scientist who pioneered astronomical studies. Galileo's observations helped dispel the belief that, in contrast to Earth, the heavens were a perfect, unchanging realm. What, if anything, does this telescope reveal about the attitudes of Galileo and his Renaissance colleagues toward scientific observation? Why? **[Infer]**

Literature

Renaissance Literature: A Branch of Rhetoric During the years of the Renaissance, literature was classified as a branch of rhetoric—the art of using spoken language to teach, give pleasure, and persuade. Literature was therefore closely related to the art of speechmaking, and it is not surprising that Renaissance writing is full of elaborate speeches. As a branch of rhetoric, literature also had the function of persuading readers to do good. Its purpose was to train the will by increasing our horror of evil and by strengthening our resolve to act well.

Machiavelli: Do Well, Not Good One major exception to literature in the service of the good is *The Prince*, a book of political philosophy by Niccolò Machiavelli (nē kô lō´ mak´ ē ə vel´ ē). While other theorists said that public deeds should reflect private morality, Machiavelli insisted that personal morality has no place in politics. Rulers are saved not by their goodness but by their strength, cunning, and ability. Because he took this approach, the adjective *Machiavellian* has come to mean "crafty and deceitful."

Literature and the Vernacular In the Middle Ages, literature in native languages, or the vernacular, had already begun to emerge. The Renaissance, however, saw a new emphasis on Italian, French, Spanish, German, Dutch, and English. In this period of linguistic patriotism, many of the great works of the period were written in the vernacular: in Italian, the sonnets of Petrarch, Boccaccio's prose tales in the *Decameron*, and Machiavelli's *The Prince*; in French, the poetry of Pierre de Ronsard (pē er´ də rōn sår´); and in Spanish, the novel *Don Quixote* by Miguel de Cervantes (mē gel´ *the ther* vän´ tes).

Latin, however, still served an important function. The Dutch scholar Erasmus, who translated the New Testament into Latin, Sir Thomas More, and many of the great Humanists wrote primarily in Latin.

Originality Through Imitation: "as the bees make honey" Rather than inventing new stories or forms, Renaissance authors often altered old

▼ **Critical Viewing**
Which details in this portrait of Lorenzo de' Medici, an Italian Renaissance merchant prince, suggest that he had the leadership qualities recommended by Machiavelli? Explain. **[Connect]**

Lorenzo il Magnifico, G. Vasari, Scala

Art in the Historical Context

The Invention of Perspective

You may assume that viewing a painting should always give you the illusion of looking into three-dimensional space. Yet it was Renaissance artists who invented perspective, the method for conveying this illusion. In the Middle Ages, paintings did not convey an accurate sense of depth. The Renaissance architect Brunelleschi (broo´ nel les´ kē) devised the system by which lines of sight, perpendicular to the vertical plane of the picture, seem to converge at a vanishing point on the horizon within the picture.

In 1425, Masaccio (mä säch´ ē ō) became the first artist to use perspective in a fresco, or wall painting. His work *The Holy Trinity with the Virgin and St. John* shows Jesus being crucified in a space that is truly three-dimensional. (See this painting to the right.) From this time on, flat surfaces could open into imaginary but realistic worlds. The scholar Eugene F. Rice, Jr., compares the invention of perspective in art to the newly acquired historical perspective by which Renaissance thinkers viewed classical antiquity as a separate period in history. Medieval scholars, says Rice, could not make such a distinction.

The Trinity (detail), Masaccio, Nicolo Orsi Battaglini

▲ **Critical Viewing** Masaccio painted this picture on a church wall so that the platform supporting the cross is about at eye level. Where is the point at which all sight-lines going "into" the picture seem to converge? Explain. **[Analyze]**

forms to give them new meanings. Many authors, for example, wrote epics modeled in part on Virgil's *Aeneid*, odes modeled on the odes of Horace, and histories modeled on the work of Pliny and Tacitus. Yet just as the Romans copied and changed the forms of Greek literature to fit their own culture, so the writers of Renaissance Europe changed classical forms. Petrarch, for instance, asserted that "we must write just as the bees make honey, not keeping the flowers [works of other writers] but turning them into a sweetness all our own, blending many different flavors into one, which shall be unlike them all, and better."

The Classics in the Age of Reason Like Renaissance Humanists, Enlightenment writers admired ancient Greek and Roman literature. The English poet John Milton (1608–1674), for example, mastered Greek, Latin, and Hebrew, as well as several modern European languages. Not only was he widely read in the classics, but he used Homer's *Iliad* and *Odyssey* and Virgil's *Aeneid* as models for his own Christian epic, *Paradise Lost*.

The Classics Pay Alexander Pope (1688–1744), an English Neoclassical (or "new classical") poet, translated Homer's *Iliad* and *Odyssey* into elegant eighteenth-century verse. His efforts earned him the princely sum of £10,000 and assured his financial independence.

In France, Jean de La Fontaine (zhän´ də là fōn ten´) based many of his fables in verse on the prose fables of the Greek author Aesop (ē´ səp). In addition, the grace and restraint of La Fontaine's style are qualities that mark his writing as classical in spirit.

Reason Rolls Up Its Sleeves Invention, the use of reason to solve life's problems, affected reading habits as well as navigation and industry. The creation of movable type by Johannes Gutenberg in the mid-1400s had made possible the printing and widespread distribution of the Bible for the first time, paving the way for the Protestants' emphasis on biblical authority. Then, in the 1600s, the new methods of printing helped foster the growth of newspapers. The first English daily newspaper appeared in 1702, and a few years later, the English authors Addison and Steele founded *The Tatler* and *The Spectator*. These periodicals served up humorous essays and witty commentaries on current topics. The growth of newspapers and periodicals created a new entity called Public Opinion.

The Encyclopedia Is Born In France, Denis Diderot (dē′ də rō′) brought to a public hungry for knowledge the world's first *encyclopedia*—a word based on the Greek for "instruction in the circle of arts and sciences." Because its commentary often clashed with accepted principles, this multivolume work suffered repeated censorship. Yet upon its completion in 1772 after long years of toil, the *Encyclopedia* became a major achievement of the Enlightenment.

Pascal and Voltaire: Reason's Differing Children Finally, it is worth remembering that in an age of reason, not every thinker reasoned in the same way. Blaise Pascal (blez′ pas kal′), for example, was a French mathematician and physicist whose credentials as a rationalist were as good as anyone's. Yet in his book *Pensées* ("Thoughts"), he emphasizes human frailty and urges readers to approach God through feelings, not thought. His fellow Frenchman Voltaire (1694–1778), author of the novel *Candide*, disapproved of Pascal's concern with finding happiness in heaven. Voltaire stressed the use of reason to foster progress and happiness on Earth.

▼ **Critical Viewing**
This illustration, showing the composing room of a print shop, was an engraving in Diderot's *Encyclopedia*. In a sense, Diderot was demonstrating the very technology that helped bring his own work to a wider reading public. What do the various details in the engraving reveal about the process of printing during the eighteenth century? Explain. **[Infer]**

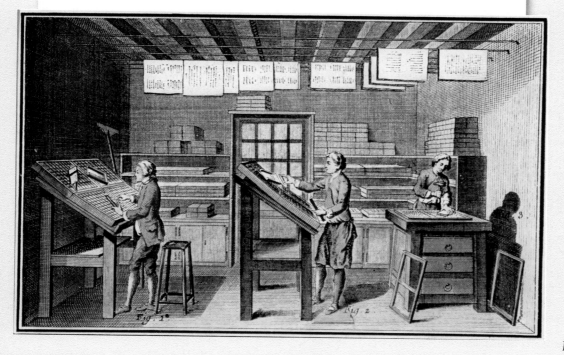

Prepare to Read

Laura ◆ The White Doe ◆ Spring ◆ To Hélène ◆ Roses

Petrarch (1304–1374)

Francesco Petrarca, whom the English called Petrarch (pē´ trärk´), was the greatest Italian poet of the fourteenth century. His talent set a pattern for lyric poetry over the next three centuries. Born in 1304, Petrarch traveled extensively throughout his life. While studying law, he began reading classical works and writing poetry. In 1327, in Avignon, France, he first saw the Laura whom he celebrates in his love poetry.

Literary Inspiration Little is known about the Laura who inspired Petrarch to write some of the world's greatest love poetry. She may have been Laura de Noyes, the wife of Hugues de Sade. Petrarch himself creates a picture of her as golden-haired, beautiful, and rich. Whoever she was, Petrarch loved her hopelessly for twenty years, and her beauty inspired the *Canzoniere* (kän tsô nyer´ ē), a vast collection of hundreds of love lyrics that Petrarch wrote and revised until the end of his life.

After his first trip to Rome in 1337, Petrarch composed two ambitious projects in Latin, leading a new Latin cultural flowering and prompting the city of Rome to crown him poet laureate. After years of travel through France and Italy, he finally completed his two major Italian works: the *Triumphs* and the *Canzoniere*.

Petrarch's prose—Latin letters, dialogues, and treatises—centers on himself, examining his own thoughts and emotions with extraordinary subtlety and depth, while his poetry exhaustively analyzes his uncertainties about love. It is this self-analysis and self-proclamation that made him a model for subsequent Renaissance writers.

Pierre de Ronsard (1524–1585)

Pierre de Ronsard (pē er´ də rōn sàr´) was called the "Prince of Poets" by his contemporaries, and the title suited his range and ambition. He wrote verse of many different kinds—epics, satires, political commentaries, and the odes and sonnets for which he is famous.

A Poet's Career Ronsard was the youngest son of a noble French family. When illness ended his chances for a life of diplomatic service, he turned to writing. He was slow to publish his work, but in 1550 he released his first four books of odes, modeled on the works of the classical poets Pindar and Horace. In 1552, he published a book of love poetry addressed largely to a woman named Cassandre. From then on, he worked prolifically, writing books of odes, hymns, and love poetry alike. Ronsard saw poetry as a kind of inspired discipline, with the poet acting as a receiver and transmitter of divine energies. At times, this vision could lead to self-importance and heavy-handedness, but it often resulted in exciting and vibrant work. His verse is marked by intensity, energy, and deep feelings for the natural world.

In 1572, he published the first four books of his *Franciade*, a patriotic epic about France that he never completed. His last major sequence of love poems, the *Sonnets pour Hélène*, appeared in 1578. Ronsard's devotion to his calling made him an untiring reviser of his poetry. During his later years, he revised his collected works over and over, preparing a final edition just before his death in 1585.

Preview

Connecting to the Literature

Today, love is the subject of all genres of popular music, from country to rap to heavy metal. Despite the passage of centuries, the similarities you find between your favorite love songs and these poems may be striking.

Literary Analysis

The Sonnet

Petrarch established the **sonnet** as the dominant form of lyric poetry during the Italian Renaissance. A sonnet is a fourteen-line poem focused on a single theme. The following characteristics are typical of the highly structured Petrarchan sonnet:

- It is divided into an eight-line *octave* followed by a six-line *sestet*.
- The octave usually has a rhyme scheme of *abba abba*.
- The sestet usually has one of three rhyme patterns: *cdecde, cdcdcd,* or *cdedce*.
- The octave often poses a question or makes a statement that is then brought to closure in the sestet.

Look for these characteristics as you read the poems in this grouping.

Comparing Literary Works

All five poems in this grouping are Petrarchan sonnets, and all share the subject of love, but the poets use a variety of images to describe their beloved. **Imagery** is descriptive language that re-creates sensory experiences. For example, Ronsard uses the image of a rose to describe his young beloved. Use a chart like the one shown to compare imagery in the five poems and to determine the overall effect the imagery produces.

Senses	Image
Touch	
Sight	
Hearing	
Smell	
Taste	
Overall Effect of the Images	

Reading Strategy

Reading in Sentences

Reading in sentences will help you understand the meaning of a poem. Although these poems are written in sentences, the end of each sentence does not always coincide with the end of the poetic line. A sentence may extend for several lines or end in the middle of a line. To read in sentences, notice the punctuation. Do not pause or make a full stop at the end of a line unless there is a period, comma, colon, semicolon, or dash.

Vocabulary Development

sated (sāt´ ed) *v.* completely satisfied (p. 676)

exults (eg zults´) *v.* rejoices greatly (p. 677)

sojourn (sō´ jʉrn) *n.* visit (p. 677)

crone (krōn) *n.* very old woman (p. 678)

languishing (laŋ´ gwish iŋ) *v.* becoming weak (p. 680)

reposes (ri pōz´ əz) *v.* puts to rest (p. 680)

from CANZONIERE

Petrarch

Background

Petrarch's *Canzoniere* features 366 poems dedicated to his beloved Laura. Although Petrarch gives no clue about her real identity, many scholars agree that Laura was a married woman whom he supposedly first saw on April 6, 1327. Even though she apparently gave his affection no encouragement, at least so far as he describes in his poetry, Petrarch loved Laura all his life—even after her death in 1348.

The *Canzoniere* is divided into two parts—those poems to Laura "in life" and those to her "in death." Her importance in the sequence of poems lies in her effect on the poet, whose desire for her is never fulfilled. This "Petrarchan" scenario, in which the lovers' relationship is never fully realized, would become a standard model for generations to come.

Three Graces (detail), Botticelli, Giraudon

◀ **Critical Viewing**
Compare the visual details in this painting with the imagery in "Laura." **[Compare]**

Laura

Petrarch

translated by Morris Bishop

She used to let her golden hair fly free
    For the wind to toy and tangle and molest;
    Her eyes were brighter than the radiant west.
    (Seldom they shine so now.) I used to see
5 Pity look out of those deep eyes on me.
    ("It was false pity," you would now protest.)
    I had love's tinder[1] heaped within my breast;
    What wonder that the flame burned furiously?
She did not walk in any mortal way,
10   But with angelic progress; when she spoke,
    Unearthly voices sang in unison.
She seemed divine among the dreary folk
    Of earth. You say she is not so today?
    Well, though the bow's unbent,[2] the wound bleeds on.

---

1. **tinder** (tin′ dər) *n.* dry, easily flammable material used for starting a fire.
2. **though the bow's unbent** though she is older and does not have her original beauty; the bow is Cupid's.

Reading Strategy
Reading in Sentences
In the octave, which lines require you to read on to the next line without stopping? Why?

✔ **Reading Check**

What emotion did Laura once feel for the speaker?

The White Doe

Petrarch
translated by Anna Maria Armi

A pure-white doe in an emerald glade
Appeared to me, with two antlers of gold,
Between two streams, under a laurel's shade,
At sunrise, in the season's bitter cold.

5   Her sight was so suavely[1] merciless
That I left work to follow her at leisure,
Like the miser who looking for his treasure
Sweetens with that delight his bitterness.

Around her lovely neck "Do not touch me"
10 Was written with topaz[2] and diamond stone,
"My Caesar's will has been to make me free."

Already toward noon had climbed the sun,
My weary eyes were not <u>sated</u> to see,
When I fell in the stream and she was gone.

---

1. **suavely** (swäv′ lē) in a smoothly gracious manner.
2. **topaz** (tō′ paz) yellow gem.

Themes in World Literature

Allegory

An **allegory** is an extended metaphor or a story line with both a literal and a symbolic level. The poem "The White Doe," for example, is an allegory in which the speaker sees his beloved in the form of "a pure-white doe in an emerald glade." Like his beloved Laura, Petrarch's doe is beautiful, pure, and untouchable. In the end, the doe disappears from sight, just as the real Laura disappears in death.

Italian poet Dante Alighieri wrote one of the most famous allegories, the *Divine Comedy*, in the early 1300s. In *Moby-Dick* (1851), American novelist Herman Melville incorporated allegorical elements concerning the human struggle against evil and fate. Although the message in Petrarch's "The White Doe" seems lighter in comparison with these other allegories, the fleeting nature of love remains a powerful theme despite the passage of centuries.

Literary Analysis
The Sonnet and Imagery
Identify two visual images in the octave.

sated (sāt′ ed) *v.* completely satisfied

Spring

Petrarch

translated by Morris Bishop

Zephyr¹ returns, and scatters everywhere
   New flowers and grass, and company does bring,
   Procne and Philomel,² in sweet despair,
   And all the tender colors of the Spring.
5 Never were fields so glad, nor skies so fair;
   And Jove <u>exults</u> in Venus'³ prospering.
   Love is in all the water, earth, and air,
   And love possesses every living thing.
   But to me only heavy sighs return
10   For her who carried in her little hand
   My heart's key to her heavenly <u>sojourn</u>.
   The birds sing loud above the flowering land;
   Ladies are gracious now.—Where deserts burn
   The beasts still prowl on the ungreening sand.

Reading Strategy
Reading in Sentences
In what way does the third sentence relate to the entire octave?

exults (eg zults´) *v.* rejoices greatly

sojourn (sō´ jʉrn) *n.* visit

---

1. **Zephyr** (zef´ ər) the west wind.
2. **Procne** (präk´ nē) **and Philomel** (fil´ ō mel´) In Greek mythology, Philomel was a princess of Athens who was raped by Tereus, husband of her sister Procne. The gods changed Philomel into a nightingale, Procne into a swallow, and Tereus into a hawk.
3. **Jove . . . Venus'** Jove was the chief god in Roman mythology, and Venus was the goddess of love.

Review and Assess

Thinking About the Selections

1. **Respond:** What do you imagine Petrarch's Laura was like?
2. **(a) Recall:** List four details about Laura that the speaker recalls in "Laura." **(b) Analyze:** What are the common qualities of the details that he remembers about her?
3. **(a) Recall:** In "The White Doe," which details of time does the speaker mention? **(b) Interpret:** What do you think these references to time mean? Explain.
4. **Interpret:** In "Spring," in what ways is the speaker's "heart's key" responsible for these contrasting images he sees?
5. **Relate:** Do you think the feelings or situations Petrarch describes in his poems are still relevant today? Why or why not?

To Hélène

Pierre de Ronsard

translated by Norman Shapiro

Background

The Latin phrase *carpe diem* means "seize the day"—in other words, make use of the present time and enjoy life while you can. This popular theme acknowledges the brevity and uncertainties of life and provides encouragement to grasp the good that the world has to offer. In "To Hélène," for example, the speaker urges his beloved to "Gather life's roses while still fresh they grow."

When you are very old, by candle's flame,
Spinning beside the fire, at end of day,
Singing my verse, admiring, you will say:
"When I was fair, Ronsard's muse I became."

5 Your servant then, some weary old beldame[1]—
Whoever she may be—nodding away,
Hearing "Ronsard," will shake off sleep, and pray
Your name be blessed, to live in deathless fame.

Buried, I shall a fleshless phantom be,
10 Hovering by the shadowed myrtle tree;
You, by the hearth, a pining <u>crone</u>, bent low,

Whose pride once scorned my love, much to your sorrow.
Heed me, live for today, wait not the morrow:
Gather life's roses while still fresh they grow.

Literary Analysis
The Sonnet What is the rhyme scheme of the octave?

crone (krōn) *n.* very old woman

---

1. **beldame** (bel′ dam) old woman.

▲ **Critical Viewing** Look closely at the expression on this woman's face. Compare and contrast her attitude with your perception of Hélène. **[Compare and Contrast]**

Roses

Pierre de Ronsard
translated by Vernon Watkins

As one sees on the branch in the month of May the rose
In her beautiful youth, in the dawn of her flower,
When the break of day softens her life with the shower,
Make jealous the sky of the damask¹ bloom she shows:
5　Grace lingers in her leaf and love sleeping glows
Enchanting with fragrance the trees of her bower,
But, broken by the rain or the sun's oppressive power,
<u>Languishing</u> she dies, and all her petals throws.
Thus in thy first youth, in thy awakening fair
10　When thy beauty was honored by lips of Earth and Air,
Atropos² has killed thee and dust thy form <u>reposes</u>.
O take, take for obsequies³ my tears, these poor showers,
This vase filled with milk, this basket strewn with flowers,
That in death as in life thy body may be roses.

1. **damask** (dam´ əsk) deep pink or rose.
2. **Atropos** (a´ trə päs) in Greek and Roman mythology, the goddess who cuts the thread of life.
3. **obsequies** (äb´ si kwēz) funeral rites or ceremonies.

Literary Analysis
The Sonnet and Imagery
What image does the speaker use to describe his love?

languishing (laŋ´ gwish iŋ) *v.* becoming weak

reposes (ri pōz´ əz) *v.* puts to rest

Review and Assess

Thinking About the Selections

1. **Respond:** How do you think Hélène might have responded to the poem about her? Explain.

2. **(a) Recall:** Describe the scene that the speaker presents in the octave of "To Hélène." **(b) Speculate:** What feelings might have prompted the speaker's emotions in this poem? Explain.

3. **(a) Recall:** Which phrases in the first six lines of "Roses" describe the gentleness of nature? **(b) Interpret:** What change has nature brought in line seven? **(c) Draw Conclusions:** What does this suggest about the well-being of the speaker's beloved?

4. **Hypothesize:** If Ronsard were alive today, what famous person might the poet immortalize in verse? Why?

Review and Assess

Literary Analysis

The Sonnet

1. In what way does the two-part structure of the **sonnet** "Laura" reflect the speaker's recollections of Laura?

2. (a) What is the rhyme scheme of "The White Doe"? (b) In what ways does the pattern vary from that of a typical sonnet?

3. How do the poems "The White Doe" and "Roses" reflect the popular Petrarchan scenario in which the lovers' relationship will never be fully realized?

Comparing Literary Works

4. (a) List three **images** describing the doe in "The White Doe" that relate to images of Laura in "Laura." (b) Why might the speaker choose to associate Laura with a white doe?

5. (a) What is the condition of the speaker in "To Hélène"? (b) In what ways do the speaker and the object of his desire differ from those in the other poems in this grouping?

6. Which of Ronsard's two sonnets is most like Petrarch's three sonnets in imagery and feeling? Explain.

Reading Strategy

Reading in Sentences

7. (a) To analyze how **reading in sentences** affects the meaning in a poem, choose sentences from the poem "Spring" to complete the chart below. (b) Then, explain the meaning of each sentence and relate its meaning to the poem.

Sentence	Meaning	Relationship to Poem

8. (a) How many complete sentences are in "The White Doe"? (b) How does the arrangement of complete sentences in the poem reflect the imagery?

Extend Understanding

9. **Psychology Connection:** Do you think that writing these poems comforted the poets or caused them more suffering? Explain.

Quick Review

A **sonnet** is a fourteen-line poem focused on a single theme. A sonnet has two parts and a structured rhyme scheme.

Imagery is descriptive language that re-creates sensory experiences.

To **read in sentences,** note the punctuation in a poem, and stop at the end of a line only if there is a period, comma, semicolon, colon, or dash.

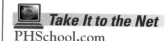

Take It to the Net
PHSchool.com

Take the interactive test online to check your understanding of these poems.

Integrate Language Skills

Vocabulary Development Lesson

Related Words: *languish*

The word *languish* means "to become weak," or "to fail in vitality and health." Other words related to *languish* include the following:

languishing (participle and verb form): "becoming weak"

languor (noun): "the feeling of being weak"

languid (adjective): "weak; without energy or vitality"

Complete each of the following sentences with one of the related words listed above.

1. The deep sadness he felt at her death left him feeling _____.
2. His _____ prevents him from working on his poetry.
3. She is _____ and very near death.

Fluency: Sentence Completion

Fill in the blanks below with the correct word from the vocabulary list on page 673.

1. He felt _____ after the great feast.
2. She _____ upon the satin pillows.
3. The old _____ sat knitting by the fire.
4. He _____ in knowing that she loves him.
5. He is _____ still, though the worst of his illness has passed.
6. A short _____ restored his spirits.

Spelling Strategy

The letters *ui* can represent several sounds: long *i* as in *guide*; short *i* as in *biscuit*; *oo* as in *fruit*; and *wi* as in *languish*. Indicate which sound is found in each of these words.

1. distinguish   2. suit   3. circuit

Grammar and Style Lesson

Predicate Adjective

A **predicate adjective** appears only with a linking verb and describes the subject of a sentence. Common linking verbs include *is, am, are, was, were, sound, taste, appear, feel, look,* and *seem*.

Ladies are *gracious* now. (modifies Ladies)

Practice Underline the subject in each item below, and draw an arrow from the predicate adjective to the word it modifies.

1. Her eyes were brighter than the sun.
2. She seemed divine among the dreary folk of earth.
3. I was fair, [and] Ronsard's muse I became.
4. Her sight was so . . . merciless that I left work to follow her at leisure.
5. He seems languid since her death.

Writing Application Write four sentences describing a great beauty. In each sentence, underline the subject and draw an arrow from the predicate adjective to the word it modifies. Note that action verbs do not take predicate adjectives.

 Prentice Hall Writing and Grammar Connection: Diamond Level, Chapter 18, Section 3

Writing Lesson

Journal Passage

For Petrarch and Ronsard, writing poems was much like keeping a journal—the poetry preserved the thoughts and feelings each poet experienced. Write a journal passage responding to any of these poems, using the voice of the love object in the poem. Use details from the poem to establish the personality of the beloved.

Prewriting   Begin by choosing one of the poems. Then, list details that reveal both the relationship the speaker shared with his beloved and how the love object might respond to the poem.

Drafting   In the voice of the beloved, state your feelings about the poem and the poet. Add details from your list along with fictitious but logical encounters or conversations between the love object and the speaker.

Model: Incorporating Details

When I was young, I inspired every great poet I

though I am old,

knew. Even now, I am considered a great beauty.

> Adding details makes writing more interesting and provides a more complete picture.

Revising   Check your finished draft against the details in your list. Replace any vague words or phrases with concrete details that reflect the voice of the beloved.

WG Prentice Hall Writing and Grammar Connection: Diamond Level, Chapter 4, Section 3

Extension Activities

Listening and Speaking Working with a partner, perform a **dramatic reading** of "Laura" and "To Hélène." As you rehearse, consider these tips:

- Adjust your voice to reflect the speaker of each poem.
- Consider the emotions expressed in the poem, and try to reflect them in your voice.
- Remember to read in complete sentences.

Perform your reading for your class, and invite questions from the audience. **[Group Activity]**

Research and Technology Compose an **informative essay** on William Butler Yeats's poem "When You Are Old" using your library's Internet or electronic sources. Address the relationship between this poem and Ronsard's. Be sure to cite your sources and include Yeats's poem.

 **Take It to the Net** PHSchool.com

Go online for an additional research activity using the Internet.

The fourteen-line poem called the *sonnet* has traditionally been a poem of love. Petrarch, whose sonnets to Laura set the thematic course of the genre, uses an octave (eight lines) and a sestet (six lines) to give his poems a kind of statement/response structure: The octave often takes a position that the sestet contradicts or modifies. The Petrarchan sonnets in this unit, selected from a sonnet sequence charting the pangs of a speaker's unfulfilled love for an idealized lady, provide an interesting take on the ups and downs of someone in love.

Elizabethan Variations Shakespeare's sonnets 29 and 116, presented here, have also been selected from a sonnet sequence. Shakespeare uses a variation of Petrarch's sonnet form: three quatrains (four lines each) and a couplet (two lines), with the couplet often a dramatic statement that resolves, restates, or redefines the central problem of the sonnet. Like Petrarch, Shakespeare creates a speaker who addresses his beloved. Both speaker and beloved, however, are less ideal and more real than the lovers in Petrarch's sonnets.

Though Petrarch wrote in fourteenth-century Italy and Shakespeare in sixteenth- and seventeenth-century England, the pain and exultation, longing and joy, despair and hope in their poetry will be familiar to anyone who has ever been in love.

Sonnet 29
William Shakespeare

When in disgrace with fortune and men's eyes,
I all alone beweep my outcast state,
And trouble deaf heaven with my bootless[1] cries,
And look upon myself and curse my fate,
5 Wishing me like to one more rich in hope,
Featured like him, like him with friends possessed,
Desiring this man's art, and that man's <u>scope</u>,
With what I most enjoy contented least.
Yet in these thoughts myself almost despising,
10 Haply[2] I think on thee, and then my state,
Like to the lark at break of day arising
From <u>sullen</u> earth, sings hymns at heaven's gate;
    For thy sweet love remembered such wealth brings
    That then I scorn to change my state with kings.

scope *n.* range of perception or understanding

sullen *adj.* gloomy; dismal

1. **bootless** *adj.* futile.
2. **haply** *adv.* by chance.

Sonnet 116

William Shakespeare

The Storm at Sea, Pieter Bruegel the Elder

Let me not to the marriage of true minds
Admit <u>impediments.</u> Love is not love
Which alters when it alteration finds,
Or bends with the remover to remove.
5 O, no! It is an ever-fixèd mark
That looks on tempests and is never shaken;
It is the star to every wandering bark,[1]
Whose worth's unknown, although his height be taken.[2]
Love's not Time's fool, though rosy lips and cheeks
10 Within his bending sickle's compass[3] come;
Love <u>alters</u> not with his brief hours and weeks,
But bears it out even to the edge of doom.[4]
     If this be error, and upon me proved,
     I never writ, nor no man ever loved.

---

1. **star . . . bark** the star that guides every wandering ship: the North Star.
2. **Whose . . . be taken** whose value is unmeasurable, although navigators measure its height in the sky.
3. **compass** *n.* range; scope.
4. **doom** Judgment Day.

▲ **Critical Viewing**
What connections do you see between this painting and "Sonnet 116"? **[Connect]**

impediments *n.* obstacles
alters *v.* changes

William Shakespeare

(1564–1616)

William Shakespeare was born in the country town of Stratford-on-Avon, England, and probably attended the town's free grammar school. Well known as an actor and a playwright, Shakespeare was part own-er of a London theater, the Globe, where many of his plays were performed. From 1592 to 1594, London's theaters were closed be-cause of the plague—this period may have provided an opportunity for Shakes-peare to write some of his 154 sonnets.

Connecting Literature Past and Present

1. Compare the speaker's attitude toward his beloved in "Laura" with the speaker's attitude in "Sonnet 29." (a) Which speaker is more optimistic? (b) Is the central figure in each poem the speaker or the beloved? (c) Indicate the specific lines that provide that information.

2. (a) In what way is the speaker's perspective on the inevitable changes of time in "Sonnet 116" similar to the perspective of the speaker in "Laura"? (b) In what way are the perspectives different?

3. Of the three poems by Petrarch and the two by Shakespeare, which one is your favorite? Explain.

Prepare to Read

from the Decameron

Giovanni Boccaccio (1313–1375)

Born in 1313, Giovanni Boccaccio [bô kä´ chō] was the illegitimate son of a Florentine merchant, an associate of a well-known banking family. His father sent him at the age of ten to work in one of his firm's banks in Naples. This southern Italian city was ruled by the Frenchman Robert of Anjou, whose court was known for its splendor and sophistication. As a member of the banking firm that lent this ruler money, Boccaccio was able to attend court functions, and he later remembered this period of his life as a time of happiness and pleasure.

Boccaccio's father encouraged his son to become a businessman and, later, a lawyer specializing in church law; Boccaccio showed little interest in either field. He did, however, begin to write while at the Neapolitan court, and he continued to write prolifically for the rest of his life. His early works, written mostly in Italian, include several long narratives. One of them, *Filocolo*, demonstrates Boccaccio's deep insights into human motives and behaviors.

A Wider Worldview In 1340, financial problems caused Boccaccio's family to recall him to Florence, and he had to leave behind the cultivated court that he loved. His letters suggest that the return to what seemed at first a petty, middle-class, money-grubbing environment was difficult. However, this change provided essential experience for the future author of the *Decameron*, a book dealing with all kinds and classes of people. As time passed, Boccaccio became more sympathetic to Florence and its citizens—he actively engaged in Florentine politics, serving as an ambassador to other countries.

Scholar and Poet In 1350, Boccaccio met the celebrated Italian poet Francesco Petrarch, the only contemporary whose gifts matched his own. This meeting was the start of a lifelong friendship. Boccaccio admired Petrarch greatly, and Petrarch's example encouraged Boccaccio in his own writings. Boccaccio produced a series of scholarly Latin works arising out of his vast reading in classical literature. In addition, with the help of a Greek collaborator, he produced the first European translation of Homer's works into Latin. He also wrote a biography of poet Dante Alighieri. In Boccaccio's last year, he began an important commentary on Dante's great work, the *Divine Comedy*.

Greatest Achievements Although Boccaccio was famous for his Latin works—and he would have regarded them as his greatest achievement—the *Decameron* is a collection of amusing and artful stories that reveal Boccaccio's impressive literary versatility. Far from being a musty old classic, the *Decameron* has delighted readers and inspired writers for half a millennium. Like many best-selling novels of our own time, it has been the inspiration for numerous full-length film adaptations.

The men and women who narrate the tales within the *Decameron* share the harrowing experience of escaping an outbreak of bubonic plague, similar to the 1348 epidemic that killed Boccaccio's parents as well as more than half of Florence's population. Framed by their medieval setting, the narratives in the *Decameron* feature a multitude of characters representing an array of social classes. Boccaccio explores deeply human themes of love, loss, deception, fortune, and more, creating a work of universality and timelessness.

Preview

Connecting to the Literature

Cherished items are keepsakes, objects you might not willingly give away. In Boccaccio's story, the main character's generous sacrifice of such an item may seem noble to some readers but very foolish to others.

Literary Analysis

Novella

A **novella** is a short prose tale. First written as early as the fourteenth century, the novella influenced the later development of the novel and the modern short story. Boccaccio's *Decameron* is a group of one hundred novellas, including "Federigo's Falcon." Like other short prose stories, these novellas share the following elements:

- a setting
- well-developed characters
- a theme, or a message about life
- a plot that includes the main events, conflicts, a climax or turning point in the story, and a final resolution

Use a chart like the one shown to identify details of these elements in "Federigo's Falcon."

Novella "Federigo's Falcon"
Setting:
Characters:
Plot:
Theme:

Connecting Literary Elements

Rather than tell his stories directly, Boccaccio creates a fictional background, or **frame,** surrounding the novellas of the *Decameron*. In the frame, ten young people leave Florence to escape the bubonic plague. To pass the time, they tell each other stories—including "Federigo's Falcon"—that fit within the shared frame. As you read, look for characters and dialogue from the frame and watch for the transition into the novella itself.

Reading Strategy

Identifying With Characters

Identifying with characters helps you connect to your reading. To identify with characters, put yourself into a character's place and relate his or her thoughts, feelings, and experiences to your own life. Note each character's situations and choices and consider the ways you might act in similar circumstances.

Vocabulary Development

courtly (kôrt′ lē) *adj.* dignified; polite; elegant (p. 689)

sumptuous (sump′ choo əs) *adj.* costly; lavish (p. 689)

frugally (froo′ gə lē) *adv.* thriftily; economically (p. 689)

deference (def′ ər əns) *n.* courteous regard or respect (p. 692)

affably (af′ ə blē) *adv.* in a friendly manner (p. 692)

impertinence (im purt′ 'n əns) *n.* insolence; impudence (p. 692)

despondent (di spän′ dənt) *adj.* dejected; hopeless (p. 693)

from the
Decameron
Giovanni Boccaccio

translated by G. H. McWilliam

Background

In the *Decameron*, a group of ten young aristocrats—seven women and three men—take up residence at a country estate to wait out an outbreak of the plague. To entertain themselves, each of them tells one story a day for ten days—hence, the name *Decameron*, which means "ten days." Each day, they elect a "king" or "queen" from among their number to preside over the day's storytelling. "Federigo's Falcon" is told on the fifth day.

▲ **Critical Viewing**
What physical attributes enable falcons, like this one, to find and capture quarry such as rabbits and game birds? **[Analyze]**

Federigo's Falcon

Once Filomena had finished, the queen, finding that there was no one left to speak apart from herself (Dioneo being excluded from the reckoning because of his privilege), smiled cheerfully and said:

It is now my own turn to address you, and I shall gladly do so, dearest ladies, with a story similar in some respects to the one we have just heard. This I have chosen, not only to acquaint you with the power of your beauty over men of noble spirit, but so that you may learn to choose for yourselves, whenever necessary, the persons on whom to bestow your largesse,[1] instead of always leaving these matters to be decided for you by Fortune, who, as it happens, nearly always scatters her gifts with more abundance than discretion.

You are to know, then, that Coppo di Borghese Domenichi, who once used to live in our city and possibly lives there still, one of the most highly respected men of our century, a person worthy of eternal fame, who achieved his position of pre-eminence by dint of his character and

Literary Analysis
Novella and Frame Which character from the frame is the narrator of the novella?

---

1. largesse (lär jes´) *n.* generous gifts.

abilities rather than by his noble lineage, frequently took pleasure during his declining years in discussing incidents from the past with his neighbors and other folk. In this pastime he excelled all others, for he was more coherent, possessed a superior memory, and spoke with greater eloquence. He had a fine repertoire, including a tale he frequently told concerning a young Florentine called Federigo, the son of Messer Filippo Alberighi, who for his deeds of chivalry and <u>courtly</u> manners was more highly spoken of than any other squire in Tuscany. In the manner of most young men of gentle breeding, Federigo lost his heart to a noble lady, whose name was Monna[2] Giovanna, and who in her time was considered one of the loveliest and most adorable women to be found in Florence. And with the object of winning her love, he rode at the ring, tilted, gave <u>sumptuous</u> banquets, and distributed a large number of gifts, spending money without any restraint whatsoever. But since she was no less chaste than she was fair, the lady took no notice, either of the things that were done in her honor, or of the person who did them.

In this way, spending far more than he could afford and deriving no profit in return, Federigo lost his entire fortune (as can easily happen) and reduced himself to poverty, being left with nothing other than a tiny little farm, which produced an income just sufficient for him to live very <u>frugally</u>, and one falcon of the finest breed in the whole world. Since he was as deeply in love as ever, and felt unable to go on living the sort of life in Florence to which he aspired, he moved out to Campi, where his little farm happened to be situated. Having settled in the country, he went hunting as often as possible with his falcon, and, without seeking assistance from anyone, he patiently resigned himself to a life of poverty.

Now one day, while Federigo was living in these straitened circumstances, the husband of Monna Giovanna happened to fall ill, and, realizing that he was about to die, he drew up his will. He was a very rich man, and in his will he left everything to his son, who was just growing up, further stipulating that, if his son should die without legitimate issue, his estate should go to Monna Giovanna, to whom he had always been deeply devoted.

Shortly afterward he died, leaving Monna Giovanna a widow, and every summer, in accordance with Florentine custom, she went away with her son to a country estate of theirs, which was very near Federigo's farm. Consequently this young lad of hers happened to become friendly with Federigo, acquiring a

2. **Monna** Lady.

Critical Viewing ▶ In what ways might this portrait be an accurate representation of Federigo? [**Analyze**]

courtly (kôrt´ lē) *adj.* dignified; polite; elegant

sumptuous (sump´ choo əs) *adj.* costly; lavish

Literary Analysis
Novella Identify the setting of the novella.

frugally (froo´ gə lē) *adv.* thriftily; economically

☑**Reading Check**

What remains of Federigo's fortune after pursuing Monna Giovanna's affection?

Robert Cheseman, Hans Holbein the Younger, Scala

passion for birds and dogs; and, having often seen Federigo's falcon in flight, he became fascinated by it and longed to own it, but since he could see that Federigo was deeply attached to the bird, he never ventured to ask him for it.

And there the matter rested, when, to the consternation of his mother, the boy happened to be taken ill. Being her only child, he was the apple of his mother's eye, and she sat beside his bed the whole day long, never ceasing to comfort him. Every so often she asked him whether there was anything he wanted, imploring him to tell her what it was, because if it was possible to acquire it, she would move heaven and earth to obtain it for him.

After hearing this offer repeated for the umpteenth time, the boy said:

"Mother, if you could arrange for me to have Federigo's falcon, I believe I should soon get better."

On hearing this request, the lady was somewhat taken aback, and began to consider what she could do about it. Knowing that Federigo had been in love with her for a long time, and that she had never deigned to cast so much as a single glance in his direction, she said to herself: "How can I possibly go to him, or even send anyone, to ask him for this falcon, which to judge from all I have heard is the finest that ever flew, as well as being the only thing that keeps him alive? And how can I be so heartless as to deprive so noble a man of his one remaining pleasure?"

Reading Strategy
Identifying With Characters What might you be willing to do if you were in Monna Giovanna's place?

Departure for the Hunt, 16th century, Réunion des Musées Nationaux, Paris

◀ **Critical Viewing** Medieval and Renaissance tapestries, like the one shown, often tell stories or depict specific events. What detailed story might this tapestry narrate? [Speculate]

Her mind filled with reflections of this sort, she remained silent, not knowing what answer to make to her son's request, even though she was quite certain that the falcon was hers for the asking.

At length, however, her maternal instincts gained the upper hand, and she resolved, come what may, to satisfy the child by going in person to Federigo to collect the bird, and bring it back to him. And so she replied:

"Bear up, my son, and see whether you can start feeling any better. I give you my word that I shall go and fetch it for you first thing tomorrow morning."

Next morning, taking another lady with her for company,[3] his mother left the house as though intending to go for a walk, made her way to Federigo's little cottage, and asked to see him. For several days, the weather had been unsuitable for hawking, so Federigo was attending to one or two little jobs in his garden, and when he heard, to his utter astonishment, that Monna Giovanna was at the front door and wished to speak to him, he happily rushed there to greet her.

When she saw him coming, she advanced with womanly grace to meet him. Federigo received her with a deep bow, whereupon she said:

"Greetings, Federigo!" Then she continued: "I have come to make amends for the harm you have suffered on my account, by loving me more than you ought to have done. As a token of my esteem, I should like to take breakfast with you this morning, together with my companion here, but you must not put yourself to any trouble."

"My lady," replied Federigo in all humility, "I cannot recall ever having suffered any harm on your account. On the contrary I have gained so much that if ever I attained any kind of excellence, it was entirely because of your own great worth and the love I bore you. Moreover I can assure you that this visit which you have been generous enough to pay me is worth more to me than all the money I ever possessed, though I fear that my hospitality will not amount to very much."

So saying, he led her unassumingly into the house, and thence into his garden, where, since there was no one else he could call upon to chaperon her, he said:

"My lady, as there is nobody else available, this good woman, who is the wife of the farmer here, will keep you company whilst I go and see about setting the table."

Though his poverty was acute, the extent to which he had squandered his wealth had not yet been fully borne home to Federigo; but on this particular morning, finding that he had nothing to set before the lady for whose love he had entertained so lavishly in the past, his eyes were well and truly opened to the fact. Distressed beyond all measure, he silently cursed his bad luck and rushed all over the house like one possessed, but could find no trace of either money or valuables. By now the morning was well advanced, he was still determined to entertain

Literary Analysis
Novella What fear motivates Monna Giovanna to ask Federigo for the falcon?

✔**Reading Check**

What does Monna Giovanna seek for her son?

---

3. **taking . . . company** A young woman of the upper classes would not go out by herself.

the gentlewoman to some sort of meal, and, not wishing to beg assistance from his own farmer (or from anyone else, for that matter), his gaze alighted on his precious falcon, which was sitting on its perch in the little room where it was kept. And having discovered, on picking it up, that it was nice and plump, he decided that since he had nowhere else to turn, it would make a worthy dish for such a lady as this. So without thinking twice about it he wrung the bird's neck and promptly handed it over to his housekeeper to be plucked, dressed, and roasted carefully on a spit. Then he covered the table with spotless linen, of which he still had a certain amount in his possession, and returned in high spirits to the garden, where he announced to his lady that the meal, such as he had been able to prepare, was now ready.

The lady and her companion rose from where they were sitting and made their way to the table. And together with Federigo, who waited on them with the utmost <u>deference</u>, they made a meal of the prize falcon without knowing what they were eating.

On leaving the table they engaged their host in pleasant conversation for a while, and when the lady thought it time to broach the subject she had gone there to discuss, she turned to Federigo and addressed him <u>affably</u> as follows:

"I do not doubt for a moment, Federigo, that you will be astonished at my <u>impertinence</u> when you discover my principal reason for coming here, especially when you recall your former mode of living and my virtue, which you possibly mistook for harshness and cruelty. But if you had ever had any children to make you appreciate the power of parental love, I should think it certain that you would to some extent forgive me.

"However, the fact that you have no children of your own does not exempt me, a mother, from the laws common to all other mothers. And being bound to obey those laws, I am forced, contrary to my own wishes and to all the rules of decorum and propriety, to ask you for something to which I know you are very deeply attached—which is only natural, seeing that it is the only consolation, the only pleasure, the only recreation remaining to you in your present extremity of fortune. The gift I am seeking is your falcon, to which my son has taken so powerful a liking, that if I fail to take it to him I fear he will succumb to the illness from which he is suffering, and consequently I shall lose him. In imploring you to give me this falcon, I appeal, not to your love, for you are under no obligation to me on that account, but rather to your noble heart, whereby you have proved yourself superior to all others in the practice of courtesy. Do me this favor, then, so that I may claim that through your generosity I have saved my son's life, thus placing him forever in your debt."

Literary Analysis
Novella What does the phrase "without thinking twice" reveal about Federigo's character?

deference (def′ ər əns) *n.* courteous regard or respect

affably (af′ ə blē) *adv.* in a friendly manner

impertinence (im purt′ 'n əns) *n.* insolence; impudence

▼ Critical Viewing
Which details from "Federigo's Falcon" are aptly represented in this painting? Explain. **[Interpret]**

When he heard what it was that she wanted, and realized that he could not oblige her because he had given her the falcon to eat, Federigo burst into tears in her presence before being able to utter a single word in reply. At first the lady thought his tears stemmed more from his grief at having to part with his fine falcon than from any other motive, and was on the point of telling him that she would prefer not to have it. But on second thoughts she said nothing, and waited for Federigo to stop crying and give her his answer, which eventually he did.

"My lady," he said, "ever since God decreed that you should become the object of my love, I have repeatedly had cause to complain of Fortune's hostility towards me. But all her previous blows were slight by comparison with the one she has dealt me now. Nor shall I ever be able to forgive her, when I reflect that you have come to my poor dwelling, which you never deigned to visit when it was rich, and that you desire from me a trifling favor which she has made it impossible for me to concede. The reason is simple, and I shall explain it in few words.

"When you did me the kindness of telling me that you wished to breakfast with me, I considered it right and proper, having regard to your excellence and merit, to do everything within my power to prepare a more sumptuous dish than those I would offer to my ordinary guests. My thoughts therefore turned to the falcon you have asked me for and, knowing its quality, I reputed it a worthy dish to set before you. So I had it roasted and served to you on the trencher this morning, and I could not have wished for a better way of disposing of it. But now that I discover that you wanted it in a different form, I am so distressed by my inability to grant your request that I shall never forgive myself for as long as I live."

In confirmation of his words, Federigo caused the feathers, talons and beak to be cast on the table before her. On seeing and hearing all this, the lady reproached him at first for killing so fine a falcon, and serving it up for a woman to eat; but then she became lost in admiration for his magnanimity[4] of spirit, which no amount of poverty had managed to diminish, nor ever would. But now that her hopes of obtaining the falcon had vanished she began to feel seriously concerned for the health of her son, and after thanking Federigo for his hospitality and good intentions, she took her leave of him, looking all <u>despondent</u>, and returned to the child. And to his mother's indescribable sorrow, within the space of a few days, whether through his disappointment in not being able to have the falcon, or because he was in any case suffering from a mortal illness, the child passed from this life.

---

4. **magnanimity** (mag' nə nim' ə tē) *n.* noble generosity.

Themes in World Literature

Boccaccio's Influence on Geoffrey Chaucer

Boccaccio's *Decameron* became a model for many subsequent writers. The English poet Geoffrey Chaucer (1340?–1400) made use of this narrative model to write *The Canterbury Tales.*

Chaucer's frame features twenty-nine pilgrims who embark on a pilgrimage to the cathedral at Canterbury, England. To pass the time, the pilgrims agree to a story-telling contest in which each traveler tells two tales along the way to Canterbury and two more tales on the return journey. The winner will receive a free dinner at the Tabard Inn upon return. Like Boccaccio's *Decameron, The Canterbury Tales* features richly developed characters whose flaws and strengths make them very human.

Literary Analysis
Novella In what way is Monna Giovanna's visit a deeply bittersweet occasion for Federigo?

despondent (di spän' dənt) *adj.* dejected; hopeless

✓ Reading Check

What emotional response does Federigo have to Monna Giovanna's request?

After a period of bitter mourning and continued weeping, the lady was repeatedly urged by her brothers to remarry, since not only had she been left a vast fortune but she was still a young woman. And though she would have preferred to remain a widow, they gave her so little peace that in the end, recalling Federigo's high merits and his latest act of generosity, namely to have killed such a fine falcon in her honor, she said to her brothers:

"If only it were pleasing to you, I should willingly remain as I am; but since you are so eager for me to take a husband, you may be certain that I shall never marry any other man except Federigo degli Alberighi."

Her brothers made fun of her, saying:

"Silly girl, don't talk such nonsense! How can you marry a man who hasn't a penny with which to bless himself?"

"My brothers," she replied, "I am well aware of that. But I would sooner have a gentleman without riches, than riches without a gentleman."

Seeing that her mind was made up, and knowing Federigo to be a gentleman of great merit even though he was poor, her brothers fell in with her wishes and handed her over to him, along with her immense fortune. Thenceforth, finding himself married to this great lady with whom he was so deeply in love, and very rich into the bargain, Federigo managed his affairs more prudently, and lived with her in happiness to the end of his days.

Review and Assess

Thinking About the Selection

1. **Respond:** Do you think Federigo was noble or misguided in serving up the falcon? Explain.

2. **(a) Recall:** What early efforts does Federigo make to win Monna Giovanna's love? **(b) Infer:** What does the narrator mean when she says Monna Giovanna's chastity compelled her to take no notice of Federigo?

3. **(a) Recall:** What gestures of hospitality does Federigo make when Monna Giovanna visits? **(b) Connect:** In what ways do his efforts reflect his former life as a wealthy gentleman? **(c) Speculate:** Do you think Monna Giovanna expected such behavior from him? Why or why not?

4. **(a) Recall:** How does Monna Giovanna respond to the news of the falcon's death? **(b) Infer:** What does her response indicate about her character?

5. **Apply:** In what ways do the ideals of love expressed in this story differ from current notions of romantic love?

Review and Assess

Literary Analysis

Novella

1. Do you think "Federigo's Falcon" contains all the elements of a **novella**? Why or why not?
2. How does the setting reflect Federigo's change of fortune?
3. What lesson about loss and restoration does this story teach? Use details from the tale to support your answer.

Connecting Literary Elements

4. (a) In the *Decameron's* **frame,** what does the queen claim her story teaches? (b) Which details in the novella might her listening audience relate to their own lives? Explain.
5. (a) Who is Coppo di Borghese Domenichi? (b) What credibility does he add to the novella and its narrator?

Reading Strategy

Identifying With Characters

6. Using a chart like the one shown, choose two events involving Federigo and two involving Monna Giovanna. Then, **identifying with each character,** explain what your reaction might be if you experienced similar events.

	Their Experiences	My Reactions
Federigo	1.	1.
	2.	2.
Monna Giovanna	1.	1.
	2.	2.

7. (a) For which character do you feel the most sympathy? (b) In what way does identifying with the character influence your ability to sympathize? Explain.

Extend Understanding

8. **Cultural Connection:** What can you infer from the characters' behavior about love, marriage, and the status of women during this period? Explain.

Quick Review

A **novella** is a short prose tale.

A **frame** is a unifying background that links together a series of stories.

When you **identify with characters,** you relate to their thoughts and feelings and connect them to your own experiences.

Take It to the Net
PHSchool.com

Take the interactive self-test online to check your understanding of this selection.

Integrate Language Skills

Vocabulary Development Lesson

Word Analysis: Latin Suffix -ence

The Latin suffix *-ence* means "quality of" or "state of being." To change an adjective ending in *-ent* to a noun, replace the *-ent* suffix with *-ence*. For example, the adjective *impertinent*, meaning "insolent or impudent," becomes *impertinence*, meaning "the quality of being impertinent."

Change the following adjectives to nouns by replacing the suffix *-ent* with *-ence*.

1. turbulent   2. insistent   3. munificent

Spelling Strategy

Many words end in an unstressed syllable spelled with a consonant + *-le*, as in *remarkable*. To add *-ly*, drop the *-le*: *remarkable* becomes *remarkably*. Rewrite these words, adding *-ly*.

1. affable   2. gentle   3. sparkle

Concept Development: Synonym or Antonym?

Review the vocabulary words on page 687 and notice the use of the words in context in the selections. Then, for each pair of words below, write S for *synonym* if the words have similar meanings or A for *antonym* if they have opposite meanings.

1. courtly, impolite
2. sumptuous, expensive
3. frugally, lavishly
4. deference, respect
5. affably, nastily
6. impertinence, rudeness
7. despondent, cheerful

Grammar and Style Lesson

Varying Sentence Beginnings

By **varying sentence beginnings,** an author adds interest to the text and helps avoid repetition. In addition to starting sentences with a subject, writers can vary sentence beginnings by using prepositional phrases, transitions, or dependent clauses.

Prepositional Phrase: *In due time,* Federigo lost his heart to a noble lady.

Transition: *Now one day* . . . the husband of Monna Giovanna happened to fall ill.

Dependent Clause: *Though his poverty was acute,* the extent of it was yet unknown.

Practice Revise the following sentences so they begin with a prepositional phrase, a transition, or a dependent clause. Underline your new sentence beginnings and identify each by type.

1. She was shocked on hearing his request.
2. He died leaving Monna Giovanna a widow shortly afterward.
3. She advanced with womanly grace to meet him when she saw him coming.
4. He took breakfast with her as a token of his esteem.
5. They had a pleasant conversation after leaving the table.

Writing Application Write a short letter of invitation. Use a variety of sentence beginnings, underlining each and identifying its type.

W̶G̶ Prentice Hall Writing and Grammar Connection: Diamond Level, Chapter 20, Section 3

Writing Lesson

Literary Analysis

One theme, or universal message, in "Federigo's Falcon" is that people should preserve their nobility of spirit at all costs. Write an essay supporting this theme, or choose a different one and defend its presence in the novella.

Prewriting	Begin by explaining the theme you have chosen and the ways in which it relates to readers today. Reread the story, listing points and specific quotations that support your idea.
Drafting	In your introduction, include a statement of the theme and its meaning. Then, in the body of your essay, identify specific details from the novella and explain how each example supports your point.
Revising	Revise your draft to include enough evidence to defend your main point. Consider strengthening your point by adding relevant citations.

Model: Using Relevant Citations

Federigo shows remarkable nobility of spirit as he faces his dwindling wealth. He never complains about sacrificing his fortune in vain. ∧ *As the narrator describes, "he patiently resigned himself to a life of poverty."*

> One effective way to cite details from a literary work is to use a direct quotation.

W̶G̶ Prentice Hall Writing and Grammar Connection: Diamond Level, Chapter 14, Section 3

Extension Activities

Listening and Speaking With a small group, organize a **storytelling circle.** Choose a central idea, such as generosity, love, or trickery. Have each group member create a story exemplifying this idea. Use the following tips as you prepare:

- Choose events that illustrate the theme.
- Add details to the story to make it vivid.
- Consider exaggerating the details to make your point more strongly.

Take turns telling your stories to the class. Then, invite the class to identify the central theme. **[Group Activity]**

Research and Technology Use library and Internet resources to research falconry. Find images from both Boccaccio's time and the present that show how falcons are handled and how they are used to hunt. Create a **classroom display** that compares or contrasts the use of falconry through the centuries, including captions that explain each image. Share your display with the class.

 Take It to the Net PHSchool.com

Go online for an additional research activity using the Internet.

Prepare to Read

from Don Quixote

Miguel de Cervantes Saavedra (1547–1616)

Miguel de Cervantes Saavedra (sər vanˊ tēz säˊ ə väˊ drə) led a life that was every bit as exciting as that of his famous character, knight-errant Don Quixote (dänˊ kē hōtˊ ē). Cervantes also displayed, on occasion, the almost foolhardy bravery that was so characteristic of his absurd knight.

Military Career Born into a poor family, Cervantes received little education. In 1570, he joined the Spanish army and shortly afterward fought in the battle of Lepanto against the Turks. This naval battle saw the destruction of the Turkish fleet by the combined forces of Spain and Italy.

Cervantes was among the 30,000 soldiers transported by the Spanish and Italian galleys. Although he was ill when the battle began, he plunged into the fighting and was wounded twice in the chest and once in the left arm. For the rest of his life, he regarded his maimed left arm as a badge of honor.

Cervantes went on to fight in a number of other battles, but he was captured by Barbary pirates while sailing home from the wars. Sold into slavery in Algiers, he repeatedly tried to escape. Although he was always recaptured, his bravery so impressed the Algerians that they did not put him to death. Believing that Cervantes was a citizen of great importance, his captors demanded a considerable ransom for his release. After he had been a prisoner for five years, the ransom was finally paid, and Cervantes was free to return to Madrid.

Difficult Times Back in Spain, Cervantes pursued an ambitious goal: to become Spain's most successful dramatist. Although he wrote prolifically, his significant collection of theatrical works was largely overlooked. Cervantes braved difficult economic circumstances during his years as a playwright and eventually found a bookkeeping job with the government to support his large household. Problems with his account books, however, led to his imprisonment on two occasions. According to legend, Cervantes began writing *Don Quixote* during one of these spells in prison.

A Wealth of Imagination When the first part of the novel appeared in 1605, it was a great success. Within only a few years, the novel had been translated into English, French, and a number of other European languages. When a false, or unauthorized, sequel to *Don Quixote* appeared on the market, Cervantes quickly embarked upon the continuation of his story—*Don Quixote, Part II*—which was published in 1615. Despite his appreciable success, Cervantes received only a small sum from his publisher for the works. At the time of his death in 1616, he was still a poor man.

It is clear that Cervantes invested his true wealth—his keen observation, playfulness, and imagination—in the creation of his novel. That is why it remains, as one translator called it, "one of the best adventure stories in the world." To date, Cervantes's masterpiece has been published in more than sixty languages, and the novel continues to be studied, critiqued, and debated by scholars around the world.

Preview

Connecting to the Literature

Literature is filled with dreamers—people who hook their wagons to a star or try to lasso the moon. Perhaps the best-known dreamer of all is Don Quixote de la Mancha, an unlikely hero who gets swept away by the stories he reads and the dreams they inspire.

Literary Analysis

Parody

A **parody** is a humorous imitation of another, usually serious, work. Most often, a parody uses exaggeration or distortion to ridicule the work, its style, or its author. *Don Quixote* affectionately parodies the literature of chivalry—elaborate stories about knights; their code of honor, courage, and chastity; and their adventures. The central character, for example, makes swords out of oak branches and helmets of cardboard, yet he considers himself a well-dressed knight. As you read, look for details that parody chivalric romances.

Connecting Literary Elements

Parodies lend themselves to discussions of **theme,** the central message or idea revealed through a literary work. *Don Quixote* uses parody to explore the idea of reality versus fantasy, prompting readers to ask:

- At what point do flights of fancy interfere with reality?
- Is a life of hard-nosed realism more rewarding than a life filled with fantastic adventures?

Note thematic questions like these as you read.

Reading Strategy

Comparing and Contrasting

Comparing and contrasting an ideal knight and Don Quixote's version means looking for similarities and differences between the two. Before you read, use a chart like the one shown to list the details you know about an ideal knight, such as his armor, squire, horse, and adventures. Then, as you read, record the details from Don Quixote's world. Identify any conclusions you can draw from comparing and contrasting those details.

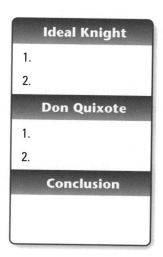

Ideal Knight
1.
2.
Don Quixote
1.
2.
Conclusion

Vocabulary Development

constitution (kän′ stə too′ shən) *n.* structure or makeup of a person or thing (p. 700)

conjectures (kən jek′ chərz) *n.* guesses (p. 700)

infatuation (in fach′ oo ā′ shən) *n.* foolish or shallow feelings of affection (p. 702)

ingenuity (in′ jə noo′ ə tē) *n.* cleverness; inventiveness (p. 704)

incongruous (in kän′ groo əs) *adj.* inconsistent; lacking in harmony (p. 707)

appropriate (ə prō′ prē āt′) *v.* take for one's own use (p. 708)

illustrious (i lus′ trē əs) *adj.* distinguished or outstanding (p. 710)

from Don Quixote

Miguel de Cervantes   translated by Samuel Putnam

Background

In traditional courtly romances, a knight-errant is a great fighter who has earned renown in jousting and tournaments. He spends his life wandering the land, performing deeds of bravery in the name of a noble woman who can never return his affection. This impossible love and its accompanying code of honor justify the knight's death-defying adventures. Don Quixote sees himself as such a knight, and no reality can resist his fabulous imagination.

Chapter I

Which treats of the station in life and the pursuits of the famous gentleman, Don Quixote de la Mancha.

In a village of La Mancha[1] the name of which I have no desire to recall, there lived not so long ago one of those gentlemen who always have a lance in the rack, an ancient buckler, a skinny nag, and a greyhound for the chase. A stew with more beef than mutton in it, chopped meat for his evening meal, scraps for a Saturday, lentils on Friday, and a young pigeon as a special delicacy for Sunday, went to account for three-quarters of his income. The rest of it he laid out on a broadcloth greatcoat and velvet stockings for feast days, with slippers to match, while the other days of the week he cut a figure in a suit of the finest homespun. Living with him were a housekeeper in her forties, a niece who was not yet twenty, and a lad of the field and market place who saddled his horse for him and wielded the pruning knife.

This gentleman of ours was close on to fifty, of a robust <u>constitution</u> but with little flesh on his bones and a face that was lean and gaunt. He was noted for his early rising, being very fond of the hunt. They will try to tell you that his surname was Quijada or Quesada—there is some difference of opinion among those who have written on the subject—but according to the most likely <u>conjectures</u> we are to understand

---

1. **La Mancha** province in south central Spain.

Literary Analysis
Parody In what way do Don Quixote's age and physical appearance parody the typical heroic knight?

constitution (kän′ stə too′ shən) *n.* structure or makeup of a person or thing

conjectures (kən jek′ chərz) *n.* guesses

Don Quixote, Honoré Daumier, Scala

▲ **Critical Viewing** Which details from this painting match the description in Chapter I of Don Quixote and his horse? **[Analyze]**

that it was really Quejana. But all this means very little so far as our story is concerned, providing that in the telling of it we do not depart one iota from the truth.

You may know, then, that the aforesaid gentleman, on those occasions when he was at leisure, which was most of the year around, was in the habit of reading books of chivalry with such pleasure and devotion as to lead him almost wholly to forget the life of a hunter and even the administration of his estate. So great was his curiosity and <u>infatuation</u> in this regard that he even sold many acres of tillable land in order to be able to buy and read the books that he loved, and he would carry home with him as many of them as he could obtain.

Of all those that he thus devoured none pleased him so well as the ones that had been composed by the famous Feliciano de Silva, whose lucid prose style and involved conceits[2] were as precious to him as pearls; especially when he came to read those tales of love and amorous challenges that are to be met with in many places, such a passage as the following, for example: "The reason of the unreason that afflicts my reason, in such a manner weakens my reason that I with reason lament me of your comeliness." And he was similarly affected when his eyes fell upon such lines as these: ". . . the high Heaven of your divinity divinely fortifies you with the stars and renders you deserving of that desert your greatness doth deserve."

The poor fellow used to lie awake nights in an effort to disentangle the meaning and make sense out of passages such as these, although Aristotle himself would not have been able to understand them, even if he had been resurrected for that sole purpose. He was not at ease in his mind over those wounds that Don Belianís gave and received; for no matter how great the surgeons who treated him, the poor fellow must have been left with his face and his entire body covered with marks and scars. Nevertheless, he was grateful to the author for closing the book with the promise of an interminable adventure to come; many a time he was tempted to take up his pen and literally finish the tale as had been promised, and he undoubtedly would have done so, and would have succeeded at it very well, if his thoughts had not been constantly occupied with other things of greater moment.

▲ **Critical Viewing**
Which details in this picture might Don Quixote find fascinating? Explain. **[Speculate]**

infatuation (in fach′ o͞o a′ shən) *n.* foolish or shallow feelings of affection

---

2. conceits elaborate comparisons or metaphors.

He often talked it over with the village curate,[3] who was a learned man, a graduate of Sigüenza,[4] and they would hold long discussions as to who had been the better knight, Palmerin of England or Amadis of Gaul; but Master Nicholas, the barber of the same village, was in the habit of saying that no one could come up to the Knight of Phoebus, and that if anyone *could* compare with him it was Don Galaor, brother of Amadis of Gaul, for Galaor was ready for anything—he was none of your finical[5] knights, who went around whimpering as his brother did, and in point of valor he did not lag behind him.

In short, our gentleman became so immersed in his reading that he spent whole nights from sundown to sunup and his days from dawn to dusk in poring over his books, until, finally, from so little sleeping and so much reading, his brain dried up and he went completely out of his mind. He had filled his imagination with everything that he had read, with enchantments, knightly encounters, battles, challenges, wounds, with tales of love and its torments, and all sorts of impossible things, and as a result had come to believe that all these fictitious happenings were true; they were more real to him than anything else in the world. He would remark that the Cid Ruy Díaz[6] had been a very good knight, but there was no comparison between him and the Knight of the Flaming Sword, who with a single backward stroke had cut in half two fierce and monstrous giants. He preferred Bernardo del Carpio, who at Roncesvalles had slain Roland despite the charm the latter bore, availing himself of the stratagem which Hercules employed when he strangled Antaeus, the son of Earth, in his arms.

He had much good to say for Morgante who, though he belonged to the haughty, overbearing race of giants, was of an affable disposition and well brought up. But, above all, he cherished an admiration for Rinaldo of Montalbán, especially as he beheld him sallying forth from his castle to rob all those that crossed his path, or when he thought of him overseas stealing the image of Mohammed which, so the story has it, was all of gold. And he would have liked very well to have had his fill of kicking that traitor Galalón, a privilege for which he would have given his housekeeper with his niece thrown into the bargain.

At last, when his wits were gone beyond repair, he came to conceive the strangest idea that ever occurred to any madman in this world. It now appeared to him fitting and necessary, in order to win a greater amount of honor for himself and serve his country at the same time, to become a knight-errant and roam the world on horseback, in a suit of armor; he would go in quest of adventures, by way of putting into practice all that he had read in his books; he would right every manner of wrong, placing himself in situations of the greatest peril such as would

---

3. **curate** clergyman in charge of a parish.
4. **Sigüenza** (se gwän´ sä) one of a group of "minor universities" granting degrees that were often laughed at by Spanish humorists.
5. **finical** (fin´i kəl) finicky.
6. **Cid Ruy Díaz** (cēd rōō´ ē dē´ äs) famous Spanish soldier Ruy Diaz de Vivar: called the Cid, a derivation of the Arabic word for *lord*.

Reading Strategy
Comparing and Contrasting Compare and contrast Don Quixote's current lifestyle with that of the knights described in this passage.

**Reading Check**

What activity consumes Don Quixote's time from dawn to dusk each day?

redound to the eternal glory of his name. As a reward for his valor and the might of his arm, the poor fellow could already see himself crowned Emperor of Trebizond[7] at the very least; and so, carried away by the strange pleasure that he found in such thoughts as these, he at once set about putting his plan into effect.

The first thing he did was to burnish up some old pieces of armor, left him by his great-grandfather, which for ages had lain in a corner, moldering and forgotten. He polished and adjusted them as best he could, and then he noticed that one very important thing was lacking: there was no closed helmet, but only a morion, or visorless headpiece, with turned up brim of the kind foot soldiers wore. His <u>ingenuity</u>, however, enabled him to remedy this, and he proceeded to fashion out of cardboard a kind of half-helmet, which, when attached to the morion, gave the appearance of a whole one. True, when he went to see if it was strong enough to withstand a good slashing blow, he was somewhat disappointed; for when he drew his sword and gave it a couple of thrusts, he succeeded only in undoing a whole week's labor. The ease with which he had hewed it to bits disturbed him no little, and he decided to make it over. This time he placed a few strips of iron on the inside, and then, convinced that it was strong enough, refrained from putting it to any further test; instead, he adopted it then and there as the finest helmet ever made.

After this, he went out to have a look at his nag; and although the animal had more *cuartos*, or cracks, in its hoof than there are quarters in a real, [8] and more blemishes than Gonela's steed which *tantum pellis et ossa fuit*,[9] it nonetheless looked to its master like a far better horse than Alexander's Bucephalus or the Babieca of the Cid.[10] He spent all of four days in trying to think up a name for his mount; for—so he told himself—seeing that it belonged to so famous and worthy a knight, there was no reason why it should not have a name of equal renown. The kind of name he wanted was one that would at once indicate what the nag had been before it came to belong to a knight-errant and what its present status was; for it stood to reason that, when the master's worldly condition changed, his horse also ought to have a famous, high-sounding appellation, one suited to the new order of things and the new profession that it was to follow.

After he in his memory and imagination had made up, struck out, and discarded many names, now adding to and now subtracting from the list, he finally hit upon "Rocinante," a name that impressed him as being sonorous and at the same time indicative of what the steed had

ingenuity (in′je no͞o′ ə tē) *n.* cleverness; inventiveness

Reading Strategy
Comparing and Contrasting Compare and contrast Don Quixote's armor with that of a traditional knight.

---

7. **Trebizond** (treb′ i zänd) in medieval times, a Greek empire off the southeast coast of the Black Sea.
8. **real** (rā äl′) former coin of Spain. In a real, there were eight *cuartos,* which means both "quarters" and "cracks."
9. **tantum pellis et ossa fuit** (tän′ tum pel′ is et äs′ə fo͞o′ it) Latin: "It was nothing but skin and bones."
10. **Alexander's Bucephalus** (byo͞o sef′ ə ləs) **or the Babieca** (bäb ē ā′kä) **of the Cid** Bucephalus was Alexander the Great's war horse; Babieca was the Cid's war horse.

Don Quixote Preparing His Armor; scene from the novel by Cervantes, Zacarías Velázquez González, Caylus Anticuario, Madrid, Spain

◀ **Critical Viewing**
In most cases, only the wealthy could afford the costly armor, horse, and training necessary to become a knight. Which details in this painting suggest that Don Quixote did not possess such wealth? **[Interpret]**

been when it was but a hack,[11] whereas now it was nothing other than the first and foremost of all the hacks in the world.

Having found a name for his horse that pleased his fancy, he then desired to do as much for himself, and this required another week, and by the end of that period he had made up his mind that he was henceforth to be known as Don Quixote, which, as has been stated, has led the authors of this veracious history to assume that his real name

---

11. hack horse used in all kinds of work and usually well worn out in service.

✔ **Reading Check**

Whose armor does Don Quixote use?

Dulcinea del Toboso from *Don Quixote* by Cervantes, 1839, Charles Robert Leslie

must undoubtedly have been Quijada, and not Quesada as others would have it. But remembering that the valiant Amadis was not content to call himself that and nothing more, but added the name of his kingdom and fatherland that he might make it famous also, and thus came to take the name Amadis of Gaul, so our good knight chose to add his place of origin and become "Don Quixote de la Mancha"; for by this means, as he saw it, he was making very plain his lineage and was conferring honor upon his country by taking its name as his own.

And so, having polished up his armor and made the morion over into a closed helmet, and having given himself and his horse a name, he naturally found but one thing lacking still: he must seek out a lady of whom he could become enamored; for a knight-errant without a lady-love was like a tree without leaves or fruit, a body without a soul.

"If," he said to himself, "as a punishment for my sins or by a stroke of fortune I should come upon some giant hereabouts, a thing that very commonly happens to knights-errant, and if I should slay him in a hand-to-hand encounter or perhaps cut him in two, or, finally, if I should vanquish and subdue him, would it not be well to have someone to whom I may send him as a present, in order that he, if he is living, may come in, fall upon his knees in front of my sweet lady, and say in a humble and submissive tone of voice, 'I, lady, am the giant Caraculiam-bro, lord of the island Malindrania, who has been overcome in single combat by that knight who never can be praised enough, Don Quixote de la Mancha, the same who sent me to present myself before your Grace that your Highness may dispose of me as you see fit'?"

Oh, how our good knight reveled in this speech, and more than ever when he came to think of the name that he should give his lady! As the story goes, there was a very good-looking farm girl who lived near by, with whom he had once been smitten, although it is generally believed that she never knew or suspected it. Her name was Aldonza Lorenzo, and it seemed to him that she was the one upon whom he should bestow the title of mistress of his thoughts. For her he wished a name that should not be <u>incongruous</u> with his own and that would convey the suggestion of a princess or a great lady; and, accordingly, he resolved to call her "Dulcinea del Toboso," she being a native of that place. A musical name to his ears, out of the ordinary and significant, like the others he had chosen for himself and his appurtenances.

Literary Analysis
Parody List three details from chivalric romances that are parodied in this paragraph.

incongruous (in´ kän´ groo əs) *adj.* inconsistent; lacking in harmony

Review and Assess

Thinking About the Selection

1. **Respond:** What do you find most humorous about Don Quixote's behavior? Why?

2. **(a) Recall:** What name does Don Quixote choose for his horse? **(b) Infer:** Identify two considerations Don Quixote makes as he chooses names. **(c) Speculate:** In what way might a simple change of name affect Don Quixote's entire world?

3. **(a) Recall:** Who is Aldonza Loreno? **(b) Analyze:** What role will she play in Don Quixote's adventures? **(c) Compare:** In what way does she fulfill the stereotype of a knight's ladylove?

4. **(a) Make a Judgment:** What theme do you think Don Quixote embodies? **(b) Support:** Which details in Chapter I reflect that theme?

5. **Evaluate:** Do you consider Don Quixote insane or the noble victim of an overactive imagination? Explain.

Chapter VII

Of the second sally of our good knight, Don Quixote de la Mancha.

. . . He remained at home very tranquilly for a couple of weeks, without giving sign of any desire to repeat his former madness. During that time he had the most pleasant conversations with his two old friends, the curate and the barber, on the point he had raised to the effect that what the world needed most was knights-errant and a revival of chivalry. The curate would occasionally contradict him and again would give in, for it was only by means of this artifice that he could carry on a conversation with him at all.

In the meanwhile Don Quixote was bringing his powers of persuasion to bear upon a farmer who lived near by, a good man—if this title may be applied to one who is poor—but with very few wits in his head. The short of it is, by pleas and promises, he got the hapless rustic to agree to ride forth with him and serve him as his squire.[1] Among other things, Don Quixote told him that he ought to be more than willing to go, because no telling what adventure might occur which would win them an island, and then he (the farmer) would be left to be the governor of it. As a result of these and other similar assurances, Sancho Panza forsook his wife and children and consented to take upon himself the duties of squire to his neighbor.

Next, Don Quixote set out to raise some money, and by selling this thing and pawning that and getting the worst of the bargain always, he finally scraped together a reasonable amount. He also asked a friend of his for the loan of a buckler and patched up his broken helmet as well as he could. He advised his squire, Sancho, of the day and hour when they were to take the road and told him to see to laying in a supply of those things that were most necessary, and, above all, not to forget the saddlebags. Sancho replied that he would see to all this and added that he was also thinking of taking along with him a very good ass that he had, as he was not much used to going on foot.

With regard to the ass, Don Quixote had to do a little thinking, trying to recall if any knight-errant had ever had a squire thus asininely mounted. He could not think of any but nevertheless he decided to take Sancho with the intention of providing him with a nobler steed as soon as occasion offered; he had but to <u>appropriate</u> the horse of the first discourteous knight he met. Having furnished himself with shirts and all

> **Literary Analysis**
> **Parody** In what ways is Sancho Panza a parody of an ideal knight's squire?

> **appropriate** (ə prō′ prē āt′)
> v. take for one's own use

---

1. **squire** (skwīr) knight's attendant.

the other things that the innkeeper had recommended, he and Panza rode forth one night unseen by anyone and without taking leave of wife and children, housekeeper or niece. They went so far that by the time morning came they were safe from discovery had a hunt been started for them.

✔Reading Check

What service does Don Quixote persuade Sancho Panza to provide?

Don Quixote and Sancho Panza Riding Clavileno, Zacarias Velazquez Gonzalez, Caylus Antiquario, Madrid, Spain

▲ **Critical Viewing** Compare and contrast the preparations for knighthood that Don Quixote makes to the training depicted in this painting. [**Compare and Contrast**]

Mounted on his ass, Sancho Panza rode along like a patriarch, with saddlebags and flask, his mind set upon becoming governor of that island that his master had promised him. Don Quixote determined to take the same route and road over the Campo de Montiel[2] that he had followed on his first journey; but he was not so uncomfortable this time, for it was early morning and the sun's rays fell upon them slantingly and accordingly did not tire them too much.

"Look, Sir Knight-errant," said Sancho, "your Grace should not forget that island you promised me; for no matter how big it is, I'll be able to govern it right enough."

"I would have you know, friend Sancho Panza," replied Don Quixote, "that among the knights-errant of old it was a very common custom to make their squires governors of the islands or the kingdoms that they won, and I am resolved that in my case so pleasing a usage shall not fall into desuetude.[3] I even mean to go them one better; for they very often, perhaps most of the time, waited until their squires were old men who had had their fill of serving their masters during bad days and worse nights, whereupon they would give them the title of count, or marquis at most, of some valley or province more or less. But if you live and I live, it well may be that within a week I shall win some kingdom with others dependent upon it, and it will be the easiest thing in the world to crown you king of one of them. You need not marvel at this, for all sorts of unforeseen things happen to knights like me, and I may readily be able to give you even more than I have promised."

"In that case," said Sancho Panza, "if by one of those miracles of which your Grace was speaking I should become king, I would certainly send for Juana Gutiérrez, my old lady, to come and be my queen, and the young ones could be infantes."[4]

"There is no doubt about it," Don Quixote assured him.

"Well, I doubt it," said Sancho, "for I think that even if God were to rain kingdoms upon the earth, no crown would sit well on the head of Mari Gutiérrez,[5] for I am telling you, sir, as a queen she is not worth two maravedis.[6] She would do better as a countess, God help her."

"Leave everything to God, Sancho," said Don Quixote, "and he will give you whatever is most fitting; but I trust you will not be so pusillanimous[7] as to be content with anything less than the title of viceroy."

"That I will not," said Sancho Panza, "especially seeing that I have in your Grace so <u>illustrious</u> a master who can give me all that is suitable to me and all that I can manage."

illustrious (i lus´ trē əs) *adj.* distinguished or outstanding

2. **Campo de Montiel** (käm´ po dā mōn tyēl´) site of a major battle in Spain in 1369.
3. **desuetude** (des´ wi tood) *n.* disuse.
4. **infantes** (in fan´ tāz) sons of Spanish or Portuguese monarchs.
5. **Mari Gutiérrez** Sancho Panza's wife (also called Juana Gutiérrez).
6. **maravedis** (mar´ ə vä dēz) former Spanish coin of trivial monetary value.
7. **pusillanimous** (pyoo´ si lan´ ə məs) *adj.* cowardly.

Chapter VIII

Of the good fortune which the valorous Don Quixote had in the terrifying and never-before-imagined adventure of the windmills, along with other events that deserve to be suitably recorded.

At this point they caught sight of thirty or forty windmills which were standing on the plain there, and no sooner had Don Quixote laid eyes upon them than he turned to his squire and said, "Fortune is guiding our affairs better than we could have wished; for you see there before you, friend Sancho Panza, some thirty or more lawless giants with whom I mean to do battle. I shall deprive them of their lives, and with the spoils from this encounter we shall begin to enrich ourselves; for this is righteous warfare, and it is a great service to God to remove so accursed a breed from the face of the earth."

"What giants?" said Sancho Panza.

"Those that you see there," replied his master, "those with the long arms some of which are as much as two leagues[8] in length."

"But look, your Grace, those are not giants but windmills, and what appear to be arms are their wings which, when whirled in the breeze, cause the millstone to go."

"It is plain to be seen," said Don Quixote, "that you have had little experience in this matter of adventures. If you are afraid, go off to one side and say your prayers while I am engaging them in fierce, unequal combat."

Saying this, he gave spurs to his steed Rocinante, without paying any heed to Sancho's warning that these were truly windmills and not giants that he was riding forth to attack. Nor even when he was close upon them did he perceive what they really were, but shouted at the top of his lungs, "Do not seek to flee, cowards and vile creatures that you are, for it is but a single knight with whom you have to deal!"

At that moment a little wind came up and the big wings began turning.

"Though you flourish as many arms as did the giant Briareus," said Don Quixote when he perceived this, "you still shall have to answer to me."

He thereupon commended himself with all his heart to his lady Dulcinea, beseeching her to succor him in this peril; and, being well covered with his shield and with his lance at rest, he bore down upon them at a full gallop and fell upon the first mill that stood in his way, giving a thrust at the wing, which was whirling at such a speed that his lance was broken into bits and both horse and horseman went rolling over the plain, very much battered indeed. Sancho upon his donkey came hurrying to his master's assistance as fast as he could, but when he reached the spot, the knight was unable to move, so great was the shock with which he and Rocinante had hit the ground.

---

8. **league** unit of distance measuring approximately 3.5 miles.

Reading Strategy
Comparing and Contrasting Do you think that, as a knight, Don Quixote is an effective role model for his squire? Why or why not?

Reading Strategy
Comparing and Contrasting Do you think the outcome of Don Quixote's battle is different from that which a real knight would experience? Explain.

✔Reading Check

What are the giants that Don Quixote intends to fight?

"God help us!" exclaimed Sancho, "did I not tell your Grace to look well, that those were nothing but windmills, a fact which no one could fail to see unless he had other mills of the same sort in his head?"

"Be quiet, friend Sancho," said Don Quixote. "Such are the fortunes of war, which more than any other are subject to constant change. What is more, when I come to think of it, I am sure that this must be the work of that magician Frestón, the one who robbed me of my study and my books, and who has thus changed the giants into windmills in order to deprive me of the glory of overcoming them, so great is the enmity that he bears me; but in the end his evil arts shall not prevail against this trusty sword of mine."

"May God's will be done," was Sancho Panza's response. And with the aid of his squire the knight was once more mounted on Rocinante, who stood there with one shoulder half out of joint. And so, speaking of the adventure that had just befallen them, they continued along the Puerto Lápice highway; for there, Don Quixote said, they could not fail to find many and varied adventures, this being a much traveled thoroughfare. The only thing was, the knight was exceedingly downcast over the loss of his lance.

"I remember," he said to his squire, "having read of a Spanish knight by the name of Diego Pérez de Vargas, who, having broken his sword in battle, tore from an oak a heavy bough or branch and with it did such feats of valor that day, and pounded so many Moors, that he came to be known as Machuca, and he and his descendants from that day forth have been called Vargas y Machuca. I tell you this because I too intend to provide myself with just such a bough as the one he wielded, and with it I propose to do such exploits that you shall deem yourself fortunate to have been found worthy to come with me and behold and witness things that are almost beyond belief."

"God's will be done," said Sancho. "I believe everything that your Grace says; but straighten yourself up in the saddle a little, for you seem to be slipping down on one side, owing, no doubt, to the shaking-up that you received in your fall."

"Ah, that is the truth," replied Don Quixote, "and if I do not speak of my sufferings, it is for the reason that it is not permitted knights-errant to complain of any wound whatsoever, even though their bowels may be dropping out."

"If that is the way it is," said Sancho, "I have nothing more to say; but, God knows, it would suit me better if your Grace did complain when something hurts him. I can assure you that I mean to do so, over the least little thing that ails me—that is, unless the same rule applies to squires as well."

Don Quixote laughed long and heartily over Sancho's simplicity, telling him that he might complain as much as he liked and where and when he liked, whether he had good cause or not; for he had read nothing to the contrary in the ordinances of chivalry.[9] Sancho then called

Literary Analysis
Parody List three "things that are almost beyond belief" that Don Quixote has already experienced.

---

9. ordinances of chivalry codes, or rules, of knighthood.

712 ◆ *The Renaissance and Rationalism*

Don Quixote and the Windmill, Francisco J. Torrome, Bonhams, London

◀ **Critical Viewing**
Which details from the story has the artist incorporated to make this work humorous? **[Analyze]**

his master's attention to the fact that it was time to eat. The knight replied that he himself had no need of food at the moment, but his squire might eat whenever he chose. Having been granted this permission, Sancho seated himself as best he could upon his beast, and, taking out from his saddlebags the provisions that he had stored there, he rode along leisurely behind his master, munching his victuals and taking a good, hearty swig now and then at the leather flask in a manner that might well have caused the biggest-bellied tavernkeeper of Málaga to envy him. Between drafts he gave not so much as a thought to any promise that his master might have made him, nor did he look upon it as any hardship, but rather as good sport, to go in quest of adventures however hazardous they might be.

The short of the matter is, they spent the night under some trees, from one of which Don Quixote tore off a withered bough to serve him as a lance, placing it in the lance head from which he had removed the broken one. He did not sleep all night long for thinking of his lady Dulcinea; for this was in accordance with what he had read in his books, of men of arms in the forest or desert places who kept a wakeful vigil, sustained by the memory of their ladies fair. Not so with Sancho, whose stomach was full, and not with chicory water. He fell into a dreamless slumber, and had not his master called him, he would not have been awakened either by the rays of the sun in his face or by the many birds who greeted the coming of the new day with their merry song.

Upon arising, he had another go at the flask, finding it somewhat more flaccid than it had been the night before, a circumstance which grieved his heart, for he could not see that they were on the way to remedying the deficiency within any very short space of time. Don Quixote did not wish any breakfast; for, as has been said, he was in the habit of nourishing himself on savorous memories. They then set out once more

Reading Strategy
Comparing and Contrasting In what ways do Don Quixote and Sancho Panza accurately imitate the lifestyle of a knight and his squire?

✔**Reading Check**
Where did Don Quixote spend the night?

along the road to Puerto Lápice, and around three in the afternoon they came in sight of the pass that bears that name.

"There," said Don Quixote as his eyes fell upon it, "we may plunge our arms up to the elbow in what are known as adventures. But I must warn you that even though you see me in the greatest peril in the world, you are not to lay hand upon your sword to defend me, unless it be that those who attack me are rabble and men of low degree, in which case you may very well come to my aid; but if they be gentlemen, it is in no wise permitted by the laws of chivalry that you should assist me until you yourself shall have been dubbed a knight."

"Most certainly, sir," replied Sancho, "your Grace shall be very well obeyed in this; all the more so for the reason that I myself am of a peaceful disposition and not fond of meddling in the quarrels and feuds of others. However, when it comes to protecting my own person, I shall not take account of those laws of which you speak, seeing that all laws, human and divine, permit each one to defend himself whenever he is attacked."

"I am willing to grant you that," assented Don Quixote, "but in this matter of defending me against gentlemen you must restrain your natural impulses."

"I promise you I shall do so," said Sancho. "I will observe this precept as I would the Sabbath day."

Review and Assess

Thinking About the Selection

1. **Respond:** Which aspects of Don Quixote's appearance or behavior—if any—do you find endearing? Explain.

2. **(a) Recall:** What promise does Don Quixote make to convince Sancho Panza to be his squire? **(b) Speculate:** Do you think this promise will be fulfilled? Why or why not?

3. **(a) Recall:** What reasons does Don Quixote give for fighting the windmills? **(b) Infer:** What characteristics of the windmills convince him that they are worthy foes? **(c) Interpret:** What does Sancho Panza mean when he says Don Quixote has "other mills of the same sort in his head"?

4. **(a) Infer:** Why is Sancho Panza a particularly helpful squire to Don Quixote? **(b) Draw Conclusions:** Why do you think Sancho Panza stays with Don Quixote even after realizing that Don Quixote has lost touch with reality?

5. **Speculate:** For which careers might it be considered an asset to have a vivid imagination like that of Don Quixote?

Review and Assess

Literary Analysis

Parody

1. (a) List three characteristics of a medieval romance that *Don Quixote* **parodies.** (b) What details indicate that the parody is affectionate or gentle? (c) In what way does Cervantes suggest his admiration for chivalric tales? Explain.

2. Using the chart shown below, identify details from the selection that parody elements of a real knight's life. Indicate how Don Quixote's personality or circumstances influence the parody.

Real Knight	Details	Don Quixote's Influence
Training		
Weapons		
Ladylove		

Connecting Literary Elements

3. (a) Identify three events that suggest a struggle between reality and fantasy. (b) What **theme** or insight into life do these events reveal?

4. (a) In what ways does Don Quixote embody the theme that a vivid imagination makes a life richer? (b) Do you agree with this theme? Why or why not?

5. (a) List two ways in which Sancho Panza is a realist—someone who sees the world as it is. (b) What theme does he embody?

Reading Strategy

Comparing and Contrasting

6. (a) **Compare and contrast** the appearance, attitude, and motives of Don Quixote and Sancho Panza as they embark on their quest. (b) Do you think their personalities complement each other, or are their differences obstacles to be overcome? Explain.

7. In what ways is Don Quixote, at least in his own mind, similar to the knights of old?

Extend Understanding

8. **Career Connection:** What careers require the kind of determination Don Quixote needed to become a knight? Explain.

Quick Review

A **parody** is an imitation of another work of literature for amusement or for instruction.

A **theme** is a central message or idea revealed through a literary work.

To **compare and contrast,** note the similarities and differences between two things.

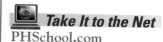 **Take It to the Net**
PHSchool.com

Take the interactive self-test online to check your understanding of this selection.

Integrate Language Skills

Vocabulary Development Lesson

Word Analysis: Latin Root *-ject-*

The Latin root *-ject-* means "to throw." If you make a *conjecture*, you "throw in," or offer, a thought or a guess. Each numbered word below contains the root *-ject-*. Match each word with the letter of the correct definition.

1. rejection
   (*re-* = back)
2. inject
   (*in-* = to bring in)
3. project
   (*pro-* = before, or forward)
4. trajectory
   (*tra-* = across)

a. to throw forward
b. the condition of being thrown back
c. the path of something thrown through space
d. to throw or put into

Concept Development: Synonyms

Review the vocabulary list on page 699. Then, for each item below, identify the vocabulary word with the closest meaning.

1. theories
2. confiscate
3. shallow affection
4. composition
5. imagination
6. famous
7. unsuitable

Spelling Strategy

The prefix *im-* or *in-*, meaning "not," changes to *ir-* when it is added to words beginning with *r*: *irreparable* = not able to be repaired; *irregular* = not regular. Use the prefix *ir-* to write the words for each definition below.

1. not reverent
2. not refutable

Grammar and Style Lesson

Gerunds

A **gerund** is a verb form ending in *-ing* that acts as a noun. Gerunds can perform all the roles of a noun in a sentence: subject, direct or indirect object, object of a preposition, and predicate nominative.

Subject: *Jousting* becomes a challenge, for he owns no lance.

Direct Object: Sancho Panza wants *fighting* the windmills to end peacefully.

Object of a Preposition: Don Quixote is an early riser and fond of *hunting*.

Predicate Nominative: Don Quixote's favorite pastime is *reading*.

Practice Identify each gerund below, and name its function in the sentence.

1. Smashing the makeshift armor with his sword gave Don Quixote no pleasure.
2. He commends the author's way of ending his books.
3. On his journey, Don Quixote tries attacking windmills.
4. Eating is one of Sancho's greatest pleasures.
5. The foremost goal of a squire is supporting his knight.

Writing Application Write four sentences describing the activities of a knight-errant. Use a gerund in each sentence, underlining the gerund and identifying its use in the sentence.

WG *Prentice Hall Writing and Grammar Connection: Diamond Level, Chapter 19, Section 2*

Writing Lesson

Profile of a Comic Hero

A hero in literature is often a very serious character on an important quest. In *Don Quixote*, however, Cervantes reinvented this character by creating a comic hero. In the spirit of *Don Quixote*, create your own comic hero and write a profile of his or her idiosyncrasies and achievements.

Prewriting Start by creating a chart like the one shown to categorize the traits of your comic hero. Then, give an example of each trait in action.

Model: Gathering Details

Trait	Trait in Action

Drafting Begin your profile with a catchy introduction, such as a quotation or an anecdote that illustrates a humorous quality of your hero. Then, present the traits of your hero and specific examples of each.

Revising Compare the details you gathered in your chart against your draft. Keep Cervantes's model in mind, and make sure that you have provided enough information to convey your hero's comic qualities. If necessary, add further details to develop those traits.

WG Prentice Hall Writing and Grammar Connection: Diamond Level, Chapter 6, Section 4

Extension Activities

Listening and Speaking Work with a partner to **role-play** the scene in which Sancho Panza tries to talk Don Quixote out of attacking the windmills. Use the following tips to prepare your scene:

- Make a few notes to capture the personality of the character you will role-play.
- Adjust your voice to reflect the emotions being expressed.
- Decide how, if at all, you will refer to his transformation.
- Speak directly to your partner as if you are having a conversation.

Present the scene for the class. **[Group Activity]**

Research and Technology Create a **visual essay** on the subject of heroes. Use computer programs such as music or imaging software to enhance your essay. Include scanned or downloaded images, and write captions that illustrate how your examples relate to the central message about heroes. Display your essay for the class.

 **Take It to the Net** PHSchool.com

Go online for an additional research activity using the Internet.

Prepare to Read

The Fox and the Crow ◆ The Oak and the Reed

Jean de La Fontaine (1621–1695)

An early French example of the somewhat absent-minded professor, Jean de La Fontaine (zhän de là fōn ten′) delighted his seventeenth-century audience, as well as later generations, with his outpouring of short stories, poems, and fables. While learning to compose verses, La Fontaine dabbled with the possibilities of studying law, entering the priesthood, or following his father's profession of forest ranger before he finally settled on a literary career. An admirer of ancient poets and playwrights, La Fontaine began publishing his own stories in his early thirties and continued to write for nearly forty years.

Patrons of the Arts Like many creative people of the era, La Fontaine depended upon patrons for his room and board. He enjoyed the semipermanent patronage of various hosts and hostesses, choosing to remain in the stimulating circles of Paris rather than with his wife and son in his quiet hometown of Château Thierry. During his long residency in the French capital, he met and befriended some of the greatest minds of the age, including Racine, Molière, and Boileau. In 1683, after many years of failed attempts, the poet was finally elected to the French Academy, the inner circle to which French writers aspired.

La Fontaine wrote in a variety of genres and styles, including prose tales, religious poetry, letters, and even an epitaph for his friend Molière. It is his vast collections of verse fables, however, for which La Fontaine is best remembered.

Words of Wisdom La Fontaine was a voracious reader of histories and literature. In fact, his own writings reflect the influences of Homer, Plato, and Boccaccio, among others. Many of La Fontaine's poems are adaptations of other works. Most contain quirky statements of ethics and philosophy, often in the form of homilies, or wise sayings. One of the major sources of his stories is Aesop, a sixth-century B.C. Greek storyteller of beast fables. A much-loved work by both authors, "The Ant and the Grasshopper," is a moralistic yet entertaining tale that contrasts the frolicsome grasshopper with the frugal, hard-working ant who collects stores of food to carry him through the winter.

Virtues and Vices La Fontaine's succinct, homespun animal stories address human idiosyncrasies, such as cowardice, curiosity, greed, and laziness. Stopping short of heavy-handed preaching, the stories contain common-sense reminders that delight as they instruct. La Fontaine used a wide range of nonhuman characters in his fables: ants, cats, wolves, trees, and mice are just a few. By putting animals in the place of humans, La Fontaine creates droll restatements of themes that continue to capture the imagination of his readers.

La Fontaine's 238 fables are so popular that French schoolchildren memorize them in their entirety and dramatize them as recital pieces. The French language is heavily salted with La Fontaine's witty aphorisms, such as "The sign brings customers," "A hungry stomach cannot hear," and "On the wings of Time grief flies away."

Preview

Connecting to the Literature

Winnie the Pooh, Snoopy, Garfield, Roadrunner, Wile E. Coyote, and the animal characters of Dr. Seuss—all figures from children's literature and cartoons—pass along useful bits of wisdom wrapped in laughter and entertainment. The seventeenth-century poetry of La Fontaine presents advice in a similar format.

Literary Analysis

Fables

Whether in the form of a poem or a short story, a **fable** dramatizes a simple lesson or principle of behavior. Most fables share the following elements:

- creatures—animals or inanimate objects—who speak and interact as though they were human
- a clearly worded moral at either the beginning or the end
- a single compressed episode
- an implied frailty or fault of character that is often the object of satire

Look for these characteristics in the fables of La Fontaine.

Comparing Literary Works

Because many fables include creatures as main characters, these works often employ **personification,** a type of figurative language in which a nonhuman subject is given human characteristics. For example, in "The Oak and the Reed," the oak tree has a conversation with his neighbor, the reed. By giving human qualities to nonhumans, La Fontaine subtly charms his readers, teaching them valuable life lessons from the experiences of imaginary beings. As you read the poems in this grouping, note the variety and degree of human responses the creatures possess.

Reading Strategy

Drawing Conclusions

La Fontaine does not directly state a moral or lesson to be learned from his fables. Instead, he allows readers to **draw conclusions** about the meaning of his works. To draw conclusions, consider the details of the fable, and use them to infer a larger message or meaning. Use a chart like the one shown to determine the moral, or general truth, that La Fontaine's fable teaches.

Vocabulary Development

buffeted (buf´ it id) *v.* struck sharply (p. 723)

hazards (haz´ ərdz) *n.* dangers (p. 723)

impervious (im pʉr´ vē əs) *adj.* not affected by, or unable to be damaged (p. 724)

prone (prōn) *adj.* lying face downward (p. 724)

The Fox and the Crow

Jean de La Fontaine *translated by Marianne Moore*

Background

La Fontaine's fables were well suited to the Age of Reason. In them, he instructs the reader in prudent living, basing his aphorisms on the mind-over-emotions philosophy of seventeenth-century moralists. A key feature of these fables is the logical and carefully worded statement of advice—or moral—on such ethical issues as integrity, diligence, compromise, and pride. Although his poems seem simple and light, La Fontaine characteristically dwells on the dangers that lurk in seemingly innocent surroundings.

On his airy perch among the branches
    Master Crow was holding cheese in his beak.
Master Fox, whose pose suggested fragrances,[1]
    Said in language which of course I cannot speak,
5   "Aha, superb Sir Ebony, well met.
How black! who else boasts your metallic jet!
        If your warbling[2] were unique,
        Rest assured, as you are sleek,
One would say that our wood had hatched nightingales."
10 All aglow, Master Crow tried to run a few scales,
        Risking trills and intervals,
Dropping the prize as his huge beak sang false.
The fox pounced on the cheese and remarked, "My dear sir,
        Learn that every flatterer
15   Lives at the flattered listener's cost:
A lesson worth more than the cheese that you lost."
        The tardy learner, smarting under ridicule,
Swore he'd learned his last lesson as somebody's fool.

---

1. **fragrances** false and devious charm.
2. **warbling** melodious singing.

The Crow and the Fox, illustration for *Fables* by Jean de La Fontaine, Private Collection

▲ **Critical Viewing** Identify details in this illustration that might interest young readers of La Fontaine's poems. **[Analyze]**

The Oak and the Reed

Jean de La Fontaine
translated by **Marianne Moore**

The oak said to the reed, "You grow
Too unprotectedly. Nature has been unfair;
A tiny wren[1] alights, and you are bending low;
    If a fitful breath of air
5   Should freshen till ripples show,
    You heed her and lower your head;
My form not only makes shade where the sun would play
But like the Caucasus[2] it does not sway.
    However it is <u>buffeted</u>.
10 Your so-called hurricanes are too faint to fear.
Would that you'd been born beneath this towering tent I've made,
    Which could afford you ample shade;
    Your <u>hazards</u> would not be severe:
    I'd shield you when the lightning played;
15   But grow you will, time and again,
On the misty fringe of the wind's domain.
I perceive that you are grievously oppressed."

---

1. **wren** (ren) small, sparrowlike songbird.
2. **Caucasus** (kô′ kə səs) mountain range between southeastern Europe and western Asia.

buffeted (buf′ it id) *v.* struck sharply

hazards (haz′ ərdz) *n.* dangers

Literary Analysis
Fables What human foible, or weakness, does the oak possess?

✔ Reading Check
From what would the oak shield the reed?

◀ **Critical Viewing** Which images in the poem match details visible in the photograph? Explain. **[Connect]**

The rush[3] said, "Bless you for fearing that I might be distressed;
    It is you alone whom the winds should alarm.
20 I bend and do not break. You've seemed consistently
    <u>Impervious</u> to harm—
    Erect when blasts rushed to and fro;
As for the end, who can foresee how things will go?"
Relentless wind was on them instantly—
25   A fury of destruction
Which the North had nursed in some haunt known to none.
    The bulrush bent, but not the tree.
    Confusion rose to a roar,
    Until the hurricane threw <u>prone</u>
30 That thing of kingly height whose head had all but touched God's
                  throne—

Who had shot his root to the threshold of Death's door.

---

3. **rush** *n.* reed.

impervious (im pur′ vē əs) *adj.* not affected by, or unable to be damaged

prone (prōn) *adj.* lying face downward

Review and Assess

Thinking About the Selections

1. **Respond:** Which of these fables do you think has the more important or useful moral? Why?

2. **(a) Recall:** What is the situation in "The Fox and the Crow"? **(b) Interpret:** What is the fox's strategy for getting what he wants? **(c) Draw Conclusions:** Do you think the crow learned the value of humility from his experience? Why or why not?

3. **(a) Recall:** Which of the fox's physical traits does the fable reveal? **(b) Interpret:** Why is the fox's intelligence a featured characteristic? **(c) Speculate:** Why do you think the speaker uses a fox in this fable?

4. **(a) Recall:** Which of the two characters in "The Oak and the Reed" speaks more? **(b) Infer:** What does this suggest about the character of the oak tree?

5. **(a) Recall:** Is the oak or the reed better able to withstand the storm? **(b) Analyze:** What physical trait does the reed possess that the oak does not? **(c) Speculate:** What does this fable suggest about the traits necessary for survival in a harsh world?

6. **Connect:** In what ways do the morals of these two fables apply to life today?

Review and Assess

Literary Analysis

Fables

1. (a) Compare the elements of a **fable** found in each of the poems using a Venn diagram like the one shown below. (b) In what ways do the poems differ?

The Fox and the Crow   The Oak and the Reed

2. Which lines in "The Fox and the Crow" make it clear that the poem is a fable?

3. (a) Besides the oak and the reed, what nonhuman contributes to the moral in "The Oak and the Reed"? (b) What moral does this character teach?

Comparing Literary Works

4. (a) List three examples of **personification** in "The Fox and the Crow." (b) In what typically human way does the crow respond to the fox's flattery? (b) What type of person might the fox represent?

5. (a) Besides physical traits, what other methods of personification are used in "The Oak and the Reed"? (b) In what way is the sun personified?

6. In what ways does the use of personification help these fables teach ethical issues?

Reading Strategy

Drawing Conclusions

7. (a) Why does the crow consider himself "somebody's fool"? (b) What **conclusions** can you draw from his experience?

8. (a) What role does extreme weather play in the lesson the oak learns? (b) What conclusions can you draw from the fable about man's ability to withstand the forces of nature?

Extend Understanding

9. **Science Connection:** Like the reed, which plants possess highly specialized abilities to survive in difficult circumstances?

Quick Review

A **fable** is a brief work that dramatizes a simple lesson or principle of behavior.

Personification is the literary technique of applying human characteristics to nonhuman or inanimate objects.

To **draw conclusions,** note details in a work and infer a larger message or meaning from them.

 **Take It to the Net**
PHSchool.com

Take the interactive self-test online to check your understanding of these selections.

Integrate Language Skills

Vocabulary Development Lesson

Word Analysis: Latin Prefix *im-*

The word *impervious* contains the prefix *im-*, meaning "no, not, without." *Impervious*, therefore, means "not affected by." Use the meaning of this prefix to define the words below.

1. immature
2. immortal
3. imprudent
4. immoderate

Spelling Strategy

The ending *-ious* is used to form an adjective, like the word *impervious*. Although the spelling *ious* is more common, some adjectives are spelled with *eous*. Add *-ious* or *-eous* to each item below. Use a dictionary to check your work.

1. subterran-   2. delic-   3. prodig-

Fluency: Sentence Completions

Review the words from the vocabulary list on page 719. Then, copy each sentence below, filling in the blanks with the appropriate vocabulary word.

1. The old tree had faced many _____, yet it remained strong.
2. The tree seemed _____ to the forces of nature.
3. Despite being _____ by the wind and rain, the oak stood straight and tall.
4. The delicate reeds, however, were often laid _____ by the gales, but their resilient stems soon straightened again.

Grammar and Style Lesson

Adjective Clauses Using *who, whom,* and *whose*

Subordinate clauses contain a subject and a verb, and they act as a single part of speech. **Adjective clauses** are subordinate clauses that modify nouns or pronouns. They are often introduced by the relative pronouns *who, whom,* and *whose*.

> **Example:** Master Fox, *whose pose suggested fragrances*, said in language which of course I cannot speak . . . (modifies "Master Fox")

Practice Identify the adjective clause and the word it modifies in each of the following sentences.

1. The crow, who was as black as ebony, sat holding cheese in his beak.
2. The crow was flattered by the fox, whom the crow never suspected of being sly and deceitful.
3. The reed, whose slender form bent to the earth, waited for the storm to pass.
4. The mighty gale, whose fury blasted the tree and the tender reeds, finally destroyed the great oak.
5. After the storm passed, the reed, who was once again standing straight, saw that the tree had fallen.

Writing Application Write four sentences about animals. Include an adjective clause in each sentence, and identify both the clause and the noun it modifies.

WG Prentice Hall Writing and Grammar Connection: Diamond Level, Chapter 19, Section 3

Writing Lesson

A Children's Story

Fables and stories with animal characters have always been popular with children. Use one of La Fontaine's poems as a basis for a fully developed children's story that teaches the same lesson as the original poem. Use additional characters if you wish.

Prewriting Start by writing an outline of the plot, or main events, of La Fontaine's fable. Then, jot down notes about his characters, adding your own ideas to describe how they sound, look, and move.

Drafting As you draft, use vivid details and dialogue to make your story entertaining. Include descriptions of each character.

Revising Compare your draft with the original poem to be sure the moral of the story is clear. Make certain that all the dialogue is set in quotation marks and that other punctuation in your fable is used correctly.

Writing Model: Punctuating for Dialogue

"I see you have a lovely piece of cheese," said the fox in a greasy voice. "It must surely be delicious!"

"Grt hgach tuk," garbled the crow, whose beak was full of cheddar.

"Tell me, Sir Ebony," said the fox, "was that your beautiful warbling I heard this morning?"

> To make dialogue clear, all punctuation that is part of the dialogue is set inside the quotation marks.

WG Prentice Hall Writing and Grammar Connection: Diamond Level, Chapter 27, Section 4

Extension Activities

Listening and Speaking Work with a partner to prepare a **dramatic reading** of one of La Fontaine's poems. Use these storytelling strategies to enliven your reading:

- Sit at eye level with your audience.
- Adjust your voice and your facial expressions to reflect the characters.
- Use props, such as plants or stuffed animals, to add interest.

Present the reading to the kindergarten class at a local school. **[Group Activity]**

Research and Technology Use the Internet or library resources to compose a **research report** on fables. Describe the types of animals that the stories feature and the lessons that they teach. Compare your findings with La Fontaine's pieces.

 **Take It to the Net** PHSchool.com

Go online for an additional research activity using the Internet.

Great Minds Do Not Think Alike

The power of the mind itself fascinated the greatest thinkers of the Age of Rationalism.

Toward the end of the sixteenth century, the French essayist Michel de Montaigne created a medallion with a motto encapsulating his life and work: *Que scay-je?* or "What do I know?"

If Montaigne had lived during the Middle Ages, he might have asked, "What do I *believe*?" If he had lived during the Romantic Age, he might have asked, "What do I *feel*?" His question "What do I *know*?" is the central theme of his time—the Age of Rationalism.

During the Renaissance, artists and thinkers celebrated human potential. The creative explosion of the fourteenth, fifteenth, and sixteenth centuries reflected a new confidence in human nature. By the seventeenth and eighteenth centuries, Europeans recognized the vast power of the mind itself. The power of thought forced tradition and complacency deeper into the shadows.

Niccolò Machiavelli—The Mind as Weapon The idea of the mind as a political tool found practical expression in the writings of Niccolò Machiavelli (1469–1527). As a diplomat for the Florentine republic, Machiavelli observed firsthand how governments should, and should not, be run. After enduring prison and exile, he settled down on a small farm, where he wrote one of the world's most influential books of political theory—*The Prince.*

In Machiavelli's fiercely realistic view, a ruler maintains control not with goodness but with strength and mental agility. A Machiavellian ruler must possess both force and cunning and use them without sentiment. For Renaissance humanists, a good king had been an ideal Christian who loved his subjects and cherished peace. By contrast, Machiavelli's prince seeks first and foremost to retain and extend his power by any means that will work. He is wily, aggressive, and ruthless, and his greatest weapon is his mind.

Blaise Pascal—The Dialogue of Reason and Religion Blaise Pascal (1623–1662), French mathematician, physicist, and religious philosopher, pondered problems both earthly and heavenly. He manifested his mathematical genius at the age of twelve by independently rediscovering Euclid's first thirty-two propositions of geometry. He also engineered the world's first calculator.

Pascal sought harmony between mathematical certainty and moral truth. In 1657, he began writing his *Pensées*, short philosophical "thoughts" that integrate science and spirituality. Some of Pascal's *pensées* reveal his logical mind, while others reveal his more poetic side. All argue his fundamental idea that the true nature of humanity is a paradox—a logical contradiction.

Pascal's paradox is that the mind has vast power but is virtually powerless in comparison with the infinite. Human beings are, therefore, "incapable of absolute ignorance and of certain knowledge." As if to answer Montaigne's "What do I know?" Pascal believed that we do know many things, and yet we do not really know much at all. The *pensées* are a rational and beautifully articulated balance of humility and pride: "Man is but a reed, the weakest in nature, but he is a thinking reed."

John Locke—Reason and Revolution To the English philosopher John Locke (1632–1704), the human mind is a *tabula rasa*, or blank slate, and people are not born with innate ideas or moral precepts. Locke believed that everything we experience makes impressions on that blank slate. We then develop ideas by reflecting on those experiences. In this approach, called empiricism, the consciousness of every human being develops independently, based on personal experience, reflections, and decisions.

Locke was also a highly influential political philosopher. In his *Two Treatises of Government* (1690), Locke argued that people are free to choose their own government. Locke reasoned that government is not based on "myth, mysticism, and mystery"; rather, it has a rational purpose—to protect life, liberty, and property. If it fails, it may be overthrown. Thomas Jefferson and other founders of the American Republic were deeply influenced by Locke's ideas.

Jean-Jacques Rousseau—The Social Contract The most extraordinarily multifaceted mind to emerge during the Age of Rationalism was that of Jean-Jacques Rousseau (1712–1778). Orphan, footman, music teacher, tutor, encyclopedia writer, political philosopher, social critic, novelist, autobiographer, wanderer, radical, free spirit—Rousseau was all of these and more.

For Rousseau, civilization corrupted humanity's natural goodness. He believed that people are fundamentally noble and virtuous, but society has made it impossible for the best in human nature to flourish; therefore, a new social order needs to be created. In *The Social Contract* (1762), Rousseau outlined what that society ought to be—a state in which a ruler leads at the will of the people, who can revoke their support if they wish. This social contract achieved its most complete embodiment in American democracy.

Rousseau's belief in reason and his efforts to formulate the idea of a democratic society place him at the pinnacle of Enlightenment thought. His devotion to nature and his belief in the unique and passionate individual make him the intellectual bridge to the Age of the Romantics.

▼ **Critical Viewing**
In what way does this portrait of Rousseau reflect the philosopher's ideas? [Connect]

Prepare to Read

from Candide

Voltaire (1694–1778)

A lifelong social critic and champion of liberty, tolerance, and truth, François-Marie Arouet—who wrote under the pen name Voltaire (vôl ter′)—often invited trouble by questioning authority. Although he was imprisoned twice and spent many years in exile from his native land, he is still regarded as one of France's greatest writers and thinkers.

Man-About-Paris Voltaire grew up in the French capital of Paris in the waning years of King Louis XIV's reign. Although his family expected him to study law, he was more interested in literature and the theater. Clever and witty, he was an immediate success when his godfather introduced him to the best of Paris society after he left school. He attended all the trendy gatherings, and his short satirical poems were much quoted by fashionable Parisians.

Fame—and Prison In 1715, Louis XIV died, and his five-year-old great-grandson came to the French throne as Louis XV. Two years later, Voltaire was accused of penning satirical barbs criticizing the late king and the Duc d'Orléans, who was serving as regent, or acting ruler, for young Louis XV. As punishment, Voltaire was at first exiled, and then he was sent to the Bastille, the notorious Paris prison, for nearly a year.

He made the most of his prison stay by completing *Oedipe,* the first of his many tragic dramas, and beginning work on the *Henriade,* his epic poem in tribute to Henry IV. After Voltaire's release from prison, *Oedipe* was staged in Paris to much acclaim. It was also around this time that Voltaire adopted his famous pen name.

Voltaire's favor in Paris was short-lived, however. In 1725, never one to hold his tongue, he made the mistake of quarreling with the powerful Chevalier de Rohan. When Voltaire challenged Rohan to a duel, Voltaire was sent briefly to the Bastille again and then into exile from his homeland.

The English Influence Voltaire spent his exile in England, a nation he found more tolerant and open-minded than the France of his day. He especially admired the achievements of English scientist Sir Isaac Newton and the ideas of English philosopher John Locke, whose principles of liberty had helped justify England's Glorious Revolution of 1688. Voltaire concluded that the freedom of thought he found in England encouraged scientific advancement and thus helped the nation prosper. When he was allowed to return home, he produced his *Lettres philosophiques,* in which he compared England favorably to France. With its emphasis on reason, religious tolerance, and freedom of thought, the work is considered a landmark of the eighteenth-century Age of Enlightenment.

Later Years Voltaire considered himself an enemy of injustice; his determination to help others, his strong opinions, and his argumentative disposition caused him trouble throughout his life. In 1750, he was invited to Berlin by the Prussian leader Frederick the Great, but three years later he angered Frederick by mocking one of Prussia's leading scientists. In Geneva, Switzerland, the Calvinist religious leaders who at first welcomed him as a champion of religious tolerance were disturbed by some of his more radical ideas.

In 1758, just after writing his best-known work, the satirical novel *Candide,* Voltaire retired to Ferney, a property he had bought near Geneva. There, he lived in semiretirement for the last two decades of his life—writing, running the estate, instituting agricultural reforms, and, of course, getting into arguments with the locals.

Preview

Connecting to the Literature

Moviemakers and authors entertain the public with wildly comedic characters. *Candide* features such personalities, yet they serve a higher purpose: to expose social inequities and to suggest a means of escaping them.

Literary Analysis

Satire

Satire is writing that uses humor to expose and ridicule human foolishness. Although satirists take aim at individuals, institutions, types of behavior, or humanity in general, the ultimate goal of a satirical piece is to inspire positive change. *Candide* prompts readers to question the conditions of their lives by calling attention to social injustices such as corrupt political systems. As you read this selection, note cases of injustice or inhumanity just under the humorous surface of this work.

Connecting Literary Elements

Satirists ridicule their subjects by using tools such as **exaggeration, understatement,** and **faulty logic.** Consider these examples from the selection:

- *Exaggeration:* ". . . The Baron's castle was the best of castles. . . ."
- *Understatement:* ". . . the next day he drilled not so badly and received only twenty strokes [of the lash]."
- *Faulty logic:* "Observe that noses were made to wear spectacles: and so we have spectacles."

As you read, notice how the repeated use of these tools contributes to the humor and persuades a reader toward the speaker's point of view.

Reading Strategy

Connecting to Historical Context

When you **connect a work to its historical context,** you identify the ideas and events in a piece that may be responses to its era. To make the connection, use a chart like the one shown to list details from the story that reflect the time period. Then, consider the way the details connect to history.

Vocabulary Development

endowed (en dou̇d´) *v.* given, or provided with (p. 732)

candor (kan´ dər) *n.* open honesty and frankness (p. 732)

vivacity (vī vas´ ə tē) *n.* liveliness or animation (p. 734)

prodigy (präd´ ə jē) *n.* person of very great ability (p. 735)

clemency (klem´ ən sē) *n.* mercy toward an enemy or offender (p. 736)

from Candide

Voltaire *translated by Richard Aldington*

Background

Subtitled "Optimism," *Candide* is deeply rooted in historical events and ideas close to Voltaire's heart. For example, his work alludes to a devastating earthquake in Lisbon in 1755 and to a popular philosophy claiming that this world is the best of all possible worlds.

Candide is an innocent youth who suffers severe hardships as he searches for his beloved, Cunegonde. Along the way, Candide learns firsthand that life is often shaped by incomprehensible forces and by the cruelty and frivolity of the ruling classes.

CHAPTER I

*How Candide was brought up in a noble castle
and how he was expelled from the same*

In the castle of Baron Thunder-ten-tronckh in Westphalia[1] there lived a youth, <u>endowed</u> by Nature with the most gentle character. His face was the expression of his soul. His judgment was quite honest and he was extremely simple-minded; and this was the reason, I think, that he was named Candide. Old servants in the house suspected that he was the son of the Baron's sister and a decent honest gentleman of the neighborhood, whom this young lady would never marry because he could only prove seventy-one quarterings[2] and the rest of his genealogical tree was lost, owing to the injuries of time.

The Baron was one of the most powerful lords in Westphalia, for his castle possessed a door and windows. His Great Hall was even decorated with a piece of tapestry. The dogs in his stable-yards formed a pack of hounds when necessary; his grooms were his huntsmen; the village curate was his Grand Almoner. They all called him "My Lord," and laughed heartily at his stories.

The Baroness weighed about three hundred and fifty pounds, was therefore greatly respected, and did the honors of the house with a dignity which rendered her still more respectable. Her daughter Cunegonde, aged seventeen, was rosy-cheeked, fresh, plump and tempting. The Baron's son appeared in every respect worthy of his father. The tutor Pangloss was the oracle of the house, and little Candide followed his lessons with all the <u>candor</u> of his age and character.

endowed (en doud´) *v.* given, or provided with

**Literary Analysis
Satire** Identify two tools of satire in the first paragraph.

candor (kan´ dər) *n.* open honesty and frankness

---

1. **Baron . . . Westphalia** The Baron is a lesser member of nobility in a historic region of northwestern Germany.
2. **quarterings** divisions on a coat-of-arms indicating generations of noble or distinguished ancestry.

Pangloss taught metaphysico-theologo-cosmolonigology.[3] He proved admirably that there is no effect without a cause and that in this best of all possible worlds, My Lord the Baron's castle was the best of castles and his wife the best of all possible Baronesses.

"'Tis demonstrated," said he, "that things cannot be otherwise; for, since everything is made for an end, everything is necessarily for the best end. Observe that noses were made to wear spectacles; and so we have spectacles. Legs were visibly instituted to be breeched, and we have breeches. Stones were formed to be quarried and to build castles; and My Lord has a very noble castle; the greatest Baron in the province should have the best house; and as pigs were made to be eaten, we eat pork all the year round; consequently, those who have asserted that all is well talk nonsense; they ought to have said that all is for the best."

Candide listened attentively and believed innocently; for he thought Mademoiselle Cunegonde extremely beautiful, although he was never bold enough to tell her so. He decided that after the happiness of being born Baron of Thunder-ten-tronckh, the second degree of happiness was to be Mademoiselle Cunegonde; the third, to see her every day; and the fourth to listen to Doctor Pangloss, the greatest philosopher of the province and therefore of the whole world.

One day when Cunegonde was walking near the castle, in a little wood which was called The Park, she observed Doctor Pangloss in the bushes, giving a lesson in experimental physics to her mother's waiting-maid, a very pretty and docile brunette. Mademoiselle Cunegonde had a great inclination for science and watched breathlessly the reiterated experiments she witnessed; she observed clearly the Doctor's sufficient reason, the effects and the causes, and returned home very much excited, pensive, filled with the desire of learning, reflecting that she might be the sufficient reason of young Candide and that he might be hers.

On her way back to the castle she met Candide and blushed; Candide also blushed. She bade him good-morning in a hesitating voice; Candide replied without knowing what he was saying. Next day, when they left the table after dinner, Cunegonde and Candide found themselves behind a

▲ **Critical Viewing**
Which details in this engraving illustrate action from the story? **[Connect]**

✔**Reading Check**
What service does Pangloss provide to Candide and the Baron's family?

---

3. **metaphysico-theologo-cosmolonigology** Voltaire satirizes philosophical studies by inventing an entirely fake school of thought.

screen; Cunegonde dropped her handkerchief, Candide picked it up; she innocently held his hand; the young man innocently kissed the young lady's hand with remarkable <u>vivacity</u>, tenderness and grace; their lips met, their eyes sparkled, their knees trembled, their hands wandered. Baron Thunder-ten-tronckh passed near the screen, and, observing this cause and effect, expelled Candide from the castle by kicking him in the backside frequently and hard. Cunegonde swooned; when she recovered her senses, the Baroness slapped her in the face; and all was in consternation in the noblest and most agreeable of all possible castles.

CHAPTER II

What happened to Candide among the Bulgarians

Candide, expelled from the earthly paradise, wandered for a long time without knowing where he was going, turning up his eyes to Heaven, gazing back frequently at the noblest of castles which held the most beautiful of young Baronesses; he lay down to sleep supperless between two furrows in the open fields: it snowed heavily in large flakes. The next morning the shivering Candide, penniless, dying of cold and exhaustion, dragged himself towards the neighboring town, which was called Waldberghoff-trarbk-dikdorff. He halted sadly at the door of an inn. Two men dressed in blue noticed him.

"Comrade," said one, "there's a well-built young man of the right height." They went up to Candide and very civilly invited him to dinner.

"Gentlemen," said Candide with charming modesty, "you do me a great honor, but I have no money to pay my share."

"Ah, sir," said one of the men in blue, "persons of your figure and merit never pay anything; are you not five feet five tall?"

"Yes, gentlemen," said he, bowing, "that is my height."

"Ah, sir, come to table; we will not only pay your expenses, we will never allow a man like you to be short of money; men were only made to help each other."

"You are in the right," said Candide, "that is what Doctor Pangloss was always telling me, and I see that everything is for the best."

They begged him to accept a few crowns,[4] he took them and wished to give them an IOU, they refused to take it and all sat down to table.

"Do you not love tenderly . . ."

"Oh, yes," said he. "I love Mademoiselle Cunegonde tenderly."

"No," said one of the gentlemen." "We were asking if you do not tenderly love the King of the Bulgarians."

"Not a bit," said he, "for I have never seen him."

"What! He is the most charming of Kings, and you must drink his health."

"Oh, gladly, gentlemen."

And he drank.

vivacity (vī vas´ ə tē) *n.* liveliness or animation

Literary Analysis
Satire and Exaggeration
Which details in the paragraph might be exaggerations? Why?

---

4. **crowns** monetary units.

"That is sufficient," he was told. "You are now the support, the aid, the defender, the hero of the Bulgarians, your fortune is made and your glory assured."

They immediately put irons on his legs and took him to a regiment. He was made to turn to the right and left, to raise the ramrod[5] and return the ramrod, to take aim, to fire, to march double time, and he was given thirty strokes with a stick; the next day he drilled not quite so badly, and received only twenty strokes; the day after, he only had ten and was looked on as a <u>prodigy</u> by his comrades.

Candide was completely mystified and could not make out how he was a hero. One fine spring day he thought he would take a walk, going straight ahead, in the belief that to use his legs as he pleased was a

---

5. **ramrod** long rod used to tamp the charge of a muzzle-loading firearm.

Reading Strategy
Connecting to Historical Context In what way is bitterness toward Prussia reflected in this characterization of Prussia's military training?

prodigy (präd′ ə jē) *n.* person of very great ability

☑**Reading Check**
Which army does Candide join?

▼ **Critical Viewing**
Why might Candide consider it the best of all worlds to live in a castle such as this one? **[Speculate]**

from *Candide* 735

privilege of the human species as well as of animals. He had not gone two leagues when four other heroes, each six feet tall, fell upon him, bound him and dragged him back to a cell. He was asked by his judges whether he would rather be thrashed thirty-six times by the whole regiment or receive a dozen lead bullets at once in his brain. Although he protested that men's wills are free and that he wanted neither one nor the other, he had to make a choice; by virtue of that gift of God which is called *liberty*, he determined to run the gauntlet[6] thirty-six times and actually did so twice. There were two thousand men in the regiment. That made four thousand strokes which laid bare the muscles and nerves from his neck to his backside. As they were about to proceed to a third turn, Candide, utterly exhausted, begged as a favor that they would be so kind as to smash his head; he obtained this favor; they bound his eyes and he was made to kneel down. At that moment the King of the Bulgarians came by and inquired the victim's crime, and as this King was possessed of a vast genius, he perceived from what he learned about Candide that he was a young metaphysician[7] very ignorant in worldly matters, and therefore pardoned him with a <u>clemency</u> which will be praised in all newspapers and all ages. An honest surgeon healed Candide in three weeks with the ointments recommended by Dioscorides.[8] He had already regained a little skin and could walk when the King of the Bulgarians went to war with the King of the Abares.[9]

clemency (klem´ ən sē) *n.* mercy toward an enemy or offender

---

6. **gauntlet** (gônt´ lit) double row of soldiers armed with clubs or weapons used to strike an individual who ran between them.
7. **metaphysician** one who studies worldly matters, such as the order and nature of the universe.
8. **Dioscorides** (dī´ əs kor´ ə dēz´) Greek physician (c. 40–c. 90) and author of *De materia medica*, the definitive text about botany and pharmacology for more than 1500 years.
9. **Bulgarians . . . Abares** (ab ar ās´) In *Candide,* the Bulgarians are Frederic the Great's Prussian army, and the Abares are the French.

Review and Assess

Thinking About the Selection

1. **Respond:** Do you think that Candide's world is "the best of all possible worlds"? Why or why not?

2. **(a) Recall:** What details concerning the Baron and his family have earned them great respect? **(b) Analyze:** In what ways is Pangloss the perfect tutor for this family?

3. **(a) Recall:** Who are the "men dressed in blue" whom Candide meets at the inn? **(b) Analyze:** In what ways does Candide reveal his innocence as he speaks with them? **(c) Evaluate:** Why do you think Candide is made to look like such a simpleton?

4. **Apply:** What kinds of writing do authors use today to address social injustices like those satirized in *Candide*?

Review and Assess

Literary Analysis

Satire

1. (a) Identify two kinds of social injustices that are **satirized** in *Candide*. (b) What types of social reform do you think the work attempts to inspire? Explain.
2. What attitude is satirized in the statement, ". . . Doctor Pangloss, the greatest philosopher of the province and therefore of the whole world"?
3. What satirical message about political freedom does Candide reveal by choosing to run the gauntlet rather than be shot for deserting the Bulgarian army?

Connecting Literary Elements

4. (a) Use a chart like the one shown to identify at least one example of each of the tools of satire—**exaggeration, understatement,** and **faulty logic**—used in *Candide*.

Detail From *Candide*	Tool of Satire Used

   (b) What conclusions can you draw about the use of satirical tools in this work?
5. (a) Describe the ways in which humor is used as a tool of satire in this selection. (b) What risks do you think satirists take when using this tool to address serious issues? Explain.

Reading Strategy

Connecting to Historical Context

6. Connect two details about the Baron's family to the **historical context** of Voltaire's era.
7. (a) What philosophy of the day does Pangloss teach? (b) What effect might this philosophy have on a society that practices it over time? Explain.
8. Why do you think the Bulgarian army is represented in a critical light?

Extend Understanding

9. **Social Studies Connection:** In what ways is a satire such as *Candide* similar to political cartoons you might find in today's newspapers and magazines?

Quick Review

Satire uses humor to ridicule or criticize a specific subject and to inspire change.

To create satire, authors use various tools, such as **exaggeration, understatement,** and **faulty logic.**

To **connect works to their historical contexts,** note ideas, assumptions, and events that are specific to the selection's era.

 **Take It to the Net**
PHSchool.com

Take the interactive self-test online to check your understanding of this selection.

Integrate Language Skills

Vocabulary Development Lesson

Word Analysis: Latin Suffix -ity

The Latin suffix -ity means "quality or state of." For example, the word *vivacity* means "a quality or state of liveliness." Use your understanding of this suffix to define the following words:

1. anonymity
2. ingenuity
3. seniority
4. authenticity

Spelling Strategy

Although the word ending -er is more common, words that name a quality or a role, such as *candor* and *juror*, usually end in -or. Add the correct word ending to each item below. Use a dictionary to check your answers.

1. exhibit-
2. trait-
3. chamb-
4. mann-

Fluency: Sentence Completion

Review the words from the vocabulary list on page 731. Then, complete each sentence below with the correct word from the vocabulary list.

1. The volunteers' enthusiasm and _____ make difficult work more enjoyable for everyone.
2. She spoke with _____ about her hurt feelings.
3. The judge granted _____ to the remorseful offender.
4. The piano, flute, and violin were a few of the instruments mastered by the child _____.
5. Little money remained in the trust fund _____ by her parents.

Grammar and Style Lesson

Parallel Structure

Parallel structure, or parallelism, is the repetition of equal ideas in a similar grammatical form. Parallelism can involve the repeated use of words, phrases, clauses, or sentences.

Their lips met, *their* eyes sparkled, *their* knees trembled. . . .

Candide *listened attentively* and *believed innocently*. . . .

Practice Identify the parallel structures in the following sentences.

1. The Baron's castle was the best of castles and his wife, the best of Baronesses.
2. According to Dr. Pangloss, noses were made to wear glasses and legs were made to wear breeches.
3. While he was in the army, he learned to take aim, to fire, and to double up.
4. You are now the support, the aid, the defender, the hero of Bulgarians.
5. Your fortune is made and your glory is assured.

Writing Application Write four sentences describing your impression of Candide and Cunegonde, using parallel structures in each one. Then, identify the parallelism in your sentences.

Writing Lesson

Short Satirical Story

Satirists write about something they would like to change in the world. Choose a foolish behavior, a social injustice, or an institution you believe worthy of reform, and write a **short satirical story** that encourages people to bring about change.

Prewriting Use a chart like the one shown to organize your story. Start by identifying a subject. Then, list specific details that you want to satirize. Finally, state the suggested reform you hope your satire will inspire.

Writing Model: Organizing Details

| Subject | Details to Be Satirized | Reform |

Drafting As you draft your satire, use a variety of tools, such as exaggeration, faulty logic, and understatement. Remember that to be effective, the satire should be humorous.

Revising Check your finished draft against your prewriting chart, noting any details you may have omitted. Be sure that your story ends in a way that supports the purpose of your satire. Add more details or alter the ending if necessary.

W̶G̶ Prentice Hall Writing and Grammar Connection: Diamond Level, Chapter 5, Section 2

Extension Activities

Listening and Speaking Listen to selections from a musical version of *Candide*. Then, participate in a **group discussion** to determine the ways in which the music reflects Voltaire's written work. Be sure to address these questions:

- Does the music add to or detract from the story?
- Do the lyrics accurately represent the characters and events?

Compare your group's reactions to other groups' opinions. **[Group Activity]**

Research and Technology Find three political cartoons that use satire to make a point. You might check the editorial pages of major newspapers or some online magazines that cover politics and world events. Use the cartoons to create a **visual report** that explains what satire is and what is satirized in the cartoons.

 **Take It to the Net** PHSchool.com

Go online for an additional research activity using the Internet.

READING INFORMATIONAL MATERIALS

Feature Articles

About Feature Articles

Most people turn to newspapers for current information about recent events. Daily papers include news articles on local and world events, but they also include a variety of other types of information. For example, **feature articles** showcase various topics of interest and are written to inform and entertain the public. Unlike news articles that present information formally and objectively, features can be written in a more informal style. In addition, feature articles often include the opinion of the writer.

Because they are meant to entertain, feature articles usually present the lighter side of life, and they address topics that are less time-sensitive than those found in straightforward news articles. Here are some common topics for feature writers:

- The Arts
- Fashion
- Health
- Entertainment
- Unusual occurrences
- Family
- Leisure
- People

"Leonardo: The Eye, The Hand, The Mind" is a feature on an exhibit of the works of Leonardo da Vinci, one of the great masters of art in Renaissance Italy.

Reading Strategy

Evaluating Support

In addition to the information they showcase, feature articles often present a writer's opinion or evaluation of a topic. These opinions must be supported with evidence such as facts, statistics, observations, and examples. To determine whether you agree with the writer's opinions, **evaluate the support,** deciding whether or not the evidence is persuasive and valid. Use a chart like the one shown to list each opinion in the following feature. For each one, identify the details that support that opinion. Then, evaluate the support to decide whether the writer's opinion is valid.

Opinion	Support	Evaluation of Support
Cotter says Leonardo's strengths lie in art, science, engineering, and aesthetic theory.	Cotter lists Leonardo's accomplishments in hydrodynamics, anatomy, physics, astronomy, invention, and art.	The list of accomplishments supports Cotter's opinion that Leonardo's strengths lie in many areas.

The New York Times

January 24, 2003

Leonardo: The Eye, the Hand, the Mind

By Holland Cotter

> In the opening sentence, the writer expresses an opinion, an element that is often found in a feature article.

LEONARDO DA VINCI (1452–1519) is the Great Oz of European art. At least that's the way he sometimes seems, glimpsed through the fogs and fumes of history: a cultural force more than a man, a colossal brain and a sovereign hand at the controls of a multidisciplinary universe.

> This paragraph introduces an opinion about Leonardo da Vinci's accomplishments and supports it with examples.

Where did his supreme gift lie? In art? Science? Engineering? Aesthetic theory? All of the above. We all have our strengths; I have mastered MetroCard dispensers and a home computer. Yet Leonardo understood, described and illustrated the principles of hydrodynamics, gross anatomy, physics and astronomy. He invented the helicopter, the armored tank and the submarine. He painted like an angel and despite being phobic about deadlines, wrote often and well. In addition, according to Vasari, he was drop-dead gorgeous.

And, perhaps most confounding, he generated all this near-magical accomplishment from behind a curtain of personal discretion so dense and insulating that no historian or psychologist—and dozens, maybe hundreds, have tried—has been able to pull it aside to reveal the person behind the personage.

"Leonardo da Vinci, Master Draftsman" at the Metropolitan Museum of Art also tries, and manages to part the curtain just a crack. We may not learn exactly what made this artist tick, but we can see him ticking away, at length and in some depth.

Naturally, the show had blockbuster written all over it from the word go. With 118 Leonardo drawings, it is the largest gathering of his work in America. The lending institutions are a superstarry lot: the Uffizi, the Louvre,

A Rider on a Rearing Horse in a Profile View, Leonardo da Vinci, Fitzwilliam Museum, University of Cambridge, England

the Vatican, the Royal Library at Windsor Castle. And the Met has given it the imperial treatment: crimson walls, acres of space, a catalog as thick as *The Physician's Desk Reference*.

Are the drawings worth the fuss? In a word, totally. Individually, many are glorious; some are workmanlike; a few are just weird, so weird you find yourself wondering: what planet was this guy from? As a package, though, as the datastream output of a single sensibility, they're huge. They are also very alive. People always say that you can't know painting from a book, that you have to experience it. This is at least as true of drawing, a profoundly physical medium, where a smudge or erasure can be a heart-catching event, and a pen stroke can leap like a solar flare.

The show comes with some fresh scholarship, not blindingly revealing, but solid and worthwhile. The curators Carmen C. Bambach and George R. Goldner, both of the Met's department of drawings and prints, have avoided a hit parade approach in their selection, opting instead for some less familiar material. They've also brought related drawings—10 studies for the Florentine mural "The Battle of Anghiari" alone—together, in some cases for the first time. Finally, by arranging the work chronologically, they've created something like an organic picture of the history of one man's polymathic life.

Leonardo was born in 1452 and started life with certain disadvantages. He was a small-town kid, . . . indifferently educated and—a liability for an artist, you would think—left-handed. But he also had luck. His supportive father took him to Florence, by then a major node on the information highway of Renaissance Europe. There he was apprenticed to Andrea del Verrocchio, a leading sculptor but also a painter (five gorgeous drawings of his open the show) from whom Leonardo learned much.

For one thing, he learned to draw sculpturally. This meant drawing with a command of volume, as several early drapery studies demonstrate. It also meant executing fleet, notational sketches to capture the look of real things viewed from many angles in actual space, as seen in Leonardo's serial depictions of squirming babies and wide-awake cats. From Verrocchio he also learned to carry a notebook with him at all times and to use it, so that whatever went in through the eye came out through his hand.

In 1481, he landed a substantial job, an altarpiece painting of "The Adoration of the Magi." And at that point, he seemed to have settled on a work pattern that, for better or worse, he would follow thereafter. Basically, it entailed conceiving pictorial designs so complex and technically demanding that he would never complete them.

For "The Adoration," for example, he planned to place more than 60 figures in an elaborate perspectival setting. He drew and drew; several well-known studies, one of them madly

Head of the Virgin, Leonardo da Vinci, The Metropolitan Museum of Art

In this paragraph, the writer provides support for his evaluation of da Vinci's work pattern.

complicated, are in the show. But the ideas never really gelled, and he eventually headed to Milan in search of different work, leaving an unfinished painting behind.

He stayed in Milan, employed by the city's ruler, Ludovico Sforza, for 15 years, which were among the most productive of his life. His first commission—he proposed it himself—was an outsize equestrian monument to Ludovico's father. Again, he produced studies galore, dashed off and spirited, fastidious and polished. But the monument never materialized, and the plans were abandoned.

In any case, Leonardo was, as usual, working on several other things. One was the unfinished painting, now owned by the Vatican, titled "St. Jerome in the Wilderness." It's at the Met and gives a stark, almost agonizing sense of how he carried his obsessive, draftsmanlike self-correction right into

what should have been the final stages of a painting.

And there was "The Last Supper," painted from 1493 to 1498 in the refectory of Santa Maria della Grazie. One renowned sheet from Windsor carries what could be a preliminary sketch of that painting's composition, mixed in with geometric and architectural designs. And from the Albertina in Vienna comes a powerfully resolved drawing on blue paper of an old man who is sometimes identified as St. Peter. Whatever his identity, he is animated by the tense, urgent gravitas of the painting itself.

When French troops invaded Milan in 1499, Leonardo made his way back to Florence. There he whipped up a large-scale drawing titled "Virgin and Child With Saint Anne" and gave himself a one-man show. The drawing—now lost, though later versions on the same theme exist—was rapturously received and resulted in a commission from the city government for the Battle of Anghiari mural, to be painted in the Palazzo della Signoria. Its subject was a Florentine military victory.

Details in this paragraph continue to support the writer's evaluation of da Vinci's work pattern.

The assignment was a very big, very public deal; Michelangelo, the local reigning prince of art, was to paint the opposite wall. Once more, Leonardo feverishly poured out ideas on paper, and the studies in the show are fantastic, from an explosive drawing of a horse in motion (several legs, many heads) to a hyperrealistic depiction of a screaming soldier. As for the mural, Leonardo designed a cartoon and expensive scaffolding, then left town, heading back to Milan.

Once there, he did what he had always done: many things simultaneously. He painted; he taught; he studied anatomy and geometry. He designed maps, architectural plans and stage sets. He conducted scientific experiments and recorded his findings in notebooks, writing from right to left and in mirror image, which, as a lefty, he had always done.

And he sketched. Small drawings of grotesque human heads flowed from his hand like telephone pad doodles. His famous "Deluge" pictures date to this time. Imaginary scenes of tidal waves overwhelming minute towns, they are both aquatic studies and apocalyptic visions. In 1516, the French king Francis I, who collected trophy artists as well as art, invited him to live at his court. Leonardo,

old at 64, moved to France and died there three years later.

He left behind a godlike reputation, worshipful disciples, a scant handful of paintings—about 15 survive—and the 4,000 works on paper that are his primary visual legacy. Some of his drawings are art historical icons; the face of Mary in a study for the painting of "The Virgin and Child With St. Anne," now in the Louvre, is one. He invented this expressive type, with its interior smile and apparitional draftsmanship, and with it a Western ideal of human perfection.

My favorite drawings, though, are of a different kind. They're ones where everything is happening, nonlinearly, all at once, and anything goes: double-sided sheets filled with animals, armaments, allegorical scenes, geometrical diagrams, exploding buildings, . . . dissected muscles, wheels and bridges, flowing water, reminder notes, sums, scratches, spots and stains.

In these, for me, the curtain parts that little bit, to reveal an artist who always preferred to dream and draw rather than to do, who remained at some level a venturesome child controlling his world by taking it apart, piece by piece, to see how the whole thing worked. By thinking big, Leonardo became big; illusions sometimes work that way. And the neat thing is that in his company, we get to think big, too.

The language of this conclusion reflects the informal style of a feature article.

Check Your Comprehension

1. According to Cotter, what are Leonardo da Vinci's supreme gifts?
2. What three things did Leonardo invent?

Applying the Reading Strategy

Evaluating Support

3. (a) What support does Cotter give to prove that da Vinci did not always finish a commission? (b) Is the support convincing? Explain.
4. (a) What is Cotter's overall message in this article? (b) Evaluate two examples of details that support the overall message.
5. Does Cotter offer enough support to persuade you to accept his perspective on Leonardo da Vinci? Explain.

Activity

Conducting a Survey on Newspaper Reading

With a group, design and conduct a survey to find out how people get their news. Use a format like the one shown here. Tally the answers and share them with the class.

Model Questionnaire

Name: _____

Choose the category that describes you and answer the question that follows.

☐ Student: What grade are you in?_____
☐ Adult: What is your occupation? _____

1. How often do you read a newspaper? Check one:
☐ Less than once a week ☐ 1 or 2 times a week
☐ 3–5 times a week ☐ Every day

2. When you read a newspaper, which sections do you regularly read? Check all that apply:
☐ Front page ☐ Local news ☐ National news
☐ Sports ☐ Business ☐ Editorials/Opinion
☐ Classified section ☐ Lifestyle ☐ Entertainment
☐ Other, please indicate _____

Contrasting Informational Materials

News Articles and Feature Articles

Review a current newspaper to identify both a news report and a feature article. Compare the two, using questions like these to focus your analysis:

- What bias, or writer's opinions, do you detect in each article? Explain.
- Which one contains more facts? Explain.
- From the lead, or opening, paragraph, are you able to identify the most important idea of each article? Explain.
- What details does each provide to support its claims?
- Which article might become outdated first? Why?

Share your findings with the class.

Writing About Literature

Analyze Literary Periods

The literature of the Renaissance and the Age of Rationalism was influenced by the cultural movement known as humanism. During the Renaissance, humanists celebrated the rediscovered ideals of classical antiquity. Scholars studied the classics in their original languages: Greek, Latin, and Hebrew. The humanist belief in the value of an active life of involvement with the world overtook the medieval ideal of a contemplative life devoted to God. Humanity's achievements and faculties—knowledge, love, and reason—took center stage. The arts and sciences took on new life, while traditional religious authority was questioned.

To explore the influences of humanism on the selections in this unit, complete the assignment described in the box at right.

Prewriting

Find a focus. Begin by reviewing the discussion of humanism and rationalism in the Unit Introduction on pages 662–671. Then, review the literature in this unit and relate it to humanism. Fill out a chart similar to the one shown below, using these questions as a guide:

- What is the theme of the selection?
- How do the characters and plot reveal the theme?
- How does the theme relate to humanism?

> **Assignment: Humanism in the Literature of the Renaissance and the Age of Rationalism**
>
> Write an analytical essay that traces the influence of humanism on the writings of the Renaissance authors—Petrarch, Boccaccio, Ronsard, and Cervantes—or the Rationalist authors—La Fontaine and Voltaire—whose works are excerpted in this unit.
>
> **Criteria:**
> - Include a thesis statement that defines humanism and explains its influence on the works you discuss.
> - Support your thesis with detailed analyses of the works.
> - Cite examples from each work you explore.
> - Approximate length: 1,500 words

Model: Charting Humanism in Renaissance and Rationalist Literature

Selection	Characteristic of Humanism	Example/Quote
"The White Doe"	speaker's ideals are expressed in a vision of his human beloved, not in a religious vision	"A pure-white doe in an emerald glade/Appeared to me . . ."

Gather evidence. After you have filled in the chart, review the chart carefully. Choose those examples you have listed that most strongly express characteristics of humanism. Then, look for other examples illustrating the same characteristics.

Write a working thesis. After you have decided which characteristics of humanism will be the focus of your paper, write a working thesis. Introduce the characteristics you will discuss, and explain why they were central to the selections.

 **Read to Write**

As you reread the texts, keep in mind that the writer may be reacting *against* the values of humanism. Look for both positive and negative influences of humanism in the selections.

Drafting

Clarify your thesis statement. As you write your first draft, make sure that your thesis statement explains clearly the characteristics of humanism that you are discussing in your paper.

> ### Model: Focusing a Thesis Statement
>
> Literature of the Renaissance and the Age of Rationalism ~~was influenced by humanism, so it was different from medieval literature, which was written before this point of view was popular.~~ *reflected a major shift from the medieval ideal of the contemplative life to the humanist notion of taking action in the world.*

Choose examples for maximum effect. Illustrate the characteristics of humanism that you discuss with specific quotations from the selections. For each example, ask yourself whether it clearly supports the point you are making. Use only examples that give strong support.

Revising and Editing

Review content: Check connections. Underline each example you use, and draw an arrow to the general point it illustrates. For any example that does not clearly support a general point, either replace it with a stronger example or add a sentence clarifying the connection.

Review style: Combine sentences and use transition words. Review your draft for choppy passages made up of short sentences. Revise these passages by combining sentences and adding transitions.

> **Original:** Petrarch's "Spring" shows the influence of humanism. Humanism looks for inspiration in classical antiquity. This poem includes several references to Greek and Roman mythology. It mentions Zephyr, Procne, Philomel, Jove, and Venus.

> **Revised:** Petrarch's "Spring" shows the influence of humanism, which looks for inspiration in classical antiquity. Petrarch emphasizes this inspiration with references to characters of Greek and Roman myths: Zephyr, Procne, Philomel, Jove, and Venus.

Publishing and Presenting

Present an informal summary. List the main points of your paper, and explain each in an informal talk to your classmates. Encourage the audience to ask questions.

W͜G Writing and Grammar Connection: Diamond Level, Chapter 14

Write to Learn
If you have difficulty writing a thesis statement, you may need to do some additional research on the values and characteristics of humanism. The more you know about this cultural movement, the easier it will be to write your thesis statement.

Write to Explain
To make every example and quotation in your paper count, directly connect these details to the point you are trying to make about humanism. Don't expect your readers to infer connections that you don't explain clearly.

Writing WORKSHOP

Exposition: Comparison-and-Contrast Essay

A **comparison-and-contrast essay** is an expository piece that describes similarities and differences between two or more items. In this workshop, you will plan, draft, and revise a comparison-and-contrast essay about a topic of your choice.

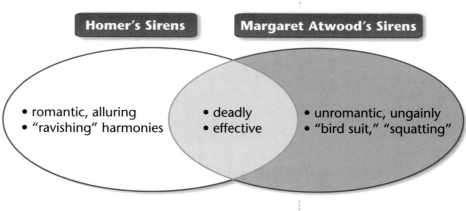

Assignment Criteria Your comparison-and-contrast essay should feature the following elements:

- A purpose for comparing and contrasting two or more items
- A thesis statement
- Evidence to support the thesis, consisting of descriptions of similarities and differences among the items
- A logical organizational plan suited to the topic
- Focused paragraphs that employ effective transitions

To preview the criteria on which your comparison-and-contrast essay may be assessed, refer to the Rubric on page 751.

Prewriting

Choose a topic. One way to choose a topic for a comparison-and-contrast essay is to make a **list**. First, choose a general subject area of interest, such as music, sports, presidents, or novels. Next, brainstorm for issues within this broad area that intrigue you. Choose a topic for your essay from your list.

Evaluate the topic. To decide whether your subjects have sufficient points of comparison for an effective comparison-and-contrast essay, use a Venn diagram similar to the one shown. If your diagram suggests too few connections, consider choosing a richer topic.

Write a thesis statement. Write a thesis statement that identifies your topic and sets out a clear rationale for your essay. Include this statement in the introductory paragraph of your essay.

Gather details. Make notes about similarities and differences between your subjects. Conduct any research necessary to provide a detailed comparison.

Homer's Sirens

Margaret Atwood's Sirens

- romantic, alluring
- "ravishing" harmonies

- deadly
- effective

- unromantic, ungainly
- "bird suit," "squatting"

Student Model

Before you begin drafting, read this student model and review the characteristics of a successful comparison-and-contrast essay.

Anna Lvovsky
Rockville, MD

Sirens: His and Hers

Femininity in classical myth has been treated differently by men and women. Men tend to romanticize mythic females, while women tend to reject such fictionalization. These divergent viewpoints are exemplified by Homer's and Margaret Atwood's portrayals of the legendary Sirens. Homer's *Odyssey* relays an idealized vision of alluring, powerful females, whereas Atwood's "Siren Song" bluntly depicts the Sirens as miserable victims of their own condition.

> In her introduction, Anna identifies the subjects she will compare.

The *Odyssey* is narrated from a masculine perspective and presents a romantic but superficial impression of the Sirens. The speaker remarks on the "ravishing" quality of their harmonies, suggesting their power to overcome. His reference to "honeyed" voices evokes sweetness and appeal. The creatures' very song is stirring; the speaker refers to the music as "thrilling." As a man, the speaker of the poem responds in the expected fashion to these stimuli: He is seduced. His reaction completes an image of the Sirens as powerful, enthralling creatures, capable of manipulating all men. Homer's creatures compel a reader's awed respect.

> Anna uses a subject-by-subject organization and begins by discussing Homer.

Immune to the Sirens' feminine allure, Atwood takes a tersely unromantic approach. By adopting the perspective of a Siren, she portrays the creatures, not as deadly beauties, but as helpless victims. Atwood's narrator presents herself as trapped in a "bird suit" and "squatting" on an island, depictions that strip away dignity and beauty. "Beached skulls" convey the destructiveness and barrenness of her occupation. Whereas Homer's narrator finds the song exciting, she herself dismisses it as "boring."

> The essay offers equivalent depth and detail in discussing the second subject.

Exciting or boring, the song's lethal efficiency does provide one point of agreement between Homer and Atwood: The song induces men to leap to their deaths and, as Atwood writes, "it works every time." Ultimately, though, Atwood conjures an image diametrically opposed to Homer's idealized suggestion of alluring women. Her Sirens are dejected creatures who merit not our awe or respect but our pity.

> Anna acknowledges a similarity between her subjects; then, she sharpens the contrast between them.

It is unsurprising that men of traditional literature judge women entirely by external attributes. Homer's *Odyssey* epitomizes this tendency, representing the Sirens as powerful, desirable creatures on the basis of a brief impression. It is up to Margaret Atwood in "Siren Song" to rebut such a shallow interpretation and portray the true vulnerability of these idealized figures.

> The essay ends with a strong conclusion.

Drafting

Organize your essay. Comparison-and-contrast essays are generally organized in one of two ways: subject by subject or point by point. In subject-by-subject organization, you first discuss all the features of one item and then discuss all the features of the second, the third, and so on. Using point-by-point organization, in contrast, you begin by discussing the same point about all of the items and then move on to the second, third, and subsequent points. The outlines to the right illustrate these two kinds of organization.

Elaborate. Provide evidence to support all of the important points you make in your essay. Supporting evidence may take any or all of the following forms:

- **Examples:** Use examples that illustrate the similarities and differences between the items.
- **Facts:** Whenever possible, use detailed, factual evidence that will help readers gain a clear understanding of each item.
- **Quotations:** Quotations from experts on your topic lend authority to your arguments.

Organizational Plans

Point by Point
Point 1
- Subject A
- Subject B
Point 2
- Subject A
- Subject B
Point 3
- Subject A
- Subject B

Subject by Subject
Subject A
- Point 1
- Point 2
- Point 3
Subject B
- Point 1
- Point 2
- Point 3

Revising

Revise for clarity. Because the essay compares two or more items, clear organization is essential. The reader must know which item is under discussion in each part of the essay, so be sure to revise the essay to achieve this clarity. Reorder details, grouping related points, or add transitions as needed.

Revise for balance. As you reread your draft, highlight your supporting evidence, using a different color for each item you compare and contrast. Determine whether you have included approximately the same amount of detail about every item. If not, add or delete examples, facts, quotations, and other supporting details.

Model: Revising to Balance Comparisons

The speaker remarks on the "ravishing" quality of their harmonies, suggesting their power to overcome. His reference to "honeyed" voices evokes sweetness and appeal. *The creatures' very song is stirring; the speaker refers to the music as "thrilling."*

Anna matches Atwood's reference to the Sirens' "boring song" with a contrasting reference in Homer.

Revise for effective transitions. Review your draft to make sure that you have used effective transitions between sentences and paragraphs. Use words and phrases that signal and clarify transitions, such as *by contrast* and *on the other hand*.

No transition: The theme of the first story emphasizes acceptance of one's lot in life. The theme of the second focuses on struggling against one's fate.

Transition: The theme of the first story emphasizes acceptance of one's lot in life. **By contrast,** the theme of the second focuses on struggling against one's fate.

Compare the model and the nonmodel.

Nonmodel	Model
. . . the song induces men to leap to their deaths and, as Atwood writes, "it works every time." Atwood conjures an image diametrically opposed to Homer's idealized suggestion of alluring women.	. . . the song induces men to leap to their deaths and, as Atwood writes, "it works every time." Ultimately, though, Atwood conjures an image diametrically opposed to Homer's idealized suggestion of alluring women.

Publishing and Presenting

Choose one of the following ways to share your writing.

Give an oral presentation. Outline your essay and present the main points orally to the class. Use charts, diagrams, or other visual aids to help clarify your message.

Publish your essay electronically. Post your essay on a Web site or upload it onto a classroom computer.

WG Writing and Grammar Connection: Diamond Level, Chapter 14

Rubric for Self-Assessment

Evaluate your comparison-and-contrast essay using the following criteria and rating scale:

Criteria	Rating Scale				
	Not very				Very
Does the essay include a thesis statement in the introductory paragraph?	1	2	3	4	5
Is the thesis supported by adequate evidence?	1	2	3	4	5
Do all the items have the same amount of support?	1	2	3	4	5
Is the organization logical and consistent?	1	2	3	4	5
Does the essay use transitions effectively?	1	2	3	4	5

Listening and Speaking WORKSHOP

Presenting a Literary Interpretation

In a **literary interpretation,** a speaker analyzes an element of a work of literature such as theme, characterization, language, or plot, persuading an audience to accept his or her views. Use the strategies on this page to develop and deliver an effective literary interpretation.

Plan Your Content

Analyze literature that intrigues you and about which you have strong feelings or ideas. An interpretation that shows a work in a dramatically new light is sure to pique your audience's interest.

Choose a topic. Ask yourself: What have I read recently that made my mind race? Which selections raised the most questions in my mind? Which ones generated the liveliest discussions? Choose your topic from among those works that come to mind.

Formulate a thesis statement. Your presentation should focus on a strong thesis, or a central point. Start by reviewing the features—or the questions—that led you to select the work. Formulate your main point about the work in a clear sentence, and build your talk around this thesis statement.

Gather ammunition. As with all persuasive presentations, rely on supporting details to make your case. For most literary presentations, you will rely on the work under discussion, though you may want to cite other works or biographical information about the author. Select quotes and specific references. Be accurate!

> ### Feedback Form for Literary Interpretation
>
> **Rating System**
> + = Excellent   ✓= Average   − = Weak
>
> **Content**
> Organization _____
> Appeal to reason _____
> Appeal to emotion _____
> Addresses counterarguments _____
>
> Evaluate the quality of the supporting evidence:
> _____
>
> **Delivery**
> Volume _____
> Pacing _____
> Eye contact _____
> Body language _____
>
> Suggestions for improvement: _____
> _____

Prepare Your Presentation

Use these speaking techniques to make sure your presentation is a success.

- **Control volume and pace.** Your most important responsibility for any oral presentation is to speak clearly and slowly enough so that everyone can hear you and understand what you say. Vary your volume and pace to emphasize key points.

- **Practice your presentation.** You can't practice too often! Experiment with tone of voice, pacing, gestures, and eye contact. Memorize your talk, or use notes for the main points and improvise.

(Activity: Presentation and Feedback**)** Select one or more works of literature to interpret that most of your audience has read, and prepare a three-minute presentation. Practice with a partner or in a small group, videotaping the practice sessions if possible. Have your partners fill out a Feedback Form like the one above to use as a basis for discussing your content and delivery.

Critical Reasoning

In the reading sections of many tests, you may be required to use critical reasoning skills. Use the following strategies to help you answer questions testing these skills:

- Identify a writer's implicit assumptions: Ask yourself what else must be true for the writer's claims to be true.
- Read actively, making inferences based on the passage and testing those inferences against your own knowledge.

Test-Taking Strategies

- Read the test questions before you read the passage.
- After you have read the passage, jot down a sentence summarizing the main idea.

Sample Test Item

Directions: Read "The White Doe" by Petrarch, below, and then answer the question.

A pure-white doe in an emerald glade
Appeared to me, with two antlers of gold,
Between two streams, under a laurel's shade,
At sunrise, in the season's bitter cold.

5 Her sight was so suavely merciless
That I left work to follow her at leisure,
Like the miser who looking for his treasure
Sweetens with that delight his bitterness.

Around her lovely neck "Do not touch me"
10 Was written with topaz and diamond stone,
"My Caesar's will has been to make me free."

Already toward noon had climbed the sun,
My weary eyes were not sated to see,
When I fell in the stream and she was gone.

1. The poet assumes that the reader will

A recognize the poem as an allegory.

B have seen all the things the speaker mentions.

C know about the behavior of deer.

D all of the above

Answer and Explanation

The correct answer is **A**. Answers **B, C,** and **D** are incorrect because the reader will be able to understand the poem even without direct experience of what it describes.

▶ Practice

Directions: Read "Spring" by Petrarch, below, and then answer the questions.

Zephyr returns, and scatters everywhere
New flowers and grass, and company does bring,
Procne and Philomel, in sweet despair,
And all the tender colors of the Spring.
5 Never were fields so glad, nor skies so fair;
And Jove exults in Venus' prospering.
Love is in all the water, earth, and air,
And love possesses every living thing.
But to me only heavy sighs return
10 For her who carried in her little hand
My heart's key to her heavenly sojourn.
The birds sing loud above the flowering land;
Ladies are gracious now.—Where deserts burn
The beasts still prowl on the ungreening sand.

1. Which adjective best describes the speaker's feelings about spring?

A delighted

B indifferent

C curious

D bitter

2. The "ungreening sand" refers to

A spring.

B summer.

C the speaker's unrequited love.

D the speaker's beloved.

Romanticism and Realism

Terrace at Sainte-Adresse, Claude Monet, The Metropolitan Museum of Art

66**Would you realize
what Revolution is,
call it Progress;
and would you realize
what Progress is,
call it Tomorrow.**99

— Victor Hugo

Timeline 1800–1890

1800   1820   1840

European Events

- **1800** Wordsworth and Coleridge publish *Lyrical Ballads*, 2nd edition.

- **1804** Napoleon declares himself emperor. ◀

- **1804** Beethoven completes Symphony No. 3, the first Romantic symphony.

- **1808** Goethe publishes Part I of *Faust*.

- **1812** Napoleon invades Russia.

- **1825** In Russia, the forces of the czar crush an uprising by army officers.

- **1827** Heinrich Heine publishes *The Book of Songs*.

- **1829** In England, George Stephenson creates a better steam locomotive.

- **1831** Victor Hugo publishes his novel *Notre-Dame de Paris*. ▼

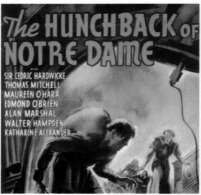

- **1848** Insurrections break out across Europe; the Second French Republic is declared.

- **1849** Gustave Courbet paints *The Stone Breakers*, a Realist work. ▼

- **1852** Second French Republic ends; the Second Empire begins.

- **1856** In England, Robert Bessemer develops process for mass-producing steel.

- **1857** Flaubert publishes *Madame Bovary*, a masterpiece of Realist fiction.

World Events

- **1803 (United States)** The Louisiana Purchase doubles the size of the country. ▼

- **1808 (Sierra Leone)** Britain acquires Sierra Leone as a colony; goes on to acquire Gambia (1816) and Gold Coast (1874).

- **1818 (India)** British control most of India.

- **1820–1821 (Egypt)** Muhammad Ali, ruler of Egypt, begins creating an African empire.

- **1825 (United States)** Erie Canal opens.

- **1825 (United States)** An organized baseball club exists in upstate New York.

- **1828 (Japan)** Poet Kobayashi Issa dies.

- **1842 (China)** China loses to Western powers in the Opium War.

- **1842 (United States)** Dr. Crawford Long begins using ether as an anesthetic.

- **1853–1854 (Japan)** Commander Matthew Perry forces Japan to trade with the West. ◀

European and World Events

- **1861** In Russia, the serfs are freed.

- **1861** A united Italy is established.

- **1864** Fyodor Dostoyevsky publishes *Notes from the Underground*.

- **1867** Karl Marx publishes the first volume of *Das Kapital*, a criticism of capitalism.

- **1869** Leo Tolstoy completes his novel *War and Peace*.

- **1870** The Franco-Prussian War begins.

- **1871** The Franco-Prussian War ends with France's defeat; the Third French Republic is established.

- **1871** The German empire begins.

- **1873** Arthur Rimbaud stops writing poetry, at the age of 19.

- **1880s** Swedish chemist Alfred Nobel builds dynamite factories.

- **1881** In Russia, Czar Alexander II is assassinated.

- **1885** Émile Zola publishes the novel *Germinal*, which depicts life in a mining town. ◄

- **1896** Alfred Nobel's will endows the Nobel Prizes.

- **1861 (United States)** The American Civil War begins.

- **1864 (China)** A destructive civil war ends.

- **1865 (United States)** The Civil War ends; President Lincoln is assassinated.

- **1869 (Egypt)** Suez Canal opens.

- **1876 (United States)** Alexander Graham Bell invents the telephone. ◄

- **1883 (Tunisia)** France gains control over Tunisia. ►

- **c. 1884 (United States)** Hiram Stevens Maxim uses smokeless powder in a new type of machine gun.

- **1886 (United States)** John Pemberton invents Coca-Cola.

- **1890 (United States)** In the West, fenced pasture has largely replaced range land.

- **1898 (Palestine)** Theodor Herzl visits Palestine to look into setting up a Jewish state.

Romanticism and Realism

(1800–1890)

Historical Background

Throughout Europe, the nineteenth century was marked by political and industrial revolutions, progress, and hope for the future. Yet it was also an era characterized by unfulfilled expectations and by the emergence of new problems.

The Seeds of Revolution Inspired by the ideas of political and social philosophers such as John Locke (1632–1704) and Jean-Jacques Rousseau (zhän zhäk´ rōō sō´) (1712–1778), the American colonists revolted against British rule and declared their independence in 1776. The success of the American Revolution helped stir up political unrest throughout Europe, especially in France. There, revolutionary activities that had begun in 1787 reached their first high point in 1789 when a Paris mob attacked and destroyed the prison known as the Bastille. In the years that followed, the monarchy was abolished, and France was declared a republic. On January 21, 1793, the leaders of the newly established French republican government

---

Point/Counterpoint

Do people have a right to revolt against their rulers?
Stirred by the French Revolution (1787–1799), two important thinkers of the time expressed opposing views on this question.

No! Men have a right . . . to justice. . . . They have a right to the fruits of their industry; . . . They have a right to the acquisitions of their parents; to the nourishment and improvement of their offspring; to instruction in life, and to consolation in death. . . . [A]nd as to the share of power, authority, and direction which each individual ought to have in the management of the state, that I must deny to be amongst the direct original rights of man in civil society. . . .

—from *Reflections on the Revolution in France* by Edmund Burke

Yes! There never did, there never will, and there never can exist a parliament, or any description of men, or any generation of men, in any country, possessed of the right or the power of binding and controlling posterity to the "end of time," or of commanding for ever how the world shall be governed, or who shall govern it; and therefore, all such clauses, . . . are . . . null and void. . . . Man has no property in man. . . .

—from *Rights of Man: Being an Answer to Mr. Burke's Attack on the French Revolution* by Thomas Paine

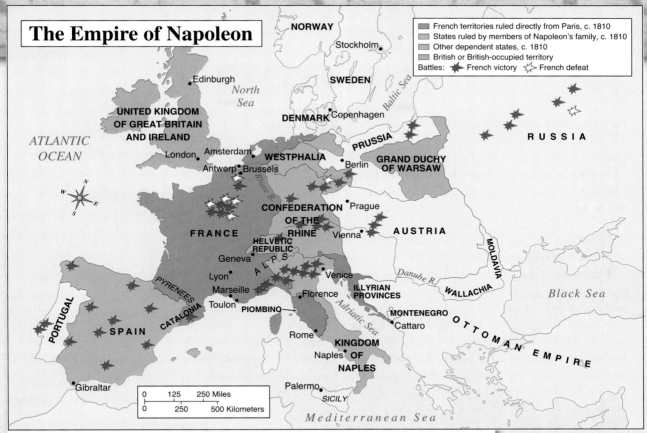

The Empire of Napoleon

Legend:
- French territories ruled directly from Paris, c. 1810
- States ruled by members of Napoleon's family, c. 1810
- Other dependent states, c. 1810
- British or British-occupied territory
- Battles: ★ French victory ☆ French defeat

executed the king. Then, from September 5, 1793, to July 27, 1794, there was a period in France known as the Reign of Terror, during which the revolutionary government executed 17,000 people.

Napoleon In 1799, a successful and popular young general, Napoleon Bonaparte (nə pō´ lē ən bō´ nə pärt´), assumed political power in France. Five years later, he made himself emperor. Although in many respects Napoleon ruled as a military dictator, he did accomplish many domestic reforms. In addition, he aroused a strong sense of nationalism among the French people.

Europe at War Between 1792 and 1815, France was almost constantly at war with other nations. At first, France defended itself against monarchies that were frightened by the Revolution and hoped to destroy it. Later, as Napoleon came to power, France embarked on a series of military conquests in which it seized control of nearly all of Europe as far east as the Russian border (see map above).

In 1812, however, Napoleon overextended himself by invading Russia. There, his army suffered a disastrous defeat. Napoleon's final defeat came in 1815 at the Battle of Waterloo, when his forces were overpowered by an allied army led by Great Britain.

Although Napoleon dominated Europe for only a brief period, his conquests had lasting effects. His armies spread many of the achievements of the French Revolution throughout Europe.

▲ **Critical Viewing**
In 1810, which countries or territories were part of the French empire, dependent on it, or ruled by members of Napoleon's family? Explain. [**Read a Map**]

While such reforms were welcomed by many, public opinion turned against Napoleon when his occupying forces began assessing high taxes and conscripting local men into his armies.

Revolutions and Reactions Following the collapse of Napoleon's empire, a large group of national delegates gathered in Vienna to reestablish the traditions that had existed before the French Revolution. Although they were able to restore royal authority throughout Europe, they were unable to erase the desire for political and social justice. As a result, the rest of the century was marked by an ongoing conflict between traditional political beliefs and democratic ideals.

Nowhere was this conflict more apparent than in France. In the aftermath of Napoleon's downfall, royal rule had been reestablished. In 1830, however, when the king took measures to restrict the people's freedom, the people revolted and forced him out of power. Although this revolt brought about a number of important reforms, it did not bring an end to the monarchy. The new king, however, was a member of the upper middle class rather than the aristocracy. When another revolution occurred in 1848, however, a second French republic was established. Yet the Second Republic lasted only four years, and it was not until 1871 that the Third French Republic was born.

The French uprising of 1848 was one of several armed rebellions breaking out in Europe that year. Others took place in Italy, Austria, and Germany, but unlike the rebellion in France, they did not lead to the abolition of absolute monarchy. Meanwhile, in Denmark, Belgium, and the Netherlands, the spirit of the age manifested itself in reform rather than armed revolt.

The Unification of Germany Also in 1848, a movement arose among the German people that was aimed at unifying the many German states into a single nation controlled by a democratic government. Like the revolts in the other European nations, this movement was thwarted. In 1871, however, after Prussia defeated France in the Franco-Prussian War, the Prussian prime minister, Otto von Bismarck (biz´ märk´), did succeed in unifying the German states. While the newly established German empire was a source of pride for nationalists, it was a major disappointment for reformers.

Similarly, Russian reformers had little success in bringing about political and social changes. Russia remained a repressive, autocratic state throughout the nineteenth century.

The Industrial Revolution Like the French Revolution, the Industrial Revolution took shape in the 1700s. In the British textile industry, inventors produced new machines that reduced the time needed to spin and weave cloth. The new machines led to the growth of the factory system, which brought workers and machinery together in one place to manufacture goods.

▼ **Critical Viewing**
Does this portrait of Bismarck offer any evidence that his government was authoritarian and militaristic? Why or why not? **[Interpret]**

Prince Otto von Bismarck in uniform with Prussian helmet, Franz von Lenbach

Industry got a further boost with the invention of the steam engine. By the 1850s, steam was the main source of power, not only in factories but also in new means of transportation such as the railroad and the steamship.

By the end of the century, the Industrial Revolution had transformed Europe's entire way of life. Scientists and inventors had developed countless new products, including the first automobiles. Electricity became an important new source of power.

Industrial Hardships The Industrial Revolution brought many benefits. It created millions of new jobs and produced a variety of goods more cheaply than ever before. At the same time, the rise of industry brought new problems. Early industrial workers often faced great hardships. Pay was low, hours were long, and working conditions were often dangerous. As people moved from the countryside to the growing industrial cities, they crowded into unhealthy urban slums.

Gare Saint-Lazare, Claude Oscar Monet

▲ **Critical Viewing** Which details in this picture reveal the influence of the Industrial Revolution? Explain. **[Infer]**

By the end of the century, reformers were at work to raise wages, outlaw child labor, and win better conditions in factories and slums. Gradually, the standard of living for workers and their families improved.

The Middle Class and Women's Rights Industry and the growth of cities sparked the rise of a new middle class. The values of this new class—values that influenced all of society—included duty, thrift, honesty, hard work, and, above all, respectability.

By the middle of the century, some reformers had begun to protest restrictions on women. Even in the most democratic nations, such as Britain, women could not vote. They were banned from most schools, and married women could not legally control their own property.

A Controversial New Idea In the mid-nineteenth century, the theories of British biologist Charles Darwin created a tremendous uproar that shook the entire Western world. According to Darwin, all forms of life evolve, or change, over a long period of time. Simpler forms of life evolve into more complex forms, and new forms evolve out of older ones. Some people attacked Darwin's theories, believing that they contradicted the Bible. Today, however, evolution is (according to the *Encyclopedia Britannica*) "one of the fundamental keystones of modern biological theory."

Literature

Shaped by the major events and developments of the time, four major artistic movements dominated nineteenth-century literature: Romanticism, Realism, Naturalism, and Symbolism.

Romanticism: The French Revolution on a Page The first of these movements, Romanticism, rejected the objectivity, rationality, and harmony that many eighteenth-century writers admired in ancient Greek and Roman artists. Romantic writers, painters, and musicians responded not to an idealized image of ancient civilization but to the real unrest of their own times: the fervor of political revolution and the squalor of the Industrial Revolution. Rebelling against Neoclassical values, they prized subjectivity, the imagination, and the wildness associated with untamed nature.

Although there were many differences in the concerns and approaches of the various writers associated with this movement, they generally shared a desire to discard the dominant forms and approaches of the eighteenth century and to forge a new type of literature. In this sense, Romanticism might be called the French Revolution carried over to the literary page. The English poet William Wordsworth, a pioneer of literary Romanticism, was at first inspired by the French Revolution and its emphasis on the worth of the ordinary person. Later, when he became disillusioned with the violence in France, he began plotting the literary revolution known as Romanticism. He would uphold the dignity of ordinary people by writing about them with imagination and respect.

In his preface to *Lyrical Ballads* (1798), a collection of poetry he co-authored with his friend Samuel Taylor Coleridge, Wordsworth outlined the dominant principles of Romanticism. He stressed the need to employ "language really used by men" in describing "situations from common life," emphasized the role of nature as a source of inspiration, and asserted that poetry should be a "spontaneous overflow of powerful feelings." These principles contrasted with the practice of eighteenth-century Neoclassical writers, who used witty language to portray upper-class people in social rather than natural settings.

The Lure of the Exotic and the Supernatural Among the other important characteristics of the Romantics were their fascination with folklife in general and the folklore of the Middle Ages specifically, their attraction to exotic cultures and the supernatural, their sense of optimism, their emphasis on individualism, their refusal to accept human limitations, and their desire for social change. Again, most of these characteristics contrast with those of Neoclassical writers.

▼ **Critical Viewing** Which details in this painting suggest that it is a Romantic work? Explain. **[Connect]**

The Wanderer Over the Sea of Clouds, 1818, Caspar David Friedrich, Kunsthalle, Hamburg

Music in the Historical Context

Beethoven Writes the First Romantic Symphony

It is 1802 and the virtuoso pianist and promising composer Ludwig von Beethoven (loot' viH vän bā' tō' vən) can no longer deny that he is growing deaf. He retreats to a country village to write a confession of his deepest fears: ". . . reflect now that for six years I have been in a hopeless case, made worse by ignorant doctors, yearly betrayed in the hope of getting better, finally forced to face the prospect of a permanent malady. . . ." He will soon have to end his career as a pianist, focusing more and more on composing.

It is 1802 and Napoleon, commanding the armies of the French Revolution, has recently defeated the Austrians and forced a peace treaty with the British. At home, a grateful populace votes him consul, or ruler, for life.

Soon, Beethoven begins working on his Symphony No. 3, which will inaugurate a musical revolution. It will be the first Romantic symphony, an expression of thought and feeling on a more ambitious scale than can be found in symphonies of the previous century. Unlike these classical works, it will have an audience wider than a small circle of aristocrats. Beethoven labors on this composition in his sketchbooks, leaving empty spaces where he will fill in melodies later. Heroic in defiance of his "malady," the composer will dedicate his work to the hero who is bringing freedom to all of Europe: Napoleon.

It is 1804 and Napoleon's agents have just discovered an assassination plot against him. An influential adviser whispers that by making himself emperor, Napoleon will discourage future conspiracies. The consul agrees. The empire begins.

It is 1804 and Symphony No. 3 is complete. When he learns that Napoleon has declared himself emperor, Beethoven angrily strikes the leader's name from the dedication. This will be the *Eroica* ("Heroic") Symphony, dedicated not to a great man but, in disillusionment and defiance, to "the memory of a great man."

Ludwig von Beethoven, Joseph Karl Stieler, 1820, Beethoven–Haus, Bonn

▲ **Critical Viewing** Which details in this portrait of Beethoven suggest aspects of the new Romantic music—for example, the powerful expression of emotion and the heroic stature of the composer? Explain. [Interpret]

In addition to Wordsworth and Coleridge, the Romantic movement included the German poet and dramatist Johann Wolfgang von Goethe (yō' hän vôlf' gäŋ fôn gö' tə), the Russian poet Alexander Pushkin, the German poet Heinrich Heine (hīn' riH hī' nə), and the French author Victor Hugo (hyoo' gō).

Realism: The Discovery of Contemporary Life During the middle of the nineteenth century in France, a new literary movement known as Realism emerged, partly as a reaction against Romanticism and partly as a result of the industrial and scientific developments that were transforming society. Just as the Romantics had focused on humble people ignored by the Neoclassicists, Realists sought to portray previously ignored figures in contemporary life, such as middle- and working-class city dwellers.

The French writer Honoré de Balzac (ô nô *rä'* dae bál zàk') (1799–1850) anticipated Realism in scores of novels that give a vast and detailed picture of nineteenth-century French society, from criminals and lowlifes to upper-class women. Balzac's compatriot Gustave Flaubert (güs tàv' flō ber') (1821–1880) wrote the classic Realist novel, *Madame Bovary*, which dissects the life of an unhappy middle-class woman. Other Realists were the English novelist Charles Dickens (1812–1870) and the Russian novelists Feodor Dostoyevsky (fyô' dôr dôs' tô yef' skē) (see below) and Leo Tolstoy. In the latter part of the century, Henrik Ibsen wrote the first realistic prose dramas.

Naturalism and Greek Tragedy Realism eventually gave birth to the literary movement known as Naturalism. One of the leaders of this movement was the French writer Émile Zola (ā mēl' zō' lä') (1840–1902). Like realists, Naturalists attempted to depict life accurately, but Naturalists were even more pessimistic than their forebears. They were reacting to the worst excesses of the Industrial Revolution and to misinterpretations of Darwinian theory that viewed society as a jungle in which only the fittest survived. As a result, they believed that the scientific laws governing heredity and society, like the Fates in ancient Greek mythology, determined the course of a person's life. Characters in naturalistic novels are therefore shaped

A Living Tradition

Feodor Dostoyevsky and Ralph Ellison

One nineteenth-century work with many literary descendants is *Notes from the Underground* (1864) by Russian author Feodor Dostoyevsky. In this novel, a nameless first-person narrator begins by announcing, "I am a sick man. . . . I am a spiteful man." This narrator is an angry stepchild of the Industrial Revolution, a nasty disbeliever in the progress of science and reason.

A literary descendant of this character is the narrator of Ralph Ellison's novel *Invisible Man*, written nearly 100 years after *Notes*. Ellison, who had been studying Dostoyevsky's work, created an African American protagonist who feels "invisible" in white society and therefore does not share that society's belief in progress:

> I am an invisible man. No, I am not a spook like those who haunted Edgar Allan Poe; nor am I one of your Hollywood-movie ectoplasms. I am a man of substance, of flesh and bone, fiber and liquids—and I might even be said to possess a mind. I am invisible, understand, simply because people refuse to see me. Like the bodiless heads you see sometimes in circus sideshows, it is as though I have been surrounded by mirrors of hard, distorting glass. When they approach me they see only my surroundings, themselves, or figments of their imagination—indeed, everything and anything except me.

by forces they can neither understand nor control. In a sense, these novels are like Greek tragedies rendered in prose, with characters who live in slums, not palaces, and with scientific laws replacing the decrees of the gods.

The Symbolist Movement Throughout the nineteenth century, literary movements reacted to previous movements as well as to social conditions: Realism was a response to Romanticism, and Naturalism grew out of Realism. The Symbolist movement, proclaimed in an 1886 manifesto in France but based on the work of earlier writers, followed this same pattern. It rejected the fate-driven world of the Naturalist novel and the Realist drama. In a sense, it was a rebellion of poets against novelists and dramatists.

On the Bank of the Seine, Bennecourt, 1868, Claude Monet, The Art Institute of Chicago

Led by Stéphane Mallarmé (stā fàn´ mà làr mā´) (1842–1898), these poets were looking for an exit from the materialistic nineteenth century. Dismayed by the drabness of everyday life and the vulgar taste of the rising middle class, they searched for an otherworldly spiritual reality. Taking the earlier French poet Charles Baudelaire (shàrl bōd ler´) as their guide, Symbolist poets sought to suggest this reality through musical phrasing and unusual figurative language.

In addition to Baudelaire, poets who anticipated this movement were Paul Verlaine (pôl ver len´) and Arthur Rimbaud (àr tür´ ram bō´). Verlaine, famous for the musicality of his verse, expressed a Symbolist credo when he wrote in "The Art of Poetry," "Let there be music, again and forever!" Rimbaud, a visionary poet who believed he could create a new world and a new language in his verse, stopped writing poetry when he was still a teenager!

The Visual Arts: From Splendor to Strangeness Some of the same movements influencing literature affected the visual arts, as well. Romantic painters like Caspar David Friedrich (frē´ driH) (page 762) depicted mysterious, lonely views of natural splendor. Then, as in literature, Realists rebelled against Romantics. Gustave Courbet (güs tàv´ kōōr be´), for example, painted such gritty subjects as laborers breaking stones (page 756). He declared, "I cannot paint an angel because I have never seen one." In their turn, Impressionists rebelled against Realists. Trying to capture fleeting impressions of shimmering light and color, they treated their paintings less like windows onto reality and more like colorful flat surfaces. Still later, Symbolists like Odilon Redon (ô dē lōn´ rə dōn´) painted such strange and unreal subjects as a drifting balloon in the form of a gigantic eyeball.

▲ **Critical Viewing**
In what ways might this Impressionist painting by Monet differ from a photograph of the same scene? Explain. **[Compare and Contrast]**

Prepare to Read

from Faust

Johann Wolfgang von Goethe (1749–1832)

Because of the tremendous diversity of his talents and interests, Johann (yō hän′) Wolfgang von Goethe (gö′ tə) is best described as a true Renaissance man. He was not only a gifted writer but also a scientist, a painter, a statesman, a philosopher, and an educator.

The son of a wealthy lawyer, Goethe was born in the German town of Frankfurt am Main. After receiving a thorough education from private tutors, he was sent to the University of Leipzig to study law. More interested in the arts than in law, Goethe spent most of his free time writing poetry, studying art, and attending concerts. Nonetheless, he finished his legal studies in 1771.

A Developing Novelist Goethe practiced law for a brief period, during which he wrote *The Sorrows of Young Werther* (1774), an autobiographical novel inspired by an unhappy love affair and the suicide of one of his friends. One of the most important novels of the eighteenth century, *The Sorrows of Young Werther* earned Goethe international fame.

A year after the novel's publication, Goethe accepted an invitation to the court of the reigning duke of Weimar, Charles Augustus. Developing a close friendship with the duke, Goethe lived in Weimar for the rest of his life, and for ten years he served as the duke's chief minister. In 1786, he traveled to Italy in an effort to dedicate time and energy to his writing. He remained there for two years, writing, traveling, painting, and studying classical culture.

Shortly after returning to Weimar, Goethe fell in love with Christiane Vulpius, whom he later married. He also became the director of the court theater and began devoting much of his energy to scientific studies. Through a close friendship with the noted German writer Friedrich von Schiller (1759–1805), Goethe gained valuable guidance and advice concerning his writing and assistance in revising a number of his important works.

A Legendary Figure Probably the most notable of these works was *Faust*. With Schiller's advice and direction, Goethe revised an early draft of the play, adding a prologue. Unfortunately, Schiller died three years before *Faust, Part I* (1808) was published.

The final and greatest achievement of Goethe's literary career was the completion of *Faust, Part II*. The poet's vision of the legendary Faust transformed the traditional character into a newer, more sympathetic one that has fascinated readers and scholars for centuries. Goethe had begun his work on *Part II* while still a young man; because he contributed to the piece throughout his life, *Faust, Part II* ultimately reflects the deep philosophy of life and wry wisdom of the poet's mature years. Goethe never knew of the success of *Faust, Part II*, as it was published late in 1832, a few months after his death.

Faust was by no means the only literary work that Goethe completed. Among his other notable works are his novels—*Wilhelm Meister's Apprenticeship* (1795), *Elective Affinities* (1809), and *Wilhelm Meister's Travels* (1821–1829)—and his autobiographical work *Poetry and Truth* (1811–1832). By the time of his death, Goethe had become a legendary figure throughout the Western world.

Preview

Connecting to the Literature

The Devil lurks in many forms in literature across time and cultures, often trying to convince victims to sell their souls in exchange for their heart's desire. Compare Faust's dilemma to the situation of other characters from books or movies who were tempted by the Devil.

Literary Analysis

Romanticism

Romanticism is a literary and artistic movement that is characterized by the following elements:

- The Romantics favored emotion over reason, intuition over intellect, the subjective over the objective.
- They celebrated creativity, individuality, and imagination.
- Their writings reflect nature, self-knowledge, folklore, and the mysterious and exotic.

Look for these characteristics of Romanticism in *Faust*.

Connecting Literary Elements

A **legend** is a traditional story, handed down through many generations. It usually deals with a hero, a saint, or a national leader. Often, legends reflect a people's cultural values. Notice how Goethe uses facts from the real Faust's life to develop his story.

Reading Strategy

Drawing Inferences

Drawing inferences means making educated guesses based on specific details the author provides.

- Read between the lines to look for any implied meaning.
- Explore passages for clues about characters, setting, plot, and mood.
- Examine significant word choices, patterns of events, and other clues to help you understand the writer's implied message.

Use an organizer like the one shown as you read.

Passage
"I work as the cat does with the mouse."

↓

What Can Be Inferred
Mephistopheles is sly, using man's weaknesses and catching man when he's unaware of his predicament.

Vocabulary Development

envoys (än′ voiz′) *n.* messengers (p. 769)

fervent (fur′ vənt) *adj.* intensely devoted or earnest (p. 770)

primal (prī′ məl) *adj.* original; fundamental (p. 771)

obstinate (äb′ stə nət) *adj.* determined to have one's way; stubborn (p. 775)

fetters (fet′ ərz) *n.* shackles, chains (p. 780)

tenacity (tə nas′ ə tē) *n.* persistence; stubbornness (p. 783)

insatiableness (in sā′ shə bəl nəs) *n.* the quality of being impossible to fill (p. 784)

from Faust

JOHANN WOLFGANG VON GOETHE
translated by Louis MacNeice

Background

Few historical figures have fueled the imagination of the Western world as much as the German scholar and traveling magician Georg Faust (or Faustus), who lived from about 1480 to 1540. According to legend, Faust sold his soul to the Devil in exchange for youth, knowledge, and magical powers. At the time of its origin, the Faust legend was widely thought to be true. In contrast, when Goethe's *Faust* was published, few people believed that the type of events it depicted could actually happen.

Many versions of the Faust legend portray Faust as a man with an unquenchable thirst for knowledge. In Faust's time, only the very wealthy could afford to dedicate their lives to learning. Faust's quest, though noble in theory, drives him into a contract with the Devil. Goethe's version transforms Faust into something of a Romantic hero, embodying the ideal of limitless spiritual aspirations.

Prologue in Heaven

The LORD. *The* HEAVENLY HOSTS. MEPHISTOPHELES[1] *following.*
The THREE ARCHANGELS[2] *step forward.*

RAPHAEL: The chanting sun, as ever, rivals
The chanting of his brother spheres
And marches round his destined circuit—
A march that thunders in our ears.
5 His aspect cheers the Hosts of Heaven
Though what his essence none can say;
These inconceivable creations

---

1. **Mephistopheles** (mef′ ə stäf′ ə lēz′) the Devil.
2. **three archangels** the three chief angels—Raphael, Gabriel, and Michael.

Keep the high state of their first day.

     GABRIEL: And swift, with inconceivable swiftness,
10   The earth's full splendor rolls around,
     Celestial radiance alternating
     With a dread night too deep to sound;
     The sea against the rocks' deep bases
     Comes foaming up in far-flung force,
15   And rock and sea go whirling onward
     In the swift spheres' eternal course.

     MICHAEL: And storms in rivalry are raging
     From sea to land, from land to sea,
     In frenzy forge the world a girdle
20   From which no inmost part is free.
     The blight of lightning flaming yonder
     Marks where the thunder-bolt will play;
     And yet Thine <u>envoys</u>, Lord, revere
     The gentle movement of Thy day.

25 **CHOIR OF ANGELS:** Thine aspect cheers the Hosts of Heaven
     Though what Thine essence none can say,
     And all Thy loftiest creations
     Keep the high state of their first day.

     [*Enter* MEPHISTOPHELES.]

     MEPHISTOPHELES: Since you, O Lord, once more approach and ask
30   If business down with us be light or heavy—
     And in the past you've usually welcomed me—
     That's why you see me also at your levee.[3]

---

3. levee (lev´ ē) *n.* morning reception held by a person of high rank.

▲ **Critical Viewing**
Which of the archangels' words could describe the scene in this photograph? **[Connect]**

Literary Analysis
Romanticism Which words in Michael's dialogue are charged with emotional intensity?

envoys (än´ voiz´) *n.* messengers

☑**Reading Check**
According to Michael, what girdles, or imprisons, the earth?

Excuse me, I can't manage lofty words—
Not though your whole court jeer and find me low;
35 My pathos[4] certainly would make you laugh
Had you not left off laughing long ago.
Your suns and worlds mean nothing much to me;
How men torment themselves, that's all I see.
The little god of the world, one can't reshape, reshade him;
40 He is as strange to-day as that first day you made him.
His life would be not so bad, not quite,
Had you not granted him a gleam of Heaven's light;
He calls it Reason, uses it not the least
Except to be more beastly than any beast.
45 He seems to me—if your Honor does not mind—
Like a grasshopper—the long-legged kind—
That's always in flight and leaps as it flies along
And then in the grass strikes up its same old song.
I could only wish he confined himself to the grass!
50 He thrusts his nose into every filth, alas.

LORD: Mephistopheles, have you no other news?
Do you always come here to accuse?
Is nothing ever right in your eyes on earth?

MEPHISTOPHELES: No, Lord! I find things there as downright bad
      as ever.
55 I am sorry for men's days of dread and dearth;
Poor things, *my* wish to plague 'em isn't <u>fervent</u>.

LORD: Do you know Faust?

MEPHISTOPHELES: The Doctor?[5]

LORD: Aye, my servant.

MEPHISTOPHELES: Indeed! He serves you oddly enough, I think.
The fool has no earthly habits in meat and drink.
60 The ferment in him drives him wide and far,
That he is mad he too has almost guessed;
He demands of heaven each fairest star
And of earth each highest joy and best,
And all that is new and all that is far
65 Can bring no calm to the deep-sea swell of his breast.

LORD: Now he may serve me only gropingly,
Soon I shall lead him into the light.
The gardener knows when the sapling first turns green
That flowers and fruit will make the future bright.

---

4. pathos (pā′ thäs) *n.* suffering.
5. Doctor Doctor of Philosophy.

Reading Strategy
Drawing Inferences
What does Mephistopheles imply that Faust is unable to accomplish with his ability to reason?

fervent (fur′ vənt) *adj.* intensely devoted or earnest

Literary Analysis
Romanticism Explain how these lines reflect the Romantics' attitude toward the importance of the individual and the value of unbounded spiritual aspirations.

Mephistopheles, 1863, Eugène Delacroix, Giraudon

▲ **Critical Viewing**
What impression of Mephistopheles does the artist convey? **[Explain]**

70 **MEPHISTOPHELES:** What do you wager?
        You will lose him yet,
    Provided *you* give *me* permission
    To steer him gently the course I set.

    LORD: So long as he walks the earth alive,
    So long you may try what enters your head;
75 Men make mistakes as long as they strive.

    MEPHISTOPHELES: I thank you for that; as regards the dead,
    The dead have never taken my fancy.
    I favor cheeks that are full and rosy-red;
    No corpse is welcome to my house;
80 I work as the cat does with the mouse.

    LORD: Very well; you have my full permission.
    Divert this soul from its <u>primal</u> source
    And carry it, if you can seize it,
    Down with you upon your course—
85 And stand ashamed when you must needs admit:
    A good man with his groping intuitions
    Still knows the path that is true and fit.

    MEPHISTOPHELES: All right—but it won't last for long.
    I'm not afraid my bet will turn out wrong.
90 And, if my aim prove true and strong,
    Allow me to triumph wholeheartedly.
    Dust shall he eat—and greedily—
    Like my cousin the Snake[6] renowned in tale and song.

primal (prī´ məl) *adj.* original; fundamental

☑️ **Reading Check**
What wager has Mephistopheles made with the Lord?

---

6. my cousin the Snake In Genesis, the devil assumes the form of a serpent in order to tempt Eve to eat from the Tree of Knowledge.

LORD: That too you are free to give a trial;
95 I have never hated the likes of you.
Of all the spirits of denial
The joker is the last that I eschew.
Man finds relaxation too attractive—
Too fond too soon of unconditional rest;
100 Which is why I am pleased to give him a companion
Who lures and thrusts and must, as devil, be active.
But ye, true sons of Heaven, it is your duty
To take your joy in the living wealth of beauty.
The changing Essence which ever works and lives
105 Wall you around with love, serene, secure!
And that which floats in flickering appearance
Fix ye it firm in thoughts that must endure.

CHOIR OF ANGELS: Thine aspect cheers the Hosts of Heaven
Though what Thine essence none can say,
110 And all Thy loftiest creations
Keep the high state of their first day.

[*Heaven closes.*]

MEPHISTOPHELES [*alone*]: I like to see the Old One now and then
And try to keep relations on the level.
It's really decent of so great a person
115 To talk so humanely even to the Devil.

Reading Strategy
Drawing Inferences
What can you infer about the purpose of the Devil from the Lord's words?

Review and Assess

Thinking About the Selection

1. **Respond:** What do you imagine will be the outcome of Mephistopheles's wager with the Lord? Explain your answer.

2. **(a) Recall:** How would you characterize Mephistopheles as he appears in "Prologue in Heaven"? **(b) Infer:** What is his attitude toward humanity?

3. **(a) Recall:** How does Mephistopheles describe Faust? **(b) Deduce:** Based on Mephistopheles's description, what type of person do you imagine Faust to be?

4. **(a) Recall:** What is the Lord's attitude toward Mephistopheles? **(b) Support:** How is this attitude conveyed?

5. **Take a Position:** Do you agree with the Lord's statement that "Men make mistakes as long as they strive" (line 75)? Explain.

from Faust

Background

In "Prologue in Heaven," Mephistopheles and the Lord disagree about Faust's true soul, and the Lord gives Mephistopheles permission to compete for Faust's soul. Only a great test will determine whether Faust recognizes the value of the life he currently lives or whether greed and irrationality will drive him to sell his soul to the Devil. Mephistopheles knows Faust's weakness—an unquenchable desire for knowledge—and seeks to use it as his means of luring Faust into a high-stakes bargain. Will Faust be tempted? Will Mephistopheles be forced to admit that Faust is like other good men who know "the path that is true and fit"? Look for the answers to these questions in "The First Part of the Tragedy."

from The First Part of the Tragedy

NIGHT

In a high-vaulted narrow Gothic[1] room FAUST, *restless, in a chair at his desk.*

> **FAUST:** Here stand I, ach, Philosophy
> Behind me and Law and Medicine too
> And, to my cost, Theology—
> All these I have sweated through and through
> 5 And now you see me a poor fool
> As wise as when I entered school!
> They call me Master, they call me Doctor,
> Ten years now I have dragged my college
> Along by the nose through zig and zag

---

1. **Gothic** (gäth´ ik) *adj.* of a style of architecture characterized by the use of ribbed vaulting, flying buttresses, pointed arches, and steep, high roofs.

✔Reading Check

Why does Faust consider himself a "poor fool"?

10   Through up and down and round and round
And this is all that I have found—
The impossibility of knowledge!
It is this that burns away my heart;
Of course I am cleverer than the quacks,
15   Than master and doctor, than clerk and priest,
I suffer no scruple or doubt in the least,
I have no qualms about devil or burning,
Which is just why all joy is torn from me,
I cannot presume to make use of my learning,
20   I cannot presume I could open my mind
To proselytize² and improve mankind.

Besides, I have neither goods nor gold,
Neither reputation nor rank in the world;
No dog would choose to continue so!
25   Which is why I have given myself to Magic
To see if the Spirit may grant me to know
Through its force and its voice full many a secret,
May spare the sour sweat that I used to pour out
In talking of what I know nothing about,
30   May grant me to learn what it is that girds
The world together in its inmost being,
That the seeing its whole germination, the seeing
Its workings, may end my traffic in words.

After summoning the Earth Spirit and finding it unwilling to assist him in his quest for knowledge, Faust lapses into a state of despair. He decides to end his life by drinking a cup of poison but abruptly changes his mind when he hears the tolling of church bells and the singing of choruses, celebrating the arrival of Easter. Setting out on a walk through the countryside with Wagner, his assistant, Faust is inspired by the beauty of spring and soothed by the peasants' expressions of admiration and affection for him. When he returns to his study, however, his sense of contentment quickly dissipates. Alerted by the growling of his dog, Faust becomes aware of another presence in the room. When Faust threatens to use magic to defend himself against the unseen intruder, Mephistopheles comes forward from behind the stove, disguised as a traveling scholar. Faust soon becomes aware of Mephistopheles's true identity, and he is intrigued by the possibility of establishing a contract with the devil. However, Faust falls asleep before the two can reach an agreement. In the following scene, Mephistopheles returns to the study to resume his discussion with Faust.

---

2. **proselytize** (präs´ ə li tīz´) v. to try to convert.

Literary Analysis
Romanticism and Legends How does Faust's speech reflect what you know about the real Faust from the Background on page 768?

▼ **Critical Viewing**
Why might Faust sympathize with the man in this painting? **[Hypothesize]**

[The same room. Later.]

FAUST: Who's knocking? Come in! *Now* who wants to annoy me?

35 **MEPHISTOPHELES** [*outside door*]: It's I.

FAUST: Come in!

MEPHISTOPHELES [*outside door*]:
You must say "Come in" three times.

FAUST: Come in then!

MEPHISTOPHELES [*entering*]:
Thank you; you overjoy me.
We two, I hope, we shall be good friends;
40 To chase those megrims[3] of yours away
I am here like a fine young squire to-day,
In a suit of scarlet trimmed with gold
And a little cape of stiff brocade,
With a cock's feather in my hat
45 And at my side a long sharp blade,
And the most succinct advice I can give
Is that you dress up just like me,
So that uninhibited and free
You may find out what it means to live.

50 **FAUST:** The pain of earth's constricted life, I fancy,
Will pierce me still, whatever my attire;
I am too old for mere amusement,
Too young to be without desire,
How can the world dispel my doubt?
55 You must do without, you must do without!
That is the everlasting song
Which rings in every ear, which rings,
And which to us our whole life long
Every hour hoarsely sings.
60 I wake in the morning only to feel appalled,
My eyes with bitter tears could run
To see the day which in its course
Will not fulfil a wish for me, not one;
The day which whittles away with <u>obstinate</u> carping
65 All pleasures—even those of anticipation,
Which makes a thousand grimaces to obstruct
My heart when it is stirring in creation.
And again, when night comes down, in anguish
I must stretch out upon my bed

---

3. megrims (mē′ grəmz) *n.* low spirits.

Reading Strategy
Drawing Inferences Why has Mephistopheles changed his costume from that of a traveling scholar to "a suit of scarlet trimmed with gold"?

obstinate (äb′ stə nət) *adj.* determined to have one's way; stubborn.

✔**Reading Check**
What torments Faust every day?

70 And again no rest is granted me,
For wild dreams fill my mind with dread.
The God who dwells within my bosom
Can make my inmost soul react;
The God who sways my every power
75 Is powerless with external fact.
And so existence weighs upon my breast
And I long for death and life—life I detest.

MEPHISTOPHELES: Yet death is never a wholly welcome guest.

FAUST: O happy is he whom death in the dazzle of victory
80 Crowns with the bloody laurel in the battling swirl!
Or he whom after the mad and breakneck dance
He comes upon in the arms of a girl!
O to have sunk away, delighted, deleted,
Before the Spirit of the Earth, before his might!

85 **MEPHISTOPHELES:** Yet I know someone who failed to drink
A brown juice on a certain night.

FAUST: Your hobby is espionage—is it not?

MEPHISTOPHELES: Oh I'm not omniscient[4]—but I know a lot.

FAUST: Whereas that tumult in my soul
90 Was stilled by sweet familiar chimes
Which cozened the child that yet was in me
With echoes of more happy times,
I now curse all things that encompass
The soul with lures and jugglery
95 And bind it in this dungeon of grief
With trickery and flattery.
Cursed in advance be the high opinion
That serves our spirit for a cloak!
Cursed be the dazzle of appearance
100 Which bows our senses to its yoke!
Cursed be the lying dreams of glory,
The illusion that our name survives!
Cursed be the flattering things we own,
Servants and ploughs, children and wives!
105 Cursed be Mammon[5] when with his treasures
He makes us play the adventurous man
Or when for our luxurious pleasures
He duly spreads the soft divan![6]

Literary Analysis
Romanticism In what way does this passage exhibit the Romantics' interest in emotion and the individual?

---

4. **omniscient** (äm nish′ ənt) *adj.* knowing all things.
5. **Mammon** (mam′ ən) Generally, Mammon refers to riches regarded as an object of worship and greedy pursuit; here, the word is used to refer to the Devil, as an embodiment of greed.
6. **divan** (di van′) *n.* large, low couch or sofa, usually without armrests or a back.

◀ **Critical Viewing**
How does the study por-
trayed here fit Faust's
personality? [**Connect**]

A curse on the balsam of the grape!
110 A curse on the love that rides for a fall!
A curse on hope! A curse on faith!
And a curse on patience most of all!

[*The* INVISIBLE SPIRITS *sing again.*]

SPIRITS: Woe! Woe!
You have destroyed it,
115   The beautiful world;
By your violent hand
'Tis downward hurled!
A half-god has dashed it asunder!
From under
120   We bear off the rubble to nowhere
And ponder
Sadly the beauty departed.
Magnipotent
One among men,

Reading Strategy
Drawing Inferences
Which details help you
determine whether these
invisible spirits are on the
side of good or evil?

Reading Check

What has Faust
destroyed?

125 Magnificent
Build it again,
Build it again in your breast!
Let a new course of life
Begin
130 With vision abounding
And new songs resounding
To welcome it in!

MEPHISTOPHELES: These are the juniors
Of my faction.
Hear how precociously[7] they counsel
135 Pleasure and action.
Out and away
From your lonely day
Which dries your senses and your juices
Their melody seduces.

Literary Analysis
Romanticism In what ways does Mephistopheles's speech reflect the Romantics' interest in emotions?

140 Stop playing with your grief which battens
Like a vulture on your life, your mind!
The worst of company would make you feel
That you are a man among mankind.
Not that it's really my proposition
145 To shove you among the common men;
Though I'm not one of the Upper Ten,
If you would like a coalition
With me for your career through life,
I am quite ready to fit in,
150 I'm yours before you can say knife.
I am your comrade;
If you so crave,
I am your servant, I am your slave.

FAUST: And what have I to undertake in return?

155 **MEPHISTOPHELES:** Oh it's early days to discuss what that is.

FAUST: No, no, the devil is an egoist
And ready to do nothing gratis
Which is to benefit a stranger.
Tell me your terms and don't prevaricate![8]
160 A servant like you in the house is a danger.

Reading Strategy
Drawing Inferences What does Faust mean when he refers to Mephistopheles as "a servant like you"?

MEPHISTOPHELES: I will bind myself to your service in this world,
To be at your beck and never rest nor slack;

---

7. **precociously** (pri kō′ shəs lē) *adv.* exhibiting maturity to a point beyond that which is normal for the age.
8. **prevaricate** (pri var′ i kāt) *v.* to tell an untruth.

When we meet again on the other side,
In the same coin you shall pay me back.

165 **FAUST:** The other side gives me little trouble;
First batter this present world to rubble,
Then the other may rise—if that's the plan.
This earth is where my springs of joy have started,
And this sun shines on me when broken-hearted;
170 If I can first from them be parted,
Then let happen what will and can!
I wish to hear no more about it—
Whether there too men hate and love
Or whether in those spheres too, in the future,
175 There is a Below or an Above.

MEPHISTOPHELES: With such an outlook you can
risk it.
Sign on the line! In these next days you will get
Ravishing samples of my arts;
I am giving you what never man saw yet.

180 **FAUST:** Poor devil, can *you* give anything ever?
Was a human spirit in its high endeavor
Even once understood by one of your breed?
Have you got food which fails to feed?
Or red gold which, never at rest,
185 Like mercury runs away through the hand?
A game at which one never wins?
A girl who, even when on my breast,
Pledges herself to my neighbor with her eyes?
The divine and lovely delight of honor
190 Which falls like a falling star and dies?
Show me the fruits which, before they are plucked,
decay
And the trees which day after day renew their green!

MEPHISTOPHELES: Such a commission doesn't
alarm me,
I have such treasures to purvey.
195 But, my good friend, the time draws on when we
Should be glad to feast at our ease on something good.

FAUST: If ever I stretch myself on a bed of ease,
Then I am finished! Is that understood?
If ever your flatteries can coax me
200 To be pleased with myself, if ever you cast
A spell of pleasure that can hoax me—
Then let *that* day be my last!
That's my wager!

Themes in World Literature

The Terrible Bargain
Over the years, the Faust legend has appeared in many variations and adaptations. Each retelling involves a person who trades his soul for experience, knowledge, or treasure. "The Devil and Tom Walker" by Washington Irving is just one of these variations. Set in colonial Massachusetts, the short story features the miser Tom Walker and his overbearing wife. Wishing for untold wealth, Tom makes a pact with the Devil, whom he encounters in a swampy forest. Like other fictional characters who sell their souls, he obtains his heart's desire in exchange.

Adaptations do not share the same ending—in some, such as "The Devil and Tom Walker," the protagonist is doomed; in others, such as "The Devil and Daniel Webster" by Stephen Vincent Benét, he is redeemed. Variations of the legend appear across genres and generations as well. In Oscar Wilde's novel *A Picture of Dorian Gray* (1891), Gray trades his soul for perpetual youth. In *Bedazzled*, a Hollywood film released in 2000, the terrible bargain is reinvented when a man trades his soul to the Devil—who appears in the form of a beautiful woman—in exchange for seven wishes. Look for variations of the Faust legend in art, movies, music, and, of course, literature.

Reading Check
What will Mephistopheles show Faust when he signs the agreement?

MEPHISTOPHELES: Done!

FAUST: Let's shake!
205   If ever I say to the passing moment
    "Linger a while! Thou art so fair!"
    Then you may cast me into <u>fetters</u>,
    I will gladly perish then and there!
    Then you may set the death-bell tolling,
210   Then from my service you are free,
    The clock may stop, its hand may fall,
    And that be the end of time for me!

MEPHISTOPHELES: Think what you're saying, we shall not
      forget it.

FAUST: And you are fully within your rights;
215   I have made no mad or outrageous claim.
    If I stay as I am, I am a slave—
    Whether yours or another's, it's all the same.

MEPHISTOPHELES: I shall this very day at the College Banquet[9]
    Enter your service with no more ado,
220   But just one point—As a life-and-death insurance
    I must trouble you for a line or two.

FAUST: So you, you pedant, you too like things in writing?
    Have you never known a man? Or a man's word? Never?
    Is it not enough that my word of mouth
225   Puts all my days in bond for ever?
    Does not the world rage on in all its streams
    And shall a promise hamper *me?*
    Yet this illusion reigns within our hearts
    And from it who would be gladly free?
230   Happy the man who can inwardly keep his word;
    Whatever the cost, he will not be loath to pay!
    But a parchment, duly inscribed and sealed,
    Is a bogey[10] from which all wince away.
    The word dies on the tip of the pen
235   And wax and leather lord it then.
    What do you, evil spirit, require?
    Bronze, marble, parchment, paper?
    Quill or chisel or pencil of slate?
    You may choose whichever you desire.

240 **MEPHISTOPHELES:** How can you so exaggerate
    With such a hectic rhetoric?

fetters (fet´ ərz) *n.* shackles, chains

Reading Strategy
Drawing Inferences
Why does Mephistopheles want the agreement recorded in writing?

Critical Viewing ▶
How does this painting convey the powers of nature that Faust has experienced? **[Analyze]**

---

9. **the College Banquet** the *Doctorschmaus*, a dinner given by a successful candidate for a Ph.D. degree.
10. **bogey** (bō´ gē) *n.* anything one especially, and often needlessly, fears.

Any little snippet is quite good—
And you sign it with one little drop of blood.

FAUST: If that is enough and is some use,
245   One may as well pander to your fad.

MEPHISTOPHELES: Blood is a very special juice.

FAUST: Only do not fear that I shall break this contract.
What I promise is nothing more
Than what all my powers are striving for.
250   I have puffed myself up too much, it is only
Your sort that really fits my case.
The great Earth Spirit has despised me
And Nature shuts the door in my face.
The thread of thought is snapped asunder,
255   I have long loathed knowledge in all its fashions.
In the depths of sensuality

✓ **Reading Check**

Why does Mephistopheles want Faust to sign the agreement in blood?

Dunstanburgh Castle in a Thunderstorm, Thomas Girtin, Ashmolean Museum, Oxford, UK

Let us now quench our glowing passions!
And at once make ready every wonder
Of unpenetrated sorcery!
260   Let us cast ourselves into the torrent of time,
Into the whirl of eventfulness,
Where disappointment and success,
Pleasure and pain may chop and change
As chop and change they will and can;
265   It is restless action makes the man.

MEPHISTOPHELES: No limit is fixed for you, no bound;
If you'd like to nibble at everything
Or to seize upon something flying round—
Well, may you have a run for your money!
270   But seize your chance and don't be funny!

FAUST: I've told you, it is no question of happiness.
The most painful joy, enamored hate, enlivening
Disgust—I devote myself to all excess.
My breast, now cured of its appetite for knowledge,
275   From now is open to all and every smart,
And what is allotted to the whole of mankind
That will I sample in my inmost heart,
Grasping the highest and lowest with my spirit,
Piling men's weal and woe upon my neck,
280   To extend myself to embrace all human selves
And to founder in the end, like them, a wreck.

MEPHISTOPHELES: O believe *me,* who have been
    chewing
These iron rations many a thousand year,
No human being can digest
285   This stuff, from the cradle to the bier[11]
This universe—believe a devil—
Was made for no one but a god!
He exists in eternal light
But *us* he has brought into the darkness
290   While *your* sole portion is day and night.

FAUST: I will all the same!

MEPHISTOPHELES: That's very nice.
There's only one thing I find wrong;
Time is short, art is long.
You could do with a little artistic advice.
295   Confederate with one of the poets
And let him flog his imagination

---
11. bier (bir) *n.* coffin and its supporting platform.

▼ **Critical Viewing**
What arts and sciences represented in this still life would Faust find interesting? **[Speculate]**

Vanitas, Edwaert Collier, Johnny van Haeften Gallery, London, UK

To heap all virtues on your head,
A head with such a reputation:
Lion's bravery,
300 Stag's velocity,
Fire of Italy,
Northern <u>tenacity</u>.
Let *him* find out the secret art
Of combining craft with a noble heart
305 And of being in love like a young man,
Hotly, but working to a plan.
Such a person—*I'd* like to meet him;
"Mr. Microcosm"[12] is how I'd greet him.

FAUST: What am I then if fate must bar
310 My efforts to reach that crown of humanity
After which all my senses strive?

MEPHISTOPHELES: You are in the end . . . what you are.
You can put on full-bottomed wigs with a million locks,
You can put on stilts instead of your stocks,
315 You remain for ever what you are.

FAUST: I feel my endeavors have not been worth a pin
When I raked together the treasures of the human mind,
If at the end I but sit down to find
No new force welling up within.
320 I have not a hair's breadth more of height,
I am no nearer the Infinite.

MEPHISTOPHELES: My very good sir, you look at things
Just in the way that people do;
We must be cleverer than that
325 Or the joys of life will escape from you.
Hell! You have surely hands and feet,
Also a head and you-know-what;
The pleasures I gather on the wing,
Are they less mine? Of course they're not!
330 Suppose I can afford six stallions,
I can add that horse-power to my score
And dash along and be a proper man
As if my legs were twenty-four.
So good-bye to thinking! On your toes!
335 The world's before us. Quick! Here goes!
I tell you, a chap who's intellectual
Is like a beast on a blasted heath
Driven in circles by a demon
While a fine green meadow lies round beneath.

12. **Mr. Microcosm** man regarded as the epitome of the world.

---

tenacity (tə nas′ ə tē) *n.* persistence; stubborness

Reading Strategy
Drawing Inferences
What can you infer about Faust from line 312?

Literary Analysis
Romanticism and Legends Do you think Faust hopes to become a legendary figure? Explain.

Reading Check

After all Faust's efforts to gain knowledge, what will he become in the end?

340 **FAUST:** How do we start?

MEPHISTOPHELES: We just say go—and skip.
But please get ready for this pleasure trip.

[*Exit* FAUST.]

Only look down on knowledge and reason,
The highest gifts that men can prize,
345 Only allow the spirit of lies
To confirm you in magic and illusion,
And then I have you body and soul.
Fate has given this man a spirit
Which is always pressing onward, beyond control,
350 And whose mad striving overleaps
All joys of the earth between pole and pole.
Him shall I drag through the wilds of life
And through the flats of meaninglessness,
I shall make him flounder and gape and stick
355 And to tease his <u>insatiableness</u>
Hang meat and drink in the air before his watering lips;
In vain he will pray to slake his inner thirst,
And even had he not sold himself to the devil
He would be equally accursed.

Reading Strategy
Drawing Inferences
What does Mephistopheles mean by "meat and drink"?

insatiableness (in sā′ shə bəl nəs) *n.* the quality of being impossible to fill

Review and Assess

Thinking About the Selection

1. **Respond:** Which of Faust's feelings in the selection, if any, surprised you? Explain.
2. **(a) Recall:** What is Faust's state of mind in the opening scene? **(b) Deduce:** What does Faust mean when he says that he has discovered "the impossibility of knowledge"?
3. **(a) Recall:** What are the terms of the agreement between Faust and Mephistopheles? **(b) Evaluate:** Which character has the better part of the bargain?
4. **(a) Recall:** What does Faust use to sign his agreement with Mephistopheles? **(b) Infer:** What can you infer about Faust's attitude regarding the afterlife from his willingness to sign the agreement?
5. **Hypothesize:** Would Faust be a more satisfied person if he were living in today's world? Explain.

Review and Assess

Literary Analysis

Romanticism

1. Use a chart like the one shown to cite passages from *Faust* that demonstrate key features of **Romanticism.**

Features of Romanticism	Passage from *Faust*
favoring emotion over reason	
favoring intuition over intellect	
favoring the subjective over the objective	
celebrating the individual	

2. (a) Identify three details from *Faust* that express the Romantics' love of the mysterious and exotic. (b) Why is this characteristic of Romantic writing particularly suitable for *Faust*?
3. In what way does the treatment of Mephistopheles reflect the idealism and optimism of the Romantics? Explain.

Connecting Literary Elements

4. Which details in *Faust* point to the fact that Goethe embellishes the truth about the real Faust and adds to the **legend** about him?
5. What does this version of *Faust* tell you about the values and beliefs of Goethe's society?

Reading Strategy

Drawing Inferences

6. By **drawing inferences** from lines 10–24 of "The First Part of the Tragedy," explain why Faust makes a pact with the Devil.
7. In lines 180–192, what crucial knowledge does Faust imply is missing in Mephistopheles?
8. What can you infer about Mephistopheles's true character from lines 343–359, lines that are spoken after Faust has exited?

Extend Understanding

9. **Cultural Connection:** In Goethe's *Faust*, the Devil offers the temptation of knowledge. (a) Do you think this offer would be valuable in all cultures? (b) What other prizes might tempt people?

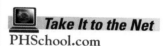

Integrate Language Skills

Vocabulary Development Lesson

Related Words: *prime*

The word *prime*, from a Latin root meaning "first," is the basis for many related words.

From the following list, choose the related word that best completes each sentence below. Use a dictionary to check your responses.

a. primal   b. primitive   c. primary   d. primeval

1. She is held back by the ___ nature of the technology she uses.
2. One of our ___ instincts is the need to protect our young.
3. He lives on one hundred acres of ___ forest, untouched by an ax.
4. The doctor's ___ concern is for the health of his patients.

Concept Development: Synonyms

Match each vocabulary word on the left to the word on the right that has a similar meaning.

1. envoys
2. fervent
3. primal
4. obstinate
5. fetters
6. tenacity
7. insatiableness

a. shackles
b. basic
c. greediness
d. eager
e. messengers
f. stubborn
g. persistence

Spelling Strategy

In English, the suffix *-ity*, as used in the word *laity*, is more common than the suffix *-ety*. For each of the following words, write its noun form ending in *-ity*.

1. tenacious   2. scarce   3. possible

Grammar and Style Lesson

Usage: *who* and *whom*

The words *who* and *whom* are often used incorrectly. *Who*, like *he* or *she*, is used as a subject or subject complement. *Whom*, like *him* or *her*, is used as a direct object or as an object of a preposition. Study these examples:

"The God <u>who</u> dwells within my bosom . . ."

"Happy is he <u>whom</u> death . . . Crowns with the bloody laurel . . ."

Practice Copy each item below, adding *who* or *whom* as needed. Then, identify the word's function in the phrase or sentence.

1. "*Now* ___ wants to annoy me?"

2. "The God ___ sways my every power /Is powerless with external fact."
3. "O happy is he . . . ___ after the mad and breakneck dance / He comes upon . . ."
4. "Yet I know someone ___ failed to drink / A brown juice on a certain night."
5. It is the Devil ___ Faust meets in the study.

Writing Application Write a paragraph in which you predict how this play might end. Include two sentences in which you use *who* and *whom* correctly.

W/G **Prentice Hall Writing and Grammar Connection: Diamond Level, Chapter 22, Section 2**

Writing Lesson

Writing a Film Script

Imagine that you are a screenwriter who has been hired to create a film adaptation of Goethe's *Faust*. Think about the ways in which the original text should be expanded in preparation for filming. Your script should focus only on the parts of Goethe's poetic drama that you have read.

Prewriting   Begin by imagining what the scene would look like on a movie screen. List any special effects that you would expect to see, such as lighting, sound effects, and camera angles.

Drafting   Once you have a good idea of the adaptations that should be made, begin writing your screenplay. Format the script like the model below.

Model: Writing Stage Directions

[*Camera on Faust, deep in study. Candlelight on him and his books. Sound of knocking on door.*]

Faust: Who's knocking? [*Camera close-up on Faust's face as he looks up.*] Come in! *Now* who wants to annoy me?

Mephistopheles: [*Camera shot of Mephistopheles.*] It's I.

> Stage directions describe actions, camera angles, sound effects, lighting, and special effects.

Revising   Ask a classmate to read your finished screenplay to see if your stage directions are clear. Finally, keeping your classmate's comments in mind, revise your screenplay, and prepare a final copy.

WG *Prentice Hall Writing and Grammar Connection: Diamond Level, Chapter 2, Section 2*

Extension Activities

Listening and Speaking With a partner, rehearse and present a **brief dialogue** based on the play. As you rehearse, keep the following elements consistent:

- the tone and mood of the work
- the character development
- the culture in which the dialogue is set

As you prepare your presentation, be sure to use your voice and facial expressions effectively.
[Group Activity]

Research and Technology Using a video camera, make a **film** version of a segment from the play. Your short film might include unusual camera angles, sound effects, planned lighting, and other special effects.

 **Take It to the Net**   PHSchool.com

Go online for an additional research activity using the Internet.

from # The Tragical History of Doctor Faustus

Christopher Marlowe

Great literature often grows from legendary events and characters. Goethe's *Faust*, for example, was inspired by the folk legend of an actual person: Johann Faust (or Faustus), who lived in Wittenberg, Germany, from 1480 to 1540. According to the legend, Faust had sold his soul to the devil for youth, knowledge, and magical powers. Like the real person, Goethe's Faust willingly sacrifices his soul to have all his wishes fulfilled. In fact, he focuses so intently on power and riches in this life that he is willing to risk eternal damnation in the next.

Doomed Forever Goethe was not the first writer to be inspired by the Faust legend. Christopher Marlowe's *The Tragical History of Doctor Faustus* was written in the sixteenth century, not long after the death of the real Johann Faust. Like Goethe's Faust, Marlowe's Doctor Faustus learns the awful majesty and inevitable doom of the bargain he makes with the devil.

ACT I. SCENE III. IN A GROVE.

Enter FAUSTUS.

FAUSTUS: Now that the gloomy shadow of the earth,
    Longing to view Orion's drizzling look,
    Leaps from th' antarctic world unto the sky,
    And dims the welkin[1] with her pitchy breath,
5   Faustus, begin thine incantations,
    And try if devils will obey thy hest,
    Seeing thou hast pray'd and sacrific'd to them.
    Within this circle is Jehovah's name,
    Forward and backward anagrammatiz'd,[2]
10   The breviated names of holy saints,
    Figures of every adjunct to the heavens,
    And characters of signs and erring stars,
    By which the spirits are enforc'd to rise:
    Then fear not, Faustus, but be resolute,
15   And try the uttermost magic can perform.—
       Sint mihi dei Acherontis propitii! Valeat numen
    triplex Jehovœ! Ignei, aërii, aquatani spiritus, salvete!
    Orientis princeps Belzebub, inferni ardentis monarcha, et
    Demogorgon, propitiamus vos, ut appareat et surgat
    Mephistophilis: quid tu moraris? Per Jehovam, Gehennam,
20   *et consecratam aquam quam nunc spargo, signumque*
    crucis quod nunc facio, et per vota nostra, ipse nunc surgat
    nobis dicatus Mephistophilis![3]

Enter MEPHISTOPHILIS.

    I charge thee to return, and change thy shape;
    Thou art too ugly to attend on me:
25   Go, and return an old Franciscan friar;
    That holy shape becomes a devil best.

Exit MEPHISTOPHILIS.

    I see there's virtue[4] in my heavenly words:
    Who would not be proficient in this art?
    How pliant is this Mephistophilis,

Thematic Connection
Why do you think the physical appearance of Mephistophilis is important to Faustus?

---

1. **welkin** sky or vault of heaven.
2. **Jehovah's name . . . anagrammatiz'd** (an´ ə gram´ ə tīzd) Jehovah, the holy name of God in the Old Testament, has been spelled backward and forward in a magical rite.
3. *Sint . . . Mephistophilis* May the gods of the underworld (Acheron) be kind to me! May the triple deity of Jehovah be gone! To the spirits of fire, air, and water, greetings. Prince of the east, Beelzebub, monarch of the fires below, and Demogorgon, we appeal to you, so that Mephistophilis may appear and rise: why do you delay? By Jehovah, hell, and the hallowed water which I now sprinkle, and the sign of the cross which I now make, and by our vows, let Mephistophilis himself now arise to serve us!
4. **virtue** power, as well as goodness.

30

Full of obedience and humility!
Such is the force of magic and my spells:
Now, Faustus, thou art conjuror laureat,[5]
That canst command great Mephistophilis:
Quin regis Mephistophilis fratris imagine.[6]

Enter MEPHISTOPHILIS (*like a Franciscan friar*).

35   **MEPHISTOPHILIS:** Now, Faustus, what wouldst thou have me do?

FAUSTUS: I charge thee wait upon me whilst I live,
To do whatever Faustus shall command,
Be it to make the moon drop from her sphere,
Or the ocean to overwhelm the world.

40   **MEPHISTOPHILIS:** I am a servant to great Lucifer,
And may not follow thee without his leave:
No more than he commands must we perform.

FAUSTUS: Did not he charge thee to appear to me?

MEPHISTOPHILIS: No, I came hither of mine own accord.

45   **FAUSTUS:** Did not my conjuring speeches raise thee? speak.

MEPHISTOPHILIS: That was the cause, but yet *per accidens:*[7]
For, when we hear one rack the name of God,
Abjure[8] the Scriptures and his Savior Christ,
We fly, in hope to get his glorious soul;
50   Nor will we come, unless he use such means
Whereby he is in danger to be damn'd.
Therefore the shortest cut for conjuring
Is stoutly to abjure the Trinity,
And pray devoutly to the prince of Hell.

55   **FAUSTUS:** So Faustus hath
Already done; and holds this principle,
There is no chief but only Belzebub;[9]
To whom Faustus doth dedicate himself.
This word "damnation" terrifies not him,
60   For he confounds hell in Elysium:
His ghost be with the old philosophers![10]
But, leaving these vain trifles of men's souls,
Tell me what is that Lucifer, thy Lord?

---

5. **conjuror laureat** the greatest magician.
6. *Quin . . . imagine* Why do you not return, Mephistophilis, in the appearance of a friar?
7. *per accidens* by the immediate, not the ultimate, cause.
8. **abjure** (ab jŏŏr´) *v.* give up; renounce.
9. **Belzebub**, variant spelling of **Beelzebub** (bē el´ zə bub´) the chief devil, whose name means "god of flies" in Hebrew.
10. **For he . . . philosophers** He thinks that hell is really Elysium. In Greek mythology, Elysium was the dwelling place of the virtuous after death. In Dante's *Inferno*, it is a pleasant abode for righteous pagans in a special part of hell.

Critical Viewing ▶
What can you infer about the different personalities of Faustus and Mephistophilis from their clothing and their attitudes in this painting? [**Infer**]

Mephistopheles Appears Before Faust, Eugène Delacroix, The Wallace Collection

MEPHISTOPHILIS: Arch-regent and commander of all spirits.

65 **FAUSTUS:** Was not that Lucifer an angel once?

MEPHISTOPHILIS: Yes, Faustus, and most dearly lov'd of God.

FAUSTUS: How comes it, then, that he is prince of devils?

MEPHISTOPHILIS: O, by aspiring pride and insolence;
For which God threw him from the face of heaven.

70 **FAUSTUS:** And what are you that live with Lucifer?

MEPHISTOPHILIS: Unhappy spirits that fell with Lucifer,
Conspir'd against our God with Lucifer,
And are for ever damn'd with Lucifer.

FAUSTUS: Where are you damn'd?

MEPHISTOPHILIS: In hell.

75 **FAUSTUS:** How comes it, then, that thou art out of hell?

MEPHISTOPHILIS: Why this is hell, nor am I out of it;
Think'st thou that I, who saw the face of God,
And tasted the eternal joys of heaven,
Am not tormented with ten thousand hells,
80 In being depriv'd of everlasting bliss?
O Faustus, leave these frivolous[11] demands,
Which strike a terror to my fainting soul!

FAUSTUS: What, is great Mephistophilis so passionate
For being deprivèd of the joys of heaven?
85 Learn thou of Faustus manly fortitude,
And scorn those joys thou never shalt possess.
Go bear these tidings to great Lucifer:
Seeing Faustus hath incurr'd eternal death
By desperate thoughts against Jove's deity,
90 Say, he surrenders up to him his soul,
So he will spare him four and twenty years,
Letting him live in all voluptuousness;[12]
Having thee ever to attend on me,
To give me whatsoever I shall ask,
95 To tell me whatsoever I demand,
To slay mine enemies, and aid my friends,
And always be obedient to my will.
Go and return to mighty Lucifer,
And meet me in my study at midnight,
100 And then resolve me of thy master's mind.

MEPHISTOPHILIS: I will, Faustus.

> **Thematic Connection**
> What is Mephistophilis's definition of hell?

---

11. **frivolous** (friv´ ə ləs) *adj.* of little value, trifling.
12. **voluptuousness** (və lup´ choo əs nis) *n.* indulgence in sensual delights and pleasures.

Exit MEPHISTOPHILIS.

FAUSTUS: Had I as many souls as there be stars,
    I'd give them all for Mephistophilis.
    By him I'll be great emperor of the world,
105   And make a bridge thorough the moving air,
    To pass the ocean with a band of men;
    I'll join the hills that bind the Afric[13] shore,
    And make that country continent to Spain,
    And both contributory to my crown:
110   The Emperor shall not live but by my leave,
    Nor any potentate of Germany.
    Now that I have obtain'd what I desire,
    I'll live in speculation of this art,[14]
    Till Mephistophilis return again.

Exit FAUSTUS.

---

13. **Afric** African.
14. **speculation of this art** deep study of this art.

Christopher Marlowe

(1564–1593)
Born the son of a shoemaker in Canterbury, England, Christopher Marlowe earned B.A. and M.A. degrees from Cambridge University and later moved to London, where he wrote a series of plays. Marlowe was unorthodox in his opinions and his life. His plays treat controversial topics, and he had a reputation for heretical opinions. In 1593, he was brought before a government council on charges of speaking against the doctrines of the Church of England. Before the case was resolved, however, he was killed in a tavern brawl.

Connecting Literature Past and Present

1. What universal human temptations are at the heart of both *Faust* and *The Tragical History of Doctor Faustus*?

2. (a) In what ways is Faustus in *The Tragical History of Doctor Faustus* like Faust in Goethe's *Faust*? (b) In what ways are these two characters different?

3. Which of these two characters do you find more sympathetic? Explain.

Prepare to Read

I Have Visited Again ◆ The Lorelei ◆ The Lotus Flower

Alexander Pushkin (1799–1837)

Russian author Alexander Pushkin was born in Moscow into an aristocratic family. As a youth, he led a life of relative privilege and wrote with a skill that would hint at his eventual fame. While working in government service in St. Petersburg, he aroused suspicion by associating with political rebels and writing poems advocating government changes. In 1820, the government acted upon its suspicions by reappointing Pushkin to a post in a remote province in southern Russia. During the five years Pushkin spent there, he enhanced his reputation as a writer and began working on his masterpiece, the verse novel *Yevgeny Onegin* (1833). Unfortunately, his unrestrained and sometimes violent behavior resulted in his dismissal from civil service in 1824 and banishment to his family's estate.

Though isolated and unhappy on the estate, Pushkin channeled most of his energy into his writing. He spent much of his time interacting with the peasants who lived on the estate, learning about their lifestyles and incorporating their legends and folklore into a number of his finest poems.

Acts of Rebellion Pushkin was allowed to return to Moscow in 1826. Yet again, he became the object of political distrust and was eventually put under police surveillance. Despite limited freedoms, Pushkin produced some of his finest works during this time, including his collection of prose tales *Tales of the Late I.P. Belkin* (1831).

After marrying Natalya Goncharova in 1831, Pushkin grudgingly returned to government service. In a final act of rebellion, Pushkin entered into a duel that cost him his life. Despite the pointless ending of his brief life, Pushkin is now regarded as the finest poet Russia has ever produced.

Heinrich Heine (1797–1856)

German poet Heinrich Heine [hīn´ rik hī´ nə] wrote brilliant love poems that have been set to music by various composers. Yet he was also a gifted satirist and political writer, and his fierce attacks on repression and prejudice made him a highly controversial figure.

Born and raised in Düsseldorf, Heine earned a law degree in 1825 but abandoned it to pursue a career as a writer. In 1827, he gained prominence as a poet with *The Book of Songs* (1827), a collection regarded by many as his finest work. Influenced by the Romantic poets, these love poems were inspired by Heine's unrequited attachment to his cousin, Amalie.

A Controversial Poet Heine moved to Paris in 1831, and from this vantage point he wrote scathing criticisms of the political and social situation in Germany. After his views were published in *The Romantic School* (1833–1835) and "On the History of Religion and Philosophy in Germany" (1834–1835), his popularity was soon overshadowed by outrage. The German government banned all his books and made it clear that he was no longer welcome in his homeland.

Even after his death in 1856, Heine remained controversial. Riots broke out in several German cities when attempts were made to erect monuments in his honor, and when the Nazis assumed power in the 1930s, many of his works were suppressed. After World War II, Heine became a controversial figure in other countries, including the United States, because his political beliefs resembled Marxism. Despite such controversy, Heine is still generally regarded as one of the finest writers of the nineteenth century.

Preview

Connecting to the Literature

Elements of nature, such as trees, rivers, flowers, and the night sky, often have an emotional effect on us. As you read, think about how you would feel if you were standing with the speaker, looking at the same sights.

Literary Analysis

Lyric Poetry

Lyric poetry, or lyrics, are brief poems that express a speaker's personal thoughts and feelings. Many early lyrics were written to be sung to the accompaniment of a lyre, which looks much like a small, modern-day harp. Most of these poems still tend to be melodic, like songs, and generally focus on producing a single, unified effect. In these lines from "The Lotus Flower," notice the melancholy effect of the words.

> With sunken head and sadly
> She dreamily waits for the night.

As you read these poems, use a chart like the one shown to record the words and phrases that contribute to a single unifying effect.

Comparing Literary Works

Each of these poems uses **symbols** to achieve a desired effect. A symbol is a person, place, or object that has its own meaning but also suggests a larger or secondary meaning. For example, in "I Have Visited Again," the growing trees symbolize the passing of time and inspire the speaker to reflect on his mortality. As you read, compare the way each speaker uses symbols to express observations and emotions.

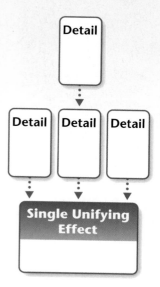

Reading Strategy

Reading Between the Lines

Reading between the lines reveals different or deeper meanings in poems, meanings that clarify a speaker's words, a character's actions, and even a poem's relevance to readers of all backgrounds. To read between the lines:

- Make inferences, or educated guesses, about the meanings of whole lines or passages.
- Find clues about the characters, setting, mood, and symbolism.
- Examine specific word choices, including words in the title.

Vocabulary Development

painstakingly (pānz′ tāk iŋ lē) *adv.* using great diligence or care (p. 796)

fathomless (fath′ əm les) *adj.* immeasurably deep (p. 797)

ancestral (an ses′ trəl) *adj.* inherited, as from an ancestor (p. 797)

morose (mə rōs′) *adj.* gloomy; in a bad or sullen mood (p. 798)

resplendent (ri splen′ dənt) *adj.* brightly shining; dazzling (p. 800)

mutely (myoot′ lē) *adv.* silently; without the capacity to speak (p. 800)

I Have Visited Again

Alexander Pushkin
translated by **D.M. Thomas**

Background

Initially, Alexander Pushkin found the inspiration to write in the politics of his homeland. His rebellious writings, as well as his unruly behavior, resulted in banishment to his family estate. Such a personality seems distantly related to the speaker of the gentle words and images in "I Have Visited Again." In this poem, the speaker revisits the estate to find that time and nature have hardly stood still in the intervening years.

> . . . I have visited again
> That corner of the earth where I spent two
> Unnoticed, exiled years. Ten years have passed
> Since then, and many things have changed for me,
> 5 And I have changed too, obedient to life's law—
> But now that I am here again, the past
> Has flown out eagerly to embrace me, claim me,
> And it seems that only yesterday I wandered
> Within these groves.
>
> Here is the cottage, sadly
> 10 Declined now, where I lived with my poor old nurse.
> She is no more. No more behind the wall
> Do I hear her heavy footsteps as she moved
> Slowly, <u>painstakingly</u> about her tasks.

Literary Analysis
Lyric Poetry Explain how Pushkin achieves a single, unifying effect in this stanza.

painstakingly (pānz′ tāk iŋ lē) *adv.* using great diligence or care

Here are the wooded slopes where often I
15 Sat motionless, and looked down at the lake,
Recalling other shores and other waves . . .
It gleams between golden cornfields and green meadows,
A wide expanse; across its <u>fathomless</u> waters
A fisherman passes, dragging an ancient net.
20 Along the shelving banks, hamlets are scattered
—Behind them the mill, so crooked it can scarcely
Make its sails turn in the wind . . .

                                    On the bounds
Of my <u>ancestral</u> acres, at the spot
Where a road, scarred by many rainfalls, climbs
25 The hill, three pine-trees stand—one by itself,
The others close together. When I rode
On horseback past them in the moonlit night,
The friendly rustling murmur of their crowns
Would welcome me. Now, I have ridden out
30 Upon that road, and seen those trees again.

fathomless (fath´ əm les)
adj. immeasurably deep

ancestral (an ses´ trəl) *adj.*
inherited, as from an
ancestor

Reading Strategy
**Reading Between the
Lines** By using words like
ancient, ancestral, and
many rainfalls in lines
19–24, what does the
speaker suggest about
the land and the people
who live there?

✔**Reading Check**

In what ways has the
estate changed since the
speaker last visited it?

▼**Critical Viewing** Which details in this landscape could serve to illustrate
Pushkin's poem? **[Support]**

Lake Scene in France, Josephine Bowes, The Bowes Museum, Barnard Castle, County Durham, UK

They have remained the same, make the same murmur—
But round their ageing roots, where all before
Was barren, naked, a thicket of young pines
Has sprouted; like green children round the shadows
35　　Of the two neighbouring pines. But in the distance
Their solitary comrade stands, <u>morose</u>,
Like some old bachelor, and round its roots
All is barren as before.

　　　　　　　　　　　I greet you, young
And unknown tribe of pine-trees! I'll not see
40　　Your mighty upward thrust of years to come
When you will overtop these friends of mine
And shield their ancient summits from the gaze
Of passers-by. But may my grandson hear
Your welcome murmur when, returning home
45　　From lively company, and filled with gay
And pleasant thoughts, he passes you in the night,
And thinks perhaps of me . . .

morose (mə rōs´) *adj.*
gloomy; in a bad or sullen
mood

Review and Assess

Thinking About the Selection

1. **Respond:** What single effect does the entire poem convey to you? Identify words that Pushkin used to evoke this feeling.

2. **(a) Recall:** Identify four familiar landmarks in the poem that have changed over the years. **(b) Infer:** How has the speaker changed in a similar fashion?

3. **(a) Recall:** In stanza three, what thoughts occupied the speaker while he looked down at the lake? **(b) Infer:** What does the speaker mean by "other shores"? **(c) Hypothesize:** Why might the speaker have yearned to be in another place?

4. **(a) Recall:** Where does the "unknown tribe of pine-trees" grow? **(b) Speculate:** What role will those pines play in the future? **(c) Interpret:** What do those pines symbolize?

5. **Apply:** Novelist Thomas Wolfe commented on how our lives change by saying that we "can't go home again," a theme shared by "I Have Visited Again." Do you agree or disagree with such a claim? Explain your answer.

The Lorelei

Heinrich Heine
translated by Aaron Kramer

Background

The lorelei is a legendary sea nymph whose irresistible singing from the rocks in the Rhine River lured unsuspecting sailors to shipwrecks. Both this poem and "The Lotus Flower" seem to be inspired by Heine's deep attachment to his cousin Amalie. Fearing her father's reaction, Amalie did not return Heine's affection. While lyric poetry often explores the joys of love, "The Lorelei" and "The Lotus Flower" focus on love's difficulties.

I cannot explain the sadness
That's fallen on my breast.
An old, old fable haunts me,
And will not let me rest.

5   The air grows cool in the twilight,
And softly the Rhine[1] flows on;
The peak of a mountain sparkles
Beneath the setting sun.

More lovely than a vision,
10 A girl sits high up there;
Her golden jewelry glistens,
She combs her golden hair.

With a comb of gold she combs it,
And sings an evensong;
15 The wonderful melody reaches
A boat, as it sails along.

The boatman hears, with an anguish
More wild than was ever known;
He's blind to the rocks around him;
20 His eyes are for her alone.

—At last the waves devoured
The boat, and the boatman's cry;
And this she did with her singing,
The golden Lorelei.

Literary Analysis
Lyric Poetry Which words convey strong emotions in the poem?

---

1. **Rhine** (rīn) river in western Europe.

The Lotus Flower

Heinrich Heine
translated by Edgar Alfred Bowring

The lotus flower is troubled
    At the sun's <u>resplendent</u> light;
With sunken head and sadly
    She dreamily waits for the night.

5   The moon appears as her wooer,
    She wakes at his fond embrace;
For him she kindly uncovers
    Her sweetly flowering face.

She blooms and glows and glistens,
10   And <u>mutely</u> gazes above;
She weeps and exhales and trembles
    With love and the sorrows of love.

resplendent (ri splen´ dənt) *adj.* brightly shining; dazzling

Reading Strategy
Reading Between the Lines What kind of person does Heine describe as "the sun"?

mutely (myo͞ot´ lē) *adv.* silently; without capacity to speak

Review and Assess
Thinking About the Selections

1. **Respond:** How do you envision the lorelei in Heine's "The Lorelei"? Explain. What is it about this vision that would seem so alluring and haunting to the boatman?

2. **(a) Recall:** What effect does the lorelei have on the boatman? **(b) Interpret:** What similarities do you see between the legend of the lorelei and Heine's situation with his uncle's daughter?

3. **(a) Recall:** What words does the speaker use in "The Lotus Flower" to give human traits to both the lotus flower and the moon? **(b) Interpret:** Whom might the moon symbolize? **(c) Apply:** Why does the lotus flower see her wooer only at night?

4. **(a) Recall:** In "The Lotus Flower," what two ideas does the speaker link in the last line? **(b) Infer:** What does the speaker mean when he refers to the "sorrows of love"?

5. **Apply:** To what types of situations in real life could you relate the legend of the lorelei? Explain your answer.

Review and Assess

Literary Analysis

Lyric Poetry

1. Which specific emotions expressed in "I Have Visited Again" qualify it as a **lyric poem**?
2. (a) What words in "The Lorelei" refer to sounds? (b) How do these words reflect the original purpose of many lyric poems?
3. What is the single effect produced in "The Lotus Flower"?

Comparing Literary Works

4. (a) Complete a chart like the one shown to analyze the **symbols** in "I Have Visited Again." Begin by listing persons, places, or objects and the words the speaker uses to describe them. (b) In the last column, use the speaker's description to determine what the symbols mean.

Person, Place, or Object	Words Describing the Image	Symbolic Meaning of the Image

5. In "The Lorelei," the girl is wearing golden jewelry, and she combs her "golden hair" with a "comb of gold." (a) What does the girl have in common with gold? (b) What does this suggest about what the girl symbolizes?

Reading Strategy

Reading Between the Lines

6. By **reading between the lines**, what deeper understanding of the speaker can you discover in the fifth stanza of "I Have Visited Again"?
7. (a) According to the first stanza of "The Lorelei," what haunts the speaker? (b) What connection might exist between the sadness he feels and the lorelei?

Extend Understanding

8. **Science Connection:** In what ways are modern ships equipped to prevent the kinds of shipwrecks described in "The Lorelei"?

Quick Review

Lyric poems are brief poems that express a speaker's personal thoughts and feelings and create a unified effect.

A **symbol** is a person, place, or object that stands for or represents something else.

When you **read between the lines,** you use clues in the text to discover deeper meaning in literature.

 **Take It to the Net**
PHSchool.com

Take the interactive self-test online to check your understanding of these selections.

Integrate Language Skills

Vocabulary Development Lesson

Word Analysis: Anglo-Saxon Suffix -less

The suffix -less, which means "without," "not able to," or "not able to be," can be added to many nouns to form an adjective. Use your understanding of -less to write the word that means the same as each of the following phrases.

1. not able to be fathomed
2. without guile
3. without pity
4. without sun

Spelling Strategy

When adding a suffix that begins with a consonant to a word that ends with a silent e, retain the silent e. On a separate piece of paper, add -ly or -ful to each of the following words.

1. scarce   2. love   3. tune

Fluency: Clarify Word Meaning

Select the word from the vocabulary list on page 795 that matches or best relates to each description below.

1. How you might respond to a surprise that left you speechless
2. The land from which your great-grandparents came
3. The way you might walk across a rocky field in the dark
4. The deepest lake ever discovered
5. A very sad child
6. A dazzling display of gold

Grammar and Style Lesson

Pronouns and Antecedents

A **pronoun** must agree with its **antecedent**—the word to which it refers—in the following ways:

- in number—singular or plural
- in gender—masculine or feminine

ANTECEDENT PRONOUN
. . . my poor old *nurse*. *She* is no more.
(feminine, singular)

Practice For each item that follows, choose the correct pronoun. Then, identify its antecedent.

1. I saw those trees again. (It, They) remained the same.
2. The solitary pine stands alone, and around (its, their) roots are no young pines.
3. A lovely girl wore a gold bracelet and necklace. (It, They) sparkled in the twilight.
4. The boatman hears the lorelei singing. The song lures (him, her) to the rocks.
5. At last the waves devoured the boat. (It, They) sank beneath the surface of the river.

Writing Application Write five sentences describing scenes in nature. In each, use a pronoun that correctly matches its antecedent.

WG *Prentice Hall Writing and Grammar Connection: Diamond Level, Chapter 23, Section 2*

Writing Lesson

Analytical Essay

Pushkin reflects on the passing of time in "I Have Visited Again." In the poem, the speaker relies on images from nature to mark the passing stages of his life. Write an essay in which you analyze the treatment of time in this poem.

Prewriting   Begin by rereading the poem and taking notes about how time progresses. You might make an informal outline with headings such as "past," "present," and "future." Under each heading, write phrases used in the poem.

Drafting   Use your informal outline or your notes as you begin writing your analytical essay.

Revising   After completing the first draft of your essay, trade papers with a partner and read each other's essay. Circle any points that lack support or seem vague, and suggest clarifying details that will strengthen each point in your partner's essay.

Model: Clarifying Meaning

The speaker sees the effects of time in the old cottage, which has "sadly / Declined" and deteriorated, *in the ten years since his exile there.*

> Specific examples or illustrations can clarify the writer's points.

 Prentice Hall Writing and Grammar Connection: Diamond Level, Chapter 13, Section 4

Extension Activities

Listening and Speaking Lyric poems have often been set to music. With a partner, find appropriate background music for either "The Lorelei" or "The Lotus Flower." As you choose the music, keep these questions in mind:

- Does the music express the same mood as the poem?
- Does the music enhance the poem's meaning?

Then, prepare and perform an **oral interpretive reading** of the poem for your classmates, using the music to enrich the performance. **[Group Activity]**

Research and Technology The term *siren* has a special meaning in literature. Use the Internet and electronic encyclopedias to research this term, and prepare a **museum exhibit** of images and artifacts related to literary sirens. Write placards that connect your findings to "The Lorelei."

 **Take It to the Net**   PHSchool.com

Go online for an additional research activity using the Internet.

Prepare to Read

from The Expiation

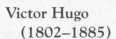

Victor Hugo
(1802–1885)

The French Romantic writer Victor Hugo was so popular that well over one million mourners flooded onto the streets of Paris to pay tribute to him following his death. Because of his beautiful, energetic lyric poetry and his vocal support for a republican government, Hugo attained hero status among the French people. In fact, their admiration for Hugo was exceeded only by Hugo's tremendous admiration for himself—a trait reflected in his suggestion that Paris be renamed *Hugo* in his honor.

A Career Blossoms Hugo was born in Besançon in 1802, the son of a high-ranking officer in Napoleon's army. Hugo's talents as a writer were first recognized during his teens, when he won a poetry contest sponsored by the French Academy. Encouraged by his success, he began focusing all of his energy on writing and studying poetry. By 1822, he had founded a literary magazine, married his childhood sweetheart, and published his first collection of poetry, *Odes et poésies diverses*.

Hugo's career as a writer continued to blossom with the publication of his first novel, *Han d'Islande* (1823), as well as two more collections of verse. Continuing to write at a prolific pace, Hugo produced three plays, *Cromwell* (1827), *Marion de Lorme* (1829), and *Hernani* (1830), which earned him public recognition and established him as the leading French Romantic writer. His fame as a writer continued to grow with the publication of one of his most popular novels, *The Hunchback of Notre-Dame* (1831).

Literature of Politics After 1831, much of Hugo's writing expressed his political and social beliefs. Overwhelming grief over the drowning of his daughter Léopoldine and a love affair with the actress Juliette Drouet drove him further from his literary career.

Following the revolution of 1848, Hugo was elected to a government position in which he acted as a champion of workers and educational reforms. However, when Napoleon III seized power and appointed himself emperor, Hugo was forced to flee to Brussels. Hugo spent nineteen years in exile, continuing his involvement in politics and producing his most stirring piece of social commentary, the novel *Les Misérables*. Published in 1862, the novel was a tremendous success, and in 1870, the year in which Napoleon III fell from power, Hugo returned to his homeland in triumph.

Following his return to France, Hugo once again became active in the French government. Although deeply shaken by the deaths of his two sons in 1871 and 1873, and suffering from serious illness by age seventy-six, he managed to continue writing until his death.

"Russia 1812" is an excerpt from Hugo's lengthy poem *The Expiation*. The piece depicts the long, tragic retreat of Napoleon's Grand Army following their unsuccessful invasion of Russia in 1812. As Napoleon's army advanced upon Moscow, the Russian forces withdrew from the city, thus avoiding major clashes with the French while luring Napoleon's army farther and farther away from its supply sources. When the French army finally reached the city in September of 1812, they found it abandoned, completely stripped of supplies, and set on fire. Realizing that it would be pointless to continue his advance, Napoleon ordered his broken troops to retreat. Hugo's poem describes the event in vivid but painful detail and with the grandeur of vision that marked the poet's career.

Preview

Connecting to the Literature

Since the dawn of the written word, authors have penned their impressions and experiences of war: triumph, defeat, upheaval, and peace. Look for timeless messages like these in this excerpt from *The Expiation*.

Literary Analysis

Mood

Mood, or atmosphere, is the feeling a literary work or passage creates in a reader through the use of descriptive details. Notice how the following lines create a mood of misery and cold despair:

> "... one saw the picket dying at his post, / still standing in his saddle, white with frost, / the stone lips frozen to the bugle's mouth!"

As you read, be aware of the details that create a specific mood.

Connecting Literary Elements

The **tone** of a literary work is the speaker's attitude toward the audience or subject. Tone can be formal or informal, friendly or distant. The speaker uses simple but very powerful words in *The Expiation*, allowing the horrific events to speak for themselves. Look for words that create the tone and mood as you read this excerpt.

Reading Strategy

Responding to Imagery

When you **respond to imagery,** you notice details in the writing that appeal to your senses, and you take special note of how those details make you feel. These strategies will help you respond to imagery as you read:

- Focus on details that create vivid pictures in your mind.
- Call on your own sense memories to see, hear, taste, smell, and touch what the words are describing.
- Picture yourself in the same situation that is being described, and imagine how you would feel.

Use a chart like the one shown as you respond to the imagery in the poem.

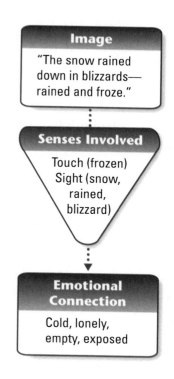

Image

"The snow rained down in blizzards—rained and froze."

Senses Involved

Touch (frozen) Sight (snow, rained, blizzard)

Emotional Connection

Cold, lonely, empty, exposed

Vocabulary Development

dregs (dregz) *n.* last, most undesirable parts (p. 806)

submerges (səb murj´ əz) *v.* covers over (p. 806)

solitude (säl´ ə tood´) *n.* seclusion, isolation, or remoteness (p. 807)

avenger (ə venj´ er) *n.* one who exacts punishment for wrongdoing (p. 807)

shroud (shroud) *n.* cloth sometimes used to wrap a corpse for burial (p. 807)

obsessed (əb sest´) *adj.* greatly preoccupied (p. 807)

leaden (led´ 'n) *adj.* depressed; dispirited (p. 808)

from The Expiation
Russia 1812

VICTOR HUGO

TRANSLATED by Robert Lowell

Background

The speaker of "Russia 1812" describes the agonized retreat of Napoleon's Grand Army from Moscow in 1812. During their march across the frigid, barren Russian plains, countless French soldiers died from frostbite, starvation, and constant attacks by Russian snipers. By the time the retreat had ended, two thirds of France's Grand Army had died. The unsuccessful invasion of Russia signaled the beginning of the end for Napoleon and his empire.

The snow fell, and its power was multiplied.
For the first time the Eagle[1] bowed its head—
dark days! Slowly the Emperor returned—
behind him Moscow! Its onion domes still burned.
5 The snow rained down in blizzards—rained and froze.
Past each white waste a further white waste rose.
None recognized the captains or the flags.
Yesterday the Grand Army, today its <u>dregs</u>!
No one could tell the vanguard[2] from the flanks.
10 The snow! The hurt men struggled from the ranks,
hid in the bellies of dead horses, in stacks
of shattered caissons.[3] By the bivouacs,[4]
one saw the picket[5] dying at his post,
still standing in his saddle, white with frost,
15 the stone lips frozen to the bugle's mouth!
Bullets and grapeshot[6] mingled with the snow,
that hailed . . . The Guard, surprised at shivering, march
in a dream now; ice rimes the gray mustache.
The snow falls, always snow! The driving mire
20 <u>submerges</u>; men, trapped in that white empire,
have no more bread and march on barefoot—gaps!
They were no longer living men and troops,

Campaign of France, 1814, Ernest Meissonier, Giraudon

---

1. **Eagle** the standard of Napoleon's military forces.
2. **vanguard** (van′ gärd′) *n.* the part of an army that goes ahead of the main body in an advance.
3. **caissons** (kā′ sänz) *n.* two-wheeled wagons used for transporting ammunition.
4. **bivouacs** (biv′ waks) *n.* temporary encampments.
5. **picket** (pik′ it) *n.* soldier responsible for guarding a body of troops from surprise attack.
6. **grapeshot** (grāp′ shät′) *n.* cluster of small iron balls fired from a cannon.

but a dream drifting in a fog, a mystery,
mourners parading under the black sky.
25   The solitude, vast, terrible to the eye,
was like a mute avenger everywhere,
as snowfall, floating through the quiet air,
buried the huge army in a huge shroud.
Could anyone leave this kingdom? A crowd—
30   each man, obsessed with dying, was alone.
Men slept—and died! The beaten mob sludged on,
ditching the guns to burn their carriages.
Two foes. The North, the Czar.[7] The North was worse.
In hollows where the snow was piling up,
35   one saw whole regiments fallen asleep.
Attila's dawn, Cannaes of Hannibal![8]
The army marching to its funeral!
Litters, wounded, the dead, deserters—swarms,
crushing the bridges down to cross a stream.
40   They went to sleep ten thousand, woke up four.
Ney,[9] bringing up the former army's rear,
hacked his horse loose from three disputing Cossacks[10] . . .
All night, the *qui vive?*[11] The alert! Attacks; retreats!
White ghosts would wrench away our guns,
45   or we would see dim, terrible squadrons,
circles of steel, whirlpools of savages,

---

7. **the Czar** (zär) the Russian emperor.
8. **Attila's . . . Hannibal** references to the defeat of Attila, the leader of the Huns, at Gaul in
A.D. 451, and to the final victory of Hannibal, the Carthaginian general who invaded Rome
in 218 B.C.
9. **Ney** (nā) the French officer in charge of defending the rear in the retreat from Moscow.
10. **Cossacks** (käs´ aks´) people of southern Russia, famous as horsemen and cavalrymen.
11. *qui vive?* (kē vēv´) French: "Who goes there?" (literally, "(long) live who?" meaning
"whose side are you on?")

solitude (säl´ ə to͞od´) *n.*
seclusion, isolation, or
remoteness

avenger (ə venj´ er) *n.* one
who exacts punishment
for wrongdoing

shroud (shro͞ud) *n.* cloth
sometimes used to wrap a
corpse for burial

obsessed (əb sest´) *adj.*
greatly preoccupied

Reading Strategy
Responding to Imagery
What is the strongest
word among the images in
lines 37–40?

✓ **Reading Check**

What conditions make it
impossible for Napoleon's
army to wage a successful
fight?

◀ **Critical Viewing**

Which details in the
painting suggest that
Napoleon's army is in
retreat? [**Analyze**]

rush sabering through the camp like dervishes.[12]
And in this way, whole armies died at night.

The Emperor was there, standing—he saw.
50 This oak already trembling from the axe,
watched his glories drop from him branch by branch:
chiefs, soldiers. Each one had his turn and chance—
they died! Some lived. These still believed his star,
and kept their watch. They loved the man of war,
55 this small man with his hands behind his back,
whose shadow, moving to and fro, was black
behind the lighted tent. Still believing, they
accused their destiny of *lèse-majesté*.[13]
His misfortune had mounted on their back.
60 The man of glory shook. Cold stupefied[14]
him, then suddenly he felt terrified.
Being without belief, he turned to God:
"God of armies, is this the end?" he cried.
And then at last the expiation[15] came,
65 as he heard some one call him by his name,
someone half-lost in shadow, who said, "No,
Napoleon." Napoleon understood,
restless, bareheaded, <u>leaden</u>, as he stood
before his butchered legions in the snow.

leaden (led´'n) *adj.* depressed; dispirited

---

12. **dervishes** (dʉr´ vish əz) *n.* Muslims dedicated to lives of poverty and chastity.
13. ***lèse-majesté*** (lez´ ma´ zhes tā´) French: treason; crime against one's sovereign (literally, "injured majesty").
14. **stupefied** (stoo´ pə fid´) *v.* stunned; made dull or lethargic.
15. **expiation** (eks´ pē ā´ shən) *n.* reparation; atonement.

Review and Assess

Thinking About the Selection

1. **Respond:** Do you find the descriptions of the suffering of the French forces convincing? Why or why not?

2. **(a) Recall:** What does the speaker mean when he says in line 1 that the snow's "power was multiplied"? **(b) Analyze:** Which words emphasize the coldness and barrenness of the landscape?

3. **(a) Recall:** In lines 50–52, what comparison does the speaker make to describe the downfall of the French army? **(b) Infer:** Why is this comparison appropriate?

4. **(a) Recall:** What seems to be the speaker's attitude toward Napoleon? **(b) Support:** Which details reveal the speaker's attitude?

5. **Apply:** What impact, if any, do literary works such as Hugo's have on your attitude toward war?

Review and Assess

Literary Analysis

Mood

1. (a) Use an organizer like the one shown to jot down details in the poem. (b) Use those details to determine the **mood**.

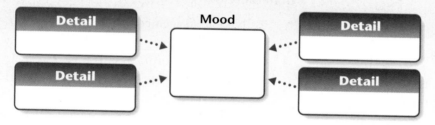

2. (a) What does the French retreat from Russia reveal about the role of nature in determining the course of human history? (b) How does this revelation contribute to the mood of the poem?

Connecting Literary Elements

3. (a) Choose one word that might describe the **tone** of the first stanza. (b) List three details that support this idea.

4. (a) What is the speaker's tone toward Napoleon in lines 49–69? (b) Support your response with two details from the poem.

Reading Strategy

Responding to Imagery

5. (a) In lines 1–24, what are the dominant colors in the speaker's descriptions? (b) How do these colors contribute to your **response to the imagery** in these lines? Explain.

6. (a) Identify one strong image in lines 1–37. (b) Which of your senses responds to the imagery?

7. How does the imagery in *The Expiation* affect your understanding of what the troops had to endure?

Extend Understanding

8. **Psychology Connection:** (a) Explain how it is possible that the French soldiers still love and believe in Napoleon despite the disastrous outcome of the Russian campaign. (b) Why is this phenomenon common in other wars, with other leaders and soldiers?

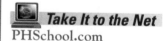

Integrate Language Skills

Vocabulary Development Lesson

Word Analysis: Latin Prefix *sub-*

The Latin prefix *sub-* means "under" or "below." Use this meaning as you define the words below.

1. submarine
2. subpar
3. subordinate
4. submerge

Spelling Strategy

Words whose final syllable includes a long vowel sound followed by a single consonant often end in a silent *e*. Identify the letter of the correct spelling of each word below.

1. (a) solitud
2. (a) inspire
3. (a) squadron

(b) solitude
(b) inspir
(b) squadrone

Word Fluency: Sentence Completion

Review the vocabulary list on page 805. Then, complete each sentence below with the best word from the list.

1. Napoleon seemed ___?___ with power.
2. The only ___?___ the dead soldier had was his own uniform.
3. Their feeling of ___?___ was intensified by the darkness of night.
4. Only the ___?___ remained of the once-great army.
5. The doctor ___?___ the soldier's cold feet in warm water.
6. Each sniper considered himself a great ___?___ for Russia.
7. The soldier, ___?___, hungry, and cold, thought of home.

Grammar and Style Lesson

Participial Phrases

A participle is a form of a verb that can act as an adjective. A **participial phrase** is made up of a participle and its modifiers and complements. The whole phrase acts as an adjective. In this example, the participle is in boldface and the participial phrase is underlined:

the stone lips **frozen** to the bugle's mouth . . . (describes *lips*)

the snowfall, **floating** through the quiet air . . . (describes *snowfall*)

Practice Identify the participles and participial phrases in the numbered items below. Then, identify the word that each participial phrase describes.

1. "men, trapped in that white empire, / have no more bread . . ."
2. "a dream drifting in a fog, a mystery . . ."
3. "mourners parading under the black sky."
4. "the Guard, surprised by the shivering . . ."
5. "each man, obsessed with dying, was alone."

Writing Application Write two sentences about an extreme weather condition using participial phrases. In each sentence, circle the participle, underline the participial phrase, and identify the word it describes.

W̶G̶ Prentice Hall Writing and Grammar Connection: Diamond Level, Chapter 19, Section 2

Writing Lesson

Writing a War Poem

The powerful events of war have inspired writers throughout history. Write a poem describing a battle or another scene from a war.

Prewriting Brainstorm about the depiction of war in books and movies or on television, noting accounts of battles by soldiers who participated in them. Develop a list of words and details that could contribute to the mood of your poem.

Model: Developing a List of Words and Details

Sound Images	Visual Images	Tactile Images	Emotions

Drafting Using these words and details, begin writing your poem. Choose vivid, precise images that will evoke an emotional response from the reader.

Revising To revise your poem, circle the words that create mood. Change repetitive words or images that do not create the mood you want.

W͞G Prentice Hall Writing and Grammar Connection: Diamond Level, Chapter 6, Section 2

Extension Activities

Listening and Speaking Learn more about Napoleon and the war with Russia by conducting an interview with your history teacher or by doing research on the topic. Prepare a **brief speech** to share some of the results of your research. As you prepare, keep these guidelines in mind:

- Make sure that you understand everything said in the interview well enough to explain it to others.
- Choose details to help your audience understand more about Napoleon.
- Choose language that has vivid imagery to make it more interesting to your audience.

Write your brief speech, and then share it with the class.

Research and Technology With a partner, prepare an **illustrated timeline** of the major events in Napoleon's life, both personal and political. You may illustrate it yourself or use software, photocopies, or printouts of appropriate art. Present your timeline by posting it on a bulletin board in your classroom. [Group Activity]

 **Take It to the Net** PHSchool.com

Go online for an additional research activity using the Internet.

Prepare to Read

Invitation to the Voyage ◆ The Albatross ◆
The Sleeper in the Valley ◆ Ophelia ◆ Autumn Song

Charles Baudelaire (1821–1867)

Charles Baudelaire (shärl bōd ler′) was one of the most colorful, startling, and innovative poets of the nineteenth century. Attempting to break away from the Romantic tradition, Baudelaire created poems that are objective rather than sentimental. Many of his works celebrate the city and the artificial rather than nature.

As a youth, Baudelaire rebelled against his family to pursue a career as a writer. To dissuade him from such a dissolute life, they sent him on an ocean voyage to India. Instead of completing the voyage, he returned to France to claim his share of his late father's fortune. Soon, extravagant living drove him into debt, a problem that would plague him for the rest of his life.

Baudelaire published short stories, translated works by Edgar Allan Poe into French, and both wrote and collected poems for *Flowers of Evil* (1857), which would become his signature work. Although his talents were not widely recognized during his lifetime, Baudelaire's reputation blossomed posthumously, and he came to be considered one of the finest nineteenth-century poets.

Arthur Rimbaud (1854–1891)

Arthur Rimbaud (är tür′ ran bō′) earned recognition for his poetry at the age of eight, was first published at age fifteen, and stopped writing altogether at nineteen. Renowned French poet Paul Verlaine introduced Rimbaud to many of the most prominent poets of the day and encouraged Rimbaud as he wrote some of his finest poetry.

Unfortunately, Verlaine and Rimbaud quarreled frequently; ultimately, Verlaine attempted to murder his young friend. After serving a two-year prison sentence for his crime, Verlaine published Rimbaud's collection of poetry, *Illuminations* (1886). The collection earned widespread acclaim among critics and writers and was applauded as the work of a mature and remarkably talented poet. By the time of his death in 1891, Rimbaud's poetry had already begun to influence other writers; during the twentieth century, his lifestyle became a model for such vagabond writers, artists, and musicians as Jack Kerouac and Bob Dylan.

Paul Verlaine (1844–1896)

Like many of his fellow poets, Paul Verlaine (ver lān′) was an accomplished writer at a very young age; his body of work includes exquisitely musical lyrics, religious verse, and sonnets. Verlaine benefited from associations with renowned authors such as Baudelaire, Rimbaud, and novelist Victor Hugo. In particular, Verlaine shared a tumultuous friendship with Rimbaud that ended badly—Verlaine shot his friend in a murder attempt that landed him in prison for two years.

Through the success of his poems, Verlaine brought early attention to the Symbolists, an emerging group of writers whose works relied on complex patterns of symbols to convey deeply personal themes.

Like so many of his fellow poets, Verlaine craved a bohemian lifestyle. Though the last years of his life were spent in poverty and dissolution, Verlaine was honored as Prince of Poets in 1895 and given a public funeral in Paris upon his death in 1896.

Preview

Connecting to the Literature

Baudelaire, Rimbaud, and Verlaine believed that personal, immediate, and emotional responses were valid subjects for poetry. Pay attention to the emotion in these poems, and notice the part nature plays in those feelings.

Literary Analysis

Romantic Poetry

Romantic poetry is part of a literary and artistic movement called Romanticism. While earlier poems often relied on wit and stylish pretense, Romantic works placed a premium on elements closer to the heart:

- imagination
- nature
- the exotic
- emotion
- individuality

As you read, notice how these elements guide a reader's imagination toward an emotional response, and identify the emotions you feel.

Comparing Literary Works

All the poems in this grouping use nature as a subject or as a way to communicate a message. Consider these questions as you read:

- Is nature something to interact with, wonder at, fear, or appreciate?
- Is nature indifferent to human suffering or sympathetic toward it?
- Is nature—especially its colors and seasons—used symbolically?

Look for the poets' attitudes toward nature and contrast the messages these poems communicate.

Reading Strategy

Judging a Poet's Message

As a reader, your job is not only to discover the point a poet is making but also to weigh what the poet says against your own experiences and past readings. When you **judge a poet's message,** you assess the validity of the poet's ideas and decide whether you agree or disagree with them.

As you read these poems, use a chart like the one shown to identify and judge the message each poet expresses.

Poet's Message

Experiences I Share With the Poet

My Unique Experiences

My Conclusions

Vocabulary Development

proffering (präf´ ər iŋ) *v.* offering (p. 815)

nonchalantly (nän´ shə länt´ lē) *adv.* in a casually indifferent manner (p. 816)

sovereign (säv´ rən) *n.* monarch or ruler (p. 816)

adroit (ə droit´) *adj.* skillful in a physical or mental way (p. 816)

flourish (flʉr´ ish) *n.* fanfare, as of trumpets (p. 819)

strains (strānz) *n.* passages of music; tunes; airs (p. 820)

monotone (män´ ə tōn´) *n.* sound or song that repeats a single note (p. 822)

Invitation to the Voyage

Charles Baudelaire
translated by Richard Wilbur

Background

There is little doubt that Charles Baudelaire's ocean voyage to India was a significant event in his life. Although the journey was cut short—lasting only eight months instead of eighteen—the experience clearly inspired him as a poet. The voyage, his desire for a life of ease and luxury, and his yearning to escape reality all find expression in his poems "Invitation to the Voyage" and "The Albatross."

> My child, my sister, dream
> How sweet all things would seem
> Were we in that kind land to live together
> And there love slow and long,
> 5   There love and die among
> Those scenes that image you, that sumptuous[1] weather.
> Drowned suns that glimmer there
> Through cloud-disheveled[2] air
> Move me with such a mystery as appears
> 10   Within those other skies
> Of your treacherous eyes
> When I behold them shining through their tears.
>
> There, there is nothing else but grace and measure,
> Richness, quietness, and pleasure.
>
> 15   Furniture that wears
> The luster of the years
> Softly would glow within our glowing chamber,

Literary Analysis
Romantic Poetry List three characteristics of Romantic poetry in lines 8–11.

Critical Viewing ▶
Which details in this seascape might inspire a poet? **[Interpret]**

---

1. **sumptuous** (sump´ choo əs) *adj.* magnificent or splendid.
2. **disheveled** (di shev´ əld) *adj.* disarranged and untidy.

Flowers of rarest bloom
<u>Proffering</u> their perfume
20   Mixed with the vague fragrances of amber;
      Gold ceilings would there be,
      Mirrors deep as the sea,
The walls all in an Eastern splendor hung—
      Nothing but should address
25   The soul's loneliness,
Speaking her sweet and secret native tongue.

There, there is nothing else but grace and measure,
Richness, quietness, and pleasure.

      See, sheltered from the swells
30   There in the still canals
Those drowsy ships that dream of sailing forth;
      It is to satisfy
      Your least desire, they ply
Hither through all the waters of the earth.
35   The sun at close of day
      Clothes the fields of hay,
Then the canals, at last the town entire
      In hyacinth and gold:
      Slowly the land is rolled
40   Sleepward under a sea of gentle fire.

There, there is nothing else but grace and measure,
Richness, quietness, and pleasure.

proffering (präf´ ər iŋ) *v.*
offering

Reading Strategy
Judging a Poet's Message What message is the speaker determined to communicate through these repeated lines?

Literary Analysis
Romantic Poetry Explain how individuality is presented in lines 32–34.

Erminia in the Rough Sea, 1869, National Trust Photographic Library

The Albatross

Charles Baudelaire *translated by* Richard Howard

Often, to pass the time on board, the crew
will catch an albatross, one of those big birds
which <u>nonchalantly</u> chaperone a ship
across the bitter fathoms of the sea.

5 Tied to the deck, this <u>sovereign</u> of space,
as if embarrassed by its clumsiness,
pitiably lets its great white wings
drag at its sides like a pair of unshipped oars.

How weak and awkward, even comical
10 this traveler but lately so <u>adroit</u>—
one deckhand sticks a pipestem in its beak,
another mocks the cripple that once flew!

The Poet is like this monarch of the clouds
riding the storm above the marksman's range;
15 exiled on the ground, hooted and jeered,
he cannot walk because of his great wings.

nonchalantly (nän´shə länt´ lē)
adv. in a casually indifferent
manner

sovereign (säv´ rən) *n.*
monarch or ruler

adroit (ə drɔit´) *adj.* skillful
in a physical or mental way

Reading Strategy
**Judging a Poet's
Message** What message
does the speaker convey
about the albatross in its
natural setting?

Review and Assess

Thinking About the Selections

1. **Respond:** Would you like to experience the type of voyage that the speaker describes in "Invitation to the Voyage"? Why or why not?

2. **(a) Recall:** Which details describe the "kind land" in "Invitation to the Voyage"? **(b) Interpret:** What impression of the land do these details convey?

3. **(a) Interpret:** What message about the life of a poet does the speaker convey in "The Albatross"? **(b) Evaluate:** Do you think this message can be applied to contemporary poets? Why or why not?

4. **(a) Connect:** Explain whether the world described in "Invitation to the Voyage" is enticing to you. **(b) Compare:** How does this place compare to your ideal world?

Critical Viewing ▶
Which images in Rimbaud's poem describe the scene in this landscape?
[Connect]

The Sleeper in the Valley

Arthur Rimbaud *translated by* William Jay Smith

This is the green wherein a river chants
Whose waters on the grasses wildly toss
Its silver tatters, where proud sunlight slants
Within a valley thick with beams like moss.

5   A youthful soldier, mouth agape, head bare,
And nape where fresh blue water cresses drain
Sleeps stretched in grass, beneath the cloud, where
On abundant green the light descends like rain.

His feet on iris roots, smiling perhaps
10 As would some tiny sickly child, he naps.
O nature, he is cold: make warm his bed.

This quiver of perfume will not break his rest;
In the sun he sleeps, his hand on quiet breast.
Upon one side there are two spots of red.

Literary Analysis
Romantic Poetry
List four visual images of nature in the first stanza.

Reading Strategy
Judging a Poet's Message
What philosophy about death does the speaker imply by referring to the soldier as being in a bed?

Ophelia

Arthur Rimbaud
translated by Daisy Aldan

▲ **Critical Viewing**   What emotions do the colors and images in this painting evoke in you? [**Respond**]

Background

Arthur Rimbaud's rare talent for poetry came at an early age. He wrote "Ophelia," for example, at age fifteen. Many critics consider it a remarkable piece—not only because of the author's youth but also because of the poem's quality as a literary piece. By the time Rimbaud's brief career ended at nineteen, novice poets were crafting their own poems in imitation of his widely recognized lyrical style.

In his poem "Ophelia," Rimbaud borrows a character from *Hamlet*. In Shakespeare's play, Ophelia is a beautiful, innocent, impressionable young maiden who is in love with Hamlet, the play's protagonist. Confused by Hamlet's sudden rejection of her, and grief-stricken by her father's death, Ophelia spirals into depression and insanity. The poem "Ophelia" presents one interpretation of Ophelia's life, the troubled relationship she endures with Hamlet, and the way in which her life ends.

I

On the calm black wave where the stars sleep
Floats white Ophelia like a great lily,
Floats very slowly, lying in her long veils . . .
—From the distant woods, the <u>flourish</u> of the kill.

5   For more than a thousand years sad Ophelia
White phantom, passes, on the long black river.
For more than a thousand years her sweet obsession
Whispers her love to the evening breeze.

The wind embraces her breasts and unfolds her great veils
10 In a corolla[1] gently rocked by the waters;
Trembling willows weep on her shoulder,
Reeds lean on her lofty pensive[2] brow.

---

1. **corolla** (kə räl′ ə) *n.* the petals, or inner floral leaves, of a flower.
2. **pensive** (pen′ siv) *adj.* thinking deeply or seriously, often of sad or melancholy things.

flourish (flʉr′ ish) *n.* fanfare, as of trumpets

Literary Analysis
Romantic Poetry
What comparison is the speaker making through the use of phrases such as "the wind embraces" and "willows weep"?

 **Reading Check**

How long has the spirit of Ophelia passed on the dark river?

Bruised water lilies sigh about her;
Sometimes in a sleeping alder tree she awakens
15 A nest; a tiny wing-flutter escapes;
Mysterious sounds fall from the golden stars.

II

O pale Ophelia! fair as snow!
You died, child, yes, carried off by a river!
Because the winds falling from the great cliffs of Norway
20 Spoke low to you of fierce freedom;

Because a wind, tearing your long hair,
Bore strange shouts to your dreaming spirit;
Because your heart listened to the <u>strains</u> of Nature
In the wails of the tree and the sighs of the nights.

▲ Critical Viewing
How do details in this painting compare and contrast with images in the poem? [**Compare and Contrast**]

strains (strānz) *n.* passages of music; tunes; airs

Because the voice of mad seas, immense rattle,
Bruised your child's heart, too sweet and too human;
Because on an April morning, a handsome pale courtier,
A sorry fool, sat mutely at your feet!

Heaven! Love! Freedom! What a dream, O Foolish girl!
30 You melted toward him as snow near flame:
Your words were strangled by your great visions
—And the terrible Infinite frightened your blue eyes!

III

And the Poet says you come at night
To gather flowers in the rays of the stars;
35 And he has seen on the water, lying in her long veils,
White Ophelia floating, like a great lily.

Reading Strategy
Judging a Poet's Message What does the speaker seem to say about people who seek nature, love, and freedom?

Review and Assess

Thinking About the Selections

1. **Respond:** What are your impressions of Ophelia after reading Rimbaud's poem? How do you feel about the choices she made? Explain.

2. **(a) Recall:** In "The Sleeper in the Valley," who appears to be sleeping? **(b) Draw Conclusions:** What evidence in the poem suggests that the sleeper is not really asleep?

3. **(a) Recall:** Identify three words or phrases the speaker uses to describe the gentle qualities of nature in "The Sleeper in the Valley." **(b) Compare and Contrast:** How does the speaker's depiction of nature contrast with the actual events that took place there? Refer to specific lines and details to support your answers.

4. **(a) Recall:** In "Ophelia," what colors are mentioned in the first four lines? **(b) Analyze:** How are these colors used to establish Ophelia's purity and innocence?

5. **(a) Apply:** In what way is nature indifferent to human affairs? **(b) Speculate:** How does nature affect people emotionally?

Autumn Song

Paul Verlaine *translated by* Louis Simpson

Violins complain
Of autumn again,
    They sob and moan.
And my heartstrings ache
5 Like the song they make,
    A <u>monotone</u>.

Suffocating, drowned,
And hollowly, sound
    The midnight chimes.
10 Then the days return
I knew, and I mourn
    For bygone times.

And I fall and drift
With the winds that lift
15   My heavy grief.
Here and there they blow,
And I rise and go
    Like a dead leaf.

Literary Analysis
Romantic Poetry
What comparison in the first stanza helps the reader understand the intense emotion the speaker feels?

monotone (män′ ə tōn′) *n.* sound or song that repeats a single note

Review and Assess

Thinking About the Selection

1. **Respond:** What advice would you give to the speaker in "Autumn Song"? Why?

2. **(a) Recall:** Identify four verbs in lines 1–12. **(b) Analyze:** What overall feeling is created by these verbs?

3. **(a) Recall:** What is the speaker mourning? **(b) Speculate:** What events or conditions in the speaker's past might be worth mourning?

4. **(a) Make a Judgment:** In what ways would this poem be different if it were called "Summer Song"? **(b) Extend:** Compose three lines of this new poem.

Review and Assess

Literary Analysis

Romantic Poetry

1. For each poem in this grouping, complete an organizer like the one below, noting details that are typical of **Romantic poetry.**

Imagination	Emotion	Nature	Individuality	The Exotic

2. In "Invitation to the Voyage," how do the images of the "kind land" in line 3 relate to the ideas expressed in the poem's refrain?
3. (a) In line 26 of "Ophelia," what does the speaker mean when he says that Ophelia was "too human"? (b) What element of Romantic poetry does this sentiment evoke?

Comparing Literary Works

4. (a) Compare the ways in which "Invitation to the Voyage" and "Autumn Song" express the emotion of longing. (b) In what ways is nature used to express this longing? Explain.
5. (a) What images from nature are associated with Ophelia in "Ophelia" and the soldier in "The Sleeper in the Valley"? (b) Identify three factors contributing to the perception that these characters deserve sympathy.

Reading Strategy

Judging a Poet's Message

6. (a) Explain how the desire to escape to an ideal or imaginary world is a message in "Invitation to the Voyage." (b) **Judge the poet's message** by explaining the possible benefits of escapism. (c) What negative consequences result from escapist behavior?
7. (a) Which details in "The Albatross" best communicate the speaker's attitude toward the crew? (b) Do you agree with this attitude? Explain.

Extend Understanding

8. **Science Connection:** How might a naturalist react to the treatment of the bird in "The Albatross"?

Integrate Language Skills

Vocabulary Development Lesson

Word Analysis: Greek Prefix *mono-*

The Greek prefix *mono-* means "alone," "one," or "single." Add the prefix *mono-* to each of the roots given below. Use your understanding of the prefix and the clues provided to define the new word.

1. _____tone (sound)
2. _____logue (speaking)
3. _____poly (commerce)

Spelling Strategy

In words like *indignant*, the *g* and the *n* each stand for a separate sound. Sometimes, *gn* stands for only the *n* sound, as in *sign*. In these cases, it usually follows the letters *ai*, *ei*, or *i*. For each word below, identify whether *gn* stands for two separate sounds or just one sound.

1. sovereign   3. arraign
2. malignant   4. sovereignty

Grammar and Style Lesson

Adjectival Modifiers

An **adjectival modifier** is a phrase or clause that describes a noun or pronoun. Adjectival modifiers can come in many different forms. Study the examples provided below.

Prepositional Phrase: "Flowers *of rarest bloom* . . ." (modifies *Flowers*)

Participial Phrase: ". . .When I behold them *shining through their tears*." (modifies *them*)

Adjective Clause: ". . . drowsy ships *that dream of sailing forth* . . ." (modifies *ships*)

Concept Development: Analogies

An *analogy* compares the relationship between word meanings. For example, in analogies, word pairs often represent these common relationships:

synonym:	*talk* is to *chat*
antonym:	*noise* is to *silence*
degree:	*cold* is to *freezing*
part to whole:	*clarinet* is to *orchestra*

Review the vocabulary list on page 813. Then, choose the word from that list that best completes each analogy below.

1. *Wanting* is to *desiring* as *offering* is to ___.
2. *Noisy* is to *loud* as *fanfare* is to ___.
3. *Fiddle* is to *violin* as *tunes* is to ___.
4. *Felicitous* is to *felicity* as *monotonous* is to ___.
5. *Elegant* is to *refined* as *casually* is to ___.
6. *Student* is to *teacher* as *subject* is to ___.
7. *Plain* is to *beautiful* as *incapable* is to ___.

Practice For each item below, underline the adjectival modifier. Then, circle the word that the adjectival modifier describes.

1. "Drowned suns that glimmer there . . ."
2. "The Poet is like this monarch . . ."
3. "Because a wind, tearing your long hair, . . ."
4. "This is the green wherein a river chants . . ."
5. "With the winds that lift / My heavy grief . . ."

Writing Application Write two sentences about a journey, using adjectival modifiers. In each sentence, underline the adjectival modifier and circle the word it describes.

W͜G Prentice Hall Writing and Grammar Connection: Diamond Level, Chapter 19, Section 1

Writing Lesson

Comparison-and-Contrast Essay

In all of the poems within this grouping, nature significantly affects both the speakers and the events in the poems. Write an essay in which you compare and contrast the treatment of nature in three of the poems you have read.

Prewriting Choose three poems and take note of how nature is depicted in each one. Make an outline of the similarities and differences, organizing your observations into points you want to make.

> ### Model: Making an Outline
>
> I. Comparisons between "Invitation to the Voyage"
>   and "The Albatross"
>   A. Nature is presented positively in both.
>   B. Examples: "Flowers of rarest bloom," albatross
>   as "monarch of the clouds"

An outline for your own use can be formal, with numerals and letters as shown here, or informal, using bullets.

Drafting Using the words and details in your outline, write your essay. Address each of the points you have outlined.

Revising Compare your finished draft to your outline. Revise your essay to add any details that were missed.

 Prentice Hall Writing and Grammar Connection: Diamond Level, Chapter 9, Section 3

Extension Activities

Listening and Speaking Read Queen Gertrude's monologue in *Hamlet* at the end of Act IV, Scene vii. Then, read section II of Rimbaud's "Ophelia." In a **discussion** with a partner:

1. Consider each speaker and each audience.
2. Note the passage of time in each.
3. Evaluate how each speaker feels about Ophelia's death.

Draw conclusions about the differences you find. **[Group Activity]**

Research and Technology Build a **multimedia travelogue** illustrating Baudelaire's sea voyage to India. Select images and music or sounds that connect to his poem. You may also be able to include scents and items to touch. Present your travelogue to the class.

 Take It to the Net PHSchool.com

Go online for an additional research activity using the Internet.

Prepare to Read

Two Friends ◆ How Much Land Does a Man Need? ◆ A Problem

Guy de Maupassant
(1850–1893)

Guy de Maupassant (gē də mō´ pä sän) first wrote under the guidance of famous French writers Gustave Flaubert and Émile Zola. Encouraged by Zola, Maupassant published his first short story in 1880. The story earned him immediate fame, establishing his career as a prolific and extremely popular writer. The royalties from his first volume of short stories, *Madame Tellier's Establishment* (1881), and his novels *A Woman's Life* (1883) and *Bel-Ami* (1885) enabled him to live a life of luxury. He traveled extensively, incorporating his recollections into his early works. Maupassant's later stories, however, reflect his growing inner turmoil, often presenting an uncomplimentary but realistic portrait of the world. In "Two Friends," for example, Maupassant presents a graphic depiction of the violence and destruction of war.

Health problems and bouts of depression plagued Maupassant. Finally, Maupassant was committed to an asylum, where he died in 1893.

Leo Tolstoy
(1828–1910)

Leo Tolstoy (tōl´ stöi) was born at his family's estate near Moscow. The tragic loss of his parents and a beloved aunt affected him profoundly, leading to a lifelong obsession with the inevitability of death.

Tolstoy's first novel was published in 1852, followed by a collection of stories in 1856. *War and Peace* (1869), a novel about Napoleon's invasion of Russia in 1812, was immediately regarded as a masterpiece for its graphic depiction of war, its insights into Russian culture, and its exploration into the meaning of life. The deeply tragic novel confirmed Tolstoy's already lofty reputation as a writer.

Struggling through a spiritual crisis, Tolstoy created his own religious faith that emphasized a natural existence, universal love, equality, and nonviolence. In accordance with his beliefs, Tolstoy renounced the rights to his works published after 1881 and gave his property to his family. In 1910, shortly after leaving his wife and family, Tolstoy died in an obscure railroad station.

Anton Chekhov
(1860–1904)

Anton Chekhov (chek´ôf) is one of only a few major writers who also studied and practiced medicine. Despite the demands of a medical career, Chekhov published a substantial body of work, including both scientific pieces and great literary works. One of his finest plays, *The Seagull* (1896), focuses on intergenerational conflict.

Toward the end of the nineteenth century, declining health forced Chekhov to move to the warmer climate of Yalta. Illness did not impair his literary output, however, and in his last years he produced two critically acclaimed plays, *The Sisters* (1901) and *The Cherry Orchard* (1904). When Chekhov finally succumbed to tuberculosis in 1904, his literary reputation had not yet extended beyond Russia. Since World War I, however, he has come to be regarded as one of the finest short-story writers the world has ever produced.

Preview

Connecting to the Literature

Sometimes, even the smallest decision can be difficult to make. The protagonists in these stories are forced to make important choices that have disastrous consequences. Look for the challenges the characters face as they make their decisions, and imagine what you might have done in their place.

Literary Analysis

Dynamic and Static Characters

Like people in life, characters in literature can change as a story progresses. A **dynamic character** experiences a change or shift in attitude and behavior during the course of a literary work. However, a **static character's** attitudes and behavior remain essentially stable throughout.

As you become acquainted with the characters in these stories, create a chart like the one shown to identify each of the characters as either dynamic or static. Consider how the contrasts between these character types add tension within each story.

Comparing Literary Works

These short stories feature characters making decisions that direct the outcomes of their lives. Every decision brings consequences—some good, some bad. These anticipated consequences often drive the choices characters make. Look at the way each character approaches his or her choices, and compare the factors each one considers before he or she acts.

Reading Strategy

Evaluating Characters' Decisions

Evaluate characters' decisions just as you would assess your own. Follow these steps to critically consider a choice and its effect on future actions:

- Consider whether the character benefits from the decision the way he or she imagined.
- Analyze the effect each decision has on other characters.
- Finally, judge whether the decision turns out to be good or bad.

Use this process to evaluate characters' decisions in each story you read.

Character Name

↓

Attitudes at Beginning of Story

↓

Attitudes at End of Story

↓

Static or Dynamic?

Vocabulary Development

pillaging (pil′ ij iŋ) *v.* plundering; looting (p. 830)

superimposed (sōō′ pər im pōzd′) *v.* placed on top of something else (p. 830)

placidly (plas′ id lē) *adv.* calmly (p. 833)

discord (dis′ kôrd) *n.* dissension; conflict (p. 837)

prostrate (präs′ trāt) *adj.* lying with one's face down (p. 845)

taciturn (tas′ ə tʉrn) *adj.* almost always silent (p. 852)

benevolent (bə nev′ ə lənt) *adj.* doing or inclined to do good; kindly; charitable (p. 852)

Two Friends

Guy de Maupassant   *translated by* Gordon R. Silber

Background

The backdrop for "Two Friends" is the Franco-Prussian War, also called the Franco-German War. In this ten-month conflict in 1870–71, a coalition of German states known as Prussia fought to defeat France and capture its emperor, Napoleon III. In one military strategy, the German army blockaded Paris, starving the city's inhabitants into compliance. As Maupassant's story begins, Paris is on the verge of surrender.

Paris was blockaded, starved, in its death agony. Sparrows were becoming scarcer and scarcer on the rooftops and the sewers were being depopulated. One ate whatever one could get.

As he was strolling sadly along the outer boulevard one bright January morning, his hands in his trousers pockets and his stomach empty, M.[1] Morissot, watchmaker by trade but local militiaman for the time being, stopped short before a fellow militiaman whom he recognized as a friend. It was M. Sauvage, a riverside acquaintance.

Every Sunday, before the war, Morissot left at dawn, a bamboo pole in his hand, a tin box on his back. He would take the Argenteuil railroad, get off at Colombes, and walk to Marante Island. As soon as he arrived at this ideal spot he would start to fish; he fished until nightfall.

Every Sunday he would meet a stout, jovial little man, M. Sauvage, a haberdasher[2] in Rue Notre-Dame-de-Lorette, another ardent fisherman. Often they spent half a day side by side, line in hand and feet dangling above the current. Inevitably they had struck up a friendship.

Some days they did not speak. Sometimes they did; but they understood one another admirably without saying anything because they had similar tastes and responded to their surroundings in exactly the same way.

Critical Viewing ▶

What might Sauvage and Morissot find enticing about the setting of this landscape? **[Speculate]**

1. **M.** abbreviation for French title *Monsieur* (mə syö´), equivalent to *Mister* or *Sir.*
2. **haberdasher** (hab´ ər dash´ ər) *n.* person who is in the business of selling men's clothing.

On a spring morning, toward ten o'clock, when the young sun was drawing up from the tranquil stream wisps of haze which floated off in the direction of the current and was pouring down its vernal warmth on the backs of the two fanatical anglers,[3] Morissot would sometimes say to his neighbor, "Nice, isn't it?" and M. Sauvage would answer, "There's nothing like it." And that was enough for them to understand and appreciate each other.

On an autumn afternoon, when the sky, reddened by the setting sun, cast reflections of its scarlet clouds on the water, made the whole river crimson, lighted up the horizon, made the two friends look as ruddy as fire, and gilded the trees which were already brown and beginning to tremble with a wintery shiver, M. Sauvage would look at Morissot with a smile and say, "Fine sight!" And Morissot, awed, would answer, "It's better than the city, isn't it?" without taking his eyes from his float.

As soon as they recognized one another they shook hands energetically, touched at meeting under such changed circumstances. M. Sauvage, with a sigh, grumbled, "What goings-on!" Morissot groaned dismally, "And what weather! This is the first fine day of the year."

The sky was, in fact, blue and brilliant.

---

3. **anglers** (aŋ′ glərz) *n.* people who fish.

Literary Analysis
Dynamic and Static Characters In what way do these opening paragraphs prepare you for changes that may occur in the main characters?

✔**Reading Check**
What hobby do Sauvage and Morissot have in common?

Les Maisons Cabassud à la Ville d'Avray, Camille Corot, The Louvre, Paris

Two Friends ◆ 829

They started to walk side by side, absent-minded and sad. Morissot went on, "And fishing! Ah! Nothing but a pleasant memory."

"When'll we get back to it?" asked M. Sauvage.

They went into a little café and had an absinthe,[4] then resumed their stroll along the sidewalks.

Morissot stopped suddenly. "How about another, eh?" M. Sauvage agreed, "If you want." And they entered another wine shop.

On leaving they felt giddy, muddled, as one does after drinking on an empty stomach. It was mild. A caressing breeze touched their faces.

The warm air completed what the absinthe had begun. M. Sauvage stopped. "Suppose we went?"

"Went where?"

"Fishing, of course."

"But where?"

"Why, on our island. The French outposts are near Colombes. I know Colonel Dumoulin; they'll let us pass without any trouble."

Morissot trembled with eagerness: "Done! I'm with you." And they went off to get their tackle.

An hour later they were walking side by side on the highway. They reached the villa which the Colonel occupied. He smiled at their request and gave his consent to their whim. They started off again, armed with a pass.

Soon they passed the outposts, went through the abandoned village of Colombes, and reached the edge of the little vineyards which slope toward the Seine. It was about eleven.

Opposite, the village of Argenteuil seemed dead. The heights of Orgemont and Sannois dominated the whole countryside. The broad plain which stretches as far as Nanterre was empty, absolutely empty, with its bare cherry trees and its colorless fields.

Pointing up to the heights, M. Sauvage murmured, "The Prussians are up there!" And a feeling of uneasiness paralyzed the two friends as they faced this deserted region.

"The Prussians!" They had never seen any, but for months they had felt their presence—around Paris, ruining France, <u>pillaging</u>, massacring, starving the country, invisible and all-powerful. And a kind of superstitious terror was <u>superimposed</u> on the hatred which they felt for this unknown and victorious people.

Morissot stammered, "Say, suppose we met some of them?"

His Parisian jauntiness coming to the surface in spite of everything, M. Sauvage answered, "We'll offer them some fish."

But they hesitated to venture into the country, frightened by the silence all about them.

Literary Analysis
Dynamic and Static Characters What is changing in the relationship between the characters?

Reading Strategy
Evaluating Characters' Decisions Which details prove that the decision to go to the island is a dangerous one?

pillaging (pil´ ij iŋ) v. plundering; looting

superimposed (soo´ pər im pōzd´) v. placed on top of something else

---

4. **absinthe** (ab´ sinth) n. bitter, anise-flavored liqueur.

Finally M. Sauvage pulled himself together: "Come on! On our way! But let's go carefully." And they climbed over into a vineyard, bent double, crawling, taking advantage of the vines to conceal themselves, watching, listening.

A stretch of bare ground had to be crossed to reach the edge of the river. They began to run, and when they reached the bank they plunged down among the dry reeds.

Morissot glued his ear to the ground and listened for sounds of anyone walking in the vicinity. He heard nothing. They were indeed alone, all alone.

Reassured, they started to fish.

Opposite them Marante Island, deserted, hid them from the other bank. The little building which had housed a restaurant was shut up and looked as if it had been abandoned for years.

M. Sauvage caught the first gudgeon,[5] Morissot got the second, and from then on they pulled in their lines every minute or two with a silvery little fish squirming on the end, a truly miraculous draught.

Skillfully they slipped the fish into a sack made of fine net which they had hung in the water at their feet. And happiness pervaded their whole being, the happiness which seizes upon you when you regain a cherished pleasure of which you have long been deprived.

The good sun was pouring down its warmth on their backs. They heard nothing more; they no longer thought about anything at all; they forgot about the rest of the world—they were fishing!

But suddenly a dull sound which seemed to come from under ground made the earth tremble. The cannon were beginning.

Morissot turned and saw, over the bank to the left, the great silhouette of Mount Valérien wearing a white plume on its brow, powder-smoke which it had just spit out.

And almost at once a second puff of smoke rolled from the summit, and a few seconds after the roar still another explosion was heard.

Then more followed, and time after time the mountain belched forth death-dealing breath, breathed out milky-white vapor which rose slowly in the calm sky and formed a cloud above the summit.

M. Sauvage shrugged his shoulders. "There they go again," he said.

As he sat anxiously watching his float bob up and down, Morissot was suddenly seized by the wrath which a peace-loving man will feel toward madmen who fight, and grumbled, "Folks sure are stupid to kill one another like that."

M. Sauvage answered, "They're worse than animals."

And Morissot, who had just pulled in a bleak, went on, "And to think that it will always be like this as long as there are governments."

M. Sauvage stopped him: "The Republic[6] wouldn't have declared war—"

---

5. **gudgeon** (guj′ ən) *n.* small European freshwater fish.
6. **The Republic** the provisional republican government that assumed control when Napoleon III was captured by the Prussians.

✓ Reading Check

Why are Sauvage and Morissot anxious while approaching their favorite spot?

Morissot interrupted: "Under kings you have war abroad; under the Republic you have war at home."

And they started a leisurely discussion, unraveling great political problems with the sane reasonableness of easy-going, limited individuals, and found themselves in agreement on the point that men would never be free. And Mount Valérien thundered unceasingly, demolishing French homes with its cannon, crushing out lives, putting an end to the dreams which many had dreamt, the joys which many had been waiting for, the happiness which many had hoped for, planting in wives' hearts, in maidens' hearts, in mothers' hearts, over there, in other lands, sufferings which would never end.

"That's life for you," opined M. Sauvage.

"You'd better say 'That's death for you,'" laughed Morissot.

But they shuddered in terror when they realized that someone had just come up behind them, and looking around they saw four men standing almost at their elbows, four tall men, armed and bearded, dressed like liveried[7] servants, with flat caps on their heads, pointing rifles at them.

The two fish lines dropped from their hands and floated off down stream.

In a few seconds they were seized, trussed up, carried off, thrown into a rowboat and taken over to the island.

And behind the building which they had thought deserted they saw a score of German soldiers.

A kind of hairy giant who was seated astride a chair smoking a porcelain pipe asked them in excellent French: "Well, gentlemen, have you had good fishing?"

Then a soldier put down at the officer's feet the sack full of fish which he had carefully brought along. The Prussian smiled: "Aha! I see that it didn't go badly. But we have to talk about another little matter. Listen to me and don't get excited.

"As far as I am concerned, you are two spies sent to keep an eye on me. I catch you and I shoot you. You were pretending to fish in order to conceal your business. You have fallen into my hands, so much the worse for you. War is like that.

Literary Analysis
Dynamic and Static Characters In what way does the characters' conversation show that the men have changed?

▼ Critical Viewing
Which details of these Prussian officers' uniforms might intimidate citizens like the two friends? **[Analyze]**

---

7. liveried (liv´ ər ēd) *adj.* uniformed.

"But—since you came out past the outposts you have, of course, the password to return. Tell me that password and I will pardon you."

The two friends, side by side, pale, kept silent. A slight nervous trembling shook their hands.

The officer went on: "No one will ever know. You will go back <u>placidly</u>. The secret will disappear with you. If you refuse, it is immediate death. Choose."

They stood motionless, mouths shut.

The Prussian quietly went on, stretching out his hand toward the stream: "Remember that within five minutes you will be at the bottom of that river. Within five minutes! You have relatives, of course?"

Mount Valérien kept thundering.

The two fishermen stood silent. The German gave orders in his own language. Then he moved his chair so as not to be near the prisoners and twelve men took their places, twenty paces distant, rifles grounded.

The officer went on: "I give you one minute, not two seconds more."

Then he rose suddenly, approached the two Frenchmen, took Morissot by the arm, dragged him aside, whispered to him, "Quick, the password? Your friend won't know. I'll pretend to relent."

Morissot answered not a word.

The Prussian drew M. Sauvage aside and put the same question.

M. Sauvage did not answer.

They stood side by side again.

And the officer began to give commands. The soldiers raised their rifles.

Then Morissot's glance happened to fall on the sack full of gudgeons which was lying on the grass a few steps away.

A ray of sunshine made the little heap of still squirming fish gleam. And he almost weakened. In spite of his efforts his eyes filled with tears.

He stammered, "Farewell, Monsieur Sauvage."

M. Sauvage answered, "Farewell, Monsieur Morissot."

They shook hands, trembling from head to foot with a shudder which they could not control.

The officer shouted, "Fire!"

The twelve shots rang out together.

M. Sauvage fell straight forward, like a log. Morissot, who was taller, tottered, half turned, and fell crosswise on top of his comrade, face up, as the blood spurted from his torn shirt.

The German gave more orders.

His men scattered, then returned with rope and stones which they tied to the dead men's feet. Then they carried them to the bank.

Mount Valérien continued to roar, its summit hidden now in a mountainous cloud of smoke.

Two soldiers took Morissot by the head and the feet, two others seized M. Sauvage. They swung the bodies for a moment then let go.

placidly (plas´ id lē) *adv.* calmly

Reading Strategy
Evaluating Characters' Decisions What will be the consequences for Paris if the two men reveal the password?

Reading Strategy
Evaluating Characters' Decisions Do you think the fate of the two friends would have been different if they had revealed the password? Explain.

✔ **Reading Check**

What does the Prussian officer demand of Sauvage and Morissot?

They described an arc and plunged into the river feet first, for the weights made them seem to be standing upright.

There was a splash, the water trembled, then grew calm, while tiny wavelets spread to both shores.

A little blood remained on the surface.

The officer, still calm, said in a low voice: "Now the fish will have their turn."

And he went back to the house.

And all at once he caught sight of the sack of gudgeons in the grass. He picked it up, looked at it, smiled, shouted, "Wilhelm!"

A soldier in a white apron ran out. And the Prussian threw him the catch of the two and said: "Fry these little animals right away while they are still alive. They will be delicious."

Then he lighted his pipe again.

Review and Assess

Thinking About the Selection

1. **Respond:** What did you find especially shocking or disturbing about this story? Explain.

2. **(a) Recall:** List three characteristics of the friendship between M. Morissot and M. Sauvage. **(b) Infer:** What motivates the two men to go fishing?

3. **(a) Recall:** Why are the villages of Colombes and Argenteuil and the surrounding areas deserted? **(b) Connect:** How does the emptiness of the landscape foreshadow, or hint at, the events that occur later in the story?

4. **(a) Recall:** What do the two men say about war in relation to republics and monarchies? **(b) Draw Conclusions:** What do their comments reveal about their own attitudes? **(c) Connect:** In what way do these attitudes affect the outcome of the story?

5. **(a) Recall:** Which words describe the physical appearance and actions of the Prussian soldiers? **(b) Support:** How does this description support the two men's earlier impressions of the Prussian forces?

6. **(a) Recall:** What strategies does the Prussian officer use to force the password from the two friends? **(b) Judge:** Would you describe the Prussian officer as an ethical soldier? Explain.

7. **(a) Relate:** If you were in the place of one of the two friends in Maupassant's story, would you have gone fishing? Why or why not? **(b) Take a Position:** Should the two friends be blamed for their own deaths? Why or why not?

How Much Land Does a Man Need?

Leo Tolstoy
translated by Louise and Aylmer Maude

Background

From the sixteenth century to the mid-nineteenth century, Russian peasants were bound by law to work land they could rent but not own. They grew food meant to feed others, cultivated crops that others would sell, and worked to exhaustion to make a profit for the landowner. Peasants could even be bought and sold with the land they worked. This story takes place after the laws were changed to allow ordinary people to purchase land. To those who had never owned it, land represented the ability to control one's destiny. Tolstoy uses land, an image close to the heart of every Russian, to explore the age-old question, "How much is enough?"

I

An elder sister came to visit her younger sister in the country. The elder was married to a tradesman in town, the younger to a peasant in the village. As the sisters sat over their tea talking, the elder began to boast of the advantages of town life: saying how comfortably they lived there, how well they dressed, what fine clothes her children wore, what good things they ate and drank, and how she went to the theater, promenades,[1] and entertainments.

The younger sister was piqued, and in turn disparaged the life of a tradesman, and stood up for that of a peasant.

"I would not change my way of life for yours," said she. "We may live roughly, but at least we are free from anxiety. You live in better style than we do, but though you often earn more than you need, you are very likely to lose all you have. You know the proverb, 'Loss and gain are brothers twain.'[2] It often happens that people who are wealthy one day are begging their bread the next. Our way is safer. Though a peasant's life is not a fat one, it is a long one. We shall never grow rich, but we shall always have enough to eat."

---

1. **promenades** (präm′ ə nädz) *n.* balls or formal dances.
2. **twain** (twān) *n.* two.

☑**Reading Check**

Which sister lives the life of a country peasant?

The elder sister said sneeringly:

"Enough? Yes, if you like to share with the pigs and the calves! What do you know of elegance or manners! However much your goodman may slave, you will die as you are living—on a dung heap—and your children the same."

"Well, what of that?" replied the younger. "Of course our work is rough and coarse. But, on the other hand, it is sure, and we need not bow to any one. But you, in your towns, are surrounded by temptations; today all may be right, but tomorrow the Evil One may tempt your husband with cards, wine, or women, and all will go to ruin. Don't such things happen often enough?"

Pakhom, the master of the house, was lying on the top of the stove and he listened to the women's chatter.

"It is perfectly true," thought he. "Busy as we are from childhood tilling mother earth, we peasants have no time to let any nonsense settle in our heads. Our only trouble is that we haven't land enough. If I had plenty of land, I shouldn't fear the Devil himself!"

The women finished their tea, chatted a while about dress, and then cleared away the tea-things and lay down to sleep.

But the Devil had been sitting behind the stove, and had heard all that was said. He was pleased that the peasant's wife had led her husband into boasting, and that he had said that if he had plenty of land he would not fear the Devil himself.

Literary Analysis
Dynamic and Static Characters In what ways does Pakhom think his life would change if he had enough land?

▲ **Critical Viewing** Compare and contrast the details in this painting with the sisters' description of peasant life. [Compare and Contrast]

"All right," thought the Devil. "We will have a tussle. I'll give you land enough; and by means of that land I will get you into my power."

II

Close to the village there lived a lady, a small landowner who had an estate of about three hundred acres. She had always lived on good terms with the peasants until she engaged as her steward an old soldier, who took to burdening the people with fines. However careful Pakhom tried to be, it happened again and again that now a horse of his got among the lady's oats, now a cow strayed into her garden, now his calves found their way into her meadows—and he always had to pay a fine.

Pakhom paid up, but grumbled, and, going home in a temper, was rough with his family. All through that summer, Pakhom had much trouble because of this steward, and he was even glad when winter came and the cattle had to be stabled. Though he grudged the fodder when they could no longer graze on the pasture-land, at least he was free from anxiety about them.

In the winter the news got about that the lady was going to sell her land and that the keeper of the inn on the high road was bargaining for it. When the peasants heard this they were very much alarmed.

"Well," thought they, "if the innkeeper gets the land, he will worry us with fines worse than the lady's steward. We all depend on that estate."

So the peasants went on behalf of their commune, and asked the lady not to sell the land to the innkeeper, offering her a better price for it themselves. The lady agreed to let them have it. Then the peasants tried to arrange for the commune to buy the whole estate, so that it might be held by them all in common. They met twice to discuss it, but could not settle the matter; the Evil One sowed <u>discord</u> among them and they could not agree. So they decided to buy the land individually, each according to his means; and the lady agreed to this plan as she had to the other.

Presently Pakhom heard that a neighbor of his was buying fifty acres, and that the lady had consented to accept one half in cash and to wait a year for the other half. Pakhom felt envious.

"Look at that," thought he, "the land is all being sold, and I shall get none of it." So he spoke to his wife.

"Other people are buying," said he, "and we must also buy twenty acres or so. Life is becoming impossible. That manager is simply crushing us with his fines."

So they put their heads together and considered how they could manage to buy it. They had one hundred rubles[3] laid by. They sold a colt and one half of their bees, hired out one of their sons as a laborer and took his wages in advance, borrowed the rest from a brother-in-law, and so scraped together half the purchase money.

discord (dis′ kôrd) n. dissension; conflict

✔**Reading Check**

What motivates Pakhom and the villagers to buy land?

---

3. rubles (rōō′ bəlz) n. Russian money.

Having done this, Pakhom chose a farm of forty acres, some of it wooded, and went to the lady to bargain for it. They came to an agreement, and he shook hands with her upon it and paid her a deposit in advance. Then they went to town and signed the deeds; he paying half the price down, and undertaking to pay the remainder within two years.

So now Pakhom had land of his own. He borrowed seed, and sowed it on the land he had bought. The harvest was a good one, and within a year he had managed to pay off his debts both to the lady and to his brother-in-law. So he became a landowner, plowing and sowing his own land, making hay on his own land, cutting his own trees, and feeding his cattle on his own pasture. When he went out to plow his fields, or to look at his growing corn, or at his grass-meadows, his heart would fill with joy. The grass that grew and the flowers that bloomed there seemed to him unlike any that grew elsewhere. Formerly, when he had passed by that land, it had appeared the same as any other land, but now it seemed quite different.

Reading Strategy
Evaluating Characters' Decisions Considering the costs of purchasing the land, do you think Pakhom made the right decision? Explain.

III

So Pakhom was well-contented, and everything would have been right if the neighboring peasants would only not have trespassed on his corn-fields and meadows. He appealed to them most civilly, but they still went on: now the communal herdsmen would let the village cows stray into his meadows, then horses from the night pasture would get among his corn. Pakhom turned them out again and again, and forgave their owners, and for a long time he forbore to prosecute anyone. But at last he lost patience and complained to the district court. He knew it was the peasants' want of land, and no evil intent on their part, that caused the trouble, but he thought:

"I cannot go on overlooking it or they will destroy all I have. They must be taught a lesson."

So he had them up, gave them one lesson, and then another, and two or three of the peasants were fined. After a time Pakhom's neighbors began to bear him a grudge for this, and would now and then let their cattle on to his land on purpose. One peasant even got into Pakhom's wood at night and cut down five young lime trees for their bark. Pakhom, passing through the wood one day, noticed something white. He came nearer and saw the stripped trunks lying on the ground, and close by stood the stumps where the trees had been. Pakhom was furious.

"If he had only cut one here and there it would have been bad enough," thought Pakhom, "but the rascal has actually cut down a whole clump. If I could only find out who did this, I would pay him out."

He racked his brains as to who it could be. Finally he decided: "It must be Simon—no one else could have done it." So he went to Simon's homestead to have a look round, but he found nothing, and only had an angry scene. However, he now felt more certain than ever that Simon had done it, and he lodged a complaint. Simon was summoned. The case was tried, and retried, and at the end of it all Simon was

Reading Strategy
Evaluating Characters' Decisions Which of Pakhom's past experiences may have influenced his decision to overlook his neighbors' behavior?

acquitted, there being no evidence against him. Pakhom felt still more aggrieved, and let his anger loose upon the elder and the judges.

"You let thieves grease your palms," said he. "If you were honest folk yourselves you would not let a thief go free."

So Pakhom quarreled with the judges and with his neighbors. Threats to burn his building began to be uttered. So though Pakhom had more land, his place in the commune was much worse than before.

About this time a rumor got about that many people were moving to new parts.

"There's no need for me to leave my land," thought Pakhom. "But some of the others may leave our village and then there would be more room for us. I would take over their land myself and make my estate a bit bigger. I could then live more at ease. As it is, I am still too cramped to be comfortable."

One day Pakhom was sitting at home when a peasant, passing through the village, happened to call in. He was allowed to stay the night, and supper was given him. Pakhom had a talk with this peasant and asked him where he came from. The stranger answered that he came from beyond the Volga,[4] where he had been working. One word led to another, and the man went on to say that many people were settling in those parts. He told how some people from his village had settled there. They had joined the commune, and had had twenty-five acres per man granted them. The land was so good, he said, that the rye sown on it grew as high as a horse, and so thick that five cuts of a sickle made a sheaf. One peasant, he said, had brought nothing with him but his bare hands, and now he had six horses and two cows of his own.

Pakhom's heart kindled with desire. He thought:

"Why should I suffer in this narrow hole, if one can live so well else-where? I will sell my land and my homestead here, and with the money I will start afresh over there and get everything new. In this crowded place one is always having trouble. But I must first go and find out all about it myself."

Toward summer he got ready and started. He went down the Volga on a steamer to Samara,[5] then walked another three hundred miles on foot, and at last reached the place. It was just as the stranger had said. The peasants had plenty of land: every man had twenty-five acres of communal land given him for his use, and any one who had money could buy, besides, at two shillings an acre as much good freehold land[6] as he wanted.

Having found out all he wished to know, Pakhom returned home as autumn came on, and began selling off his belongings. He sold his land at a profit, sold his homestead and all his cattle, and withdrew from

---

4. **Volga** (väl´ gə) the major river in western Russia.
5. **Samara** (Sə ma´ rə) city in eastern Russia.
6. **freehold land** privately owned land that the owner can lease to others for a fee.

✓Reading Check

What does Pakhom think he can find beyond the Volga River?

membership of the commune. He only waited till the spring, and then started with his family for the new settlement.

IV

As soon as Pakhom and his family reached their new abode, he applied for admission into the commune of a large village. He stood treat to the elders and obtained the necessary documents. Five shares of communal land were given him for his own and his sons' use: that is to say—125 acres (not all together, but in different fields) besides the use of the communal pasture. Pakhom put up the buildings he needed, and bought cattle. Of the communal land alone he had three times as

▼ Critical Viewing

In what ways does this painting convey the challenges Pakhom might face as an independent landowner? [Analyze]

Cornfield at Ewell, William Holman Hunt

much as at his former home, and the land was good corn-land. He was ten times better off than he had been. He had plenty of arable land and pasturage, and could keep as many head of cattle as he liked.

At first, in the bustle of building and settling down, Pakhom was pleased with it all, but when he got used to it he began to think that even here he had not enough land. The first year, he sowed wheat on his share of the communal land and had a good crop. He wanted to go on sowing wheat, but had not enough communal land for the purpose, and what he had already used was not available; for in those parts wheat is only sown on virgin soil or on fallow land. It is sown for one or two years, and then the land lies fallow till it is again overgrown with prairie grass. There were many who wanted such land and there was not enough for

all; so that people quarreled about it. Those who were better off wanted it for growing wheat, and those who were poor wanted it to let to dealers, so that they might raise money to pay their taxes. Pakhom wanted to sow more wheat, so he rented land from a dealer for a year. He sowed much wheat and had a fine crop, but the land was too far from the village—the wheat had to be carted more than ten miles. After a time Pakhom noticed that some peasant-dealers were living on separate farms and were growing wealthy; and he thought:

"If I were to buy some freehold land and have a homestead on it, it would be a different thing altogether. Then it would all be nice and compact."

The question of buying freehold land recurred to him again and again.

He went on in the same way for three years, renting land and sowing wheat. The seasons turned out well and the crops were good, so that he began to lay money by. He might have gone on living contentedly, but he grew tired of having to rent other people's land every year, and having to scramble for it. Wherever there was good land to be had, the peasants would rush for it and it was taken up at once, so that unless you were sharp about it you got none. It happened in the third year that he and a dealer together rented a piece of pasture land from some peasants; and they had already plowed it up, when there was some dispute and the peasants went to law about it and things fell out so that the labor was all lost.

Reading Strategy
Evaluating Characters' Decisions What happiness have Pakhom's decisions brought him?

✔ **Reading Check**

What thought continues to bother Pakhom?

"If it were my own land," thought Pakhom, "I should be independent, and there would not be all this unpleasantness."

So Pakhom began looking out for land which he could buy; and he came across a peasant who had bought thirteen hundred acres, but having got into difficulties was willing to sell again cheap. Pakhom bargained and haggled with him, and at last they settled the price at 1,500 rubles, part in cash and part to be paid later. They had all but clinched the matter when a passing dealer happened to stop at Pakhom's one day to get a feed for his horses. He drank tea with Pakhom and they had a talk. The dealer said that he was just returning from the land of the Bashkirs,[7] far away, where he had bought thirteen thousand acres of land, all for 1,000 rubles. Pakhom questioned him further, and the tradesman said:

"All one need do is to make friends with the chiefs. I gave away about one hundred rubles' worth of silk robes and carpets, besides a case of tea, and I gave wine to those who would drink it; and I got the land for less than a penny[8] an acre." And he showed Pakhom the title-deeds, saying:

"The land lies near a river, and the whole prairie is virgin soil."

Pakhom plied him with questions, and the tradesman said:

"There is more land there than you could cover if you walked a year, and it all belongs to the Bashkirs. They are as simple as sheep, and land can be got almost for nothing."

"There, now," thought Pakhom, "with my 1,000 rubles, why should I get only thirteen hundred acres, and saddle myself with a debt besides? If I take it out there, I can get more than ten times as much for the money."

V

Pakhom inquired how to get to the place, and as soon as the tradesman had left him, he prepared to go there himself. He left his wife to look after the homestead, and started on his journey taking his man with him. They stopped at a town on their way and bought a case of tea, some wine, and other presents, as the trademan had advised. On and on they went until they had gone more than three hundred miles, and on the seventh day they came to a place where the Bashkirs had pitched their tents. It was all just as the tradesman had said. The people lived on the steppes,[9] by a river, in felt-covered tents. They neither tilled the ground, nor ate bread. Their cattle and horses grazed in herds on the steppe. The colts were tethered behind the tents, and the mares were driven to them twice a day. The mares were milked, and from the milk kumiss[10] was made. It was the women who prepared kumiss, and they also made cheese. As far as the men were concerned,

▲ **Critical Viewing**
An iron sickle such as this might be used to clear fields of tall weeds and grasses. With this information in mind, does Pakhom's desire for more land seem foolish? Explain. **[Criticize]**

---

7. **Bashkirs** (bash kirz´) nomadic people who live in the plains of southwestern Russia.
8. **penny** here, one hundredth of a ruble.
9. **steppe** (step) *n.* high grassland of central Asia.
10. **kumiss** (koo´ mis) *n.* mare's milk that has been fermented and is used as a drink.

drinking kumiss and tea, eating mutton, and playing on their pipes, was all they cared about. They were all stout and merry, and all the summer long they never thought of doing any work. They were quite ignorant, and knew no Russian, but were good-natured enough.

As soon as they saw Pakhom, they came out of their tents and gathered round their visitor. An interpreter was found, and Pakhom told them he had come about some land. The Bashkirs seemed very glad; they took Pakhom and led him into one of the best tents, where they made him sit on some down cushions placed on a carpet, while they sat round him. They gave him some tea and kumiss, and had a sheep killed, and gave him mutton to eat. Pakhom took presents out of his cart and distributed them among the Bashkirs, and divided the tea amongst them. The Bashkirs were delighted. They talked a great deal among themselves, and then told the interpreter to translate.

"They wish to tell you," said the interpreter, "that they like you, and that it is our custom to do all we can to please a guest and to repay him for his gifts. You have given us presents, now tell us which of the things we possess please you best, that we may present them to you."

"What pleases me best here," answered Pakhom, "is your land. Our land is crowded and the soil is exhausted; but you have plenty of land and it is good land. I never saw the like of it."

The interpreter translated. The Bashkirs talked among themselves for a while. Pakhom could not understand what they were saying, but saw that they were much amused and that they shouted and laughed. Then they were silent and looked at Pakhom while the interpreter said:

"They wish me to tell you that in return for your presents they will gladly give you as much land as you want. You have only to point it out with your hand and it is yours."

The Bashkirs talked again for a while and began to dispute. Pakhom asked what they were disputing about, and the interpreter told him that some of them thought they ought to ask their chief about the land and not act in his absence, while others thought there was no need to wait for his return.

VI

While the Bashkirs were disputing, a man in a large fox-fur cap appeared on the scene. They all became silent and rose to their feet. The interpreter said, "This is our chief himself."

Pakhom immediately fetched the best dressing-gown and five pounds of tea, and offered these to the chief. The chief accepted them, and seated himself in the place of honor. The Bashkirs at once began telling him something. The chief listened for a while, then made a sign with his head for them to be silent, and addressing himself to Pakhom, said in Russian:

"Well, let it be so. Choose whatever piece of land you like; we have plenty of it."

Literary Analysis
Dynamic and Static Characters Which elements of the Bashkirs' lifestyle has Pakhom sought for himself since his days as a peasant farmer?

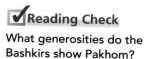

Reading Check
What generosities do the Bashkirs show Pakhom?

"How can I take as much as I like?" thought Pakhom. "I must get a deed to make it secure, or else they may say, 'It is yours,' and afterward may take it away again."

"Thank you for your kind words," he said aloud. "You have much land, and I only want a little. But I should like to be sure which bit is mine. Could it not be measured and made over to me? Life and death are in God's hands. You good people give it to me, but your children might wish to take it away again."

"You are quite right," said the chief. "We will make it over to you."

"I heard that a dealer had been here," continued Pakhom, "and that you gave him a little land, too, and signed title-deeds to that effect. I should like to have it done in the same way."

The chief understood.

"Yes," replied he, "that can be done quite easily. We have a scribe, and we will go to town with you and have the deed properly sealed."

"And what will be the price?" asked Pakhom.

"Our price is always the same: one thousand rubles a day."

Pakhom did not understand.

"A day? What measure is that? How many acres would that be?"

"We do not know how to reckon it out," said the chief. "We sell it by the day. As much as you can go around on your feet in a day is yours, and the price is one thousand rubles a day."

Pakhom was surprised.

"But in a day you can get around a large tract of land," he said.

The chief laughed.

"It will all be yours!" said he. "But there is one condition: If you don't return on the same day to the spot whence you started, your money is lost."

"But how am I to mark the way that I have gone?"

"Why, we shall go to any spot you like, and stay there. You must start from that spot and make your round, taking a spade with you. Wherever you think necessary, make a mark. At every turning, dig a hole and pile up the turf; then afterward we will go round with a plow from hole to hole. You may make as large a circuit as you please, but before the sun sets you must return to the place you started from. All the land you cover will be yours."

Pakhom was delighted. It was decided to start early next morning. They talked a while, and after drinking some more kumiss and eating some more mutton, they had tea again, and then the night came on. They gave Pakhom a feather-bed to sleep on, and the Bashkirs dispersed for the night, promising to assemble the next morning at daybreak and ride out before sunrise to the appointed spot.

VII

Pakhom lay on the feather-bed, but could not sleep. He kept thinking about the land.

"What a large tract I will mark off!" thought he. "I can easily do thirty-five miles in a day. The days are long now, and within a circuit of thirty-

Reading Strategy
Evaluating Characters' Decisions What past experiences might have influenced Pakhom's decision to obtain a deed from the Bashkirs?

five miles what a lot of land there will be! I will sell the poorer land, or let it to peasants, but I'll pick out the best and farm it. I will buy two ox-teams, and hire two more laborers. About a hundred and fifty acres shall be plowland, and I will pasture cattle on the rest."

Pakhom lay awake all night, and dozed off only just before dawn. Hardly were his eyes closed when he had a dream. He thought he was lying in that same tent and heard somebody chuckling outside. He wondered who it could be, and rose and went out, and he saw the Bashkir chief sitting in front of the tent holding his sides and rolling about with laughter. Going nearer to the chief, Pakhom asked: "What are you laughing at?" But he saw that it was no longer the chief, but the dealer who had recently stopped at his house and had told him about the land. Just as Pakhom was going to ask, "Have you been here long?" he saw that it was not the dealer, but the peasant who had come up from the Volga, long ago, to Pakhom's old home. Then he saw that it was not the peasant either, but the Devil himself with hoofs and horns, sitting there and chuckling, and before him lay a man barefoot, <u>prostrate</u> on the ground, with only trousers and a shirt on. And Pakhom dreamt that he looked more attentively to see what sort of a man it was that was lying there, and he saw that the man was dead, and that it was himself! He awoke horror-struck.

"What things one does dream," thought he.

Looking round he saw through the open door that the dawn was breaking.

"It's time to wake them up," thought he. "We ought to be starting."

He got up, roused his man (who was sleeping in his cart), bade him harness; and went to call the Bashkirs.

"It's time to go to the steppe to measure the land," he said.

The Bashkirs rose and assembled, and the chief came too. Then they began drinking kumiss again, and offered Pakhom some tea, but he would not wait.

"If we are to go, let us go. It is high time," said he.

VIII

The Bashkirs got ready and they all started; some mounted on horses, and some in carts. Pakhom drove in his own small cart with his servant and took a spade with him. When they reached the steppe, the morning red was beginning to kindle. They ascended a hillock (called by the Bashkirs a *shikhan*) and, dismounting from their carts and their horses, gathered in one spot. The chief came up to Pakhom and stretching out his arm toward the plain;

prostrate (präs´ trāt) *adj.* lying with one's face down

 **Reading Check**

How many miles does Pakhom plan to walk?

"See," said he, "all this, as far as your eye can reach, is ours. You may have any part of it you like."

Pakhom's eyes glistened: it was all virgin soil, as flat as the palm of your hand, as black as the seed of a poppy, and in the hollows different kinds of grasses grew breast high.

The chief took off his fox-fur cap, placed it on the ground and said:

"This will be the mark. Start from here, and return here again. All the land you go round shall be yours."

Pakhom took out his money and put it on the cap. Then he took off his outer coat, remaining in his sleeveless under-coat. He unfastened his girdle[11] and tied it tight below his stomach, put a little bag of bread into the breast of his coat, and tying a flask of water to his girdle, he drew up the tops of his boots, took the spade from his man, and stood ready to start. He considered for some moments which way he had better go—it was tempting everywhere.

"No matter," he concluded, "I will go toward the rising sun."

He turned his face to the east, stretched himself, and waited for the sun to appear above the rim.

"I must lose no time," he thought, "and it is easier walking while it is still cool."

The sun's rays had hardly flashed above the horizon, before Pakhom, carrying the spade over his shoulder, went down into the steppe.

Pakhom started walking neither slowly nor quickly. After having gone a thousand yards he stopped, dug a hole, and placed pieces of turf one on another to make it more visible. Then he went on; and now that he had walked off his stiffness he quickened his pace. After a while he dug another hole.

Pakhom looked back. The hillock could be distinctly seen in the sunlight, with the people on it, and the glittering tires of the cartwheels. At a rough guess Pakhom concluded that he had walked three miles. It was growing warmer; he took off his under-coat, flung it across his

---

11. girdle (gʉrd´ əl) *n.* belt or sash.

Literary Analysis
Dynamic and Static Characters In what ways has ambition changed Pakhom?

▼ **Critical Viewing**
What might Pakhom imagine for himself while looking at land such as this? **[Speculate]**

shoulder, and went on again. It had grown quite warm now; he looked at the sun, it was time to think of breakfast.

"The first shift is done, but there are four in a day, and it is too soon yet to turn. But I will just take off my boots," said he to himself.

He sat down, took off his boots, stuck them into his girdle, and went on. It was easy walking now.

"I will go on for another three miles," thought he, "and then turn to the left. This spot is so fine, that it would be a pity to lose it. The further one goes, the better the land seems."

He went straight on for a while, and when he looked round, the hillock was scarcely visible and the people on it looked like black ants, and he could just see something glistening there in the sun.

"Ah," thought Pakhom, "I have gone far enough in this direction, it is time to turn. Besides I am in a regular sweat, and very thirsty."

He stopped, dug a large hole, and heaped up pieces of turf. Next he untied his flask, had a drink, and then turned sharply to the left. He went on and on; the grass was high, and it was very hot.

Pakhom began to grow tired: he looked at the sun and saw that it was noon.

"Well," he thought, "I must have a rest."

He sat down, and ate some bread and drank some water; but he did not lie down, thinking that if he did he might fall asleep. After sitting a little while, he went on again. At first he walked easily: the food had strengthened him; but it had become terribly hot and he felt sleepy. Still he went on, thinking: "An hour to suffer, a lifetime to live."

He went a long way in this direction also, and was about to turn to the left again, when he perceived a damp hollow: "It would be a pity to leave that out," he thought. "Flax would do well there." So he went on past the hollow and dug a hole on the other side of it before he turned the corner. Pakhom looked toward the hillock. The heat made the air hazy: it seemed to be quivering, and through the haze the people on the hillock could scarcely be seen.

Reading Strategy
Evaluating Characters' Decisions What are the possible implications of Pakhom's decision to "go on for another three miles"?

☑**Reading Check**
What obstacles does Pakhom encounter as he walks?

"Ah!" thought Pakhom, "I have made the sides too long; I must make this one shorter." And he went along the third side, stepping faster. He looked at the sun: it was nearly half-way to the horizon, and he had not yet done two miles of the third side of the square. He was still ten miles from the goal.

"No," he thought, "though it will make my land lop-sided, I must hurry back in a straight line now. I might go too far, and as it is I have a great deal of land."

So Pakhom hurriedly dug a hole, and turned straight toward the hillock.

IX

Pakhom went straight toward the hillock, but he now walked with difficulty. He was exhausted from the heat, his bare feet were cut and bruised, and his legs began to fail. He longed to rest, but it was impossible if he meant to get back before sunset. The sun waits for no man, and it was sinking lower and lower.

"Oh, dear," he thought, "if only I have not blundered trying for too much! What if I am too late?"

He looked toward the hillock and at the sun. He was still far from his goal, and the sun was already near the rim.

Pakhom walked on and on; it was very hard walking but he went quicker and quicker. He pressed on, but was still far from the place. He began running, threw away his coat, his boots, his flask, and his cap, and kept only the spade which he used as a support.

"What shall I do?" he thought again. "I have grasped too much and ruined the whole affair. I can't get there before the sun sets."

And this fear made him still more breathless. Pakhom went on running, his soaking shirt and trousers stuck to him and his mouth was parched. His breast was working like a blacksmith's bellows, his heart was beating like a hammer, and his legs were giving way as if they did not belong to him. Pakhom was seized with terror lest he should die of the strain.

Though afraid of death, he could not stop. "After having run all that way they will call me a fool if I stop now," thought he. And he ran on and on, and drew near and heard the Bashkirs yelling and shouting to him, and their cries inflamed his heart still more. He gathered his last strength and ran on.

The sun was close to the rim, and cloaked in mist looked large, and red as blood. Now, yes now, it was about to set! The sun was quite low, but he was also quite near his aim. Pakhom could already see the people on the hillock waving their arms to hurry him up. He could see the fox-fur cap on the ground and the money on it, and the chief sitting on the ground holding his sides. And Pakhom remembered his dream.

"There's plenty of land," thought he, "but will God let me live on it? I have lost my life, I have lost my life! I shall never reach that spot!"

Pakhom looked at the sun, which had reached the earth: one side of it had already disappeared. With all his remaining strength he rushed on, bending his body forward so that his legs could hardly follow fast enough to keep him from falling. Just as he reached the hillock it suddenly grew dark. He looked up—the sun had already set! He gave a cry: "All my labor has been in vain," thought he, and was about to stop, but he heard the Bashkirs still shouting, and remembered that though to him, from below, the sun seemed to have set, they on the hillock could still see it. He took a long breath and ran up the hillock. It was still light there. He reached the top and saw the cap. Before it sat the chief laughing and holding his sides. Again Pakhom remembered his dream, and he uttered a cry: his legs gave way beneath him, he fell forward and reached the cap with his hands.

"Ah, that's a fine fellow!" exclaimed the chief. "He has gained much land!"

Pakhom's servant came running up and tried to raise him, but he saw that blood was flowing from his mouth. Pakhom was dead!

The Bashkirs clicked their tongues to show their pity.

His servant picked up the spade and dug a grave long enough for Pakhom to lie in, and buried him in it. Six feet from his head to his heels was all he needed.

Review and Assess

Thinking About the Selection

1. **Respond:** If you were in Pakhom's place, at what point might you be satisfied with your property? Explain.

2. **(a) Recall:** What does the younger sister say about peasant life and city life? **(b) Connect:** Considering the outcome of the story, what is ironic, or surprising, about the younger sister's comments?

3. **(a) Recall:** What changes Pakhom's attitude toward his first plot of land? **(b) Speculate:** Explain whether you think that Pakhom's attitude would have remained the same if he had not had difficulties with his neighbors.

4. **(a) Recall:** Besides Pakhom, who is featured in his dream? **(b) Infer:** What does the dream suggest about the Devil's role in the story?

5. **(a) Recall:** In the end, how much land did Pakhom need? **(b) Analyze:** What is ironic about the final line? **(c) Criticize:** Did you find the ending satisfying? Why or why not?

6. **(a) Apply:** Greek playwright Socrates wrote, "He is richest who is content with the least. He who has little and wants less is richer than he that has much and wants more." Apply this sentiment to the story. **(b) Take a Stand:** Do you agree with Socrates? Why or why not?

A Problem

Anton Chekhov *translated by* Constance Garnett

The Library at Windsor Castle, Joseph Nash, National Trust Photographic Library

▲ **Critical Viewing**   In what ways is family honor reflected in a formal study like this one? **[Analyze]**

Background

In the nineteenth century, members of the Russian aristocracy lived on wealth that had been accumulated generations earlier. For this class, honor meant more than displays of good behavior. Honor required preserving the reputation and heritage of a long-standing family name. When good fortunes changed and money became unavailable, a family name and its history of prosperity suggested the promise of stability to come. Such a promise was often all the aristocrats could rely on to save them from imminent financial disaster.

The strictest measures were taken that the Uskovs' family secret might not leak out and become generally known. Half of the servants were sent off to the theater or the circus; the other half were sitting in the kitchen and not allowed to leave it. Orders were given that no one was to be admitted. The wife of the Colonel, her sister, and the governess, though they had been initiated into the secret, kept up a pretense of knowing nothing; they sat in the dining-room and did not show themselves in the drawing-room or the hall.

Sasha Uskov, the young man of twenty-five who was the cause of all the commotion, had arrived some time before, and by the advice of kind-hearted Ivan Markovitch, his uncle, who was taking his part, he sat meekly in the hall by the door leading to the study, and prepared himself to make an open, candid explanation.

The other side of the door, in the study, a family council was being held. The subject under discussion was an exceedingly disagreeable and delicate one. Sasha Uskov had cashed at one of the banks a false promissory note[1] and it had become due for payment three days before, and now his two paternal uncles and Ivan Markovitch, the brother of his dead mother, were deciding the question whether they should pay the money and save the family honor, or wash their hands of it and leave the case to go to trial.

Literary Analysis
Dynamic and Static Characters Which clues about the character of Sasha Uskov does this paragraph present?

✔ **Reading Check**

Who is at the center of the Uskov family's secret?

---

1. **promissory note** written promise to pay a certain sum of money on demand; an IOU.

To outsiders who have no personal interest in the matter such questions seem simple; for those who are so unfortunate as to have to decide them in earnest they are extremely difficult. The uncles had been talking for a long time, but the problem seemed no nearer decision.

"My friends!" said the uncle who was a colonel, and there was a note of exhaustion and bitterness in his voice. "Who says that family honor is a mere convention? I don't say that at all. I am only warning you against a false view; I am pointing out the possibility of an unpardonable mistake. How can you fail to see it? I am not speaking Chinese; I am speaking Russian!"

"My dear fellow, we do understand," Ivan Markovitch protested mildly.

"How can you understand if you say that I don't believe in family honor? I repeat once more; fa-mil-y ho-nor false-ly un-der-stood is a prejudice! Falsely understood! That's what I say: whatever may be the motives for screening a scoundrel, whoever he may be, and helping him to escape punishment, it is contrary to law and unworthy of a gentleman. It's not saving the family honor; it's civic cowardice! Take the army, for instance. . . . The honor of the army is more precious to us than any other honor, yet we don't screen our guilty members, but condemn them. And does the honor of the army suffer in consequence? Quite the opposite!"

The other paternal uncle, an official in the Treasury, a <u>taciturn</u>, dull-witted, and rheumatic man, sat silent, or spoke only of the fact that the Uskovs' name would get into the newspapers if the case went for trial. His opinion was that the case ought to be hushed up from the first and not become public property; but, apart from publicity in the newspapers, he advanced no other argument in support of this opinion.

The maternal uncle, kind-hearted Ivan Markovitch, spoke smoothly, softly, and with a tremor in his voice. He began with saying that youth has its rights and its peculiar temptations. Which of us has not been young, and who has not been led astray? To say nothing of ordinary mortals, even great men have not escaped errors and mistakes in their youth. Take, for instance, the biography of great writers. Did not every one of them gamble, drink, and draw down upon himself the anger of right-thinking people in his young days? If Sasha's error bordered upon crime, they must remember that Sasha had received practically no education; he had been expelled from the high school in the fifth class; he had lost his parents in early childhood, and so had been left at the tenderest age without guidance and good, <u>benevolent</u> influences. He was nervous, excitable, had no firm ground under his feet, and, above all, he had been unlucky. Even if he were guilty, anyway he deserved indulgence and the sympathy of all compassionate souls. He ought, of course, to be punished, but he was punished as it was by his conscience and the agonies he was enduring now while awaiting the sentence of his relations. The comparison with the army made by the Colonel was

taciturn (tas´ə tʉrn) *adj.* almost always silent

Reading Strategy
Evaluating Characters' Decisions With which paternal uncle do you agree? Explain.

benevolent (bə nev´ ə lənt) *adj.* doing or inclined to do good; kindly; charitable

delightful, and did credit to his lofty intelligence; his appeal to their feeling of public duty spoke for the chivalry of his soul, but they must not forget that in each individual the citizen is closely linked with the Christian. . . .

"Shall we be false to civic duty," Ivan Markovitch exclaimed passionately, "if instead of punishing an erring boy we hold out to him a helping hand?"

Ivan Markovitch talked further of family honor. He had not the honor to belong to the Uskov family himself, but he knew their distinguished family went back to the thirteenth century; he did not forget for a minute, either, that his precious, beloved sister had been the wife of one of the representatives of that name. In short, the family was dear to him for many reasons, and he refused to admit the idea that, for the sake of a paltry fifteen hundred rubles[2] a blot should be cast on the escutcheon[3] that was beyond all price. If all the motives he had brought forward were not sufficiently convincing, he, Ivan Markovitch, in conclusion, begged his listeners to ask themselves what was meant by

---

2. **rubles** (roo´ bəlz) *n.* Russian unit of currency.
3. **escutcheon** (e skuch´ ən) *n.* shield on which a coat of arms is displayed.

✓ **Reading Check**

Which uncle defends the mistakes made by all men in their youth?

Ball at the Moulin de la Galette, 1876, Pierre Auguste Renoir

▲ **Critical Viewing** What do you think Sasha might find attractive about the lifestyle captured in this painting? **[Speculate]**

crime? Crime is an immoral act founded upon ill-will. But is the will of man free? Philosophy has not yet given a positive answer to that question. Different views were held by the learned. The latest school of Lombroso,[4] for instance, denies the freedom of the will, and considers every crime as the product of the purely anatomical peculiarities of the individual.

"Ivan Markovitch," said the Colonel, in a voice of entreaty, "we are talking seriously about an important matter, and you bring in Lombroso, you clever fellow. Think a little, what are you saying all this for? Can you imagine that all your thunderings and rhetoric will furnish an answer to the question?"

Sasha Uskov sat at the door and listened. He felt neither terror, shame, nor depression, but only weariness and inward emptiness. It seemed to him that it made absolutely no difference to him whether they forgave him or not; he had come here to hear his sentence and to explain himself simply because kind-hearted Ivan Markovitch had

Literary Analysis
Dynamic and Static Characters What is Sasha's attitude toward his misdeed at this point?

---

4. **Lombroso** Cesare Lombroso (1835–1909), an Italian physician and criminologist who believed that a criminal was a distinct human type, with specific physical and mental deviations, and that a criminal tendency was the result of hereditary factors.

E. Duranty, 1879, Edgar Degas, Glasgow Museums

◀ **Critical Viewing**
In what way does the expression on this man's face match what Ivan Markovitch might be feeling? **[Connect]**

begged him to do so. He was not afraid of the future. It made no difference to him where he was: here in the hall, in prison, or in Siberia.

"If Siberia, then let it be Siberia, damn it all!"

He was sick of life and found it insufferably hard. He was inextricably involved in debt; he had not a farthing[5] in his pocket; his family had become detestable to him; he would have to part from his friends and his women sooner or later, as they had begun to be too contemptuous of his sponging on them. The future looked black.

Sasha was indifferent, and was only disturbed by one circumstance; the other side of the door they were calling him a scoundrel and a criminal. Every minute he was on the point of jumping up, bursting into the study and shouting in answer to the detestable metallic voice of the Colonel:

"You are lying!"

"Criminal" is a dreadful word—that is what murderers, thieves, robbers are; in fact, wicked and morally hopeless people. And Sasha was very far from being all that. . . . It was true he owed a great deal and did not pay his debts. But debt is not a crime, and it is unusual for a man not to be in debt. The Colonel and Ivan Markovitch were both in debt. . . .

"What have I done wrong besides?" Sasha wondered.

He had discounted a forged note. But all the young men he knew did the same. Handrikov and Von Burst always forged IOU's from their parents or friends when their allowances were not paid at the regular time, and then when they got their money from home they redeemed them before they became due. Sasha had done the same, but had not redeemed the IOU because he had not got the money which Handrikov had promised to lend him. He was not to blame; it was the fault of circumstances. It was true that the use of another person's signature was considered reprehensible; but, still, it was not a crime but a generally accepted dodge, an ugly formality which injured no one and was quite harmless, for in forging the Colonel's signature Sasha had had no intention of causing anybody damage or loss.

"No, it doesn't mean that I am a criminal . . . " thought Sasha. "And it's not in my character to bring myself to commit a crime. I am soft, emotional. . . . When I have the money I help the poor. . . . "

Sasha was musing after this fashion while they went on talking the other side of the door.

"But, my friends, this is endless," the Colonel declared, getting excited. "Suppose we were to forgive him and pay the money. You know he would not give up leading a dissipated life, squandering money, making debts, going to our tailors and ordering suits in our names! Can you guarantee that this will be his last prank? As far as I am concerned, I have no faith whatever in his reforming!"

The official of the Treasury muttered something in reply; after him Ivan Markovitch began talking blandly and suavely again. The Colonel moved his chair impatiently and drowned the other's words with his

Reading Strategy
Evaluating Characters' Decisions Do you think that Sasha's line of reasoning adequately excuses the decision he made to discount the note? Explain.

✔ **Reading Check**
What terrible wrong has Sasha committed?

---

5. **farthing** (fär´ *th*in) *n.* coin of little value.

detestable metallic voice. At last the door opened and Ivan Markovitch came out of the study; there were patches of red on his lean shaven face.

"Come along," he said, taking Sasha by the hand. "Come and speak frankly from your heart. Without pride, my dear boy, humbly and from your heart."

Sasha went into the study. The official of the Treasury was sitting down; the Colonel was standing before the table with one hand in his pocket and one knee on a chair. It was smoky and stifling in the study. Sasha did not look at the official or the Colonel; he felt suddenly ashamed and uncomfortable. He looked uneasily at Ivan Markovitch and muttered:

"I'll pay it . . . I'll give it back. . . ."

"What did you expect when you discounted the IOU?" he heard a metallic voice.

"I . . . Handrikov promised to lend me the money before now."

Sasha could say no more. He went out of the study and sat down again on the chair near the door. He would have been glad to go away altogether at once, but he was choking with hatred and he awfully wanted to remain, to tear the Colonel to pieces, to say something rude to him. He sat trying to think of something violent and effective to say to his hated uncle, and at that moment a woman's figure, shrouded in the twilight, appeared at the drawing-room door. It was the Colonel's wife. She beckoned Sasha to her, and, wringing her hands, said, weeping:

"*Alexandre*, I know you don't like me, but . . . listen to me; listen, I beg you. . . . But, my dear, how can this have happened? Why, it's awful, awful! For goodness' sake, beg them, defend yourself, entreat them."

Sasha looked at her quivering shoulders, at the big tears that were rolling down her cheeks, heard behind his back the hollow, nervous voices of worried and exhausted people, and shrugged his shoulders. He had not in the least expected that his aristocratic relations would raise such a tempest over a paltry fifteen hundred rubles! He could not understand her tears nor the quiver of their voices.

An hour later he heard that the Colonel was getting the best of it; the uncles were finally inclining to let the case go for trial.

"The matter's settled," said the Colonel, sighing. "Enough."

After this decision all the uncles, even the emphatic Colonel, became noticeably depressed. A silence followed.

"Merciful Heavens!" sighed Ivan Markovitch. "My poor sister!"

And he began saying in a subdued voice that most likely his sister, Sasha's mother, was present unseen in the study at that moment. He felt in his soul how the unhappy, saintly woman was weeping, grieving, and begging for her boy. For the sake of her peace beyond the grave, they ought to spare Sasha.

The sound of a muffled sob was heard. Ivan Markovitch was weeping and muttering something which it was impossible to catch through the door. The Colonel got up and paced from corner to corner. The long conversation began over again.

But then the clock in the drawing-room struck two. The family council was over. To avoid seeing the person who had moved him to such wrath, the Colonel went from the study, not into the hall, but into the vestibule. . . . Ivan Markovitch came out into the hall. . . . He was agitated and rubbing his hands joyfully. His tear-stained eyes looked good-humored and his mouth was twisted into a smile.

▲ **Critical Viewing**
In what way are Russian rubles like these at the heart of this story's conflict? **[Analyze]**

"Capital," he said to Sasha. "Thank God! You can go home, my dear, and sleep tranquilly. We have decided to pay the sum, but on condition that you repent and come with me tomorrow into the country and set to work."

A minute later Ivan Markovitch and Sasha in their great coats and caps were going down the stairs. The uncle was muttering something edifying. Sasha did not listen, but felt as though some uneasy weight were gradually slipping off his shoulders. They had forgiven him; he was free! A gust of joy sprang up within him and sent a sweet chill to his heart. He longed to breathe, to move swiftly, to live! Glancing at the street lamps and the black sky, he remembered that Von Burst was celebrating his name-day[6] that evening at the "Bear," and again a rush of joy flooded his soul. . . .

"I am going!" he decided.

But then he remembered he had not a farthing, that the companions he was going to would despise him at once for his empty pockets. He must get hold of some money, come what may!

"Uncle, lend me a hundred rubles," he said to Ivan Markovitch.

His uncle, surprised, looked into his face and backed against a lamp-post.

"Give it to me," said Sasha, shifting impatiently from one foot to the other and beginning to pant. "Uncle, I entreat you, give me a hundred rubles."

His face worked; he trembled, and seemed on the point of attacking his uncle. . . .

"Won't you?" he kept asking, seeing that his uncle was still amazed and did not understand. "Listen. If you don't, I'll give myself up tomorrow! I won't let you pay the IOU! I'll present another false note tomorrow!"

Reading Strategy
Evaluating Characters' Decisions What consequences might occur if Ivan Markovitch gives the hundred rubles to Sasha?

✔**Reading Check**
Who agrees to pay Sasha's debt?

---

6. **name-day** feast day of the saint after whom a person is named.

Petrified, muttering something incoherent in his horror, Ivan Markovitch took a hundred-ruble note out of his pocket-book and gave it to Sasha. The young man took it and walked rapidly away from him. . . .

Taking a sledge,[7] Sasha grew calmer, and felt a rush of joy within him again. The "rights of youth" of which kind-hearted Ivan Markovitch had spoken at the family council woke up and asserted themselves. Sasha pictured the drinking party before him, and, among the bottles, the women, and his friends, the thought flashed through his mind:

"Now I see that I am a criminal; yes, I am a criminal."

---

7. **sledge** (slej) *n.* strong, heavy sled.

Review and Assess

Thinking About the Selection

1. **Respond:** With which character in "A Problem" do you sympathize most? Why?

2. **(a) Recall:** What has Sasha done that has so upset the family? **(b) Infer:** Why do you think Sasha takes his offense so lightly?

3. **(a) Recall:** What do most of the relatives want to do about Sasha and the problem he has created? **(b) Speculate:** How has Sasha's past behavior influenced his relatives' attitude toward his current situation?

4. **(a) Recall:** What does Ivan Markovitch want to do about the problem? **(b) Make a Judgment:** Do you think Uncle Ivan's attitude helps or harms Sasha?

5. **(a) Recall:** What is Ivan Markovitch's most important, and ultimately most convincing, point in his defense of Sasha? **(b) Infer:** What inferences can you make about Ivan Markovitch's character based on his tearful speech to the uncles? **(c) Analyze Cause and Effect:** Does the Colonel's reaction to the speech change your impression of him? Why or why not?

6. **(a) Recall:** What is Ivan Markovitch's emotional reaction to Sasha's final request? **(b) Interpret:** Why does Ivan Markovitch react this way?

7. **Evaluate:** Of the two choices facing the family—to let the case go to trial or to pay Sasha's debt—which would have done Sasha the most good? Why?

Review and Assess

Literary Analysis

Dynamic and Static Characters

1. Are the main characters in "Two Friends" **dynamic or static characters**? Use details from the story to support your response.
2. In "How Much Land Does a Man Need?" which details suggest that Pakhom is a static character in spite of the changes he experiences?
3. Which details in "A Problem" suggest that the character of Sasha Uskov will never change?

Comparing Literary Works

4. (a) How much consideration did Pakhom give to his family each time he decided to buy more land? (b) In what way does Pakhom's attitude compare with Sasha's in "A Problem"?
5. Do the main characters in "Two Friends" and "A Problem" pass a point of no return? Explain.

Reading Strategy

Evaluating Characters' Decisions

6. **Evaluate the characters' decisions** in the three stories by completing a chart like the one shown. Criteria for evaluating their choices are provided.

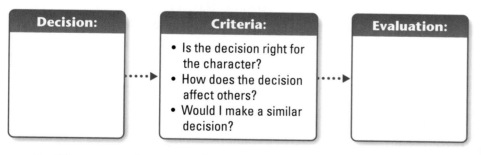

Decision:	Criteria:	Evaluation:
	• Is the decision right for the character? • How does the decision affect others? • Would I make a similar decision?	

7. Choose one character who, in your opinion, makes a bad decision. (a) What good or harmless intentions might have been at the heart of the decision? (b) Does having such good intentions make the character's behavior forgivable? Explain.

Extend Understanding

8. **Psychology Connection:** In Pakhom's culture, land is a status symbol indicating wealth, power, and social rank. What kinds of status symbols do people crave today? Explain.

Quick Review

A **dynamic character** experiences changes in behavior and attitude throughout a story.

A **static character** stays the same.

To **evaluate characters' decisions,** make judgments as to whether their decisions are good or bad.

 **Take It to the Net**
PHSchool.com

Take the interactive self-test online to check your understanding of these selections.

Integrate Language Skills

Vocabulary Development Lesson

Word Analysis: Latin Prefix *dis-*

The Latin prefix *dis-* can mean "apart" or "not," changing the meaning of a word to its opposite. Add the prefix *dis-* to each word below, and define the new words you create.

1. grace   **2.** claim   **3.** orient

Spelling Strategy

Nouns ending in *-ence* usually end in *-ent* and *-ently* in their adjective and adverb forms. Write the adjective and adverb forms of each of the following nouns.

1. violence   **2.** absence   **3.** prudence

Concept Development: Synonyms

Choose the word from the list on the right that is closest in meaning to each vocabulary word below.

1. benevolent	**a.** looting
2. discord	**b.** charitable
3. pillaging	**c.** over
4. placidly	**d.** face down
5. prostrate	**e.** calmly
6. superimposed	**f.** silent
7. taciturn	**g.** conflict

Grammar and Style Lesson

Restrictive and Nonrestrictive Adjective Clauses

Restrictive—essential—**adjective clauses** limit, or restrict, the meaning of the nouns they modify. They identify and define, and they are necessary to the meaning.

> **Restrictive:** "[He] sowed it on the land *he had bought.*" (modifies *land*)

Nonrestrictive—nonessential—**adjective clauses** give additional information about nouns. They describe, but they are not necessary to the noun's meaning. Use commas to set off these clauses.

> **Nonrestrictive:** Sasha Uskov, *who was the cause of all the trouble* . . . (modifies *Sasha Uskov*)

Practice Identify each italicized clause that follows as restrictive or nonrestrictive. Then, circle the word it modifies.

1. Anyone *who had money* could buy . . . as much freehold land as he wanted.

2. . . . a blot should be cast on the escutcheon *that was beyond all price.*

3. He borrowed seed and sowed it on the land *he had bought.*

4. Pakhom looked at the sun, *which had reached the earth.*

5. She engaged . . . an old soldier, *who took to burdening the people with fines.*

Writing Application Write two sentences about a friend. Use a restrictive clause in one sentence and a nonrestrictive clause in the other. Identify each clause and circle the word it modifies.

Writing Lesson

Analyzing a Character's Decision

For many of the characters in these stories, changing one critical decision would create an entirely new ending to the story. Write an essay analyzing a character's decision at such a major turning point.

Prewriting	Choose a character from one of the stories you have read, and identify a key decision. Then, brainstorm for a plausible alternative decision and a new, logical ending to the story.
Drafting	As you write, refer to specific moments in the text to support your new ending, and address any other characters in the story who might be affected by your character's decision.
Revising	Review your essay, identifying sentences that do not connect logically. Use transitions to build a flowing, coherent paragraph.

> ### Model: Using Transitions for Coherence
>
> Ivan Markovitch forgot that Sasha had never worked
>
> *For his nephew's own good,*
>
> for anything in life. ∧ Ivan Markovitch should force
>
> Sasha to recognize his errors.

Transitional words and phrases build paragraph coherence and establish a clear line of reasoning.

*W*G *Prentice Hall Writing and Grammar Connection: Diamond Level, Chapter 3, Section 2*

Extension Activities

Listening and Speaking Create a **monologue** in which Sasha speaks to Uncle Ivan five years after the events in "The Problem." In your monologue, address the following topics:

- how Sasha's life progressed after the events of the story
- what Sasha has learned about himself since taking the hundred rubles from Uncle Ivan
- what kind of relationship Sasha would like to have with Uncle Ivan and the family

Perform your monologue for your class.

Research and Technology With a partner, use library or Internet sources to research the topic of heraldry. Build a **coat of arms** for a character in the story based on the examples you find. Include a brief report explaining how the parts of the heraldic shield apply to the character. **[Group Activity]**

 **Take It to the Net** PHSchool.com

Go online for an additional research activity using the Internet.

Prepare to Read

A Doll House

Henrik Ibsen (1828–1906)

When the drama *Ghosts* by Henrik Ibsen (hen´ rik ib´ sən) was first performed in 1881, one critic attacked the play, calling it "an open drain, a loathsome sore, an abominable piece, a repulsive and degrading work." Critics and even audiences of his day sometimes responded negatively to Ibsen's works because he was a literary pioneer. He was not only the creator of the modern realistic prose drama but also one of the first modern writers to make drama a vehicle for social commentary by exploring issues considered socially unacceptable. Because of his bold innovation and his extraordinary talent, Ibsen is widely regarded as the greatest and most influential dramatist of the nineteenth century.

Difficult Beginnings Ibsen was born in Skien, Norway. Although his father had once been a successful merchant, bankruptcy reduced his family to poverty and social rejection. When he was fifteen, Ibsen became a druggist's apprentice. He hated the work and chose to live in virtual isolation, writing poetry in his spare time. After failing a university entrance examination, he became determined to forge a living as a writer. With two finished plays to his credit—*Catiline* (1850) and *The Burial Mound* (1850)—Ibsen was hired as a playwright by the National Theater in the city of Bergen, where he remained for six years.

A Career in Theater In 1857, Ibsen accepted an opportunity to manage a new theater. The theater went bankrupt in 1862, however, leaving Ibsen deeply in debt and in a state of despair. Two years later, he left Norway for Italy, where he wrote most of his finest plays. With the completion of *Brand* (1866), the tragedy of a misunderstood idealist, and *Peer Gynt* (1867), a dramatic fantasy based on Norwegian folklore, he established himself as a popular playwright among both critics and theatergoers.

Controversial Art Ibsen's talent blossomed, though his plays were not always greeted enthusiastically by the public. *A Doll House* (1879), for example, aroused controversy because it portrayed a woman whose actions were unacceptable for that time. In response to the public's hostile reception of *Ghosts* (1881), Ibsen wrote *An Enemy of the People* (1882), which portrays a man who comes into conflict with the inhabitants of a village.

The Problem Plays Ibsen's later work defied the prevailing tastes in theater of the day. The typical dramatic style was modeled after the Romantic movement, with plot-heavy, idealized storylines whose endings were unfailingly happy. Ibsen eventually departed completely from such a style to create psychological dramas in which the conflict is internal and the plot's action is limited. Although Ibsen's later works often earned scathing reviews from critics and even from his audiences, emerging and notable playwrights like George Bernard Shaw embraced Ibsen's talent and defended his work. Ibsen's innovative pieces, often called "Problem Plays," constitute serious drama in which the problems of human life caused by society and its accepted practices are presented as such and are not masked by unrelated details.

Ibsen wrote prolifically through the nineteenth century, completing such well-known plays as *The Wild Duck* (1884) and *Hedda Gabler* (1890). When Ibsen died in 1906, it was already clear that his controversial work challenged the traditional expectations of theater. Only later in the twentieth century did it become obvious that Isben's contributions to dialogue, plot, set design, and acting style forged an entirely new form of modern theater.

Preview
Connecting to the Literature

A nickname meant to express affection can sometimes offend or create a false impression. In Act One of *A Doll House*, Torvald has pet names for his wife, Nora, that reflect his impression of her personality and behavior.

Literary Analysis
Modern Realistic Drama

Ibsen developed the **modern realistic drama**—a type of play unlike anything audiences had seen before—which included these characteristics:

- To reflect ordinary language, it is written in prose, not verse.
- It depicts characters and situations as they really are.
- It addresses controversial issues and society's assumptions.

A Doll House (1879) focuses on the role and status of women in the late nineteenth century. As you read Act One, notice Nora's subordinate role.

Connecting Literary Elements

Like real life, modern realistic dramas include **conflict,** the struggle between two opposing forces. Conflict can be either **internal,** occurring within the mind of a character, or **external,** occurring between a character and society, nature, another person, God, or fate.

In *A Doll House*, Nora faces both internal and external conflicts as she struggles to live life by her own rules.

Reading Strategy
Reading Drama

A drama is written to be performed by actors. When **reading drama,** imagine how the scenes would look on stage, how the dialogue would sound, and how the characters would move. To get the most out of your reading:

- Picture the setting described in the stage directions.
- Imagine voice and tone as you read dialogue.
- Picture characters' gestures and movements.

Look for details in *A Doll House* that will help you envision the drama. Then, use a chart like the one shown to help you form mental images.

Detail From the Play

Torvald's nicknames for Nora: *squirrel, skylark*

Mental Image

Nora should move as though she were a small animal, with quick, skipping steps.

Vocabulary Development

spendthrift (spend´ thrift´) *n.* person who spends money carelessly (p. 865)

squandering (skwän´ dər iŋ) *v.* spending money wastefully (p. 865)

prodigal (präd´ i gəl) *n.* person who spends money wastefully (p. 867)

indiscreet (in´ di skrēt´) *adj.* unwise or not careful (p. 875)

frivolous (friv´ ə ləs) *adj.* silly and light-minded; not sensible (p. 875)

contraband (kän´ trə band´) *n.* unlawful or forbidden goods (p. 880)

subordinate (sə bôr´ də nit) *adj.* inferior; ranking under or below (p. 885)

A Doll House

Henrik Ibsen
translated by Rolf Fjelde

Background

Critics regard Nora Helmer, one of the main characters in *A Doll House*, as among the most remarkable women characters in drama, primarily because of the personal journey she experiences in the play. As the drama opens, she appears to be a picture-perfect nineteenth-century wife to her husband, Torvald. The Helmers belonged to the upper middle class, and the elaborately decorated set would represent a typical wealthy home in the Victorian period. Like most other married women of her day, Nora would have made certain that every aspect of her home reflected the Helmers' social class and supported the comfortable, almost lavish lifestyle they enjoyed.

THE CHARACTERS

TORVALD HELMER, a lawyer
NORA, his wife
DR. RANK
MRS. LINDE
NILS KROGSTAD, a bank clerk

THE HELMERS' THREE SMALL CHILDREN
ANNE-MARIE, their nurse
HELENE, a maid
A DELIVERY BOY

The action takes place in HELMER's *residence.*

ACT ONE

A comfortable room, tastefully but not expensively furnished. A door to the right in the back wall leads to the entryway; another to the left leads to HELMER's *study. Between these doors, a piano. Midway in the left-hand wall a door, and farther back a window. Near the window a round table with an armchair and a small sofa. In the right-hand wall, toward the rear, a door, and nearer the foreground a porcelain stove with two armchairs and a rocking chair beside it. Between the stove and the side door, a small table. Engravings on the walls. An étagère[1] with china fig-ures and other small art objects; a small bookcase with richly bound books; the floor carpeted; a fire burning in the stove. It is a winter day.*

A bell rings in the entryway; shortly after we hear the door being unlocked. NORA *comes into the room humming happily to herself; she is wearing street clothes and carries an armload of packages, which she puts down on the table to the right. She has left the hall door open; and through it a* DELIVERY BOY *is seen, holding a Christmas tree and a basket, which he gives to the* MAID *who let them in.*

Reading Strategy
Reading Drama List four details in the stage direc-tions that indicate the Helmers' social standing.

NORA: Hide the tree well, Helene. The children mustn't get a glimpse of it till this evening, after it's trimmed. [*To the* DELIVERY BOY, *taking out her purse:*] How much?

DELIVERY BOY: Fifty, ma'am.

NORA: There's a crown.[2] No, keep the change. [*The* BOY *thanks her and leaves.* NORA *shuts the door. She laughs softly to herself while taking off her street things. Drawing a bag of macaroons from her pocket, she eats a couple, then steals over and listens at her husband's study door.*] Yes, he's home. [*Hums again as she moves to the table right.*]

HELMER [*from the study*]: Is that my little lark twittering out there?

NORA [*busy opening some packages*]: Yes, it is.

HELMER: Is that my squirrel rummaging around?

NORA: Yes!

HELMER: When did my squirrel get in?

NORA: Just now. [*Putting the macaroon bag in her pocket and wiping her mouth.*] Do come in, Torvald, and see what I've bought.

HELMER: Can't be disturbed. [*After a moment he opens the door and peers in, pen in hand.*] Bought, you say? All that there? Has the little <u>spendthrift</u> been out throwing money around again?

NORA: Oh, but Torvald, this year we really should let ourselves go a bit. It's the first Christmas we haven't had to economize.

HELMER: But you know we can't go <u>squandering</u>.

NORA: Oh yes, Torvald, we can squander a little now. Can't we?

spendthrift (spend´ thrift´) *n.* person who spends money carelessly

squandering (skwän´ dər iŋ) *v.* spending money wastefully

✔**Reading Check**

What surprise is Nora pre-paring for her children?

---

1. **étagère** (ā tä zher´) *n.* stand with open shelves for displaying small art objects and ornaments.
2. **crown** basic monetary unit of Norway; *krone* (krō´ nə) in Norwegian.

Just a tiny, wee bit. Now that you've got a big salary and are going to make piles and piles of money.

HELMER: Yes—starting New Year's. But then it's a full three months till the raise comes through.

NORA: Pooh! We can borrow that long.

HELMER: Nora! [*Goes over and playfully takes her by the ear.*] Are your scatterbrains off again? What if today I borrowed a thousand crowns, and you squandered them over Christmas week, and then on New Year's Eve a roof tile fell on my head, and I lay there—

NORA [*putting her hand on his mouth*]: Oh! Don't say such things!

HELMER: Yes, but what if it happened—then what?

NORA: If anything so awful happened, then it just wouldn't matter if I had debts or not.

HELMER: Well, but the people I'd borrowed from?

NORA: Them? Who cared about them! They're strangers.

HELMER: Nora, Nora, how like a woman! No, but seriously, Nora, you know what I think about that. No debts! Never borrow! Something of freedom's lost—and something of beauty, too—from a home that's founded on borrowing and debt. We've made a brave stand up to now, the two of us; and we'll go right on like that the little while we have to.

NORA [*going toward the stove*]: Yes, whatever you say, Torvald.

HELMER [*following her*]: Now, now, the little lark's wings mustn't droop. Come on, don't be a sulky squirrel. [*Taking out his wallet.*] Nora, guess what I have here.

NORA [*turning quickly*]: Money!

HELMER: There, see. [*Hands her some notes.*] Good grief, I know how costs go up in a house at Christmastime.

NORA: Ten—twenty—thirty—forty. Oh, thank you, Torvald; I can manage no end on this.

HELMER: You really will have to.

NORA: Oh yes, I promise I will! But come here so I can show you everything I bought. And so cheap! Look, new clothes for Ivar here—and a sword. Here a horse and a trumpet for Bob. And a doll and a doll's bed here for Emmy; they're nothing much, but she'll tear them to bits in no time anyway. And here I have

Literary Analysis
Modern Realistic Drama
Identify two of Nora's words that reflect everyday, informal speech.

▼ **Critical Viewing**
Can you tell that Nora and Torvald share a troubled relationship? Why or why not? [**Interpret**]

dress material and handkerchiefs for the maids. Old Anne-Marie really deserves something more.

HELMER: And what's in that package there?

NORA [*with a cry*]: Torvald, no! You can't see that till tonight!

HELMER: I see. But tell me now, you little <u>prodigal</u>, what have you thought of for yourself?

NORA: For myself? Oh, I don't want anything at all.

HELMER: Of course you do. Tell me just what—within reason—you'd most like to have.

NORA: I honestly don't know. Oh, listen, Torvald—

HELMER: Well?

NORA [*fumbling at his coat buttons, without looking at him*]: If you want to give me something, then maybe you could—you could—

HELMER: Come on, out with it.

NORA [*hurriedly*]: You could give me money, Torvald. No more than you think you can spare; then one of these days I'll buy something with it.

HELMER: But Nora—

NORA: Oh, please, Torvald darling, do that! I beg you, please. Then I could hang the bills in pretty gilt paper on the Christmas tree. Wouldn't that be fun?

HELMER: What are those little birds called that always fly through their fortunes?

NORA: Oh yes, spendthrifts; I know all that. But let's do as I say, Torvald; then I'll have time to decide what I really need most. That's very sensible, isn't it?

HELMER [*smiling*]: Yes, very—that is, if you actually hung onto the money I give you, and you actually used it to buy yourself something. But it goes for the house and for all sorts of foolish things, and then I only have to lay out some more.

NORA: Oh, but Torvald—

HELMER: Don't deny it, my dear little Nora. [*Putting his arm around her waist.*] Spendthrifts are sweet, but they use up a frightful amount of money. It's incredible what it costs a man to feed such birds.

NORA: Oh, how can you say that! Really, I save everything I can.

HELMER [*laughing*]: Yes, that's the truth. Everything you can. But that's nothing at all.

NORA [*humming, with a smile of quiet satisfaction*]: Hm, if you only knew what expenses we larks and squirrels have, Torvald.

HELMER: You're an odd little one. Exactly the way your father was. You're never at a loss for scaring up money; but the moment you have it, it runs right out through your fingers; you never know what you've

prodigal (präd´ i gəl) *n.* person who spends money wastefully

Literary Analysis
Modern Realistic Drama
Explain how Torvald and Nora manage the family's money.

 **Reading Check**

What is Torvald's attitude toward borrowing money?

done with it. Well, one takes you as you are. It's deep in your blood. Yes, these things are hereditary, Nora.

NORA: Ah, I could wish I'd inherited many of Papa's qualities.

HELMER: And I couldn't wish you anything but just what you are, my sweet little lark. But wait; it seems to me you have a very—what should I call it?—a very suspicious look today—

NORA: I do?

HELMER: You certainly do. Look me straight in the eye.

NORA [*looking at him*]: Well?

HELMER [*shaking an admonitory³ finger*]: Surely my sweet tooth hasn't been running riot in town today, has she?

NORA: No. Why do you imagine that?

HELMER: My sweet tooth really didn't make a little detour through the confectioner's?

NORA: No, I assure you, Torvald—

HELMER: Hasn't nibbled some pastry?

NORA: No, not at all.

HELMER: Not even munched a macaroon or two?

NORA: No, Torvald, I assure you, really—

Reading Strategy
Reading Drama What do the stage directions suggest about Torvald's attitude toward Nora?

---

3. admonitory (ad män´ i tôr´ ē) *adj.* warning.

A Lark, Archibald Thorburn, John Spike Fine Watercolours, London, UK

◄ **Critical Viewing**
Which characteristics of a lark, like the one shown, does Torvald see in Nora?
[Connect]

HELMER: There, there now. Of course I'm only joking.

NORA [*going to the table, right*]: You know I could never think of going against you.

HELMER: No, I understand that; and you *have* given me your word. [*Going over to her.*] Well, you keep your little Christmas secrets to yourself, Nora darling. I expect they'll come to light this evening, when the tree is lit.

NORA: Did you remember to ask Dr. Rank?

HELMER: No. But there's no need for that; it's assumed he'll be dining with us. All the same, I'll ask him when he stops by here this morning. I've ordered some fine wine. Nora, you can't imagine how I'm looking forward to this evening.

NORA: So am I. And what fun for the children, Torvald!

HELMER: Ah, it's so gratifying to know that one's gotten a safe, secure job, and with a comfortable salary. It's a great satisfaction, isn't it?

NORA: Oh, it's wonderful!

HELMER: Remember last Christmas? Three whole weeks before, you shut yourself in every evening till long after midnight, making flowers for the Christmas tree, and all the other decorations to surprise us. Ugh, that was the dullest time I've ever lived through.

NORA: It wasn't at all dull for me.

HELMER [*smiling*]: But the outcome *was* pretty sorry, Nora.

NORA: Oh, don't tease me with that again. How could I help it that the cat came in and tore everything to shreds.

HELMER: No, poor thing, you certainly couldn't. You wanted so much to please us all, and that's what counts. But it's just as well that the hard times are past.

NORA: Yes, it's really wonderful.

HELMER: Now I don't have to sit here alone, boring myself, and you don't have to tire your precious eyes and your fair little delicate hands—

NORA [*clapping her hands*]: No, is it really true, Torvald, I don't have to? Oh, how wonderfully lovely to hear! [*Taking his arm.*] Now I'll tell you just how I've thought we should plan things. Right after Christmas— [*The doorbell rings.*] Oh, the bell. [*Straightening the room up a bit.*] Somebody would have to come. What a bore!

HELMER: I'm not at home to visitors, don't forget.

MAID [*from the hall doorway*]: Ma'am, a lady to see you—

NORA: All right, let her come in.

MAID [*to* HELMER]: And the doctor's just come too.

HELMER: Did he go right to my study?

MAID: Yes, he did.

Reading Strategy
Reading Drama What mental image do you have of the Helmers as Torvald makes this speech? Explain.

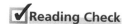**Reading Check**

Who will join the Helmers for dinner in the evening?

A Doll House, Act One ◆ 869

[HELMER *goes into his room. The* MAID *shows in* MRS. LINDE, *dressed in traveling clothes, and shuts the door after her.*]

MRS. LINDE [*in a dispirited and somewhat hesitant voice*]: Hello, Nora.

NORA [*uncertain*]: Hello—

MRS. LINDE: You don't recognize me.

NORA: No, I don't know—but wait, I think— [*Exclaiming.*] What! Kristine! Is it really you?

MRS. LINDE: Yes, it's me.

NORA: Kristine! To think I didn't recognize you. But then, how could I? [*More quietly.*] How you've changed, Kristine!

MRS. LINDE: Yes, no doubt I have. In nine—ten long years.

NORA: Is it so long since we met! Yes, it's all of that. Oh, these last eight years have been a happy time, believe me. And so now you've come in to town, too. Made the long trip in the winter. That took courage.

MRS. LINDE: I just got here by ship this morning.

NORA: To enjoy yourself over Christmas, of course. Oh, how lovely! Yes, enjoy ourselves, we'll do that. But take your coat off. You're not still cold? [*Helping her.*] There now, let's get cozy here by the stove. No, the easy chair there! I'll take the rocker here. [*Seizing her hands.*] Yes, now you have your old look again; it was only in that first moment. You're a bit more pale, Kristine—and maybe a bit thinner.

MRS. LINDE: And much, much older, Nora.

NORA: Yes, perhaps a bit older; a tiny, tiny bit; not much at all. [*Stopping short; suddenly serious.*] Oh, but thoughtless me, to sit here, chattering away. Sweet, good Kristine, can you forgive me?

MRS. LINDE: What do you mean, Nora?

NORA [*softly*]: Poor Kristine, you've become a widow.

MRS. LINDE: Yes, three years ago.

NORA: Oh, I knew it, of course; I read it in the papers. Oh, Kristine, you must believe me; I often thought of writing you then, but I kept postponing it, and something always interfered.

MRS. LINDE: Nora dear, I understand completely.

NORA: No, it was awful of me, Kristine. You poor thing, how much you must have gone through. And he left you nothing?

MRS. LINDE: No.

NORA: And no children?

MRS. LINDE: No.

NORA: Nothing at all, then?

MRS. LINDE: Not even a sense of loss to feed on.

NORA [*looking incredulously at her*]: But Kristine, how could that be?

Reading Strategy
Reading Drama What gestures might the actors use during these lines? Why?

Reading Strategy
Reading Drama What do you imagine Nora's movements might be during these lines? Explain.

MRS. LINDE [*smiling wearily and smoothing her hair*]: Oh, sometimes it happens, Nora.

NORA: So completely alone. How terribly hard that must be for you. I have three lovely children. You can't see them now; they're out with the maid. But now you must tell me everything—

MRS. LINDE: No, no, no, tell me about yourself.

NORA: No, you begin. Today I don't want to be selfish. I want to think only of you today. But there *is* something I must tell you. Did you hear of the wonderful luck we had recently?

MRS. LINDE: No, what's that?

NORA: My husband's been made manager in the bank, just think!

MRS. LINDE: Your husband? How marvelous!

Literary Analysis
Modern Realistic Drama
Identify three ways that Nora's and Mrs. Linde's social situations differ.

NORA: Isn't it? Being a lawyer is such an uncertain living, you know, especially if one won't touch any cases that aren't clean and decent. And of course Torvald would never do that, and I'm with him completely there. Oh, we're simply delighted, believe me! He'll join the bank right after New Year's and start getting a huge salary and lots of commissions. From now on we can live quite differently—just as we want. Oh, Kristine, I feel so light and happy! Won't it be lovely to have stacks of money and not a care in the world?

MRS. LINDE: Well, anyway, it would be lovely to have enough for necessities.

NORA: No, not just for necessities, but stacks and stacks of money!

MRS. LINDE [*smiling*]: Nora, Nora, aren't you sensible yet? Back in school you were such a free spender.

NORA [*with a quiet laugh*]: Yes, that's what Torvald still says. [*Shaking her finger.*] But "Nora, Nora" isn't as silly as you all think. Really, we've been in no position for me to go squandering. We've had to work, both of us.

MRS. LINDE: You too?

NORA: Yes, at odd jobs—needlework, crocheting, embroidery, and such—[*Casually.*] and other things too. You remember that Torvald left the department when we were married? There was no chance of promotion in his office, and of course he needed to earn more money. But that first year he drove himself terribly. He took on all kinds of extra work that kept him going morning and night. It wore him down, and then he fell deathly ill. The doctors said it was essential for him to travel south.

MRS. LINDE: Yes, didn't you spend a whole year in Italy?

NORA: That's right. It wasn't easy to get away, you know. Ivar had just been born. But of course we had to go. Oh, that was a beautiful trip, and it saved Torvald's life. But it cost a frightful sum, Kristine.

MRS. LINDE: I can well imagine.

☑**Reading Check**
What loss did Kristine suffer three years ago?

NORA: Four thousand, eight hundred crowns it cost. That's really a lot of money.

MRS. LINDE: But it's lucky you had it when you needed it.

NORA: Well, as it was, we got it from Papa.

MRS. LINDE: I see. It was just about the time your father died.

NORA: Yes, just about then. And, you know, I couldn't make that trip out to nurse him. I had to stay here, expecting Ivar any moment, and with my poor sick Torvald to care for. Dearest Papa, I never saw him again, Kristine. Oh, that was the worst time I've known in all my marriage.

MRS. LINDE: I know how you loved him. And then you went off to Italy?

NORA: Yes. We had the means now, and the doctors urged us. So we left a month after.

MRS. LINDE: And your husband came back completely cured?

NORA: Sound as a drum!

MRS. LINDE: But—the doctor?

NORA: Who?

MRS. LINDE: I thought the maid said he was a doctor, the man who came in with me.

NORA: Yes, that was Dr. Rank—but he's not making a sick call. He's our closest friend, and he stops by at least once a day. No, Torvald hasn't had a sick moment since, and the children are fit and strong, and I am, too. [*Jumping up and clapping her hands.*] Oh, dear God, Kristine, what a lovely thing to live and be happy! But how disgusting of me—I'm talking of nothing but my own affairs. [*Sits on a stool close by* KRISTINE, *arms resting across her knees.*] Oh, don't be angry with me! Tell me, is it really true that you weren't in love with your husband? Why did you marry him, then?

MRS. LINDE: My mother was still alive, but bedridden and helpless—and I had my two younger brothers to look after. In all conscience, I didn't think I could turn him down.

NORA: No, you were right there. But was he rich at the time?

MRS. LINDE: He was very well off, I'd say. But the business was shaky, Nora. When he died, it all fell apart, and nothing was left.

NORA: And then—?

MRS. LINDE: Yes, so I had to scrape up a living with a little shop and a little teaching and whatever else I could find. The last three years have been like one endless workday without a rest for me. Now it's over, Nora. My poor mother doesn't need me, for she's passed on. Nor the boys, either; they're working now and can take care of themselves.

NORA: How free you must feel—

MRS. LINDE: No—only unspeakably empty. Nothing to live for now. [*Standing up anxiously.*] That's why I couldn't take it any longer out in

Literary Analysis
Modern Realistic Drama
What factors motivated Mrs. Linde to marry someone she did not love?

Reading Strategy
Reading Drama What might Mrs. Linde's voice sound like in these lines?

that desolate hole. Maybe here it'll be easier to find something to do and keep my mind occupied. If I could only be lucky enough to get a steady job, some office work—

NORA: Oh, but Kristine, that's so dreadfully tiring, and you already look so tired. It would be much better for you if you could go off to a bathing resort.

MRS. LINDE [*going toward the window*]: I have no father to give me travel money, Nora.

NORA [*rising*]: Oh, don't be angry with me.

MRS. LINDE [*going to her*]: Nora dear, don't you be angry with me. The worst of my kind of situation is all the bitterness that's stored away. No one to work for, and yet you're always having to snap up your opportunities. You have to live; and so you grow selfish. When you told me the happy change in your lot, do you know I was delighted less for your sakes than for mine?

NORA: How so? Oh, I see. You think maybe Torvald could do something for you.

MRS. LINDE: Yes, that's what I thought.

NORA: And he will, Kristine! Just leave it to me; I'll bring it up so delicately—find something attractive to humor him with. Oh, I'm so eager to help you.

MRS. LINDE: How very kind of you, Nora, to be so concerned over me— double kind, considering you really know so little of life's burdens yourself.

NORA: I—? I know so little—?

MRS. LINDE [*smiling*]: Well, my heavens—a little needlework and such—Nora, you're just a child.

NORA [*tossing her head and pacing the floor*]: You don't have to act so superior.

MRS. LINDE: Oh?

NORA: You're just like the others. You all think I'm incapable of anything serious.

MRS. LINDE: Come now—

NORA: That I've never had to face the raw world.

MRS. LINDE: Nora dear, you've just been telling me all your troubles.

NORA: Hm! Trivia! [*Quietly.*] I haven't told you the big thing.

MRS. LINDE: Big thing? What do you mean?

▲ **Critical Viewing**
What type of household might pay Nora to complete needlework like that on the chair in this photograph? **[Connect]**

☑ **Reading Check**
What does Mrs. Linde hope to gain by visiting the Helmers?

NORA: You look down on me so, Kristine, but you shouldn't. You're proud that you worked so long and hard for your mother.

MRS. LINDE: I don't look down on a soul. But it *is* true: I'm proud—and happy, too—to think it was given to me to make my mother's last days almost free of care.

NORA: And you're also proud thinking of what you've done for your brothers.

MRS. LINDE: I feel I've a right to be.

NORA: I agree. But listen to this, Kristine—I've also got something to be proud and happy for.

MRS. LINDE: I don't doubt it. But whatever do you mean?

NORA: Not so loud. What if Torvald heard! He mustn't, not for anything in the world. Nobody must know, Kristine. No one but you.

MRS. LINDE: But what is it, then?

NORA: Come here. [*Drawing her down beside her on the sofa.*] It's true—I've also got something to be proud and happy for. I'm the one who saved Torvald's life.

MRS. LINDE: Saved—? Saved how?

NORA: I told you about the trip to Italy. Torvald never would have lived if he hadn't gone south—

MRS. LINDE: Of course; your father gave you the means—

NORA [*smiling*]: That's what Torvald and all the rest think, but—

MRS. LINDE: But—?

NORA: Papa didn't give us a pin. I was the one who raised the money.

MRS. LINDE: You? That whole amount?

NORA: Four thousand, eight hundred crowns. What do you say to that?

MRS. LINDE: But Nora, how was it possible? Did you win the lottery?

NORA [*disdainfully*]: The lottery? Pooh! No art to that.

MRS. LINDE: But where did you get it from then?

NORA [*humming, with a mysterious smile*]: Hmm, tra-la-la-la.

MRS. LINDE: Because you couldn't have borrowed it.

NORA: No? Why not?

MRS. LINDE: A wife can't borrow without her husband's consent.

NORA [*tossing her head*]: Oh, but a wife with a little business sense, a wife who knows how to manage—

MRS. LINDE: Nora, I simply don't understand—

NORA: You don't have to. Whoever said I *borrowed* the money? I could have gotten it other ways. [*Throwing herself back on the sofa.*] I could have gotten it from some admirer or other. After all, a girl with my ravishing appeal—

Reading Strategy
Reading Drama Why do you think the stage direction specifies that Nora draws Mrs. Linde down onto the sofa?

Reading Strategy
Reading Drama What do the stage directions suggest about Nora's attitude toward her money scheme?

◀ **Critical Viewing**
Which details in this photo suggest that Kristine and Nora enjoy each other's company? [**Interpret**]

MRS. LINDE: You lunatic.

NORA: I'll bet you're eaten up with curiosity, Kristine.

MRS. LINDE: Now listen here, Nora—you haven't done something <u>indiscreet</u>?

NORA [*sitting up again*]: Is it indiscreet to save your husband's life?

MRS. LINDE: I think it's indiscreet that without his knowledge you—

NORA: But that's the point: he mustn't know! My Lord, can't you understand? He mustn't ever know the close call he had. It was to *me* the doctors came to say his life was in danger—that nothing could save him but a stay in the south. Didn't I try strategy then! I began talking about how lovely it would be for me to travel abroad like other young wives; I begged and I cried; I told him please to remember my condition, to be kind and indulge me; and then I dropped a hint that he could easily take out a loan. But at that Kristine, he nearly exploded. He said I was <u>frivolous</u>, and it was his duty as man of the house not to indulge me in whims and fancies—as I think he called them. Aha, I thought, now you'll just have to be saved—and that's when I saw my chance.

MRS. LINDE: And your father never told Torvald the money wasn't from him?

NORA: No, never. Papa died right about then. I'd considered bringing him into my secret and begging him never to tell. But he was too sick at the time—and then, sadly, it didn't matter.

MRS. LINDE: And you've never confided in your husband since?

indiscreet (in′ di skrēt′) *adj.* unwise or not careful

frivolous (friv′ ə ləs) *adj.* silly and light-minded; not sensible

✔**Reading Check**
What secret does Nora share with Kristine?

NORA: For heaven's sake, no! Are you serious? He's so strict on that subject. Besides—Torvald, with all his masculine pride—how painfully humiliating for him if he ever found out he was in debt to me. That would just ruin our relationship. Our beautiful, happy home would never be the same.

MRS. LINDE: Won't you ever tell him?

NORA [*thoughtfully, half smiling*]: Yes—maybe sometime, years from now, when I'm no longer so attractive. Don't laugh! I only mean when Torvald loves me less than now, when he stops enjoying my dancing and dressing up and reciting for him. Then it might be wise to have something in reserve—[*Breaking off.*] How ridiculous! That'll never hap-pen—Well, Kristine, what do you think of my big secret? I'm capable of something too, hm? You can imagine, of course, how this thing hangs over me. It really hasn't been easy meeting the payments on time. In the business world there's what they call quarterly interest and what they call amortization,[4] and these are always so terribly hard to man-age. I've had to skimp a little here and there, wherever I could, you know. I could hardly spare anything from my house allowance, because Torvald has to live well. I couldn't let the children go poorly dressed; whatever I got for them, I felt I had to use up completely—the darlings!

MRS. LINDE: Poor Nora, so it had to come out of your own budget, then?

NORA: Yes, of course. But I was the one most responsible, too. Every time Torvald gave me money for new clothes and such, I never used more than half; always bought the simplest, cheapest outfits. It was a godsend that everything looks so well on me that Torvald never noticed. But it did weigh me down at times, Kristine. It *is* such a joy to wear fine things. You understand.

MRS. LINDE: Oh, of course.

NORA: And then I found other ways of making money. Last winter I was lucky enough to get a lot of copying to do. I locked myself in and sat writing every evening till late in the night. Ah, I was tired so often, dead tired. But still it was wonderful fun, sitting and working like that, earn-ing money. It was almost like being a man.

MRS. LINDE: But how much have you paid off this way so far?

NORA: That's hard to say, exactly. These accounts, you know, aren't easy to figure. I only know that I've paid out all I could scrape together. Time and again I haven't known where to turn. [*Smiling.*] Then I'd sit here dreaming of a rich old gentleman who had fallen in love with me—

MRS. LINDE: What! Who is he?

NORA: Oh, really! And that he'd died, and when his will was opened, there in big letters it said, "All my fortune shall be paid over in cash, immediately, to that enchanting Mrs. Nora Helmer."

Literary Analysis
Modern Realistic Drama
Do you think the Helmers' "beautiful, happy home" is built on the foundation of a lie? Why or why not?

Literary Analysis
Modern Realistic Drama and Conflict What type of conflict motivates Nora to maintain her house allow-ance? Explain.

---

4. **amortization** (am´ ər ti zā´ shən) *n.* putting aside money at intervals for gradual payment of a debt.

MRS. LINDE: But Nora dear—who *was* this gentleman?

NORA: Good grief, can't you understand? The old man never existed; that was only something I'd dream up time and again whenever I was at my wits' end for money. But it makes no difference now; the old fossil can go where he pleases for all I care; I don't need him or his will—because now I'm free. [*Jumping up.*] Oh, how lovely to think of that, Kristine! Care-free! To know you're carefree, utterly carefree; to be able to romp and play with the children, and to keep up a beautiful, charming home—everything just the way Torvald likes it! And think, spring is coming, with big blue skies. Maybe we can travel a little then. Maybe I'll see the ocean again. Oh yes, it *is* so marvelous to live and be happy!

[*The front doorbell rings.*]

MRS. LINDE [*rising*]: There's the bell. It's probably best that I go.

NORA: No, stay. No one's expected. It must be for Torvald.

MAID [*from the hall doorway*]: Excuse me, ma'am—there's a gentleman here to see Mr. Helmer, but I didn't know—since the doctor's with him—

NORA: Who is the gentleman?

KROGSTAD [*from the doorway*]: It's me, Mrs. Helmer.

[MRS. LINDE *starts and turns away toward the window.*]

NORA [*stepping toward him, tense, her voice a whisper*]: You? What is it? Why do you want to speak to my husband?

KROGSTAD: Bank business—after a fashion. I have a small job in the investment bank, and I hear now your husband is going to be our chief—

NORA: In other words, it's—

KROGSTAD: Just dry business, Mrs. Helmer. Nothing but that.

NORA: Yes, then please be good enough to step into the study. [*She nods indifferently as she sees him out by the hall door, then returns and begins stirring up the stove.*]

MRS. LINDE: Nora—who was that man?

NORA: That was a Mr. Krogstad—a lawyer.

MRS. LINDE: Then it really was him.

NORA: Do you know that person?

MRS. LINDE: I did once—many years ago. For a time he was a law clerk in our town.

NORA: Yes, he's been that.

Literature in context Cultural Connection

The Norwegian Krone

The krone, or crown, is a unit of Norwegian currency. Today, the forty kroner [plural form] Torvald gives Nora would be worth only about five dollars and fifty cents, less than half the price of a typical compact disc. In 1879, however, the year *A Doll House* was first produced, those forty kroner would have bought considerably more. At that time, a pound of bacon cost about eight cents in the United States; a skilled laborer brought home about ten dollars a week. So, while forty kroner does not sound like a significant sum, Torvald was being rather generous. On a larger scale, Nora would need to devote considerable time and effort to paying back four thousand eight hundred crowns. Its current equivalent is more than six hundred American dollars.

Reading Strategy
Reading Drama How does the atmosphere onstage change when Krogstad enters?

☑ **Reading Check**

What kind of work did Nora perform to pay off her debt?

MRS. LINDE: How he's changed.

NORA: I understand he had a very unhappy marriage.

MRS. LINDE: He's a widower now.

NORA: With a number of children. There now, it's burning. [*She closes the stove door and moves the rocker a bit to one side.*]

MRS. LINDE: They say he has a hand in all kinds of business.

NORA: Oh? That may be true; I wouldn't know. But let's not think about business. It's so dull.

[DR. RANK *enters from* HELMER's *study.*]

RANK [*still in the doorway*]: No, no, really—I don't want to intrude, I'd just as soon talk a little while with your wife. [*Shuts the door, then notices* MRS. LINDE.] Oh, beg pardon. I'm intruding here too.

NORA: No, not at all. [*Introducing him.*] Dr. Rank, Mrs. Linde.

RANK: Well now, that's a name much heard in this house. I believe I passed the lady on the stairs as I came.

MRS. LINDE: Yes, I take the stairs very slowly. They're rather hard on me.

RANK: Uh-hm, some touch of internal weakness?

MRS. LINDE: More overexertion, I'd say.

RANK: Nothing else? Then you're probably here in town to rest up in a round of parties?

MRS. LINDE: I'm here to look for work.

RANK: Is that the best cure for overexertion?

MRS. LINDE: One has to live, Doctor.

RANK: Yes, there's a common prejudice to that effect.

NORA: Oh, come on, Dr. Rank—you really do want to live yourself.

RANK. Yes, I really do. Wretched as I am, I'll gladly prolong my torment indefinitely. All my patients feel like that. And it's quite the same, too, with the morally sick. Right at this moment there's one of those moral invalids in there with Helmer—

MRS. LINDE [*softly*]: Ah!

NORA: Who do you mean?

RANK: Oh, it's a lawyer, Krogstad, a type you wouldn't know. His character is rotten to the root— but even he began chattering all-importantly about how he had to *live.*

NORA: Oh? What did he want to talk to Torvald about?

Literary Analysis
Modern Realistic Drama and Conflict What conflict motivates Nora to change the topic of conversation so abruptly?

▼ **Critical Viewing**
Which details in this photo reveal the economic status of the Helmers? [Interpret]

RANK: I really don't know. I only heard something about the bank.

NORA: I didn't know that Krog—that this man Krogstad had anything to do with the bank.

RANK: Yes, he's gotten some kind of berth down there. [*To* MRS. LINDE.] I don't know if you also have, in your neck of the woods, a type of person who scuttles about breathlessly, sniffing out hints of moral corruption, and then maneuvers his victim into some sort of key position where he can keep an eye on him. It's the healthy these days that are out in the cold.

MRS. LINDE: All the same, it's the sick who most need to be taken in.

RANK [*with a shrug*]: Yes, there we have it. That's the concept that's turning society into a sanatorium.

[NORA, *lost in her thoughts, breaks out into quiet laughter and claps her hands.*]

RANK: Why do you laugh at that? Do you have any real idea of what society is?

Literary Analysis
Modern Realistic Drama
In what ways do Dr. Rank's words reflect characteristics of modern realistic drama?

✔**Reading Check**

What does Dr. Rank know of Krogstad's personality?

NORA: What do I care about dreary old society? I was laughing at something quite different—something terribly funny. Tell me, Doctor—is everyone who works in the bank dependent now on Torvald?

RANK: Is that what you find so terribly funny?

NORA [*smiling and humming*]: Never mind, never mind! [*Pacing the floor.*] Yes, that's really immensely amusing: that we—that Torvald has so much power now over all those people. [*Taking the bag out of her pocket.*] Dr. Rank, a little macaroon on that?

RANK: See here, macaroons! I thought they were <u>contraband</u> here.

NORA: Yes, but these are some that Kristine gave me.

MRS. LINDE: What? I—?

NORA: Now, now, don't be afraid. You couldn't possibly know that Torvald had forbidden them. You see, he's worried they'll ruin my teeth. But hmp! Just this once! Isn't that so, Dr. Rank? Help yourself. [*Puts a macaroon in his mouth.*] And you too, Kristine. And I'll also have one, only a little one—or two, at the most. [*Walking about again.*] Now I'm really tremendously happy. Now there's just one last thing in the world that I have an enormous desire to do.

RANK: Well! And what's that?

NORA: It's something I have such a consuming desire to say so Torvald could hear.

RANK: And why can't you say it?

NORA: I don't dare. It's quite shocking.

MRS. LINDE: Shocking?

RANK: Well, then it isn't advisable. But in front of us you certainly can. What do you have such a desire to say so Torvald could hear?

NORA: I have such a huge desire to say—to hell and be damned!

RANK: Are you crazy?

MRS. LINDE: My goodness, Nora!

RANK: Go on, say it. Here he is.

NORA [*hiding the macaroon bag*]: Shh, shh, shh!

[HELMER *comes in from his study, hat in hand, overcoat over his arm.*]

contraband (kän´ trə band´) *n.* unlawful or forbidden goods

Literary Analysis
Modern Realistic Drama
What social benefits might Nora gain from Torvald's "power now over all those people"?

Literary Analysis
Modern Realistic Drama
Why are Mrs. Linde and Dr. Rank so shocked by Nora's words?

NORA [*going toward him*]: Well, Torvald dear, are you through with him?

HELMER: Yes, he just left.

NORA: Let me introduce you—this is Kristine, who's arrived here in town.

HELMER: Kristine—? I'm sorry, but I don't know—

NORA: Mrs. Linde, Torvald dear. Mrs. Kristine Linde.

HELMER: Of course. A childhood friend of my wife's, no doubt?

MRS. LINDE: Yes, we knew each other in those days.

NORA: And just think, she made the long trip down here in order to talk with you.

HELMER: What's this?

MRS. LINDE: Well, not exactly—

NORA: You see, Kristine is remarkably clever in office work, and so she's terribly eager to come under a capable man's supervision and add more to what she already knows—

HELMER: Very wise, Mrs. Linde.

NORA: And then when she heard that you'd become a bank manager—the story was wired out to the papers—then she came in as fast as she could and—Really, Torvald, for my sake you can do a little something for Kristine, can't you?

HELMER: Yes, it's not at all impossible. Mrs. Linde, I suppose you're a widow?

MRS. LINDE: Yes.

HELMER: Any experience in office work?

MRS. LINDE: Yes, a good deal.

HELMER: Well, it's quite likely that I can make an opening for you—

NORA [*clapping her hands*]: You see, you see!

HELMER: You've come at a lucky moment, Mrs. Linde.

MRS. LINDE: Oh, how can I thank you?

HELMER: Not necessary. [*Putting his overcoat on.*] But today you'll have to excuse me—

RANK: Wait, I'll go with you. [*He fetches his coat from the hall and warms it at the stove.*]

NORA: Don't stay out long, dear.

HELMER: An hour; no more.

NORA: Are you going too, Kristine?

MRS. LINDE [*putting on her winter garments*]: Yes, I have to see about a room now.

HELMER: Then perhaps we can all walk together.

Reading Strategy
Reading Drama In what ways might Nora's determination to help Mrs. Linde be apparent in Nora's body language? Explain.

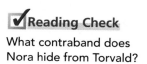
Reading Check

What contraband does Nora hide from Torvald?

NORA [*helping her*]: What a shame we're so cramped here, but it's quite impossible for us to—

MRS. LINDE: Oh, don't even think of it! Good-bye, Nora dear, and thanks for everything.

NORA: Good-bye for now. Of course you'll be back this evening. And you too, Dr. Rank. What? If you're well enough? Oh, you've got to be! Wrap up tight now.

[*In a ripple of small talk the company moves out into the hall; children's voices are heard outside on the steps.*]

NORA: There they are! There they are! [*She runs to open the door. The children come in with their nurse,* ANNE-MARIE.] Come in, come in! [*Bends down and kisses them.*] Oh, you darlings—! Look at them, Kristine. Aren't they lovely!

RANK: No loitering in the draft here.

HELMER: Come, Mrs. Linde—this place is unbearable now for anyone but mothers.

[DR. RANK, HELMER, *and* MRS. LINDE *go down the stairs.* ANNE-MARIE *goes into the living room with the children.* NORA *follows, after closing the hall door.*]

NORA: How fresh and strong you look. Oh, such red cheeks you have! Like apples and roses. [*The children interrupt her throughout the following.*] And it was so much fun? That's wonderful. Really? You pulled both Emmy and Bob on the sled? Imagine, all together! Yes, you're a clever boy, Ivar. Oh, let me hold her a bit, Anne-Marie. My sweet little doll baby! [*Takes the smallest from the nurse and dances with her.*] Yes, yes, Mama will dance with Bob as well. What? Did you throw snowballs? Oh, if I'd only been there! No, don't bother, Anne-Marie—I'll undress them myself. Oh yes, let me. It's such fun. Go in and rest; you look half frozen. There's hot coffee waiting for you on the stove. [*The nurse goes into the room to the left.* NORA *takes the children's winter things off, throwing them about, while the children talk to her all at once.*] Is that so? A big dog chased you? But it didn't bite? No, dogs never bite little, lovely doll babies. Don't peek in the packages, Ivar! What is it? Yes, wouldn't you like to know. No, no, it's an ugly something. Well? Shall we play? What shall we play? Hide-and-seek? Yes, let's play hide-and-seek. Bob must hide first. I must? Yes, let me hide first. [*Laughing and shouting, she and the children play in and out of the living room and the adjoining room to the right. At last* NORA *hides under the table. The children come storming in, search, but cannot find her, then hear her muffled laughter, dash over to the table, lift the cloth up and find her. Wild shouting. She creeps forward as if to scare them. More shouts. Meanwhile, a knock at the hall door; no one has noticed it. Now the door half opens, and* KROGSTAD *appears. He waits a moment; the game goes on.*]

KROGSTAD: Beg pardon, Mrs. Helmer—

NORA [*with a strangled cry, turning and scrambling to her knees*]: Oh! What do you want?

Literary Analysis
Modern Realistic Drama Judging by Torvald's comment, what role did men of that time seem to have in raising children?

Reading Strategy
Reading Drama How do the stage directions help clarify the relationship Nora has with her children?

▲ **Critical Viewing**   Which details in this photograph support Nora's assertions that her children did not "go poorly dressed" as she paid her debt to Krogstad? **[Connect]**

KROGSTAD: Excuse me. The outer door was ajar; it must be someone forgot to shut it—

NORA [*rising*]: My husband isn't home, Mr. Krogstad.

KROGSTAD: I know that.

NORA: Yes—then what do you want here?

KROGSTAD: A word with you.

NORA: With—? [*To the children, quietly.*] Go in to Anne-Marie. What? No, the strange man won't hurt Mama. When he's gone, we'll play some more. [*She leads the children into the room to the left and shuts the door after them. Then, tense and nervous:*] You want to speak to me?

KROGSTAD: Yes, I want to.

NORA: Today? But it's not yet the first of the month—

KROGSTAD: No, it's Christmas Eve. It's going to be up to you how merry a Christmas you have.

NORA: What is it you want? Today I absolutely can't—

KROGSTAD: We won't talk about that till later. This is something else. You do have a moment to spare, I suppose?

NORA: Oh, yes, of course—I do, except—

KROGSTAD: Good. I was sitting over at Olsen's Restaurant when I saw your husband go down the street—

NORA: Yes?

KROGSTAD: With a lady.

NORA: Yes. So?

KROGSTAD: If you'll pardon my asking: wasn't that lady a Mrs. Linde?

NORA: Yes.

KROGSTAD: Just now come into town?

NORA: Yes, today.

KROGSTAD: She's a good friend of yours?

NORA: Yes, she is. But I don't see—

KROGSTAD: I also knew her once.

NORA: I'm aware of that.

KROGSTAD: Oh? You know all about it. I thought so. Well, then let me ask you short and sweet: is Mrs. Linde getting a job in the bank?

NORA: What makes you think you can cross-examine me, Mr. Krogstad—you, one of my husband's employees? But since you ask, you might as well know—yes, Mrs. Linde's going to be taken on at the bank. And I'm the one who spoke for her, Mr. Krogstad. Now you know.

KROGSTAD: So I guessed right.

Reading Strategy
Reading Drama What gestures might Nora use to convey her "tense and nervous" emotions?

Reading Strategy
Reading Drama What tone of voice do you think Nora uses in these lines? Explain.

NORA [*pacing up and down*]: Oh, one does have a tiny bit of influence, I should hope. Just because I am a woman, don't think it means that— When one has a <u>subordinate</u> position, Mr. Krogstad, one really ought to be careful about pushing somebody who—hm—

KROGSTAD: Who has influence?

NORA: That's right.

KROGSTAD [*in a different tone*]: Mrs. Helmer, would you be good enough to use your influence on my behalf?

NORA: What? What do you mean?

KROGSTAD: Would you please make sure that I keep my subordinate position in the bank?

NORA: What does that mean? Who's thinking of taking away your position?

KROGSTAD: Oh, don't play the innocent with me. I'm quite aware that your friend would hardly relish the chance of running into me again; and I'm also aware now whom I can thank for being turned out.

NORA: But I promise you—

KROGSTAD: Yes, yes, yes, to the point: there's still time, and I'm advising you to use your influence to prevent it.

NORA: But Mr. Krogstad, I have absolutely no influence.

KROGSTAD: You haven't? I thought you were just saying—

NORA: You shouldn't take me so literally. I! How can you believe that I have any such influence over my husband?

KROGSTAD: Oh, I've known your husband from our student days. I don't think the great bank manager's more steadfast than any other married man.

NORA: You speak insolently about my husband, and I'll show you the door.

KROGSTAD: The lady has spirit.

NORA: I'm not afraid of you any longer. After New Year's, I'll soon be done with the whole business.

KROGSTAD [*restraining himself*]: Now listen to me, Mrs. Helmer. If necessary, I'll fight for my little job in the bank as if it were life itself.

NORA: Yes, so it seems.

KROGSTAD: It's not just a matter of income; that's the least of it. It's something else—All right, out with it! Look, this is the thing. You know, just like all the others, of course, that once, a good many years ago, I did something rather rash.

NORA: I've heard rumors to that effect.

KROGSTAD: The case never got into court; but all the same, every door was closed in my face from then on. So I took up those various

---

subordinate (sə bôr′ də nit) *adj.* inferior; ranking under or below

---

Literary Analysis
Modern Realistic Drama and Conflict What conflicts have troubled Krogstad for many years?

✔**Reading Check**

What favor does Krogstad ask of Nora?

activities you know about. I had to grab hold somewhere; and I dare say I haven't been among the worst. But now I want to drop all that. My boys are growing up. For their sakes, I'll have to win back as much respect as possible here in town. That job in the bank was like the first rung in my ladder. And now your husband wants to kick me right back down in the mud again.

NORA: But for heaven's sake, Mr. Krogstad, it's simply not in my power to help you.

KROGSTAD: That's because you haven't the will to—but I have the means to make you.

NORA: You certainly won't tell my husband that I owe you money?

KROGSTAD: Hm—what if I told him that?

NORA: That would be shameful of you. [*Nearly in tears.*] This secret— my joy and my pride—that he should learn it in such a crude and disgusting way—learn it from you. You'd expose me to the most horrible unpleasantness—

KROGSTAD: Only unpleasantness?

NORA [*vehemently*]: But go on and try. It'll turn out the worse for you, because then my husband will really see what a crook you are, and then you'll never be able to hold your job.

KROGSTAD: I asked if it was just domestic unpleasantness you were afraid of?

NORA: If my husband finds out, then of course he'll pay what I owe at once, and then we'd be through with you for good.

KROGSTAD [*a step closer*]: Listen, Mrs. Helmer—you've either got a very bad memory, or else no head at all for business. I'd better put you a little more in touch with the facts.

NORA: What do you mean?

KROGSTAD: When your husband was sick, you came to me for a loan of four thousand, eight hundred crowns.

NORA: Where else could I go?

KROGSTAD: I promised to get you that sum—

NORA: And you got it.

KROGSTAD: I promised to get you that sum, on certain conditions. You were so involved in your husband's illness, and so eager to finance your trip, that I guess you didn't think out all the details. It might just be a good idea to remind you. I promised you the money on the strength of a note I drew up.

NORA: Yes, and that I signed.

KROGSTAD: Right. But at the bottom I added some lines for your father to guarantee the loan. He was supposed to sign down there.

Literary Analysis
Modern Realistic Drama
In what way does this passage indicate that women in nineteenth-century Norway could not legally get loans on their own?

NORA: Supposed to? He did sign.

KROGSTAD: I left the date blank. In other words, your father would have dated his signature himself. Do you remember that?

NORA: Yes, I think—

KROGSTAD: Then I gave you the note for you to mail to your father. Isn't that so?

NORA: Yes.

KROGSTAD: And naturally you sent it at once—because only some five, six days later you brought me the note, properly signed. And with that, the money was yours.

NORA: Well, then; I've made my payments regularly, haven't I?

KROGSTAD: More or less. But—getting back to the point—those were hard times for you then, Mrs. Helmer.

NORA: Yes, they were.

KROGSTAD: Your father was very ill, I believe.

NORA: He was near the end.

KROGSTAD: He died soon after?

NORA: Yes.

KROGSTAD: Tell me, Mrs. Helmer, do you happen to recall the date of your father's death? The day of the month, I mean.

NORA: Papa died the twenty-ninth of September.

KROGSTAD: That's quite correct; I've already looked into that. And now we come to a curious thing— [*Taking out a paper.*] which I simply cannot comprehend.

NORA: Curious thing? I don't know—

KROGSTAD: This is the curious thing: that your father co-signed the note for your loan three days after his death.

NORA: How—? I don't understand.

KROGSTAD: Your father died the twenty-ninth of September. But look. Here your father dated his signature October second. Isn't that curious, Mrs. Helmer? [NORA *is silent.*] Can you explain it to me? [NORA *remains silent.*] It's also remarkable that the words "October second" and the year aren't written in your father's hand, but rather in one that I think I know. Well, it's easy to understand. Your father forgot perhaps to date his signature, and then someone or other added it, a bit sloppily, before anyone knew of his death. There's nothing wrong in that. It all comes down to the signature. And there's no question about that, Mrs. Helmer. It really *was* your father who signed his own name here, wasn't it?

NORA [*after a short silence, throwing her head back and looking squarely at him*]: No, it wasn't. *I* signed Papa's name.

Reading Strategy
Reading Drama In what ways might stage directions indicating movements or gestures add tension to this dialogue?

Literary Analysis
Modern Realistic Drama and Conflict Identify three sources of external conflict against which Nora is struggling.

Reading Check

For whose sake does Krogstad wish to build a better life?

KROGSTAD: Wait, now—are you fully aware that this is a dangerous confession?

NORA: Why? You'll soon get your money.

KROGSTAD: Let me ask you a question—why didn't you send the paper to your father?

NORA: That was impossible. Papa was so sick. If I'd asked him for his signature, I also would have had to tell him what the money was for. But I couldn't tell him, sick as he was, that my husband's life was in danger. That was just impossible.

KROGSTAD: Then it would have been better if you'd given up the trip abroad.

NORA: I couldn't possibly. The trip was to save my husband's life. I couldn't give that up.

KROGSTAD: But didn't you ever consider that this was a fraud against me?

NORA: I couldn't let myself be bothered by that. You weren't any concern of mine. I couldn't stand you, with all those cold complications you made, even though you knew how badly off my husband was.

KROGSTAD: Mrs. Helmer, obviously you haven't the vaguest idea of what you've involved yourself in. But I can tell you this: it was nothing more and nothing worse that I once did—and it wrecked my whole reputation.

NORA: You? Do you expect me to believe that you ever acted bravely to save your wife's life?

KROGSTAD: Laws don't inquire into motives.

NORA: Then they must be very poor laws.

KROGSTAD: Poor or not—if I introduce this paper in court, you'll be judged according to law.

NORA: This I refuse to believe. A daughter hasn't a right to protect her dying father from anxiety and care? A wife hasn't a right to save her husband's life? I don't know much about laws, but I'm sure that somewhere in the books these things are allowed. And you don't know anything about it—you who practice the law? You must be an awful lawyer, Mr. Krogstad.

KROGSTAD: Could be. But business—the kind of business we two are mixed up in—don't you think I know about that? All right. Do what you want now. But I'm telling you *this:* if I get shoved down a second time, you're going to keep me company. [*He bows and goes out through the hall.*]

NORA [*pensive⁵ for a moment, then tossing her head*]: Oh, really! Trying to frighten me! I'm not so silly as all that. [*Begins gathering up the*

---

5. **pensive** (pen´ siv) *adj.* thinking deeply or seriously, often of sad or melancholy things.

Literary Analysis
Modern Realistic Drama and Conflict List three points of conflict for Nora in this scene.

Literary Analysis
Modern Realistic Drama In what two ways are Krogstad's words characteristic of modern realistic drama?

children's clothes, but soon stops.] But—? No, but that's impossible! I did it out of love.

THE CHILDREN [*In the doorway, left*]: Mama, that strange man's gone out the door.

NORA: Yes, yes, I know it. But don't tell anyone about the strange man. Do you hear? Not even Papa!

THE CHILDREN. No, Mama. But now will you play again?

NORA: No, not now.

THE CHILDREN. Oh, but Mama, you promised.

NORA: Yes, but I can't now. Go inside; I have too much to do. Go in, go in, my sweet darlings. [*She herds them gently back in the room and shuts the door after them. Settling on the sofa, she takes up a piece of embroidery and makes some stitches, but soon stops abruptly.*] No! [*Throws the work aside, rises, goes to the hall door and calls out.*] Helene! Let me have the tree in here. [*Goes to the table, left, opens the table drawer, and stops again.*] No, but that's utterly impossible!

MAID [*with the Christmas tree*]: Where should I put it, ma'am?

NORA: There. The middle of the floor.

MAID: Should I bring anything else?

NORA: No, thanks. I have what I need.

[*The* MAID, *who has set the tree down, goes out.*]

Reading Strategy
Reading Drama What tone of voice do you think Nora uses here? Explain.

NORA [*absorbed in trimming the tree*]: Candles here—and flowers here. That terrible creature! Talk, talk, talk! There's nothing to it at all. The tree's going to be lovely. I'll do anything to please you, Torvald. I'll sing for you, dance for you—

[HELMER *comes in from the hall, with a sheaf of papers under his arm.*]

NORA: Oh! You're back so soon?

HELMER: Yes. Has anyone been here?

NORA: Here? No.

HELMER: That's odd. I saw Krogstad leaving the front door.

NORA: So? Oh yes, that's true. Krogstad was here a moment.

HELMER: Nora, I can see by your face that he's been here, begging you to put in a good word for him.

NORA: Yes.

HELMER: And it was supposed to seem like your own idea? You were to hide it from me that he'd been here. He asked you that, too, didn't he?

NORA: Yes, Torvald, but—

HELMER: Nora, Nora, and you could fall for that? Talk with that sort of person and promise him anything? And then in the bargain, tell me an untruth.

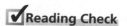**Reading Check**

What kind of lawyer does Nora believe Krogstad to be?

△ Critical Viewing Which details in this illustration depict the perfect Christmas that Nora hopes to provide for her family? [**Speculate**]

NORA: An untruth—?

HELMER: Didn't you say that no one had been here? [*Wagging his finger.*] My little songbird must never do that again. A songbird needs a clean beak to warble with. No false notes. [*Putting his arm about her waist.*] That's the way it should be, isn't it? Yes, I'm sure of it. [*Releasing her.*] And so, enough of that. [*Sitting by the stove.*] Ah, how snug and cozy it is here. [*Leafing among his papers.*]

NORA [*busy with the tree, after a short pause*]: Torvald!

HELMER: Yes.

NORA: I'm so much looking forward to the Stenborgs' costume party, day after tomorrow.

HELMER: And I can't wait to see what you'll surprise me with.

NORA: Oh, that stupid business!

HELMER: What?

NORA: I can't find anything that's right. Everything seems so ridiculous, so inane.[6]

HELMER: So my little Nora's come to *that* recognition?

NORA [*going behind his chair, her arms resting on his back*]: Are you very busy, Torvald?

HELMER: Oh—

NORA: What papers are those?

HELMER: Bank matters.

NORA: Already?

HELMER: I've gotten full authority from the retiring management to make all necessary changes in personnel and procedure. I'll need Christmas week for that. I want to have everything in order by New Year's.

NORA: So that was the reason this poor Krogstad—

HELMER: Hm.

NORA [*still leaning on the chair and slowly stroking the nape of his neck*]: If you weren't so very busy, I would have asked you an enormous favor, Torvald.

HELMER: Let's hear. What is it?

NORA: You know, there isn't anyone who has your good taste—and I want so much to look well at the costume party. Torvald, couldn't you take over and decide what I should be and plan my costume?

HELMER: Ah, is my stubborn little creature calling for a lifeguard?

NORA: Yes, Torvald, I can't get anywhere without your help.

HELMER: All right—I'll think it over. We'll hit on something.

---

6. **inane** (in ān´) *adj.* foolish; silly.

Literary Analysis
Modern Realistic Drama and Conflict What conflict makes everything else in Nora's life seem unimportant to her?

**Reading Check**

What changes at the bank is Torvald planning to make during Christmas week?

NORA: Oh, how sweet of you. [*Goes to the tree again. Pause.*] Aren't the red flowers pretty—? But tell me, was it really such a crime that this Krogstad committed?

HELMER: Forgery. Do you have any idea what that means?

NORA: Couldn't he have done it out of need?

HELMER: Yes, or thoughtlessness, like so many others. I'm not so heartless that I'd condemn a man categorically for just one mistake.

NORA: No, of course not, Torvald!

HELMER: Plenty of men have redeemed themselves by openly confessing their crimes and taking their punishment.

NORA: Punishment—?

HELMER: But now Krogstad didn't go that way. He got himself out by sharp practices, and that's the real cause of his moral breakdown.

NORA: Do you really think that would—?

HELMER: Just imagine how a man with that sort of guilt in him has to lie and cheat and deceive on all sides, has to wear a mask even with the nearest and dearest he has, even with his own wife and children. And with the children, Nora—that's where it's most horrible.

NORA: Why?

HELMER: Because that kind of atmosphere of lies infects the whole life of a home. Every breath the children take in is filled with the germs of something degenerate.

NORA [*coming closer behind him*]: Are you sure of that?

HELMER: Oh, I've seen it often enough as a lawyer. Almost everyone who goes bad early in life has a mother who's a chronic liar.

NORA: Why just—the mother?

HELMER: It's usually the mother's influence that's dominant, but the father's works in the same way, of course. Every lawyer is quite familiar with it. And still this Krogstad's been going home year in, year out, poisoning his own children with lies and pretense; that's why I call him morally lost. [*Reaching his hands out toward her.*] So my sweet little Nora must promise me never to plead his cause. Your hand on it. Come, come, what's this? Give me your hand. There, now. All settled. I can tell you it'd be impossible for me to work alongside of him. I literally feel physically revolted when I'm anywhere near such a person.

NORA [*withdraws her hand and goes to the other side of the Christmas tree*]: How hot it is here! And I've got so much to do.

HELMER [*getting up and gathering his papers*]: Yes, and I have to think about getting some of these read through before dinner. I'll think about your costume, too. And something to hang on the tree in gilt paper, I may even see about that. [*Putting his hand on her head.*] Oh you, my darling little songbird. [*He goes into his study and closes the door after him.*]

Reading Strategy
Reading Drama What emotions is Torvald experiencing as he says these lines? Explain.

Literary Analysis
Modern Realistic Drama and Conflict In what ways might Torvald's words cause Nora more inner conflict?

NORA [*softly, after a silence*]: Oh, really! It isn't so. It's impossible. It must be impossible.

ANNE-MARIE [*in the doorway, left*]: The children are begging so hard to come in to Mama.

NORA: No, no, no, don't let them in to me! You stay with them, Anne-Marie.

ANNE-MARIE: Of course, ma'am. [*Closes the door.*]

NORA [*pale with terror*]: Hurt my children—? Poison my home? [*A moment's pause; then she tosses her head.*] That's not true. Never in all the world.

Review and Assess

Thinking About Act One

1. **Respond:** Considering the Helmers' current situation, do you feel more sympathy for Torvald or for Nora? Explain.

2. **(a) Recall:** What are some of the pet names Torvald uses for Nora? **(b) Infer:** What does Torvald's use of these pet names suggest about his attitude toward his wife? **(c) Assess:** Do you think these nicknames represent Nora's entire personality? Explain.

3. **(a) Recall:** What lie concerning the macaroons does Nora tell Torvald? **(b) Interpret:** How would you describe Torvald's treatment of Nora as he questions her about the macaroons? **(c) Draw Conclusions:** What does Torvald's attitude reveal about the relationship he has with his wife?

4. **(a) Recall:** How does Nora behave toward her husband? **(b) Compare and Contrast:** How is Nora's behavior different when she is around Krogstad? **(c) Make a Judgment:** Do you think Nora is "just a child" and "incapable of anything serious," as others seem to believe? Explain.

5. **(a) Recall:** Which details in the first act indicate that Nora and her husband do not know each other very well? **(b) Interpret:** What is ironic about Nora's comment that if Torvald found out her secret, it "would just ruin [their] relationship"?

6. **Draw Conclusions:** What developments in Act One suggest that Nora is in trouble? Explain.

7. **Relate:** Based on the behavior of the characters during Act One, what differences can you see between our society and the one depicted in the play?

Review and Assess

Literary Analysis

Modern Realistic Drama

1. Use an organizer like this one to record details that establish *A Doll House* as a **modern realistic drama.**

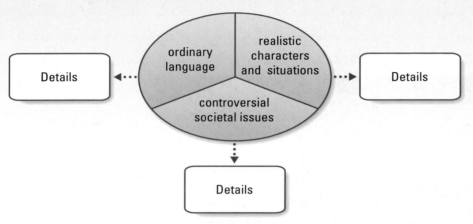

2. (a) What limitations on women does Nora find especially frustrating? (b) What strategies does she use to break through these restrictions? (c) Do you find her methods realistic? Explain.

Connecting Literary Elements

3. (a) What **conflict** has existed between Krogstad and Nora for the past few years? (b) What new circumstances does Krogstad introduce that intensify this conflict?
4. (a) What is Torvald's attitude about an "atmosphere of lies" in the home? (b) What would Nora lose if he discovered her secrets?

Reading Strategy

Reading Drama

5. (a) Explain how stage directions help clarify the relationships between characters when **reading a drama.** (b) Identify one example from the play that supports your response.
6. Select a passage in Act One that has no stage directions, and then add directions that make the passage easier to visualize.

Extend Understanding

7. **Psychology Connection:** What advice might a relationship expert offer Nora and Torvald?

Integrate Language Skills

Vocabulary Development Lesson

Word Analysis: Coined Words

Coined words are manufactured, often by combining existing words. *Spendthrift* combines *spend* and *thrift* in a new word meaning "one who spends money carelessly." Replace each phrase with a lively coined word.

1. snow-covered trees   2. someone who gossips

Spelling Strategy

Adding a prefix to a word never changes the spelling of the base word. For each item, combine the prefix and the root to form an existing word.

1. *mis-* + understand   2. *dis-* + honest

Concept Development: Antonyms

Choose the letter of the word in each item below that is opposite in meaning to the first word.

1. spendthrift: (a) miser, (b) shopper
2. squandering: (a) spending, (b) saving
3. prodigal: (a) penny-pincher, (b) party-giver
4. indiscreet: (a) shocking, (b) prudent
5. frivolous: (a) wise, (b) foolish
6. contraband: (a) loot, (b) imports
7. subordinate: (a) superior, (b) inferior

Grammar and Style Lesson

Compound Predicates

A predicate states the action or condition of the subject. A **compound predicate** has two or more verbs or verb phrases that relate to the same subject. Compound predicates are usually connected by a conjunction, such as *and* or *or*.

> S   V   V
> "The *cat* **came** in and **tore** everything to shreds. . . ."

Practice Copy the examples below. In each one, circle the subject and underline the verbs or verb phrases in each compound predicate.

1. *The maid shows in Mrs. Linde . . . and shuts the door after her.*

2. "He'll join the bank right after New Year's and start getting a huge salary. . . ."

3. ". . . [he] scuttles about breathlessly . . . and then maneuvers his victims into some sort of key position. . . ."

4. *. . . she takes up a piece of embroidery and makes some stitches, but soon stops abruptly.*

5. *Nora . . . breaks out into quiet laughter and claps her hands.*

Writing Application Write two sentences about Nora's situation in *A Doll House*. Use compound predicates in each sentence, circling the subject and underlining the verbs or verb phrases.

Extension Activities

Writing Write a **monologue** in which Nora confesses her secrets to Torvald. Use details that reflect her personality and experiences. Rehearse your piece and present it to your class.

Research and Technology With a partner, make a **rendering of the set** from Act One using art supplies or computer software. Display your work for the class. **[Group Activity]**

W̧G Prentice Hall Writing and Grammar Connection: Diamond Level, Chapter 18, Section 1

Prepare to Read

A Doll House, Act Two

Literary Analysis

Characterization in Drama

Characterization is the means by which a writer reveals a character's personality. In most fiction, characterization is developed through one or more of the following methods:

- direct statements about a character
- a character's actions, thoughts, or comments
- comments about a character made by other characters

Along with these methods, **characterization in drama** uses the additional elements of stage directions and dialogue. Look for these methods as you read Act Two of *A Doll House*.

Connecting Literary Elements

In a literary work, the main character, called the **protagonist**, is central to the action and often the one with whom the audience sympathizes. The **antagonist** is the character or force in conflict with the protagonist.

In *A Doll House*, Nora Helmer is the protagonist. Instead of a single antagonist, however, Nora encounters various adversaries. Note Nora's many antagonists as you read.

Reading Strategy

Inferring Beliefs of the Period

Inferring beliefs of the period means observing how social, religious, and cultural practices of a time period affect the characters and their choices. To infer the beliefs of the period as you read:

- Notice how husbands and wives relate to each other.
- Pay attention to the role of women in society.
- Look for clues to social, religious, or cultural practices.

Use an organizer like the one shown to infer the beliefs of a period.

What a Character Says or Does

Anne-Marie had given her daughter up for adoption.

Inferred Beliefs of the Period

Society provided little or no assistance to young, unmarried mothers.

Vocabulary Development

proclaiming (prō klām´ iŋ) *v.* announcing publicly and loudly (p. 900)

intolerable (in täl´ ər ə bəl) *adj.* unbearable; painful; cruel (p. 901)

impulsive (im pul´ siv) *adj.* sudden and unthinking (p. 904)

tactless (takt´ lis) *adj.* unskilled in dealing with people (p. 904)

excruciating (eks krōō´ shē āt´ iŋ) *adj.* causing intense mental or bodily pain (p. 904)

retribution (re´ trə byōō´ shən) *n.* punishment; revenge (p. 907)

disreputable (dis rep´ yōō tə bəl) *adj.* not fit to be seen or approved (p. 914)

Review and Anticipate

Years ago, Nora secretly borrowed money from Krogstad to help her husband Torvald recover from a serious illness. Desperate for a signature to guarantee the loan but reluctant to disturb her dying father, she forged her father's name on the document. In Act One, Nora shares her secret with Mrs. Linde, her childhood friend who hopes to get a position at Torvald's bank. Nora persuades Torvald to hire Mrs. Linde, but he can do so only by firing Krogstad. Now Krogstad threatens to expose Nora's secret if she does not urge Torvald to keep him employed at the bank. Will Krogstad expose Nora's secrets to Torvald? Will Nora buy herself enough time to solve her dilemma without involving Torvald? Find the answers to these questions in Act Two.

ACT TWO

Same room. Beside the piano the Christmas tree now stands stripped of ornament, burned-down candle stubs on its ragged branches. NORA's *street clothes lie on the sofa.* NORA, *alone in the room, moves restlessly about; at last she stops at the sofa and picks up her coat.*

NORA [*dropping the coat again*]: Someone's coming! [*Goes toward the door, listens.*] No—there's no one. Of course—nobody's coming today, Christmas Day—or tomorrow, either. But maybe—[*Opens the door and looks out.*] No, nothing in the mailbox. Quite empty. [*Coming forward.*] What nonsense! He won't do anything serious. Nothing terrible could happen. It's impossible. Why, I have three small children.

[ANNE-MARIE, *with a large carton, comes in from the room to the left.*]

ANNE-MARIE: Well, at last I found the box with the masquerade clothes.

NORA: Thanks. Put it on the table.

ANNE-MARIE [*does so*]: But they're all pretty much of a mess.

NORA: Ahh! I'd love to rip them in a million pieces!

ANNE-MARIE: Oh, mercy, they can be fixed right up. Just a little patience.

NORA: Yes, I'll go get Mrs. Linde to help me.

ANNE-MARIE: Out again now? In this nasty weather? Miss Nora will catch cold—get sick.

NORA: Oh, worse things could happen— How are the children?

Literary Analysis
Characterization in Drama What does Nora's comment to herself reveal about her character?

✔**Reading Check**
What is in the box Anne-Marie brings to Nora?

ANNE-MARIE: The poor mites are playing with their Christmas presents, but—

NORA: Do they ask for me much?

ANNE-MARIE: They're so used to having Mama around, you know.

NORA: Yes, but Anne-Marie, I *can't* be together with them as much as I was.

ANNE-MARIE: Well, small children get used to anything.

NORA: You think so? Do you think they'd forget their mother if she was gone for good?

ANNE-MARIE: Oh, mercy—gone for good!

NORA: Wait, tell me, Anne-Marie—I've wondered so often—how could you ever have the heart to give your child over to strangers?

ANNE-MARIE: But I had to, you know, to become little Nora's nurse.

NORA: Yes, but how could you *do* it?

ANNE-MARIE: When I could get such a good place? A girl who's poor and who's gotten in trouble is glad enough for that. Because that slippery fish, he didn't do a thing for me, you know.

NORA: But your daughter's surely forgotten you.

ANNE-MARIE: Oh, she certainly has not. She's written to me, both when she was confirmed and when she was married.

NORA [*clasping her about the neck*]: You old Anne-Marie, you were a good mother for me when I was little.

ANNE-MARIE: Poor little Nora, with no other mother but me.

NORA: And if the babies didn't have one, then I know that you'd— What silly talk! [*Opening the carton.*] Go in to them. Now I'll have to— Tomorrow you can see how lovely I'll look.

ANNE-MARIE: Oh, there won't be anyone at the party as lovely as Miss Nora. [*She goes off into the room, left.*]

NORA [*begins unpacking the box, but soon throws it aside*]: Oh, if I dared to go out. If only nobody would come. If only nothing would happen here while I'm out. What craziness—nobody's coming. Just don't think. This muff—needs a brushing. Beautiful gloves, beautiful gloves. Let it go. Let it go! One, two, three, four, five, six— [*With a cry.*] Oh, there they are! [*Poises to move toward the door, but remains irresolutely standing.* MRS. LINDE *enters from the hall, where she has removed her street clothes.*]

NORA: Oh, it's you, Kristine. There's no one else out there? How good that you've come.

MRS. LINDE: I hear you were up asking for me.

NORA: Yes, I just stopped by. There's something you really can help me with. Let's get settled on the sofa. Look, there's going to be a costume party tomorrow evening at the Stenborgs' right above us, and now

Reading Strategy
Inferring Beliefs of the Period In what way does Anne-Marie imply that religion and marriage were significant social concerns at this time?

Literary Analysis
Characterization in Drama Identify three of Nora's thoughts that reveal her anxiety over her situation.

Lady with a Fur Muff, Theodore Bruckner, Whitford & Hughes, London, UK

Critical Viewing ▶
In what ways might
Nora dress like the
woman in this painting?
[Interpret]

Torvald wants me to go as a Neapolitan[1] peasant girl and dance the tarantella that I learned in Capri.[2]

MRS. LINDE: Really, are you giving a whole performance?

NORA: Torvald says yes, I should. See, here's the dress. Torvald had it made for me down there; but now it's all so tattered that I just don't know—

MRS. LINDE: Oh, we'll fix that up in no time. It's nothing more than the trimmings—they're a bit loose here and there. Needle and thread? Good, now we have what we need.

NORA: Oh, how sweet of you!

MRS. LINDE [*sewing*]: So you'll be in disguise tomorrow, Nora. You know what? I'll stop by then for a moment and have a look at you all dressed up. But listen, I've absolutely forgotten to thank you for that pleasant evening yesterday.

NORA [*getting up and walking about*]: I don't think it was as pleasant as usual yesterday. You should have come to town a bit sooner, Kristine— Yes, Torvald really knows how to give a home elegance and charm.

MRS. LINDE: And you do, too, if you ask me. You're not your father's daughter for nothing. But tell me, is Dr. Rank always so down in the mouth as yesterday?

NORA: No, that was quite an exception. But he goes around critically ill all the time—tuberculosis of the spine, poor man. You know, his father was a disgusting thing who kept mistresses and so on—and that's why the son's been sickly from birth.

MRS. LINDE [*lets her sewing fall to her lap*]: But my dearest Nora, how do you know about such things?

NORA [*walking more jauntily*]: Hmp! When you've had three children, then you've had a few visits from—from women who know something of medicine, and they tell you this and that.

MRS. LINDE [*resumes sewing; a short pause*]: Does Dr. Rank come here every day?

NORA: Every blessed day. He's Torvald's best friend from childhood, and *my* good friend, too. Dr. Rank almost belongs to this house.

MRS. LINDE: But tell me—is he quite sincere? I mean, doesn't he rather enjoy flattering people?

NORA: Just the opposite. Why do you think that?

MRS. LINDE: When you introduced us yesterday, he was <u>proclaiming</u> that he'd often heard my name in this house; but later I noticed that your husband hadn't the slightest idea who I really was. So how could Dr. Rank—?

Reading Strategy
Inferring Beliefs of the Period Identify two talents or accomplishments that upper-class society of that time expected of women like Nora.

proclaiming (prō klām′ iŋ) *v.* announcing publicly and loudly

---

1. **Neapolitan** (nē ə päl′ ət 'n) of Naples, a seaport in southern Italy.
2. **Capri** (kä prē′) island near the entrance to the Bay of Naples.

NORA: But it's all true, Kristine. You see, Torvald loves me beyond words, and, as he puts it, he'd like to keep me all to himself. For a long time he'd almost be jealous if I even mentioned any of my old friends back home. So of course I dropped that. But with Dr. Rank I talk a lot about such things, because he likes hearing about them.

MRS. LINDE: Now listen, Nora; in many ways you're still like a child. I'm a good deal older than you, with a little more experience. I'll tell you something: you ought to put an end to all this with Dr. Rank.

NORA: What should I put an end to?

MRS. LINDE: Both parts of it, I think. Yesterday you said something about a rich admirer who'd provide you with money—

NORA: Yes, one who doesn't exist—worse luck. So?

MRS. LINDE: Is Dr. Rank well off?

NORA: Yes, he is.

MRS. LINDE: With no dependents?

NORA: No, no one. But—?

MRS. LINDE: And he's over here every day?

NORA: Yes, I told you that.

MRS. LINDE: How can a man of such refinement be so grasping?

NORA: I don't follow you at all.

MRS. LINDE: Now don't try to hide it, Nora. You think I can't guess who loaned you the forty-eight hundred crowns?

NORA: Are you out of your mind? How could you think such a thing! A friend of ours, who comes here every single day. What an <u>intolerable</u> situation that would have been!

MRS. LINDE: Then it really wasn't him.

NORA: No, absolutely not. It never even crossed my mind for a moment— And he had nothing to lend in those days; his inheritance came later.

MRS. LINDE: Well, I think that was a stroke of luck for you, Nora dear.

NORA: No, it never would have occurred to me to ask Dr. Rank— Still, I'm quite sure that if I had asked him—

MRS. LINDE: Which you won't, of course.

NORA: No, of course not. I can't see that I'd ever need to. But I'm quite positive that if I talked to Dr. Rank—

MRS. LINDE: Behind your husband's back?

NORA: I've got to clear up this other thing; *that's* also behind his back. I've got to clear it all up.

MRS. LINDE: Yes, I was saying that yesterday, but—

NORA [*pacing up and down*]: A man handles these problems so much better than a woman—

Reading Strategy
Inferring Beliefs of the Period What does Nora suggest about Torvald's personality?

intolerable (in täl′ ər ə bəl) *adj.* unbearable; painful; cruel

**Reading Check**

From what illness is Dr. Rank suffering?

MRS. LINDE: One's husband does, yes.

NORA: Nonsense. [*Stopping.*] When you pay everything you owe, then you get your note back, right?

MRS. LINDE: Yes, naturally.

NORA: And can rip it into a million pieces and burn it up—that filthy scrap of paper!

MRS. LINDE [*looking hard at her, laying her sewing aside, and rising slowly*]: Nora, you're hiding something from me.

NORA: You can see it in my face?

MRS. LINDE: Something's happened to you since yesterday morning. Nora, what is it?

NORA [*hurrying toward her*]: Kristine! [*Listening.*] Shh! Torvald's home. Look, go in with the children a while. Torvald can't bear all this snipping and stitching. Let Anne-Marie help you.

▲ **Critical Viewing**
In what ways does the actress portraying Nora show the faith Nora has in her husband? [**Analyze**]

MRS. LINDE [*gathering up some of the things*]: All right, but I'm not leaving here until we've talked this out. [*She disappears into the room, left, as* TORVALD *enters from the hall.*]

NORA: Oh, how I've been waiting for you, Torvald dear.

HELMER: Was that the dressmaker?

NORA: No, that was Kristine. She's helping me fix up my costume. You know, it's going to be quite attractive.

HELMER: Yes, wasn't that a bright idea I had?

NORA: Brilliant! But then wasn't I good as well to give in to you?

HELMER: Good—because you give in to your husband's judgment? All right, you little goose, I know you didn't mean it like that. But I won't disturb you. You'll want to have a fitting, I suppose.

NORA: And you'll be working?

HELMER: Yes. [*Indicating a bundle of papers.*] See. I've been down to the bank. [*Starts toward his study.*]

NORA: Torvald.

HELMER [*stops*]: Yes.

NORA: If your little squirrel begged you, with all her heart and soul, for something—?

HELMER: What's that?

NORA: Then would you do it?

HELMER: First, naturally, I'd have to know what it was.

NORA: Your squirrel would scamper about and do tricks, if you'd only be sweet and give in.

HELMER: Out with it.

NORA: Your lark would be singing high and low in every room—

HELMER: Come on, she does that anyway.

NORA: I'd be a wood nymph and dance for you in the moonlight.

HELMER: Nora—don't tell me it's that same business from this morning?

NORA [*coming closer*]: Yes, Torvald, I beg you, please!

HELMER: And you actually have the nerve to drag that up again?

NORA: Yes, yes, you've got to give in to me; you *have* to let Krogstad keep his job in the bank.

HELMER: My dear Nora, I've slated his job for Mrs. Linde.

NORA: That's awfully kind of you. But you could just fire another clerk instead of Krogstad.

HELMER: This is the most incredible stubbornness! Because you go

Reading Strategy
Inferring Beliefs of the Period What common social beliefs about men and women can you infer from Nora's comment? Explain.

Reading Strategy
Inferring Beliefs of the Period Why does Nora compare herself to a squirrel as she pleads with Torvald?

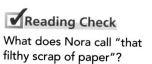

Reading Check
What does Nora call "that filthy scrap of paper"?

and give an <u>impulsive</u> promise to speak up for him, I'm expected to—

NORA: That's not the reason, Torvald. It's for your own sake. That man does writing for the worst papers; you said it yourself. He could do you any amount of harm. I'm scared to death of him—

HELMER: Ah, I understand. It's the old memories haunting you.

NORA: What do you mean by that?

HELMER: Of course, you're thinking about your father.

NORA: Yes, all right. Just remember how those nasty gossips wrote in the papers about Papa and slandered him so cruelly. I think they'd have had him dismissed if the department hadn't sent you up to investigate, and if you hadn't been so kind and open-minded toward him.

HELMER: My dear Nora, there's a notable difference between your father and me. Your father's official career was hardly above reproach. But mine is; and I hope it'll stay that way as long as I hold my position.

NORA: Oh, who can ever tell what vicious minds can invent? We could be so snug and happy in our quiet, carefree home—you and I and the children, Torvald! That's why I'm pleading with you so—

HELMER: And just by pleading for him you make it impossible for me to keep him on. It's already known at the bank that I'm firing Krogstad. What if it's rumored around now that the new bank manager was vetoed by his wife—

NORA: Yes, what then—?

HELMER: Oh yes—as long as our little bundle of stubbornness gets her way—! I should go and make myself ridiculous in front of the whole office—give people the idea I can be swayed by all kinds of outside pressure. Oh, you can bet I'd feel the effects of that soon enough! Besides— there's something that rules Krogstad right out at the bank as long as I'm the manager.

NORA: What's that?

HELMER: His moral failings I could maybe overlook if I had to—

NORA: Yes, Torvald, why not?

HELMER: And I hear he's quite efficient on the job. But he was a crony of mine back in my teens—one of those rash friendships that crop up again and again to embarrass you later in life. Well, I might as well say it straight out: we're on a first-name basis. And that <u>tactless</u> fool makes no effort at all to hide it in front of others. Quite the contrary— he thinks that entitles him to take a familiar air around me, and so every other second he comes booming out with his "Yes, Torvald!" and "Sure thing, Torvald!" I tell you, it's been <u>excruciating</u> for me. He's out to make my place in the bank unbearable.

NORA: Torvald, you can't be serious about all this.

HELMER: Oh no? Why not?

NORA: Because these are such petty considerations.

---

impulsive (im pul′ siv) *adj.* sudden and unthinking

Literary Analysis
Characterization in Drama What do Torvald's real reasons for firing Krogstad reveal about Torvald's personality?

tactless (takt′ lis) *adj.* unskilled in dealing with people

excruciating (eks krōō′ shē āt′ iŋ) *adj.* causing intense mental or bodily pain

HELMER: What are you saying? Petty? You think I'm petty!

NORA: No, just the opposite, Torvald dear. That's exactly why—

HELMER: Never mind. You call my motives petty; then I might as well be just that. Petty! All right! We'll put a stop to this for good. [*Goes to the hall door and calls.*] Helene!

NORA: What do you want?

HELMER [*searching among his papers*]: A decision. [*The* MAID *comes in.*] Look here; take this letter; go out with it at once. Get hold of a messenger and have him deliver it. Quick now. It's already addressed. Wait, here's some money.

MAID: Yes, sir. [*She leaves with the letter.*]

HELMER [*straightening his papers*]: There, now, little Miss Willful.

NORA [*breathlessly*]: Torvald, what was that letter?

HELMER: Krogstad's notice.

NORA: Call it back, Torvald! There's still time. Oh, Torvald, call it back! Do it for my sake—for your sake, for the children's sake! Do you hear, Torvald; do it! You don't know how this can harm us.

HELMER: Too late.

NORA: Yes, too late.

HELMER: Nora dear, I can forgive you this panic, even though basically you're insulting me. Yes, you are! Or isn't it an insult to think that *I* should be afraid of a courtroom hack's revenge? But I forgive you any-way, because this shows so beautifully how much you love me. [*Takes her in his arms.*] This is the way it should be, my darling Nora. What-ever comes, you'll see: when it really counts, I have strength and cour-age enough as a man to take on the whole weight myself.

NORA [*terrified*]: What do you mean by that?

HELMER: The whole weight, I said.

NORA [*resolutely*]: No, never in all the world.

HELMER: Good. So we'll share it, Nora, as man and wife. That's as it should be. [*Fondling her.*] Are you happy now? There, there, there—not these frightened dove's eyes. It's nothing at all but empty fantasies— Now you should run through your tarantella and practice your tam-bourine. I'll go to the inner office and shut both doors, so I won't hear a thing; you can make all the noise you like. [*Turning in the doorway.*] And when Rank comes, just tell him where he can find me. [*He nods to her and goes with his papers into the study, closing the door.*]

Literary Analysis
Characterization in Drama Does Torvald's decision to send the maid with Krogstad's notice reveal a cowardly person-ality? Explain.

✓**Reading Check**

Why does Torvald fire Krogstad?

NORA [*standing as though rooted, dazed with fright, in a whisper*]: He really could do it. He will do it. He'll do it in spite of everything. No, not that, never, never! Anything but that! Escape! A way out— [*The doorbell rings.*] Dr. Rank! Anything but that! *Anything*, whatever it is! [*Her hands pass over her face, smoothing it; she pulls herself together, goes over and opens the hall door.* DR. RANK *stands outside, hanging his fur coat up. During the following scene, it begins getting dark.*]

NORA: Hello, Dr. Rank. I recognized your ring. But you mustn't go in to Torvald yet; I believe he's working.

RANK: And you?

NORA: For you, I always have an hour to spare—you know that. [*He has entered, and she shuts the door after him.*]

RANK: Many thanks. I'll make use of these hours while I can.

NORA: What do you mean by that? While you can?

RANK: Does that disturb you?

NORA: Well, it's such an odd phrase. Is anything going to happen?

RANK: What's going to happen is what I've been expecting so long—but I honestly didn't think it would come so soon.

NORA [*gripping his arm*]: What is it you've found out? Dr. Rank, you have to tell me!

RANK [*sitting by the stove*]: It's all over with me. There's nothing to be done about it.

NORA [*breathing easier*]: Is it you—then—?

RANK: Who else? There's no point in lying to one's self. I'm the most miserable of all my patients, Mrs. Helmer. These past few days I've been auditing my internal accounts. Bankrupt! Within a month I'll probably be laid out and rotting in the churchyard.

NORA: Oh, what a horrible thing to say.

RANK: The thing itself is horrible. But the worst of it is all the other horror before it's over. There's only one final examination left; when I'm finished with that, I'll know about when my disintegration will begin. There's something I want to say. Helmer with his sensitivity has such a sharp distaste for anything ugly. I don't want him near my sickroom.

NORA: Oh, but Dr. Rank—

RANK: I won't have him in there. Under no condition. I'll lock my door to him— As soon as I'm completely sure of the worst, I'll send you my calling card marked with a black cross, and you'll know then the wreck has started to come apart.

NORA: No, today you're completely unreasonable. And I wanted you so much to be in a really good humor.

RANK: With death up my sleeve? And then to suffer this way for somebody else's sins. Is there any justice in that? And in every single family,

Literary Analysis
Characterization in Drama What do the stage directions reveal about Nora's concern for Dr. Rank?

in some way or another, this inevitable <u>retribution</u> of nature goes on—

NORA [*her hands pressed over her ears*]: Oh, stuff! Cheer up! Please—be gay!

RANK: Yes, I'd just as soon laugh at it all. My poor, innocent spine, serving time for my father's gay army days.

NORA [*by the table, left*]: He was so infatuated with asparagus tips and *pâté de foie gras*,[3] wasn't that it?

RANK: Yes—and with truffles.

NORA: Truffles, yes. And then with oysters, I suppose?

RANK: Yes, tons of oysters, naturally.

NORA: And then the port and champagne to go with it. It's so sad that all these delectable things have to strike at our bones.

RANK: Especially when they strike at the unhappy bones that never shared in the fun.

NORA: Ah, that's the saddest of all.

RANK [*looks searchingly at her*]: Hm.

NORA [*after a moment*]: Why did you smile?

RANK: No, it was you who laughed.

NORA: No, it was you who smiled, Dr. Rank!

RANK [*getting up*]: You're even a bigger tease than I'd thought.

NORA: I'm full of wild ideas today.

RANK: That's obvious.

NORA [*putting both hands on his shoulders*]: Dear, dear Dr. Rank, you'll never die for Torvald and me.

RANK: Oh, that loss you'll easily get over. Those who go away are soon forgotten.

NORA [*looks fearfully at him*]: You believe that?

RANK: One makes new connections, and then—

NORA: Who makes new connections?

RANK: Both you and Torvald will when I'm gone. I'd say you're well under way already. What was that Mrs. Linde doing here last evening?

NORA: Oh, come—you can't be jealous of poor Kristine?

RANK: Oh yes, I am. She'll be my successor here in the house. When I'm down under, that woman will probably—

NORA: Shh! Not so loud. She's right in there.

RANK: Today as well. So you see.

---

3. *pâté de foie gras* (pä tā´ də fwä´ grä´) paste or spread made of the livers of fattened geese.

retribution (re´ trə byoo´ shən) *n.* punishment; revenge

Reading Strategy
Inferring Beliefs of the Period What modern knowledge of health and heredity does Rank imply when he refers to his father's lavish lifestyle?

**Reading Check**

What will Dr. Rank send the Helmers when his death becomes imminent?

NORA: Only to sew on my dress. Good gracious, how unreasonable you are. [*Sitting on the sofa.*] Be nice now, Dr. Rank. Tomorrow you'll see how beautifully I'll dance; and you can imagine then that I'm dancing only for you—yes, and of course for Torvald, too—that's understood. [*Takes various items out of the carton.*] Dr. Rank, sit over here and I'll show you something.

RANK [*sitting*]: What's that?

NORA: Look here. Look.

RANK: Silk stockings.

NORA: Flesh-colored. Aren't they lovely? Now it's so dark here, but tomorrow— No, no, no, just look at the feet. Oh well, you might as well look at the rest.

RANK: Hm—

NORA: Why do you look so critical? Don't you believe they'll fit?

RANK: I've never had any chance to form an opinion on that.

NORA [*glancing at him a moment*]: Shame on you. [*Hits him lightly on the ear with the stockings.*] That's for you. [*Puts them away again.*]

RANK: And what other splendors am I going to see now?

NORA: Not the least bit more, because you've been naughty. [*She hums a little and rummages among her things.*]

RANK [*after a short silence*]: When I sit here together with you like this, completely easy and open, then I don't know—I simply can't imagine—whatever would have become of me if I'd never come into this house.

NORA [*smiling*]: Yes, I really think you feel completely at ease with us.

RANK [*more quietly, staring straight ahead*]: And then to have to go away from it all—

NORA: Nonsense, you're not going away.

RANK [*his voice unchanged*]: —and not even be able to leave some poor show of gratitude behind, scarcely a fleeting regret—no more than a vacant place that anyone can fill.

NORA: And if I asked you now for—? No—

RANK: For what?

NORA: For a great proof of your friendship—

RANK: Yes, yes?

NORA: No, I mean—for an exceptionally big favor—

▲ **Critical Viewing**
Why might a lady's sewing kit be a valued piece of property for women like Nora and Mrs. Linde? **[Hypothesize]**

RANK: Would you really, for once, make me so happy?

NORA: Oh, you haven't the vaguest idea what it is.

RANK: All right, then tell me.

NORA: No, but I can't, Dr. Rank—it's all out of reason. It's advice and help, too—and a favor—

RANK: So much the better. I can't fathom what you're hinting at. Just speak out. Don't you trust me?

NORA: Of course. More than anyone else. You're my best and truest friend, I'm sure. That's why I want to talk to you. All right, then, Dr. Rank: there's something you can help me prevent. You know how deeply, how inexpressibly dearly Torvald loves me; he'd never hesitate a second to give up his life for me.

RANK [*leaning close to her*]: Nora—do you think he's the only one—

NORA [*with a slight start*]: Who—?

RANK: Who'd gladly give up his life for you.

NORA [*heavily*]: I see.

RANK: I swore to myself you should know this before I'm gone. I'll never find a better chance. Yes, Nora, now you know. And also you know now that you can trust me beyond anyone else.

NORA [*rising, natural and calm*]: Let me by.

RANK [*making room for her, but still sitting*]: Nora—

NORA [*in the hall doorway*]: Helene, bring the lamp in. [*Goes over to the stove.*] Ah, dear Dr. Rank, that was really mean of you.

RANK [*getting up*]: That I've loved you just as deeply as somebody else? Was *that* mean?

NORA: No, but that you came out and told me. That was quite unnecessary—

RANK: What do you mean? Have you known—?
[*The* MAID *comes in with the lamp, sets it on the table, and goes out again.*]

RANK: Nora—Mrs. Helmer—I'm asking you: have you known about it?

NORA: Oh, how can I tell what I know or don't know? Really, I don't know what to say— Why did you have to be so clumsy, Dr. Rank! Everything was so good.

RANK: Well, in any case, you now have the knowledge that my body and soul are at your command. So won't you speak out?

NORA [*looking at him*]: After that?

RANK: Please, just let me know what it is.

NORA: You can't know anything now.

RANK: I have to. You mustn't punish me like this. Give me the chance to do whatever is humanly possible for you.

Literary Analysis
Characterization in Drama Why do you think Nora is willing to ask Dr. Rank for money in spite of his impending bankruptcy?

Literary Analysis
Characterization in Drama What does Nora's refusal to ask Dr. Rank for money suggest about her personality?

**Reading Check**

What does Dr. Rank claim he would give up for Nora?

NORA: Now there's nothing you can do for me. Besides, actually, I don't need any help. You'll see—it's only my fantasies. That's what it is. Of course! [*Sits in the rocker, looks at him, and smiles.*] What a nice one you are, Dr. Rank. Aren't you a little bit ashamed, now that the lamp is here?

RANK: No, not exactly. But perhaps I'd better go—for good?

NORA: No, you certainly can't do that. You must come here just as you always have. You know Torvald can't do without you.

RANK: Yes, but *you*?

NORA: You know how much I enjoy it when you're here.

RANK: That's precisely what threw me off. You're a mystery to me. So many times I've felt you'd almost rather be with me than with Helmer.

NORA: Yes—you see, there are some people that one loves most and other people that one would almost prefer being with.

RANK: Yes, there's something to that.

NORA: When I was back home, of course I loved Papa most. But I always thought it was so much fun when I could sneak down to the maids' quarters, because they never tried to improve me, and it was always so amusing, the way they talked to each other.

RANK: Aha, so it's *their* place that I've filled.

NORA [*jumping up and going to him*]: Oh, dear, sweet Dr. Rank, that's not what I meant at all. But you can understand that with Torvald it's just the same as with Papa—

[*The* MAID *enters from the hall.*]

MAID: Ma'am—please! [*She whispers to* NORA *and hands her a calling card.*]

NORA [*glancing at the card.*]: Ah! [*Slips it into her pocket.*]

RANK: Anything wrong?

NORA: No, no, not at all. It's only some—it's my new dress—

RANK: Really? But—there's your dress.

NORA: Oh, that. But this is another one—I ordered it—Torvald mustn't know—

RANK: Ah, now we have the big secret.

NORA: That's right. Just go in with him—he's back in the inner study. Keep him there as long as—

RANK: Don't worry. He won't get away. [*Goes into the study.*]

NORA [*to the* MAID]: And he's standing waiting in the kitchen?

Reading Strategy
Inferring the Beliefs of the Period What common cultural practices are revealed in the stage directions?

MAID: Yes, he came up by the back stairs.

NORA: But didn't you tell him somebody was here?

MAID: Yes, but that didn't do any good.

NORA: He won't leave?

MAID: No, he won't go till he's talked with you, ma'am.

NORA: Let him come in, then—but quietly. Helene, don't breathe a word about this. It's a surprise for my husband.

MAID: Yes, yes, I understand— [*Goes out.*]

NORA: This horror—it's going to happen. No, no, no, it can't happen, it mustn't. [*She goes and bolts* HELMER's *door. The* MAID *opens the hall door for* KROGSTAD *and shuts it behind him. He is dressed for travel in a fur coat, boots, and a fur cap.*]

NORA [*going toward him*]: Talk softly. My husband's home.

KROGSTAD: Well, good for him.

NORA: What do you want?

KROGSTAD: Some information.

NORA: Hurry up, then. What is it?

KROGSTAD: You know, of course, that I got my notice.

NORA: I couldn't prevent it, Mr. Krogstad. I fought for you to the bitter end, but nothing worked.

KROGSTAD: Does your husband's love for you run so thin? He knows everything I can expose you to, and all the same he dares to—

NORA: How can you imagine he knows anything about this?

KROGSTAD: Ah, no—I can't imagine it either, now. It's not at all like my fine Torvald Helmer to have so much guts—

NORA: Mr. Krogstad, I demand respect for my husband!

KROGSTAD: Why, of course—all due respect. But since the lady's keeping it so carefully hidden, may I presume to ask if you're also a bit better informed than yesterday about what you've actually done?

NORA: More than you ever could teach me.

KROGSTAD: Yes, I *am* such an awful lawyer.

NORA: What is it you want from me?

KROGSTAD: Just a glimpse of how you are, Mrs. Helmer. I've been thinking about you all day long. A cashier, a night-court scribbler, a—well, a type like me also has a little of what they call a heart, you know.

NORA: Then show it. Think of my children.

KROGSTAD: Did you or your husband ever think of mine? But never mind. I simply wanted to tell you that you don't need to take this thing too seriously. For the present, I'm not proceeding with any action.

Literary Analysis
Characterization in Drama What do Nora's instructions to Helene suggest about Nora's desperation?

Reading Check

Who waits for Nora in the kitchen?

NORA: Oh no, really! Well—I knew that.

KROGSTAD: Everything can be settled in a friendly spirit. It doesn't have to get around town at all; it can stay just among us three.

NORA: My husband must never know anything of this.

KROGSTAD: How can you manage that? Perhaps you can pay me the balance?

NORA: No, not right now.

KROGSTAD: Or you know some way of raising the money in a day or two?

NORA: No way that I'm willing to use.

KROGSTAD: Well, it wouldn't have done you any good, anyway. If you stood in front of me with a fistful of bills, you still couldn't buy your signature back.

NORA: Then tell me what you're going to do with it.

KROGSTAD: I'll just hold onto it—keep it on file. There's no outsider who'll even get wind of it. So if you've been thinking of taking some desperate step—

NORA: I have.

KROGSTAD: Been thinking of running away from home—

NORA: I have!

KROGSTAD: Or even of something worse—

NORA: How could you guess that?

KROGSTAD: You can drop those thoughts.

NORA: How could you guess I was thinking of *that*?

KROGSTAD: Most of us think about *that* at first. I thought about it too, but I discovered I hadn't the courage—

NORA [*lifelessly*]: I don't either.

KROGSTAD [*relieved*]: That's true, you haven't the courage? You too?

NORA: I don't have it—I don't have it.

KROGSTAD: It would be terribly stupid, anyway. After that first storm at home blows out, why, then— I have here in my pocket a letter for your husband—

NORA: Telling everything?

▲ **Critical Viewing**
In what ways do the actors in this photograph capture the tension between Nora and Krogstad? **[Interpret]**

KROGSTAD: As charitably as possible.

NORA [*quickly*]: He mustn't ever get that letter. Tear it up. I'll find some way to get money.

KROGSTAD: Beg pardon, Mrs. Helmer, but I think I just told you—

NORA: Oh, I don't mean the money I owe you. Let me know how much you want from my husband, and I'll manage it.

KROGSTAD: I don't want any money from your husband.

NORA: What do you want, then?

KROGSTAD: I'll tell you what. I want to recoup, Mrs. Helmer; I want to get on in the world—and there's where your husband can help me. For

Reading Check

What does Krogstad plan to do with the signature Nora forged?

A Doll House, Act Two ◆ 913

a year and a half I've kept myself clean of anything <u>disreputable</u>—all that time struggling with the worst conditions; but I was satisfied, working my way up step by step. Now I've been written right off, and I'm just not in the mood to come crawling back. I tell you, I want to move on. I want to get back in the bank—in a better position. Your husband can set up a job for me—

NORA: He'll never do that!

KROGSTAD: He'll do it. I know him. He won't dare breathe a word of protest. And once I'm in there together with him, you just wait and see! Inside of a year, I'll be the manager's right-hand man. It'll be Nils Krogstad, not Torvald Helmer, who runs the bank.

NORA: You'll never see the day!

KROGSTAD: Maybe you think you can—

NORA: I have the courage now—for *that.*

KROGSTAD: Oh, you don't scare me. A smart, spoiled lady like you—

NORA: You'll see; you'll see!

KROGSTAD: Under the ice, maybe? Down in the freezing, coal-black water? There, till you float up in the spring, ugly, unrecognizable, with your hair falling out—

NORA: You don't frighten me.

KROGSTAD: Nor do you frighten me. One doesn't do these things, Mrs. Helmer. Besides, what good would it be? I'd still have him safe in my pocket.

NORA: Afterwards? When I'm no longer—?

KROGSTAD: Are you forgetting that *I'll* be in control then over your final reputation? [NORA *stands speechless, staring at him.*] Good; now I've warned you. Don't do anything stupid. When Helmer's read my letter, I'll be waiting for his reply. And bear in mind that it's your husband himself who's forced me back to my old ways. I'll never forgive him for that. Good-bye, Mrs. Helmer. [*He goes out through the hall.*]

NORA [*goes to the hall door, opens it a crack, and listens*]: He's gone. Didn't leave the letter. Oh no, no, that's impossible too! [*Opening the door more and more.*] What's that? He's standing outside—not going downstairs. He's thinking it over? Maybe he'll—? [*A letter falls in the mailbox; then* KROGSTAD'*s footsteps are heard, dying away down a flight of stairs.* NORA *gives a muffled cry and runs over toward the sofa table. A short pause.*] In the mailbox. [*Slips warily over to the hall door.*] It's lying there. Torvald, Torvald—now we're lost!

MRS. LINDE [*entering with the costume from the room, left*]: There now, I can't see anything else to mend. Perhaps you'd like to try—

NORA [*in a hoarse whisper*]: Kristine, come here.

MRS. LINDE [*tossing the dress on the sofa*]: What's wrong? You look upset.

disreputable (dis rep′ yo͞o tə bəl) *adj.* not fit to be seen or approved

Literary Analysis
Characterization in Drama Does knowing Krogstad's past and his plans for the future make him seem more or less villainous? Explain.

NORA: Come here. See that letter? *There!* Look—through the glass in the mailbox.

MRS. LINDE: Yes, yes, I see it.

NORA: That letter's from Krogstad—

MRS. LINDE: Nora—it's Krogstad who loaned you the money!

NORA: Yes, and now Torvald will find out everything.

MRS. LINDE: Believe me, Nora, it's best for both of you.

NORA: There's more you don't know. I forged a name.

MRS. LINDE: But for heaven's sake—?

NORA: I only want to tell you that, Kristine, so that you can be my witness.

MRS. LINDE: Witness? Why should I—?

NORA: If I should go out of my mind—it could easily happen—

MRS. LINDE: Nora!

NORA: Or anything else occurred—so I couldn't be present here—

MRS. LINDE: Nora, Nora, you aren't yourself at all!

NORA: And someone should try to take on the whole weight, all of the guilt, you follow me—

MRS. LINDE: Yes, of course, but why do you think—?

NORA: Then you're the witness that it isn't true, Kristine. I'm very much myself; my mind right now is perfectly clear; and I'm telling you: nobody else has known about this; I alone did everything. Remember that.

MRS. LINDE: I will. But I don't understand all this.

NORA: Oh, how could you ever understand it? It's the miracle now that's going to take place.

MRS. LINDE: The miracle?

NORA: Yes, the miracle. But it's so awful, Kristine. It mustn't take place, not for anything in the world.

MRS. LINDE: I'm going right over and talk with Krogstad.

NORA: Don't go near him; he'll do you some terrible harm!

MRS. LINDE: There was a time once when he'd gladly have done anything for me.

NORA: He?

MRS. LINDE: Where does he live?

NORA: Oh, how do I know? Yes. [*Searches in her pocket.*] Here's his card. But the letter, the letter—!

HELMER [*from the study, knocking on the door*]: Nora!

NORA [*with a cry of fear*]: Oh! What is it? What do you want?

Reading Strategy
Inferring Beliefs of the Period What social realities of the time would keep Mrs. Linde from mentioning her prior relationship with Krogstad?

✓**Reading Check**

What does Krogstad leave for Torvald?

HELMER: Now, now, don't be so frightened. We're not coming in. You locked the door—are you trying on the dress?

NORA: Yes, I'm trying it. I'll look just beautiful, Torvald.

MRS. LINDE [*who has read the card*]: He's living right around the corner.

NORA: Yes, but what's the use? We're lost. The letter's in the box.

MRS. LINDE: And your husband has the key?

NORA: Yes, always.

MRS. LINDE: Krogstad can ask for his letter back unread; he can find some excuse—

NORA: But it's just this time that Torvald usually—

MRS. LINDE: Stall him. Keep him in there. I'll be back as quick as I can. [*She hurries out through the hall entrance.*]

NORA [*goes to* HELMER's *door, opens it, and peers in*]: Torvald!

HELMER [*from the inner study*]: Well—does one dare set foot in one's own living room at last? Come on, Rank, now we'll get a look— [*In the doorway.*] But what's this?

NORA: What, Torvald dear?

HELMER: Rank had me expecting some grand masquerade.

RANK [*in the doorway*]: That was my impression, but I must have been wrong.

NORA: No one can admire me in my splendor—not till tomorrow.

HELMER: But Nora, dear, you look so exhausted. Have you practiced too hard?

NORA: No, I haven't practiced at all yet.

HELMER: You know, it's necessary—

NORA: Oh, it's absolutely necessary, Torvald. But I can't get anywhere without your help. I've forgotten the whole thing completely.

HELMER: Ah, we'll soon take care of that.

NORA: Yes, take care of me, Torvald, please! Promise me that? Oh, I'm so nervous. That big party— You must give up everything this evening for me. No business—don't even touch your pen. Yes? Dear Torvald, promise?

HELMER: It's a promise. Tonight I'm totally at your service—you little helpless thing. Hm—but first there's one thing I want to— [*Goes toward the hall door.*]

NORA: What are you looking for?

HELMER: Just to see if there's any mail.

NORA: No, no, don't do that, Torvald!

Literary Analysis
Characterization in Drama Why might Torvald carry the mailbox key instead of Nora?

HELMER: Now what?

NORA: Torvald, please. There isn't any.

HELMER: Let me look, though. [*Starts out.* NORA, *at the piano, strikes the first notes of the tarantella.* HELMER, *at the door, stops.*] Aha!

NORA: I can't dance tomorrow if I don't practice with you.

HELMER [*going over to her*]: Nora dear, are you really so frightened?

NORA: Yes, so terribly frightened. Let me practice right now; there's still time before dinner. Oh, sit down and play for me, Torvald. Direct me. Teach me, the way you always have.

HELMER: Gladly, if it's what you want. [*Sits at the piano.*]

NORA [*snatches the tambourine up from the box, then a long, varicolored shawl, which she throws around herself, whereupon she springs forward and cries out*]: Play for me now! Now I'll dance! [HELMER *plays and* NORA *dances.* RANK *stands behind* HELMER *at the piano and looks on.*]

HELMER [*as he plays*]: Slower. Slow down.

NORA: Can't change it.

HELMER: Not so violent, Nora!

NORA: Has to be just like this.

HELMER [*stopping*]: No, no, that won't do at all.

NORA [*laughing and swinging her tambourine*]: Isn't that what I told you?

RANK: Let me play for her.

HELMER [*getting up*]: Yes, go on. I can teach her more easily then. [RANK *sits at the piano and plays;* NORA *dances more and more wildly.* HELMER *has stationed himself by the stove and repeatedly gives her directions; she seems not to hear them; her hair loosens and falls over her shoulders; she does not notice, but goes on dancing.* MRS. LINDE *enters.*]

MRS. LINDE [*standing dumbfounded at the door*]: Ah—!

NORA [*still dancing*]: See what fun, Kristine!

HELMER: But Nora darling, you dance as if your life were at stake.

NORA: And it is.

HELMER: Rank, stop! This is pure madness. Stop it, I say!

[RANK *breaks off playing, and* NORA *halts abruptly.*]

HELMER [*going over to her*]: I never would have believed it. You've forgotten everything I taught you.

NORA [*throwing away the tambourine*]: You see for yourself.

Literature in context — History Connection

The Tarantella

Henrik Ibsen had important dramatic reasons for choosing this specific dance for Nora to perform. Both the dance and the tarantula spider were named for the southern Italian city of Taranto. In the 1400s, it was believed that the bite of the tarantula was deadly, and the only way to counteract its fatal bite was to dance wildly to distribute the poison throughout the body and sweat it out. The folk dance itself features quick steps, teasing behavior, and a tambourine.

Associated with the tarantella was tarantism, a form of mass hysteria in which the victims, thought to be bitten by the tarantula, danced themselves into a frenzy. Two other forms of this hysteria were the St. Vitus dance, a bizarre twitching of seemingly possessed people, and the dance of death, in which a skeleton led a line of dancers across the countryside. Historians believe all three dances may have been a response to the horrors of the Black Death, the plague that killed a third of all people in Europe in the 1300s. For Nora, the frenetic dancing of the tarantella releases the fear and desperation that torture her as Torvald comes closer to discovering her secrets.

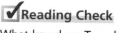

Reading Check

What key does Torvald always carry?

HELMER: Well, there's certainly room for instruction here.

NORA: Yes, you see how important it is. You've got to teach me to the very last minute. Promise me that, Torvald?

HELMER: You can bet on it.

NORA: You mustn't, either today or tomorrow, think about anything else but me; you mustn't open any letters—or the mailbox—

HELMER: Ah, it's still the fear of that man—

NORA: Oh yes, yes, that too.

HELMER: Nora, it's written all over you—there's already a letter from him out there.

NORA: I don't know. I guess so. But you mustn't read such things now; there mustn't be anything ugly between us before it's all over.

RANK [*quietly to* HELMER]: You shouldn't deny her.

HELMER [*putting his arm around her*]: The child can have her way. But tomorrow night, after you've danced—

NORA: Then you'll be free.

MAID [*in the doorway, right*]: Ma'am, dinner is served.

NORA: We'll be wanting champagne, Helene.

MAID: Very good, ma'am. [*Goes out.*]

HELMER: So—a regular banquet, hm?

NORA: Yes, a banquet—champagne till daybreak! [*Calling out.*] And some macaroons, Helene. Heaps of them—just this once.

HELMER [*taking her hands*]: Now, now, now—no hysterics. Be my own little lark again.

NORA: Oh, I will soon enough. But go on in—and you, Dr. Rank. Kristine, help me put up my hair.

RANK [*whispering, as they go*]: There's nothing wrong—really wrong, is there?

HELMER: Oh, of course not. It's nothing more than this childish anxiety I was telling you about. [*They go out, right.*]

NORA: Well?

MRS. LINDE: Left town.

NORA: I could see by your face.

MRS. LINDE: He'll be home tomorrow evening. I wrote him a note.

NORA: You shouldn't have. Don't try to stop anything now. After all, it's a wonderful joy, this waiting here for the miracle.

Literary Analysis
Characterization in Drama Explain how Nora's urgent pleading reflects her attitude toward her present situation.

MRS. LINDE: What is it you're waiting for?

NORA: Oh, you can't understand that. Go in to them; I'll be along in a moment. [MRS. LINDE *goes into the dining room.* NORA *stands a short while as if composing herself; then she looks at her watch.*]

NORA: Five. Seven hours to midnight. Twenty-four hours to the midnight after, and then the tarantella's done. Seven and twenty-four? Thirty-one hours to live.

HELMER [*in the doorway, right*]: What's become of the little lark?

NORA [*going toward him with open arms*]: Here's your lark!

Review and Assess

Thinking About Act Two

1. **Respond:** What would you advise Nora to do about her dilemma? Why?

2. **(a) Recall:** How does Nora describe her relationship with Dr. Rank? **(b) Recall:** What role did Anne-Marie fulfill for Nora in the past? **(c) Analyze:** What do Dr. Rank and Anne-Marie offer Nora that Torvald does not?

3. **(a) Recall:** What does Dr. Rank confess to Nora? **(b) Speculate:** What favor do you think Nora might have asked of Dr. Rank? **(c) Analyze:** Why do you think she changes her mind? **(d) Take a Stand:** Do you think Nora made the right decision? Why or why not?

4. **(a) Recall:** What does Krogstad say about Torvald? **(b) Infer:** What opinion of Torvald does Krogstad seem to have?

5. **(a) Interpret:** What does Nora mean when she says she has thirty-one hours left to live? **(b) Speculate:** What "miracle" do you think Nora hopes for at the end of the act? Explain.

6. **(a) Compare and Contrast:** Compare and contrast the situations of Dr. Rank, Krogstad, Torvald, and Nora as Act Two ends. **(b) Assess:** Of these four characters, which one seems most likely to experience an improved situation in the near future? **(c) Support:** Identify details in Act Two that help explain your answer.

7. **(a) Make a Judgment:** Is Mrs. Linde a loyal friend to Nora? **(b) Support:** Support your answer with evidence from the play.

8. **Extend:** What lessons can be learned about personal relationships from the problems facing Nora and Torvald?

Review and Assess

Literary Analysis
Characterization in Drama

1. (a) Using a chart like the one below, track the **characterization** of Nora through descriptions of her behavior, the comments she makes, and comments made about her by other characters.

Behavior	Comments She Makes	Comments by Other Characters

(b) Based on your findings, what conclusions can you draw about Nora?

2. When Dr. Rank says, "Those who go away are soon forgotten," what do we learn about his character?

3. Identify three details in Act Two that suggest that Krogstad was once a decent man.

Connecting Literary Elements

4. Which details in the play—or in your response to it—confirm that Nora is the **protagonist** of this work?

5. (a) In what way does Nora act as an **antagonist** to herself? (b) Does this dual nature make her character more or less realistic? Explain.

6. (a) Besides money, what does Krogstad want from the Helmers? (b) Is Krogstad a threat to Nora physically, mentally, or emotionally? Explain.

Reading Strategy
Inferring Beliefs of the Period

7. Based on the type of work that Mrs. Linde, Anne-Marie, and Nora are qualified to do, what can you **infer about beliefs of the period** regarding the importance of educating women?

8. (a) What does Nora see as her most important role in life? (b) How does this reflect the attitudes of her time?

Extend Understanding

9. **Career Connection:** If you were a judge, whom would you punish more severely—Nora, for forging her father's signature, or Krogstad, for blackmailing the Helmers? Why?

Integrate Language Skills

Vocabulary Development Lesson

Word Analysis: Latin Prefix *re-*

The prefix *re-*, which means "again" or "back," can help you define many words. For example, the Latin word *tribuere* means "to pay," and *retribution* can be defined as "payback for evil done." Match each word in the left column with its definition in the right column.

1. reproach   **a.** to restore
2. reinstate   **b.** to accuse

Spelling Strategy

The long *a* sound can be spelled in several different ways—for example, *ei* (*deign*), *ai* (*train*), *ey* (*they*), *a* (*apron*), and *ay* (*essay*). Complete the spelling of each word below.

1. ob___   2. del___   3. b___by

Fluency: Words in Context

Explain why each statement is true or false.

1. An *impulsive* shopper buys without first considering his or her budget.
2. An employee seeks *retribution* when awarded a day off from work.
3. A library is a place for *proclaiming* your thoughts to all of the patrons.
4. For their *disreputable* behavior, criminals are sent to prison.
5. A sleepy child finds a warm bed *intolerable*.
6. Many consider it *tactless* to compliment a friend on her new clothes.
7. *Excruciating* pain in a tooth would need a dentist's immediate care.

Grammar and Style Lesson

Commas After Introductory Words

Use commas to set off a mild interjection or another interrupter that introduces a sentence.

Examples: "Oh, of course not. . . ."

"Now, now, don't be frightened. . . ."

Practice Add commas to set off introductory words. If a sentence is correct as is, write *Correct*.

1. Hey did you ever see *A Doll House*?
2. Yes I saw a film version of the stage play.
3. Well which actors played the major roles?
4. I must say that I found the play very disturbing.
5. Perhaps but you could learn a great deal from the play.

Writing Application Using dialogue, write a brief scene that involves two or more characters. Use commas to set off at least three introductory words.

Extension Activities

Writing Put yourself in Krogstad's place and write the **letter** that he mailed to Torvald. Proofread your letter, prepare a final copy, and share it with your classmates.

Listening and Speaking With a group, prepare a **radio play** based on a scene from Act Two. Use language that is appropriate to each character. **[Group Activity]**

Prentice Hall Writing and Grammar Connection: Diamond Level, Chapter 27, Section 2

Prepare to Read

A Doll House, Act Three

Literary Analysis

Theme

A **theme** is a central message, idea, or insight into life that is revealed by a literary work. In a drama, a theme may be stated directly or suggested through dialogue and actions. A complex play like *A Doll House* may have several themes:

- Real love has little to do with physical beauty or social status.
- A successful relationship is based on trust, equality, individuality.
- Every person has the right to individuality.

As you read Act Three, pay close attention to how the characters' actions or dialogue convey the theme.

Connecting Literary Elements

To prepare readers to recognize key themes, Ibsen uses **foreshadowing,** a technique of incorporating details that suggest events or conditions to come. In Act Two, for example, Nora tells Torvald that he will soon be free, but she does not indicate from what he will be free. The outcome is revealed in Act Three. Note how foreshadowing keeps you guessing.

Reading Strategy

Recognizing Dramatic Tension

Dramatic tension is the sense of suspense that an audience feels while watching a drama unfold. To **recognize dramatic tension,** monitor the anticipation you feel while reading each scene. Ask questions such as these:

- Why are these characters in conflict with one another?
- In what way are the stakes being raised, making it clear that the protagonist stands to lose more and more as the play progresses?

Record moments of conflict or mystery in a chart like the one shown. For each one, write a question to reflect the suspense you experience in that moment.

Vocabulary Development

calculating (kal′ kyoo lāt′ iŋ) *adj.* shrewd or cunning (p. 924)

evasions (ē vā′ zhənz) *n.* attempts to avoid duties or questions (p. 926)

naturalistic (nach′ ər əl is′ tik) *adj.* faithful to nature (p. 928)

proprieties (prō prī′ ə tēz) *n.* conformities with what is considered fitting, suitable, or proper (p. 928)

hypocrite (hip′ ə krit′) *n.* someone who merely pretends to be virtuous (p. 935)

grafter (graft′ ər) *n.* someone who takes advantage of his or her position to gain money or property dishonestly (p. 935)

bewildered (bē wil′ dərd) *adj.* puzzled; confused (p. 937)

Moment of Conflict or Mystery

Mrs. Linde asks Krogstad to speak with her about Nora's debt.

↓

Question

Will Mrs. Linde reveal Nora's desperation?

Review and Anticipate

In Act Two, Torvald's misgivings prompt him to fire Krogstad in spite of Nora's pleas to retain him. Not to be bested, Krogstad arrives with a letter for Torvald that reveals Nora's deception. Krogstad plans to blackmail Torvald into giving him back his job at the bank and leaves the letter in the Helmers' locked mailbox.

Desperate to protect her home and marriage, Nora exhausts every available tactic to change Krogstad's mind and to prevent Torvald from reading the letter. Will Nora salvage Torvald's good name or allow him to take the blame for her actions? What, if anything, will she learn from her mistakes? As you read, look for answers to these questions in the conclusion to Ibsen's *A Doll House*.

ACT THREE

Same scene. The table, with chairs around it, has been moved to the center of the room. A lamp on the table is lit. The hall door stands open. Dance music drifts down from the floor above. MRS. LINDE *sits at the table, absently paging through a book, trying to read, but apparently unable to focus her thoughts. Once or twice she pauses, tensely listening for a sound at the outer entrance.*

MRS. LINDE [*glancing at her watch*]: Not yet—and there's hardly any time left. If only he's not—[*Listening again.*] Ah, there he is. [*She goes out in the hall and cautiously opens the outer door. Quiet footsteps are heard on the stairs. She whispers.*] Come in. Nobody's here.

KROGSTAD [*in the doorway*]: I found a note from you at home. What's back of all this?

MRS. LINDE: I just *had* to talk to you.

KROGSTAD: Oh? And it just *had* to be here in this house?

MRS. LINDE: At my place it was impossible; my room hasn't a private entrance. Come in; we're all alone. The maid's asleep, and the Helmers are at the dance upstairs.

KROGSTAD [*entering the room*]: Well, well, the Helmers are dancing tonight? Really?

MRS. LINDE: Why not?

KROGSTAD: How true—why not?

MRS. LINDE: All right, Krogstad, let's talk.

Reading Strategy
Recognizing Dramatic Tension What effect does time have on the dramatic tension in this scene?

✔**Reading Check**

Who left a note for Krogstad at his home?

KROGSTAD: Do we two have anything more to talk about?

MRS. LINDE: We have a great deal to talk about.

KROGSTAD: I wouldn't have thought so.

MRS. LINDE: No, because you've never understood me, really.

KROGSTAD: Was there anything more to understand—except what's all too common in life? A <u>calculating</u> woman throws over a man the moment a better catch comes by.

MRS. LINDE: You think I'm so thoroughly calculating? You think I broke it off lightly?

KROGSTAD: Didn't you?

MRS. LINDE: Nils—is that what you really thought?

KROGSTAD: If you cared, then why did you write me the way you did?

MRS. LINDE: What else could I do? If I had to break off with you, then it was my job as well to root out everything you felt for me.

KROGSTAD [*wringing his hands*]: So that was it. And this—all this, simply for money!

MRS. LINDE: Don't forget I had a helpless mother and two small brothers. We couldn't wait for you, Nils; you had such a long road ahead of you then.

KROGSTAD: That may be; but you still hadn't the right to abandon me for somebody else's sake.

MRS. LINDE: Yes—I don't know. So many, many times I've asked myself if I did have that right.

KROGSTAD [*more softly*]: When I lost you, it was as if all the solid ground dissolved from under my feet. Look at me; I'm a half-drowned man now, hanging onto a wreck.

MRS. LINDE: Help may be near.

KROGSTAD: It was near—but then you came and blocked it off.

MRS. LINDE: Without my knowing it, Nils. Today for the first time I learned that it's you I'm replacing at the bank.

KROGSTAD: All right—I believe you. But now that you know, will you step aside?

MRS. LINDE: No, because that wouldn't benefit you in the slightest.

KROGSTAD: Not "benefit" me, hm! I'd step aside anyway.

MRS. LINDE: I've learned to be realistic. Life and hard, bitter necessity have taught me that.

KROGSTAD: And life's taught me never to trust fine phrases.

MRS. LINDE: Then life's taught you a very sound thing. But you do have to trust in actions, don't you?

KROGSTAD: What does that mean?

calculating (kal´ kyoo lāt´ iŋ) *adj.* shrewd or cunning

Literary Analysis
Theme and Foreshadowing What action on Mrs. Linde's part might these words foreshadow?

MRS. LINDE: You said you were hanging on like a half-drowned man to a wreck.

KROGSTAD: I've good reason to say that.

MRS. LINDE: I'm also like a half-drowned woman on a wreck. No one to suffer with; no one to care for.

KROGSTAD: You made your choice.

MRS. LINDE: There wasn't any choice then.

KROGSTAD: So—what of it?

MRS. LINDE: Nils, if only we two shipwrecked people could reach across to each other.

KROGSTAD: What are you saying?

MRS. LINDE: Two on one wreck are at least better off than each on his own.

KROGSTAD: Kristine!

MRS. LINDE: Why do you think I came into town?

KROGSTAD: Did you really have some thought of me?

MRS. LINDE: I have to work to go on living. All my born days, as long as I can remember, I've worked, and it's been my best and my only joy. But now I'm completely alone in the world; it frightens me to be so empty and lost. To work for yourself—there's no joy in that. Nils, give me something—someone to work for.

KROGSTAD: I don't believe all this. It's just some hysterical feminine urge to go out and make a noble sacrifice.

MRS. LINDE: Have you ever found me to be hysterical?

KROGSTAD: Can you honestly mean this? Tell me—do you know everything about my past?

MRS. LINDE: Yes.

KROGSTAD: And you know what they think I'm worth around here.

MRS. LINDE: From what you were saying before, it would seem that with me you could have been another person.

KROGSTAD: I'm positive of that.

MRS. LINDE: Couldn't it happen still?

KROGSTAD: Kristine—you're saying this in all seriousness? Yes, you are! I can see it in you. And do you really have the courage, then—?

MRS. LINDE: I need to have someone to care for; and your children need a mother. We both need each other. Nils, I have faith that you're good at heart—I'll risk everything together with you.

KROGSTAD [*gripping her hands*]: Kristine, thank you, thank you— Now I know I can win back a place in their eyes. Yes—but I forgot—

MRS. LINDE [*listening*]: Shh! The tarantella. Go now! Go on!

Reading Strategy
Recognizing Dramatic Tension If Krogstad rejects Mrs. Linde, will it raise the dramatic tension in this scene? Why or why not?

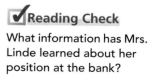

Reading Check

What information has Mrs. Linde learned about her position at the bank?

KROGSTAD: Why? What is it?

MRS. LINDE: Hear the dance up there? When that's over, they'll be coming down.

KROGSTAD: Oh, then I'll go. But—it's all pointless. Of course, you don't know the move I made against the Helmers.

MRS. LINDE: Yes, Nils, I know.

KROGSTAD: And all the same, you have the courage to—?

MRS. LINDE: I know how far despair can drive a man like you.

KROGSTAD: Oh, if I only could take it all back.

MRS. LINDE: You easily could—your letter's still lying in the mailbox.

KROGSTAD: Are you sure of that?

MRS. LINDE: Positive. But—

KROGSTAD [looks at her searchingly]: Is that the meaning of it, then? You'll save your friend at any price. Tell me straight out. Is that it?

MRS. LINDE: Nils—anyone who's sold herself for somebody else once isn't going to do it again.

KROGSTAD: I'll demand my letter back.

MRS. LINDE: No, no.

KROGSTAD: Yes, of course. I'll stay here till Helmer comes down; I'll tell him to give me my letter again—that it only involves my dismissal—that he shouldn't read it—

MRS. LINDE: No, Nils, don't call the letter back.

KROGSTAD: But wasn't that exactly why you wrote me to come here?

MRS. LINDE: Yes, in that first panic. But it's been a whole day and night since then, and in that time I've seen such incredible things in this house. Helmer's got to learn everything; this dreadful secret has to be aired; those two have to come to a full understanding; all these lies and evasions can't go on.

KROGSTAD: Well, then, if you want to chance it. But at least there's one thing I can do, and do right away—

MRS. LINDE [listening]: Go now, go quick! The dance is over. We're not safe another second.

KROGSTAD: I'll wait for you downstairs.

MRS. LINDE: Yes, please do; take me home.

KROGSTAD: I can't believe it; I've never been so happy. [He leaves by way of the outer door; the door between the room and the hall stays open.]

MRS. LINDE [straightening up a bit and getting together her street clothes]: How different now! How different! Someone to work for, to live for—a home to build. Well, it is worth the try! Oh, if they'd only come! [Listening.] Ah, there they are. Bundle up. [She picks up her hat and coat. NORA's and HELMER's voices can be heard outside; a key turns in

Reading Strategy
Recognizing Dramatic Tension In what way does the music of the tarantella affect the dramatic tension in this scene?

Literary Analysis
Theme What general theme about people or life does Mrs. Linde express?

evasions (ē vā′ zhənz) n. attempts to avoid duties or questions

the lock, and HELMER *brings* NORA *into the hall almost by force. She is wearing the Italian costume with a large black shawl about her; he has on evening dress, with a black domino[1] open over it.*]

NORA [*struggling in the doorway*]: No, no, no, not inside! I'm going up again. I don't want to leave so soon.

HELMER: But Nora dear—

NORA: Oh, I beg you, please, Torvald. From the bottom of my heart, *please*—only an hour more!

HELMER: Not a single minute, Nora darling. You know our agreement. Come on, in we go; you'll catch cold out here. [*In spite of her resistance, he gently draws her into the room.*]

MRS. LINDE: Good evening.

NORA: Kristine!

HELMER: Why, Mrs. Linde—are you here so late?

MRS. LINDE: Yes, I'm sorry, but I did want to see Nora in costume.

NORA: Have you been sitting here, waiting for me?

MRS. LINDE: Yes. I didn't come early enough; you were all upstairs; and then I thought I really couldn't leave without seeing you.

HELMER [*removing* NORA'S *shawl*]: Yes, take a good look. She's worth looking at, I can tell you that, Mrs. Linde. Isn't she lovely?

MRS. LINDE: Yes, I should say—

HELMER: A dream of loveliness, isn't she? That's what everyone thought at the party, too. But she's horribly stubborn—this sweet little thing. What's to be done with her? Can you imagine, I almost had to use force to pry her away.

NORA: Oh, Torvald, you're going to regret you didn't indulge me, even for just a half hour more.

HELMER: There, you see. She danced her tarantella and got a tumultuous [2] hand—which was well earned, although the performance may have

▲ **Critical Viewing**
In what way does Nora's attitude in Act Three match the expression of the actress in this picture? [**Connect**]

Reading Check

What does Mrs. Linde want Krogstad to do with the letter to Torvald?

---

1. **domino** (däm′ ə nō′) *n.* loose cloak or robe with wide sleeves and hood, worn with a mask at masquerades.
2. **tumultuous** (tōō mul′ chōō əs) *adj.* wild and noisy.

been a bit too <u>naturalistic</u>—I mean it rather overstepped the <u>proprieties</u> of art. But never mind—what's important is, she made a success, an overwhelming success. You think I could let her stay on after that and spoil the effect? Oh no; I took my lovely little Capri girl—my capricious[3] little Capri girl, I should say—took her under my arm; one quick tour of the ballroom, a curtsy to every side, and then—as they say in novels—the beautiful vision disappeared. An exit should always be effective, Mrs. Linde, but that's what I can't get Nora to grasp. Phew, its hot in here. [*Flings the domino on a chair and opens the door to his room.*] Why's it dark in here? Oh, yes, of course. Excuse me. [*He goes in and lights a couple of candles.*]

NORA [*in a sharp, breathless whisper*]: So?

MRS. LINDE [*quietly*]: I talked with him.

NORA: And—?

MRS. LINDE: Nora—you must tell your husband everything.

NORA [*dully*]: I knew it.

MRS. LINDE: You've got nothing to fear from Krogstad, but you have to speak out.

NORA: I won't tell.

MRS. LINDE: Then the letter will.

NORA: Thanks, Kristine. I know now what's to be done. Shh!

HELMER [*reentering*]: Well, then, Mrs. Linde—have you admired her?

MRS. LINDE: Yes, and now I'll say good night.

HELMER: Oh, come, so soon? Is this yours, this knitting?

MRS. LINDE: Yes, thanks. I nearly forgot it.

HELMER: Do you knit, then?

MRS. LINDE: Oh yes.

HELMER: You know what? You should embroider instead.

MRS. LINDE: Really? Why?

HELMER: Yes, because it's a lot prettier. See here, one holds the embroidery so, in the left hand, and then one guides the needle with the right—so—in an easy, sweeping curve—right?

MRS. LINDE: Yes, I guess that's—

HELMER: But, on the other hand, knitting—it can never be anything but ugly. Look, see here, the arms tucked in, the knitting needles going up and down, there's something Chinese about it. Ah, that was really a glorious champagne they served.

---

3. **capricious** (kə prish′ əs) *adj.* erratic; flighty.

MRS. LINDE: Yes, good night, Nora, and don't be stubborn anymore.

HELMER: Well put, Mrs. Linde!

MRS. LINDE: Good night, Mr. Helmer.

HELMER [*accompanying her to the door*]: Good night, good night. I hope you get home all right. I'd be very happy to—but you don't have far to go. Good night, good night. [*She leaves. He shuts the door after her and returns.*] There, now, at last we got her out the door. She's a deadly bore, that creature.

NORA: Aren't you pretty tired, Torvald?

HELMER: No, not a bit.

NORA: You're not sleepy?

HELMER: Not at all. On the contrary, I'm feeling quite exhilarated. But you? Yes, you really look tired and sleepy.

NORA: Yes, I'm very tired. Soon now I'll sleep.

HELMER: See! You see! I was right all along that we shouldn't stay longer.

NORA: Whatever you do is always right.

HELMER [*kissing her brow*]: Now my little lark talks sense. Say, did you notice what a time Rank was having tonight?

NORA: Oh, was he? I didn't get to speak with him.

HELMER: I scarcely did either, but it's a long time since I've seen him in such high spirits. [*Gazes at her a moment, then comes nearer her.*] Hm— it's marvelous, though, to be back home again—to be completely alone with you. Oh, you bewitchingly lovely young woman!

NORA: Torvald, don't look at me like that!

HELMER: Can't I look at my richest treasure? At all that beauty that's mine, mine alone—completely and utterly.

NORA [*moving around to the other side of the table*]: You mustn't talk to me that way tonight.

HELMER [*following her*]: The tarantella is still in your blood, I can see— and it makes you even more enticing. Listen. The guests are beginning to go. [*Dropping his voice.*] Nora—it'll soon be quiet through this whole house.

NORA: Yes, I hope so.

HELMER: You do, don't you, my love? Do you realize—when I'm out at a party like this with you—do you know why I talk to you so little, and keep such a distance away; just send you a stolen look now and then— you know why I do it? It's because I'm imagining then that you're my secret darling, my secret young bride-to-be, and that no one suspects there's anything between us.

NORA: Yes, yes; oh, yes, I know you're always thinking of me.

Literary Analysis
Theme What does Mrs. Linde suggest about everyone's right to become an individual when she tells Nora not to be stubborn?

Literary Analysis
Theme In what way is Torvald preventing Nora from finding happiness in their marriage?

Reading Check

What advice does Mrs. Linde give Nora regarding Torvald?

HELMER: And then when we leave and I place the shawl over those fine young rounded shoulders—over that wonderful curving neck—then I pretend that you're my young bride, that we're just coming from the wedding, that for the first time I'm bringing you into my house—that for the first time I'm alone with you—completely alone with you, your trembling young beauty! All this evening I've longed for nothing but you. When I saw you turn and sway in the tarantella—my blood was pounding till I couldn't stand it—that's why I brought you down here so early—

NORA: Go away, Torvald! Leave me alone. I don't want all this.

HELMER: What do you mean? Nora, you're teasing me. You will, won't you? Aren't I your husband—?

[*A knock at the outside door.*]

NORA [*startled*]: What's that?

HELMER [*going toward the hall*]: Who is it?

RANK [*outside*]: It's me. May I come in a moment?

HELMER [*with quiet irritation*]: Oh, what does he want now? [*Aloud.*] Hold on. [*Goes and opens the door.*] Oh, how nice that you didn't just pass us by!

RANK: I thought I heard your voice, and then I wanted so badly to have a look in. [*Lightly glancing about.*] Ah, me, these old familiar haunts. You have it snug and cozy in here, you two.

HELMER: You seemed to be having it pretty cozy upstairs, too.

RANK: Absolutely. Why shouldn't I? Why not take in everything in life? As much as you can, anyway, and as long as you can. The wine was superb—

HELMER: The champagne especially.

RANK: You noticed that too? It's amazing how much I could guzzle down.

NORA: Torvald also drank a lot of champagne this evening.

RANK: Oh?

NORA: Yes, and that always makes him so entertaining.

RANK: Well, why shouldn't one have a pleasant evening after a well-spent day?

HELMER: Well spent? I'm afraid I can't claim that.

RANK [*slapping him on the back*]: But I can, you see!

NORA: Dr. Rank, you must have done some scientific research today.

RANK: Quite so.

HELMER: Come now—little Nora talking about scientific research!

NORA: And can I congratulate you on the results?

RANK: Indeed you may.

Literary Analysis
Theme and Foreshadowing What personality change in Nora might be fore-shadowed when she speaks up to Torvald?

Reading Strategy
Recognizing Dramatic Tension What effect does Torvald's irritation have on the dramatic tension in this scene?

NORA: Then they were good?

RANK: The best possible for both doctor and patient—certainty.

NORA [*quickly and searchingly*]: Certainty?

RANK: Complete certainty. So don't I owe myself a gay evening afterwards?

NORA: Yes, you're right, Dr. Rank.

HELMER: I'm with you—just so long as you don't have to suffer for it in the morning.

RANK: Well, one never gets something for nothing in life.

NORA: Dr. Rank—are you very fond of masquerade parties?

RANK: Yes, if there's a good array of odd disguises—

NORA: Tell me, what should we two go as at the next masquerade?

HELMER: You little featherhead—already thinking of the next!

RANK: We two? I'll tell you what: you must go as Charmed Life—

HELMER: Yes, but find a costume for *that*!

RANK: Your wife can appear just as she looks every day.

HELMER: That was nicely put. But don't you know what you're going to be?

RANK: Yes, Helmer, I've made up my mind.

HELMER: Well?

RANK: At the next masquerade I'm going to be invisible.

HELMER: That's a funny idea.

RANK: They say there's a hat—black, huge—have you never heard of the hat that makes you invisible? You put it on, and then no one on earth can see you.

HELMER [*suppressing a smile*]: Ah, of course.

Reading Check

What does Dr. Rank tell Nora regarding the results of his scientific research?

Critical Viewing ▶
What information has Dr. Rank learned that might explain the serious demeanor of the actor in this picture? [**Connect**]

RANK: But I'm quite forgetting what I came for. Helmer, give me a cigar, one of the dark Havanas.

HELMER: With the greatest pleasure. [*Holds out his case.*]

RANK: Thanks. [*Takes one and cuts off the tip.*]

NORA [*striking a match*]: Let me give you a light.

RANK: Thank you. [*She holds the match for him; he lights the cigar.*] And now good-bye.

HELMER: Good-bye, good-bye, old friend.

NORA: Sleep well, Doctor.

RANK: Thanks for that wish.

NORA: Wish me the same.

RANK: You? All right, if you like— Sleep well. And thanks for the light. [*He nods to them both and leaves.*]

HELMER [*his voice subdued*]: He's been drinking heavily.

NORA [*absently*]: Could be. [HELMER *takes his keys from his pocket and goes out in the hall.*] Torvald—what are you after?

HELMER: Got to empty the mailbox; it's nearly full. There won't be room for the morning papers.

NORA: Are you working tonight?

HELMER: You know I'm not. Why—what's this? Someone's been at the lock.

NORA: At the lock—?

HELMER: Yes, I'm positive. What do you suppose—? I can't imagine one of the maids—? Here's a broken hairpin. Nora, it's yours—

NORA [*quickly*]: Then it must be the children—

HELMER: You'd better break them of that. Hm, hm—well, opened it after all. [*Takes the contents out and calls into the kitchen.*] Helene! Helene, would you put out the lamp in the hall. [*He returns to the room, shutting the hall door, then displays the handful of mail.*] Look how it's piled up. [*Sorting through them.*] Now what's this?

NORA [*at the window*]: The letter! Oh, Torvald, no!

HELMER: Two calling cards—from Rank.

NORA: From Dr. Rank?

HELMER [*examining them*]: "Dr. Rank, Consulting Physician." They were on top. He must have dropped them in as he left.

NORA: Is there anything on them?

HELMER: There's a black cross over the name. See? That's a gruesome notion. He could almost be announcing his own death.

NORA: That's just what he's doing.

Reading Strategy
Recognizing Dramatic Tension Do you think Dr. Rank's secrecy about his illness creates dramatic tension in this scene? Why or why not?

Literary Analysis
Theme and Foreshadowing What possible confrontation might be foreshadowed when Torvald goes to the mailbox?

HELMER: What! You've heard something? Something he's told you?

NORA: Yes. That when those cards came, he'd be taking his leave of us. He'll shut himself in now and die.

HELMER: Ah, my poor friend! Of course I knew he wouldn't be here much longer. But so soon— And then to hide himself away like a wounded animal.

NORA: If it has to happen, then it's best it happens in silence—don't you think so, Torvald?

HELMER [*pacing up and down*]: He'd grown right into our lives. I simply can't imagine him gone. He with his suffering and loneliness—like a dark cloud setting off our sunlit happiness. Well, maybe it's best this way. For him, at least. [*Standing still.*] And maybe for us too, Nora. Now we're thrown back on each other, completely. [*Embracing her.*] Oh you, my darling wife, how can I hold you close enough? You know what, Nora—time and again I've wished you were in some terrible danger, just so I could stake my life and soul and everything, for your sake.

NORA [*tearing herself away, her voice firm and decisive*]: Now you must read your mail, Torvald.

HELMER: No, no, not tonight. I want to stay with you, dearest.

NORA: With a dying friend on your mind?

HELMER: You're right. We've both had a shock. There's ugliness between us—these thoughts of death and corruption. We'll have to get free of them first. Until then—we'll stay apart.

NORA [*clinging about his neck*]: Torvald—good night! Good night!

HELMER [*kissing her on the cheek*]: Good night, little songbird. Sleep well, Nora. I'll be reading my mail now. [*He takes the letters into his room and shuts the door after him.*]

NORA [*with bewildered glances, groping about, seizing* HELMER's *domino, throwing it around her, and speaking in short, hoarse, broken whispers*]: Never see him again. Never, never. [*Putting her shawl over her head.*] Never see the children either—them, too. Never, never. Oh, the freezing black water! The depths—down—Oh, I wish it were over—He has it now; he's reading it—now. Oh no, no, not yet. Torvald, good-bye, you and the children—[*She starts for the hall; as she does,* HELMER *throws open his door and stands with an open letter in his hand.*]

HELMER: Nora!

NORA [*screams*]: Oh—!

HELMER: What is this? You know what's in this letter?

NORA: Yes, I know. Let me go! Let me out!

HELMER [*holding her back*]: Where are you going?

NORA [*struggling to break loose*]: You can't save me, Torvald!

Literary Analysis
Theme and Foreshadowing Do you think Torvald's lines foreshadow that he will take the blame for Nora? Explain.

**Reading Check**

What discovery does Torvald make when he empties the mailbox?

HELMER [*slumping back*]: True! Then it's true what he writes? How horrible! No, no it's impossible—it can't be true.

NORA: It *is* true. I've loved you more than all this world.

HELMER: Ah, none of your slippery tricks.

NORA [*taking one step toward him*]: Torvald—!

HELMER: What is this you've blundered into!

NORA: Just let me loose. You're not going to suffer for my sake. You're not going to take on my guilt.

HELMER: No more playacting. [*Locks the hall door.*] You stay right here and give me a reckoning. You understand what you've done? Answer! You understand?

NORA [*looking squarely at him, her face hardening*]: Yes. I'm beginning to understand everything now.

▲ **Critical Viewing**
In what ways does this photograph capture the change in the relationship between Torvald and Nora? [**Interpret**]

HELMER [*striding about*]: Oh, what an awful awakening! In all these eight years—she who was my pride and joy—a <u>hypocrite</u>, a liar—worse, worse—a criminal! How infinitely disgusting it all is! The shame! [NORA *says nothing and goes on looking straight at him. He stops in front of her.*] I should have suspected something of the kind. I should have known. All your father's flimsy values— Be still! All your father's flimsy values have come out in you. No religion, no morals, no sense of duty— Oh, how I'm punished for letting him off! I did it for your sake, and you repay me like this.

NORA: Yes, like this.

HELMER: Now you've wrecked all my happiness—ruined my whole future. Oh, it's awful to think of. I'm in a cheap little <u>grafter</u>'s hands; he can do anything he wants with me, ask for anything, play with me like a puppet—and I can't breathe a word. I'll be swept down miserably into the depths on account of a featherbrained woman.

NORA: When I'm gone from this world, you'll be free.

HELMER: Oh, quit posing. Your father had a mess of those speeches too. What good would that ever do me if you were gone from this world, as you say? Not the slightest. He can still make the whole thing known; and if he does, I could be falsely suspected as your accomplice. They might even think that I was behind it—that I put you up to it. And all that I can thank you for—you that I've coddled the whole of our marriage. Can you see now what you've done to me?

NORA [*icily calm*]: Yes.

HELMER: It's so incredible, I just can't grasp it. But we'll have to patch up whatever we can. Take off the shawl. I said, take it off! I've got to appease him somehow or other. The thing has to be hushed up at any cost. And as for you and me, it's got to seem like everything between us is just as it was—to the outside world, that is. You'll go right on living in this house, of course. But you can't be allowed to bring up the children; I don't dare trust you with them— Oh, to have to say this to someone I've loved so much! Well, that's done with. From now on happiness doesn't matter; all that matters is saving the bits and pieces, the appearance— [*The doorbell rings.* HELMER *starts.*] What's that? And so late. Maybe the worst—? You think he'd—? Hide, Nora! Say you're sick. [NORA *remains standing motionless.* HELMER *goes and opens the door.*]

MAID [*half dressed, in the hall*]: A letter for Mrs. Helmer.

HELMER: I'll take it. [*Snatches the letter and shuts the door.*] Yes, it's from him. You don't get it; I'm reading it myself.

NORA: Then read it.

HELMER [*by the lamp*]: I hardly dare. We may be ruined, you and I. But—I've got to know. [*Rips open the letter, skims through a few lines, glances at an enclosure, then cries out joyfully.*] Nora! [NORA *looks inquiringly at him.*] Nora! Wait!—better check it again— Yes, yes, it's true. I'm saved. Nora, I'm saved!

hypocrite (hip´ə krit´) *n.* someone who merely pretends to be virtuous

grafter (graft´ər) *n.* someone who takes advantage of his or her position to gain money or property dishonestly

Literary Analysis
Theme and Foreshadowing In what way might Nora's "icily calm" reaction foreshadow her behavior from this point on?

**Reading Check**

Other than Krogstad, whom does Torvald now consider a criminal and a grafter?

NORA: And I?

HELMER: You too, of course. We're both saved, both of us. Look. He's sent back your note. He says he's sorry and ashamed—that a happy development in his life—oh, who cares what he says! Nora, we're saved! No one can hurt you. Oh, Nora, Nora—but first, this ugliness all has to go. Let me see— [*Takes a look at the note.*] No, I don't want to see it; I want the whole thing to fade like a dream. [*Tears the note and both letters to pieces, throws them into the stove and watches them burn.*] There—now there's nothing left— He wrote that since Christmas Eve you— Oh, they must have been three terrible days for you, Nora.

NORA: I fought a hard fight.

HELMER: And suffered pain and saw no escape but— No, we're not going to dwell on anything unpleasant. We'll just be grateful and keep on repeating: it's over now, it's over! You hear me, Nora? You don't seem to realize—it's over. What's it mean—that frozen look? Oh, poor little Nora, I understand. You can't believe I've forgiven you. But I have Nora; I swear I have. I know that what you did, you did out of love for me.

NORA: That's true.

HELMER: You loved me the way a wife ought to love her husband. It's simply the means that you couldn't judge. But you think I love you any the less for not knowing how to handle your affairs? No, no—just lean on me; I'll guide you and teach you. I wouldn't be a man if this feminine helplessness didn't make you twice as attractive to me. You mustn't mind those sharp words I said—that was all in the first confusion of thinking my world had collapsed. I've forgiven you, Nora; I swear I've forgiven you.

NORA: My thanks for your forgiveness. [*She goes out through the door, right.*]

HELMER: No, wait— [*Peers in.*] What are you doing in there?

NORA [*inside*]: Getting out of my costume.

HELMER [*by the open door*]: Yes, do that. Try to calm yourself and collect your thoughts again, my frightened little songbird. You can rest easy now; I've got wide wings to shelter you with. [*Walking about close by the door.*] How snug and nice our home is, Nora. You're safe here; I'll keep you like a hunted dove I've rescued out of a hawk's claws. I'll bring peace to your poor, shuddering heart. Gradually it'll happen, Nora; you'll see. Tomorrow all this will look different to you; then everything will be as it was. I won't have to go on repeating I forgive you; you'll feel it for yourself. How can you imagine I'd ever conceivably want to disown you—or even blame you in any way? Ah, you don't know a man's heart, Nora. For a man there's something indescribably sweet and satisfying in knowing he's forgiven his wife—and forgiven her out of a full and open heart. It's as if she belongs to him in two ways now: in a sense he's given her fresh into the world again, and she's become his wife and his child as well. From now on that's what you'll be to me—you little,

Reading Strategy
Recognizing Dramatic Tension In what ways does Torvald change when the dramatic tension breaks?

Literary Analysis
Theme and Foreshadowing Do you think Torvald recognizes his wife's individuality? Explain.

bewildered, helpless thing. Don't be afraid of anything, Nora; just open your heart to me, and I'll be conscience and will to you both—[NORA *enters in her regular clothes.*] What's this? Not in bed? You've changed your dress?

NORA: Yes, Torvald, I've changed my dress.

HELMER: But why now, so late?

NORA: Tonight I'm not sleeping.

HELMER: But Nora dear—

NORA [*looking at her watch*]: It's still not so very late. Sit down, Torvald; we have a lot to talk over. [*She sits at one side of the table.*]

HELMER: Nora—what is this? That hard expression—

NORA: Sit down. This'll take some time. I have a lot to say.

HELMER [*sitting at the table directly opposite her*]: You worry me, Nora. And I don't understand you.

NORA: No, that's exactly it. You don't understand me. And I've never understood you either—until tonight. No, don't interrupt. You can just listen to what I say. We're closing out accounts, Torvald.

HELMER: How do you mean that?

NORA [*after a short pause*]: Doesn't anything strike you about our sitting here like this?

HELMER: What's that?

NORA: We've been married now eight years. Doesn't it occur to you that this is the first time we two, you and I, man and wife, have ever talked seriously together?

HELMER: What do you mean—seriously?

NORA: In eight whole years—longer even—right from our first acquaintance, we've never exchanged a serious word on any serious thing.

HELMER: You mean I should constantly go and involve you in problems you couldn't possibly help me with?

NORA: I'm not talking of problems. I'm saying that we've never sat down seriously together and tried to get to the bottom of anything.

HELMER: But dearest, what good would that ever do you?

NORA: That's the point right there: you've never understood me. I've been wronged greatly, Torvald—first by Papa, and then by you.

HELMER: What! By us—the two people who've loved you more than anyone else?

NORA [*shaking her head*]: You never loved me. You've thought it fun to be in love with me, that's all.

HELMER: Nora, what a thing to say!

bewildered (bē wil′dərd) *adj.* puzzled, confused

Literary Analysis
Theme and Foreshadowing What do you think Nora's change of dress foreshadows? Explain.

Literary Analysis
Theme In what way do these lines reflect the theme that a successful relationship is based on equality and partnership?

**Reading Check**
According to Torvald, what motivated Nora to get involved with Krogstad?

NORA: Yes, it's true now, Torvald. When I lived at home with Papa, he told me all his opinions, so I had the same ones too; or if they were different I hid them, since he wouldn't have cared for that. He used to call me his doll-child, and he played with me the way I played with my dolls. Then I came into your house—

HELMER: How can you speak of our marriage like that?

NORA [*unperturbed*]: I mean, then I went from Papa's hands into yours. You arranged everything to your own taste, and so I got the same taste as you—or I pretended to; I can't remember. I guess a little of both, first one, then the other. Now when I look back, it seems as if I'd lived here like a beggar—just from hand to mouth. I've lived by doing tricks for you, Torvald. But that's the way you wanted it. It's a great sin what you and Papa did to me. You're to blame that nothing's become of me.

HELMER: Nora, how unfair and ungrateful you are! Haven't you been happy here?

NORA: No, never. I thought so—but I never have.

HELMER: Not—not happy!

NORA: No, only lighthearted. And you've always been so kind to me. But our home's been nothing but a playpen. I've been your doll-wife here, just as at home I was Papa's doll-child. And in turn the children have been my dolls. I thought it was fun when you played with me, just as they thought it fun when I played with them. That's been our marriage, Torvald.

HELMER: There's some truth in what you're saying—under all the raving exaggeration. But it'll all be different after this. Playtime's over; now for the schooling.

NORA: Whose schooling—mine or the children's?

HELMER: Both yours and the children's, dearest.

NORA: Oh, Torvald, you're not the man to teach me to be a good wife to you.

HELMER: And you can say that?

NORA: And I—how am I equipped to bring up children?

HELMER: Nora!

NORA: Didn't you say a moment ago that that was no job to trust me with?

HELMER: In a flare of temper! Why fasten on that?

NORA: Yes, but you were so very right. I'm not up to the job. There's another job I have to do first. I have to try to educate myself. You can't help me with that. I've got to do it alone. And that's why I'm leaving you now.

HELMER [*jumping up*]: What's that?

Literary Analysis
Theme Which of the play's themes is Nora stating in these lines? Explain.

Reading Strategy
Recognizing Dramatic Tension What does Torvald stand to lose if Nora leaves him?

NORA: I have to stand completely alone, if I'm ever going to discover myself and the world out there. So I can't go on living with you.

HELMER: Nora, Nora!

NORA: I want to leave right away. Kristine should put me up for the night—

HELMER: You're insane! You've no right! I forbid you!

NORA: From here on, there's no use forbidding me anything. I'll take with me whatever is mine. I don't want a thing from you, either now or later.

HELMER: What kind of madness is this?

NORA: Tomorrow I'm going home—I mean, home where I came from. It'll be easier up there to find something to do.

HELMER: Oh, you blind, incompetent child!

NORA: I must learn to be competent, Torvald.

HELMER: Abandon your home, your husband, your children! And you're not even thinking what people will say.

NORA: I can't be concerned about that. I only know how essential this is.

HELMER: Oh, it's outrageous. So you'll run out like this on your most sacred vows.

NORA: What do you think are my most sacred vows?

HELMER: And I have to tell you that! Aren't they your duties to your husband and children?

NORA: I have other duties equally sacred.

HELMER: That isn't true. What duties are they?

NORA: Duties to myself.

HELMER: Before all else, you're a wife and a mother.

NORA: I don't believe in that anymore. I believe that, before all else, I'm a human being, no less than you—or anyway, I ought to try to become one. I know the majority thinks you're right, Torvald, and plenty of books agree with you, too. But I can't go on believing what the majority says, or what's written in books. I have to think over these things myself and try to understand them.

HELMER: Why can't you understand your place in your own home? On a point like that, isn't there one everlasting guide you can turn to? Where's your religion?

NORA: Oh, Torvald, I'm really not sure what religion is.

HELMER: What—?

NORA: I only know what the minister said when I was confirmed. He told me religion was this thing and that. When I get clear and away by

Literature in context — History Connection

Independent Women, 1879

A Doll House shocked its original audience because it addressed a controversial issue: the status of women. In 1879, when the play was written, it was virtually unthinkable in Europe and America that a middle-class wife could be a wholly independent person. Few women were highly educated or had careers of their own. Women in Norway could not vote until 1913—in the United States and Britain, women did not win full voting rights until 1920 and 1928, respectively.

When Nora tells Torvald she is leaving him and her children, they both recognize the difficulties she will face on her own. Torvald—and Ibsen's audience—would find Nora's choice shocking, and perhaps even foolhardy.

Literary Analysis
Theme Who or what is the "majority" whose opinion Nora questions?

✔Reading Check
What decision has Nora made about her life with Torvald?

myself, I'll go into that problem too. I'll see if what the minister said was right, or, in any case, if it's right for me.

HELMER: A young woman your age shouldn't talk like that. If religion can't move you, I can try to rouse your conscience. You do have some moral feeling? Or, tell me—has that gone too?

NORA: It's not easy to answer that, Torvald. I simply don't know. I'm all confused about these things. I just know I see them so differently from you. I find out, for one thing, that the law's not at all what I'd thought—but I can't get it through my head that the law is fair. A woman hasn't a right to protect her dying father or save her husband's life! I can't believe that.

HELMER: You talk like a child. You don't know anything of the world you live in.

NORA: No, I don't. But now I'll begin to learn for myself. I'll try to discover who's right, the world or I.

HELMER: Nora, you're sick; you've got a fever. I almost think you're out of your head.

NORA: I've never felt more clearheaded and sure in my life.

HELMER: And—clearheaded and sure—you're leaving your husband and children?

NORA: Yes.

HELMER: Then there's only one possible reason.

NORA: What?

HELMER: You no longer love me.

NORA: No. That's exactly it.

HELMER: Nora! You can't be serious!

NORA: Oh, this is so hard, Torvald—you've been so kind to me always. But I can't help it. I don't love you anymore.

HELMER [*struggling for composure*]: Are you also clearheaded and sure about that?

NORA: Yes, completely. That's why I can't go on staying here.

HELMER: Can you tell me what I did to lose your love?

NORA: Yes, I can tell you. It was this evening when the miraculous thing didn't come—then I knew you weren't the man I'd imagined.

HELMER: Be more explicit; I don't follow you.

NORA: I've waited now so patiently eight long years—for, my Lord, I know miracles don't come every day. Then this crisis broke over me, and such a certainty filled me: *now* the miraculous event would occur. While Krogstad's letter was lying out there, I never for an instant dreamed that you could give in to his terms. I was so utterly sure you'd

Literary Analysis
Theme and Foreshadowing What future conflicts might Nora's lines foreshadow?

Reading Strategy
Recognizing Dramatic Tension In what way does Nora raise the stakes, making it clear that she and Torvald may lose more than Torvald imagined?

◀ **Critical Viewing**
What characteristics does
Nora share with this china
doll? In what ways is Nora
very different? [**Compare
and Contrast**]

say to him: go on, tell your tale to the whole wide world. And when he'd
done that—

HELMER: Yes, what then? When I'd delivered my own wife into shame
and disgrace—!

NORA: When he'd done that, I was so utterly sure that you'd step forward, take the blame on yourself and say: I am the guilty one.

HELMER: Nora—!

NORA: You're thinking I'd never accept such a sacrifice from you? No, of
course not. But what good would my protests be against you? That was
the miracle I was waiting for, in terror and hope. And to stave that off, I
would have taken my life.

HELMER: I'd gladly work for you day and night, Nora—and take on pain
and deprivation. But there's no one who gives up honor for love.

NORA: Millions of women have done just that.

HELMER: Oh, you think and talk like a silly child.

NORA: Perhaps. But you neither think nor talk like the man I could join
myself to. When your big fright was over—and it wasn't from any threat
against me, only for what might damage you—when all the danger was
past, for you it was just as if nothing had happened. I was exactly the
same, your little lark, your doll, that you'd have to handle with double
care now that I'd turned out so brittle and frail. [*Gets up.*] Torvald—in
that instant it dawned on me that for eight years I've been living here
with a stranger, and that I'd even conceived three children—oh, I can't
stand the thought of it! I could tear myself to bits.

Reading Strategy
**Recognizing Dramatic
Tension** In what ways
does Nora's speech
explain the increasing dramatic tension throughout
the play?

✓**Reading Check**
How long has Nora waited
for some "miraculous"
change to occur in her life?

The Customs, National Gallery, London

▲ **Critical Viewing** Which details in this painting suit this final scene of *A Doll House*? **[Interpret]**

HELMER [*heavily*]: I see. There's a gulf that's opened between us—that's clear. Oh, but Nora, can't we bridge it somehow?

NORA: The way I am now, I'm no wife for you.

HELMER: I have the strength to make myself over.

NORA: Maybe—if your doll gets taken away.

HELMER: But to part! To part from you! No, Nora, no—I can't imagine it.

NORA [*going out, right*]: All the more reason why it has to be. [*She reenters with her coat and a small overnight bag, which she puts on a chair by the table.*]

HELMER: Nora, Nora, not now! Wait till tomorrow.

NORA: I can't spend the night in a strange man's room.

HELMER: But couldn't we live here like brother and sister—

NORA: You know very well how long that would last. [*Throws her shawl about her.*] Good-bye, Torvald. I won't look in on the children. I know they're in better hands than mine. The way I am now, I'm no use to them.

HELMER: But someday, Nora—someday—?

NORA: How can I tell? I haven't the least idea what'll become of me.

HELMER: But you're my wife, now and wherever you go.

NORA: Listen, Torvald—I've heard that when a wife deserts her husband's house just as I'm doing, then the law frees him from all responsibility. In any case, I'm freeing you from being responsible. Don't feel yourself bound, any more than I will. There has to be absolute freedom for us both. Here, take your ring back. Give me mine.

HELMER: That too?

NORA: That too.

HELMER: There it is.

NORA: Good. Well, now it's all over, I'm putting the keys here. The maids know all about keeping up the house—better than I do. Tomorrow, after I've left town, Kristine will stop by to pack up everything that's mine from home. I'd like those things shipped up to me.

HELMER: Over! All over! Nora, won't you ever think about me?

NORA: I'm sure I'll think of you often, and about the children and the house here.

HELMER: May I write you?

NORA: No—never. You're not to do that.

HELMER: Oh, but let me send you—

NORA: Nothing. Nothing.

HELMER: Or help you if you need it.

Reading Strategy
Recognizing Dramatic Tension Which of Nora's words in this line best reveals the dramatic tension in the scene?

Literary Analysis
Theme and Foreshadowing Identify three details in Acts One and Two that foreshadow Nora's realization that she knows very little about her own home.

**Reading Check**
From what is Nora freeing Torvald?

NORA: No. I accept nothing from strangers.

HELMER: Nora—can I never be more than a stranger to you?

NORA [*picking up the overnight bag*]: Ah, Torvald—it would take the greatest miracle of all—

HELMER: Tell me the greatest miracle!

NORA: You and I both would have to transform ourselves to the point that— Oh, Torvald, I've stopped believing in miracles.

HELMER: But I'll believe. Tell me! Transform ourselves to the point that?

NORA: That our living together could be a true marriage. [*She goes out down the hall.*]

HELMER [*sinks down on a chair by the door, face buried in his hands*]: Nora! Nora! [*Looking about and rising.*] Empty. She's gone. [*A sudden hope leaps in him.*] The greatest miracle—?

[*From below, the sound of a door slamming shut.*]

Review and Assess

Thinking About Act Three

1. **Respond:** What is your response to Nora's decision to leave her husband and children? Explain.

2. **(a) Recall:** What plan does Mrs. Linde propose for herself and Krogstad? **(b) Analyze:** How does Mrs. Linde manage to solve several problems at once with this plan? **(c) Compare and Contrast:** What advantages do Mrs. Linde and Krogstad have over Torvald and Nora?

3. **(a) Recall:** What is Torvald's reaction when he reads the first letter from Krogstad? **(b) Draw Conclusions:** What does Torvald's reaction indicate to Nora about her husband's personality?

4. **(a) Recall:** What help does Nora agree to accept from Torvald in the future? **(b) Speculate:** Why do you think Nora refuses his help? **(c) Make a Judgment:** Do you think Torvald truly understands Nora's reasons for leaving? Why or why not?

5. **(a) Synthesize:** In what way does the play's title relate to Nora's discoveries about Torvald and to her decision to leave him? **(b) Speculate:** Do you think Nora might find happiness in another relationship in the future? Explain.

6. **Relate:** Which of Nora's experiences are still relevant today? Explain.

Review and Assess

Literary Analysis

Theme

1. (a) One **theme** of *A Doll House* relates to discovering the keys to a successful relationship. Use a chart like the one shown to cite three examples of dialogue from Act Three that relate to this theme.

Character	Dialogue	Keys to a Successful Relationship

   (b) What conclusions about a successful relationship can you draw from the dialogue you noted?

2. Identify three details supporting the theme that society and authority hinder the development of the individual.

3. Which characters embody the theme that all people must live their lives according to their convictions? Explain.

Connecting Literary Elements

4. Mrs. Linde says to Krogstad, "Anyone who's sold herself for somebody else once isn't going to do it again." In what way does this comment **foreshadow** Nora's decision to leave Torvald?

5. (a) What events are foreshadowed when Torvald remarks that "an exit should always be effective, Mrs. Linde, but that's what I can't get Nora to grasp"? (b) What is ironic or unexpected about Torvald's statement?

Reading Strategy

Recognizing Dramatic Tension

6. (a) Which moment in Act Three marks the height of **dramatic tension**? (b) Which conflicts are resolved when the dramatic tension breaks? (c) Which conflicts remain unresolved?

7. (a) What is at stake for Nora if she remains with Torvald? (b) List three lines in Act Three that show the extent to which Torvald fails to understand what Nora stands to lose. (c) Explain the way in which those lines increase the dramatic tension.

Extend Understanding

8. **Career Connection:** Consider the résumé Nora might build. What marketable skills has Nora acquired during her years with Torvald that will allow her to support herself without his help?

Integrate Language Skills

Vocabulary Development Lesson

Word Analysis: Greek Prefix *hypo-*

The Greek prefix *hypo-* means "under," "less than," or "slightly." Use your understanding of the meaning of *hypo-* to identify the word that best completes each sentence below.

a. hypocrite   **b.** hypothermia

1. After being rescued from the cold river, she suffered from ___.
2. The ___ pretended to be someone that he was not.

Spelling Strategy

Both the letter *i* and the letter *y* can represent either the short or long *i* sound in words. Complete each word below with either the letter *i* or the letter *y*.

1. h___pocrite
2. m___stery
3. tr___logy
4. v___carious

Grammar and Style Lesson

Infinitives and Infinitive Phrases

An **infinitive** is a verb form consisting of the base form of a verb, usually with the word *to*. An **infinitive phrase** combines an infinitive plus its complements or modifiers to act as a single part of speech. Infinitive phrases function as nouns, adjectives, or adverbs.

> **As a Noun:** "Life's taught me never <u>to trust fine phrases</u>. . . ." (direct object of the verb *taught*)
>
> **As an Adjective:** "Someone <u>to work for</u>, <u>to live for</u>. . . ." (modifying the pronoun *someone*)
>
> **As an Adverb:** "How am I equipped <u>to bring up children</u>?" (modifying the verb *equipped*)

Fluency: Context

Review the vocabulary words on page 922. Then, complete each of the following sentences.

1. The ____ looted a local business.
2. She used her____ ways to convince her brother to finish her chores.
3. By paying attention to social ___, he earned a spotless reputation.
4. The child seemed ___ by the unjust punishment.
5. The suspect responded with ___ to all questions.
6. The lawyer was branded a ___ when he committed perjury on the witness stand.
7. The audience was shocked by the ___ appearance of the robot.

Practice Copy each item below, underlining the infinitive phrase and identifying its function in the sentence.

1. "Do we two have anything more to talk about?"
2. ". . . you hadn't the right to abandon me for somebody else's sake."
3. "I've learned to be realistic."
4. ". . . I did want to see Nora in costume."
5. "That is why I brought you down to sit with me."

Writing Application Write a paragraph about Nora in which you use three infinitive phrases. Underline each phrase, and identify its function.

W/G Prentice Hall Writing and Grammar Connection: Diamond Level, Chapter 19, Section 2

Writing Lesson

Writing a Persuasive Essay

When one is faced with a difficult choice, it can be extremely hard to make the right decision. Write a persuasive essay in which you argue for or against Nora's decision to leave Torvald, basing your arguments on events or lines from the play.

Prewriting Review the play and decide whether or not you agree with Nora's decision. Create an outline, listing points that confirm your opinion and including references to the play that support each point.

Drafting As you write, anticipate your readers' objections to the position you are taking. For example, if you think Nora's decision is the right one, you might consider who will take care of Nora's children or how she might support herself. Answer each objection, and write your counterarguments clearly and effectively.

Revising Review your draft, removing any empty or unnecessary words or phrases that do not add to your argument.

Model: Removing Unnecessary Words or Phrases

~~It seems to me that~~ Nora could never be happy if her marriage continued in the same pattern. Her husband's weaknesses and her own shortcomings force her to seek ~~a sense of~~ independence.

> Removing unnecessary words and phrases focuses your sentences and makes them more effective.

WG *Prentice Hall Writing and Grammar Connection: Diamond Level, Chapter 7, Section 4*

Extension Activities

Listening and Speaking In a small group, participate in a **round-table discussion** of the themes in *A Doll House.* Follow these rules of courtesy:

1. Pay attention as others speak.
2. Do not interrupt.
3. Speak clearly.

Compare the opinions shared in the discussion with those of other groups in your class.
[Group Activity]

Research and Technology Choose one character and scene from *A Doll House* and develop a **costume design display.** Begin by researching the dress of the time. Make a sketch of the character wearing a costume appropriate for the scene. Choose fabric swatches and include them in a display that you share with your class.

 **Take It to the Net** PHschool.com

Go online for an additional research activity using the Internet.

A Closer Look

The Slamming of the Door

The slamming of the door at the end of *A Doll House* was a sound heard round the world.

The last words of Henrik Ibsen's play *A Doll House* are not spoken by any of the characters. Rather, they are a single stage direction: "From below, the sound of a door slamming shut."

In 1879, when the play was first performed, that sound—a symbol of Nora's escape from her constrictive marriage—represented a direct challenge to the existing beliefs concerning the roles of men and women. In the decades after the publication of the play, the status of women in Western society began undergoing a dramatic transformation. Today, many scholars view Nora's slamming of the door as a pivotal point in the evolution of the modern feminist movement. In fact, as the great British playwright George Bernard Shaw wrote, the slamming of the door can be regarded as "the end of a chapter in human history."

Women in the Nineteenth Century At the time Ibsen wrote *A Doll House*, the idea that a woman might choose to leave her husband and children in order to live independently was not merely unacceptable—it was inconceivable for the vast majority of people. Common belief suggested that women were inferior to men, a notion that was supported by the laws of that time. As a result, women did not enjoy the same rights and privileges as men. Few women were educated. They could not own property. They could not vote. They had severely limited career opportunities. Women were expected to marry and to devote their lives to serving their husbands and raising their children. They were expected to obey their husbands without question.

Nora's Rebellion When Nora leaves Torvald and her children in order to educate herself and seek her own fulfillment, she rebels not only against Torvald's authority but also against the expectations of society as a whole. She first tells Torvald that she is leaving him, and he forbids her to go. Then, he warns her that she is "not even thinking about what people will say." Nora responds that she is not concerned with other people's opinions, adding that her duty to herself is more important than her duties as a wife and mother. She declares, "I'm a human being, no less than you—or anyway, I ought to try to become one. I know the majority thinks you're right, Torvald, and plenty of books agree with you, too. But I can't go on believing what the majority says, or what's written in books."

The Impact of Nora's Rebellion When Nora finally leaves and she slams the door shut behind her, Torvald remains in a state of shock and dismay. Similarly, Ibsen's first audiences were shocked and dismayed by what they saw

and heard. Yet, this sense of shock forced many people to reevaluate their ideas about men and women; in the years that followed the play's first performances, women began to gain some of the rights and privileges that they had previously been denied. For example, one historian points out that "within five years of the publication of *A Doll House*, women were being admitted to the private Liberal Club in the tradition-bound city of Oslo" in Ibsen's native land of Norway.

During the course of the twentieth century, the status of women in most countries of the world continued to improve. Women gained the right to vote and to own property. In addition, the educational and professional opportunities available to women expanded tremendously. Many women became involved in politics; in a number of countries, including Great Britain, Pakistan, and the Philippines, women were elected to the highest government posts.

Ibsen and Feminism Because of the stories he tells in *A Doll House* and other works, Ibsen is often regarded as one of the pioneering spirits in the feminist movement. Although Ibsen himself might have argued that he did not deserve this label, it cannot be denied that he was one of the first men to openly express concern about the status of women. Ibsen's notes to *A Doll House* clearly indicate that he wanted the play to capture the ways in which society restricted women's freedom and growth. He wrote, "There are two kinds of spiritual law, two kinds of conscience, one in man and another, altogether different, in women. They do not understand each other; but in practical life the woman is judged by man's law, as though she were not a woman but a man. . . . A woman cannot be herself in the society of the present day, which is exclusively a masculine society. . . ."

Today, many questions about gender remain unanswered. For example, are the psyches of men and women fundamentally different, as Ibsen suggests? Yet, even without answers to these questions, common attitudes and laws no longer support the notion that women are inferior. Nora's slamming of the door may no longer shock, but the echoes it created continue to resonate.

▲ Critical Viewing
In what ways can doors, like those shown above, serve as symbols for ideas or emotions? [Generalize]

READING INFORMATIONAL MATERIALS

Critical Reviews

About Critical Reviews

A critical review analyzes and evaluates a product, an artistic performance, or even the behavior of a person or group. As the name suggests, critical reviews usually contain strong opinions. In this context, however, the word *critical* can mean either a positive or a negative judgment. Most critical reviews will contain the following:

- a brief summary of the subject matter
- a carefully thought-out and stated opinion
- supporting evidence

Because the purpose of a critical review is often to persuade, expect to find argumentative presentations and powerful language.

Reading Strategy

Comparing and Contrasting Critical Reviews

Opinions can vary greatly from person to person. For objectivity, you should read multiple critical reviews on a single subject to arrive at the "big picture" of what is being reviewed. Compare the reviews to determine where critics share the same point of view. Then, note the contrasts—points where the critics differ. Making these comparisons and contrasts will help you evaluate both the critical reviews and their subject matter.

As critics, the writers of the following critical reviews saw the same performance of Ibsen's *A Doll's House*. Yet their impressions of the show—particularly the performance of the leading actress—range from glowing praise to lukewarm acceptance. To determine an overall impression of the show, complete the following chart by filling in the critics' names and opinions as you read the reviews.

Critical Reviews			
Critic			
Lead Actress's Performance			
Director and/or Script			
Overall Evaluation (+ or -)			

CurtainUp Review: A Doll's House

by Judd Hollander & Sue Feinberg

From the moment she steps onto the stage of the Belasco Theater, Janet McTeer delivers a riveting performance as Nora Helmer, the heroine of Henrik Ibsen's *A Doll's House,* currently playing at the Belasco Theatre.

Set in a small Norwegian town during Christmas 1879 (and inspired by actual events), the play tells the story of a young wife (McTeer) and mother who's still pretty much a child herself. This time out, however, the 118-year-old work has been given a 1990s feel. McTeer's Nora is a whirling dervish, full of life and laughter, a woman who would be more at home on the stage of an English Music Hall than with her husband Torvald (Owen Teale) and three children. (Her idea of a perfect life is having "pots and pots and pots of money.")

After years of struggle, the couple has finally achieved a measure of financial security, thanks to Torvald's new job as a bank manager. But then a ghost from Nora's past appears in the form of Nils Krogstad (Peter Gowen). Several years earlier, Nora secretly borrowed money for a trip to a warmer climate to allow her desperately ill husband to recover. In order to guarantee the loan, she forged a signature on a contract. Krogstad wants his money back and Nora, not able to give it, is terrified that Torvald will learn the truth.

As events unfold, Nora slowly comes to realize that the "perfect" life she has led is nothing but a fairy tale. Her life has been that of a *doll* to be pampered and protected, first by her father and then by her husband. But even as she's forced to face reality, she tries to do the *right* thing, only to realize that what she loves the most is the biggest lie of all.

Ibsen's work caused quite a shock when it first premiered in 1879 and was heralded as one of the first modern, post-Shakespeare "women's plays." McTeer takes the role of Ibsen's

> This critical review begins with a brief summary of the subject matter.

---

* **CurtainUp.com is an online theater magazine. URL: www.curtainup.com**

doll wife and brilliantly makes it her own. Her Nora runs the gamut of emotions from fear to rage to loathing to desperation. Even her demeanor and manner alter and she seems to age before our eyes, gaining not experience or wisdom, but the understanding that these are the qualities she must find. Just before the show ends, there's a scene where she mocks her former "sing-song" persona. That Nora is light-years removed from the one we first met only three hours or, according to the play's time frame, three days before.

While McTeer is the play's linchpin, she does not have the toughest role in the piece. That honor goes to Owen Teale. His Torvald at first glance seems the stereotypical nineteenth-century husband, a man with a keen sense of propriety who *knows* that a man is ruler of his home. He unquestionably loves Nora, and Teale lets us see and feel the passion beneath the propriety of the

character—as well as a mean streak that makes him dangerous if crossed.

Many of Teale's lines, which would not have raised an eyebrow in 1879 Norway, drew roars of contemptuous laughter from the 1997 audience. Yet when his whole world comes crashing down and he's forced (after much prodding) to confront the lie his life has become, he makes a subtle, almost unnoticed, transformation. Slowly he begins to understand his wife's pain and the role he has played in letting it continue. When he says to Nora "I have the strength in me to become another man," we're seeing a soul laid bare in a way that's totally convincing.

Director Anthony Page keeps the pace moving during the more active scenes, and he and the actors managed to hold the audience's interest even during the slow sections, which consist of lengthy, two-person conversations with very little action (though they do provide vital plot information).

The script, taken from a literal translation of the work, could probably have been cut by a half-hour. However, the cast and producers seemed more interested in presenting a definitive version of the Ibsen work rather than adapting it to suit a 90s audience. And in this, they have succeeded admirably. Despite its wordiness, the play gradually draws you into its emotional web and delivers a knockout punch of a payoff.

Quibbles about slow-pacing aside, *A Doll's House* is an intense and compelling journey through the human spirit and well worth the trip.

A thorough critical review covers all the parts of what is being reviewed. Here, the critics discuss the director, the actors, the producers, and the script.

The review ends with a positive recommendation to potential theatergoers.

Sunday, April 20, 1997

A Lot of Baggage for Nora to Carry

After a History of Misinterpretation, Ibsen's Leave-Taking Heroine Finally Gets Her Due

By Lloyd Rose
Washington Post Staff Writer

As Nora in the London-produced *A Doll's House* now playing on Broadway, the tall, rangy Janet McTeer is as gawkily graceful as a young swan. This Nora is a six-foot bundle of adorability—and she knows it. Everything in her movement and manner—especially her hoarse, self-conscious giggle—says to the men in her life, "Aren't I silly, aren't I scatterbrained, aren't I helpless, don't you adore me?" And they do.

A Doll's House, the story of a pampered bourgeois wife who rebelliously leaves her domineering husband, has a problematic reputation. . . . At least one reviewer felt constrained to point out that the New York production is more than "a feminist screed." Henrik Ibsen . . . has been getting bopped with accusations of feminism since the play's debut in 1880. When Nora realized her life was a lie and walked out on her husband and children, nineteenth-century audiences were scandalized.

McTeer and director Anthony Page bring this production very close to what I've always thought is the essential truth of *A Doll's House*. . . .

McTeer's Nora doesn't realize so much that Torvald is a cad (Owen Teale's honorable, grounded performance makes that impossible anyway) as that she has constructed a fantasy about his being a hero. The mistake is hers, for being a grown woman who believes in a fairy tale. This discovery doesn't put Nora in a lecturing mood. She's staggered, a little dazed, as if she'd been punched in the head by reality.

As McTeer plays it, the last speech isn't superior and scolding; she doesn't even don her coat until toward the end. Her Nora is tentative, feeling her way through the revelations that have been forced upon her, realizing what she has done. As a result, the character is fascinating, surprising, disturbing, instead of being all dreary and moral and right.

This production doesn't go quite as far as it could—Nora still scores some too-easy points over Torvald— but it goes a long, brave way. In London McTeer won an Olivier Award for her performance, beating out such powerhouse talents as Diana Rigg and Vanessa Redgrave, and you certainly see why. She's not as luminous as Redgrave. She's not as witty and fierce as Rigg. But she is certainly, as Ralph Richardson used to say of Laurence Olivier, "bold . . . very, very bold."

A Doll's House

By Henrik Ibsen
A New Version by Frank McGuiness

Reviewed by David Spencer

The first thing you have to understand about this so-called revival of *A Doll's House*—which comes to Broadway by way of London—is that it's not a revival at all. It follows the general outline of Ibsen's famous drama about a woman's coming of age—it contains the same characters and the same events—but it's essentially a new play by Frank ("Someone Who'll Watch over Me") McGuiness. Note his credit: not "translation by" but "a new version by." It's a credit I note with particular emphasis because I have one such on my own resumé. . . . So as you read all the pæans to Janet McTeer's performance as a devastating "new" Nora, keep in mind that a new Nora is precisely, *literally*, what's on offer. And it starts not with the actress, but with the script—whose spin on Ibsen is both compelling and subversive.

That [Janet McTeer] is vivacious, sensual, charismatic, explosive—everything you want a "star" to be—is undeniable. Her Nora trembles with suppressed giggles, bursts with surprise, teases mercilessly, touches, hugs, whispers conspiratorially, revels in her own outrageousness. In the play's first act, this electrifies the audience—palpably. At first, it all but overwhelms Owen Teale's performance as her husband Torvald (a portrayal of a vigorously insecure martinet wannabe) . . . but it creates a buzz of excitement and discovery.

It's not a buzz that sustains, though. Because after intermission, with Acts Two and Three (performed in one stretch), the vivacity turns to a jittery desperation and finally to out-and-out hysteria. It seems like a perfectly logical progression: once the tight rein on Nora's sense of stability is released by the threat of blackmail and ruination, her energy *would* fly out of control, she *would* find herself without moorings. But in the playing, it is merely relentless.

Happily, in Acts Two and Three, with the shock of the new Nora no longer a novelty, we do get to concentrate on the others in the ensemble—and they are fine within the parameters of the script.

They don't, however, bring the audience closer to the play. Yes, with this *Doll's House* being so different, so modern of intent, it is endlessly fascinating—but it's a fascination experienced from a distance. You are always *aware* of the revisionist take on things, always pausing to *note* the controversial new choices, to *compare* them to Ibsen's original . . . rather than just experiencing them on a visceral level.

I don't mean to condemn this production—or, for that matter, Ms. McTeer. McGuiness' revisionist take is a fine and noble experiment, and his Nora is clearly a magnificent actress. I just feel as if—in the final analysis, in the grand karmic sweep of the universe—this *A Doll's House* is *not* the be-all, end-all revelation the hype would have you believe, but rather an intermediary step.

Notice the powerful words Spencer uses to communicate his opinion of the performance.

The writer identifies both positive and negative aspects of the production.

Check Your Comprehension

1. According to critic David Spencer, why is the 1997 production of *A Doll's House* "not the be-all, end-all" version of the play?
2. What evidence do the *CurtainUp* critics use to prove that the role of Torvald is the toughest one to portray in *A Doll's House*? Explain.

Applying the Reading Strategy

Comparing and Contrasting Critical Reviews

3. The *CurtainUp* review describes the show as having a "1990s feel" to it. Which critic would most likely agree with this assessment?
4. This 1997 production of *A Doll's House* won the Tony Award for Best Revival of a Play. (a) Which review supports this choice? (b) Which critic would probably disagree with this choice? Explain.
5. Complete a chart like the one shown to identify the points on which the reviewers agree and disagree.

Shared Opinions	Differing Opinions

Activity

Writing a Critical Review

Write a critical review of a movie or television show. Before you write, watch the movie or show and take notes on the following elements:

- acting
- costumes
- script
- overall quality

Address each element in your critical review, supporting your opinions with evidence.

Contrasting Informational Materials

Critical Reviews and Advertisements

Critical reviews share several elements with advertisements. In fact, it is a common practice in the theater to incorporate statements from critical reviews into a play's advertisements. Using the information in the three critical reviews, create a print advertisement for this production of *A Doll's House*. Then, answer these questions:

1. What elements do reviews and ads share?
2. What information from a critical review would *not* be present in an ad?
3. What words or phrases from a review would be effective in your ad?

Writing About Literature

Compare and Contrast Literary Periods

Two movements, Romanticism and Realism, define the literature of the nineteenth century. Romantic writers—often inspired by nature—turned inward to tap spontaneous emotions. At the same time, they turned outward to celebrate the lives, language, and folk-lore of ordinary people. Realism, which emerged later, continued the Romantics' interest in ordinary life, but the Realists' pessimistic view of the suffering of the working class contrasted sharply with the Romantic vision of simple, contented folk.

Write an essay comparing Romantic and Realist literature with the literature of another literary period of your choice. See the box at the right for details of the assignment.

Prewriting

Find a focus. Review the literature both in this unit and in the unit against which you will compare these selections. For an overview of the periods, read the Unit Introduction for each unit as well. Use a chart similar to the one below to take notes. As you review selections, consider these questions to narrow your focus:

- Which aspects of a literary movement does this work reflect?
- Which parts of the work illustrate these aspects?
- What historical developments influenced this work?
- Which other works or literary trends influenced this work?

Model: Focus to Compare and Contrast Literary Periods

Selection	Literary Period	Evidence
"The Lorelei"	Romantic	Influence of folklore; irrational power of desire
"The Fox and the Crow"	Age of Reason	Rational analysis of motives; teaches a lesson

Review your chart, and select two works from each period on which you will focus. In making your choice, consider interesting contrasts as well as similarities between works.

Gather details. Go back to each work you have chosen and gather specific details of plot, setting, and characterization for comparison.

Write a working thesis. Write a single sentence summing up the main points of comparison and contrast between the work of the 1800s that you will discuss and the ones you have chosen from another literary era.

Assignment: Different Times, Different Literature

Write an analytical essay that compares and contrasts Romantic and Realist works of the nineteenth century with works of another literary period. Suggest how events of the period and reactions to other literary works influenced the works you analyze.

Criteria:

- Include a thesis statement drawn from your analysis of the works of two different literary eras.
- Support your thesis with detailed analyses of at least two works from each era.
- Highlight likenesses and differences among the works of different periods.
- Approximate length: 1,500 words

Read to Write

As you reread the texts, identify the themes and decide how these themes reflect the interests and values of the era in which the works were written.

Drafting

Write an outline. Preparing a detailed outline will help you organize your thoughts and will guide you as you draft. Each main heading of the outline indicated by a capital letter will become a paragraph. Numbered subheadings indented under each heading will be supporting sentences.

Model: Making a Detailed Outline

B. Elements of Realism in Tolstoy story
1. simple language
2. main character is a peasant
3. realistic details about Russia

C. Comparison to elements in Romantic story
1. courtly language
2. main characters are aristocrats
3. some realistic details

Write to Learn
Each time you reread the selections that you are analyzing in your paper, you will find additional nuances of meaning. Don't hesitate to add more information to your essay as your understanding of the works deepens.

Write to Explain
Make sure that you have a good reason for including the details and quotations that you use in your essay. Explain those reasons clearly to your readers.

Revising and Editing

Review content: Eliminate unnecessary details. Identify the main idea in each paragraph. No matter how "interesting" they might be, details in a paragraph that do not support the main idea should be eliminated.

Review style: Strengthen word choice. Alter dull sentences to make them more interesting, replacing vague words with ones that are more expressive and words you use repeatedly with synonyms.

Original: Pakhom's enemy is his greed. He doesn't get greedy all at once—he becomes greedy little by little. When he has some land, he wants more. When he gets more land, he wants even more. His greed makes the devil happy.

Revised: Pakhom's enemy is his greed. His avarice doesn't sweep over him all at once—it creeps up on him little by little. When he has a modest amount of land, he craves more. His dissatisfaction delights the devil.

Publishing and Presenting

Submit your essay to a literary magazine. Revise your essay, adding necessary background to help a general audience who may be unfamiliar with your topic. Then, submit your essay to the school literary magazine.

W͏G Writing and Grammar Connection: Diamond Level, Chapter 9

Writing WORKSHOP

Response to Literature

A **response to literature** presents an individual's reaction to one aspect of a work of literature, such as its theme, plot, characterization, or use of language. Responses to literature may range from formal and academic to informal and personal. In this workshop, you will write a formal response to a favorite literary work.

Assignment Criteria Your response to literature should display the following characteristics:

- A discussion of the themes or significant ideas of a piece of literature
- Accurate references to the text, including examples, quotations, and allusions
- A personal response drawn from your ideas and experiences
- A logical organizational plan
- A thesis statement, introduction, and conclusion

To preview the criteria on which your response to literature may be assessed, refer to the Rubric on page 961.

Prewriting

Choose a topic. **Brainstorm** to generate ideas. List works of literature you have read lately that most fully engaged your attention or related most strongly to your own life. Consider also works that raised many questions for you. Choose the piece from your list that sparks the most ideas, one that you would like to explore in depth.

Gather evidence. Make sure you have enough ideas about the work you chose to construct an interesting essay with sufficient supporting details. To generate ideas, consider using the technique of **hexagonal writing,** in which you explore six aspects of a piece of literature. Make a hexagonal chart similar to the one shown here, and follow the directions in the example to complete a hexagon based on your topic.

Consider your audience. Identify the interests and level of sophistication of your audience. To help you choose supporting evidence and decide how much explanation to provide, decide how familiar your audience is with the literature you intend to discuss. Then, shape your material in order to convince your audience that the work and its theme are relevant to them.

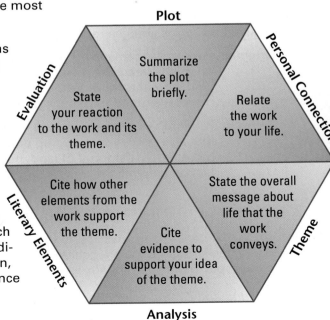

Plot — Summarize the plot briefly.

Personal Connection — Relate the work to your life.

Theme — State the overall message about life that the work conveys.

Analysis — Cite evidence to support your idea of the theme.

Literary Elements — Cite how other elements from the work support the theme.

Evaluation — State your reaction to the work and its theme.

Student Model

Before you begin your first draft, read this student model and review the characteristics of a response to literature.

Nick Groesch
Decatur, Illinois

The Tarantella in Ibsen's *A Doll House*

Many great playwrights have used performing arts as a way to exemplify themes in their works. Shakespeare, for example, uses a play within *Hamlet* to reveal the guilt of Claudius and to deplore the evil of regicide. In *A Doll House,* Ibsen makes use of the tarantella, an Italian folk dance, in several dramatic ways. In Act Two, Ibsen uses the tarantella to increase suspense, to reveal a deeply flawed marriage, and to symbolize Nora's utter desperation.

On a practical level, Nora's dancing serves as a distraction. By deliberately dancing badly, Nora draws Helmer's attention away from the arrival of Krogstad's letter, which will shatter her world. "Yes, you see how important [the tarantella] is. You've got to teach me to the very last minute" (Act Two). Nora successfully delays the reading of the letter, increasing the play's suspense.

On another level, Ibsen uses the tarantella rehearsal to reveal problems in the Helmers' marriage. As he instructs Nora, Helmer shows that he views his wife as a "doll," a performing toy to be played with and shown off to his friends. Among his significant remarks: "you little helpless thing"; "Be my own little lark again"; "It's nothing more than this childish anxiety I was telling you about." By showing Helmer's patronizing attitude in this scene, Ibsen prepares the viewer for Nora's explosion of resentment and rebellion.

Finally, Nora's wild dancing is a symbol of her desperation. The tarantella was believed to cure its dancer from the poison of a tarantula. Krogstad's threats and letter are poison to Nora's happiness and marriage. Nora takes it upon herself to practice the tarantella because she wishes to rid herself of this "poison." Unfortunately, the tarantella does not cure poison, nor does Nora's dance solve her problems. She realizes this and, at the end of Act Two, she says, "Seven hours to midnight. Twenty-four hours to the midnight after, and then the tarantella's done. Seven and twenty-four? Thirty-one hours to live."

Ibsen uses the tarantella for plot reasons, as a ruse that distracts Helmer; to develop character, as a picture of a troubled marriage; and finally as a symbol of Nora's life spinning out of control. Though it does not "cure" anything, the tarantella sets up and intensifies the final showdown between Helmer and Nora, an epic climax that defines *A Doll House* as Ibsen's most influential play.

Nick's thesis statement clearly defines the scope of his response essay.

Nick accurately quotes lines of dialogue from the play to support his points.

Nick gives essential background information in order to explore the tarantella as a symbol.

Nick concludes his response with a summary and a forceful statement on the importance of the scene to Ibsen's play.

Drafting

Draft a thesis statement. Review your notes, and decide which critical point you want to make about the piece of literature. Then, write a thesis statement that introduces your ideas. Include the thesis statement as the main idea of your introductory paragraph.

Organize your essay. Follow a logical plan of organization to write your first draft. Consider a basic three-part organization, as shown at the right.

Elaborate. Give reasons for your analysis of the themes and for your response to them. Cite evidence from the work, from other pieces of literature, and from your life experience.

Revising

Revise the introduction and conclusion. Read through the introduction and conclusion of your essay. Revise so that the conclusion restates or further explains the main points of the introduction in an interesting way.

Organization of a Response to Literature

Introduction
- State thesis.
- Introduce work of literature, theme, and response.

Body
- Elaborate on thesis statement.
- Provide evidence: examples, quotations, personal reactions.

Conclusion
- Summarize main ideas and provide final insight.

Model: Revise Introduction and Conclusion

Introduction

In Act Two, Ibsen uses the tarantella to increase suspense, to reveal a deeply flawed marriage, and to symbolize Nora's utter desperation.

Conclusion

~~Ibsen uses the tarantella both practically as a ruse to distract Helmer and as a symbol of Nora's life spinning out of control.~~ *Ibsen uses the tarantella for plot reasons, as a ruse that distracts Helmer; to develop character, as a picture of a troubled marriage; and finally as a symbol of Nora's life spinning out of control. Though it does not "cure" anything, the tarantella sets up and intensifies the final showdown between Helmer and Nora, an epic climax that defines A Doll House as Ibsen's most influential play.*

> Nick revised his conclusion to better match his introduction and to add a final insight.

Revise for clarity. Remember that your readers are most likely not as familiar as you are with the work of literature that is the subject of your essay. Provide enough background information to help all your readers follow your essay.

Compare the model and the nonmodel below to evaluate the clarity of each one.

Nonmodel	Model
On a practical level, Nora's dancing serves as a distraction. By dancing badly, Nora draws Helmer's attention away from the arrival of Krogstad's letter.	On a practical level, Nora's dancing serves as a distraction. By deliberately dancing badly, Nora draws Helmer's attention away from the arrival of Krogstad's letter, which will shatter her world.

Publishing and Presenting

Choose one of the following ways to share your writing with classmates or a wider audience.

Present to a book group. Invite a group of classmates or friends to read the work of literature that is the topic of your essay. After everyone has read the piece, get the group together and present a summary of your essay. Afterwards, have a discussion in which group members compare their own reactions to the work.

Publish an online review of the work. Post your response to the work on a student or bookstore Web site. Be sure to follow the submission requirements for the site to make sure your submission is accepted and posted.

W̶G̶ Writing and Grammar Connection: Diamond Level, Chapter 14

Rubric for Self-Assessment

Evaluate your response to literature using the following criteria and rating scale:

Criteria	Rating Scale				
	Not very				Very
How clear and accurate is my thesis statement?	1	2	3	4	5
How well have I explained the significant ideas of the piece?	1	2	3	4	5
How well have I supported my personal reactions with evidence from the text?	1	2	3	4	5
How logical is the organization of my essay?	1	2	3	4	5
How accurately does the conclusion summarize my ideas?	1	2	3	4	5
How well does my conclusion reflect and extend my introduction?	1	2	3	4	5

Delivering an Oral Response to Literature

An **oral response to literature** might be an offhand comment to a friend about a bestseller you read, a panel discussion about the relevance of literature to the critical issues of the day, or a formal presentation on a theme in the work of a great author. The following strategies will help you prepare and present an effective formal oral response to a work.

Prepare Your Content

Choose a topic that excites you. What have you read recently that made you angry, puzzled, or elated? That piece would make an excellent subject for your presentation.

Narrow your focus. What will be the main idea or theme of your talk? Keep that most important idea in mind as you prepare your presentation. Assume that you must persuade your audience to accept your viewpoint. Anticipate and address potential objections.

Support your ideas. Your ideas will be most convincing if they are supported with quotations from and references to the text under discussion and other relevant works. Read over the work several times. Then, carefully choose the evidence that supports your viewpoint.

Prepare Your Delivery

Use the following techniques to prepare your presentation of a response to literature:

- **Choose a logical structure.** Which structure will work most effectively for your presentation: chronological order, order of importance, part to whole, comparison and contrast? Select a specific pattern and use it consistently throughout your talk.

- **Develop an effective opening and conclusion.** The impact of your talk as a whole is only as strong as its introduction and conclusion. An intriguing beginning snares the attention of the audience, and a dramatic conclusion leaves your main point etched in the audience's memory. Revise the opening and conclusion of your presentation until they are effective.

- **Rehearse your presentation.** Practice to make your delivery conversational and comfortable. Try to avoid reading an essay word for word. Instead, use your notes as a guide.

Feedback Form for an Oral Response to Literature

Rating System
+ = Excellent   ✓ = Average   − = Weak

Content
Clarity of main idea _____
Persuasiveness of viewpoint _____
Supporting evidence _____

Suggestions for improvement: _____
_____

Delivery
Organization _____
Opening _____
Conclusion _____

Other comments on delivery: _____
_____

Activity: Presentation and Feedback Choose a short story or a short piece of non-fiction. Prepare a three-minute oral response to the work. Have a partner use the Feedback Form to evaluate your preparation, and revise your work based on your partner's observations. Present your response to your class.

Assessment WORKSHOP

Strategy, Organization, and Style

On some tests, you may be asked to read a passage with numbered sentences or paragraphs and to answer questions about its organization and use of language. Use these strategies to help you answer such questions:

- Summarize, in logical order, the events or ideas in the passage. Next to each event or idea, write the number of the sentence or paragraph in which it appears. Use your outline to help you answer questions about reordering parts of the passage.

- Note the purpose of the passage—to persuade readers to hold an opinion, to inform them about a topic, or to entertain them. Recall this purpose when answering questions about main ideas, supporting details, and irrelevant sentences.

Test-Taking Strategies

- Read the entire passage before answering the questions.
- Eliminate any answers that are obviously incorrect.

Sample Test Item

Directions: Read the passage, and then choose the letter of the best answer to the question.

(1) In five years the plague, which had no cure, caused a gruesome death for 25 million people—one third of Europe's population. (2) The fleas on rodents soon carried the plague from China throughout Europe. (3) Smaller outbreaks of the plague continued until the 1600s. (4) In the 1330s, China was stricken by the bubonic plague, which got its name from buboes, the swellings of the lymph glands.

1. Which sentence sequence makes the most sense?

   A 4, 2, 1, 3
   B 2, 4, 3, 1
   C 3, 1, 2, 4
   D 1, 2, 3, 4

Answer and Explanation

The correct answer is *A* because it arranges the sentences describing the outbreak and spread of the plague in sequential order. Each of the other choices presents events out of sequence.

► Practice

Directions: Read the passage, and then choose the letter of the best answer to the question.

(1) Beginning in the late ninth century, Viking raids from the north, Magyar raids from the east, and Muslim raids from the south endangered Europe. (2) After Charlemagne's death in 814, Europe once again faced the threat of invasion. (3) As a result of these attacks, the feudal system was born: a system of mutual defense pacts between lords and vassals. (4) The Holy Roman Empire, ruled by Charlemagne, returned some semblance of security to Europe. (5) The Roman Empire was overrun by Germanic tribes in the fifth century A.D., and its fall left Europe vulnerable to more invaders.

1. Which sentence sequence makes the most sense?

   A 1, 3, 2, 5, 4
   B 5, 4, 2, 1, 3
   C 4, 1, 3, 2, 5
   D 2, 1, 3, 5, 4

The Modern World

> **Almost all of the affairs of men remain a terrible uncertainty. We think of what has disappeared, and we are almost destroyed by what has been destroyed; we do not know what will be born, and we fear the future, not without reason. . . .**
>
> — Paul Valéry

Timeline 1890–1945

Historical and Cultural Events

- **1890** Ohio inventor builds first internal combustion automobile in the United States.

- **1899** Sigmund Freud publishes *The Interpretation of Dreams.* ▼

- **1901** Marconi sends a message across the Atlantic via wireless telegraphy.

- **1903** Orville Wright makes the first successful flight in an airplane. ▼

- **1903** Henri Becquerel and Pierre and Marie Curie win a Nobel Prize for work on radioactivity.

- **1905** Einstein proposes his theory of special relativity.

- **1907** Pablo Picasso completes *The Young Women of Avignon.*

- **1907** Tungsten filament lamps first used in the United States.

- **1908** Henry Ford starts producing standardized Model T automobiles.

- **1911** Marie Curie wins second Nobel Prize, for isolating pure radium.

- **1914–1918** World War I is fought, killing millions. ▼

- **1917** Communists seize power in Russia.

- **1919** U. S. Senate rejects League of Nations.

Literary Events

- **1890** Japanese author Mori Ōgai publishes his story "The Dancing Girl."

- **1893** Nicaraguan poet Rubén Darío becomes Colombian consul in Buenos Aires, Argentina.

- **1896** Alfred Nobel dies; his will endows the Nobel Prize in Literature.

- **1896** French author Paul Valéry publishes *An Evening With Monsieur Teste.*

- **1900** French novelist Colette publishes *Claudine at School.*

- **1900** Spanish poet Juan Ramón Jiménez comes to Madrid at the invitation of Rubén Darío.

- **1907–1908** Austro-German poet Rainer Maria Rilke publishes *New Poems.*

- **1911–1913** Mori Ōgai publishes his novel *The Wild Goose.*

- **c. 1912** Ezra Pound and others create the Imagist movement. ◄

- **1913** Rabindranath Tagore receives the Nobel Prize in Literature.

- **1913** Marcel Proust publishes the first volume of *Remembrance of Things Past.*

- **1913** French poet Guillaume Apollinaire publishes *Alcools.*

World Events

- **1927** Charles Lindbergh makes a successful solo flight across the Atlantic.
- **1928** Stalin begins forcing peasants onto collective farms, killing those who resist.
- **1929** Great Depression begins, lasting until about 1939. ▼

- **1931** Japan seizes Manchuria from China.
- **1932** Franklin Roosevelt elected President of the U. S. (serves 1932–1945). ▼

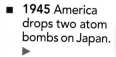

- **1933** Hitler becomes chancellor of Germany.
- **1934** Stalin begins a campaign of terror against those who are "disloyal."
- **1937** Japan launches a full-scale war against China.
- **1939** Hitler invades Poland, starting World War II.

- **1940** Churchill becomes Prime Minister of Great Britain.
- **1940** Japanese enter the war on the side of the Axis Powers.
- **1941** Germany invades the Soviet Union.
- **1941** The United States enters the war on the side of the Allies.
- **1945** America drops two atom bombs on Japan. ▶
- **1945** The Allies defeat the Axis Powers, ending World War II.

- **1921** André Breton meets Sigmund Freud.
- **1921** Italian author Luigi Pirandello publishes the play *Six Characters in Search of an Author.*
- **1922** James Joyce publishes *Ulysses.*
- **1922** Russian poet Boris Pasternak publishes *My Sister—Life.*
- **1923** Rainer Maria Rilke publishes *Duino Elegies* and *Sonnets to Orpheus.*
- **1924** Franz Kafka dies of tuberculosis.

- **1935–1940** Anna Akhmatova composes *Requiem.*
- **1936** Federico García Lorca (portrayed here by actor Andy Garcia) is assassinated by fascists. ▼

- **1942** Albert Camus publishes his novel *The Stranger.*
- **1944** Colette publishes her novel *Gigi.*
- **1945** Gabriela Mistral becomes the first Latin American to win the Nobel Prize in Literature.

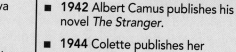
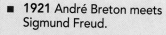

The Modern World

(1890–1945)

Historical Background

Breakthroughs in Technology and Science Sparked by the efforts of brilliant scientists and inventors, major technological advances began occurring in the late nineteenth and early twentieth centuries that would permanently alter the ways in which people lived. Within a period of just a few decades, the airplane, the automobile, the radio, and the telephone were introduced, making travel and communication faster and easier than ever before. At the same time, other discoveries and inventions, such as electricity, central heating, movies, and new medical remedies, were improving the quality of people's lives. Still other advances, such as the development of the machine gun and the tank, made it easier for people to destroy one another.

Scientific breakthroughs rivaled these technological advances. The husband and wife team of Marie and Pierre Curie, for example, pioneered in studying radioactivity. Then, in 1905, German-born physicist Albert Einstein proposed his special theory of relativity, showing that calculations of time and motion depend on an observer's relative position. Einstein also proved that energy and matter can be converted into each other, as expressed by the famous formula $E = mc^2$.

Understanding Human Behavior Austrian psychiatrist Sigmund Freud (froid) proposed an equally radical theory of human behavior. Using a method of gathering information about mental processes known as psychoanalysis, Freud concluded that people's behavior is largely shaped by unconscious influences stemming from experiences during infancy and early childhood. Because Freud's theories challenged the belief that human activity sprang from rational thought, they initially sparked controversy. Yet as time passed, his ideas gained increasing acceptance. World War I itself seemed the greatest proof that humans were basically irrational!

World War I Encouraged by advances in science and technology, many people became increasingly optimistic about the future of humanity. To some, it even seemed possible that people could ultimately solve all their problems and establish lasting peace. This sense of optimism was utterly shattered, however, by the horrifying realities of World War I.

▼ **Critical Viewing** This photograph shows Marie Curie in her laboratory, where she studied radioactivity. What positive and negative results have come from the study of radioactivity? Explain. **[Draw Conclusions]**

Art in the Historical Context

The Art of Colonized Lands Conquers the West

In the late nineteenth and early twentieth centuries, Western colonizers sought new markets and mineral wealth in Africa, the Pacific Islands, and other so-called primitive places. Western artists sought a different kind of wealth in these same lands. They realized how much they could learn from the art of tribal peoples, from sculptures and masks that broke up the human figure and face in startling ways. Instead of imitating nature as Western works did, tribal art used abstractions—geometric shapes and fantastic forms—to convey spiritual realities.

In 1906–7, Pablo Picasso incorporated the abstractions of tribal art in a painting that made people gasp, *Les Demoiselles d'Avignon* ("The Young Women of Avignon"). Picasso himself was so uncertain about the canvas that he put it aside for a while. Today, it is recognized as the work that revolutionized Western art. With his slashing lines, Picasso attacked ideals of beauty and techniques of perspective that dated back to the Renaissance.

Les Demoiselles d'Avignon (detail), 1907, Pablo Picasso, The Museum of Modern Art, New York, NY

Beginning late in the summer of 1914, the war was a conflict between the Allies (France, Russia, Great Britain, Italy, and Japan, joined later by the United States) and the Central Powers (Germany, Austria-Hungary, and Turkey). This war eventually involved much of the world.

Throughout most of the conflict, neither side was able to make any significant advances. Having reached a stalemate early in the war, the opposing armies settled into trenches protected by mines and barbed wire. For the next few years, the two sides took turns rushing the opposing trenches. With each of these charges, hundreds of soldiers would be mowed down by machine-gun fire. By the time the war ended in 1918 with the Allies victorious, about eight and a half million soldiers had died of wounds or disease and about thirteen million civilians had lost their lives from a variety of war-related causes.

The Rise of Nazism In the aftermath of the war, the Allies drafted a treaty that required Germany to accept full blame and pay reparations for the total cost of the war. Germany signed the treaty, but its harsh terms created strong feelings of resentment among the German people. These feelings, coupled with the inflation caused by war reparations that Germany had to pay, generated unrest that plagued the nation throughout the 1920s.

The Great Depression In 1929, a severe economic slump hit the United States and, soon afterward, other industrialized nations such as Germany. Known as the Great Depression, it lasted through the 1930s and contributed to the rise of Hitler and other political extremists. In the early 1930s, the Nazis exploited the turmoil resulting from political unrest and economic decline to seize control of Germany.

▲ **Critical Viewing**
Compare and contrast this mask from the South Pacific island of New Britain (top) with the head of a young woman in Picasso's painting (bottom). Use details from each work to support your points. **[Compare and Contrast]**

Persecution of Jews Hitler quickly molded the nation into a totalitarian state, brutally suppressing all dissent. The word *totalitarian* refers to "a state in which one party or group retains total authority under a dictator." The Nazis assumed control of every aspect of German life, including religion, schools, and the press. They burned books and destroyed works of art they judged to be "un-German," and they forced radio stations to play military music and Nazi speeches. At the same time, they began ruthlessly persecuting German Jews, stripping them of their citizenship and expelling them from government posts and teaching positions.

▲ **Critical Viewing**
Which details in these pictures suggest the charismatic power that Hitler exercised over the German people? Explain. [Interpret]

Other Totalitarian Regimes Hitler's government was only one of a number of totalitarian regimes to emerge during the first half of the twentieth century. In Russia, where communists had seized power in the November Revolution of 1917, a totalitarian state was established after Joseph Stalin rose to power in the early 1920s. Like Hitler, Stalin brutally suppressed all dissent, executing millions of people who resisted his policies. Another totalitarian ruler, Benito Mussolini, gained control of Italy and later became one of Hitler's chief allies. In Spain, Francisco Franco established a fascist regime after winning a bloody civil war.

The German Invasion of Poland During the Spanish Civil War (1936–1939), both the Germans and the Italians provided Franco with military support. Pablo Picasso's painting *Guernica* (see pages 964–965) is a reaction to news of a German bombing raid on the Spanish city of Guernica in 1937. Because the democratic powers did little to discourage German and Italian involvement in Spain, Hitler and Mussolini did not hesitate to engage in further acts of military aggression. On September 1, 1939, German forces invaded Poland, subduing the country in little over a month. Britain and France responded by declaring war on Germany. Another world conflict had begun.

World War II pitted the Axis Powers (led by Germany, Italy, and Japan) against the Allies (led by Britain, France, the Soviet Union, and the United States). It is important to remember, however, that France was under German Occupation from 1940 to 1944, the Soviet Union was originally on Germany's side, Japan did not join the Axis immediately, and the United States did not enter the war until late in 1941.

The Russian Campaign Only weeks before the German invasion of Poland, Hitler had signed a Nonaggression Pact with the Soviet Union. On June 22, 1941, this famous "friendship" of dictators ended as German forces staged a surprise invasion of the Soviet Union.

German forces advanced rapidly at first but could not achieve victory by the winter of 1941. Like Napoleon, Hitler would pay dearly for hurling his armies eastward. The German dictator would not be able to contend with the huge reserves of Soviet manpower or with the icy assaults of "General Winter," as historians have sometimes called the Russian winter.

The Attack on Pearl Harbor On July 27, 1940, the Japanese aligned themselves with the Germans and the Italians. At the time the Japanese officially entered the war, the United States had not become directly involved in the conflict. On December 7, 1941, however, the Japanese drew the United States into the war by launching a surprise air attack on the American naval base at Pearl Harbor in Hawaii.

The End of the War and the Beginning of the Atomic Age In May of 1945, after years of savage fighting, the Nazis surrendered to the Allies. About three months later, Japan also surrendered, after the United States had dropped atomic bombs on the Japanese cities of Hiroshima and Nagasaki. With the defeat of Japan, peace had finally arrived. Yet so had the atomic age.

The destruction caused by World War II was staggering. It is estimated that some 50 million people lost their lives as a result of the war. In addition, bombing raids reduced much of Europe and Japan to rubble, and millions of people were uprooted from their homes.

The Holocaust One of the most shocking aspects of the war was not fully discovered until the Allied forces marched into Germany. In response to Hitler's diabolical plan to exterminate the Jewish people, the Nazis had imprisoned and executed about six million Jews in concentration camps. They had also executed millions of others, including people of Slavic descent and Gypsies. This systematic slaughter of Jews and others is one of the most tragic events in human history. It has come to be known as the Holocaust, from the Greek *holokauston*, a translation of the Hebrew '*olah*, meaning "burnt sacrifice offered to God." Jews also refer to this event as the Shoah, a Hebrew word meaning "catastrophe."

▼ **Critical Viewing** This view of the Nazis' Terezin concentration camp was painted by an inmate who suffered its horrors. Does anything in the painting reveal the harsh realities of the camp? Why or why not? **[Interpret]**

View of Terezin, Hanus Weinberg, State Jewish Museum, Prague

Literature

The modern age was one of the most turbulent and violent periods of human history. Yet it was also an era of tremendous artistic and literary achievement. Responding to the events and developments of their time and experimenting with new literary forms and approaches, modern writers from across the world created a fresh and remarkably diverse body of literature.

Worldwide Literary Connections With the advances in travel and communication, the various regions of the world became increasingly intertwined during the modern age. Consequently, the literary world became more interconnected than ever before, as writers from all countries were exposed to the literary movements and traditions of other cultures.

For the first time, writers from non-Western and less developed countries began to receive worldwide attention. The modern Indian writer Rabindranath Tagore (rə bēn′ drə nät′ tə gôr′), for example, earned a Nobel Prize in Literature. The Chilean poet Gabriela Mistral (gä brē ā′ lä mēs träl′) also won a Nobel Prize in Literature, after the Nicaraguan poet Rubén Darío (rōō ben′ dä rē′ ō) had drawn the attention of the literary world to Latin America. Darío not only received worldwide acclaim but also influenced a number of important European poets.

The Birth of Modernism The term *Modernism* refers to a movement or group of movements in all the arts that occurred in the late nineteenth and early twentieth centuries. Modernist writers, painters, and composers sensed

Close-up on Culture

Nobel Launches "World Literature" With a Bang!

Alfred Nobel (1833–1896), the Swedish inventor of dynamite, was also the founder of the famous Nobel Prizes. One of these, the Nobel Prize in Literature, helped launch the modern idea of "World Literature." This world-class prize confirmed that writers were part of an international fellowship of the imagination, whether they worked in Chile or Nigeria, France or Australia.

Nobel had invented dynamite to serve peaceful uses, but it was later used to kill people in wars. Not wanting to be associated with death and destruction, the Swedish inventor set up a fund in his will to endow five Nobel Prizes (more were added later). One of the original five, the Nobel Prize in Literature is awarded by the Swedish Academy. Each winner receives a gold medal, a diploma, and a sum of money—by 1996, it was more than one million dollars! Not only has the prize established a standard by which all writers can be judged equally, but it has also helped publicize individual authors and groups of authors. For example, the 2002 prize awarded to Hungarian author Imre Kertész brought renewed attention to Holocaust literature.

that dramatic changes in society—advances in transportation and communication, the growth of cities, devastating new modes of warfare—were calling into question the values and traditions of the past. In response, these artists began to question artistic traditions as well. They wanted to create works of art that expressed the radically different *modern* world in which they lived.

The first flowering of Modernism was in pre-World War I Paris and London. Paris especially was a laboratory for artistic experimentation. There, in 1906, the young Spanish painter Pablo Picasso looked to primitive art as a means of challenging Western traditions (see page 969).

Art That Provoked Riots If Picasso's work caused astonishment, the music of Russian-born composer Igor Stravinsky provoked riots. In 1913, the performance of his ballet piece *The Rite of Spring* at a Paris theater caused an uproar in the audience that drowned out the music. The audience was reacting to the changing rhythms and the lack of traditional harmony in a work that, like Picasso's, drew on primitive sources for inspiration.

In the field of literature, two great experimenters were the poet Guillaume Apollinaire (gē yōm´ à pô lē ner´) (1880–1918) and the novelist Marcel Proust (mär sel´ proost´) (1871–1922). Apollinaire astonished readers with unexpected associations, and Proust explored the meaning of time and memory in his multivolume novel *Remembrance of Things Past* (1913–1927).

An Imagist's Marching Orders Meanwhile, across the Channel in London, a group of poets that included the American Ezra Pound were struggling to make poetry in English more colloquial and concrete. In a literary manifesto expressing the beliefs of this new Imagist movement, Pound gave twentieth-century poets their marching orders: In presenting images or clear pictures, he commanded, "Use no superfluous word, . . . Go in fear of abstractions. . . . Don't make each line stop dead at the end . . . "

The War and a Second Flowering of Modernism The unprecedented destruction during World War I finally proved—to anyone who still doubted—that a new historical age had arrived. The war forever divided what came to seem like an innocent time from a modern era whose innocence was another battlefield casualty.

▲ **Critical Viewing**
This illustration for the bound sheet music of Stravinsky's ballet *Pétrouchka* contains Russian words because the dance was performed by the Russian Ballet. Which visual details suggest that the dance will be new and boldly imaginative? Explain. **[Interpret]**

To many artists who participated in the second flowering of Modernism during the 1920s, the war was the ultimate proof of human irrationality. It seemed to verify Freud's theories about the irrational motivations of human behavior, and these theories gained in influence during the postwar period. For example, they were the basis for the literary and artistic movement called Surrealism, which viewed the unconscious as a source of inspiration. The French poet André Breton (än drā´ brə tôn´) (1896–1966), who led the movement, advocated writing quickly and without thinking. This technique would enable authors to bypass the rational mind and write directly from the unconscious.

Eliminating the Traditional Links Other great Modernists of the 1920s, while not Surrealists themselves, shared the Surrealists' tendency to remove connecting language and structures from their work—all the expositions, transitions, resolutions, and explanations that readers had come to expect. To reflect the disjointedness and irrationality of the modern world, they often

A Living Tradition

James Joyce's *Ulysses* and Homer's *Odyssey*

In searching for new techniques to record modern realities, twentieth-century writers often returned to age-old sources. Irishman James Joyce, for example, went as far back as ancient Greece. In his novel *Ulysses*, besides pioneering a stream-of-consciousness narrative that reveals characters' thoughts directly, Joyce organizes events according to the episodes of Homer's ancient epic the *Odyssey*. (Ulysses is the Roman name of that epic's hero, Odysseus.) The epic describes the ten-year homeward journey of Odysseus from the Trojan War and his reunion with his son, Telemachus, and his faithful wife, Penelope.

Joyce's book follows two characters—young Irishman Stephen Dedalus and middle-aged Jew Leopold Bloom—as they traverse Dublin on June 16, 1904. Following in Odysseus' footsteps, Bloom goes on a one-day journey to meet his spiritual son, Stephen, and reunite with his wife, Molly. His thoughts and adventures humorously parallel the Greek hero's encounters with mythological characters. The result is a detailed realistic narrative with mythological dimensions.

For example, Bloom's casual thoughts as he passes a tea-merchant's window recall the lotus-eaters, who tempt Odysseus' men to taste the sleep-inducing lotus plant and forget their homeward journey:

> . . . The far east. Lovely spot it must be: the garden of the world, big lazy leaves to float about on, cactuses, flowery meads, snaky lianas they call them. Wonder is it like that. Those Cinghalese [people of Sri Lanka] lobbing around in the sun, in *dolce far niente* [Italian for "sweet doing nothing"]. Not doing a hand's turn all day. Sleep six months out of twelve. . . .

built their work from fragments. James Joyce, for example, used a stream-of-consciousness narration to immerse readers in the flow of a character's fragmentary thoughts. Yet even as he did so, he created a new type of structure (see page 974).

Implied Themes, Elusive Realities In keeping with the uncertainties of modern life, Modernist writers tended to imply, rather than directly state, the themes of their works. This approach forced readers to draw their own conclusions. For example, at the beginning of Franz Kafka's novel *The Trial*, a man named Joseph K. (his last name is never more than an initial) wakes up one morning to find that he has been accused of a crime. Neither he nor the reader ever discovers the reason for the accusation. What is even stranger, this Austrian novelist describes the most bizarre events using prose suitable for a bland business report.

As Kafka's novel suggests, Modernists questioned the nature of reality itself. They no longer assumed that it was comprehensible, let alone comforting. In Luigi Pirandello's drama *Six Characters in Search of an Author*, for example, fictional characters that the author has discarded take over the stage.

La condition humaine (The Human Condition), 1933, René Magritte, National Gallery of Art, Washington, D.C.

▲ **Critical Viewing** Belgian artist René Magritte often painted scenes as strange as those evoked by authors like Kafka and Pirandello. Which details in this painting are strangely unreal? Why? **[Interpret]**

"'Can you describe this?'...'I can.'" The turbulent events of the first half of the twentieth century directly affected the lives of many writers. It made them both victims and witnesses, falling prey to wars and the persecutions of tyrants but also nobly recording injustices. The Spanish poet Federico García Lorca (fe´ de rē´ kô gär sē´ ə lôr´ kə) was murdered by supporters of Franco during the early stages of the Spanish Civil War. The Russian poet Anna Akhmatova (ukh mät´ ə və), like many of her compatriots, suffered grievously at the hands of Stalin. In the poem *Requiem*, she laments the dictator's imprisonment of her son but also bears witness to the pain of all oppressed Russians. Likewise, her introduction to the poem could serve as a testament for all modern writers who battled injustice with their pens. In it, she describes how another woman waiting to see an imprisoned relative asks her, "Can you describe this?" She answers, "I can."

Beyond the Modern Age Although the end of World War II marks the official close of the modern age, the literary innovations and accomplishments of this era did not end in 1945. Many modern writers, including Albert Camus (ka mo͞o´), Gabriela Mistral, Boris Pasternak (pas´ tər nak´), and Anna Akhmatova remained productive long after the end of the war. At the same time, a new generation of talented writers arose across the globe, bringing with them fresh ideas and approaches.

The Metamorphosis

Franz Kafka (1883–1924)

In a letter to a friend, Franz Kafka once wrote, "I think we ought to read only the kind of books that wound and stab us.... We need the books that affect us like a disaster, that grieve us deeply, like the death of someone we loved more than ourselves, like being banished into forests far from everyone.... A book must be the axe for the frozen sea inside us." Although he was not discussing his own writing at the time, Kafka's description of a book's potential power probably fits his own fiction better than that of any other writer. In fact, few writers have created literary works more tragic, disturbing, and unsettling than Kafka's.

The Writer's Beginnings Born in Prague, which is now the capital of the Czech Republic, Kafka was one of four children and the only son. His father was a successful and domineering businessman, and Kafka spent a good part of his life alternately longing for his father's approval and resenting his strictness. Kafka lived with his family until he was thirty-one, and his relationship with his father, along with his feelings of familial obligation, guilt, and duty, are reflected in much of his writing. In *Letter to My Father* (1919) Kafka wrote: "My writing was all about you; all I did there, after all, was to bemoan what I could not bemoan upon your breast. It was an intentionally long-drawn-out leave-taking from you."

Kafka began writing short stories and plays at a very young age. Despite his interest in writing, however, he chose to study law at the University of Prague. After serving a legal internship, he took a job as a lawyer with an Italian insurance company. A year later, he was offered a position with the state Worker's Accident Insurance Institute, where he remained employed until 1922. Kafka's career never hindered his writing. In fact, the bureaucratic chaos that he observed in the business world actually served as an inspiration for his fiction.

Being an Outsider As a German-speaking Jew in a country inhabited mainly by Czech-speaking gentiles, Kafka knew what it meant to be an outsider. His sense of alienation is apparent in nearly all his fiction. In his early works, including "The Metamorphosis" (1915), he explored the awful consequences of ignoring one's true desires and aspirations and living according to the expectations of others. During the later stages of his career, Kafka depicted the conflict of the individual who rejects society yet truly longs for its acclaim. In his story "A Hunger Artist" (1924), for example, the protagonist attracts the attention of the public by sitting in a cage and refusing to eat. Eventually, however, people lose interest in him, and he starves to death in obscurity and despair.

Posthumous Acclaim In 1917, Kafka was diagnosed with tuberculosis. Shortly before his death in 1924, he told his friend Max Brod to destroy all his papers and personal documents, as well as his unfinished and unpublished works. Brod did not believe that Kafka had truly wanted his work destroyed, so he ignored the request. Instead, he arranged for the publication of Kafka's unfinished novels, *The Trial*, *The Castle*, and *America*, along with his personal diaries, *Letter to My Father*, and a number of unpublished short stories. The publication of these works earned Kafka critical acclaim and public acceptance, neither of which he had known during his lifetime. Kafka's reputation continued to grow, and he is now widely recognized as one of the finest and most influential writers of the twentieth century.

Preview

Connecting to the Literature

Imagine that when you woke up one day, your friends did not recognize you, found you repulsive, and could not understand you when you spoke. In this story, the main character experiences just such a terrible transformation.

Literary Analysis

Modernism

In the late nineteenth and early twentieth centuries, many writers began turning away from the style, form, and content of nineteenth-century literature in favor of new themes and techniques. While this movement, known as **Modernism,** encompassed a vast number of smaller literary movements, most Modernist works share certain characteristics:

- They attempt to capture the realities of modern life.
- They express a sense of uncertainty and alienation.
- They leave readers to draw their own conclusions.

Consider how these and other Modernist views and techniques are at work in Kafka's story.

Connecting Literary Elements

The first paragraph of this story drops you into a world in which something impossible has happened. The presence of this imaginative element in an otherwise realistic story makes "The Metamorphosis" an example of **literature of the fantastic,** a genre that mixes imagination and reality to entertain and challenge readers. As you read, note the presence of both imaginative and realistic details, and think about the effects they create.

Reading Strategy

Applying the Author's Biography

"The Metamorphosis" is not an autobiography, but **applying the author's biography**—making connections to Kafka's life—can shed light on its meaning. For example, Kafka's troubled relationship with his father probably helped him write realistically about the father and son in this story. Use a diagram like the one shown to record facts from Kafka's life that you think shed light on "The Metamorphosis."

Vocabulary Development

impracticable (im prak´ ti kə bəl) *adj.* not capable of being put into practice (p. 978)

obstinacy (äb´ stə nə sē) *n.* stubbornness (p. 985)

exuded (ig zo͞od´ id) *v.* discharged a liquid through the skin (p. 986)

rectify (rek´ tə fī) *v.* to set things right or restore balance (p. 988)

imminent (im´ ə nənt) *adj.* ready to happen at any moment (p. 989)

gyration (jī rā´ shən) *n.* circular or spiral motion (p. 990)

pallid (pal´ id) *adj.* pale (p. 992)

debacle (di bäk´ əl) *n.* overwhelming failure or defeat (p. 1015)

THE Metamorphosis

FRANZ KAFKA   *translated by* Stanley Corngold

Background

Many authors produce great writing that moves, challenges, and inspires readers. Only a few, however, make such distinctive contributions that their names become synonymous with specific literary qualities. Such is the case with Kafka. The term *kafkaesque* describes a nightmarish mood—specifically, the feeling that one is trapped in an intense, distorted world and that danger or doom is close at hand. As you read "The Metamorphosis," decide how well the adjective *kafkaesque* describes this tale, which many scholars consider one of the greatest stories of the twentieth century.

Part I

When Gregor Samsa woke up one morning from unsettling dreams, he found himself changed in his bed into a monstrous vermin. He was lying on his back as hard as armor plate, and when he lifted his head a little, he saw his vaulted brown belly, sectioned by arch-shaped ribs, to whose dome the cover, about to slide off completely, could barely cling. His many legs, pitifully thin compared with the size of the rest of him, were waving helplessly before his eyes.

"What's happened to me?" he thought. It was no dream. His room, a regular human room, only a little on the small side, lay quiet between the four familiar walls. Over the table, on which an unpacked line of fabric samples was all spread out—Samsa was a traveling salesman— hung the picture which he had recently cut out of a glossy magazine and lodged in a pretty gilt frame. It showed a lady done up in a fur hat and a fur boa, sitting upright and raising up against the viewer a heavy fur muff in which her whole forearm had disappeared.

Gregor's eyes then turned to the window, and the overcast weather— he could hear raindrops hitting against the metal window ledge— completely depressed him. "How about going back to sleep for a few minutes and forgetting all this nonsense," he thought, but that was completely <u>impracticable</u>, since he was used to sleeping on his right side and in his present state could not get into that position. No matter

Literary Analysis
Modernism From the very first paragraph, what seems new or different about Kafka's approach to telling this story?

impracticable (im prak´ ti kə bəl) *adj.* not capable of being put into practice

how hard he threw himself onto his right side, he always rocked onto his back again. He must have tried it a hundred times, closing his eyes so as not to have to see his squirming legs, and stopped only when he began to feel a slight, dull pain in his side, which he had never felt before.

"Oh God," he thought, "what a grueling job I've picked. Day in, day out—on the road. The upset of doing business is much worse than the actual business in the home office, and besides, I've got the torture of traveling, worrying about changing trains, eating miserable food at all hours, constantly seeing new faces, no relationships that last or get more intimate. To the devil with it all!" He felt a slight itching up on top of his belly; shoved himself slowly on his back closer to the bedpost, so as to be able to lift his head better; found the itchy spot, studded with small white dots which he had no idea what to make of; and wanted to touch the spot with one of his legs but immediately pulled it back, for the contact sent a cold shiver through him.

He slid back again into his original position. "This getting up so early," he thought, "makes anyone a complete idiot. Human beings have to have their sleep. Other traveling salesmen live like harem women. For instance, when I go back to the hotel before lunch to write up the business I've done, these gentlemen are just having breakfast. That's all I'd have to try with my boss; I'd be fired on the spot. Anyway, who knows if that wouldn't be a very good thing for me. If I didn't hold back for my parents' sake, I would have quit long ago, I would have marched up to the boss and spoken my piece from the bottom of my heart. He would have fallen off the desk! It is funny, too, the way he sits on the desk and talks down from the heights to the employees, especially when they have to come right up close on account of the boss's being hard of hearing. Well, I haven't given up hope completely; once I've gotten the money together to pay off my parents' debt to him—that will probably take another five or six years—I'm going to do it without fail. Then I'm going to make the big break. But for the time being I'd better get up, since my train leaves at five."

And he looked over at the alarm clock, which was ticking on the chest of drawers. "God Almighty!" he thought. It was six-thirty, the hands were

Reading Strategy
Applying the Author's Biography In what ways might Kafka's career as an accident-insurance lawyer have helped him to write this scene?

✓**Reading Check**

Into what kind of creature has Gregor Samsa been transformed?

quietly moving forward, it was actually past the half-hour, it was already nearly a quarter to. Could it be that the alarm hadn't gone off? You could see from the bed that it was set correctly for four o'clock; it certainly had gone off, too. Yes, but was it possible to sleep quietly through a ringing that made the furniture shake? Well, he certainly hadn't slept quietly, but probably all the more soundly for that. But what should he do now? The next train left at seven o'clock; to make it, he would have to hurry like a madman, and the line of samples wasn't packed yet, and he himself didn't feel especially fresh and ready to march around. And even if he did make the train, he could not avoid getting it from the boss, because the messenger boy had been waiting at the five-o'clock train and would have long ago reported his not showing up. He was a tool of the boss, without brains or backbone. What if he were to say he was sick? But that would be extremely embarrassing and suspicious because during his five years with the firm Gregor had not been sick even once. The boss would be sure to come with the health-insurance doctor, blame his parents for their lazy son, and cut off all excuses by quoting the health-insurance doctor, for whom the world consisted of people who were completely healthy but afraid to work. And, besides, in this case would he be so very wrong? In fact, Gregor felt fine, with the exception of his drowsiness, which was really unnecessary after sleeping so late, and he even had a ravenous appetite.

Just as he was thinking all this over at top speed, without being able to decide to get out of bed—the alarm clock had just struck a quarter to seven—he heard a cautious knocking at the door next to the head of his bed. "Gregor," someone called—it was his mother—"it's a quarter to seven. Didn't you want to catch the train?" What a soft voice! Gregor was shocked to hear his own voice answering, unmistakably his own voice, true, but in which, as if from below, an insistent distressed chirping intruded, which left the clarity of his words intact only for a moment really, before so badly garbling them as they carried that no one could be sure if he had heard right. Gregor had wanted to answer in detail and to explain everything, but, given the circumstances, confined himself to saying, "Yes, yes, thanks, Mother, I'm just getting up." The wooden door must have prevented the change in Gregor's voice from being noticed outside, because his mother was satisfied with this explanation and shuffled off. But their little exchange had made the rest of the family aware that, contrary to expectations, Gregor was still in the house, and already his father was knocking on one of the side doors, feebly but with his fist. "Gregor, Gregor," he called, "what's going on?" And after a little while he called again in a deeper, warning voice, "Gregor! Gregor!" At the other side door, however, his sister moaned gently, "Gregor? Is something the matter with you? Do you want anything?" Toward both sides Gregor answered: "I'm all ready," and made

▲ Critical Viewing
In what ways does this image of a jangling alarm clock reflect the urgency of Gregor's situation? **[Connect]**

Literary Analysis
Modernism In what ways does the change in Gregor's voice suggest the Modernist theme of alienation?

an effort, by meticulous pronunciation and by inserting long pauses between individual words, to eliminate everything from his voice that might betray him. His father went back to his breakfast, but his sister whispered, "Gregor, open up, I'm pleading with you." But Gregor had absolutely no intention of opening the door and complimented himself instead on the precaution he had adopted from his business trips, of locking all the doors during the night even at home.

First of all he wanted to get up quietly, without any excitement; get dressed; and the main thing, have breakfast, and only then think about what to do next, for he saw clearly that in bed he would never think things through to a rational conclusion. He remembered how even in the past he had often felt some kind of slight pain, possibly caused by lying in an uncomfortable position, which, when he got up, turned out to be purely imaginary, and he was eager to see how today's fantasy would gradually fade away. That the change in his voice was nothing more than the first sign of a bad cold, an occupational ailment of the traveling salesman, he had no doubt in the least.

It was very easy to throw off the cover; all he had to do was puff himself up a little, and it fell off by itself. But after this, things got difficult, especially since he was so unusually broad. He would have needed hands and arms to lift himself up, but instead of that he had only his numerous little legs, which were in every different kind of perpetual motion and which, besides, he could not control. If he wanted to bend one, the first thing that happened was that it stretched itself out; and if he finally succeeded in getting this leg to do what he wanted, all the others in the meantime, as if set free, began to work in the most intensely painful agitation. "Just don't stay in bed being useless," Gregor said to himself.

First he tried to get out of bed with the lower part of his body, but this lower part—which by the way he had not seen yet and which he could not form a clear picture of—proved too difficult to budge; it was taking so long; and when finally, almost out of his mind, he lunged forward with all his force, without caring, he had picked the wrong direction and slammed himself violently against the lower bedpost, and the searing pain he felt taught him that exactly the lower part of his body was, for the moment anyway, the most sensitive.

He therefore tried to get the upper part of his body out of bed first and warily turned his head toward the edge of the bed. This worked easily, and in spite of its width and weight, the mass of his body finally followed, slowly, the movement of his head. But when at last he stuck his head over the edge of the bed into the air, he got too scared to continue any further, since if he finally let himself fall in this position, it would be a miracle if he didn't injure his head. And just now he had better not for the life of him lose consciousness; he would rather stay in bed.

But when, once again, after the same exertion, he lay in his original position, sighing, and again watched his little legs struggling, if possible more fiercely, with each other and saw no way of bringing peace and

Literary Analysis
Modernism and Literature of the Fantastic In what ways does this scene combine realistic details with fantastic ones in order to express a Modernist sense of alienation?

 **Reading Check**

What does each member of Gregor's family urge him to do?

order into this mindless motion, he again told himself that it was impossible for him to stay in bed and that the most rational thing was to make any sacrifice for even the smallest hope of freeing himself from the bed. But at the same time he did not forget to remind himself occasionally that thinking things over calmly—indeed, as calmly as possible—was much better than jumping to desperate decisions. At such moments he fixed his eyes as sharply as possible on the window, but unfortunately there was little confidence and cheer to be gotten from the view of the morning fog, which shrouded even the other side of the narrow street. "Seven o'clock already," he said to himself as the alarm clock struck again, "seven o'clock already and still such a fog." And for a little while he lay quietly, breathing shallowly, as if expecting, perhaps, from the complete silence the return of things to the way they really and naturally were.

But then he said to himself, "Before it strikes a quarter past seven, I must be completely out of bed without fail. Anyway, by that time someone from the firm will be here to find out where I am, since the office opens before seven." And now he started rocking the complete length of his body out of the bed with a smooth rhythm. If he let himself topple out of bed in this way, his head, which on falling he planned to lift up sharply, would presumably remain unharmed. His back seemed to be hard; nothing was likely to happen to it when it fell onto the car-pet. His biggest misgiving came from his concern about the loud crash that was bound to occur and would probably create, if not terror, at least anxiety behind all the doors. But that would have to be risked.

When Gregor's body already projected halfway out of bed—the new method was more of a game than a struggle, he only had to keep on rocking and jerking himself along— he thought how simple everything would be if he could get some help. Two strong persons—he thought of his father and the maid—would have been completely sufficient; they would only have had to shove their arms under his arched back, in this way scoop him off the bed, bend down with their burden, and then just be careful and patient while he managed to swing himself down onto the floor, where his little legs would hope-fully acquire some purpose. Well, leaving out the fact that the doors were locked, should he really call for help? In spite of all his miseries, he could not repress a smile at this thought.

He was already so far along that when he rocked more strongly he could hardly keep his balance, and very soon he would have to commit himself, because in five minutes it would be a quarter past seven—

Literary Analysis
Modernism In what ways does the view from Gregor's window reflect a Modernist perception of twentieth-century life?

▼ Critical Viewing
Which elements of this sculpture of a business-man seem to express an attitude toward work that is similar to Gregor's? Explain. **[Analyze]**

Walking Man, bronze statue 150 x 60 x 133 cm, Rick Amor, Niagara Galleries

when the doorbell rang. "It's someone from the firm," he said to himself and almost froze, while his little legs only danced more quickly. For a moment everything remained quiet. "They're not going to answer," Gregor said to himself, captivated by some senseless hope. But then, of course, the maid went to the door as usual with her firm stride and opened up. Gregor only had to hear the visitor's first word of greeting to know who it was—the office manager himself. Why was only Gregor condemned to work for a firm where at the slightest omission they immediately suspected the worst? Were all employees louts without exception, wasn't there a single loyal, dedicated worker among them who, when he had not fully utilized a few hours of the morning for the firm, was driven half-mad by pangs of conscience and was actually unable to get out of bed? Really, wouldn't it have been enough to send one of the apprentices to find out—if this prying were absolutely necessary—did the manager himself have to come, and did the whole innocent family have to be shown in this way that the investigation of this suspicious affair could be entrusted only to the intellect of the manager? And more as a result of the excitement produced in Gregor by these thoughts than as a result of any real decision, he swung himself out of bed with all his might. There was a loud thump, but it was not a real crash. The fall was broken a little by the carpet, and Gregor's back was more elastic than he had thought, which explained the not very noticeable muffled sound. Only he had not held his head carefully enough and hit it; he turned it and rubbed it on the carpet in anger and pain.

"Something fell in there," said the manager in the room on the left. Gregor tried to imagine whether something like what had happened to him today could one day happen even to the manager; you really had to grant the possibility. But, as if in rude reply to this question, the manager took a few decisive steps in the next room and made his patent leather boots creak. From the room on the right his sister whispered, to inform Gregor, "Gregor, the manager is here." "I know," Gregor said to himself; but he did not dare raise his voice enough for his sister to hear.

"Gregor," his father now said from the room on the left, "the manager has come and wants to be informed why you didn't catch the early train. We don't know what we should say to him. Besides, he wants to speak to you personally. So please open the door. He will certainly be so kind as to excuse the disorder of the room." "Good morning, Mr. Samsa," the manager called in a friendly voice. "There's something the matter with him," his mother said to the manager while his father was still at the door, talking. "Believe me, sir, there's something the matter with him. Otherwise how would Gregor have missed a train? That boy has nothing on his mind but the business. It's almost begun to rile me that he never goes out nights. He's been back in the city for eight days now, but every night he's been home. He sits there with us at the table, quietly reading the paper or studying timetables. It's already a distraction for him when he's busy working with his fretsaw.[1] For instance, in

---

1. **fretsaw** (fret′ sô) *n.* saw with a long, narrow, fine-toothed blade.

Reading Strategy
Applying the Author's Biography Do you think Gregor's anger toward his employers may reflect Kafka's work experiences? Explain?

☑Reading Check

Who arrives to speak with Gregor?

the span of two or three evenings he carved a little frame. You'll be amazed how pretty it is; it's hanging inside his room. You'll see it right away when Gregor opens the door. You know, I'm glad that you've come, sir. We would never have gotten Gregor to open the door by ourselves; he's so stubborn. And there's certainly something wrong with him, even though he said this morning there wasn't." "I'm coming right away," said Gregor slowly and deliberately, not moving in order not to miss a word of the conversation. "I haven't any other explanation myself," said the manager. "I hope it's nothing serious. On the other hand, I must say that we businessmen—fortunately or unfortunately, whichever you prefer—very often simply have to overcome a slight indisposition[2] for business reasons." "So can the manager come in now?" asked his father, impatient, and knocked on the door again. "No," said Gregor. In the room on the left there was an embarrassing silence; in the room on the right his sister began to sob.

Why didn't his sister go in to the others? She had probably just got out of bed and not even started to get dressed. Then what was she crying about? Because he didn't get up and didn't let the manager in, because he was in danger of losing his job, and because then the boss would start hounding his parents about the old debts? For the time being, certainly, her worries were unnecessary. Gregor was still here and hadn't the slightest intention of letting the family down. True, at the moment he was lying on the carpet, and no one knowing his condition could seriously have expected him to let the manager in. But just because of this slight discourtesy, for which an appropriate excuse would easily be found later on, Gregor could not simply be dismissed. And to Gregor it seemed much more sensible to leave him alone now than to bother him with crying and persuasion. But it was just the uncertainty that was tormenting the others and excused their behavior.

"Mr. Samsa," the manager now called, raising his voice, "what's the matter? You barricade yourself in your room, answer only 'yes' and 'no,' cause your parents serious, unnecessary worry, and you neglect—I mention this only in passing—your duties to the firm in a really shocking manner. I am speaking here in the name of your par-

Literary Analysis
Modernism Why do Gregor's parents try to impress the office manager with a sense of Gregor's individuality?

▼ **Critical Viewing**
What mood do you think this image of a traveling salesman conveys? Explain. **[Interpret]**

---

2. indisposition (in´ dis pə zish´ ən) *n.* slight illness.

ents and of your employer and ask you in all seriousness for an immediate, clear explanation. I'm amazed, amazed. I thought I knew you to be a quiet, reasonable person, and now you suddenly seem to want to start strutting about, flaunting strange whims. The head of the firm did suggest to me this morning a possible explanation for your tardiness—it concerned the cash payments recently entrusted to you—but really, I practically gave my word of honor that this explanation could not be right. But now, seeing your incomprehensible <u>obstinacy</u>, I am about to lose even the slightest desire to stick up for you in any way at all. And your job is not the most secure. Originally I intended to tell you all this in private, but since you make me waste my time here for nothing, I don't see why your parents shouldn't hear too. Your performance of late has been very unsatisfactory; I know it is not the best season for doing business, we all recognize that; but a season for not doing any business, there is no such thing, Mr. Samsa, such a thing cannot be tolerated."

"But sir," cried Gregor, beside himself, in his excitement forgetting everything else, "I'm just opening up, in a minute. A slight indisposition, a dizzy spell, prevented me from getting up. I'm still in bed. But I already feel fine again. I'm just getting out of bed. Just be patient for a minute! I'm not as well as I thought yet. But really I'm fine. How something like this could just take a person by surprise! Only last night I was fine, my parents can tell you, or wait, last night I already had a slight premonition.[3] They must have been able to tell by looking at me. Why didn't I report it to the office! But you always think that you'll get over a sickness without staying home. Sir! Spare my parents! There's no basis for any of the accusations that you're making against me now; no one has ever said a word to me about them. Perhaps you haven't seen the last orders I sent in. Anyway, I'm still going on the road with the eight o'clock train; these few hours of rest have done me good. Don't let me keep you, sir. I'll be at the office myself right away, and be so kind as to tell them this, and give my respects to the head of the firm."

And while Gregor hastily blurted all this out, hardly knowing what he was saying, he had easily approached the chest of drawers, probably as a result of the practice he had already gotten in bed, and now he tried to raise himself up against it. He actually intended to open the door, actually present himself and speak to the manager; he was eager to find out what the others, who were now so anxious to see him, would say at the sight of him. If they were shocked, then Gregor had no further responsibility and could be calm. But if they took everything calmly, then he, too, had no reason to get excited and could, if he hurried, actually be at the station by eight o'clock. At first he slid off the polished chest of drawers a few times, but at last, giving himself a final push, he stood upright; he no longer paid any attention to the pains in his abdomen, no matter how much they were burning. Now he let himself fall against the back of a nearby chair, clinging to its slats with his

---

3. premonition (prēm´ ə nish´ ən) *n.* a warning in advance of an event.

obstinacy (äb´ stə nə sē) *n.* stubbornness

Literary Analysis
Modernism According to the office manager, how is Gregor's odd behavior alienating him from daily life?

Literary Analysis
Modernism In opening the door and showing himself, what does Gregor hope to learn about his own state of mind?

✔**Reading Check**
What is the warning the office manager gives Gregor about his job?

little legs. But by doing this he had gotten control of himself and fell silent, since he could now listen to what the manager was saying.

"Did you understand a word?" the manager was asking his parents. "He isn't trying to make fools of us, is he?" "My God," cried his mother, already in tears, "maybe he's seriously ill, and here we are, torturing him. Grete! Grete!" she then cried. "Mother?" called his sister from the other side. They communicated by way of Gregor's room. "Go to the doctor's immediately. Gregor is sick. Hurry, get the doctor. Did you just hear Gregor talking?" "That was the voice of an animal," said the manager, in a tone conspicuously soft compared with the mother's yelling. "Anna!" "Anna!" the father called through the foyer into the kitchen, clapping his hands, "get a locksmith right away!" And already the two girls were running with rustling skirts through the foyer—how could his sister have gotten dressed so quickly?—and tearing open the door to the apartment. The door could not be heard slamming; they had probably left it open, as is the custom in homes where a great misfortune has occurred.

But Gregor had become much calmer. It was true that they no longer understood his words, though they had seemed clear enough to him, clearer than before, probably because his ear had grown accustomed to them. But still, the others now believed that there was something the matter with him and were ready to help him. The assurance and confidence with which the first measures had been taken did him good. He felt integrated into human society once again and hoped for marvelous, amazing feats from both the doctor and the locksmith, without really distinguishing sharply between them. In order to make his voice as clear as possible for the crucial discussions that were approaching, he cleared his throat a little—taking pains, of course, to do so in a very muffled manner, since this noise, too, might sound different from human coughing, a thing he no longer trusted himself to decide. In the next room, meanwhile, everything had become completely still. Perhaps his parents were sitting at the table with the manager, whispering; perhaps they were all leaning against the door listening.

Gregor slowly lugged himself toward the door, pushing the chair in front of him, then let go of it, threw himself against the door, held himself upright against it—the pads on the bottom of his little legs exuded a little sticky substance—and for a moment rested there from the exertion. But then he got started turning the key in the lock with his mouth. Unfortunately it seemed that he had no real teeth—what was he supposed to grip the key with?—but in compensation his jaws, of course, were very strong; with their help he actually got the key moving and paid no attention to the fact that he was undoubtedly hurting himself in some way, for a brown liquid came out of his mouth, flowed over the key, and dripped onto the floor. "Listen," said the manager in the next room, "he's turning the key." This was great encouragement to Gregor; but everyone should have cheered him on, his father and mother too. "Go, Gregor," they should have called, "keep going, at that lock, harder, harder!" And in the delusion that they were all following his efforts with suspense, he clamped his jaws madly on the key with all the strength he could muster.

Critical Viewing ▶
Does this image from a dramatic adaptation of "The Metamorphosis" effectively capture both Gregor's physical transformation and his social alienation? Explain. **[Evaluate]**

Literary Analysis
Modernism In what ways might Gregor's confidence in the locksmith and the doctor reflect society's misplaced faith in both technology and medicine?

exuded (ig zōōd' id) v. discharged a liquid through the skin

Depending on the progress of the key, he danced around the lock; holding himself upright only by his mouth, he clung to the key, as the situation demanded, or pressed it down again with the whole weight of his body. The clearer click of the lock as it finally snapped back literally woke Gregor up. With a sigh of relief he said to himself, "So I didn't need the locksmith after all," and laid his head down on the handle in order to open wide one wing of the double doors.

Since he had to use this method of opening the door, it was really opened very wide while he himself was still invisible. He first had to edge slowly around the one wing of the door, and do so very carefully if he was not to fall flat on his back just before entering. He was still busy with this difficult maneuver and had no time to pay attention to anything else when he heard the manager burst out with a loud "Oh!"—it sounded like a rush of wind—and now he could see him, standing closest to the door, his hand pressed over his open mouth, slowly backing away, as if repulsed by an invisible, unrelenting force. His mother—in spite of the manager's presence she stood with her hair still unbraided from the night, sticking out in all directions—first looked at his father with her hands clasped, then took two steps toward Gregor, and sank down in the midst of her skirts spreading out around her, her face completely hidden on her breast. With a hostile expression his father clenched his fist, as if to drive Gregor back into his room, then looked

Literary Analysis
Modernism How do his parents' reactions to seeing Gregor underscore key Modernist ideas?

✔ **Reading Check**

What does Gregor finally succeed in doing after great effort?

uncertainly around the living room, shielded his eyes with his hands, and sobbed with heaves of his powerful chest.

Now Gregor did not enter the room after all but leaned against the inside of the firmly bolted wing of the door, so that only half his body was visible and his head above it, cocked to one side and peeping out at the others. In the meantime it had grown much lighter; across the street one could see clearly a section of the endless, grayish-black building opposite—it was a hospital—with its regular windows starkly piercing the façade; the rain was still coming down, but only in large, separately visible drops that were also pelting the ground literally one at a time. The breakfast dishes were laid out lavishly on the table; since for his father breakfast was the most important meal of the day, which he would prolong for hours while reading various newspapers. On the wall directly opposite hung a photograph of Gregor from his army days, in a lieutenant's uniform, his hand on his sword, a carefree smile on his lips, demanding respect for his bearing and his rank. The door to the foyer was open, and since the front door was open too, it was possible to see out onto the landing and the top of the stairs going down.

"Well," said Gregor—and he was thoroughly aware of being the only one who had kept calm—"I'll get dressed right away, pack up my samples, and go. Will you, will you please let me go? Now, sir, you see, I'm not stubborn and I'm willing to work; traveling is a hardship, but without it I couldn't live. Where are you going, sir? To the office? Yes? Will you give an honest report of everything? A man might find for a moment that he was unable to work, but that's exactly the right time to remember his past accomplishments and to consider that later on, when the obstacle has been removed, he's bound to work all the harder and more efficiently. I'm under so many obligations to the head of the firm, as you know very well. Besides, I also have my parents and my sister to worry about. I'm in a tight spot, but I'll also work my way out again. Don't make things harder for me than they already are. Stick up for me in the office, please. Traveling salesmen aren't well liked there, I know. People think they make a fortune leading the gay life. No one has any particular reason to <u>rectify</u> this prejudice. But you, sir, you have a better perspective on things than the rest of the office, an even better perspective, just between the two of us, than the head of the firm himself, who in his capacity as owner easily lets his judgment be swayed against an employee. And you also know very well that the traveling salesman, who is out of the office practically the whole year round, can so easily become the victim of gossip, coincidences, and unfounded accusations, against which he's completely unable to defend himself, since in most cases he knows nothing at all about them except

when he returns exhausted from a trip, and back home gets to suffer on his own person the grim consequences, which can no longer be traced back to their causes. Sir, don't go away without a word to tell me you think I'm at least partly right!"

But at Gregor's first words the manager had already turned away and with curled lips looked back at Gregor only over his twitching shoulder. And during Gregor's speech he did not stand still for a minute but, without letting Gregor out of his sight, backed toward the door, yet very gradually, as if there were some secret prohibition against leaving the room. He was already in the foyer, and from the sudden movement with which he took his last step from the living room, one might have thought he had just burned the sole of his foot. In the foyer, however, he stretched his right hand far out toward the staircase, as if nothing less than an unearthly deliverance were awaiting him there.

Gregor realized that he must on no account let the manager go away in this mood if his position in the firm were not to be jeopardized in the extreme. His parents did not understand this too well; in the course of the years they had formed the conviction that Gregor was set for life in this firm; and furthermore, they were so preoccupied with their immediate troubles that they had lost all consideration for the future. But Gregor had this forethought. The manager must be detained, calmed down, convinced, and finally won over; Gregor's and the family's future depended on it! If only his sister had been there! She was perceptive; she had already begun to cry when Gregor was still lying calmly on his back. And certainly the manager, this ladies' man, would have listened to her; she would have shut the front door and in the foyer talked him out of his scare. But his sister was not there, Gregor had to handle the situation himself. And without stopping to realize that he had no idea what his new faculties of movement were, and without stopping to realize either that his speech had possibly—indeed, probably—not been understood again, he let go of the wing of the door; he shoved himself through the opening, intending to go to the manager, who was already on the landing, ridiculously holding onto the banisters with both hands; but groping for support, Gregor immediately fell down with a little cry onto his numerous little legs. This had hardly happened when for the first time that morning he had a feeling of physical well-being; his little legs were on firm ground; they obeyed him completely, as he noted to his joy; they even strained to carry him away wherever he wanted to go; and he already believed that final recovery from all his sufferings was <u>imminent</u>. But at that very moment, as he lay on the floor rocking with repressed motion, not far from his mother and just opposite her, she, who had seemed so completely self-absorbed, all at once jumped up, her arms stretched wide, her fingers spread, and cried, "Help, for God's sake, help!" held her head bent as if to see Gregor better, but inconsistently darted madly backward instead; had forgotten that the table laden with the breakfast dishes stood behind her; sat down on it hastily, as if her thoughts were elsewhere, when she

Reading Strategy
Applying the Author's Biography How might Gregor's reactions reflect Kafka's feelings about his financial responsibilities for his family?

imminent (im´ ə nənt) *adj.* ready to happen at any moment

**Reading Check**

Once his door is open, what does Gregor insist he be permitted to do?

reached it; and did not seem to notice at all that near her the big coffee-pot had been knocked over and coffee was pouring in a steady stream onto the rug.

"Mother, Mother," said Gregor softly and looked up at her. For a minute the manager had completely slipped his mind; on the other hand at the sight of the spilling coffee he could not resist snapping his jaws several times in the air. At this his mother screamed once more, fled from the table, and fell into the arms of his father, who came rushing up to her. But Gregor had no time now for his parents; the manager was already on the stairs; with his chin on the banister, he was taking a last look back. Gregor was off to a running start, to be as sure as possible of catching up with him; the manager must have suspected something like this, for he leaped down several steps and disappeared; but still he shouted "Agh," and the sound carried through the whole staircase. Unfortunately the manager's flight now seemed to confuse his father completely, who had been relatively calm until now, for instead of running after the manager himself, or at least not hindering Gregor in his pursuit, he seized in his right hand the manager's cane, which had been left behind on a chair with his hat and overcoat, picked up in his left hand a heavy newspaper from the table, and stamping his feet, started brandishing the cane and the newspaper to drive Gregor back into his room. No plea of Gregor's helped, no plea was even understood; however humbly he might turn his head, his father merely stamped his feet more forcefully. Across the room his mother had thrown open a window in spite of the cool weather, and leaning out, she buried her face, far outside the window, in her hands. Between the alley and the staircase a strong draft was created, the window curtains blew in, the newspapers on the table rustled, single sheets fluttered across the floor. Pitilessly his father came on, hissing like a wild man. Now Gregor had not had any practice at all walking in reverse, it was really very slow going. If Gregor had only been allowed to turn around, he could have gotten into his room right away, but he was afraid to make his father impatient by this time-consuming gyration, and at any minute the cane in his father's hand threatened to come down on his back or his head with a deadly blow. Finally, however, Gregor had no choice, for he noticed with horror that in reverse he could not even keep going in one direction; and so, incessantly throwing uneasy side-glances at his father, he began to turn around as quickly as possible, in reality turning only very slowly. Perhaps his father realized his good intentions, for he did not interfere with him; instead, he even now and then directed the maneuver from afar with the tip of his cane. If only his father did not keep making this intolerable hissing sound! It made Gregor lose his head completely. He had almost finished the turn when— his mind continually on this hissing—he made a mistake and even started turning back around to his original position. But when he had at last successfully managed to get his head in front of the opened door, it turned out that his body was too broad to get through as it was. Of course in his father's present state of mind it did not even remotely occur to him

Reading Strategy
Applying the Author's Biography In what ways does this description of Gregor's father reflect your knowledge about Kafka's father?

gyration (jī rā′ shən) n. circular or spiral motion

to open the other wing of the door in order to give Gregor enough room to pass through. He had only the fixed idea that Gregor must return to his room as quickly as possible. He would never have allowed the complicated preliminaries Gregor needed to go through in order to stand up on one end and perhaps in this way fit through the door. Instead he drove Gregor on, as if there were no obstacle, with exceptional loudness; the voice behind Gregor did not sound like that of only a single father; now this was really no joke anymore, and Gregor forced himself—come what may—into the doorway. One side of his body rose up, he lay lop-sided in the opening, one of his flanks was scraped raw, ugly blotches marred the white door, soon he got stuck and could not have budged anymore by himself, his little legs on one side dangled tremblingly in midair, those on the other were painfully crushed against the floor—when from behind his father gave him a hard shove, which was truly his salvation, and bleeding profusely, he flew far into his room. The door was slammed shut with the cane, then at last everything was quiet.

Review and Assess

Thinking About Part I

1. **Respond:** In what ways, if any, did the characters in this story remind you of people whom you have met?

2. **(a) Recall:** What is Gregor's first reaction to his transformation? **(b) Generalize:** How does Gregor's family react to his transformation? **(c) Analyze:** In what ways do the differences in their reactions set up a challenge for this family?

3. **(a) Recall:** Who visits Gregor on the first morning of his transformation? **(b) Generalize:** How would you describe Gregor's relationship to this person? Explain. **(c) Analyze:** Was Gregor happy in his life before his transformation? Explain.

4. **(a) Recall:** In what ways are Gregor's parents indebted to Gregor's boss? **(b) Analyze Cause and Effect:** What does Gregor seem to fear will happen to his family if he loses his job?

5. **(a) Speculate:** Why do you think neither his family nor the office manager ever questions whether the creature before them is actually Gregor? **(b) Support:** Which details, if any, in Part I suggest that Gregor's physical transformation is an outward expression of an alienation he has already experienced both at home and at work? Explain.

6. **Analyze:** Do you think Gregor's inner sense of self has changed as a result of his physical transformation? Explain.

Part I of "The Metamorphosis" ends with Gregor being driven back into his room by his cane-wielding father. The office manager has fled in horror, the family is in shock, and Gregor himself is wounded and bloody. Do you think Gregor will be able to overcome his family's revulsion? Do you think he will become normal and human again, or will he grow increasingly alienated and different? Read Part II to see what happens as the first day of Gregor's strange transformation continues.

Part II

It was already dusk when Gregor awoke from his deep, comalike sleep. Even if he had not been disturbed, he would certainly not have woken up much later, for he felt that he had rested and slept long enough, but it seemed to him that a hurried step and a cautious shutting of the door leading to the foyer had awakened him. The light of the electric street-lamps lay in <u>pallid</u> streaks on the ceiling and on the upper parts of the furniture, but underneath, where Gregor was, it was dark. Groping clumsily with his antennae, which he was only now beginning to appreciate, he slowly dragged himself toward the door to see what had been happening there. His left side felt like one single long, unpleasantly tautening scar, and he actually had to limp on his two rows of legs. Besides, one little leg had been seriously injured in the course of the morning's events—it was almost a miracle that only one had been injured—and dragged along lifelessly.

Only after he got to the door did he notice what had really attracted him—the smell of something to eat. For there stood a bowl filled with fresh milk, in which small slices of white bread were floating. He could almost have laughed for joy, since he was even hungrier than he had been in the morning, and he immediately dipped his head into the milk, almost to over his eyes. But he soon drew it back again in disappointment; not only because he had difficulty eating on account of the soreness in his left side—and he could eat only if his whole panting body cooperated—but because he didn't like the milk at all, although it used to be his favorite drink, and that was certainly why his sister had put it in the room; in fact, he turned away from the bowl almost with repulsion and crawled back to the middle of the room.

In the living room, as Gregor saw through the crack in the door, the gas had been lit, but while at this hour of the day his father was in the habit of reading the afternoon newspaper in a loud voice to his mother and sometimes to his sister too, now there wasn't a sound. Well, perhaps this custom of reading aloud, which his sister was always telling

pallid (pal´ id) *adj.* pale

Literary Analysis
Modernism In what ways does Gregor's rejection of the food brought by Grete symbolize his growing alienation?

him and writing him about, had recently been discontinued altogether. But in all the other rooms too it was just as still, although the apartment certainly was not empty. "What a quiet life the family has been leading," Gregor said to himself, and while he stared rigidly in front of him into the darkness, he felt very proud that he had been able to provide such a life in so nice an apartment for his parents and his sister. But what now if all the peace, the comfort, the contentment were to come to a horrible end? In order not to get involved in such thoughts, Gregor decided to keep moving, and he crawled up and down the room.

During the long evening first one of the side doors and then the other was opened a small crack and quickly shut again; someone had probably had the urge to come in and then had had second thoughts. Gregor now settled into position right by the living-room door, determined somehow to get the hesitating visitor to come in, or at least to find out who it might be; but the door was not opened again, and Gregor waited in vain. In the morning, when the doors had been locked, everyone had wanted to come in; now that he had opened one of the doors and the others had evidently been opened during the day, no one came in, and now the keys were even inserted on the outside.

It was late at night when the light finally went out in the living room, and now it was easy for Gregor to tell that his parents and his sister had stayed up so long, since, as he could distinctly hear, all three were now retiring on tiptoe. Certainly no one would come in to Gregor until the morning; and so he had ample time to consider undisturbed how best to rearrange his life. But the empty high-ceilinged room in which he was forced to lie flat on the floor made him nervous, without his being able to tell why—since it was, after all, the room in which he had lived for the past five years—and turning half unconsciously and not without a slight feeling of shame, he scuttled under the couch where, although his back was a little crushed and he could not raise his head anymore, he immediately felt very comfortable and was only sorry that his body was too wide to go completely under the couch.

There he stayed the whole night, which he spent partly in a sleepy trance, from which hunger pangs kept waking him with a start, partly in worries and vague hopes, all of which, however, led to the conclusion that for the time being he would have to lie low and, by being patient and showing his family every possible consideration, help them bear

FRANZ KAFKA
DIE VERWANDLUNG

DER JÜNGSTE TAG ★ 22/23
KURT WOLFF VERLAG · LEIPZIG
1916

▲ **Critical Viewing**
Why do you think Kafka insisted that the illustration for the cover of the first edition of "The Metamorphosis," shown above, not depict the insect itself? [Speculate]

☑**Reading Check**
Where have the keys to Gregor's room been moved?

the inconvenience which he simply had to cause them in his present condition.

Early in the morning—it was still almost night—Gregor had the opportunity of testing the strength of the resolutions he had just made, for his sister, almost fully dressed, opened the door from the foyer and looked in eagerly. She did not see him right away, but when she caught sight of him under the couch—God, he had to be somewhere, he couldn't just fly away—she became so frightened that she lost control of herself and slammed the door shut again. But, as if she felt sorry for her behavior, she immediately opened the door again and came in on tiptoe, as if she were visiting someone seriously ill or perhaps even a stranger. Gregor had pushed his head forward just to the edge of the couch and was watching her. Would she notice that he had left the milk standing, and not because he hadn't been hungry, and would she bring in a dish of something he'd like better? If she were not going to do it of her own free will, he would rather starve than call it to her attention, although, really, he felt an enormous urge to shoot out from under the couch, throw himself at his sister's feet, and beg her for something good to eat. But his sister noticed at once, to her astonishment, that the bowl was still full, only a little milk was spilled around it; she picked it up immediately—not with her bare hands, of course, but with a rag— and carried it out. Gregor was extremely curious to know what she would bring him instead, and he racked his brains on the subject. But he would never have been able to guess what his sister, in the goodness of her heart, actually did. To find out his likes and dislikes, she brought him a wide assortment of things, all spread out on an old newspaper: old, half-rotten vegetables; bones left over from the evening meal, caked with congealed white sauce; some raisins and almonds; a piece of cheese, which two days before Gregor had declared inedible; a plain slice of bread, a slice of bread and butter, and one with butter and salt. In addition to all this she put down some water in the bowl apparently permanently earmarked for Gregor's use. And out of a sense of delicacy, since she knew that Gregor would not eat in front of her, she left hurriedly and even turned the key, just so that Gregor should know that he might make himself as comfortable as he wanted. Gregor's legs began whirring now that he was going to eat. Besides, his bruises must have completely healed, since he no longer felt any handicap, and marveling at this he thought how, over a month ago he had cut his finger very slightly with a knife and how this wound was still hurting him only the day before yesterday. "Have I become less sensitive?" he thought, already sucking greedily at the cheese, which had immediately and forcibly attracted him ahead of all the other dishes. One right after the other, and with eyes streaming with tears of contentment, he devoured the cheese, the vegetables, and the sauce; the fresh foods, on the other hand, he did not care for; he couldn't even stand their smell and even dragged the things he wanted to eat a bit further away. He had finished with everything long since and was just lying lazily at the same spot when his sister slowly turned the key as a sign for him to withdraw.

Literary Analysis
Modernism Do Gregor's thoughts reflect a realistic viewpoint on his life and prospects? Explain.

Literary Analysis
Modernism What evidence does this passage describing his meal provide for the view that Gregor is more alienated from the world of humans than he realizes?

That immediately startled him although he was almost asleep, and he scuttled under the couch again. But it took great self-control for him to stay under the couch even for the short time his sister was in the room, since his body had become a little bloated from the heavy meal, and in his cramped position he could hardly breathe. In between slight attacks of suffocation he watched with bulging eyes as his unsuspecting sister took a broom and swept up, not only his leavings, but even the foods which Gregor had left completely untouched—as if they too were no longer usable—and dumping everything hastily into a pail, which she covered with a wooden lid, she carried everything out. She had hardly turned her back when Gregor came out from under the couch, stretching and puffing himself up.

This, then, was the way Gregor was fed each day, once in the morning, when his parents and the maid were still asleep, and a second time in the afternoon after everyone had had dinner, for then his parents took a short nap again, and the maid could be sent out by his sister on some errand. Certainly they did not want him to starve either, but perhaps they would not have been able to stand knowing any more about his meals than from hearsay, or perhaps his sister wanted to spare them even what was possibly only a minor torment, for really, they were suffering enough as it was.

Gregor could not find out what excuses had been made to get rid of the doctor and the locksmith on that first morning, for since the others could not understand what he said, it did not occur to any of them, not even to his sister, that he could understand what they said, and so he had to be satisfied, when his sister was in the room, with only occasionally hearing her sighs and appeals to the saints. It was only later, when she had begun to get used to everything—there could never, of course, be any question of a complete adjustment—that Gregor sometimes caught a remark which was meant to be friendly or could be interpreted as such. "Oh, he liked what he had today," she would say when Gregor had tucked away a good helping, and in the opposite case, which gradually occurred more and more frequently, she used to say, almost sadly, "He's left everything again."

But if Gregor could not get any news directly, he overheard a great deal from the neighboring rooms, and as soon as he heard voices, he would immediately run to the door concerned and press his whole body against it. Especially in the early days, there was no conversation that was not somehow about him, if only implicitly. For two whole days there were family consultations at every mealtime about how they should cope; this was also the topic of discussion between meals, for at least two members of the family were always at home, since no one probably wanted to stay home alone and it was

Themes in World Literature

The Modernist Revolution

During the late nineteenth and early twentieth centuries, major scientific, technological, and industrial developments occurred that dramatically altered the way people lived. Not only did this period witness such breakthroughs as the invention of the automobile, the airplane, the telephone, and the machine gun, but it also saw the emergence of brilliant thinkers and scientists, including Sigmund Freud, Albert Einstein, and Friedrich Nietzsche, whose ideas reshaped people's understanding of themselves and the world around them. This period of rapid change culminated in World War I, a bloody conflict that wiped out almost an entire generation of European men. As a result of these events and developments, many people felt the need to discard the ideas and values of the past and to find new ideas that more appropriately reflected twentieth-century life. Franz Kafka's disturbing fictional world is one of the best literary examples of this new vision, but the Modernist movement affected every creative discipline. The Modernists' vibrant, unsettling, and profound artistic experiments continue to resonate in our culture to this day.

☑ Reading Check

What kinds of food does Gregor now prefer?

impossible to leave the apartment completely empty. Besides, on the very first day the maid—it was not completely clear what and how much she knew of what had happened—had begged his mother on bended knees to dismiss her immediately; and when she said goodbye a quarter of an hour later, she thanked them in tears for the dismissal, as if for the greatest favor that had ever been done to her in this house, and made a solemn vow, without anyone asking her for it, not to give anything away to anyone.

Now his sister, working with her mother, had to do the cooking too; of course that did not cause her much trouble, since they hardly ate anything. Gregor was always hearing one of them pleading in vain with one of the others to eat and getting no answer except, "Thanks, I've had enough," or something similar. They did not seem to drink anything either. His sister often asked her father if he wanted any beer and gladly offered to go out for it herself; and when he did not answer, she said, in order to remove any hesitation on his part, that she could also send the janitor's wife to get it, but then his father finally answered with a definite "No," and that was the end of that.

In the course of the very first day his father explained the family's financial situation and prospects to both the mother and the sister. From time to time he got up from the table to get some kind of receipt or notebook out of the little strongbox he had rescued from the collapse of his business five years before. Gregor heard him open the complicated lock and secure it again after taking out what he had been looking for. These explanations by his father were to some extent the first pleasant news Gregor had heard since his imprisonment. He had always believed that his father had not been able to save a penny from the business, at least his father had never told him anything to the con-

▼ **Critical Viewing**
In this photograph of Mikhail Baryshnikov as Gregor Samsa, what information do you think Gregor might be overhearing? Explain. **[Hypothesize]**

trary, and Gregor, for his part, had never asked him any questions. In those days Gregor's sole concern had been to do everything in his power to make the family forget as quickly as possible the business disaster which had plunged everyone into a state of total despair. And so he had begun to work with special ardor[4] and had risen almost overnight from stock clerk to traveling salesman, which of course had opened up very different money-making possibilities, and in no time his successes on the job were transformed, by means of commissions, into hard cash that could be plunked down on the table at home in front of his astonished and delighted family. Those had been wonderful times, and they had never returned, at least not with the same glory, although later on Gregor earned enough money to meet the expenses of the entire family and actually did so. They had just gotten used to it, the family as well as Gregor, the money was received with thanks and given with pleasure, but no special feeling of warmth went with it any more. Only his sister had remained close to Gregor, and it was his secret plan that she who, unlike him, loved music and could play the violin movingly, should be sent next year to the Conservatory, regardless of the great expense involved, which could surely be made up for in some other way. Often during Gregor's short stays in the city, the Conservatory would come up in his conversations with his sister, but always merely as a beautiful dream which was not supposed to come true, and his parents were not happy to hear even these innocent allusions; but Gregor had very concrete ideas on the subject and he intended solemnly to announce his plan on Christmas Eve.

Thoughts like these, completely useless in his present state, went through his head as he stood glued to the door, listening. Sometimes out of general exhaustion he could not listen anymore and let his head bump carelessly against the door, but immediately pulled it back again, for even the slight noise he made by doing this had been heard in the next room and made them all lapse into silence. "What's he carrying on about in there now?" said his father after a while, obviously turning toward the door, and only then would the interrupted conversation gradually be resumed.

Gregor now learned in a thorough way—for his father was in the habit of often repeating himself in his explanations, partly because he himself had not dealt with these matters for a long time, partly, too, because his mother did not understand everything the first time around—that in spite of all their misfortunes a bit of capital, a very little bit, certainly, was still intact from the old days, which in the meantime had increased a little through the untouched interest. But besides that, the money Gregor had brought home every month—he had kept only a few dollars for himself—had never been completely used up and had accumulated into a tidy principal. Behind his door Gregor nodded emphatically, delighted at this unexpected foresight and thrift. Of course he actually could have paid off more of his father's debt to the

4. ardor (är′ dər) *n.* emotional warmth.

Reading Strategy
Applying the Author's Biography Kafka's father did not support his son's literary aspirations. How does that information add meaning to this discussion about the Conservatory?

Reading Check

What event, five years before, had plunged the family into financial distress?

boss with this extra money, and the day on which he could have gotten rid of his job would have been much closer, but now things were undoubtedly better the way his father had arranged them.

Now this money was by no means enough to let the family live off the interest; the principal was perhaps enough to support the family for one year, or at the most two, but that was all there was. So it was just a sum that really should not be touched and that had to be put away for a rainy day; but the money to live on would have to be earned. Now his father was still healthy, certainly, but he was an old man who had not worked for the past five years and who in any case could not be expected to undertake too much; during these five years, which were the first vacation of his hard-working yet unsuccessful life, he had gained a lot of weight and as a result had become fairly sluggish. And was his old mother now supposed to go out and earn money, when she suffered from asthma, when a walk through the apartment was already an ordeal for her, and when she spent every other day lying on the sofa under the open window, gasping for breath? And was his sister now supposed to work—who for all her seventeen years was still a child and whom it would be such a pity to deprive of the life she had led until now, which had consisted of wearing pretty clothes, sleeping late, help-ing in the house, enjoying a few modest amusements, and above all playing the violin? At first, whenever the conversation turned to the necessity of earning money, Gregor would let go of the door and throw himself down on the cool leather sofa which stood beside it, for he felt hot with shame and grief.

Often he lay there the whole long night through, not sleeping a wink and only scrabbling on the leather for hours on end. Or, not balking at the huge effort of pushing an armchair to the window, he would crawl up to the window sill and, propped up in the chair, lean against the window, evidently in some sort of remembrance of the feeling of free-dom he used to have from looking out the window. For, in fact, from day to day he saw things even a short distance away less and less dis-tinctly; the hospital opposite, which he used to curse because he saw so much of it, was now completely beyond his range of vision, and if he had not been positive that he was living in Charlotte Street—a quiet but still very much a city street—he might have believed that he was look-ing out of his window into a desert where the gray sky and the gray earth were indistinguishably fused. It took his observant sister only twice to notice that his armchair was standing by the window for her to push the chair back to the same place by the window each time she had finished cleaning the room, and from then on she even left the inside casement of the window open.

If Gregor had only been able to speak to his sister and thank her for everything she had to do for him, he could have accepted her services more easily; as it was, they caused him pain. Of course his sister tried to ease the embarrassment of the whole situation as much as possible, and as time went on, she naturally managed it better and better, but in time Gregor, too, saw things much more clearly. Even the way she came

Literary Analysis
Modernism In what ways does this information about their finances and work skills emphasize the entire family's alienation from the world at large?

Reading Strategy
Applying the Author's Biography How would living in a city have helped Kafka write this description?

in was terrible for him. Hardly had she entered the room than she would run straight to the window without taking time to close the door—though she was usually so careful to spare everyone the sight of Gregor's room— then tear open the casements with eager hands, almost as if she were suffocating, and remain for a little while at the window even in the coldest weather, breathing deeply. With this racing and crashing she frightened Gregor twice a day; the whole time he cowered under the couch, and yet he knew very well that she would certainly have spared him this if only she had found it possible to stand being in a room with him with the window closed.

One time—it must have been a month since Gregor's metamorphosis, and there was certainly no particular reason any more for his sister to be astonished at Gregor's appearance—she came a little earlier than usual and caught Gregor still looking out the window, immobile and so in an excellent position to be terrifying. It would not have surprised Gregor if she had not come in, because his position prevented her from immediately opening the window, but not only did she not come in, she even sprang back and locked the door; a stranger might easily have thought that Gregor had been lying in wait for her, wanting to bite her. Of course Gregor immediately hid under the couch, but he had to wait until noon before his sister came again, and she seemed much more uneasy than usual. He realized from this that the sight of him was still repulsive to her and was bound to remain repulsive to her in the future, and that she probably had to overcome a lot of resistance not to run away at the sight of even the small part of his body that jutted out from under the couch. So, to spare her even this sight, one day he carried the sheet on his back to the couch—the job took four hours—and arranged it in such a way that he was now completely covered up and his sister could not see him even when she stooped. If she had considered this sheet unnecessary, then of course she could have removed it, for it was clear enough that it could not be for his own pleasure that Gregor shut himself off altogether, but she left the sheet the way it was, and Gregor thought that he had even caught a grateful look when one time he cautiously lifted the sheet a little with his head in order to see how his sister was taking the new arrangement.

During the first two weeks, his parents could not bring themselves to come in to him, and often he heard them say how much they appreciated his sister's work, whereas until now they had frequently been annoyed with her because she had struck them as being a little useless. But now both of them, his father and his mother, often waited outside Gregor's room while his sister straightened it up, and as soon as she came out she had to tell them in great detail how the room looked, what Gregor had eaten, how he had behaved this time, and whether he had perhaps shown a little improvement. His mother, incidentally, began relatively soon to want to visit Gregor, but his father and his sister at first held her back with reasonable arguments to which Gregor listened very attentively and of which he wholeheartedly approved. But later she had to be restrained by force, and then when she cried out,

Literary Analysis
Modernism What does Gregor now do, deliberately, to alienate himself? Why does he do this?

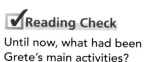

Reading Check
Until now, what had been Grete's main activities?

The Metamorphosis, Part II ◆ 999

"Let me go to Gregor, he is my unfortunate boy! Don't you understand that I have to go to him?" Gregor thought that it might be a good idea after all if his mother did come in, not every day of course, but perhaps once a week; she could still do everything much better than his sister, who, for all her courage, was still only a child and in the final analysis had perhaps taken on such a difficult assignment only out of childish flightiness.

Gregor's desire to see his mother was soon fulfilled. During the day Gregor did not want to show himself at the window, if only out of consideration for his parents, but he couldn't crawl very far on his few square yards of floor space, either; he could hardly put up with just lying still even at night; eating soon stopped giving him the slightest pleasure, so, as a distraction, he adopted the habit of crawling crisscross over the walls and the ceiling. He especially liked hanging from the ceiling; it was completely different from lying on the floor; one could breathe more freely; a faint swinging sensation went through the body; and in the almost happy absent-mindedness which Gregor felt up there, it could happen to his own surprise that he let go and plopped onto the floor. But now, of course, he had much better control of his body than before and did not hurt himself even from such a big drop. His sister immediately noticed the new entertainment Gregor had discovered for himself—after all, he left behind traces of his sticky substance wherever he crawled—and so she got it into her head to make it possible for Gregor to crawl on an altogether wider scale by taking out the furniture which stood in his way—mainly the chest of drawers and the desk. But she was not able to do this by herself; she did not dare ask her father for help; the maid would certainly not have helped her, for although this girl, who was about sixteen, was bravely sticking it out after the previous cook had left, she had asked for the favor of locking herself in the kitchen at all times and of only opening the door on special request. So there was nothing left for his sister to do except to get her mother one day when her father was out. And his mother did come, with exclamations of excited joy, but she grew silent at the door of Gregor's room. First his sister looked to see, of course, that everything in the room was in order; only then did she let her mother come in. Hurrying as fast as he could, Gregor had pulled the sheet down lower still and pleated it more tightly—it really looked just like a sheet accidentally thrown over the couch. This time Gregor also refrained from spying from under the sheet; he renounced seeing

Literature in context Science Connection

What Kind of Insect Is Gregor Samsa?

Readers of "The Metamorphosis" have long debated what kind of "vermin" Gregor has become. American novelist John Updike writes: "Popular belief has him a cockroach. . . . But, as Vladimir Nabokov, who knew his entomology, pointed out . . . , Gregor is too broad and convex to be a cockroach. . . . Gregor Samsa, awaking, sees 'numerous legs, which were pitifully thin compared to the rest of his bulk.' If 'numerous' is more than six, then he must be a centipede—not an insect at all.

From evidence in the story he is brown in color and about as long as the distance between a doorknob and the floor. He has a kind of voice at first . . . which disappears as the story progresses. His jaws don't work as ours do but he has eyelids, nostrils, and a neck. He is, in short, impossible to picture except when the author wants to evoke his appearance, to bump the reader up against some astounding, poignant new aspect of Gregor's embodiment. . . ."

his mother for the time being and was simply happy that she had come after all. "Come on, you can't see him," his sister said, evidently leading her mother in by the hand. Now Gregor could hear the two frail women moving the old chest of drawers—heavy for anyone—from its place and his sister insisting on doing the harder part of the job herself, ignoring the warnings of her mother, who was afraid that she would overexert herself. It went on for a long time. After struggling for a good quarter of an hour, his mother said that they had better leave the chest where it was, because, in the first place, it was too heavy, they would not finish before his father came, and with the chest in the middle of the room, Gregor would be completely barricaded; and, in the second place, it was not at all certain they were doing Gregor a favor by removing his furniture. To her the opposite seemed to be the case; the sight of the bare wall was heart-breaking; and why shouldn't Gregor also have the same feeling, since he had been used to his furniture for so long and would feel abandoned in the empty room. "And doesn't it look," his mother concluded very softly—in fact she had been almost whispering the whole time, as if she wanted to avoid letting Gregor, whose exact where-abouts she did not know, hear even the sound of her voice, for she was convinced that he did not understand the words—"and doesn't it look as if by removing his furniture we were showing him that we have given up all hope of his getting better and are leaving him to his own devices without any consideration? I think the best thing would be to try to keep the room exactly the way it was before, so that when Gregor comes back to us again, he'll find everything unchanged and can forget all the more easily what's happened in the meantime."

When he heard his mother's words, Gregor realized that the monot-ony of family life, combined with the fact that not a soul had addressed a word directly to him, must have addled[5] his brain in the course of the past two months, for he could not explain to himself in any other way how in all seriousness he could have been anxious to have his room cleared out. Had he really wanted to have his warm room, comfortably fitted with furniture that had always been in the family, changed into a cave, in which, of course, he would be able to crawl around unham-pered in all directions but at the cost of simultaneously, rapidly, and totally forgetting his human past? Even now he had been on the verge of forgetting, and only his mother's voice, which he had not heard for so long, had shaken him up. Nothing should be removed; everything had to stay; he could not do without the beneficial influence of the furniture on his state of mind; and if the furniture prevented him from carrying on this senseless crawling around, then that was no loss but rather a great advantage.

But his sister unfortunately had a different opinion; she had become accustomed, certainly not entirely without justification, to adopt with her parents the role of the particularly well-qualified expert whenever Gre-gor's affairs were being discussed; and so her mother's advice was now

---

5. **addled** (ad′ ′ld) v. muddled or confused.

Literary Analysis
Modernism What does the removal of the furniture suggest to Gregor's mother about the permanence of her son's alienation from the family?

☑Reading Check

What change to Gregor's room does Grete decide to make?

sufficient reason for her to insist, not only on the removal of the chest of drawers and the desk, which was all she had been planning at first, but also on the removal of all the furniture with the exception of the indispensable couch. Of course it was not only childish defiance and the self-confidence she had recently acquired so unexpectedly and at such a cost that led her to make this demand; she had in fact noticed that Gregor needed plenty of room to crawl around in; and on the other hand, as best as she could tell, he never used the furniture at all. Perhaps, however, the romantic enthusiasm of girls her age, which seeks to indulge itself at every opportunity, played a part, by tempting her to make Gregor's situation even more terrifying in order that she might do even more for him. Into a room in which Gregor ruled the bare walls all alone, no human being besides Grete was ever likely to set foot.

And so she did not let herself be swerved from her decision by her mother, who, besides, from the sheer anxiety of being in Gregor's room, seemed unsure of herself, soon grew silent, and helped her daughter as best she could to get the chest of drawers out of the room. Well, in a pinch Gregor could do without the chest, but the desk had to stay. And hardly had the women left the room with the chest, squeezing against it and groaning, than Gregor stuck his head out from under the couch to see how he could feel his way into the situation as considerately as possible. But unfortunately it had to be his mother who came back first, while in the next room Grete was clasping the chest and rocking it back and forth by herself, without of course budging it from the spot. His mother, however, was not used to the sight of Gregor, he could have made her ill, and so Gregor, frightened, scuttled in reverse to the far end of the couch but could not stop the sheet from shifting a little at the front. That was enough to put his mother on the alert. She stopped, stood still for a moment, and then went back to Grete.

Although Gregor told himself over and over again that nothing special was happening, only a few pieces of furniture were being moved, he soon had to admit that this coming and going of the women, their little calls to each other, the scraping of the furniture along the floor had the effect on him of a great turmoil swelling on all sides, and as much as he tucked in his head and his legs and shrank until his belly touched the floor, he was forced to admit that he would not be able to stand it much longer. They were clearing out his room; depriving him of everything that he loved; they had already carried away the chest of drawers, in which he kept the fretsaw and other tools; were now budging the desk firmly embedded in the floor, the desk he had done his homework on when he was a student at business college, in high school, yes, even in public school—now he really had no more time to examine the good intentions of the two women, whose existence, besides, he had almost forgotten, for they were so exhausted that they were working in silence, and one could hear only the heavy shuffling of their feet.

And so he broke out—the women were just leaning against the desk in the next room to catch their breath for a minute—changed his course four times, he really didn't know what to salvage first, then he saw hang-

Literary Analysis
Modernism Do you think this explanation for Grete's desire to intensify Gregor's alienation is valid? Explain.

ing conspicuously on the wall, which was otherwise bare already, the picture of the lady all dressed in furs, hurriedly crawled up on it and pressed himself against the glass, which gave a good surface to stick to and soothed his hot belly. At least no one would take away this picture, while Gregor completely covered it up. He turned his head toward the living-room door to watch the women when they returned.

They had not given themselves much of a rest and were already coming back; Grete had put her arm around her mother and was practically carrying her. "So what should we take now?" said Grete and looked around. At that her eyes met Gregor's as he clung to the wall. Probably only because of her mother's presence she kept her self-control, bent her head down to her mother to keep her from looking around, and said, though in a quavering and thoughtless voice: "Come, we'd better go back into the living room for a minute." Grete's intent was clear to Gregor, she wanted to

Lady in Yellow (Eleanor Reeves), ca. 1905, Susan Watkins, Chrysler Museum of Art, Norfolk, VA

bring his mother into safety and then chase him down from the wall. Well, just let her try! He squatted on his picture and would not give it up. He would rather fly in Grete's face.

But Grete's words had now made her mother really anxious; she stepped to one side, caught sight of the gigantic brown blotch on the flowered wallpaper, and before it really dawned on her that what she saw was Gregor, cried in a hoarse, bawling voice: "Oh, God, Oh, God!"; and as if giving up completely, she fell with outstretched arms across the couch and did not stir. "You, Gregor!" cried his sister with raised fist and piercing eyes. These were the first words she had addressed directly to him since his metamorphosis. She ran into the next room to get some kind of spirits to revive her mother; Gregor wanted to help

▲ **Critical Viewing**
In what ways do you think this portrait is both similar to and different from Gregor's picture of a lady "all dressed in furs"? [Compare and Contrast]

☑ **Reading Check**
What does Gregor do in reaction to the removal of his furniture?

too—there was time to rescue the picture—but he was stuck to the glass and had to tear himself loose by force; then he too ran into the next room, as if he could give his sister some sort of advice, as in the old days; but then had to stand behind her doing nothing while she rummaged among various little bottles; moreover, when she turned around she was startled, a bottle fell on the floor and broke, a splinter of glass wounded Gregor in the face, some kind of corrosive medicine flowed around him; now without waiting any longer, Grete grabbed as many little bottles as she could carry and ran with them inside to her mother; she slammed the door behind her with her foot. Now Gregor was cut off from his mother, who was perhaps near death through his fault; he could not dare open the door if he did not want to chase away his sister, who had to stay with his mother; now there was nothing for him to do except wait; and tormented by self-reproaches and worry, he began to crawl, crawled over everything, walls, furniture and ceiling, and finally in desperation, as the whole room was beginning to spin, fell down onto the middle of the big table.

A short time passed; Gregor lay there prostrate; all around, things were quiet, perhaps that was a good sign. Then the doorbell rang. The maid, of course, was locked up in her kitchen and so Grete had to answer the door. His father had come home. "What's happened?" were his first words; Grete's appearance must have told him everything. Grete answered in a muffled voice, her face was obviously pressed against her father's chest; "Mother fainted, but she's better now. Gregor's broken out." "I knew it," his father said. "I kept telling you, but you women don't want to listen." It was clear to Gregor that his father had put the worst interpretation on Grete's all-too-brief announcement and assumed that Gregor was guilty of some outrage. Therefore Gregor now had to try to calm his father down, since he had neither the time nor the ability to enlighten him. And so he fled to the door of his room and pressed himself against it for his father to see, as soon as he came into the foyer, that Gregor had the best intentions of returning to his room immediately and that it was not necessary to drive him back; if only the door were opened for him, he would disappear at once.

But his father was in no mood to notice such subtleties; "Ah!" he cried as he entered, in a tone that sounded as if he were at once furious and glad. Gregor turned his head away from the door and lifted it toward his father. He had not really imagined his father looking like this, as he stood in front of him now; admittedly Gregor had been too absorbed recently in his newfangled crawling to bother as much as before about events in the rest of the house and should really have been prepared to find some changes. And yet, and yet—was this still his father? Was this the same man who in the old days used to lie wearily buried in bed when Gregor left on a business trip; who greeted him on his return in the evening, sitting in his bathrobe in the armchair, who actually had difficulty getting to his feet but as a sign of joy only lifted up his arms; and who, on the rare occasions when the whole family went out for a walk, on a few Sundays in June and on the major hol-

Literary Analysis
Modernism How does this scene capture key Modernist themes, especially those of helplessness and alienation?

Literary Analysis
Modernism and Literature of the Fantastic In what ways does Gregor's surprise about his father's changed appearance reflect the fantastic nature of this story?

idays, used to shuffle along with great effort between Gregor and his mother, who were slow walkers themselves, always a little more slowly than they, wrapped in his old overcoat, always carefully planting down his crutch-handled cane, and, when he wanted to say something, nearly always stood still and assembled his escort around him? Now, however, he was holding himself very erect, dressed in a tight-fitting blue uniform with gold buttons, the kind worn by messengers at banking concerns; above the high stiff collar of the jacket his heavy chin protruded; under his bushy eyebrows his black eyes darted bright, piercing glances; his usually rumpled white hair was combed flat, with a scrupulously exact, gleaming part. He threw his cap—which was adorned with a gold monogram, probably that of a bank—in an arc across the entire room onto the couch, and with the tails of his long uniform jacket slapped back, his hands in his pants pockets, went for Gregor with a sullen look on his face. He probably did not know himself what he had in mind; still he lifted his feet unusually high off the floor, and Gregor staggered at the gigantic size of the soles of his boots. But he did not linger over this, he had known right from the first day of his new life that his father considered only the strictest treatment called for in dealing with him. And so he ran ahead of his father, stopped when his father stood still, and scooted ahead again when his father made even the slightest movement. In this way they made more than one tour of the room, without anything decisive happening; in fact the whole movement did not even have the appearance of a chase because of its slow tempo. So Gregor kept to the floor for the time being, especially since he was afraid that his father might interpret a flight onto the walls or the ceiling as a piece of particular nastiness. Of course Gregor had to admit that he would not be able to keep up even this running for long, for whenever his father took one step, Gregor had to execute countless movements. He was already beginning to feel winded, just as in the old days he had not had very reliable lungs. As he now staggered around, hardly keeping his eyes open in order to gather all his strength for the running; in his obtuseness[6] not thinking of any escape other than by running; and having almost forgotten that the walls were at his disposal, though here of course they were blocked up with elaborately carved furniture full of notches and points—at that moment a lightly flung object hit the floor right near him and rolled in front of him. It was an apple; a second one came flying right after it; Gregor stopped dead with fear; further running was useless, for his father was determined to bombard him. He had filled his pockets from the fruit bowl on the buffet and was now pitching one apple after another, for the time being without taking good aim. These little red apples rolled around on the floor as if electrified, clicking into each other. One apple, thrown weakly, grazed Gregor's back and slid off harmlessly. But the very next one that came flying after it literally forced its way into Gregor's back;

Reading Strategy
Applying the Author's Biography How might Kafka have drawn on personal experience to describe this encounter between Gregor and his father?

Reading Check
What objects does Mr. Samsa throw at Gregor?

---

6. **obtuseness** (ăb tōōs´ nəs) n. slowness to understand or perceive.

Gregor tried to drag himself away, as if the star-tling, unbelievable pain might disappear with a change of place; but he felt nailed to the spot and stretched out his body in a complete con-fusion of all his senses. With his last glance he saw the door of his room burst open, as his mother rushed out ahead of his screaming sis-ter, in her chemise, for his sister had partly undressed her while she was unconscious in order to let her breathe more freely; saw his mother run up to his father and on the way her unfastened petticoats slide to the floor one by one; and saw as, stumbling over the skirts, she forced herself onto his father, and embracing him, in complete union with him—but now Gregor's sight went dim—her hands clasping his father's neck, begged for Gregor's life.

Review and Assess

Thinking About Part II

1. **Respond:** Do you primarily feel sympathy or disgust for Gregor? Explain your answer.

2. **(a) Recall:** What surprising news about the family's finances does Gregor learn? **(b) Interpret:** With what mixed feelings does Gregor react to this news? **(c) Analyze:** What does this news suggest about Gregor's alienation from his family even before his metamorphosis?

3. **(a) Interpret:** Each time Grete enters Gregor's room, how does she react? **(b) Draw Conclusions:** What does her reaction sug-gest about the condition and smell of the room? **(c) Analyze:** In what ways does this situation emphasize Gregor's isolation from humanity?

4. **(a) Recall:** Which item in his room is Gregor determined to keep? **(b) Interpret:** What emotions, relationships, or desires might this item symbolize to him? Explain.

5. **(a) Generalize:** Why might Grete's parents have seen her as "useless" prior to Gregor's transformation? **(b) Compare and Contrast:** In what ways has Grete changed as a result of Gregor's transformation? **(c) Evaluate:** Are these changes positive or negative? Explain.

Review and Anticipate

By the end of Part II, Gregor's situation has reached a crisis. His enraged father has attacked Gregor, causing a severe injury. His furious sister has tried both to care for Gregor and to protect her parents. Although the sight of him sickens her, Gregor's mother now pleads for his life. Do you think Gregor can survive in this environment? Do you think the family can tolerate the strain? If not, what does their future hold? Read Part III, in which the story concludes, to find out.

Part III

Gregor's serious wound, from which he suffered for over a month—the apple remained imbedded in his flesh as a visible souvenir since no one dared to remove it—seemed to have reminded even his father that Gregor was a member of the family, in spite of his present pathetic and repulsive shape, who could not be treated as an enemy; that, on the contrary, it was the commandment of family duty to swallow their disgust and endure him, endure him and nothing more.

And now, although Gregor had lost some of his mobility probably for good because of his wound, and although for the time being he needed long, long minutes to get across his room, like an old war veteran—crawling above ground was out of the question—for this deterioration of his situation he was granted compensation which in his view was entirely satisfactory: every day around dusk the living-room door—which he was in the habit of watching closely for an hour or two beforehand—was opened, so that, lying in the darkness of his room, invisible from the living room, he could see the whole family sitting at the table under the lamp and could listen to their conversation, as it were with general permission; and so it was completely different from before.

Of course these were no longer the animated conversations of the old days, which Gregor used to remember with a certain nostalgia in small hotel rooms when he'd had to throw himself wearily into the damp bedding. Now things were mostly very quiet. Soon after supper his father would fall asleep in his armchair; his mother and sister would caution each other to be quiet; his mother, bent low under the light, sewed delicate lingerie for a clothing store; his sister, who had taken a job as a salesgirl, was learning shorthand and French in the evenings in order to attain a better position some time in the future. Sometimes his father woke up, and as if he had absolutely no idea that he had been asleep, said to his mother, "Look how long you're sewing again today!" and went right back to sleep, while mother and sister smiled wearily at each other.

Literary Analysis

Modernism Would you consider this after-supper scene a slice of real modern life? Why or why not?

✔ Reading Check

What does the family now allow Gregor to do every day around dusk?

With a kind of perverse obstinacy his father refused to take off his official uniform even in the house; and while his robe hung uselessly on the clothes hook, his father dozed, completely dressed, in his chair, as if he were always ready for duty and were waiting even here for the voice of his superior. As a result his uniform, which had not been new to start with, began to get dirty in spite of all the mother's and sister's care, and Gregor would often stare all evening long at this garment, covered with stains and gleaming with its constantly polished gold buttons, in which the old man slept most uncomfortably and yet peacefully.

As soon as the clock struck ten, his mother tried to awaken his father with soft encouraging words and then persuade him to go to bed, for this was no place to sleep properly, and his father badly needed his sleep, since he had to be at work at six o'clock. But with the obstinacy that had possessed him ever since he had become a messenger, he always insisted on staying at the table a little longer, although he invariably fell asleep and then could be persuaded only with the greatest effort to exchange his armchair for bed. However much mother and sister might pounce on him with little admonitions,[7] he would slowly shake his head for a quarter of an hour at a time, keeping his eyes closed, and would not get up. Gregor's mother plucked him by the sleeves, whispered blandishments into his ear, his sister dropped her homework in order to help her mother, but all this was of no use. He only sank deeper into his armchair. Not until the women lifted him up under his arms did he open his eyes, look alternately at mother and sister, and usually say, "What a life. So this is the peace of my old age." And leaning on the two women, he would get up laboriously, as if he were the greatest weight on himself, and let the women lead him to the door, where, shrugging them off, he would proceed independently, while Gregor's mother threw down her sewing and his sister her pen as quickly as possible so as to run after his father and be of further assistance.

Who in this overworked and exhausted family had time to worry about Gregor any more than was absolutely necessary? The household was stinted more and more; now the maid was let go after all; a gigantic bony cleaning woman with white hair fluttering about her head came mornings and evenings to do the heaviest work; his mother took care of everything else, along with all her sewing. It even happened that various pieces of family jewelry, which in the old days his mother and sister had been overjoyed to wear at parties and celebrations, were sold, as Gregor found out one evening from the general discussion of the prices they had fetched. But the biggest complaint was always that they could not give up the apartment, which was much too big for their present needs, since no one could figure out how Gregor was supposed to be moved. But Gregor understood easily that it was not only consideration for him which prevented their moving, for he could easily have been transported in a suitable crate with a few air holes; what mainly

Literary Analysis
Modernism and Literature of the Fantastic
In what ways does this discussion of the family's struggles mix reality and fantasy?

---

7. admonitions (ad´ mə nish´ ənz) *n.* mild rebukes; reprimands.

prevented the family from moving was their complete hopelessness and the thought that they had been struck by a misfortune as none of their relatives and acquaintances had ever been hit. What the world demands of poor people they did to the utmost of their ability; his father brought breakfast for the minor officials at the bank, his mother sacrificed herself to the underwear of strangers, his sister ran back and forth behind the counter at the request of the customers; but for anything more than this they did not have the strength. And the wound in Gregor's back began to hurt anew when mother and sister, after getting his father to bed, now came back, dropped their work, pulled their chairs close to each other and sat cheek to cheek; when his mother, pointing to Gregor's room, said, "Close that door, Grete"; and when Gregor was back in darkness, while in the other room the women mingled their tears or stared dry-eyed at the table.

Gregor spent the days and nights almost entirely without sleep. Sometimes he thought that the next time the door opened he would take charge of the family's affairs again, just as he had done in the old days; after this long while there again appeared in his thoughts the boss and the manager, the salesmen and the trainees, the handyman who was so dense, two or three friends from other firms, a chambermaid in a provincial hotel—a happy fleeting memory—a cashier in a millinery store,[8] whom he had courted earnestly but too slowly—they all appeared, intermingled with strangers or people he had already forgotten; but instead of helping him and his family, they were all inaccessible, and he was glad when they faded away. At other times he was in no mood to worry about his family, he was completely filled with rage at his miserable treatment, and although he could not imagine anything that would pique his appetite, he still made plans for getting into the pantry to take what was coming to him, even if he wasn't hungry. No longer considering what she could do to give Gregor a special treat, his sister, before running to business every morning and afternoon, hurriedly shoved any old food into Gregor's room with her foot; and in the evening, regardless of whether the food had only been toyed with or—the most usual case—had been left completely untouched, she swept it out with a swish of the broom. The cleaning up of Gregor's room, which she now always did in the evenings, could not be done more hastily. Streaks of dirt ran along the walls, fluffs of dust and filth lay here and there on the floor. At first, whenever his sister came in, Gregor would place himself in those corners which were particularly offending, meaning by his position in a sense to reproach her. But he could probably have stayed there for weeks without his sister's showing any improvement; she must have seen the dirt as clearly as he did, but she had just decided to leave it. At the same time she made sure—with an irritableness that was completely new to her and which had in fact infected the whole family—that the cleaning of Gregor's room remain her province. One time his mother had submitted Gregor's room to a major housecleaning, which she managed

Literary Analysis
Modernism How do the conditions in which Gregor is now living suggest that his alienation from his family and his former life has reached a new low?

Reading Check

For what reason does the family say they cannot move from their current apartment?

---

8. **millinery** (mil´ ə ner´ ē) **store** one that sells women's hats.

only after employing a couple of pails of water—
all this dampness, of course,
irritated Gregor too and he
lay prostrate, sour and
immobile, on the couch—
but his mother's punish-
ment was not long in coming.
For hardly had his sister
noticed the difference in Gregor's
room that evening than, deeply
insulted, she ran into the living room
and, in spite of her mother's imploringly
uplifted hands, burst out in a fit of crying, which his parents—his father had
naturally been startled out of his armchair—at first watched in helpless
amazement; until they too got going; turning to the right, his father blamed his mother for
not letting his sister clean Gregor's room; but turning to the left, he screamed at his sister that she
would never again be allowed to clean Gregor's room;
while his mother tried to drag his father, who was out
of his mind with excitement, into the bedroom, his sister, shaken with sobs, hammered the table with her
small fists; and Gregor hissed loudly with rage because it
did not occur to any of them to close the door and spare
him such a scene and a row.

But even if his sister, exhausted from her work at the
store, had gotten fed up with taking care of Gregor as she
used to, it was not necessary at all for his mother to take her
place and still Gregor did not have to be neglected. For now the
cleaning woman was there. This old widow, who thanks to her
strong bony frame had probably survived the worst in a long life,
was not really repelled by Gregor. Without being in the least inquisitive, she had once accidentally opened the door of Gregor's room,
and at the sight of Gregor—who, completely taken by surprise, began to
race back and forth although no one was chasing him—she had
remained standing, with her hands folded on her stomach, marveling.
From that time on she never failed to open the door a crack every
morning and every evening and peek in hurriedly at Gregor. In the
beginning she also used to call him over to her with words she probably
considered friendly, like, "Come over here for a minute, you old dung
beetle!" or "Look at that old dung beetle!" To forms of address like these
Gregor would not respond but remained immobile where he was, as if
the door had not been opened. If only they had given this cleaning
woman orders to clean up his room every day, instead of letting her
disturb him uselessly whenever the mood took her. Once, early in the
morning—heavy rain, perhaps already a sign of approaching spring,

▲ **Critical Viewing**
Which aspects of Gre-
gor's transformation does
this ballet adaptation
emphasize? Explain.
[Interpret]

was beating on the window panes—Gregor was so exasperated when the cleaning woman started in again with her phrases that he turned on her, of course slowly and decrepitly, as if to attack. But the cleaning woman, instead of getting frightened, simply lifted up high a chair near the door, and as she stood there with her mouth wide open, her intention was clearly to shut her mouth only when the chair in her hand came crashing down on Gregor's back. "So, is that all there is?" she asked when Gregor turned around again, and she quietly put the chair back in the corner.

Gregor now hardly ate anything anymore. Only when he accidentally passed the food laid out for him would he take a bite into his mouth just for fun, hold it in for hours, and then mostly spit it out again. At first he thought that his grief at the state of his room kept him off food, but it was the very changes in his room to which he quickly became adjusted. His family had gotten into the habit of putting in this room things for which they could not find any other place, and now there were plenty of these, since one of the rooms in the apartment had been rented to three boarders. These serious gentlemen—all three had long beards, as Gregor was able to register once through a crack in the door—were obsessed with neatness, not only in their room, but since they had, after all, moved in here, throughout the entire household and especially in the kitchen. They could not stand useless, let alone dirty junk. Besides, they had brought along most of their own household goods. For this reason many things had become superfluous, and though they certainly weren't salable, on the other hand they could not just be thrown out. All these things migrated into Gregor's room. Likewise the ash can and the garbage can from the kitchen. Whatever was not being used at the moment was just flung into Gregor's room by the cleaning woman, who was always in a big hurry; fortunately Gregor generally saw only the object involved and the hand that held it. Maybe the cleaning woman intended to reclaim the things as soon as she had a chance or else to throw out everything together in one fell swoop, but in fact they would have remained lying wherever they had been thrown in the first place if Gregor had not squeezed through the junk and set it in motion, at first from necessity, because otherwise there would have been no room to crawl in, but later with growing pleasure, although after such excursions, tired to death and sad, he did not budge again for hours.

Since the roomers sometimes also had their supper at home in the common living room, the living-room door remained closed on certain evenings, but Gregor found it very easy to give up the open door, for on many evenings when it was opened he had not taken advantage of it, but instead, without the family's noticing, had lain in the darkest corner of his room. But once the cleaning woman had left the living-room door slightly open, and it also remained opened a little when the roomers came in in the evening and the lamp was lit. They sat down at the head of the table where in the old days his father, his mother, and Gregor had eaten, unfolded their napkins, and picked up their knives

Literary Analysis
Modernism Which details in this discussion of the state of his room suggest that Gregor has become useless or disposable? Explain.

**Reading Check**
To whom has a room in the Samsa apartment been rented?

and forks. At once his mother appeared in the doorway with a platter of meat, and just behind her came his sister with a platter piled high with potatoes. A thick vapor steamed up from the food. The roomers bent over the platters set in front of them as if to examine them before eating, and in fact the one who sat in the middle, and who seemed to be regarded by the other two as an authority, cut into a piece of meat while it was still on the platter, evidently to find out whether it was tender enough or whether it should perhaps be sent back to the kitchen. He was satisfied, and mother and sister, who had been watching anxiously, sighed with relief and began to smile.

The family itself ate in the kitchen. Nevertheless, before going into the kitchen, his father came into this room and, bowing once, cap in hand, made a turn around the table. The roomers rose as one man and mumbled something into their beards. When they were alone again, they ate in almost complete silence. It seemed strange to Gregor that among all the different noises of eating he kept picking up the sound of their chewing teeth, as if this were a sign to Gregor that you needed teeth to eat with and that even with the best make of toothless jaws you couldn't do a thing. "I'm hungry enough," Gregor said to himself, full of grief, "but not for these things. Look how these roomers are gorging themselves, and I'm dying!"

On this same evening—Gregor could not remember having heard the violin during the whole time—the sound of violin playing came from the kitchen. The roomers had already finished their evening meal, the one in the middle had taken out a newspaper, given each of the two others a page, and now, leaning back, they read and smoked. When the violin began to play, they became attentive, got up, and went on tiptoe to the door leading to the foyer, where they stood in a huddle. They must have been heard in the kitchen, for his father called, "Perhaps the playing bothers you, gentlemen? It can be stopped right away." "On the contrary," said the middle roomer. "Wouldn't the young lady like to come in to us and play in here where it's much roomier and more comfortable?" "Oh, certainly," called Gregor's father, as if he were the violinist. The boarders went back into the room and waited. Soon Gregor's father came in with the music stand, his mother with the sheet music, and his sister with the violin. Calmly his sister got everything ready for playing; his parents—who had never rented out rooms before and therefore behaved toward the roomers with excessive politeness—did not even dare sit down on their own chairs; his father leaned against the door, his right hand inserted between two buttons of his uniform coat, which he kept closed; but his mother was offered a chair by one of the roomers, and since she left the chair where the roomer just happened to put it, she sat in a corner to one side.

His sister began to play. Father and mother, from either side, attentively followed the movements of her hands. Attracted by the playing, Gregor had dared to come out a little further and already had his head in the living room. It hardly surprised him that lately he was showing so little consideration for the others; once such consideration had been

Literary Analysis
Modernism In what ways does the family's behavior toward the boarders reveal changes in their sense of identity?

his greatest pride. And yet he would never have had better reason to keep hidden; for now, because of the dust which lay all over his room and blew around at the slightest movement, he too was completely covered with dust; he dragged around with him on his back and along his sides fluff and hairs and scraps of food; his indifference to everything was much too deep for him to have gotten on his back and scrubbed himself clean against the carpet, as once he had done several times a day. And in spite of his state, he was not ashamed to inch out a little farther on the immaculate living-room floor.

Admittedly no one paid any attention to him. The family was completely absorbed by the violin-playing; the roomers, on the other hand, who at first had stationed themselves, hands in pockets, much too close behind his sister's music stand, so that they could all have followed the score, which certainly must have upset his sister, soon withdrew to the window, talking to each other in an undertone, their heads lowered, where they remained, anxiously watched by his father. It now seemed only too obvious that they were disappointed in their expectation of hearing beautiful or entertaining violin-playing, had had enough of the whole performance, and continued to let their peace be disturbed only out of politeness. Especially the way they all blew the cigar smoke out of their nose and mouth toward the ceiling suggested great nervousness. And yet his sister was playing so beautifully. Her face was inclined to one side, sadly and probingly her eyes followed the lines of music. Gregor crawled forward a little farther, holding his head close to the floor, so that it might be possible to catch her eye. Was he an animal, that music could move him so? He felt as if the way to the unknown nourishment he longed for were coming to light. He was determined to force himself on until he reached his sister, to pluck at her skirt, and to let her know in this way that she should bring her violin into his room, for no one here appreciated her playing the way he would appreciate it. He would never again let her out of his room—at least not for as long as he lived; for once, his nightmarish looks would be of use to him; he would be at all the doors of his room at the same time and hiss and spit at the aggressors; his sister, however, should not be forced to stay with him, but would do so of her own free will; she should sit next to him on the couch, bending her ear down to him, and then he would confide to her that he had had the firm intention of sending her to the Conservatory, and that, if the catastrophe had not intervened, he would have announced this to everyone last Christmas—certainly Christmas had come and gone?—without taking notice of any objections. After this declaration his sister would burst into tears of emotion, and Gregor would raise himself up to her shoulder and kiss her on the neck which, ever since she started going out to work, she kept bare, without a ribbon or collar.

Themes in World Literature

Magical Realism

Franz Kafka tells Gregor Samsa's tale by mixing reality and fantasy. Many critics consider Kafka's approach a forerunner of **magical realism,** a literary movement that has gained popularity in the past few decades. Magical realism is especially strong in Latin America, where its best-known authors include Jorge Luis Borges, Julio Cortázar, Gabriel García Márquez, and Isabel Allende.

Magical realists create worlds that are based in reality and describe everyday settings. However, reality is often punctuated by "magical" elements—fantastic characters, events, or both. For example, in the García Márquez story "A Very Old Man With Enormous Wings," a couple takes captive an elderly, shabby-looking angel. Such magical elements can help readers gain deeper, more vivid insights into the nature of the world and human relationships.

Literary Analysis
Modernism The music appears to move Gregor to reach out for some meaning to his situation. Do you think that he will find that meaning? Explain.

✔**Reading Check**

What does Gregor's sister do to entertain the boarders?

"Mr. Samsa!" the middle roomer called to Gregor's father and without wasting another word pointed his index finger at Gregor, who was slowly moving forward. The violin stopped, the middle roomer smiled first at his friends, shaking his head, and then looked at Gregor again. Rather than driving Gregor out, his father seemed to consider it more urgent to start by soothing the roomers although they were not at all upset, and Gregor seemed to be entertaining them more than the violin-playing. He rushed over to them and tried with outstretched arms to drive them into their room and at the same time with his body to block their view of Gregor. Now they actually did get a little angry—it was not clear whether because of his father's behavior or because of their dawning realization of having had without knowing it such a next door neighbor as Gregor. They demanded explanations from his father; in their turn they raised their arms, plucked excitedly at their beards, and, dragging their feet, backed off toward their room. In the meantime his sister had overcome the abstracted mood into which she had fallen after her playing had been so suddenly interrupted; and all at once, after holding violin and bow for a while in her slackly hanging hands and continuing to follow the score as if she were still playing, she pulled herself together, laid the instrument on the lap of her mother—who was still sitting in her chair, fighting for breath, her lungs violently heaving—and ran into the next room, which the roomers, under pressure from her father, were nearing more quickly than before. One could see the covers and bolsters on the beds, obeying his sister's practiced hands, fly up and arrange themselves. Before the boarders had reached the room, she had finished turning down the beds and had slipped out. Her father seemed once again to be gripped by his perverse obstinacy to such a degree that he completely forgot any respect still due his tenants. He drove them on and kept on driving until, already at the bedroom door, the middle boarder stamped his foot thunderingly and thus brought him to a standstill. "I herewith declare," he said, raising his hand and casting his eyes around for Gregor's mother and sister too, "that in view of the disgusting conditions prevailing in this apartment and family"—here he spat curtly and decisively on the floor—"I give notice as of now. Of course I won't pay a cent for the days I have been living here, either; on the contrary, I shall consider taking some sort of action against you with claims that—believe me—will be easy to substantiate." He stopped and looked straight in front of him, as if he were expecting something. And in fact his two friends at once chimed in with the words, "We too give notice as of now." Thereupon he grabbed the door knob and slammed the door with a bang.

Gregor's father, his hands groping, staggered to his armchair and collapsed into it; it looked as if he were stretching himself out for his usual evening nap, but the heavy drooping of his head, as if it had lost all support, showed that he was certainly not asleep. All this time Gregor had lain quietly at the spot where the roomers had surprised him. His disappointment at the failure of his plan—but perhaps also the weakness caused by so much fasting—made it impossible for him to

Literary Analysis
Modernism How do the boarders' words and actions create new uncertainty for the Samsas?

move. He was afraid with some certainty that in the very next moment a general <u>debacle</u> would burst over him, and he waited. He was not even startled by the violin as it slipped from under his mother's trembling fingers and fell off her lap with a reverberating clang.

"My dear parents," said his sister and by way of an introduction pounded her hand on the table, "things can't go on like this. Maybe you don't realize it, but I do. I won't pronounce the name of my brother in front of this monster, and so all I say is: we have to try to get rid of it. We've done everything humanly possible to take care of it and to put up with it; I don't think anyone can blame us in the least."

"She's absolutely right," said his father to himself. His mother, who still could not catch her breath, began to cough dully behind her hand, a wild look in her eyes.

His sister rushed over to his mother and held her forehead. His father seemed to have been led by Grete's words to more definite thoughts, had sat up, was playing with the cap of his uniform among the plates which were still lying on the table from the roomers' supper, and from time to time looked at Gregor's motionless form.

"We must try to get rid of it," his sister now said exclusively to her father, since her mother was coughing too hard to hear anything. "It will be the death of you two, I can see it coming. People who already have to work as hard as we do can't put up with this constant torture at home, too. I can't stand it anymore either." And she broke out crying so bitterly that her tears poured down onto her mother's face, which she wiped off with mechanical movements of her hand.

"Child," said her father kindly and with unusual understanding, "but what can we do?"

Gregor's sister only shrugged her shoulders as a sign of the bewildered mood that had now gripped her as she cried, in contrast with her earlier confidence.

"If he could understand us," said her father, half questioning; in the midst of her crying Gregor's sister waved her hand violently as a sign that that was out of the question.

"If he could understand us," his father repeated and by closing his eyes, absorbed his daughter's conviction of the impossibility of the idea, "then maybe we could come to an agreement with him. But the way things are——"

"It has to go," cried his sister. "That's the only answer, Father. You just have to try to get rid of the idea that it's Gregor. Believing it for so long, that is our real misfortune. But how can it be Gregor? If it were Gregor, he would have realized long ago that it isn't possible for human beings to live with such a creature, and he would have gone away of his own free will. Then we wouldn't have a brother, but we'd be able to go on living and honor his memory. But as things are, this animal persecutes us, drives the roomers away, obviously wants to occupy the whole apartment and for us to sleep in the gutter. Look, Father," she suddenly shrieked, "he's starting in again!" And in a fit of terror that was completely incomprehensible to Gregor, his sister abandoned even her

Literary Analysis
Modernism Do you agree with Grete that Gregor could have gone away of his own free will? Why or why not?

**Reading Check**

What action against Gregor does Grete insist the family take?

mother, literally shoved herself off from her chair, as if she would rather sacrifice her mother than stay near Gregor, and rushed behind her father, who, upset only by her behavior, also stood up and half-lifted his arms in front of her as if to protect her.

But Gregor had absolutely no intention of frightening anyone, let alone his sister. He had only begun to turn around in order to trek back to his room; certainly his movements did look peculiar, since his ailing condition made him help the complicated turning maneuver along with his head, which he lifted up many times and knocked against the floor. He stopped and looked around. His good intention seemed to have been recognized; it had only been a momentary scare. Now they all watched him, silent and sad. His mother lay in her armchair, her legs stretched out and pressed together, her eyes almost closing from exhaustion; his father and his sister sat side by side, his sister had put her arm around her father's neck.

Now maybe they'll let me turn around, Gregor thought and began his labors again. He could not repress his panting from the exertion, and from time to time he had to rest. Otherwise no one harassed him, he was left completely on his own. When he had completed the turn, he immediately began to crawl back in a straight line. He was astonished at the great distance separating him from his room and could not understand at all how, given his weakness, he had covered the same distance a little while ago almost without realizing it. Constantly intent only on rapid crawling, he hardly noticed that not a word, not an excla-mation from his family interrupted him. Only when he was already in the doorway did he turn his head—not completely, for he felt his neck stiffening; nevertheless he still saw that behind him nothing had changed except that his sister had gotten up. His last glance ranged over his mother, who was now fast asleep.

He was hardly inside his room when the door was hurriedly slammed shut, firmly bolted, and locked. Gregor was so frightened at the sudden noise behind him that his little legs gave way under him. It was his sis-ter who had been in such a hurry. She had been standing up straight, ready and waiting, then she had leaped forward nimbly. Gregor had not even heard her coming, and she cried "Finally!" to her parents as she turned the key in the lock.

"And now?" Gregor asked himself, looking around in the darkness. He soon made the discovery that he could no longer move at all. It did not surprise him; rather, it seemed unnatural that until now he had actually been able to propel himself on these thin little legs. Otherwise he felt relatively comfortable. He had pains, of course, throughout his whole body, but it seemed to him that they were gradually getting fainter and fainter and would finally go away altogether. The rotten apple in his back and the inflamed area around it, which were com-pletely covered with fluffy dust, already hardly bothered him. He thought back on his family with deep emotion and love. His conviction that he would have to disappear was, if possible, even firmer than his sister's. He remained in this state of empty and peaceful reflection until

Literary Analysis

Modernism How does this description of Gregor's struggles reveal that his family no longer regards him as even remotely human? Explain.

the tower clock struck three in the morning. He still saw that outside the window everything was beginning to grow light. Then, without his consent, his head sank down to the floor, and from his nostrils streamed his last weak breath.

When early in the morning the cleaning woman came—in sheer energy and impatience she would slam all the doors so hard although she had often been asked not to, that once she had arrived, quiet sleep was no longer possible anywhere in the apartment— she did not at first find anything out of the ordinary on paying Gregor her usual short visit. She thought that he was deliberately lying motionless, pretending that his feelings were hurt; she credited him with unlimited intelligence. Because she happened to be holding the long broom, she tried from the doorway to tickle Gregor with it. When this too produced no results, she became annoyed and jabbed Gregor a little, and only when she had shoved him without any resistance to another spot did she begin to take notice. When she quickly became aware of the true state of things, she opened her eyes wide, whistled softly, but did not dawdle; instead, she tore open the door of the bedroom and shouted at the top of her voice into the darkness: "Come and have a look, it's croaked; it's lying there, dead as a doornail!"

The couple Mr. and Mrs. Samsa sat up in their marriage bed and had a struggle overcoming their shock at the cleaning woman before they could finally grasp her message. But then Mr. and Mrs. Samsa hastily scrambled out of bed, each on his side, Mr. Samsa threw the blanket around his shoulders, Mrs. Samsa came out in nothing but her nightgown; dressed this way, they entered Gregor's room. In the meantime the door of the living room had also opened, where Grete had been sleeping since the roomers had moved in; she was fully dressed, as if she had not been asleep at all; and her pale face seemed to confirm this. "Dead?" said Mrs. Samsa and looked inquiringly at the cleaning woman, although she could scrutinize everything for herself and could recognize the truth even without scrutiny. "I'll say," said the cleaning woman, and to prove it she pushed Gregor's corpse with her broom a good distance sideways. Mrs. Samsa made a movement as if to hold the broom back but did not do it. "Well," said Mr. Samsa, "now we can thank God!" He crossed himself, and the three women followed his example. Grete, who never took her eyes off the corpse, said, "Just look how thin he was. Of course he didn't eat anything for such a long time. The food came out again just the way it went in." As a matter of fact, Gregor's body was completely flat and dry; this was obvious now for the first time, really, since the body was no longer raised up by his little legs and nothing else distracted the eye.

▲ **Critical Viewing**
Compare and contrast this depiction of the scene in which the cleaning woman discovers Gregor's body with Kafka's description of the event. **[Compare and Contrast]**

✔**Reading Check**
Before he dies, what final thoughts about his family does Gregor have?

"Come in with us for a little while, Grete," said Mrs. Samsa with a melancholy smile, and Grete, not without looking back at the corpse, followed her parents into their bedroom. The cleaning woman shut the door and opened the window wide. Although it was early in the morning, there was already some mildness mixed in with the fresh air. After all, it was already the end of March.

The three boarders came out of their room and looked around in astonishment for their breakfast; they had been forgotten. "Where's breakfast?" the middle roomer grumpily asked the cleaning woman. But she put her finger to her lips and then hastily and silently beckoned the boarders to follow her into Gregor's room. They came willingly and then stood, their hands in the pockets of their somewhat shabby jackets, in the now already very bright room, surrounding Gregor's corpse.

At that point the bedroom door opened, and Mr. Samsa appeared in his uniform, his wife on one arm, his daughter on the other. They all looked as if they had been crying; from time to time Grete pressed her face against her father's sleeve.

"Leave my house immediately," said Mr. Samsa and pointed to the door, without letting go of the women. "What do you mean by that?" said the middle roomer, somewhat nonplussed, and smiled with a sugary smile. The two others held their hands behind their back and incessantly rubbed them together, as if in joyful anticipation of a big argument, which could only turn out in their favor. "I mean just what I say," answered Mr. Samsa and with his two companions marched in a straight line toward the roomer. At first the roomer stood still and looked at the floor, as if the thoughts inside his head were fitting themselves together in a new order. "So, we'll go, then," he said and looked up at Mr. Samsa as if, suddenly overcome by a fit of humility, he were asking for further permission even for this decision. Mr. Samsa merely nodded briefly several times, his eyes wide open. Thereupon the roomer actually went immediately into the foyer, taking long strides; his two friends had already been listening for a while, their hands completely still, and now they went hopping right after him, as if afraid that Mr. Samsa might get into the foyer ahead of them and interrupt the contact with their leader. In the foyer all three took their hats from the coatrack, pulled their canes from the umbrella stand, bowed silently, and left the apartment. In a suspicious mood which proved completely unfounded, Mr. Samsa led the two women out onto the landing; leaning over the banister, they watched the three roomers slowly but steadily going down the long flight of stairs, disappearing on each landing at a particular turn of the stairway and a few moments later emerging again; the farther down they got, the more the Samsa family's interest in them wore off, and when a butcher's boy with a carrier on his head came climbing up the stairs with a proud bearing, toward them and then up on past them, Mr. Samsa and the women quickly left the banister and all went back, as if relieved, into their apartment.

Literary Analysis
Modernism and Literature of the Fantastic
Does this scene following Gregor's death strike you as realistic? Explain.

Literary Analysis
Modernism What is surprising about the effects of Gregor's death on the family?

They decided to spend this day resting and going for a walk; they not only deserved a break in their work, they absolutely needed one. And so they sat down at the table and wrote three letters of excuse, Mr. Samsa to the management of the bank, Mrs. Samsa to her employer, and Grete to the store owner. While they were writing, the cleaning woman came in to say that she was going, since her morning's work was done. The three letter writers at first simply nodded without looking up, but as the cleaning woman still kept lingering, they looked up, annoyed. "Well?" asked Mr. Samsa. The cleaning woman stood smiling in the doorway, as if she had some great good news to announce to the family but would do so only if she were thoroughly questioned. The little ostrich feather which stood almost upright on her hat and which had irritated Mr. Samsa the whole time she had been with them swayed lightly in all directions. "What do you want?" asked Mrs. Samsa, who inspired the most respect in the cleaning woman. "Well," the cleaning woman answered, and for good-natured laughter could not immediately go on, "look, you don't have to worry about getting rid of the stuff next door. It's already been taken care of." Mrs. Samsa and Grete bent down over their letters, as if to continue writing; Mr. Samsa, who noticed that the cleaning woman was now about to start describing everything in detail, stopped her with a firmly outstretched hand. But since she was not going to be permitted to tell her story, she remembered that she was in a great hurry, cried, obviously insulted, "So long, everyone," whirled around wildly, and left the apartment with a terrible slamming of doors.

"We'll fire her tonight," said Mr. Samsa, but did not get an answer from either his wife or his daughter, for the cleaning woman seemed to have ruined their barely regained peace of mind. They got up, went to the window, and stayed there, holding each other tight. Mr. Samsa turned around in his chair toward them and watched them quietly for a while. Then he called, "Come on now, come over here. Stop brooding over the past. And have a little consideration for me, too." The women obeyed him at once, hurried over to him, fondled him, and quickly finished their letters.

Then all three of them left the apartment together, something they had not done in months, and took the trolley into the open country on the outskirts of the city. The car, in which they were the only

▼ Critical Viewing
Which aspects of this photograph of Prague, Kafka's home, reflect the mood of this story? Explain.
[Connect]

✔ Reading Check
After Gregor's death, what does Mr. Samsa tell the boarders?

passengers, was completely filled with warm sunshine. Leaning back comfortably in their seats, they discussed their prospects for the time to come, and it seemed on closer examination that these weren't bad at all, for all three positions—about which they had never really asked one another in any detail—were exceedingly advantageous and especially promising for the future. The greatest immediate improvement in their situation would come easily, of course, from a change in apartments; they would now take a smaller and cheaper apartment, but one better situated and in every way simpler to manage than the old one, which Gregor had picked for them. While they were talking in this vein, it occurred almost simultaneously to Mr. and Mrs. Samsa, as they watched their daughter getting livelier and livelier, that lately, in spite of all the troubles which had turned her cheeks pale, she had blossomed into a good-looking, shapely girl. Growing quieter and communicating almost unconsciously through glances, they thought that it would soon be time, too, to find her a good husband. And it was like a confirmation of their new dreams and good intentions when at the end of the ride their daughter got up first and stretched her young body.

Review and Assess

Thinking About Part III

1. **Respond:** How do you feel about the Samsa family's treatment of Gregor? Explain.

2. **(a) Recall:** What does Gregor do when he hears Grete playing the violin? **(b) Interpret:** How does he explain his own actions to himself? **(c) Analyze:** In what ways might this scene represent Gregor's desire to hold onto his humanity?

3. **(a) Recall:** What do Gregor's parents and sister discuss when they leave the apartment at the end of the story? **(b) Make a Judgment:** Is the family better off without Gregor? Explain.

4. **(a) Describe:** At the story's end, what is the state of Gregor's body? **(b) Support:** Which details in the story support the statement that Gregor suffers from a profound lack of nourishment, both physically and emotionally?

5. **Analyze:** The early spring setting and the Samsas' uplifted mood seem to set up a traditional happy ending. What makes this ending neither traditional nor happy?

6. **Modify:** How might an author portray similar relationship problems in a fictional family without the use of fantastic or supernatural details?

Review and Assess

Literary Analysis

Modernism

1. Before the rise of **Modernism,** works of fiction often began with expositions, or background information. Why would an exposition make this story less effective?

2. Using a chart like the one shown, discuss two details from Part I of "The Metamorphosis" that show the realities of modern life.

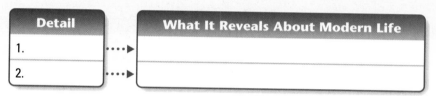

Detail	What It Reveals About Modern Life
1.	
2.	

3. In a typical Modernist work, the narrator neither judges characters nor interprets events. Is this true of "The Metamorphosis"? Explain.

4. (a) How do Gregor's perceptions shape the portrayal of other characters? (b) Is Gregor's point of view reliable? Why or why not?

Connecting Literary Elements

5. (a) Which details in the opening scene, in which Gregor's parents and the office manager speak through the closed door, are realistic? (b) Which details are fantastic? (c) In what ways is this scene an example of **literature of the fantastic**?

6. (a) How does Gregor feel about his job? (b) Might his transformation be something he unconsciously wanted? Explain.

Reading Strategy

Applying the Author's Biography

7. Kafka's father was a domineering man who instilled in his son a sense of duty, as well as feelings of fear and guilt. (a) **Apply the author's biography** by stating whether Kafka's father served as a model for Mr. Samsa. (b) Which details support your point of view?

8. Kafka's father took a dim view of his son's literary aspirations. Does this story symbolically express this conflict? Explain.

Extend Understanding

9. **Cultural Connection:** Stories in which humans are changed into animals abound in mythology, literature, and popular culture. Select one such story, and discuss the emotions and personality traits that are associated with the transformation.

Quick Review

Modernism was a literary movement that expressed the uncertainties of modern life. Modernists used experimental techniques, avoided traditional plot structures, and drew no final conclusions or meaning.

Literature of the fantastic mixes imaginative and realistic elements to entertain and challenge readers.

When you **apply the author's biography** to his or her work, you think about the writing as an expression of the author's life and times.

Take It to the Net
PHSchool.com

Take the interactive self-test online to check your understanding of this selection.

Integrate Language Skills

Vocabulary Development Lesson

Word Analysis: Latin Prefix *im-*

The Latin prefix *im-* means "not," as in *immature*, or "into" or "toward," as in *impact*. Use your knowledge of this prefix to define each of the following words.

1. impatient
2. immigration
3. impressed
4. imbalance

Spelling Strategy

When words end in *-le* or *-el*, their ending sound is the same. When a *k* sound precedes the ending, as in *debacle*, *-le* usually is the correct spelling. For each word below, write the correct spelling. If the spelling is correct, write *correct*.

1. tickle
2. excel
3. chuckel

Concept Development: Analogies

In each item below, match the relationship between the first two words by selecting a word from the vocabulary list on page 977.

1. *Wisdom* is to *owl* as ___?___ is to *donkey*.
2. *Dull* is to *sparkling* as ___?___ is to *colorful*.
3. *Near* is to *place* as ___?___ is to *time*.
4. *Exhaled* is to *breath* as ___?___ is to *sweat*.
5. *Spiral* is to *shape* as ___?___ is to *movement*.
6. *Offend* is to *insult* as ___?___ is to *apology*.
7. *Achievement* is to *success* as ___?___ is to *failure*.
8. *Improbable* is to *true* as ___?___ is to *possible*.

Grammar and Style Lesson

Adverb Clauses

Adverb clauses are subordinate clauses—groups of words containing a subject and a verb that cannot stand by themselves as sentences—that modify verbs, adjectives, or adverbs. Adverb clauses often begin with conjunctions such as *when, where, if, as if, as, because,* or *since* and explain *how, where, when, why, to what extent,* or *under what circumstances*.

> CONJ.   S   V
> **Example:** *When Gregor Samsa awoke one morning from unsettling dreams,* he found himself changed into a monstrous vermin. [**Tells when**]

Practice Identify the adverb clause in each item below. Indicate whether it tells *how, where, when, why, to what extent,* or *under what circumstances*.

1. If I didn't hold back for my parents' sake, I would have quit long ago.
2. I'd better go, since my train leaves at five.
3. When he reached the edge, he stopped.
4. I'm obligated to the firm, as you know.
5. His little legs strained to carry him away wherever he wanted to go.

Writing Application Write four sentences about Gregor Samsa. Use an adverb clause in each one.

W̶G̶ Prentice Hall Writing and Grammar Connection: Diamond Level, Chapter 19, Section 3

Writing Lesson

Essay Responding to a Critical Perspective

In an essay about "The Metamorphosis," Vladimir Nabokov wrote: "Kafka's art consists in accumulating on the one hand, Gregor's insect features, all the sad detail of his insect disguise, and on the other hand, in keeping vivid and limpid before the reader's eyes Gregor's sweet and subtle human nature." Write an essay in response to this statement. Agree or disagree with Nabokov, but defend your view.

Prewriting   Review the story. Make one list of details that describe Gregor's insectlike traits. Make a second list that suggests Gregor's human qualities. Decide whether you agree or disagree with Nabokov.

Drafting   Express and defend your opinion. Include details from the text that support your view.

Model: Elaborating to Add Support

Gregor Samsa looks like an insect, but he still has human compassion. For example, when the office manager criticizes Gregor's work, Gregor fears for his parents. He calls out, "Sir! Spare my parents!"

> Using quotations from the story can strengthen your ideas.

Revising   As you reread your essay, make sure that your supporting details are accurate and easy to follow. Remove any ideas or details that stray from the main purpose of each paragraph.

WG Prentice Hall Writing and Grammar Connection: Diamond Level, Chapter 14, Section 3

Extension Activities

Listening and Speaking Memorial services often include a **eulogy,** or speech of praise, about the deceased. Use these tips to write a eulogy about Gregor Samsa:

- Skim the story and make notes about any traits in Gregor that you find praiseworthy.
- Decide how, if at all, you will refer to his transformation.

Present the eulogy for the class.

Research and Technology In a small group, research Modernism in the visual arts, music, drama, and architecture. Prepare a **multimedia classroom presentation** that identifies similarities among various expressions of Modernism. **[Group Activity]**

 **Take It to the Net**   PHSchool.com

Go online for an additional research activity using the Internet.

READING INFORMATIONAL MATERIALS

Scientific Texts

About Scientific Texts

Science is systematic knowledge, acquired through observation and experimentation, of the structure and behavior of our physical world. **Scientific texts** contain detailed information about science for those who wish to study it. The typical scientific text contains the following:

- Facts about a variety of science topics
- *Hypotheses,* or theories, to explain scientific facts
- Descriptions of experiments conducted to verify these hypotheses
- Opportunities to duplicate these experiments in other environments
- Diagrams of relevant scientific details

In the section of a scientific text that you are about to read, you can expect to learn facts and details about insects and the process of metamorphosis.

Reading Strategy

Analyzing Text Features

Textbook reading is a complex process. Because your goal as you read a textbook is to understand, to learn, and to remember what you have read, you should read more carefully and more thoughtfully than when you are reading for other purposes.

Analyzing text features will help you meet your goal. Here are some tips to help you analyze text features:

- Find and preview the major headings, charts, diagrams, and pictures.
- Read the introductory and summary paragraphs.
- Study the review questions.
- Note any text that is printed in bold or italics.

As you read this excerpt from a biology textbook, use a chart like the one shown to help you record each text feature, describe its use, and determine how it helps you learn.

Text Feature	How It Is Used	How It Helps Me Learn
Checkpoint	Asks questions about the content	Checks to see that I remember and have understood what I have read

What Is an Insect?

Like all arthropods, insects have a segmented body, an exoskeleton, and jointed appendages. They also have several features that are specific to insects. **Insects have a body divided into three parts—head, thorax, and abdomen. Three pairs of legs are attached to the thorax.** The beetle in **Figure 28–15** exhibits these characteristics. In many insects such as ants, the body parts are clearly separated from each other by narrow connections. In other insects, such as grasshoppers, the divisions between the three body parts are not as sharply defined. A typical insect also has a pair of antennae and a pair of compound eyes on the head, two pairs of wings on the thorax, and tracheal tubes that are used for respiration.

The essential life functions in insects are carried out in basically the same ways as they are in other arthropods. However, insects have a variety of interesting adaptations that deserve a closer look.

✓**CHECKPOINT** *What are the names of the three parts of an insect's body?*

Responses to Stimuli Insects use a multitude of sense organs to respond to stimuli. Compound eyes are made of many lenses that detect minute changes in color and movement. The brain assembles this information into a single, detailed image. Compound eyes produce an image that is less detailed than what we see. However, eyes with multiple lenses are far better at detecting movement—one reason it is so hard to swat a fly!

Insects have chemical receptors for taste and smell on their mouthparts, as might be expected, and also on their antennae and legs. When a fly steps in a drop of water, it knows immediately whether the water contains salt or sugar. Insects also have sensory hairs that detect slight movements in the surrounding air or water. As objects move toward insects, the insects can feel the movement of the displaced air or water and respond appropriately. Many insects also have well-developed ears that hear sounds far above the human range. These organs are located in what we would consider odd places—behind the legs in grasshoppers, for example.

Guide for Reading

🔑 **Key Concepts**
- What are the distinguishing features of insects?
- What two types of development can insects undergo?
- What types of insects form societies?

Vocabulary
incomplete metamorphosis
nymph
complete metamorphosis
pupa

An italicized question helps readers check their understanding of what they have read.

This diagram shows the three divisions of an insect's body.

Head

Thorax

Abdomen

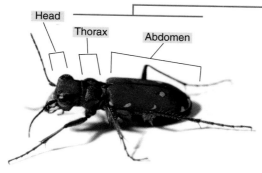

◀ **Figure 28–15** 🔑 **Insects have a body divided into three parts—head, thorax, and abdomen. Three pairs of legs are attached to the thorax.** In addition to these features, this green tiger beetle has other characteristics of a typical insect—wings, antennae, compound eyes, and tracheal tubes for respiration.

Metamorphosis 🔑 **The growth and development of insects usually involve metamorphosis, which is a process of changing shape and form. Insects undergo either incomplete metamorphosis or complete metamorphosis.** Both complete and incomplete metamorphosis are shown in **Figure 28–18**. The immature forms of insects that undergo gradual or **incomplete metamorphosis,** such as the chinch bug, look very much like the adults. These immature forms are called **nymphs** (NIMFS). Nymphs lack functional sexual organs and other adult structures, such as wings. As they molt several times and grow, the nymphs gradually acquire adult structures. This type of development is characterized by a similar appearance throughout all stages of the life cycle.

Many insects, such as bees, moths, and beetles, undergo a more dramatic change in body form during a process called **complete metamorphosis.** These animals hatch into larvae that look and act nothing like their parents. They also feed in completely different ways from adult insects. The larvae typically feed voraciously and grow rapidly. They molt a few times and grow larger but change little in appearance. Then they undergo a final molt and change into a **pupa** (PYOO-puh; plural: pupae)—the stage in which an insect changes from larva to adult. During the pupal stage, the body is completely remodeled inside and out. The adult that emerges seems like a completely different animal. Unlike the larva, the adult typically can fly and is specialized for reproduction. **Figure 28–18** shows the complete metamorphosis of a ladybug beetle.

A heading and the definition in bold-face type provide basic information about what readers will learn on this page.

Figure 28–18 🔑 The growth and development of insects usually involve metamorphosis, which is a process of changing shape and form. Insects undergo incomplete metamorphosis or complete metamorphosis. The chinch bug (left) undergoes incomplete metamorphosis, and the developing nymphs look similar to the adult. The ladybug (right) undergoes complete metamorphosis, and during the early stages the developing larva and pupa look completely different from the adult.

✓CHECKPOINT *What is a pupa?*

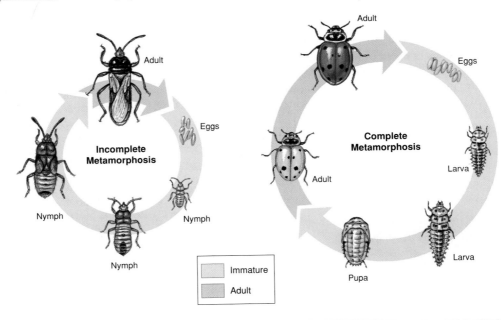

Incomplete Metamorphosis: Adult, Eggs, Nymph, Nymph, Nymph

Complete Metamorphosis: Adult, Eggs, Larva, Larva, Pupa, Adult

Immature
Adult

Check Your Comprehension

1. Into how many parts is an insect's body divided?
2. What types of changes can compound eyes detect?
3. What is the definition of *metamorphosis*?

Applying the Reading Strategy

Analyzing Text Features

4. (a) How many sections does this selection have? (b) Why is this organization particularly well suited to this subject matter?
5. Why are some of the sentences printed in boldface type?
6. What information did you learn from Figure 28–18 on page 1026?

Activity

Generating Questions for Research

1. (a) To find out more about insects, prepare a chart like the one below to focus your research. In the first column, record the details you already know about insects. In the second column, list questions that you still have about insects.

What I Know	Questions for Research
The life cycle of an insect usually involves metamorphosis.	What types of insects do not go through metamorphosis?

(b) Next, choose two of the questions that interest you the most. Consult reliable Internet sources, library reference books, and other nonfiction materials to find the answers to your questions. Record the answers and identify where you found them.

Contrasting Informational Materials

Fact or Fiction?

Sometimes, works of fiction such as short stories or novels present scientific, historical, or other information that seems accurate and true—but is not. For example, in Franz Kafka's short story *The Metamorphosis*, Gregor Samsa transforms into a gigantic, hideous vermin. Kafka's detailed description of Samsa's metamorphosis is vivid and convincing—but scientifically impossible.

1. Why are you more likely to trust the accuracy of the scientific information in the biology textbook pages?
2. Do you think an author writing fiction should be scientifically accurate? Why or why not?

Prepare to Read

Poems by Anna Akhmatova, Boris Pasternak, Rainer Maria Rilke, and Paul Valéry

Anna Akhmatova
(1889–1966)

Anna Akhmatova (äk mä´ tō və) was born on June 11, 1889, in Odessa, a small town on the coast of the Black Sea. Throughout her career, she wrote about the people she knew and the events she witnessed. The Russo-Japanese War, the two World Wars, and Stalin's totalitarianism greatly affected her. During Stalin's purge of writers and intellectuals in the late 1930s, Akhmatova's work was banned and her life was threatened. Despite these pressures, she continued to write. In 1940, when the ban was lifted, she published the collections *Poems* and *From Six Books*.

Boris Pasternak
(1890–1960)

One of Russia's greatest writers, Boris Pasternak (pas´ tər nak´) was born in Moscow on February 10, 1890. During the two World Wars and the years of Stalinist oppression, most Russian writers emigrated, were exiled, or suffered in prison camps, but Pasternak led a fairly calm life. He did not, however, avoid persecution entirely. In 1956, when he completed his great novel *Doctor Zhivago*, Soviet authorities forbade its publication. (The novel was published throughout the world to great acclaim, but it was not published in Russia until 1988.) When Pasternak received the Nobel Prize in Literature in 1958, Soviet authorities forced him to decline the honor. The writer spent the remaining two years of his life in near exile in an artists' community outside Moscow.

Rainer Maria Rilke
(1875–1926)

Rainer Maria Rilke (rī´ nər mä rē´ ä ril´ kə) is considered one of the most important poets of the twentieth century. He spent his childhood in Prague and later lived in Russia, France, and Switzerland. An air of solitude, along with a sense of the urgency and intensity of the inner life, fills his poetry. Rilke published many poetry collections, including *Sonnets to Orpheus* (1923) and *Duino Elegies* (1923). He also published a short-story collection, *Stories of God* (1904), and a novel, *The Tale of the Love and Death of Cornet Christopher Rilke* (1906), which earned him both critical and popular success.

Paul Valéry
(1871–1945)

Paul Valéry (pôl và lā rē´) was born on October 30, 1871, in Sète, a small Mediterranean coastal town in France. He attended law school in Montpellier, where he met the Symbolist poet Stéphane Mallarmé (stä fan´ mà làr mā´), who would greatly influence him. Valéry was also inspired by the work of American writer Edgar Allan Poe, whose work taught him about the melodious verbal combinations that are possible in poetry.

From 1892 to 1917, Valéry faded into reclusive investigations of creativity, mathematics, and psychology. When he emerged from this "silent period," he received numerous awards, appointments, and honorary degrees.

Preview

Connecting to the Literature

Many poets who wrote during the first half of the twentieth century lived through turbulent times that forced them to question everything—people's relationships to society, the divine, nature, nation, and their own inner lives. These poems ask the important questions about what it means to be human.

Literary Analysis

Speaker in a Poem

Like a narrator in a story, the **speaker in a poem** is the one who "says" its words. There are several kinds of poetic speakers:

- The speaker may be the voice of the poet him- or herself.
- The speaker may be a fictional character.
- The speaker may be a human being, a nonhuman entity, or even an inanimate object.

In order to fully understand a poem, it is important to identify the speaker. To do so, answer these questions as you read: Who is the speaker? Whom is the speaker addressing? Why does the speaker want to share his or her thoughts?

Comparing Literary Works

Every poem expresses some aspect of the **poet's vision**—the writer's view of the world. As you read these poems, identify the ideas each poet finds important, as well as his or her feelings about people, society, and nature. Together, these elements suggest a vision or worldview that is distinctive to each poet. After you have grasped each poet's vision, compare the ways in which they are similar and the ways in which they are different.

Reading Strategy

Analyzing Images

Poets often use imagery—language that appeals to one or more of the five senses—to express ideas. **Analyzing images,** therefore, is a key to interpreting poems. As you read, rephrase each image in the most literal, or plain, way you can. The literal meanings can lead you to a better understanding of deeper meanings. Use a chart like the one shown to state the literal meanings of the images you find.

> **Image**
>
> ". . . the gloomy eyes/ Pregnant with eagles and battles of foreseen fall"

⬇

> **Literal Meaning**
>
> Even though he looks ahead to victory in battle, he is sad or troubled.

Vocabulary Development

plundered (plun´ dərd) *adj.* stripped of possessions (p. 1030)

opaque (ō pāk´) *adj.* not shining or lustrous; dull (p. 1034)

tremulous (trem´ yo͞o ləs) *adj.* trembling; quivering (p. 1035)

accolade (ak´ ə lād´) *n.* anything done as a sign of praise or respect (p. 1037)

profusion (prō fyo͞o´ zhən) *n.* abundance; rich or lavish supply (p. 1037)

imperishable (im per´ ish ə bəl) *adj.* indestructible (p. 1038)

despond (di spänd´) *v.* to lose courage or hope (p. 1038)

omnipotent (äm nip´ ə tənt) *adj.* having unlimited power or authority (p. 1040)

Everything Is Plundered

Anna Akhmatova
translated by *Stanley Kunitz*

Background

Anna Akhmatova was part of a group of poets known as the Acmeists. Unlike the Symbolists, who used poetry to transcend reality, the Acmeists used poetry to understand and embrace the present moment. As Amanda Haight writes of the Acmeists in *Anna Akhmatova: A Poetic Pilgrimage*, " . . . there was to be no escape for them from the world's realities as these grew harsher. It was necessary for them to try to reach God and to understand His purposes through understanding, living, and loving life." In the following two poems, consider Akhmatova's responses to the tragically harsh reality of war.

Everything is <u>plundered</u>, betrayed, sold,
Death's great black wing scrapes the air,
Misery gnaws to the bone.
Why then do we not despair?

5 By day, from the surrounding woods,
cherries blow summer into town;
at night the deep transparent skies
glitter with new galaxies.

And the miraculous comes so close
10 to the ruined, dirty houses—
something not known to anyone at all,
but wild in our breast for centuries.

plundered (plun´ dərd) *adj.*
stripped of possessions

Starry Night, 1923–1924, Edvard Munch, The Munch Museum/The Munch-Ellingsen Group

Critical Viewing ▶
In what ways might this painting suggest a meeting of the miraculous and the ordinary? Explain. **[Interpret]**

I Am Not One of Those Who Left the Land

Anna Akhmatova
translated by Stanley Kunitz

Starting Over, Western Russia, 1941–45, Tretyakov Gallery

I am not one of those who left the land
to the mercy of its enemies.
Their flattery leaves me cold,
my songs are not for them to praise.

5 But I pity the exile's lot.
Like a felon, like a man half-dead,
dark is your path, wanderer;
wormwood[1] infects your foreign bread.

But here, in the murk of conflagration,[2]
10 where scarcely a friend is left to know,
we, the survivors, do not flinch
from anything, not from a single blow.

Surely the reckoning will be made
after the passing of this cloud.
15 We are the people without tears,
straighter than you . . . more proud . . .

1. **wormwood** (wʉrm´ wood´) *n.* bitter herb that often symbolizes grief.
2. **conflagration** (kän´ flə grā´ shən) *n.* destructive fire.

▲ Critical Viewing
Does this image portray those who left the land or those who remained? Explain. **[Distinguish]**

Review and Assess

Thinking About the Selections

1. **Respond:** Did you feel optimistic or pessimistic after reading these poems? Explain.

2. **(a) Recall:** In stanza 1 of "Everything Is Plundered," what abstract idea has a "great black wing"? **(b) Analyze:** What is the effect of the poet's describing this idea as a living creature?

3. **(a) Interpret:** In stanza 3, what is "wild in our breast"? **(b) Analyze:** How do stanzas 2 and 3 answer the question posed in line 4?

4. **(a) Define:** In line 3 of "I Am Not One of Those Who Left the Land," to whom does the pronoun "their" refer? **(b) Analyze:** Why might the speaker not enjoy their flattery?

5. **Extend:** What do you think Akhmatova would say to refugees of recent or current wars?

The Weeping Orchard

Boris Pasternak

translated by **Mark Rudman with Bohdan Boychuk**

Background

Both of these poems by Boris Pasternak are thick with imagery and met-aphorical meaning that reaches beyond their immediate subject matter. This density of images reflects Pasternak's involvement with a literary move-ment in Russia known as Imagism. As their name suggests, the Imagists stressed the use of imagery and believed that the true basis of poetry was the metaphor—language that reveals similarities between dissimilar things. Imagist poems, like the two here, offer little explanation, instead focusing the reader's attention on a single, sharply defined moment in time.

It's eerie—how the orchard drips and listens:
    is it the only one in the world
to crumple a branch on this window like lace,
    or is there a witness?

5   The spongy, bruised earth heaves
    and chokes under the burden.
In the distances you can hear, as in August,
    midnight ripen in the fields.

Not a sound. No one looks on.
10   Assured there's no one there
it reverts to old tricks—rolls down roof
    to gutter, and spills over.

I will bring it to my lips and listen:
    am I the only one in the world,
15 ready to weep on the slightest occasion,
    or is there a witness?

Silence. No breath of leaf, nothing
    in the dark but this weird
gulping, and flapping of slippers,
20   and sighs, broken by tears.

Literary Analysis
Speaker in a Poem In the first stanza, where do you think the speaker is and what is the speaker doing? Explain.

Literary Analysis
Speaker in a Poem In the fourth stanza, how do the reader's impressions of the speaker become more precise?

The Drowsy Garden

Boris Pasternak
translated by Babette Deutsch

The drowsy garden scatters insects
Bronze as the ash from braziers[1] blown.
Level with me and with my candle,
Hang flowering worlds, their leaves full-grown.

5   As into some unheard-of dogma[2]
I move across into this night,
Where a worn poplar age has grizzled
Screens the moon's strip of fallow[3] light,

Where the pond lies, an open secret,
10 Where apple bloom is surf and sigh,
And where the garden, a lake dwelling,
Holds out in front of it the sky.

---

1. **braziers** (brā′ zhərz) *n.* metal pans or bowls used to hold burning coals or charcoal.
2. **dogma** (dôg′ mə) *n.* doctrine or belief, or a set of doctrines and beliefs.
3. **fallow** (fal′ ō) *adj.* pale-yellow; brownish-yellow.

Review and Assess
Thinking About the Selections

1. **Respond:** Which images in these poems were the most vivid for you? Explain.
2. **(a) Recall:** In stanza 2 of "The Weeping Orchard," what words does the speaker use to describe the earth? **(b) Interpret:** Which emotions do these words suggest the speaker feels?
3. **(a) Recall:** What objects and sounds are described in the final stanza? **(b) Analyze:** How does this stanza suggest that the speaker has projected his own emotions onto nature? Explain.
4. **(a) Recall:** In lines 5–6 of "The Drowsy Garden," to what abstract idea does the speaker compare his entrance into the garden? **(b) Analyze:** What might this garden symbolize for the speaker?
5. **(a) Interpret:** In what sense does the final image move the reader from the garden into the larger world? **(b) Summarize:** Summarize the philosophy that the poem expresses.

The GROWNUP

Rainer Maria Rilke
translated by Randall Jarrell

Background

In 1899, Rainer Maria Rilke traveled to Russia, where he met the great writer and religious mystic Leo Tolstoy. As a result of this encounter, Rilke came to see all things as saturated with a mystical, divine energy. His association with French sculptor Auguste Rodin, who believed that the work of an artist held religious meaning, reinforced that philosophy. Rilke applied this view not only to elements of nature but even to inanimate objects. Look for signs of Rilke's philosophy in the three poems that follow.

All this stood on her and was the world
And stood on her with all things, pain and grace,
As trees stand, growing and erect, all image
And imageless as the ark of the Lord God,[1]
5 And solemn, as if set upon a state.

And she bore it, bore, somehow, the weight
Of the flying, fleeting, faraway,
The monstrous and the still unmastered,
Unmoved, serene, as the water bearer
10 Stands under a full jar. Till in the midst
        of play,
Transfiguring,[2] preparing for the other,
The first white veil fell smoothly, softly,

Over her opened face, almost <u>opaque</u>,
Never to raise itself again, and giving
        somehow
15 To all her questions one vague answer:
In thee, thou once a child, in thee.

opaque (ō pāk´) *adj.* not shining or lustrous; dull

▲ **Critical Viewing**

Which words and phrases from "The Grownup" might be used to describe the woman in this painting? **[Connect]**

---

1. **all image . . . the Lord God** The Ark of the Covenant, the sacred chest of the Hebrews that contained the Tablets of the Law, represented God. Because the Jews had been commanded by God not to reproduce His image, the chest was not adorned with the image of God.
2. **transfiguring** (trans fig´ yər iŋ) *v.* changing in form or appearance.

INTERIOR OF THE Rose

Rainer Maria Rilke *translated by* Kate Flores

Where, for this within,
Is there a without? And upon what wound
Lies a weft[1] so thin?
What heavens are reflected
5   In the inward seas
Of these opening roses
Thus reposing?[2] See
How loosely in looseness
They lie, as though never
10   A <u>tremulous</u> hand could spill them.
They cannot hold themselves still;
Many are filling
Up unto their brim and flowing
Over with interior space
15   Into days, which seem ever
Grown fuller and fuller,
Until all of summer a room
Has become, a room enclosed in a dream.

1. **weft** (weft) *n.* something woven.
2. **reposing** (ri pōz´ iŋ) *v.* resting.

Literary Analysis
Speaker in a Poem What do you think the speaker in this poem is doing?

tremulous (trem´ yo͞o ləs) *adj.* trembling; quivering

Review and Assess

Thinking About the Selections

1. **Respond:** Do you find either of these poems surprising? Explain.

2. **(a) Recall:** In "The Grownup," what happens to the person at "play"? **(b) Interpret:** What change does this event symbolize?

3. **(a) Recall:** In stanza 2, which words describe the nature of the weight "she" bears? **(b) Classify:** Which two adjectives and one image describe how she bears the weight? **(c) Contrast:** How does her attitude toward the weight differ from the weight itself?

4. **(a) Define:** In lines 1–2 of "Interior of the Rose," note two words that have opposite meanings. **(b) Distinguish:** In lines 2–7, what other words or phrases suggest a similar opposition? **(c) Support:** Using these details, support the idea that the roses symbolize both the physical and the spiritual worlds.

Archaic Torso of Apollo[1]

Rainer Maria Rilke
translated by *Stephen Mitchell*

We cannot know his legendary head
with eyes like ripening fruit. And yet his torso
is still suffused[2] with brilliance from inside,
like a lamp, in which his gaze, now turned to low,

5　gleams in all its power. Otherwise
the curved breast could not dazzle you so, nor could
a smile run through the placid hips and thighs
to that dark center where procreation[3] flared.

Otherwise this stone would seem defaced
10　beneath the translucent cascade of the shoulders
and would not glisten like a wild beast's fur:

would not, from all the borders of itself,
burst like a star: for here there is no place
that does not see you. You must change your life.

---

1. **Archaic . . . Apollo:** The Archaic period of Greek art lasted from the late seventh century to about 480 B.C. Apollo was the Greek god of music, poetry, prophecy, and medicine. He was associated with the sun and portrayed as a handsome, athletic young man.
2. **suffused** (sə fyōōzd´) *v.* filled with a glow, color, or liquid.
3. **procreation** (prō´ krē ā´ shən) *n.* the process of producing or bringing into existence.

Literary Analysis
Speaker and Poet's Vision
How closely do you think the speaker's words reflect Rilke's personal worldview? Explain.

Review and Assess
Thinking About the Selection

1. **Respond:** Do you find it easy to picture the statue? Explain.
2. **(a) Recall:** In line 1, which part of the statue does the speaker say is missing? **(b) Identify:** In line 4, which word suggests sight? **(c) Analyze:** How does this surprising contrast relate to the idea expressed in the poem's final two lines?
3. **(a) Classify:** Which words in the poem relate to light? **(b) Analyze:** How might the energy of the statue relate to the god that it depicts?
4. **Take a Position:** Do you think works of art have the power to transform individual lives in a permanent way? Why or why not?

Palm

Paul Valéry
translated by Barbara Gibbs

Background

Paul Valéry was influenced by the literary movement known as Symbolism. The Symbolists rebelled against the Realist writers' goal of representing life factually and accurately. Instead, the Symbolists used symbols (images that represent abstract ideas and thus express deeper meanings) to suggest key ideas and to manipulate reality. The purpose of poetry, according to the Symbolists, is to take the reader beyond the poem itself to another level of meaning or experience. See if you can detect that purpose at work in the following three poems.

An angel sets at my place
—Barely screening the <u>accolade</u>
Of his formidable grace—
Fresh milk, new-baked bread;
5 With his lids he makes a sign
That is like a petition
That says to my vision:
Calm, calm, be calm,
Know the heaviness of a palm
10 Bearing its <u>profusion</u>!

Even as it bends
Under abundant good things
The shape perfectly rounds,
The heavy fruits are strings.
15 Wonder how it sheds
Vibrancy, how a slow thread
That parcels out the moment
Adjudicates[1] without mystery
The heaviness of the sky
20 And the earth's enticement!

accolade (ak´ ə lād´) *n.* anything done as a sign of praise or respect

profusion (prō fyōō´ zhən) *n.* abundance; rich or lavish supply

✔ **Reading Check**

What gifts does the angel set at the speaker's place?

---

1. adjudicates (ə jōō´ də kāts) *v.* serves as a judge.

This fair mobile arbitress
Between shadow and sunlight
Wears the sibyl's² dress,
Wisdom of day, sleep of night.
25 All round the one spot
The wide palm wearies not
Of welcomes and farewells . . .
How noble and soft it is
And worthy to dispose
30 The comforts of immortals!

The faint gold it sighs
Rings like a mere finger of air
Burdening the desert skies
With a silken signature.
35 An <u>imperishable</u> sound
Which it gives to the sandy wind
That waters it with its grains
Serves it as oracle³
And foretells the miracle
40 Of the chanting pain.

Between sand and sky,
Ignorant of its own nature,
Each brightening day
Adds honey to its store.
45 This gentleness is ordered by
The divine continuity
Which does not mark passing time
But rather hides it
In a juice wherein secretes
50 All of love's perfume.

If you sometimes <u>despond</u>—
If the ardored⁴ rigor
In spite of tears responds
Under a shadow of languor⁵—
55 Never blame of avarice⁶
A Wisdom that is nurse
To so much gold and authority:
An everlasting hope
Rises through the dark sap
60 To maturity! . . .

𝒯hemes in
World Literature

Poe's Influence on Valéry
The French Symbolists
greatly admired American
author Edgar Allan Poe,
whose works Charles Baudelaire had translated into French
between 1848 and 1857. Much of
Valéry's literary philosophy reflects
Poe's theories and beliefs about literature. In addition, Valéry's style
often shows Poe's influence. In
"Palm," for example, Valéry's focus
on the musicality of words is
strongly reminiscent of the creative
use of sound in Poe's poetry.

imperishable (im per′ ish ə
bəl) *adj.* indestructible

Reading Strategy
Analyzing Images To
what senses do the
images in lines 45–50
appeal? Explain.

despond (di spänd′) *v.* to
lose courage or hope

Literary Analysis
Speaker and Poet's Vision
Based on the final stanza,
how would you describe
the poet's view of the
human condition?

---

2. **sibyl's** (sib′ əlz) In ancient Greece and Rome, sibyls were female prophets.
3. **oracle** (ôr′ ə kəl) *n.* person of great knowledge or wisdom, especially in revealing mysteries.
4. **ardored** (är′ dərd) *adj.* passionate.
5. **languor** (laŋ′ gər) *n.* lack of interest or spirit.
6. **avarice** (av′ ə ris) *n.* greed for riches.

The Friendly Wood

Paul Valéry   *translated by* Vernon Watkins

Meditations pure were ours
Side by side, along the ways;
We held each other's hand without
Speaking, among the hidden flowers.

5   Alone we walked as if betrothed,
Lost in the green night of the fields;
We shared this fruit of fairy reels,
The moon, to madmen well disposed.

And then, we were dead upon the moss,
10   Far, quite alone, among the soft
Shades of this intimate, murmuring wood;

And there, in the vast light aloft,
We found ourselves with many a tear,
O my companion of silence dear!

Literary Analysis
Speaker in a Poem
Whom is the speaker addressing?

Review and Assess

Thinking About the Selections

1. **Respond:** "Palm" was part of a collection entitled *Charmes*, or "songs." In what ways is "Palm" like a song?

2. **(a) Recall:** According to the first line of "Palm," with which being is the speaker in contact? **(b) Interpret:** What message does the being bring in stanza 1?

3. **(a) Recall:** In lines 21–22, what does the palm stand "between"? **(b) Classify:** What other words in stanza 3 suggest a similar balance? **(c) Analyze:** What does the speaker admire about the palm?

4. **(a) Deduce:** In "The Friendly Wood," note three activities that the speaker does with a companion. **(b) Interpret:** How would you describe the relationship between the speaker and the companion?

5. **Generalize:** Why do you think the natural world moves some people more than others?

CAESAR[1]

Paul Valéry
translated by C. F. MacIntyre

Caesar, serene Caesar, your foot on all,
The hard fists in the beard, and the gloomy eyes
Pregnant with eagles and battles of foreseen fall,
Your heart swells, feeling itself <u>omnipotent</u> cause.

5   In vain the lake trembles, licking its rosy bed,
Vainly glistens the gold of the young wheat straws.
You harden in the knots of your gathered body
The word which must finally rive[2] your tight-clenched jaws.

The spacious world, beyond the immense horizon,
10 The Empire awaits the torch, the order, the lightning
Which will turn the evening to a furious dawn.

Happily there on the waves, and cradled in hazard,
A lazy fisherman is drifting and singing,
Not knowing what thunder collects in the center of Caesar.

omnipotent (äm nip´ ə tənt)
adj. having unlimited
power or authority

---

1. **Caesar** (sē´ zər) here, any emperor or dictator.
2. **rive** (rīv) *v.* tear apart; rend.

Review and Assess
Thinking About the Selection

1. **Respond:** Did this poem suggest a new way of thinking about war or military leadership? Why or why not?

2. **(a) Recall:** In line 3, with which visions are Caesar's eyes "pregnant"? **(b) Analyze Cause and Effect:** How will these private visions alter the world?

3. **(a) Compare and Contrast:** In what ways do the images in lines 5–6 differ from those that describe Caesar? **(b) Deduce:** Why are the efforts of these items made "in vain"?

4. **(a) Speculate:** How might the fisherman's life change because of Caesar? **(b) Modify:** If "Caesar" ended with the third stanza, would the poem lose its effectiveness? Explain.

5. **Make a Judgment:** Is leadership of the kind Caesar displays admirable? Explain.

Review and Assess

Literary Analysis

Speaker in a Poem

1. (a) What information about the **speaker's** identity do the details in "Everything Is Plundered" suggest? (b) Do you think the speaker in this poem is Akhmatova herself? Why or why not?

2. In "Archaic Torso of Apollo," what do we learn about the speaker through the description of the statue? Explain.

3. Use a chart like the one shown to examine how the sensory details used in "The Weeping Orchard" reveal the speaker's thoughts and feelings.

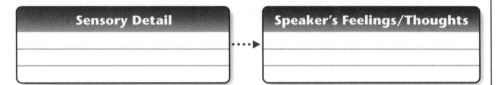

Sensory Detail		Speaker's Feelings/Thoughts
	····▶	

Comparing Literary Works

4. Both "Everything Is Plundered" and "Caesar" could be described as war poems. How are the two **poets' visions** of war both similar and different?

5. (a) Compare and contrast the lessons each speaker learns through close observation of an object in "Archaic Torso of Apollo" and "Palm." (b) What worldviews do these lessons express?

Reading Strategy

Analyzing Images

6. (a) Begin to **analyze images** by noting one example of a pleasant image and one example of a disturbing image in "Caesar." (b) What does the use of both types of images suggest about the meaning of the poem?

7. (a) Identify images of water and the feelings or moods they create in each of the poems by Pasternak. (b) Explain a possible symbolic meaning for the images of water in each poem.

Extend Understanding

8. **Career Connection:** From this grouping, choose one poem whose topic might interest a journalist. Explain how the journalist's approach would differ from the poet's.

Quick Review

The **speaker** in a poem is the poem's "voice," the one who "tells" the poem to the reader.

The speaker's words might suggest the **poet's vision** — the poet's view of life.

To **analyze images,** think carefully about the purpose and meaning of sensory language in literary works.

 **Take It to the Net**
PHSchool.com

Take the interactive self-test online to check your understanding of these selections.

Integrate Language Skills

Vocabulary Development Lesson

Word Analysis: Latin Word Part *omni-*

The word part *omni-* means "all," "unlimited," or "universally," as in *omnipotent,* which means "all-powerful." Match each numbered word below with its definition.

1. omnipresent
2. omniscient
3. omnivore

   a. creature that eats everything
   b. having unlimited knowledge
   c. existing in all places at all times

Spelling Strategy

Words beginning with an *ak* sound often contain the Latin prefix *ad-,* which means "to," "toward," or "akin to." That prefix is spelled *ac* before the letter *c* or *q* (as in *accident* and *acquire*).

Each of the following words is misspelled. In your notebook, write the correct spelling.

1. acept
2. acompany
3. aquaint
4. aclaim
5. acqord
6. aquiesce

Fluency: Sentence Completions

Review the vocabulary list on page 1029. Then, using the context clues in the following passage, fill in each blank in the paragraph below with a word from the vocabulary list.

It was a battle royal: our Centerburg Panthers against the Jackson Tigers. The ancient, ___?___ rivalry between our schools was alive and well—and we were losing. No ray of cheer was passing through the ___?___ cloud of doom above my head. "I must not ___?___," I said. "Those Tigers will be ___?___ of their trophy. Our ___?___ Panthers will win!" Just then a ___?___ cry ran through the crowd: We had the ball! One basket and then another scored as the buzzer sounded. There were cries of jubilation. Cheers rang out in ___?___, for we had won! The Panthers waved to acknowledge the crowd's ___?___, while the defeated Tigers straggled off the court.

Grammar and Style Lesson

Concrete Nouns and Abstract Nouns

Concrete nouns name things that people can physically see, touch, taste, hear, or smell. **Abstract nouns** name things that cannot be perceived through the physical senses.

Examples:
Concrete: *trees, child, lace, lightning, perfume*
Abstract: *questions, life, vibrancy, miracle*

Practice Identify whether each noun below is concrete or abstract.

1. gentleness
2. fisherman
3. wisdom
4. garden
5. flattery
6. dogma
7. eagles
8. tears

Writing Application Write four sentences about a natural scene. In each sentence, use at least one concrete noun and one abstract noun.

W̶G Prentice Hall Writing and Grammar Connection: Diamond Level, Chapter 17, Section 1

Writing Lesson

Reflective Essay

In a reflective essay, a writer relates ideas about a subject to his or her personal experience. Write a reflective essay in which you discuss Rilke's poem "The Grownup" and offer your interpretation of its meaning. Then, discuss your perspective on the process of maturing from a child into an adult.

Prewriting   As you reread "The Grownup," take notes about its meaning and any personal experience it brings to mind.

Drafting   Begin by summarizing "The Grownup." Then, write at least one paragraph on its meaning and at least another paragraph on your perspective. Tie your ideas together in your conclusion.

Revising   As you review your draft, underline your main ideas. Then, make sure that the personal experiences you describe clearly relate to and support those ideas.

Model: Revising to Connect Literature to Life

Rilke's speaker says that growing up happens "in the midst of play." *That comment reminds me of the first time that I felt childish while playing "house." The game suddenly seemed foolish.* Clearly, maturity can come as a shock.

> A reflective essay uses personal experience to support ideas.

W̶G̶ *Prentice Hall Writing and Grammar Connection: Diamond Level, Chapter 14, Section 2*

Extension Activities

Listening and Speaking   Rilke wrote "Archaic Torso of Apollo" in response to a sculpture. Following his example, write and present a **poem** in response to a work of art. Consider these suggestions:

- Skim through art books or electronic art resources to find a work you like.
- Note details about the work and the thoughts and feelings that it inspires in you.
- Write a poem that will inspire similar thoughts and feelings in others.

Present both the poem and the art to the class.

Research and Technology   During the 1920s, the Russian art world gave rise to many literary movements, including Futurism, Acmeism, and Constructivism. In a small group, research two such movements. Then, choose one poem that best represents each movement, and create a **comparison-and-contrast report** for the class. **[Group Activity]**

Take It to the Net   PHSchool.com

Go online for an additional research activity using the Internet.

Prepare to Read

The Bracelet

Colette (1873–1954)

No other writer captured what it was like to be a woman in France in the late nineteenth and early twentieth centuries better than Colette (kō let´). Yet Colette herself was in no way typical of her time. The women's rights movement was still in its infancy during her lifetime; nevertheless, Colette proved that a woman could be strong, independent, and successful.

First Marriage Colette was born in the small village of St. Sauveur-en-Puisaye (sen´ sō vër´ än püē zä) in the French province of Burgundy. As a child, she was taught by her mother to savor the sights, sounds, and textures of country life, an appreciation that her fiction would later reflect. After her twentieth birthday, she married Henri Gauthier-Villars (än rē´ gō tyä´ vē lär´), a mediocre writer fourteen years her senior. By providing her with encouragement and support and by introducing her to many of the most prominent French writers of the time, Gauthier-Villars played a vital role in launching Colette's literary career. In fact, her husband published her first series of books, known as the "Claudine" novels, under the pseudonym Willy. The "Claudine" novels centered on the misadventures of a teenage girl and became a huge popular success. They inspired numerous related projects and products, including a musical, Claudine clothing, and Claudine soap, perfume, and cigars.

After her marriage ended in 1906, Colette lived alone for several years. During this period, she continued to develop her literary skills while also indulging in a number of other creative endeavors, including singing, dancing, and hairdressing. Colette's experiences during this period of her life inspired two successful books, *The Vagabond* (1910) and *Recaptured* (1913).

Her Star Rises In 1912, Colette married Henri de Jouvenel (də zhōō və nel´), a prominent journalist. The marriage ended in divorce in 1925. As her second marriage failed, however, Colette's fame grew. She published such highly regarded works as *Chéri* (1920), *My Mother's House* (1922), *The Ripening* (1923), *The Last of Chéri* (1926), and *Sido* (1929). Two of these works—*Chéri* and *The Last of Chéri*—focus on a tragic love affair between a young man and an older woman, while the other works deal with the experiences of childhood and adolescence.

Colette married her third husband, Maurice Goudeket (mô rēs´ gōō də kā´), another writer, in 1935. Unlike her first two marriages, her marriage to Goudeket brought her great contentment and lasted for the remainder of her life. Unfortunately, her happiness was tainted by the onset of crippling arthritis and by her husband's arrest and imprisonment by the Nazis during World War II. These setbacks did not affect her productivity as a writer, however, and in the 1930s and 1940s she wrote many successful books, including *The Cat* (1933), *Duo* (1934), *Gigi* (1944), and *The Blue Light* (1949).

A Literary Legend By the time of her death in 1954, Colette had written more than fifty novels or novellas and an even greater number of short stories. Among the French public, she had established herself as a literary legend, and she had received a number of distinguished honors, including her induction into both the Royal Belgian Academy and the French Goncourt Academy. During the years since her death, her reputation has continued to grow, and she is now regarded by many as the outstanding French fiction writer of her time.

Preview

Connecting to the Literature

If we are unhappy, we sometimes think back with fondness to a better time in our lives. Such is the case of the wealthy but dissatisfied Madame Augelier, whose childhood memory becomes a driving force in her life.

Literary Analysis

Epiphany

An **epiphany** is a sudden flash of insight that a person has about himself or herself, another person, a situation, or life itself. That revelation may be positive, but it may also be negative. In traditional plots, a series of events leads to the resolution of a conflict. However, in many modern stories, the series of events leads to an epiphany that may alter the conflict without resolving it. As you read, use a chart like the one shown to identify details that suggest the nature of the epiphany Madame Augelier experiences. Then, decide whether the conflict is resolved or merely changed.

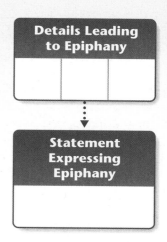

Connecting Literary Elements

An author's choice of the best words to convey meaning contributes to the power and beauty of a work of writing. Colette's use of precise **descriptive details**—words and phrases that appeal to the senses—is one reason her story is so vivid and clear. Compare these two phrases:

Apples in a bowl   Calville apples in a silver bowl

While their meaning is essentially the same, the second phrase creates an image, or word picture, that is both more informative and more suggestive of emotion. As you read, notice the many descriptive details Colette employs.

Reading Strategy

Drawing Conclusions

When you **draw conclusions,** you use your reasoning to reach logical decisions on the basis of evidence. For example, if someone comes inside shaking out a wet umbrella, you might draw the conclusion that it is raining. When reading, you draw conclusions by applying your knowledge and experiences to details from the work. As you read "The Bracelet," draw conclusions about Madame Augelier's life and character.

Vocabulary Development

supple (sup´ əl) *adj.* easily bent; flexible (p. 1046)

connoisseur (kän´ ə sʉr´) *n.* person with expert judgment and taste (p. 1046)

convalescent (kän´ və les´ ənt) *n.* person who is recovering health after illness (p. 1049)

enraptured (en rap´ chərd) *adj.* filled with great pleasure (p. 1049)

iridescent (ir´ i des´ ənt) *adj.* showing rainbowlike shifts in color (p. 1049)

serpentine (sʉr´ pən tēn´) *adj.* resembling a snake (p. 1049)

congealed (kən jēld´) *v.* thickened; solidified (p. 1049)

The Bracelet

Colette

translated by Matthew Ward

Background

At the turn of the twentieth century, the women's rights movement was very new. Women in the West were just beginning to enjoy educational and employment opportunities, and marriage generally was the best guarantee of economic security. Like most of Colette's fiction, "The Bracelet" touches on the changing role of women in France in the early twentieth century. The main character, Madame Augelier, is married to a wealthy business executive. In a subtle fashion, the story asks whether the security and predictability of such a marriage is enough for happiness.

". . . Twenty-seven, twenty-eight, twenty-nine . . . There really are twenty-nine . . ."

Madame Augelier mechanically counted and recounted the little *pavé*[1] diamonds. Twenty-nine square brilliants, set in a bracelet, which slithered between her fingers like a cold and <u>supple</u> snake. Very white, not too big, admirably matched to each other—the pretty bijou[2] of a <u>connoisseur</u>. She fastened it on her wrist, and shook it, throwing off blue sparks under the electric candles; a hundred tiny rainbows, blazing with color, danced on the white tablecloth. But Madame Augelier was looking more closely instead at the other bracelet, the three finely engraved creases encircling her wrist above the glittering snake.

"Poor François . . . what will he give me next year, if we're both still here?"

François Augelier, industrialist, was traveling in Algeria at the time, but, present or absent, his gift marked both the year's end and their wedding anniversary. Twenty-eight jade bowls, last year; twenty-seven old enamel plaques mounted on a belt, the year before . . .

"And the twenty-six little Royal Dresden[3] plates . . . And the twenty-four meters of antique Alençon lace[4] . . ." With a slight effort of memory

supple (sup´ əl) *adj.* easily bent; flexible

connoisseur (kän´ ə sur´) *n.* person with expert judgment and taste

Reading Strategy
Drawing Conclusions
What conclusions might you draw about the Augeliers' relationship, based on Madame's comment about her husband?

✔**Reading Check**

For what occasion has Madame Augelier received a diamond bracelet from her husband?

---

1. *pavé* (pa vā´) jewelry setting in which the gems are placed close together so that no metal shows.
2. **bijou** (bē zhoo´) *n.* jewel.
3. **Royal Dresden** (drez´ dən) fine, decorated porcelain or chinaware made near Dresden, a city in southeast-central Germany.
4. **Alençon** (ə len´ sän´) **lace** needlepoint lace with a solid design on a net background.

Madame Mayden, Amedeo Modigliani

▲ **Critical Viewing** In what ways is this portrait similar to and different from your image of Madame Augelier? Explain. **[Compare and Contrast]**

Madame Augelier could have gone back as far as four modest silver place settings, as far as three pairs of silk stockings . . .

"We weren't rich back then. Poor François, he's always spoiled me so . . ." To herself, secretly, she called him "poor François," because she believed herself guilty of not loving him enough, underestimating the strength of affectionate habits and abiding fidelity.

Madame Augelier raised her hand, tucked her little finger under, extended her wrist to erase the bracelet of wrinkles, and repeated intently, "It's so pretty . . . the diamonds are so white . . . I'm so pleased . . ." Then she let her hand fall back down and admitted to herself that she was already tired of her new bracelet.

"But I'm not ungrateful," she said naïvely with a sigh. Her weary eyes wandered from the flowered tablecloth to the gleaming window. The smell of some Calville apples in a silver bowl made her feel slightly sick and she left the dining room.

In her boudoir[5] she opened the steel case which held her jewels, and adorned her left hand in honor of the new bracelet. Her ring had on it a black onyx band and a blue-tinted brilliant; onto her delicate, pale, and

---

5. **boudoir** (bōō′ dwär′) *n.* woman's bedroom, dressing room, or private sitting room.

Reading Strategy
Drawing Conclusions
Based on her comments about her husband and her feelings about his gifts, what conclusions can you draw about Madame Augelier's happiness with her life? Explain.

▼ **Critical Viewing**
Do you think Monsieur Augelier would have given jewels like these to his wife earlier or later in their marriage? Explain. **[Connect]**

somewhat wrinkled little finger, Madame Augelier slipped a circle of dark sapphires. Her prematurely white hair, which she did not dye, appeared even whiter as she adjusted amid slightly frizzy curls a narrow fillet sprinkled with a dusting of diamonds, which she immediately untied and took off again.

"I don't know what's wrong with me. I'm not feeling all that well. Being fifty is a bore, basically . . ."

She felt restless, both terribly hungry and sick to her stomach, like a <u>convalescent</u> whose appetite the fresh air has yet to restore.

"Really now, is a diamond actually as pretty as all that?"

Madame Augelier craved a visual pleasure which would involve the sense of taste as well; the unexpected sight of a lemon, the unbearable squeaking of the knife cutting it in half, makes the mouth water with desire . . .

"But I don't want a lemon. Yet this nameless pleasure which escapes me does exist, I know it does, I remember it! Yes, the blue glass bracelet . . ."

A shudder made Madame Augelier's slack cheeks tighten. A vision, the duration of which she could not measure, granted her, for a second time, a moment lived forty years earlier, that incomparable moment as she looked, <u>enraptured</u>, at the color of the day, the <u>iridescent</u>, distorted image of objects seen through a blue glass bangle, moved around in a circle, which she had just been given. That piece of perhaps Oriental glass, broken a few hours later, had held in it a new universe, shapes not the inventions of dreams, slow, <u>serpentine</u> animals moving in pairs, lamps, rays of light <u>congealed</u> in an atmosphere of indescribable blue . . .

The vision ended and Madame Augelier fell back, bruised, into the present, into reality.

But the next day she began searching, from antique shops to flea markets, from flea markets to crystal shops, for a glass bracelet, a certain color of blue. She put the passion of a collector, the precaution, the dissimulation[6] of a lunatic into her search. She ventured into what she called "impossible districts," left her car at the corner of strange streets, and in the end, for a few centimes, she found a circle of blue glass which she recognized in the darkness, stammered as she paid for it, and carried it away.

---

6. **dissimulation** (di sim′ yoo lā′ shən) *n.* hiding of one's feelings or motives by pretense.

Literature in context World Events Connection

Algeria and France

At the time of this story, France governed much of western and west-central Africa. Algeria, a French colony since 1834, played an important role in France's economy, partly through its production and export of citrus fruit and wine. Yet the relationship between Algeria and France was never an easy one. Cultural and economic conflicts between the country's poor Muslim majority and wealthy Europeans erupted into armed conflict in 1954, the year of Colette's death. After eight years of struggle, Algeria finally secured its independence from France in July of 1962. In this story, Colette subtly places Madame Augelier's life within a broader cultural context by mentioning the absent Monsieur Augelier's travels in Algeria.

convalescent (kän′ və les′ ənt) *n.* person who is recovering health after illness

enraptured (en rap′ chərd) *adj.* filled with great pleasure

iridescent (ir′ i des′ ənt) *adj.* showing rainbowlike shifts in color

serpentine (sʉr′ pən tēn′) *adj.* resembling a snake

congealed (kən jēld′) *adj.* thickened; solidified

✓Reading Check

What object does Madame Augelier long to find?

In the discreet light of her favorite lamp she set the bracelet on the dark field of an old piece of velvet, leaned forward, and waited for the shock . . . But all she saw was a round piece of bluish glass, the trinket of a child or a savage, hastily made and blistered with bubbles; an object whose color and material her memory and reason recognized; but the powerful and sensual genius who creates and nourishes the marvels of childhood, who gradually weakens, then dies mysteriously within us, did not even stir.

Resigned, Madame Augelier thus came to know how old she really was and measured the infinite plain over which there wandered, beyond her reach, a being detached from her forever, a stranger, turned away from her, rebellious and free even from the bidding of memory: a little ten-year-old girl wearing on her wrist a bracelet of blue glass.

Review and Assess

Thinking About the Selection

1. **Respond:** Do you sympathize with Madame Augelier? Why or why not?

2. **(a) Recall:** As the story begins, with what attitude does Madame Augelier count the diamonds in her bracelet? **(b) Analyze:** How does this description show that the bracelet was given and received with little true feeling? **(c) Define:** What does the beginning of the story tell you about the nature of Madame Augelier's world?

3. **(a) Recall:** What gifts did Madame Augelier receive from her husband in their third and fourth years of marriage? **(b) Generalize:** How has the couple's relationship and lifestyle changed since then? Explain.

4. **(a) Recall:** What object does Madame Augelier suddenly remember from her childhood? **(b) Infer:** Why does she go shopping? **(c) Deduce:** What is Madame Augelier truly hoping to find when she goes shopping?

5. **(a) Compare and Contrast:** When Madame Augelier examines the glass bracelet at home, how does it compare with the vision from her childhood? **(b) Interpret:** What has changed since her childhood?

6. **Make a Judgment:** Do you think the title of this story refers to the diamond bracelet or to the blue bracelet? Support your answer.

Review and Assess

Literary Analysis

Epiphany

1. Colette provides an **epiphany** instead of a resolution to the conflict in this story. (a) What is the main conflict in "The Bracelet"? (b) At the end of the story, Madame Augelier is "resigned." Why is that an important term in understanding Madame Augelier and the conflict?

2. (a) What sudden realization does Madame Augelier experience in "The Bracelet"? (b) How does she react to that epiphany?

3. Early in the story, how do Madame Augelier's memories of past anniversary presents help prepare readers for her epiphany?

4. Does Madame Augelier's epiphany seem believable? Explain.

Connecting Literary Elements

5. What **descriptive details** about anniversary gifts of the past help draw the reader into the story?

6. (a) What details about the blue glass bracelet does Madame Augelier remember? (b) In what ways do these details lead to the story's epiphany?

Reading Strategy

Drawing Conclusions

7. Use a chart like the one shown to identify details that allow you to **draw the conclusion** that Madame Augelier is unhappy.

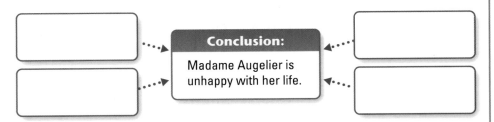

Conclusion:
Madame Augelier is unhappy with her life.

8. (a) At the beginning of the story, how does Madame Augelier feel about getting older? (b) Do her feelings change at the end of the story? (c) Which details led you to draw each of these conclusions?

Extend Understanding

9. **Social Studies Connection:** What does this story reveal about upper-class life in France in the early twentieth century? Explain.

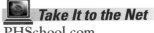

Integrate Language Skills

Vocabulary Development Lesson

Word Analysis: Latin Prefix *en-*

The prefix *en-* has several related meanings, including "to put into or cover," "to cause to be," or "to provide with." The vocabulary word *enraptured* literally means "put into a state of rapture." Use the meanings of *en-* to define each of the following words.

1. encourage
2. endanger
3. enlarge
4. enrobed
5. enlighten
6. encumbered

Spelling Strategy

If a noun ends in *-ence*, the adjective form of the word ends in *-ent*. For example, the noun *iridescence* becomes the adjective *iridescent*. Write the adjective form of each of the following nouns.

1. absence
2. impatience
3. opulence
4. eloquence

Fluency: Sentence Completions

Complete each sentence below with a word from the vocabulary list on page 1045.

1. The ___?___ struggled to his feet and, with some assistance, took a few steps.
2. He gave a(n) ___?___ grin at finally being able to walk again.
3. She admired the sparkling, ___?___ beads that decorated the gown.
4. At the five-star restaurant, the ___?___ examined his dessert with a scowl.
5. "This ___?___ chocolate sauce is inedible!" he complained to the waiter.
6. The lioness took a ___?___ path as she followed the herd.
7. Her ___?___ body glided through the grass with ease.

Grammar and Style Lesson

Commonly Confused Words: *sit* and *set*

Be careful to distinguish between **sit** and **set**, two easily confused verbs. *Sit* means "to be seated or resting in a particular spot." *Set* means "to put (something) in a certain place."

> . . . He asked her to *sit* down.

> . . . she *set* the bracelet on an old piece of velvet . . .

The main forms of *sit* are *sit*, *sitting*, *sat*, and *(have) sat*. The main forms of *set* are *set*, *setting*, *set*, and *(have) set*.

Practice Identify the correct verb in each of the following sentences.

1. Twenty-nine square stones (sat, set) in the bracelet.
2. Madame Augelier (sat, set) the bracelet in the box.
3. She was (sitting, setting) in her bedroom.
4. She had (sat, set) the box on the dresser.
5. She paced around the room and then (sat, set) down again.

Writing Application Write a paragraph about things you think you might own someday. Five times in the paragraph, use a form of the verb *sit* or *set* correctly.

WG Prentice Hall Writing and Grammar Connection: Diamond Level, Chapter 21, Section 1

Writing Lesson

Analytical Essay

Write an essay in which you analyze how Colette's use of images—words or phrases that appeal to the senses and create word pictures—helps convey the theme, or message about life, in "The Bracelet."

Prewriting In one sentence, state the story's theme or message. Then, reread the story, listing images that you associate with that theme. Use a chart like the one shown to explore each image.

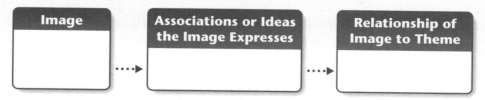

Image	Associations or Ideas the Image Expresses	Relationship of Image to Theme

Drafting Begin with a general statement about the theme, or main idea, of "The Bracelet." Then, cite specific examples of images in the story that suggest or develop that theme or main idea.

Revising As you review your draft, underline your main ideas and check that each one is clearly stated and well supported. Add examples of images as needed to illustrate your points.

W̶G Prentice Hall Writing and Grammar Connection: Diamond Level, Chapter 14, Section 2

Extension Activities

Listening and Speaking Adapt "The Bracelet" as a **monologue** given by Madame Augelier. Use these tips to prepare:

- Decide whether Madame Augelier will address the audience or will speak as if she is alone and thinking aloud.
- Determine what confessions Madame Augelier might make.
- Include her epiphany in some way.

Deliver the monologue to a small group or to the class.

Research and Technology "The Bracelet" takes place in France at the turn of the twentieth century. With a partner, research the clothing and decorating styles of that era. Then, prepare a **set and costume design** that accurately reflect Madame Augelier's clothing and home and that could be used for a dramatic performance of the story. **[Group Activity]**

 **Take It to the Net** PHSchool.com

Go online for an additional research activity using the Internet.

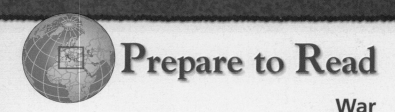
Luigi Pirandello (1867–1936)

With the completion of his masterpiece, *Six Characters in Search of an Author* (1921)—a play about a group of characters who, in their quest to find an author to tell their story, interrupt a group of actors rehearsing another play—Luigi Pirandello (lo͞o ē′ jē pir′ ən del′ ō) established himself as one of the most innovative dramatists of his time. Unfortunately, however, Pirandello's success as a playwright has overshadowed his numerous accomplishments as a fiction writer. Today, many people are unaware that in Italy, his native land, Luigi Pirandello is widely recognized as the master of the short story.

Early Trials The son of a successful sulfur merchant, Pirandello was born on the island of Sicily, off the southern tip of Italy. After high school, he attended the University of Rome and later received a doctorate from the University of Bonn in Germany. In 1894, he married the daughter of another sulfur merchant, and with the financial support of both his parents and his in-laws, he devoted the next ten years entirely to writing. When the sulfur mines collapsed in 1903, however, the fortunes of both families were wiped out, and Pirandello became a teacher in order to earn a living. At about the same time, his wife showed symptoms of the mental illness for which she would later be institutionalized.

First Triumphs Despite these setbacks, Pirandello continued to write. Having already established himself as a gifted short-story writer, Pirandello published his best-known novel, *The Late Mattia Pascal*, in 1904. Like many of his early stories, the novel explored the complexities of personal identity and questioned the distinction between appearance and reality. These themes were also the focus of *It Is So (If You Think So)* (1917), Pirandello's first successful play, and were fully developed in his greatest dramatic works, *Six Characters in Search of an Author* and *Henry IV* (1922).

An International Star Having established a worldwide reputation as a playwright, Pirandello was able to open his own theater company in 1924. At the same time, he continued to write and publish prolifically. Although his later works did not achieve the popularity of his early successful plays, Pirandello received the ultimate recognition for his achievements in 1934 when he was awarded the Nobel Prize in Literature. He died two years later in Rome.

A Great Legacy At the time of his death, it was already clear that Luigi Pirandello's artistic vision had exerted a great influence on the theater, as well as on the literary world in general. However, the full force of his influence did not become clear until the emergence of new generations of playwrights, who found in his work an ideal reflection of modern uncertainties. Perhaps Pirandello summed up his work best when he wrote, "Life is full of infinite absurdities, which, strangely enough, do not even need to appear plausible, since they are true." Because of his originality and his influence on other writers, Luigi Pirandello will be remembered as one of the most important writers of the twentieth century.

Preview

Connecting to the Literature

While war can have a powerful effect upon the soldiers who see combat, it also affects the families who worry about their loved ones on the front lines. This story focuses on those whom the soldiers leave behind.

Literary Analysis

Setting

The **setting** of a literary work is the time and place in which it occurs. Some settings provide a mere backdrop for the action, while others present a force, such as a winter storm or a cultural bias, that affects the characters. In "War," Pirandello establishes the setting with these words:

> At dawn, in a stuffy and smoky second-class carriage . . .

As you read "War," think about the role the setting itself plays in driving the story.

Connecting Literary Elements

Characterization is the art of creating and developing characters. There are two types of characterization:

- **Direct characterization:** The writer simply states what a character is like.

- **Indirect characterization:** The writer reveals what a character is like by describing his or her appearance, words, and actions and by noting what other characters say about him or her.

As you meet the characters in "War," consider not only *what* you learn about them but *how* you learn it.

Reading Strategy

Comparing and Contrasting Characters

"War" is populated by characters who share similar concerns but react in very different ways. Clarify their similarities and differences by **comparing and contrasting the characters.** To do so, use a chart like the one shown.

Character	1	2
Appearance		
Behavior		
Words		
Emotions		
Beliefs		

Vocabulary Development

plight (plīt) *n.* sad or difficult situation (p. 1057)

paternal (pə tʉr′ nəl) *adj.* like a father (p. 1057)

discrimination (di skrim′ i nā′ shən) *n.* show of partiality or prejudice (p. 1057)

vitality (vī tal′ ə tē) *n.* energy; life force (p. 1058)

retorted (ri tôrt′ id) *v.* replied, especially in a sharp or challenging way (p. 1058)

stoically (stō′ i klē) *adv.* done with indifference to pain or pleasure (p. 1059)

incongruous (in kän′ grōō əs) *adj.* not fitting a situation; inappropriate (p. 1060)

harrowing (har′ ō iŋ) *adj.* disturbing; frightening (p. 1060)

War

Luigi Pirandello *translated by* Samuel Putnam

Background

In the late nineteenth and early twentieth centuries, political tensions in Europe led to alliances among several major powers. Germany, Austria-Hungary, and Italy formed the Triple Alliance; Great Britain, France, and Russia formed the Triple Entente. When World War I broke out in 1914, however, Italy did not join in on the side of its allies. Instead, Italian officials made a secret treaty with the Triple Entente, promising Italy's military help in return for land gains at the war's end. Italy then declared war on its former allies. In the years of fighting that followed, approximately 650,000 Italians died—nearly 2 percent of the country's population—and almost 950,000 more were wounded. It is against this bitter cultural landscape that Pirandello's story unfolds.

The passengers who had left Rome by the night express had had to stop until dawn at the small station of Fabriano[1] in order to continue their journey by the small old-fashioned "local" joining the main line with Sulmona.[2]

At dawn, in a stuffy and smoky second-class carriage in which five people had already spent the night, a bulky woman in deep mourning, was hoisted in—almost like a shapeless bundle. Behind her—puffing and moaning, followed her husband—a tiny man, thin and weakly, his face death-white, his eyes small and bright and looking shy and uneasy.

Having at last taken a seat he politely thanked the passengers who had helped his wife and who had made room for her; then he turned round to the woman trying to pull down the collar of her coat and politely enquired:

"Are you all right, dear?"

The wife, instead of answering, pulled up her collar again to her eyes, so as to hide her face.

"Nasty world," muttered the husband with a sad smile.

And he felt it his duty to explain to his travelling companions that the poor woman was to be pitied for the war was taking away from her her only son, a boy of twenty to whom both had devoted their entire life,

Literary Analysis
Setting Which details in this description of the setting suggest closeness and discomfort? Explain.

1. **Fabriano** (fä′ brē ä′ nō) city in eastern Italy, approximately 100 miles from Rome.
2. **Sulmona** (so͞ol mō′ na) city in eastern Italy, approximately 75 miles from Rome.

even breaking up their home at Sulmona to follow him to Rome where he had to go as a student, then allowing him to volunteer for war with an assurance, however, that at least for six months he would not be sent to the front and now, all of a sudden, receiving a wire saying that he was due to leave in three days' time and asking them to go and see him off.

The woman under the big coat was twisting and wriggling, at times growling like a wild animal, feeling certain that all those explanations would not have aroused even a shadow of sympathy from those people who—most likely—were in the same <u>plight</u> as herself. One of them, who had been listening with particular attention, said:

"You should thank God that your son is only leaving now for the front. Mine has been sent there the first day of the war. He has already come back twice wounded and been sent back again to the front."

"What about me? I have two sons and three nephews at the front," said another passenger.

"Maybe, but in our case it is our *only* son," ventured the husband.

"What difference can it make? You may spoil your only son with excessive attentions, but you cannot love him more than you would all your other children if you had any. <u>Paternal</u> love is not like bread that can be broken into pieces and spilt amongst the children in equal shares. A father gives all his love to each one of his children without <u>discrimination</u>, whether it be one or ten, and if I am suffering now for my two sons, I am not suffering half for each of them but double. . . ."

"True . . . true . . . " sighed the embarrassed husband, "but suppose (of course we all hope it will never be your case) a father has two sons at the front and he loses one of them, there is still one left to console him . . . while . . . "

"Yes," answered the other, getting cross, "a son left to console him but also a son left for whom he must survive, while in the case of

plight (plīt) *n.* sad or difficult situation

paternal (pə tʉr´ nəl) *adj.* like a father

discrimination (di skrim´ i nā´ shən) *n.* show of partiality or prejudice

✓**Reading Check**

According to her husband, why is the woman in the big coat to be pitied?

Critical Viewing ▶
Do you think this painting of a World War I battlefield suggests hope or terror? Explain.

A Star Shell, exh. 1916, Christopher R.W. Nevinson, Tate Gallery, London

the father of an only son if the son dies the father can die too and put an end to his distress. Which of the two positions is the worse? Don't you see how my case would be worse than yours?"

"Nonsense," interrupted another traveller, a fat, red-faced man with bloodshot eyes of the palest grey.

He was panting. From his bulging eyes seemed to spurt inner violence of an uncontrolled <u>vitality</u> which his weakened body could hardly contain.

"Nonsense," he repeated, trying to cover his mouth with his hand so as to hide the two missing front teeth. "Nonsense. Do we give life to our children for our own benefit?"

The other travellers stared at him in distress. The one who had had his son at the front since the first day of the war sighed: "You are right. Our children do not belong to us, they belong to the Country. . . ."

"Bosh," <u>retorted</u> the fat traveller. "Do we think of the Country when we give life to our children? Our sons are born because . . . well, because they must be born and when they come to life they take our own life with them. This is the truth. We belong to them but they never belong to us. And when they reach twenty they are exactly what we were at their age. We too had a father and mother, but there were so many other things as well . . . girls, cigarettes, illusions, new ties . . . and the Country, of course, whose call we would have answered—when we were twenty—even if father and mother had said no. Now, at our age, the love of our Country is still great, of course, but stronger than it is the love for our children. Is there any one of us here who wouldn't gladly take his son's place at the front if he could?"

There was a silence all round, everybody nodding as to approve.

"Why then," continued the fat man, "shouldn't we consider the feelings of our children when they are twenty? Isn't it natural that at their age they should consider the love for their Country (I am speaking of decent boys, of course) even greater than the love for us? Isn't it natural that it should be so, as after all they must look upon us as upon old boys who cannot move any more and must stay at home? If Country exists, if Country is a natural necessity like bread, of which each of us must eat in order not to die of hunger, somebody must go to defend it. And our sons go, when they are twenty, and they don't want tears, because if they die, they die inflamed and happy (I am speaking, of

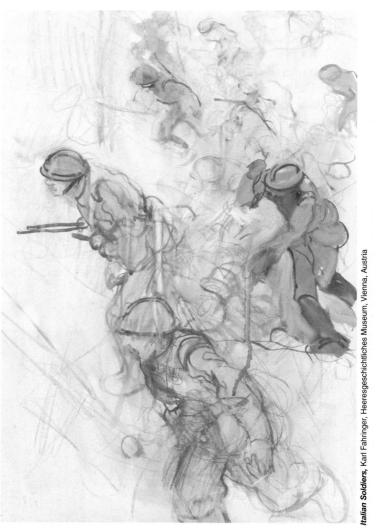

Italian Soldiers, Karl Fahringer, Heeresgeschichtliches Museum, Vienna, Austria

▲ **Critical Viewing**
Which aspects of war does this drawing emphasize? **[Interpret]**

vitality (vī tal′ ə tē) *n.* energy; life force

retorted (ri tôrt′ id) *v.* replied, especially in a sharp or challenging way

course, of decent boys). Now, if one dies young and happy, without having the ugly sides of life, the boredom of it, the pettiness, the bitterness of disillusion . . . what more can we ask for him? Everyone should stop crying: everyone should laugh, as I do . . . or at least thank God—as I do—because my son, before dying, sent me a message saying that he was dying satisfied at having ended his life in the best way he could have wished. That is why, as you see, I do not even wear mourning. . . ."

He shook his light fawn³ coat as to show it; his livid⁴ lip over his missing teeth was trembling, his eyes were watery and motionless and soon after he ended with a shrill laugh which might well have been a sob.

"Quite so . . . quite so . . ." agreed the others.

The woman who, bundled in a corner under her coat, had been sitting and listening had—for the last three months—tried to find in the words of her husband and her friends something to console her in her deep sorrow, something that might show her how a mother should resign herself to send her son not even to death but to a probable danger of life. Yet not a word had she found amongst the many which had been said . . . and her grief had been greater in seeing that nobody—as she thought—could share her feelings.

But now the words of the traveller amazed and almost stunned her. She suddenly realized that it wasn't the others who were wrong and could not understand her but herself who could not rise up to the same height of those fathers and mothers willing to resign themselves, without crying, not only to the departure of their sons but even to their death.

She lifted her head, she bent over from her corner trying to listen with great attention to the details which the fat man was giving to his companions about the way his son had fallen as a hero, for his King and his Country, happy and without regrets. It seemed to her that she had stumbled into a world she had never dreamt of, a world so far unknown to her and she was so pleased to hear everyone joining in congratulating that brave father who could so <u>stoically</u> speak of his child's death.

---

3. **fawn** (fôn) pale, yellowish brown.
4. **livid** (liv´ id) discolored, as from a bruise; black-and-blue.

Critical Viewing ▶ In what ways do you think the couple in this drawing are similar to and different from the couple in this story?
[Compare and Contrast]

Reading Strategy
Comparing and Contrasting Characters In what ways does the fat man seem different from the other passengers?

stoically (stō´ i klē) *adv.* done with indifference to pain or pleasure

✔**Reading Check**

What message did the fat man's son send to him?

Then suddenly, just as if she had heard nothing of what had been said and almost as if waking up from a dream, she turned to the old man, asking him:

"Then . . . is your son really dead?"

Everybody stared at her. The old man, too, turned to look at her, fixing his great, bulging, horribly watery light grey eyes, deep in her face. For some little time he tried to answer, but words failed him. He looked and looked at her, almost as if only then—at that silly, <u>incongruous</u> question—he had suddenly realized at last that his son was really dead . . . gone for ever . . . for ever. His face contracted, became horribly distorted, then he snatched in haste a handkerchief from his pocket and, to the amazement of everyone, broke into <u>harrowing</u>, heart-rending, uncontrollable sobs.

Review and Assess

Thinking About the Selection

1. **Respond:** How did you feel about the fat man's emotional breakdown at the end of the story? Explain.

2. **(a) Recall:** What is the "bulky" woman wearing? **(b) Connect:** In what way does her clothing reflect her mental and emotional state?

3. **(a) Recall:** What message did the son send by "wire" to his parents? **(b) Recall:** What assurance had the parents received when their son joined the military? **(c) Draw Conclusions:** What is suggested about the nature of war when this promise is not kept?

4. **(a) Recall:** According to the husband, why is his suffering worse than the suffering of those with more than one child?
   (b) Infer: Do the other passengers agree with him? Explain.
   (c) Assess: Is this an argument that can be won? Why or why not?

5. **(a) Recall:** According to the fat man, what love is greater than the love of country? **(b) Compare and Contrast:** How do the feelings of young people toward their country differ from the feelings of their parents? **(c) Analyze:** How does the fat man use reason to explain away his own personal tragedy? Explain.

6. **(a) Recall:** What question does the mother ask the fat man?
   (b) Analyze Cause and Effect: How does he react to her question? **(c) Draw Conclusions:** Why does he react as he does? Explain.

7. **Synthesize:** In what ways might this story help you react toward people who have suffered a personal loss?

Review and Assess

Literary Analysis

Setting

1. Using a chart like the one shown below, clarify the **setting** of "War" by naming two details about the time, two details about the place, and two details about the passengers' cultural attitudes.

Time	Place	Attitudes
1.	1.	1.
2.	2.	2.

2. (a) How does the historical context—Italy during World War I—affect the characters in this story? (b) In what ways does that context help suggest the theme, or message, of the story? Explain.

3. (a) In what ways might the setting of this story be similar to a combat zone? (b) In what ways might such a setting motivate characters to interact with one another?

Connecting Literary Elements

4. (a) Cite two examples of **indirect characterization** that Pirandello uses to present the husband and wife. (b) What information about the characters does each of these examples provide? Explain.

5. Write one sentence of **direct characterization** for each of the three main characters—the mother, the father, and the fat traveler.

Reading Strategy

Comparing and Contrasting Characters

6. (a) **Compare and contrast the characters** by examining Pirandello's descriptions of the eyes and the clothes of both the mother and the fat man. (b) How do those descriptions suggest similarities and differences between the two characters?

7. (a) For which character do you feel the most sympathy? (b) What do you think sets him or her apart from the others?

Extend Understanding

8. **Cultural Connection:** (a) According to the fat man, why is the attention of young people "fragmented"? (b) Do you see that kind of fragmentation in today's youth culture? Explain.

Quick Review

The **setting** of a literary work is the time and place of the action.

Characterization is the art of creating and developing characters. In **direct characterization,** the author simply states what a character is like. In **indirect characterization,** the author implies what a character is like through details.

When you **compare and contrast characters,** you look for similarities and differences among them.

 **Take It to the Net**
PHSchool.com

Take the interactive self-test online to check your understanding of this selection.

Integrate Language Skills

Vocabulary Development Lesson

Word Analysis: Latin Root -patr-

The root -patr-, found in the word *paternal*, comes from the Latin word *pater*, which means "father." Complete each sentence below by filling in the blank with one of the words listed.

> patrician   patriotic   patriarch

1. Grandfather is the family's ___?___.
2. ___?___ people love their homeland.
3. A person of high birth is a ___?___.

Spelling Strategy

Words that contain a long *i* sound followed by a *t* are often, but not always, spelled with the letter combination *ight*. In each pair of words below, select the word that is spelled correctly.

1. delight/delite   2. foresight/foresyte

Concept Development: Synonyms

Review the vocabulary list on page 1055. Then, select the word in the right column that is similar in meaning to the vocabulary word in the left column.

1. plight   a. vigor
2. paternal   b. impassively
3. discrimination   c. distressing
4. vitality   d. retaliated
5. retorted   e. fatherly
6. stoically   f. absurd
7. incongruous   g. favoritism
8. harrowing   h. difficulty

Grammar and Style Lesson

Adjective Clauses

Adjective clauses are subordinate clauses that modify nouns or pronouns and often begin with the word *that*, *which*, *who*, *whom*, or *whose*. Restrictive adjective clauses are essential to the meaning of the sentence and are not set off by commas. Nonrestrictive adjective clauses are not essential to the meaning and are set off by commas.

Examples:

Restrictive: The passengers <u>who had left Rome on the night express</u> had had to stop . . . [modifies *passengers*]

Nonrestrictive: One of them, <u>who had been listening with particular attention</u>, said . . . [modifies *one*]

Practice Identify the adjective clause in each sentence below. Then, indicate whether it is restrictive or nonrestrictive, and name the word it modifies.

1. He thanked the men who had helped.
2. The unhappy woman, whom everyone was watching, listened to the conversation.
3. They discussed a topic that grieved her.
4. The war, which had claimed many lives, soon might claim her son.
5. Combat brings grief to many parents whose children are in the military.

Writing Application Write a paragraph about the characters in "War." Include at least two restrictive and two nonrestrictive adjective clauses.

Writing Lesson
Newspaper Article

Imagine yourself in the setting of "War." As a journalist on the train, you have witnessed the exchange among the passengers. Write a newspaper article reporting what you observed. Include a general statement about the impact of the war on ordinary people.

Prewriting   Write a rough outline of the events described in the story and the statements the characters make. Review the outline, circling the items that you want to include in the article.

Drafting   Begin with a lead, a strong first paragraph that introduces the subject in an interesting way. Follow with a logically ordered report of the events that you witnessed.

Revising   Review your draft. To maintain objectivity, remove material that is not factual and replace language that suggests a personal bias.

Model: Revising to Maintain Objectivity

an older
Then ~~a foolish old~~ man interrupted. With great animation,

said
he ~~babbled~~ that young men naturally love their country

and want to fight. ~~It was crazy talk.~~

> A newspaper article sticks to the facts and does not express bias.

WG Prentice Hall Writing and Grammar Connection: Diamond Level, Chapter 2, Section 2

Extension Activities

Listening and Speaking In a small group, prepare a **dramatic reading** of this story. Use these tips to help your planning:

- Select readers for the narrator, the husband, the wife, the fat man, and the two passengers who speak.
- Vary the volume and tone of your voice to capture the characters' emotions.
- Use eye contact and appropriate gestures.

Deliver the dramatic reading in class. **[Group Activity]**

Research and Technology Using print and electronic sources, prepare a **multimedia report** about a typical soldier's experience in battle during World War I. Include information about military technology, trench warfare, standard-issue equipment, and attitudes toward the war. Present the report to the class, using appropriate handouts to clarify information.

 **Take It to the Net**   PHSchool.com

Go online for an additional research activity using the Internet.

The mother in Pirandello's short story "War," in this unit, feels desperate and distraught when she thinks of her only son in battle. Human responses to anxiety and grief, however, are individual and unique. On the train with the mother are other travelers who also have sons in combat. These parents have come up with various ways to calm their fears and worries—and even to deal with the ultimate tragedy of losing a child.

Love and Grief The parents of Will Hutchenson in "The Corn Planting" are, like the mother and father in "War," parents of an only son. Their lives revolve around Will, and when they suffer a crushing loss, they have their own special way of dealing with their sorrow. You may notice these parents' similarities to the parents in Pirandello's story, but take note of their differences as well.

The Corn Planting

Sherwood Anderson

The farmers who come to our town to trade are a part of the town life. Saturday is the big day. Often the children come to the high school in town.

It is so with Hatch Hutchenson. Although his farm, some three miles from town, is small, it is known to be one of the best-kept and best-worked places in all our section. Hatch is a little gnarled old figure of a man. His place is on the Scratch Gravel Road and there are plenty of poorly kept places out that way.

Hatch's place stands out. The little frame house is always kept painted, the trees in his orchard are whitened with lime halfway up the trunks, and the barn and sheds are in repair, and his fields are always clean-looking.

Hatch is nearly seventy. He got a rather late start in life. His father, who owned the same farm, was a Civil War man and came home badly wounded, so that, although he lived a long time after the war, he couldn't work much. Hatch was the only son and stayed at home, working the place until his father died. Then, when he was nearing fifty, he married a schoolteacher of forty, and they had a son. The schoolteacher was a small one like Hatch. After they married, they both stuck close to the land. They seemed to fit into their farm life as certain people fit into the clothes they wear. I have noticed something about people who make a go of marriage. They grow more and more alike. Then even grow to look alike.

Their one son, Will Hutchenson, was a small but remarkably strong boy. He came to our high school in town and pitched on our town baseball team. He was a fellow always cheerful, bright and alert, and a great favorite with all of us.

For one thing, he began as a young boy to make amusing little drawings. It was a talent. He made drawings of fish and pigs and cows, and they looked like people you knew. I never did know, before, that people could look so much like cows and horses and pigs and fish.

When he had finished in the town high school, Will went to Chicago, where his mother had a cousin living, and he became a student in the Art Institute out there. Another young fellow from our town was also in Chicago. He really went two years before Will did. His name was Hal Weyman, and he was a student at the University of Chicago. After he graduated, he came home and got a job as principal of our high school.

Hal and Will Hutchenson hadn't been close friends before, Hal being several years older than Will, but in Chicago they got together, went together to see plays, and, as Hal later told me, they had a good many long talks.

I got it from Hal that, in Chicago, as at home here when he was a young boy, Will was immediately popular. He was good-looking, so the girls in the art school liked him, and he had a straightforwardness that made him popular with all the young fellows.

Hal told me that Will was out to some party nearly every night, and

Thematic Connection
Why do you think the description of Will is so positive?

◀ **Critical Viewing**
In what ways does the farm setting impact the characters in this story? **[Connect]**

right away he began to sell some of his amusing little drawings and to make money. The drawings were used in advertisements, and he was well paid.

He even began to send some money home. You see, after Hal came back here, he used to go quite often out to the Hutchenson place to see Will's father and mother. He would walk or drive out there in the afternoon or on summer evenings and sit with them. The talk was always of Will.

Hal said it was touching how much the father and mother depended on their one son, how much they talked about him and dreamed of his future. They had never been people who went about much with the town folks or even with their neighbors. They were of the sort who work all the time, from early morning till late in the evenings, and on moonlight nights, Hal said, and after the little old wife had got the supper, they often went out into the fields and worked again.

You see, by this time old Hatch was nearing seventy and his wife would have been ten years younger. Hal said that whenever he went out to the farm they quit work and came to sit with him. They might be in one of the fields, working together, but when they saw him in the road, they came running. They had got a letter from Will. He wrote every week.

The little old mother would come running following the father. "We got another letter, Mr. Weyman," Hatch would cry, and then his wife, quite breathless, would say the same thing, "Mr. Weyman, we got a letter."

The letter would be brought out at once and read aloud. Hal said the letters were always delicious. Will larded them with little sketches. There were humorous drawings of people he had seen or been with, rivers of automobiles on Michigan Avenue in Chicago, a policeman at a street crossing, young stenographers hurrying into office buildings. Neither of the old people had ever been to the city and they were curious and eager. They wanted the drawings explained, and Hal said they were like two children wanting to know every little detail Hal could remember about their son's life in the big city. He was always at them to come there on a visit and they would spend hours talking of that.

"Of course," Hatch said, "we couldn't go."

"How could we?" he said. He had been on that one little farm since he was a boy. When he was a young fellow, his father was an invalid and so Hatch had to run things. A farm, if you run it right, is very exacting. You have to fight weeds all the time. There are the farm animals to take care of. "Who would milk our cows?" Hatch said. The idea of anyone but him or his wife touching one of the Hutchenson cows seemed to hurt him. While he was alive, he didn't want anyone else plowing one of his fields, tending his corn, looking after things about the barn. He felt that way about his farm. It was a thing you couldn't explain, Hal said. He seemed to understand the two old people.

Thematic Connection
In what way does Will's parents' reaction to his letters indicate his importance in their lives?

The Hailstorm, Thomas Hart Benton, Joslyn Art Museum, Omaha, Nebraska

It was a spring night, past midnight, when Hal came to my house and told me the news. In our town we have a night telegraph operator at the railroad station and Hal got a wire. It was really addressed to Hatch Hutchenson, but the operator brought it to Hal. Will Hutchenson was dead, had been killed. It turned out later that he was at a party with some other young fellows and there might have been some drinking. Anyway, the car was wrecked, and Will Hutchenson was killed. The operator wanted Hal to go out and take the message to Hatch and his wife, and Hal wanted me to go along.

I offered to take my car, but Hal said no, "Let's walk out," he said. He wanted to put off the moment, I could see that. So we did walk. It was early spring, and I remember every moment of the silent walk we took, the little leaves just coming on the trees, the little streams we crossed, how the moonlight made the water seem alive. We loitered and loitered, not talking, hating to go on.

▲ **Critical Viewing**
In what ways does the storm in this painting reflect the blow that the Hutchensons are about to receive? [**Connect**]

Then we got out there, and Hal went to the front door of the farmhouse while I stayed in the road. I heard a dog bark, away off somewhere. I heard a child crying in some distant house. I think that Hal, after he got to the front door of the house, must have stood there for ten minutes, hating to knock.

Then he did knock, and the sound his fist made on the door seemed terrible. It seemed like guns going off. Old Hatch came to the door, and I heard Hal tell him. I know what happened. Hal had been trying, all the way out from town, to think up words to tell the old couple in some gentle way, but when it came to the scratch, he couldn't. He blurted everything right out, right into old Hatch's face.

That was all. Old Hatch didn't say a word. The door was opened, he stood there in the moonlight, wearing a funny long white nightgown, Hal told him, and the door went shut again with a bang, and Hal was left standing there.

He stood for a time, and then came back out into the road to me. "Well," he said, and "Well," I said. We stood in the road looking and listening. There wasn't a sound from the house.

And then—it might have been ten minutes or it might have been a half-hour—we stood silently, listening and watching, not knowing what to do—we couldn't go away—"I guess they are trying to get so they can believe it," Hal whispered to me.

▲ **Critical Viewing**
In what way might this couple be similar to the Hutchensons? [**Compare**]

I got his notion all right. The two old people must have thought of their son Will always only in terms of life, never of death.

We stood watching and listening, and then, suddenly, after a long time, Hal touched me on the arm. "Look," he whispered. There were two white-clad figures going from the house to the barn. It turned out, you see, that old Hatch had been plowing that day. He had finished plowing and harrowing a field near the barn.

The two figures went into the barn and presently came out. They went into the field, and Hal and I crept across the farmyard to the barn and got to where we could see what was going on without being seen.

It was an incredible thing. The old man had got a hand corn-planter out of the barn and his wife had got a bag of seed corn, and there, in the moonlight, that night, after they got that news, they were planting corn.

It was a thing to curl your hair—it was so ghostly. They were both in their nightgowns. They would do a row across the field, coming quite close to us as we stood in the shadow of the barn, and then, at the end of each row, they would kneel side by side by the fence and stay silent for a time. The whole thing went on in silence. It was the first time in my life I ever understood something, and I am far from sure now that I can put down what I understood and felt that night—I mean something about the connection between certain people and the earth—a kind of silent cry, down into the earth, of these two old people, putting corn down into the earth. It was as though they were putting death down into the ground that life might grow again—something like that.

They must have been asking something of the earth, too. But what's the use? What they were up to in connection with the life in their field and the lost life in their son is something you can't very well make clear in words. All I know is that Hal and I stood the sight as long as we could, and then we crept away and went back to town, but Hatch Hutchenson and his wife must have got what they were after that night, because Hal told me that when he went out in the morning to see them and to make the arrangements for bringing their dead son home, they were both curiously quiet and Hal thought in command of themselves. Hal said he thought they had got something. "They have their farm and they have still got Will's letters to read," Hal said.

Sherwood Anderson

(1876–1941)

Born the third of seven children, Sherwood Anderson grew up in a small town in Ohio. His father, a harness maker and house painter, was not always able to earn enough to support the family. Anderson dropped out of school at fourteen to work but finished high school in his twenties, after a year in the army. Much of Anderson's writing, which uses everyday speech to capture the essence of characters, features small-town life in the rural Midwest.

Connecting Literature Past and Present

1. (a) What do Hatch Hutchenson and his wife have in common with the man and woman who enter the train at Fabriano in Pirandello's "War"? (b) In what ways are the two couples' lives different?

2. In what way does nature help Hatch and his wife cope with their devastating loss?

3. (a) What do you think the parents in "War" would say to Hatch Hutchenson and his wife? (b) What do you think Hatch Hutchenson and his wife would say to the parents in "War"?

Prepare to Read

The Guitar ◆ *from* Lament for Ignacio Sánchez Mejías: Absent Soul ◆ Ithaka ◆ The Soul With Boundaries

Federico García Lorca (1898–1936)

In August 1936, one month after the start of the Spanish Civil War, the Spanish newspaper *El Diario de Albacete* broke the shocking story that Federico García Lorca had been assassinated. Subsequent reports confirmed that he had been murdered by right-wing Nationalists, who deemed his writings politically offensive.

Ironically, García Lorca did not write explicitly political poetry. His inspiration came from the people and culture of rural Andalusia, where the poet was born. Andalusia is the homeland of the gypsies, or flamencos. With the exception of the poems collected in *Poet in New York*, all of García Lorca's work reflects the dark beauty of Andalusian culture.

García Lorca also wrote several major plays, including *Blood Wedding* and *The House of Bernarda Alba*. Although his writing career was tragically cut short, García Lorca is considered one of Spain's greatest poets and playwrights.

Constantine Cavafy (1863–1933)

Constantine Cavafy [kə´ vä´ fē] was born in 1863 in Alexandria, Egypt. Although he lived in Greece only briefly, he became a Greek citizen as soon as he was of age. Today, he is considered the most original and influential Greek poet of the twentieth century.

In his poems, Cavafy combines two distinct kinds of Greek: demotic Greek, the language of the common people, and purist Greek, the official language of the church and state. Although the distinctions between the two do not translate into English, Cavafy's use of both forms of Greek can be seen as a political statement.

During his lifetime, Cavafy published poems privately. However, when *The Poems of Constantine P. Cavafy* was published posthumously in 1935, Cavafy began to draw the attention of the world. Ever since then, his reputation—both in Greece and abroad—has continued to grow.

Fernando Pessoa (1888–1935)

Fernando Pessoa [pes´ wä] was born in Lisbon, Portugal, on June 13, 1888. While many writers publish under pseudonyms, or false names, Pessoa's creative use of poetic identities is unique in the history of literature.

In a letter to a friend, Pessoa described the birth of his first literary alter ego: ". . . I wrote thirty-odd poems straight off, in a kind of ecstasy whose nature I cannot define. . . . I started with a title—'The Keeper of Sheep.' And what followed was the apparition of somebody in me, to whom I at once gave the name of Alberto Caeiro."

Alberto Caeiro was one of four personas, whom Pessoa called *heteronyms*, who wrote and published poems. The others were Ricardo Reis, Alvaro de Campos, and Fernando Pessoa himself. For each of these heteronyms, Pessoa invented a biography, personality, beliefs, physical appearance, and literary style. One critic wrote, "Pessoa was a poet who wrote poets as well as poems."

Over the course of his life, Pessoa created at least seventy distinct identities who wrote thousands of literary works. His many books of poetry and prose include *Antinous* (1918), *Sonnets* (1918), and *English Poems* (1921).

Preview

Connecting to the Literature

When traveling, you can journey by car or by plane; you might walk, take a bus, or even ride a horse. If life itself is a journey, how should one travel? These poems look at the long journey of life and express ideas about the best ways to make the trip.

Literary Analysis

Lyric Poetry and Epiphany

Lyric poetry is melodic verse that expresses the observations of a single speaker. Unlike narrative poems, lyric poems do not tell complete stories. Instead, they build to express a moment of insight—an **epiphany,** or revelation. The poet Dante Gabriel Rossetti called the sonnet, which is a type of lyric poem, a "moment's monument." Because of this emphasis on the moment, lyric poems exclude details that a narrative would supply. As you read, look for the moment of insight captured by each poem.

Comparing Literary Works

A **metaphor** is an implied comparison between two seemingly different things. In the example below, García Lorca likens the sound of a guitar to a woeful utterance, and he then characterizes the sky as a kind of building:

> Now begins <u>the cry</u> / <u>Of the guitar,</u> / Breaking <u>the vaults</u> / <u>Of dawn</u>.

While most metaphors are brief, an **extended metaphor** flows throughout a literary work. Several comparisons may be made along the way, combining to create a larger meaning. All of the poems in this grouping contain metaphors, some of which are extended. As you read, compare the use of metaphor in each poem.

Reading Strategy

Reading Stanzas as Units of Meaning

Many poems take the form of stanzas, or formal groupings of lines. Like a paragraph in a work of prose, a stanza usually expresses one main idea. To aid your understanding of poetry, **read stanzas as units of meaning** in the same way that you read paragraphs. You might pause after each stanza and consider its main thought. Use a chart like the one shown to record statements expressing these ideas.

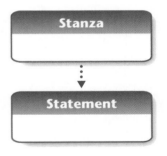

Vocabulary Development

monotonously (mə nät′'n əs lē) *adv.* done in a way that goes on and on without variation (p. 1073)

posterity (päs ter′ ə tē) *n.* future generations of people (p. 1074)

exalted (eg zôlt′ id) *adj.* lifted high because of dignity or honor (p. 1076)

sensual (sen′ shōō əl) *adj.* pleasing to the senses (p. 1077)

summit (sum′ it) *n.* highest point (p. 1079)

dispersed (di spurst′) *adj.* broken up and scattered (p. 1079)

divergent (dī vur′ jənt) *adj.* differing from each other (p. 1080)

The Guitar

Federico García Lorca
translated by
Elizabeth du Gué Trapier

The Old Guitarist, 1903, Pablo Picasso, The Art Institute of Chicago

Background

García Lorca did not accept the label of "Gypsy Poet." Instead, he insisted, "I could just as well be a poet of sewing needles and hydraulic landscapes. . . ." Nevertheless, Gypsy culture pervades García Lorca's work, providing him with images that transcend the local and become universal.

"The Guitar" captures the flamenco music of the Gitanos, the Gypsy population of Andalusia. Some flamenco music is festive, but García Lorca admired the *cante jondo* (kan´ tä hōn´ dō), a deeper and more somber tradition. "Absent Soul" is the final section of "Lament for Ignacio Sánchez Mejías," an elegy to a famous bullfighter who was a friend of García Lorca's. Sánchez Mejías died in 1934 after having been gored during a bullfight.

◀ **Critical Viewing**
Does the mood of this painting fit the mood of the poem? Explain.
[Interpret]

Now begins the cry
Of the guitar,
Breaking the vaults
Of dawn.
5 Now begins the cry
Of the guitar.
Useless
To still it.
Impossible
10 To still it.
It weeps <u>monotonously</u>
As weeps the water,
As weeps the wind
Over snow.
15 Impossible
To still it.
It weeps
For distant things,
Warm southern sands
20 Desiring white camellias[1]
It mourns the arrow without a target,
The evening without morning,
And the first bird dead
Upon a branch.
25 O guitar!
A wounded heart,
Wounded by five swords.

---

1. **camellias** (kə mēl´ yəz) showy, roselike flowers of an ornamental evergreen shrub native to eastern Asia.

Literary Analysis
Lyric Poetry and Epiphany Which words and individual sounds help give lines 7–16 a musical feeling?

monotonously (me nät´n es lē) *adv.* done in a way that goes on and on without variation

Review and Assess

Thinking About the Selection

1. **Respond:** Which image in this poem do you find most striking?

2. **(a) Recall:** In lines 3–4, what effect does the guitar's cry have upon the "vaults / Of dawn"? **(b) Interpret:** What does this image suggest about the intensity of emotion expressed by the guitar?

3. **(a) Recall:** In lines 21–24, for what three things does the speaker say the guitar mourns? **(b) Analyze:** How does each of these things capture a sense of unfulfilled promise? Explain.

4. **(a) Recall:** In lines 25–27, which objects wound the guitar? **(b) Interpret:** What is your interpretation of this image? Explain.

5. **Extend:** What musical instrument seems most like a person to you? Explain.

from "Lament for Ignacio Sánchez Mejías"

Absent Soul

Federico García Lorca
translated by Stephen Spender and J. L. Gili

The bull does not know you, nor the fig tree,
nor the horses, nor the ants in your own house.
The child and the afternoon do not know you
because you have died for ever.

5 The back of the stone does not know you,
nor the black satin in which you crumble.
Your silent memory does not know you
because you have died for ever.

The autumn will come with small white snails,
10 misty grapes and with clustered hills,
but no one will look into your eyes
because you have died for ever.

Because you have died for ever,
like all the dead of the Earth,
15 like all the dead who are forgotten
in a heap of lifeless dogs.

Nobody knows you. No. But I sing of you.
For <u>posterity</u> I sing of your profile and grace.
Of the signal[1] maturity of your understanding.
20 Of your appetite for death and the taste of its mouth.
Of the sadness of your once valiant gaiety.

It will be a long time, if ever, before there is born
an Andalusian[2] so true, so rich in adventure.
I sing of his elegance with words that groan,
25 and I remember a sad breeze through the olive trees.

Reading Strategy
Stanzas as Units of Meaning What is the main idea expressed in the fourth stanza?

posterity (päs ter´ ə tē) *n.* future generations of people

---

1. **signal** (sig´ nel) *adj.* extraordinary; distinguished.
2. **Andalusian** inhabitant of Andalusia, a region of Spain bordering both the Atlantic Ocean and the Mediterranean Sea.

▲ **Critical Viewing** Based on this photograph of an olive grove, why might olive trees be an appropriate image in a poem of lament? **[Analyze]**

Review and Assess

Thinking About the Selection

1. **Respond:** After reading this poem, do you feel that you know Sánchez Mejías? Explain.

2. **(a) Recall:** In the first stanza, what six things do not know Sánchez Mejías? **(b) Generalize:** In what ways might each of these things reflect some aspect of Sánchez Mejías's life?

3. **(a) Infer:** Whom does the speaker address in the first five stanzas? **(b) Interpret:** How does that address change in the last stanza? **(c) Analyze:** What emotional shift might this change reflect? Explain.

4. **(a) Distinguish:** In line 20, what trait of Sánchez Mejías does the speaker celebrate? **(b) Interpret:** What do you think García Lorca is saying about how to live life to the fullest? Explain.

Ithaka

Constantine Cavafy

translated by
**Edmund Keeley
and Philip Sherrard**

Background

Constantine Cavafy found special inspiration in the Homeric epics—the *Iliad* and the *Odyssey*—and paid tribute to them in at least nine poems and an essay. "Ithaka," published in 1911, is the last of these tributes.

In Homer's *Odyssey*, the hero Odysseus spends twenty years struggling to return to his home, the city of Ithaka. Along the way, he meets monsters and goddesses, suffers losses, and experiences rapture. In this poem, Cavafy uses Odysseus' legendary tale to describe a way to live one's life.

Reading Strategy
Reading Stanzas as Units of Meaning In the first stanza, what attitude toward their journey does the speaker advise travelers to take?

exalted (eg zôlt´ id) *adj.* lifted high because of dignity or honor

When you set out for Ithaka[1]
Pray that your road's a long one,
full of adventure, full of discovery.
Laistrygonians, Cyclops,
5   angry Poseidon[2]—don't be scared of them:
you won't find things like that on your way
as long as your thoughts are <u>exalted,</u>
as long as a rare excitement
stirs your spirit and your body.
10 Laistrygonians, Cyclops,
wild Poseidon—you won't encounter them
unless you bring them along inside you,
unless your soul raises them up in front of you.

Pray that your road's a long one.
15 May there be many a summer morning when—
full of gratitude, full of joy—
you come into harbors seen for the first time;
may you stop at Phoenician[3] trading centers
and buy fine things,
20 mother of pearl and coral, amber and ebony,

---

1. Ithaka often spelled Ithaca; one of a group of islands off the west coast of Greece; the legendary home of Odysseus.
2. Laistrygonians (les trə gōn´ ē ənz), **Cyclops, angry Poseidon** In Homer's *Odyssey*, the Laistrygonians are a race of giants, the Cyclops is a one-eyed monster, and Poseidon is the sea god. All of these characters pose varying threats to Odysseus and his crew.
3. Phoenician of or relating to Phoenicia, the ancient name for a narrow strip of land, now largely modern Lebanon, on the eastern coast of the Mediterranean Sea. The Phoenicians were famous as traders and sailors.

sensual perfumes of every kind,
as many sensual perfumes as you can;
may you visit numerous Egyptian cities
to fill yourself with learning from the wise.

25 Keep Ithaka always in mind.
Arriving there is what you're destined for.
But don't hurry the journey at all.
Better if it goes on for years
so you're old by the time you reach the island,
30 wealthy with all you've gained on the way,
not expecting Ithaka to make you rich.

Ithaka gave you the marvelous journey.
Without her you wouldn't have set out.
She hasn't anything else to give.

35 And if you find her poor, Ithaka won't have fooled you.
Wise as you'll have become, and so experienced,
you'll have understood by then what an Ithaka means.

sensual (sen´ shoo əl) *adj.*
pleasing to the senses

Literary Analysis
Lyric Poetry and Epiphany In what ways do the details in lines 20–22 help convey the excitement of the journey?

Review and Assess

Thinking About the Selection

1. **Respond:** How do you feel about the journey that this poem describes? Explain your answer.

2. **(a) Recall:** In the first stanza, what three characters from the *Odyssey* does the speaker say the traveler need not fear? **(b) Infer:** According to the speaker in lines 12–13, under what circumstances might such characters appear? **(c) Analyze:** What real-life experiences might these characters represent? Explain.

3. **(a) Infer:** In the second stanza, identify two places that the speaker urges travelers to visit. **(b) Interpret:** What values do these places represent to the speaker? **(c) Evaluate:** Do you think these values are critical to happiness in life? Explain your answer.

4. **(a) Recall:** In line 31, what expectation does the speaker say one should not have of Ithaka? **(b) Draw Conclusions:** What, then, is the value of Ithaka?

5. **Analyze:** In the poem's final line, the poet refers to "an Ithaka," rather than to "Ithaka." In what way does this change suggest that Ithaka has taken on new meaning?

6. **Evaluate:** "Ithaka" was a favorite poem of Jacqueline Kennedy Onassis, the widow of President John F. Kennedy, and it was read at her funeral. In your opinion, is "Ithaka" a good memorial poem? Why or why not?

The Soul With Boundaries

Fernando Pessoa
translated by Richard Zenith

Background

Fernando Pessoa believed that the human self is fundamentally divided. It is no surprise, therefore, that many of his poems ponder one or both of two questions that are basic to modern literature: *Who am I? What is real?* This poem considers both questions.

The soul with boundaries
Is for the deaf and blind;
I want to feel everything
In every possible way.

5   From the <u>summit</u> of being conscious,
I gaze at the earth and sky,
Looking at them with innocence:
Nothing I see is mine.

But I see them so intently
10 And am so <u>dispersed</u> in them
That every thought I think
Makes me into someone else.

Since every dispersed facet[1]
Is another sliver of being,
15 I break my soul into pieces
And into various persons.

And if my very own soul
I see with a varying gaze,
How can I have anything
20 Definite to say?

---

1. facet (fas´ it) any of a number of sides or aspects of a whole.

summit (sum´ it) *n.* highest point

Literary Analysis
Lyric Poetry and Epiphany In lines 5–12, what single experience or moment is the speaker describing?

dispersed (di spʉrst´) *adj.* broken up and scattered

☑ **Reading Check**
According to the first stanza, what does the speaker want?

◀ **Critical Viewing**

In what ways does this photograph suggest the idea of the "summit of being conscious"? [**Analyze**]

If I think I belong to me,
I'm merely self-deceived.
I'm diverse and not my own,
Like sky and land and sea.

25 If all things are but slivers
Of the universal intelligence,
Then let me be my parts,
Scattered and <u>divergent</u>.

If from myself I'm absent
30 And whatever I feel is distant,
How did my soul come to have
An individual existence?

I've learned to adapt my self
To the world God has made.
35 His mode of being is different;
My being has different modes.

Thus I imitate God,
Who, when he made what is,
Took from it the infinite
40 And even its unity.

Reading Strategy
Reading Stanzas as Units of Meaning Restate the idea expressed in this stanza—lines 21–24—in your own words.

divergent (dī vʉr´ jənt) *adj.* differing from each other

Review and Assess

Thinking About the Selection

1. **Respond:** Would you like to have the speaker of this poem as a friend? Why or why not?

2. **(a) Recall:** In the first stanza, to whom does the speaker say a "soul with boundaries" belongs? **(b) Compare and Contrast:** By contrast, what does the speaker want to experience?

3. **(a) Recall:** According to the speaker in lines 11–12, what happens in the process of thinking different thoughts? **(b) Analyze Cause and Effect:** How does the question asked in lines 19–20 directly relate to this process?

4. **(a) Interpret:** According to the speaker in lines 25–26, all things might be "slivers" of what entity? **(b) Interpret:** Based on lines 33–36, how does the speaker's sense of self mirror his view of God?

5. **Evaluate:** Is "The Soul With Boundaries" a poem that can instruct readers in a practical way, or is it intended primarily as a mental exercise? Explain your answer.

Review and Assess

Literary Analysis

Lyric Poetry and Epiphany

1. (a) What is the **epiphany,** or moment of perception, that García Lorca explores in his **lyric poem** "The Guitar"? (b) What perception does Cavafy share in "Ithaka"?
2. (a) In lines 9–10 of "Absent Soul," what letter sounds are repeated? (b) How do these sounds create a musical feeling?
3. In what sense do the observations in "The Soul With Boundaries" celebrate the poet's vision of life?

Comparing Literary Works

4. (a) Use a chart like the one shown below to examine the meaning of one **metaphor** from each of the poems in this grouping.

Poem	Metaphor	Two Things Compared	Meaning

   (b) How does each metaphor express or clarify an abstract, or intangible, idea?
5. (a) What is the **extended metaphor** in "Ithaka"? (b) What brief comparisons build to create the extended metaphor? (c) What does Ithaka itself represent?

Reading Strategy

Reading Stanzas as Units of Meaning

6. Begin to **read stanzas as units of meaning** by writing a one-sentence statement expressing the main idea for each stanza of "Absent Soul."
7. Would you recommend this reading strategy to a friend who was struggling with poetry? Why or why not?

Extend Understanding

8. **Geography Connection:** If you were to update "Ithaka," omitting the Homeric references, what modern locations might you use? Why?

Integrate Language Skills

Vocabulary Development Lesson

Word Analysis: Latin Prefix *dis-*

The prefix *dis-* can mean "away or apart," "cause to be the opposite of," "fail to," and "not." Complete the definitions below with the correct word from the following list.

disable   disbelieve

disagreeable   digress

1. You _____ when you stray from a topic.
2. You _____ when you do not have faith.
3. You are _____ when you quarrel.
4. You _____ something when you break it.

Spelling Strategy

The *sh* sound can be spelled with *su* (*sensual*), *ti* (*caution*), *si* (*session*), or *ci* (*delicious*). For each of the words below, spell the *sh* sound correctly.

1. electri__an   3. pa__ently
2. vi__al   4. expul__on

Concept Development: Synonyms or Antonyms?

Review the vocabulary list on page 1071. Then, classify each of the following pairs of words as either synonyms (words with similar meanings) or antonyms (words with opposite meanings).

1. monotonously, tediously
2. posterity, ancestry
3. exalted, uplifted
4. sensual, repugnant
5. summit, apex
6. dispersed, gathered
7. divergent, similar

Grammar and Style Lesson

The Understood *You* in Imperative Sentences

Imperative sentences are sentences that give orders or directions. Often in such sentences, the subject is not stated explicitly but is understood to be *you*, or the person being addressed.

Examples:

Pray that your road's a long one. [*You* pray that . . .]

Keep Ithaka always in mind. [*You* keep Ithaka always in mind.]

Practice Rewrite each sentence below so that it contains the understood *you* as its subject.

1. You listen to the sound of the guitar.
2. Don't you be afraid of its sad melody.
3. While the music plays, you hear its grief.
4. You ask the guitarist about the song, but don't you be surprised at his answer.
5. Don't you hurry the journey at all.

Writing Application Write four imperative sentences of advice. Use the understood *you* as the subject in each sentence.

*W*G *Prentice Hall Writing and Grammar Connection: Diamond Level, Chapter 18, Section 2*

Writing Lesson

Sentence Outline and Summary

In "The Soul With Boundaries," Fernando Pessoa constructs a carefully reasoned train of thought that explains his ideas about the nature of the self. Clarify Pessoa's ideas by writing a sentence outline—an outline that states ideas in complete sentences—of the poem. Then, write a one-paragraph summary of the poem.

Prewriting Reread "The Soul With Boundaries," stanza by stanza. After each stanza, write a sentence that expresses its main idea.

Drafting Review the sentences that you wrote. Then, look for points in the poem in which Pessoa's focus shifts slightly, and add a sentence that clarifies that shift. Finally, write a paragraph that summarizes the main points of the poem.

Revising As you review your work, highlight any vague words and phrases. Consider replacing them with more precise choices.

Model: Revising to Clarify Key Ideas

        wonders   *with authority*

The speaker ~~asks~~ how he can speak if he has such

  fragmented   *The question*

a ~~strange~~ view of existence and of himself. ~~He really~~

      bother him.

does not ~~care.~~ Indeed, being "scattered and divergent"

is a quality that he celebrates

~~makes him happy~~. . . .

> Precise words and phrases clarify the writer's ideas.

WG *Prentice Hall Writing and Grammar Connection: Diamond Level, Chapter 31, Section 1*

Extension Activities

Listening and Speaking Lyric poems were originally sung to music. Using García Lorca's "The Guitar," connect to that tradition by delivering a **reading to music.** Follow these tips to prepare:

- Find examples of classical Spanish or Gypsy guitar music.
- Choose one piece that matches the mood of the poem.
- Play the music for the class—once by itself and once as you read "The Guitar" aloud.

After the reading, explain to listeners why you chose the music you did.

Research and Technology Cavafy's poem includes allusions, or references, to Homer's epic poem the *Odyssey*. With a partner, research three of these allusions—the Laistrygonians, Cyclops, and Poseidon—and create an **allusion chart.** Identify the characters' qualities, the challenges that they created for Odysseus, and specific meanings that they add to Cavafy's poem "Ithaka." **[Group Activity]**

 **Take It to the Net** PHschool.com

Go online for an additional research activity using the Internet.

A Closer Look

The Nobel Prize: A Dynamite Idea

Alfred Nobel, the inventor of dynamite, was—surprisingly—a pacifist who sought to honor hope, creativity, and the pursuit of peace.

"If I have a thousand ideas a year, and only one turns out to be good, I'm satisfied," Alfred Bernhard Nobel once said. Nobel exceeded his goal many times. The Swedish scientist who invented dynamite and the blasting cap is also the founder of the most distinguished of all international honors—the Nobel Prize.

A Scientist With the Soul of a Poet Alfred Nobel was born in Stockholm on October 21, 1833. Although he had a deep interest in literature, he was trained as a chemist and physicist and pursued a career that successfully combined science with business. In the 1850s, Nobel became interested in the problems presented by nitroglycerine, an invention of the Italian chemist Ascanio Sobrero. Nitroglycerine is an extremely volatile liquid that can explode unpredictably under heat or pressure. Nobel wanted to find a way to tame nitroglycerine and put it to practical use in construction work.

Nobel's experiments with nitroglycerine were often unsuccessful and deadly. In one accident, Nobel's brother Emil and several other people were killed. Yet, Nobel remained undeterred in his quest. In 1866, he finally found a successful formula that stabilized nitroglycerine and allowed it to be shaped into rods. He patented the material under the name of dynamite. In order to detonate the dynamite, he also invented a detonator, or blasting cap, which could be ignited by lighting a fuse. These inventions helped dramatically reduce the costs of construction work, especially where large-scale excavations were required.

A Man of Peace The invention of dynamite was a huge success. It made Nobel wealthy, and it transformed the construction industry, but Nobel was not happy. A man who valued literature, wrote his own poetry, and held pacifist views, Nobel was deeply disturbed that dynamite was being used in the making of weapons. Nobel held himself responsible for the deaths his invention had caused and would cause. To redeem his legacy, he established a fund of $9 million; after his death, the interest from this fund was to be used to generate an annual prize honoring actions promoting peace, as well as achievements in literature, physics, chemistry, medicine, and economics. Nobel died in 1896, and the first prizes were awarded in 1901.

▲ ▼ Critical Viewing
While these photographs of Nobel laureates V. S. Naipaul, above, and José Saramago, below, show similar moments in the lives of these two men, they capture very different emotions. Compare and contrast the moods these pictures convey.
[Compare and Contrast]

The Literature Prize The Nobel Prize in Literature, which recognizes the most distinguished body of literary work created by a single author, is one of the most highly publicized of all the prizes. The prize represents an international literary standard, and it has helped bring both individual authors and entire countries to the world's attention. For example, Nobel Prizes awarded to Chilean poet Pablo Neruda (1971) and Colombian author Gabriel García Márquez (1982) placed Latin American literature at the forefront of public awareness; Wole Soyinka's prize (1986) created new appreciation of African literature, and Naguib Mahfouz's prize (1988) placed Egyptian literature in the public spotlight. The same has happened for Japanese literature, with awards to Yasunari Kawabata (1968) and Kenzaburo Oe (1994).

Controversies and Criticism At the same time, however, the Nobel Prize in Literature has had its share of controversy. The Nobel committee is made up of four to five members, most of whom are Swedish citizens. Scandinavian countries have received the Nobel Prize in Literature most often, gaining 14.9 percent of the prizes. France is runner-up, taking home 12.9 percent of the prizes. In the past two decades, however, the awards have honored writers from countries around the globe, including Guatemala, the Czech Republic, Poland, Italy, China, and Iceland.

Some critics claim that the decisions of the Nobel committee are politically motivated, honoring the most acceptable rather than the best. These critics cite the omission of some of the greatest and most influential writers of the twentieth century, such as Marcel Proust, Franz Kafka, and James Joyce, from the list of prize winners. Yet, the good that Alfred Nobel achieved in the establishment of the prize that bears his name far outweighs any controversies or criticisms. Imperfect as it may be, the Nobel Prize in Literature positions literature in the forefront of human experience and accomplishment. When the prize is announced, the news makes headlines, stirs debate, and causes celebrations. For a brief moment every year, Nobel achieves his dream of bringing the world together, not for purposes of war or commerce but simply to honor human goodness, creativity, and achievement.

▲ **Critical Viewing**
Which elements in this photograph of the ceremony for the Nobel laureates of 2001 indicate the importance of the occasion? Explain. **[Deduce]**

Prepare to Read

The Glass of Milk

Manuel Rojas (1896–1973)

A man of great strength and vigor, Manuel Rojas (män wel′ rō′ häs) is known for his forceful and moving prose. Not only is he regarded as the master of the modern Chilean short story, but he is also considered to be one of the finest of all the modern Latin American fiction writers.

Years of Hard Labor Although he was of Chilean descent, Manuel Rojas was born and reared in Argentina. His father died when Rojas was not yet five years old, leaving the child in poverty. When he reached his early teens, Rojas began working as a laborer in order to support himself. At the age of sixteen, he moved to Chile, where he worked as a sailor, housepainter, bargeman, night watchman, typographer, and railroad worker. Then, in 1924, he settled permanently in Santiago, the Chilean capital, and his life changed. He began devoting his energies to journalism and creative writing. Two years later, he published his first collection of short stories, *Men of the South* (1926).

Rojas's early stories, and many that he wrote later, mined his own life experiences for inspiration. The stories in *Men of the South* described characters, like Rojas himself, who worked as laborers in both Argentina and Chile. The book immediately established Rojas as one of the most promising Latin American writers of his generation.

Laborer Turned Writer In 1931, Rojas was named the director of the University of Chile Press. This appointment, along with the publication of his novel *Launches in the Bay* (1932), contributed to his growing stature in the Latin American literary community. Throughout the next three decades, his reputation among critics, writers, and the general public continued to grow.

The works he produced during this period include *The Biretta From Maule* (1943), *Son of a Thief* (1951), and *Better Than Wine* (1958).

His Greatest Novel Regarded as Rojas's finest work, the novel *Son of a Thief* is an account of the sufferings of a young Argentine boy. Following his father's arrest and imprisonment for burglary, the boy spends his childhood in poverty. Like Rojas himself, the boy later works as a laborer to support himself and makes a lone journey to Chile in search of a better life. There, he accidentally becomes involved in a street riot and is unjustly imprisoned. Rojas describes the boy's experiences in a graphically realistic manner. More than any other quality, however, it is Rojas's penetrating insights into the inner workings of the boy's mind that have established this novel as one of the best ever produced in Latin America. The book was translated into the major European languages and established Rojas as an international literary figure. In 1964, Rojas's novel *Shadows Against the Wall*, which features many of the characters from *Son of a Thief*, was published to international acclaim.

A Major Influence Rojas's contributions to Latin American fiction in the twentieth century cannot be overestimated. Influenced by the American writer William Faulkner, Rojas incorporated some of the experimental devices—interior monologues, flashbacks, and stream-of-consciousness techniques—that Faulkner used in his novels and short stories. Rojas did not use these techniques simply because they were different or dazzling but rather to intensify the portrayals of his characters. These techniques later caught the interest of a new generation of Latin American writers, including Gabriel García Márquez, who used them to great effect. Rojas's fiction displays a simplicity, restraint, and deep humanity that is as affecting today as when it was first written.

Preview

Connecting to the Literature

Imagine being alone in a strange city, with no money, friends, or food. The boy in this story faces precisely this predicament and must figure out a way to survive.

Literary Analysis

Autobiographical Fiction

Autobiographical fiction is storytelling that is based on the writer's life. Unlike autobiography or memoir, autobiographical fiction does not try to relate events exactly as they happened. Instead, it may

- exaggerate, minimize, or omit events.
- change names, omit characters, or add fictional characters.
- change the setting.

Regardless of such changes, the essence of the story remains rooted in the author's experience. Manuel Rojas was known for his autobiographical fiction. As you read, note details that seem to emerge from Rojas's own life.

Connecting Literary Elements

Point of view refers to the perspective assumed by the narrator in a story. Three commonly used types of point of view are first person, third-person omniscient, and third-person limited.

- *First person:* The narrator is a character in the story who uses the pronouns "I," "me," "we," and "us."
- *Third person:* The narrator uses the pronouns "he," "she," "it," or "them." The *omniscient* narrator relates the thoughts of all the characters; the *limited* narrator relates those of a single character.

This story uses the third-person limited point of view. As you read, notice the kinds of information this perspective both reveals and conceals.

Reading Strategy

Judging Characters' Actions

When you judge characters' actions, you evaluate their behavior in light of specific criteria, such as your values, experience, and sense of what is reasonable. As you read, use a chart like the one shown to analyze characters' behavior and decide whether you find their actions defensible.

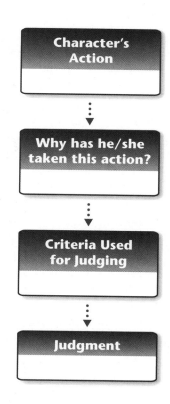

Vocabulary Development

gaudy (gôd´ ē) *adj.* cheaply bright and showy (p. 1090)

timidity (tə mid´ ə tē) *n.* quality of being shy and easily frightened (p. 1090)

drudgery (druj´ ər ē) *n.* hard, tiresome work (p. 1090)

anguished (aŋ´ gwisht) *adj.* showing worry, grief, or pain (p. 1093)

acute (ə kyōot´) *adj.* very serious; sharp; intense (p. 1093)

entrails (en´ trālz) *n.* intestines; guts (p. 1093)

The Glass of Milk

Manuel Rojas

translated by Zoila Nelken

Background

The setting for this story is an unnamed port city north of Punta Arenas in southern Chile. Chile is a long, narrow country on the Pacific coast of South America. With 2,700 miles of coastline, Chile relies on shipping as one of its main industries. Although the Chilean economy has enjoyed periods of prosperity, the country has always had a sizable population of poor, unskilled laborers like the main character in this story.

Propped on the starboard[1] rail, the sailor seemed to be waiting for someone. A bundle wrapped in white paper, grease-spotted, was in his left hand; his right tended his pipe.

From behind some freight-cars, a thin youth appeared; he paused a moment, looked out to sea, and then walked on along the edge of the wharf with his hands in his pockets, idling or thinking.

When he passed in front of the ship, the sailor called out to him in English:

"I say, look here!"

The youth raised his head, and without stopping, answered in the same language:

"Hello! What?"

"Are you hungry?"

There was a brief silence during which the youth seemed to be thinking, and took one shorter step as if to stop, but then replied, smiling feebly at the sailor:

"No. I'm not hungry. Thanks, sailor."

---

1. starboard (stär′ bərd) *adj.* on the right-hand side of a ship.

Puerto de Villefranche, Joaquim Torres-Garcia, Christie's, New York

▲ **Critical Viewing** Which details in this painting of a South American port city help convey a mood similar to that of the opening scene of the story? Explain. **[Analyze]**

"All right."

The sailor took his pipe out of his mouth, spat, and replacing it, looked away. The youth, ashamed that he had seemed to need charity, walked a little faster, as if afraid he might change his mind.

A moment later, a <u>gaudy</u> tramp with a long, blond beard and blue eyes, dressed in odd rags and oversized, torn shoes, passed before the sailor, who without greeting called to him:

"Are you hungry?"

He had not yet finished the phrase when the tramp looked with shining eyes at the package the sailor held in his hand and answered hurriedly:

"Yes, sir; I'm very much hungry!"

The sailor smiled. The package flew through the air and landed in the eager hands. The hungry fellow did not even say "thanks," but sat right down on the ground, opened the still-warm bundle, and happily rubbed his hands as he saw what it contained. A port loafer might not speak English well, but he would never forgive himself if he didn't know enough to ask food from someone who did speak it.

The youth who passed by first had stopped nearby, and had seen what happened.

He was hungry too. He had not eaten for exactly three days, three long days. And more from <u>timidity</u> and shame than from pride, he refused to wait by the gangways at mealtimes, hoping the generosity of the sailors would produce some package of left-overs and bits of meat. He could not do it, he would never be able to do it. And when, as just now, someone did offer him a handout, the boy refused it heroically, though he felt his hunger increase with the refusal.

He had been wandering for six days around the side-streets and docks of that port. An English vessel had left him there after bringing him from Punta Arenas,² where he had jumped a previous ship on which he had served as captain's mess boy. He had spent a month there helping an Austrian crabber and then had stowed away on the first ship bound north.

He was discovered the day after sailing, and put to work in the boiler room. At the first large port of call, he had been put off, and there he had remained, like a bale without a label, without an acquaintance, without a penny, and without a trade.

As long as the ship was in port, the boy managed to eat, but after that . . . The great city that rose up beyond the back streets with their taverns and cheap inns did not attract him; it seemed a place of slavery: stale, dark, without the grand sweep of the sea; among its high walls and narrow streets people lived and died bewildered by agonizing <u>drudgery</u>.

The boy was gripped by that fascination of the sea which molds the most peaceful and orderly lives as a strong arm a thin rod. Although

gaudy (gôd′ ē) *adj.* cheaply bright and showy

timidity (tə mid′ ə tē) *n.* quality of being shy and easily frightened

**Reading Strategy
Judging Characters' Actions** Is the young man's decision to refuse the food wise? Explain your answer.

drudgery (druj′ ər ē) *n.* hard, tiresome work

---

2. Punta Arenas (pōōn′ tä ä *re*′ näs) southernmost seaport in Chile.

very young, he had already made several trips along the coast of South America on various ships, doing odd jobs and tasks, tasks and odd jobs which were almost useless on land.

After the ship left him, the boy walked and walked, hoping to chance upon something that would enable him to live somehow until he could get back to his home grounds; but he found nothing. The port was not very busy, and the few ships that had work would not take him on.

The docks were swarming with confirmed tramps: sailors on the beach, like himself, who had either jumped ship or were fleeing some crime; loafers given to idleness, who kept alive one knows not how, by begging or stealing, spending their days as if they were the beads of some grimy rosary,[3] waiting for who knows what extraordinary events, or not expecting anything; people of the strangest and most exotic races and places, and even some in whose existence one doesn't believe until one sees a living example.

Retrato de un Joven, Leonor Fini, Christie's, New York

The following day, convinced that he could not hold out much longer, the youth decided to resort to any means to get some food.

Walking along, he found himself in front of a ship that had docked the night before, and was loading wheat. A line of men, heavy sacks on their shoulders, shuttled from the freight-cars, across the gangplank to the hatchways of the ship's hold where the stevedores[4] received the cargo.

He watched for a while, until he dared to speak to the foreman, offering his services. He was accepted, and enthusiastically he took his place in the long line of dock workers.

During the first period of the day he worked well; but later, he began to feel tired and dizzy; he swayed as he crossed the gangplank, the heavy load on his shoulder, on seeing at his feet the opening between

▲ **Critical Viewing**
Does the boy depicted in this portrait seem like someone who would be too timid to accept an offer of food? [**Make a Judgment**]

☑ **Reading Check**
For how many days has the boy gone without food?

---

3. **rosary** (rō´ zər ē) *n.* string of beads used to keep count in saying prayers.
4. **stevedores** (stē´ və dôrz´) *n.* people employed at loading and unloading ships.

Trabajadores, Hector Poleo

▲ **Critical Viewing** Which figure in this painting best represents the boy in the story? Explain your answer. **[Interpret]**

the side of the ship and the thick wall of the wharf, at the bottom of which the sea, stained with oil and littered with garbage, lapped quietly.

There was a brief pause at lunch time, and while some of the men went off to the nearby eating places, and others ate what they had brought, the boy stretched out on the ground to rest, hiding his hunger.

He finished the day's work feeling completely exhausted, covered with sweat, at the end of his rope. While the laborers were leaving, the boy sat on some sacks, watching for the foreman, and when the last man had gone, approached him; confused and stuttering, he asked, without explaining what was happening to him, if he could be paid immediately, or if it were possible to get an advance on his earnings.

The foreman answered that it was customary to pay at the end of the job, and that it would still be necessary to work the following day in order to finish loading the ship. One more day! On the other hand, they never paid a cent in advance.

"But," he said, "if you need it, I could lend you about forty cents . . . That's all I have."

The boy thanked him for his offer with an <u>anguished</u> smile, and left.

Then the boy was seized by <u>acute</u> despair. He was hungry, hungry, hungry! Hunger doubled him over, like a heavy, broad whiplash. He saw everything through a blue haze, and he staggered like a drunk when he walked. Nevertheless, he would not have been able to complain or to shout, for his suffering was deep and exhausting; it was not pain, but anguish, the end! It seemed to him that he was flattened out by a great weight.

Suddenly he felt his <u>entrails</u> on fire, and he stood still. He began to bend down, down, doubling over forcibly like a rod of steel, until he thought that he would drop. At that instant, as if a window opened before him, he saw his home, the view from it, the faces of his mother, brothers and sisters, all that he wanted and loved appeared and disappeared before his eyes shut by fatigue. . . Then, little by little, the giddiness passed and he began to straighten up, while the burning subsided gradually. Finally, he straightened up, breathing deeply. One more hour and he would drop unconscious to the ground.

He quickened his step, as if fleeing another dizzy spell, and, as he walked, he made up his mind to eat anywhere, without paying, even if they shamed him, beat him, sent him to jail, anything; the main thing was to eat, eat, eat. A hundred times he mentally repeated the word: eat, eat, eat, until it lost its meaning, leaving his head feeling hot and empty.

He did not intend to run away; he would simply say to the owner, "Sir, I was hungry, hungry, hungry, and I can't pay . . . Do what you want."

He came to the outskirts of the city, and on one of the first streets he found a milk bar. It was a small, clean, and airy place, with little tables with marble tops. Behind the counter stood a blonde lady in a very white apron.

Literary Analysis
Autobiographical Fiction
How do you think Rojas was able to describe the boy's discomfort with such detail and intensity?

anguished (aŋ´ gwisht) *adj.* showing worry, grief, or pain

acute (ə kyōōt´) *adj.* very serious; sharp; intense

entrails (en´ trālz) *n.* intestines; guts

Reading Check
What does the boy ask the foreman?

He chose that place. There were few passersby. He could have eaten at one of the cheap grills near the wharves but they were always full of people who gambled and drank.

There was only one customer in the milk bar. He was a little old man with glasses, who sat reading, his nose stuck between the pages of a newspaper, motionless, as if glued to his chair. On the little table there was a half-empty glass of milk.

While he waited for him to leave, the boy walked up and down the sidewalk; he felt the burning sensation in his stomach returning little by little; and he waited five, ten, up to fifteen minutes. He grew tired, and stood to one side of the door, from where he cast glances like stones at the old man.

What the devil could he be reading with such attention? The boy even imagined the old man was his enemy, who knew his intentions and had decided to frustrate them. He felt like entering and saying something insulting that would force the old man to leave, a rude word or phrase that would show him he had no right to sit there reading for an hour for so small a purchase.

Finally, the client finished what he was reading, or at least, interrupted it. He downed the rest of the milk in one gulp, rose slowly, paid, and walked toward the door. He went out. He was a stoop-shouldered old man, probably a carpenter or varnisher.

Once in the street, the old man put on his glasses, stuck his nose in the newspaper again, and walked slowly away, stopping every ten steps to read more closely.

The youth waited until he was some distance away, and then entered. For a moment the boy stood by the entrance, undecided, not knowing where to sit. Finally, he chose a table and walked toward it, but halfway there he changed his mind, walked backed, tripped over a chair, and finally installed himself in a corner.

The lady came, wiped the tabletop with a rag, and in a soft voice that had a trace of Castilian[5] accent, asked him:

"What will you have?"

"A glass of milk."

"Large?"

"Yes, large."

"Is that all?"

"Are there any biscuits?"

"No. Vanilla wafers."

"Well, vanilla wafers."

When the lady had turned away, he wiped his hands on his knees, rejoicing, as if he were cold and were about to drink something hot.

---

5. Castilian (kas til′ yən) of Castile, a region in northern and central Spain.

The lady returned, and placed before him a large glass of milk, and a dish full of vanilla wafers; then she went back to her place behind the counter.

His first impulse was to drink the milk in one gulp and then eat the vanilla wafers; but he immediately changed his mind. He felt the woman's eyes watching him with curiosity and attention. He did not dare to look at her; he felt that if he did she would guess his situation and his shameful intentions, and he would have to get up and leave without touching what he had ordered.

Slowly, he took a vanilla wafer and moistening it in the milk, he took a bite; he took a sip of milk, and he felt the burning in his stomach diminishing, dying away. But he became aware of the reality of his desperate situation at once, and he felt something tight and hot well up inside, choking him. He realized that he was about to cry, to sob aloud, and although he knew that the lady was looking at him, he could neither hold back nor undo the burning knot of tears that grew tighter and tighter. He fought it, and as he fought he ate hurriedly, as if frightened, afraid that crying would keep him from eating. When he had finished the milk and the wafers, his eyes clouded and something hot rolled down his nose and into the glass. A terrible sob racked his whole body.

He held his head in his hands, and for a long time he cried, cried with rage, cried with shame, crying as he had never cried before.

Literary Analysis
Autobiographical Fiction and Point of View In what ways does the use of the third-person limited point of view heighten the tension when the boy first receives the food?

He was hunched over crying when he felt a hand caress his tired head, and heard a woman's voice with a sweet Castilian accent say to him:

"Cry, son, cry . . ."

Again his eyes filled with tears and he cried as intensely as before, but this time, not with pain but with joy; he felt a great refreshing sensation spread inside him, extinguishing the hot something that had nearly strangled him. As he cried, it seemed to him that his life and feelings were cleansed like a glass under a stream of water, recovering the clearness and firmness of former days.

When the crying spell passed, he wiped his eyes and face with his handkerchief, feeling relieved. He raised his head and looked at the lady, but she was no longer looking at him, she was gazing out at the street, at a distant point in space, and her face seemed sad.

On the table before him there was another glass of milk and another dish heaped with vanilla wafers. He ate slowly, without thinking about anything, as if nothing had happened to him, as if he were at home and his mother were that woman who was standing behind the counter.

When he had finished, it had grown dark, and the place was lit by an electric light. He remained seated for a while, wondering what he would say to the lady when he left, without thinking of anything appropriate.

At last he got up and said simply,

"Thank you very much, ma'am; goodbye . . ."

✓Reading Check
What food does the boy finally obtain?

"Goodbye, son," she answered.

He went out. The wind blowing from the sea refreshed his face, still hot from crying. He walked about aimlessly for a while, then went down a street that led to the docks. It was a very beautiful night, and large stars gleamed in the summer sky.

He thought about the blonde lady who had treated him so generously, resolving to repay her, to reward her as she deserved, when he got some money. But these thoughts of gratitude vanished with the burning of his face, until not one remained, and the recent event receded and was lost in the recesses of his past life.

Suddenly, he surprised himself humming. He straightened up happily, strode on with assurance and determination.

He came to the edge of the sea, and walked back and forth with a spring in his step; he felt like a new man, as if his inner forces, previously scattered, had reassembled and united solidly.

Then he sat down on a pile of burlap sacks; fatigue, like a tingling sensation, climbed up his legs. He looked at the sea. The lights of the wharf and ships spread over the water in a reddish-gold ripple, trembling softly. He stretched out on his back, looking up at the sky for a long time. He did not feel like thinking, or singing, or talking. He just felt alive, that was all. Then he fell asleep with his face toward the sea.

Review and Assess

Thinking About the Selection

1. **Respond:** Do you feel sympathy for the boy? Why or why not?

2. **(a) Recall:** What is in the white bundle that the sailor offers, first to the boy and then to the tramp? **(b) Interpret:** Why does the boy refuse it? **(c) Compare and Contrast:** Based on their responses to the sailor, compare and contrast the boy and the tramp.

3. **(a) Recall:** What assistance does the foreman offer to the boy at the end of the day? **(b) Deduce:** Why does the youth refuse the foreman's help?

4. **(a) Interpret:** With what emotions does the boy react to his first bite of food? Explain your answer. **(b) Analyze:** Why do you think he reacts in this way?

5. **(a) Interpret:** How does the waitress respond to the boy's expression of emotion? **(b) Analyze Cause and Effect:** As a result of her behavior toward him, what does the boy resolve to do? **(c) Analyze:** Which details suggest that the boy will not keep these resolutions? Explain.

6. **Evaluate:** Is the boy a better person at the end of the story than he was at the beginning? Give evidence to support your opinion.

Review and Assess

Literary Analysis

Autobiographical Fiction

1. Rojas was known for writing **autobiographical fiction.** Based on this story, do you think that he went hungry as a young man? Explain your answer.

2. Would Rojas have been able to describe the milk bar so convincingly if he had not visited a place like it? Explain.

3. (a) What might motivate an author to write a story based on his or her own life? (b) What are some of the advantages and disadvantages of using one's own life as a creative source?

Connecting Literary Elements

4. In what ways does the use of the third-person limited **point of view** affect the kinds of details Rojas uses to convey the waitress's feelings toward the boy?

5. In what ways does the third-person limited point of view affect the choice of details in the scene between the foreman and the boy?

6. Select two scenes from this story. Then, use a chart like the one shown to explore the ways in which each scene would be different if Rojas had written it from the boy's first-person point of view or from the third-person omniscient point of view.

Scene	First-Person Point of View	Third-Person Omniscient
1.		
2.		

Reading Strategy

Judging Characters' Actions

7. (a) What do you think of the woman's behavior in the milk bar? (b) What criteria did you use to **judge** this **character's actions**?

8. How do you think the boy would justify his decision to obtain food by illegal means when he had already turned down the sailor's food and refused the foreman's loan? Explain your answer.

Extend Understanding

9. **Social Studies Connection:** In the United States, government agencies have taken some responsibility for assisting people who are hungry. Is this a proper role for government? Explain.

Integrate Language Skills

Vocabulary Development Lesson

Word Analysis: Latin Suffix -ity

The suffix -ity means "state, quality, or condition." It is added to an adjective to form a noun. Hence, timidity means "the state or condition of being timid." Add the suffix -ity to each of the words below. Then, write a definition of each word.

1. human
2. pure
3. general
4. curious

Spelling Strategy

The j sound may be spelled with a g, as in drudgery. Write the correct spelling of the underlined word in each sentence.

1. The sailor did not budje from the railing.
2. The youth did not hold a grudje.

Fluency: Words in Context

Using the italicized word, write a one-sentence answer for each question below.

1. Why do many performers wear gaudy clothing?
2. Under what circumstances can people be overcome with timidity?
3. What task do many people consider a form of drudgery?
4. Under what circumstances might someone give an anguished smile?
5. How might a person express acute sadness?
6. Where would an injury to an animal's entrails be located?

Grammar and Style Lesson

Conjunctive Adverbs

A **conjunctive adverb** is a word that joins only independent clauses—clauses that contain a subject and a verb and express a complete idea—not single words, phrases, or subordinate clauses. Conjunctive adverbs include the words accordingly, also, besides, consequently, finally, however, indeed, moreover, nevertheless, then, otherwise, and therefore.

Examples:

The lady returned, and placed before him a glass of milk; then she went back to her place behind the counter.

The boy refused the food; consequently, he felt his hunger increase.

Practice Complete each sentence below with a conjunctive adverb.

1. The boy had not eaten; ___?___, his stomach began to burn like fire.
2. He had no skills; ___?___, no one would hire him.
3. He needed to eat; ___?___, he could die.
4. He waited as long as he could; ___?___, he resolved to steal food.
5. The boy was broke; ___?___, he ordered food.

Writing Application Write five sentences about the boy in this story. Use a different conjunctive adverb in each sentence.

Writing Lesson
Character Analysis

In Manuel Rojas's story, the boy's actions say a great deal about his personality, values, and sense of self. Write an essay in which you analyze the boy's character based on his actions.

Prewriting   Reread the story, taking notes about the boy's decisions and actions. Identify the events that led the boy into his predicament, the reasons for his choices, and the ways in which he relates to other people.

Drafting   Write an introduction in which you state your main idea. To build each paragraph that follows, state a supporting idea in one sentence, elaborate upon it in the next sentence or two, and add supporting details in the final sentence.

Revising   Review your draft, highlighting the main ideas and underlining the supporting sentences in each paragraph. If sentences do not support the main idea, consider deleting or moving them.

Model: Revising to Create Unity

The boy was timid around other people. <u>For example, even though he was starving, it took him a long time to work up his nerve to ask for work.</u> ~~He did work very hard after he got the job.~~

> Every sentence in a paragraph should support the main idea.

W̶G Prentice Hall Writing and Grammar Connection: Diamond Level, Chapter 5, Section 3

Extension Activities

Listening and Speaking With a partner, write and deliver to the class a retelling of the story from the waitress's point of view. Use these tips to prepare:

- Reread the story, looking for clues about the waitress's thoughts and feelings.
- Answer these questions: What is the waitress's life like? What does she think of the boy? What does she do after he leaves?

As you write, try to match the mood of Rojas's story. Then, present your work to the class. **[Group Activity]**

Research and Technology Use electronic and print resources to research how long a person can survive without food. Identify the effects of hunger, and examine how these effects build up as time passes. Using a computer program, create a **human hunger chart** in which you present your findings.

 Take It to the Net   PHSchool.com

Go online for an additional research activity using the Internet.

Prepare to Read

Fear ◆ The Prayer ◆ Time ◆ Green ◆ Lightness

Gabriela Mistral
(1889–1957)

When Gabriela Mistral (gä´ brē ā´ lä mēs träl´) heard the news that she had won the Nobel Prize in Literature in 1945, she declared, "Perhaps it was because I was the candidate of the women and children." Ever since Mistral began writing poetry, women and children were her primary subjects. As an educator and diplomat, she devoted herself to improving their lives.

A Poet and Teacher Mistral's real name was Lucila Godoy Alcayaga (loo sē´ lə gō doï´ al kī ä´ gə). At the age of fifteen, she began two of her careers—teacher and poet. Fearing that she might lose her teaching jobs because of the content of her poetry, Mistral published her work under pseudonyms. The name Gabriela Mistral came from the archangel Gabriel and the fierce mistral wind that blows over the south of France. It was under this name that Mistral became the first South American to win the Nobel Prize in Literature.

A Great Loss Mistral's fame spread to the United States in 1922 with the publication of her first book of poetry, *Desolación*. Mistral wrote *Desolación* shortly after the death of her fiancé. Many believe that his death became the driving force behind her creativity.

International Role The poet's literary fame and reputation as a champion of women and children drew the attention of politicians. In 1922, the Mexican minister of education invited Mistral to develop a program of education reform in his country. Mistral later became Chile's delegate to the Institute of Intellectual Cooperation, an organization that was part of the League of Nations—a precursor of today's United Nations. She also taught in the United States and served in many diplomatic posts. Mistral spent the last years of her life on Long Island in New York State.

Juan Ramón Jiménez
(1881–1958)

Juan Ramón Jiménez is widely viewed as one of Spain's finest poets. Ironically, he spent much of his life in exile from his native land.

Becoming a Poet Jiménez was a law student at the University of Seville when he first published his poems in a magazine. These poems caught the attention of the celebrated Nicaraguan poet Ruben Darío, who was then living in the Spanish capital of Madrid. Soon, Jiménez moved to Madrid, where he became the editor of two literary magazines. In 1900, he published two volumes of poetry, though he later thought these so awful that he sought out and destroyed every copy he could. Within a few years, however, he had developed a lyrical power more to his liking. That skill is evident in poetry collections like *Pure Elegies* (1908) and in *Platero and I* (1914–1917), his popular prose poems about a man roaming the countryside with his donkey.

Love and Exile In 1913, Jiménez fell in love with Zenobia Camprubi Aymar, an American living in Madrid. When she returned to New York, he followed, and the two married. The couple returned to live in Spain until the 1930s, when Jiménez was asked to serve as the ambassador to the United States for Spain's democratic royalist government. After the fascists defeated the royalists in the Spanish Civil War (1936–1939), Jiménez refused to return home. Instead, he and Zenobia settled in Puerto Rico, where they lived out their remaining days. In 1956, Jiménez was awarded the Nobel Prize in Literature.

Preview

Connecting to the Literature

It has been said that great music is about love—whether it is love of a person, a place, an object, or life in general. These poems suggest that, in its essence, poetry also is about love.

Literary Analysis

Imagery

Imagery is language that appeals to one or more of the five senses—sight, hearing, taste, smell, and touch. In literature, imagery conveys meaning and evokes emotion. For example, in "The Prayer," the speaker describes the man she loves with these images:

> my cup of freshness, honeycomb of my mouth, //
> lime of my bones, . . . / bird-trill to my ears . . .

Notice that these images appeal to the senses, convey different shades of meaning, and express emotions. As you read, use a chart like the one shown to identify the senses to which specific images appeal. Then, think about the meaning and emotions each image conveys.

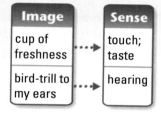

Comparing Literary Works

Tone is the speaker's attitude toward his or her audience or subject and can be described with the same words one uses to describe emotions, such as *humorous, sad, angry,* or *joyful.* For example, these lines from "Lightness" create a contemplative and joy-filled tone:

> My window-curtain, / in the majestic stillness and the silence /
> of the unruffled early morning, / moving softly to light breezes.

As you read these poems, compare each speaker's tone and identify the details that convey distinct attitudes.

Reading Strategy

Restating for Understanding

Some poems contain passages that are especially challenging. To clarify the meaning of such passages, **restate** them in your own words. As you read these poems, pause whenever you are uncertain about the meaning of a line or passage and restate it for understanding.

Vocabulary Development

invokes (in vōks´) *v.* calls on (p. 1103)

anoint (ə noint´) *v.* to rub oil or ointment on (p. 1103)

sheaves (shēvz) *n.* bundles of cut stalks of grain (p. 1105)

cascade (kas kād´) *n.* small, steep waterfall (p. 1106)

primeval (prī mē´ vəl) *adj.* having to do with the earliest times (p. 1110)

impetus (im´ pə təs) *n.* driving force (p. 1110)

Fear

Gabriela Mistral *translated by* Doris Dana

I don't want them to turn
my little girl into a swallow.
She would fly far away into the sky
and never· fly again to my straw bed,
5   or she would nest in the eaves[1]
where I could not comb her hair.
I don't want them to turn
my little girl into a swallow.

I don't want them to make
10 my little girl a princess.
In tiny golden slippers
how could she play on the meadow?
And when night came, no longer
would she sleep at my side.
15 I don't want them to make
my little girl a princess.

And even less do I want them
one day to make her queen.
They would put her on a throne
20 where I could not go to see her.
And when nighttime came
I could never rock her . . .
I don't want them to make
my little girl a queen!

---

1. **eaves** (ēvz) *n.* lower edge(s) of a roof, usually
projecting beyond the sides of a building.

Woman and Child, Pablo Picasso, Estate of
Pablo Picasso/Artists Rights Society (ARS), New
York. Museo Picasso, Barcelona, Spain. Scala

▲ **Critical Viewing**
Which details in this
woman's expression and
posture suggest a mother's
concern for her child?
Explain. **[Interpret]**

The Prayer

Gabriela Mistral
translated by John A. Crowe

Background

When Gabriela Mistral was seventeen years old, she met Romelio Ureta, who became the love of her life. Unfortunately, the relationship ended with Ureta's early death, a loss from which Mistral never fully recovered. *Desolación* (1922), the collection in which "Fear" and "The Prayer" appear, reflects her intense sadness and despair over Ureta's death. It is her first great collection of poetry, one that brought her international fame.

Thou knowest, Lord, with what flaming boldness,
my word <u>invokes</u> Thy help for strangers.
I come now to plead for one who was mine,
my cup of freshness, honeycomb of my mouth,

5 lime of my bones, sweet reason of life's journey,
bird-trill to my ears, girdle of my garment.
Even those who are no part of me are in my care.
Harden not Thine eyes if I plead with Thee for this one!

He was a good man, I say he was a man
10 whose heart was entirely open; a man
gentle in temper, frank as the light of day,
as filled with miracles as the spring of the year.

Thou answerest harshly that he is unworthy of entreaty[1]
who did not <u>anoint</u> with prayer his fevered lips,
15 who went away that evening without waiting for Thy sign,
his temples shattered like fragile goblets.

---

1. entreaty (en trēt′ ē) *n.* earnest request.

Literary Analysis
Imagery and Tone What attitude toward her subject does the speaker express in the first stanza?

invokes (in vōks′) *v.* calls on

anoint (ə noint′) *v.* to rub oil or ointment on

**Reading Check**

For whom does the speaker say she now comes "to plead"?

The Revolution, Manuel Rodríguez Lozano, Museo Nacional de Arte Moderno, Mexico City

But I, my Lord, protest that I have touched,—
just like the spikenard[2] of his brow,—
his whole gentle and tormented heart:
20   and it was silky as a nascent[3] bud!

Thou sayest that he was cruel? Thou forgettest, Lord, that I loved
     him,
and that he knew my wounded heart was wholly his.
He troubled forever the waters of my gladness?
It does not matter! Thou knowest: I loved him, I loved him!

25   And to love (Thou knowest it well) is a bitter exercise;
a pressing of eyelids wet with tears,
a kissing-alive of hairshirt tresses,[4]
keeping, below them, the ecstatic eyes.

▲ **Critical Viewing**
Do you think these women are expressing the same emotions as the speaker in the poem? Explain. **[Interpret]**

Reading Strategy
Restating for Understanding Restate this stanza in your own words.

---

2. **spikenard** (spīk´ nərd) *n.* perennial North American plant with whitish flowers, purplish berries, and fragrant roots.
3. **nascent** (nas´ ənt) *adj.* coming into being.
4. **tresses** (tres´ əz) *n.* woman's or girl's hair.

The piercing iron has a welcome chill,
30 when it opens, like <u>sheaves</u> of grain, the loving flesh.
And the cross (Thou rememberest, O King of the Jews!)
is softly borne, like a spray of roses.

Here I rest, Lord, my face bowed down
to the dust, talking with thee through the twilight,
35 through all the twilights that may stretch through life,
if Thou art long in telling me the word I await.

I shall weary Thine ears with prayers and sobs;
a timid greyhound, I shall lick Thy mantle's hem,
Thy loving eyes cannot escape me,
40 Thy foot avoid the hot rain of my tears.

Speak at last the word of pardon! It will scatter
in the wind the perfume of a hundred fragrant vials
as it empties; all waters will be dazzling;
the wilderness will blossom, the cobblestones will sparkle.

45 The dark eyes of wild beasts will moisten,
and the conscious mountain that Thou didst forge from stone
will weep through the white eyelids of its snowdrifts;
Thy whole earth will know that Thou hast forgiven!

sheaves (shēvz) *n.* bundles of cut stalks of grain

Review and Assess

Thinking About the Selections

1. **Respond:** Which poem did you find more moving? Why?

2. **(a) Recall:** In "Fear," what three things does the speaker say she does not want to happen? **(b) Infer:** What kind of life can you infer the speaker does not want for her child?

3. **(a) Interpret:** Who might "they" be in the poem? **(b) Connect:** In what ways does the title of the poem connect to the speaker's attitude toward "them"?

4. **(a) Recall:** In "The Prayer," for whom is the speaker of the poem pleading? **(b) Analyze:** What does the speaker want?

5. **(a) Interpret:** In stanza six, what two charges against the lost loved one does the speaker attribute to God? **(b) Generalize:** With what single argument does the speaker respond?

6. **(a) Interpret:** What does the speaker say will happen if God does as she asks? **(b) Draw Conclusions:** Why do you think the speaker believes the details noted in the final two stanzas will sway God? Explain.

7. **Make a Judgment:** How important do you think it is to be forgiven and to forgive? Explain your answer.

Time

Gabriela Mistral *translated by* Doris Dana

DAYBREAK

My heart swells that the Universe
like a fiery cascade may enter.
The new day comes. Its coming
leaves me breathless.
5   I sing. Like a cavern brimming
I sing my new day.

For grace lost and recovered
I stand humble. Not giving. Receiving.
Until the Gorgon¹ night,
10 vanquished, flees.

MORNING

She has returned! She has returned!
Each morning the same and new.
Awaited every yesterday,
she must return this morning.

15 Mornings of empty hands
that promised and betrayed.
Behold this new morning unfold,
leap like a deer from the East,
awake, happy and new,
20 alert, eager and rich with deeds.

Brother, raise up your head
fallen to your breast. Receive her.
Be worthy of her who leaps up,
soars and darts like a halcyon,²
25 golden halcyon plunging earthward singing
Alleluia, alleluia, alleluia!

cascade (kas kād´) *n.*
small, steep waterfall

Reading Strategy
**Restating for Under-
standing** In your own
words, what do the first
two lines of the second
stanza mean?

---

1. Gorgon (gôr´ gən) any of three sisters with snakes for hair, so
horrible that any beholder is turned to stone.
2. halcyon (hal´ sē ən) bird that, according to legend, nests on the
sea and calms the waters.

AFTERNOON

I feel my heart melt like wax
in this sweetness:
slow oil, not wine,
my veins,
30   I feel my life fleeting
silent and sweet as a gazelle.³

NIGHT

Mountain ranges dissolve,
cattle wander astray,
35   the sun returns to its forge,⁴
all the world slips away.

Orchard and garden are fading,
the farmhouse already immersed.
My mountains submerge their crests
40   and their living cry.

All creatures are sliding aslant
down toward forgetfulness and sleep.
You and I, also, my baby,
tumble down toward night's keep.

---

3. gazelle (gə zel´) small, swift, graceful antelope native to Africa and Asia.
4. forge (fôrj) furnace for heating metal.

Review and Assess

Thinking About the Selection

1. **Respond:** Based on these descriptions, which time of day do you find most attractive? Explain.

2. **(a) Recall:** Which parts of a day does Mistral describe?
   (b) Classify: At which times of day does the speaker seem to be exhilarated? Explain. **(c) Compare and Contrast:** At which times of day does the speaker seem more thoughtful? Explain.

3. **(a) Interpret:** Does this poem describe a particular day or one of many days? Explain. **(b) Generalize:** If you were to draw a picture of this poem, what geometric shape would it take? Explain.

4. **(a) Compare and Contrast:** Compare and contrast the depictions of night in the first section and in the final section of the poem.
   (b) Generalize: What does the speaker seem to feel about night?

5. **(a) Synthesize:** If this poem describes an entire human life, what stages of life might each section symbolize? Explain. **(b) Draw Conclusions:** Does this poem suggest a way in which one should live one's life? Explain.

Green

Juan Ramón Jiménez
translated by J. B. Trend

Green was the maiden, green, green!
Green her eyes were, green her hair.

The wild rose in her green wood
was neither red nor white, but green.

5   Through the green air she came.
(The whole earth turned green for her).

The shining gauze of her garment
was neither blue nor white, but green.

Over the green sea she came.
10   (And even the sky turned green then).

My life will always leave unlatched
a small green gate to let her in.

Woman Under an Apple Tree, 1966, David Brayne, © The Grand Design, Leeds, England

Literary Analysis
Imagery and Tone What attitude toward the subject is suggested in the last two lines? Explain.

◀ **Critical Viewing**
In what ways are the uses of the color green in the poem and in the painting similar and different? [**Compare and Contrast**]

Lightness

Juan Ramón Jiménez
translated by J. B. Trend

Background

Juan Ramón Jiménez was a poet for whom the visual world was extremely important. He was especially fond of color, which he found to be not merely decorative but full of emotion and meaning. Early in Jiménez's career, his poetry was dominated by green and yellow. However, as his style evolved, it became more formal and rigorous, matched by a change in his color palette to pure white. That evolution is evident in this poem.

My window-curtain,
in the majestic stillness and the silence
of the unruffled early morning,
moving softly to light breezes.

5   Oh, lovely moment
that makes the living brother to the dead,
one like another (there's no telling
which is the dead and which the living)
in the one great intensity of breathing!
10 . . . All the world must be dead now, or else all
living still.

And those light breezes of the early morning
move the white, waving curtain
of my wide-open window . . .

✓Reading Check

What object does the speaker observe in the early morning?

15   I think
  this gentle movement of my curtain
  is the life of the universe, all the breath
  of the earth, all the strength
  remaining with us
20 of earth's <u>primeval</u> <u>impetus</u>, the light sound
  of its whirling, heavenly orbit.

   And the curtain's
  moving now,
  in the light breezes of the early morning,
25 all white . . .

   Oh, how full is the least thing
  that fills the world, and fixes
  the boundless contemplation
  of such uncertainty: the leaf
30 that falls, the drop
  that sparkles,
  the scent that passes . . . !

   And the curtain
  that's blue now and not white
35 —for it has been all night now
  with me, to watch its swaying uncertainty—
  is moving softly, still, in the light breeze.

primeval (prī mē´ vəl) *adj.* having to do with the earliest times

impetus (im´ pə təs) *n.* driving force

Review and Assess

Thinking About the Selections

1. **Respond:** Have you ever had an experience similar to those described in either of these poems? Explain.

2. **(a) Recall:** In "Green," what color is the maiden's hair?
   (b) Interpret: Is the speaker describing a real person? Explain.

3. **(a) Recall:** What does the speaker leave open for the maiden?
   (b) Analyze: Why do you think the speaker wants to let the maiden in?

4. **(a) Recall:** In "Lightness," what object does the speaker observe? **(b) Interpret:** Why does this object remind the speaker of something breathing?

5. **(a) Recall:** What examples does Jiménez give of the "least thing that fills the world"? **(b) Compare and Contrast:** How is the curtain like each of these examples?

6. **Make a Judgment:** Does Jiménez's symbolic use of color aid your understanding of these poems? Support your answer.

Review and Assess

Literary Analysis

Imagery

1. (a) In "Fear," in what ways does Mistral's **imagery** of a swallow provide a vivid sense of the mother's worries? (b) How are the images of the princess and queen both similar to and different from those of the swallow?

2. (a) In "The Prayer," identify one image that appeals to each of the five senses. (b) To which sense does the imagery in the poem appeal the most? Explain.

3. (a) What image does Jiménez use to describe the breathing of the universe in "Lightness"? (b) Create an outline of the poem that traces Jiménez's development of the meaning of this image.

Comparing Literary Works

4. (a) Which details in "Fear" and "Green" are reminiscent of fairy tales? (b) How is the **tone** of each poem similar and different?

5. (a) In what ways are the tones of "Lightness" and "Time" similar? (b) Which poem has more variation in tone? Why?

Reading Strategy

Restating for Understanding

6. **Restate** this passage from "The Prayer":
   Thou answerest harshly that he is unworthy of entreaty/
   who did not anoint with prayer his fevered lips, . . .

7. (a) Use a chart like the one shown to clarify two passages from "Lightness" that are unclear to you.

Passage	Restatement
1.	
2.	

(b) Do you think this reading strategy is better suited to reading poetry or prose? Explain.

Extend Understanding

8. **Psychology Connection:** Do you think poems such as these can express more complex emotions than can other kinds of writing or art? Why or why not?

Quick Review

Imagery is language that appeals to one or more of the five senses.

Tone refers to the speaker's attitude toward his or her audience or subject.

To **restate for understanding** as you read, pause after challenging lines or passages and express them in your own words.

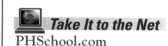 **Take It to the Net**
PHSchool.com

Take the interactive self-test online to check your understanding of these selections.

Integrate Language Skills

Vocabulary Development Lesson

Word Analysis: Latin Root -prim-

The Latin root -prim- means "first." Thus, *primeval* means "having to do with the earliest times." Complete the sentences that follow with the correct word from the list.

primary   primal   primate

1. The ___?___ specialist studied gorillas.
2. The ___?___ reason to sing is enjoyment.
3. In the dark woods, his ___?___ fears kicked in.

Spelling Strategy

For words ending in silent *e*, drop the *e* before suffixes starting with vowels (*cascade* + *-ing* = *cascading*); keep the *e* for suffixes starting with consonants (*amuse* + *-ment* = *amusement*). Add the suffix shown to each word below.

1. invoke + *-ing*
2. chastise + *-ed*
3. abate + *-ment*
4. debate + *-able*

Concept Development: Analogies

An analogy is a comparison of the relationships between two different sets of ideas. Review the vocabulary list on page 1101. Then, complete each analogy that follows with the most appropriate word from the list.

invokes   cascade

anoint   primeval

sheaves   impetus

1. bales : hay :: ___?___ : grain
2. ___?___ : force :: impact : collision
3. ___?___ : contemporary :: A : Z
4. speak : podium :: ___?___ : altar
5. ___?___ : waterfall :: pamphlet : book
6. ___?___ : asks :: confesses : tells

Grammar and Style Lesson

Direct Address

When the speaker in a literary work talks directly to someone or something, the form of speech is called **direct address.** Commas are used to separate the word or phrase of the direct address from the rest of the sentence, regardless of its position in the sentence.

Examples:

Middle: Here I rest, *Lord*, my face bowed down. . . .

Beginning: *Brother*, raise up your head. . . .

End: Do not forget me, *my love*.

Practice Identify the word or phrase of direct address in each sentence below. Add punctuation where needed.

1. You forget Lord that I loved him. . . .
2. My friend it was good to see you.
3. I assure you that I am well sister.
4. Together my baby we tumble toward sleep.
5. I will do as you suggest sir.

Writing Application Write five sentences using direct address. Underline the words of direct address and punctuate correctly.

W\G Prentice Hall Writing and Grammar Connection: Diamond Level, Chapter 27, Section 2

Writing Lesson

Interpretive Essay

In the citation for Gabriela Mistral's Nobel Prize in Literature, the Nobel committee described her work as "poems of love dedicated to death." In an essay, discuss what you think this phrase means and how it applies to one of Mistral's poems.

Prewriting	Generate ideas by writing about the quotation for five minutes without stopping. After five minutes, review what you have written, circling ideas you want to develop further.
Drafting	To organize your essay, state your main idea in one sentence. Then, list the ideas and details that support it. Elaborate upon each of these ideas in a paragraph. Organize the paragraphs in a logical order, and finish with a strong conclusion.
Revising	As you review your essay, check that each paragraph flows logically into the next. Consider reordering paragraphs that seem out of place.

Model: Reordering Paragraphs for Coherence

The speaker admits that her lover was cruel, but then she says it doesn't matter because she loved him. That is reason enough to forgive him.

"The Prayer" is a poem about love and death. The speaker prays to God to forgive her dead lover. She offers God many reasons, but the strongest one is her love.

> In an essay that is coherent, paragraphs flow in a logical order.

WG Prentice Hall Writing and Grammar Connection: Diamond Level, Chapter 14, Section 4

Extension Activities

Listening and Speaking Choose the poem from this grouping that you like best. Then, prepare and deliver an **oral interpretation** of the poem. Use these tips to prepare:

- Vary the speed, rhythm, and pitch of your voice.
- Pause to emphasize ideas or add drama.
- Identify words and phrases that should be stressed.

As you deliver the poem for the class, use body language that expresses your feelings.

Research and Technology With a small group, use print and nonprint resources to research the symbolic meanings of colors. Select quotations from visual artists and writers and incorporate them into a **color chart.** Use the chart as the basis of a class discussion about the meaning of color in Jiménez's work. **[Group Activity]**

 Take It to the Net PHSchool.com

Go online for an additional research activity using the Internet.

Fear / The Prayer / Time / Green / Lightness ◆ 1113

Prepare to Read

Under Reconstruction

Mori Ōgai (1862–1922)

When he was appointed to the post of surgeon general in 1907, Mori Ōgai (mō´ rē´ ō´ gä´ ē´) became the highest-ranking doctor in Japan. He held that position for nearly ten years. Yet, Ōgai is remembered far more for his contributions to literature than for his achievements as a doctor. Today, he is regarded not only as one of the leading writers of his time but also as one of the pioneers of modern Japanese literature.

Years in Germany Ōgai, whose father was also a doctor, earned his medical degree from Tokyo University. After enlisting in the Japanese imperial army, he was sent to Germany in 1884 to continue his studies in medicine.

During his four-year stay in Germany, Ōgai focused most of his studies in the areas of hygiene and bacteriology, which were then new frontiers in medicine. He excelled in his work and even published a paper documenting his research, in a German medical journal.

While in Germany, Ōgai also developed a passionate interest in both German literature and the German way of life. Many of his earliest literary works were translations of German poems and short stories. Ōgai wrote the first Japanese translations of works by Rainer Maria Rilke, August Strindberg, Henrik Ibsen, Gustave Flaubert, and many other great European writers. Perhaps his greatest accomplishment was the completion of the first Japanese translation of Johann Wolfgang von Goethe's *Faust* (1913). These works by European masters profoundly affected new generations of Japanese writers, thus helping to create modern Japanese literature.

Man of Many Talents A man of tremendous energy and intelligence, Ōgai quickly achieved success as both a writer and a doctor following his return to Japan. In his role as an army surgeon, he served in both the Sino-Japanese War (1895) and the Russo-Japanese War (1904–1905) before being promoted to the rank of surgeon general. As a writer, he became a literary celebrity in the 1890s when he published autobiographical works of fiction based on his experiences in Germany. His reputation as a writer continued to grow throughout the early part of the twentieth century with the publication of such well-known works as his novel *The Wild Goose* (1911–1913). During the final stage of his literary career, he wrote historical novels, stories, and biographies, which some readers and critics consider his finest works.

Lasting Influence In addition to his achievements as a fiction writer, Ōgai also made important contributions as a dramatist and a literary critic. As a dramatist, he not only wrote a number of Western-style plays but also strongly supported traditional Kabuki theater, a dramatic form dating back to the 1600s. As a critic, he played an important role in shaping the direction of Japanese poetry, drama, and fiction. Because of the wide scope of Ōgai's literary contributions, some contemporary critics consider him to be the most important Japanese literary figure of the entire twentieth century.

Preview

Connecting to the Literature

Even though the end results may be beneficial, change can often be traumatic. This story focuses on a period of profound and unsettling change in the lives of not just one man but an entire nation.

Literary Analysis

Social Commentary

Literary works often provide writers with a means of expressing their views about society. Such **social commentary** may simply be informative, offering insight into a society's values, customs, beliefs, or trends. For example, in these lines, Ōgai's narrator notices a departure from Japanese tradition:

> By the door was a pile of little cloths for wiping one's shoes and next to these a large Western doormat. . . . Apparently in this restaurant one was supposed to observe the Western custom and wear one's shoes indoors.

Social commentary may also be critical, exposing a society's hypocrisies, limitations, or failures. As you read, look for details that describe, explain, or criticize specific trends, customs, or values.

Connecting Literary Elements

Description is writing that presents details about the people, places, and things that populate a literary work. In works of fiction, descriptive writing usually includes

- sensory details—language that appeals to the five senses.
- details about characters' thoughts, appearance, and mannerisms.

Effective description can reveal more about the characters and setting than mere explanations provide. As you read, notice how Ōgai's use of description creates vivid pictures of the characters and their environment.

Reading Strategy

Recognizing Cultural Details

Cultural details are those elements of daily life that signal how people in a specific place and time live, think, or worship. In this story, the author's use of cultural details shows a society in transition, suggesting that the story is about more than just a relationship between two people. As you read, use a chart like the one shown to record and interpret cultural details.

Detail

Watanabé has the title of "Councilor"

Interpretation

This is an ordered society with formal ranks and titles.

Vocabulary Development

oblique (ə blēk´) *adj.* inclined; slanted (p. 1117)

truncated (trun´ kāt əd) *adj.* cut short; with an angle cut off (p. 1117)

imposingly (im pō´ ziŋ lē) *adv.* making a strong, forceful impression (p. 1119)

nonchalantly (nän´ shə länt´ lē) *adv.* with a lack of concern (p. 1119)

Under Reconstruction

Mori Ōgai
translated by Ivan Morris

▲ **Critical Viewing**   In what ways might Western influences change this Japanese scene? **[Speculate]**

Background

Today, Japan is one of the most highly developed countries in the world, with trade and technological links to all parts of the globe. In the mid-nineteenth century, however, it was an isolated society that still functioned under the feudal system, a decentralized form of government in which individual lords ruled over separate regions. Only with the visit of American naval officer Matthew C. Perry in 1853 and a change of government in the late 1860s did Japan open itself to contact and trade with the West. A period of rapid transformation and modernization followed. "Under Reconstruction" was written in 1910, while Japan was in the throes of these changes.

Ouda, Hironaga Takehiko, Courtesy of the Trustees of the British Museum

It had just stopped raining when Councilor Watanabé got off the tram in front of the Kabuki[1] playhouse. Carefully avoiding the puddles, he hurried through the Kobiki district in the direction of the Department of Communications. Surely that restaurant was somewhere around here, he thought as he strode along the canal; he remembered having noticed the signboard on one of these corners.

The streets were fairly empty. He passed a group of young men in Western clothes. They were talking noisily and looked as if they had all just left their office. Then a girl in a kimono[2] and a gaily-colored sash hurried by, almost bumping into him. She was probably a waitress from some local teahouse, he thought. A rickshaw[3] with its hood up passed him from behind.

Finally he caught sight of a small signboard with the inscription written horizontally in the Western style: *Seiyōken Hotel*. The front of the building facing the canal was covered with scaffolding. The side entrance was on a small street. There were two <u>oblique</u> flights of stairs outside the restaurant, forming a sort of <u>truncated</u> triangle. At the head of each staircase was a glass door; after hesitating a moment, Watanabé entered the one on the left on which were written the characters for *Entrance*.

---

1. **Kabuki** (kä bōō′ kē) *n.* a form of Japanese drama.
2. **kimono** (kə mō′ nō) *n.* traditional Japanese outer garment with short, wide sleeves and a sash.
3. **rickshaw** (rik′ shô′) *n.* small, two-wheeled carriage with a hood, pulled by one or two people.

Reading Strategy
Recognizing Cultural Details Which details in the first two paragraphs reveal some of the changes Japanese society is undergoing at the time of the story? Explain.

oblique (ə blēk′) *adj.* inclined; slanted

truncated (truŋ′ kāt əd) *adj.* cut short; with an angle cut off

☑**Reading Check**

What business establishment does Councilor Watanabé enter?

Inside he found a wide passage. By the door was a pile of little cloths for wiping one's shoes and next to these a large Western doormat. Watanabé's shoes were muddy after the rain and he carefully cleaned them with both implements. Apparently in this restaurant one was supposed to observe the Western custom and wear one's shoes indoors.

There was no sign of life in the passage, but from the distance came a great sound of hammering and sawing. The place was under reconstruction, thought Watanabé.

He waited awhile, but as no one came to receive him, he walked to the end of the passage. Here he stopped, not knowing which way to turn. Suddenly he noticed a man with a napkin under his arm leaning against the wall a few yards away. He went up to him.

"I telephoned yesterday for a reservation."

The man sprang to attention. "Oh yes, sir. A table for two, I believe? It's on the second floor. Would you mind coming with me, sir."

The waiter followed him up another flight of stairs. The man had known immediately who he was, thought Watanabé. Customers must be few and far between with the repairs underway. As he mounted the stairs, the clatter and banging of the workmen became almost deafening.

"Quite a lively place," said Watanabé, looking back at the waiter.

"Oh no, sir. The men go home at five o'clock. You won't be disturbed while you're dining, sir."

When they reached the top of the stairs, the waiter hurried past Watanabé and opened a door to the left. It was a large room overlooking the canal. It seemed rather big for just two people. Round each of the three small tables in the room were squeezed as many chairs as could possibly be fitted. Under the window was a huge sofa and next to it a potted vine about three feet high and a dwarfed plant with large hothouse grapes.

The waiter walked across the room and opened another door. "This is your dining room, sir." Watanabé followed him. The room was small—just right, in fact, for a couple. In the middle a table was elaborately set with two covers and a large basket of azaleas and rhododendrons.

With a certain feeling of satisfaction, Watanabé returned to the large room. The waiter withdrew and Watanabé again found himself alone. Abruptly the sound of hammering stopped. He looked at his watch: yes, it was exactly five o'clock. There was still half an hour till his appointment. Watanabé took a cigar from an open box on the table, pierced the end, and lit it.

Strangely enough, he did not have the slightest feeling of anticipation. It was as if it did not matter who was to join him in this room, as if he did not care in the slightest whose face it was that he would soon be seeing across that flower basket. He was surprised at his own coolness.

Puffing comfortably at his cigar, he walked over to the window and opened it. Directly below were stacked huge piles of timber. This was the main entrance. The water in the canal appeared completely stationary.

Literary Analysis
Social Commentary and Description In what ways might this description of the hotel under repair express the author's feelings about the state of Japanese society?

On the other side he could see a row of wooden buildings. They looked like houses of assignation. Except for a woman with a child on her back, walking slowly back and forth outside one of the houses, there was no one in sight. At the far right, the massive redbrick structure of the Naval Museum <u>imposingly</u> blocked his view.

Watanabé sat down on the sofa and examined the room. The walls were decorated with an ill-assorted collection of pictures: nightingales on a plum tree, an illustration from a fairy tale, a hawk. The scrolls were small and narrow, and on the high walls they looked strangely short as if the bottom portions had been tucked under and concealed. Over the door was a large framed Buddhist text. And this is meant to be the land of art, thought Watanabé.

For a while he sat there smoking his cigar and simply enjoying a sensation of physical well-being. Then he heard the sound of voices in the passage and the door opened. It was she.

She wore a large Anne-Marie straw hat decorated with beads. Under her long gray coat he noticed a white embroidered batiste blouse. Her skirt was also gray. She carried a tiny umbrella with a tassel. Watanabé forced a smile to his face. Throwing his cigar in an ashtray, he got up from the sofa.

The German woman removed her veil and glanced back at the waiter, who had followed her into the room and who was now standing by the door. Then she turned her eyes to Watanabé. They were the large, brown eyes of a brunette. They were the eyes into which he had so often gazed in the past. Yet he did not remember those mauve shadows from their days in Berlin. . . .

"I'm sorry I kept you waiting," she said abruptly in German.

She transferred her umbrella to her left hand and stiffly extended the gloved fingers of her right hand. No doubt all this was for the benefit of the waiter, thought Watanabé as he courteously took the fingers in his hand.

"You can let me know when dinner is ready," he said, glancing at the door. The waiter bowed and left the room.

"How delightful to see you," he said in German.

The woman <u>nonchalantly</u> threw her umbrella on a chair and sat down on the sofa with a slight gasp of exhaustion. Putting her elbows on the table, she gazed silently at Watanabé. He drew up a chair next to the table and sat down.

"It's very quiet here, isn't it?" she said after a while.

"It's under reconstruction," said Watanabé. "They were making a terrible noise when I arrived."

"Oh, that explains it. The place does give one rather an unsettled feeling. Not that I'm a particularly calm sort of person at best."

imposingly (im pō′ ziŋ lē) *adv.* making a strong, forceful impression

nonchalantly (nän′ shə länt′ lē) *adv.* with a lack of concern

✔**Reading Check**

With whom does Councilor Watanabé have an appointment?

"When did you arrive in Japan?"

"The day before yesterday. And then yesterday I happened to see you on the street."

"And why did you come?"

"Well, you see, I've been in Vladivostok[4] since the end of last year."

"I suppose you've been singing in that hotel there, whatever it's called."

"Yes."

"You obviously weren't alone. Were you with a company?"

"No, I wasn't with a company. But I wasn't alone either. . . . I was with a man. In fact you know him." She hesitated a moment. "I've been with Kosinsky."

"Oh, that Pole. So I suppose you're called Kosinskaya now."

"Don't be silly! It's simply that I sing and Kosinsky accompanies me."

"Are you sure that's all?"

"You mean, do we have a good time together? Well, I can't say it never happens."

"That's hardly surprising. I suppose he's in Tokyo with you?"

"Yes, we're both at the Aikoku-san Hotel."

"But he lets you come out alone."

"My dear friend, I only let him accompany me in singing, you know." She used the word *begleiten.*[5] If he accompanied her on the piano, thought Watanabé, he accompanied her in other ways too.

"I told him that I'd seen you on the Ginza," she continued, "and he's very anxious to meet you."

"Allow me to deprive myself of that pleasure."

"Don't worry. He isn't short of money or anything."

Woman With a Black Hat, Kees van Dongen, © Scala

---

4. **Vladivostok** (vlad´ i väs´ täk)
   seaport in southeastern Siberia,
   on the Sea of Japan.
5. *begleiten* (bə glī´ tən) German:
   accompany.

"No, but he probably will be before long if he stays here," said Watanabé with a smile. "And where do you plan to go next?"

"I'm going to America. Everyone tells me that Japan is hopeless, so I'm not going to count on getting work here."

"You're quite right. America is a good place to go after Russia. Japan is still backward. . . . It's still under reconstruction, you see."

"Good heavens! If you aren't careful, I'll tell them in America that a Japanese gentleman admitted his country was backward. In fact, I'll say it was a Japanese government official. You are a government official, aren't you?"

"Yes, I'm in the government."

"And behaving yourself very correctly, no doubt?"

"Frighteningly so! I've become a real *Fürst*,[6] you know. Tonight's the only exception."

"I'm very honored!" She slowly undid the buttons of her long gloves, took them off, and held out her right hand to Watanabé.
It was a beautiful, dazzlingly white hand. He clasped it firmly, amazed at its coldness. Without removing her hand from Watanabé's grasp, she looked steadily at him. Her large, brown eyes seemed with their dark shadows to have grown to twice their former size.

"Would you like me to kiss you?" she said.

Watanabé made a wry face. "We are in Japan," he said.

Without any warning, the door was flung open and the waiter appeared. "Dinner is served, sir."

"We are in Japan," repeated Watanabé. He got up and led the woman into the little dining room. The waiter suddenly turned on the glaring overhead lights.

The woman sat down opposite Watanabé and glanced round the room. "They've given us a *chambre séparée*,[7] she said laughing. "How exciting!" She straightened her back and looked directly at Watanabé as if to see how he would react.

"I'm sure it's quite by chance," he said calmly.

Three waiters were in constant attendance on the two of them. One poured sherry, the other served slices of melon, and the third bustled about ineffectually.

"The place is alive with waiters," said Watanabé.

"Yes, and they seem to be a clumsy lot," she said, squaring her elbows as she started on her melon. "They're just as bad at my hotel."

"I expect you and Kosinsky find they get in your way. Always barging in without knocking. . . ."

"You're wrong about all that, you know. Well, the melon is good anyway."

6. *Fürst* (fürst) German: Duke.
7. *chambre séparée* (shän′ br′ sä pä rä′) French: separate room.

Literary Analysis
Social Commentary What is the effect of Watanabé's repeating the statement, "We are in Japan"?

Reading Strategy
Recognizing Cultural Details What does the bustling of the waiters tell you about Japanese culture?

✔**Reading Check**

What is the German woman's profession?

"In America you'll be getting stacks of food to eat every morning as soon as you wake up."

The conversation drifted along lightly. Finally the waiters brought in fruit salad and poured champagne.

"Aren't you jealous—even a little?" the woman suddenly asked. All the time they had been eating and chatting away. She had remembered how they used to sit facing each other like this after the theater at the little restaurant above the Blühr Steps. Sometimes they had quarreled, but they had always made it up in the end. She had meant to sound as if she were joking; but despite herself, her voice was serious and she felt ashamed.

Watanabé lifted his champagne glass high above the flowers and said in a clear voice: "Kosinsky *soll leben!*"[8]

The woman silently raised her glass. There was a frozen smile on her face. Under the table her hand trembled uncontrollably.

It was still only half past eight when a solitary, black car drove slowly along the Ginza through an ocean of flickering lights. In the back sat a woman, her face hidden by a veil.

---

8. *soll leben* (zōl lā′ bən) German: shall live.

Review and Assess

Thinking About the Selection

1. **Respond:** How do you think you might feel if you saw your hometown undergoing changes like those taking place in the city in this story? Explain.

2. **(a) Recall:** What does Watanabé discover inside the door of the hotel? **(b) Generalize:** In what ways does this detail reflect larger issues in the society?

3. **(a) Recall:** What is happening at the hotel as Watanabé arrives? **(b) Analyze:** In what ways might the activity at the hotel symbolize larger trends in the society as a whole? Explain.

4. **(a) Infer:** What kind of relationship do you think Watanabé and the German woman shared in the past? **(b) Support:** Which details support your inference?

5. **(a) Distinguish:** What memory does the German woman have of her time with Watanabé in Germany? **(b) Analyze:** In what ways do you think Watanabé has changed now that he has returned to Japan?

6. **Assess:** Do you think "Under Reconstruction" is a good title for this story? Why or why not?

Review and Assess

Literary Analysis

Social Commentary

1. (a) Which details about the sign announcing the Seiyoken Hotel does Watanabé observe? (b) In what ways might his observations, taken together, be an example of **social commentary**?

2. (a) With what statement does Watanabé sum up his study of the restaurant's decor? (b) How do you interpret this statement?

3. (a) How does the meeting between Watanabé and the German woman parallel the changes taking place in early twentieth-century Japan? (b) Is this story an example of social commentary that describes, explains, or criticizes? Explain.

Connecting Literary Elements

4. Use a chart like the one shown to examine the **description** of the setting. Identify details describing both the exterior and interior of the hotel.

5. (a) Identify two details each that describe the German woman's appearance, her actions, and the qualities of her speech. (b) What impression of her personality does this description create? Explain.

Reading Strategy

Recognizing Cultural Details

6. (a) Identify four **cultural details** that Watanabé observes on his way to the hotel. (b) What do these details reveal about the nature of Japanese culture at this time?

7. What does the behavior of the waiters suggest about Japanese culture?

Extend Understanding

8. **Social Studies Connection:** Do you think technological advances, which make global communication easier, increase or decrease the need for awareness of cultural differences? Explain.

Quick Review

Social commentary is writing that describes, explains, or criticizes aspects of society or society as a whole.

Description is writing that provides details, often using sensory language, about the people, places, and things that populate a literary work.

To **recognize cultural details** as you read, notice the mention of objects, customs, religious practices, and other elements that paint a picture of life in a specific time and place.

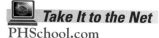
Take It to the Net
PHSchool.com

Take the interactive self-test online to check your understanding of this selection.

Integrate Language Skills

Vocabulary Development Lesson

Word Analysis: Latin Prefix *non-*

The adverb *nonchalantly* combines the prefix *non-*, which means "not," and the word part *calere*, which means "to be warm." Thus, a nonchalant person is cool or indifferent about something. Use the meanings of the roots in parentheses to match each word with its definition.

1. nondescript (describe)   **a.** without rival

2. nonpareil (equal)   **b.** lacking qualities

3. nonsense (logic)   **c.** without meaning

Spelling Strategy

In most words ending in *-que,* the long *e* sound preceding the *q* is spelled with an *i.* Use the clues on the left to finish the spelling of each incomplete word below.

1. old furnishings: ant_____

2. summary of opinion: crit_____

3. air of mystery: myst_____

Fluency: True or False?

After reviewing the vocabulary list on page 1115, determine whether each of the following statements is true or false. Then, explain your answer.

1. If a policeman looks at someone *imposingly,* he wants the person to relax.

2. If a shopper *nonchalantly* strolls through the mall, he might be window-shopping.

3. If a story is *truncated,* it spins out at great length.

4. If the support beams of a house tilt at an *oblique* angle, the home is probably not safe for habitation.

Grammar and Style Lesson

Gerunds

A **gerund** is a verb form that ends in *-ing* and acts like a noun. Gerunds can function as either subjects or objects in a sentence.

Subject: The clatter and <u>banging</u> of the workmen became almost deafening.

Object of Preposition: From the distance came a great sound of <u>hammering</u> and <u>sawing</u>.

Direct Object: Would you mind <u>coming</u> with me, sir?

Practice In each sentence below, identify the gerund and indicate its function.

1. With no warning, the door swung open.

2. With a feeling of satisfaction, he returned.

3. The sound of hammering stopped.

4. The place gives one an unsettled feeling.

5. I let him accompany me in singing.

Writing Application Write a paragraph describing what you learned about Japan in this story. Use and underline at least three gerunds.

 Prentice Hall Writing and Grammar Connection: Diamond Level, Chapter 19, Section 2

Writing Lesson

Character Sketch

In "Under Reconstruction," some information is stated directly, while much is revealed indirectly. For example, Watanabé does not often make direct statements, yet the details he notices, his speech, and his actions reveal his feelings. Write a character sketch of Watanabé, basing your ideas on what he observes, says, and does.

Prewriting Reread the story, taking notes about Watanabé's observations, actions, and speech. Write a sentence summarizing these notes, which you will then refine into a thesis statement.

Drafting Write an introduction in which you state your thesis. Then, write a paragraph for each of your ideas, supporting each one with details from the story. Finish with a memorable conclusion.

Revising As you review your draft, highlight words and phrases that seem vague or imprecise. Consider replacing them with choices that are clearer and more specific.

Model: Revising to Replace Vague Words With Precise Ones

cautious

While in Japan, Watanabé is a very ~~nice~~ man. He

hurries   *hotel*

~~goes~~ to the ~~place~~ early because he does not think it

proper

~~okay~~ to be late.

> Precise language makes writing more meaningful and informative.

Prentice Hall Writing and Grammar Connection: Diamond Level, Chapter 5, Section 4

Extension Activities

Listening and Speaking With a partner, write and perform the **dialogue** that might have occurred between Kosinsky and the German woman after her dinner with Watanabé. Use these tips to plan:

- Brainstorm for a list of questions or statements the two might say to each other.
- Role-play the encounter.

Write the dialogue. As you perform it for the class, use appropriate body language and eye contact. **[Group Activity]**

Research and Technology Japan is known for its distinctive design aesthetic. Use electronic and print resources to research examples of Japanese design, such as cars or ceramics. Use a computer program to create a **slide show presentation** that provides an overview of Japanese design.

 **Take It to the Net**   PHSchool.com

Go online for an additional research activity using the Internet.

Prepare to Read

My Old Home

Lu Hsun (1881–1936)

The most important event in Lu Hsun's (lōō shunz) life may have occurred in 1905 when he saw a film that showed a Chinese man, who had been accused of spying for the Russians, being executed by the Japanese during the Russo-Japanese War (1904 –1905). For Lu Hsun, the meaning of this incident was all too clear—China, once the dominant force in the Far East, was now a backward, powerless country. China existed at the mercy not only of powerful Western nations but also of such emerging Asian powers as Japan. Although he had once been interested in medicine, Lu Hsun now believed that the real illness in Chinese society lay in the spirit of the people. He felt that literature, more than any other discipline, could provide the cure for the culture's apathy. He vowed to become a writer and to use his pen to help promote change in his country. He spent the rest of his life fulfilling this promise.

A Difficult Upbringing Lu Hsun was born into a wealthy family that stressed the ancient Chinese values of respect for education and learning. During his childhood, however, his family suffered severe financial setbacks that left them in poverty. Despite their financial problems, Lu Hsun attended a private school and later went to Japan to study medicine. However, after seeing the film of the Chinese man's execution, he abandoned the study of medicine to pursue his literary career.

The Foundations of a Writer To be a great writer, Lu Hsun understood that he needed to know more about the world and its literature. He learned to speak German and Russian, which enabled him to read original works by such writers as the Russians Nikolai Gogol and Anton Chekhov and the German Friedrich Nietzsche. He began publishing a journal called *New Life*, in which he included translations of stories by Western writers, along with articles encouraging the Chinese people to read the works of such influential Western thinkers as Nietzsche and Charles Darwin.

The New Culture Movement In 1918, Lu Hsun joined a rebellious circle of Chinese writers that came to be known as the New Culture Movement. Encouraged by the other members of this group, he wrote his first short story, "Diary of a Madman" (1918). The story is considered to be the first modern Chinese short story because it uses the real language of ordinary people rather than the scholarly language of most Chinese literature up to that time. Lu Hsun went on to become a prolific and successful writer, composing poems and essays as well as short stories. His most famous story, "The Story of Ah Q" (1921), is a satirical attack on contemporary Chinese society. His collection of stories *Old Stories Retold* (1935) also offers a darkly satirical portrait of Chinese society.

Support for the Revolution During the final years of his life, Lu Hsun's writing became increasingly political. Having witnessed the corruption and failure of China's republican government, Lu Hsun became convinced that a revolution was necessary. His work portrayed the plight of the poor and powerless and gave voice to rising revolutionary feeling. Because of his sympathy for the revolution, Lu Hsun's work has remained popular in contemporary China, even during periods when most literature was being suppressed by the government. Today, most scholars consider him to be the most important Chinese fiction writer of his time.

Preview

Connecting to the Literature

Think what it might be like to return to a place from which you had moved. When the narrator of this story returns to his childhood village, his visit is full of both sadness and hope.

Literary Analysis

Atmosphere

Emotions color perceptions. For example, when one is cheerful, the world looks quite different from the way it looks when one is dejected. In literature, this quality of reflected emotion is called **atmosphere**—the emotional nature of the world the author creates. Atmosphere arises from descriptions, especially those of the setting. As you read, use a chart like the one shown to interpret the atmosphere of this story.

Connecting Literary Elements

A **flashback** is a section of a literary work that interrupts the present action of a story to relate an event from an earlier time. A flashback may take the form of a dream, a memory, a story, or an actual switch to a past time. Writers use flashbacks to provide background on events and characters in the present. In "My Old Home," Lu Hsun transitions evenly into a long flashback:

> At this point a strange picture suddenly flashed into my mind: a golden moon suspended in a deep blue sky . . .

As you read, identify the ways in which the flashback clarifies the narrator's perspective on the events he is experiencing in the present.

Reading Strategy

Applying the Historical Context

In many literary works, the setting includes a **historical context** that shapes characters' attitudes and behavior. The historical context includes the elements of the setting, such as social attitudes, politics, and economics, that are particular to that place and time. As you read, apply the historical context to determine how the attitudes of the characters reflect the events and ideas of their day.

Vocabulary Development

somber (säm′ bər) *adj.* dark, gloomy; serious (p. 1128)

talisman (tal′ is mən) *n.* charm or token; lucky object (p. 1130)

stealthily (stel′ thə lē) *adv.* secretly (p. 1131)

ken (ken) *n.* range of understanding; comprehension (p. 1131)

contemptuously (kən temp′ choo əs lē) *adv.* scornfully; disrespectfully (p. 1132)

indignantly (in dig′ nənt lē) *adv.* angrily (p. 1133)

gentry (jen′ trē) *n.* landowning families ranked just below the nobility (p. 1135)

dissipation (dis′ ə pā′ shən) *n.* wasteful or immoral behavior; overindulgence (p. 1136)

Excerpt

It was late winter. As we drew near my former home, the day became overcast and a cold wind blew. . . .

⬇

Telling Details

winter; overcast; cold wind

⬇

Atmosphere

gloomy, depressed

MY OLD HOME

Lu Hsun
translated by Yang Hsien-yi and Gladys Yang

Background

The Chinese Empire lasted for more than two thousand years, surviving wars, invasions, and rebellions. It produced some of the greatest cultural achievements in world history and fostered a deep respect for tradition. Yet, the society also suffered from sharp class distinctions, with an impoverished and uneducated majority who spent their lives in servitude to the rich.

From 1911 to 1912, a revolution replaced rule by an emperor with a republic. Unfortunately, the republic proved highly inefficient and weak. It was unable to centralize power effectively and factional fighting broke out, leading to widespread political instability. Poverty continued to plague the country, and many of the old social barriers remained in place. It is during this turbulent time in Chinese history that the events in this story unfold.

Braving the bitter cold, I traveled more than seven hundred miles back to the old home I had left over twenty years before.

It was late winter. As we drew near my former home the day became overcast and a cold wind blew into the cabin of our boat, while all one could see through the chinks in our bamboo awning were a few desolate villages, void of any sign of life, scattered far and near under the <u>somber</u> yellow sky. I could not help feeling depressed.

Ah! Surely this was not the old home I had remembered for the past twenty years?

The old home I remembered was not in the least like this. My old home was much better. But if you asked me to recall its peculiar charm or describe its beauties, I had no clear impression, no words to describe it. And now it seemed this was all there was to it. Then I rationalized the matter to myself, saying: Home was always like this, and although it has not improved, still it is not so depressing as I imagine; it is only my mood that has changed, because I am coming back to the country this time with no illusions.

This time I had come with the sole object of saying goodbye. The old house our clan had lived in for so many years had already been sold to another family, and was to change hands before the end of the year. I had to hurry there before New Year's Day to say goodbye forever to the familiar old house, and to move my family to another place where I was working, far from my old home town.

At dawn on the second day I reached the gateway of my home. Broken stems of withered grass on the roof, trembling in the wind, made very clear the reason why this old house could not avoid changing hands. Several branches of our clan had probably already moved away, so it was unusually quiet. By the time I reached the house my mother was already at the door to welcome me, and my eight-year-old nephew, Hung-erh, rushed out after her.

Though mother was delighted, she was also trying to hide a certain feeling of sadness. She told me to sit down and rest and have some tea, letting the removal wait for the time being. Hung-erh, who had never seen me before, stood watching me at a distance.

But finally we had to talk about the removal. I said that rooms had already been rented elsewhere, and I had bought a little furniture; in addition it would be necessary to sell all the furniture in the house in order to buy more things. Mother agreed, saying that the luggage was nearly all packed, and about half the furniture that could not easily be moved had already been sold. Only it was difficult to get people to pay up.

"You must rest for a day or two, and call on our relatives, and then we can go," said mother.

"Yes."

Reading Strategy
Applying Historical Context Based on your knowledge of the political situation in China at the time, why might the family have had financial trouble?

✔**Reading Check**
Why has the narrator returned home?

Landscape, Zhu Qizhan, Photo Courtesy of Joan Lebold Cohen

"Then there is Jun-tu. Each time he comes here he always asks after you, and wants very much to see you again. I told him the probable date of your return home, and he may be coming any time."

At this point a strange picture suddenly flashed into my mind: a golden moon suspended in a deep blue sky and beneath it the seashore, planted as far as the eye could see with jade-green watermelons, while in their midst a boy of eleven or twelve, wearing a silver necklet and grasping a steel pitchfork in his hand, was thrusting with all his might at a *zha*[1] which dodged the blow and escaped between his legs.

This boy was Jun-tu. When I first met him he was just over ten—that was thirty years ago, and at that time my father was still alive and the family well off, so I was really a spoiled child. That year it was our family's turn to take charge of a big ancestral sacrifice, which came round only once in thirty years, and hence was an important one. In the first month the ancestral images were presented and offerings made, and since the sacrificial vessels were very fine and there was such a crowd of worshippers, it was necessary to guard against theft. Our family had only one part-time laborer. (In our district we divide laborers into three classes: those who work all the year for one family are called full-timers; those who are hired by the day are called dailies; and those who farm their own land and only work for one family at New Year, during festivals or when rents are being collected are called part-timers.) And since there was so much to be done, he told my father that he would send for his son Jun-tu to look after the sacrificial vessels.

When my father gave his consent I was overjoyed, because I had long since heard of Jun-tu and knew that he was about my own age, born in the intercalary month,[2] and when his horoscope was told it was found that of the five elements[3] that of earth was lacking, so his father called him Jun-tu (Intercalary Earth). He could set traps and catch small birds.

I looked forward every day to New Year, for New Year would bring Jun-tu. At last, when the end of the year came, one day mother told me that Jun-tu had come, and I flew to see him. He was standing in the kitchen. He had a round, crimson face and wore a small felt cap on his head and a gleaming silver necklet round his neck, showing that his father doted on him and, fearing he might die, had made a pledge with the gods and buddhas,[4] using the necklet as a <u>talisman</u>. He was very shy, and I was the only person he was not afraid of. When there was no one else there, he would talk with me, so in a few hours we were fast friends.

I don't know what we talked of then, but I remember that Jun-tu was in high spirits, saying that since he had come to town he had seen many new things.

---

1. *zha* (ja) badgerlike animal.
2. **intercalary month** Each year in the Chinese lunar calendar consists of 360 days, divided into twelve months of twenty-nine or thirty days. To compensate for the five additional days included in the traditional Western calendar, a thirteenth, or intercalary, month is added to the Chinese calendar every few years.
3. **the five elements** metal, water, fire, wood, and earth.
4. **buddhas** (boo´ dəz) In the Buddhist religion, buddhas are figures who embody divine wisdom and virtue.

Literary Analysis
Atmosphere and Flashback Which clues in the text suggest that a flashback has begun?

Literary Analysis
Atmosphere and Flashback What information does the flashback provide about the narrator's relationship with Jun-tu?

talisman (tal´ is mən) *n.* charm or token; lucky object

The next day I wanted him to catch birds.

"Can't be done," he said. "It's only possible after a heavy snowfall. On our sands, after it snows, I sweep clear a patch of ground, prop up a big threshing basket with a short stick, and scatter husks of grain beneath. When the birds come there to eat, I tug a string tied to the stick, and the birds are caught in the basket. There are all kinds: wild pheasants, woodcocks, wood-pigeons, 'blue-backs.' . . ."

Accordingly I looked forward very eagerly to snow.

"Just now it is too cold," said Jun-tu another time, "but you must come to our place in summer. In the daytime we'll go to the seashore to look for shells, there are green ones and red ones, besides 'scare-devil' shells and 'buddha's hands.' In the evening when dad and I go to see to the watermelons, you shall come too."

"Is it to look out for thieves?"

"No. If passers-by are thirsty and pick a watermelon, folk down our way don't consider it as stealing. What we have to look out for are badgers, hedgehogs and *zha*. When under the moonlight you hear the crunching sound made by the *zha* when it bites the melons, then you take your pitchfork and creep <u>stealthily</u> over. . . ."

I had no idea then what this thing called *zha* was—and I am not much clearer now for that matter—but somehow I felt it was something like a small dog, and very fierce.

"Don't they bite people?"

"You have a pitchfork. You go across, and when you see it you strike. It's a very cunning creature and will rush toward you and get away between your legs. Its fur is as slippery as oil. . . ."

I had never known that all these strange things existed: at the seashore there were shells all colors of the rainbow; watermelons were exposed to such danger, yet all I had known of them before was that they were sold in the greengrocer's.

"On our shore, when the tide comes in, there are lots of jumping fish, each with two legs like a frog. . . ."

Jun-tu's mind was a treasure-house of such strange lore, all of it outside the <u>ken</u> of my former friends. They were ignorant of all these things and, while Jun-tu lived by the sea, they like me could see only the four corners of the sky above the high courtyard wall.

Unfortunately, a month after New Year Jun-tu had to go home. I burst into tears and he took refuge in the kitchen, crying and refusing to come out, until finally his father carried him off. Later he sent me by his father a packet of shells and a few very beautiful feathers, and I sent him presents once or twice, but we never saw each other again.

Now that my mother mentioned him, this childhood memory sprang into life like a flash of lightning, and I seemed to see my beautiful old home. So I answered:

"Fine! And he—how is he?"

stealthily (stel´ thə lē) *adv.* secretly

Literary Analysis
Atmosphere and Flashback How would you describe the atmosphere created in this flashback? Explain your answer.

ken (ken) *n.* range of understanding; comprehension

☑ **Reading Check**
Which childhood friend does the narrator fondly recall?

"He? . . . He's not at all well off either," said mother. And then, looking out of the door: "Here come those people again. They say they want to buy our furniture; but actually they just want to see what they can pick up. I must go and watch them."

Mother stood up and went out. The voices of several women could be heard outside. I called Hung-erh to me and started talking to him, asking him whether he could write, and whether he would be glad to leave.

"Shall we be going by train?"

"Yes, we shall go by train."

"And boat?"

"We shall take a boat first."

"Oh! Like this! With such a long mustache!" A strange shrill voice suddenly rang out.

I looked up with a start, and saw a woman of about fifty with prominent cheekbones and thin lips. With her hands on her hips, not wearing a skirt but with her trousered legs apart, she stood in front of me just like the compass in a box of geometrical instruments.

I was flabbergasted.

"Don't you know me? Why, I have held you in my arms!"

I felt even more flabbergasted. Fortunately my mother came in just then and said:

"He has been away so long, you must excuse him for forgetting. You should remember," she said to me, "this is Mrs. Yang from across the road. . . . She has a beancurd shop."

Then, to be sure, I remembered. When I was a child there was a Mrs. Yang who used to sit nearly all day long in the beancurd shop across the road, and everybody used to call her Beancurd Beauty. She used to powder herself, and her cheekbones were not so prominent then nor her lips so thin; moreover she remained seated all the time, so that I had never noticed this resemblance to a compass. In those days people said that, thanks to her, that beancurd shop did very good business. But, probably on account of my age, she had made no impression on me, so that later I forgot her entirely. However, the Compass was extremely indignant and looked at me most contemptuously, just as one might look at a Frenchman who had never heard of Napoleon or an American who had never heard of Washington, and smiling sarcastically she said:

"You had forgotten? Naturally I am beneath your notice. . . ."

Literary Analysis
Atmosphere and Flashback In what ways does the atmosphere of the flashback differ from the present? Explain.

▼ **Critical Viewing**
Do you think this photograph resembles the narrator's family during his affluent childhood or after they suffered financial hardship? Explain. [Distinguish]

contemptuously
(kən temp′ chōō əs lē) *adv.*
scornfully; disrespectfully

"Certainly not . . . I . . ." I answered nervously, getting to my feet.

"Then you listen to me, Master Hsun. You have grown rich, and they are too heavy to move, so you can't possibly want these old pieces of furniture anymore. You had better let me take them away. Poor people like us can do with them."

"I haven't grown rich. I must sell these in order to buy. . . ."

"Oh, come now, you have been made the intendant of a circuit,[5] how can you still say you're not rich? You have three concubines now, and whenever you go out it is in a big sedan-chair with eight bearers. Do you still say you're not rich? Hah! You can't hide anything from me."

Knowing there was nothing I could say, I remained silent.

"Come now, really, the more money people have the more miserly they get, and the more miserly they are the more money they get . . ." remarked the Compass, turning <u>indignantly</u> away and walking slowly off, casually picking up a pair of mother's gloves and stuffing them into her pocket as she went out.

After this a number of relatives in the neighborhood came to call. In the intervals between entertaining them I did some packing, and so three or four days passed.

One very cold afternoon, I sat drinking tea after lunch when I was aware of someone coming in, and turned my head to see who it was. At the first glance I gave an involuntary start, hastily stood up and went over to welcome him.

The newcomer was Jun-tu. But although I knew at a glance that this was Jun-tu, it was not the Jun-tu I remembered. He had grown to twice his former size. His round face, once crimson, had become sallow and acquired deep lines and wrinkles; his eyes too had become like his father's, the rims swollen and red, a feature common to most peasants who work by the sea and are exposed all day to the wind from the ocean. He wore a shabby felt cap and just one very thin padded jacket, with the result that he was shivering from head to foot. He carried a paper package and a long pipe, nor was his hand the plump red hand I remembered, but coarse and clumsy and chapped, like the bark of a pine tree.

Delighted as I was, I did not know how to express myself, and could only say:

"Oh! Jun-tu—so it's you? . . ."

After this there were so many things I wanted to talk about, they should have poured out like a string of beads: woodcocks, jumping fish, shells, *zha*. . . . But I was tongue-tied, unable to put all I was thinking into words.

He stood there, mixed joy and sadness showing on his face. His lips moved, but not a sound did he utter. Finally, assuming a respectful attitude, he said clearly:

"Master! . . ."

---

5. **intendant of a circuit** an official position between the county and provincial levels.

Reading Strategy
Applying Historical Context In what ways do the Compass's remarks reflect the historical realities of the period?

indignantly (in dig´ nənt lē) *adv.* angrily

**Reading Check**

What level of status and wealth does the Compass believe the narrator has attained?

I felt a shiver run through me; for I knew then what a lamentably thick wall had grown up between us. Yet I could not say anything.

He turned his head to call:

"Shui-sheng, bow to the master." Then he pulled forward a boy who had been hiding behind his back, and this was just the Jun-tu of twenty years before, only a little paler and thinner, and he had no silver necklet.

"This is my fifth," he said. "He's not used to company, so he's shy and awkward."

Mother came downstairs with Hung-erh, probably after hearing our voices.

"I got your letter some time ago, madam," said Jun-tu. "I was really so pleased to know the master was coming back. . . ."

"Now, why are you so polite? Weren't you playmates together in the past?" said mother gaily. "You had better still call him Brother Hsun as before."

"Oh, you are really too. . . . What bad manners that would be. I was a child then and didn't understand." As he was speaking Jun-tu motioned Shui-sheng to come and bow, but the child was shy, and stood stock-still behind his father.

"So he is Shui-sheng? Your fifth?" asked mother. "We are all strangers, you can't blame him for feeling shy. Hung-erh had better take him out to play."

When Hung-erh heard this he went over to Shui-sheng, and Shui-sheng went out with him, entirely at his ease. Mother asked Jun-tu to sit down, and after a little hesitation he did so; then leaning his long pipe against the table he handed over the paper package, saying:

"In winter there is nothing worth bringing; but these few beans we dried ourselves, if you will excuse the liberty, sir."

When I asked him how things were with him, he just shook his head.

"In a very bad way. Even my sixth can do a little work, but still we haven't enough to eat . . . and then there is no security . . . all sorts of people want money, there is no fixed rule . . . and the harvests are bad. You grow things, and when you take them to sell you always have to pay several taxes and lose money, while if you don't try to sell, the things may go bad. . . ."

He kept shaking his head; yet, although his face was lined with wrinkles, not one of them moved, just as if he were a stone statue. No doubt he felt intensely bitter, but could not express himself. After a pause he took up his pipe and began to smoke in silence.

From her chat with him, mother learned that he was busy at home and had to go back the next day; and since he had had no lunch, she told him to go to the kitchen and fry some rice for himself.

Themes in World Literature

The Vernacular

A vibrant popular literature is only possible if the language in which books are written is familiar to the ordinary person. For example, if contemporary American writers restricted themselves to ancient Greek, it is unlikely that they would sell many books. The vernacular, or language of the common people, is critical for the flowering of popular literature.

Lu Hsun is considered the first modern Chinese writer because he used the vernacular and wrote about topics of concern to ordinary people. In Japan, Mori Ōgai (p. 1114) is credited with similar innovations.

Use of the vernacular in the West has a longer history. In the seventeenth century, Shakespeare combined the formal rhythms spoken by his heroes with the more casual language of his lower-class characters. In the nineteenth century, English Romantics used the ordinary diction of daily speech.

Today, one measure of the success of a literary work is that the dialogue sounds true-to-life. The wealth of contemporary literature worldwide is due, in large part, to the use of the vernacular.

After he had gone out, mother and I both shook our heads over his hard life: many children, famines, taxes, soldiers, bandits, officials and landed <u>gentry</u>, all had squeezed him as dry as a mummy. Mother said that we should offer him all the things we were not going to take away, letting him choose for himself.

That afternoon he picked out a number of things: two long tables, four chairs, an incense burner and candlesticks, and one balance. He also asked for all the ashes from the stove (in our part we cook over straw, and the ashes can be used to fertilize sandy soil), saying that when we left he would come to take them away by boat.

That night we talked again, but not of anything serious; and the next morning he went away with Shui-sheng.

After another nine days it was time for us to leave. Jun-tu came in the morning. Shui-sheng did not come with him—he had just brought a little girl of five to watch the boat. We were very busy all day, and had no time to talk. We also had quite a number of visitors, some to see us off, some to fetch things, and some to do both. It was nearly evening when we left by boat, and by that time everything in the house, however old or shabby, large or small, fine or coarse, had been cleared away.

As we set off, in the dusk, the green mountains on either side of the river became deep blue, receding toward the stern of the boat.

Hung-erh and I, leaning against the cabin window, were looking out together at the indistinct scene outside, when suddenly he asked:

"Uncle, when shall we go back?"

"Go back? Do you mean that before you've left you want to go back?"

"Well, Shui-sheng has invited me to his home. . . ." He opened wide his black eyes in anxious thought.

Mother and I both felt rather sad, and so Jun-tu's name came up again. Mother said that ever since our family started packing up, Mrs. Yang from the beancurd shop had come over every day, and the day before in the ash-heap she had unearthed a dozen bowls and plates, which after some discussion she insisted must have been buried there by Jun-tu, so that when he came to remove the ashes he could take them home at the same time. After making this discovery Mrs. Yang was very pleased with herself, and flew off taking the dog-teaser with her. (The dog-teaser is used by poultry keepers in our parts. It is a wooden cage inside which food is put, so that hens can stretch their necks in to eat but dogs can only look on furiously.) And it was a marvel, considering the size of her feet, how fast she could run.

I was leaving the old house farther and farther behind, while the hills and rivers of my old home were also receding gradually ever farther in the distance. But I felt no regret. I only felt that all round me was an invisible high wall, cutting me off from my fellows, and this depressed me thoroughly. The vision of that small hero with the silver necklet among the watermelons had formerly been as clear as day, but now it suddenly blurred, adding to my depression.

Mother and Hung-erh fell asleep.

gentry (jen′ trē) *n.* landowning families ranked just below the nobility

Reading Strategy
Applying Historical Context How have the political and economic realities of the time affected Jun-tu?

✓**Reading Check**

What title of respect does Jun-tu use to address the narrator?

I lay down, listening to the water rippling beneath the boat, and knew that I was going my way. I thought: although there is such a barrier between Jun-tu and myself, the children still have much in common, for wasn't Hung-erh thinking of Shui-sheng just now? I hope they will not be like us, that they will not allow a barrier to grow up between them. But again I would not like them, because they want to be akin, all to have a treadmill existence like mine, nor to suffer like Jun-tu until they become stupefied,[6] nor yet, like others, to devote all their energies to <u>dissipation</u>. They should have a new life, a life we have never experienced.

The access of hope made me suddenly afraid. When Jun-tu asked for the incense burner and candlesticks I had laughed up my sleeve at him to think that he still worshiped idols and could not put them out of his mind. Yet what I now called hope was no more than an idol I created myself. The only difference was that what he desired was close at hand, while what I desired was less easily realized.

As I dozed, a stretch of jade-green seashore spread itself before my eyes, and above a round golden moon hung in a deep blue sky. I thought: hope cannot be said to exist, nor can it be said not to exist. It is just like roads across the earth. For actually the earth had no roads to begin with, but when many men pass one way, a road is made.

dissipation (dis′ ə pā′ shən) *n.* wasteful or immoral behavior; overindulgence

---

6. stupefied (stoo′ pə fīd) *v.* stunned; made dull or lethargic.

Review and Assess

Thinking About the Selection

1. **Respond:** Do you think the narrator should have tried to help Jun-tu? Explain.

2. **(a) Recall:** In what state of repair does the narrator find his old house? **(b) Infer:** How have the family's circumstances changed since the narrator was a child? Explain.

3. **(a) Classify:** Describe the narrator's relationship with Jun-tu when they were children. **(b) Compare and Contrast:** As adults, how has their relationship changed? **(c) Analyze Cause and Effect:** What do you think is the main reason for this change? Explain.

4. **(a) Interpret:** At the end of the story, to what emotion does the narrator compare Jun-tu's worship of idols? **(b) Analyze:** In what ways does the narrator wish the next generation will be different from his own?

5. **Evaluate:** Do you think this story is more effective as a work of fiction or as a document advocating political change? Explain.

Review and Assess

Literary Analysis

Atmosphere

1. (a) How would you describe the **atmosphere** of this story? (b) Identify five details in the setting and action that create this atmosphere.

2. (a) How does the atmosphere created in the section describing the narrator's friendship with Jun-tu contrast with the atmosphere of the present time of the story? (b) What circumstances account for this difference?

3. (a) In what ways does this story suggest that the failure of Chinese society has damaged individuals? (b) How does the atmosphere of the story reinforce that message?

Connecting Literary Elements

4. (a) What prompts the narrator's **flashback** to his childhood friendship with Jun-tu? (b) How does the flashback help you understand the narrator's feelings when he meets the adult Jun-tu?

5. (a) What other techniques might the author have used to convey the information revealed in the flashback? (b) Why do you think the author used a flashback instead of another explanatory technique?

Reading Strategy

Applying the Historical Context

6. (a) Use a chart like this to **apply the historical context** to this story.

Historical Context	Details Revealing Historical Context
1. People are poor.	
2. People maintain feudal code.	

(b) Based on this story, how might the reading of fiction enhance one's understanding of history? Explain.

7. At the time of the story, China was experiencing overpopulation. How are Jun-tu's troubles indicative of this problem?

Extend Understanding

8. **Social Studies Connection:** Does American society suffer from any of the same problems that are evident in this story? Explain.

Quick Review

Atmosphere is the emotional quality of the world the author creates.

A **flashback** is a section of a literary work that interrupts the relating of events in the present to tell about an event from an earlier time.

When you **apply the historical context**, you determine how the circumstances and attitudes of the characters reflect the events and ideas of their day.

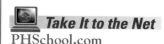
Take It to the Net
PHSchool.com

Take the interactive self-test online to check your understanding of this selection.

Integrate Language Skills

Vocabulary Development Lesson

Word Analysis: Latin Root *-dign-*

The root of *indignant* is *-dign-*, which means "worth" or "worthy" in Latin. Therefore, *indignant* means "angry at being treated in an unworthy way." Match each word below with its definition.

1. dignified
2. dignity
3. dignitary

a. person of great worth
b. honor or respect
c. behaving with a strong sense of self-worth

Spelling Strategy

When a word ends in a consonant plus *y*, change the *y* to *i* before adding most suffixes: *stealthy* + *-ly* = *stealthily*. Add the suffix indicated to each of the words below.

1. plenty + *-ful*
2. defy + *-ance*
3. hasty + *-ly*
4. beauty + *-fy*

Fluency: Clarify Meaning

Answer each question below with a complete sentence, and then explain your reasoning.

1. When would you see a *somber* sky?
2. Why might someone become *indignant*?
3. If you speak *contemptuously*, how might people react?
4. Does the population of the United States include members of the *gentry*?
5. When might an animal move *stealthily*?
6. What object might be considered a modern-day *talisman*?
7. Why might someone who lives a life of *dissipation* have problems?
8. Will space travel remain outside the *ken* of most people?

Grammar and Style Lesson

Commonly Confused Words: *than* and *then*

Than and *then* are two words that are often confused. The word *than* is a conjunction and is used in comparisons, while the word *then* is an adverb used to show time or sequence of events.

Than: I traveled more *than* seven hundred miles back to the old home I had left. (*comparison*)

Then: You hear the crunching sound, *then* you take your pitchfork and creep stealthily over. (*sequencing*)

Practice Identify the word that correctly completes each sentence below.

1. The narrator last saw his home more (than, then) twenty years ago.
2. Everyone was younger (than, then).
3. The narrator first travels by train and (than, then) boards a boat.
4. The house seems shabbier (than, then) it did when he was a child.
5. The narrator pauses briefly to look around; (than, then) he leaves his old house.

Writing Application Write five sentences about your home. Use either *than* or *then* in each sentence.

WG Prentice Hall Writing and Grammar Connection: Diamond Level, Chapter 25, Section 2

Writing Lesson

Comparison-and-Contrast Essay

In "My Old Home," the narrator juxtaposes his memories of the past with the realities of the present. Following his example, write a comparison-and-contrast essay exploring the differences between the world of the narrator's childhood and that of his adulthood. Focus your essay by discussing one element, such as people, things, ideas, or emotions.

Prewriting Make a two-column chart in which you list the two things you are comparing and contrasting. Then, record specific details that reveal the similarities and differences between them.

Drafting In your introduction, state your topic and your main idea. In the body of your essay, present the details that support your ideas. Address each point of comparison and contrast thoroughly.

Revising Review your essay, making sure that your ideas flow logically. If the connections between ideas are unclear, add appropriate transitions.

Model: Revising to Add Transitions

The narrator saw a broken-down house with a
  In contrast,
damaged roof. When he was a child, the house was
  While it had once been full of relatives,
well kept. Only his mother and nephew lived there now.

> Appropriate transitional words and phrases clarify the relationships between ideas.

W_G *Prentice Hall Writing and Grammar Connection: Diamond Level, Chapter 9, Sections 1–5*

Extension Activities

Listening and Speaking With a small group, research China's revolution of 1911–1912 and deliver an **oral report** on the subject. Use these tips to prepare:

- Organize the topic into categories, and assign independent research tasks.
- Choose a facilitator, and divide up responsibilities for the presentation.

As you prepare your report, create smooth transitions between topics and speakers. **[Group Activity]**

Research and Technology In this story, Jun-tu is born in the "intercalary" month. Using both electronic and print resources, research a calendar system created by another culture. Then, create a **visual display** that compares and contrasts the system you have researched with the one used in the West.

 **Take It to the Net** PHSchool.com

Go online for an additional research activity using the Internet.

Prepare to Read

The Artist

Rabindranath Tagore (1861–1941)

In 1915, the Indian writer Rabindranath Tagore (rə bēn´ drə nät´ tä´ gôr) was knighted by the British government in recognition of his literary contributions. This was one of the British Empire's highest honors, yet four years later Tagore renounced his title. He did so to protest the Amritsar (əm rit´ sər) Massacre, in which British troops fired on a group of unarmed Indian protesters.

A Gifted Family Tagore was born in Bengal, which was then a province of British India. Tagore's family was highly accomplished. His father was a famous Hindu philosopher and religious reformer. Other members of Tagore's family distinguished themselves in art, music, and finance. A gifted child with a wide range of intellectual and artistic talents, Tagore began writing at the age of eight. He composed both poems and short stories, producing a series of books while he was still in his twenties. This highly productive period culminated with the publication of *Manasi* (mä nä´ sē), one of his finest collections of verse, in 1890.

A Witness to Suffering In 1891, Tagore moved to his father's estate in a rural section of Bengal, where he developed a deep awareness of the poverty and other hardships faced by so many of India's inhabitants. From that point on, his social concerns became the dominant focus of his life. Among the many contributions that he made to Indian society were his establishment of a university and a progressive, open-air school in western Bengal. He was also a vocal supporter of human rights and personal freedom, though he did not press for Indian independence from Britain.

A Prolific Writer Despite involvement in other activities, Tagore remained a productive writer throughout his life. Altogether he produced more than one thousand poems, two dozen plays, eight novels, and several collections of short stories.

Generally, Tagore's poems and stories are considered to be his strongest works. His poems are characterized by a quiet simplicity and dignity, and his short stories are noted for their irony, subtle humor, and social and philosophical themes. Among his most famous collections of poems and short stories are *The Golden Boat* (1894), *Late Harvest* (1896), *Dreams* (1896), *Song Offerings* (1910), and *Bunches of Tales* (1912).

Fame in the West With the publication of the English version of *Gitanjali: Song Offerings* in 1912, Tagore's reputation was firmly established in the West. In his introduction to the English translation, the great Irish poet William Butler Yeats commented, "These lyrics—which are in the original . . . full of subtlety of rhythm, untranslatable delicacies of color, of metrical invention—display in their thought a world I have dreamed of all my life long." The English translation of *Song Offerings*, along with his role in introducing Indian literature to the Western world, earned Tagore the Nobel Prize in Literature in 1913.

A Man of Many Talents Although it is not a well-known fact outside India, Tagore's artistic talents were by no means limited to writing. A gifted musician and composer, he wrote more than two thousand songs and helped create a new style of Indian music. In addition, he was also a talented painter, considered by many art critics to be the finest Indian artist of his time.

Preview

Connecting to the Literature

The struggle between the pursuit of money and the pursuit of happiness is as ancient as civilization itself. In this story, that struggle becomes the dominant theme in the life of one family.

Literary Analysis

Conflict

Conflict, the struggle between opposing forces, is a key element of fiction because most plots develop from conflict. While there are many different types of literary conflict, they can be divided into two general categories:

- *Internal conflict* occurs within the mind of a character and involves a struggle with ideas, beliefs, attitudes, or emotions.
- *External conflict* takes place between a character and an outside force, such as another person, society, nature, fate, or God.

As you read, use a chart like the one shown to examine the conflicts in this story and to categorize them as either internal or external.

Conflicts	
External	**Internal**
1. Govinda's conflict with Satyabati	1.
2.	2.

Connecting Literary Elements

Characters are the people or animals who take part in the action of a literary work. Like a real person, **round characters** are complex and multi-faceted, displaying both good and bad qualities. By contrast, **flat characters** are one-dimensional. As you read, analyze the characters and determine whether they are round and multifaceted or flat and one-dimensional.

Reading Strategy

Identifying Cause and Effect

A **cause** is an event, an action, or a feeling that produces a result. An **effect** is the result that is produced. Sometimes, words like *because, so,* and *therefore* signal causes and effects. However, fiction writers often develop events without presenting such obvious connections. As you read this story, identify the causes and effects of each character's feelings, thoughts, and actions.

Vocabulary Development

meager (mē´ gər) *adj.* thin; lean (p. 1142)

terminology (tur´ mə näl´ ə jē) *n.* terms used in a specific discipline (p. 1142)

frugality (froo gal´ ə tē) *n.* thrift (p. 1144)

connotations (kän´ ə tā´ shənz) *n.* ideas suggested by a word that go beyond its concrete meaning (p. 1144)

equable (ek´ wə bəl) *adj.* steady; uniform (p. 1144)

squandered (skwän´ dərd) *v.* wasted (p. 1144)

disdain (dis dān´) *n.* strong dislike (p. 1146)

myriad (mir´ ē əd) *adj.* many; varied (p. 1147)

enumerating (ē noo´ mər āt´ iŋ) *v.* counting; listing (p. 1147)

THE ARTIST

Rabindranath Tagore

translated by Mary Lago, Tarun Gupta, and Amiya Chakravarty

Background

Rabindranath Tagore is best known as a writer and painter, but he was also a teacher whose theories of education have had an international impact. For Tagore, creativity was the essence of both human beings and the natural world. He believed that traditional education, with its emphasis on uniformity and facts, encouraged children to ignore both their natural creativity and their connections to the world around them. To address this issue, Tagore established a school in Bengal in 1901. Classes were held outdoors. Each day began and ended with an artistic activity. This story reflects these same views about the importance of creativity in people's lives and provides an indictment of modern materialistic values.

Govinda came to Calcutta after graduation from high school in Mymensingh.[1] His widowed mother's savings were <u>meager</u>, but his own unwavering determination was his greatest resource. "I *will* make money," he vowed, "even if I have to give my whole life to it." In his <u>terminology</u>, wealth was always referred to as *pice*.[2] In other words he had in mind a very concrete image of something that could be seen, touched, and smelled; he was not greatly fascinated with fame, only with the very ordinary *pice*, eroded by circulation from market to market, from hand to hand, the tarnished *pice*, the *pice* that smells of copper, the original form of Kuvera,[3] who assumes the assorted guises of silver, gold, securities, and wills, and keeps men's minds in a turmoil.

After traveling many tortuous roads and getting muddied repeatedly in the process, Govinda had now arrived upon the solidly paved embankment of his wide and free-flowing stream of money. He was firmly seated in the manager's chair at the MacDougal Gunnysack Company. Everyone called him MacDulal.

When Govinda's lawyer-brother, Mukunda,[4] died, he left behind a wife, a four-year-old son, a house in Calcutta, and some cash savings.

meager (mē´ gər) *adj.* thin; lean

terminology (tur´ mə näl´ ə jē) *n.* terms used in a specific discipline

---

1. **Calcutta** (kal kut´ ə) ... **Mymensingh** (mī´ mən siŋ´) Calcutta is a seaport in northeastern India; Mymensingh, now in Bangladesh, is about 190 miles northeast of Calcutta.
2. *pice* (pīs) Indian coin.
3. **Kuvera** (koo ver´ ä) Hindu god of wealth, usually spelled Kubera.
4. **Mukunda** (mə koon´ də).

Reading Check

After graduating from high school, what did Govinda vow?

▲ **Critical Viewing** This collage includes a postage stamp and an architectural detail. What do these images suggest about the role of art in daily Indian life? Explain. **[Draw Conclusions]**

In addition to his property there was some debt; therefore, provision for his family's needs depended upon <u>frugality</u>. Thus his son, Chunilal,[5] was brought up in circumstances that were undistinguished in comparison with those of the neighbors.

Mukunda's will gave Govinda entire responsibility for this family. Ever since Chunilal was a baby, Govinda had bestowed spiritual initiation upon his nephew with the sacred words: "Make money."

The main obstacle to the boy's initiation was his mother, Satyabati.[6] She said nothing outright; her opposition showed in her behavior. Art had always been her hobby. There was no limit to her enthusiasm for creating all sorts of original and decorative things from flowers, fruits and leaves, even foodstuffs, from paper and cloth cutouts, from clay and flour, from berry juices and the juices of other fruits, from *jaba-* and *shiuli-*flower stems. This activity brought her considerable grief, because anything unessential or irrational has the character of flash floods in July: it has considerable mobility, but in relation to the utilitarian[7] concerns of life it is like a stalled ferry. Sometimes there were invitations to visit relatives; Satyabati forgot them and spent the time in her bedroom with the door shut, kneading a lump of clay. The relatives said, "She's terribly stuck-up." There was no satisfactory reply to this. Mukunda had known, even on the basis of his bookish knowledge, that value judgments can be made about art too. He had been thrilled by the noble <u>connotations</u> of the word "art," but he could not conceive of its having any connection with the work of his own wife.

This man's nature had been very <u>equable.</u> When his wife <u>squandered</u> time on unessential whims, he had smiled at it with affectionate delight. If anyone in the household made a slighting remark, he had protested immediately. There had been a singular self-contradiction in Mukunda's makeup; he had been an expert in the practice of law, but it must be conceded that he had had no worldly wisdom with regard to his household affairs. Plenty of money had passed through his hands, but since it had not preoccupied his thoughts, it had left his mind free. Nor could he have tyrannized over his dependents in order to get his own way. His living habits had been very simple; he had never made any unreasonable demands for the attention or services of his relatives.

Mukunda had immediately silenced anyone in the household who cast an aspersion[8] upon Satyabati's disinterest in housework. Now and

Themes in World Literature

Obsessions With Wealth

Literature throughout the world expresses the uneasy relationship people have with money.

For Tagore, money is decidedly negative. Wealth and its pursuit is a distraction from the values of creativity and spirituality that really matter. In *The Canterbury Tales*, the English poet Geoffrey Chaucer adopted the biblical viewpoint that the love of money is the root of all evil.

Other writers treat the issue more gently. For example, Jane Austen, the English novelist, described characters who marry for love but gain fortune as a bonus. Likewise, Charles Dickens writes of characters who gain wealth without losing their virtue. For example, in his novel *Great Expectations*, a fortune comes to the kind, loyal, and industrious Pip. For Pip, riches are a blessing, not an evil.

frugality (fro͞o gal´ ə tē) *n.* thrift

connotations (kän´ ə tā´ shənz) *n.* ideas suggested by a word that go beyond its concrete meaning

equable (ek´ wə bəl) *adj.* steady; uniform

squandered (skwän´ dərd) *v.* wasted

---

5. **Chunilal** (cho͞o´ nē lal)
6. **Satyabati** (sət´ yə bə´ tē)
7. **utilitarian** (yo͞o til ə ter´ ē ən) *adj.* stressing usefulness.
8. **aspersion** (ə spʉr´ zhən) *n.* damaging or disparaging remark.

then, on his way home from court, he would stop at Radhabazar to buy some paints, some colored silk and colored pencils, and stealthily[9] he would go and arrange them on the wooden chest in his wife's bedroom. Sometimes, picking up one of Satyabati's drawings, he would say, "Well, this one is certainly very beautiful."

One day he had held up a picture of a man, and since he had it upside down, he had decided that the legs must be a bird's head. He had said, "Satu, this should be framed—what a marvelous picture of a stork!" Mukunda had gotten a certain delight out of thinking of his wife's artwork as child's play, and the wife had taken a similar pleasure in her husband's judgment of art. Satyabati had known perfectly well that she could not hope for so much patience, so much indulgence, from any other family in Bengal.[10] No other family would have made way so lovingly for her overpowering devotion to art. So, whenever her husband had made extravagant remarks about her painting, Satyabati could scarcely restrain her tears.

One day Satyabati lost even this rare good fortune. Before his death her husband had realized one thing quite clearly: the responsibility for his debt-ridden property must be left in the hands of someone astute enough to skillfully steer even a leaky boat to the other shore. This is how Satyabati and her son came to be placed completely under Govinda's care. From the very first day Govinda made it plain to her that the *pice* was the first and foremost thing in life. There was such profound degradation in his advice that Satyabati would shrink with shame.

Nevertheless, the worship of money continued in diverse forms in their daily life. If there had been some modesty about it, instead of such constant discussion, it wouldn't have been so bad. Satyabati knew in her heart that all of this lowered her son's standard of values, but there was nothing to do but endure it. Since those delicate emotions endowed with uncommon dignity are the most vulnerable, they are very easily hurt or ridiculed by rude or insensitive people.

The study of art requires all sorts of supplies. Satyabati had received these for so long without even asking that she had felt no reticence[11] with regard to them. Amid the new circumstances in the family she felt terribly ashamed to charge all these unessential items to the housekeeping budget. So she would save money by economizing on her own food and have the supplies purchased and brought in secretly. Whatever work she did was done furtively,[12] behind closed

Literary Analysis
Round and Flat Characters Would you describe Mukunda as a round or flat character? Explain.

Literary Analysis
Conflict What is the nature of the conflict between Satyabati and Govinda?

✓**Reading Check**

To what activity is Satyabati devoted?

---

9. **stealthily** (stel´ the lē) *adv.* secretly or slyly.
10. **Bengal** (ben gôl´) region in northeastern India.
11. **reticence** (ret´ ə səns) *n.* quality or state of being habitually silent or uncommunicative.
12. **furtively** (fʉr´ tiv lē) *adv.* slyly; secretively.

doors. She was not afraid of a scolding, but the stares of insensitive observers embarrassed her.

Now Chuni was the only spectator and critic of her artistic activity. Gradually he became a participant. He began to feel its intoxication. The child's offense could not be concealed, since it overflowed the pages of his notebook onto the walls of the house. There were stains on his face, on his hands, on the cuffs of his shirt. Indra,[13] the king of the gods, does not spare even the soul of a little boy in the effort to tempt him away from the worship of money.

On the one hand the restraint increased, on the other hand the mother collaborated in the violations. Occasionally the head of the company would take his office manager, Govinda, along on business trips out of town. Then the mother and son would get together in unrestrained joy. This was the absolute extreme of childishness! They drew pictures of animals that God has yet to create. The likeness of the dog would get mixed up with that of the cat. It was difficult to distinguish between fish and fowl. There was no way to preserve all these creations; their traces had to be thoroughly obliterated before the head of the house returned. Only Brahma, the Creator, and Rudra, the Destroyer, witnessed the creative delight of these two persons; Vishnu,[14] the heavenly Preserver, never arrived.

The compulsion for artistic creation ran strong in Satyabati's family. There was an older nephew, Rangalal, who rose overnight to fame as an artist. That is to say, the connoisseurs of the land roared with laughter at the unorthodoxy of his art. Since their stamp of imagination did not coincide with his, they had a violent scorn for his talent. But curiously enough, his reputation thrived upon <u>disdain</u> and flourished in this atmosphere of opposition and mockery. Those who imitated him most

Two Gazelle, From the Babar Nama, 1530, New Delhi National Museum, Borromeo

▲ Critical Viewing
Do you think this painting effectively captures Satyabati's and Chunilal's love of art? **[Evaluate]**

disdain (dis dān´) *n.* strong dislike

---

13. **Indra** (in´ drə) chief god of the early Hindu religion.
14. **Brahma** (brä´ mə) . . . **Rudra** (rōō´ drə) . . . **Vishnu** (vish´ nōō) In the Hindu religion, Brahma is the creator of the universe, Rudra is the god of destruction and reproduction, and Vishnu is the god of preservation.

took it upon themselves to prove that the man was a hoax as an artist, that there were obvious defects even in his technique.

This much-maligned artist came to his aunt's home one day, at a time when the office manager was absent. After persistent knocking and shoving at the door he finally got inside and found that there was nowhere to set foot on the floor. The cat was out of the bag.

"It is obvious," said Rangalal, "that the image of creation has emerged anew from the soul of the artist; this is not random scribbling. He and that god who creates form are the same age. Get out all the drawings and show them to me."

Where should they get the drawings? That artist who draws pictures all over the sky in <u>myriad</u> colors, in light and shadow, calmly discards his mists and mirages. Their creations had gone the same way. With an oath Rangalal said to his aunt, "From now on, I'll come and get whatever you make."

There came another day when the office manager had not returned. Since morning the sky had brooded in the shadows of July; it was raining. No one monitored the hands of the clock and no one wanted to know about them. Today Chuni began to draw a picture of a sailing boat while his mother was in the prayer room. The waves of the river looked like a flock of hungry seals just on the point of swallowing the boat. The clouds seemed to cheer them on and float their shawls overhead, but the seals were not conventional seals, and it would be no exaggeration to say of the clouds: "Light and mist merge in the watery waste." In the interests of truth it must be said that if boats were built like this one, insurance companies would never assume such risks. Thus the painting continued; the sky-artist drew fanciful pictures, and inside the room the wide-eyed boy did the same.

No one realized that the door was open. The office manager appeared. He roared in a thunderous voice, "What's going on?"

The boy's heart jumped and his face grew pale. Now Govinda perceived the real reason for Chunilal's examination errors in historical dates. Meanwhile the crime became all the more evident as Chunilal tried unsuccessfully to hide the drawing under his shirt. As Govinda snatched the picture away, the design he saw on it further astonished him. Errors in historical dates would be preferable to this. He tore the picture to pieces. Chunilal burst out crying.

From the prayer room Satyabati heard the boy's weeping, and she came running. Both Chunilal and the torn pieces of the picture were on the floor. Govinda went on <u>enumerating</u> the reasons for his nephew's failure in the history examination and suggesting dire remedies.

Satyabati had never said a word about Govinda's behavior toward them. She had quietly endured everything, remembering that this was the person on whom her husband had relied. Now her eyes were wet with tears, and shaking with anger, she said hoarsely, "Why did you tear up Chuni's picture?"

myriad (mir′ ē əd) *adj.* many; varied

enumerating (ē noō′ mər āt′ iŋ) *v.* counting; listing

✔**Reading Check**

Who gradually becomes a participant in Satyabati's artistic activity?

Govinda said, "Doesn't he have to study? What will become of him in the future?"

" Even if he becomes a beggar in the street," answered Satyabati, "he'll be better off in the future. But I hope he'll never be like you. May his pride in his God-given talent be more than your pride in *pices*. This is my blessing for him, a mother's blessing."

"I can't neglect my responsibility," said Govinda. "I will not tolerate this. Tomorrow I'll send him to a boarding school; otherwise, you'll ruin him."

The office manager returned to the office. The rain fell in torrents and the streets flowed with water.

Holding her son's hand, Satyabati said, "Let's go, dear."

Chuni said, "Go where, Mother?"

"Let's get out of this place."

The water was knee-deep at Rangalal's door. Satyabati came in with Chunilal. She said, "My dear boy, you take charge of him. Keep him from the worship of money."

Review and Assess

Thinking About the Selection

1. **Respond:** Which perspective of the world do you think is more realistic—Satyabati's or Govinda's? Explain.

2. **(a) Recall:** What did Govinda show an "unwavering determination" to obtain? **(b) Interpret:** How does he regard Satyabati's art? **(c) Compare and Contrast:** Compare and contrast Mukunda's attitude toward both money and art with Govinda's.

3. **(a) Recall:** How do "the connoisseurs of the land" regard Rangalal's art? **(b) Connect:** In what ways are Rangalal's art and that of Satyabati and Chunilal similar? **(c) Analyze:** Based on these descriptions, do you think the author values art more as a product or as an activity? Explain.

4. **(a) Interpret:** Who is the sky-artist? **(b) Analyze:** What is Tagore suggesting about the relationship between artistic expression and spirituality?

5. **(a) Interpret:** Why does Govinda take on the responsibility for Satyabati and Chunilal? **(b) Evaluate:** What does this arrangement suggest about Indian culture, particularly the roles of women, at the time of the story?

6. **Make a Judgment:** Do you think Satyabati's actions at the end of the story are wise? Explain.

Review and Assess

Literary Analysis

Conflict

1. (a) What values does Govinda try to instill in Chunilal? (b) In what ways do his values create an **external conflict** with Satyabati?
2. What **internal conflicts** does Satyabati experience as a result of her external conflict with Govinda?
3. (a) When does the conflict between Govinda and Satyabati reach its point of greatest intensity? (b) How is the conflict resolved?
4. Both Govinda and Satyabati embody specific values. (a) What values does each character represent? (b) Based on these values, what conflict in society as a whole does this story express? Explain.

Connecting Literary Elements

5. (a) When he was alive, how did Mukunda manage his work, his relationship with Satyabati, and his dealings with their relatives? (b) Is Mukunda a **flat** or a **round character**? Explain.
6. Both Govinda and Satyabati have obsessions. (a) Compare and contrast the effects these obsessions have on their lives. (b) Do you think either Govinda or Satyabati is a flat character? Explain.

Reading Strategy

Identifying Cause and Effect

7. (a) Use a chart like the one shown to **identify causes and effects** in this story, beginning with Mukunda's death.

Mukunda's Death		
Effect	**Effect**	**Effect**

   (b) Choose one of these effects and describe how it, in turn, becomes the cause of another series of events.
8. (a) What is the cause of Satyabati's decision to practice her art in secret? (b) What effect does this secrecy have on her son?

Extend Understanding

9. **Cultural Connection:** How might this story be different if it were set in contemporary America? Explain your answer.

Integrate Language Skills

Vocabulary Development Lesson

Word Analysis: Greek Word Part *-logy*

The Greek word part *-logy* means "the science, theory, or study of." Therefore, *terminology* means the "system of words used in a specific field." Match the word containing the word part *-logy* in the left column with its definition in the right column.

1. theology   **a.** study of life
2. geology   **b.** study of Earth's physical history
3. biology   **c.** study of religion

Spelling Strategy

In words ending in a consonant preceded by two vowels, do not double the final consonant before adding a suffix: *disdain + -ed = disdained.* Add the indicated suffix to each of the words below.

1. certain + *-ly*   2. claim + *-ed*

Fluency: Words in Context

Review the vocabulary list on page 1141. Then, fill in the blanks in the paragraph with the appropriate words from the list.

The book was so successful, it created a whole new ___?___. Kids used their ___?___ funds to buy copies. While some adults looked on with ___?___, believing that their kids had ___?___ their money, others had more ___?___ feelings. They felt that the book fostered good values and had no negative ___?___. They encouraged ___?___, but they also knew that their children would find a ___?___ of products they wanted to buy.

Grammar and Style Lesson
Appositives and Appositive Phrases

An **appositive** is a noun or pronoun placed near another noun or pronoun to provide additional information about it. When an appositive is accompanied by its own modifiers, it forms an **appositive phrase.**

If an appositive is essential to the meaning of a sentence, commas are not used. If an appositive can be omitted without affecting the meaning, it is set off with commas.

> **Nonessential:** Indra, <u>the king of the gods</u>, does not spare even the soul of a little boy . . .
>
> **Essential:** The story "<u>The Artist</u>" condemns materialism.

Practice Rewrite each sentence below, incorporating the information given as an appositive.

1. Govinda worshipped money. (*the villain*)
2. He tried to influence his nephew. (*Chunilal*)
3. Satyabati pursued her dream. (*an artist*)
4. Rangalal encouraged Satyabati. (*a painter*)
5. Satyabati turned to her nephew for help. (*Rangalal*)

Writing Application Write a paragraph in which you use an appositive or an appositive phrase to describe each character from "The Artist."

 Prentice Hall Writing and Grammar Connection: Diamond Level, Chapter 19, Section 1

Writing Lesson

Newspaper Editorial

Newspaper editorials provide a public forum for citizens to express their opinions about pressing issues. As Satyabati, write an editorial in which you argue for a different emphasis in society's values.

Prewriting   Reread the story, taking notes about the values that Satyabati holds dear. Identify experiences in her life that demonstrate the importance of these values. Note ways in which Govinda's worship of money is damaging to himself, his family, and society as a whole.

Drafting   Write an introduction with a vivid anecdote or quotation. Then, clearly state Satyabati's thesis. As you build your body paragraphs, anticipate and address opposing viewpoints.

Model: Drafting to Address Opposing Viewpoints

Of course, we need a strong economy. We need people who can run businesses successfully. However, we also need creative people. Art does not detract from our financial success. Rather, it helps us be successful.

> Anticipating and addressing opposing viewpoints strengthens an argument.

Revising   Read your editorial to identify sections that could be more persuasive. Add or eliminate details to strengthen the overall impression.

W̶G̶ Prentice Hall Writing and Grammar Connection: Diamond Level, Chapter 7, Section 7

Extension Activities

Research and Technology In this story, Govinda assumes responsibility for his brother's family after the brother's death. With a small group, research and deliver a **group report** on the traditions and laws that dictate such after-death arrangements in India. Follow these tips to prepare:

- Use photographs, illustrations, or other visual aids.
- Organize the material so that ideas flow smoothly between speakers.

If necessary, do additional research to fill in gaps in your information. **[Group Activity]**

Listening and Speaking Find a collection of Tagore's poetry, and select two or three poems that share a similar theme. Write an introduction and conclusion, and deliver a **themed reading.** To prepare, read the poems aloud, stressing different words to emphasize meaning. Find an appropriate tone, and pace your delivery.

 **Take It to the Net**   PHSchool.com

Go online for an additional research activity using the Internet.

Writing About Literature

Compare and Contrast Literary Trends Across Cultures

The Modern Era, from 1890 to 1945, was a period remade by catastrophic wars, economic upheaval, and revolutionary discoveries in science and technology. Both the form and the content of the work of writers around the world reflected these turbulent times.

The literary movement known as Modernism focused on the themes of uncertainty, alienation, and despair. Write an essay that compares the treatment of these themes in selected works in this unit. Details of the assignment are outlined in the box at the right.

Prewriting

Review the selections. Review the works in this unit, answering the following questions:

- Is the theme of alienation or despair stated or strongly implied in this work?

- In what ways does the writer develop this theme?

- Do formal aspects of this work—for example, the lack of exposition, transitions, and resolution or the use of free verse—reflect this theme?

- In what way does the writer's culture affect the treatment of the theme?

Gather evidence. After you have chosen the works you will discuss in your paper, begin comparing and contrasting the selections by filling in a chart similar to the one below. Use your chart to begin sorting similarities and differences among the works by culture. Then, return to the works to select quotations and specific details of content or form to support your analysis.

Assignment: Alienation Across Cultures

Write an essay comparing the themes of uncertainty, alienation, and despair in works of at least two of the cultures in this unit.

Criteria:

- Include a thesis statement that defines these themes and draws from your analysis of the literature.
- Support your thesis with detailed analyses of at least two works, each from a different culture.
- Cite evidence of each similarity and difference you explore.
- Approximate length: 1,500 words

Read to Write

As you reread the texts, look for the theme in the setting, the plot, or the characters. In poetry, also look for the theme in symbols and in formal elements, such as the use of fragmented sentences.

Model: Charting to Compare and Contrast Treatments of Theme

Selection	How Work Demonstrates Theme	Cultural Tie
"Interior of the Rose"	mystery of a rose	rose common subject in poetry of Europe
"Everything Is Plundered"	acknowledges and rejects despair	destruction of homeland caused by war

Write three focus statements. Based on your review of the literature, write three focus statements. In the first, *define the themes* that you will explore in your essay. In the second, *explain the impact of the theme on form* (if any) in the works you have chosen. In the third, *explain the effect of culture on theme* in these works. Build the introduction for your essay around these three focus statements.

Drafting

Outline. Use information from your chart to make a working outline. In the major headings, list the similarities and differences you will discuss. In the subheadings, list the evidence from the literature.

> **Model: Making a Working Outline**
>
> I. World is strange, not set up in human terms
>   A. "Interior of the Rose"
>   1. Interior of the rose changes world
>   a. ". . . a room enclosed in a dream"
>   B. "Under Reconstruction"
>   1. Construction work in hotel represents unsettledness of postwar life

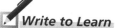

Write to Learn

Remember that your outline is only a guide. Include information that supports your arguments even if it doesn't fit neatly into your outline.

Refer to historical events. Be as specific as you can in describing historical events that shaped the writer's perspective and in explaining their significance.

Revising and Editing

Review content: Check for accuracy. Did the character wear a red jacket? Did the speaker say, "Oh, my aching heart" or "Oh, my breaking heart"? Absolute accuracy is essential if you want readers to take your ideas seriously. Check each reference in your paper for accuracy.

Write to Explain

Connect your thoughts clearly so that readers can follow your arguments. Do not leave out any logical steps. The more closely your readers can follow your thinking, the more persuasive your ideas will be.

Review style: Vary sentence structure. Choose varied sentence structures to add variety to your writing.

Choppy: The love of nature is a universal theme in poetry. It is a theme that appears in all eras. But the tone of Rilke's "Interior of the Rose" is Modernist. The tone of pain and uncertainty in the poem shows this.

Varied: The love of nature is a universal theme in poetry, one that appears in all eras. But the tone of pain and uncertainty in Rilke's "Interior of the Rose" places the poem well within the Modernist camp.

Publishing and Presenting

Give a dramatic reading. Read excerpts for the class from two of the selections you discussed in your essay. Then, explain why you compared these selections.

𝒲𝒢 *Writing and Grammar Connection: Diamond Level, Chapter 9*

Writing WORKSHOP

Exposition: Multimedia Report

In a **multimedia report,** a presenter shares information, enhancing narration and explanation with media, such as video images, slides, audiotape recordings, music, and art. In this workshop, you will plan, draft, and revise a multimedia report.

Assignment Criteria Your multimedia report should feature the following elements:

- Well-integrated, varied audio and visual features
- A clear and logical organization
- Innovative use of relevant media to convey key concepts
- Effective pacing of media with smooth transitions between elements to create a comprehensible whole
- An enticing introduction and memorable conclusion

To preview the criteria on which your multimedia report may be assessed, refer to the Rubric on page 1157.

Prewriting

Choose a topic. A good topic for a multimedia report is one that interests you and for which appropriate multimedia material is available. If no topic comes readily to mind, **browse** through magazines for inspiration. List possible topics, and then choose the one that offers the most possibilities for a multimedia presentation.

Create a media checklist. In a chart similar to the one shown here, list the various categories of media that you believe will be available for your topic. In the right-hand column, note your ideas about how to use the various media.

Research the topic. As you research your topic, jot down ideas about creative ways to engage your audience. Consult your library for audio or video clips of interviews and for documentaries, music, and art resources. Search the Internet for similar resources. Consider using any medium that will help bring your topic to life.

Media Checklist	
☑ Music	Pachelbel *Canon in D*
☑ Videos	democracy flowchart
☑ Art	Rockwell's *Freedom of Speech* painting
☑ Photographs	various government images and symbols
☐ Computer Presentation	

Review for varied media. After your initial research, review the media you have located. If you find that most items fall into one category—for instance, still images—look for additional items to ensure that your report is rich in a variety of media, including sound clips, video, and still images.

Identify a thesis. Review your notes and materials. Develop a statement of the key ideas you intend to cover, and be guided by it as you draft.

Student Model

Before you begin drafting, read this student model and review the characteristics of an effective multimedia presentation.

Mark Sueyoshi
Palm Springs, California

The Government of the United States

Text	Audio and Video
[Cue AUDIO] There are three types of democracy. [Cue VIDEO]	AUDIO: Pachelbel *Canon in D* VIDEO CHART: A flowchart of democracy branching into different types, drawn out as the audience watches.
[Cue TRANSITION ZOOM] In democratic centralism, leaders (not elected by popular vote) decide what is best for the people. Examples of this form of democracy are the Soviet Union and China. [Cue SLIDES]	TRANSITION ZOOM: Zooms into Democratic Centralism rectangle. Democratic Centralism SLIDES: Rapid sequence showing flags or national symbols of USSR and China
[Cue VIDEO CHART, pause, then cue TRANSITION ZOOM] In direct democracy, each citizen participates directly in policy making. Governments that have used this form of democracy are ancient Greece and colonial New England. [Cue SLIDES]	TRANSITION ZOOM: Zooms into Direct Democracy rectangle. Direct Democracy SLIDES: Rapid sequence of images of ancient Athens, Norman Rockwell's *Freedom of Speech* painting of a New England town meeting, colonial Maryland
[Cue VIDEO CHART, pause, then cue TRANSITION ZOOM] And in representative democracy, citizens elect leaders to create policy. The United States maintains this form of government. [Cue SLIDES]	TRANSITION ZOOM: Zooms into Representative Democracy rectangle D.C. SLIDES: Rapid sequence of Washington images: Capitol Hill, White House, Lincoln Memorial
Direct democracy, appropriate for a town meeting, is not practical on a national level. [Cue VIDEO, AUDIO]	Busy People VIDEO: crowd scenes, such as city pedestrians at rush hour Crowd AUDIO: roar of a crowd
[Cue Timeline SLIDE] And so, for over 225 years the United States government has protected and served its citizens. [Cue VIDEO]	Timeline SLIDE: show major events in U.S. history Fireworks VIDEO: images of Fourth of July celebrations

Classical music establishes a formal tone appropriate to the subject.

Use of zoom technique adds motion and interest to charts on governments.

Mark provides clear directions to keep the flow of the presentation smooth.

Audiovisual elements provide a vivid and memorable conclusion.

Drafting

Outline your report. Create a broad working outline to organize your ideas in a logical fashion. The chart shown here outlines an effective sequence for a multimedia presentation.

Draft a script. Use your outline and notes to draft a script and plan your delivery. Write cues in your script to indicate what media to use and when to use them. Strive for a balance between the narrative, audio, and visual elements.

Prepare the equipment. Assemble all the equipment you will need for your presentation. Follow these suggestions for getting organized:

- Plan a logical arrangement of props and technology so you can reach each type of media easily.
- Cue pieces of equipment so you can run each with one touch at the appropriate moment in your script.
- Make sure everything is functioning properly.
- Work with an assistant if necessary.

Organize Your Report

Introduction: Present the topic and a thesis statement about it. Include a dramatic or vivid media element to win viewers' interest.

Body: Develop the thesis through exposition and examples, the text of which should be enhanced in places by other media.

Conclusion: Reiterate research that supports thesis.

Revising

Revise to clarify transitions and sequence. Make sure your report will flow smoothly when you present it to an audience.

1. Give a partner a copy of your script to follow as you present your report.
2. Ask your partner to place a check mark next to any points that were confusing, out of order, or that required transitions.
3. Rewrite as necessary to clarify sequence and connections among ideas. Eliminate awkward transitions.

Model: Revising to Improve Transitions

Direct democracy, appropriate for a town meeting, is not practical on a national level. [Cue repeat of Direct Democracy SLIDES] [Cue Busy People VIDEO]

~~Direct democracy SLIDES~~ ∧ *Busy People VIDEO: series of crowd scenes, such as city pedestrians at rush hour*

Mark deletes repetitive images and adds a more appropriate video to match his text.

Revise to improve variety of media. Review your script for overuse of a particular form of media and revise for variety.

Without variety: Play audio of interview with actor.
Play audio of interview with artist.
Play audio of interview with musician.

With variety: Play video footage of actor in performance.
Play audio footage of interview with artist to accompany slides of work.
Play CD by musician.

The plans below show the multimedia element of part of a presentation. Compare the model and the nonmodel.

Nonmodel	Model
SLIDE: chart of representative democracy SLIDES: Washington, D.C., images SLIDE: picture of crowd of pedestrians	TRANSITION ZOOM: chart of representative democracy SLIDES: Washington, D.C., images VIDEO: crowd scenes, such as rush hour AUDIO: roar of a crowd

Publishing and Presenting

Present your report. Deliver your multimedia report to your class, following these guidelines:

- Practice to familiarize yourself with your script.
- Have a backup plan in case any piece of equipment fails.
- Speak at an appropriate pace and volume, and maintain eye contact.

WG Writing and Grammar Connection: Diamond Level, Chapter 12

Rubric for Self-Assessment

Evaluate your mutimedia report using the following criteria and rating scale:

Criteria	Rating Scale Not very Very				
How varied are the media?	1	2	3	4	5
How well do media convey key ideas?	1	2	3	4	5
How well organized is the report?	1	2	3	4	5
How smooth are the transitions among media?	1	2	3	4	5
How effective is the pacing?	1	2	3	4	5

Listening and Speaking WORKSHOP

Analyze a Media Presentation

People are bombarded with information from various media sources daily. How can you wade through this deluge to evaluate the quality, thoroughness, and objectivity of the information that comes your way? The strategies on this page can help you **analyze media presentations**.

Evaluate the Content

News reports, documentaries, newsmagazines, editorials, and other types of media presentations have a specific purpose—to inform, to persuade, to entertain, or any combination of these. Consider the following points as you analyze news media presentations:

Identify the main idea. Like a headline in a newspaper, the first line of a broadcast report usually relates the most important idea of a news story. Pay careful attention to the type of story being reported and identify the viewpoint of the reporter.

Evaluate supporting evidence. Facts, statistics, quotations, and other evidence should give a sense of the diverse perspectives on an issue. Remember that so-called "objective" evidence can be used selectively to support a particular point of view.

Evaluate the Presentation

Following are some techniques that can be used to influence audience response:

- **Images** A photograph captures a moment in time, but an editor can choose among many photographs. The choice of a particular image can strongly influence an audience's feelings about a topic.
- **Slanted language** Commentators can present their views by means of explicit statements of opinion and subtle choices of words. Compare these sentences:

  The City Council approved the budget today. (objective)

  After avoiding the issues for a month, the City Council finally approved the budget today. (implies impatience)

- **"Experts"** Remember that the experts chosen to analyze news events have opinions. For example, an expert discussing a controversy in city policy may show bias by presenting the views of one side more sympathetically than the views of another. When you listen to an expert, consider that person's qualifications and motivations.

Feedback Form for a Media Presentation

Rating System
+ = Excellent   ✓ = Average   – = Weak

Content
Topic of story _____
Main point _____

Supporting Evidence
Expert interviews (with whom? to what effect?)
_____

Photographs/video (what is shown? to what effect?)
_____

Language (slanted language? to what effect?)
_____

What visual aids, if any, are used?
_____

Production Values
Effects of set _____
Effects of graphics _____
Effects of music/sound effects _____
Behavior of anchors/reporters _____

Activity: Analysis and Discussion Analyze a television news story using the Feedback Form above as a guide. Share your analysis in a class discussion.

Assessment WORKSHOP

Writer's Point of View

In the reading sections of some tests, you may be required to read a passage and interpret the writer's point of view. Use the following strategies to help you answer questions testing this skill:

- As you read, look for clues to the writer's attitude toward the subject.
- Remember that a writer can reveal his or her attitude in direct statements or indirectly through word choice or choice of details.
- The writer can reveal his or her attitude through tone. Ask yourself whether the tone of the passage is humorous, serious, or neutral.
- Look for changes in the writer's point of view.

Sample Test Item

Directions: Read the passage, and then answer the question that follows.

To me, Mr. Smith exemplifies the quiet heroism that characterizes many of the men of his generation. When he learned of his fatal illness, he carried on with his life, going to the office every day that he was well enough. He celebrated the holidays with his family and enjoyed choosing the perfect gift for each family member. Mr. Smith died shortly after the first of the year on the day after his birthday. He died at home in the early evening—peacefully and with dignity, just as he had lived.

1. What is the writer's attitude toward Mr. Smith?

A amusement

B amazement

C annoyance

D admiration

Answer and Explanation

The correct answer is **D**. From the first sentence, the writer clearly expresses admiration for Mr. Smith. At no point does the writer express a negative response, surprise, or humor, so responses **A**, **B**, and **C** are clearly incorrect.

Practice

Directions: Read the passage, and then answer the question that follows.

We all love wilderness areas, but did you know that Winnebago County already has 4,800 acres of wilderness? That's out of a county that has a total of only 53,000 acres! Fellow citizens, we will be going to the polls soon to vote on a referendum to add Parker's Bayou in perpetuity to the wilderness areas that remain undeveloped. Think twice, friends! Our county is having financial problems. Companies are leaving our area, in part because of a lack of land on which to build. Let's open Parker's Bayou to development. We could use more boating areas. We could use more industrial areas. We do not need more wilderness areas. Vote NO to additional wilderness acres on Tuesday.

1. Which statement best expresses the writer's point of view?

A Winnebago County already has enough wilderness areas.

B Winnebago County is a great place in which to live.

C Parker's Bayou is an unimportant part of Winnebago County.

D Winnebago County needs more wilderness areas.

Jazz le Cheval l'Écuyère et le Clown, Henri Matisse

(1946–Present)

❝*Liberty is the possibility of doubting, the possibility of making a mistake, the possibility of searching and experimenting....*❞

— Ignazio Silone,
from *The God That Failed*

Timeline 1946–Present

1946   **1956**   **1966**

Political and Cultural Events

- **1947** The transistor is invented.
- **1947** India and Pakistan gain independence.
- **1948** UN approves the Universal Declaration of Human Rights.
- **1948** The state of Israel is born.
- **1949** Communists seize power in China.
- **1950–1953** The Korean War is fought.
- **1952** United States explodes first hydrogen bomb.
- **1953** Watson and Crick discover the chemical basis of DNA. ◀

- **1957** The Russian satellite *Sputnik* goes into orbit. ▼

- **1959** A communist revolution is successful in Cuba.
- **1962** The Cuban missile crisis occurs.

- **1968** Many nations sign the Nuclear Non-Proliferation Treaty.
- **1969** The United States lands a man on the moon. ▼
- **1970s** The feminist movement is active in Western countries.
- **1971** The first microprocessor chip is introduced in the United States.
- **1975** After 20 years, the Vietnam War ends.
- **1975** The communist regime in Cambodia begins killing millions of Cambodians.

Literary Events

- **1947** French author Albert Camus publishes his novel *The Plague*. ▼
- **1947** Italian author Primo Levi publishes *Survival in Auschwitz*.

- **1958** African novelist Chinua Achebe publishes *Things Fall Apart*. ▲
- **1958** Romanian-born Elie Wiesel publishes his Holocaust novel *Night*.
- **1963** The Latin American "Boom" begins with the publication of Julio Cortázar's novel *Hopscotch*.

- **1966** German poet Nelly Sachs receives the Nobel Prize in Literature.
- **1967** Colombian Gabriel García Márquez publishes his novel *One Hundred Years of Solitude*.
- **1968** Japanese novelist Yasunari Kawabata wins the Nobel Prize in Literature.
- **1971** Pablo Neruda wins the Nobel Prize in Literature.
- **1972** Italian author Italo Calvino publishes *Invisible Cities*.

World Events

- **1977** The first mass-produced personal computers appear in the United States. ◄

- **1980** From 1950 until this year, more than 50 new nations have emerged in Africa.

- **1981** The disease known as AIDS is first reported by United States investigators.

- **1982–1983** World music becomes a genre.

- **1980s** More than 50,000 nuclear weapons exist.

- **1980s** European nations form the European Union (EU).

- **1989** Chinese government suppresses student demonstration in Tiananmen Square. ▼

- **1990–1991** The United States and allies defeat Iraq in first Persian Gulf War.

- **1990s** Apartheid ends in South Africa. ▼

- **1991** Soviet Union collapses.

- **1994** About 500,000 civilians killed in Rwanda ethnic conflicts.

- **1997** The Kyoto Protocol is formulated to control global warming.

- **2000** The Internet, a worldwide computer network, thrives.

- **2001** On September 11, hijackers crash planes into the World Trade Center and the Pentagon.

- **2003** The United States defeats Iraq in the second Gulf War.

- **1982** Gabriel García Márquez wins the Nobel Prize in Literature.

- **1983** Indian novelist R. K. Narayan publishes *A Tiger for Malgudi*.

- **1983** Caribbean author Jamaica Kincaid publishes her first book, *At the Bottom of the River*.

- **1986** Nigerian Wole Soyinka is the first black African to receive the Nobel Prize in Literature.

- **1992** Caribbean writer Derek Walcott wins Nobel Prize in Literature.

- **1996** Jamaica Kincaid publishes *The Autobiography of My Mother*.

- **1998** Bei Dao publishes a book of poems entitled *Blue House*.

- **1999** Günter Grass receives the Nobel Prize in Literature.

- **2001** R. K. Narayan dies.

- **2001** Lebanese poet Vénus Khoury-Ghata publishes *Here There Was Once a Country*.

The Contemporary World

(1946–PRESENT)

Historical Background

Perhaps the most important photograph of the postwar period is the picture of Earth from the moon. It shows a cloud-wrapped blue jewel of a planet, alone in the darkness of outer space. That jewel is ours. If we—the people of the world—do not learn how to cherish Earth and live in peace with one another, then our treasure will be lost. The history of the contemporary world reveals our failures and successes in this struggle.

The End of Colonialism and the Cold War In the postwar period, the colonial empires built by Western powers during the Age of Imperialism crumbled. In Asia and Africa, people demanded and won freedom. Between 1950 and 1980, more than 50 new nations arose in Africa alone. The new nations emerged into a world dominated and divided by the Cold War, a more than 40-year struggle between the United States and the Soviet Union. Each of these superpowers wanted new countries to adopt its ideology, or system of thought or belief—either capitalism or socialism.

Set up at the end of World War II as a forum for settling disputes, the United Nations (UN) played a vital role in decolonization. It has also tried to act as a peacekeeper and to provide valuable health, educational, and other services for the world's people.

Deadly Weapons Since the United States first exploded two atomic bombs in 1945, nations have been building nuclear weapons. The number of these weapons grew from 3 in 1945 to more than 50,000 in the 1980s. During the Cold War, efforts to curb the arms race had only limited success. Yet, in 1968, many nations signed the Nuclear Non-Proliferation Treaty (NPT), agreeing to halt the spread of nuclear weapons. In 1995, the treaty was renewed, but some nations still refused to sign.

Human Rights and Intervention In 1948, UN members approved the Universal Declaration of Human Rights, which proclaims that all people are entitled to basic freedoms. Nevertheless, human rights abuses, including torture and arbitrary arrest, continue to occur around the world. People have debated whether the world community should intervene to protect individual rights in a sovereign nation. The UN has a mixed record on intervention. In the 1990s, the UN sent peacekeepers to northern Iraq to protect the Kurds from persecution by the Iraqi government. The UN, however, was slow to move against Serbs who persecuted Muslims in Bosnia and did not intervene when Hutus massacred about one million Tutsis in Rwanda.

▲ **Critical Viewing** This photograph shows Earth as seen from the moon. What thoughts does it inspire in you? Explain. **[Respond]**

Terrorism: Deadly Politics Terrorism is the deliberate use of violence, especially against civilians, to achieve political results. Since the 1960s, incidents of terrorism have increased around the world. In 2001, an especially deadly incident occurred on United States soil when suicide bombers opposed to American policies in the Middle East crashed several hijacked airplanes into the World Trade Center in New York and the Pentagon in Washington, D.C., killing thousands.

The Global North and South The Cold War created an ideological split between the communist East and the capitalist West. Today, an economic gulf divides the world into two spheres—the relatively rich nations of the global North and the relatively poor nations of the global South. Nations of the North control much of the world's capital, trade, and technology. Yet, they depend increasingly on low-paid workers in developing states to provide manufactured goods as inexpensively as possible.

The Environment For both rich and poor nations, economic development has taken a heavy toll on the environment. In addition, over the last century, world temperatures have steadily increased. Scientists blame this global warming on the emission of gases into the upper atmosphere. Many warn that unless the world takes action, global warming will continue and cause great harm to the environment.

Old Ways and New In the Western world, industrialization and urbanization began during the Industrial Revolution. In the past fifty years, the rest of the world has experienced similar upheavals. Since 1945, people in the developing world have flocked to cities to find jobs and escape rural poverty. Many, settling in urban slums, have only changed the location of their poverty.

In recent times, religious revivals have swept many religions. Some religious reformers have been called fundamentalists because they stress what they see as the fundamental, or basic, values of their faiths. Many have sought political power to resist changes that they think undermine their beliefs.

▲ **Critical Viewing**
In this photograph, three firemen raise the American flag at Ground Zero, where the World Trade Center had stood on September 11, 2001. What roles did firefighters, police officers, and emergency workers play during and after the terrorist attacks that took place on that day? **[Connect]**

Women's Rights After 1945, women's movements brought changes to both the Western and the developing nations. The UN Charter supported "equal rights for men and women." By 1950, women had won the right to vote in many countries. In the industrialized world, more and more women worked outside the home; by the 1970s, the feminist movement sought equal rights for working women.

Science and Technology Since 1945, the computer has brought an information revolution. By 2000, a huge computer network, the Internet, linked individuals, governments, and businesses around the world, changing the way people learn, shop, and keep in touch with each other. (See Close-up on Culture, page 1170.)

In the field of medicine, vaccines helped prevent the spread of diseases. Recently, however, the spread of new deadly diseases, such as acquired immune deficiency syndrome (AIDS), has challenged researchers. In 1953, James Watson and Francis Crick analyzed the structure of DNA, the chemical underlying genetic inheritance. This discovery made possible the Human Genome Project (1990–present), whose goal is to locate every human gene and identify its chemical makeup.

The space age started in 1957 when the Soviet Union launched *Sputnik*, the first artificial satellite, into orbit. *Sputnik* set off a frantic "space race" between the superpowers. In 1969, the United States landed the first man on the moon. Since the Cold War ended, however, the United States and Russia have cooperated in joint space ventures.

Music in the Historical Context

The Growth of "World Music"

Portuguese fado, Brazilian samba, and Pakistani *qawwali* are diverse musical styles with something important in common. You can probably find all of them at a CD superstore under the category "world music." This grab bag of a genre includes traditional music from every corner of the globe, sometimes spiced with state-of-the-art technology or combined with current Western styles.

Almost every culture has been making music for countless years, but "world music," as such, is only about twenty years old. This genre was the brainchild of store owners and media executives in the United States and Britain who wanted to sell foreign music to Western consumers. Starting out as a marketing idea, it gained momentum with the establishment of a world music chart in 1990 and a world music Grammy Award in 1991.

Today, this category goes beyond CD ratings and sales. Like world literature, world music helps different cultures understand and appreciate one another.

So, if you want to learn about other cultures by adding new flavors to your musical diet, try feasting on Polynesian choirs, the epic songs of Baluchistan bards, or the calypsos of Costa Rica.

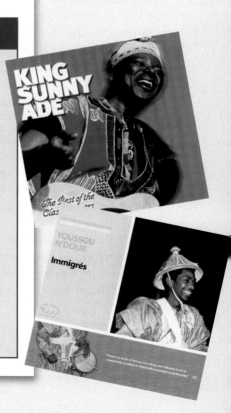

Despite the importance of global issues and trends, not every region experienced the postwar period in the same way. The following summaries focus on specific areas.

Latin America Despite setbacks, Latin American nations have tried to sustain economic growth and overcome a legacy of poverty and social inequality. Marxism, military rule, and the Roman Catholic Church have been continuing influences in the region. The United States has also exerted a strong influence on Latin American politics. After the communist revolution in Cuba in 1959, the region became the focus of intense Cold War rivalries. Of the larger nations, Mexico enjoyed economic gains, but most of its people remained in poverty. As of 2003, Argentina was facing an economic crisis, and Brazil had just elected a leftist president.

Europe, West and East Many Western European nations joined with the United States in NATO (North Atlantic Treaty Organization), the alliance that opposed the Soviet Union during the Cold War. Protected by NATO's umbrella, Western Europe enjoyed strong economic growth. Many nations introduced the welfare state, although in the 1980s, economic slowdowns forced cuts in social programs. European nations formed the European Community (EC) in 1957 and the European Union (EU) in the 1980s and 1990s. In 1999, the EU launched a single currency called the euro.

Efforts to reform inefficiencies in government and the economy led to the collapse of the Soviet Union in 1991. After shaking off Soviet domination, nations of Eastern Europe faced economic challenges and ethnic conflicts. Many of them will join the EU. Yugoslavia, a Soviet ally, experienced a breakup into warring nations and ethnic groups, with NATO military pressure resolving crises in Bosnia and Kosovo.

The Middle East Nationalistic and religious struggles have made this region a trouble spot. Israel's declaration of statehood in 1948 represented a rebirth of the Jewish spirit after the Holocaust, the systematic destruction of Jews by the Nazis. Since 1948, however, Israelis and Arabs have engaged in a long struggle punctuated by several wars. In addition, the United States fought two wars against Iraq, in 1990–1991 and again in 2003, when it finally toppled the regime of Saddam Hussein. Both Islamic fundamentalism and pro-democratic movements are significant forces in this region.

Africa Leaders of new African nations set out to build strong central governments, achieve economic growth, and raise standards of living. They have faced a variety of obstacles, including economic dependency and political instability. After independence, a number of new nations experienced military or one-party rule. Many have since introduced multiparty democracy. African nations also experimented with different

Los Papagayos ("The Parrots") (detail), 1986, Beatriz Gonzalez, Courtesy of the artist, Bogota, Colombia

▲ **Critical Viewing**
The Parrots, a painting by Beatriz Gonzalez, is a commentary on Latin American politics. Judging by the images and colors in this detail from the painting, what statement is the artist making? Explain.
[Interpret]

economic systems, including socialism and mixed economies, which combine capitalism and central control. In the 1990s, after decades of conflict, South Africa abandoned its system of apartheid, or racial separation, and made a transition to democratic rule.

Asia After its defeat in World War II, Japan introduced democratic reforms and by the 1960s emerged as an economic superpower. Similarly, nations such as Taiwan, Singapore, and South Korea underwent rapid industrialization. In 1949, Mao Zedong led a communist takeover of power in China. Since Mao's death in 1976, communist leaders have attempted to modernize China economically. The violent suppression of student demonstrations in Tiananmen Square (1989), however, showed the regime's determination to keep individual freedoms in check.

Cold War tensions sparked devastating conflicts in Korea, Vietnam, and Cambodia. The Korean War (1950–1953) pitted North Korea and China against South Korea and United Nations forces led by the United States. In the Vietnam War (1955–1975), which was also fought in Cambodia and Laos, the United States failed to prevent communist North Vietnam from taking over South Vietnam. Cambodian communists who seized power after winning a civil war (1975) killed millions of Cambodians.

Since gaining independence in 1947, India and Pakistan have faced rapid urbanization, population growth, and border conflicts with one another. India has built on the legacy of British rule to create the world's largest democracy, although it is still troubled by conflicts between Muslims and Hindus. In Muslim Pakistan, the military has periodically seized power from corrupt civilian regimes, and Islamic parties have gained in recent elections.

▲ **Critical Viewing**
This photograph was taken in Nairobi National Park, Kenya. What messages does it convey about a contemporary African nation? Explain. **[Interpret]**

Literature

No one knows which of today's works will become tomorrow's classics. (See the Point/Counterpoint feature, below.) What is sure, however, is that writers from many nations are producing exciting and challenging literature.

The Latin American "Boom" The postwar upsurge of literature in Latin America was so dramatic that it was called the "Boom." One of the leading figures of this "Boom" was Argentinian fiction writer Julio Cortázar (hoo͞ lē̆ ō kôr tə zär). His experimental novel *Hopscotch* (1963) may be the work that first gained attention for Latin authors. Another landmark novel was *One Hundred Years of Solitude* (1967), by the Colombian Gabriel García Márquez (gäv rē el gär sē ä mär kəs). Poets Pablo Neruda (pä blō ne ro͞o də) of Chile and Octavio Paz (ôk tä vyô päs) of Mexico also gained international reputations, and each won the Nobel Prize in Literature.

National and Literary Independence In the newly independent nations of Africa, Asia, and the Caribbean, political independence has gone hand in hand with literary accomplishment. It often seemed as if gifted writers from former British colonies were reconquering the colonizer's language, adding to it the richness of their own traditions.

Nigerians Wole Soyinka (wō lā shô yiŋ kə), a playwright and poet, and Chinua Achebe (chin wä ä chā bā), a fiction writer, have enhanced their works with African mythology and proverbs.

Point/Counterpoint

To Preserve or to Change the Literary Canon

Should contemporary multicultural writers be added to the literary canon, the authors accepted for serious study? Two scholars disagree.

Yes! "I'm a cultural historian, and I have been in education all my life. But I didn't know when I began reading for this book [on curriculum] that 'Western Civ' as a subject is as new as it is. The aura it has as the undying, indelible basis of American education is nonsense. . . . There is no final answer, I imagine, to . . . what the curriculum should be."

—Lawrence W. Levine, in *The Chronicle of Higher Education*

No! ". . . the Canon's true question remains: What shall the individual . . . read, this late in history? . . . When our English and other literature departments shrink to the dimensions of our current Classics departments . . . we will perhaps be able to return to the study of the inescapable, to Shakespeare and his few peers, who after all, invented all of us."

—Harold Bloom, *The Western Canon*

The Indian writer R. K. Narayan painted a vivid, humorous portrait of everyday Indian life. Nobel Prize-winner Derek Walcott, from the Caribbean, has explored his complex relationship to the West Indies in elegant poetry. Fellow Caribbean author Jamaica Kincaid has written about family relationships and the colonial legacy in Antigua.

The Two Europes: Writers Without Illusions The West has produced such outstanding writers as Albert Camus (ka mōō´) of France, Günter Grass (gōōn´ tər gräs) of Germany, and Italo Calvino (ē tä´ lō käl vē´ nō) of Italy. These authors are familiar with the ravages of war and the temptations to escape into a material, unreflective existence in postwar society.

Worthy of special mention are Holocaust authors like poet Nelly Sachs and prose writers Prìmo Levi (prē´ mō lä´ vē) and Elie Wiesel (el´ ē wi zel´). These writers experienced the attempt of the Nazis to exterminate European Jewry and have borne witness to one of history's most terrifying episodes.

Writers from Eastern Europe contended with censorship and the disapproval of authoritarian governments. Their options were few. The Russian poet Yevgeny Yevtushenko (yev gen´ ē yev´ tōō sheŋ´ kō) stayed and campaigned for more liberal policies. Another choice, with its own set of problems, was emigration and exile. The Polish poet Czesław Miłosz (ches´ wäf mē´ wōsh) went into exile, defecting to the West. Russia's Alexander Solzhenitsyn (sōl´ zhə nēt´ sin), however, was forced into exile.

Close-up on Culture

World Literature and the Internet

World literature, like so much else in today's culture, lives on the Internet. Here are a few ways to pursue foreign authors in the realms of cyberspace:

• Authors or Works To find a helpful site, key the name of an author or work into a search engine. The more famous the entry, the greater your chances of finding information. Bypass .com sites that often want to sell you something, and look for those sponsored by universities (.edu) or reputable organizations (.org).

• Organizations Two organizations whose sites have information on world literature are the Nobel Foundation and the Academy of American Poets. The Nobel site provides background on winners of the Nobel Prize in Literature. The Academy's site has information on many foreign poets, including Anna Akhmatova, C. P. Cavafy, Czesław Miłosz, and Octavio Paz.

• Literary Databases Many literary databases, like the one entitled Literary Resources at Rutgers University, are now available on the Internet. Under "Literary Resources—Other National Literatures," the Rutgers database has links to sites about authors from Australia, France, Germany, Italy, Japan, Russia, and other countries. For additional databases, key "literary databases" into a search engine.

Embattled Writers Eastern Europe was not the only region where writers were censored and harassed. Nadine Gordimer, who is white, stayed in South Africa and attacked the policy of racial segregation and discrimination known as apartheid (ə pär´ tāt´). In China, Bei Dao (bā´ dou) wrote poetry and prose that inspired the student leaders of the Tiananmen Square demonstration. When that demonstration was suppressed, however, Bei Dao went into exile.

The Middle East, torn by political and religious conflict, has wounded its writers both literally and figuratively. In 1994, Nobel Prize-winning Egyptian novelist Naguib Mahfouz (nä´ hēb´ mä füz´) was stabbed by an Islamic fundamentalist angered by Mahfouz's portrayal of God in a novel. The Turkish government imprisoned poet Nazim Hikmet (nä zəm´ hik met´) for years because of his leftist political beliefs. Both Palestinian Taha Muhammad Ali and Israeli poet Yehuda Amichai (yə hoō´ də ä´ mi khī) wrote of the pain brought by war.

Another witness to war is Vietnamese poet Nguyen Thi Vinh (noō´ yin tī vin). She expresses in a few simple words the pain of the Vietnam War, which divided a country, families, and friends: "How can this happen to us / my friend / my foe?"

"The One Great Heart" World literature takes on a new meaning in an era when we can view Earth from the moon. Never before have all the cultures of the world talked to each other so directly and immediately. (See Close-up on Culture, page 1170.) Solzhenitsyn, noting this fact, has called world literature "the one great heart," and he looks to writers as a force for truth and justice.

Solzhenitsyn's vision is menaced in two different ways: by those who would censor or suppress books and by the forces of hunger, poverty, and illiteracy that make it difficult or impossible to read. These warnings aside, however, we should celebrate the achievements of contemporary authors. In few other eras have writers contended with such rapid changes or such breakdowns of traditional ways and truths. In no other era have they searched for identity and meaning with greater persistence or passion. Their spirited, playfully serious poems, essays, and novels are "the one great heart" of our time.

▼ **Critical Viewing** What links do you see between this painting by Picasso and Solzhenitsyn's concept of world literature as "the one great heart"? [Connect]

Round of Friendship . . . , Pablo Picasso

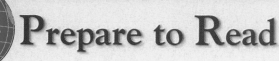

Prepare to Read

The Handsomest Drowned Man in the World ◆ House Taken Over

Gabriel García Márquez (b. 1928)

Colombian author Gabriel García Márquez (gä´ vrē el gär sē´ ä mär´ kes) is one of the originators of magical realism, a literary genre that combines realistic storytelling with elements of folklore and fantasy. In his fiction, he depicts the sharp contrasts of life in Latin America, a continent known not only for its vibrant culture but also for terrible political violence.

Childhood Full of Stories García Márquez was born in Aracataca, a small village on Colombia's Caribbean coast. Because his parents were poor and struggling, García Márquez lived with his grandparents until he was eight years old. He loved listening to the mysterious fables recounted by his grandmother and the tales of military adventure narrated by his grandfather. Later, he adapted for his own work some of these stories he had heard as a child.

Worlds of Solitude In 1955, García Márquez published *Leaf Storm*, the collection of stories that introduced Macondo, a fictional town based on Aracataca. His later masterpiece, *One Hundred Years of Solitude* (1967), chronicles a century of life in Macondo. One of the finest examples of magical realism, the novel earned García Márquez the Nobel Prize in Literature in 1982.

Undoing Death "The Handsomest Drowned Man in the World" is typical of García Márquez's work in many ways. It marries real events with flights of fantasy. It also presents a dead person as the hero. While death is often lurking in García Márquez's work, the author's vision transforms it. Through the vitality of the story itself, the exuberance of its language, and the sheer power of imagination, death is undone.

Julio Cortázar (1914–1984)

Standing six feet tall, with long hair and a beard, the Argentinian Julio Cortázar (hōō´ lē ō kôr tä´ zər) was an imposing figure. He was also a towering presence as a writer, producing novels, short stories, and poetry and translating into Spanish the works of authors such as Edgar Allan Poe. He is best known, however, for his experimental fiction.

An International Sense of Identity Cortázar was born in Brussels, Belgium, to Argentinian parents. Although he returned to Argentina when he was a small boy, his sense of belonging to both Europe and Latin America was an important theme in his life.

In his early thirties, Cortázar landed a job as a translator for the United Nations and moved to Paris. While he had already begun writing the fiction that would make him famous, he did not publish it until 1951, when *Bestiary*, a collection of stories, appeared. *Cronopias and Famas* followed eleven years later. Experimental and playful, the volume opens with a selection entitled "The Instruction Manual," which provides detailed and wacky directions for such habitual actions as combing one's hair or descending a staircase.

Involving the Reader In 1963, Cortázar published his most remarkable novel, *Hopscotch*. Other experimental novels, including *62: A Model Kit* (1968) and *Last Round* (1969), also invite reader participation.

Cortázar once summarized his theory of fiction as follows: "The man of the future . . . will have to find the bases of a reality which is truly his and, at the same time, maintain the capacity of dreaming and playing . . . since it is through those doors that the Other, the fantastic dimension, and the unexpected will always slip. . . ." When you read "House Taken Over," you will step through one of "those doors."

Preview

Connecting to the Literature

Reality and dreams are not always opposites. Powerful dreams can have the force of real events, while real events can seem like the product of a dreamer's imagination. In these stories, dream and reality come together.

Literary Analysis

Magical Realism

As its name suggests, **magical realism** combines realistic events with elements of myth, magic, and marvels of the natural world. Born out of the conflicts and beauty of Latin American culture, the style mixes reality and fantasy to create a rich sense of life's possibilities and limitations. For example, "The Handsomest Drowned Man in the World" begins with a grimly believable event: a dead body washes up on a beach. Soon, however, García Márquez's descriptions of the body give it mythic proportions:

> Not only was he the tallest, strongest, most virile, and best built man they had ever seen, but even though they were looking at him there was no room for him in their imagination.

As you read these stories, pay close attention to details. Think about which elements are realistic and which are strangely unreal.

Comparing Literary Works

Magical realist tales often use **archetypes**—universal symbols that evoke deep, even unconscious responses. For example, in "The Handsomest Drowned Man in the World," the archetype of the sea plays a critical role. As you read, identify other archetypes that García Márquez and Cortázar use, and compare the ways in which each adds to the mythic feeling of the stories.

Reading Strategy

Hypothesizing

When you **hypothesize**, you make informed guesses or propose ideas based on clues in a text. Additional details in the text then prove your hypothesis true or false. As you read these stories, use a chart like the one shown to hypothesize.

Vocabulary Development

bountiful (boun′ tə fəl) *adj.* generous; abundant (p. 1175)

labyrinths (lab′ ə rinths) *n.* structures with an intricate network of winding passages (p. 1175)

haggard (hag′ ərd) *adj.* wasted; worn; gaunt (p. 1175)

resistant (ri zis′ tənt) *adj.* strong; firm (p. 1178)

destitute (des′ tə tōōt′) *adj.* completely poor (p. 1178)

replete (ri plēt′) *adj.* well-filled; stocked (p. 1184)

dexterity (deks ter′ ə tē) *n.* skillfulness in the use of one's hands (p. 1184)

brusquely (brusk′ lē) *adv.* in an abrupt manner (p. 1187)

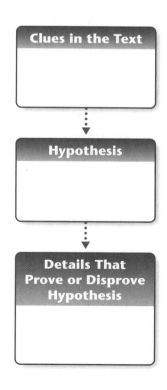

Clues in the Text

↓

Hypothesis

↓

Details That Prove or Disprove Hypothesis

The Handsomest Drowned Man in the World

A Tale for Children

Gabriel García Márquez *translated by Gregory Rabassa*

Background

This story about an unlikely hero is set in a poor Colombian seaside village that closely resembles the author's home village of Aracataca. In this work and others, García Márquez re-creates and expands upon his grandmother's storytelling style. According to García Márquez, her memorable tales related "things that sounded supernatural and fantastic, but she told them with complete naturalness."

The first children who saw the dark and slinky bulge approaching through the sea let themselves think it was an enemy ship. Then they saw it had no flags or masts and they thought it was a whale. But when it washed up on the beach, they removed the clumps of seaweed, the jellyfish tentacles, and the remains of fish and flotsam, and only then did they see that it was a drowned man.

They had been playing with him all afternoon, burying him in the sand and digging him up again, when someone chanced to see them and spread the alarm in the village. The men who carried him to the nearest house noticed that he weighed more than any dead man they had ever known, almost as much as a horse, and they said to each other that maybe he'd been floating too long and the water had got into his bones. When they laid him on the floor they said he'd been taller than all other men because there was barely enough room for him in the house, but they thought that maybe the ability to keep on growing after death was part of the nature of certain drowned men. He had the smell of the sea about him and only his shape gave one to suppose that it was the corpse of a human being, because the skin was covered with a crust of mud and scales.

They did not even have to clean off his face to know that the dead man was a stranger. The village was made up of only twenty-odd wooden houses that had stone courtyards with no flowers and which were spread about on the end of a desertlike cape. There was so little land that mothers always went about with the fear that the wind would carry off their children and the few dead that the years had caused among them had to be

Literary Analysis
Magical Realism Which details in the description of the drowned man are so exaggerated that they seem unreal?

thrown off the cliffs. But the sea was calm and <u>bountiful</u> and all the men fit into seven boats. So when they found the drowned man they simply had to look at one another to see that they were all there.

That night they did not go out to work at sea. While the men went to find out if anyone was missing in neighboring villages, the women stayed behind to care for the drowned man. They took the mud off with grass swabs, they removed the underwater stones entangled in his hair, and they scraped the crust off with tools used for scaling fish. As they were doing that they noticed that the vegetation on him came from faraway oceans and deep water and that his clothes were in tatters, as if he had sailed through <u>labyrinths</u> of coral. They noticed too that he bore his death with pride, for he did not have the lonely look of other drowned men who came out of the sea or that <u>haggard</u>, needy look of men who drowned in rivers. But only when they finished cleaning him off did they become aware of the kind of man he was and it left them breathless. Not only was he the tallest, strongest, most virile, and best built man they had ever seen, but even though they were looking at him there was no room for him in their imagination.

They could not find a bed in the village large enough to lay him on nor was there a table solid enough to use for his wake. The tallest men's

Waves, 1917, Christopher Nevinson, Phillips, The International Fine Art Auctioneers, UK

⚠ **Critical Viewing** Does this painting depict the sea as being "calm and bountiful," as it is described in the story? Why or why not? **[Evaluate]**

The Handsomest Drowned Man in the World ◆ 1175

▲ **Critical Viewing** In what ways does this painting reflect the kinds of emotions expressed by the women caring for the drowned man? **[Connect]**

holiday pants would not fit him, nor the fattest ones' Sunday shirts, nor the shoes of the one with the biggest feet. Fascinated by his huge size and his beauty, the women then decided to make him some pants from a large piece of sail and a shirt from some bridal brabant[1] linen so that he could continue through his death with dignity. As they sewed, sitting in a circle and gazing at the corpse between stitches, it seemed to them that the wind had never been so steady nor the sea so restless as on that night and they supposed that the change had something to do with the dead man. They thought that if that magnificent man had lived in the village, his house would have had the widest doors, the highest ceiling, and the strongest floor, his bedstead would have been made from a midship frame held together by iron bolts, and his wife would have been the happiest woman. They thought that he would have had so much authority that he could have drawn fish out of the sea simply by calling their names and that he would have put so much work into his land that springs would have burst forth from among the rocks so that he would have been able to plant flowers on the cliffs. They secretly compared him to their own men, thinking that for all their lives theirs were incapable of doing what he could do in one night, and they ended up dismissing them deep in their hearts as the weakest, meanest, and most useless creatures on earth. They were wandering through that maze of fantasy when the oldest woman, who as the oldest had looked upon the drowned man with more compassion than passion, sighed:

"He has the face of someone called Esteban."

It was true. Most of them had only to take another look at him to see that he could not have any other name. The more stubborn among them, who were the youngest, still lived for a few hours with the illusion that when they put his clothes on and he lay among the flowers in patent leather shoes his name might be Lautaro. But it was a vain illusion. There had not been enough canvas, the poorly cut and worse sewn pants were too tight, and the hidden strength of his heart popped the buttons on his shirt. After midnight the whistling of the wind died down and the sea fell into its Wednesday drowsiness. The silence put an end to any last doubts: he was Esteban. The women who had dressed him, who had combed his hair, had cut his nails and shaved him were unable to hold back a shudder of pity when they had to resign themselves to his being dragged along the ground. It was then that they understood how unhappy he must have been with that huge body since it bothered him even after death. They could see him in life, condemned to going through doors sideways, cracking his head on crossbeams, remaining on his feet during visits, not

---

1. **brabant** (brə bant´) region in Belgium and the Netherlands famous for its textile products.

Reading Strategy
Hypothesizing In what ways do you think the arrival of the drowned man will affect life in this village? Explain.

☑ **Reading Check**

What name do the village women give the drowned man?

knowing what to do with his soft, pink, sea lion hands while the lady of the house looked for her most <u>resistant</u> chair and begged him, frightened to death, sit here, Esteban, please, and he, leaning against the wall, smiling, don't bother, ma'am, I'm fine where I am, his heels raw and his back roasted from having done the same thing so many times whenever he paid a visit, don't bother, ma'am, I'm fine where I am, just to avoid the embarrassment of breaking up the chair, and never knowing perhaps that the ones who said don't go, Esteban, at least wait till the coffee's ready, were the ones who later on would whisper the big boob finally left, how nice, the handsome fool has gone. That was what the women were thinking beside the body a little before dawn. Later, when they covered his face with a handkerchief so that the light would not bother him, he looked so forever dead, so defenseless, so much like their men that the first furrows of tears opened in their hearts. It was one of the younger ones who began the weeping. The others, coming to, went from sighs to wails, and the more they sobbed the more they felt like weeping, because the drowned man was becoming all the more Esteban for them, and so they wept so much, for he was the most <u>destitute</u>, most peaceful, and most obliging man on earth, poor Esteban. So when the men returned with the news that the drowned man was not from the neighboring villages either, the women felt an opening of jubilation in the midst of their tears.

"Praise the Lord," they sighed, "he's ours!"

resistant (ri zis´ tənt) *adj.* strong; firm

destitute (des´ tə tōōt´) *adj.* completely poor

▼ **Critical Viewing**
In what ways does this undersea photograph support the narrator's description of "labyrinths" of coral? **[Support]**

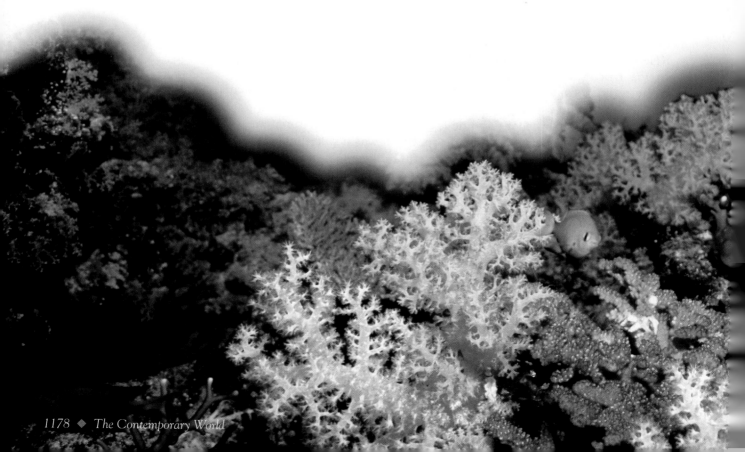

The men thought the fuss was only womanish frivolity. Fatigued because of the difficult nighttime inquiries, all they wanted was to get rid of the bother of the newcomer once and for all before the sun grew strong on that arid, windless day. They improvised a litter with the remains of foremasts and gaffs,[2] tying it together with rigging[3] so that it would bear the weight of the body until they reached the cliffs. They wanted to tie the anchor from a cargo ship to him so that he would sink easily into the deepest waves, where fish are blind and divers die of nostalgia, and bad currents would not bring him back to shore, as had happened with other bodies. But the more they hurried, the more the women thought of ways to waste time. They walked about like startled hens, pecking with the sea charms on their breasts, some interfering on one side to put a scapular[4] of the good wind on the drowned man, some on the other side to put a wrist compass on him, and after a great deal of *get away from there, woman, stay out of the way, look, you almost made me fall on top of the dead man,* the men began to feel mistrust in their lives and started grumbling about why so many main-altar decorations for a stranger, because no matter how many nails and holy-water jars he had on him, the sharks would chew him all the same, but the women kept piling on their junk relics, running back and forth, stumbling, while they released in sighs what they did not in tears, so that the men finally exploded with *since when has there*

2. **gaffs** poles that are part of a ship's mast.
3. **rigging** ropes and other gear used to control the sails of a vessel.
4. **scapular** (skap´ yə lər) religious medal.

Reading Check

Why do the women cover the drowned man's face with a handkerchief?

ever been such a fuss over a drifting corpse, a drowned nobody, a piece of cold Wednesday meat. One of the women, mortified by so much lack of care, then removed the handkerchief from the dead man's face and the men were left breathless too.

He was Esteban. It was not necessary to repeat it for them to recognize him. If they had been told Sir Walter Raleigh,[5] even they might have been impressed with his gringo accent, the macaw on his shoulder, his cannibal-killing blunderbuss, but there could be only one Esteban in the world and there he was, stretched out like a sperm whale, shoeless, wearing the pants of an undersized child, and with those stony nails that had to be cut with a knife. They had only to take the handkerchief off his face to see that he was ashamed, that it was not his fault that he was so big or so heavy or so handsome, and if he had known that this was going to happen, he would have looked for a more discreet place to drown in, seriously, I even would have tied the anchor off a galleon around my neck and staggered off a cliff like someone who doesn't like things in order not to be upsetting people now with this Wednesday dead body, as you people say, in order not to be bothering anyone with this filthy piece of cold meat that doesn't have anything to do with me. There was so much truth in his manner that even the most mistrustful men, the ones who felt the bitterness of endless nights at sea fearing that their women would tire of dreaming about them and begin to dream of drowned men, even they and others who were harder still shuddered in the marrow of their bones at Esteban's sincerity.

That was how they came to hold the most splendid funeral they could conceive of for an abandoned drowned man. Some women who had gone to get flowers in the neighboring villages returned with other women who could not believe what they had been told, and those women went back for more flowers when they saw the dead man, and they brought more and more until there were so many flowers and so many people that it was hard to walk about. At the final moment it pained them to return him to the waters as an orphan and they chose a father and mother from among the best people, and aunts and uncles and cousins, so that through him all the inhabitants of the village became kinsmen. Some sailors who heard the weeping from a distance went off course and people heard of one who had himself tied to the mainmast, remembering ancient fables about sirens. While they fought for the privilege of carrying him on their shoulders along the steep escarpment[6] by the cliffs, men and women became aware for the first time of the desolation of their streets, the dryness of their courtyards, the narrowness of their dreams as they faced the splendor and beauty of their drowned man. They let him go without an anchor so that he could come back if he wished and whenever he wished, and they all held their breath for the fraction of centuries the body took to fall into the abyss. They did not need to look at one another to realize that they were no longer all present, that

---

5. **Sir Walter Raleigh** English explorer (1552–1618) known for his charm and boldness; organized expeditions to North and South America.
6. **escarpment** (e skärp´ mənt) slope.

Themes in
World Literature

García Márquez and William Faulkner

The fictional world of Gabriel García Márquez was strongly influenced by the American author William Faulkner, who wrote many stories and novels set in the imaginary Mississippi county of Yoknapatawpha (yŏk´ nə pə tô´ fə). Inspired by Faulkner's rich and intimate descriptions of Yoknapatawpha and its residents, García Márquez created his own fictional village of Macondo. He also decided that his earlier works had been "simply intellectual elaborations, nothing to do with my reality." To address this flaw, he changed his writing style, incorporating personal imagery, details, and knowledge.

While Macondo is clearly modeled on García Márquez's hometown of Aracataca, it is not merely the product of Márquez's observant eye. Rather, as a fictional setting, the town rests on a deep undercurrent of fantasy and magic, which frequently erupts. As it does, readers travel to a haunting landscape, where reality still holds sway but dream and imagination are equally powerful.

Reading Strategy
Hypothesizing Do you think the village will remember Esteban after his funeral? Explain.

they would never be. But they also knew that everything would be different from then on, that their houses would have wider doors, higher ceilings, and stronger floors so that Esteban's memory could go everywhere without bumping into beams and so that no one in the future would dare whisper the big boob finally died, too bad, the handsome fool has finally died, because they were going to paint their house fronts gay colors to make Esteban's memory eternal and they were going to break their backs digging for springs among the stones and planting flowers on the cliffs so that in future years at dawn the passengers on great liners would awaken, suffocated by the smell of gardens on the high seas, and the captain would have to come down from the bridge in his dress uniform, with his astrolabe[7] his pole star, and his row of war medals and, pointing to the promontory of roses on the horizon, he would say in fourteen languages, look there, where the wind is so peaceful now that it's gone to sleep beneath the beds, over there, where the sun's so bright that the sunflowers don't know which way to turn, yes, over there, that's Esteban's village.

---

7. **astrolabe** (as´ trō lāb´) old-fashioned instrument used in navigating a ship.

Review and Assess

Thinking About the Selection

1. **Respond:** Which aspect of this story do you find most surprising? Explain.

2. **(a) Recall:** As the village men carry the drowned man from the beach, what do they observe about his size and weight?
   (b) Contrast: How does the drowned man's size contrast with the size of the village? **(c) Interpret:** What does this size relationship suggest about the importance of the drowned man?

3. **(a) Recall:** After the men bring the body to town, what do the women do with it? **(b) Analyze Cause and Effect:** As a result of their actions, what qualities do the women notice about the dead man?

4. **(a) Interpret:** With what emotions do the men first react to the women's fuss over the body? Explain. **(b) Analyze Cause and Effect:** What happens to change their minds? Explain.

5. **(a) Generalize:** In what ways does the town change as a result of its encounter with Esteban? **(b) Analyze:** What do these changes suggest about Esteban's symbolic value to the town?

6. **Evaluate:** Do you think that García Márquez intends his subtitle, "A Tale for Children," to be interpreted literally? Why or why not?

7. **Apply:** Philosophers have sometimes expressed the idea that the key to releasing human potential is to expand people's imagination. Explain how this story supports that notion.

HOUSE TAKEN OVER

Julio Cortázar *translated by* Paul Blackburn

Background

Cortázar wrote this story while still in the grip of a frightening nightmare. Critic Evelyn Picon Garfield describes the story's origin, explaining that Cortázar "dreamt that he was alone in a house full of passageways when suddenly he heard a noise from the depths of the corridor. He had a sensation of nightmarish terror. After quickly closing the door and bolting it tight, for a few minutes he felt safe and thought that the nightmare would become a peaceful dream. All of a sudden the noise sounded on his side of the door. He woke up, and still in his pajamas, without taking time to brush his teeth or comb his hair, he sat down at the typewriter. In about an hour and a half 'House Taken Over' was written."

We liked the house because, apart from its being old and spacious (in a day when old houses go down for a profitable auction of their construction materials), it kept the memories of great-grandparents, our paternal grandfather, our parents and the whole of childhood.

Irene and I got used to staying in the house by ourselves, which was crazy, eight people could have lived in that place and not have gotten in each other's way. We rose at seven in the morning and got the cleaning done, and about eleven I left Irene to finish off whatever rooms and went to the kitchen. We lunched at noon precisely; then there was nothing left to do but a few dirty plates. It was pleasant to take lunch and commune with[1] the great hollow, silent house, and it was enough for us just to keep it clean. We ended up thinking, at times, that that was what had kept us from marrying. Irene turned down two suitors for no particular reason, and María Esther went and died on me before we could manage to get engaged. We were easing into our forties with the unvoiced concept that the quiet, simple marriage of sister and

> **Literary Analysis**
> **Magical Realism and Archetypes** Based on the first paragraph, what might a house represent for an individual?

> ✔**Reading Check**
> With whom does the narrator live?

---

1. **commune** (kə myoon′) **with** be in close rapport or harmony with.

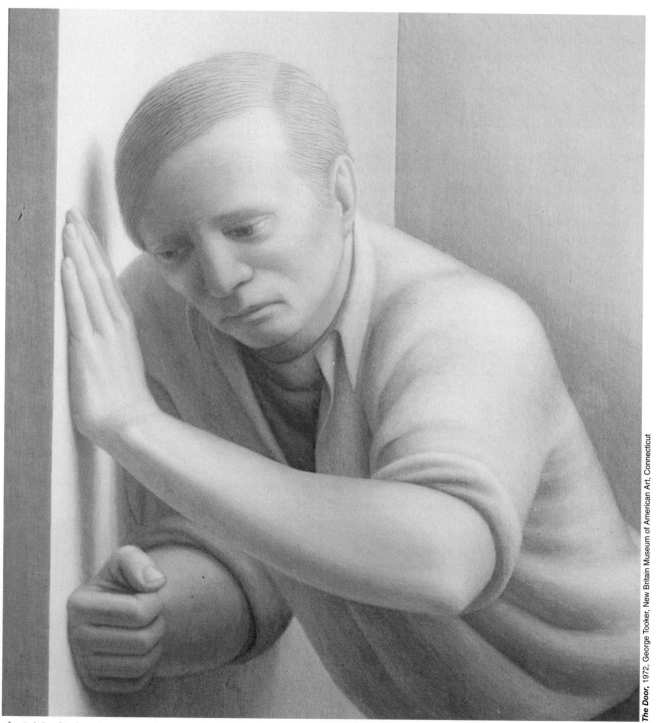

The Door, 1972, George Tooker, New Britain Museum of American Art, Connecticut

▲ **Critical Viewing**   Based on the title of the story and the man's posture and expression in this painting, what kinds of events do you think this story will include? **[Hypothesize]**

brother was the indispensable end to a line established in this house by our grandparents. We would die here someday, obscure and distant cousins would inherit the place, have it torn down, sell the bricks and get rich on the building plot; or more justly and better yet, we would topple it ourselves before it was too late.

Irene never bothered anyone. Once the morning housework was finished, she spent the rest of the day on the sofa in her bedroom, knitting. I couldn't tell you why she knitted so much; I think women knit when they discover that it's a fat excuse to do nothing at all. But Irene was not like that, she always knitted necessities, sweaters for winter, socks for me, handy morning robes and bedjackets for herself. Sometimes she would do a jacket, then unravel it the next moment because there was something that didn't please her; it was pleasant to see a pile of tangled wool in her knitting basket fighting a losing battle for a few hours to retain its shape. Saturdays I went downtown to buy wool; Irene had faith in my good taste, was pleased with the colors and never a skein[2] had to be returned. I took advantage of these trips to make the rounds of the bookstores, uselessly asking if they had anything new in French literature. Nothing worthwhile had arrived in Argentina since 1939.[3]

But it's the house I want to talk about, the house and Irene, I'm not very important. I wonder what Irene would have done without her knitting. One can reread a book, but once a pullover is finished you can't do it over again, it's some kind of disgrace. One day I found that the drawer at the bottom of the chiffonier, <u>replete</u> with mothballs, was filled with shawls, white, green, lilac. Stacked amid a great smell of camphor—it was like a shop; I didn't have the nerve to ask her what she planned to do with them. We didn't have to earn our living, there was plenty coming in from the farms each month, even piling up. But Irene was only interested in the knitting and showed a wonderful <u>dexterity</u>, and for me the hours slipped away watching her, her hands like silver sea-urchins, needles flashing, and one or two knitting baskets on the floor, the balls of yarn jumping about. It was lovely.

How not to remember the layout of that house. The dining room, a living room with tapestries, the library and three large bedrooms in the section most recessed, the one that faced toward Rodríguez Peña.[4] Only a corridor with its massive oak door separated that part from the front wing, where there was a bath, the kitchen, our bedrooms and the hall. One entered the house through a vestibule with enameled tiles, and a wrought-iron grated door opened onto the living room. You had to come in through the vestibule and open the gate to go into the living room; the doors to our bedrooms were

replete (ri plēt´) *adj.* well-filled; stocked

dexterity (deks ter´ ə tē) *n.* skillfulness in the use of one's hands

---

2. **skein** (skān) *n.* quantity of thread or yarn wound in a coil.
3. **Nothing . . . 1939** When World War II began in 1939, communications between Argentina and Europe were disrupted.
4. **Rodríguez Peña** (ro drē´ gəz pā´ nyə) fashionable street in Buenos Aires.

La Nuit (Night), René Magritte, Private Collection/Herscovici/Art Resource, New York, NY

on either side of this, and opposite it was the corridor leading to the back section; going down the passage, one swung open the oak door beyond which was the other part of the house; or just before the door, one could turn to the left and go down a narrower passageway which led to the kitchen and the bath. When the door was open, you became aware of the size of the house; when it was closed, you had the impression of an apartment, like the ones they build today, with barely enough room to move around in. Irene and I always lived in this part of the house and hardly ever went beyond the oak door except to do the cleaning. Incredible how much dust collected on the furniture. It may be Buenos Aires[5] is a clean city, but she owes it to her population and nothing else. There's too much dust in the air, the slightest breeze and it's back on the marble console tops and in the diamond patterns of the tooled-leather desk set. It's a lot of work to get it off with a feather duster; the motes[6] rise and hang in the air, and settle again a minute later on the pianos and the furniture.

---

5. **Buenos Aires** (bwā′ nəs er′ ēz) capital of Argentina.
6. **motes** specks of dust or other tiny particles.

▲ **Critical Viewing**
Which details in this painting help convey a mood similar to that of the story? [**Connect**]

Literary Analysis
Magical Realism and Archetypes What universal human needs does the archetype of a house suggest?

☑ **Reading Check**
In which part of the house do Irene and the narrator spend most of their time?

I'll always have a clear memory of it because it happened so simply and without fuss. Irene was knitting in her bedroom, it was eight at night, and I suddenly decided to put the water up for *mate*.[7] I went down the corridor as far as the oak door, which was ajar, then turned into the hall toward the kitchen, when I heard something in the library or the dining room. The sound came through muted and indistinct, a chair being knocked over onto the carpet or the muffled buzzing of a conversation. At the same time, or a second later, I heard it at the end of the passage which led from those two rooms toward the door. I hurled myself against the door before it was too late and shut it, leaned on it with the weight of my body; luckily, the key was on our side; moreover, I ran the great bolt into place, just to be safe.

I went down to the kitchen, heated the kettle, and when I got back with the tray of *mate*, I told Irene:

"I had to shut the door to the passage. They've taken over the back part."

She let her knitting fall and looked at me with her tired, serious eyes.

"You're sure?"

I nodded.

"In that case," she said, picking up her needles again, "we'll have to live on this side."

I sipped at the *mate* very carefully, but she took her time starting her work again. I remember it was a gray vest she was knitting. I liked that vest.

The first few days were painful, since we'd both left so many things in the part that had been taken over. My collection of French literature, for example, was still in the library. Irene had left several folios of stationery and a pair of slippers that she used a lot in the winter. I missed my briar pipe, and Irene, I think, regretted the loss of an ancient bottle of Hesperidin.[8] It happened repeatedly (but only in the first few days) that we would close some drawer or cabinet and look at one another sadly.

"It's not here."

One thing more among the many lost on the other side of the house.

But there were advantages, too. The cleaning was so much simplified that, even when we got up late, nine-thirty for instance, by eleven we were sitting around with our arms folded. Irene got into the habit of coming to the kitchen with me to help get lunch. We thought about it and decided on this: while I prepared the lunch, Irene would cook up dishes that could be eaten cold in the evening. We were happy with the arrangement because it was

Literary Analysis
Magical Realism Which do you find more fantastic—the noises in the house or the narrator's reaction to them? Explain.

Still Life Reviving, Remedios Varos, Collection of Beatriz Varo de Cano, Valencia, Spain

▲ **Critical Viewing**
How is this painting similar to and different from your image of the mysterious happenings in this story? [**Compare and Contrast**]

---

7. ***mate*** (mä´ tā´) beverage made from the dried leaves of a South American evergreen tree.
8. **Hesperidin** (hes per´ i din) vitamin that comes from the rind of green citrus fruits and is used for various medicinal purposes.

always such a bother to have to leave our bedrooms in the evening and start to cook. Now we made do with the table in Irene's room and platters of cold supper.

Since it left her more time for knitting, Irene was content. I was a little lost without my books, but so as not to inflict myself on my sister, I set about reordering papa's stamp collection; that killed some time. We amused ourselves sufficiently, each with his own thing, almost always getting together in Irene's bedroom, which was the more comfortable. Every once in a while, Irene might say:

"Look at this pattern I just figured out, doesn't it look like clover?"

After a bit it was I, pushing a small square of paper in front of her so that she could see the excellence of some stamp or another from Eupen-et-Malmédy.[9] We were fine, and little by little we stopped thinking. You can live without thinking.

(Whenever Irene talked in her sleep, I woke up immediately and stayed awake. I never could get used to this voice from a statue or a parrot, a voice that came out of the dreams, not from a throat. Irene said that in my sleep I flailed about enormously and shook the blankets off. We had the living room between us, but at night you could hear everything in the house. We heard each other breathing, coughing, could even feel each other reaching for the light switch when, as happened frequently, neither of us could fall asleep.

Aside from our nocturnal rumblings, everything was quiet in the house. During the day there were the household sounds, the metallic click of knitting needles, the rustle of stamp-album pages turning. The oak door was massive, I think I said that. In the kitchen or the bath, which adjoined the part that was taken over, we managed to talk loudly, or Irene sang lullabies. In a kitchen there's always too much noise, the plates and glasses, for there to be interruptions from other sounds. We seldom allowed ourselves silence there, but when we went back to our rooms or to the living room, then the house grew quiet, half-lit, we ended by stepping around more slowly so as not to disturb one another. I think it was because of this that I woke up irremediably[10] and at once when Irene began to talk in her sleep.)

Except for the consequences, it's nearly a matter of repeating the same scene over again. I was thirsty that night, and before we went to sleep, I told Irene that I was going to the kitchen for a glass of water. From the door of the bedroom (she was knitting) I heard the noise in the kitchen; if not the kitchen, then the bath, the passage off at that angle dulled the sound. Irene noticed how <u>brusquely</u> I had paused, and

---

9. **Eupen-et-Malmédy** (yo͞o pen´ ā mäl mā´ dē) districts in eastern Belgium.
10. **irremediably** (ir´ ri mē´ dē ə blē) *adv.* in a way that cannot be helped or corrected.

Themes in
World Literature

Political Unrest in Latin America

The histories of Latin American countries are filled with violent change and dramatic shifts in political ideology. In the twentieth century, many Latin American countries experienced *coups* (co͞oz)—revolutions in which military leaders wrested power from civilian authorities and took control of the government. For example, from the mid-1940s through 1956, the dictator Juan Peron ruled Argentina. Intolerant of opposition, the government jailed critics and used violence to suppress dissension. In his Nobel Prize acceptance speech, Gabriel García Márquez described the plight of Latin America, saying that as of the early 1980s, hundreds of thousand of people throughout Latin America had simply disappeared or been killed for political reasons.

Because direct criticism of their governments was so dangerous, many Latin American writers resorted to indirect methods, such as the use of symbols and parables, to comment on the politics of their countries. As a result, many Latin American stories can be read on at least two levels. For example, while "House Taken Over" can be read as a mystery or a dreamlike ghost story, it can also be read as a parable about an aggressive new generation replacing an older, more placid one.

---

brusquely (brusk´ lē) *adv.* in an abrupt manner

 **Reading Check**

What does the narrator hear from the library or dining room?

---

came up beside me without a word. We stood listening to the noises, growing more and more sure that they were on our side of the oak door, if not the kitchen then the bath, or in the hall itself at the turn, almost next to us.

We didn't wait to look at one another. I took Irene's arm and forced her to run with me to the wrought-iron door, not waiting to look back. You could hear the noises, still muffled but louder, just behind us. I slammed the grating and we stopped in the vestibule. Now there was nothing to be heard.

"They've taken over our section," Irene said. The knitting had reeled off from her hands and the yarn ran back toward the door and disappeared under it. When she saw that the balls of yarn were on the other side, she dropped the knitting without looking at it.

"Did you have time to bring anything?" I asked hopelessly.

"No, nothing."

We had what we had on. I remembered fifteen thousand pesos[11] in the wardrobe in my bedroom. Too late now.

I still had my wrist watch on and saw that it was 11 P.M. I took Irene around the waist (I think she was crying) and that was how we went into the street. Before we left, I felt terrible; I locked the front door up tight and tossed the key down the sewer. It wouldn't do to have some poor devil decide to go in and rob the house, at that hour and with the house taken over.

---

11. **fifteen thousand pesos** large sum of money at that time, equivalent to over a thousand dollars.

Review and Assess

Thinking About the Selection

1. **(a) Recall:** What daily activities do the narrator and his sister engage in before the house is invaded? **(b) Draw Conclusions:** Based on their daily habits, what are these characters like? Explain.

2. **(a) Recall:** What does the narrator do when he hears the muffled sounds from the library or dining room? **(b) Compare and Contrast:** In what ways does the narrator's physical reaction differ from his outward emotional reaction to the invasion? Explain.

3. **(a) Recall:** After the intruders are in the house, what do the narrator and Irene do in their sleep? **(b) Infer:** What do the differences between their sleeping and waking lives suggest about their true reactions to the invasion of their house?

4. **Take a Position:** Some critics have suggested that the noises symbolize a social revolution overtaking the outdated lifestyle of this upper-class family. Others suggest that they represent the mysterious forces that can attack the mind. Which of these two interpretations do you favor? Why?

Review and Assess

Literary Analysis

Magical Realism

1. (a) For each story, use a chart like the one shown to identify realistic and fantastic details.

	Realistic Details	Fantastic Details
Characters		
Setting		
Events		

    (b) Describe specific ways in which each story begins firmly rooted in the real and slowly develops a fantastic dimension. (c) Why do you think this structure is common in works of **magical realism**?

2. (a) In "The Handsomest Drowned Man in the World," how do the children's actions suggest that the world of the story is not quite the world of reality?

3. In "House Taken Over," how might the division of the house into a front and back section relate to the changing balance of reality and fantasy in the story?

Comparing Literary Works

4. (a) Which details in "The Handsomest Drowned Man in the World" present the **archetype** of the sea as the source of life? (b) Which details suggest the sea is a taker of life?

5. (a) In what ways does "House Taken Over," present the archetype of a shelter as a symbol for the individual? (b) In what ways does the house represent an entire family line?

Reading Strategy

Hypothesizing

6. (a) State one **hypothesis** you formed as you began to read "House Taken Over." (b) In what ways did the events of the story prove or disprove your hypothesis?

7. In what ways can hypothesizing increase your involvement in a work of literature? Explain.

Extend Understanding

8. **Psychology Connection:** Julio Cortázar believed that ". . . the fantastic dimension, and the unexpected" are important in both literature and life. Do you agree? Explain your answer.

Integrate Language Skills

Vocabulary Development Lesson

Word Analysis: Latin Prefix *re-*

The Latin prefix *re-* can mean "again" or "back." The word *replete*, which means "well filled," combines this prefix with the Latin root *-plete*, which means "filled." Add the prefix *re-* to each word below. Then, write a definition for each new word.

1. absorb
2. occurrence
3. current
4. animate
5. appraisal
6. construction

Spelling Strategy

The suffix *-ety /-ity* means "the state or quality of," but *-ity* is the more common variation in English. Add *-ety* or *-ity* to complete each word below.

1. hered_____
2. soci_____
3. scarc_____
4. generos_____

Concept Development: Synonyms or Antonyms?

Review the vocabulary words and definitions on page 1173, and notice the way the words are used in the context of each selection. Then, identify each of the following pairs of words as either synonyms (words with similar meanings) or antonyms (words with opposite meanings).

1. labyrinths, mazes
2. brusquely, abruptly
3. dexterity, clumsiness
4. replete, lacking
5. resistant, frail
6. haggard, exhausted
7. bountiful, scarce
8. destitute, prosperous

Grammar and Style Lesson

Punctuating Dialogue

In "The Handsomest Drowned Man in the World," García Márquez includes dialogue without punctuation, allowing the story to shift seamlessly from the observations of the villagers to those of the dead man. However, in most pieces of writing, correct **punctuation of dialogue** is essential. To correctly punctuate dialogue, place quotation marks around the speaker's exact words. Locate periods and commas inside the quotation marks.

Examples:

"In that case," she said, picking up her needles again, "we'll have to live on this side."

"Did you have time to bring anything?" I asked hopelessly.

Practice Rewrite each item below, using correct punctuation.

1. Who is it asked the children
2. We must bury him said the men
3. Don't go, Esteban said the women
4. If they have come said Irene we must leave at once
5. I looked at my sister and said Yes

Writing Application Suppose that the narrator of "House Taken Over" and his sister return to the house ten years later. Write a short dialogue that they share as they look over their old home. Punctuate each line of dialogue correctly.

 Prentice Hall Writing and Grammar Connection: Diamond Level, Chapter 27, Section 4

Writing Lesson

Essay Tracing the Development of a Character

In García Márquez's masterful story, the drowned man undergoes a surprising transformation from a less-than-human thing into a fully realized character. Write an essay in which you describe how the author achieves this unlikely feat of characterization.

Prewriting   As you reread the story, collect details about the drowned man that appear in the beginning, middle, and end. Identify points at which the drowned man's character takes on new shades of personality and identity.

Drafting   Write an introduction that describes the subject of the essay and includes a statement expressing your main idea. Then, in your body paragraphs, follow the chronology of the story to present your insights.

Model: Using Transitions to Clarify Order of Events

At the beginning of the story, the children treat the body as a toy. Then, the village men carry the body to town. There, the women clean and care for the body and make an amazing discovery—they realize that this is not a typical drowned man but a hero.

> Transitions like *at the beginning* and *then* help readers follow the order of events.

Revising   Reread your essay, making sure that you have clearly shown the development of the drowned man's character. Consider adding transitional words and phrases to clarify the logical flow of your ideas.

*W*_G *Prentice Hall Writing and Grammar Connection: Diamond Level, Chapter 9, Section 4*

Extension Activities

Listening and Speaking Storytellers often use ideas from their listeners when they spin stories. Julio Cortázar creates a similar feeling of audience participation in many of his written works. Follow those models by creating and delivering an **interactive story** of your own.

- Begin by describing characters, a setting, and a conflict.
- At key moments, pause and ask for suggestions from your audience.

Continue telling your story until the conflict is resolved. [**Group Activity**]

Research and Technology Use design software or paper and colored pencils to create a detailed **layout** of the house described in "House Taken Over." Show the location of rooms and furniture, and identify the locations where key story events occur. Choose a specific symbol to represent the mysterious forces that take over the house.

 **Take It to the Net** PHSchool.com

Go online for an additional research activity using the Internet.

Prepare to Read

Fable ◆ Concord ◆ Sonnet 49 ◆ Sonnet 71 ◆
from Omeros

Octavio Paz (1914–1998)

Mexican poet Octavio Paz (ok täv´ yō päs) was born in a suburb of Mexico City. As a writer and diplomat, he spent time in Paris, Japan, India, and the United States. In each country, he discovered elements of art or culture that influenced his own work.

For example, his exposure to French Surrealism encouraged him to write imaginatively, without worrying about logical meaning. While the Mexican ambassador to India, he studied Indian religions and philosophies. These studies found their way into some of his poems, including "Blanco," which Paz arranged to mimic the sections of the sacred Indian diagram called a *mandala*.

Even though Paz embraced the cultures of other countries, he never compromised his Mexican identity. While he continued to write poetry, he also turned his attention to nonfiction examinations of Mexican culture. His book *The Labyrinth of Solitude* (1950) expresses these observations and has been hailed as a "Latin American classic."

Throughout the 1970s, Paz taught at Harvard University and other American colleges. He received the Nobel Prize in Literature in 1990.

Pablo Neruda (1904–1973)

The poet Pablo Neruda (pä´ blō ne rōō´ thä) drew inspiration from objects that most people barely notice: "It is well . . . to look closely at the world of objects at rest. Wheels that have crossed long, dusty distances with their mineral and vegetable burdens, sacks from coalbins, barrels and baskets . . . From them flow the contacts of the man with the earth. . . ." Neruda was born in Parral, Chile, the son of a railway worker. When he was just twenty, his book *Twenty Love Poems and a Desperate Song* earned him recognition as one of his country's best poets. The Chilean government often sent promising writers abroad, and Neruda was assigned to various diplomatic positions. For the next twelve years, he traveled extensively, discovering artistic and cultural movements, including French Surrealism, that influenced his work.

In his later years, Neruda became increasingly involved in politics and expressed his opinions in his poems. Even his political opponents conceded his enormous talent. In 1971, Neruda received the Nobel Prize in Literature.

Derek Walcott (b. 1930)

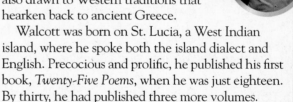

As a Caribbean islander, Derek Walcott has experienced a sense of cultural division: He owes allegiance to his own rich native traditions, which can be traced back to African sources, yet he is also drawn to Western traditions that hearken back to ancient Greece.

Walcott was born on St. Lucia, a West Indian island, where he spoke both the island dialect and English. Precocious and prolific, he published his first book, *Twenty-Five Poems*, when he was just eighteen. By thirty, he had published three more volumes.

Walcott is also a distinguished theater director and playwright. In his dramatic works, he explores his Caribbean roots more deeply than he does in his poetry. For example, one of Walcott's most famous plays, *Dream on Monkey Mountain*, is set in the back country of a Caribbean island. It portrays a world in which superstition and myth dominate.

Walcott divides his time between St. Lucia and the United States, where he teaches creative writing at Boston University. In 1992, Walcott received the Nobel Prize in Literature for his achievements as both poet and playwright.

Preview

Connecting to the Literature

Most of our daily activities emphasize logical thinking. However, these beautiful, surprising poems prove that the mind is far more mysterious and alive than our daily lives usually reveal.

Literary Analysis

Surrealism

Surrealism, which means "beyond realism," is an artistic movement that emphasizes the irrational side of human nature. While Surrealists begin with familiar, everyday objects and experiences, they move quickly to the vivid, imaginative associations of the unconscious mind. Surrealists often rely on surprising juxtapositions, as these lines from Paz's "Fable" demonstrate:

> Rain was a willow with unpinned hair
> A tree grew in the palm of your hand . . .

Surrealist works can seem like dreams in which ordinary objects become extraordinary. As you read these poems, use a chart like the one shown to record common things that the poet's vision transforms.

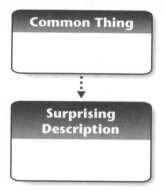

Common Thing

Surprising Description

Comparing Literary Works

To emphasize the connections between the real and the imagined, Surrealists often use **personification,** a type of figurative language in which a nonhuman subject is given human traits. These poems are very different, but all use personification. For example, Neruda describes Tomorrow's "green footsteps," while Walcott refers to the "language's desire."

As you read, compare the ways in which each poet uses personification, and determine how it adds to the effect and meaning of each poem.

Reading Strategy

Reading Verse for Meaning

When you **read verse for meaning,** focus on the sentences in poems, not the line breaks. Pause after commas and stop after periods. In poems in which punctuation has been omitted, imagine it there to guide your reading. Once you understand a poem's basic meaning, note the ways in which line breaks, stanza length, or omitted punctuation can emphasize certain ideas. Apply these techniques as you read these selections.

Vocabulary Development

prophesied (präf´ə sīd) v. predicted (p. 1194)

divinations (div´ə nā´ shənz) n. divine predictions (p. 1194)

nocturnal (näk tʉr´ nəl) adj. relating to or occurring during the night (p. 1196)

carnivorous (kär niv´ ə rəs) adj. meat-eating (p. 1197)

entwined (en twīnd´) v. twisted together (p. 1197)

FABLE

OCTAVIO PAZ

translated by Eliot Weinberger

Background

In his famous poem "Ode on a Grecian Urn," the British poet John Keats
wrote that a great work of art can "tease us out of thought." The poetry of
Octavio Paz does just that—inviting the reader into a new world where the
imagination and the unconscious dominate. Instead of focusing on the
rational and the realistic, Paz encourages readers to see the world with a
deeper, more emotional logic, as these two poems demonstrate.

Reading Strategy
Read Verse for Meaning
Where would you temporarily place punctuation
marks to aid your understanding of this poem?
Explain.

Ages of fire and of air
Youth of water
From green to yellow
        From yellow to red
From dream to watching
        From desire to act
5 It was only one step and you took it so lightly
Insects were living jewels
The heat rested by the side of the pond
Rain was a willow with unpinned hair
A tree grew in the palm of your hand
10 And that tree laughed sang <u>prophesied</u>
Its <u>divinations</u> filled the air with wings
There were simple miracles called birds
Everything was for everyone
        Everyone was everything
There was only one huge word with no back to it
15 A word like a sun
One day it broke into tiny pieces
They were the words of the language we now speak
Pieces that will never come together
Broken mirrors where the world sees itself shattered

prophesied (präf′ ə sīd) *v.*
predicted

divinations (div ə nā′ shənz)
n. divine predictions

Concord

OCTAVIO PAZ

translated by Eliot Weinberger

Kaukola Ridge at Sunset, 1889, Albert Edelfelt, Ateneum Art Museum, Helsinki, The Central Art Archives

For Carlos Fuentes

Water above
Grove below
Wind on the roads

Quiet well
5   Bucket's black   Spring water

Water coming down to the trees
Sky rising to the lips

Review and Assess

Thinking About the Selections

1. **Respond:** Which images, if any, in either poem remind you of something you have seen or felt before? Explain.

2. **(a) Recall:** In line 13 of "Fable," what does the speaker say "Everything" was for? **(b) Recall:** How does the speaker define "Everyone"? **(c) Deduce:** In what ways do the images in lines 6–12 provide examples of the generalizations in line 13?

3. **(a) Recall:** In line 16, what happens to the "one huge word" mentioned in line 14? **(b) Analyze Cause and Effect:** What is the result of this event, as described in the final four lines of the poem?

4. **(a) Recall:** In "Concord," identify two images in the first two lines. **(b) Infer:** In what ways do these images invert logic?

5. **(a) Recall:** What natural event is happening in the final two lines of the poem? **(b) Analyze:** How does Paz transform this everyday event into something extraordinary?

▲ **Critical Viewing**
Do you think this painting captures the spirit of this poem? Why or why not? **[Assess]**

Sonnet 49

Pablo Neruda *translated by* Stephen Tapscott

After Rain, 1998, Roger Winter, Fischbach Gallery, New York

◀ **Critical Viewing**
The poet describes a sky with folded "wings." Does this painting create a similar image? Explain. **[Connect]**

Background

Neruda included these sonnets in his collection *One Hundred Love Sonnets*, written for his third wife, Matilde Urrutia, while he and Matilde were living in Isla Negra, a small Chilean fishing village. Images of the natural world, particularly the sea, fill these sonnets, which many critics consider to be among the greatest love poems ever written.

It's today: all of yesterday dropped away
among the fingers of the light and the sleeping eyes.
Tomorrow will come on its green footsteps;
no one can stop the river of the dawn.

5 No one can stop the river of your hands,
your eyes and their sleepiness, my dearest.
You are the trembling of time, which passes
between the vertical light and the darkening sky.

The sky folds its wings over you,
10 lifting you, carrying you to my arms
with its punctual, mysterious courtesy.

That's why I sing to the day and to the moon,
to the sea, to time, to all the planets,
to your daily voice, to your <u>nocturnal</u> skin.

Literary Analysis
Surrealism and Personification In lines 9 and 10, which human qualities does Neruda give to the sky?

nocturnal (näk tʉr´ nəl) *adj.* relating to or occurring during the night.

Sonnet 71

Pablo Neruda
translated by Stephen Tapscott

Love crosses its islands, from grief to grief,
it sets its roots, watered with tears,
and no one—no one—can escape the heart's progress
as it runs, silent and <u>carnivorous</u>.

5 You and I searched for a wide valley, for another planet
where the salt wouldn't touch your hair,
where sorrows couldn't grow because of anything I did,
where bread could live and not grow old.

A planet <u>entwined</u> with vistas and foliage,
10 a plain, a rock, hard and unoccupied:
we wanted to build a strong nest

with our own hands, without hurt or harm or speech,
but love was not like that: love was a lunatic city
with crowds of people blanching[1] on their porches.

carnivorous (kär niv´ ə rəs)
adj. meat-eating

entwined (en twīnd´) *v.*
twisted together

---

1. **blanching** (blanch´ iŋ) becoming pale; bleaching.

Review and Assess

Thinking About the Selections

1. **Respond:** Do you think these poems are more effective when read silently or aloud? Explain.

2. **(a) Recall:** In line 5 of "Sonnet 49," how does the speaker describe the loved one's hands? **(b) Infer:** Which other details in the poem suggest that love and the beloved are part of the natural world?

3. **(a) Recall:** What does the sky do in lines 9–11? **(b) Analyze:** In what ways does this image create a sense of the harmony between human beings and nature?

4. **(a) Recall:** In the first stanza of "Sonnet 71," what three things does love do? **(b) Analyze:** What is the speaker suggesting about the relationship between love and sadness?

5. **(a) Recall:** To what does the speaker compare love in the final image of the poem? **(b) Draw Conclusions:** In what ways is love different from the speaker's expectations?

from OMEROS
Chapter XIII

Derek Walcott

Background

Omeros is a book-length epic poem that describes the wanderings of a present-day Odysseus and the sufferings of others who are displaced and seeking home. The title of the poem is the Greek form of Homer's name. Walcott ties themes from Homer's ancient epics to his own experiences growing up on the Caribbean island of St. Lucia. In this excerpt, the ghost of Walcott's father describes his life on St. Lucia. He also gives his son a goal to strive for in his writing; that goal becomes one of the main themes of Omeros.

I

"I grew up where alleys ended in a harbor
and Infinity wasn't the name of our street;
where the town anarchist was the corner barber

with his own flagpole and revolving Speaker's seat.
5 There were rusted mirrors in which we would look back
on the world's events. There, toga'd[1] in a pinned sheet,

the curled hairs fell like commas. On their varnished rack,
The World's Great Classics read backwards in his mirrors
where he doubled as my chamberlain.[2] I was known

10 for quoting from them as he was for his scissors.
I bequeath you that clean sheet and an empty throne."
We'd arrived at that corner where the barber-pole

---

1. **toga'd** (tō´ gəd) *v.* dressed like an ancient Roman, in a long, one-piece outer garment.
2. **chamberlain** (chām´ bər lin) *n.* personal attendant of a ruler or lord.

Reading Strategy
Read Verse for Meaning
In what ways do the quotation marks help you understand what is happening in the poem?

**Reading Check**

Where does the speaker's father say the alleys of his hometown ended?

Barber Shop, 1942, Cundo Bermudez, The Museum of Modern Art

▲ **Critical Viewing** Does the barber portrayed in this painting seem similar to the barber described in the poem? Why or why not? **[Compare and Contrast]**

angled from the sidewalk, and the photographer,
who'd taken his portrait, and, as some think, his soul,
15 leant from a small window and scissored his own hair

in a mime, suggesting a trim was overdue
to my father, who laughed and said "Wait" with one hand.
Then the barber mimed a shave with his mouth askew,

and left the window to wait by his wooden door
20 framed with dead portraits, and he seemed to understand
something in the life opposite not seen before.

"The rock he lived on was nothing. Not a nation
or a people," my father said, and, in his eyes,
this was a curse. When he raged, his indignation

25 jabbed the air with his scissors, a swift catching flies,
as he pumped the throne serenely round to his view.
He gestured like Shylock: "Hath not a Jew eyes?"[3]

making his man a negative. An Adventist,
he's stuck on one glass that photograph of Garvey's
30 with the braided tricorne and gold-fringed epaulettes,

and that is his other Messiah.[4] His paradise
is a phantom Africa. Elephants. Trumpets.
And when I quote Shylock silver brims in his eyes.

II

"Walk me down to the wharf."
                                    At the corner of Bridge
35 Street, we saw the liner as white as a mirage,
its hull bright as paper, preening with privilege.

"Measure the days you have left. Do just that labor
which marries your heart to your right hand: simplify
your life to one emblem, a sail leaving harbor

Literary Analysis
Surrealism and Personification Which word in line 36 gives human characteristics to the ocean liner? Explain.

---

3. **Shylock: "Hath . . . eyes?"** question asked by Shylock, a Jewish character in Shakespeare's *The Merchant of Venice.* Shylock's point is that a Jew does, of course, have eyes and is just as human as a Christian.
4. **an Adventist** (ad´ vənt´ist) **. . . other Messiah** (mə sī´ ə) An Adventist is a member of a Christian sect that believes the world will soon come to an end. Marcus Garvey (1887–1940), an African American of Jamaican descent, believed that blacks around the world should unite and return to Africa. That is why some regard him as a messiah, or savior of his people.

40 and a sail coming in. All corruption will cry
to be taken aboard. Fame is that white liner
at the end of your street, a city to itself,

taller than the Fire Station, and much finer,
with its brass-ringed portholes, mounting shelf after shelf,
45 than anything Castries[5] could ever hope to build."

The immaculate hull insulted the tin roofs
beneath it, its pursers[6] were milk, even the bilge
bubbling from its stern in quietly muttering troughs

and its humming engines spewed expensive garbage
50 where boys balanced on logs or, riding old tires,
shouted up past the hull to tourists on the rails

to throw down coins, as cameras caught their black cries,
then jackknife or swan-dive—their somersaulting tails
like fishes flipped backwards—as the coins grew in size

55 in the wobbling depth; then, when they surfaced, fights
for possession, their heads butting like porpoises,
till, like a city leaving a city, the lights

blazed in its moving rooms, and the liner would glide
over its own phosphorus, and wash hit the wharves
60 long after stewards had set the service inside

the swaying chandeliered salons, and the black waves
settle down to their level. The stars would renew
their studded diagrams over Achille's canoe.[7]

From here, in his boyhood, he had seen women climb
65 like ants up a white flower-pot, baskets of coal
balanced on their torchoned[8] heads, without touching them,

up the black pyramids, each spine straight as a pole,
and with a strength that never altered its rhythm.
He spoke for those Helens[9] from an earlier time:

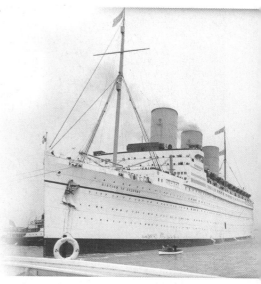

---

5. **Castries** (kas trēz´) capital of St. Lucia and Walcott's hometown.
6. **pursers** (pʉrs´ ərz) *n.* ships' officers in charge of freight, tickets, and similar matters.
7. **Achille's** (ə shēlz´) **canoe** Achille, a fisherman, is one of the main characters in Walcott's *Omeros*, which is loosely based on the epics of the ancient Greek poet Homer (*Omeros* is Greek for Homer). Achille is named for Achilles (a kil´ ēz´), a hero whose exploits are described by Homer
8. **torchoned** (tôr´ shänd) *adj.* wrapped around with a cloth.
9. **Helens** Helen is one of the main characters in Homer's epic the *Iliad*. A beautiful Greek queen, she was kidnapped by a Trojan prince, and this deed provoked a war between the Greeks and the Trojans.

Reading Check
What impressive object is visible at the corner of Bridge Street?

70   "Hell was built on those hills. In that country of coal
    without fire, that inferno the same color
    as their skins and shadows, every laboring soul

    climbed with her hundredweight basket,[10] every load for
    one copper penny, balanced erect on their necks
75   that were tight as the liner's hawsers[11] from the weight.

    The carriers were women, not the fair, gentler sex.
    Instead, they were darker and stronger, and their gait
    was made beautiful by balance, in their ascending

    the narrow wooden ramp built steeply to the hull
80   of a liner tall as a cloud, the unending
    line crossing like ants without touching for the whole

    day. That was one section of the wharf, opposite
    your grandmother's house where I watched the silhouettes
    of these women, while every hundredweight basket

▲ Critical Viewing

Derek Walcott painted this watercolor of St. Lucia. Compare and contrast this view of the island with the descriptions in the poem. **[Compare and Contrast]**

---

10. **hundredweight basket** basket weighing one hundred pounds.
11. **hawsers** (hô´ zərz) *n.* large ropes used for towing or securing a ship.

85   was ticked by two tally clerks in their white pith-helmets,[12]
and the endless repetition as they climbed the
infernal anthracite hills[13] showed you hell, early."

III

"Along this coal-blackened wharf, what Time decided
to do with my treacherous body after this,"
90   he said, watching the women, "will stay in your head

as long as a question you have no right to ask,
only to doubt, not hate our infuriating
silence. I am only the shadow of that task

as much as their work, your pose of a question waiting,
95   as you crouch with a writing lamp over a desk,
remains in the darkness after the light has gone,

and whether night is palpable between dawn and dusk
is not for the living; so you mind your business,
which is life and work, like theirs, but I will say this:

100   O Thou, my Zero, is an impossible prayer,
utter extinction is still a doubtful conceit.
Though we pray to nothing, nothing cannot be there.[14]

Kneel to your load, then balance your staggering feet
and walk up that coal ladder as they do in time,
105   one bare foot after the next in ancestral rhyme.

Because Rhyme remains the parentheses of palms
shielding a candle's tongue, it is the language's
desire to enclose the loved world in its arms;

or heft a coal-basket; only by its stages
110   like those groaning women will you achieve that height
whose wooden planks in couplets lift your pages

higher than those hills of infernal anthracite.
There, like ants or angels, they see their native town,
unknown, raw, insignificant. They walk, you write;

---

12. **two tally clerks . . . pith-helmets** The clerks who tallied, or counted, the baskets wore light, bell-shaped hats as protection from the sun.
13. **anthracite** (an´ thrə sīt´) **hills** mounds of hard coal.
14. **O Thou . . . conceit** (kən sēt´) **. . . be there** You cannot address a prayer to nothingness as if you were praying to God. The conceit, or idea, of nothingness probably does not correspond to anything real.

Reading Check

How much money did the women receive for each load of coal?

115 keep to that narrow causeway without looking down,
     climbing in their footsteps, that slow, ancestral beat
     of those used to climbing roads; your own work owes them

     because the couplet of those multiplying feet
     made your first rhymes. Look, they climb, and no one knows them;
120 they take their copper pittances, and your duty

     from the time you watched them from your grandmother's house
     as a child wounded by their power and beauty
     is the chance you now have, to give those feet a voice."

     We stood in the hot afternoon. My father took
125 his fob-watch[15] from its pocket, replaced it, then said,
     lightly gripping my arm,
                            "He enjoys a good talk,

     a serious trim, and I myself look ahead
     to our appointment." He kissed me. I watched him walk
     through a pillared balcony's alternating shade.

---

15. **fob-watch** (fäb´ wäch) watch carried in a small front pocket of a pair of trousers.

Review and Assess

Thinking About the Selection

1. **Respond:** Which images in this excerpt did you find most striking? Explain.

2. **(a) Recall:** In line 46, what does the speaker say the ocean liner does to the town? **(b) Compare and Contrast:** In what ways does the ocean liner differ from the town? **(c) Infer:** What mixed feelings do you think the townspeople might have for the ocean liner and its passengers? Explain.

3. **(a) Classify:** In his boyhood, what work did the father watch local women perform? **(b) Interpret:** When the father calls the women "Helens," he alludes to the Greek queen whose beauty helped spark the Trojan War. What does this comparison suggest about the women? **(c) Analyze:** In what ways is this comparison both surprising and not surprising?

4. **(a) Distinguish:** In lines 103–123, which details compare the women's labor to the art of writing poetry? **(b) Draw Conclusions:** According to the father, why is the son obligated to the women?

5. **(a) Infer:** What specific advice does the father give the son regarding the use of rhyme? **(b) Speculate:** What evidence does this excerpt provide that the son heeded the father's advice? Explain.

Review and Assess

Literary Analysis

Surrealism

1. Explain specific ways in which lines 8–14 of Paz's poem "Fable" contain two essential elements of **Surrealism**—surprising juxtapositions and extraordinary transformations of everyday objects.

2. Is Paz's poem "Concord" also an example of Surrealism? Explain.

3. (a) Which details in stanza two of Neruda's "Sonnet 71" could be classified as Surrealist? Explain. (b) Which details in the poem's final stanza could be considered Surrealist? Explain.

4. Using these poems as examples, describe specific ways in which Surrealist writers ground their fantastic visions in realistic details.

Comparing Literary Works

5. (a) Use a chart like the one shown to analyze examples of **personification** in these selections. (b) Which examples describe objects and which describe ideas?

Poem	Example	Human Trait	Emotional Effect

6. Based on these poems, explain how the use of personification to describe an abstraction, such as love, can help a reader perceive the author's ideas.

7. Using these poems as examples, why do you think Surrealist works often include examples of personification?

Reading Strategy

Reading Verse for Meaning

8. (a) When you **read** the excerpt from *Omeros* **for meaning,** where do you pause and where do you come to a full stop? (b) Explain how the three-line stanzas organize the speaker's ideas.

9. In lines 64–69 of the excerpt from *Omeros*, explain how the punctuation helps you understand what is happening in the poem.

Extend Understanding

10. **Mathematics Connection:** In what ways do you think scientists or mathematicians might make use of the kinds of whimsical thinking demonstrated by the Surrealists? Explain.

Quick Review

Surrealism is an artistic movement that emphasizes the irrational side of human nature. Surrealist works go beyond a realistic depiction of the world to portray the vivid, imaginative associations of the unconscious mind.

Personification is a type of figurative language in which a nonhuman subject is given human traits.

When you **read verse for meaning,** you first focus on the sentences rather than the line breaks of poems, using punctuation as a guide.

 **Take It to the Net**
PHSchool.com

Take the interactive self-test online to check your understanding of these selections.

Integrate Language Skills

Vocabulary Development Lesson

Word Analysis: Latin Suffix -al

The Latin suffix -al means "of," "like," or "suited for." It combines with the root -nocturn-, meaning "night," to form the adjective *nocturnal*, meaning "suited for or living at night." Use your knowledge of -al to define each adjective below.

1. paternal
2. anecdotal
3. recreational
4. fraternal

Spelling Strategy

The letter combination *gn* can be pronounced in two ways. In some words, both the *g* and the *n* are voiced *(signal)*. In many others, the *g* is silent *(gnarl)*. Complete the spelling of the words below. Then, identify those in which the *g* is silent.

1. si___
2. i___orant
3. fei___ing
4. forei___er

Grammar and Style Lesson

Correct Use of *between* and *among*

Both of the prepositions *between* and *among* are used to show connections. *Between*, however, is used to show connections between two, and only two, things. *Among* always suggests connections among three or more things.

> **Examples:**
> You are the trembling of time, which passes <u>between</u> the vertical light and the darkening sky. *(connects no more than two things)*
>
> . . . all of yesterday dropped away <u>among</u> the fingers of the light . . . *(connects three or more things)*

Concept Development: Synonyms

Review the vocabulary list on page 1193. Then, select the letter of the word that is closest in meaning to each of the numbered vocabulary words.

1. prophesied: (a) prejudged, (b) benefited, (c) forecasted
2. nocturnal: (a) annual, (b) nighttime, (c) periodic
3. carnivorous: (a) all-consuming, (b) hungry, (c) meat-eating
4. divinations: (a) separations, (b) constitutions, (c) predictions
5. entwined: (a) tangled, (b) complimentary, (c) compartmentalized

Practice Correctly complete each sentence below with *between* or *among*.

1. Some Surrealist poems create links __?__ the rational and the subconscious.
2. "Sonnet 49" appears __?__ ninety-nine other poems.
3. Walcott examines the conflict __?__ responsibility and obsession.
4. There are many similarities __?__ the visions of Paz, Neruda, and Walcott.
5. There are differences in interpretations __?__ the readers of any poem.

Writing Application Write a paragraph comparing and contrasting two poems in this grouping. Use *between* and *among* at least once each.

WG Prentice Hall Writing and Grammar Connection: Diamond Level, Chapter 25, Section 2

Writing Lesson

Letter to a Poet

Select the poem from this grouping that you like best and write a letter to the poet. In your letter, explain what you enjoyed about the poem and how it made you feel, and include any questions you would like to ask the poet.

Prewriting   Select a poem and brainstorm for words and phrases that express the ways in which the poem affects you. Explore connections between the poem and your own life. Also, jot down any questions about the poem that you would like to ask the poet.

Drafting   Begin by explaining your reason for writing. Then, discuss your personal impressions of the poem. End with your questions.

Revising   Review your letter, making sure that you have maintained a tone of appropriate respect. Highlight informal words or phrases and replace them with more formal alternatives.

Model: Revising to Create an Appropriate Tone

truly enjoyed reading   *The image of the tree growing*
~~I really got~~ "Fable." ~~The part where the tree grew~~

I once had.
out of someone's hand reminded me of a dream ~~of~~

my dream
~~mine. In it,~~ my fingertips turned into roses.

> A more formal tone shows an appropriate level of respect.

W_G *Prentice Hall Writing and Grammar Connection: Diamond Level, Chapter 6, Section 4*

Extension Activities

Listening and Speaking   With a partner, select two of these poems that seem very different in subject, tone, or imagery and deliver **contrasting readings** for the class. Use these tips to prepare:

- Discuss how each poem should be read to clarify its meaning and tone for an audience.
- Select suitable sound effects or music.

As you deliver your readings, vary the volume and tone of your voice and use body language that enhances your presentation. **[Group Activity]**

Research and Technology   Neruda's sonnets are part of a tradition of such poems. Use print and electronic sources to locate a variety of sonnets and create an **anthology.** Organize the sonnets by type or by theme. Write an introduction in which you define a sonnet and explain the process you used to make your selections. Choose appropriate illustrations for both the cover and the interior.

 **Take It to the Net**   PHSchool.com

Go online for an additional research activity using the Internet.

A Closer Look

I, WITNESS

In the twentieth century, a new literature arose that gave voice to the victim and empowered the powerless.

In 1970, Alexander Solzhenitsyn, whose writing testified to the tyranny of the government of the Soviet Union, wrote a Nobel Prize acceptance speech called "The One Great Heart." The Soviet government would not allow Solzhenitsyn to travel to Sweden to deliver the speech, but it was published and widely read. In his speech, the author declared that "world literature is no longer an abstraction or a generalized concept invented by literary critics, but a common body and common spirit, a living, heartfelt unity reflecting the growing spiritual unity of mankind." More and more, Solzhenitsyn believed, readers and writers in even the most remote countries are connected to people around the globe. Where once there was sporadic communication, now there is dialogue and community.

New World Literature The concept of world literature is not new. In fact, the German writer Goethe used the phrase some 200 years ago. However, it was not until the twentieth century that two essential factors—decolonization and globalization—helped make the concept of world literature a reality. With decolonization, former colonies declared independence from colonial powers. For example, in 1947, India declared independence from Great Britain, becoming a self-governing country for the first time since 1757. As similar events took place around the globe, new forms of literature arose that emphasized the voices of former colonial subjects who had traditionally been ignored or silenced.

With globalization, new technologies such as television, the movies, the Internet, and rapid forms of travel have made the disparate cultures of the world increasingly accessible. The cultural cross-pollination that enriches our lives today allows new literary voices to spread far beyond their original geographical borders. For example, the Antiguan writer Jamaica Kincaid is lauded for her autobiographical novels about a girl growing up on a Caribbean island and leaving home for the United States. Vénus Khoury-Ghata, a Lebanese writer living in France, has achieved international recognition for her poems in French about her Arab heritage.

Witnesses to History Although the twentieth century ushered in a glorious parade of technological innovations, it also saw bloodshed on an unprecedented scale. Writers from all over the world have borne witness to these evils. During World War I, fighting forces routinely used machine guns, tanks, and chemical weapons. From the battlefields came the frank, anguished voices of young American and European poets turned soldiers, many of whom were killed in the conflict. Their work did not glorify the bloody battles, nor did it flinch from representing the human cost of the first truly modern war. Following World War II, European writers like Primo Levi, an Italian Jewish chemist who survived Auschwitz, and Paul Celan, a Romanian Jewish poet whose parents were deported and killed, documented the destruction of Europe's Jews at the hands of the Nazis.

Italian Landscape, Ben Shahn, © Estate of Ben Shahn/Licensed by VAGA, New York, NY

▲ **Critical Viewing**
How can literature help refugees like those depicted in this painting? **[Synthesize]**

Subjectivity and Truth Perhaps we look to writers to bear witness because they have the power to convey truths that fact can only suggest. Reading Chinua Achebe's short story "Marriage Is a Private Affair," we grasp the importance of tribal differences in rural Nigeria, not because they are explained to us but because we see what happens when a young man marries a woman his father refuses to accept. Through the poetry of Taha Muhammad Ali, who is Palestinian, and of Yehuda Amichai, who is an Israeli Jew, we begin to feel how deeply the conflict in the Middle East wounds the spirits of the people who live there.

In some of the most powerful twentieth-century literature, individual writers bear witness for those who can no longer speak. When we read Elie Wiesel's account of his father's death in a concentration camp and his own survival, we are reminded of the millions of people murdered by the Nazis who took their stories to the grave. Reading the Misty Poets, we think of the Chinese writers who have been imprisoned or killed for criticizing the Communist government.

Somewhere, Somebody Is Writing Because good writers tell the truth even when it is unwelcome, many of them are forced to write in secret or in exile. At this very moment, someone may be scribbling forbidden words that tell the truth of his or her experience. Some writers risk their lives again and again to share what they have witnessed. The words of writers like Vaclav Havel in Czechoslovakia and Leopold Sedar Senghor in Senegal carry such weight that the authors are chosen for political leadership, enabling them to embody the ideas they express. Wherever it is written, wherever it is read, world literature serves to remind us of our common humanity; in its pages, we hear the steady beat of "One Great Heart."

Prepare to Read

A Walk to the Jetty *from* Annie John

Jamaica Kincaid (b. 1949)

"I've never really written about anyone except myself and my mother," says author Jamaica Kincaid. Drawn from her childhood experiences on the Caribbean island of Antigua, Kincaid's fiction explores the complex relationship between mother and daughter and the ways in which it changes, sometimes painfully, during a daughter's passage into adulthood.

Rural Childhood Jamaica Kincaid was born Elaine Potter Richardson on May 25, 1949, in St. John's, Antigua. Like most rural Antiguans, Kincaid grew up in a home without electricity or running water. Nonetheless, her early childhood was happy, primarily because of the deep connection she felt to her mother. That attachment changed, however, when Kincaid was nine years old and the first of her three younger brothers was born. The writer was devastated by this threat to a mother's love that she perceived as hers alone.

Salvation in Books Kincaid was highly intelligent, but her intellectual gifts went largely unrecognized by her teachers. Today, she attributes this oversight to the colonial system under which she grew up. At the time, Antigua was a British dependency. It became an independent nation in 1981. Racism and economic oppression ensured that expectations for young black women remained low. In the face of indifference both at home and at school, Kincaid retreated into the world of books, where she discovered a passion that was missing in other areas of her life. One of her favorite novels was Charlotte Brontë's *Jane Eyre*.

Struggle for Education By the time she was a teenager, Kincaid was determined to leave Antigua. At the age of sixteen, she secured a job as a nanny for a wealthy family living in a New York City suburb. From that position she moved on to a series of unskilled jobs and later to an unsuccessful attempt at getting a college degree. Despite educational and career setbacks, Kincaid made a number of connections in the New York City publishing world, and by the early 1970s she was publishing articles in several magazines for teens.

Hard-Won Success Eventually, Kincaid became a staff writer for *The New Yorker*, in which many of her stories first appeared. In 1983, she published *At the Bottom of the River*, a collection of short stories. While its imaginative metaphors seemed too obscure to some reviewers, others praised the book's lyrical prose and keen insights. Kincaid admits that the stories in the collection may be difficult to grasp; in writing them, she says she sometimes fell into a kind of hallucinatory state. Her later works demonstrate a more traditional narrative style.

Fictionalizing Her Life Kincaid's critically acclaimed novels *Annie John* (1985) and *Lucy* (1990) are both clearly autobiographical. *Annie John* relates the experiences of a young girl growing up on a Caribbean island. "A Walk to the Jetty," in which Annie leaves her childhood home—and, by inference, her childhood self—serves as the book's final scene. *Lucy* picks up the same story by relating the tale of a young Caribbean girl who travels to the United States to take a job caring for the children of a wealthy American couple. Both books are classic Jamaica Kincaid, rich in memories and charged with emotional intensity.

Preview

Connecting to the Literature

If you have ever made a big change, such as moving across the country or even to another town, you will understand how the main character in this story feels. As Annie John prepares to leave her childhood home, she follows a road of bittersweet memories.

Literary Analysis

Point of View

All works of fiction are related by a narrator who speaks from a distinct perspective, or **point of view.** Most stories are told from either a first-person or one of two types of third-person point of view. These are defined by the narrator's relationship to the action and by his or her knowledge of other characters' thoughts and feelings. This story is told from the first-person point of view, which has the following characteristics:

- The narrator is a character who is involved in the story.
- The narrator uses the pronouns "I," "we," "me," "our," and "us."

Point of view controls the information the reader receives. For example, the first-person point of view allows Annie John to share her thoughts and feelings, but it prevents other characters from doing the same. As you read, notice the ways in which the point of view shapes your understanding of the story.

Connecting Literary Elements

The first-person point of view lends itself to the use of **flashback**—a section of a literary work that relates an incident from the past. Flashbacks may take the form of dreams, memories, stories, or actual shifts in time. As you read, identify the details that spark Annie John's flashbacks, and notice the ways in which her memories suggest reasons for her decision to leave the island.

Reading Strategy

Understanding Spatial Relationships

As Annie John walks to the jetty, landmarks along the way trigger her memories. In order to better appreciate Annie John's experience, it is helpful to **understand spatial relationships**—the arrangement of physical features within a setting. As you read, use a chart like the one shown to gain a clear picture of Annie John's walk.

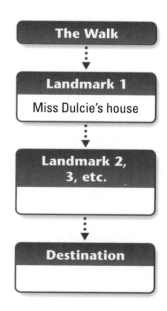

Vocabulary Development

jetty (jet´ē) *n.* wall or barrier built into a body of water to protect a harbor (p. 1213)

loomed (lo͞omd) *v.* appeared in a large or threatening form (p. 1213)

wharf (wôrf) *n.* structure built as a landing place for boats (p. 1217)

scorn (skôrn) *n.* contempt; open dislike or derision (p. 1217)

stupor (sto͞op´ ər) *n.* mental dullness, as if drugged (p. 1218)

cue (kyo͞o) *n.* prompt or reminder (p. 1218)

A Walk to the Jetty

from **Annie John**

Jamaica Kincaid

Background

At the beginning of *Annie John*, the novel from which "A Walk to the Jetty" is excerpted, Annie John is a happy ten-year-old. She loves both her parents, but she is especially close to her mother. However, when Annie is almost twelve, her mother's affections mysteriously sour. In front of Annie's father, "We were politeness and kindness and love and laughter." Alone, the enmity between the two deepens. When she is sixteen years old, Annie John decides to move to England. The final section of the novel, "A Walk to the Jetty" begins as she prepares to leave the island of her childhood.

▼ **Critical Viewing**
Does the woman in this painting seem to be departing, like the narrator in the story, or does she seem to be waiting? Explain. **[Make a Judgment]**

Vista II, 1987, Hughie Lee-Smith, June Kelly Gallery

My mother had arranged with a stevedore[1] to take my trunk to the <u>jetty</u> ahead of me. At ten o'clock on the dot, I was dressed, and we set off for the jetty. An hour after that, I would board a launch that would take me out to sea, where I then would board the ship. Starting out, as if for old time's sake and without giving it a thought, we lined up in the old way: I walking between my mother and my father. I <u>loomed</u> way above my father and could see the top of his head. We must have made a strange sight: a grown girl all dressed up in the middle of a morning, in the middle of the week, walking in step in the middle between her two parents, for people we didn't know stared at us. It was all of half an hour's walk from our house to the jetty, but I was passing through most of the years of my life. We passed by the house where Miss Dulcie, the seamstress that I had been apprenticed to for a time, lived, and just as I was passing by, a wave of bad feeling for her came over me, because I suddenly remembered that the months I spent with her all she had me do was sweep the floor, which was always full of threads and pins and needles, and I never seemed to sweep it clean enough to please her. Then she would send me to the store to buy buttons or thread, though I was only allowed to do this if I was given a sample of the button or thread, and then she would find fault even though they were an exact match of the samples she had given me. And all the while she said to me, "A girl like you will never learn to sew properly, you know." At the time, I don't suppose I minded it, because it was customary to treat the first-year apprentice with such scorn, but now I placed on the dustheap of my life Miss Dulcie and everything that I had had to do with her.

We were soon on the road that I had taken to school, to church, to Sunday school, to choir practice, to Brownie meetings, to Girl Guide meetings, to meet a friend. I was five years old when I first walked on this road unaccompanied by someone to hold my hand. My mother had placed three pennies in my little basket, which was a duplicate of her bigger basket, and sent me to the chemist's shop to buy a pennyworth of senna leaves, a pennyworth of eucalyptus leaves, and a pennyworth of camphor.[2] She then instructed me on what side of the road to walk, where to make a turn, where to cross, how to look carefully before I crossed, and if I met anyone that I knew to politely pass greetings and keep on my way. I was wearing a freshly ironed yellow dress that had printed on it scenes of acrobats flying through the air and swinging on a trapeze. I had just had a bath, and after it, instead of powdering me with my baby-smelling talcum powder, my mother had, as a special favor, let me use her own talcum powder, which smelled quite perfumy and came in a can that had painted on it people going out to dinner in nineteenth-century London and was called Mazie. How it pleased me to walk out the door and bend my head down to sniff at myself and see

jetty (jet′ ē) *n.* wall or barrier built into a body of water to protect a harbor

loomed (lōōmd) *v.* appeared in a large or threatening form

Reading Strategy
Understanding Spatial Relationships Where are Annie and her parents, and where are they headed?

---

1. **stevedore** (stē′ və dôr) *n.* person whose job is the loading and unloading of ships.
2. **chemist's shop . . . camphor** (kam′ fər) *chemist's shop* is the British term for *pharmacy*; the items mentioned are small amounts of plant matter that are used in remedies.

**Reading Check**

Why is the narrator going to the jetty?

that I smelled just like my mother. I went to the chemist's shop, and he had to come from behind the counter and bend down to hear what it was that I wanted to buy, my voice was so little and timid then. I went back just the way I had come, and when I walked into the yard and presented my basket with its three packages to my mother, her eyes filled with tears and she swooped me up and held me high in the air and said that I was wonderful and good and that there would never be anybody better. If I had just conquered Persia, she couldn't have been more proud of me.

We passed by our church—the church in which I had been christened and received[3] and had sung in the junior choir. We passed by a house in which a girl I used to like and was sure I couldn't live without had lived. Once, when she had mumps, I went to visit her against my mother's wishes, and we sat on her bed and ate the cure of roasted, buttered sweet potatoes that had been placed on her swollen jaws, held there by a piece of white cloth. I don't know how, but my mother found out about it, and I don't know how, but she put an end to our friendship. Shortly after, the girl moved with her family across the sea to somewhere else. We passed the doll store, where I would go with my mother when I was little and point out the doll I wanted that year for Christmas. We passed the store where I bought the much-fought-over shoes I wore to church to be received in. We passed the bank. On my sixth birthday, I was given, among other things, the present of a sixpence.[4] My mother and I then went to this bank, and with the sixpence I opened my own savings account. I was given a little gray book with my name in big letters on it, and in the balance column it said "6d." Every Saturday morning after that, I was given a sixpence—later a shilling, and later a two-and-sixpence piece—and I would take it to the bank for deposit. I had never been allowed to withdraw even a farthing from my bank account until just a few weeks before I was to leave; then the whole account was closed out, and I received from the bank the sum of six pounds ten shillings and two and a half pence.

We passed the office of the doctor who told my mother three times that I did not need glasses, that if my eyes were feeling weak a glass of carrot juice a day would make them strong again. This happened when I was eight. And so every day at recess I would run to my school gate and meet my mother, who was waiting for me with a glass of juice from carrots she had just grated and then squeezed, and I would drink it and then run back to meet my chums. I knew there was nothing at all

San Antonio de Oriente, José Antonio Velásquez, Museum of Modern Art of Latin America

▲ Critical Viewing
How is this painting of a Caribbean village similar to and different from your image of the narrator's home in the story? Explain. [Compare and Contrast]

Literary Analysis
Point of View and Flashback What information about Annie's relationship with her mother does this flashback provide?

---

3. **received** *v.* accepted into the congregation as a mature Christian.
4. **sixpence** *n.* former monetary unit in the British commonwealth, worth six pennies (about 12 U.S. cents). A shilling was worth two sixpence, a two-and-sixpence was two and one-half shillings (two shillings and one sixpence), a pound was twenty shillings, and a farthing was a "fourthing": one fourth of a penny.

wrong with my eyes, but I had recently read a story in *The Schoolgirl's Own Annual* in which the heroine, a girl a few years older than I was then, cut such a figure to my mind with the way she was always adjusting her small, round, horn-rimmed glasses that I felt I must have a pair exactly like them. When it became clear that I didn't need glasses, I began to complain about the glare of the sun being too much for my eyes, and I walked around with my hands shielding them—especially in my mother's presence. My mother then bought for me a pair of sunglasses with the exact horn-rimmed frames I wanted, and how I enjoyed the gestures of blowing on the lenses, wiping them with the hem of my uniform, adjusting the glasses when they slipped down my nose, and just removing them from their case and putting them on. In three weeks, I grew tired of them and they found a nice resting place in a drawer, along with some other things that at one time or another I couldn't live without.

We passed the store that sold only grooming aids, all imported from England. This store had in it a large porcelain dog—white, with black spots all over and a red ribbon of satin tied around its neck. The dog sat in front of a white porcelain bowl that was always filled with fresh water, and it sat in such a way that it looked as if it had just taken a long drink. When I was a small child, I would ask my mother, if ever we were near this store, to please take me to see the dog, and I would stand in front of it, bent over slightly, my hands resting on my knees, and stare at it and stare at it. I thought this dog more beautiful and more real than any actual dog I had ever seen or any actual dog I would ever see. I must have outgrown my interest in the dog, for when it disappeared I never asked what became of it. We passed the library, and if there was anything on this walk that I might have wept over leaving, this most surely would have been the thing. My mother had been a member of the library long before I was born. And since she took me everywhere with her when I was quite little, when she went to the library she took me along there, too. I would sit in her lap very quietly as she read books that she did not want to take home with her. I could not read the words yet, but just the way they looked on the page was interesting to me. Once, a book she was reading had a large picture of a man in it, and when I asked her who he was she told me that he was Louis Pasteur[5] and that the book was about his life. It stuck in my mind, because she said it was because of him that she boiled my milk to purify it before I was allowed to drink it, that it was his idea, and that that was why the process was called pasteurization. One of the things I had put away in my mother's old trunk in which she kept all my childhood things was my library card. At that moment, I owed sevenpence in overdue fees.

5. **Louis Pasteur** (pas tʉr´) French chemist and bacteriologist (1822–1895) who developed pasteurization, the process for using heat to kill disease-causing bacteria in milk.

Literary Analysis
Point of View In what ways does the first-person point of view allow the narrator to share specific private thoughts and feelings?

✔ **Reading Check**

Which landmark from her childhood does the narrator almost weep over leaving?

As I passed by all these places, it was as if I were in a dream, for I didn't notice the people coming and going in and out of them, I didn't feel my feet touch ground, I didn't even feel my own body—I just saw these places as if they were hanging in the air, not having top or bottom, and as if I had gone in and out of them all in the same moment. The sun was bright; the sky was blue and just above my head. We then arrived at the jetty.

My heart now beat fast, and no matter how hard I tried, I couldn't keep my mouth from falling open and my nostrils from spreading to the ends of my face. My old fear of slipping between the boards of the jetty and falling into the dark-green water where the dark-green eels lived came over me. When my father's stomach started to go bad, the doctor had recommended a walk every evening right after he ate his dinner. Sometimes he would take me with him. When he took me with him, we usually went to the jetty, and there he would sit and talk to the night watchman about cricket[6] or some other thing that didn't interest me, because it was not personal; they didn't talk about their wives, or their children, or their parents, or about any of their likes and dislikes. They talked about things in such a strange way, and I didn't see what they found funny, but sometimes they made each other laugh so much that their guffaws would bound out to sea and send back an echo. I was always sorry when we got to the jetty and saw that the night watchman on duty was the one he enjoyed speaking to; it was like being locked up in a book filled with numbers and diagrams and what-ifs. For the thing about not being able to understand and enjoy what they were saying was I had nothing to take my mind off my fear of slipping in between the boards of the jetty.

Now, too, I had nothing to take my mind off what was happening to me. My mother and my father—I was leaving them forever. My home on an island—I was leaving it forever. What to make of everything? I felt a familiar hollow space inside. I felt I was being held down against my will. I felt I was burning up from head to toe. I felt that someone was tearing me up into little pieces and soon I would be able to see all the little pieces as they floated out into nothing in the deep blue sea. I didn't know whether to laugh or cry. I could see that it would be better not to think too clearly about any one thing. The launch was being made ready to take me, along with some other passengers, out to the ship that was anchored in the sea. My father paid our fares, and we joined a line of people waiting to board. My mother checked my bag to make sure that I had my passport, the money she had given me, and a sheet of paper placed between some pages in my Bible on which were

The Landscape and Climate of Antigua
White sand beaches, spectacular coral reefs, and an average temperature of 80 degrees make Antigua a popular vacation spot. There are 365 beaches on Antigua—one for each day of the year! The island is approximately 14 miles long and 11 miles wide, covering 108 square miles. With an average rainfall of only 40 inches per year, the island is one of the sunniest in the eastern Caribbean. While the steady supply of sunshine is a pleasure for tourists, the constant threat of drought can be devastating to the property and livelihoods of native Antiguans.

Reading Strategy
Understanding Spatial Relationships What is the connection between Annie's physical location and her emotions?

6. **cricket** *n.* British game, similar to baseball but played with a flat bat and eleven players on each team.

written the names of the relatives—people I had not known existed—with whom I would live in England. Across from the jetty was a <u>wharf</u>, and some stevedores were loading and unloading barges. I don't know why seeing that struck me so, but suddenly a wave of strong feeling came over me, and my heart swelled with a great gladness as the words "I shall never see this again" spilled out inside me. But then, just as quickly, my heart shriveled up and the words "I shall never see this again" stabbed at me. I don't know what stopped me from falling in a heap at my parents' feet.

When we were all on board, the launch headed out to sea. Away from the jetty, the water became the customary blue, and the launch left a wide path in it that looked like a road. I passed by sounds and smells that were so familiar that I had long ago stopped paying any attention to them. But now here they were, and the ever-present "I shall never see this again" bobbed up and down inside me. There was the sound of the sea-gull diving down into the water and coming up with something silverish in its mouth. There was the smell of the sea and the sight of small pieces of rubbish floating around in it. There were boats filled with fishermen coming in early. There was the sound of their voices as they shouted greetings to each other. There was the hot sun, there was the blue sea, there was the blue sky. Not very far away, there was the white sand of the shore, with the run-down houses all crowded in next to each other, for in some places only poor people lived near the shore. I was seated in the launch between my parents, and when I realized that I was gripping their hands tightly I glanced quickly to see if they were looking at me with <u>scorn</u>, for I felt sure that they must have known of my never-see-this-again feelings. But instead my father kissed me on the forehead and my mother kissed me on the mouth, and they both gave over their hands to me, so that I could grip them as much as I wanted. I was on the verge of feeling that it had all been a mistake, but I remembered that I wasn't a child anymore, and that now when I made up my mind about something I had to see it through. At that moment, we came to the ship, and that was that.

The goodbyes had to be quick, the captain said. My mother introduced herself to him and then introduced me. She told him to keep an eye on me, for I had never gone this far away from home on my own. She gave him a letter to pass on to the captain of the next ship that I would board in Barbados.[7] They walked me to my cabin, a small space that I would share with someone else—a woman I did not know. I had never before slept in a room with someone I did not know. My father kissed me goodbye and told me to be good and to write home often. After he said this, he looked at me, then looked at the floor and swung his left foot, then looked at me again. I could see that he

---

7. **Barbados** (bär bā′ dōs) easternmost island in the West Indies, southeast of Antigua.

wharf (wôrf) *n.* structure built as a landing place for boats

scorn (skôrn) *n.* contempt; open dislike or derision

▼ **Critical Viewing**
In what ways does this painting of a ship express the kinds of emotions the narrator experiences as she leaves her home? **[Connect]**

✔ **Reading Check**
What phrase is "ever present" in the narrator's mind?

wanted to say something else, something that he had never said to me before, but then he just turned and walked away. My mother said, "Well," and then she threw her arms around me. Big tears streamed down her face, and it must have been that—for I could not bear to see my mother cry—which started me crying, too. She then tightened her arms around me and held me to her close, so that I felt that I couldn't breathe. With that, my tears dried up and I was suddenly on my guard. "What does she want now?" I said to myself. Still holding me close to her, she said, in a voice that raked across my skin, "It doesn't matter what you do or where you go, I'll always be your mother and this will always be your home."

I dragged myself away from her and backed off a little, and then I shook myself, as if to wake myself out of a <u>stupor</u>. We looked at each other for a long time with smiles on our faces, but I know the opposite of that was in my heart. As if responding to some invisible <u>cue</u>, we both said, at the very same moment, "Well." Then my mother turned around and walked out the cabin door. I stood there for I don't know how long, and then I remembered that it was customary to stand on deck and wave to your relatives who were returning to shore. From the deck, I could not see my father, but I could see my mother facing the ship, her eyes searching to pick me out. I removed from my bag a red cotton handkerchief that she had earlier given me for this purpose, and I waved it wildly in the air. Recognizing me immediately, she waved back just as wildly, and we continued to do this until she became just a dot in the matchbox-size launch swallowed up in the big blue sea.

I went back to my cabin and lay down on my berth. Everything trembled as if it had a spring at its very center. I could hear the small waves lap-lapping around the ship. They made an unexpected sound, as if a vessel filled with liquid had been placed on its side and now was slowly emptying out.

stupor (stōōp´ ər) *n.* mental dullness, as if drugged

cue (kyōō) *n.* prompt or reminder

Review and Assess

Thinking About the Selection

1. **Respond:** Do you admire Annie John? Why or why not?
2. **(a) Recall:** Identify four places that Annie John passes.
   (b) Interpret: In what ways is Annie John walking through time as well as through space?
3. **(a) Recall:** As Annie John approaches the jetty, what old feeling does she experience? **(b) Analyze:** Why does she experience this feeling as she prepares to leave the island?
4. **(a) Recall:** In the story's final image, to what does Annie John compare the sound of the waves? **(b) Analyze:** In what ways does this image mirror her emotional state? Explain.
5. **Speculate:** Do you think Annie John will be successful in her new life? Why or why not?

Review and Assess

Literary Analysis

Point of View

1. Which elements of the text show that "A Walk to the Jetty" is narrated from the first-person **point of view**? Explain.
2. (a) Cite three passages in the text in which you learn something about Annie John's parents. (b) What do you learn? (c) In what specific ways does the first-person point of view limit information about characters other than the narrator?
3. Why might the first-person point of view generate more sympathy for the narrator than would another point of view?

Connecting Literary Elements

4. Each **flashback** in this excerpt is triggered as Annie John passes a familiar place. Use a chart like the one shown to analyze four of her flashbacks.

Place	Triggered Memory	What We Learn

5. What information do the flashbacks provide about Annie John's reasons for leaving home?

Reading Strategy

Understanding Spatial Relationships

6. (a) Describe the ways in which the **spatial relationships** between Annie John and her parents change as they begin their journey, travel on the launch, board the ship, and say goodbye. (b) In what ways do their spatial relationships express their emotional relationships?
7. In what ways does Annie John's physical journey relate to her emotional journey?

Extend Understanding

8. **Social Studies Connection:** While not a formal ceremony, Annie John's departure from home is a rite of passage—an event signifying that a child has become an adult. What rites of passage exist in American culture?

Quick Review

Point of view is the perspective from which a story is told. With a **first-person** point of view, a story is told by a narrator who is part of the action and uses the pronouns "I," "me," "we," "our," and "us."

A **flashback** is a section of a literary work that interrupts the sequence of events to relate an incident from the past.

To **understand spatial relationships** as you read, pay attention to details that describe the physical arrangements of elements in a setting.

 **Take It to the Net**
PHSchool.com

Take the interactive self-test online to check your understanding of this selection.

Integrate Language Skills

Vocabulary Development Lesson

Word Analysis: Latin Root -stup-

The word *stupor* contains the Latin root *-stup-*, which means "stunned or amazed." Use the meaning of this root to match each numbered word to its synonym.

1. stupefy
2. stupendous
3. stupefaction

a. bewilderment
b. numb
c. astonishing

Spelling Strategy

In most English words, when a *c* comes before the vowel *u*, it has a *k* sound, as in the word *cue*. In some words, the *c* before a *u* is doubled. Correctly complete the spelling of each word below with letters representing the *k* sound.

1. ___uriosity
2. o___upant
3. va___uum
4. con___ur

Grammar and Style Lesson

Adjective Clauses

An **adjective clause** is a type of subordinate clause—one that contains a subject and a verb but cannot stand alone as a sentence. Adjective clauses modify nouns or pronouns and are introduced with relative pronouns, such as *who* or *whom*, *whose*, *which*, or *that*.

> **Example:**
>
> We were soon on the road *that I had taken to* *school* . . . (*modifies road*)
>
> My mother had placed three pennies in my little basket, *which was a duplicate of her bigger* *basket* . . . (*modifies basket*)

Concept Development: Analogies

Analogies present words in pairs to emphasize their relationships. Common links include synonym, antonym, degree of intensity, and part to whole. For each numbered item below, study the relationship presented in the first pair. Then, use the vocabulary words on page 1211 to complete word pairs that express the same relationship.

1. *Strength* is to *weakness* as ___?___ is to *admiration*.
2. *Advice* is to *guidance* as ___?___ is to *prompt*.
3. *Bumper* is to *automobile* as ___?___ is to *harbor*.
4. *Frenzy* is to *calmness* as ___?___ is to *lucidity*.
5. *Encouraged* is to *supported* as ___?___ is to *threatened*.
6. *Hangar* is to *airplane* as ___?___ is to *boat*.

Practice Identify the adjective clause and the word it modifies in each of the following sentences.

1. Annie walked past the store, which reminded her of her mother.
2. Miss Dulcie did not respect Annie, whose chores included sweeping.
3. The family walked down the road that they had traveled many times before.
4. Annie remembered the watchman who often talked with her father.
5. The waves that lapped against the boat made a sad sound.

Writing Application Write a paragraph to describe Annie's memories on the day she leaves home. Include one adjective clause in each sentence.

WG Prentice Hall Writing and Grammar Connection: Diamond Level, Chapter 19, Section 3

Writing Lesson

A Reminiscence

Imagine that you are walking through a familiar landscape, such as your neighborhood, a shopping mall, or your school. Write a reminiscence—a narrative that relates events from the past—in which memories are triggered by elements of the setting. You may write as yourself or as a fictional character.

Prewriting Brainstorm for memories and sensory details—elements that relate to the senses—by using a cluster diagram like the one shown. Try to identify larger themes or ideas that the memories capture.

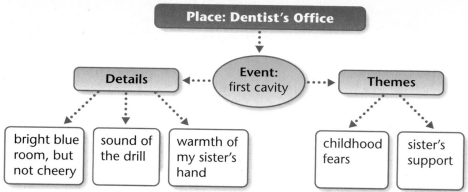

Drafting Begin by describing the purpose of your journey. Then, use the landscape itself to order the narrative. Describe each place you pass, and explain the memory it triggers.

Revising As you review your writing, make sure that you have used vivid sensory details. Consider adding details to enliven your reminiscence.

W̶G̶ Prentice Hall Writing and Grammar Connection: Diamond Level, Chapter 4, Section 2

Extension Activities

Listening and Speaking Conduct a **discussion** about the benefits and challenges of traveling or schooling abroad. Use these tips to prepare:

- Invite someone in your school to speak to your class about travel or education in another country.
- Generate a list of questions in advance.

You may wish to take notes about the discussion and write a report or interview for your school newspaper. **[Group Activity]**

Research and Technology Using details from the text, create a **map** showing Annie's walk to the jetty. Include landmarks, illustrations, and other references to help make your map a vivid representation of Kincaid's narrative. Include a key so that viewers can connect the illustrations with the related site on Annie's journey.

 **Take It to the Net** PHSchool.com

Go online for an additional research activity using the Internet.

Prepare to Read

The Guest

Albert Camus
(1913–1960)

When a now-famous Polish writer was an unknown student in Paris, he often wandered around the city at all hours. Late one night, he met a solitary man in a cheap café and the two shared a stimulating philosophical discussion. Only later, when he was home in bed, did he realize that he had been talking with the celebrated French author Albert Camus (ka mōō´). This remarkable anecdote illustrates several of Camus's most endearing qualities: his modesty, his searching intelligence, and his restless night-owl habits.

Early Hardship Camus was born in Mondovi, Algeria, to parents of European descent. His family was desperately poor and his mother was deaf. Camus's childhood became even more difficult when his father died in World War I.

Despite his poverty, Camus's intelligence shone; his teachers recognized his gifts and encouraged him in his studies. Although Camus had to work at odd jobs while attending the University of Algiers, he was an excellent scholar. In addition to his main studies in literature, he also helped found a small theater group that staged plays of interest to working-class people. Years later, when he wrote plays such as *Caligula* (1944), the drama of a Roman emperor who resembles modern dictators like Hitler and Mussolini, Camus drew on this early theatrical experience.

Tests of Integrity A man of strong moral principles, Camus sometimes suffered for his convictions. For instance, when he publicly criticized the French colonial government of Algiers, he was forced to leave the country. He emigrated to France, where he worked as an investigative reporter for a Parisian newspaper.

Camus's integrity was tested again when the Germans occupied France during World War II. At the risk of his life, Camus supported the French Resistance Movement by serving as the principal editor of *Combat,* an illegal newspaper. As an underground journalist, he won recognition for his independent views and the emphasis he placed on moral behavior.

First Important Works Despite the turmoil of World War II, Camus published two of his most influential works, the novel *The Stranger* (1942) and the essay "The Myth of Sisyphus" (1942), during the war years. The novel describes a man who realizes that conventional values are ultimately senseless and absurd—humans are uninvited guests in an indifferent universe. In 1947, Camus published another novel that deals with similar themes but in a more positive way. Set in the Algerian city of Oran, *The Plague* describes an epidemic that symbolizes both the German Occupation of France and all the other evils that beset humankind. In combating the plague, several of the characters learn the importance of honor and compassion.

Acknowledged as a major twentieth-century writer, Camus spent part of the late 1940s touring and lecturing in North and South America. On returning to Paris, he withdrew from public life and continued to produce essays and plays. In 1957, he received the Nobel Prize in Literature. Camus's death in an auto accident three years later cut short his brilliant career. However, in 1994, *The First Man,* a manuscript that had been found in the wreckage of his car, was published in France. English publication of the book followed in 1995. An autobiographical work-in-progress, the book reveals Camus in all his brilliance, modesty, and humanity.

Preview

Connecting to the Literature

If you have ever resisted pressure to do something you felt was wrong, you will understand how the main character in this story feels. Caught between hostile parties as a revolution begins, Daru stands alone.

Literary Analysis

Existentialism

Existentialism is a philosophy that teaches the importance of personal choice, not universal codes, in creating values. The various forms of Existentialism agree on these essential points:

- The universe is indifferent and can provide no answers.
- Our lives matter because of our own actions, not because we are part of a greater plan.
- The individual has total freedom to choose and to act.
- Human life is inherently valuable; freedom is an end in itself.

Although Camus did not accept the label of Existentialist, he is widely regarded as one of its foremost literary practitioners. As you read this story, look for details that suggest an Existentialist outlook.

Connecting Literary Elements

The **setting** of a story is the time and place of the action. In many stories, the setting is merely a context, like a painted backdrop on a stage. Sometimes, however, the setting adds meaning. For example, in "The Guest," the stark, windswept vistas reflect the **theme**—the story's central message. As you read, think about how the setting and theme are intertwined.

Reading Strategy

Inferring Cultural Attitudes

Cultural attitudes are the customs, values, and beliefs that are held by people living in a distinct place and time. In most literary works, the author does not spell out these attitudes. Instead, he or she provides details, such as dialogue, actions, and descriptions, that allow readers to infer cultural attitudes. As you read, use a chart like the one shown to identify details and to infer the cultural attitudes they express.

Detail

Daru offers mint tea to the visitors.

↓

Cultural Attitude

Hospitality is important.

Vocabulary Development

plateau (pla tō´) *n.* elevated tract of relatively level land (p. 1225)

siege (sēj) *n.* the surrounding of a fortified place by an opposing force, such as an army (p. 1226)

foretaste (fôr´ tāst´) *n.* slight experience or hint of something that is still to come (p. 1227)

mobilized (mō´ bə līzd´) *v.* ready for action or battle (p. 1229)

denounce (dē nouns´) *v.* accuse publicly (p. 1231)

fraternized (frat´ ər nīzd´) *v.* associated in a brotherly way; socialized (p. 1234)

furtive (fur´ tiv) *adj.* done in a secret or sneaky way (p. 1234)

The Guest

Albert Camus

translated by Justin O'Brien

▲ **Critical Viewing**   What details of this image capture the isolation of the setting Camus describes? **[Connect]**

Background

In 1954, a war for independence began in the North African country of Algeria, which had been a colony of France since 1848. More than a century of colonialism had created a deeply divided society with a wealthy European elite, a small European working class, and a large Muslim majority that was mostly poor. The independence struggle began with terrorist attacks on police posts by a radical Muslim group, the National Liberation Front (FLN). As the revolt spread, the French military retaliated with severe reprisals. The early stages of the rebellion provide the historical context for this story.

The schoolmaster was watching the two men climb toward him. One was on horseback, the other on foot. They had not yet tackled the abrupt rise leading to the schoolhouse built on the hillside. They were toiling onward, making slow progress in the snow, among the stones, on the vast expanse of the high, deserted <u>plateau</u>. From time to time the horse stumbled. Without hearing anything yet, he could see the breath issuing from the horse's nostrils. One of the men, at least, knew the region. They were following the trail although it had disappeared days ago under a layer of dirty white snow. The schoolmaster calculated that it would take them half an hour to get onto the hill. It was cold; he went back into the school to get a sweater.

Literary Analysis
Existentialism; Setting and Theme Why might this setting be appropriate in a story expressing Existentialist views?

plateau (pla tō´) *n.* elevated tract of relatively level land

✔**Reading Check**

Why is the trail to the schoolhouse difficult for the men to follow?

He crossed the empty, frigid classroom. On the blackboard the four rivers of France, drawn with four different colored chalks, had been flowing toward their estuaries for the past three days. Snow had suddenly fallen in mid-October after eight months of drought without the transition of rain, and the twenty pupils, more or less, who lived in the villages scattered over the plateau had stopped coming. With fair weather they would return. Daru now heated only the single room that was his lodging, adjoining the classroom and giving also onto the plateau to the east. Like the class windows, his window looked to the south too. On that side the school was a few kilometers[1] from the point where the plateau began to slope toward the south. In clear weather could be seen the purple mass of the mountain range where the gap opened onto the desert.

Somewhat warmed, Daru returned to the window from which he had first seen the two men. They were no longer visible. Hence they must have tackled the rise. The sky was not so dark, for the snow had stopped falling during the night. The morning had opened with a dirty light which had scarcely become brighter as the ceiling of clouds lifted. At two in the afternoon it seemed as if the day were merely beginning. But still this was better than those three days when the thick snow was falling amidst unbroken darkness with little gusts of wind that rattled the double door of the classroom. Then Daru had spent long hours in his room, leaving it only to go to the shed and feed the chickens or get some coal. Fortunately the delivery truck from Tadjid,[2] the nearest village to the north, had brought his supplies two days before the blizzard. It would return in forty-eight hours.

Besides, he had enough to resist a <u>siege</u>, for the little room was cluttered with bags of wheat that the administration left as a stock to distribute to those of his pupils whose families had suffered from the drought. Actually they had all been victims because they were all poor. Every day Daru would distribute a ration to the children. They had missed it, he knew, during these bad days. Possibly one of the fathers or big brothers would come this afternoon and he could supply them with grain. It was just a matter of carrying them over to the next harvest. Now shiploads of wheat were arriving from France and the worst was over. But it would be hard to forget that poverty, that army of ragged ghosts wandering in the sunlight, the plateaus burned to a cinder month after month, the earth shriveled up little by little, literally scorched, every stone bursting into dust under one's foot. The sheep had died then by thousands and even a few men, here and there, sometimes without anyone's knowing.

In contrast with such poverty, he who lived almost like a monk in his remote schoolhouse, nonetheless satisfied with the little he had and with the rough life, had felt like a lord with his white-washed walls, his

Literary Analysis
Existentialism In what ways does the description of Daru's circumstances during the blizzard reflect Existentialist ideas?

siege (sēj) *n.* the surrounding of a fortified place by an opposing force, such as an army

Reading Strategy
Inferring Cultural Attitudes What cultural attitudes toward wealth are suggested by this discussion of drought and poverty?

---

1. **kilometers** (kil´ ə mēt´ ərz) *n.* measures of distance, each of which is equal to 1,000 meters, or about five eighths of a mile.
2. **Tadjid** (tä jēd´)

narrow couch, his unpainted shelves, his well, and his weekly provision of water and food. And suddenly this snow, without warning, without the <u>foretaste</u> of rain. This is the way the region was, cruel to live in, even without men—who didn't help matters either. But Daru had been born here. Everywhere else, he felt exiled.

He stepped out onto the terrace in front of the schoolhouse. The two men were now halfway up the slope. He recognized the horseman as Balducci, the old gendarme[3] he had known for a long time. Balducci was holding on the end of a rope an Arab who was walking behind him with hands bound and head lowered. The gendarme waved a greeting to which Daru did not reply, lost as he was in contemplation of the Arab dressed in a faded blue jellaba,[4] his feet in sandals but covered with socks of heavy raw wool, his head surmounted by a narrow, short *chèche*.[5] They were approaching. Balducci was holding back his horse in order not to hurt the Arab, and the group was advancing slowly.

Within earshot, Balducci shouted: "One hour to do the three kilometers from El Ameur!"[6] Daru did not answer. Short and square in his thick sweater, he watched them climb. Not once had the Arab raised his head. "Hello," said Daru when they got up onto the terrace. "Come in and warm up." Balducci painfully got down from his horse without letting go the rope. From under his bristling mustache he smiled at the schoolmaster. His little dark eyes, deep-set under a tanned forehead,

Arab at the Door of His House, Eugène Delacroix, Rijksmuseum, Amsterdam

foretaste (fôr´ tāst´) *n.* slight experience or hint of something that is still to come

Reading Strategy
Inferring Cultural Attitudes
What can you infer about Daru based on his interest in the Arab's clothing?

✔**Reading Check**

Who are the two men who approach Daru's schoolhouse?

◀ **Critical Viewing**
How is this dwelling similar to or different from your image of Daru's schoolhouse? [**Compare and Contrast**]

and his mouth surrounded with wrinkles made him look attentive and studious. Daru took the bridle, led the horse to the shed, and came back to the two men, who were now waiting for him in the school. He led them into his room. "I am going to heat up the classroom," he said. "We'll be more comfortable there." When he entered the room again, Balducci was on the couch. He had undone the rope tying him to the Arab, who had squatted near the stove. His hands still bound, the *chèche* pushed back on his head, he was looking toward the window. At first Daru noticed only his huge lips, fat, smooth, almost Negroid; yet his nose was straight, his eyes were dark and full of fever. The *chèche* revealed an obstinate forehead and, under the weathered skin now rather discolored by the cold, the whole face had a restless and rebellious look that struck Daru when the Arab, turning his face toward him, looked him straight in the eyes. "Go into the other room," said the schoolmaster, "and I'll make you some mint tea." "Thanks," Balducci said. "What a chore! How I long for retirement." And addressing his prisoner in Arabic: "Come on, you." The Arab got up and, slowly, holding his bound wrists in front of him, went into the classroom.

▲ **Critical Viewing**
Does this image convey a feeling of poverty, like that suffered by Daru's students, or merely a feeling of simplicity? Explain. **[Make a Judgment]**

With the tea, Daru brought a chair. But Balducci was already enthroned on the nearest pupil's desk and the Arab had squatted against the teacher's platform facing the stove, which stood between the desk and the window. When he held out the glass of tea to the prisoner, Daru hesitated at the sight of his bound hands. "He might perhaps be untied." "Sure," said Balducci. "That was for the trip." He started to get to his feet. But Daru, setting the glass on the floor, had knelt beside the Arab. Without saying anything, the Arab watched him with his feverish eyes. Once his hands were free, he rubbed his swollen wrists against each other, took the glass of tea, and sucked up the burning liquid in swift little sips.

"Good," said Daru. "And where are you headed?"

Balducci withdrew his mustache from the tea. "Here, son."

"Odd pupils! And you're spending the night?"

"No. I'm going back to El Ameur. And you will deliver this fellow to Tinguit.[7] He is expected at police headquarters."

Balducci was looking at Daru with a friendly little smile.

"What's this story?" asked the schoolmaster. "Are you pulling my leg?"

"No, son. Those are the orders."

"The orders? I'm not . . ." Daru hesitated, not wanting to hurt the old Corsican.[8] "I mean, that's not my job."

Reading Strategy
Inferring Cultural Attitudes
Based on Daru's response to Balducci's instruction, what inference can you draw about his attitudes toward authority? Explain.

---

7. Tinguit (ting´ wēt)
8. Corsican (kôr´ si kən) native of Corsica, a Mediterranean island.

"What! What's the meaning of that? In wartime people do all kinds of jobs."

"Then I'll wait for the declaration of war!"

Balducci nodded.

"O.K. But the orders exist and they concern you too. Things are brewing, it appears. There is talk of a forthcoming revolt. We are <u>mobilized</u>, in a way."

Daru still had his obstinate look.

"Listen, son," Balducci said. "I like you and you must understand. There's only a dozen of us at El Ameur to patrol throughout the whole territory of a small department[9] and I must get back in a hurry. I was told to hand this guy over to you and return without delay. He couldn't be kept there. His village was beginning to stir; they wanted to take him back. You must take him to Tinguit tomorrow before the day is over. Twenty kilometers shouldn't faze a husky fellow like you. After that, all will be over. You'll come back to your pupils and your comfortable life."

Behind the wall the horse could be heard snorting and pawing the earth. Daru was looking out the window. Decidedly, the weather was clearing and the light was increasing over the snowy plateau. When all the snow was melted, the sun would take over again and once more would burn the fields of stone. For days, still, the unchanging sky would shed its dry light on the solitary expanse where nothing had any connection with man.

"After all," he said, turning around toward Balducci, "what did he do?" And, before the gendarme had opened his mouth, he asked: "Does he speak French?"

"No, not a word. We had been looking for him for a month, but they were hiding him. He killed his cousin."

"Is he against us?"

"I don't think so. But you can never be sure."

"Why did he kill?"

"A family squabble, I think. One owed the other grain, it seems. It's not at all clear. In short, he killed his cousin with a billhook.[10] You know, like a sheep, *kreezk!*"

Balducci made the gesture of drawing a blade across his throat and the Arab, his attention attracted, watched him with a sort of anxiety. Daru felt a sudden wrath against the man, against all men with their rotten spite, their tireless hates, their blood lust.

But the kettle was singing on the stove. He served Balducci more tea, hesitated, then served the Arab again, who, a second time, drank avidly. His raised arms made the jellaba fall open and the schoolmaster saw his thin, muscular chest.

"Thanks, kid," Balducci said. "And now, I'm off."

He got up and went toward the Arab, taking a small rope from his pocket.

---

9. **department** administrative district in France and certain other countries, similar to a state.
10. **billhook** tool with a carved or hooked blade, used for pruning or cutting.

Literary Analysis
Existentialism How does Balducci's statement that "the orders exist" represent a choice for Daru?

mobilized (mō´ bə līzd´) v. ready for action or battle

✓**Reading Check**
What crime has the Arab prisoner committed?

Album Afrique 1835–1845. Arab of Constantine, Auguste Raffet, Musée Condé, Chantilly, France

◀ **Critical Viewing**
Imagine that this Arab is Balducci's prisoner. What might he be thinking? **[Speculate]**

"What are you doing?" Daru asked dryly.

Balducci, disconcerted, showed him the rope.

"Don't bother."

The old gendarme hesitated. "It's up to you. Of course, you are armed?"

"I have my shotgun."

"Where?"

"In the trunk."

"You ought to have it near your bed."

"Why? I have nothing to fear."

"You're crazy, son. If there's an uprising, no one is safe, we're all in the same boat."

"I'll defend myself. I'll have time to see them coming."

Balducci began to laugh, then suddenly the mustache covered the white teeth.

"You'll have time? O.K. That's just what I was saying. You have always been a little cracked. That's why I like you, my son was like that."

At the same time he took out his revolver and put it on the desk.

"Keep it; I don't need two weapons from here to El Ameur."

The revolver shone against the black paint of the table. When the gendarme turned toward him, the schoolmaster caught the smell of leather and horseflesh.

"Listen, Balducci," Daru said suddenly, "every bit of this disgusts me, and first of all your fellow here. But I won't hand him over. Fight, yes, if I have to. But not that."

The old gendarme stood in front of him and looked at him severely.

Reading Strategy
Inferring Cultural Attitudes
What does Balducci mean when he says, "we're all in the same boat"? Explain.

"You're being a fool," he said slowly. "I don't like it either. You don't get used to putting a rope on a man even after years of it, and you're even ashamed—yes, ashamed. But you can't let them have their way."

"I won't hand him over," Daru said again.

"It's an order, son, and I repeat it."

"That's right. Repeat to them what I've said to you: I won't hand him over."

Balducci made a visible effort to reflect. He looked at the Arab and at Daru. At last he decided.

"No, I won't tell them anything. If you want to drop us, go ahead; I'll not <u>denounce</u> you. I have an order to deliver the prisoner and I'm doing so. And now you'll just sign this paper for me."

"There's no need. I'll not deny that you left him with me."

"Don't be mean with me. I know you'll tell the truth. You're from hereabouts and you are a man. But you must sign, that's the rule."

Daru opened his drawer, took out a little square bottle of purple ink, the red wooden penholder with the "sergeant-major" pen he used for making models of penmanship, and signed. The gendarme carefully folded the paper and put it into his wallet. Then he moved toward the door.

"I'll see you off," Daru said.

"No," said Balducci. "There's no use being polite. You insulted me."

He looked at the Arab, motionless in the same spot, sniffed peevishly, and turned away toward the door. "Good-by, son," he said. The door shut behind him. Balducci appeared suddenly outside the window and then disappeared. His footsteps were muffled by the snow. The horse stirred on the other side of the wall and several chickens fluttered in fright. A moment later Balducci reappeared outside the window leading the horse by the bridle. He walked toward the little rise without turning around and disappeared from sight with the horse following him. A big stone could be heard bouncing down. Daru walked back toward the prisoner, who, without stirring, never took his eyes off him. "Wait," the schoolmaster said in Arabic and went toward the bedroom. As he was going through the door, he had a second thought, went to the desk, took the revolver, and stuck it in his pocket. Then, without looking back, he went into his room.

For some time he lay on his couch watching the sky gradually close over, listening to the silence. It was this silence that had seemed painful to him during the first days here, after the war. He had requested a post in the little town at the base of the foothills separating the upper plateaus from the desert. There, rocky walls, green and black to the north, pink and lavender to the south, marked the frontier of eternal summer. He had been named to a post farther north, on the plateau itself. In the beginning, the solitude and the silence had been hard for him on these wastelands peopled only by stones. Occasionally, furrows suggested cultivation, but they had been dug to uncover a certain kind of stone good for building. The only plowing here was to harvest rocks. Elsewhere a thin layer of soil accumulated in the hollows would be

denounce (dē nouns')
v. accuse publicly

Reading Strategy
Inferring Cultural Attitudes
What cultural attitudes are suggested by Balducci's statement, "I know you'll tell the truth. You're from hereabouts and you are a man"?

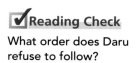
Reading Check
What order does Daru refuse to follow?

scraped out to enrich paltry village gardens. This is the way it was: bare rock covered three quarters of the region. Towns sprang up, flourished, then disappeared; men came by, loved one another or fought bitterly, then died. No one in this desert, neither he nor his guest, mattered. And yet, outside this desert neither of them, Daru knew, could have really lived.

When he got up, no noise came from the classroom. He was amazed at the unmixed joy he derived from the mere thought that the Arab might have fled and that he would be alone with no decision to make. But the prisoner was there. He had merely stretched out between the stove and the desk. With eyes open, he was staring at the ceiling. In that position, his thick lips were particularly noticeable, giving him a pouting look. "Come," said Daru. The Arab got up and followed him. In the bedroom, the schoolmaster pointed to a chair near the table under the window. The Arab sat down without taking his eyes off Daru.

"Are you hungry?"

"Yes," the prisoner said.

Daru set the table for two. He took flour and oil, shaped a cake in a frying-pan, and lighted the little stove that functioned on bottled gas. While the cake was cooking, he went out to the shed to get cheese, eggs, dates, and condensed milk. When the cake was done he set it on the window sill to cool, heated some condensed milk diluted with water, and beat up the eggs into an omelette. In one of his motions he knocked against the revolver stuck in his right pocket. He set the bowl down, went into the classroom, and put the revolver in his desk drawer. When he came back to the room, night was falling. He put on the light and served the Arab. "Eat," he said. The Arab took a piece of the cake, lifted it eagerly to his mouth, and stopped short.

"And you?" he asked.

"After you. I'll eat too."

The thick lips opened slightly. The Arab hesitated, then bit into the cake determinedly.

The meal over, the Arab looked at the schoolmaster. "Are you the judge?"

"No, I'm simply keeping you until tomorrow."

"Why do you eat with me?"

"I'm hungry."

The Arab fell silent. Daru got up and went out. He brought back a folding bed from the shed, set it up between the table and the stove, perpendicular to his own bed. From a large suitcase which, upright in a corner, served as a shelf for papers, he took two blankets and arranged them on the camp bed. Then he stopped, felt useless, and sat down on his bed. There was nothing more to do or to get ready. He had to look at this man. He looked at him, therefore, trying to imagine his face bursting with rage. He couldn't do so. He could see nothing but the dark yet shining eyes and the animal mouth.

"Why did you kill him?" he asked in a voice whose hostile tone surprised him.

The Arab looked away.

Literary Analysis
Existentialism; Setting and Theme In what ways does the statement that "no one in this desert . . . mattered" reflect Existentialist thought?

Literary Analysis
Existentialism Which personal choices and values does Daru's replacing the revolver demonstrate? Explain.

Seated Arab, Eugène Delacroix, Réunion des Musées Nationaux

◄ **Critical Viewing**
Is this man's clothing appropriate for the setting Camus describes? Why or why not? **[Assess]**

"He ran away. I ran after him."

He raised his eyes to Daru again and they were full of a sort of woeful interrogation. "Now what will they do to me?"

"Are you afraid?"

He stiffened, turning his eyes away.

"Are you sorry?"

The Arab stared at him openmouthed. Obviously he did not understand. Daru's annoyance was growing. At the same time he felt awkward and self-conscious with his big body wedged between the two beds.

"Lie down there," he said impatiently. "That's your bed."

The Arab didn't move. He called to Daru:

"Tell me!"

The schoolmaster looked at him.

"Is the gendarme coming back tomorrow?"

"I don't know."

"Are you coming with us?"

"I don't know. Why?"

The prisoner got up and stretched out on top of the blankets, his feet toward the window. The light from the electric bulb shone straight into his eyes and he closed them at once.

"Why?" Daru repeated, standing beside the bed.

The Arab opened his eyes under the blinding light and looked at him, trying not to blink.

"Come with us," he said.

In the middle of the night, Daru was still not asleep. He had gone to bed after undressing completely; he generally slept naked. But when he suddenly realized that he had nothing on, he hesitated. He felt vulnerable and the temptation came to him to put his clothes back on. Then he shrugged his shoulders; after all, he wasn't a child and, if need be,

Reading Strategy
Inferring Cultural Attitudes
Does the prisoner fail to grasp Daru's question ("Are you sorry?") because he holds different cultural attitudes, or is it simply a matter of his personality? Explain.

☑ **Reading Check**
How does Daru feel at the thought his prisoner might have fled?

he could break his adversary in two. From his bed he could observe him, lying on his back, still motionless with his eyes closed under the harsh light. When Daru turned out the light, the darkness seemed to coagulate all of a sudden. Little by little, the night came back to life in the window where the starless sky was stirring gently. The schoolmaster soon made out the body lying at his feet. The Arab still did not move, but his eyes seemed open. A faint wind was prowling around the schoolhouse. Perhaps it would drive away the clouds and the sun would reappear.

During the night the wind increased. The hens fluttered a little and then were silent. The Arab turned over on his side with his back to Daru, who thought he heard him moan. Then he listened for his guest's breathing, become heavier and more regular. He listened to that breath so close to him and mused without being able to go to sleep. In this room where he had been sleeping alone for a year, this presence bothered him. But it bothered him also by imposing on him a sort of brotherhood he knew well but refused to accept in the present circumstances. Men who share the same rooms, soldiers or prisoners, develop a strange alliance as if, having cast off their armor with their clothing, they <u>fraternized</u> every evening, over and above their differences, in the ancient community of dream and fatigue. But Daru shook himself; he didn't like such musings, and it was essential to sleep.

A little later, however, when the Arab stirred slightly, the schoolmaster was still not asleep. When the prisoner made a second move, he stiffened, on the alert. The Arab was lifting himself slowly on his arms with almost the motion of a sleepwalker. Seated upright in bed, he waited motionless without turning his head toward Daru, as if he were listening attentively. Daru did not stir; it had just occurred to him that the revolver was still in the drawer of his desk. It was better to act at once. Yet he continued to observe the prisoner, who, with the same slithery motion, put his feet on the ground, waited again, then began to stand up slowly. Daru was about to call out to him when the Arab began to walk, in a quite natural but extraordinarily silent way. He was heading toward the door at the end of the room that opened into the shed. He lifted the latch with precaution and went out, pushing the door behind him but without shutting it. Daru had not stirred. "He is running away," he merely thought. "Good riddance!" Yet he listened attentively. The hens were not fluttering; the guest must be on the plateau. A faint sound of water reached him, and he didn't know what it was until the Arab again stood framed in the doorway, closed the door carefully, and came back to bed without a sound. Then Daru turned his back on him and fell asleep. Still later he seemed, from the depths of his sleep, to hear <u>furtive</u> steps around the schoolhouse. "I'm dreaming! I'm dreaming!" he repeated to himself. And he went on sleeping.

fraternized (frat´ ər nīzd´) *v.* associated in a brotherly way; socialized

furtive (fur´ tiv) *adj.* done in a secret or sneaky way

When he awoke, the sky was clear; the loose window let in a cold, pure air. The Arab was asleep, hunched up under the blankets now, his mouth open, utterly relaxed. But when Daru shook him, he started dreadfully, staring at Daru with wild eyes as if he had never seen him and such a frightened expression that the schoolmaster stepped back. "Don't be afraid. It's me. You must eat." The Arab nodded his head and said yes. Calm had returned to his face, but his expression was vacant and listless.

The coffee was ready. They drank it seated together on the folding bed as they munched their pieces of the cake. Then Daru led the Arab under the shed and showed him the faucet where he washed. He went back into the room, folded the blankets and the bed, made his own bed and put the room in order. Then he went through the classroom and out onto the terrace. The sun was already rising in the blue sky; a soft, bright light was bathing the deserted plateau. On the ridge the snow was melting in spots. The stones were about to reappear. Crouched on the edge of the plateau, the schoolmaster looked at the deserted expanse. He thought of Balducci. He had hurt him, for he had sent him off in a way as if he didn't want to be associated with him. He could still hear the gendarme's farewell and, without knowing why, he felt strangely empty and vulnerable. At that moment, from the other side of the schoolhouse, the prisoner coughed. Daru listened to him almost despite himself and then, furious, threw a pebble that whistled through the air before sinking into the snow. That man's stupid crime revolted him, but to hand him over was contrary to honor. Merely thinking of it made him smart with humiliation. And he cursed at one and the same time his own people who had sent him this Arab and the Arab too who had dared to kill and not managed to get away. Daru got up, walked in a circle on the terrace, waited motionless, and then went back into the schoolhouse.

The Arab, leaning over the cement floor of the shed, was washing his teeth with two fingers. Daru looked at him and said: "Come." He went back into the room ahead of the prisoner. He slipped a hunting-jacket on over his sweater and put on walking-shoes. Standing, he waited until the Arab had put on his *chèche* and sandals. They went into the classroom and the schoolmaster pointed to the exit, saying: "Go ahead." The fellow didn't budge. "I'm coming," said Daru. The Arab went out. Daru went back into the room and made a package of pieces of rusk,[11] dates, and sugar. In the classroom, before going out, he hesitated a second in front of his desk, then crossed the threshold and locked the door. "That's the way," he said. He started toward the east, followed by the prisoner. But, a short distance from the schoolhouse, he thought he heard a slight sound behind them. He retraced his steps and examined the surroundings of the house; there was no one there. The Arab watched him without seeming to understand. "Come on," said Daru.

---

11. **rusk** (rusk) *n.* sweet bread or cake, toasted or baked until crisp.

Literary Analysis
Existentialism; Setting and Theme In what ways does Daru's throwing the pebble into the desert reflect Existentialist views?

✔**Reading Check**
What does Daru hear "from the depths of his sleep"?

They walked for an hour and rested beside a sharp peak of lime-stone. The snow was melting faster and faster and the sun was drinking up the puddles at once, rapidly cleaning the plateau, which gradually dried and vibrated like the air itself. When they resumed walking, the ground rang under their feet. From time to time a bird rent the space in front of them with a joyful cry. Daru breathed in deeply the fresh morning light. He felt a sort of rapture before the vast familiar expanse, now almost entirely yellow under its dome of blue sky. They walked an hour more, descending toward the south. They reached a level height made up of crumbly rocks. From there on, the plateau sloped down, eastward, toward a low plain where there were a few spindly trees and, to the south, toward outcroppings of rock that gave the landscape a chaotic look.

Daru surveyed the two directions. There was nothing but the sky on the horizon. Not a man could be seen. He turned toward the Arab, who was looking at him blankly. Daru held out the package to him. "Take it," he said. "There are dates, bread, and sugar. You can hold out for two days. Here are a thousand francs[12] too." The Arab took the package and the money but kept his full hands at chest level as if he didn't

---

12. **a thousand francs** (fraŋks) *n.* at that time, monetary units of France and certain other countries, 1,000 francs being enough money for a few days' food and travel.

Literary Analysis
Existentialism; Setting and Theme In what ways does the setting reflect both a change in Daru's mood and Existentialist ideas about personal freedom?

▼ **Critical Viewing**
Imagine that this man is the prisoner, walking toward the police station. What might he be thinking as he turns himself in? **[Speculate]**

know what to do with what was being given him. "Now look," the schoolmaster said as he pointed in the direction of the east, "there's the way to Tinguit. You have a two-hour walk. At Tinguit you'll find the administration and the police. They are expecting you." The Arab looked toward the east, still holding the package and the money against his chest. Daru took his elbow and turned him rather roughly toward the south. At the foot of the height on which they stood could be seen a faint path. "That's the trail across the plateau. In a day's walk from here you'll find pasturelands and the first nomads. They'll take you in and shelter you according to their law." The Arab had now turned toward Daru and a sort of panic was visible in his expression. "Listen," he said. Daru shook his head: "No, be quiet. Now I'm leaving you." He turned his back on him, took two long steps in the direction of the school, looked hesitantly at the motionless Arab, and started off again. For a few minutes he heard nothing but his own step resounding on the cold ground and did not turn his head. A moment later, however, he turned around. The Arab was still there on the edge of the hill, his arms hanging now, and he was looking at the schoolmaster. Daru felt something rise in his throat. But he swore with impatience, waved vaguely, and started off again. He had already gone some distance when he again stopped and looked. There was no longer anyone on the hill.

Reading Strategy
Inferring Cultural Attitudes
Based on Daru's statement about the nomads, what can you infer about their cultural attitudes?

✔**Reading Check**
What items does Daru give the prisoner before he departs?

Daru hesitated. The sun was now rather high in the sky and was beginning to beat down on his head. The schoolmaster retraced his steps, at first somewhat uncertainly, then with decision. When he reached the little hill, he was bathed in sweat. He climbed it as fast as he could and stopped, out of breath, at the top. The rock-fields to the south stood out sharply against the blue sky, but on the plain to the east a steamy heat was already rising. And in that slight haze, Daru, with heavy heart, made out the Arab walking slowly on the road to prison.

A little later, standing before the window of the classroom, the schoolmaster was watching the clear light bathing the whole surface of the plateau, but he hardly saw it. Behind him on the blackboard, among the winding French rivers, sprawled the clumsily chalked-up words he had just read: "You handed over our brother. You will pay for this." Daru looked at the sky, the plateau, and, beyond, the invisible lands stretching all the way to the sea. In this vast landscape he had loved so much, he was alone.

Review and Assess

Thinking About the Selection

1. **Respond:** Did you find the end of the story surprising? Why or why not?

2. **(a) Recall:** Who are the two men who arrive at Daru's home? **(b) Interpret:** As the men approach, what details in their appearance and behavior does Daru observe? **(c) Analyze:** What do these details suggest about the characters and status of the men?

3. **(a) Recall:** What demand does Balducci make of Daru with regard to the Arab prisoner? **(b) Infer:** Why is Daru expected to take orders delivered to him by Balducci? **(c) Analyze:** Why do you think Daru refuses to comply?

4. **(a) Recall:** Why did the police feel it necessary to remove the Arab prisoner from custody in his village? **(b) Draw Conclusions:** How does this situation emphasize the danger of Daru's position?

5. **(a) Infer:** What is Daru's opinion of the Arab? Support your answer. **(b) Interpret:** Do Daru's feelings about the Arab affect his treatment of the man? Explain.

6. **(a) Interpret:** How does Daru resolve his dilemma over the Arab? **(b) Make a Judgment:** Do you think this was a good resolution?

7. **Speculate:** Would Daru have acted differently if he had known the Arab's friends might seek revenge? Why or why not?

Review and Assess

Literary Analysis

Existentialism

1. Daru shows the Arab two paths and leaves him to make his own choice. In what ways does this decision reflect **Existentialist** ideas?

2. (a) How does Daru feel about the Arab's crime? (b) How does he treat the Arab? (c) What values do Daru's feelings and actions reflect? Explain.

3. What does the end of the story suggest about the difficulties of living one's life according to Existentialist principles? Explain.

Connecting Literary Elements

4. (a) Use a chart like the one shown to identify details about the

Weather	Location	Cultural Conflict

climate, the landscape, and the cultural conflict in this story. (b) Discuss the ways in which these details of the **setting** reflect ideas that are central to the story's meaning, or **theme.**

5. (a) Why do you think Daru feels that "outside this desert neither of them [Daru or the Arab] . . . could have really lived"? (b) In what ways does this statement contribute to the story's theme?

6. Who is the guest in this story—the Arab prisoner in Daru's house or Daru in Algeria? Explain.

Reading Strategy

Inferring Cultural Attitudes

7. Daru's blackboard shows the four rivers of France. **Infer cultural attitudes** by describing what this statement reveals about the mind-set of Europeans living in Algeria.

8. What cultural attitudes can you infer from the message the Arab's supporters leave on Daru's blackboard? Explain.

Extend Understanding

9. **Literature Connection:** Camus believed that he had a responsibility to serve humanity through his writing. In what ways do you think that literature can accomplish this goal?

Quick Review

Existentialism is a philosophy that emphasizes the value of personal choice in an indifferent world.

The **setting** is the time and the place in which a story occurs. The **theme** is the central message or insight about life that is communicated in a literary work.

To **infer cultural attitudes** when reading, look for clues about the values and customs of a group of people.

Take It to the Net
PHSchool.com

Take the interactive self-test online to check your understanding of this selection.

Integrate Language Skills

Vocabulary Development Lesson

Word Analysis: Anglo-Saxon Prefix *fore-*

The prefix *fore-*, as in *foretaste*, means "before in time, place, order, or rank." Add the prefix *fore-* to each of the words below. Then, write a definition for each new word.

1. word   **2.** sight   **3.** runner

Spelling Strategy

When *i* and *e* spell the long *e* sound, the letters usually appear as *ie*, as in *siege*. For each sentence below, write the correct spelling of the underlined word.

1. The Arab did not feel any <u>greef</u>.
2. Balducci stayed for a <u>breef</u> time.
3. Balducci wanted Daru to <u>releeve</u> him.
4. The Arab was not a <u>theef</u>.
5. Daru did not <u>acheeve</u> peace.

Fluency: Sentence Completion

Review the vocabulary list on page 1223. Then, complete the sentences below with words from the list.

1. As the battle neared, the village ___?___ its forces.
2. The house overlooked a vast ___?___.
3. The clash between Daru and the officer gave a ___?___ of conflicts to come.
4. The criminal feared that his friend would ___?___ him.
5. He had enough food to survive a ___?___.
6. He had never befriended his neighbor or ___?___ with him.
7. Because he distrusted the prisoner, he kept a ___?___ eye on him all night.

Grammar and Style Lesson

Prepositional Phrases as Adjectives and Adverbs

A **prepositional phrase** is a group of words made up of a preposition and a noun or pronoun. When a prepositional phrase modifies a noun or pronoun, it is called an adjective phrase; when it modifies a verb, adjective, or adverb, it is called an adverb phrase.

Adverb: Snow had suddenly fallen . . . <u>after eight months</u>. (modifies *fallen*)

Adjective: It had disappeared under a layer <u>of dirty white snow</u>. (modifies *layer*)

Practice Identify the prepositional phrase in each sentence below, note the word it modifies, and state whether it is an adjective or adverb phrase.

1. The prisoner walked along the trail.
2. Daru studied the man with the jellaba.
3. With quick movements, Daru served tea.
4. Balducci said goodbye in a hurt tone.
5. The Arabs from the village were angry.

Writing Application Write a paragraph describing Daru's home. Identify adjective phrases and adverb phrases, circling the word each phrase modifies.

W͞G Prentice Hall Writing and Grammar Connection: Diamond Level, Chapter 19, Section 1

Writing Lesson

Essay Evaluating Fiction as an Expression of Philosophy

Although Camus refused the label of Existentialist, his work has often been read as an expression of that philosophy. Write an essay in which you discuss the ways in which Daru's situation, thoughts, and actions in "The Guest" do or do not reflect an Existentialist stance.

Prewriting Scan the story for details describing Daru's circumstances, actions, thoughts, and statements. Use a chart like the one shown to analyze how each detail does or does not reflect Existentialist views.

Model: Using a Chart to Compare Fiction to Philosophy

Details		Existentialist Ideas
Daru's Situation: Daru is isolated and alone.	·····▶	Human beings are alone in an indifferent universe.
Daru's Thoughts:	·····▶	
Daru's Actions:	·····▶	

Drafting Choose point-by-point or block organization for your essay. With the former, introduce each detail and discuss it in relationship to Existentialism. With the latter, discuss all the details that reflect Existentialist ideas. Then, discuss all of those that do not.

Revising As you reread your draft, underline your main ideas. If a paragraph lacks a clear main idea, add one or combine it with another paragraph. If a paragraph has more than one main idea, create two paragraphs.

W̶G̶ Prentice Hall Writing and Grammar Connection: Diamond Level, Chapter 9, Section 2

Extension Activities

Listening and Speaking With a small group, adapt and perform "The Guest" as a **play.** Use these tips to prepare:

- Reread the story, listing details about the characters.
- Write roles for the three characters, a narrator, and a director.
- Include stage directions.

Rehearse the play and then perform it for the class. **[Group Activity]**

Research and Technology Conduct research on the Internet to learn about the history of Algeria. Then, create a **timeline** that identifies important events and people. Include a notation identifying Camus's birth and the probable time during which the events in this story took place.

 **Take It to the Net** PHSchool.com

Go online for an additional research activity using the Internet.

Prepare to Read

Folding Chairs ◆ Food for Prophets ◆ The Garden of Stubborn Cats

Günter Grass (b. 1927)

Günter Grass (gün´ tər gräs) survived the most problematic period in modern German history, the era of Adolf Hitler's dictatorship (1933–1945). Grass's experience of that nightmare period—and the lessons he drew from it—are at the heart of his writing and political activities. Today, Grass is viewed as the foremost voice of postwar German literature.

Facing Horror Grass was born in Danzig, now the Polish city of Gdansk (g' dänsk´), where the first shots of World War II were fired. At sixteen, Grass was drafted. Later, he witnessed the horrors of the German concentration camp at Dachau, an experience that led him to reject Nazism.

Released from service in the spring of 1946, Grass pursued his interest in the arts. He apprenticed as a stonemason and then studied sculpting and graphics at the Düsseldorf Academy of Art. In the evenings, he worked as a jazz drummer.

A Triumph In 1954, after moving to Berlin, Grass married Anna Schwarz, a Swiss dancer. Anna encouraged Grass's writing, submitting some of his poems to a radio competition. Grass began publishing his poems, plays, and essays and started work on a novel. The result was his renowned work *The Tin Drum*, a survey of the Nazi era that mixes fairy tale, fantasy, and realism. The novel won Grass much praise and a number of literary prizes.

Facing the Future During the Cold War, when Germany was divided into two antagonistic countries, Grass organized meetings of writers from East Germany and West Germany and spoke out for peace. He has said that the one reliable ally literature has is the future, and both his writings and political activities reflect his faith in human possibility. In 1999, Grass's literary achievements earned him the Nobel Prize in Literature.

Italo Calvino (1923–1985)

The parents of Italo Calvino (ē´ täl ō kal vē´ nō´) were botanists, but although they had hoped he would become a scientist, Calvino said that he was "attracted to another kind of vegetation, that of the written word." Like a good botanist, Calvino spent time collecting "specimens": He edited a famous collection of Italian folk tales. It is his own novels and stories, however, that have earned him a reputation as one of Italy's most inventive writers.

Fighting Fascism Born in Cuba, Calvino grew up on the Italian Riviera at San Remo, where his father was curator of the botanical gardens. During World War II, Calvino fought in a partisan movement against Fascist control of Italy. His experience as a partisan was the basis for his first novel, *The Path to the Nest of Spiders* (1947). The war was also an inspiration for his short-story collection *Adam, One Afternoon, and Other Stories* (1949).

At the end of the war, Calvino studied literature in Turin. After graduating, he joined Einaudi, a publishing venture begun by Cesare Pavese, who shared literary and leftist political ideas with Calvino.

A New Vision While many postwar Italian writers worked within a harsh vision of society known as Neorealism, Calvino's work from the 1950s on is notable for its fairy-tale qualities. He believed that the pattern of the fable is the formula for all stories. Like heroes of fairy tales, lost in an enchanted wood, Calvino's characters face a mysterious, challenging environment. In Calvino's stories, however, a modern city often replaces an enchanted wood as the setting. Mixing imagination and humor with philosophy and science, Calvino has created true modern fairy tales.

Preview

Connecting to the Literature

The walls of a home hold warmth and memories in; they keep out rain and the feeling of being a stranger. These writers consider what it means to be "inside"—to feel at home—and whether even a city needs an "outside"—a place beyond human rules.

Literary Analysis

Symbolism

Symbolism is the use of concrete images that stand for abstract meanings. An image may be given symbolic meaning in a number of ways:

- The meaning may be evoked by emphasizing ordinary associations. For example, a folding chair is meant to be moved from place to place. In "Folding Chairs," Grass emphasizes this association. He employs images of folding chairs to symbolize the lack of a true home.

- Symbolic meaning may be evoked through the traditional associations of an image. For example, the locusts in "Food for Prophets" recall a biblical story: a plague of locusts sent as divine punishment.

As you read the selections, identify and interpret images used symbolically.

Comparing Literary Works

Symbolism is one device that writers use to express a theme. The **theme** of a work is the message it sends or the question it poses. In "Folding Chairs," Grass's title image symbolizes impermanence—the theme of the poem.

As you read, notice the ways the writers use symbols to probe themes.

Reading Strategy

Recognizing Symbols

To **recognize symbols,** look for characters, places, or objects that are

- emphasized by repeated appearances or vivid descriptions.
- rich in common associations that suggest a theme (for instance, Calvino's cats call up associations with nature's mysterious side).

Use a chart like the one shown to interpret symbols as you read.

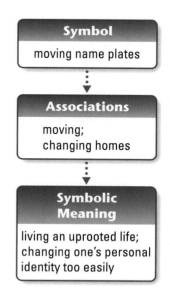

Symbol

moving name plates

Associations

moving;
changing homes

Symbolic Meaning

living an uprooted life;
changing one's personal
identity too easily

Vocabulary Development

emigrate (em´ i grāt´) v. leave one place to live in another (p. 1244)

laden (lād´ 'n) adj. carrying a heavy load (p. 1244)

environs (en vī´ rənz) n. surrounding area; vicinity (p. 1247)

convergent (kən vʉr´ jənt) adj. coming together at a point (p. 1248)

squalid (skwäl´ id) adj. foul, especially as the result of neglect; wretched (p. 1248)

altruistic (al´ trōo is´ tik) adj. motivated by unselfish concern for the welfare of others (p. 1248)

Chairs of Paris, 1927, André Kertész

Folding Chairs

Günter Grass

translated by
Michael Hamburger

Background

During World War II, many Jews fled Nazi persecution in Germany, emigrating to other nations. The end of the war flooded Europe with an estimated 21 million refugees, including former prisoners of war. Millions left the devastated cities of Europe to search for a new life. In "Folding Chairs," Grass may be reflecting on this massive uprooting of Europeans.

How sad these changes are.
People unscrew the name plates from the doors,
take the saucepan of cabbage
and heat it up again, in a different place.

5   What sort of furniture is this
that advertises departure?
People take up their folding chairs
and <u>emigrate</u>.

Ships <u>laden</u> with homesickness and the urge to vomit
10   carry patented seating contraptions
and unpatented owners
to and fro.

Now on both sides of the great ocean
there are folding chairs;
15   how sad these changes are.

Literary Analysis
Symbolism What associations with folding chairs does Grass introduce in lines 5–8?

emigrate (em´ i grāt´) *v.* leave one place to live in another

laden (lād´ 'n) *adj.* carrying a heavy load

Food for Prophets

Günter Grass

translated by Anselm Hollo

Background

Grass adds authority and symbolic resonance to this poem by referring to two well-known biblical images. *Prophets* are religious leaders of Israel who are gifted with visions and healing powers. *Locusts* are grasshopperlike insects that emerge periodically in swarms, devastating crops.

When the locusts occupied our town,
no milk came to the door, the dailies suffocated,
our jails were opened to release
all prophets.
5   They streamed through the streets,
3800 prophets,
talking and teaching without restriction,
and eating their fill of that gray
& jumpy mess
10   we called the plague.
So everything was fine and up to expectations.

Soon our milk came again; our papers reappeared;
and prophets filled our jails.

Reading Strategy
Recognizing Symbols
Which two routines does Grass use to represent ordinary life?

Review and Assess

Thinking About the Selections

1. **Respond:** Do you agree that changing homes is sad? Explain.
2. **(a) Recall:** In line 6 of "Folding Chairs," what do folding chairs "advertise"? **(b) Analyze:** Why does the idea of portable furniture contradict some of our associations with home?
3. **Interpret:** In what sense are there now folding chairs "on both sides of the great ocean"?
4. **(a) Recall:** In "Food for Prophets," who is released from jail when the plague occurs? **(b) Hypothesize:** Why are these people released?
5. **(a) Recall:** Who is put in jail at the end of "Food for Prophets"? **(b) Draw Conclusions:** What contrast does the poem suggest between society in crisis and society in ordinary times?

The Garden of Stubborn Cats

Italo Calvino
translated by William Weaver

Background

The worldwide rebuilding that took place after World War II led to two parallel trends: modernization and urbanization. Bombed-out buildings were replaced using new technologies. In cities once dominated by stone buildings from the Middle Ages, concrete and steel office buildings bloomed. Advances in engineering led to higher and higher skyscrapers. At the same time, people flooded urban areas in search of employment. In this selection, Calvino looks at one side effect of this urban boom—the crowding out of wild spaces in which nature might lead its own life.

▲ **Critical Viewing**
On the basis of this image, predict how the story will contrast the wildness of cats with architectural orderliness. **[Predict]**

The city of cats and the city of men exist one inside the other, but they are not the same city. Few cats recall the time when there was no distinction: the streets and squares of men were also streets and squares of cats, and the lawns, courtyards, balconies, and fountains: you lived in a broad and various space. But for several generations now domestic felines have been prisoners of an uninhabitable city: the streets are uninterruptedly overrun by the mortal traffic of cat-crushing automobiles; in every square foot of terrain where once a garden extended or a vacant lot or the ruins of an old demolition, now condominiums loom up, welfare housing, brand-new skyscrapers; every entrance is crammed with parked cars; the courtyards, one by one, have been roofed by reinforced concrete and transformed into garages or movie houses or storerooms or workshops. And where a rolling plateau of low roofs once extended, copings, terraces, water tanks, balconies, skylights, corrugated-iron sheds, now one general superstructure rises wherever structures can rise; the intermediate differences in height, between the low ground of the street and the supernal[1] heaven of the penthouses, disappear; the cat of a recent litter seeks in vain the itinerary[2] of its fathers, the point from which to make the soft leap from balustrade to cornice to drainpipe, or for the quick climb on the roof-tiles.

But in this vertical city, in this compressed city where all voids tend to fill up and every block of cement tends to mingle with other blocks of cement, a kind of counter-city opens, a negative city, that consists of empty slices between wall and wall, of the minimal distances ordained by the building regulations between two constructions, between the rear of one construction and the rear of the next; it is a city of cavities, wells, air conduits, driveways, inner yards, accesses to basements, like a network of dry canals on a planet of stucco and tar, and it is through this network, grazing the walls, that the ancient cat population still scurries.

On occasion, to pass the time, Marcovaldo would follow a cat. It was during the work-break, between noon and three, when all the personnel except Marcovaldo went home to eat, and he—who brought his lunch in his bag—laid his place among the packing-cases in the warehouse, chewed his snack, smoked a half-cigar, and wandered around, alone and idle, waiting for work to resume. In those hours, a cat that peeped in at a window was always welcome company, and a guide for new explorations. He had made friends with a tabby, well fed, a blue ribbon around its neck, surely living with some well-to-do family. This tabby shared with Marcovaldo the habit of an afternoon stroll right after lunch; and naturally a friendship sprang up.

Following his tabby friend, Marcovaldo had started looking at places as if through the round eyes of a cat and even if these places were the usual <u>environs</u> of his firm he saw them in a different light, as settings for cattish stories, with connections practicable only by light, velvety paws. Though from the outside the neighborhood seemed poor in cats, every day on his rounds Marcovaldo made the acquaintance of some new face, and a miau, a hiss, a stiffening of fur on an arched back was enough for him to sense ties and intrigues and rivalries among them. At those moments he thought he had already penetrated the secrecy of the felines' society: and then he felt himself scrutinized by pupils that became slits, under the surveillance of the antennae of taut whiskers,

Literature
in context Design Connection

Traditional Architecture
Traditional architectural features are at risk in modern cities, although some survive. Calvino uses terms for a few such features:

- **balustrade** railing supported by small ornamental posts

- **belvedere** open, roofed gallery in an upper story, opening onto a view

- **capitals** tops of columns

- **copings** top layers of a stone or brick wall, sloped to carry off water

- **cornice** horizontal molding projecting from the top of a wall or building; overhanging part of a roof

- **transom** small window or shutter over a door or window

environs (en vi´ rənz) *n.* surrounding area; vicinity

✔**Reading Check**

What does Marcovaldo do on his lunchbreak?

---

1. **supernal** (sə pʉrn´ əl) *adj.* celestial or divine.
2. **itinerary** (ī tin´ ər er´ ē) *n.* route.

and all the cats around him sat impassive as sphinxes, the pink triangles of their noses <u>convergent</u> on the black triangles of their lips, and the only things that moved were the tips of the ears, with a vibrant jerk like radar. They reached the end of a narrow passage, between <u>squalid</u> blank walls; and, looking around, Marcovaldo saw that the cats that had led him this far had vanished, all of them together, no telling in which direction, even his tabby friend, and they had left him alone. Their realm had territories, ceremonies, customs that it was not yet granted to him to discover.

On the other hand, from the cat city there opened unsuspected peepholes onto the city of men: and one day the same tabby led him to discover the great Biarritz Restaurant.

Anyone wishing to see the Biarritz Restaurant had only to assume the posture of a cat, that is, proceed on all fours. Cat and man, in this fashion, walked around a kind of dome, at whose foot some low, rectangular little windows opened. Following the tabby's example, Marcovaldo looked down. They were transoms through which the luxurious hall received air and light. To the sound of gypsy violins, partridges and quails swirled by on silver dishes balanced by the white-gloved fingers of waiters in tailcoats. Or, more precisely, above the partridges and quails the dishes whirled, and above the dishes the white gloves, and poised on the waiters' patent-leather shoes, the gleaming parquet[3] floor, from which hung dwarf potted palms and tablecloths and crystal and buckets like bells with the champagne bottle for their clapper: everything was turned upside-down because Marcovaldo, for fear of being seen, wouldn't stick his head inside the window and confined himself to looking at the reversed reflection of the room in the tilted pane.

But it was not so much the windows of the dining-room as those of the kitchens that interested the cat: looking through the former you saw, distant and somehow transfigured, what in the kitchens presented itself—quite concrete and within paw's reach—as a plucked bird or a fresh fish. And it was toward the kitchens, in fact, that the tabby wanted to lead Marcovaldo, either through a gesture of <u>altruistic</u> friendship or else because it counted on the man's help for one of its raids. Marcovaldo, however, was reluctant to leave his belvedere over the main room: first as he was fascinated by the luxury of the place, and then because something down there had riveted his attention. To such an extent that, overcoming his fear of being seen, he kept peeking in, with his head in the transom.

In the midst of the room, directly under that pane, there was a little glass fish-tank, a kind of aquarium, where some fat trout were swimming. A special customer approached, a man with a shiny bald pate, black suit, black beard. An old waiter in tailcoat followed him, carrying a little net as if he were going to catch butterflies. The gentleman in black looked at the trout with a grave, intent air; then he raised one

convergent (kən vʉr´ jənt) *adj.* coming together at a point

Reading Strategy
Recognizing Symbols
What words in Calvino's description of the cats suggest that the animals have symbolic meaning?

squalid (skwäl´ id) *adj.* foul, especially as the result of neglect; wretched

Literary Analysis
Symbolism Based on this description, what might the Biarritz Restaurant symbolize?

altruistic (al´ trōō is´ tik) *adj.* motivated by unselfish concern for the welfare of others

---

3. **parquet** (pär kā´) inlaid woodwork in geometric forms.

hand and with a slow, solemn gesture singled out a fish. The waiter dipped the net into the tank, pursued the appointed trout, captured it, headed for the kitchens, holding out in front of him, like a lance, the net in which the fish wriggled. The gentleman in black, solemn as a magistrate who has handed down a capital sentence, went to take his seat and wait for the return of the trout, sautéed "à la meunière."[4]

If I found a way to drop a line from up here and make one of those trout bite, Marcovaldo thought, I couldn't be accused of theft; at worst, of fishing in an unauthorized place. And ignoring the miaus that called him toward the kitchens, he went to collect his fishing tackle.

Nobody in the crowded dining-room of the Biarritz saw the long, fine line, armed with hook and bait, as it slowly dropped into the tank. The fish saw the bait, and flung themselves on it. In the fray one trout managed to bite the worm: and immediately it began to rise, rise, emerge from the water, a silvery flash, it darted up high, over the laid tables and the trolleys of hors d'oeuvres, over the blue flames of the crêpes Suzette,[5] until it vanished into the heavens of the transom.

Winter: Cat on a Cushion, Théophile-Alexandre Steinlen, The Metropolitan Museum of Art, New York

Marcovaldo had yanked the rod with the brisk snap of the expert fisherman, so the fish landed behind his back. The trout had barely touched the ground when the cat sprang. What little life the trout still had was lost between the tabby's teeth. Marcovaldo, who had abandoned his line at that moment to run and grab the fish, saw it snatched from under his nose, hook and all. He was quick to put one foot on the rod, but the snatch had been so strong that the rod was all the man had left, while the tabby ran off with the fish, pulling the line after it. Treacherous kitty! It had vanished.

▲ **Critical Viewing**
Drawing on details in the painting, explain what it suggests about the nature of cats. [Interpret]

But this time it wouldn't escape him: there was that long line trailing after him and showing the way he had taken. Though he had lost sight of the cat, Marcovaldo followed the end of the line: there it was, running along a wall; it climbed a parapet, wound through a doorway, was swallowed up by a basement . . . Marcovaldo, venturing into more and more cattish places, climbed roofs, straddled railings, always managed to catch a glimpse—perhaps only a second before it disappeared—of that moving trace that indicated the thief's path.

Now the line played out down a sidewalk, in the midst of the traffic, and Marcovaldo, running after it, almost managed to grab it. He flung himself down on his belly: there, he grabbed it! He managed to seize one end of the line before it slipped between the bars of a gate.

---

4. **sautéed "à la meunière"** (sô tād´ ä lä mə nyer´) describes fish prepared by being rolled in flour, fried in butter, and sprinkled with lemon juice and chopped parsley.
5. **hors d'oeuvres** (ôr´ dʉrvz´) . . . **crêpes Suzette** (krep sü zet´) Hors d'oeuvres are appetizers; crêpes Suzette are thin pancakes rolled or folded in a sauce and served in flaming brandy.

☑**Reading Check**
How is Marcovaldo able to fish at the Biarritz Restaurant?

Beyond a half-rusted gate and two bits of wall buried under climbing plants, there was a little rank[6] garden, with a small, abandoned-looking building at the far end of it. A carpet of dry leaves covered the path, and dry leaves lay everywhere under the boughs of the two plane-trees, forming actually some little mounds in the yard. A layer of leaves was yellowing in the green water of a pool. Enormous buildings rose all around, skyscrapers with thousands of windows, like so many eyes trained disapprovingly on that little square patch with two trees, a few tiles, and all those yellow leaves, surviving right in the middle of an area of great traffic.

And in this garden, perched on the capitals and balustrades, lying on the dry leaves of the flower-beds, climbing on the trunks of the trees or on the drainpipes, motionless on their four paws, their tails making a question-mark, seated to wash their faces, there were tiger cats, black cats, white cats, calico cats, tabbies, angoras, Persians, house cats and stray cats, perfumed cats and mangy cats. Marcovaldo realized he had finally reached the heart of the cats' realm, their secret island. And, in his emotion, he almost forgot his fish.

It had remained, that fish, hanging by the line from the branch of a tree, out of reach of the cats' leaps; it must have dropped from its kidnapper's mouth at some clumsy movement, perhaps as it was defended from the others, or perhaps displayed as an extraordinary prize. The line had got tangled, and Marcovaldo, tug as he would, couldn't manage to yank it loose. A furious battle had meanwhile been joined among the cats, to reach that unreachable fish, or rather, to win the right to try and reach it. Each wanted to prevent the others from leaping: they hurled themselves on one another, they tangled in mid-air, they rolled around clutching each other, and finally a general war broke out in a whirl of dry, crackling leaves.

After many futile yanks, Marcovaldo now felt the line was free, but he took care not to pull it: the trout would have fallen right in the midst of that infuriated scrimmage of felines.

It was at this moment that, from the top of the walls of the gardens, a strange rain began to fall: fish-bones, heads, tails, even bits of lung and lights.[7] Immediately the cats' attention was distracted from the suspended trout and they flung themselves on the new delicacies. To Marcovaldo, this seemed the right moment to pull the line and regain his fish. But, before he had time to act, from a blind of the little villa, two yellow, skinny hands darted out: one was brandishing scissors; the other, a frying-pan. The hand with the scissors was raised above the trout, the hand with the frying-pan was thrust under it. The scissors cut the line, the trout fell into the pan; hands, scissors and pan withdrew, the blind closed: all in the space of a second. Marcovaldo was totally bewildered.

"Are you also a cat-lover?" A voice at his back made him turn round. He was surrounded by little old women, some of them ancient, wearing

6. **rank** (raŋk) *adj.* growing vigorously and coarsely.
7. **lights** term for animal organs used for catfood.

Literary Analysis
Symbolism and Theme
What theme does the opposition between the garden and the modern city suggest?

old-fashioned hats on their heads; others, younger, but with the look of spinsters; and all were carrying in their hands or their bags packages of left-over meat or fish, and some even had little pans of milk. "Will you help me throw this package over the fence, for those poor creatures?"

All the ladies, cat-lovers, gathered at this hour around the garden of dry leaves to take food to their protégés.[8]

The Big White Cat, Gertrude Halsband, Private Collection

"Can you tell me why they are all here, these cats?" Marcovaldo inquired.

"Where else could they go? This garden is all they have left! Cats come here from other neighborhoods, too, from miles and miles around . . ."

"And birds, as well," another lady added. "They're forced to live by the hundreds and hundreds on these few trees . . ."

"And the frogs, they're all in that pool, and at night they never stop croaking . . . You can hear them even on the eighth floor of the buildings around here."

"Who does this villa belong to anyway?" Marcovaldo asked. Now, outside the gate, there weren't just the cat-loving ladies but also other people: the man from the gas pump opposite, the apprentices from a mechanic's shop, the postman, the grocer, some passers-by. And none of them, men and women, had to be asked twice: all wanted to have their say, as always when a mysterious and controversial subject comes up.

"It belongs to a Marchesa.[9] She lives there, but you never see her . . ."

"She's been offered millions and millions, by developers, for this little patch of land, but she won't sell . . ."

"What would she do with millions, an old woman all alone in the world? She wants to hold on to her house, even if it's falling to pieces, rather than be forced to move . . ."

"It's the only undeveloped bit of land in the downtown area . . . Its value goes up every year . . . They've made her offers—"

"Offers! That's not all. Threats, intimidation, persecution . . . You don't know the half of it! Those contractors!"

"But she holds out. She's held out for years . . ."

"She's a saint. Without her, where would those poor animals go?"

"A lot she cares about the animals, the old miser! Have you ever seen her give them anything to eat?"

"How can she feed the cats when she doesn't have food for herself? She's the last descendant of a ruined family!"

▲ **Critical Viewing**
Contrast the way this cat fits in with a natural scene with the way cats fit in with the city in Calvino's story.
[Compare and Contrast]

---

8. protégés (prōt′ ə zhāz′) *n.* those guided and helped by another.
9. Marchesa (mär kā′ sə) title of an Italian noblewoman.

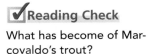
Reading Check
What has become of Marcovaldo's trout?

"She hates cats! I've seen her chasing them and hitting them with an umbrella!"

"Because they were tearing up her flowerbeds!"

"What flowerbeds? I've never seen anything in this garden but a great crop of weeds!"

Marcovaldo realized that with regard to the old Marchesa opinions were sharply divided: some saw her as an angelic being, other as an egoist and a miser.

"It's the same with the birds; she never gives them a crumb!"

"She gives them hospitality. Isn't that plenty?"

"Like she gives the mosquitoes, you mean. They all come from here, from that pool. In the summertime the mosquitoes eat us alive, and it's all the fault of that Marchesa!"

"And the mice? This villa is a mine of mice. Under the dead leaves they have their burrows, and at night they come out . . ."

"As far as the mice go, the cats take care of them . . ."

"Oh, you and your cats! If we had to rely on them . . ."

"Why? Have you got something to say against cats?"

Here the discussion degenerated into a general quarrel.

"The authorities should do something: confiscate the villa!" one man cried.

"What gives them the right?" another protested.

"In a modern neighborhood like ours, a mouse-nest like this . . . it should be forbidden . . ."

"Why, I picked my apartment precisely because it overlooked this little bit of green . . ."

"Green, hell! Think of the fine skyscraper they could build here!"

Marcovaldo would have liked to add something of his own, but he couldn't get a word in. Finally, all in one breath, he exclaimed: "The Marchesa stole a trout from me!"

The unexpected news supplied fresh ammunition to the old woman's enemies, but her defenders exploited it as proof of the indigence[10] to which the unfortunate noblewoman was reduced. Both sides agreed that Marcovaldo should go and knock at her door to demand an explanation.

It wasn't clear whether the gate was locked or unlocked; in any case, it opened, after a push, with a mournful creak. Marcovaldo picked his way among the leaves and cats, climbed the steps to the porch, knocked hard at the entrance.

At a window (the very one where the frying-pan had appeared), the blind was raised slightly and in one corner a round, pale blue eye was seen, and a clump of hair dyed an undefinable color, and a dry skinny hand. A voice was heard, asking: "Who is it? Who's at the door?", the words accompanied by a cloud smelling of fried oil.

▲ **Critical Viewing**
Which characteristic of cats described in the story is emphasized by this image? [Connect]

---

10. indigence (in´ di jəns) poverty.

"It's me, Marchesa. The trout man," Marcovaldo explained. "I don't mean to trouble you. I only wanted to tell you, in case you didn't know, that the trout was stolen from me, by that cat, and I'm the one who caught it. In fact the line . . ."

"Those cats! It's always those cats . . ." the Marchesa said, from behind the shutter, with a shrill, somewhat nasal voice. "All my troubles come from the cats! Nobody knows what I go through! Prisoner night and day of those horrid beasts! And with all the refuse people throw over the walls to spite me!"

"But my trout . . ."

"Your trout! What am I supposed to know about your trout!" The Marchesa's voice became almost a scream, as if she wanted to drown out the sizzle of the oil in the pan, which came through the window along with the aroma of fried fish. "How can I make sense of anything, with all the stuff that rains into my house?"

"I understand, but did you take the trout or didn't you?"

"When I think of all the damage I suffer because of the cats! Ah, fine state of affairs! I'm not responsible for anything! I can't tell you what I've lost! Thanks to those cats, who've occupied house and garden for years! My life at the mercy of those animals! Go and find the owners! Make them pay damages! Damages? A whole life destroyed! A prisoner here, unable to move a step!"

"Excuse me for asking: but who's forcing you to stay?"

From the crack in the blind there appeared sometimes a round, pale blue eye, sometimes a mouth with two protruding teeth; for a moment the whole face was visible, and to Marcovaldo it seemed, bewilderingly, the face of a cat.

"They keep me prisoner, they do, those cats! Oh, I'd be glad to leave! What wouldn't I give for a little apartment all my own, in a nice clean modern building! But I can't go out . . . They follow me, they block my path, they trip me up!" The voice became a whisper, as if to confide a secret. "They're afraid I'll sell the lot . . . They won't leave me . . . won't allow me . . . When the builders come to offer me a contract, you should see them, those cats! They get in the way, pull out their claws; they even chased a lawyer off! Once I had the contract right here, I was about to sign it, and they dived in through the window, knocked over the inkwell, tore up all the pages . . ."

All of a sudden Marcovaldo remembered the time, the shipping department, the boss. He tiptoed off over the dried leaves, as the voice continued to come through the slats of the blind, enfolded in that cloud apparently from the oil of a frying-pan. "They even scratched me . . . I still have the scar . . . All alone here at the mercy of these demons . . ."

Winter came. A blossoming of white flakes decked the branches and capitals and the cats' tails. Under the snow, the dry leaves disolved into mush. The cats were rarely seen, the cat-lovers even less; the packages of fish-bones were consigned only to cats who came to the door. Nobody, for quite a while, had seen anything of the Marchesa. No smoke came now from the chimneypot of the villa.

Literary Analysis
Symbolism In what way does Marcovaldo's perception of the Marchesa as a cat add symbolic meaning to her character?

Reading Strategy
Recognizing Symbols Why does the relationship of the Marchesa to the cats suggest that she is a symbolic character?

**Reading Check**
According to the Marchesa, why do the cats interfere with her business?

One snowy day, the garden was again full of cats, who had returned as if it were spring, and they were miauing as if on a moonlight night. The neighbors realized that something had happened: they went and knocked at the Marchesa's door. She didn't answer: she was dead.

In the spring, instead of the garden, there was a huge building site that a contractor had set up. The steam shovels dug down to great depths to make room for the foundations, cement poured into the iron armatures, a very high crane passed beams to the workmen who were making the scaffoldings. But how could they get on with their work? Cats walked along all the planks, they made bricks fall and upset buckets of mortar, they fought in the midst of the piles of sand. When you started to raise an armature, you found a cat perched on the top of it, hissing fiercely. More treacherous pusses climbed onto the masons' backs as if to purr, and there was no getting rid of them. And the birds continued making their nests in all the trestles, the cab of the crane looked like an aviary[11] . . . And you couldn't dip up a bucket of water that wasn't full of frogs, croaking and hopping . . .

---

11. **aviary** (ā´ vē er´ ē) large bird cage or building for housing many birds.

Review and Assess

Thinking About the Selection

1. **Respond:** With whom did you sympathize most—the Marchesa or the cats? Explain.

2. **(a) Recall:** What is the "negative city"? **(b) Infer:** How have changes in the city altered the way cats live?

3. **(a) Recall:** How does Marcovaldo find the secret garden of the cats? **(b) Analyze:** Cite three details from Calvino's descriptions that explain why this garden is unique in the city.

4. **(a) Analyze:** Identify two descriptive details that make the Marchesa seem mysterious. **(b) Draw Conclusions:** Does the Marchesa somehow belong to the "city of cats," or is she just a prisoner there? Explain.

5. **Make a Generalization:** Given what happens after the Marchesa's death, make a generalization about the two opposing forces in this story, and explain what Calvino suggests about their relationship.

6. **Make a Judgment:** Do you think that some spaces in a city should be used in unforeseen, improvised ways, or should all space be used only according to plan? Explain.

Review and Assess

Literary Analysis

Symbolism

1. (a) What is the **symbolism** of the folding chair in "Folding Chairs"? (b) Given the emigration of Europeans to America in the 1940s, explain how the final image expands on this symbolism.

2. (a) Explain what the locusts symbolize in "Food for Prophets." (b) Is the release of prophets from jail a solution to this problem? Explain.

3. (a) What is the relationship of the cats to the city in "The Garden of Stubborn Cats"? (b) Explain what symbolic meaning the final event of the story adds to the cats.

Comparing Literary Works

4. Starting from the symbols in which they are expressed, compare the **theme** of "Food for Prophets" with that of Calvino's story. Use a chart like the one shown to organize your ideas.

Image	Symbolism	Theme: What It Shows About Society
Locusts		
Cats		

5. Based on the problems with society that these selections address, list four characteristics of your ideal city. Explain how your ideal city would solve these problems.

Reading Strategy

Recognizing Symbols

6. In "Folding Chairs," what similarities among the images of name plates, cooking, and chairs help you **recognize** these images as **symbols**?

7. (a) Identify a symbol in Calvino's story. (b) Explain what clues helped you recognize the object or character as a symbol.

Extend Understanding

8. **Technology Connection:** (a) In what ways is the Internet a "folding chair," or a symbol of people's lack of a true home? (b) In what ways does the Internet create "gardens of cats," nurturing mystery or spontaneity? (c) Do you think the Internet is more isolating or nurturing? Explain.

Integrate Language Skills

Vocabulary Development Lesson

Word Analysis: Latin Prefix *e-*

The Latin prefix *e-* (a form of the prefix *ex-* used before certain consonants) means "away from" or "out of." The word *emigrate* means "to move away from one place to live in another."

Complete each of the sentences that follow with one of the words provided below. Then, write a definition of each word, incorporating the meaning of *e-*.

emerge   emission   evacuate   evaporate

1. During World War II, many were forced by bombing raids to _____ their homes.
2. Some compared the _____ of toxic chemicals from the factory to a plague of locusts.
3. After a storm, the cats usually _____ from their hiding places.
4. The sun came out, and the puddles started to _____, disappearing by evening.

Fluency: Context

Review the vocabulary list on page 1243. Then, match each word listed to the correct clue below.

1. someone who volunteers for charities
2. describing three roads that meet
3. when people do this, they often become citizens of a new country
4. suburbs, in relation to cities
5. conditions in a run-down neighborhood
6. someone carrying two full grocery bags

Spelling Strategy

The suffix *-ence* is used to form a noun from an adjective that ends in *-ent*. For example, *convergent* becomes *convergence*.

Change each of these nouns to form an adjective. Use the suffix *-ence*.

independent   confident   emergent

Grammar and Style Lesson

Usage: *lay* and *lie*

Lay means "to put or set something down" and is used with a direct object. Its principal parts are *lay*, *laying*, *laid*, and *laid*.

> DIR. OBJ.
> . . . he *laid* his place among the packing cases in the warehouse. . . .

Lie means "to rest" or "to recline" and is never used with a direct object. Its principal parts are *lie*, *lying*, *lay*, and *lain*.

> A carpet of dry leaves covered the path, and dry leaves *lay* everywhere under the boughs of the two plane-trees. . . .

Practice For each item below, choose the correct word.

1. After (lying, laying) the plate down, the waiter left the room.
2. The old woman went to (lie, lay) down.
3. The workers had (laid, lain) their tools on the ground by 5:00 P.M.
4. Marcovaldo (lies, lays) the fish down.
5. Cats were (lying, laying) everywhere.

Writing Application Using forms of *lay* twice and forms of *lie* twice, write four sentences describing Marcovaldo's visit to the cats' garden.

Writing Lesson

Location Scout's Report

Imagine that shooting is about to begin for a film based on "The Garden of Stubborn Cats." As a location scout, write a description of a place you would recommend for filming a particular scene. To help the film director decide, include vivid descriptive details and a clear argument for using your location.

Prewriting   Choose a scene from the story. Then, think of a place you know that corresponds to the setting of the scene. Use a cluster diagram like the one shown to collect details that describe your location and to show why it is appropriate.

Model: Gathering Details With a Cluster Diagram

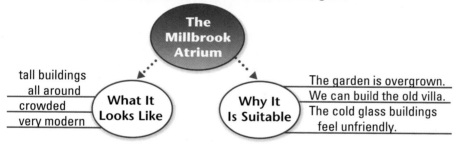

Drafting   Make your chosen location come to life for the film's director by using exact details from your notes. Explain why the place is appropriate for the setting described in the story.

Revising   Ask a partner to read your report and draw the scene you describe. If the sketch is inconsistent in parts with your location, add greater details to the corresponding parts of your report.

W *Prentice Hall Writing and Grammar Connection: Diamond Level, Chapter 6, Section 2*

Extension Activities

Listening and Speaking Divide a group into two teams, and hold a **debate** on this resolution: *We need to control urban development.* With teammates, develop the follow elements to support your position:

- logical arguments
- effective language
- illustrations from Grass's poems and Calvino's story

Hold your debate for the class. **[Group Activity]**

Research and Technology Develop a **visual display** that illustrates the characteristics and origins of several breeds of cats. Include breeds mentioned in "The Garden of Stubborn Cats." To make your chart both informative and easy to read, use annotations and symbols.

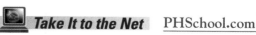 **Take It to the Net**   PHSchool.com

Go online for an additional research activity using the Internet.

Prepare to Read

from Survival in Auschwitz ◆ *from* Night ◆ When in early summer . . .

Primo Levi (1919–1987)

Both a chemist and a writer, Primo Levi had more than one side. Yet his fate hinged on a single fact: He was Jewish. This fact alone was enough to send Levi, like millions of other Jews in the 1930s and 1940s, to a brutal concentration camp.

Captured When the Nazis occupied Italy in 1943, Levi, a native of Turin, joined a resistance group. In December, the Nazis captured the young chemist and deported him to the camp at Auschwitz, in Poland. Levi was freed when the Allies liberated the camp in 1945. He achieved fame when his early memoir of the experience, *Survival in Auschwitz* (1947), was republished in 1958.

Writer and Chemist Levi worked as a chemist until 1977, when he retired to write full time. In books such as *The Periodic Table* (1975), he explores science, literature, and history. In his last book, *The Drowned and the Saved* (1986), he returns to the Holocaust with a darker, less hopeful eye.

Elie Wiesel (b. 1928)

Convinced that he had survived the Holocaust in order to "bear witness" to its horrors, Elie Wiesel nonetheless waited a decade to relate his experiences. "I didn't want to use the wrong words," he recalls. Finally, in 1956, Wiesel published *Night*, his renowned memoir of the Holocaust.

A Family Broken Wiesel grew up in the small Romanian town of Sighet. As World War II raged, the Nazis shipped Sighet's Jews to Auschwitz. The family was split up. The sixteen-year-old Wiesel ended up with his father in Buchenwald, a concentration camp in Germany.

Remembering In 1945, American troops liberated the camp. Orphaned by the war, Wiesel went to France, where he began his career as a journalist and spokesperson against oppression. Over the decades, he has spoken out against apartheid in South Africa, "ethnic cleansing" in Bosnia, and other practices he found to resemble Nazism. For his humanitarian efforts, Wiesel was awarded the Nobel Peace Prize in 1986.

Nelly Sachs (1891–1970)

As a teenager in Berlin, Germany, Nelly Sachs wrote a letter to a favorite author, Sweden's Selma Lagerlöf. That fateful letter began a correspondence that eventually saved Sachs's life.

History Interrupts By the 1920s, Sachs, with Lagerlöf's encouragement, was publishing her poetry in a Berlin newspaper. She might have continued on to moderate literary success, but history intervened. The Nazis came to power in 1933, and Sachs, who was Jewish, watched as the world turned dark. In 1940, threat became reality: She learned that she was to be sent to a concentration camp.

A Friend Helps When Lagerlöf heard of her friend's danger, she lobbied Sweden's royalty for the permission Sachs and her mother needed to move to Sweden. The Swedish government issued visas to Sachs and her mother, and the two escaped Germany. Haunted by friends and relatives killed in the Holocaust, Sachs devoted much of her poetry to the event. Though she eventually became a Swedish citizen, she continued to write in German. In 1966, Sachs, like Selma Lagerlöf before her, was awarded the Nobel Prize in Literature.

Preview

Connecting to the Literature

Being somebody looks easy: "I'm somebody who jogs." "I'm somebody who likes rock music." Watch a former friend ignore you, though, and it's not hard to feel like a nobody. In the 1940s, a nation tried to turn these writers into nobodies. Their words speak for the nobody in all of us.

Literary Analysis

Autobiography

An **autobiography** is a nonfiction work in which a person tells his or her own life story. An autobiography may be written for a number of reasons:

- Famous people may write autobiographies to satisfy readers' curiosity and to ensure accuracy about their lives.
- People who have shaped or witnessed historic events may write autobiographies to give insight into those events.

In their autobiographical writings, Primo Levi and Elie Wiesel give readers insight into the Holocaust. As you read, note ways in which the writers' purposes shape their autobiographies.

Comparing Literary Works

One form of autobiography is the **memoir,** a first-person account that focuses on one person or series of events in the writer's life, rather than telling the writer's full life story. Like many memoirs, Levi's and Wiesel's works offer an understanding of the meaning of events.

Use a chart like the one shown to compare the writers' insights.

Reading Strategy

Connecting to Historical Context

Holocaust narratives offer universal truths, but they are also rooted in history. To understand these works fully, **connect to historical context,** linking the work to events of the time. For instance, to understand why Levi, an Italian, is a prisoner of the Germans, you need to know that the Nazis occupied Italy in 1943. As you read, connect the background information on pages 1258, 1260, and 1267 with events and images in the selections.

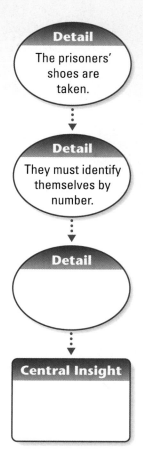

Detail

The prisoners' shoes are taken.

Detail

They must identify themselves by number.

Detail

Central Insight

Vocabulary Development

sordid (sôr´ did) *adj.* filthy; depressingly wretched (p. 1265)

prophetic (prō fet´ ik) *adj.* giving a prediction of the future (p. 1265)

intuition (in´ tōō ish´ ən) *n.* instinctive understanding (p. 1265)

affinity (ə fin´ i tē) *n.* close relationship; natural liking (p. 1265)

plaintive (plān´ tiv) *adj.* expressing sorrow; mournful (p. 1269)

beseeching (bē sēch´ iŋ) *adj.* asking for something earnestly (p. 1269)

liquidated (lik´ wi dāt´ id) *adj.* disposed of; ended; killed (p. 1274)

deportees (dē´ pôr tēz´) *n.* people ordered to leave a country (p. 1274)

from Survival in Auschwitz

Primo Levi
translated by Stuart Woolf

Background

The Holocaust was the systematic persecution and murder of millions of Jews and others deemed unfit by Germany's Nazi party. The Nazis came to power in Germany in 1933. During World War II (1939–1945), Nazi forces rounded up Jews throughout German-occupied lands and shot them or shipped them to concentration camps. Here, the prisoners were worked or starved to death or killed, often by poison gas. In this excerpt, Primo Levi describes his arrival at the complex of three camps at Auschwitz, in Poland.

▲ **Critical Viewing**
Explain how a prisoner such as Levi might react to the sight of this sign, "Work Gives Freedom," over the gate of Auschwitz. **[Connect]**

On the Bottom

The journey did not last more than twenty minutes. Then the lorry[1] stopped, and we saw a large door, and above it a sign, brightly illuminated (its memory still strikes me in my dreams): _Arbeit Macht Frei_,[2] work gives freedom.

---

1. lorry (lor´ ē) _n._ British term for "truck."
2. _Arbeit Macht Frei_ (ar´ bĭt mäkt frī)

We climb down, they make us enter an enormous empty room that is poorly heated. We have a terrible thirst. The weak gurgle of the water in the radiators makes us ferocious; we have had nothing to drink for four days. But there is also a tap—and above it a card which says that it is forbidden to drink as the water is dirty. Nonsense. It seems obvious that the card is a joke, "they" know that we are dying of thirst and they put us in a room, and there is a tap, and *Wassertrinken Verboten.*[3] I drink and I incite my companions to do likewise, but I have to spit it out, the water is tepid and sweetish, with the smell of a swamp.

This is hell. Today, in our times, hell must be like this. A huge, empty room: we are tired, standing on our feet, with a tap which drips while we cannot drink the water, and we wait for something which will certainly be terrible, and nothing happens and nothing continues to happen. What can one think about? One cannot think anymore, it is like being already dead. Someone sits down on the ground. The time passes drop by drop.

We are not dead. The door is opened and an SS[4] man enters, smoking. He looks at us slowly and asks, *"Wer kann Deutsch?"*[5] One of us whom I have never seen, named Flesch, moves forward; he will be our interpreter. This SS man makes a long calm speech; the interpreter translates. We have to form rows of five, with intervals of two yards between man and man; then we have to undress and make a bundle of the clothes in a special manner, the woolen garments on one side, all the rest on the other; we must take off our shoes but pay great attention that they are not stolen.

Stolen by whom? Why should our shoes be stolen? And what about our documents, the few things we have in our pockets, our watches? We all look at the interpreter, and the interpreter asks the German, and the German smokes and looks him through and through as if he were transparent, as if no one had spoken.

I had never seen old men naked. Mr. Bergmann wore a truss[6] and asked the interpreter if he should take it off, and the interpreter hesitated. But the German understood and spoke seriously to the interpreter pointing to someone. We saw the interpreter swallow and then he said: "The officer says, take off the truss, and you will be given that of Mr. Coen." One could see the words coming bitterly out of Flesch's mouth; this was the German manner of laughing.

Literary Analysis
Autobiography Why does Levi tell some of his autobiography in the first-person plural (*we*)?

▼ **Critical Viewing**
What does this image of wedding rings taken from concentration camp prisoners suggest about the treatment Levi will receive? **[Interpret]**

---

3. ***Wassertrinken Verboten*** (väs´ ər trink´ 'n fer bōt´ 'n) German: "It is forbidden to drink the water."
4. **SS** abbreviation for the *Shutzstaffel* (shōotz´ shtäf el), a quasi-military unit of the Nazi party, used as a secret police.
5. ***Wer kann Deutsch?*** (ver kän dóich) German: "Who knows German?"
6. **truss** *n.* padded strap worn to support a hernia (an abdominal muscle rupture).

☑**Reading Check**
What happens to the prisoners' shoes after they are warned to guard them from theft?

Now another German comes and tells us to put the shoes in a certain corner, and we put them there, because now it is all over and we feel outside this world and the only thing is to obey. Someone comes with a broom and sweeps away all the shoes, outside the door in a heap. He is crazy, he is mixing them all together, ninety-six pairs, they will be all mixed up. The outside door opens, a freezing wind enters and we are naked and cover ourselves up with our arms. The wind blows and slams the door; the German reopens it and stands watching with interest how we writhe[7] to hide from the wind, one behind the other. Then he leaves and closes it.

Now the second act begins. Four men with razors, soapbrushes and clippers burst in; they have trousers and jackets with stripes, with a number sewn on the front; perhaps they are the same sort as those others of this evening (this evening or yesterday evening?); but these are robust[8] and flourishing. We ask many questions but they catch hold of us and in a moment we find ourselves shaved and sheared. What comic faces we have without hair! The four speak a language which does not seem of this world. It is certainly not German, for I understand a little German.

Concentration Camp Inmates, February 1945, Pencil and watercolor on paper, Hellmut Bachrach-Barée. Gift of the artist. Courtesy of the Yad Vashem Art Museum, Jerusalem

Finally another door is opened: here we are, locked in, naked, sheared and standing, with our feet in water—it is a shower-room. We are alone. Slowly the astonishment dissolves, and we speak, and everyone asks questions and no one answers. If we are naked in a shower-room, it means that we will have a shower. If we have a shower it is because they are not going to kill us yet. But why then do they keep us standing, and give us nothing to drink, while nobody explains anything, and we have no shoes or clothes, but we are all naked with our feet in the water, and we have been traveling five days and cannot even sit down.

And our women?

Mr. Levi asks me if I think that our women are like us at this moment, and where they are, and if we will be able to see them again. I say yes, because he is married and has a daughter; certainly we will see them again. But by now my belief is that all this is a game to mock and

▲ Critical Viewing

What details of style— color, texture, clarity, line—help this drawing of concentration camp prisoners convey a sad or even grim mood? Explain. [Analyze]

---

7. writhe (rīth)*v.* twist the body about, as in pain.

8. robust (rō bust´) *adj.* strong and healthy; full of vigor.

sneer at us. Clearly they will kill us, whoever thinks he is going to live is mad, it means that he has swallowed the bait, but I have not; I have understood that it will soon all be over, perhaps in this same room, when they get bored of seeing us naked, dancing from foot to foot and trying every now and again to sit down on the floor. But there are two inches of cold water and we cannot sit down.

We walk up and down without sense, and we talk, everybody talks to everybody else, we make a great noise. The door opens, and a German enters; it is the officer of before. He speaks briefly, the interpreter translates. "The officer says you must be quiet, because this is not a rabbinical school."[9] One sees the words which are not his, the bad words, twist his mouth as they come out, as if he was spitting out a foul taste. We beg him to ask what we are waiting for, how long we will stay here, about our women, everything; but he says no, that he does not want to ask. This Flesch, who is most unwilling to translate into Italian the hard cold German phrases and refuses to turn into German our questions because he knows that it is useless, is a German Jew of about fifty, who has a large scar on his face from a wound received fighting the Italians on the Piave.[10] He is a closed, taciturn[11] man, for whom I feel an instinctive respect as I feel that he has begun to suffer before us.

The German goes and we remain silent, although we are a little ashamed of our silence. It is still night and we wonder if the day will ever come. The door opens again, and someone else dressed in stripes comes in. He is different from the others, older, with glasses, a more civilized face, and much less robust. He speaks to us in Italian.

By now we are tired of being amazed. We seem to be watching some mad play, one of those plays in which the witches, the Holy Spirit and the devil appear. He speaks Italian badly, with a strong foreign accent. He makes a long speech, is very polite, and tries to reply to all our questions.

We are at Monowitz, near Auschwitz, in Upper Silesia, a region inhabited by both Poles and Germans. This camp is a work-camp, in German one says *Arbeitslager*,[12] all

Reading Strategy
Connecting to Historical Context In what way do these difficulties over language reflect the actions and policies of the Nazis in Europe?

▼ Critical Viewing
Explain which aspect of Levi's experience the faceless figures in this image capture. [Connect]

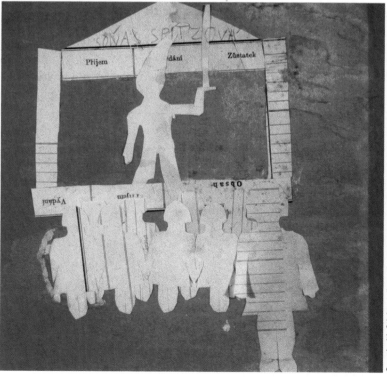

Guard with Stick, a collage of paper cut from an office ledger, Soña Spitzova, Jewish Museum in Prague, Courtesy of the United States Holocaust Memorial Museum

---

9. **rabbinical school** school for the training of rabbis (scholars and teachers of Jewish law). The comment is a negative reference to the practice in such schools of orally disputing issues of law.
10. **Piave** (pyä′ vā) river in northeastern Italy, located between Padua and Venice.
11. **taciturn** (tas′ ə tʉrn′) *adj.* habitually silent; uncommunicative.
12. **Arbeitslager** (är′ bīts läg′ r)

the prisoners (there are about ten thousand) work in a factory which produces a type of rubber called Buna, so that the camp itself is called Buna.

We will be given shoes and clothes—no, not our own—other shoes, other clothes, like his. We are naked now because we are waiting for the shower and the disinfection, which will take place immediately after the reveille, because one cannot enter the camp without being disinfected.

Certainly there will be work to do, everyone must work here. But there is work and work: he, for example, acts as doctor. He is a Hungarian doctor who studied in Italy and he is the dentist of the Lager.[13] He has been in the Lager for four and a half years (not in this one: Buna has only been open for a year and a half), but we can see that he is still quite well, not very thin. Why is he in the Lager? Is he Jewish like us? "No," he says simply, "I am a criminal."

We ask him many questions. He laughs, replies to some and not to others, and it is clear that he avoids certain subjects. He does not speak of the women: he says they are well, that we will see them again soon, but he does not say how or where. Instead he tells us other things, strange and crazy things, perhaps he too is playing with us. Perhaps he is mad—one goes mad in the Lager. He says that every Sunday there are concerts and football matches. He says that whoever boxes well can become cook. He says that whoever works well receives prize-coupons with which to buy tobacco and soap. He says that the water is really not drinkable, and that instead a coffee substitute is distributed every day, but generally nobody drinks it as the soup itself is sufficiently watery to quench thirst. We beg him to find us something to drink, but he says that he cannot, that he has come to see us secretly, against SS orders, as we still have to be disinfected, and that he must leave at once; he has come because he has a liking for Italians, and because, he says, he "has a little heart." We ask him if there are other Italians in the camp and he says there are some, a few, he does not know how many; and he at once changes the subject. Meanwhile a bell

---

13. **Lager** (läg' r) German: "camp."

▼ **Critical Viewing**

In what way does this image capture the "demolition of a man" discussed by Levi? **[Connect]**

Drawing for the Transportation Bas Relief, Dee Clements

rang and he immediately hurried off and left us stunned and disconcerted. Some feel refreshed but I do not. I still think that even this dentist, this incomprehensible person, wanted to amuse himself at our expense, and I do not want to believe a word of what he said.

At the sound of the bell, we can hear the still dark camp waking up. Unexpectedly the water gushes out boiling from the showers—five minutes of bliss; but immediately after, four men (perhaps they are the barbers) burst in yelling and shoving and drive us out, wet and steaming, into the adjoining room which is freezing; here other shouting people throw at us unrecognizable rags and thrust into our hands a pair of broken-down boots with wooden soles; we have no time to understand and we already find ourselves in the open, in the blue and icy snow of dawn, barefoot and naked, with all our clothing in our hands, with a hundred yards to run to the next hut. There we are finally allowed to get dressed.

When we finish, everyone remains in his own corner and we do not dare lift our eyes to look at one another. There is nowhere to look in a mirror, but our appearance stands in front of us, reflected in a hundred livid faces, in a hundred miserable and <u>sordid</u> puppets. We are transformed into the phantoms glimpsed yesterday evening.

Then for the first time we became aware that our language lacks words to express this offense, the demolition of a man. In a moment, with almost <u>prophetic</u> <u>intuition</u>, the reality was revealed to us: we had reached the bottom. It is not possible to sink lower than this; no human condition is more miserable than this, nor could it conceivably be so. Nothing belongs to us anymore; they have taken away our clothes, our shoes, even our hair; if we speak, they will not listen to us, and if they listen, they will not understand. They will even take away our name: and if we want to keep it, we will have to find in ourselves the strength to do so, to manage somehow so that behind the name something of us, of us as we were, still remains.

We know that we will have difficulty in being understood, and this is as it should be. But consider what value, what meaning is enclosed even in the smallest of our daily habits, in the hundred possessions which even the poorest beggar owns: a handkerchief, an old letter, the photo of a cherished person. These things are part of us, almost like limbs of our body; nor is it conceivable that we can be deprived of them in our world, for we immediately find others to substitute the old ones, other objects which are ours in their personification and evocation of our memories.

Literary Analysis
Autobiography Identify one technique Levi uses to put "the demolition of a man" into words.

Imagine now a man who is deprived of everyone he loves, and at the same time of his house, his habits, his clothes, in short, of everything he possesses: he will be a hollow man, reduced to suffering and needs, forgetful of dignity and restraint, for he who loses all often easily loses himself. He will be a man whose life or death can be lightly decided with no sense of human <u>affinity</u>, in the most fortunate of cases, on the basis of a pure judgment of utility. It is in this way that one can understand

 **Reading Check**
What does Levi say the prisoners are left with?

the double sense of the term "extermination camp," and it is now clear what we seek to express with the phrase: "to lie on the bottom."

Häftling:[14] I have learnt that I am a Häftling. My number is 174517; we have been baptized, we will carry the tattoo on our left arm until we die.

The operation was slightly painful and extraordinarily rapid: they placed us all in a row, and one by one, according to the alphabetical order of our names, we filed past a skillful official, armed with a sort of pointed tool with a very short needle. It seems that this is the real, true initiation: only by "showing one's number" can one get bread and soup. Several days passed, and not a few cuffs and punches, before we became used to showing our number promptly enough not to disorder the daily operation of food-distribution; weeks and months were needed to learn its sound in the German language. And for many days, while the habits of freedom still led me to look for the time on my wristwatch, my new name ironically appeared instead, its number tattooed in bluish characters under the skin.

---

14. *Häftling* (heft´ liŋ) German: "prisoner."

Literary Analysis
Autobiography and Memoir By telling the reader about his number, what insight does Levi suggest? Explain.

Review and Assess

Thinking About the Selection

1. **Respond:** To what audience would you recommend Levi's autobiography? Why?

2. **(a) Recall:** Describe three ways in which the prisoners are mistreated when they arrive at Auschwitz. **(b) Interpret:** What do you think Levi means when he writes "Today, in our times, hell must be like this"?

3. **(a) Recall:** Describe the way in which Flesch fulfills his role as translator. **(b) Infer:** Why is he reluctant to translate the German officer's comments into Italian?

4. **(a) Recall:** Explain the way in which the prisoners are "renamed" at the camp. **(b) Analyze:** What does Levi feel is the significance of this renaming?

5. **(a) Infer:** According to Levi, what makes up human identity? **(b) Draw Conclusions:** What does Levi suggest are the primary goals of the concentration camp?

6. **Draw Conclusions:** Referring to the Nazi treatment of the prisoners, Levi writes that "our language lacks words to express this offense, the demolition of a man." What does this remark imply about Levi's task of writing a memoir of this experience?

from Night

Elie Wiesel

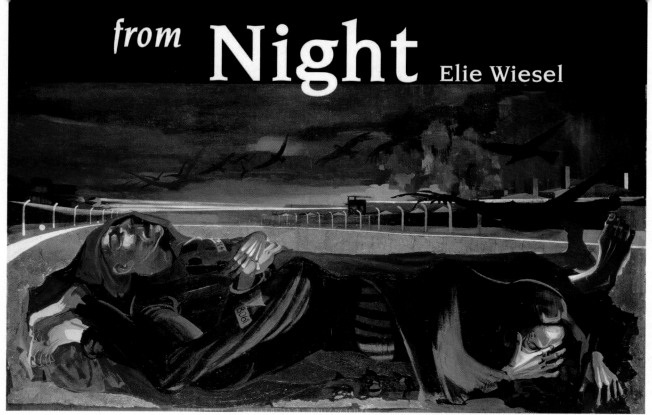

translated by Stella Rodway

Background

Toward the end of World War II (1939–1945), as the Allied armies fighting the Germans gained territory, German forces evacuated the inmates of the concentration camps in forced "death marches" and in "death trains." They hoped to send the prisoners deeper into Germany to prevent their liberation. In this excerpt from *Night,* Wiesel describes his experiences as a sixteen-year-old sent on such a journey with his father.

▲ **Critical Viewing**
What does this painting suggest about the mood of Wiesel's memoir? **[Predict]**

That same evening, we reached our destination.

It was late at night. The guards came to unload us. The dead were abandoned in the train. Only those who could still stand were able to get out.

Meir Katz stayed in the train. The last day had been the most murderous. A hundred of us had got into the wagon. A dozen of us got out—among them, my father and I.

We had arrived at Buchenwald.[1]

**Reading Check**
What happened to many of Elie's fellow passengers?

---

1. **Buchenwald** (bōōk´ 'n wôld´) village in Germany that was the site of a Nazi concentration camp and extermination center.

At the gate of the camp, SS[2] officers were waiting for us. They counted us. Then we were directed to the assembly place. Orders were given us through loudspeakers:

"Form fives!" "Form groups of a hundred!" "Five paces forward!"

I held onto my father's hand—the old, familiar fear: not to lose him.

Right next to us the high chimney of the crematory oven[3] rose up. It no longer made any impression on us. It scarcely attracted our attention.

An established inmate of Buchenwald told us that we should have a shower and then we could go into the blocks. The idea of having a hot bath fascinated me. My father was silent. He was breathing heavily beside me.

"Father," I said. "Only another moment more. Soon we can lie down—in a bed. You can rest. . . ."

He did not answer. I was so exhausted myself that his silence left me indifferent. My only wish was to take a bath as quickly as possible and lie down in a bed.

But it was not easy to reach the showers. Hundreds of prisoners were crowding there. The guards were unable to keep any order. They struck out right and left with no apparent result. Others, without the strength to push or even to stand up, had sat down in the snow. My father wanted to do the same. He groaned.

"I can't go on. . . . This is the end. . . . I'm going to die here. . . ."

He dragged me toward a hillock of snow from which emerged human shapes and ragged pieces of blanket.

"Leave me," he said to me. "I can't go on. . . . Have mercy on me. . . . I'll wait here until we can get into the baths. . . . You can come and find me."

I could have wept with rage. Having lived through so much, suffered so much, could I leave my father to die now? Now, when we could have a good hot bath and lie down?

"Father!" I screamed. "Father! Get up from here! Immediately! You're killing yourself. . . ."

I seized him by the arm. He continued to groan.

"Don't shout, son. . . . Take pity on your old father. . . . Leave me to rest here. . . . Just for a bit, I'm so tired . . . at the end of my strength. . . ."

He had become like a child, weak, timid, vulnerable.

"Father," I said. "You can't stay here."

I showed him the corpses all around him; they too had wanted to rest here.

"I can see them, son. I can see them all right. Let them sleep. It's so long since they closed their eyes. . . . They are exhausted . . . exhausted. . . ."

His voice was tender.

I yelled against the wind:

<hr>

2. **SS** quasi-military unit of the Nazi party, used as a special police.
3. **crematory oven** large oven in which the corpses of Holocaust victims were burned. In some cases, victims were burned while still alive.

Literary Analysis
Autobiography In what way does Wiesel's use of dialogue enrich his autobiography?

"They'll never wake again! Never! Don't you understand?"

For a long time this argument went on. I felt that I was not arguing with him, but with death itself, with the death that he had already chosen.

The sirens began to wail. An alert. The lights went out throughout the camp. The guards drove us toward the blocks. In a flash, there was no one left on the assembly place. We were only too glad not to have had to stay outside longer in the icy wind. We let ourselves sink down onto the planks. The beds were in several tiers. The cauldrons of soup at the entrance attracted no one. To sleep, that was all that mattered.

It was daytime when I awoke. And then I remembered that I had a father. Since the alert, I had followed the crowd without troubling about him. I had known that he was at the end, on the brink of death, and yet I had abandoned him.

I went to look for him.

▲ Critical Viewing
Does Wiesel's memoir suggest any possibility of understanding why a group of people reduced others to the condition of these inmates? Explain. [Apply]

But at the same moment this thought came into my mind: "Don't let me find him! If only I could get rid of this dead weight, so that I could use all my strength to struggle for my own survival, and only worry about myself." Immediately I felt ashamed of myself, ashamed forever.

I walked for hours without finding him. Then I came to the block where they were giving out black "coffee." The men were lining up and fighting.

A <u>plaintive</u>, <u>beseeching</u> voice caught me in the spine:

"Eliezer . . . my son . . . bring me . . . a drop of coffee. . . ."

I ran to him.

"Father! I've been looking for you for so long. . . . Where were you? Did you sleep? . . . How do you feel?"

He was burning with fever. Like a wild beast, I cleared a way for myself to the coffee cauldron. And I managed to carry back a cupful. I had a sip. The rest was for him. I can't forget the light of thankfulness in his eyes while he gulped it down—an animal gratitude. With those few gulps of hot water, I probably brought him more satisfaction than I had done during my whole childhood.

He was lying on a plank, livid,[4] his lips pale and dried up, shaken by tremors. I could not stay by him for long. Orders had been given to

plaintive (plān′ tiv) *adj.* expressing sorrow; mournful

beseeching (bē sēch′ iŋ) *adj.* asking for something earnestly

✓**Reading Check**

What problem with his father does Eliezer have to confront?

---

4. **livid** (liv′ id) *adj.* here, bruised; grayish blue or pale.

clear the place for cleaning. Only the sick could stay.

We stayed outside for five hours. Soup was given out. As soon as we were allowed to go back to the blocks, I ran to my father.

"Have you had anything to eat?"

"No."

"Why not?"

"They didn't give us anything . . . they said that if we were ill we should die soon anyway and it would be a pity to waste the food. I can't go on any more. . . ."

I gave him what was left of my soup. But it was with a heavy heart. I felt that I was giving it up to him against my will. No better than Rabbi Eliahou's son[5] had I withstood the test.

He grew weaker day by day, his gaze veiled, his face the color of dead leaves. On the third day after our arrival at Buchenwald, everyone had to go to the showers. Even the sick, who had to go through last.

1943 A.D., c.1943, Ben Shahn, Courtesy of the Syracuse University Art Collection, © Estate of Ben Shahn/Licensed by VAGA, New York, NY

▲ **Critical Viewing**
Given what you have read in Wiesel's memoir, explain what thoughts might preoccupy this prisoner. **[Apply]**

On the way back from the baths, we had to wait outside for a long time. They had not yet finished cleaning the blocks.

Seeing my father in the distance, I ran to meet him. He went by me like a ghost, passed me without stopping, without looking at me. I called to him. He did not come back. I ran after him:

"Father, where are you running to?"

He looked at me for a moment, and his gaze was distant, visionary; it was the face of someone else. A moment only and on he ran again.

Struck down with dysentery,[6] my father lay in his bunk, five other invalids with him. I sat by his side, watching him, not daring to believe that he could escape death again. Nevertheless, I did all I could to give him hope.

Suddenly, he raised himself on his bunk and put his feverish lips to my ear:

"Eliezer . . . I must tell you where to find the gold and the money I buried . . . in the cellar. . . . You know. . . ."

He began to talk faster and faster, as though he were afraid he would not have time to tell me. I tried to explain to him that this was not the

---

5. **Rabbi Eliahou's son** Earlier in the book, Elie has witnessed a son abandoning his father, Rabbi Eliahou, by pretending not to notice when his father falls behind on a forced march.

6. **dysentery** (dis´ ən ter´ ē) *n.* disease of the intestines.

end, that we would go back to the house together, but he would not listen to me. He could no longer listen to me. He was exhausted. A trickle of saliva, mingled with blood, was running from between his lips. He had closed his eyes. His breath was coming in gasps.

For a ration of bread, I managed to change beds with a prisoner in my father's bunk. In the afternoon the doctor came. I went and told him that my father was very ill.

"Bring him here!"

I explained that he could not stand up. But the doctor refused to listen to anything. Somehow, I brought my father to him. He stared at him, then questioned him in a clipped voice:

"What do you want?"

"My father's ill," I answered for him. "Dysentery . . ."

"Dysentery? That's not my business. I'm a surgeon. Go on! Make room for the others."

Protests did no good.

"I can't go on, son. . . . Take me back to my bunk. . . ."

I took him back and helped him to lie down. He was shivering.

"Try and sleep a bit, father. Try to go to sleep. . . ."

His breathing was labored, thick. He kept his eyes shut. Yet I was convinced that he could see everything, that now he could see the truth in all things.

Another doctor came to the block. But my father would not get up. He knew that it was useless.

Besides, this doctor had only come to finish off the sick. I could hear him shouting at them that they were lazy and just wanted to stay in bed. I felt like leaping at his throat, strangling him. But I no longer had the courage or the strength. I was riveted to my father's deathbed. My hands hurt, I was clenching them so hard. Oh, to strangle the doctor and the others! To burn the whole world! My father's murderers! But the cry stayed in my throat.

When I came back from the bread distribution, I found my father weeping like a child:

"Son, they keep hitting me!"

"Who?"

I thought he was delirious.

"Him, the Frenchman . . . and the Pole . . . they were hitting me."

Another wound to the heart, another hate, another reason for living lost.

"Eliezer . . . Eliezer . . . tell them not to hit me. . . . I haven't done anything . . . . Why do they keep hitting me?"

I began to abuse his neighbors. They laughed at me. I promised them bread, soup. They laughed. Then they got angry; they could not stand

✔ Reading Check

Give an example of a way in which Eliezer takes care of his father.

from *Night* ◆ 1271

my father any longer, they said, because he was now unable to drag himself outside to relieve himself.

The following day he complained that they had taken his ration of bread.

"While you were asleep?"

"No. I wasn't asleep. They jumped on top of me. They snatched my bread . . . and they hit me . . . again. . . . I can't stand any more, son . . . a drop of water. . . ."

I knew that he must not drink. But he pleaded with me for so long that I gave in. Water was the worst poison he could have, but what else could I do for him? With water, without water, it would all be over soon anyway. . . .

"You, at least, have some mercy on me. . . ."

Have mercy on him! I, his only son!

A week went by like this.

"This is your father, isn't it?" asked the head of the block.

"Yes."

"He's very ill."

"The doctor won't do anything for him."

"The doctor *can't* do anything for him, now. And neither can you."

He put his great hairy hand on my shoulder and added:

"Listen to me, boy. Don't forget that you're in a concentration camp. Here, every man has to fight for himself and not think of anyone else. Even of his father. Here, there are no fathers, no brothers, no friends. Everyone lives and dies for himself alone. I'll give you a sound piece of advice—don't give your ration of bread and soup to your old father. There's nothing you can do for him. And you're killing yourself. Instead, you ought to be having his ration."

I listened to him without interrupting. He was right, I thought in the most secret region of my heart, but I dared not admit it. It's too late to save your old father, I said to myself. You ought to be having two rations of bread, two rations of soup. . . .

Only a fraction of a second, but I felt guilty. I ran to find a little soup to give my father. But he did not want it. All he wanted was water.

"Don't drink water . . . have some soup. . . ."

"I'm burning . . . why are you being so unkind to me, my son? Some water. . . ."

I brought him some water. Then I left the block for roll call. But I turned around and came back again. I lay down on the top bunk. Invalids were allowed to stay in the block. So I would be an invalid myself. I would not leave my father.

There was silence all round now, broken only by groans. In front of the block, the SS were giving orders. An officer passed by the beds. My father begged me:

"My son, some water. . . . I'm burning. . . . My stomach. . . ."

"Quiet, over there!" yelled the officer.

"Eliezer," went on my father, "some water. . . ."

Reading Strategy
Connecting to Historical Context Using facts about life in the concentration camps, explain why Wiesel was led to such dark thoughts.

The officer came up to him and shouted at him to be quiet. But my father did not hear him. He went on calling me. The officer dealt him a violent blow on the head with his truncheon.

I did not move. I was afraid. My body was afraid of also receiving a blow.

Then my father made a rattling noise and it was my name: "Eliezer."

I could see that he was still breathing—spasmodically.[7]

I did not move.

When I got down after roll call, I could see his lips trembling as he murmured something. Bending over him, I stayed gazing at him for over an hour, engraving into myself the picture of his blood-stained face, his shattered skull.

Then I had to go to bed. I climbed into my bunk, above my father, who was still alive. It was January 28, 1945.

I awoke on January 29 at dawn. In my father's place lay another invalid. They must have taken him away before dawn and carried him to the crematory. He may still have been breathing.

There were no prayers at his grave. No candles were lit to his memory. His last word was my name. A summons, to which I did not respond.

I did not weep, and it pained me that I could not weep. But I had no more tears. And, in the depths of my being, in the recesses of my weakened conscience, could I have searched it, I might perhaps have found something like—free at last!

I had to stay at Buchenwald until April eleventh. I have nothing to say of my life during this period. It no longer mattered. After my father's death, nothing could touch me any more.

I was transferred to the children's block, where there were six hundred of us.

The front was drawing nearer.

I spent my days in a state of total idleness. And I had but one desire—to eat. I no longer thought of my father or of my mother.

---

7. **spasmodically** (spaz mäd′ ik ə lē) *adv.* in spasms; intermittently; irregularly.

▲ **Critical Viewing**
Explain what Wiesel's memoir adds to your reaction to this image of a young prisoner of Buchenwald. **[Respond]**

Literary Analysis
Autobiography and Memoir By focusing on his father, what basic human concerns does Wiesel dramatize?

✔**Reading Check**
What eventually happens to Eliezer's father?

From time to time I would dream of a drop of soup, of an extra ration of soup. . . .

On April fifth, the wheel of history turned.

It was late in the afternoon. We were standing in the block, waiting for an SS man to come and count us. He was late in coming. Such a delay was unknown till then in the history of Buchenwald. Something must have happened.

Two hours later the loudspeakers sent out an order from the head of the camp: all the Jews must come to the assembly place.

This was the end! Hitler was going to keep his promise.

The children in our block went toward the place. There was nothing else we could do. Gustav, the head of the block, made this clear to us with his truncheon. But on the way we met some prisoners who whispered to us:

"Go back to your block. The Germans are going to shoot you. Go back to your block, and don't move."

We went back to our block. We learned on the way that the camp resistance organization had decided not to abandon the Jews and was going to prevent their being <u>liquidated</u>.

As it was late and there was great upheaval—innumerable Jews had passed themselves off as non-Jews—the head of the camp decided that a general roll call would take place the following day. Everybody would have to be present.

The roll call took place. The head of the camp announced that Buchenwald was to be liquidated. Ten blocks of <u>deportees</u> would be evacuated each day. From this moment, there would be no further distribution of bread and soup. And the evacuation began. Every day, several thousand prisoners went through the camp gate and never came back.

liquidated (lik′ wi dāt′ id) *adj.* disposed of; ended; killed

deportees (dē′ pôr tēz′) *n.* people ordered to leave a country

▼ **Critical Viewing**
What does Wiesel's account of daily life in Buchenwald add to your appreciation of the spirit of an inmate (see photograph) in drawing this portrait of another inmate? **[Interpret]**

On April tenth, there were still about twenty thousand of us in the camp, including several hundred children. They decided to evacuate us all at once, right on until the evening. Afterward, they were going to blow up the camp.

So we were massed in the huge assembly square, in rows of five, waiting to see the gate open. Suddenly, the sirens began to wail. An alert! We went back to the blocks. It was too late to evacuate us that evening. The evacuation was postponed again to the following day.

We were tormented with hunger. We had eaten nothing for six days, except a bit of grass or some potato peelings found near the kitchens.

At ten o'clock in the morning the SS scattered through the camp, moving the last victims toward the assembly place.

Then the resistance movement decided to act. Armed men suddenly rose up everywhere. Bursts of firing. Grenades exploding. We children stayed flat on the ground in the block.

The battle did not last long. Toward noon everything was quiet again. The SS had fled and the resistance had taken charge of the running of the camp.

At about six o'clock in the evening, the first American tank stood at the gates of Buchenwald.

Review and Assess

Thinking About the Selection

1. **Respond:** Describe your reaction when sixteen-year-old Wiesel was liberated.

2. **(a) Recall:** In what ways does Wiesel change during his time in the camp? **(b) Analyze Cause and Effect:** What causes these changes?

3. **(a) Recall:** How does Wiesel respond to his father's illness? **(b) Compare and Contrast:** Contrast Wiesel's response with those of the doctor and his father's blockmates. **(c) Generalize:** What does this contrast show about basic human values in the camp?

4. **(a) Analyze:** While Wiesel's father is alive, what conflicting feelings does Wiesel experience? **(b) Infer:** Citing details, explain what Wiesel feels, in addition to sorrow, at his father's death.

5. **(a) Evaluate:** Do you think Wiesel's complicated feelings about his father show selfishness, or might anyone have experienced them? Explain.

6. **Extend:** Why might guilt be a common emotion experienced by the survivors of a tragedy? In your answer, draw on details from Wiesel's memoir.

When in Early Summer

Nelly Sachs

translated by
Ruth and Matthew Mead

When in early summer the moon sends out secret signs,
the chalices of lilies scent of heaven,
some ear opens to listen
beneath the chirp of the cricket
5 to earth turning and the language of spirits set free.

But in dreams fish fly in the air
and a forest takes firm root in the floor of the room.

But in the midst of enchantment a voice speaks clearly and amazed:
World, how can you go on playing your games
10 and cheating time—
World, the little children were thrown like butterflies,
wings beating into the flames—

and your earth has not been thrown like a rotten apple
into the terror-roused abyss—

15 And sun and moon have gone on walking—
two cross-eyed witnesses who have seen nothing.

Review and Assess

Thinking About the Selection

1. **Respond:** Which image evoked your strongest response? Why?
2. **(a) Recall:** What natural events does the speaker describe in the first two lines? **(b) Interpret:** Describe the relationship between the poet and nature that is suggested by these opening lines.
3. **(a) Recall:** What does the "voice" accuse the world of doing in lines 9–10? **(b) Infer:** According to the voice, what event should prevent the world from doing these things? **(c) Interpret:** In what sense does the voice break the enchantment of the opening?
4. **Speculate:** What might Sachs's speaker say to a poet who, after the Holocaust, continued to write poetry about nature?

Review and Assess

Literary Analysis

Autobiography

1. (a) What might Levi's purpose be in writing an **autobiography**? Cite supporting details. (b) Identify one example of a way in which Levi draws the reader into events.

2. (a) What do you think Wiesel's purpose is in writing an **autobiography**? Cite supporting details. (b) Explain two ways in which Wiesel's report of his difficulties with his father helps readers understand concentration camp life.

3. Imagine that another writer has written an account of the lives of Levi and Wiesel. Identify two ways in which this account would differ from these autobiographies.

Comparing Literary Works

4. Compare and contrast the central insights of Levi's and Wiesel's **memoirs,** using a chart like the one shown.

	Events	Insights	Similarities/ Differences
Levi			
Wiesel			

5. (a) Explain Levi's insight into ways the concentration camp stripped people of words. (b) In Sachs's poem, what point is made about consequences of the Holocaust for poetry? (c) Using these insights, explain why it is difficult but important to put the Holocaust into words.

Reading Strategy

Connecting to Historical Context

6. Explain the way in which **historical context** adds to your understanding of the different nationalities of the people Levi first meets.

7. What historical facts help you understand the conclusion of the selection from *Night*? Explain.

Extend Understanding

8. **Social Studies Connection:** In today's world, what steps might people take to prevent governments from treating people in dehumanizing ways? Explain your answer.

Integrate Language Skills

Vocabulary Development Lesson

Word Analysis: Latin Root *-port-*

The Latin root *-port-* means "carry" or "move." The word *deportees* means "people who are moved away," or expelled from a country. Explain what *-port-* adds to the meaning of these words:

1. importer
2. portable
3. deportment

Spelling Strategy

The *-tion* ending, found in *intuition*, makes the *shun* sound. The ending *-sion* is generally pronounced *zhun*, as in *diversion*. The ending *-ssion*, pronounced *shun*, is common with base words that end in *-ss*—for example, *possess, possession*. Complete each word with the correct ending: *-tion, -sion,* or *-ssion.*

1. liquida____
2. indeci____
3. succe____

Concept Development: Antonyms

In each item, choose the antonym, or word opposite in meaning, of the first word.

1. affinity: (a) similarity, (b) hatred, (c) friendliness
2. deportees: (a) teachers, (b) immigrants, (c) promises
3. intuition: (a) payment, (b) thoughtfulness, (c) incomprehension
4. liquidated: (a) made, (b) destroyed, (c) ate
5. prophetic: (a) commemorative, (b) intelligent, (c) strong
6. beseeching: (a) answering, (b) asking, (c) wondering
7. sordid: (a) ugly, (b) clean, (c) jumbled
8. plaintive: (a) old, (b) fancy, (c) cheerful

Grammar and Style Lesson

Absolute Phrases

An **absolute phrase,** or nominative absolute, consists of a noun or a pronoun modified by a participle or a participial phrase. Unlike a participial phrase, an absolute phrase does not modify a subject or an object elsewhere in the sentence. It has no grammatical relationship to the rest of the sentence. Study this example from *Night*, noting how the phrase adds descriptive detail in few words.

> **Absolute Phrase:** My father grew weaker day by day, his gaze veiled.
> NOUN PART.

> **Participial (Not Absolute) Phrase:**
> Having lived through so much, . . . could I leave my father to die now?

Practice Identify the absolute phrase in each item, or write *none* if the item lacks such a phrase.

1. . . . my new name ironically appeared instead, its number tattooed in bluish characters under the skin.
2. Imagine now a man who is deprived of everyone he loves. . . .
3. He was lying on a plank, livid, his lips [being] pale and dried up. . . .
4. Seeing my father in the distance, I ran to meet him.
5. . . . the little children were thrown like butterflies, / wings beating into the flames. . . .

Writing Application Use two absolute phrases in a description of Wiesel's liberation.

W̶G̶ Prentice Hall Writing and Grammar Connection: Diamond Level, Chapter 19, Section 2

Writing Lesson

Persuasive Essay

Imagine that your school is planning a curriculum unit to teach students about the Holocaust. Write an essay supporting the inclusion in the unit of Levi's or Wiesel's memoir or Sachs' poem. In your essay, explain your choice, using reasons suited to your audience—the teachers at your school.

Prewriting	First, choose the selection you will propose. You might choose a work on the basis of its emotional impact or its strong historical insight. Then, list at least three reasons that this selection should be included in a unit about the Holocaust.
Drafting	Begin your draft with a clear statement of your opinion. Then, provide supporting arguments in a logical order. Use strong, direct language that will reinforce your points.
Revising	Review your essay to ensure that you have included details and used language appropriate to your audience and purpose. Replace words that are weak or that might not be suitable. Add details that your audience will find persuasive.

Model: Revising for Audience and Purpose

Finally, ~~I thought~~ what Levi says about identity is ~~cool.~~ He shows
profound.

how important respect for the identity of others is.
In addition to learning

history, students reading the memoir will reflect on basic values.

WG *Prentice Hall Writing and Grammar Connection: Diamond Level, Chapter 7, Section 4*

Extension Activities

Research and Technology Using the Web site for the United States Holocaust Memorial Museum in Washington, D.C., research Holocaust memorials around the world. Then, create a **multimedia presentation,** using a slide-show program. Compare the following aspects of each memorial:

- main purpose, including commemoration or documentation, and any specific focus
- distinctive features, including art, architecture, exhibits, and archives

Give your presentation to the class.

Listening and Speaking Hold a **group discussion** in which you compare Wiesel's and Levi's memoirs. For instance, you might compare their use of certain types of sentences for effect, as well as their themes. In your discussion, listen actively to build on the contributions of others. **[Group Activity]**

 **Take It to the Net** PHSchool.com

Go online for an additional research activity using the Internet.

READING INFORMATIONAL MATERIALS

Press Releases

About Press Releases

A **press release** is a brief document circulated to news agencies that announces or responds to an event or a trend. By distributing a press release, individuals or organizations encourage the news media to report on the event or viewpoint discussed in the release.

Press releases are often written not simply to inform reporters, but to influence the way in which a news story is presented. In fact, journalists are invited to reprint material in a press release as part of an article. A responsible reporter will always attribute words from a press release to the organization or individual in whose name the release is issued.

Reading Strategy

Distinguishing Fact From Opinion

In using press releases, journalists must carefully **distinguish between fact and opinion**—between statements that can be verified and statements that express a viewpoint on the facts. Like a responsible journalist, you should distinguish facts from opinions when reading a press release or other public statement.

As you read the press release on pages 1281 and 1282, **distinguish between facts and opinions** by using the information in the chart below.

Identifying Facts and Opinions

Claims of Fact
• can be verified through experiment or proof or can be confirmed by an authoritative source
• are either true or false
Example: Imre Kertész's first novel was originally published in 1975.

Statements of Opinion
• are judgments that may depend on claims of fact but that present a viewpoint on the facts, not just the facts themselves
• reflect the values of the opinion holder
• may be defended by persuasive appeals to facts and to shared values
Example: Kertész ". . . inspires a singular freedom of thought."

Who Is Imre Kertész?

Born in Budapest, Hungary, Imre Kertész was a teenager in 1944, a time when Hungary was collaborating with Germany's Nazi government to confine Jews to ghettos, confiscate their property, and deport them to concentration camps such as Auschwitz and Buchenwald. Kertész's experiences in Auschwitz pervade his writing. Two of his novels that have been translated into English are *Fateless* and *Kaddish for a Child not Born*. Like the great philosophers and writers mentioned in this press release, Kertész's works deal with fundamental issues related to life, death, and human existence.

The Swedish Academy
PRESS RELEASE
10 October 2002

SVENSKA AKADEMIEN

The Nobel Prize in Literature 2002
Recipient: Imre Kertész

The Nobel Prize in Literature for 2002 is awarded to the Hungarian writer Imre Kertész

> "for writing that upholds the fragile experience of the individual against the barbaric arbitrariness of history."

In his writing Imre Kertész explores the possibility of continuing to live and think as an individual in an era in which the subjection of human beings to social forces has become increasingly complete. His works return unremittingly to the decisive experience of his life: the period spent in Auschwitz, to which he was taken as a teenage boy during the Nazi persecution of Hungary's Jews. For him, Auschwitz is not an exceptional occurrence that, like an alien body, subsists outside the normal history of Western Europe. It is the ultimate truth about human degradation in modern existence.

Kertész's first novel, *Sorstalanság*, 1975 (*Fateless*, 1992), deals with the young Köves, who is arrested and taken to a concentration camp but conforms and survives. The novel uses the alienating device of taking the reality of the camp completely for granted, an everyday existence like any other, admittedly with conditions that are thankless, but not without moments of happiness. Köves regards events as a child would, without completely understanding them and without finding them unnatural or disquieting. He lacks our ready-made answers.

> Key biographical facts describing experiences that shaped Kertész's life and work appear near the beginning of the article.

Sentences like this one include an opinion of Kertész's novel. A journalist may then adapt such subjective material to describe Kertész's work to readers.

The shocking credibility of the description derives perhaps from this very absence of any element of the moral indignation or metaphysical protest that the subject cries out for. The reader is confronted not only with the cruelty of the atrocities but just as much with the thought-lessness that characterized their execution. Both perpetrators and victims were preoccupied with insistent practical problems; the major questions did not exist. Kertész's message is that *to live is to conform.* The capacity of the captives to come to terms with Auschwitz is one outcome of the same principle that finds expression in everyday human coexistence.

In thinking like this, the author concurs with a philosophical tradition in which life and human spirit are enemies. In *Kaddis a meg nem született gyermekért,* 1990 (*Kaddish for a Child not Born,* 1997), Kertész presents a consistently negative picture of childhood and from this pre-history derives the paradoxical feeling of being at home in the concentration camp. He completes his implacable existential analysis by depicting love as the highest stage of conformism, total capitulation to the desire to exist at any cost. For Kertész the spiritual dimension of man lies in his inability to adapt to life. Individual experience seems useless as soon as it is considered in the light of the needs and interests of the human collective.

In his collection of fragments, *Gályanapló* ("*Galley Diary*"), 1992, Kertész demonstrates his full intellectual scope. "Theoretical justifications are merely constructions," he writes, but nevertheless he conducts an untiring dialogue with the great tradition of cultural criticism – Pascal, Goethe, Schopenhauer, Nietzsche, Kafka, Camus, Beckett, Bernhard. In essence, Imre Kertész is a minority consisting of one individual. He regards his kinship with the concept of a Jew as a definition inflicted on him by the enemy. But through its consequences this arbitrary categorization has nevertheless been his initiation into the deepest knowledge of humanity and the age in which he lives.

The publication dates for each novel are facts that appear earlier in the press release, but the press release repeats the dates here to make it easier for an editor to take this paragraph exactly as it is and incorporate it into a news article.

The novels that succeeded *Sorstalanság,* 1975 (*Fateless,* 1992), *A kudarc* ("*Fiasco*"), 1988, and *Kaddis a meg nem született gyermekért,* 1990 (*Kaddish for a Child not Born,* 1997), can almost be characterized as comments and additions to the first and decisive work. This provides the theme of *A kudarc.* While he waits for an expected refusal of his real novel, the one about Auschwitz, the aging author spends his days writing a contemporary novel in the style of Kafka, a claustrophobic description of socialist Eastern Europe. In the end, he is informed that his previous book will, in spite of everything, be published, but all he can feel is emptiness. On display in the literary marketplace, his personality is transformed into an object, his secrets into banalities.

This opinion of Kertész's style might provide a writer with an apt quotation for a review or book jacket blurb.

The refusal to compromise in Kertész's stance can be perceived clearly in his style, which is reminiscent of a thickset hawthorn hedge, dense and thorny for unsuspecting visitors. But he relieves his readers of the burden of compulsory emotions and inspires a singular freedom of thought.

Check Your Comprehension

1. What is Kertész's country of origin?
2. What harrowing experience marked his teenage years?
3. According to the press release, what is distinctive about the way in which Kertész presents a similar experience in his first novel, *Fateless*?

Applying the Reading Strategy

Distinguishing Fact From Opinion

4. Cite an example of a fact in the press release.
5. (a) Cite an example of a statement of opinion in the press release. (b) Explain which values or tastes this statement reflects. Record your responses in a chart like the one shown.

Statement of Opinion	
Statement: _____ _____	
☐ Does statement express a judgment of taste or value? ☐ Is statement open to being proved as fact? ☐ Does statement explain facts?	**Values** What does the statement assume is good or valuable?

Activity

Writing a News Article

Using this press release and additional research, write a newspaper article on the award of the 2002 Nobel Prize in Literature to Imre Kertész. Your news article should include an informative headline and address the questions *Who? What? When? Where?* and *Why?* As you work, follow these guidelines for responsible journalism:

- Confirm claims in one source by checking them against another source.
- Avoid reporting opinions as if they were facts.
- Attribute quotations to a source.

Comparing Informational Materials

Press Releases and Book Reviews

Book reviews, which appear in magazines and newpapers, usually provide a brief summary of the book along with the reviewer's evaluation of it. Consider the ways in which this press release about Kertész would be similar to or different from a book review of one of his novels.

Write a brief essay explaining the similarities and differences between this press release and a book review. Discuss which details from the press release might appear in a book review and what new details might be added. Also, discuss any differences in format.

Prepare to Read

A Song on the End of the World ◆
The End and the Beginning

Czesław Miłosz (b. 1911)

Poet, essayist, and novelist Czeslaw Miłosz (chez´ wäf mē´ wōsh) has lived as many lives as the legendary cat. From a young writer haunted by "gloomy visions" to a diplomat in Washington, D.C., to a university professor in California, Miłosz is widely known today as a distinguished Nobel Prize winner.

Born in the Lithuanian city of Wilno (also known as Vilna), young Miłosz decided to study law. Hitler had just seized control in Germany, and Miłosz rejected the Nazi glorification of the state. Communism seemed like an antidote, yet Miłosz questioned the rigidity of its doctrines. His early poetry captures the violence-haunted atmosphere of the 1930s.

Defiance and Resignation After World War II broke out, Miłosz moved to Warsaw, Poland, where he participated in underground publishing activities carried on in defiance of the Nazi occupiers. After the war, when the Communist U.S.S.R. dominated Poland, Miłosz served as a diplomat for Poland in Washington, D.C. Miłosz was not a hard-line Communist; he hoped for reform. In 1951, though, he gave up hopes of working for change from within and broke with the Communist government. Moving first to France, he later became a professor of literature at the University of California at Berkeley.

Leading by Example Although he says he is uncomfortable in the role of moral leader, Miłosz's independence of mind has been widely admired by younger generations of Poles. His poems have carried a great deal of moral authority in Poland. In 1980, his international stature was confirmed when he received the Nobel Prize in Literature.

Wisława Szymborska (b. 1923)

For Wisława Szymborska (vīs wa´ va shim boor´ ska), inspiration begins when a poet says "I don't know." Her work centers around the rediscovery of astonishment. "[I]n the language of poetry," she said in her 1996 Nobel Prize acceptance speech, "where every word is weighed, nothing is usual or normal. Not a single stone or a single cloud above it."

Born in the small town of Bnin, Poland (now a part of Kórnik), Szymborska moved in 1931 to Krakow, where she still lives today. In 1945, her first published poem appeared in a daily newspaper. In 1953, she became the poetry editor at a literary magazine.

Privacy and Politics Unlike her fellow Pole Miłosz, Szymborska has led much of her life out of the public eye. Still, politics left an inevitable mark on her work.

In the early 1950s, Szymborska wrote in the government-permitted style of the time. A relaxation of government regulations allowed her to publish in her own voice, but in the 1980s, the government again cracked down on dissent. During that time, Szymborska contributed to underground and exile periodicals. The triumph of Poland's Solidarity movement in 1989 brought an end to strict government oversight of culture.

A Distinguished Honor Szymborska has published more than sixteen collections of poetry, as well as a collection of essays. She has refused to give readings, however, out of her dislike for publicity. When told she had won the 1996 Nobel Prize in Literature, Szymborska said it felt as if the world "came crashing down on me." Although she valued the honor, she told Miłosz at the time, "I am a private person."

Preview

Connecting to the Literature

If you have ever rediscovered your first-grade class picture or revisited a long-forgotten childhood playground, then you know that, as these poets show, time is measured by how much we forget more than by what we remember.

Literary Analysis

Irony

Irony occurs when writers create a contrast between what is stated and what is meant or between what is expected to happen and what actually happens. Irony can take the following forms:

- **Situational irony** is an opposition between events and expectations. In his poem, Miłosz insists that the day the world ends will be like any other, although we expect it to be more dramatic.

- **Verbal irony** is a clash between the words used for a thing and its reality. Szymborska writes "After every war / someone has to tidy up," ironically understating the damage caused by war.

As you read, note the poets' use of verbal and situational irony.

Comparing Literary Works

These poets use irony to challenge our ideas of history. They take **history as a theme,** looking for a meaning or a pattern in historical events.

- Miłosz's irony makes us reconsider just what an ordinary day is.
- Szymborska's irony suggests that progress means forgetting, not learning from, the past.

As you read, compare the lessons about history in these poems. Consider whether history appears as a cycle that repeats itself or as a straight line.

Reading Strategy

Evaluating the Writer's Statement of Philosophy

To **evaluate a writer's philosophy,** first identify the writer's view of life. Begin by analyzing patterns in the work, such as similarities in details that point to a common meaning. Then, decide whether the writer's view is supported by your own ideas and experiences.

As you read, evaluate each poet's philosophy, using a chart like this one.

Vocabulary Development

glimmering (glim´ ər iŋ) v. flickering; giving a faint, unsteady light (p. 1286)

prophet (präf´ ət) n. inspired person who speaks great truths or foretells the future (p. 1287)

shards (shärdz) n. sharp fragments (p. 1288)

glaze (glāz) v. fit glass to a window; cover with a shiny finish (p. 1288)

gawking (gôk´ iŋ) v. staring foolishly; gaping (p. 1290)

Details

"A Song on the End of the World"
"A bee circles clover . . ."
"A fisherman mends a glimmering net."

↓

Meanings They Suggest

Ordinary events seem extraordinary on the day the world ends.

↓

Philosophy

Ordinary life is precious; we just forget how precious.

↓

Evaluation

A Song on the End of the World

Czesław Miłosz   *translated by Anthony Miłosz*

Background

Written in 1944, this poem reflects historical events: A world *did* come to an end in the Polish capital of Warsaw during World War II. In 1939, Nazi Germany and the Soviet Union invaded Poland and divided the country between them. In the summer of 1944, as the Polish resistance movement rebelled against Nazi rule, Warsaw was nearly leveled.

Miłosz thought it unlikely that he would survive the war, but he found wisdom in the advice of Martin Luther, a leader of the Protestant movement for religious reform: "[W]hen asked what he would do if he knew tomorrow was going to be the end of the world, he said, 'I would plant apple trees.'"

The calm conviction of Miłosz's poem reflects this insight into the value of the ordinary. It also reflects Poland's long history as the target of invasion and occupation, a history that also echoes in Szymborska's poem "The End and the Beginning."

On the day the world ends
A bee circles a clover,
A fisherman mends a <u>glimmering</u> net.
Happy porpoises jump in the sea,
5 By the rainspout young sparrows are playing
And the snake is gold-skinned as it should always be.

On the day the world ends
Women walk through the fields under their umbrellas,
A drunkard grows sleepy at the edge of a lawn,
10 Vegetable peddlers shout in the street
And a yellow-sailed boat comes nearer the island,
The voice of a violin lasts in the air
And leads into a starry night.

glimmering (glim´ ər iŋ) v. flickering; giving a faint, unsteady light

Literary Analysis
Irony Explain why the details in these two stanzas are ironic, given the situation.

And those who expected lightning and thunder
15   Are disappointed.
And those who expected signs and archangels' trumps[1]
Do not believe it is happening now.
As long as the sun and the moon are above,
As long as the bumblebee visits a rose,
20   As long as rosy infants are born
No one believes it is happening now.

Only a white-haired old man, who would be a <u>prophet</u>
Yet is not a prophet, for he's much too busy,
Repeats while he binds his tomatoes:
25   There will be no other end of the world,
There will be no other end of the world.

Warsaw, 1944

---

1. trumps *n.* trumpets.

Reading Strategy
Evaluating the Writer's Statement of Philosophy
What do these lines suggest about the writer's view of how we ordinarily live?

prophet (präf′ ət) *n.* inspired person who speaks great truths or foretells the future

Review and Assess

Thinking About the Selection

1. **Respond:** Are you disturbed or comforted by Miłosz's poem? Explain.

2. **(a) Recall:** With what phrase do the first two stanzas begin? **(b) Compare:** What do the details that follow each phrase have in common? **(c) Analyze:** What is surprising about them?

3. **(a) Recall:** In the third stanza, what does the speaker say that some people are expecting? **(b) Infer:** What traditional views about the end of the world do these expectations reflect? **(c) Draw Conclusions:** Why do these people not believe that the world is ending?

4. **(a) Infer:** Why do you think the old man binds tomatoes if he believes the world is ending? **(b) Interpret:** What is the meaning of the poem's last line? **(c) Analyze:** What is the effect of repeating this line?

5. **(a) Generalize:** In what sense might one appreciate every day as if it were the last day? **(b) Draw Conclusions:** What point does the poet make about the value of ordinary things?

6. **(a) Compare:** What do the speaker and the white-haired "prophet" have in common? **(b) Evaluate:** Prophets are said to foresee fateful events, such as the end of the world. In what sense does the writer of this poem play the role of a prophet?

The End and the Beginning

Wisława Szymborska

translated by Stanislaw Baranczak and Clare Cavanagh

After every war
someone has to tidy up.
Things won't pick
themselves up, after all.

5　Someone has to shove
the rubble to the roadsides
so the carts loaded with corpses
can get by.

Someone has to trudge
10　through sludge and ashes,
through the sofa springs,
the <u>shards</u> of glass,
the bloody rags.

Someone has to lug the post
15　to prop the wall,
someone has to <u>glaze</u> the window,
set the door in its frame.

No sound bites, no photo opportunities,
and it takes years.
20　All the cameras have gone
to other wars.

The bridges need to be rebuilt,
the railroad stations, too.
Shirtsleeves will be rolled
25　to shreds.

shards (shärdz) *n.* sharp fragments

glaze (glāz) *v.* fit glass to a window; cover with a shiny finish

Critical Viewing ▶
Might this woman represent the "someone" in the poem, or does that "someone" have a different spirit? Explain. **[Connect]**

Reading Strategy
Evaluating the Writer's Statement of Philosophy
What view of modern life does the speaker express in these lines?

Aftermath, 1945, Karl Hofer, Hamburg Kunsthalle, Hamburg, Germany

Someone, broom in hand,
still remembers how it was.
Someone else listens, nodding
his unshattered head.
30   But others are bound to be bustling nearby
who'll find all that
a little boring.

From time to time someone still must
dig up a rusted argument
35   from underneath a bush
and haul it off to the dump.

Those who knew
what this was all about
must make way for those
40   who know little.
And less than that.
And at last nothing less than nothing.

Someone has to lie there
in the grass that covers up
45   the causes and effects
with a cornstalk in his teeth,
<u>gawking</u> at clouds.

Literary Analysis
Irony and History as a Theme According to the speaker, what pattern does history follow after a war?

gawking (gôk´ iŋ) v. staring foolishly; gaping

Review and Assess

Thinking About the Selection

1. **Respond:** Does this poem cause you to rethink your own feelings about history, or does it leave them unchanged? Explain.

2. **(a) Recall:** What event has taken place before the poem begins? **(b) Generalize:** Identify what kinds of tasks the aftermath of this event requires. **(c) Interpret:** What is the ultimate result of this work? Cite details to support your answer.

3. **(a) Recall:** What repeated word indicates who must do this work? **(b) Infer:** To whom is the speaker referring? **(c) Interpret:** What does the use of this word indicate about the reason that people do the work and, eventually, forget the event?

4. **(a) Interpret:** What is the attitude of the "others" in line 30? **(b) Connect:** In what way does the attitude of the "others" allow "someone" to just lie in the grass?

5. **Make a Judgment:** Does the conclusion of the poem represent a healing of society or does it conceal a danger? Explain.

Review and Assess

Literary Analysis

Irony

1. (a) Identify an example of **verbal irony** in lines 22–26 of "A Song on the End of the World." (b) Explain what the irony in your example involves.

2. In what way is the central idea of the poem—that the day the world ends will be an ordinary day—an example of **situational irony**?

3. (a) Explain one verbal irony in the first stanza of "The End and the Beginning." (b) Explain the irony in the last stanza. (c) In what way does the irony in the first and last stanzas relate to the poem's title?

4. Explain the way in which each poem might be different if its message were stated directly, without irony.

Comparing Literary Works

5. (a) Compare **history as a theme** in each poem, using a chart like the one shown.

Events Described	"Final" Event	Pattern of History	Optimistic/ Pessimistic

(b) In your opinion, which poem presents the more optimistic view? Explain.

6. (a) In what sense does the speaker in each poem remember something that others forget or ignore? (b) What role in history does each poem suggest that poets have? Explain.

Reading Strategy

Evaluating the Writer's Statement of Philosophy

7. (a) What **philosophical statement** does Miłosz make about the value of an ordinary day? Give details from the poem in support. (b) What philosophical statement does Szymborska make about our ability to learn from the past? Support your answer with details.

8. With which philosophy do you agree? Explain.

Extend Understanding

9. **Social Studies Connection:** In the early twentieth century, many believed progress was making the world a better place. How do these late-twentieth-century poems challenge that idea?

Integrate Language Skills

Vocabulary Development Lesson

Related Words: *glaze* and *glimmering*

Glaze and *glimmering* are related to the Indo-European root *ĝhel*, meaning "to shine or to glow." To *glaze* is to fit glass, a shiny substance, to a window. A *glimmering* is a faint shining. Explain how the root meaning "to shine" adds to the meaning of each of these related words:

1. glimpse
2. gold
3. glint

Spelling Strategy

If a word is spelled with a doubled consonant preceded by a single vowel, the vowel sound is short. *Glimmering* has a short *i* sound. In contrast, if a single consonant appears between two vowels, the first vowel sound is often long. *Glaze* has a long *a* sound. Explain whether the boldface vowel in each of these words is short or long.

1. d**a**pper
2. v**a**cate
3. p**o**tential

Concept Development: Analogies

For each item below, study the relationship presented in the first pair. Then, complete the analogies by using the vocabulary words on page 1285 to build word pairs expressing the same relationship.

1. *Storyteller* is to *tale* as ____?____ is to *prediction*.
2. *Upholster* is to *cloth* as ____?____ is to *glass*.
3. *Drizzling* is to *rain* as ____?____ is to *light*.
4. *Rocks* are to *stones* as ____?____ are to *fragments*.
5. *Yelling* is to *whispering* as ____?____ is to *peeking*.

Grammar and Style Lesson

Indefinite and Demonstrative Pronouns

An **indefinite pronoun** is used to refer to persons, places, or things without specifying which one. Indefinite pronouns include such words as *each*, *everything*, and *someone*. A **demonstrative pronoun** is used to point out a specific person, place, or thing. These pronouns include *this*, *that*, *these*, and *those*.

> **Indefinite:** <u>Someone</u> has to shove / the rubble to the roadsides. . . .
>
> **Demonstrative:** . . . <u>those</u> who expected thunder and lightning . . .

Practice For each item, identify the indefinite or demonstrative pronouns, and label each *I* or *D*.

1. No one believes it is happening now.
2. Someone, broom in hand, / still remembers how it was.
3. But others are bound to be bustling nearby / who'll find all that / a little boring.
4. Those who knew / what this was all about / must make way for those / who know little.
5. And less than that.

Writing Application Write four sentences about an event from history, using at least one indefinite and one demonstrative pronoun.

 Prentice Hall Writing and Grammar Connection: Diamond Level, Chapter 17, Section 1

Writing Lesson

Narrative About a Quiet Hero

The old man in Miłosz's poem shows heroic devotion to ordinary pursuits in the midst of danger. Write an account of a person, real or fictional, with such a devotion, showing why he or she deserves your admiration.

Prewriting   Begin by listing details that describe the dangerous situation and the way in which your subject managed to keep a sense of quiet dignity. Circle those that are most vivid or significant.

Model: Listing Relevant Details

(tornado alarm)
kids yelling in the hall
Mrs. Clark stayed calm.
(She moved slowly.)
She touched me on the
shoulder as I passed by.

She said, "We will be
fine."
She reminded us
where to go in the
building.

> Details about the situation and the hero will help bring the event to life.

Drafting   As you draft, remember that understatement is often more effective than exaggeration. Choose precise verbs and adjectives to *show* the quiet heroism of your character, rather than announcing it.

Revising   As you revise your account, add specific details that will help the reader imagine the scene.

WG Prentice Hall Writing and Grammar Connection: Diamond Level, Chapter 6, Section 2

Extension Activities

Listening and Speaking With a partner, present a **multimedia reading** of one of the poems. Accompany your reading with appropriate audiovisuals, such as music or slides. Use these tips to prepare:

- Select musical and visual qualities of the poem to emphasize, such as repetition.
- Practice the timing of your presentation before you perform it for the class.

After your presentation, ask audience members to evaluate the effectiveness of each of its elements. **[Group Activity]**

Research and Technology In their poems, Miłosz and Szymborska respond to Poland's difficult history. Create a **map or set of maps** showing Poland's shifting boundaries over time. Clearly indicate which nations have ruled Poland, as well as the birthplace or main city of residence of each poet.

Take It to the Net PHSchool.com

Go online for an additional research activity using the Internet.

Prepare to Read

Freedom to Breathe ◆ *from* Nobel Lecture ◆ Visit

Alexander Solzhenitsyn (b. 1918)

Alexander Solzhenitsyn (sōl′ zhə nēt′ sin) spent years in Soviet prison camps. There, he resolved to survive as a witness to oppression. His unsparing accounts of the camps are among the most important documents of the twentieth century.

Early Imprisonment Born in Kislovodsk, a city in southern Russia, Solzhenitsyn served in the Soviet army during World War II. While a soldier, he was convicted of treason—he had written letters critical of Josef Stalin, the Soviet leader. Solzhenitsyn found himself in a windswept camp in central Asia, where prisoners did backbreaking work on a meager diet.

Released in 1953, Solzhenitsyn eventually wrote a novel about life in the camps, *One Day in the Life of Ivan Denisovich* (1962). Although the government encouraged this novel's publication, the political tide soon shifted. After 1963, the government banned further publication of Solzhenitsyn's books.

Exile Officially rejected in Russia, Solzhenitsyn began to publish his novels in the West. The faster his prestige grew abroad, the worse his fortunes were at home. When he was awarded the Nobel Prize in Literature in 1970, Solzhenitsyn would not travel to accept it, fearing that the Soviet government would not let him return. Finally, in 1973, Solzhenitsyn published the first volume of *The Gulag Archipelago, 1918–1956*, a chronicle of the prison camps. Within months, he was deported by the Soviet government.

Solzhenitsyn eventually settled in the United States, where he continued to speak out on behalf of freedom. He returned to Russia in 1994. His life and work bear witness to the power of words—a power mighty enough to upset a nation.

Yevgeny Yevtushenko (b. 1933)

Perhaps the best introduction to Russian poet Yevgeny Yevtushenko (yev gen′ ē yev′ tōō shen′ kō) is one of his recordings. Yevtushenko is a remarkable performer, his voice fit to calm a child or storm a barricade. He has not been afraid to raise this voice against injustice.

The Celebrity Poet Born in 1933 in Zima Junction, along the Trans-Siberian Railroad, Yevtushenko published his first book, *Prospectors of the Future* (1952), while he was still in college. Over the next nine years, his poems and his public readings made him a celebrity in the Soviet Union, as popular as any movie star in the West. Yevtushenko did not merely read his poems: He acted them, lived them—lowering his voice to a whisper, then breaking out in a mighty roar, all the while gesturing dramatically.

Breaking Silence In 1961, Yevtushenko's fame became international with the poem "Babi Yar." It was at Babi Yar, near Kiev, that German troops murdered 34,000 Jews during two days in 1941. In his poem, Yevtushenko boldly referred to Russian anti-Semitism, a forbidden subject in Soviet Russia. The editor of the Russian *Literary Gazette* agonized over the poem, knowing that printing it could cost him his job. As the magazine's presses began to roll, and after consulting with his wife, he decided to take the risk. The poem's passionate attack on prejudice won Yevtushenko admirers in the West.

Elected in 1989 to the Congress of People's Deputies, Yevtushenko supported Mikhail Gorbachev's *perestroika*, or restructuring of Soviet society. His most recent work is *Don't Die Before You're Dead* (1993), a novel concerning life after the dismantling of the Soviet Union.

Preview

Connecting to the Literature

Perhaps you have awakened early on a spring morning and, in the unfamiliar stillness, found the person you have always been. Perhaps you felt then how far a day might carry you—how large the future is. Literature, as these writers show, is also a moment to rediscover freedom and the future.

Literary Analysis

Speaker

The **speaker** of a work is the character who "says" its words, or the voice of the work. There are various types of speaker. A speaker may be

- a distinctive fictional character.
- a character bearing a close resemblance to the writer.
- a writer's representation of himself or herself.
- a generalized, impersonal voice, as in a factual essay.

In Yevtushenko's poem "Visit," the speaker has an intimate, personal voice and uses details from the poet's experience. In this poem, the speaker is the poet's representation of himself. Solzhenitsyn himself is the speaker in his Nobel Lecture, yet he carefully crafts a particular public voice for himself. As you read, note the qualities of the speaker in each work.

Comparing Literary Works

As each of these works develops, the speaker takes on a new role, ensuring a dramatic conclusion. In Solzhenitsyn's Nobel Lecture, for example, the speaker turns from his role as award recipient to a role as spokesperson for truth. In Yevtushenko's poem, the speaker shifts from one who remembers the past to one who is confronted by it. As you read, compare the speakers' changes, noting ways in which they add drama to the works.

Reading Strategy

Inferring the Speaker's Attitude

To fully understand a work, use the details to **infer the speaker's attitude,** determining the speaker's views of ideas and events. Use a chart like the one shown to list and interpret clues to the speaker's attitude.

Vocabulary Development

glistens (glis´ enz) v. shines or sparkles with reflected light (p. 1296)

reciprocity (res´ ə präs´ ə tē) n. mutual exchange (p. 1297)

assimilate (ə sim´ ə lāt´) v. absorb; incorporate into a greater body (p. 1298)

inexorably (in eks´ ə rə blē´) adv. relentlessly (p. 1299)

oratory (ôr´ ə tôr´ ē) n. skillful public speaking (p. 1299)

fungus (fuŋ´ gəs) n. mildew; any of a group of plants lacking leaves and roots (p. 1302)

clenched (klencht) adj. gripped firmly or tightly (p. 1302)

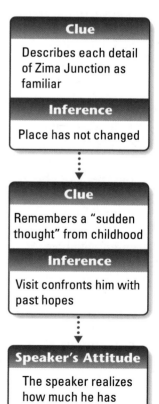

Clue

Describes each detail of Zima Junction as familiar

Inference

Place has not changed

Clue

Remembers a "sudden thought" from childhood

Inference

Visit confronts him with past hopes

Speaker's Attitude

The speaker realizes how much he has changed.

Freedom to Breathe

Alexander Solzhenitsyn
translated by Michael Glenny

Background

In this brief essay and in his Nobel Lecture, Alexander Solzhenitsyn argues for the power of freedom and of truth. During the Soviet period in Russia, freedom of speech was curtailed. Writers could publish legally only with the approval of the state. Dissenting opinions and alternative literature circulated secretly, as typewritten manuscript, in a literary underground. Solzhenitsyn himself was exiled for his dissent. Clearly, the Soviet government would have agreed with Solzhenitsyn's assessment—freedom is our truth, and truth is dangerous to an oppressive government.

A shower fell in the night and now dark clouds drift across the sky, occasionally sprinkling a fine film of rain.

I stand under an apple tree in blossom and I breathe. Not only the apple tree but the grass round it <u>glistens</u> with moisture; words cannot describe the sweet fragrance that pervades the air. I inhale as deeply as I can, and the aroma invades my whole being; I breathe with my eyes open, I breathe with my eyes closed—I cannot say which gives me the greater pleasure.

This, I believe, is the single most precious freedom that prison takes away from us: the freedom to breathe freely, as I now can. No food on earth, no wine, not even a woman's kiss is sweeter to me than this air steeped in the fragrance of flowers, of moisture and freshness.

No matter that this is only a tiny garden, hemmed in by five-story houses like cages in a zoo. I cease to hear the motorcycles backfiring, radios whining, the burble of loudspeakers. As long as there is fresh air to breathe under an apple tree after a shower, we may survive a little longer.

glistens (glis′ enz) v. shines or sparkles with reflected light

Literary Analysis
Speaker and Dramatic Conclusion Why is it surprising to learn these details about the setting at the conclusion?

from *Nobel Lecture*

Alexander Solzhenitsyn
translated by F. D. Reeve

I am, however, encouraged by a keen sense of WORLD LITERATURE as the one great heart that beats for the cares and misfortunes of our world, even though each corner sees and experiences them in a different way.

In past times, also, besides age-old national literatures there existed a concept of world literature as the link between the summits of national literatures and as the aggregate[1] of reciprocal literary influences. But there was a time lag: readers and writers came to know foreign writers only belatedly, sometimes centuries later, so that mutual influences were delayed and the network of national literary high points was visible not to contemporaries but to later generations.

Today, between writers of one country and the readers and writers of another, there is an almost instantaneous <u>reciprocity</u>, as I myself know. My books, unpublished, alas, in my own country, despite hasty and often bad translations have quickly found a responsive world readership. Critical analysis of them has been undertaken by such leading Western writers as Heinrich Böll.[2] During all these recent years, when both my work and my freedom did not collapse, when against the laws of gravity they held on seemingly in thin air, seemingly ON NOTHING, on the invisible, mute surface tension of sympathetic people, with warm gratitude I learned, to my complete surprise, of the support of the world's writing fraternity. On my fiftieth birthday I was astounded to receive greetings from well-known European writers. No pressure put on me now passed unnoticed. During the dangerous weeks when I was

reciprocity (res´ ə präs´ ə tē) *n.* mutual exchange

✔Reading Check

According to Solzhenitsyn, what is the main difference between world literature in the past and in the present?

---

1. **aggregate** (ag´ rə git) *n.* group of things gathered together and considered as a whole.
2. **Heinrich Böll** (hīn´ riH böl) German novelist (1917–1985) and winner of the Nobel Prize in Literature.

being expelled from the Writers' Union,[3] THE PROTECTIVE WALL put forward by prominent writers of the world saved me from worse persecution, and Norwegian writers and artists hospitably prepared shelter for me in the event that I was exiled from my country. Finally, my being nominated for a Nobel Prize was originated not in the land where I live and write but by François Mauriac[4] and his colleagues. Afterward, national writers' organizations expressed unanimous support for me.

As I have understood it and experienced it myself, world literature is no longer an abstraction or a generalized concept invented by literary critics, but a common body and common spirit, a living, heartfelt unity reflecting the growing spiritual unity of mankind. State borders still turn crimson, heated red-hot by electric fences and machine-gun fire; some ministries of internal affairs still suppose that literature is "an internal affair" of the countries under their jurisdiction; and newspaper headlines still herald, "They have no right to interfere in our internal affairs!" Meanwhile, no such thing as INTERNAL AFFAIRS remains on our crowded Earth. Mankind's salvation lies exclusively in everyone's making everything his business, in the people of the East being anything but indifferent to what is thought in the West, and in the people of the West being anything but indifferent to what happens in the East. Literature, one of the most sensitive and responsive tools of human existence, has been the first to pick up, adopt, and <u>assimilate</u> this sense of the growing unity of mankind. I therefore confidently turn to the world literature of the present, to hundreds of friends whom I have not met face to face and perhaps never will see.

Bust of Soviet leader V. I. Lenin.

My friends! Let us try to be helpful, if we are worth anything. In our own countries, torn by differences among parties, movements, castes, and groups, who for ages past has been not the dividing but the uniting force? This, essentially, is the position of writers, spokesmen of a national language, of the chief tie binding the nation, the very soil which the people inhabit, and, in fortunate circumstances, the nation's spirit too.

I think that world literature has the power in these frightening times to help mankind see itself accurately despite what is advocated by partisans[5] and by parties. It has the power to transmit the condensed experience of one region to another, so that different scales of values

---

assimilate (ə sim´ ə lāt´) v. absorb; incorporate into a greater body

---

3. **Writers' Union** official Soviet writers' organization. In addition to being expelled from this union, Solzhenitsyn was forbidden to live in Moscow.
4. **François Mauriac** (frän swä´ mô´ rē ak´) French novelist and essayist (1885–1970).
5. **partisans** (pärt´ i zənz) n. emotional supporters of a party or viewpoint.

are combined, and so that one people accurately and concisely knows the true history of another with a power of recognition and acute awareness as if it had lived through that history itself—and could thus be spared repeating old mistakes. At the same time, perhaps we ourselves may succeed in developing our own WORLD-WIDE VIEW, like any man, with the center of the eye seeing what is nearby but the periphery[6] of vision taking in what is happening in the rest of the world. We will make correlations[7] and maintain world-wide standards.

Who, if not writers, are to condemn their own unsuccessful governments (in some states this is the easiest way to make a living; everyone who is not too lazy does it) as well as society itself, whether for its cowardly humiliation or for its self-satisfied weakness, or the lightheaded escapades of the young, or the youthful pirates brandishing knives?

We will be told: What can literature do against the pitiless onslaught of naked violence? Let us not forget that violence does not and cannot flourish by itself; it is inevitably intertwined with LYING. Between them there is the closest, the most profound and natural bond: nothing screens violence except lies, and the only way lies can hold out is by violence. Whoever has once announced violence as his METHOD must <u>inexorably</u> choose lying as his PRINCIPLE. At birth, violence behaves openly and even proudly. But as soon as it becomes stronger and firmly established, it senses the thinning of the air around it and cannot go on without befogging itself in lies, coating itself with lying's sugary <u>oratory</u>. It does not always or necessarily go straight for the gullet; usually it demands of its victims only allegiance to the lie, only complicity in the lie.

The simple act of an ordinary courageous man is not to take part, not to support lies! Let *that* come into the world and even reign over it, but not through me. Writers and artists can do more: they can VANQUISH LIES! In the struggle against lies, art has always won and always will. Conspicuously, incontestably for everyone. Lies can stand up against much in the world, but not against art.

Once lies have been dispelled, the repulsive nakedness of violence will be exposed—and hollow violence will collapse.

That, my friends, is why I think we can help the world in its red-hot hour: not by the naysaying of having no armaments, not by abandoning oneself to the carefree life, but by going into battle!

---

6. **periphery** (pə rif′ ər ē) surrounding area; boundary; perimeter.
7. **correlations** (kôr′ ə lā′ shənz) analysis of relationships or connections.

Literary Analysis
Speaker In addition to the role of award recipient, what other role does Solzhenitsyn assume through this speech?

inexorably (in eks′ ə rə blē) *adv.* relentlessly

oratory (ôr′ ə tôr′ ē) *n.* skillful public speaking

▼ **Critical Viewing**
What do stamps such as the ones on these pages suggest about the role of modern communications in creating a world literature? [Draw a Conclusion]

✓**Reading Check**
Identify one reason that, according to Solzhenitsyn, writers have the power to serve justice.

In Russian, proverbs about TRUTH are favorites. They persistently express the considerable, bitter, grim experience of the people, often astonishingly:

ONE WORD OF TRUTH OUTWEIGHS THE WORLD.

On such a seemingly fantastic violation of the law of the conservation of mass and energy[8] are based both my own activities and my appeal to the writers of the whole world.

---

8. **the law of the conservation of mass and energy** law of physics stating that in any physical or chemical change, the sum of mass and energy must remain constant: Energy and matter are not created by nature from nothing.

Review and Assess

Thinking About the Selections

1. **Respond:** Have you found that your own readings in world literature have broadened your understanding of the world? Explain.

2. **(a) Recall:** In the first paragraph of "Freedom to Breathe," what details does the writer use to set the scene? **(b) Interpret:** Describe the mood of this setting. **(c) Evaluate:** Does the description of the surrounding area help you appreciate the speaker's delight? Explain.

3. **(a) Recall:** What fundamental freedom does prison take away, according to "Freedom to Breathe"? **(b) Compare:** With what does the speaker contrast this freedom?

4. **Evaluate:** Do you agree that "freedom to breathe" is a basic necessity? Explain.

5. **(a) Recall:** Name two ways in which, according to Solzhenitsyn's Nobel Lecture, European writers showed support for Solzhenitsyn. **(b) Connect:** How does Solzhenitsyn's own career exemplify his idea of a modern world literature?

6. **(a) Infer:** Why does Solzhenitsyn say in his Nobel Lecture that a nation's literature is a "uniting force"? **(b) Interpret:** In what sense does he call world literature "the one great heart"?

7. **Evaluate:** Is Solzhenitsyn's claim about the power of literature to contest violence valid? Explain.

8. **Apply:** Give a modern instance in which people are discouraged from speaking their minds, and explain what Solzhenitsyn might say about this situation.

Visit

Yevgeny Yevtushenko
translated by
Robin Milner-Gulland
and Peter Levi, S.J.

Going to Zima Junction,[1] quiet place.
Watching out for it in the distance
with the window of the carriage wide open,
familiar houses, ornamental carving.
5 The jump down from the train before it stops,
crunching along on the warm slag;[2]
the linesman working with a hose
cursing and swearing in the stifling heat.
The ducks in midstream with their heads buried,
10 the perches where the poultry crow at dawn,
along the sidings ornamental stars
of white and colored bricks set in the wall.
Walking along the dusty paving-boards,
passing the clock that sits on the town hall,
15 hearing behind the fence of the old market
rustle of oats and clink of weights and measures:
and there the painted wooden fruit-baskets,
the cranberries wet on the low counters,
and the bright yellow butter-balls afloat
20 in basins made of flower-painted china.
Same cranny where the birds are still nesting,
and, most familiar, the faded gate.
And the house is exactly the same size,
the log fence still mended with boards,
25 the same broom leaning upon the stove,

---

1. **Zima** (zē′ mə) **Junction** town in the Asian part of Russia (formerly part of the Soviet Union), just west of Lake Baikal and north of Mongolia.
2. **slag** (slag) refuse separated from a metal in the process of smelting.

Reading Check

What is the speaker's likely connection to the place he describes?

the same tinned mushrooms on the window-sill,
the crack in the stairs is not different,
darkening deeply down, feeding <u>fungus</u>. . . .
Some nut or bolt or other I'd picked up
30   just as I always picked something up
was <u>clenched</u> happily in my hand
and dropped again as I went hurrying
down to the river and the river-mist,
and wandering sometimes in the woods
35   by a path choked in a tangle of tall weeds
in search of some deep-colored country flower,
and working with the freckled ferry girl,
heaving the glossy hawser hand by hand.
Trying the quality of "old honey"
40   where the beehives rear up above the pond,
rocking along slow-motion in the cart,
slow rhythms of the whip's lazy flicking.
Wandering through the cranberry patches
with a casual crowd of idle lads,
45   and fishing beneath bridges with the noise
of trains thundering above your head,
joking, throwing your shirt off in the grass,
and diving in high from the river-bank,
with one sudden thought, how little I
50   have done in life, how much I can do.

fungus (fun´ gəs) n. mildew;
any of a group of plants
lacking leaves and roots

clenched (klencht) v.
gripped firmly or tightly

**Reading Strategy
Inferring the Speaker's
Attitude** Confronted by
this concluding memory,
what questions might the
speaker ask about his
present life?

Review and Assess

Thinking About the Selection

1. **Respond:** Do you like revisiting places where you once spent a great deal of time? Why or why not?

2. **(a) Recall:** Identify three scenes described by the speaker as he moves through the town toward his old home. **(b) Infer:** At what point does the poem shift from the speaker's present visit to his memories of the past? Explain your response.

3. **Interpret:** In what sense do the speaker's memories of the past lead him to confront his present and his future?

4. **Relate:** Imagine that, ten years from now, you are remembering today, as the adult speaker remembers his childhood. What reactions might you have?

Review and Assess

Literary Analysis

Speaker

1. (a) For each of the three works, identify statements in the following categories: personal details, public facts, generalizations, and exclamations. (b) Characterize each **speaker,** explaining whether he speaks in a personal voice, a public voice, or a mixed voice.

2. (a) Identify two ways in which Solzhenitsyn's Nobel Lecture links general themes to personal experience. (b) Why does this link add authority to the speaker's general points?

3. In "Visit," what contrast does the speaker suggest between his present and his past? Explain your answer, citing details.

Comparing Literary Works

4. (a) Compare the dramatic endings created by the call to action in the Nobel Lecture and the turn from *I* to *we* in "Freedom to Breathe." (b) In what way do these endings extend the speakers' preceding points?

5. Compare the shift in the speaker's role in "Freedom to Breathe" and in "Visit," analyzing details with a chart like the one shown.

Speaker's Role		Meaning of Events	
Beginning	End	Beginning	End

Reading Strategy

Inferring the Speaker's Attitude

6. What is the **speaker's attitude** toward city life in "Freedom to Breathe"? Give details in support.

7. What is Solzhenitsyn's attitude toward literature in his Nobel Lecture? Identify two details supporting your answer.

8. From images and direct statements in Yevtushenko's "Visit," what can you infer about the speaker's attitude toward his visit?

Extend Understanding

9. **Science Connection:** Explain why Solzhenitsyn thinks literature "violates" the law of the conservation of mass and energy.

Quick Review

The **speaker** is the character or voice that "says" the words of a literary work. A change in the speaker's role or purpose in a work can add drama.

To **infer the speaker's attitude,** look for details that suggest how a speaker views his or her subject.

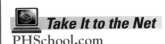 **Take It to the Net**
PHSchool.com

Take the interactive self-test online to check your understanding of these selections.

Integrate Language Skills

Vocabulary Development Lesson

Usage: Forms of *reciprocity*

The noun *reciprocity*, meaning "mutual exchange," has adjective, adverb, and verb forms. Complete each item with a form of *reciprocity*.

a. reciprocally   **b.** reciprocal   **c.** reciprocate

1. Pen pals have a ___?___ arrangement.
2. Although he could not ___?___, he appreciated the support of other writers.
3. Just as others supported his rights, he acts ___?___ to support the rights of others.

Spelling Strategy

In some nouns derived from Latin, such as *fungus*, the final sound *us* is spelled *us*. In an adjective, this final sound is usually spelled *ous*. For each word below, add the correct ending.

1. stimul__   **2.** camp__   **3.** adventur__

Concept Development: Synonyms

Review the vocabulary list on page 1295. Then, for each numbered vocabulary word listed below, select the letter of its synonym, the word closest to it in meaning.

1. assimilate: (a) calculate, (b) absorb, (c) compare
2. glistens: (a) glides, (b) shines, (c) speaks
3. oratory: (a) eloquence, (b) radiance, (c) benevolence
4. clenched: (a) kissed, (b) soaked, (c) gripped
5. inexorably: (a) inevitably, (b) endlessly, (c) bluntly
6. fungus: (a) rash, (b) shrub, (c) mildew
7. reciprocity: (a) suburb, (b) exchange, (c) cookery

Grammar and Style Lesson

Using Dashes

A **dash** (—) indicates a longer, more emphatic pause than a comma does. A dash usually signals an interruption in the sequence of ideas and may be used to indicate an abrupt shift of focus, a dramatic exclamation, or a break from listing details to generalizing about them. Review this sentence from "Freedom to Breathe":

> . . . I breathe with my eyes open, I breathe with my eyes closed—I cannot say which gives me the greater pleasure.

Writers can use dashes to set up distinctive rhythms in their writing, achieving the feeling of a living voice that wanders off or bursts into digressions, exclamations, and explanations.

Practice Insert dashes where necessary in the following sentences.

1. Solzhenitsyn whose life was saved by his readers writes of the power of literature.
2. The speaker and this is the strange part is actually in a small inner-city garden.
3. Scenes at the railroad station, scenes along the road each is as familiar as the next.
4. The speaker remembers discovering that he had a future but now he *is* that future!
5. Three Russian writers Pushkin, Pasternak, and Solzhenitsyn have all believed in the writer's role as social critic.

Writing Application Write a brief description of a garden, using dashes correctly in three sentences.

W͞G Prentice Hall Writing and Grammar Connection: Diamond Level, Chapter 27, Section 5

Writing Lesson

Persuasive Speech

The written word may seem without force, but in his Nobel Lecture, Solzhenitsyn argues that the word can conquer violence. Write a persuasive speech in which you support or refute Solzhenitsyn's view of the power of words and truth. To persuade your readers, use precise and powerful language.

Prewriting   Reread the Nobel Lecture, jotting down each important point Solzhenitsyn makes. Write a one-sentence summary of his idea of truth, and decide whether or not you agree with it. Then, list reasons, examples, and other details to support your position.

Drafting   Begin your essay with a statement of your position. As you draft, make sure you use charged, precise words to add persuasive force.

Model: Choose Effective Persuasive Language

A man of (profound moral authority,) Solzhenitsyn uses

(compelling) examples from his personal experience to

support his claims.

> Charged words and phrases, such as *profound moral authority* and *compelling,* add persuasive force.

Revising   Review your speech. Identify any weak or unclear wording, and replace it with stronger phrasing.

Prentice Hall Writing and Grammar Connection: Diamond Level, Chapter 7, Section 3

Extension Activities

Listening and Speaking Using "Freedom to Breathe" or "Visit" as a model, present an **oral description** of the sights and smells of one of your favorite places. Use these tips to prepare:

- Before you write, brainstorm for vivid imagery appealing to the five senses.
- As you practice, pay special attention to your tempo, speaking slowly enough to be understood, but not dragging.
- Give a dress rehearsal for a small audience.

Present your description to the class.

Research and Technology Solzhenitsyn is a famous Nobel Prize winner. Working in a small group, compile an **annotated list** of Nobel Prize winners in literature. For each writer, include a capsule biography and a brief description of his or her works. Post your list in the classroom. **[Group Activity]**

 **Take It to the Net** PHSchool.com

Go online for an additional research activity using the Internet.

Half a Day

Naguib Mahfouz (b. 1911)

A writer may become so closely associated with a place that the two seem inseparable. Charles Dickens seems to have created Victorian England just for his novels; the American Dust Bowl itself seems to speak through John Steinbeck's works. Novelist Naguib Mahfouz (nä´ heb´ mä fōoz´) has just such a special relationship with Egypt. For his vivid depictions of twentieth-century Cairo, the Egyptian capital, Western literary critics have compared him to Dickens and to Honoré de Balzac, the great chronicler of French life. Strangely, the very country for which Mahfouz is a voice forced him to find new, indirect ways to speak his mind.

Dangerous Times Mahfouz was born in 1911 in an old quarter of Cairo. In 1930, he entered the University of Cairo, where he studied philosophy. Throughout his undergraduate career, he contributed essays on philosophical subjects to various magazines. Although his readings in literature were slim, classes at the University of Cairo were in English and French, and Mahfouz's access to those languages increased the scope of his reading. Among his favorite authors were Tolstoy, Chekhov, Kafka, and Ibsen.

Mahfouz began his career as a novelist in a politically dangerous, repressive period. In 1930, Ismail Sidki, the new prime minister, had suspended Egypt's 1923 constitution. Once in power, Sidki brutally crushed any attempt to question his authority. Two of Mahfouz's main influences, the writers Taha Hussein and Abbas al-Akkad, were persecuted during this time: Hussein was accused of heresy, and al-Akkad was imprisoned.

Telling the Truth The harsh treatment of Hussein, al-Akkad, and others made Mahfouz realize the futility of direct criticism of the government. He turned instead to narrative. During World War II, he wrote three historical novels set in ancient Egypt.

Mixing history with symbolism, Mahfouz's tales of tyrannical rule and foreign occupation had strong contemporary implications. At the time Mahfouz was writing, Egypt was ruled by a despot, dominated by an aristocracy of foreign (largely Turkish) origins, and occupied by British troops. Yet because the novels were not "about" the present, telling instead of ancient history, Mahfouz escaped censorship. In the end, these novels express a tragic vision that extends beyond their specific political implications.

Master of Many Styles Mahfouz wrote prolifically through the 1940s, withdrew from writing for much of the 1950s, and returned to literature in the 1960s. During his career, he has experimented widely with style. Some of his short stories of the 1960s are surrealistic. Later novels, such as *Arabian Nights and Days* (1982), have an open-ended structure reminiscent of traditional Arabic narratives.

Mahfouz is perhaps most celebrated, though, for mastering the novel, a Western genre, and making it relevant to Egyptian life. He also modernized the literary language of the Arab tradition. By shaping classical Arabic into a vehicle of popular speech, he created an authoritative voice in which to tell of the lives of ordinary Egyptians.

The Master Honored In 1988, Mahfouz won the Nobel Prize. The award, he remarked, made way for a new international recognition of Arab literature: "Egypt and the Arab world also get the Nobel Prize with me. . . . [I]n the future, literate people will look for Arab literature, and Arab literature deserves that recognition." Now almost deaf and partially blind, Mahfouz claims to live only to write; he has said, "If the urge should ever leave me, I want that day to be my last."

Preview

Connecting to the Literature

"If you take out the trash every day, then we'll talk about getting a dog." Sometimes, life seems like one big detour. But what if all of life really *is* a detour, and we can never get to what we wanted in the first place? In this story, Mahfouz plays a trick with time to confront us with this question.

Literary Analysis

Surrealism

Surrealism, meaning "beyond realism," refers to works that use realism to create a dreamlike world. Surrealist works generally portray people and objects in realistic detail. By connecting realistic elements in strange ways, though, surrealistic works break rules of logic and sequence. In this passage from "Half a Day," for example, realistic details create a dreamlike situation—in one day, the world has changed:

> I proceeded a few steps, then came to a startled halt. . . . Where was the street lined with gardens? Where had it disappeared to?

As you read, use a chart like this one to note realistic elements and the ways they become dreamlike.

Connecting Literary Elements

By causing confusion and surprise, Mahfouz's surrealism pushes the reader to see life from a shocking new angle. In this way, Mahfouz uses surrealism to convey his **theme,** or message about life. As you read, note ways in which your reactions to events help you better appreciate the theme.

Realistic Details
Surrealistic Connections

Reading Strategy

Determining the Author's Purpose

To **determine the author's purpose** in writing, think about the effect the work is meant to have on readers. For example, in "Half a Day," Mahfouz includes details that make readers think about the way life works. His purpose is to convey an insight into life. To fully understand Mahfouz's purpose, connect his choice of details to possible insights as you read.

Vocabulary Development

unmarred (un märd´) *adj.* unspoiled; unimpaired (p. 1309)

intimacy (in´ tə mə sē) *n.* familiarity; warmth (p. 1309)

intricate (in´ tri kit) *adj.* complicated; elaborate (p. 1310)

presumed (prē zoomd´) *v.* expected; supposed (p. 1310)

throngs (thrôŋz) *n.* crowds (p. 1311)

hordes (hôrdz) *n.* large moving crowds; wandering tribes (p. 1311)

hastened (hās´ ənd) *v.* hurried; moved swiftly (p. 1312)

Half a Day

Naguib Mahfouz
translated by Denys Johnson-Davies

Background

"Half a Day" is set in Cairo, the capital of Egypt and the city in which Naguib Mahfouz grew up. Cairo itself embodies the mysteries of time that Mahfouz explores in the story. Ancient and modern exist there side by side. Along the skyline, contemporary hotels rub shoulders with the ancient pyramids. Narrow, twisting streets where camels, horses, and pedestrians once jostled are now choked with vehicular traffic. Modern Western influences are visible in people's clothing and in the fast-food restaurants, alongside traditional garb and open-air markets. As you read Mahfouz's story, you will encounter hints of the changes that brought the modern world to ancient Cairo.

I proceeded alongside my father, clutching his right hand, running to keep up with the long strides he was taking. All my clothes were new: the black shoes, the green school uniform, and the red tarboosh.[1] My delight in my new clothes, however, was not altogether <u>unmarred</u>, for this was no feast day but the day on which I was to be cast into school for the first time.

My mother stood at the window watching our progress, and I would turn toward her from time to time, as though appealing for help. We walked along a street lined with gardens; on both sides were extensive fields planted with crops, prickly pears, henna trees, and a few date palms.

"Why school?" I challenged my father openly. "I shall never do anything to annoy you."

"I'm not punishing you," he said, laughing. "School's not a punishment. It's the factory that makes useful men out of boys. Don't you want to be like your father and brothers?"

I was not convinced. I did not believe there was really any good to be had in tearing me away from the <u>intimacy</u> of my home and throwing me into this building that stood at the end of the road like some huge, high-walled fortress, exceedingly stern and grim.

When we arrived at the gate we could see the courtyard, vast and crammed full of boys and girls. "Go in by yourself," said my father, "and join them. Put a smile on your face and be a good example to others."

I hesitated and clung to his hand, but he gently pushed me from him. "Be a man," he said. "Today you truly begin life. You will find me waiting for you when it's time to leave."

I took a few steps, then stopped and looked but saw nothing. Then the faces of boys and girls came into view. I did not know a single one of them, and none of them knew me. I felt I was a stranger who had lost his way. But glances of curiosity were directed toward me, and one boy approached and asked, "Who brought you?"

---

unmarred (un märd´) *adj.* unspoiled; unimpaired

Literary Analysis
Surrealism What ordinary details give the opening descriptions a realistic quality?

intimacy (in´ tə mə sē) *n.* familiarity; warmth

◀ **Critical Viewing**
What does this photograph suggest about contrasts between ancient and modern in the setting of the story? **[Connect]**

✔**Reading Check**
Why is the day an important one for the boy?

---

1. **tarboosh** (tär bōōsh´) *n.* brimless cap of felt or other cloth shaped like a truncated cone.

"My father," I whispered.

"My father's dead," he said quite simply.

I did not know what to say. The gate was closed, letting out a pitiable screech. Some of the children burst into tears. The bell rang. A lady came along, followed by a group of men. The men began sorting us into ranks. We were formed into an intricate pattern in the great courtyard surrounded on three sides by high buildings of several floors; from each floor we were overlooked by a long balcony roofed in wood.

"This is your new home," said the woman. "Here too there are mothers and fathers. Here there is everything that is enjoyable and beneficial to knowledge and religion. Dry your tears and face life joyfully."

We submitted to the facts, and this submission brought a sort of contentment. Living beings were drawn to other living beings, and from the first moments my heart made friends with such boys as were to be my friends and fell in love with such girls as I was to be in love with, so that it seemed my misgivings had had no basis. I had never imagined school would have this rich variety. We played all sorts of different games: swings, the vaulting horse, ball games. In the music room we chanted our first songs. We also had our first introduction to language. We saw a globe of the Earth, which revolved and showed the various continents and countries. We started learning the numbers. The story of the Creator of the universe was read to us, we were told of His present world and of His Hereafter, and we heard examples of what He said. We ate delicious food, took a little nap, and woke up to go on with friendship and love, play and learning.

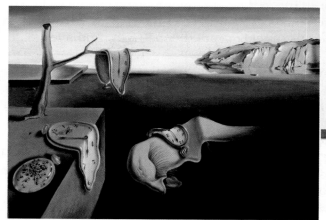

The Persistence of Memory, Salvador Dali, 1931, The Museum of Modern Art / Artists Rights Society (ARS), New York

As our path revealed itself to us, however, we did not find it as totally sweet and unclouded as we had presumed. Dust-laden winds and unexpected accidents came about suddenly, so we had to be watchful, at the ready, and very patient. It was not all a matter of playing and fooling around. Rivalries could bring about pain and hatred or give rise to fighting. And while the lady would sometimes smile, she would often scowl and scold. Even more frequently she would resort to physical punishment.

In addition, the time for changing one's mind was over and gone and there was no question of ever returning to the paradise of home. Nothing lay ahead of us but exertion, struggle, and perseverance. Those who

intricate (in´ tri kit) *adj.* complicated; elaborate

presumed (prē zōōmd´) *v.* expected; supposed

were able took advantage of the opportunities for success and happiness that presented themselves amid the worries.

The bell rang announcing the passing of the day and the end of work. The <u>throngs</u> of children rushed toward the gate, which was opened again. I bade farewell to friends and sweethearts and passed through the gate. I peered around but found no trace of my father, who had promised to be there. I stepped aside to wait. When I had waited for a long time without avail, I decided to return home on my own. After I had taken a few steps, a middle-aged man passed by, and I realized at once that I knew him. He came toward me, smiling, and shook me by the hand, saying, "It's a long time since we last met—how are you?"

With a nod of my head, I agreed with him and in turn asked, "And you, how are you?"

"As you can see, not all that good, the Almighty be praised!"

Again he shook me by the hand and went off. I proceeded a few steps, then came to a startled halt. . . . Where was the street lined with gardens? Where had it disappeared to? When did all these vehicles invade it? And when did all these <u>hordes</u> of humanity come to rest upon its surface? How did these hills of refuse come to cover its sides? And where were the fields that bordered it? High buildings had taken over, the street surged with children, and disturbing noises shook the air. At various points stood conjurers showing off their tricks and making snakes appear from baskets. Then there was a band announcing

▲ **Critical Viewing**
Explain which part of the story this image illustrates—the world before or the world after the narrator's day at school.
[Connect]

throngs (thrôŋz) *n.* crowds

hordes (hôrdz) *n.* large moving crowds; wandering tribes

✓**Reading Check**
What is the reason for the narrator's confusion?

the opening of a circus, with clowns and weight lifters walking in front. A line of trucks carrying central security troops crawled majestically by. The siren of a fire engine shrieked, and it was not clear how the vehicle would cleave its way to reach the blazing fire. A battle raged between a taxi driver and his passenger, while the passenger's wife called out for help and no one answered. . . . I was in a daze. My head spun. I almost went crazy. How could all this have happened in half a day, between early morning and sunset? I would find the answer at home with my father. But where was my home? I could see only tall buildings and hordes of people. I <u>hastened</u> on to the crossroads between the gardens and Abu Khoda. I had to cross Abu Khoda to reach my house, but the stream of cars would not let up. The fire engine's siren was shrieking at full pitch as it moved at a snail's pace, and I said to myself, "Let the fire take its pleasure in what it consumes." Extremely irritated, I wondered when I would be able to cross. I stood there a long time, until the young lad employed at the ironing shop on the corner came up to me. He stretched out his arm and said gallantly, "Grandpa, let me take you across."

hastened (hās′ ənd) v. hurried; moved swiftly

Reading Strategy
Determining the Author's Purpose What does the final sentence suggest about the writer's purpose?

Review and Assess

Thinking About the Selection

1. **Respond:** At the story's conclusion, did you feel sympathy for the narrator? Why or why not?

2. **(a) Recall:** Where does the father take the narrator?
   (b) Interpret: How does the narrator feel as he faces this change?

3. **(a) Recall:** What does the narrator learn from the first boy with whom he speaks? **(b) Infer:** What is the effect of the boy's statement on the narrator? **(c) Connect:** In what sense does this statement point to the end of the story?

4. **(a) Recall:** What discovery does the narrator make in the paragraph beginning, "As our path revealed itself . . . " ? **(b) Interpret:** What view of people's paths through life underlies this passage?

5. **(a) Recall:** After the bell rings and the narrator goes outside the gates, whom does he meet? **(b) Hypothesize:** Who might this person be? Explain your answer.

6. **(a) Analyze:** What has happened to the narrator by the end of the story? Give two details in support of your answer.
   (b) Draw Conclusions: What does the story suggest about people's ability to make a home for themselves in the world?

7. **Make a Judgment:** Explain whether you think adulthood can be fulfilling or whether you agree with Mahfouz's suggestion that adulthood cannot replace the lost paradise of childhood.

Review and Assess

Literary Analysis

Surrealism

1. (a) What everyday event does "Half a Day" explore? (b) At what point in the story do events turn **surreal**? Explain.

2. (a) Identify two dreamlike details, descriptions, or events in the story. (b) For each example, explain the way in which an ordinary, realistic context adds to its dreamlike quality.

3. Is the ending of the story realistic, surreal, or both? Explain your answer.

Connecting Literary Elements

4. (a) Explain in what way the following passage reflects the story's **theme:** "[T]he time for changing one's mind was over and gone and there was no question of ever returning to the paradise of home." (b) What insight about life is expressed in the narrator's final attempt to return home?

5. Do you think the surprise ending of the story helps a reader grasp the story's insight into time? Explain why or why not.

Reading Strategy

Determining the Author's Purpose

6. How does the story's title, repeated in the last paragraph, help you determine the **author's purpose**?

7. Use a chart like the one below to list three details that serve as clues to the author's purpose. For each, explain what the detail indicates about that purpose.

Detail	What It Shows About the Author's Purpose

Extend Understanding

8. **Cultural Connection:** What lesson does the story suggest about modern times, when new technology may change the world dramatically during one person's lifetime?

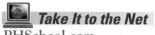

Integrate Language Skills

Vocabulary Development Lesson

Connotations: Words for Crowds

The word *throngs* is one of several words meaning "crowds." Each of these words has different connotations, or associations. For example, *horde* has negative associations, suggesting a destructive crowd, whereas *assembly* has positive ones, suggesting an orderly decision-making group. Identify the connotations of each of the following "crowd" words.

   1. masses   **2.** throngs   **3.** swarms

Spelling Strategy

When adding the suffix *-ed* to a word ending "consonant + vowel + consonant," double the final consonant only if the last syllable is stressed. For example, *re fer´* + *-ed* becomes *referred.* If the last syllable is not stressed, make no change. For example, *has´ ten* + *-ed* becomes *hastened.* Copy the following words, adding the suffix *-ed* to each.

   1. occur   **2.** benefit   **3.** repel

Fluency: Words in Context

Use your knowledge of the italicized words to answer the following questions:

1. Is an *unmarred* piece of furniture likely to cost more than a marred piece? Explain.
2. Would you feel "on guard" in an atmosphere of *intimacy*? Why or why not?
3. Is an *intricate* dance step easy to learn? Explain.
4. If someone is *presumed* to be innocent, should he or she be punished? Explain.
5. Would you be likely to see *throngs* on a desert island? Why or why not?
6. If *hordes* are coming to dinner, how much food will you have to make? Explain.
7. If a person *hastened* to your side, would you have to wait a long time? Explain.

Grammar and Style Lesson

Agreement in Inverted Sentences

In an **inverted sentence,** the subject follows the verb. As in any sentence, the subject and verb must agree. Common examples are sentences beginning with *here* or *there,* such as this model from "Half a Day":

> **Example:** . . . there <u>was</u> a <u>band</u> announcing the opening of a circus . . .

Writers may choose to invert sentences to create emphasis or vary the rhythm of their prose. When Mahfouz writes, "At various points stood conjurers . . .", he creates a small build-up to the word *conjurers,* adding a sense of surprise.

Practice Rewrite each sentence below to correct errors in subject-verb agreement. For any sentence without an error, write *correct.*

1. There was many moments when the boy enjoyed school.
2. Here was a few students he had not met yet.
3. There were lessons in geography and science.
4. There were the boy's father, outside the school.
5. From the street comes loud noises.

Writing Application Write a paragraph about your neighborhood. Include at least two inverted sentences. Check that subjects and verbs agree.

𝒲𝒢 Prentice Hall Writing and Grammar Connection: Diamond Level, Chapter 23, Section 1

Writing Lesson

Surrealistic Descriptive Essay

In "Half a Day," Mahfouz writes about ordinary life using the logic of a dream. Using this surrealistic logic, write a description of an object or event. Make sure to provide enough precise details to support your surrealistic effects.

Prewriting   Once you have a topic, make a T-chart, listing realistic details on the left and surrealistic connections between them on the right.

Drafting   As you draft, focus on providing complete, vividly realistic descriptions to support your surrealistic flights of fantasy.

Revising   Reread your description. Mark passages in which your descriptions are vague. Consider adding specific details to those passages.

Model: Revising to Add Descriptive Detail

freckled   *,bending its neck with a queen's grace,*

The giraffe unclipped its long nose and left it

piercing

hanging on the tree. The modest tree shed three

musical notes, bringing the night to peer out from

crystal

the cracks in its mountain. Soon, the world was

plunged into gloom.

> Adding vivid, descriptive details supports the surrealistic logic of this description.

WG *Prentice Hall Writing and Grammar Connection: Diamond Level, Chapter 6, Section 4*

Extension Activities

Listening and Speaking Mahfouz's story suggests that change makes it impossible to reach what one wants. Form a **discussion panel** with classmates to talk about the effects of change.

- Have one member moderate, ensuring that all have a fair chance to contribute.
- Appoint a notetaker.
- Listen actively to other panelists' ideas, responding with questions for clarification.

Post a summary of your discussion in class.
[Group Activity]

Research and Technology Prepare and present a **multimedia presentation** on the culture of Egypt, Mahfouz's homeland, including daily life, religion, and the arts, using photographs, videos, maps, and music. Familiarize yourself beforehand with the equipment you will use, and test it to make sure it works properly.

 **Take It to the Net**   PHSchool.com

Go online for an additional research activity using the Internet.

Prepare to Read

Pride ◆ The Diameter of the Bomb ◆
From the Book of Esther I Filtered the Sediment

Dahlia Ravikovitch (b. 1936)

"Can't you write about me without me?" poet Dahlia Ravikovitch once asked an interviewer. Painfully shy, Ravikovitch has always shunned the limelight. Yet her poems are filled with intense feeling, fusing emotional revelation with images of history, religion, and mythology. Ravikovitch is probably Israel's most prominent female poet.

A Traumatic Childhood Ravikovitch was born in Ramat Gan, a suburb of Tel Aviv, twelve years before Israel became a nation. When she was six, her father was killed in a hit-and-run accident, and she moved with the rest of her family to an Israeli communal farm, or kibbutz. Her father's death left a lifelong scar, but it also made her deeply sympathetic to the suffering of others. "Because I know what it is like to be hurt," she explains, "I try not to hurt anyone."

Turning Pain to Poetry Poetry became the means by which Ravikovitch expressed her deepest feelings. Drawing on the Bible as well as the English literature she had studied in college, she published her first full volume of poetry in 1959. Two collections, *A Dress of Fire* (1978) and *The Window* (1989), have been translated into English.

Working for Peace Ravikovitch's compassion also marks her involvement in the Israeli peace movement. Israel has an uneasy, sometimes violent, relationship with the Palestinian inhabitants of the region. In 1997, when uprisings drove many Israelis away from Palestinian areas, the sixty-year-old Ravikovitch continued to visit the city of Hebron, bringing chocolates and cheer to a ten-year-old Palestinian boy she had met there.

Yehuda Amichai (1924–2000)

In modern Israel, the language of the streets and shops is Hebrew, the ancient language of the Bible. As the Israeli poet Yehuda Amichai observes, "Every word we use carries in and of itself connotations from the Bible. . . . Every word reverberates through the halls of Jewish history." Amichai's genius lay in his ear for both the traditional and modern resonances of the language.

Rebellion and Loss Amichai was born in Germany. Before the outbreak of World War II, however, his Orthodox Jewish family emigrated to Palestine, the region in which Israel was later (1948) to be established. Eventually, the family settled in Jerusalem. The young Amichai rebelled against his father's strict religious practices, yet his great love for his father survived the conflict.

Apprenticeships As a young man, Amichai served in World War II and in Israel's War of Independence. An early collection of short stories is based in part on his wartime experiences. During this period, he began reading the English poets W. H. Auden and T. S. Eliot. Both poets, especially Auden, inspired him to use colloquial language in his work.

Speaking for Others Amichai published his first collection of poems in 1955, but it was with his second book of poetry, *Two Hopes Away* (1958), that Amichai was embraced as the spokesperson for his generation, capturing its disillusionment. In this book, Amichai introduced what one critic called the characteristic themes of his subsequent work: "love, war, the passage of time, his relationship with his father, his father's death, and his own undefined guilt."

Preview

Connecting to the Literature

"What would I do if I had total control?" Most people have a quick answer—they would win every time. These poems ask a trickier question: "What happens when we want to control life—but find we can't?"

Literary Analysis

Imagery

Imagery is descriptive language that re-creates sensory experience. An **image** is a specific word picture created using such language. For example, "Pride" contains powerful images of movement and rest:

> And so the moss flourishes, the seaweed / whips around, / the sea pushes through and rolls back—/ the rocks seem motionless.

A **sustained image** is one that is extended over a number of lines. As you read, note the effects of both brief and sustained images.

Comparing Literary Works

Poets often use imagery to develop **figurative language,** or language that is not meant to be taken literally. Figures of speech include

- **metaphor,** in which one thing is spoken of as if it were another kind of thing
- **simile,** in which one thing is compared to another using *like* or *as*
- **personification,** in which a nonhuman subject is given human characteristics.

For example, in "From the Book of Esther . . . ," the poet speaks of numbing oneself to the pains and joys of life as "filtering sediment." In this metaphor, a habit of mind is described as if it were a physical act. As you read, compare the poets' uses of figurative language to probe life.

Reading Strategy

Evaluating a Writer's Message

To **evaluate a writer's message,** identify the work's main insight. Then, consider whether the insight makes sense and whether it is well supported. For example, in "The Diameter of the Bomb," Amichai's message concerns the effects of a single act. He supports his message with a vivid, sustained image. As you read, use a chart like this one to evaluate the writers' messages.

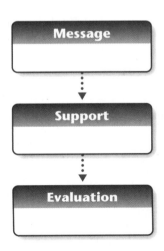

Vocabulary Development

flourishes (flʉrʹ ish ez) *v.* thrives; grows vigorously (p. 1318)

considerably (kən sidʹ er ə blē) *adv.* to a great degree (p. 1319)

solitary (sälʹ ə ter ē) *adj.* lone; single; sole (p. 1319)

sediment (sedʹ ə mənt) *n.* waste material that settles to the bottom of a liquid (p. 1320)

vulgar (vulʹ gər) *adj.* coarse; common (p. 1320)

Pride

Dahlia Ravikovitch
translated by Chana Bloch *and* Ariel Bloch

Background

Before the onset of World War II, Jews had begun to return to Palestine, the Jewish homeland in biblical times. Violence flared up between the Arab inhabitants of Palestine and the new immigrants. In 1948, the United Nations divided Palestine, creating the state of Israel for Jewish settlers, who now included refugees from the Holocaust. Palestinians and their Arab allies were outraged, and the region was plunged into a series of wars and uprisings. The work of these poets suggests that, exposed day after day to threats and horrors, people in the region face a kind of moral weariness.

> I tell you, even rocks crack,
> and not because of age.
> For years they lie on their backs
> in the heat and the cold,
> 5   so many years,
> it almost seems peaceful.
> They don't move, so the cracks stay hidden.
> A kind of pride.
> Years pass over them, waiting.
> 10   Whoever is going to shatter them
> hasn't come yet.
> And so the moss <u>flourishes</u>, the seaweed
> whips around,
> the sea pushes through and rolls back—
> 15   the rocks seem motionless.
> Till a little seal comes to rub against them,
> comes and goes away.
> And suddenly the rock has an open wound.
> I told you, when rocks break, it happens by surprise.
> 20   And people, too.

Literary Analysis
Imagery and Figurative Language Identify two words or phrases that personify the rocks, giving them human qualities.

flourishes (flur´ ish ez) v. thrives; grows vigorously

The Diameter of the Bomb

Yehuda Amichai
translated by Chana Bloch

The diameter of the bomb was thirty centimeters
and the diameter of its effective range about seven meters,
with four dead and eleven wounded.
And around these, in a larger circle
5 of pain and time, two hospitals are scattered
and one graveyard. But the young woman
who was buried in the city she came from,
at a distance of more than a hundred kilometers,
enlarges the circle <u>considerably</u>,
10 and the <u>solitary</u> man mourning her death
at the distant shores of a country far across the sea
includes the entire world in the circle.
And I won't even mention the crying of orphans
that reaches up to the throne of God and
15 beyond, making
a circle with no end and no God.

Literary Analysis
Imagery How does the visual image of the circle change in lines 1–6?

considerably (kən sid′ er ə blē) *adv.* to a great degree

solitary (säl′ ə ter ē) *adj.* lone; single; sole

Review and Assess

Thinking About the Selections

1. **Respond:** In each poem, what most surprised you? Explain.
2. **(a) Recall:** What happens to the rocks at the end of "Pride"?
   (b) Analyze Cause and Effect: Compare the apparent cause of this event with its deeper causes.
3. **(a) Interpret:** What does the expansion of the circle in the poem suggest about human suffering? **(b) Draw Conclusions:** What lesson about justice does the poem suggest?

From the Book of Esther I Filtered the Sediment

Yehuda Amichai

translated by Chana Bloch

From the Book of Esther I filtered the <u>sediment</u>
of <u>vulgar</u> joy, and from the Book of Jeremiah
the howl of pain in the guts. And from
the Song of Songs the endless
5 search for love, and from Genesis the dreams
and Cain, and from Ecclesiastes
the despair, and from the Book of Job: Job.
And with what was left, I pasted myself a new Bible.
Now I live censored and pasted and limited and in peace.

10 A woman asked me last night on the dark street
how another woman was
who'd already died. Before her time—and not
in anyone else's time either.
Out of a great weariness I answered,
15 "She's fine, she's fine."

sediment (sed´ ə mənt) *n.* waste material that settles to the bottom of a liquid

vulgar (vul´ gər) *adj.* coarse; common

Reading Strategy
Evaluating a Writer's Message What do these lines suggest about the speaker's reason for living a life "censored and pasted and limited and in peace"?

Review and Assess

Thinking About the Selection

1. **Respond:** How did you react to the speaker's "weariness"?
2. **(a) Recall:** List three examples of the "sediment" that the speaker filters from the Bible. **(b) Connect:** Explain the connection between the "sediment" the speaker removes and the type of life mapped out in his "new Bible."
3. **(a) Analyze:** What does the speaker's "great weariness" lead him to do in the last line? **(b) Infer:** What is the probable source of his attitude? Cite details to support your answer.
4. **Apply:** What advice might you offer someone in the speaker's position?

Review and Assess

Literary Analysis

Imagery

1. (a) Identify three **images** in "Pride," explaining to which sense each one appeals. (b) Explain the connection between each image and the "pride" to which the title refers.

2. (a) What **sustained image** is central to "The Diameter of the Bomb"? (b) Using a chart like this one, explain how the development of this image moves from a specific event to a general idea.

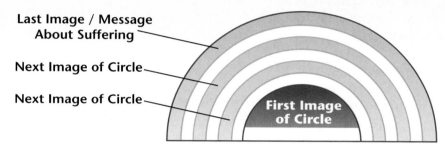

Last Image / Message About Suffering

Next Image of Circle

Next Image of Circle

First Image of Circle

3. (a) How is the image of "sediment" in "From the Book of Esther . . . " contradicted by the experiences it symbolizes? (b) In using this image, what attitude does the speaker reveal? Explain.

Comparing Literary Works

4. Identify the types of **figurative language** used in "Pride" and "The Diameter of the Bomb."

5. Compare the image of the circle in "The Diameter of the Bomb" with the image of sediment in "From the Book of Esther . . . ."
   (a) Which image expands the reader's vision of the world? Explain.
   (b) Which gives more insight into the poem's speaker? Explain.

Reading Strategy

Evaluating a Writer's Message

6. (a) Identify the **writer's message** in each of the three poems.
   (b) For each one, identify the way in which the poet supports it (makes it understandable and compelling).

7. In your judgment, which message is best supported? Explain.

Extend Understanding

8. **Math Connection:** (a) Using the terms *circumference* and *diameter,* describe the last circle in Amichai's poem. (b) Do you think such a circle can be defined using a mathematical equation? Explain.

Integrate Language Skills

Vocabulary Development Lesson

Latin Word Origins: *vulgar*

The word *vulgar*, meaning "common" or "coarse," is related to the Latin word *vulgus*, meaning "the common people" or "the public." Historically, *vulgar* also came to refer to the spoken language of a country (as opposed to Latin, used by the church and in government). Today, *vulgar* is often used to mean "improper." The original meaning of the root *-vulg-* can be detected, though, in words such as *divulge*, meaning "to make public."

For each item below, write a sentence that includes the word *vulgar*.

1. the language spoken by medieval farmers
2. a common pleasure, such as sharing a meal
3. an audience member who sniffs, yawns, and stretches loudly throughout a performance

Grammar and Style Lesson

Elliptical Clauses

Elliptical comes from the word *ellipsis*, meaning "omission." In an **elliptical clause,** some words are left out, but the clause is understood as if they were present. Review the following example:

Elliptical Clause: The diameter of the bomb was thirty centimeters / and the <u>diameter of its effective range</u> [. . .] <u>about seven meters</u>, . . . (*was* is understood)

Practice For each item below, write the elliptical clauses and the understood words.

1. "I tell you, even rocks crack, / and not because of age."

Concept Development: Synonyms and Antonyms

Synonyms are words that are the same or nearly the same in meaning. Antonyms are opposites. Identify each synonym or antonym pair below.

1. flourishes / withers
2. considerably / slightly
3. solitary / sole
4. sediment / residue
5. vulgar / courtly

Spelling Strategy

When adding the suffix *-ly* to a word ending in a consonant + *le*, drop the *le*. Add *-ly* to each of the following words.

1. comfortable   2. miserable   3. agreeable

2. "From the Book of Esther I filtered the sediment / of vulgar joy, and from the Book of Jeremiah / the howl of pain in the guts."
3. Amichai's images are more abstract; Ravikovitch's, more concrete.
4. Amichai writes with a keen eye; Ravikovitch, with a large heart.
5. They might agree on this idea: Art is born of suffering; great art, of great suffering.

Writing Application Write a paragraph about people's responses to misfortune. Include two sentences with elliptical clauses.

Writing Lesson

Poem With a Strong Central Image

Following the examples of Ravikovitch and Amichai, write a poem with a strong central image that conveys a message about life. For the best effect, make sure that your poem is focused, with each detail supporting your central image.

Prewriting   Select a topic, such as *kindness*, and write several sentences about it. Use these sentences to develop a message for your poem. Next, list images that will help convey this message. Circle the strongest one.

Drafting   As you draft, keep your central image and message in mind. Bring the image to life by using words that appeal to the senses.

Revising   Underline in one color those details in your poem that develop the central image. Use another color to underline details that distract from it. Consider eliminating distracting details and elaborating on those that strengthen the central image.

Model: Revising to Strengthen Your Central Image

A smile, a word of kindness, a needed hug—

(a seed), planted in the soil of someone's day

it holds a waiting flower,

unfurling it sunward,

~~leaving its mark~~ after you have gone.

> Eliminating distracting details and providing additional support help clarify the central image.

Prentice Hall Writing and Grammar Connection: Diamond Level, Chapter 6, Section 4

Extension Activities

Listening and Speaking The speaker in "From the Book of Esther . . ." has a sharp, ironic understanding of his own "weariness." Give an **oral interpretation** of the poem, using these tips:

- Jot down notes on the speaker's attitude toward life.
- Identify the reaction to that attitude—does the speaker feel self-contempt? Resignation?
- Experiment with various tones of voice and pacing to convey the speaker's personality.

Present your interpretation to the class.

Research and Technology The rocks in "Pride" lie along the ocean shore. In a group, produce a **multimedia presentation** on seaside geology. Divide tasks and conduct research on the following subtopics: Types of Rocks, Rock Formation, and Erosion. Use visuals to present your information to the class. **[Group Activity]**

 **Take It to the Net**   PHSchool.com

Go online for an additional research activity using the Internet.

from Hiroshima

JOHN HERSEY

In Yehuda Amichai's poem "The Diameter of the Bomb" (p. 1319), the circle of devastation that is described extends physically and metaphorically in all directions and for eternal distances. Modern and contemporary literature has all too often had occasion to address issues related to war, bombing, and destruction, as well as their dramatic effect on the everyday lives of individuals.

The Ultimate Weapon John Hersey's account of the dropping of the atomic bomb on Hiroshima in 1945 provides a deceptively calm and objective account of horror. In this excerpt from *Hiroshima*, the specific details of Miss Toshiko Sasaki's normal morning activities form the story of a step-by-step journey toward disaster. In this nonfiction account, as in the fiction, poetry, and other nonfiction in this unit, similar mundane details serve as reminders that ordinary lives can become extraordinary in an instant and that those directly affected by violence and tragedy are—up to that moment—just like everyone else.

At exactly fifteen minutes past eight in the morning, on August 6, 1945, Japanese time, at the moment when the atomic bomb flashed above Hiroshima, Miss Toshiko Sasaki, a clerk in the personnel department of the East Asia Tin Works, had just sat down at her place in the plant office and was turning her head to speak to the girl at the next desk. At that same moment, Dr. Masakazu Fujii was settling down cross-legged to read the Osaka *Asahi* on the porch of his private hospital, overhanging one of the seven deltaic rivers which divide Hiroshima; Mrs. Hatsuyo Nakamura, a tailor's widow, stood by the window of her kitchen, watching a neighbor tearing down his house because it lay in the path of an air-raid-defense fire lane; . . . and the Reverend Mr. Kiyoshi Tanimoto, pastor of the Hiroshima Methodist Church, paused at the door of a rich man's house in Koi, the city's western suburb, and prepared to unload a handcart full of things he had <u>evacuated</u> from town in fear of the massive B-29 raid which everyone expected Hiroshima to suffer. A hundred thousand people were killed by the atomic bomb, and these [four] were among the survivors. They still wonder why they lived when so many others died. Each of them counts many small items of chance or <u>volition</u>—a step taken in time, a decision to go indoors, catching one streetcar instead of the next—that spared him. And now each knows that in the act of survival he lived a dozen lives and saw more death than he ever thought he would see. At the time, none of them knew anything. . . .

▲ **Critical Viewing**
There are no people shown in this photo-graph—nor in many others depicting the devastation wrought by the Hiroshima bomb. Does the lack of hu-manity lessen or intensify the power of the image? Explain. **[Assess]**

evacuated (ē vak′ yōō āt′ əd) *v.* made empty; withdrawn

volition (vō lish′ ən) *n.* act of using the will

Miss Toshiko Sasaki, the East Asia Tin Works clerk, . . . got up at three o'clock in the morning on the day the bomb fell. There was extra housework to do. Her eleven-month-old brother, Akio, had come down the day before with a serious stomach upset; her mother had taken him to the Tamura Pediatric Hospital and was staying there with him. Miss Sasaki, who was about twenty, had to cook breakfast for her father, a brother, a sister, and herself, and—since the hospital, because of the war, was unable to provide food—to prepare a whole day's meals for her mother and the baby, in time for her father, who worked in a factory making rubber earplugs for artillery crews, to take the food by on his way to the plant. When she had finished

▼ **Critical Viewing**
How effectively do these remains of the sacred tree of a Hiroshima temple convey the physical and emotional devastation of the blast? Explain. **[Evaluate]**

and had cleaned and put away the cooking things, it was nearly seven. The family lived in Koi, and she had a forty-five-minute trip to the tin works, in the section of town called Kannonmachi. She was in charge of the personnel records in the factory. She left Koi at seven, and as soon as she reached the plant, she went with some of the other girls from the personnel department to the factory auditorium. A prominent local Navy man, a former employee, had committed suicide the day before by throwing himself under a train—a death considered honorable enough to warrant a memorial service, which was to be held at the tin works at ten o'clock that morning. In the large hall, Miss Sasaki and the others made suitable preparations for the meeting. This work took about twenty minutes.

Miss Sasaki went back to her office and sat down at her desk. She was quite far from the windows, which were off to her left, and behind her were a couple of tall bookcases containing all the books of the factory library, which the personnel department had organized. She settled herself at her desk, put some things in a drawer, and shifted papers. She thought that before she began to make entries in her lists of new employees, discharges, and departures for the Army, she would chat for a moment with the girl at her right. Just as she turned her head away from the windows, the room was filled with a blinding light. She was paralyzed by fear, fixed still in her chair for a long moment (the plant was 1,600 yards from the center).

Everything fell, and Miss Sasaki lost consciousness. The ceiling dropped suddenly and the wooden floor above collapsed in splinters and the people up there came down and the roof above them gave way; but principally and first of all, the bookcases right behind her swooped forward and the contents threw her down, with her left leg horribly twisted and breaking underneath her. There, in the tin factory, in the first moment of the atomic age, a human being was crushed by books.

John Hersey

(1914–1993)

Born in China to American parents and raised there until age ten, John Hersey returned repeatedly to East Asia during his long career as a war correspondent, novelist, and essayist. During the 1940s, Hersey traveled to China and Japan as a correspondent for *The New Yorker* and *Time* magazines. He also used these visits to gather material for his most famous and acclaimed book, *Hiroshima*. This remarkable report of the devastation caused by the atomic bomb first appeared in *The New Yorker*, when Wallace Shawn, the editor at that time, made the unprecedented decision to bump all of the magazine's other editorial content to publish Hersey's work as a four-part article.

Connecting Literature Past and Present

1. (a) In what way are the everyday details that Hersey provides about Miss Toshiko Sasaki's life similar to those provided in Amichai's poem "The Diameter of the Bomb"? (b) How do they differ?

2. Which has a stronger impact on you—the poetic account of a terrorist's bomb or this nonfiction account of a wartime bombing? Explain.

3. In what other literary works that you have read have tiny, ordinary decisions made the difference between life and death? Explain.

Prepare to Read

Twigs ◆ My mother would lose herself . . . ◆ She used to throw her old crockery . . . ◆ On Living

Taha Muhammad Ali (b. 1931)

Galilee, the native land of Taha Muhammad Ali (ta´ Ha mσo Ham´ id a lē´), is a bit of history come to life. According to the Bible, Jesus grew up and preached in the region. Now a part of Israel, the land also bears the scars where history has been violently erased. Saffuriya, the small Galilean village in which Ali was born, was largely destroyed in the first Arab-Israeli war of 1948.

Escape Ali and his family escaped the destruction of their village by fleeing to Lebanon. A year later, Ali crossed back into Israel and resettled in the city of Nazareth, also in Galilee.

Memory It is perhaps ironic that, although part of his past had been destroyed, Ali turned to the work of memory. By day, he operated a souvenir shop in the old quarter of Nazareth, selling items to tourists who wanted to remember the city. At night, Ali educated himself in classical Arabic poetry. Eventually, he began writing poems himself. Today, Ali is among the foremost contemporary Palestinian poets.

Nazim Hikmet (1902–1963)

As an old empire crumbled, Nazim Hikmet (nä zəm´ hik met´) turned to a radical vision of the future. The son of a Turkish diplomat, Hikmet was born in Salonika, Greece. The collapse of Turkey's Ottoman Empire at the end of World War I prompted Hikmet to join the cause of Turkish nationalism. Later, he traveled to the Soviet Union, where he studied radical political theory.

Dangerous Rebellions Hikmet returned home to fight injustice, publishing essays, plays, and poetry.

A rebel in more than politics, Hikmet wrote free verse in defiance of literary conventions. The authoritarian Turkish government prosecuted him for his political views, and he served years in prison.

Prison and Exile In 1938, Hikmet was accused of inciting a military revolt—soldiers had been found reading his poetry. Imprisoned again, he was not released until 1950. A year later, further persecution forced him to flee Turkey by motorboat in a storm. Hikmet spent the rest of his life in exile. Today, he is considered modern Turkey's greatest poet.

Vénus Khoury-Ghata (b. 1937)

Vénus Khoury-Ghata (vā nōōs´ khσur´ ē gha´ ta) has lived up to her first name, taken from the Roman goddess of love and beauty—she was honored as Miss Beirut in 1959! Today, however, this accomplished poet is better remembered for the literary awards she has won, such as the prestigious Prix Apollinaire.

Becoming Inspired Khoury-Ghata was born in Lebanon when that nation was still under French rule. She grew up in Beirut, the capital, but spent summers in her mother's village, the hometown of renowned poet Kahlil Gibran. Stories about Gibran brought out Khoury-Ghata's interest in poetry. She began writing poems in French.

Becoming Famous One day, a Beirut neighbor who was also a poet read her poems. Impressed, he took them to a small publisher, who put out a volume of Khoury-Ghata's verse. A French scholar visiting Beirut brought the book to a larger publisher. Eventually, Khoury-Ghata and her husband, a French scientist, moved to Paris. There, she began winning prizes for her poetry. She has also published more than a dozen novels.

Preview

Connecting to the Literature

The beating sun, the thud of waves—a shocking rush of cold water . . .
Afterward, riding home, you realize how dazzling the day was—just when it
is over. These poets look at loss to show how dazzling life itself is.

Literary Analysis

Free Verse

Free verse is poetry not unified by a regular, rhythmical pattern, or meter.
To unify their poems, free-verse writers use other strategies, including these:

- creating a lively voice using conversational speech
- writing in fragments, each of which, like a saying or a riddle,
  combines ideas and images to provoke thought
- weaving together vivid images using dreamlike associations

Note the techniques these free-verse poets use to unify their work.

Comparing Literary Works

One source of unity in a free-verse poem is a **theme,** or central message.
These three poems share a theme: The ordinary routines, pleasures, and
needs of life are actually the most extraordinary—they are immeasurably
valuable. In "Twigs," for example, the poet muses that

> it has taken me / all of sixty years / to understand / that water
> is the finest drink, / and bread the most delicious food, . . .

As you read, use a chart like this one to compare ways in which the
poets develop the theme of the extraordinary in the ordinary.

Reading Strategy

Listening

To appreciate a poem, **listen** to the music the poet (or translator) has
created with words. Read the poem aloud, listening for the following:

- rhythms of the lines, whether soothing or rousing, lazy or busy
- echoes, such as repeated phrases or repeated consonant sounds
- contrasts in sound, such as between long and short vowels
- texture of words, such as the "crunchiness" of *crunchy*

Vocabulary Development

consolation (kän′ sə lā′ shən) *n.* comfort; something that eases disappointment or sadness (p. 1330)

brevity (brev′ ə tē) *n.* briefness (p. 1330)

putrefy (pyo͞o′ trə fī) *v.* rot (p. 1331)

foundering (foun′ dər iŋ) *n.* stumbling; sinking; becoming stuck (p. 1332)

self-abnegation (self ab′ nə gā′ shən) *n.* self-denial; lack of consideration for oneself or one's own interests (p. 1332)

contrary (kän′ trer′ ē) *adj.* unfavorable; opposing (p. 1333)

dubious (do͞o′ bē əs) *adj.* doubtful; uncertain; suspect (p. 1333)

Twigs

Taha Muhammad Ali
translated by Peter Cole,
Yahya Hijazi, Gabriel Lévin

Background

Although Taha Muhammad Ali's Galilean hometown of Saffuriya was destroyed in the Arab-Israeli war of 1948, the language of that village—a spoken dialect of Arabic—is very much alive in Ali's poems. Ali is known for using both spoken Arabic and traditional literary Arabic (a descendant of the language of the Qur'an) in his works. This synthesis makes his poems at once intensely personal and powerfully universal.

Neither music
fame nor wealth,
not even poetry itself,
could provide <u>consolation</u>
5   for life's <u>brevity</u>,
or the fact that *King Lear*
is a mere eighty pages long, and comes to an end,
and for the thought that one might suffer greatly
on account of a rebellious child.

            *

10 My love for you
is what's magnificent,
but I, you, and the others,
most likely,
are ordinary people.

            *

15 My poem
goes beyond poetry
because you
exist
beyond the realm of women.

Literary Analysis
Free Verse Identify two characteristics of this stanza that show that the poem is in free verse.

consolation (kän´ sə lā´ shən) *n.* comfort; something that eases disappointment or sadness

brevity (brəv´ ə tē) *n.* briefness

20   And so
     it has taken me
     all of sixty years
     to understand
     that water is the finest drink,
25   and bread the most delicious food,
     and that art is worthless
     unless it plants
     a measure of splendor in people's hearts.

                    *

     After we die,
30   and the weary heart
     has lowered its final eyelid
     on all that we've done,
     and on all that we've longed for,
     on all that we've dreamt of,
35   all we've desired
     or felt,
     hate will be
     the first thing
     to <u>putrefy</u>
40   within us.
                    1989–1991

putrefy (py$\overline{oo}$′ trə fī) v. rot

Review and Assess

Thinking About the Selection

1. **Respond:** Do you find this poem comforting? Why or why not?

2. **(a) Recall:** Name the three facts in the first stanza that make the speaker inconsolable. **(b) Connect:** What do these three facts have in common?

3. **(a) Recall:** In the second stanza, what is called "magnificent" and what "ordinary"? **(b) Interpret:** In what sense does what is magnificent go beyond the ordinary, yet stay within it? **(c) Connect:** Given this magnificence in ordinary life, explain why the person addressed in this stanza exists "beyond the realm of women."

4. **(a) Interpret:** Restate the messages of the fourth and fifth stanzas in your own words. **(b) Draw Conclusions:** In what sense are these stanzas answers to the first stanza?

5. **Connect:** Explain the sense in which each stanza is like a "twig" growing from a larger, common branch.

Themes in World Literature

Writers in Exile

Ali, Khoury-Ghata, and Hikmet all have lived through exile in one form or another. For some writers, exile is voluntary. In other cases, like Hikmet's, the exiled writer has been forced to leave a politically troubled nation where honest, critical writing is dangerous. Among these prominent writers-in-exile are:

• ancient Latin poet Ovid (43 B.C.– A.D. 17?), who offended the Roman emperor Augustus and was sent to live in a fishing village by the Black Sea, far from his beloved Rome. (For more on Ovid, see page 514.)

• contemporary Russian novelist Alexander Solzhenitsyn (b. 1918), who was deported from the U.S.S.R. in 1973 after publishing *The Gulag Archipelago*, his history of Soviet forced labor camps. After living in the United States for years, he returned to Russia in 1994. (For more on Solzhenitsyn, see page 1294.)

• contemporary African poet Abena Busia (b. 1953). Busia followed her father, one of Ghana's first modern leaders, into exile when his government was overturned. Today, she lives, writes, and teaches in New Jersey.

My mother would lose herself . . .

Vénus Khoury-Ghata
translated by Marilyn Hacker

Background

In summers as a child, Vénus Khoury-Ghata would visit her mother's vil-lage, a joyful escape from city life. There, she read the works of the village's most famous son, poet Kahlil Gibran, and watched the mountain women go about their daily chores with steady industry. Her memories of these visits have sustained her as an adult. The grown-up Khoury-Ghata realized one day that despite her material wealth, her life was lacking in joy. She says, "I had to produce something, and live the way my mother had lived. . . . After seven hours of writing I'm glad to do some ironing." These poems by Khoury-Ghata will introduce you both to her mother and to her magical memories of summers in a beloved village.

My mother would lose herself in the puffing movements of her
    broom
battling the sand which she called desert
the dampness she called crumbled water
swamp

5 remote from the world her sweeper's hands
exhumed invisible corpses
pursued the least <u>foundering</u> of the wind
the slightest stain of darkness
she swept with so much <u>self-abnegation</u>
10 and burst out laughing in the worst storm
for fear of appearing ill-tempered

Mother you were so modest
you took no credit for the wind which blew just for your arms as
    they swept.

Reading Strategy
Listening Find a phrase in lines 1–4 with a distinctive sound texture and describe that texture.

foundering (foun′dər iŋ) *n.* stumbling; sinking; becoming stuck

self-abnegation (self ab′nə gā′ shən) *n.* self-denial; lack of consideration for one-self or one's own interests

She used to throw her old crockery …

Vénus Khoury-Ghata *translated by* Marilyn Hacker

She used to throw her old crockery at the moon
which mends chipped plates
darns wedding sheets
and sorts lamplight-yellowed snapshots by degrees of sadness

5   The whole universe shared my mother's household chores
<u>contrary</u> winds blew into her bureau drawers
bargained between her shutters
and swept towards town the dream-crumbs she nibbled in her
        sleep

Negligent mother
10 clouds of a <u>dubious</u> whiteness dried out on your clothesline
provoking the nightingales' sarcasm and saddening the sun
you reported them missing to the police when the wind carried
        them out of the valley
called the wind a thief of sheets and cattle
then withdrew your complaint when the clouds came home to you,
        fog kneeling on your doorstep.

Literary Analysis
Free Verse In what way
do lines 2–4 echo one
another?

contrary (kän′ trer′ ē) *adj.*
unfavorable; opposing

dubious (doo′ bē əs) *adj.*
doubtful; uncertain;
suspect

Review and Assess

Thinking About the Selections

1. **Respond:** Would you like to meet the poet's mother? Explain.

2. **(a) Recall:** In line 1 of "My mother would lose herself … ," what
   does the poet say her mother would do? **(b) Infer:** What does this
   phrase suggest about the mother's personality?

3. **(a) Interpret:** Explain why the images in the second stanza make
   her sweeping seem like a serious task. **(b) Connect:** In what sense
   do the last two lines of the poem turn around the idea that the
   mother disappears into her sweeping?

4. **(a) Recall:** What does the universe do in the second stanza of
   "She used to throw her old crockery … "? **(b) Interpret:** How
   does this image capture a child's idea of his or her mother?

5. **Connect:** Explain the way in which the concluding image of fog
   builds on the notion of the mother's relation to the world.

On Living

Nazım Hikmet

translated by Randy Blasing *and* Mutlu Konuk

Background

Nazım Hikmet was one of Turkey's greatest modern poets. His commitment to a grand political vision, his influence on later poets, and his expansive style are comparable to those of the nineteenth-century American poet Walt Whitman. His poems, including the one that appears here, are at once personal and public. They speak of the poet's self while speaking simultaneously of his beloved country and of the wider world.

I

Living is no laughing matter:
        you must live with great seriousness
        like a squirrel, for example—
I mean without looking for something beyond and above living,
5   I mean living must be your whole occupation.
Living is no laughing matter:
        you must take it seriously,
        so much so and to such a degree
that, for example, your hands tied behind your back,
10   your back to the wall,
        or else in a laboratory
        in your white coat and safety glasses,
        you can die for people—
        even for people whose faces you've never seen,
15   even though you know living
        is the most real, the most beautiful thing.
I mean, you must take living so seriously
        that even at seventy, for example, you'll plant olive trees—
        and not for your children, either,
20   but because although you fear death you don't believe it,
        because living, I mean, weighs heavier.

II

Let's say we're seriously ill, need surgery—
which is to say we might not get up
            from the white table.
25 Even though it's impossible not to feel sad
           about going a little too soon,
we'll still laugh at the jokes being told,
we'll look out the window to see if it's raining,
or still wait anxiously
30   for the latest newscast . . .
Let's say we're at the front—
        for something worth fighting for, say.
There, in the first offensive, on that very day,
        we might fall on our face, dead.
35 We'll know this with a curious anger,
        but we'll still worry ourselves to death
        about the outcome of the war, which could last years.
Let's say we're in prison
and close to fifty,
40 and we have eighteen more years, say,
        before the iron doors will open.
We'll still live with the outside,
with its people and animals, struggle and wind—
        I mean with the outside beyond the walls.
45 I mean, however and wherever we are,
        we must live as if we will never die.

Literary Analysis
Free Verse Identify two phrases that make the poem sound conversational.

Reading Check

According to the speaker, what might one do in old age, showing that one takes life "seriously"?

On Living ◆ 1335

This earth will grow cold,
a star among stars
        and one of the smallest,
50   a gilded mote on blue velvet—
        I mean *this*, our great earth.
This earth will grow cold one day,
not like a block of ice
or a dead cloud even
55   but like an empty walnut it will roll along
        in pitch-black space . . .
You must grieve for this right now
—you have to feel this sorrow now—
for the world must be loved this much
60   if you're going to say "I lived". . .

                 February 1948

Reading Strategy
Listening Describe the contrasting vowel sounds in line 50.

Review and Assess

Thinking About the Selection

1. **Respond:** What do you like or dislike about the poet's style? Explain.

2. **(a) Recall:** In the first stanza, what are the three examples of a person living "seriously"? **(b) Analyze:** What do the three examples have in common?

3. **(a) Recall:** What three situations are described in the second stanza? **(b) Connect:** How does each support the idea in line 45 that "we must live as if we will never die"?

4. **Generalize:** In the poem, what does the nearness of death emphasize about life?

5. **(a) Compare and Contrast:** Describe the main difference between the last stanza and the first two. **(b) Connect:** Discuss a way in which this stanza supports the message of the previous two, as well as a way in which it makes that message more general.

6. **Evaluate:** Do you think the poet's use of phrases such as "I mean" and "Let's say" helps convey the seriousness of his subject? Explain.

7. **(a) Apply:** Describe an event or a circumstance you have encountered in literature, film, or your own life in which life appeared in all its "seriousness." **(b) Compare:** Compare this circumstance to a situation described by Hikmet.

Review and Assess

Literary Analysis

Free Verse

1. (a) In the **free-verse** poem "Twigs," in what way do the irregular line lengths in the first stanza match the pacing of the speaker's ideas?
2. (a) Identify four references to wind or air in "My mother would lose herself. . . ." (b) In what way is the last reference different from the first? (c) Explain how this pattern of imagery helps the reader see the mother as her child sees her—at the center of the world.
3. (a) In "She used to throw her old crockery . . . ," identify two images in which the poet weaves the natural world into her mother's housekeeping. (b) Explain how the last stanza turns this relationship between nature and mother into a small drama.
4. (a) Identify two repeated phrases in "On Living" that give it a conversational tone. (b) Why is this tone suited to a poem about the "seriousness" of even the small things in life?

Comparing Literary Works

5. Compare the speaker's **theme** in "Twigs" with the discoveries about life in one of the other poems.
6. Explain the way in which death helps Hikmet see the extraordinary value of the ordinary, whereas Khoury-Ghata finds this value in memories of her vanished childhood.

Reading Strategy

Listening

7. Using a chart like the one shown, examine sound devices in each of the four poems. In the first column, quote an example of a sound device and identify it (repetition, rhythm, or contrast). In the second column, explain which idea or image this device emphasizes.

Sound Device	Idea or Image Emphasized

Extend Understanding

8. **Cultural Connection:** Identify three ways individuals or groups in the United States may show respect for the beauty of everyday life.

Quick Review

Free verse is poetry that is not unified by a regular, rhythmical pattern. Writers of free verse may unify their poems by writing a series of thought-provoking fragments, by following the dream logic of images, or by creating a lively, conversational voice.

A **theme** is a central message or insight revealed by a literary work.

To **listen** to a work of poetry, notice the rhythm of its lines, repeated words or sounds, contrasting sounds, and the texture of words.

Take It to the Net
PHSchool.com

Take the interactive self-test online to check your understanding of these selections.

Integrate Language Skills

Vocabulary Development Lesson

Word Analysis: Latin Prefixes *con-* and *contra-*

The prefix *con-* means "with" or "together." The prefix appears in the word *consolation*, which refers to a thing that "brings a person together with" comfort.

Do not confuse *con-* with the prefix *contra-*, meaning "against." This prefix appears in the word *contrary*, meaning "opposing or against something else."

With the help of a dictionary, define each of these words, using *with*, *together*, *against*, or *opposite* in each definition.

1. confluence
2. contradict
3. concoct
4. contraband
5. contact

Fluency: Words in Context

To practice using the vocabulary words listed on page 1329, write one sentence on each of the following topics, using the word given.

1. sad event (*consolation*)
2. party (*brevity*)
3. vegetable (*putrefy*)
4. football game (*foundering*)
5. injustice (*self-abnegation*)
6. evidence (*contrary*)
7. weather (*dubious*)

Spelling Strategy

When adding a suffix to a verb ending in *e*, the *e* is usually dropped or changed to another vowel. For example, *console* becomes *consolation*. Add the suffix *-tion* to each of these words:

1. oppose   2. compose   3. declare

Grammar and Style Lesson

Linking Verbs and Subject Complements

A **linking verb**—such as *be, become, seem,* or *feel*—expresses a state of being. To determine whether a verb is a linking verb, replace it with a form of *be*. If the sentence still makes sense, then usually the verb is a linking verb.

A **subject complement** is the noun, pronoun, adjective, or clause that follows a linking verb and identifies or describes the subject of the sentence.

>   LV   SUBJ. COMP.
> **Examples:** My love for you / is what's magnificent, . . .
>   LV   SUBJ. COMP.
>   This earth will grow cold one day, . . .

Practice Copy each item below. Double-underline any linking verbs and single-underline any subject complements. Write *none* if there are none.

1. . . . but I, you, and the others, / most likely, / are ordinary people.
2. . . . you took no credit for the wind. . . .
3. Living is no laughing matter: . . .
4. . . . living . . . weighs heavier.
5. . . . it's impossible not to feel sad. . . .

Writing Application Write a four-line poem describing a person or an object. Use a linking verb and a subject complement in each line.

*W*G *Prentice Hall Writing and Grammar Connection: Diamond Level, Chapter 18, Section 3*

Writing Lesson

Comparison-and-Contrast Essay

In "Twigs" and "On Living," Ali and Hikmet offer powerful messages about life. Write an essay in which you compare and contrast the two poems. For each point in your essay, quote relevant, supporting passages from the poems.

Prewriting   Reread the poems, gathering details that will support your comparison. Begin by listing questions that will help you focus your search.

Model: Answering Questions to Gather Details

- What is each poet saying about life's ending?

  Ali: Life is too short; "not even poetry itself, / could provide consolation for life's brevity, . . ."

- In what ways are the poets' voices similar?

> Answering questions such as these makes reviewing the poems and organizing a comparison a more efficient, focused task.

Drafting   As you draft, answer the questions you identified in your prewriting. Follow a logical order, focusing on the questions that you find most important.

Revising   Reread your essay, marking each comparison you have made, and check to make sure you have quoted sufficient support from the poems.

W̷G̷ Prentice Hall Writing and Grammar Connection: Diamond Level, Chapter 9, Section 2

Extension Activities

Listening and Speaking With a partner, conduct research to find paintings or photographs that echo the situation, events, mood, or images of Vénus Khoury-Ghata's poems. Choose a series of strong images, and then incorporate them into an **illustrated reading** of the poems. Use these tips:

- Consider various presentation methods, such as projecting slides or hanging posters.
- Practice the timing of your reading, coordinating the display of images with the text.
- Present your reading to the class. Afterward, explain your choices of images.

[Group Activity]

Research and Technology Even in the contemporary world, a writer's attempts to tell the truth or express an opinion can lead to a prison sentence, or worse. Conduct research on another writer who, like Hikmet, has been imprisoned or exiled for his or her work. Compose a persuasive **letter to the world,** arguing that the author's rights be restored. Use stirring language and the specific details you find in researching the case.

 **Take It to the Net** PHSchool.com

Go online for an additional research activity using the Internet.

Prepare to Read

Prayer to Masks ◆ Season

Léopold Sédar Senghor
(1906–2001)

Poets are often thought to live dreamy, impractical lives, but Léopold Sédar Senghor (lā ô pôld´ sā där´ sän gôr´) is a clear exception. One of the greatest African poets writing in French, he also served as president of the West African nation of Senegal from its independence in 1960 until his retirement at the end of 1980.

Studying Abroad Senghor was born in the small village of Joal on the coast of Senegal, a predominantly Muslim country. In 1928, he traveled to France and studied literature at the Sorbonne, France's equivalent to Harvard.

Returning to the Past During his student years, Senghor and other young black writers launched the Negritude Movement, aimed at promoting traditional African cultural values in literature. At the same time, Senghor strongly believed that black literature in French was possible and that by writing in French, he could reach a large audience. He looked to the success of Harlem Renaissance writers such as Langston Hughes, who wedded African consciousness with English literary forms.

Traditions United After graduating from the Sorbonne, Senghor taught in France until World War II, when he joined the French army. In 1940, he was captured by the Germans and held prisoner for two years. During this decade, Senghor wrote his first two books of poetry, *Chants d'ombre* (1945; *Shadow Songs)* and *Hosties noires* (1948; *Black Hosts).* In 1948, Senghor also published a ground-breaking anthology of Caribbean and African poetry. He was elected in 1983 to the Académie Française, the first black member since this prestigious literary institution's founding in 1635.

Wole Soyinka
(b. 1934)

Travel sometimes helps people rediscover the value of what they have left behind. Wole Soyinka (wō´ lā shô yiŋ´ kə), perhaps Nigeria's finest contemporary dramatist, studied and worked in England for a time. When he returned to Nigeria in 1960, he was ready to begin a literary campaign in celebration of traditional African culture.

Mining His Heritage Soyinka belongs to the Yoruba people of Nigeria. He has long argued for the value of traditional African culture in solving the problems of post-colonial Africa. Many of his plays, including *The Swamp Dwellers* (performed 1958), depict the conflict between Yoruba and European values. Yoruba proverbs, dance, and music feature prominently in his plays.

Trouble at Home In 1966, a group of northern Nigerians seized power and divided Nigeria into twelve states. The eastern region rebelled, forming the Republic of Biafra. Civil war followed, causing widespread famine and destruction. The war ended in 1970 with the surrender of Biafra.

Speaking Up In 1967, Soyinka was imprisoned because of his outspoken criticism of the impending civil war. He recorded his two-year prison experience in *Poems from Prison* (1969) and in a memoir, *The Man Died* (1972). Many of his later plays, including *A Play of Giants* (1984), are satires decrying the succession of military regimes that have ruled Nigeria.

Soyinka is truly an African writer, one whose work is immersed both in traditional West African culture and in contemporary West African politics. In 1986, he became the first African to receive the Nobel Prize in Literature.

Preview

Connecting to the Literature

You can call a rainy Saturday a drag. Or you can call it an opportunity—your chance to bake a cake, say. What you call a thing can affect how you see it. These poets call the past and future of Africa by hopeful new names.

Literary Analysis

Rhetorical Devices

Poets, like persuasive speakers, use rhetorical devices, patterns of words and ideas that create emphasis. Rhetorical devices include the following:

- **repetition,** the repeating of words or sentence patterns
- **elaboration,** the addition of details that extend a key idea
- **paradox,** a self-contradictory idea that reveals a deeper truth

Soyinka uses all three of these devices in the opening lines of "Season":

> Rust is ripeness, rust, / and the wilted corn-plume

He repeats the word *rust*, emphasizing the decline of plants in autumn. He elaborates by joining "wilted corn-plume" to "rust." In addition, he uses a paradox, setting decay equal to ripeness to suggest that an ending is a beginning. As you read, note the use and impact of rhetorical devices.

Comparing Literary Works

Poets and other writers may use rhetorical devices so they can freshly imagine a situation. For instance, Senghor confronts a situation in which African culture seems secondary to European culture. Throughout "A Prayer to Masks," he uses rhetorical devices to affirm the central importance of African culture. As you read, compare the situations confronted by the speakers and the writers' uses of rhetorical devices.

Reading Strategy

Applying Literary Background Information

To **apply literary background information,** use biographical and historical information to help you interpret details in a writer's work. Review the information in the author biographies on page 1340 and in the Background note on page 1342. As you read, apply the information in these features to the poems, using a chart like the one shown.

Vocabulary Development

despotism (des′ pət iz′ əm) *n.* tyranny; system of government in which the ruler has absolute power (p. 1342)

pitiable (pit′ ē ə bəl) *adj.* inspiring pity (may be used scornfully) (p. 1342)

immobile (i mō′ bəl) *adj.* not moving; unchanging (p. 1343)

laden (lād′'n) *adj.* loaded (p. 1344)

Detail in Work

The speaker's face is an "image" of traditional African masks.

Literary Background

Senghor, educated in Europe, founded the Negritude Movement, promoting black culture.

Interpretation

Senghor asserts his African identity—his resemblance to the masks—over his European education.

Prayer to Masks

Léopold Sédar Senghor
translated by Gerald Moore
and Ulli Beier

Background

Begun by Léopold Sédar Senghor and other French-speaking black students in Paris in 1932, the Negritude Movement was originally a response to the French government policy toward native cultures. In their colonies, the French tried to assimilate, or absorb, Africans into French culture. Negritude was a bold assertion that African culture was as valuable as French culture. As it spread, the Negritude Movement helped revitalize pride in African cultural identity among blacks worldwide.

Black mask, red mask, you black and white masks,
Rectangular masks through whom the spirit breathes,
I greet you in silence!
And you too, my lionheaded ancestor.
5   You guard this place, that is closed to any feminine laughter, to
    any mortal smile.
You purify the air of eternity, here where I breathe the air of my
    fathers.
Masks of markless faces, free from dimples and wrinkles,
You have composed this image, this my face that bends over the
    altar of white paper.
In the name of your image, listen to me!
10 Now while the Africa of <u>despotism</u> is dying—it is the agony of a
    <u>pitiable</u> princess

Like that of Europe to whom she is connected through the navel[1]—
Now fix your <u>immobile</u> eyes upon your children who have been
    called
And who sacrifice their lives like the poor man his last garment
So that hereafter we may cry "here" at the rebirth of the world
    being the leaven[2] that the white flour needs.

15 For who else would teach rhythm to the world that has died of
    machines and cannons?
For who else should ejaculate the cry of joy, that arouses the dead
    and the wise in a new dawn?
Say, who else could return the memory of life to men with a
    torn hope?
They call us cotton heads, and coffee men, and oily men,
They call us men of death.

20 But we are the men of the dance whose feet only gain power when
    they beat the hard soil.

---

1. **navel** (nā′ vəl) *n.* scar marking the place where the umbilical cord, which supplies oxygen and nutrients from the mother, attached the baby to its mother while in the womb.
2. **leaven** (lev′ ən) *n.* small piece of fermenting dough that is added to a larger batch of dough to make it rise.

immobile (i mō′ bəl) *adj.*
not moving; unchanging

Reading Strategy
Applying Literary Background Information In lines 18–19, who are "they"?

Review and Assess

Thinking About the Selection

1. **Respond:** If you, like the speaker of "Masks," were to address a symbol of your ancestors, what might you say?

2. **(a) Recall:** Name three things that the speaker calls on in the opening of the poem. **(b) Interpret:** What is the mood of the place where these things are located? Give details in support.

3. **(a) Recall:** In line 8, over what does the speaker bend? **(b) Hypothesize:** Where might he be writing? Explain.

4. **(a) Recall:** According to the speaker, what is the relationship between the masks and the speaker's own face? **(b) Interpret:** What does this relationship suggest about his connection to the values and traditions of his ancestors? Explain.

5. **(a) Analyze:** Explain the difference between the first part of the poem and lines 9–14. **(b) Interpret:** What event does the speaker call on the masks to witness?

6. **(a) Infer:** According to the speaker, what values might African culture teach Europeans? Support your answer with details from the poem. **(b) Draw Conclusions:** Explain the sort of "rebirth of the world" that the speaker envisions.

7. **Apply:** What values do you think American culture has adapted from African culture?

Season Wole Soyinka

Rust is ripeness, rust,
And the wilted corn-plume;
Pollen is mating-time when swallows
Weave a dance
5   Of feathered arrows
Thread corn-stalks in winged
Streaks of light. And, we loved to hear
Spliced phrases of the wind, to hear
Rasps[1] in the field, where corn-leaves
10 Pierce like bamboo slivers.

Now, garnerers[2] we
Awaiting rust on tassels, draw
Long shadows from the dusk, wreathe
Dry thatch in wood-smoke. Laden stalks
15 Ride the germ's[3] decay—we await
The promise of the rust.

1. **rasps** (rasps) *n.* rough, grating tones (usually a verb).
2. **garnerers** (gär´ nər ərz) *n.* harvesters; gatherers.
3. **germ's** *n.* here, of a seed or bud.

Literary Analysis
Rhetorical Devices In what way does the speaker elaborate on the description of the swallows?

laden (lād´ 'n) *adj.* loaded

Review and Assess

Thinking About the Selection

1. **Respond:** Describe your own associations with autumn.
2. **(a) Recall:** Identify two signs of ripeness in the poem.
   (b) Intepret: In what way does harvest time combine decay and ripeness?
3. **(a) Recall:** What "time" does pollen symbolize? **(b) Infer:** What is the relationship between this season and the time of ripeness?
4. **(a) Recall:** Identify two images used to describe the flight of sparrows. **(b) Compare:** In what way do these images contrast with the images of shadows and smoke in the second stanza?
5. **(a) Classify:** Divide the images in lines 3–10 between those that involve joining together and those that involve cutting.
   (b) Compare: Contrast these activities with those in the second stanza.
6. **(a) Infer:** What is the literal "promise of the rust" for which the harvesters wait? **(b) Connect:** In what larger sense might a society look for hope in a time of "rust"?

Review and Assess

Literary Analysis

Rhetorical Devices

1. (a) Identify two uses of the **rhetorical device** of word **repetition** in "Prayer to Masks." (b) Identify one instance in which a sentence pattern is repeated. (c) Explain what effect each instance of repetition has on the impact of the poem.

2. (a) Find an instance of **elaboration** in "Prayer to Masks." (b) Explain why the poem might have lacked energy if the poet had not added details to his main idea.

3. Interpret the **paradox** in the last two lines of "Season," explaining why the idea seems like a self-contradiction but actually expresses a truth.

Comparing Literary Works

4. Using a chart like the one shown, compare the ways in which each of the two poems imaginatively transforms a situation or problem.

Poem	Old Situation	New Interpretation	Rhetorical Devices Used

5. Compare the poets' attitudes toward the past and the future, given their present situation.

Reading Strategy

Applying Literary Background Information

6. Use your knowledge of the Negritude Movement to interpret two ideas or images in "Prayer to Masks."

7. Explain why "Season" might be read as a comment on Nigeria's history—from its independence from Britain in 1960, to its civil war in 1967, to the periods of dictatorship that followed. In your answer, give details from the poem.

Extend Understanding

8. **Psychology Connection:** Give an example from your own experience of a mask—a role or an image—with which people identify.

Integrate Language Skills

Vocabulary Development Lesson

Word Analysis: Greek suffix *-ism*

The Greek suffix *-ism* often means "the doctrine, belief, or practice of." The word *despotism* means "the practice of absolute rule." In Senghor's poem, the word refers specifically to the absolute power of European powers over regions of Africa during the colonial period.

Using the meaning of the suffix, define each of the following words. Check your definitions using a dictionary.

1. minimalism
2. pacifism
3. feminism
4. athleticism
5. pietism

Concept Development: Synonyms

For each of the numbered vocabulary words below, write the letter of the correct synonym, or word closest to it in meaning.

1. despotism   a. paralyzed
2. pitiable   b. burdened
3. immobile   c. dictatorship
4. laden   d. helpless

Spelling Strategy

When a word ends in a consonant and a *y*, change the *y* to *i* before adding most suffixes. For example, *pity* becomes *pitiable*. Add the suffix in parentheses to each of the following words.

1. amplify (*-er*)   2. defy (*-ant*)   3. verify (*-able*)

Grammar and Style Lesson

Correct Use of *who* and *whom*

The correct use of *who* and *whom* helps a poet refer clearly to people or groups of people. **Who,** like *he* or *she,* is used as a subject or a subject complement. **Whom,** like *him* or *her,* is used as an object or an object of a preposition. Study these examples:

> **Subject:** Now fix your immobile eyes upon your children <u>who</u> have been called / And <u>who</u> sacrifice their lives. . . .
> [*Who* is the subject of the verbs *have been called* and *sacrifice*.]

> **Object:** Rectangular masks through <u>whom</u> the spirit breathes, / I greet you in silence! [*Whom* is the object of the preposition *through*.]

Practice Identify which word, *who* or *whom*, correctly completes each sentence below.

1. The Africans (who, whom) Europeans educated were caught between cultures.
2. The Europeans (who, whom) educated them rarely valued African culture.
3. The writers (who, whom) formed the Negritude Movement celebrated black culture.
4. Some were inspired by Langston Hughes, for (who, whom) both European and African traditions were important.
5. For a writer such as Soyinka, (who, whom) speaks out for both tradition and reform, the future is as important as the past.

Writing Application Write a poem about the past, using both *who* and *whom* correctly twice.

WG Prentice Hall Writing and Grammar Connection: Diamond Level, Chapter 22, Section 2

Writing Lesson

Descriptive Essay

As "Prayer to Masks" suggests, masks have important symbolic value in African culture, as they do in many other societies around the world. Conduct research on the use of masks in several cultures. Then, write an essay describing one of the masks you have studied. In your essay, include enough specific details to help readers visualize the mask and imagine the feelings that it projects.

Prewriting   Begin by listing details about the mask, using a chart like the one shown.

Model: Listing Details by Category

Expression	Colors	Materials	Textures	Used for . . .

Drafting   In your first paragraph, use a striking detail to introduce the mask and identify its culture of origin. As you draft the body of your essay, include descriptive details from among those you listed in your prewriting.

Revising   Reread your essay, circling any passages that seem vague or general. Consider adding descriptive details to strengthen these passages.

W͟G͟ *Prentice Hall Writing and Grammar Connection: Diamond Level, Chapter 6, Section 2*

Extension Activities

Listening and Speaking Divide a group into two sides, and hold a **debate** on this issue: Did European colonialism in Africa have more negative or more positive consequences? To prepare, research specific historical examples of European colonies in Africa. Choose evidence that supports your persuasive purpose. In your arguments, include persuasive devices of these types:

- appeals to logic, such as cause-and-effect arguments
- appeals to ethics, such as arguments about fairness and morality
- charged language appealing to emotions

Hold your debate before the class.
[Group Activity]

Research and Technology Conduct research on the Negritude Movement, the authors associated with it, and the works that it fostered. Note the influence of the movement in the United States and in the Caribbean, as well as in Africa. Then, compile an **annotated bibliography** of works influenced by the movement. For each work you list, include publication information, a brief description of the work, and a summary of its significance to the movement.

 **Take It to the Net** PHSchool.com

Go online for an additional research activity using the Internet.

Prepare to Read

Comrades ◆ Marriage Is a Private Affair

Nadine Gordimer (b. 1923)

Most of Nadine Gordimer's fiction is set in her native country of South Africa. During the years of apartheid—South Africa's official policy of racial segregation that ended in 1990—Gordimer wrote passionately in favor of racial justice. In her fiction, she demonstrates how institutionalized racism damages everyone in a society. It harms the oppressed by denying their rights to health, education, economic security, and political determination; it harms the oppressors by distorting their deepest human feelings.

Early Bloomer Born in Springs, South Africa, Gordimer grew up in a profoundly segregated society. Like most other white middle-class children in South Africa at the time, she attended private, all-white schools and lived in all-white neighborhoods. Her mother believed her daughter had a delicate constitution and often kept her home. As a result, Gordimer turned to writing to occupy herself. Her literary gifts bore fruit, and by the time she was fifteen years old, Gordimer was publishing regularly. As she grew older and became more aware of her country's problems, she applied her talents to describing the damage suffered by all South Africans under apartheid.

International Stardom Today, Gordimer is one of the most successful writers in the world. Her many literary works include *The Soft Voice of the Serpent* (1952), *Not for Publication* (1965), *The Conservationist* (1974), *The Essential Gesture: Writing, Politics, and Place* (1988), *Jump and Other Stories* (1991), and *The House Gun* (1998). In 1991, Gordimer added the Nobel Prize in Literature to her long list of honors.

Chinua Achebe (b. 1930)

During the Nigerian civil war, which lasted from 1967 to 1970, Chinua Achebe (chin wä´ ə cheb´ ā) survived the bombing of his house by fleeing for his life, leaving behind an unpublished manuscript. When Achebe eventually returned home, he found one remaining copy, which someone had managed to save. This manuscript—*How the Leopard Got His Claws*, Achebe's parable about Nigeria—was published in 1972.

Living in Two Worlds Achebe was born in the Ibo village of Ogidi, Nigeria. His parents named him Albert, after Prince Albert, the husband of England's Queen Victoria. As a university student, Achebe later abandoned his English name in favor of Chinua, his Ibo name. The duality reflected in Achebe's names permeates his work, which describes the effects of Western customs and values on traditional African society.

Writing in English One legacy of British colonialism in Nigeria is the widespread use of English in education and government. As an educated Nigerian, Achebe writes in English, but he uses Ibo parables, words, and attitudes to convey a distinctly Nigerian sensibility. His keen ear and satiric sensibility have made him one of the most highly esteemed African writers in English.

A Landmark Work Achebe's signature work, the novel *Things Fall Apart*, was published to international acclaim in 1958. Many critics consider the book to be the first major work of fiction to emerge from Africa. Both a critical and popular success, the novel has been translated into more than fifty languages and has exerted a major influence on other African writers.

Preview

Connecting to the Literature

Most people who have known only peace and comfort develop a view of reality quite different from that of those who have known war and suffering. In these selections, characters struggle to bridge their differences.

Literary Analysis

Atmosphere

In literature, **atmosphere** refers to the emotional quality of the world the author creates. Atmosphere arises from descriptive details, setting, or plot and often mirrors the emotions of the characters themselves. In "Marriage Is a Private Affair," for example, descriptions of the weather reflect the pain and confusion in an old man's heart:

> He leaned against a window and looked out. The sky was overcast with heavy black clouds and a high wind began to blow. . . .

As you read these stories, look for descriptive details that reflect the characters' emotions and create distinctive atmospheres.

Comparing Literary Works

Both of these selections explore the ways in which intense cultural tensions can distort the kind feelings and good intentions of well-meaning people. As you read, identify the cultural tensions each story examines. Then, compare the ways in which both stories show that the damage caused by such tensions can be private and subtle but still devastating.

Reading Strategy

Identifying With a Character

You may better appreciate each of these stories if you **identify with a character** who appears in the work. To do so, imagine yourself in the character's situation. Think about what you would do and feel. As you read, use a chart like the one shown to explore similarities between yourself and a key character.

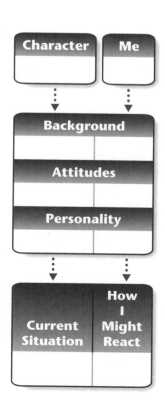

Vocabulary Development

assent (ə sent´) *n.* expression of agreement (p. 1351)

euphemisms (yōō´ fə miz´ əmz) *n.* words or phrases that are less expressive or direct but considered less distasteful or offensive than others (p. 1353)

furtively (fur´ tiv lē) *adv.* in a sneaky manner, as if to hinder observation (p. 1354)

revelation (rev´ ə lā´ shən) *n.* striking disclosure of something (p. 1354)

disposed (di spōzd´) *adj.* inclined; tending toward (p. 1356)

vehemently (vē´ ə mənt lē) *adv.* forcefully; intensely (p. 1357)

deference (def´ ər əns) *n.* submission to the desires or opinions of another; courteous respect (p. 1359)

perfunctorily (pər fuŋk´ tôr i lē) *adv.* indifferently; with little interest or care (p. 1360)

Comrades

Nadine Gordimer

Background

From 1948 until 1990, the country of South Africa operated under the apartheid system—the government policy that called for strict racial segregation and political and economic discrimination against nonwhites. Many South Africans, both white and black, fought against the apartheid system. While much of the dissent was political and peaceful, the tensions sometimes boiled over into violence. It is against this backdrop of painful political and cultural divisions that this story takes place.

As Mrs. Hattie Telford pressed the electronic gadget that deactivates the alarm device in her car a group of youngsters came up behind her. Black. But no need to be afraid; this was not a city street. This was a non-racial enclave of learning, a place where tended flowerbeds and trees bearing botanical identification plates civilized the wild reminder of campus guards and dogs. The youngsters, like her, were part of the crowd loosening into dispersion after a university conference on People's Education. They were the people to be educated; she was one of the committee of white and black activists (convenient generic for revolutionaries, leftists secular and Christian, fellow-travelers and liberals) up on the platform.

—Comrade . . . — She was settling in the driver's seat when one so slight and slim he seemed a figure in profile came up to her window. He drew courage from the friendly lift of the woman's eyebrows above blue eyes, the tilt of her freckled white face: —Comrade, are you going to town?—

No, she was going in the opposite direction, home . . . but quickly, in the spirit of the hall where these young people had been somewhere, somehow present with her (ah no, she with them) stamping and singing Freedom songs, she would take them to the bus station their spokesman named. —Climb aboard!—

The others got in the back, the spokesman beside her. She saw the nervous white of his eyes as he glanced at and away from her. She searched for talk to set them at ease. Questions, of course. Older people always start with questioning young ones. Did they come from Soweto?

They came from Harrismith, Phoneng Location.

Literary Analysis
Atmosphere In the first paragraph, which descriptive details contribute to an atmosphere of tension?

Reading Strategy
Identifying With a Character Can you identify with Mrs. Telford's mixed feelings as she agrees to take the boys to town? Why or why not?

She made the calculation: about two hundred kilometers distant. How did they get here? Who told them about the conference?

—We are Youth Congress in Phoneng.—

A delegation. They had come by bus; one of the groups and stragglers who kept arriving long after the conference had started. They had missed, then, the free lunch?

At the back, no one seemed even to be breathing. The spokesman must have had some silent communication with them, some obligation to speak for them created by the journey or by other shared experience in the mysterious bonds of the young—these young. —We are hungry.— And from the back seats was drawn an <u>assent</u> like the suction of air in a compressing silence.

She was silent in response, for the beat of a breath or two. These large gatherings both excited and left her overexposed, open and vulnerable to the rub and twitch of the mass shuffling across rows of seats and loping up the aisles, babies' fudge-brown soft legs waving as their napkins are changed on mothers' laps, little girls with plaited loops on their heads listening like old crones, heavy women swaying to chants, men with fierce, unreadably black faces breaking into harmony tender and deep as they sing to God for his protection of Umkhonto weSizwe,

Reading Strategy
Identifying With a Character What do you think the boys are feeling as they sit in the back of Mrs. Telford's car?
assent (ə sent´) *n.* expression of agreement

✔**Reading Check**
What gathering have Mrs. Telford and the group of boys just attended?

▲ **Critical Viewing** In what ways do you think this scene of an anti-apartheid demonstration might resemble the event attended by Mrs. Telford and the students? Explain. **[Connect]**

as people on both sides have always, everywhere, claimed divine protection for their soldiers, their wars. At the end of a day like this she wanted a drink, she wanted the depraved luxury of solitude and quiet in which she would be restored (enriched, oh yes! by the day) to the familiar limits of her own being.

Hungry. Not for iced whiskey and feet up. It seemed she had scarcely hesitated: —Look. I live nearby, come back to my house and have something to eat. Then I'll run you into town.—

—That will be very nice. We can be glad for that.— And at the back the tight vacuum relaxed.

They followed her in through the gate, shrinking away from the dog—she assured them he was harmless but he was large, with a fancy collar by which she held him. She trooped them in through the kitchen because that was the way she always entered her house, something she would not have done if they had been adult, her black friends whose sophistication might lead them to believe the choice of entrance was an unthinking historical slight. As she was going to feed them, she took them not into her living-room with its sofas and flowers but into her dining-room, so that they could sit at table right away. It was a room in confident taste that could afford to be spare: bare floorboards, matching golden wooden ceiling, antique brass chandelier, reed blinds instead of stuffy curtains. An African wooden sculpture represented a lion marvelously released from its matrix in the grain of a Mukwa tree-trunk. She pulled up the chairs and left the four young men while she went back to the kitchen to make coffee and see what there was in the refrigerator for sandwiches. They had greeted the maid, in the language she and they shared, on their way through the kitchen, but when the maid and the lady of the house had finished preparing cold meat and bread, and the coffee was ready, she suddenly did not want them to see that the maid waited on her. She herself carried the heavy tray into the dining-room.

They are sitting round the table, silent, and there is no impression that they stopped an undertone exchange when they heard her approaching. She doles out plates, cups. They stare at the food but their eyes seem focused on something she can't see; something that overwhelms. She urges them—Just cold meat, I'm afraid, but there's chutney[1] if you like it . . . milk everybody? . . . is the coffee too strong, I have a heavy hand, I know. Would anyone like to add some hot water?—

They eat. When she tries to talk to one of the others, he says *Ekskuus?* And she realizes he doesn't understand English, of the white man's languages knows perhaps only a little of that of the Afrikaners in the rural town he comes from. Another gives his name, as if in some delicate acknowledgement of the food. —I'm Shadrack Nsutsha.— She repeats the surname to get it right. But he does not speak again. There

---

1. chutney (chŭt′ nē) *n.* relish or sauce of Indian origin, typically combining sweet and sour ingredients, such as fruit and vinegar, with sugar and spices.

Literary Analysis
Atmosphere Which details contribute to an atmosphere of tension or suspense in Mrs. Telford's house? Explain.

is an urgent exchange of eye-language, and the spokesman holds out the emptied sugar-bowl to her. —Please.— She hurries to the kitchen and brings it back refilled. They need carbohydrate, they are hungry, they are young, they need it, they burn it up. She is distressed at the inadequacy of the meal and then notices the fruit bowl, her big copper fruit bowl, filled with apples and bananas and perhaps there is a peach or two under the grape leaves with which she likes to complete an edible still life. —Have some fruit. Help yourselves.—

They are stacking their plates and cups, not knowing what they are expected to do with them in this room which is a room where apparently people only eat, do not cook, do not sleep. While they finish the bananas and apples (Shadrack Nsutsha had seen the single peach and quickly got there first) she talks to the spokesman, whose name she has asked for: Dumile. —Are you still at school, Dumile?— Of course he is not at school—*they* are not at school; youngsters their age have not been at school for several years, they are the children growing into young men and women for whom school is a battleground, a place of boycotts and demonstrations, the literacy of political rhetoric, the education of revolt against having to live the life their parents live. They have pompous titles of responsibility beyond childhood: he is chairman of his branch of the Youth Congress, he was expelled two years ago—for leading a boycott? Throwing stones at the police? Maybe burning the school down? He calls it all—quietly, abstractly, doesn't know many ordinary, concrete words but knows these <u>euphemisms</u>— "political activity." No school for two years? No. —So what have you been able to do with yourself, all that time?—

She isn't giving him a chance to eat his apple. He swallows a large bite, shaking his head on its thin, little-boy neck. —I was inside. Detained from this June for six months.—

She looks round the others. —And you?—

Shadrack seems to nod slightly. The other two look at her. She should know, she should have known, it's a common enough answer from youths like them, their color. They're not going to be saying they've been selected for the 1st Eleven at cricket or that they're off on a student tour to Europe in the school holidays.

The spokesman, Dumile, tells her he wants to study by correspondence, "get his matric" that he was preparing for two years ago; two years ago when he was still a child, when he didn't have the hair that is now appearing on his face, making him a man, taking away the childhood. In the hesitations, the silences of the table, where there is nervously spilt coffee among plates of banana skins, there grows the certainty that he will never get the papers filled in for the correspondence college, he will never get the two years back. She looks at them all and cannot believe what she knows: that they, suddenly here in her house, will carry the AK-47s[2] they only sing about, now, miming death as they sing. They will have a career of wiring explosives to the under-

---

2. **AK-47s** military assault rifles.

Reading Strategy
Identifying With a Character With whom do you identify more strongly— the students or Mrs. Telford? Explain.

euphemisms (yōō′ fə miz′ əmz) *n.* words or phrases that are less expressive or direct but considered less distasteful or offensive than others

✓**Reading Check**
For how long have the boys not attended school?

sides of vehicles, they will go away and come back through the bush to dig holes not to plant trees to shade home, but to plant land-mines. She can see they have been terribly harmed but cannot believe they could harm. They are wiping their fruit-sticky hands <u>furtively</u> palm against palm.

She breaks the silence; says something, anything.

—How d'you like my lion? Isn't he beautiful? He's made by a Zimbabwean artist, I think the name's Dube.—

But the foolish interruption becomes <u>revelation</u>. Dumile, in his gaze—distant, lingering, speechless this time—reveals what has overwhelmed them. In this room, the space, the expensive antique chandelier, the consciously simple choice of reed blinds, the carved lion: all are on the same level of impact, phenomena undifferentiated, undecipherable. Only the food that fed their hunger was real.

furtively (fur′ tiv lē) *adv.* in a sneaky manner, as if to hinder observation

revelation (rev′ ə lā′ shən) *n.* striking disclosure of something

Review and Assess

Thinking About the Selection

1. **Respond:** As you read the story, what outcome did you hope for?

2. **(a) Recall:** When the students approach Mrs. Telford, what event has just ended? **(b) Distinguish:** What different roles did Mrs. Telford and the students play at the event? **(c) Infer:** What does her participation in the event reveal about Mrs. Telford's politics?

3. **(a) Recall:** When the student first approaches Mrs. Telford in her car, which details in her appearance give him courage? **(b) Generalize:** What do these details suggest about her character? Explain. **(c) Analyze:** Why do you think the student needs courage to speak with Mrs. Telford?

4. **(a) Recall:** Why does Mrs. Telford take the students to her house instead of to town? **(b) Interpret:** What emotion or idea might the students' physical hunger represent? Explain.

5. **(a) Classify:** Which details in the description of Mrs. Telford's home suggest her affluence? **(b) Infer:** In what ways does Mrs. Telford's home stand in sharp contrast to the environment in which the students live? **(c) Support:** Which details in the text support your answer? Explain.

6. **(a) Deduce:** Why do the boys no longer attend school? **(b) Infer:** What realization does Mrs. Telford have about the students' futures? **(c) Take a Position:** Do you think the harm the boys have suffered justifies any harm they will do in the future? Explain.

7. **Synthesize:** Why might shared political struggles involve groups with otherwise very different backgrounds and beliefs?

Marriage Is a Private Affair

Chinua Achebe

Background

The main characters in this story belong to two different Nigerian ethnic groups, the Ibo (ē´ bō´) (also called the Igbo) and the Ibibio (ib´ ə bē´ ō´). The Ibo are the largest ethnic group in southeastern Nigeria and one of the largest in the nation. During Britain's colonial rule of Nigeria, many Ibo were educated in British missionary schools, and today most of the Ibo population is Christian. The Ibo strongly supported the independence of southeastern Nigeria during the civil war of 1967–1970, and as a result, they earned the resentment of powerful Nigerian ethnic groups in the north. The Ibibio, also of southeastern Nigeria, are a smaller but nevertheless powerful group. Conflict between traditional Ibo values and those of modern life are at the center of this story.

"Have you written to your dad yet?" asked Nene[1] one afternoon as she sat with Nnaemeka[2] in her room at 16 Kasanga Street, Lagos.[3]

"No. I've been thinking about it. I think it's better to tell him when I get home on leave!"

"But why? Your leave is such a long way off yet—six whole weeks. He should be let into our happiness now."

Nnaemeka was silent for a while, and then began very slowly as if he groped for his words: "I wish I were sure it would be happiness to him."

"Of course it must," replied Nene, a little surprised. "Why shouldn't it?"

"You have lived in Lagos all your life, and you know very little about people in remote parts of the country."

---

1. **Nene** (nā´ nā´)
2. **Nnaemeka** ('n nē´ mə kə)
3. **Lagos** (lā´ gäs´) former capital city of Nigeria.

Reading Check

What has Nnaemaka been thinking about doing?

"That's what you always say. But I don't believe anybody will be so unlike other people that they will be unhappy when their sons are engaged to marry."

"Yes. They are most unhappy if the engagement is not arranged by them. In our case it's worse—you are not even an Ibo."

This was said so seriously and so bluntly that Nene could not find speech immediately. In the cosmopolitan atmosphere of the city it had always seemed to her something of a joke that a person's tribe could determine whom he married.

At last she said, "You don't really mean that he will object to your marrying me simply on that account? I had always thought you Ibos were kindly <u>disposed</u> to other people."

"So we are. But when it comes to marriage, well, it's not quite so simple. And this," he added, "is not peculiar to the Ibos. If your father were alive and lived in the heart of Ibibio-land he would be exactly like my father."

"I don't know. But anyway, as your father is so fond of you, I'm sure he will forgive you soon enough. Come on then, be a good boy and send him a nice lovely letter . . ."

"It would not be wise to break the news to him by writing. A letter will bring it upon him with a shock. I'm quite sure about that."

"All right, honey, suit yourself. You know your father."

As Nnaemeka walked home that evening he turned over in his mind the different ways of overcoming his father's opposition, especially now that he had gone and found a girl for him. He had thought of showing his letter to Nene but decided on second thoughts not to, at least for the moment. He read it again when he got home and couldn't help smiling to himself. He remembered Ugoye[4] quite well, an Amazon[5] of a girl who used to beat up all the boys, himself included, on the way to the stream, a complete dunce at school.

I have found a girl who will suit you admirably—Ugoye Nweke,[6] the eldest daughter of our neighbor, Jacob Nweke. She has a proper Christian upbringing. When she stopped schooling some years ago her father (a man of sound judgment) sent her to live in the house of a pastor where she has received all the training a wife could need. Her Sunday School teacher has told me that she reads her Bible very fluently. I hope we shall begin negotiations when you come home in December.

On the second evening of his return from Lagos Nnaemeka sat with his father under a cassia tree. This was the old man's retreat where he went to read his Bible when the parching December sun had set and a fresh, reviving wind blew on the leaves.

"Father," began Nnaemeka suddenly, "I have come to ask forgiveness."

"Forgiveness? For what, my son?" he asked in amazement.

"It's about this marriage question."

---

4. **Ugoye** (yōō gō′ yə)
5. **Amazon** (am′ ə zän) large, strong, masculine woman. In Greek mythology, the Amazons were a race of female warriors.
6. **Nweke** (′n wā′ kā)

Reading Strategy
Identifying With a Character With which character do you identify most—the one who wants to share the news or the one who fears doing so?

disposed (di spōzd′) *adj.* inclined; tending toward

Critical Viewing ▶
Do you think this painting captures the characters and mood of this story? Why or why not? **[Generalize]**

"Which marriage question?"

"I can't—we must—I mean it is impossible for me to marry Nweke's daughter."

"Impossible? Why?" asked his father.

"I don't love her."

"Nobody said you did. Why should you?" he asked.

"Marriage today is different . . ."

"Look here, my son," interrupted his father, "nothing is different. What one looks for in a wife are a good character and a Christian background."

Nnaemeka saw there was no hope along the present line of argument.

"Moreover," he said, "I am engaged to marry another girl who has all of Ugoye's good qualities, and who . . ."

His father did not believe his ears. "What did you say?" he asked slowly and disconcertingly.

"She is a good Christian," his son went on, "and a teacher in a Girls' School in Lagos."

"Teacher, did you say? If you consider that a qualification for a good wife I should like to point out to you, Emeka, that no Christian woman should teach. St. Paul in his letter to the Corinthians[7] says that women should keep silence." He rose slowly from his seat and paced forwards and backwards. This was his pet subject, and he condemned <u>vehemently</u> those church leaders who encouraged women to teach in their

---

7. **St. Paul . . . Corinthians** reference to the Bible's New Testament (1 Corinthians 14:34), in which Paul writes, "Let your women keep silent in the churches."

Literary Analysis
Atmosphere What atmosphere do Nnaemeka's disturbed emotions create?

vehemently (vē´ ə mənt lē) *adv.* forcefully; intensely

✓**Reading Check**

What arrangement has Nnaemeka's father made for his son's marriage?

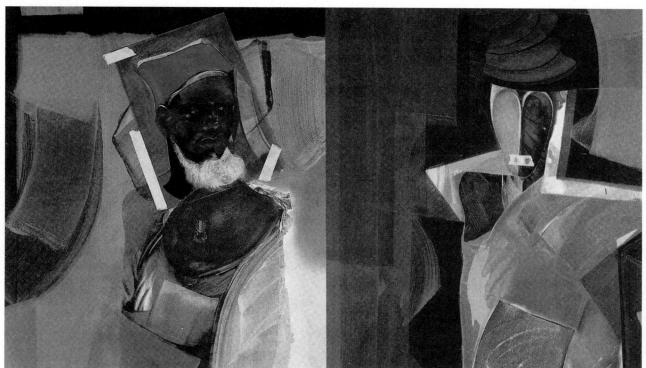

The Old African, The Medal, and the Statue, 1988, Fodé Camara, Museum of African American Art

schools. After he had spent his emotion on a long homily[8] he at last came back to his son's engagement, in a seemingly milder tone.

"Whose daughter is she, anyway?"

"She is Nene Atang."

"What!" All the mildness was gone again. "Did you say Neneataga, what does that mean?"

"Nene Atang from Calabar.[9] She is the only girl I can marry." This was a very rash reply and Nnaemeka expected the storm to burst. But it did not. His father merely walked away into his room. This was most unexpected and perplexed Nnaemeka. His father's silence was infinitely more menacing than a flood of threatening speech. That night the old man did not eat.

When he sent for Nnaemeka a day later he applied all possible ways of dissuasion. But the young man's heart was hardened, and his father eventually gave him up as lost.

"I owe it to you, my son, as a duty to show you what is right and what is wrong. Whoever put this idea into your head might as well have cut your throat. It is Satan's work." He waved his son away.

"You will change your mind, Father, when you know Nene."

"I shall never see her," was the reply. From that night the father scarcely spoke to his son. He did not, however, cease hoping that he would realize how serious was the danger he was heading for. Day and night he put him in his prayers.

Nnaemeka, for his own part, was very deeply affected by his father's grief. But he kept hoping that it would pass away. If it had occurred to him that never in the history of his people had a man married a woman who spoke a different tongue, he might have been less optimistic. "It has never been heard," was the verdict of an old man speaking a few weeks later. In that short sentence he spoke for all of his people. This man had come with others to commiserate with Okeke[10] when news went round about his son's behavior. By that time the son had gone back to Lagos.

"It has never been heard," said the old man again with a sad shake of his head.

"What did Our Lord say?" asked another gentleman. "Sons shall rise against their Fathers; it is there in the Holy Book."

"It is the beginning of the end," said another.

The discussion thus tending to become theological, Madubogwu, a highly practical man, brought it down once more to the ordinary level.

"Have you thought of consulting a native doctor about your son?" he asked Nnaemeka's father.

"He isn't sick," was the reply.

"What is he then? The boy's mind is diseased and only a good

Themes in World Literature

Arranged Marriages

Until the twentieth century, arranged marriages were common in almost all cultures of the world. It is no surprise, then, that this nuptial custom has been both chronicled and critiqued by countless writers throughout history. The author of the Old Testament book of Genesis, for example, describes the arranged marriage between Isaac, son of Abraham, and Rebekah. Two millennia later, Shakespeare treats the same theme—but far less objectively—in his tragedy *Romeo and Juliet* (1595). More recently, writers from India and other parts of Asia have tackled this difficult subject, most notably Chitra Divakaruni in her collection of short stories *Arranged Marriage* (1995). The theme also appears in Yasunari Kawabata's short story "The Jay" (p. 1382).

Literary Analysis
Atmosphere In what ways does this paragraph intensify the sense of Nnaemeka's isolation?

---

8. homily (häm´ ə lē) *n.* religious speech.
9. Calabar (kal´ ə bär) seaport in southeast Nigeria.
10. Okeke (o kā´ kā)

herbalist can bring him back to his right senses. The medicine he requires is *Amalile*, the same that women apply with success to recapture their husbands' straying affection."

"Madubogwu is right," said another gentleman. "This thing calls for medicine."

"I shall not call in a native doctor." Nnaemeka's father was known to be obstinately ahead of his more superstitious neighbors in these matters. "I will not be another Mrs. Ochuba. If my son wants to kill himself let him do it with his own hands. It is not for me to help him."

"But it was her fault," said Madubogwu. "She ought to have gone to an honest herbalist. She was a clever woman, nevertheless."

"She was a wicked murderess," said Jonathan who rarely argued with his neighbors because, he often said, they were incapable of reasoning. "The medicine was prepared for her husband, it was his name they called in its preparation and I am sure it would have been perfectly beneficial to him. It was wicked to put it into the herbalist's food, and say you were only trying it out."

Six months later, Nnaemeka was showing his young wife a short letter from his father:

> *It amazes me that you could be so unfeeling as to send me your wedding picture. I would have sent it back. But on further thought I decided just to cut off your wife and send it back to you because I have nothing to do with her. How I wish that I had nothing to do with you either.*

When Nene read through this letter and looked at the mutilated picture her eyes filled with tears, and she began to sob.

"Don't cry, my darling," said her husband. "He is essentially good-natured and will one day look more kindly on our marriage." But years passed and that one day did not come.

For eight years, Okeke would have nothing to do with his son, Nnaemeka. Only three times (when Nnaemeka asked to come home and spend his leave) did he write to him.

"I can't have you in my house," he replied on one occasion. "It can be of no interest to me where or how you spend your leave—or your life, for that matter."

The prejudice against Nnaemeka's marriage was not confined to his little village. In Lagos, especially among his people who worked there, it showed itself in a different way. Their women, when they met at their village meeting, were not hostile to Nene. Rather, they paid her such excessive <u>deference</u> as to make her feel she was not one of them. But as time went on, Nene gradually broke through some of this prejudice and even began to make friends among them. Slowly and grudgingly they began to admit that she kept her home much better than most of them.

The story eventually got to the little village in the heart of the Ibo country that Nnaemeka and his young wife were a most happy couple. But his father was one of the few people who knew nothing about this.

Literary Analysis
Atmosphere How does the discussion between the old men show that Nnaemeka's conflict with his father is part of a much larger societal conflict?

Reading Strategy
Identifying With a Character Can you identify with Nene's reaction to the letter and photograph? Explain.

deference (def´ ər əns) *n.* submission to the desires or opinions of another; courteous respect

Reading Check
For how long does Okeke avoid all contact with his son?

He always displayed so much temper whenever his son's name was mentioned that everyone avoided it in his presence. By a tremendous effort of will he had succeeded in pushing his son to the back of his mind. The strain had nearly killed him but he had persevered, and won.

Then one day he received a letter from Nene, and in spite of himself he began to glance through it <u>perfunctorily</u> until all of a sudden the expression on his face changed and he began to read more carefully.

> . . . *Our two sons, from the day they learnt that they have a grand-father, have insisted on being taken to him. I find it impossible to tell them that you will not see them. I implore you to allow Nnaemeka to bring them home for a short time during his leave next month. I shall remain here in Lagos . . .*

The old man at once felt the resolution he had built up over so many years falling in. He was telling himself that he must not give in. He tried to steel his heart against all emotional appeals. It was a re-enactment of that other struggle. He leaned against a window and looked out. The sky was overcast with heavy black clouds and a high wind began to blow filling the air with dust and dry leaves. It was one of those rare occasions when even Nature takes a hand in a human fight. Very soon it began to rain, the first rain in the year. It came down in large sharp drops and was accompanied by the lightning and thunder which mark a change of season. Okeke was trying hard not to think of his two grandsons. But he knew he was now fighting a losing battle. He tried to hum a favorite hymn but the pattering of large rain drops on the roof broke up the tune. His mind immediately returned to the children. How could he shut his door against them? By a curious mental process he imagined them standing, sad and forsaken, under the harsh angry weather—shut out from his house.

That night he hardly slept, from remorse—and a vague fear that he might die without making it up to them.

perfunctorily (pər fuŋk′ tôr i lē) *adv.* indifferently; with little interest or care

Literary Analysis
Atmosphere In what ways does Nene's letter change the story's atmosphere?

Review and Assess

Thinking About the Selection

1. **Respond:** What would you like to say to Nnaemeka's father at the end of the story? Explain.

2. **(a) Recall:** What criteria does Nnaemeka's father use to judge the suitability of a wife? **(b) Infer:** What criteria has Nnaemeka used to choose Nene? **(c) Evaluate:** Does the author seem to favor one set of criteria over the other? Explain.

3. **(a) Analyze Cause and Effect:** Which event triggers the father's emotional trauma at the end of the story? **(b) Predict:** Based on the story's final scene, what do you think the father will do?

4. **Take a Position:** Should marriage be an entirely private affair or should the opinions of friends and relatives play a role? Explain.

Review and Assess

Literary Analysis

Atmosphere

1. (a) How would you describe the **atmosphere** in the opening paragraph of "Comrades"? (b) Use a chart like the one shown to identify descriptive details that contribute to this atmosphere.

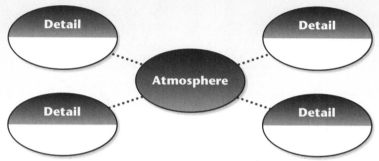

2. (a) After Mrs. Telford carries the tray into the dining room, how does the story's verb tense change? (b) What is the effect of this change on the story's atmosphere?
3. (a) In "Marriage Is a Private Affair," which details contribute to the story's atmosphere of intense but restrained emotion? Explain. (b) At what point does the atmosphere change, and why?

Comparing Literary Works

4. Which specific cultural pressures or tensions are at work in each of these stories?
5. (a) In what ways do both Mrs. Telford and Nnaemeka's father try to behave honorably? (b) Do they succeed? Why or why not?
6. What does each story say about the cruelties of prejudice? Explain.

Reading Strategy

Identifying With a Character

7. With which character or situation in each story do you most strongly **identify**? Explain.
8. At which point in each story would you have felt or acted differently than the character did? Explain.

Extend Understanding

9. **Career Connection:** Mediators are professionals who help people settle disputes peacefully. If you were a mediator, what advice would you give to Nnaemeka and his father?

Quick Review

Atmosphere is the emotional quality of the world the author creates in a work of literature.

To **identify with a character** as you read, imagine yourself in the place of a character and try to experience events through his or her eyes.

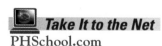 **Take It to the Net**
PHSchool.com

Take the interactive self-test online to check your understanding of these selections.

Integrate Language Skills

Vocabulary Development Lesson

Word Analysis: Greek Prefix *eu-*

The prefix *eu-* means "good" or "well." Use the clues in parentheses and your knowledge of the meaning of the prefix *eu-* to write a definition of both words below.

1. eulogy (*-logy* = word or speech)
2. euphonious (*-phonious* = sounding)

Spelling Strategy

In many English words of Greek origin, *ph* is used to spell the *f* sound, as in *euphemism*, *telephone*, and *graph*. For each of the following pairs, choose the correct spelling.

1. apostrofe/apostrophe
2. megafone/megaphone
3. sorrowful/sorrowphul
4. grafite/graphite

Fluency: Words in Context

Answer *yes* or *no* to each question below. Explain each response.

1. If you are *disposed* to eating fish, would you try salmon?
2. Is *deference* proper when meeting a queen?
3. If Lee studies *perfunctorily*, can she expect to earn an A?
4. If you *assent* to more, will you be busier?
5. Could a phone call made *furtively* be easily overheard?
6. If Mike *vehemently* dislikes soccer, will he choose to play the game?
7. Would the *revelation* of a password help you gain access to something?
8. Could you use *euphemisms* to avoid disturbing someone?

Grammar and Style Lesson

Noun Clauses

A subordinate clause is a group of words with a subject and a verb that cannot stand by itself as a complete sentence. A **noun clause** is a subordinate clause that functions as a noun. It can serve as the subject of a verb, a direct object, or the object of a preposition. Noun clauses are often introduced by the words *that*, *what*, *which*, *how*, and *why*.

> **Subject:** "What one looks for in a wife are a good character and a Christian background."
>
> **Direct Object:** They're not going to be saying . . . that they're off on a student tour in Europe.

Practice For each item below, identify the noun clause and explain its function in the sentence.

1. She went to the kitchen to see what was in the refrigerator.
2. The women saw how nicely she kept her home.
3. She cannot believe what she knows.
4. She did not know that the letter would change his feelings.
5. He understood why she was upset.

Writing Application Write a summary of the events in one of these stories. Include at least two noun clauses.

WG Prentice Hall Writing and Grammar Connection: Diamond Level, Chapter 19, Section 3

Writing Lesson

Manual on How to Change a Story's Atmosphere

Gordimer uses precise descriptive details to create an intense and vivid atmosphere in "Comrades." Using her story as an example, write a manual for young authors on how to create various types of atmosphere in a story.

Prewriting   Reread "Comrades" and list details Gordimer uses to create a tense atmosphere. Then, brainstorm for other types of atmosphere that a story might create and the kinds of details that would be effective.

Drafting   Explain the concept of atmosphere. Follow with three sections, each of which describes how to create a different type of atmosphere and provides examples. Introduce each example.

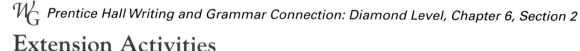

Model: Drafting to Introduce Example Text

For example, notice how altered details change the atmosphere from one of tension to one of friendliness:
Original Text: The others got in the back, the spokes-man beside her. She saw the nervous white of his eyes.
New Text: The others tumbled into the back, the spokesman beside her. She saw weary gratitude in his eyes as he sent her a silent *thanks*.

> A clear introduction to an example clarifies its purpose.

Revising   As you review your work, make sure that your examples clearly evoke the types of atmospheres you specify. Consider altering details as needed to create the desired effect.

WG Prentice Hall Writing and Grammar Connection: Diamond Level, Chapter 6, Section 2

Extension Activities

Listening and Speaking With a small group, write and perform a **dramatization** of a scene from "Comrades." Use these tips to prepare:

- As a group, choose a scene to dramatize.
- Review the scene, noting details that suggest characters' posture and attitudes.
- Write the dramatization in script form.

Use both dialogue and body language to re-create the story's tension. **[Group Activity]**

Research and Technology Conduct research on the nation of Nigeria. Focus your research by organizing it into the following categories: geography; population; economy; art and culture; and history. Share your findings in a five-minute **presentation** for the class.

 *Take It to the Net*   PHSchool.com

Go online for an additional research activity using the Internet.

Prepare to Read

An Astrologer's Day ◆ By Any Other Name

R. K. Narayan (1906–2001)

Indian writer R. K. Narayan once said, "If one pauses to think, one realizes that there is little one could say about one's self." Others, however, have much to say about Narayan. For instance, critic John Upside called Narayan "the foremost Indian writer of fiction in English." English novelist Graham Greene said, "It was Mr. Narayan with his *Swami and Friends* who first brought India . . . alive to me." Throughout his career, Narayan's work met with critical acclaim and was translated into every European language as well as Hebrew.

A Grandmother's Influence Narayan was born in Madras, India, on October 10, 1906. His father traveled frequently for his work, and his mother was frail. As a result, Narayan was raised by his grandmother and an uncle. After school, Narayan's grandmother recited stories and poetry in Tamil, an Indian language. She also received numerous visitors—local people seeking advice on marriages, treatment for scorpion bites, or horoscope readings. These colorful characters became the subjects of Narayan's early fiction.

First Success After graduating from college, Narayan worked as a teacher, but he soon devoted himself entirely to writing. His first major effort, the novel *Swami and Friends*, became an international success. In the novel, Narayan created the fictional setting of Malgudi, which was based on the town of Mysore. Like William Faulkner's Yoknapatawpha (yōk´ nə pə tô´ fə) County or Gabriel García Márquez's Macondo, Malgudi is a literary microcosm—a little world that represents both the local concerns of Indians and the universal concerns of people everywhere.

Narayan was one of the finest writers to depict India from an insider's perspective. He chose his characters from the middle class—street vendors, holy men, students, teachers—and wrote about them with wit and sympathy. His work demonstrates the valiant struggle to harmonize ancient traditions with the confusions of contemporary life.

Santha Rama Rau (b. 1923)

Born to an affluent family in Madras, India, Santha Rama Rau has traveled the world and lived far from her homeland for many years. However, she never forgot her Indian roots, which infuse her work with color and wisdom.

Daughter of India Rama Rau's father was a prominent diplomat and her mother, a noted social reformer. Born when India was still a British colony, Rama Rau was sent to school in England and graduated in 1939 from the St. Paul's School for Girls in London. Two years later, she enrolled at Wellesley College in the United States. In between, she made a trip back to India that became the basis of her first nonfiction book, *Home to India*. Published in 1945, the book became an international bestseller.

Resettling in America When India won independence in 1947, Rama Rau's father was appointed as his nation's first ambassador to Japan. While traveling with her father to Tokyo, Rama Rau met her first husband, an American. The couple settled in New York City, where she published nonfiction and novels and also adapted E. M. Forster's novel *A Passage to India* into a Broadway play.

A Writing Philosophy Rama Rau was once asked for her advice on writing. "Really, in the end," she explained, "the only thing that can make you a writer is the person that you are, the intensity of your feeling, the honesty of your vision, the unsentimental acknowledgement of the endless interest of the life around and within you."

Preview

Connecting to the Literature

One's name and history are basic to one's sense of self. Imagine, then, what it would feel like to simply be assigned a new name or to have to abandon one's past. That is the experience of the characters in these selections.

Literary Analysis

Plot

Plot is the sequence of events in a literary work. Most plots involve characters and a conflict and follow a specific pattern:

- *Exposition:* The basic situation is introduced.
- *Inciting Incident:* The conflict is revealed.
- *Development:* The conflict increases in intensity.
- *Climax:* The conflict reaches its highest point.
- *Falling Action:* Events that occur after the climax are described.
- *Resolution:* The story ends with details that reveal insight.

In these selections, both the falling action and the resolution provide new information. As you read, identify the climax in each selection. Then, notice the surprising information you learn as each selection concludes.

Comparing Literary Works

In both Narayan's short story and Rama Rau's memoir, the main characters experience an identity crisis. As you read, determine what each story suggests about the extent to which one's identity can truly be altered.

Reading Strategy

Recognizing Ironic Details

Verbal irony involves a contrast between what is stated and what is meant. *Situational irony* involves a contrast between what is expected and what actually happens. As you read, use a chart like the one shown to **recognize ironic details.** Note details that create expectations in your mind. Then, decide whether your expectations are fulfilled.

Vocabulary Development

prophetic (prō fet´ ik) *adj.* having to do with predicting the future (p. 1366)

ancestral (an ses´ trəl) *adj.* relating to the people from whom one is descended (p. 1368)

paraphernalia (par´ ə fər nāl´ yə) *n.* articles of equipment (p. 1368)

incantations (in´ kan tā´ shənz) *n.* chants sung as part of a ritual (p. 1369)

provincial (prō vin´ shəl) *adj.* lacking in sophistication (p. 1372)

insular (in´ sə lər) *adj.* having a narrow viewpoint (p. 1372)

wizened (wiz´ ənd) *adj.* dried up and wrinkled due to age (p. 1374)

Detail

The astrologer makes a deal with a challenging client.

Expected Outcome

The astrologer will fail.

Actual Outcome

An Astrologer's Day

R. K. Narayan

Background

The English word *astrology* combines the Greek word *astro-*, which means "star or other heavenly body," with the Greek suffix *-logy*, which means "the study of." Hence, astrology is the study of the ways in which heavenly bodies, such as the sun, moon, stars, and planets, affect life on Earth. Some people believe that the stars and planets exert influences that affect individuals and can reveal the future. However, unlike astronomy, which is a hard science, astrology is considered by many people to be a body of superstitions and the arena of frauds. In this selection, the astrologer may or may not be one such fraud.

Punctually at midday he opened his bag and spread out his professional equipment, which consisted of a dozen cowrie shells,[1] a square piece of cloth with obscure mystic charts on it, a notebook, and a bundle of palmyra writing. His forehead was resplendent with sacred ash and vermilion,[2] and his eyes sparkled with a sharp abnormal gleam which was really an outcome of a continual searching look for customers, but which his simple clients took to be a <u>prophetic</u> light and felt comforted. The power of his eyes was considerably enhanced by their position—placed as they were between the painted forehead and the dark whiskers which streamed down his cheeks: even a half-wit's eyes would sparkle in such a setting. To crown the effect he wound a saffron-colored turban around his head. This color scheme never failed. People were attracted to him as bees are attracted to cosmos or dahlia stalks. He sat under the boughs of a spreading tamarind tree which flanked a path running through the town hall park. It was a remarkable place in many ways: a surging crowd was always moving up and down this narrow road morning till night. A variety of trades

Reading Strategy
Recognizing Ironic Details In what ways do the details about the astrologer's appearance provide the reader with information that his clients do not have?

prophetic (prō fet´ ik) *adj.* having to do with predicting the future

---

1. **cowrie** (kou´ rē) **shells** brightly colored, glossy seashells.
2. **sacred ash and vermilion** religious marking originally used only by Brahmins, the highest caste in Indian society.

and occupations was represented all along its way: medicine sellers, sellers of stolen hardware and junk, magicians, and, above all, an auctioneer of cheap cloth, who created enough din all day to attract the whole town. Next to him in vociferousness came a vendor of fried groundnut, who gave his ware a fancy name each day, calling it "Bombay Ice Cream" one day, and on the next "Delhi Almond," and on the third "Raja's Delicacy," and so on and so forth, and people flocked to him. A considerable portion of this crowd dallied before the astrologer too. The astrologer transacted his business by the light of a flare which crackled and smoked up above the groundnut heap nearby. Half the enchantment of the place was due to the fact that it did not have the benefit of municipal lighting. The place was lit up by shop lights. One or two had hissing gaslights, some had naked flares stuck on poles, some were lit up by old cycle lamps, and one or two, like the astrologer's, managed without lights of their own. It was a bewildering crisscross of light rays and moving shadows. This suited the astrologer very well, for the simple reason that he had not in the least intended to be an astrologer when he began life; and he knew no more of what was going to happen to others than he knew what was going to happen to himself next minute. He was as much a stranger to the stars as were his innocent customers. Yet he said things which pleased and astonished everyone: that was more a matter of study, practice, and shrewd guesswork. All the same, it was as much an honest man's labor as any other, and he deserved the wages he carried home at the end of a day.

Reading Strategy
Recognizing Ironic Details In what ways is the information about the astrologer's true abilities ironic?

☑**Reading Check**
Where does the astrologer conduct his business?

▲ **Critical Viewing** In what ways is the market shown in this photograph both similar to and different from the site where the astrologer does business? [**Compare and Contrast**]

He had left his village without any previous thought or plan. If he had continued there he would have carried on the work of his fore-fathers—namely, tilling the land, living, marrying, and ripening in his cornfield and <u>ancestral</u> home. But that was not to be. He had to leave home without telling anyone, and he could not rest till he left it behind a couple of hundred miles. To a villager it is a great deal, as if an ocean flowed between.

He had a working analysis of mankind's troubles: marriage, money, and the tangles of human ties. Long practice had sharpened his per-ception. Within five minutes he understood what was wrong. He charged three paise[3] per question, never opened his mouth till the other had spoken for at least ten minutes, which provided him enough stuff for a dozen answers and advices. When he told the person before him, gazing at his palm, "In many ways you are not getting the fullest results for your efforts," nine out of ten were disposed to agree with him. Or he questioned: "Is there any woman in your family, maybe even a distant relative, who is not well disposed towards you?" Or he gave an analysis of character: "Most of your troubles are due to your nature. How can you be otherwise with Saturn where he is? You have an impetuous[4] nature and a rough exterior." This endeared him to their hearts immediately, for even the mildest of us loves to think that he has a forbidding exterior.

The nuts vendor blew out his flare and rose to go home. This was a signal for the astrologer to bundle up too, since it left him in darkness except for a little shaft of green light which strayed in from somewhere and touched the ground before him. He picked up his cowrie shells and <u>paraphernalia</u> and was putting them back into his bag when the green shaft of light was blotted out; he looked up and saw a man standing before him. He sensed a possible client and said, "You look so care-worn. It will do you good to sit down for a while and chat with me." The other grumbled some reply vaguely. The astrologer pressed his invita-tion; whereupon the other thrust his palm under his nose, saying, "You call yourself an astrologer?" The astrologer felt challenged and said, tilting the other's palm towards the green shaft of light, "Yours is a nature . . ." "Oh, stop that," the other said. "Tell me something worthwhile. . . ."

Our friend felt piqued.[5] "I charge only three paise per question, and what you get ought to be good enough for your money. . . ." At this the other withdrew his arm, took out an anna, and flung it out to him, saying, "I have some questions to ask. If I prove you are bluffing, you must return that anna to me with interest."

"If you find my answers satisfactory, will you give me five rupees?"

"No."

---

3. **paise** (pīˈ se), *plural of* **paisa** (pīˈ säˈ) monetary unit of India or Pakistan, equal to one hundredth of a rupee.
4. **impetuous** (im pechˈ o͞o əs) *adj.* rash; impulsive.
5. **piqued** (pēkt) *adj.* displeased; resentful.

ancestral (an sesˊ trəl) *adj.* relating to the people from whom one is descended

paraphernalia (par´ ə fər nālˊ yə) *n.* articles of equipment

▼ **Critical Viewing**
In what way does this pho-tograph affect your mental picture of the characters in this story? **[Connect]**

"Or will you give me eight annas?"

"All right, provided you give me twice as much if you are wrong," said the stranger. This pact was accepted after a little further argument. The astrologer sent up a prayer to heaven as the other lit a cheroot. The astrologer caught a glimpse of his face by the match light. There was a pause as cars hooted on the road, jutka[6] drivers swore at their horses, and the babble of the crowd agitated the semidarkness of the park. The other sat down, sucking his cheroot, puffing out, sat there ruthlessly. The astrologer felt very uncomfortable. "Here, take your anna back. I am not used to such challenges. It is late for me today. . . ." He made preparations to bundle up. The other held his wrist and said, "You can't get out of it now. You dragged me in while I was passing." The astrologer shivered in his grip; and his voice shook and became faint. "Leave me today. I will speak to you tomorrow." The other thrust his palm in his face and said, "Challenge is challenge. Go on." The astrologer proceeded with his throat drying up, "There is a woman . . ."

"Stop," said the other. "I don't want all that. Shall I succeed in my present search or not? Answer this and go. Otherwise I will not let you go till you disgorge all your coins." The astrologer muttered a few <u>incantations</u> and replied, "All right. I will speak. But will you give me a rupee if what I say is convincing? Otherwise I will not open my mouth, and you may do what you like." After a good deal of haggling the other agreed. The astrologer said, "You were left for dead. Am I right?"

"Ah, tell me more."

"A knife has passed through you once?" said the astrologer.

"Good fellow!" He bared his chest to show the scar. "What else?"

"And then you were pushed into a well nearby in the field. You were left for dead."

"I should have been dead if some passerby had not chanced to peep into the well," exclaimed the other, overwhelmed by enthusiasm. "When shall I get at him?" he asked, clenching his fist.

"In the next world," answered the astrologer. "He died four months ago in a far-off town. You will never see any more of him." The other groaned on hearing it. The astrologer proceeded:

"Guru Nayak—"

"You know my name!" the other said, taken aback.

"As I know all other things. Guru Nayak, listen carefully to what I have to say. Your village is two days' journey due north of this town. Take the next train and begone. I see once again great danger to your life if you go from home." He took out a pinch of sacred ash and held it to him. "Rub it on your forehead and go home. Never travel southward again, and you will live to be a hundred."

"Why should I leave home again?" the other said reflectively. "I was only going away now and then to look for him and to choke out his life if I met him." He shook his head regretfully. "He has escaped my hands.

Literary Analysis
Plot Which details intensify the conflict the astrologer is experiencing? Explain.

incantations (in´ kan tā´ shənz) *n.* chants sung as part of a ritual

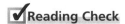

Reading Check
What single question does the client want the astrologer to answer?

---

6. **jutka** (jut´ kə) Hindi word for a one-horse vehicle, hired out as a taxi.

I hope at least he died as he deserved." "Yes," said the astrologer. "He was crushed under a lorry." The other looked gratified to hear it.

The place was deserted by the time the astrologer picked up his articles and put them into his bag. The green shaft was also gone, leaving the place in darkness and silence. The stranger had gone off into the night, after giving the astrologer a handful of coins.

It was nearly midnight when the astrologer reached home. His wife was waiting for him at the door and demanded an explanation. He flung the coins at her and said, "Count them. One man gave all that."

"Twelve and a half annas," she said, counting. She was overjoyed. "I can buy some jaggery[7] and coconut tomorrow. The child has been asking for sweets for so many days now. I will prepare some nice stuff for her."

"The swine has cheated me! He promised me a rupee," said the astrologer. She looked up at him. "You look worried. What is wrong?"

"Nothing."

After dinner, sitting on the pyol,[8] he told her, "Do you know a great load is gone from me today? I thought I had the blood of a man on my hands all these years. That was the reason why I ran away from home, settled here, and married you. He is alive."

She gasped. "You tried to kill!"

"Yes, in our village, when I was a silly youngster. We drank, gambled, and quarreled badly one day—why think of it now? Time to sleep," he said, yawning, and stretched himself on the pyol.

---

7. **jaggery** (jag´ ər ē) *n.* dark, crude sugar from the sap of certain palm trees.
8. **pyol** (pī´ əl) collection of material on which a person can sit or sleep.

Review and Assess

Thinking About the Selection

1. **Respond:** Do you find the astrologer amusing? Why or why not?

2. **(a) Recall:** Does the astrologer actually read the stars or predict the future? **(b) Summarize:** What methods does he use to tell people's fortunes? **(c) Evaluate:** Do you agree with the narrator that the astrologer performs "an honest man's labor"? Explain.

3. **(a) Recall:** What is the last piece of advice that the astrologer gives Nayak? **(b) Deduce:** What is the astrologer's true motive in giving Nayak this advice? **(c) Make a Judgment:** Do you think the astrologer acts ethically? Explain.

4. **(a) Speculate:** What might the astrologer have told Nayak if he had not recognized him? **(b) Evaluate:** Would Nayak have been satisfied with such a message? Explain.

5. **Take a Position:** Do you think justice is served in the case of the astrologer and Nayak? Why or why not?

Reading Strategy
Recognizing Ironic Details Is the astrologer's statement about being cheated ironic? Explain.

By Any Other Name

Santha Rama Rau

Background

India was under direct British control from about 1860 until 1947, when it became an independent country. During that time, the British set up a school system geared mostly to middle- and upper-class Indian students. The goals of this system were to instill British beliefs and values into Indian youth and to train students for jobs in government and various other professions. It was expected that these students would champion British policies among the rest of the population, an approach that was largely successful. Remnants of the British education system remain in India today.

At the Anglo-Indian day school in Zorinabad to which my sister and I were sent when she was eight and I was five and a half, they changed our names. On the first day of school, a hot, windless morning of a north Indian September, we stood in the headmistress's[1] study and she said, "Now you're the *new* girls. What are your names?"

My sister answered for us. "I am Premila, and she"—nodding in my direction—"is Santha."

The headmistress had been in India, I suppose, fifteen years or so, but she still smiled her helpless inability to cope with Indian names. Her rimless half-glasses glittered, and the precarious bun on the top of her head trembled as she shook her head. "Oh, my dears, those are much too hard for me. Suppose we give you pretty English names. Wouldn't that be more jolly? Let's see, now—Pamela for you, I think." She shrugged in a baffled way at my sister. "That's as close as I can get. And for *you*," she said to me, "how about Cynthia? Isn't that nice?"

My sister was always less easily intimidated than I was, and while she kept a stubborn silence, I said, "Thank you," in a very tiny voice.

Literary Analysis
Plot In what ways does the first sentence establish the conflict as relating to an identity crisis?

✓ **Reading Check**
What new names does the headmistress give to Premila and Santha?

---

1. **headmistress** woman in charge of a school; principal, especially of a private school.

We had been sent to that school because my father, among his responsibilities as an officer of the civil service, had a tour of duty to perform in the villages around that steamy little <u>provincial</u> town, where he had his headquarters at that time. He used to make his shorter inspection tours on horseback, and a week before, in the stale heat of a typically postmonsoon day[2] we had waved goodbye to him and a little procession—an assistant, a secretary, two bearers,[3] and the man to look after the bedding rolls and luggage. They rode away through our large garden, still bright green from the rains, and we turned back into the twilight of the house and the sound of fans whispering in every room.

Up to then, my mother had refused to send Premila to school in the British-run establishments of that time, because, she used to say, "you can bury a dog's tail for seven years and it still comes out curly, and you can take a Britisher away from his home for a lifetime and he still remains <u>insular</u>." The examinations and degrees from entirely Indian schools were not, in those days, considered valid. In my case, the question had never come up, and probably never would have come up if Mother's extraordinary good health had not broken down. For the first time in my life, she was not able to continue the lessons she had been giving us every morning. So our Hindi books were put away, the stories of the Lord Krishna[4] as a little boy were left in mid-air, and we were sent to the Anglo-Indian school.

That first day at school is still, when I think of it, a remarkable one. At that age, if one's name is changed, one develops a curious form of dual personality. I remember having a certain detached and disbelieving concern in the actions of "Cynthia," but certainly no responsibility. Accordingly, I followed the thin, erect back of the headmistress down the veranda to my classroom feeling, at most, a passing interest in what was going to happen to me in this strange, new atmosphere of School.

The building was Indian in design, with wide verandas opening onto a central courtyard, but Indian verandas are usually white-washed, with stone floors. These, in the tradition of British schools, were painted dark brown and had matting on the floors. It gave a feeling of extra intensity to the heat.

I suppose there were about a dozen Indian children in the school—which contained perhaps forty children in all—and four of them were in my class. They were all sitting at the back of the room, and I went to join them. I sat next to a small, solemn girl who didn't smile at me. She had long, glossy-black braids and wore a cotton dress, but she still kept on her Indian jewelry—a gold chain around her neck, thin gold bracelets, and tiny ruby studs in her ears. Like most Indian children, she had a rim of black kohl[5] around her eyes. The cotton dress should

Indian Clothing

Many Indian women and girls wear a sari (sä´rē), a long piece of brightly colored cloth wrapped over a blouse around the body. One end of the sari forms an ankle-length skirt, and the other is draped over the shoulder or sometimes the head. Saris woven into colorful patterns have been worn by Indian women for many centuries. Saris are sometimes made of silk, but cotton is more common.

provincial (prō vin´ shəl) *adj.* lacking in sophistication

insular (in´ sə lər) *adj.* having a narrow viewpoint

Literary Analysis
Plot In what ways does the little girl's clothing and jewelry exemplify the conflict Premila and Santha are experiencing?

---

2. **postmonsoon day** day that follows a heavy rainfall.
3. **bearers** porters; people who carry luggage.
4. **Lord Krishna** incarnation of Vishnu, one of the three most important gods in Hinduism.
5. **kohl** (kōl) *n.* cosmetic eyeliner worn by women in some parts of Asia. It is applied with the fingers, rather than a pencil or a brush.

have looked strange, but all I could think of was that I should ask my mother if I couldn't wear a dress to school, too, instead of my Indian clothes.

I can't remember too much about the proceedings in class that day, except for the beginning. The teacher pointed to me and asked me to stand up. "Now, dear, tell the class your name."

I said nothing.

"Come along," she said, frowning slightly. "What's your name, dear?"

"I don't know," I said, finally.

The English children in the front of the class—there were about eight or ten of them—giggled and twisted around in their chairs to look at me. I sat down quickly and opened my eyes very wide, hoping in that way to dry them off. The little girl with the braids put out her hand and very lightly touched my arm. She still didn't smile.

Most of that morning I was rather bored. I looked briefly at the children's drawings pinned to the wall, and then concentrated on a lizard clinging to the ledge of the high, barred window behind the teacher's head. Occasionally it would shoot out its long yellow tongue for a fly, and then it would rest, with its eyes closed and its belly palpitating, as though it were swallowing several times quickly. The lessons were mostly concerned with reading and writing and simple numbers—things that my mother had already taught me—and I paid very little attention. The teacher wrote on the easel blackboard words like "bat" and "cat," which seemed babyish to me; only "apple" was new and incomprehensible.

When it was time for the lunch recess, I followed the girl with braids out onto the veranda. There the children from the other classes were assembled. I saw Premila at once and ran over to her, as she had charge of our lunchbox. The children were all opening packages and sitting down to eat sandwiches. Premila and I were the only ones who had Indian food—thin wheat chapatties,[6] some vegetable curry, and a bottle of buttermilk. Premila thrust half of it into my hand and whispered fiercely that I should go and sit with my class, because that was what the others seemed to be doing.

The enormous black eyes of the little Indian girl from my class looked at my food longingly, so I offered her some. But she only shook her head and plowed her way solemnly through her sandwiches.

I was very sleepy after lunch, because at home we always took a siesta.[7] It was usually a pleasant time of day, with the bedroom darkened against the harsh afternoon sun, the drifting off into sleep with the sound of Mother's voice reading a story in one's mind, and, finally, the shrill, fussy voice of the ayah[8] waking one for tea.

At school, we rested for a short time on low, folding cots on the veranda, and then we were expected to play games. During the hot part

Reading Strategy
Recognizing Ironic Details What is ironic about Santha's answer to the question of what her name is?

---

6. **chapatties** (chə pät´ ēz) *n.* round, flat, unleavened breads baked in a dry skillet; a staple of Indian cuisine.
7. **siesta** (sē es´ tə) *n.* afternoon nap or rest.
8. **ayah** (ä´ yə) *n.* nursemaid or lady's maid.

Reading Check

Why are Premila and Santha sent to the British-run school?

of the afternoon we played indoors, and after the shadows had begun to lengthen and the slight breeze of the evening had come up we moved outside to the wide courtyard.

I had never really grasped the system of competitive games. At home, whenever we played tag or guessing games, I was always allowed to "win"—"because," Mother used to tell Premila, "she is the youngest, and we have to allow for that." I had often heard her say it, and it seemed quite reasonable to me, but the result was that I had no clear idea of what "winning" meant.

When we played twos-and-threes that afternoon at school, in accordance with my training, I let one of the small English boys catch me, but was naturally rather puzzled when the other children did not return the courtesy. I ran about for what seemed like hours without ever catching anyone, until it was time for school to close. Much later I learned that my attitude was called "not being a good sport," and I stopped allowing myself to be caught, but it was not for years that I really learned the spirit of the thing.

When I saw our car come up to the school gate, I broke away from my classmates and rushed toward it yelling, "Ayah! Ayah!" It seemed like an eternity since I had seen her that morning—a <u>wizened</u>, affectionate figure in her white cotton sari, giving me dozens of urgent and useless instructions on how to be a good girl at school. Premila followed more sedately, and she told me on the way home never to do that again in front of the other children.

When we got home we went straight to Mother's high, white room to have tea with her, and I immediately climbed onto the bed and bounced gently up and down on the springs. Mother asked how we had liked our first day in school. I was so pleased to be home and to have left that peculiar Cynthia behind that I had nothing whatever to say about school, except to ask what "apple" meant. But Premila told Mother about the classes, and added that in her class they had weekly tests to see if they had learned their lessons well.

I asked, "What's a test?"

Premila said, "You're too small to have them. You won't have them in your class for donkey's years." She had learned the expression that day and was using it for the first time. We all laughed enormously at her wit. She also told Mother, in an aside, that we should take sandwiches to school the next day. Not, she said, that *she* minded. But they would be simpler for me to handle.

That whole lovely evening I didn't think about school at all. I sprinted barefoot across the lawns with my favorite playmate, the cook's son, to the stream at the end of the garden. We quarreled in our usual way, waded in the tepid water under the lime trees, and waited for the night to bring out the smell of the jasmine. I listened with fascination to his stories of ghosts and demons, until I was too frightened to cross the garden alone in the semidarkness. The ayah found me, shouted at the cook's son, scolded me, hurried me in to supper—it was an entirely usual, wonderful evening.

wizened (wiz´ ənd) *adj.* dried up and wrinkled due to age

Literary Analysis
Plot Why does Premila want to take sandwiches to school?

It was a week later, the day of Premila's first test, that our lives changed rather abruptly. I was sitting at the back of my class, in my usual inattentive way, only half listening to the teacher. I had started a rather guarded friendship with the girl with the braids, whose name turned out to be Nalini (Nancy, in school). The three other Indian children were already fast friends. Even at that age it was apparent to all of us that friendship with the English or Anglo-Indian children was out of the question. Occasionally, during the class, my new friend and I would draw pictures and show them to each other secretly.

The door opened sharply and Premila marched in. At first, the teacher smiled at her in a kindly and encouraging way and said, "Now, you're little Cynthia's sister?"

Premila didn't even look at her. She stood with her feet planted firmly apart and her shoulders rigid, and addressed herself directly to me. "Get up," she said. "We're going home."

I didn't know what had happened, but I was aware that it was a crisis of some sort. I rose obediently and started to walk toward my sister.

"Bring your pencils and your notebook," she said.

I went back for them, and together we left the room. The teacher started to say something just as Premila closed the door, but we didn't wait to hear what it was.

In complete silence we left the school grounds and started to walk home. Then I asked Premila what the matter was. All she would say was "We're going home for good."

It was a very tiring walk for a child of five and a half, and I dragged along behind Premila with my pencils growing sticky in my hand. I can still remember looking at the dusty hedges, and the tangles of thorns in the ditches by the side of the road, smelling the faint fragrance from the eucalyptus trees and wondering whether we would ever reach home. Occasionally a horse-drawn tonga[9] passed us, and the women, in their pink or green silks, stared at Premila and me trudging along on the side of the road. A few coolies[10] and a line of women carrying baskets of vegetables on their heads smiled at us. But it was nearing the hottest time of day, and the road was almost deserted. I walked more and more slowly, and shouted to Premila, from time to time, "Wait for me!" with increasing peevishness. She spoke to me only once, and that was to tell me to carry my notebook on my head, because of the sun.

▲ **Critical Viewing**
Does this photograph of a street in Bombay, India, seem like the "little provincial town" Rama Rau describes in this memoir? Explain. **[Evaluate]**

**Reading Check**
Why does the narrator fail to grasp the idea of competition?

---

9. tonga (täŋˊ gə) *n.* two-wheeled, horse-drawn carriage.
10. coolies (ko͞oˊ lēz) *n.* unskilled laborers who work for low wages.

When we got to our house the ayah was just taking a tray of lunch into Mother's room. She immediately started a long, worried questioning about what are you children doing back here at this hour of the day.

Mother looked very startled and very concerned, and asked Premila what had happened.

Premila said, "We had our test today, and She made me and the other Indians sit at the back of the room, with a desk between each one."

Mother said, "Why was that, darling?"

"She said it was because Indians cheat," Premila added. "So I don't think we should go back to that school."

Mother looked very distant, and was silent a long time. At last she said, "Of course not, darling." She sounded displeased.

We all shared the curry she was having for lunch, and afterward I was sent off to the beautifully familiar bedroom for my siesta. I could hear Mother and Premila talking through the open door.

Mother said, "Do you suppose she understood all that?"

Premila said, "I shouldn't think so. She's a baby."

Mother said, "Well, I hope it won't bother her."

Of course, they were both wrong. I understood it perfectly, and I remember it all very clearly. But I put it happily away, because it had all happened to a girl called Cynthia, and I never was really particularly interested in her.

Review and Assess

Thinking About the Selection

1. **Respond:** Do you find Premila's actions surprising? Explain.

2. **(a) Recall:** Why were the two girls sent to the British school?
   (b) Interpret: What explanation does the girls' mother give for not wanting to send them there? **(c) Infer:** In what ways does her statement foreshadow, or hint at, what the school will be like?

3. **(a) Recall:** What does Premila tell Santha to do at lunch recess?
   (b) Interpret: What concerns or fears does her statement reveal?
   (c) Analyze Cause and Effect: In what ways does the test change her feelings?

4. **(a) Recall:** At the end of the story, what does the narrator say she put "happily away"? **(b) Analyze:** Why is she able to dismiss the experience so easily?

5. **(a) Speculate:** What attitudes toward both themselves and the British might the Indian children who remain at the school develop? **(b) Make a Judgment:** Do you think their experience will have long-term effects on Premila or on Santha? Explain.

6. **Generalize:** What does this story suggest about the ways in which people of different cultures should relate to each other?

Review and Assess

Literary Analysis

Plot

1. Use a chart like the one shown to analyze the **plot** of "An Astrologer's Day." (a) Which events lead to the *climax*? (b) What is the *conflict*? (c) Which events form the *falling action*?

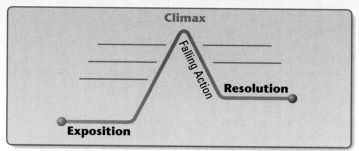

2. Why is the information about the astrologer that is revealed in the falling action important for a complete understanding of the story?
3. (a) In "By Any Other Name," which events build up to the climax? (b) Summarize Rama Rau's reaction to events as she describes it in the *resolution*.

Comparing Literary Works

4. (a) In "An Astrologer's Day," what measures does the astrologer take to conceal his identity? (b) What are his motives?
5. In "By Any Other Name," does the headmistress give the girls new identities simply because she cannot pronounce their names? Explain.
6. What statement about personal identity might both the astrologer and Premila offer?

Reading Strategy

Recognizing Ironic Details

7. Which details in the resolution of "An Astrologer's Day" are examples of situational **irony** because they contradict your expectations?
8. (a) In "By Any Other Name," identify three details that demonstrate *verbal irony*. (b) How is the narrator's reaction to her experience at the British school an example of *situational irony*? Explain.

Extend Understanding

9. **History Connection:** In what ways might an imperial power like England leave its mark on former colonies or dependencies?

Integrate Language Skills

Vocabulary Development Lesson

Word Analysis: Latin Root -cant-

The Latin root -cant-, which appears in the word *incantations*, means "sing" or "chant." Use this information to match each word on the left with its definition on the right.

1. cantor
2. canto
3. cantata

a. division of a long poem
b. singer of religious music
c. song or hymn

Spelling Strategy

The *r* sound at the end of many adjectives is spelled *ar*, as in the word *insular*. Write the adjective ending in *ar* that is related to each noun below.

1. pole
2. globule
3. molecule
4. spectacle

Concept Development: Synonyms

For each numbered word below, choose the letter of the word that is its synonym.

1. paraphernalia: (a) garbage, (b) equipment, (c) whistle
2. incantations: (a) chants, (b) books, (c) injections
3. insular: (a) isolated, (b) trendy, (c) waterlogged
4. prophetic: (a) ignored, (b) ancient, (c) predictive
5. wizened: (a) decrepit, (b) angry, (c) foolish
6. provincial: (a) old, (b) unsophisticated, (c) evil
7. ancestral: (a) familial, (b) wealthy, (c) stolen

Grammar and Style Lesson

Correct Use of Adjectives and Adverbs

An **adjective** modifies a noun or pronoun. Always use an adjective after a linking verb (*is*, *are*, *seems*, and *feels*) if the modifier describes the subject. An **adverb** modifies a verb, an adjective, or another adverb. Always use an adverb to modify an action verb.

Adjective after a linking verb:

    S   LV   ADJ
His forehead was <u>resplendent</u> with sacred ash. . . .

Adverb after an action verb:

S V   ADV
I sat down <u>quickly</u>. . . .

Practice Rewrite each sentence below, correcting errors in adjective and adverb use.

1. The astrologer felt anxiously when he recognized the man.
2. He was lucky to have escaped him for such an extraordinary long time.
3. He did good in describing the man's life because he knew him.
4. Premila and Santha felt badly about changing their names.
5. The headmistress spoke gentle but her words stung.

Writing Application Write a paragraph describing how you would feel about changing your name. Correctly use at least three adjectives and three adverbs.

W̶G Prentice Hall Writing and Grammar Connection: Diamond Level, Chapter 17, Section 3

Writing Lesson

Personal Essay With a Surprise Ending

In "An Astrologer's Day," R. K. Narayan reveals information at the end of the story that changes our understanding of the characters and events. Write a personal essay that tells a story and offers readers a similar surprise ending.

Prewriting   Choose an experience that centers on an interesting problem. Brainstorm for details about the people, setting, and events. Then, list the details in chronological order.

Drafting   Begin with an introduction that states the problem. As you tell the story, use your list of details to bring it to life. By the end of the story, show how the problem was resolved in a surprising way.

Revising   As you review your essay, make sure that you have not presented telltale details too early. Remove or revise your hints if they disclose too much information, spoiling the surprise.

Model: Revising to Avoid Revealing a Surprise Ending

Although her five brothers usually showed up, cousin Jill never came to our family reunions. ~~This year, she thought she might make it.~~ When my cousins arrived, I was sort of surprised that the guys were toting a floral suitcase. . . .

> The omission of certain details preserves the surprise of the ending.

Prentice Hall Writing and Grammar Connection: Diamond Level, Chapter 5, Section 4

Extension Activities

Listening and Speaking Conduct research on the most common names in several countries, including India. Create and deliver an **oral report on names** for your class. Use these tips to prepare:

- Create an introduction that will grab listeners' attention.
- Use photographs, maps, and other visual aids to spark interest.

As you speak, help your listeners follow the flow of information by creating smooth transitions between sections of the report.

Research and Technology With a small group, prepare a **multimedia presentation** about R. K. Narayan's life and works. Use the Internet and other sources to locate pictures of Narayan and the places he wrote about. Then, combine them into a video or slide show. Select passages from his works and Indian music to accompany the images. **[Group Activity]**

 **Take It to the Net**   PHSchool.com

Go online for an additional research activity using the Internet.

Yasunari Kawabata (1899–1972)

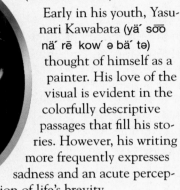

Early in his youth, Yasunari Kawabata (yä´ sōō nä´ rē kow´ ə bä´ tə) thought of himself as a painter. His love of the visual is evident in the colorfully descriptive passages that fill his stories. However, his writing more frequently expresses sadness and an acute perception of life's brevity.

Early Sorrows Many critics see Kawabata's pensive fiction as a reflection of a very difficult childhood. By the time he was sixteen years old, Kawabata was entirely alone in the world. His father had died when the writer was only two years old, and his mother died the following year. Kawabata lived with his grandfather until the elder's death twelve years later. After his grandfather's death, Kawabata attended the elite First High School in Tokyo and Tokyo Imperial University, where he studied Japanese literature.

A Young Writer's Diary Although it was not published for years, Kawabata's first important work was *Diary of a Sixteen-Year-Old.* According to the author, he composed the diary in 1914, during twelve days in May. He stopped writing in the diary a week before his grandfather died. The memories of his grandfather's last days often recur in Kawabata's fiction, but the *Diary* has the most evocative passages. Some scholars question the *Diary*'s authenticity, arguing that it was probably written in 1925, the year it was published. But Kawabata insists that he found the manuscript on student composition paper in an uncle's warehouse. He said, "The strangest thing was that I had not the least recollection of the events described in the diary. . . . I confronted honest emotions of a forgotten past. But the grandfather I had described was uglier than the grandfather of my memory. For ten years my mind had been constantly cleansing my grandfather's image."

First Successes Kawabata's first published story, "A View of the Yasukuni Festival," attracted favorable attention. It was an auspicious beginning for his career because it impressed several important figures in the Japanese literary world. As a result of these contacts, Kawabata started work on a literary magazine, *Bungei Shunju.* He also met the novelist Riichi Yokomitsu, who became a close friend and influenced Kawabata's writing for the rest of his career. Yokomitsu and Kawabata eventually became the two major Japanese novelists of the era.

Encouraging Free Speech For years, Kawabata led an extremely private life, but in 1933 he began to participate more actively in the literary world. He joined the staff of magazines, and he was appointed to the Literary Discussion Group, an organization that tried to foster cooperation between writers and the repressive Japanese government. While Kawabata willingly cooperated with the government's strictures, he continued to publish articles in which he argued for free speech and encouraged a spirit of rebellion against social conventions. In his words, "Without rebellion against conventional morality there can be no pure literature." Kawabata proved that point with his own work, including the novel *Snow Country* (1937), which many critics consider his masterpiece.

In later life, Kawabata's influence on Japanese literature was fully recognized. He won numerous awards and served as one of the judges of Japan's most prestigious literary prize. His starring role in Japanese literature was confirmed in 1968 when he became the first Japanese writer to win the Nobel Prize in Literature.

Preview

Connecting to the Literature

Sometimes, even in company, we can feel more alone than when we are by ourselves. That is the plight of the young woman in this story, who holds quiet but deeply felt emotions.

Literary Analysis

Thematic Imagery

Images are word pictures created through language that appeals to one or more of the five senses. Imagery provides concrete representations of ideas or emotions. For example, in "The Jay," imagery of a distraught mother bird and her lost nestling reflects the story's human drama of a young woman separated from both her real mother and her stepmother:

> The jay flew to the chestnut, skimmed the ground, and flew back again, calling out all the while.
> Would the nestling still be near, that the mother was so reluctant to leave?

When imagery in a work extends beyond a single moment and connects to the central message, it is called **thematic imagery.** As you read, consider ways in which the imagery of the birds suggests larger, thematic concepts.

Connecting Literary Elements

Imagery is one tool a writer can use to create **mood**—the feeling that a literary work evokes in a reader. A mood of fragility and isolation pervades much of "The Jay." As you read, notice how the mood is connected to the descriptions of the birds, and identify the point at which the mood abruptly shifts.

Reading Strategy

Judging Characters' Actions

The characters in this story are caught in a complicated family web, which has caused them to react in different ways. When you **judge characters' actions,** you measure a character's behavior against certain criteria, such as your personal experiences, values, and understanding of human nature. As you read, use a chart like the one shown to identify each character's thoughts and feelings and the actions he or she takes. Then, form a judgment about each character.

Vocabulary Development

reluctant (ri luk´ tənt) *adj.* showing hesitation; unwilling (p. 1383)

deficiency (dē fish´ ən sē) *n.* shortage of a necessary substance (p. 1383)

extravagant (ek strav´ ə gənt) *adj.* excessive; spending much more than is necessary (p. 1383)

prospective (prō spek´ tiv) *adj.* likely to be or to become in the future (p. 1385)

forlornly (fôr lôrn´ lē) *adv.* in a sad or lonely manner because of isolation or desertion (p. 1386)

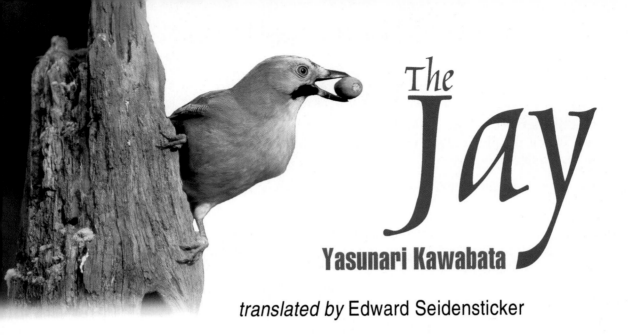

The Jay

Yasunari Kawabata

translated by Edward Seidensticker

Background

From the mid-1800s until the end of World War II, arranged marriages were common in Japanese society. Marital partners were chosen by one's parents, sometimes with the help of relatives or other close associates. When arranging marriages, matchmakers evaluated the social standing of the prospective spouse's family and his or her financial circumstances. Usually, the bride and groom were at least introduced before the wedding day, but they had no chance to get to know each other, and their feelings were secondary to issues of status and wealth. In this story, Yoshiko's father's failed first marriage has shaped the lives of all the characters.

The jay was noisy from dawn.

It seemed to have flown from a lower branch of the pine tree as Yoshiko was opening the shutters and then come back again. They could hear its wings from the breakfast table.

"What a racket," said her brother, starting to get up.

"Leave it alone," said her grandmother. "I think the little one must have fallen from the nest yesterday. I could still hear the mother last night after dark. I suppose she couldn't find it. And isn't that nice, here she is back again this morning."

"Are you sure?" asked Yoshiko.

Save for a liver attack some ten years before, her grandmother had never been ill, but she had suffered from cataracts[1] ever since she was

Reading Strategy
**Judging Characters'
Actions** What judgments can you make about the brother and the grandmother based on their differing reactions to the jay? Explain.

---

1. **cataracts** (kat′ ə rakts′) eye disease in which the lens or its capsule becomes opaque, causing partial or total blindness.

very young. Now she could barely see, and with the left eye only. She had to be handed her food. She could grope her way around the house, but she never went out alone into the garden.

She would sometimes stand or sit at the glass door and gaze at her fingers, spread out in the sunlight. Her whole life seemed to be concentrated in the gaze.

Yoshiko would be afraid of her. She would want to call from behind, and then she would slip away.

Yoshiko was filled with admiration that her blind grandmother could talk about the jay as if she had seen it.

When she went out to do the breakfast dishes, the jay was calling from the roof next door.

There were a chestnut and several persimmons in the back yard. She could see against them that a gentle rain was falling, so gentle that she could not make it out except against the dark background.

The jay flew to the chestnut, skimmed the ground, and flew back again, calling out all the while.

Would the nestling still be near, that the mother was so <u>reluctant</u> to leave?

Yoshiko went to her room. She must be ready by noon.

Her mother and father would be bringing her fiancé's mother.

As she sat down before the mirror she glanced at the white dots on her fingernails. They were said to be a sign that someone would come with gifts, but she had read in a newspaper that they really showed a <u>deficiency</u> in vitamin C or something of the sort. She was pleased with her face when she had finished making herself up. She thought her eyebrows and lips rather charming. She liked the set of her kimono.[2]

She had thought she would wait for her mother to help her, and then she was glad that she had dressed by herself.

Her father and mother, actually her stepmother, did not live with them.

Her father had divorced her mother when Yoshiko was four and her brother two. It was said that her mother had been gaudy and <u>extravagant</u>, but Yoshiko suspected that there had been deeper causes.

Her father had said nothing when her brother had found a picture of their mother and shown it to him. He had frowned and torn the picture to pieces.

When Yoshiko was thirteen her new mother came into the house. Later Yoshiko was to think it rather remarkable of her father to have waited almost ten years. Her new mother was a kind woman and they lived a quiet, happy life.

When her brother entered high school and went to live in a dormitory, it was plain to all of them that his attitude toward his stepmother was changing.

"I've seen Mother," he said to Yoshiko. "She is married and living in Azabu.[3] She is very beautiful. She was glad to see me."

---

2. **kimono** (kə mō′ nō′) *n.* robe with wide sleeves and a sash, part of the traditional costume of Japanese men and women.
3. **Azabu** (ä′ zä′ bo͞o′) street in Tokyo.

Literary Analysis
Thematic Imagery and Mood What mood does this description of the grandmother create? Explain.

reluctant (ri luk′ tənt) *adj.* showing hesitation; unwilling

deficiency (dē fish′ ən sē) *n.* shortage of a necessary substance

Literary Analysis
Thematic Imagery In what ways does Yoshiko's situation mirror that of the lost nestling?

extravagant (ek strav′ ə gənt) *adj.* excessive; spending much more than is necessary

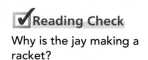
Reading Check

Why is the jay making a racket?

Yuki, 1929, Kotondo, Courtesy Ronin Gallery, New York

▲ **Critical Viewing** Do you think this painting of a Japanese woman captures Yoshiko's character and circumstances? Why or why not? **[Assess]**

Yoshiko was too startled to answer. She was sure that she had turned white, and she was trembling.

Her stepmother came in from the next room.

"It's all right. There's nothing wrong at all with his seeing his own mother. It's only natural. I knew it would happen. It doesn't bother me at all."

Her stepmother seemed drained of strength, and so tiny that Yoshiko felt somehow protective.

Her brother got up and went out. Yoshiko wanted to slap him.

"You are not to say anything, Yoshiko," said her stepmother softly. "It would only make things worse."

Yoshiko was in tears.

Her father brought her brother home from the dormitory. She thought that would be the end of the matter; and then her father and stepmother moved away.

She was frightened. She felt that she had had the full force of—a man's anger, perhaps, or vengefulness? She wondered if she and her brother had something of the same thing in them. She had felt certain, as he had left the room, that her brother had inherited that terrible masculine something.

Yet she felt too that she knew her father's loneliness those ten years he had waited to take a new wife.

She was startled when her father came with talk of a <u>prospective</u> bridegroom.

"You have had a hard time of it, Yoshiko, and I am sorry. I have told his mother that I want you to have the girlhood you never had."

There were tears in Yoshiko's eyes.

With Yoshiko married, there would be no one to take care of her grandmother and brother, and so it was decided that they would live with her father and stepmother. The decision was what touched Yoshiko most. Because of what her father had been through she had been frightened of marriage, but now that it was coming it did not seem so frightening after all.

She went to her grandmother when she had finished dressing.

"Can you see the red, Grandmother?"

"I can see that there is something red." She pulled Yoshiko to her and looked intently at her kimono and obi.[4] "I have forgotten what you look like, Yoshiko. How nice if I could see you again."

Embarrassed, Yoshiko put her hand to her grandmother's head.

She went out into the garden. She wanted to run and meet her father and stepmother. She opened a hand, but the rain was scarcely enough to wet it. Lifting her skirts she looked through the shrubs and bamboo, and found the nestling jay in the grass under the *hagi*.[5]

She stole up to it. Head pulled in, it was a tight little ball. It seemed without strength and she had no trouble taking it. She looked around but could not find the mother.

---

4. **obi** (ō′ bē) *n.* broad sash with a bow in the back, worn with a kimono.
5. *hagi* (hä′ gē′) Japanese name for the bush-clover plant.

The Jay ◆ 1385

Themes in World Literature

Linked Verse

Some critics feel that the structure of Kawabata's stories resembles a poetic form known as linked verse. In linked verse, brief moments are strung together in a meandering, seemingly irrational way. This stringing together of fleeting feelings and brief snippets of dialogue works to convey a strong sense of the characters' emotional states, their memories and desires, and their conections to the natural world. Thus, while stories like "The Jay" may be devoid of heavy plotting, they create moments of intense meaning.

prospective (prō spek′ tiv) *adj.* likely to be or to become in the future

Reading Strategy
Judging Characters' Actions Do you think Yoshiko's father has arranged her marriage out of anger, kindness, or another emotion? Explain.

✔**Reading Check**

Whom does the brother go to visit?

She ran to the house.

"I've found it, Grandmother. It seems very weak."

"Really? You must give it water."

Her grandmother was very calm.

She brought a cup of water and put its beak in, and it drank most prettily, swelling its small throat.

"Kikikikiki." It quickly revived.

Hearing, the mother jay called from a power line.

"Kikiki." The nestling struggled in Yoshiko's hand.

"How very nice," said her grandmother. "You must give it back."

Yoshiko went into the garden. The mother jay left the power line and sat watching Yoshiko from the cherry tree.

Raising her hand to show the nestling, Yoshiko put it on the ground.

She watched from inside the glass door. The nestling called <u>forlornly</u> up. The mother came nearer and then was at the lower branches of the pine tree just above. The nestling flapped its wings as if it were about to take flight, and fell forward, calling out to its mother.

Very cautious, the mother still did not alight.

Then, in a swoop, it was beside the nestling, whose joy was boundless. The head shook, the outstretched wings were trembling, it was like a spoiled child. The mother seemed to be feeding it.

Yoshiko wished that her father and stepmother would hurry. She wanted them to see.

Literary Analysis

Thematic Imagery and Mood In what ways does the bird's response to its mother change the mood of the story? Explain.

forlornly (fôr lôrn′ lē) *adv.* in a sad or lonely manner because of isolation or desertion

Review and Assess

Thinking About the Selection

1. **Respond:** Were you satisfied with the ending of this story? Why or why not?

2. **(a) Recall:** From what physical ailment does Yoshiko's grandmother suffer? **(b) Interpret:** In what ways does the grandmother's physical ailment isolate her? **(c) Analyze:** Is the grandmother completely isolated because of her ailment? Why or why not?

3. **(a) Recall:** With what action does Yoshiko's father respond when the brother shows him a picture of the mother? **(b) Infer:** What do the father's actions suggest about his feelings?

4. **(a) Recall:** Whom does the brother visit while he is living in the school dormitory? **(b) Analyze Cause and Effect:** What are some of the results of this visit?

5. **(a) Deduce:** Why will the grandmother and brother live with the father and stepmother after Yoshiko marries? **(b) Draw Conclusions:** What does this suggest about Yoshiko's life up to this point? Explain.

6. **Speculate:** After her marriage, how do you think Yoshiko will react if there is conflict with her husband? Explain.

Review and Assess

Literary Analysis

Thematic Imagery

1. (a) Describe the plight of the mother bird and nestling in this story. (b) In what specific ways do descriptions of the birds serve as **thematic imagery** that mirrors the situation of the human family?
2. (a) How does the brother react to the birds? (b) What do his reactions suggest about his relationship with his family?
3. At the end of the story, why do you think Yoshiko wants her father and stepmother to see the birds?

Connecting Literary Elements

4. (a) How would you define the **mood** of this story? Explain. (b) Use a chart like the one shown to identify details that contribute to this mood.

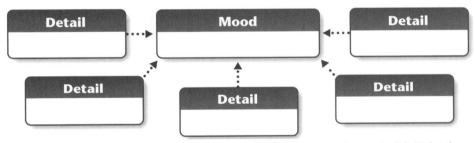

5. (a) At what point does the mood of the story change? (b) Which details convey this change?

Reading Strategy

Judging Characters' Actions

6. (a) Express your **judgment** of Yoshiko, her brother, her father, her stepmother, and her grandmother in one sentence each. (b) Explain the criteria you used to make each judgment.
7. Based on her experiences with her father, does Yoshiko's fear of a "terrible masculine something" seem realistic? Explain.

Extend Understanding

8. **Humanities Connection:** (a) What does this story suggest about the nature of relationships between young people and their elders in Japanese society? (b) How do such relationships compare to those in American culture?

Quick Review

Images are word pictures created through language that appeals to the senses. **Thematic imagery** repeats throughout a literary work and helps express its theme, or central message.

Mood is the feeling that a literary work evokes in a reader.

To **judge characters' actions,** evaluate their behavior against a set of criteria, such as your personal experience, values, and understanding of human nature.

 **Take It to the Net**
PHSchool.com

Take the interactive self-test online to check your understanding of this selection.

Integrate Language Skills

Vocabulary Development Lesson

Word Analysis: Latin Root *-spec-*

The word *prospective* combines the prefix *pro-* ("before" or "forward") with the root *-spec-* ("see" or "look"). Thus, *prospective* means "foreseen, or expected." Use your knowledge of the root *-spec-* and the definitions of the prefixes given in parentheses to define each word below.

1. introspective (*intro* = into; inside)
2. retrospective (*retro* = backward)

Spelling Strategy

When the *sh* or *ch* sound is spelled *c*, it may be followed by *ie*, as in the word *deficiency*, but not by *ei*. Complete the following words with *ie* or *ei*.

1. consc __ nce
2. omnisc __ nt
3. c __ ling
4. dec __ ve

Concept Development: Antonyms

Review the vocabulary words listed on page 1381 and notice their use in the selection. Then, for each numbered word below, select the letter of the word that is its antonym, or word of opposite meaning.

1. prospective: **(a)** visible, **(b)** previous, **(c)** hopeful
2. reluctant: **(a)** enthusiastic, **(b)** uncertain, **(c)** recent
3. deficiency: **(a)** surplus, **(b)** lack, **(c)** sorrow
4. forlornly: **(a)** uselessly, **(b)** quickly, **(c)** happily
5. extravagant: **(a)** large, **(b)** frugal, **(c)** calm

Grammar and Style Lesson

The Conditional and the Subjunctive

To express the fact that one event might happen if another event happens first, writers use the **conditional,** formed by using the helping verb *could, should,* or *would* with the main verb.

> **Conditional:** "You are not to say anything, Yoshiko," said her stepmother softly. "It *would* only *make* things worse."

Writers can also express a "what-if" relationship between events using the **subjunctive mood,** which can convey what is logically possible but actually contrary to fact.

> **Subjunctive:** The nestling flapped its wings as if it *were* about *to take* flight. . . .

To use the subjunctive form of *to be* to express "what-if" or "as-if" relationships, use *were* for all subjects. For most other verbs, use the subjunctive *were* with the infinitive form of the verb, as in the example above.

Practice Replace the underlined words in each item, rewriting conditional constructions as subjunctive and subjunctive constructions as conditional.

1. If Yoshiko <u>were to choose</u> anything she wanted, it would be harmony.
2. If he <u>should</u> arrive late, he would call first.
3. Yoshiko knew that her brother might relax if her father <u>were to stop</u> criticizing him.
4. Her sadness might decrease if he <u>were to be</u> more loving.
5. If her father <u>should leave</u>, she knew her brother would suffer.

Writing Application Write a paragraph about your friends. Include at least three examples of the subjunctive mood using *could, would,* or *should.*

W̶G *Prentice Hall Writing and Grammar Connection: Diamond Level, Chapter 21, Section 3*

Writing Lesson

Proposal for a Program for the Elderly

Elderly people such as the grandmother in "The Jay" often benefit from community programs designed to make their days more interesting. Write a proposal explaining how such a program could be set up and administered. Use the grandmother in this story as a case study, or model, to defend your ideas.

Prewriting   Write an outline that organizes the sections of your proposal. Include notes about the supporting information that you will use in each section.

Model: Outlining for Organization and Clarity

III. Activities (support: quotation from national study on aging)
    A. Creative Activities
        1. Writing (support: Self-expression can be vital.)
        2. Crafts, such as quilt-making
    B. Physical Activities
        1. Dance
        2. Outdoor sports; walking

> Notes about supporting information make an outline even more effective.

Drafting   Begin with an introduction that states your purpose and asserts the importance of this program. As you follow your outline, use details from the story to support your ideas.

Revising   Review your proposal, making sure that you have organized your ideas logically. Consider reordering sections to create a better flow.

Prentice Hall Writing and Grammar Connection: Diamond Level, Chapter 11, Connected Assignment

Extension Activities

Listening and Speaking Prepare an **oral report** on the literary history of Japan. Use both print and electronic sources, including the Internet, to gather information. Follow these tips as you prepare:

- Organize your material in chronological order.
- Summarize the lives of important writers and the plots of key works.

As you deliver your presentation, use effective body language and speak with enthusiasm.

Research and Technology With a small group, prepare a **science report** about birds. Consider the various types of bird nests, as well as migration instincts and patterns. Augment your report with illustrations, recordings, charts, and diagrams, and then present it to the class. **[Group Activity]**

 **Take It to the Net**   PHSchool.com

Go online for an additional research activity using the Internet.

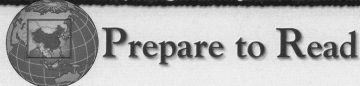

Prepare to Read

Thoughts of Hanoi ◆ All ◆ Also All ◆ Assembly Line

Nguyen Thi Vinh (b. 1924)

Nguyen Thi Vinh (noō´ yin tī vin) was born in Ha Dong Province in the Red River Delta of North Vietnam. She is a novelist, poet, and editor, but most of all she is a writer of short stories. Her first and most famous work is the novel *Two Sisters,* published in 1953. She is also the author of six other books of fiction, as well as a collection of poetry.

In 1954, the country of Vietnam was divided into two independent countries: communist North Vietnam and democratic South Vietnam. Prior to the installation of the communist government in the North, nearly one million North Vietnamese fled south. Among these was Nguyen Thi Vinh. In 1975, North Vietnam defeated South Vietnam and invaded Saigon, the country's capital. Up until that moment, Nguyen had been a prominent member of the Saigon community of writers. After the fall of Saigon, she remained in Vietnam but refused to play any public role. In 1983, Nguyen joined her family in Norway, thus becoming a refugee once again.

Bei Dao (b. 1949)

Bei Dao (bā dou) was born just two months before China's communists founded the People's Republic. He attended one of China's best schools and seemed destined for a position in the communist bureaucracy. Instead, in 1965, he became a member of the Red Guard, the quasi-military group that enforced the Cultural Revolution. At first, this movement sought to revitalize revolutionary fervor, but it soon degenerated into wholesale persecution of artists, teachers, and intellectuals.

Disillusioned, Bei Dao turned to poetry. Bold, questioning, and vivid, his poems express a deep dissatisfaction with Chinese society. Eventually, he became associated with a like-minded group of writers called the Misty Poets.

When a new wave of discontent swept China in 1976, Bei Dao's poem "Answer" became a rallying cry for change. In 1978, students set up large bulletin boards in public spaces, where they posted dissident writings. This unusual form of publication became known as the Democracy Wall Movement, and it brought Bei Dao's work to a wide audience.

During the Tiananmen Square massacre in 1989, Bei Dao was traveling abroad. The period of repression that followed the massacre prevented his return home. Today, he lives and works in the West, separated from his wife and daughter, who remain in China.

Shu Ting (b. 1952)

Shu Ting (shoō tiŋ) was born in Jinjiang County of Fujian Province. Still in middle school during China's Cultural Revolution, she was forced to leave her home, abandon her education, and go to live in a small, impoverished peasant village. When she returned to Fujian in 1973, she worked on construction sites and in factories. In spite of these experiences, she began writing poetry and, while still in her twenties, gained nationwide fame as a poet. Shu Ting became associated with the Misty Poets when her work appeared in the underground literary magazine *Today.* Shu Ting still lives in China, in the seaport city of Xiamen.

Preview

Connecting to the Literature

If you are like most American students, you had no direct experience of political violence before September 11, 2001. Think of what life must be like for people who face the ravages of war daily, whose right to free speech is stifled. The authors of these poems offer some insights.

Literary Analysis

Political Poetry

Political poetry connects the realm of private emotion to the political or social arena. While political poems often tell stories and express personal feelings, they are written in reaction to political events or as commentary about a political situation. For example, in "Thoughts of Hanoi," the speaker expresses the personal pain caused by the Vietnam War:

> Brother, I am afraid
> that one day I'll be with the March-North Army
> meeting you on your way to the South.
> I might be the one to shoot you then. . . .

As you read these poems, think about how each one examines the effects of political events or conditions on the private lives of individuals.

Comparing Literary Works

People respond to the suffering caused by war or repression in different ways. Some become hopeless, while others hold on to a belief in the human spirit. As you read these poems, compare each speaker's attitude toward both the sufferings of the present and the promise of the future.

Reading Strategy

Connecting to Historical Context

Political poems will carry deeper meaning for you if you **connect to the historical context** that they reflect. Use a chart like the one shown to list details from each poem that pertain to the historical situation from which it arose. Then, form an overall sense of the writer's message. Use the poets' biographies and the background notes to help you as you read.

Vocabulary Development

jubilant (jōō′ bə lənt) *adj.* extremely happy; exultant (p. 1394)

obsolete (äb′ sə lēt′) *adj.* out of date; out of use (p. 1395)

lamentation (lam′ ən tā′ shən) *n.* outward expression of grief; weeping or wailing (p. 1396)

heralds (her′ əldz) *v.* announces; introduces (p. 1396)

reverberates (ri vʉr′ bə rātz′) *v.* echoes; sounds again (p. 1396)

chasm (kaz′ əm) *n.* deep crack in Earth's surface (p. 1397)

monotony (mə nät′ 'n ē) *n.* tedious sameness (p. 1398)

tempo (tem′ pō) *n.* rate of speed; pace (p. 1398)

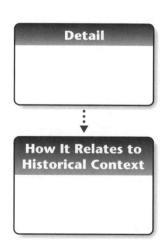

Detail

How It Relates to Historical Context

THOUGHTS OF HANOI

Nguyen Thi Vinh

translated by Nguyen Ngoc Bich *with* Burton Raffel *and* W. S. Merwin

Morning Rain, 2001, Bich Nguyet, Courtesy of Galeria La Vong Ltd.

▲ **Critical Viewing** Does this scene of people in the morning rain seem like a memory for which the speaker of this poem might yearn? Why or why not? **[Connect]**

Background

Vietnam was a colony of France until 1954, when the French suffered a major defeat at the hands of Vietnamese insurgent leader Ho Chi Minh. A cease-fire agreement divided the country into communist North Vietnam and democratic South Vietnam, with Ho ruling the North from Hanoi. The cease-fire called for elections to determine the fate of the country, but they were never held. Ho Chi Minh's troops, the Viet Cong, who were supported by Russia and China, battled the South Vietnamese government and its American backers. In the war that ensued, members of the same family sometimes fought on different sides. It was in this climate that Nguyen Thi Vinh wrote "Thoughts of Hanoi," her personal lyric about the Vietnam War from the perspective of a North Vietnamese living in the South.

The night is deep and chill
as in early autumn. Pitchblack,
it thickens after each lightning flash.
I dream of Hanoi:
5 Co-ngu[1] Road
ten years of separation
the way back sliced by a frontier of hatred.
I want to bury the past
to burn the future
10 still I yearn
still I fear
those endless nights
waiting for dawn.

Brother,
15 how is Hang Dao[2] now?
How is Ngoc Son[3] temple?
Do the trains still run
each day from Hanoi
to the neighboring towns?
20 To Bac-ninh, Cam-giang, Yen-bai,[4]
the small villages, islands
of brown thatch in a lush green sea?

The girls
bright eyes
25 ruddy cheeks
four-piece dresses

Reading Strategy
Connecting to Historical Context What "past" do you think the speaker wishes to "bury"?

✔**Reading Check**

For how many years has the speaker been away from Hanoi?

---

1. Co-ngu (cô g$\overline{oo}$)
2. Hang Dao (häŋ dou)
3. Ngoc Son (nōk sōn)
4. Bac-ninh (bäk nin), **Cam-giang** (käm gyäŋ), **Yen-bai** (ēŋ bī)

Peacefulness, Tran Nguyen Dan, Indochina Arts Project

◀ **Critical Viewing**
What image of Vietnamese
society does this painting
convey? [Interpret]

            raven-bill scarves
         sowing harvesting
            spinning weaving
30   all year round,
      the boys
            plowing
               transplanting
         in the fields
35   in their shops
         running across
               the meadow at evening
         to fly kites
               and sing alternating songs.

40   Stainless blue sky,
          jubilant voices of children
      stumbling through the alphabet,
          village graybeards strolling to the temple,
      grandmothers basking in twilight sun,
45   chewing betel leaves
      while the children run—

jubilant (jōō´ bə lənt) *adj.*
extremely happy; exultant

Brother,
how is all that now?
Or is it <u>obsolete</u>?
50   Are you like me,
reliving the past,
imagining the future?
Do you count me as a friend
or am I the enemy in your eyes?
55   Brother, I am afraid
that one day I'll be with the March-North Army
meeting you on your way to the South.
I might be the one to shoot you then
or you me
60   but please
not with hatred.

For don't you remember how it was,
you and I in school together,
plotting our lives together?
65   Those roots go deep!

Brother, we are men,
conscious of more
than material needs.
How can this happen to us
70   my friend
my foe?

obsolete (äb´ sə lēt´) *adj.*
out of date; out of use

Literary Analysis
Political Poetry What
truth about the people
fighting the Vietnam War
does this stanza express?

Review and Assess

Thinking About the Selection

1. **Respond:** Which images do you find the most vivid? Explain.

2. **(a) Recall:** In the first three lines, which details describe the night in which the speaker is dreaming? **(b) Generalize:** How would you describe the mood the speaker establishes in these lines?

3. **(a) Recall:** By what boundary does the speaker say the "way back" is sliced? **(b) Interpret:** Is this a physical boundary, an emotional boundary, or both? Explain.

4. **(a) Interpret:** Which experiences has the speaker shared with the "Brother"? Explain. **(b) Infer:** What emotional bond do these experiences suggest? **(c) Analyze:** How has that bond been tested by war?

5. **Take a Position:** While all war is terrible, do you think that civil war, like the one in Vietnam, is especially devastating? Why or why not?

All

Bei Dao   *translated by* Donald Finkel *and* Xueliang Chen

Background

In 1980, a Chinese poet named Gu Cheng published a poem that depicted two children in bright colors emerging from a world of gray. At that time, Chinese life was very regimented: People's jobs and even their style of dress were dictated by the state. Gu Cheng's poem seemed to criticize the dull grayness of that life and of the kind of literature the state prescribed: realistic, supportive of communism, and not subjective or personal. When a state literary critic attacked Gu Cheng's poem as "misty," Gu Cheng and some of his fellow poets adopted the term as a badge of honor, calling themselves the Misty Poets. Bei Dao and Shu Ting are two of the best known of the Misty Poets.

All is fated,
all cloudy,

all an endless beginning,
all a search for what vanishes,

5 all joys grave,
all griefs tearless,

every speech a repetition,
every meeting a first encounter,

all love buried in the heart,
10 all history prisoned in a dream,

all hope hedged with doubt,
all faith drowned in <u>lamentation.</u>

Every explosion <u>heralds</u> an instant of stillness,
every death <u>reverberates</u> forever.

Literary Analysis
Political Poetry Within the context of a repressive government, why might "every speech" be a "repetition"?

lamentation (lam ən tā´ shən) *n.* outward expression of grief; weeping or wailing

heralds (her´ əldz) *v.* announces; introduces

reverberates (ri vʉr´ bə rātz´) *v.* echoes; sounds again

Also All

In Answer to Bei Dao's "All"

Shu Ting *translated by* Donald Finkel *and* Jinsheng Yi

Not all trees are felled by storms.
Not every seed finds barren soil.
Not all the wings of dream are broken,
nor is all affection doomed
5   to wither in a desolate heart.

No, not all is as you say.

Not all flames consume themselves,
shedding no light on other lives.
Not all stars announce the night
10   and never dawn. Not every song
will drift past every ear and heart.

No, not all is as you say.

Not every cry for help is silenced,
nor every loss beyond recall.
15   Not every chasm spells disaster.
Not only the weak will be brought to their knees,
nor every soul be trodden under.

It won't all end in tears and blood.
Today is heavy with tomorrow—
20   the future was planted yesterday.
Hope is a burden all of us shoulder
though we might stumble under the load.

Literary Analysis
Political Poetry Which people in Chinese society might the speaker be describing as "flames"? Explain.

chasm (kaz´ əm) *n.* deep crack in Earth's surface

Review and Assess

Thinking About the Selections

1. **(a) Recall:** In lines 5–6 of "All," which adjective describes "joys"?
   (b) Recall: Which adjective describes "griefs"? **(c) Analyze:** What is the speaker saying about the kinds of emotions that are possible in a repressive society? Explain.

2. **(a) Recall:** According to the subtitle of "Also All," to whom and to what is the speaker responding in this poem? **(b) Generalize:** Which repeated line suggests the poet's motivation for writing this poem?

3. **Make a Judgment:** Do you think "Also All" can be read independently of "All" and still carry the same meaning? Why or why not?

Assembly Line

Shu Ting *translated by* Carolyn Kizer

In time's assembly line
Night presses against night.
We come off the factory night-shift
In line as we march towards home.
5 Over our heads in a row
The assembly line of stars
Stretches across the sky.
Beside us, little trees
Stand numb in assembly lines.

10 The stars must be exhausted
After thousands of years
Of journeys which never change.
The little trees are all sick,
Choked on smog and <u>monotony</u>,
15 Stripped of their color and shape.
It's not hard to feel for them;
We share the same <u>tempo</u> and rhythm.

Yes, I'm numb to my own existence
As if, like the trees and stars
20 —perhaps just out of habit
—perhaps just out of sorrow,
I'm unable to show concern
For my own manufactured fate.

Reading Strategy
Connecting to Historical Context What does the first stanza suggest about the lives of Chinese citizens at this time?

monotony (mə nät′ 'n ē) *n.* tedious sameness

tempo (tem′ pō) *n.* rate of speed; pace

Review and Assess

Thinking About the Selection

1. **Respond:** Describe the mental picture you formed while reading this poem.
2. **(a) Recall:** In lines 6–9, what natural objects does the speaker notice? **(b) Analyze:** How are the speaker and the natural objects alike?
3. **(a) Analyze:** Why is the speaker's fate "manufactured"? **(b) Analyze Cause and Effect:** What is the speaker saying about the ways in which an "assembly line" existence harms the human spirit?

Review and Assess

Literary Analysis
Political Poetry

1. (a) Use a chart like the one shown to identify personal and political details in each poem. (b) Which poem speaks to a specific political event most directly? Explain.

	Thoughts of Hanoi	All	Also All	Assembly Line
Personal details				
Political details				

2. (a) How does each of these examples of **political poetry** express the speaker's powerlessness in the face of terrible circumstances? (b) How do these examples suggest the power of a single voice?

Comparing Literary Works

3. In lines 10–11 of "Thoughts of Hanoi," the speaker describes both yearning and fear. Which emotion is stronger in the poem? Explain.

4. (a) Cite images in "Also All" that present a balance between hope and destruction. (b) How are the emotions of yearning and fear that Nguyen expresses also expressed in the poems by Shu Ting? (c) Does Bei Dao convey a similar mix of emotions? Explain.

Reading Strategy
Connecting to Historical Context

5. What information in the poet's biography or the background helps you **connect to the historical context** of "Thoughts of Hanoi"? Explain.

6. Choose a single line from "All" or "Also All" that you think best expresses the historical context of China's repressive rule. Explain your choice.

Extend Understanding

7. **Social Studies Connection:** In what ways do you think works of literature can affect political or social change? Explain.

Quick Review

Political poetry is verse that is written in response to or as commentary about political events or circumstances.

To **connect to the historical context** as you read, decide how details in the poem reflect the specific circumstances of the political climate in which they were written.

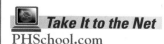 **Take It to the Net**
PHSchool.com

Take the interactive self-test online to check your understanding of these selections.

Integrate Language Skills

Vocabulary Development Lesson

Word Analysis: Latin Root -temp-

Some time-related words in English contain the root -temp-, which is based on the Latin word *tempus*, meaning *time*. Thus, *tempo* refers to a rate of speed. Use your knowledge of the root to match each word below with its definition.

1. temporal
2. temporize
3. extemporaneous

a. delay; evade
b. done without preparation
c. worldly

Spelling Strategy

In many words of Greek origin that begin with a *k* sound, the sound is spelled *ch*, as in *chasm*. Complete the spelling of the words in each sentence below.

1. She took courses in __emistry.
2. His life was busy and __aotic.

Concept Development: Synonyms or Antonyms?

Review the vocabulary list on page 1391 and notice the way each word is used in the context of the selections. Then, determine whether the words in each pair below are synonyms (words with similar meanings) or antonyms (words with opposite meanings).

1. monotony/excitement
2. heralds/greets
3. chasm/mountaintop
4. jubilant/distressed
5. reverberates/echoes
6. tempo/pace
7. obsolete/new
8. lamentations/rejoicings

Grammar and Style Lesson

Parallelism

Parallelism is the repeated expression of similar ideas in a similar grammatical form—words, phrases, clauses, or whole sentences. Parallelism is used to emphasize equal relationships between ideas and to create a smooth, musical flow of language.

Examples:

Not every cry for help is silenced,
nor every loss beyond recall. (parallel repetition of similar words)

the boys / plowing / transplanting / in the fields (parallel use of participles)

Practice Identify and explain the uses of parallelism in each item below.

1. still I yearn / still I fear /
2. —perhaps just out of habit / —perhaps just out of sorrow,
3. village greybeards strolling . . . / grandmothers basking . . .
4. all love buried in the heart, / all history prisoned in a dream,
5. Choked on smog and monotony, / Stripped of their color and shape.

Writing Application Write a few lines of poetry. Include at least two examples of parallelism.

*W*G *Prentice Hall Writing and Grammar Connection: Diamond Level, Chapter 20, Section 6*

Writing Lesson

Literary Analysis

Write a literary analysis of one of the poems in this group. In your literary analysis, explore how elements of the poem work together to support its overall theme.

Prewriting   Choose a poem and reread it carefully. As you read, jot down details that seem especially important or powerful. Identify ways in which the details combine to express a single message, or theme.

Drafting   Begin with an introduction stating your thesis—a brief statement summarizing the poem's overall effect or theme and the elements that contribute to it. In the body of the paper, support your thesis with specific details from the poem.

Revising   As you reread your work, double-check the structure of your sentences. If you have too many short, choppy sentences, combine them to achieve variety.

Model: Revising Sentences to Create Variety and Interest

In "Thoughts of Hanoi,"

Nguyen uses images like a series of frames in a film

~~in "Thoughts of Hanoi." She does this~~ to re-create a

untroubled

sense of the life of the past. ~~That life was untroubled.~~

> Combining short, repetitive sentences creates a more interesting flow.

Prentice Hall Writing and Grammar Connection: Diamond Level, Chapter 20, Section 3

Extension Activities

Listening and Speaking With a partner, prepare a **dialogue** that might have occurred between the speaker in "Thoughts of Hanoi" and her friend after the war. Use these tips to prepare:

- Make a list of questions the two might ask each other and their likely responses.
- Decide whether the two will rediscover their friendship or will remain hostile.

Practice until your dialogue sounds natural and spontaneous. Then, present it to the class.

Research and Technology With a small group, prepare a **multimedia report** on the events that occurred at Tiananmen Square in 1989. Use books, magazines, and the Internet to gather information about government leaders, leaders of the democracy movement, and the Democracy Wall. **[Group Activity]**

 **Take It to the Net** PHSchool.com

Go online for an additional research activity using the Internet.

Writing About Literature

Compare and Contrast Literary Themes Across Cultures

For many writers, the world wars, totalitarian states, and consumer economy of our era mark the failure of society to give meaningful form to life. The individual seems left on his or her own to make sense of the world, as in Camus's "The Guest." Yet the global scale of current events emphasizes the interconnections among lives. In this spirit, some writers chart the ways individual lives are shaped by the history of a group, as Derek Walcott does in *Omeros*. Camus, Walcott, and others share a general insight: The place where individual and society meet is haunted by unsettled—and unsettling—questions.

Write an essay in which you compare this theme across cultures. Refer to the box at right for details of the assignment.

Prewriting

Choose selections. Review the selections to identify those with themes that relate to the individual's place in society. Choose at least two works from two cultures for your analysis. Ask questions such as the following to help guide your search:

- What does this selection suggest about the relationship between society and the individual?
- How is this theme revealed: through the plot, setting, characterization, language, or a combination of elements?
- In what ways is the relationship between individual and society in this selection like or unlike their relationship in other works?

Drawing on your notes, fill out a chart like the one shown. Then, review the chart and choose four or more selections, at least two from each of two cultures. To ensure that your essay will be interesting and rich in detail, choose works that show striking similarities or contrasts.

Model: Charting to Compare and Contrast Themes

Selection	Theme	Evidence of Theme
"The Handsomest Drowned Man in the World"	Individuals perceive and imagine together, collectively.	Women agree the drowned man's name is Esteban.

Write a working thesis. After you have decided which aspects of the theme appear in the works you have chosen, write a working thesis. Introduce the selections you will compare and contrast and the specific ways they present the individual in society.

Assignment: Who Am I? The Individual Across Cultures

Write an analytical essay that compares the theme of the individual in society in works from two of the following cultures included in this unit: the Americas, Western Europe, Eastern Europe, the Middle East, Africa, and Asia.

Criteria:

- Include a thesis statement drawn from your analysis of the literature of the two cultures.
- Support your thesis with detailed comparisons and contrasts of at least two selections from each culture.
- Cite several examples from each work.
- Approximate length: 1,500 words

Read to Write

As you reread the texts, analyze the tone. Tone, the author's attitude toward the subject and the reader, can help you understand the theme of a work.

Drafting

Prepare an outline. Make an outline to help you organize your essay. Each main heading preceded by a Roman numeral should stand for an important idea that you plan to explore in its own paragraph. Under each subheading, list supporting examples.

> **Model: Using a Working Outline**
>
> **I.** Writers of the Americas emphasize family and heritage
>   **A.** "Handsomest Drowned Man in the World"
>   **1.** Groups of men and women think alike
>   **2.** Village agrees on what to do with drowned man
>   **B.** "House Taken Over"
>   **1.** Brother and sister live in family house

Refer to history. To strengthen your arguments, support them with references to historical events or cultural movements. Explain, where appropriate, the effect of historical circumstances on the works.

Revising and Editing

Review content: Reformulate points for accuracy. Reread your draft. Circle each sentence in which you state a main point. Then, review your circled points. For each, consider whether it accurately sums up an insight to which your paper leads. Rewrite as necessary to ensure that you have used just the right terms to explain your ideas.

Review style: Delete unnecessary words. Make sure that you have communicated your ideas in the simplest, most straightforward way possible. Take out any unnecessary words that you may have used.

Wordy: Very obviously, the title of the story gives a strong hint about its nature and tone. From the very first sentence, the reader knows that the story will not be completely realistic and will probably include elements of fantasy.

Revised: The title gives a strong hint about the tone of the story. From the first sentence, the reader knows that the story will include elements of fantasy.

Publishing and Presenting

Have a discussion. Gather with classmates who wrote about the same selections you did. Compare group members' interpretations of the literature.

W͠G Writing and Grammar Connection: Diamond Level, Chapter 9

Write to Learn
As you write your first draft, you may notice that some examples from the selections do not adequately support your ideas. Look back at the selections to make sure you have chosen the details or quotations that best illustrate the theme of the individual in society.

Write to Explain
Use parallel construction to make your comparisons and contrasts as clear as possible to readers.

Writing WORKSHOP

Workplace Writing: Job Portfolio

A **job portfolio** consists of the materials a candidate submits to a potential employer. Core elements are the **résumé,** a summary of qualifications and experience, and a cover letter that introduces the job seeker. Other materials may include references and writing or other work samples. In this workshop, you will write an effective résumé.

Assignment Criteria Your résumé should include the following elements:

- Prominently displayed name, address, and contact information
- Summaries of work history, education, and related experience tailored for the job under consideration
- Consistent style and precise language, including active verbs
- Easy-to-follow, consistent résumé format

To preview the criteria on which your résumé may be assessed, refer to the Rubric for Self-Assessment on page 1407.

Prewriting

List information. List all of your work experience. Include exact dates of employment, employers' names and addresses, and your duties. Also note relevant extra-curricular, volunteer, and educational experiences, as well as any special skills, such as word processing.

Choose a place to which to apply. Determine the type of job you wish to obtain, and apply to suitable employers. To conduct a thorough, well-informed job search, follow these steps:

- Consult library resources, visit employment agencies, and speak with guidance counselors, friends, and family to familiarize yourself with various types of jobs.
- Review print or Web guides to local businesses, and list employers of interest to you.
- Consult job listings at your school, at an employment agency, and in the Help Wanted section of the newspaper.

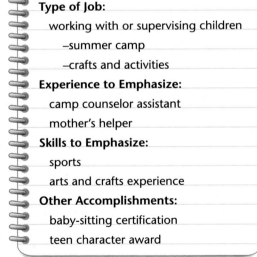

Type of Job:
    working with or supervising children
        –summer camp
        –crafts and activities
Experience to Emphasize:
    camp counselor assistant
    mother's helper
Skills to Emphasize:
    sports
    arts and crafts experience
Other Accomplishments:
    baby-sitting certification
    teen character award

Match your experience to the job. Determine which of your experiences will be of most interest for a given application. Emphasize those experiences in your cover letter and résumé. For example, a store advertising for help with displays might want to see evidence of creativity. A store looking for a cashier might be more interested in mathematical skills.

Student Model

Before you begin drafting your résumé, read this student model and review the characteristics of an effective résumé.

Megan Mary Mahoney
1234 Anystreet
Hickory, NC 28601
(888) 555-5555
e-mail@e-mail.com

> Name and contact information are placed prominently at the top of the page and set in a larger font size.

OBJECTIVE
To obtain a position as a camp counselor in order to work with children

EDUCATION

August 2001 to Present

St. Stephen High School, Hickory, NC
Expected graduation date: June 2005. Honor student.
Special courses: Journalism; Advanced Placement English
Extracurricular activities: Beta Club, yearbook staff, varsity tennis, JV soccer, and JV basketball

> Megan uses clear headings to label her education, work, and other relevant experiences.

WORK EXPERIENCE

Summer 2002 and 2003

Counselor's Assistant
Camp Joy, Hickory, NC
Helped campers with arts, sports, games, and social interaction at this nonprofit camp for underprivileged children.

> Megan provides specific details about experiences related to her objective.

2002 to Present

Part-time Mother's Helper
Sue Smith, Hickory, NC
Assist mother of severely handicapped daughter. Help with feeding and medications and watch over the child when the mother does errands.

2000 to Present

Baby Sitter
Hickory, NC
Care for several different children; regular duties include feeding, bathing, playing games, and reading bedtime stories.

SKILLS

- Sports: tennis, soccer, basketball, volleyball
- Arts and crafts, piano
- Computer skills: word processing, Internet research

SPECIAL ACHIEVEMENTS

- Received Baby-Sitting Certification at Frye Regional Hospital in December 2001. Was trained in basic first aid and baby-sitting.
- Received the Teen Character Award from the local YMCA in May 2001. Nominated for this award by teachers.

> Bullets and bold-face headings make Megan's information clear and easy to follow. Headings, dates, and bulleted items are aligned consistently.

Drafting

Select a style. Choose a résumé style, and apply the style consistently as you draft your résumé. For example, you may choose to use either sentences or phrases in the descriptions of your job history, or to mix the two in each entry. Select one of these styles, and use it consistently.

- **Whole sentences:** Responsibilities included routing copy, running errands, and assisting reporters.
- **Phrases:** Routed copy; ran errands; assisted reporters

Select a format. Résumés can follow several possible formats. The model on page 1405 shows one format. The key to an effective format is an easy-to-follow organization. No matter what format you choose, follow it consistently. Always include these features:

- Name, address, phone number, e-mail address, and other contact information, displayed prominently at the top of the document
- List of work and other applicable experiences and accomplishments, beginning with the most recent
- Names and addresses of employers in boldface or otherwise set off
- Dates of terms of employment with each employer
- Brief description of responsibilities for each job listing

Follow résumé language conventions. Do not use the pronoun *I*. Write, for example, "Took responsibility for" or "Responsible for" instead of "I took responsibility for."

Revising

Revise for consistency. Make sure you have followed a consistent organizational strategy, as well as format and style. Mark any inconsistencies as you scan your résumé.

1. Make sure the entries are aligned consistently.
2. Make sure the headings are boldfaced and capitalized.
3. Make sure all the information in a section is organized following the same pattern.

Correct any inconsistencies that you note.

Résumé Conventions

- **Heading** includes the candidate's name, address, and contact information.
- **Objective** or **Summary** provides a brief statement about the candidate and his or her professional goals.
- **Experience** lists details of work and other relevant history.
- **Education** provides a history of the candidate's schooling and other training.
- **Skills** section notes special abilities, such as computer training or fluency in a foreign language.
- **Honors/Activities/Memberships** is a flexible category that includes applicable activities that do not fit into other sections of the résumé.

Model: Revise for Consistency

August 2001 (to) Present	**St. Stephen High School,** Hickory, NC	
to		
2000 — Present	**Baby Sitter**	

The use of *to* in the first entry and the dash in the second are inconsistent. Choose one style or the other.

Revise language. Avoid vague words and passive verbs.

Vague: Was assigned work on brochures

Specific: Researched and wrote copy for four-color brochures for advertising agency

Compare the model and the nonmodel. Ask yourself: Why is the model more effective?

Nonmodel	Model
Employed by a mother of a severely handicapped child.	Assist mother of severely handicapped daughter. Help with feeding and medications and watch over the child when the mother does errands.

Publishing and Presenting

Put together a job portfolio. To accompany your résumé and complete your job portfolio, write a cover letter. Include the following elements:

- A brief, pertinent statement about yourself
- An expression of your interest in the job
- An overview of your qualifications for the job
- Contact information
- Thanks for consideration of your résumé

Follow standard business-letter format for your cover letter. Proofread your draft carefully to ensure that the final copy is free of errors.

WG Writing and Grammar Connection: Diamond Level, Chapter 16

Rubric for Self-Assessment

Evaluate your résumé using the following criteria and rating scale:

Criteria	Rating Scale				
	Not very				Very
How visible are the name, address, and contact information?	1	2	3	4	5
How well does the résumé describe qualifications and experiences?	1	2	3	4	5
How consistent is the format?	1	2	3	4	5
How precise and active is the language?	1	2	3	4	5
How clear is the organization?	1	2	3	4	5

Delivering a Multimedia Presentation

Many presentations can be enhanced through the use of sounds and visuals. When you give a **multimedia presentation,** you might use an overhead projector, a slide projector, a video or audio player, a computer, or another electronic device. The following strategies will help you develop and deliver an effective multimedia presentation.

Prepare Your Content

The suggestions below will help you develop your multimedia presentation:

- Outline your presentation, and decide which parts can be effectively presented through, or with the support of, visual or sound media.
- Choose media that suit your topic. For example, if your topic is American life during World War II, you might play popular music of the time as background.
- Use audio or visual support throughout your presentation, not just at the beginning or at the end.

Prepare Your Delivery

Multimedia presentations can be wonderful experiences for presenter and audience alike—but only if all the technology functions as intended. These tips may help you prepare to use audio and visual technology in your presentation:

- Rehearse your presentation with the multimedia equipment you will use. Become familiar with the equipment, and learn how to make volume, focus, and other adjustments to it.
- Before the presentation, double-check the equipment to make sure that all of it is functioning properly.
- Make sure visuals will be seen and the audio portion will be heard by the entire audience.
- Have a backup plan, in case the equipment fails. For example, you might have on hand photocopies of charts and graphs to pass out to the audience in case the overhead projector fails.

Feedback Form for Multimedia Presentation

Rating System
+ = Excellent   ✓ = Average   – = Weak

Content
Match of media and topic _____
Media enhance topic _____
Media used at appropriate points _____

Delivery
Smoothness of presentation _____
Ability to adjust equipment _____
Ability to work around glitches in equipment _____

Activity:
Presentation and Feedback Prepare a multimedia presentation in which you explain how to make or do something at which you excel. Practice your presentation with a partner, using the Feedback Form shown to evaluate your content and delivery. Use the evaluation to help you polish your presentation, and then deliver it to the class.

Analyzing an Author's Meaning

In the reading sections of some tests, you may be required to read a passage and interpret the author's ideas or opinions.

- Identify the main idea and supporting details of the passage.
- Select the correct answers to questions about the passage, based on your own knowledge and the information in the passage.
- Eliminate answer choices that are unrelated to information in the passage.

Test-Taking Strategies

- To interpret parts a passage, restate the ideas in your own words.
- Read all the words in a passage carefully. Even small details may give clues to correct answers.

Sample Test Question

Directions: Read the passage, and then answer the question that follows.

America is experiencing an epidemic of obesity. Assign much of the blame to our frenetic lifestyles. We are too busy to prepare and eat home-cooked meals very often, and besides, fast food is delicious. Also, have you taken a good look at portion sizes lately? They are enormous! Hamburgers, which used to weigh 4 ounces, now weigh 8, 12, or even 16 ounces. Popcorn sold in movie theaters, which used to come in small bags or dainty boxes, is now served in huge vats—and with "free" refills. This trend is probably good for the fast-food and movie-theaters profits, but it's wreaking havoc on Americans' waistlines and health.

1. With which statement would the writer of the passage clearly agree?

   A We need to make fast food more tasty.

   B We need to eat less fast food.

   C We need to close down fast-food restaurants.

   D We need to install gyms in fast-food restaurants.

Answer and Explanation

The correct answer is *B*. The writer believes people should eat less fast food. The writer does not discuss either option *C* or *D*, and *A* is contradicted in the passage.

▶ Practice

Directions: Read the following, and then complete the item that follows.

The mayor's plan to drain the swamp behind the Mayville town park is a sound one, but you may be surprised to learn the strongest reason for it. You might think at first of the mosquitoes that breed in the swamp. It is true that draining the swamp will help greatly, but pesticides could be used to eliminate mosquito larvae instead. You might think of the town's need for land on which to build a new school. The town has recently acquired three properties through tax foreclosures, however, any one of which would be suitable for a school.

The truth is that our town has hit hard times. A project such as draining the swamp, financed in part by state grants, is just what Mayville's unemployed need to find temporary work until there is a full economic recovery.

1. The author's main point is that

   A the mosquitoes should be killed.

   B Mayville has hit hard times.

   C the swamp should be drained to give Mayville's unemployed work.

   D the swamp should be drained for many reasons.

Resources

Handbooks

Indexes

Following are some suggestions for longer works that will give you the opportunity to experience the fun of sustained reading. Each of the suggestions further explores one of the time periods, themes, or literary movements in this book. Many of the titles are included in the **Prentice Hall Library,** featuring the **Penguin Literature Library**.

You may want to consult your teacher before choosing one of these longer works.

Unit One

The Bible's Greatest Stories
Paul Roche, *translator and reteller, Signet Classic, 2001*

The stories of Noah and the flood and of Ruth's loyalty to Naomi are only two of the many classic Bible tales related in this comprehensive collection. In this publication, translator and reteller Paul Roche includes maps of Palestine and the Greco-Roman world to help readers place major events that occur in the stories. Introductory material links related tales while, at the same time, making them accessible to today's readers. All the themes of great literature can be found in these stories: love, honor, war, pride, celebration, and death. These themes emerge in dramatic episodes— such as the birth of Moses or the story of Joseph's coat of many colors—gathered from such biblical books as Genesis, the four Gospels, and Acts of the Apostles.

Tales of Ancient Egypt
Selected and retold by Roger Lancelyn Green, *Puffin Classic, 1996*

Ancient Egypt is a land of fables. In *Tales of Ancient Egypt,* Roger Lancelyn Green retells twenty of these stories. Some are as close to us as our own childhoods— "The Girl with the Red-Rose Slippers," for instance, is the earliest version of the Cinderella story. Others, such as the story of how the goddess Isis tricked the god Ra, give glimpses of faraway ancient beliefs—beliefs in the power of names and in a person's immortal double. Discovered carved in temple walls or written on papyrus scrolls, some of these tales explain why a particular monument was built. Others tell of life's fundamentals—of love, of the desire to be remembered, of the struggle for justice. In these tales, readers will encounter some familiar themes; they may also rediscover the strange scent of mystery that makes tales from the past so fascinating.

The Epic of Gilgamesh
Anonymous, *translated by N. K. Sandars, Penguin Classic, 1960*

If sampling a portion of this work has given you an appetite for more, treat yourself to the complete book.

Related British Literature: Early Irish Myths and Sagas
Anonymous, *translated by Jeffrey Gantz, Penguin Classic, 1982*

The Celtic people who told the stirring tales in this book lived at about the same time as the ancient Mesopotamians, Egyptians, and Hebrews.

Related American Literature: The Conquest of New Spain
Bernal Díaz del Castillo, *translated by J. M. Cohen, Penguin Classic, 1963*

The author provides a vivid firsthand account of how the Spaniard Hernán Cortés conquered the Aztecs, one of the ancient peoples of Mexico.

Unit Two

A Tiger for Malgudi
R. K. Narayan, *Penguin Classic, 1994*

This novel by one of India's most celebrated authors features an unusual first-person narrator: a tiger. Set in the fictional South-Indian territory of Malgudi, *A Tiger for Malgudi* traces the life of a tiger named Raja from his days as a cub in the jungle to his misery as a circus animal to his eventual happiness in the care of a kind master. As the old tiger—now living in a zoo—reflects on his life and his experiences, readers gain a glimpse into Indian culture and even learn some Hindu philosophy. Raja also points out how absurd some human behaviors can seem when viewed through the eyes of a wild animal.

The Penguin Gandhi Reader
Mohandas K. Gandhi, *Penguin, 1995*

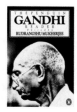

Gandhi was one of the most important political leaders of the twentieth century. His method of uncompromising yet peaceful protest helped gain India's freedom from British rule and inspired the world. This reader presents many of Gandhi's most important writings. The book is divided into eight sections, focusing on the following themes that occupied Gandhi's work and life: his

Unit Two (continued)

criticism of modern culture and rejection of materialism; the principles of *swaraj* (independence, or self-rule) and *swadeshi* (responsibility to one's immediate community); the doctrine of nonviolence; his participation in mass protest movements; his opinions about the role of women; his arguments against the Indian caste system; his thoughts on economic and social systems; his belief in religious tolerance; his commitment to a united India; and his struggle for Indian independence.

The Ramayana

R. K. Narayan, editor and reteller, *Penguin Classic, 1972*

If sampling a portion of this work has given you an appetite for more, treat yourself to the complete book.

Related British Literature:
Kim

Rudyard Kipling, *Penguin Classic, 1987*

This novel by a Nobel Prize-winning British author tells how a young boy learns the deadly game of espionage in nineteenth-century India.

Related American Literature:
Why We Can't Wait

Martin Luther King, Jr., *Signet Classic, 2000*

Dr. King describes his use of nonviolent action, a principle he learned from the life and writings of Indian leader Mohandas K. Gandhi.

Unit Three

Treason by the Book

Jonathan D. Spence, *Penguin, 2002*

Part history and part mystery, *Treason by the Book* details a plot to overthrow Yong-zheng, the Manchu emperor of China. This true story begins in 1728 when a treasonous letter addressed to the emperor is passed to one of the emperor's generals. After reading the letter, Yongzheng launches a massive investigation to find its author. When the guilty party is identified, Yongzheng does something quite unexpected. Inspired by Confucian ideas about leading by example, the emperor decides to engage in a public written dialogue with the letter's author in order to disprove his accusations and stem the tide of rebellion. *Treason by the Book* is a study not only of imperial power but also of the power of the written word.

The Narrow Road to the Deep North

Matsuo Bashō, *translated by Nobuyuki Yuasa, Penguin Classic, 1967*

As you read this book, you will be traveling through seventeenth-century Japan with an adventurous and sensitive companion, the poet Matsuo Bashō. He is more concerned with the spiritual benefits of his journey than he is with material comforts. Being poor, he cannot pay much for lodgings, but he is always ready to "pay" with a poem for the beauty he sees. For example, on finding a famous ruined castle, he sits on his hat, weeps, and writes, "A thicket of summer grass / Is all that remains / Of the dreams and ambitions / Of ancient warriors." Share sights and insights with this poet who, three hundred years before the highway adventures of America's beatniks, knew how to travel with an empty wallet and a full spirit.

The Analects

Confucius, *translated by Arthur Waley, Penguin Classic, 1979*

If sampling a portion of this work has given you an appetite for more, treat yourself to the complete book.

Related British Literature:
Across the Nightingale Floor

Lian Hearn, *Riverhead, 2003*

This novel by a British author tells about an orphan boy and his magical destiny in medieval Japan.

Related American Literature:
The Joy Luck Club

Amy Tan, *Putnam, 1989*

In her celebrated first novel, Amy Tan weaves together the stories of Chinese Americans living in San Francisco.

Unit Four

The Three Theban Plays

Sophocles, *translated by Robert Fagles, Penguin Classic, 1984*

This collection contains Sophocles' three tragedies about the royal house of Thebes. In addition to *Oedipus the King*, which appears in Unit 4 of *Prentice Hall World Masterpieces*, the collection includes the plays *Oedipus at Colonus* and *Antigone*. *Oedipus at Colonus* focuses on the end of Oedipus' life, following his downfall in *Oedipus the*

King. In *Antigone*, Oedipus is gone, but his legacy remains. His daughter, Antigone, refuses to compromise her ideals and submit to the orders of Creon, the new king of Thebes. Like her father, Antigone is strong-willed, and like him, she meets a tragic fate. These three plays are considered to be not only the greatest works by Sophocles but also the finest examples of Greek tragedy. They are ably translated by Robert Fagles, who also translated Homer's *Iliad* and *Odyssey*.

The Fall of the Roman Republic (Six Lives)
Plutarch, *translated by Rex Warner, Penguin Classic, 1954*

The Roman historian Plutarch was especially interested in the biographies of great men and the moral lessons that could be drawn from them. In this volume, he narrates the lives of six prominent Romans involved in the violence leading to the fall of the Roman republic: Marius, Sulla, Crassus, Pompey, Caesar, and Cicero. Plutarch had a flair for capturing vivid details. That is why Shakespeare relied so heavily on *Plutarch's Lives* while writing plays like *Julius Caesar*. Note, for example, how dramatically Plutarch describes the assassination of Julius Caesar: "when he [Caesar] saw that Brutus had drawn his dagger, he covered his head with his toga and sank down to the ground." Opening this book is like pulling aside the curtains of a stage and viewing the most dramatic events of Roman history.

The Iliad
Homer, *translated by Robert Fagles, Penguin Classic, 1991*

If sampling a portion of this work has given you an appetite for more, treat yourself to the complete book.

The Aeneid
Virgil, *translated by Patric Dickinson, Signet Classic, 2002*

If sampling a portion of this work has given you an appetite for more, treat yourself to the complete book.

Related British Literature:
The Extraordinary Voyage of Pytheas the Greek
Barry Cunliffe

A British archaeologist tells the true story of a Greek who, more than 2,000 years ago, made a dangerous sea voyage all the way to Iceland.

Related American Literature:
The Federalist Papers
Alexander Hamilton et al., *Penguin Classic, 1987*

Looking to the classical world as their model, three of America's greatest founding fathers set forth the principles of government that still guide us today.

Unit Five

The Divine Comedy: Paradiso
Dante Alighieri, *translated by Mark Musa, Penguin Classic, 1986*

The *Paradiso* is the last of the three volumes that form *The Divine Comedy*, Dante's allegory of his journey through the afterlife. In the *Inferno*, Dante travels through Hell under the guidance of the Roman poet Virgil. In the *Purgatorio*, Dante and Virgil ascend the Mount of Purgatory. At the mountain's summit, Virgil departs, and Beatrice, a woman Dante had loved before her death, becomes his guide. The *Paradiso* begins as Dante soars into Heaven with Beatrice. Like Hell and Purgatory, Dante's Heaven has its own geography and order. The lowest level is the Moon, followed by Mercury, Venus, the Sun, Mars, Jupiter, Saturn, the Stars, and the *Primum Mobile*—the source of all time and motion. The highest level is the Empyrean, the dwelling place of God. Dante ascends to the Empyrean, where he gazes upon the radiance of God, is overwhelmed, and later cannot remember what he saw.

Egil's Saga
Snorri Sturluson, *translated by Hermann Pálsson and Paul Edwards, Penguin Classic, 1977*

Composed in the thirteenth century by a master storyteller, this tale is set in tenth-century Iceland, Norway, and England. Egil, the hero of the book, is a formidable man, even by the standards of his dangerous Viking world. A brooding outsider, he has the courage to defy kings and to battle with the crazed warriors known as berserkers. Yet behind his impressive appearance—"wide forehead, bushy eyebrows . . . great broad beard . . . far above normal height but well-proportioned . . . bald . . ."—is an equally impressive mind. Egil is loyal and intelligent, a poet who can lament the death of his son in eloquent verse. When this fierce and complex man dies shortly before Iceland is converted to Christianity, his death seems to mark the passing of an era.

Unit Five (continued)

The Nibelungenlied

Anonymous, *translated by A. T. Hatto, Penguin Classic, 1965*
If sampling a portion of this work has given you an appetite for more, treat yourself to the complete book.

The Song of Roland

Anonymous, *translated by Glyn S. Burgess, Penguin Classic, 1990*

If sampling a portion of this work has given you an appetite for more, treat yourself to the complete book.

Related British Literature:
The Canterbury Tales

Geoffrey Chaucer, *translated by Nevill Coghill, Penguin Classic, 2003*
In this array of storytellers and their rhymed stories, a great poet portrays the many-sided life of medieval England.

Related American Literature:
A Connecticut Yankee
in King Arthur's Court

Mark Twain, *Signet Classic, 1963*
Making a fictional journey backward in time, America's greatest humorist casts a satirical but affectionate eye on the doings of King Arthur's court.

Unit Six

The Prince

Niccolò Machiavelli, *translated by George Bull, Penguin Classic, 2003*
In *The Prince*, a book about statecraft, Italian Renaissance author Machiavelli stresses the degree to which his views of political morality differ from those of previous writers. Where other theorists discuss how rulers ought to act, Machiavelli says that he deals with how rulers do act. Where others say that public deeds should reflect private morality, Machiavelli insists that personal morality has no place in politics. Rulers do not survive by their goodness but by their strength, cunning, and ability. Machiavelli's success can be measured by the enduring appeal of his work and by the continued use of his name as an adjective to denote craftiness and deceit: *Machiavellian*.

Tartuffe and Other Plays

Jean-Baptiste Molière, *translated by Donald M. Frame, Signet Classic, 1960*

In Molière's comedy *Tartuffe*, religiously devout but gullible Orgon opens his home to a stranger—Tartuffe—who poses as a pious, generous humanitarian. Unbeknownst to Orgon, however, Tartuffe is a con artist and hypocrite, a trickster who is both the creator and victim of schemes and lies that draw Orgon's seventeenth-century household into riotous chaos. Along with *Tartuffe*, this edition includes additional Molière comedies such as *The Ridiculous Précieuses* and *School for Husbands*. In general, these plays feature such character types as the hypocrite, the misanthrope, and the hypochondriac, all of whom serve to expose the absurdities of the playwright's society.

Candide

François Voltaire, *translated by John Butt, Penguin Classic, 1950*
If sampling a portion of this work has given you an appetite for more, treat yourself to the complete book.

Don Quixote

Miguel de Cervantes, *translated by John Rutherford, Penguin Classic, 2003*
If sampling a portion of this work has given you an appetite for more, treat yourself to the complete book.

Related British Literature:
The Tempest

William Shakespeare, *Pearson Prentice Hall, 2000*
In his final play, England's greatest author says farewell to the theater and explores Renaissance ideas concerning savagery and civilization.

Related American Literature:
The Falcon

John Tanner, *Penguin, 2003*
The author was captured as a boy by Ojibwa Indians, and his autobiography is the fascinating story of the encounter between white and Indian cultures.

Related American Literature:
Galileo's Daughter
Dava Sobel, *Penguin, 2000*

In this biography of a great scientist's daughter, American author Dava Sobel explores religion, science, and family relations during the Renaissance.

Unit Seven

The Hunchback of Notre Dame
Victor Hugo, *translated by Walter J. Cobb, Signet Classic, 2001*

This novel is set in medieval Paris in the shadow of the majestic Notre-Dame cathedral. Its main characters are Quasimodo, an orphaned hunchback who serves as the cathedral bell-ringer; Claude Frollo, the priest who has adopted Quasimodo; and Esmerelda, the gypsy dancer to whom Frollo is desperately attracted. The story, which begins with Quasimodo being shamefully crowned the Pope of Fools by the Parisian mob, is a tragic tale of love, loyalty, and betrayal. It is filled with unforgettable images, such as the description of a mob's assault on Notre-Dame as "a layer of living monsters crawling over the stone monsters of the façade." The story also vividly conveys two of Hugo's most important Romantic beliefs—the essential value of the outcast or outsider and the close relationship between beauty and ugliness.

Diary of a Madman and Other Stories
Nikolai Gogol, *translated by Ronald Wilks, Penguin Classic, 1973*

Trudging through the mists of nineteenth-century St. Petersburg, mumbling to themselves as they go, the harried nobodies of Nikolai Gogol's stories reflect the new sorrow of the modern world—the life of the anonymous. Gogol's faceless clerks and petty bureaucrats battle their own insignificance. His genius is to make their struggle against erasure both deeply sad and outrageously funny. "The Nose" is the grotesque tale of a man who must pursue through the city his own nose, grown into a haughty official. In "The Overcoat," a poor clerk is broken and dies after he is robbed of his expensive new overcoat. In "The Diary of a Madman," an obscure bureaucrat descends into comical madness, but his delusion rescues him from insignificance—he realizes that he is the king of Spain! In these absurd yet moving tales, society's forgettable "little people" become literature's unforgettable characters.

Faust, Part One
Faust, Part Two
Johann Wolfgang von Goethe, *translated by Philip Wayne, Penguin Classic, 1950 and 1960*

If sampling a portion of this work has given you an appetite for more, treat yourself to the complete book.

Related British Literature:
Wuthering Heights
Emily Brontë, *Pearson Prentice Hall, 2000*

Set in the wild moors of northern England, this Romantic novel tells about the love between Catherine Earnshaw and the mysterious outsider Heathcliff.

Related American Literature:
The Science Fiction of Edgar Allan Poe
Edgar Allan Poe, *Penguin Classic, 1976*

These tales of time travel, hypnotism, and electromagnetism reveal that Poe was not only the inventor of the detective story, but also a pioneer of science fiction.

Unit Eight

Siddhartha
Herman Hesse, *translated by Joachim Neugroschel, Penguin Classic, 2002*

Set in India during the sixth century B.C., this novel tells the tale of the handsome and gifted Siddhartha, whose search for wisdom shapes his life. With his friend Govinda, Siddhartha joins a band of ascetics, called *samanas*, who live in poverty and spend their days in meditation. After they pass several years with the samanas, word of a great teacher—the Buddha—reaches Siddhartha and Govinda. The friends go in search of the Buddha. When they find him, Govinda chooses to follow the Buddha, but Siddhartha departs. Alone, Siddhartha discovers the beauty of the world. He settles in a town, becomes involved with a woman, and works in business. Over the course of many years, he gains wealth, but his success soon turns to decadence. Finally, he abandons his town life and resumes his search for wisdom. Read this book to learn whether he finally discovers the truth he has sought.

Unit Eight (continued)

Cyrano de Bergerac

Edmond Rostand, *translated by Lowell Bair, Signet Classic, 2003*
This verse drama in five acts, performed in 1897 and published the following year, is set in seventeenth-century Paris. The action revolves around the noble, swashbuckling Cyrano, who, despite his many gifts, feels that no woman can ever love him because he has an enormous nose. Secretly in love with the lovely Roxane, Cyrano agrees to help his inarticulate rival, Christian, win her heart by allowing him to present as his own Cyrano's love poems, speeches, and letters. Cyrano's dramatic and beautifully written protestations of love included in letters from the battlefield reinforce Roxane's love for Christian and contribute to a romantic irony that continues to fascinate critics and audiences alike.

The Transformation and Other Stories

Franz Kafka, *translated by Malcolm Pasley, Penguin Classic, 1995*
If sampling a portion of this work has given you an appetite for more, treat yourself to the complete book.

Related British Literature: A Portrait of the Artist as a Young Man

James Joyce, *Signet Classic, 1991*
In a novel closely based on his own life, Joyce describes a young man's coming of age in Catholic Ireland and his rebellion against conventional social values.

Related American Literature: My Ántonia

Willa Cather, *Pearson Prentice Hall, 2000*
Drawing from her girlhood experiences on a Nebraska ranch, Cather tells the fictional story of a young woman growing up on the prairie in the late 1800s.

Unit Nine

Things Fall Apart

Chinua Achebe, *Anchor Books, 1959*
Set in Umofia, a small Ibo village in Nigeria, this novel explores the destructive effects of European values on African culture. The story centers on Okonkwo, one of the most honored men of his village. Okonkwo is wealthy, industrious, and brave, but he also has a violent temper and is overly concerned about his status. When he accidentally kills a member of his tribe, he is sent into exile for seven years. During Okonkwo's exile, a Christian missionary arrives in Umofia and converts many of the Ibo. This development is set within the context of an escalating British presence, which includes a new government and the threat of vast military might. Under these pressures, traditional Ibo society simply collapses. When Okonkwo returns to Umofia, he tries to fight the British presence, a decision that leads to disastrous consequences.

One Day in the Life of Ivan Denisovich

Alexander Solzhenitsyn, *translated by Ralph Parker, Signet Classic, 1998*
This powerful work of fiction exposes the brutality and inhumanity of the former Soviet Union's political oppression. Set in a Siberian forced-labor prison camp, the novel details the events of an ordinary day in January 1951 as seen through the eyes of a political prisoner, Ivan Denisovich Shukhov. The prisoner, wrongfully convicted of treason during World War II and sentenced to ten years in the labor camp, manages to maintain his humanity and dignity despite the camp's relentless dehumanization. His strength and his determination to survive are moving tributes to the human spirit.

Night

Elie Wiesel, *translated by Stella Rodway, Pearson Prentice Hall, 2000*
If sampling a portion of this work has given you an appetite for more, treat yourself to the complete book.

Related British Literature: Lord of the Flies

William Golding, *Perigee, 1987*
This novel about British schoolboys stranded on an island is both an adventure story and a parable about the nature of evil.

Related American Literature: Something to Declare

Julia Alvarez, *Plume, 1999*
In this collection of amusing and insightful essays, Alvarez discusses her life as a Dominican immigrant in America and her struggles to become a writer.

abases (ä bās´ əz) v. lowers, brings down

abhor (ab hôr´) v. feel disgust for; hate

accolade (ak´ ə lād´) n. anything done as a sign of praise or respect

accordance (ə kôrd´ 'ns) n. agreement

accrue (ə krōō´) v. come to as an advantage or a right

acute (ə kyōōt´) adj. sharp; intense

adjured (a joord´) v. ordered solemnly

adroit (ə droit´) adj. skillful

affably (af´ ə blē) adv. in a friendly manner

affidavit (af´ ə dā´ vit) n. legal document containing sworn testimony

affinity (ə fin´ i tē) n. natural liking

affliction (ə flik´ shən) n. something that causes pain or distress

altruistic (al´ trōō is´ tik) adj. selfless

ancestral (an ses´ trəl) adj. relating to the people from whom one is descended

anguish (aŋ´ gwish) n. great suffering

anguished (aŋ´ gwisht) adj. showing worry, grief, or pain

anoint (ə noint´) v. rub oil or ointment on

anticipate (an tis´ ə pāt) v. expect

antiquity (an tik´ wə tē) n. early history

appropriate (ə prō´ prē āt´) v. take for one's own use

assent (ə sent´) n. expression of agreement

assertions (ə sur´ shənz) n. claims

assimilate (ə sim´ ə lāt´) v. absorb; incorporate into a greater body

avail (ə vāl´) n. benefit; use

avenged (ə venjd´) v. took revenge on behalf of

avenger (ə venj´ er) n. one who takes revenge

awe (ô) n. feelings of fear and wonder

babel (bab´ əl) n. confusion of voices

bangle (baŋ´g'l) n. decorative bracelet

bashful (bash´ fəl) adj. shy

beneficent (be nef´ ə sənt) adj. kind; helpful

benevolent (bə nev´ ə lənt) adj. charitable

bereft (bē reft´) adj. deprived or robbed

beseeching (bē sēch´ iŋ) adj. pleading

bewildered (bi wil´ dərd) adj. puzzled; confused

bias (bī´ əs) n. prejudice; partiality

bland (bland) adj. mild

blaspheming (blas fēm´ iŋ) adj. irreverent

blasphemous (blas´ fə məs) adj. showing disrespect toward God or religious teachings

blight (blīt) n. destructive disease

bountiful (boun´ tə fəl) adj. abundant

brandished (bran´ dishd) v. waved or shook in a threatening manner

brazen (brā´ zən) adj. literally, of brass; shamelessly bold

brevity (brev´ ə tē) n. briefness

brusquely (brusk´ lē) adv. abruptly

buffeted (buf´ it id) v. struck sharply

calamity (kə lam´ ə tē) n. deep trouble

calculating (kal´ kyōō lāt iŋ) adj. shrewd

candor (kan´ dər) n. open honesty

caricature (kar´ i kə chər) n. imitation that is so distorted or inferior as to seem ridiculous

carnivorous (kär niv´ ə rəs) adj. meat-eating

cascade (kas kād´) n. small, steep waterfall

chasm (kaz´ əm) n. deep crack in Earth's surface

chastised (chas´ tīzd) v. punished

chastisements (chas´ tiz mənts) n. punishments

chide (chīd) v. scold

clemency (klem´ ən sē) n. mercy

clenched (klencht) adj. gripped firmly

commiserate (kə miz´ ər āt) v. share grief

compassionate (kəm pash´ ən it) adj. feeling or showing sympathy or pity

comprised (kəm prīzd´) v. included; consisted of

conflagration (kän´ flə grā´ shən) n. large, destructive fire

congealed (kən jēld´) v. thickened; solidified

conjectures (kən jek´ chərz) n. guesses

connoisseur (kän´ ə sur´) n. person with expert judgment and taste

connotations (kän´ ə tā´ shənz) n. ideas associated with a word

considerably (kən sid´ er ə blē) adv. to a great degree

consolation (kän´ sə lā´ shən) n. comfort; something that eases sadness

consonant (kän´ sə nənt) adj. in agreement

constitution (kän stə tōō´ shən) n. structure or make-up of a person or thing

consult (kən sult´) v. seek advice from

consummation (kän´ sə mā´ shən) n. state of supreme perfection

contemplation (kän´ təm plā´ shən) n. thoughtful inspection or study

contemptuously (kən temp´ chōō əs lē) adv. scornfully; disrespectfully

contention (kən ten´ shən) n. quarreling

contraband (kän´ trə band´) n. unlawful or forbidden goods

contrary (kän´ trer ē) adj. opposing

convalescent (kän´ və les´ 'nt) n. person who is recovering health after illness

convergent (kən vur´ jənt) adj. coming together at a point

corrupt (kə rupt´) adj. spoiled by sin or dishonesty; rotten

countenance (koun´ tə nəns) n. the look on a person's face

courtly (kôrt´ lē) adj. dignified; polite

covenant (kuv´ ə nənt) n. serious, binding agreement

crone (krōn) n. very old woman

cue (kyōō) n. prompt or reminder

culmination (kul´ mə nā´ shən) n. climax

debacle (di bäk´ əl) n. overwhelming failure or defeat

deference (def´ ər əns) n. respectful submission to the desires or opinions of another

deficiency (dē fish´ ən sē) n. shortage

degree (di grē´) n. step; stage; level

demarcation (dē´ mär kā´ shən) n. boundary

denounce (dē nouns´) v. accuse publicly

deportees (dē´ pôr tēz´) n. people forced by official order to leave a country

desecrating (des´ i krāt iŋ) v. treating as not sacred

despicable (des´ pi kə bəl) adj. deserving to be despised; contemptible

despond (di spänd´) v. lose

despondent (di spän´ dənt) adj. hopeless

despotism (des´ pət iz´ əm) n. system of government in which the ruler has absolute power

destitute (des´ tə tōōt´) adj. extremely poor

dexterity (deks ter´ ə tē) n. skillfulness in the use of one's hands

diabolical (dī ə bäl´ ik əl) adj. wicked

discord (dis´ kôrd) n. dissension; conflict

discrimination (dis krim´ ə nā´ shən) n. show of partiality or prejudice

disdain (dis dān´) n. strong dislike

dispatch (di spach´) v. kill

dispel (di spel´) v. cause to vanish

dispersed (di spurst´) adj. scattered

disposed (di spōzd´) v. tending toward

disreputable (dis rep´ yōō tə bəl) adj. not fit to be seen or approved

dissipation (dis´ ə pā´ shən) n. wasteful or immoral behavior; overindulgence

distinguishing (di stiŋ´ gwish iŋ) adj. serving to mark as separate or different

divergent (də vur´ jənt) adj. differing from each other

divinations (div´ ə nā´ shənz) n. divine predictions

dominion (də min´ yən) n. area of rule

dregs (dregz) n. last, most undesirable parts

drudgery (druj´ ər ē) n. hard, tiresome work

dubious (dōō´ bē əs) adj. doubtful; suspect

duped (dōōpt) v. tricked; fooled

earnest (ur´ nist) adj. serious; not joking

ecstasy (ek´ stə sē) *n.* great joy

eddies (ed´ ēz) *n.* waters moving in circles against the main current

elated (ē lāt´ əd) *adj.* extremely happy; joyful

elixir (ē liks´ ir) *n.* magical potion that cures all ailments

eloquence (el´ ə kwəns) *n.* skillful speech

emigrate (em´ i grāt) *v.* leave one place to live in another

endeavor (en dev´ ər) *n.* earnest attempt at achievement

endowed (en doud´) *v.* provided with

enmity (en´ mə tē) *n.* state of being enemies; antagonism; hostility

enraptured (en rap´ chərd) *adj.* completely delighted; spellbound

entrails (en´ trālz) *n.* intestines; guts

entwined (en twīnd´) *v.* twisted together

entwines (en twīnz´) *v.* twists together

enumerating (ē noo´ mər āt´ iŋ) *v.* counting; listing

environs (en vī ´ rənz) *n.* surrounding area

envoys (än´ voiz) *n.* messengers

epidemic (ep´ ə dem´ ik) *n.* rapidly and widely spreading disease

equable (ek´ wə bəl) *adj.* steady; uniform

esteemed (e stēmd´) *v.* valued; respected

estranged (e strānjd´) *adj.* isolated and unfriendly; alienated

euphemisms (yoo´ fə miz´ əmz) *n.* words or phrases that are less expressive or direct but are considered less offensive than others

evasions (i vā´ shənz) *n.* attempts to avoid duties or questions

exalted (ig zôlt´ əd) *adj.* lifted high because of dignity or honor

excruciating (eks kroo´ shē āt´ iŋ) *adj.* causing intense mental or bodily pain

exhorting (eg zôrt´ iŋ) *v.* urging

exhumed (eks hyoomd´) *v.* brought up from a grave; brought to light

expanse (ek spans´) *n.* very large open area

extirpate (ek´ stər pāt´) *v.* exterminate

extortions (eks tôr´ shənz) *n.* acts of obtaining money or something else through threats, violence, or misuse of authority

extravagant (ek strav´ ə gənt) *adj.* excessive; spending more than is needed

exuded (ig zood´ id) *v.* discharged a liquid through the skin

exulting (eg zult´ iŋ) *v.* rejoicing

exults (eg zults´) *v.* rejoices greatly

fathom (fath´ əm) *v.* probe the depths of; understand

fathomless (fath´ əm les) *adj.* immeasurably deep

feigning (fān´ iŋ) *v.* pretending

fervent (fur´ vənt) *adj.* intensely devoted

fervor (fur´ vər) *n.* strong feeling; zeal

fettered (fet´ ərd) *v.* shackled; chained

fetters (fet´ ərz) *n.* shackles; chains

flittering (flit´ ər iŋ) *adj.* flapping the wings rapidly; fluttering

flounders (floun´ dərz) *v.* struggles to move

flourish (flur´ ish) *n.* fanfare, as of trumpets

flourishes (flur´ ish ez) *v.* thrives

foretaste (fôr´ tāst´) *n.* slight experience or hint of something that is still to come

forlornly (fôr lôrn´ lē) *adv.* in a sad or lonely manner because of isolation or desertion

foundering (foun´ dər iŋ) *n.* stumbling; sinking; becoming stuck

fraternized (frat´ ər nīzd´) *v.* associated in a brotherly way; socialized

frivolous (friv´ ə ləs) *adj.* silly and light-minded; not sensible

frugality (froo gal´ ə tē) *n.* thrift

frugally (froo´ gə lē) *adv.* thriftily

fungus (fuŋ´ gəs) *n.* mildew; any of a group of plants lacking leaves and roots, including mushrooms, mold, and so on

furtive (fur´ tiv) *adj.* done in a sneaky way

furtively (fur´ tiv lē) *adv.* in a sneaky manner, as if to hinder observation

gaudy (gôd´ ē) *adj.* tastelessly showy

gaunt (gônt) *adj.* thin and bony; haggard

gawking (gôk´ iŋ) *v.* staring foolishly; gaping

gentry (jen´ trē) *n.* landowning families ranked just below the nobility

glaze (glāz) *v.* fit glass to a window; cover with a shiny finish

glean (glēn) *v.* collect grain left by reapers

glimmering (glim´ ər iŋ) *v.* flickering; giving a faint, unsteady light

glistens (glis´ enz) *v.* shines or sparkles with reflected light

grafter (graft´ ər) *n.* someone who takes advantage of his or her position to gain money or property dishonestly

gratify (grat´ i fī´) *v.* please

grotesque (grō tesk´) *adj.* strangely distorted

guile (gīl) *n.* trickery

gyration (jī rā´ shən) *n.* circular motion

haggard ((hag´ ərd) *adj.* wasted; worn

harrowed (har´ ōd) *v.* distressed

harrowing (har´ ō iŋ) *adj.* frightening

hastened (hās´ ənd) *v.* hurried

hazards (haz´ ərdz) *n.* dangers

heralds (her´ əldz) *v.* announces; introduces

homage (häm´ ij) *n.* act of reverence

hordes (hôrdz) *n.* large moving crowds; tribes

hypocrite (hip´ ə krit) *n.* someone who pretends to be virtuous

illustrious (i lus´ trē əs) *adj.* outstanding

imminent (im´ ə nənt) *adj.* about to happen

immobile (i mō´ bəl) *adj.* not moving

immolation (im´ ə lā´ shən) *n.* offering or killing made as a sacrifice

immortality (im´ môr tal´ i tē) *n.* unending existence

imperceptibly (im´ pər sep´ tə blē) *adv.* without being noticed

imperishable (im per´ ish ə bəl) *adj.* indestructible

impertinence (im purt´ ′n əns) *n.* insolence

impervious (im purˊ vē əs) *adj.* not affected by, or unable to be damaged

impetus (im´ pə təs) *n.* driving force

implore (im plôr´) *v.* beg

importunity (im´ pôr toon´ i tē) *n.* persistence

imposingly (im pō´ ziŋ lē) *adv.* making a strong, forceful impression

impracticable (im prak´ ti kə bəl) *adj.* not capable of being put into practice

impudence (im´ pyoo dəns) *n.* boldness

impulsive (im pul´ siv) *adj.* sudden and unthinking

incantation (in´ kan tā´ shən) *n.* chant

incantations (in´ kan tā´ shənz) *n.* chants sung as part of a ritual

incensed (in senst´) *adj.* very angry

incongruous (in käŋ´ groo əs) *adj.* inconsistent; not fitting a situation

incredulous (in krej´ oo ləs) *adj.* disbelieving; doubtful; skeptical

incurred (in kurd´) *v.* brought about through one's own actions

indefinitely (in def´ ə nit lē) *adv.* without a specified limit

indictment (in dīt´ mənt) *n.* formal accusation

indignantly (in dig´ nənt lē) *adv.* in a way showing righteous anger or scorn

indiscreet (in di skrēt´) *adj.* unwise or not careful

induced (in doost´) *v.* persuaded; caused

inexorably (in eks´ ə rə blē) *adv.* without a chance of being stopped

infamous (in´ fə məs) *adj.* disgraceful

infatuation (in fach´ oo ā´ shən) *n.* foolish or shallow feelings of affection

infirmity (in fur´ mə tē) *n.* weakness; illness

ingenuity (in´ je noo´ ə tē) *n.* inventiveness

innuendo (in´ yoo en´ dō) *n.* indirect remark or gesture that hints at something

insatiableness (in sā´ shə bəl nəs) *n.* the quality of being impossible to fill

insular (in´ sə lər) *adj.* having a narrow viewpoint

intimacy (in´ tə mə sē) *n.* familiarity; warmth

intolerable (in täl´ ər ə bəl) *adj.* unbearable

intrepid (in trep´ id) *adj.* brave; fearless

intricate (in´ tri kit) *adj.* complicated

intuition (in´ too ish´ ən) *n.* instinctive understanding

inverted (in vurt´ id) *adj.* upside down

invoke (in vōk´) *v.* summon; cause to appear

invoked (in vōkt´) *v.* called on for help

invokes (in vōks´) *v.* calls on

iridescent (ir´ ə des´ ənt) *adj.* showing rainbowlike shifts in color

jetty (jet´ ē) *n.* wall or barrier built into a body of water to protect a harbor

jubilant (jōō´ bə lənt) *adj.* extremely happy

ken (ken) *n.* range of understanding

labyrinths (lab´ ə rinths) *n.* structures with an intricate network of winding passages

laden (lād´ 'n) *adj.* carrying a heavy load

lamentation (lam´ ən tā´ shən) *n.* outward expression of grief; weeping; wailing

lamented (lə men´ tid) *v.* felt sorrow for

languishing (laŋ´ gwish iŋ) *v.* becoming weak

leaden (led´ 'n) *adj.* depressed; dispirited

liquidated (lik´ wi dāt id) *adj.* disposed of; ended; killed

loathsome (lōth´ səm) *adj.* detestable

loomed (lōōmd) *v.* appeared in a large or threatening form

lucid (lōō´ sid) *adj.* clear; apparent

lustrous (lus´ trəs) *adj.* shining

malice (mal´ is) *n.* ill will; spite

malicious (mə lish´ əs) *adj.* intending harm

malignant (mə lig´ nənt) *adj.* very harmful

manifestations (man´ ə fes tā´ shənz) *n.* material forms

manifested (man´ ə fest´ id) *v.* proved or revealed

manifold (man´ ə fōld´) *adj.* many; various

marshals (mär´ shəlz) *v.* commands

meager (mē´ gər) *adj.* thin; lean

mediocre (mē´ dē ō´ kər) *adj.* inferior

mitigated (mit´ ə gāt´ id) *v.* eased

mobilized (mō´ bə līzd) *v.* prepared for action or battle

monotone (män´ ə tōn´) *n.* sound or song that repeats a single note

monotonously (mə nät´ 'n əs lē) *adv.* going on and on without variation

monotony (mə nät´ 'n ē) *n.* tedious sameness

morose (mə rōs´) *adj.* gloomy

munificence (myōō nif´ ə sens) *n.* great generosity

murmur (mur´ mər) *n.* low, indistinct, continuous sound

mutely (myōōt´ lē) *adv.* silently; without the capacity to speak

myriad (mir´ ē əd) *adj.* many; varied

myriads (mir´ ē ədz) *n.* great numbers of persons or things

naturalistic (nach´ ər ə lis´ tik) *adj.* faithful to nature, or in imitation of what is natural

navigated (nav´ i gāt´ əd) *v.* piloted; steered a boat

nimble (nim´ bəl) *adj.* able to move quickly and lightly; agile

nocturnal (näk tur´ nəl) *adj.* relating to or occurring during the night

nonchalantly (nän´ shə länt´ lē) *adv.* in a casually indifferent manner

notions (nō´ shənz) *n.* ideas

oblique (ə blēk´) *adj.* not straightforward

obsequiously (əb sē´ kwē əs lē) *adv.* in a manner that shows a willingness to serve

obsessed (əb sest´) *adj.* greatly preoccupied

obsolete (äb´ sə lēt´) *adj.* no longer useful

obstinacy (äb´ stə nə sē) *n.* stubbornness

obstinate (äb´ stə nət) *adj.* stubborn

ominous (äm´ ə nəs) *adj.* hinting at bad things to come

omnipotent (äm nip´ ə tənt) *adj.* having unlimited power or authority

opaque (ō pāk´) *adj.* not shining; dull

oratory (ôr´ ə tôr´ ē) *n.* public speaking

painstakingly (pānz´ tāk iŋ lē) *adv.* using great diligence or care

pallid (pal´ id) *adj.* pale

palpable (pal´ pə bəl) *adj.* able to be touched, felt, or handled

paraphernalia (par´ ə fər nāl´ yə) *n.* articles of equipment

paternal (pə tur´ nəl) *adj.* like a father

pathos (pā´ thäs´) *n.* quality in something that evokes pity or compassion

perfunctorily (pər fuŋk´ tôr i lē) *adv.* indifferently; with little interest or care

perilous (per´ ə ləs) *adj.* dangerous

perjured (pur´ jərd) *adj.* purposely false

pervades (pər vādz´) *v.* spreads throughout

pestilence (pes´ tə ləns) *n.* plague

piety (pī´ ə tē) *n.* devotion to religious duties

pillaging (pil´ ij iŋ) *v.* plundering; looting

pitiable (pit´ ē ə bəl) *adj.* inspiring or deserving of pity (may be used scornfully)

placidly (plas´ id lē) *adv.* calmly

plaintive (plān´ tiv) *adj.* expressing sorrow

plateau (pla tō´) *n.* elevated tract of relatively level land

plight (plīt) *n.* sad or difficult situation

plunder (plun´ dər) *v.* rob by force in warfare

plundered (plun´dərd) *adj.* stripped of possessions

poised (poizd) *adj.* balanced and steady, as though suspended

pomp (pämp) *n.* ceremonial splendor

portents (pôr´ tents) *n.* signs that suggest what is about to occur

posterity (päs ter´ ə tē) *n.* future generations of people

precepts (prē´ septs) *n.* rules of conduct

precipitous (prē sip´ ə təs) *adj.* steep like a precipice; sheer

presumed (prē zōōmd´) *v.* supposed

primal (prī´ məl) *adj.* original; fundamental

primeval (prī mē´ vəl) *adj.* having to do with the earliest times

pristine (pris´ tēn´) *adj.* unspoiled

proclaim (prō klām´) *v.* declare

proclaiming (prō klām´ iŋ) *v.* declaring

prodigal (präd´ i gəl) *n.* person who spends money wastefully

prodigy (präd´ ə jē) *n.* person of very great ability

proffering (präf´ ər iŋ) *v.* offering

profusion (prə fyōō´ zhən) *n.* abundance

prone (prōn) *adj.* lying face downward

prophecy (präf´ ə sē) *n.* prediction

prophesied (präf´ ə sīd) *v.* predicted

prophet (präf´ ət) *n.* inspired person who speaks great truths or foretells the future

prophetic (prō fet´ ik) *adj.* having to do with predicting the future; giving a prediction

proprieties (prə prī´ ə tēz) *n.* conformities with what is fitting, suitable, or proper

prospective (prō spek´ tiv) *adj.* likely to be or to become in the future

prostrate (präs´ trāt) *adj.* lying face downward

protracted (prō trakt´ id) *adj.* extended

provincial (prō vin´ shəl) *adj.* lacking in sophistication

prowess (prou´ is) *n.* ability

putrefy (pyōō´ trə fī) *v.* rot; decompose

putrid (pyōō´ trid) *adj.* rotten; stinking

rank (raŋk) *adj.* foul; odorous

reapers (rē´ pərz) *n.* those who gather a crop by cutting

rebuked (ri byōōkt´) *v.* scolded sharply

reciprocity (res´ ə präs´ ə tē) *n.* mutual exchange

recompense (rek´ əm pens´) *n.* payment of what is owed; reward

rectify (rek´ tə fī) *v.* right

redeem (ri dēm´) *v.* buy back; fulfill a promise

reluctant (ri luk´ tənt) *adj.* showing hesitation; unwilling

renown (ri noun´) *n.* fame

repentance (ri pen´ təns) *n.* sorrow for wrongdoing; remorse

replete (ri plēt´) *adj.* well-filled; stocked

reposes (ri´ pōz´ əz) *v.* puts to rest

reprimand (rep´ rə mand´) *v.* chastise; blame

reprobate (rep´ rə bāt) *n.* scoundrel

resistant (ri zis´ tənt) *adj.* strong; firm

resolutely (rez´ ə lōōt´ lē) *adv.* in a determined way; without hesitation

resplendent (ri splen´ dənt) *adj.* brightly shining; dazzling

retorted (ri tôrt´ id) *v.* replied, especially in a sharp or challenging way

retribution (re´ trə byōō´ shən) *n.* punishment; revenge

revelation (rev´ ə lā´ shən) *n.* striking disclosure of something

reverberates (ri vur´ bə rātz´) *v.* echoes; sounds again

reverence (rev´ rəns) *v.* show great respect

ritual (rich´ ōō əl) *n.* observance of prescribed rules

sacrosanct (sak´ rō saŋkt´) *adj.* sacred

sated (sāt´ id) *v.* completely satisfied

scorn (skôrn) *n.* contempt; open dislike or derision; *v.* reject

scruples (skrōō´ pəlz) *n.* feelings of doubt over what is ethical

scurry (skʉr´ ē) *v.* run hastily; scamper

sediment (sed´ ə mənt) *n.* waste material that settles to the bottom of a liquid

self-abnegation (self ab´ ne gā´ shən) *n.* self-denial; lack of consideration for oneself or one's own interests

sensual (sen´ shoo əl) *adj.* pleasing to the senses

sequence (sē´ kwəns) *n.* order; succession

serene (sə rēn´) *adj.* clear; calm; peaceful

serenity (sə ren´ ə tē) *n.* peace; tranquillity

serpentine (sʉr´ pən tēn´) *adj.* snakelike

shards (shärdz) *n.* sharp fragments

sheaves (shēvz) *n.* bundles of cut stalks of grain

shrewdest (shrōōd´ est) *adj.* most cunning or clever

shroud (shroud) *n.* cloth sometimes used to wrap a corpse for burial

siege (sēj) *n.* the surrounding of a fortified place by an opposing force, such as an army

sinister (sin´ is tər) *adj.* wicked

skulks (skulks) *v.* lurks in a cowardly way

sleek (slēk) *adj.* smooth; glossy

sojourn (sō´ jʉrn) *n.* visit

solitary (säl´ ə ter´ ē) *adj.* lone; single; sole

solitude (säl´ ə tood´) *n.* seclusion; isolation

somber (säm´ bər) *adj.* dark; gloomy; serious

sordid (sôr´ did) *adj.* filthy; depressingly wretched

sovereign (säv´ rən) *adj.* chief, superior; highest; *n.* monarch or ruler

spendthrift (spend´ thrift´) *n.* person who spends money carelessly

squalid (skwäl´ id) *adj.* foul, especially as the result of neglect; wretched

squandered (skwän´ dərd) *v.* wasted

squandering (skwän´ dər iŋ) *v.* spending money wastefully

steadfast (sted´ fast´) *adj.* firm; not changing

stealthily (stel´ thə lē) *adv.* secretly

stems (stemz) *v.* stops or dams up (as a river)

stinted (stint´ id) *v.* limited to a certain quantity

stoically (stō´ iklē) *adv.* done with indifference to pain or pleasure

strains (strānz) *n.* passages of music; tunes

stupor (stoop´ ər) *n.* mental dullness

submerges (səb mʉrj´ əz) *v.* covers over

submissive (sub mis´ iv) *adj.* yielding; giving in without resistance

subordinate (sə bôr´ də nit) *adj.* inferior; ranking under or below

subsided (səb sīd´ ed) *v.* settled; lessened

succor (suk´ ər) *n.* aid; relief

suffuses (sə fyōō´ zəz) *v.* overspreads; fills with a glow

summit (sum´ it) *n.* highest point

sumptuous (sump´ choo əs) *adj.* lavish

superimposed (soo´ pər im pōzd´) *v.* placed on top of something else

supple (sup´ əl) *adj.* easily bent; flexible

sustained (sə stānd´) *v.* maintained; supported

taciturn (tas´ ə tʉrn) *adj.* not given to talking; almost always silent

tactless (takt´ lis) *adj.* unskilled in dealing with people

talisman (tal´ is mən) *n.* charm or token; lucky object

tangible (tan´ jə bəl) *adj.* definite; objective

tardily (tär´ də lē) *adv.* late

teemed (tēmd) *v.* was full of; swarmed

tempest (tem´ pist) *n.* storm

tempo ((tem´ pō) *n.* rate of speed; pace

tenacity (tə nas´ ə tē) *n.* persistence

tenuous (ten´ yōō əs) *adj.* slender or fine, as a fiber

terminal (tʉr´ mə nəl) *adj.* fatal; ending in death

terminology (tʉr´mə näl´ ə jē) *n.* terms used in a specific discipline

throngs (thrôŋz) *n.* crowds

thwarted (thwôrt´ ed) *v.* hindered

timidity (tə mid´ ə tē) *n.* quality of being shy and easily frightened

tremulous (trem´ yōō ləs) *adj.* quivering; shaking; trembling

troop (trōōp) *v.* march in a group

truncated (trun´ kāt əd) *adj.* cut short; with an angle cut off

tumult (tōō´ mult´) *n.* commotion; confusion

unfettered (un fet´ ərd) *adj.* unrestrained

unhampered (un ham´ pərd) *adv.* freely; without interference

unmarred (un märd´) *adj.* unspoiled

unrestrained (un ri strānd´) *v.* not checked or controlled

vassal (vas´ əl) *n.* person who holds land under the feudal system, pledging loyalty to an overlord

vehemently (vē´ ə mənt lē) *adv.* intensely

veiled (vāld) *v.* covered or masked

vitality (vī tal´ ə tē) *n.* energy; life force

vivacity (vī vas´ ə tē) *n.* liveliness

void (void) *n.* empty space; total emptiness

vulgar (vul´ gər) *adj.* coarse; common

ward (wôrd) *v.* turn aside (something threatening)

well-being (wel bē´ iŋ) *n.* the state of being well; health, happiness, or prosperity

wharf (wôrf) *n.* structure built as a landing place for boats

whetted (wet´ id) *adj.* sharpened

wiles (wīlz) *n.* sly tricks

wizened (wiz´ ənd) *adj.* dried up and wrinkled due to age

writhes (rīthz) *v.* twists and turns the body, as in agony

zeal (zēl) *n.* ardor; fervor

ALLEGORY An *allegory* is a literary work with two or more levels of meaning—a literal level and one or more symbolic levels. The events, settings, objects, or characters in an allegory—the literal level—stand for ideas or qualities, such as goodness, tyranny, salvation, and so on. Dante's *Divine Comedy* (p. 612) is an allegory written in the Middle Ages, when allegorical writing was common. Many works can be read allegorically as well as literally, requiring a reader's effort to match every element at the literal level with a corresponding element at the symbolic level. Allegories are also written in the form of parables.

See also Fable *and* Parable.

ALLITERATION *Alliteration* is the repetition of initial consonant sounds in accented syllables. Derek Walcott uses alliteration in these lines from "Omeros" (p. 1203):

. . . higher than those hills / of infernal anthracite.

Especially in poetry, alliteration is used to emphasize and to link words, as well as to create musical sounds.

ALLUSION An *allusion* is a reference to a well-known person, place, event, literary work, or work of art. Writers often make allusions to the Bible, classical Greek and Roman myths, plays by Shakespeare, historical events, and other material with which they expect their readers to be familiar. Canto V of the *Inferno* by Dante (p. 629) contains an allusion to the story of Lancelot.

AMBIGUITY *Ambiguity* is the effect created when words suggest and support two or more divergent interpretations. Ambiguity may be used in literature to express experiences or truths that are complex or even contradictory.

See also Irony.

ANALOGY An *analogy* is an extended comparison of relationships. It is based on the idea or insight that the relationship between one pair of things is like the relationship between another pair. Unlike a metaphor, another form of comparison, an analogy involves an explicit comparison, often using the word *like* or *as*.

See also Metaphor *and* Simile.

ANAPEST *See* Meter.

ARCHETYPAL LITERARY ELEMENTS *Archetypal literary elements* are patterns in literature found around the world. For instance, the occurrence of events in threes is an archetypal element of fairy tales. *The Epic of Gilgamesh* (p. 14) presents an archetypal battle between the forces of good and the forces of evil. Certain character types, such as mysterious guides, are also archetypal elements of traditional stories. According to some critics, these elements express in symbolic form truths about the human mind.

ASSONANCE *Assonance* is the repetition of vowel sounds in stressed syllables containing dissimilar consonant sounds.

See also Consonance.

BALLAD A *ballad* is a song that tells a story, often about adventure or romance, or a poem imitating such a song. Most ballads are divided into four- or six-line stanzas, are rhymed, use simple language, and depict dramatic action. Many ballads employ a repeated refrain. Some use incremental repetition, in which the refrain is varied slightly each time it appears.

BLANK VERSE *Blank verse* is unrhymed poetry usually written in iambic pentameter (*see* Meter). Occasional variations in rhythm are introduced in blank verse to create emphasis, variety, and naturalness of sound. Because blank verse sounds much like ordinary spoken English, it is often used in drama, as by Shakespeare, and in poetry.

See also Meter.

CARPE DIEM A Latin phrase, *carpe diem* means "seize the day" or "make the most of passing time." Many great literary works have been written with the *carpe diem* theme.

CHARACTER A person (though not necessarily a human being) who takes part in the action of a literary work is known as a character. Characters can be classified in different ways. A character who plays an important role is called a *major character*. A character who does not is called a *minor character*. A character who plays the central role in a story is called the *protagonist*. A character who opposes the *protagonist* is called the *antagonist*. A *round character* has many aspects to his or her personality. A *flat character* is defined by only a few qualities. A character who changes is called *dynamic*; a character who does not change is called *static*.

See also Characterization *and* Motivation.

CHARACTERIZATION *Characterization* is the act of creating and developing a character. A writer uses *direct characterization* when he or she describes a character's traits explicitly. Writers also use *indirect characterization*. A character's traits can be revealed indirectly in what he or she says, thinks, or does; in a description of his or her appearance; or in the statements, thoughts, or actions of other characters.

See also Character *and* Motivation.

CHOKA A traditional Japanese verse form, *choka* are poems that consist of alternating lines of five and seven syllables, with an additional seven-syllable line at the end. There is no limit to the number of lines in a choka. Choka frequently end with one or more *envoys* consisting of five lines of five, seven, five, seven, and seven syllables. Generally, the envoys elaborate or summarize the theme of the main poem.

CLIMAX The *climax* is the high point of interest or suspense in a literary work. Often, the climax is also the crisis in the plot, the point at which the protagonist changes his or her understanding or situation. Sometimes, the climax coincides with the *resolution*, the point at which the central conflict is ended.

See also Plot.

COMEDY A *comedy* is a literary work, especially a play, that has a happy ending. A comedy often shows ordinary characters in conflict with their society. Types of comedy include *romantic comedy*, which involves problems between lovers, and the *comedy of manners*, which satirically challenges the social customs of a sophisticated society. Comedy is often contrasted with tragedy, in which the protagonist meets an unfortunate end.

See also Drama *and* Tragedy.

CONCEIT A *conceit* is an unusual and surprising comparison between two very different things. This special kind of metaphor or complicated analogy is often the basis for a whole poem. *Petrarchan conceits* make extravagant claims about the beloved's beauty or the speaker's suffering, with comparisons to divine beings, powerful natural forces, and objects that contain a given quality in the highest degree. See Petrarch's "Laura" (p. 675) for an example.

See also Metaphor.

CONFLICT A *conflict* is a struggle between opposing forces. Sometimes, this struggle is internal, or within a character. At other times, the struggle is external, or between the character and some outside force. The outside force may be another character, nature, or some element of society, such as a custom or a political institution. Often, the conflict in a work combines several of these possibilities.

See also Plot.

CONNOTATION *Connotation* refers to the associations that a word calls to mind in addition to its dictionary meaning. For example, the words *home* and *domicile* have the same dictionary meaning. However, the first has positive connotations of warmth and security, whereas the second does not.

See also Denotation.

CONSONANCE *Consonance* is the repetition of final consonant sounds in stressed syllables containing dissimilar vowel sounds. Following are some examples of consonance: *black/block; slip/slop; creak/croak; feat/fit; slick/slack*. When each word in the pair is used at the end of a line, the effect is one form of *slant rhyme*.

See also Assonance.

COUPLET A *couplet* is a pair of rhyming lines written in the same meter. A *heroic couplet* is a rhymed pair of iambic pentameter lines. In a *closed couplet*, the meaning and grammar are completed within the two lines.

See also Sonnet.

DACTYL *See* Meter.

DENOTATION *Denotation* is the objective meaning of a word—that to which the word refers, independent of other associations that the word calls to mind. Dictionaries list the denotative meanings of words.

See also Connotation.

DIALECT *Dialect* is the form of a language spoken by people in a particular region or group. Dialects differ from one another in grammar, vocabulary, and pronunciation.

DIALOGUE *Dialogue* is a conversation between characters. Writers use dialogue to reveal character, to present events, to add variety to narratives, and to interest readers. Dialogue in a story is usually set off by quotation marks and paragraphing. Dialogue in a play script generally follows the name of the speaker.

DIARY A *diary* is a personal record of daily events, usually written in prose. Most diaries are not written for publication; sometimes, however, interesting diaries or diaries written by influential people are published.

DICTION *Diction* is a writer's word choice. It can be a major determinant of the writer's style. Diction can be described as formal or informal, abstract or concrete, plain or ornate, ordinary or technical.

See also Style.

DIMETER *See* Meter.

DRAMA A *drama* is a story written to be performed by actors. It may consist of one or more large sections, called acts, which are made up of any number of smaller sections, called scenes.

Drama originated in the religious rituals and symbolic reenactments of primitive peoples. The ancient Greeks, who developed drama into a sophisticated art form, created such dramatic forms as tragedy and comedy.

Oedipus the King (p. 426) is a definitive example of Greek tragedy. The classical dramas of the Greeks and the Romans faded away as the Roman empire declined.

Drama revived in Europe during the Middle Ages. The Renaissance produced a number of great dramatists, most notably England's William Shakespeare. Molière's *Tartuffe* is a comedy of manners, a form of drama popular in the seventeenth century. Goethe's tragic *Faust* (p. 768) represents a peak of nineteenth-century Romanticism. Henrik Ibsen's

A Doll House (p. 864) began a trend toward realistic prose drama and away from drama in verse form. Most of the great plays of the twentieth century are written in prose.

Among the many forms of drama from non-Western cultures are the Nō plays of Japan, such as Zeami's *The Deserted Crone*.

See also Comedy *and* Tragedy.

DRAMATIC MONOLOGUE A *dramatic monologue* is a poem in which an imaginary character speaks to a silent listener. During the monologue, the speaker reveals his or her personality, usually at a moment of crisis.

ELEGY An *elegy* is a solemn and formal lyric poem about death. It may mourn a particular person or reflect on a serious or tragic theme, such as the passing of youth or beauty.

See also Lyric Poem.

END-STOPPED LINE An *end-stopped line* is a line of poetry concluding with a break in the meter and in the meaning. This pause at the end of a line is often punctuated by a period, comma, dash, or semicolon.

See also Run-on Line.

EPIC An *epic* is a long narrative poem about the adventures of gods or of a hero. A *folk epic* is one that was composed orally and passed from storyteller to storyteller. The ancient Greek epics attributed to Homer—the *Iliad* (p. 326) and the *Odyssey*—are folk epics. The *Aeneid* (p. 492), by the Roman poet Virgil, and *The Divine Comedy* (p. 612), by the Italian poet Dante Alighieri, are examples of literary epics from the Classical and Medieval periods, respectively. An epic presents an encyclopedic portrait of the culture in which it was produced.

Epic conventions are traditional characteristics of epic poems, including an opening statement of the theme; an appeal for supernatural help in telling the story (an invocation); a beginning *in medias res* (Latin: "in the middle of things"); catalogs of people and things; accounts of past events; and descriptive phrases.

EPIGRAM An *epigram* is a brief statement in prose or in verse. The concluding couplet in a sonnet may be epigrammatic. An essay may be written in an epigrammatic style.

EPIPHANY *Epiphany* is a term introduced by James Joyce to describe a moment of insight in which a character recognizes a truth. In Colette's "The Bracelet" (p. 1046), the main character's epiphany comes at the end of the story when she realizes she cannot recapture her past.

EPITAPH An *epitaph* is an inscription written on a tomb or burial place. In literature, epitaphs include serious or humorous lines written as if intended for such use. Catullus' "I Crossed Many Lands and a Lot of Ocean" (p. 508) is an example from classical literature.

ESSAY An *essay* is a short nonfiction work about a particular subject. Essays are of many types but may be classified by tone or style as formal or informal. An essay is often classed by its main purpose as descriptive, narrative, expository, argumentative, or persuasive.

EXTENDED METAPHOR *See* Metaphor.

FABLE A *fable* is a brief story, usually with animal characters, that teaches a lesson or moral. The earliest known fables are those attributed to Aesop, a Greek writer of the sixth century B.C. Jean de La Fontaine continued this tradition during the Age of Rationalism with such fables as "The Fox and the Crow" (p. 720) and "The Oak and the Reed" (p. 723).

See also Allegory *and* Parable.

FICTION *Fiction* is prose writing about imaginary characters and events. Some writers of fiction base their stories on real events, whereas others rely solely on their imaginations.

See also Narration *and* Prose.

FIGURATIVE LANGUAGE *Figurative language* is writing or speech not meant to be interpreted literally. Poets and other writers use figurative language to paint vivid word pictures, to make their writing emotionally intense and concentrated, and to state their ideas in new and unusual ways.

Figurative language is classified into various *figures of speech*, including hyperbole, irony, metaphor, metonymy, oxymoron, paradox, personification, simile, and synecdoche.

See also the entries for individual figures of speech.

FOLKLORE The stories, legends, myths, ballads, riddles, sayings, and other traditional works produced orally by a culture are known as *folklore*. Folklore influences written literature in many ways. "The Fisherman and the Jinnee," from *The Thousand and One Nights* (p. 92), is an example of folklore.

FOOT *See* Meter.

FREE VERSE *Free verse* is poetry not written in a regular, rhythmical pattern, or meter. Instead of having metrical feet and lines, free verse has a rhythm that suits its meaning and that uses the sounds of spoken language in lines of different lengths. Free verse has been widely used in twentieth-century poetry. An example is this stanza from Nguyen Thi Vinh's "Thoughts of Hanoi" (p. 1392):

> Brother, we are men,
> conscious of more
> than material needs.
> How can this happen to us
> my friend
> my foe?

GOTHIC *Gothic* is a term used to describe literary works that make extensive use of primitive, medieval, wild, mysterious, or natural elements.

HEPTAMETER *See* Meter.

HEXAMETER *See* Meter.

HYPERBOLE *Hyperbole* is a deliberate exaggeration or overstatement. In *Candide* (p. 732), Voltaire turns a philosophical idea into this figure of speech:

> Pangloss taught metaphysico-theologo-cosmolonigology. He proved admirably that there is no effect without a cause and that in this best of all possible worlds, My Lord the Baron's castle was the best of castles and his wife the best of all possible Baronesses.

Hyperbole may be used for heightened seriousness or for comic effect.

See also Figurative Language.

IAMBIC PENTAMETER *See* Meter.

IMAGE An *image* is a word or phrase that appeals to one or more of the senses—sight, hearing, touch, taste, or smell. In a famous essay on *Hamlet*, T. S. Eliot explained how a group of images can be used as an "objective correlative." By this phrase, Eliot meant that a complex emotional state can be suggested by images that are carefully chosen to evoke this state.

See also Imagery.

IMAGERY *Imagery* is the descriptive language used in literature to re-create sensory experiences. Imagery enriches writing by making it more vivid, setting a tone, suggesting emotions, and guiding readers' reactions. The following lines from Boris Pasternak's "The Weeping Orchard" (p. 1032) show how a poet can use imagery to appeal to several senses in describing the aftermath of a storm:

> Silence. No breath of leaf, nothing
>   in the dark but this weird
> gulping, and flapping of slippers,
>   and sighs, broken by tears.

IRONY *Irony* is the general name given to literary techniques that involve surprising, interesting, or amusing contradictions. In *verbal irony*, words are used to suggest the opposite of their usual meaning. In *dramatic irony*, there is a contradiction between what a character thinks and what the reader or audience knows to be true. In *irony of situation*, an event occurs that directly contradicts expectations.

LEGEND A *legend* is a widely told story about the past that may or may not be based in fact. A legend often reflects a people's identity or cultural values, generally with more historical truth than that in a myth. *The Epic of Gilgamesh* (p. 14) from Sumeria and the *Shah-nama* from Persia are both based in part on legends. In Europe, the well-known German legend

of Johann Faust inspired novels and plays, including Goethe's *Faust* (p. 768).

See also Fable *and* Myth.

LYRIC POEM A *lyric poem* is a poem expressing the observations and feelings of a single speaker. Unlike a narrative poem, it presents an experience or a single effect, but it does not tell a full story. Early Greeks defined a lyric poem as that which was expressed by a single voice accompanied by a lyre. The poems of Archilochus, Callinus, Sappho (p. 376), and Pindar (p. 380) are lyric. Although they are no longer designed to be sung to the accompaniment of a lyre, lyric poems retain a melodic quality that results from the rhythmic patterns of rhymed or unrhymed verse. Modern forms of lyric poems include the elegy, the ode, and the sonnet.

METAPHOR A *metaphor* is a figure of speech in which one thing is spoken of as though it were something else, as in "death, that long sleep." Through this identification of dissimilar things, a comparison is suggested or implied. Octavio Paz uses the following metaphor in his poem "Fable" (p. 1194): "Insects were living jewels." The metaphor suggests the similarities between insects and precious stones.

An *extended metaphor* is developed at length and involves several points of comparison. A mixed metaphor occurs when two metaphors are jumbled together, as in "The thorns of life rained down on him."

A *dead metaphor* is one that has been so overused that its original metaphorical impact has been lost. Examples of dead metaphors include "the foot of the bed" and "toe the line."

See also Figurative Language.

METER *Meter* is the rhythmical pattern of a poem. This pattern is determined by the number and types of stresses, or beats, in each line. To describe the meter of a poem, you must scan its lines. Scanning involves marking the stressed and unstressed syllables, as follows in this excerpt from "Carpe Diem" by Horace (p. 510):

> Be wíse! | Drĭnk frée, | ănd ín | sŏ shórt | ă spáce
> Dŏ nót | prŏtrác | tĕd hópes | ŏf lífe | ĕmbráce:
> Whĭlst wĕ | ăre tálk | ĭng, ĕn | vĭous tíme | dŏth slíde;
> Thĭs dáy's | thĭne ówn; | thĕ néxt | măy bé | dĕníed.

As you can see, each stressed syllable is marked with a slanted line (´) and each unstressed syllable with a horseshoe symbol (˘). The stresses are then divided by vertical lines into groups called feet. The following types of feet are common in English poetry:

1. *Iamb:* a foot with one unstressed syllable followed by one stressed syllable, as in the word *afraid*
2. *Trochee:* a foot with one stressed syllable followed by one unstressed syllable, as in the word *heather*

3. *Anapest:* a foot with two unstressed syllables followed by one stressed syllable, as in the word *disembark*

4. *Dactyl:* a foot with one stressed syllable followed by two unstressed syllables, as in the word *solitude*

5. *Spondee:* a foot with two stressed syllables, as in the word *workday*

6. *Pyrrhic:* a foot with two unstressed syllables, as in the last foot of the word *unspeak | ably*

7. *Amphibrach:* a foot with an unstressed syllable, one stressed syllable, and another unstressed syllable, as in the word *another*

8. *Amphimacer:* a foot with a stressed syllable, one unstressed syllable, and another stressed syllable, as in *up and down*

A line of poetry is described as *iambic, trochaic, anapestic,* or *dactylic* according to the kind of foot that appears most often in the line. Lines are also described in terms of the number of feet that occur in them, as follows:

1. *Monometer:* verse written in one-foot lines
2. *Dimeter:* verse written in two-foot lines
3. *Trimeter:* verse written in three-foot lines
4. *Tetrameter:* verse written in four-foot lines
5. *Pentameter:* verse written in five-foot lines
6. *Hexameter:* verse written in six-foot lines
7. *Heptameter:* verse written in seven-foot lines

A complete description of the meter of a line tells both how many feet there are in the line and what kind of foot is most common. Thus, the translated stanza from Horace's ode quoted at the beginning of this entry would be described as being made up of iambic pentameter lines. Poetry that does not have a regular meter is called *free verse*.

See also Free Verse.

METONYMY *Metonymy* is a figure of speech that substitutes something closely related for the thing actually meant. For example, in Genesis (p. 44), it is said, "By the sweat of your brow / Shall you get bread to eat." Here the word *sweat* represents hard labor.

See also Figurative Language.

MOCK EPIC A *mock epic* is a poem about a trivial matter written in the style of a serious epic. The incongruity of style and subject matter produces comic effects.

MODERNISM *Modernism* describes an international movement in the arts during the early twentieth century. Modernists rejected old forms and experimented with the new. Literary Modernists used images as symbols. They presented human experiences in fragments, rather than as a coherent whole, which led to new experiments in the forms of poetry and fiction.

MONOLOGUE A *monologue* is a speech or performance given entirely by one person or by one character.

See also Dramatic Monologue *and* Soliloquy.

MOOD *Mood*, or atmosphere, is the feeling created in the reader by a literary work or passage. Mood may be suggested by the writer's choice of words, by events in the work, or by the physical setting. Julio Cortázar's "House Taken Over" (p. 1182) begins with a description of the narrator's life that sets a mood of comfort and routine. He later introduces an element of unknown danger that contrasts with and finally overcomes the pleasant mood at the beginning.

See also Setting *and* Tone.

MOTIVATION *Motivation* is a reason that explains or partially explains a character's thoughts, feelings, actions, or speech. Characters may be motivated by their physical needs; by their wants, wishes, desires, or dreams; or by their beliefs, values, and ideals. Effective characterization involves creating motivations that make characters seem believable.

MYTH A *myth* is a fictional tale, originally with religious significance, that explains the actions of gods or heroes, the causes of natural phenomena, or both. Allusions to characters and motifs from Greek, Roman, Norse, and Celtic myths are common in English literature. In addition, mythological stories are often retold or adapted.

See also Fable *and* Legend.

NARRATION *Narration* is writing that tells a story. The act of telling a story is also called narration. The *narrative*, or story, is told by a character or speaker called the *narrator*. Biographies, autobiographies, journals, reports, novels, short stories, plays, narrative poems, anecdotes, fables, parables, myths, legends, folk tales, ballads, and epic poems are all narratives, or types of narration.

See also Point of View.

NARRATIVE POEM A *narrative poem* is a poem that tells a story in verse. Three traditional types of narrative poems are ballads, epics, and metrical romances. The *Shah-nama*, the *Iliad* (p. 326), the *Aeneid* (p. 492), and the *Song of Roland* (p. 556) are epic narrative poems. Poets who have written narrative poems include Alexander Pushkin, Victor Hugo, and Wole Soyinka.

NATURALISM *Naturalism* was a literary movement among writers at the end of the nineteenth century and during the early decades of the twentieth century. The Naturalists depicted life in its grimmer details and viewed people as hopeless victims of natural laws.

See also Realism.

NEOCLASSICISM *Neoclassicism* was a literary movement of the late seventeenth and the eighteenth centuries in which writers turned to classical Greek and Roman literary models. Like the ancients, many Neoclassical writers dealt with themes related to proper human conduct. The most popular literary forms of the day—essays, letters, early novels, epigrams, parodies, and satires—reflected this emphasis.

See also Romanticism.

NOVEL A *novel* is an extended work of fiction that often has a complicated plot, many major and minor characters, a unifying theme, and several settings. Novels can be grouped in many ways, based on the historical periods in which they are written (such as Victorian), on the subjects and themes that they treat (such as Gothic or regional), on the techniques used in them (such as stream of consciousness), or on their part in literary movements (such as in Naturalism or Realism). A *novella* is not as long as a novel but is longer than a short story.

OBJECTIVE CORRELATIVE *See* Image.

OCTAVE *See* Stanza.

ODE An *ode* is a long, formal lyric poem with a serious theme. It may have a traditional structure with stanzas grouped in threes, called the *strophe*, the *antistrophe*, and the *epode*. Odes often honor people, commemorate events, or respond to natural scenes. The ancient Greek poet Pindar is famous for odes such as "Olympia 11" (p. 380), praising victorious athletes.

See also Lyric Poem.

ONOMATOPOEIA *Onomatopoeia* is the use of words that imitate sounds. Examples of such words are *buzz*, *hiss*, *murmur*, and *rustle*. In the line ". . . to hear / Rasps in the field," from Wole Soyinka's "Season" (p. 1344), *Rasps* is onomatopoeic. Onomatopoeia creates musical effects and reinforces meaning.

ORAL TRADITION *Oral tradition* is the body of songs, stories, and poems preserved by being passed from generation to generation by word of mouth. Folk epics, ballads, myths, legends, folk tales, folk songs, proverbs, and nursery rhymes are all products of the oral tradition.

See also Ballad, Folklore, Legend, *and* Myth.

OXYMORON An *oxymoron* is a figure of speech that fuses two contradictory ideas, such as "freezing fire" or "happy grief," thus suggesting a paradox in just a few words.

See also Figurative Language *and* Paradox.

PARABLE A *parable* is a short, simple story from which a moral or religious lesson can be drawn. The most famous parables are those in the New Testament. Leo Tolstoy's "How Much Land Does a Man Need?" (p. 835) echoes a biblical parable.

PARADOX A *paradox* is a statement that seems to be contradictory but that actually presents a truth. Wole Soyinka's "Season" (p. 1344) presents this paradox, "Rust is ripeness, rust / And the wilted-corn plume. . . ." Because rust is often associated with metallic corrosion, the statement seems contradictory. However, in the context of the color of harvested crops, the statement makes sense. Because a paradox is surprising or even shocking, it draws the reader's attention to what is being said.

See also Figurative Language *and* Oxymoron.

PARODY A *parody* is a humorous imitation of another work or of a type of work.

PASTORAL *Pastoral* refers to literary works that deal with the pleasures of a simple rural life or with escape to a simpler place and time. The tradition of pastoral literature began in ancient Greece with the poetic idylls of Theocritus. The Roman poet Virgil also wrote a famous collection of pastoral poems, the *Eclogues*.

PENTAMETER *See* Meter.

PERSONA *Persona* means, literally, "a mask." A persona is a fictional self created by an author—a self through whom the narrative of a poem or story is told.

See also Speaker.

PERSONIFICATION *Personification* is a figure of speech in which a nonhuman subject is given human characteristics. Effective personification of things or ideas makes their qualities seem unified, like the characteristics of a person, and their relationship with the reader seem closer.

See also Figurative Language *and* Metaphor.

PLOT *Plot* is the sequence of events in a literary work. The two primary elements of any plot are characters and a conflict. Most plots can be analyzed into many or all of the following parts:

1. The *exposition* introduces the setting, the characters, and the basic situation.
2. The *inciting incident* introduces the central conflict.
3. During the *development*, the conflict runs its course and usually intensifies.
4. At the *climax*, the conflict reaches a high point of interest or suspense.
5. The *denouement* ties up loose ends that remain after the climax of the conflict.
6. At the *resolution*, the story is resolved and an insight is revealed.

There are many variations on the standard plot structure. Some stories begin *in medias res* ("in the middle of things"), after the inciting incident has already occurred. In some stories, the expository material appears toward the middle, in flashbacks. In many stories, there is no denouement. Occasionally, the conflict is left unresolved.

POETRY *Poetry* is one of the three major types, or genres, of literature, the others being prose and drama. Poetry defies simple definition because there is no single characteristic that is found in all poems and not found in all nonpoems.

Often, poems are divided into lines and stanzas. Poems such as sonnets, odes, villanelles, and sestinas are governed by rules regarding the number of lines, the number and placement of stressed syllables in each line, and the rhyme scheme. In the case of villanelles and sestinas, the repetition of words at the ends of lines or of entire lines is required. However, some poems are written in free verse. Most poems make use of highly concise, musical, and emotionally charged language. Many also use imagery, figurative language, and devices of sound like rhyme.

Types of poetry include *narrative poetry* (ballads, epics, and metrical romances); *dramatic poetry* (dramatic monologues and dramatic dialogues); *lyrics* (sonnets, odes, elegies, and love poems); and *concrete poetry* (a poem presented on the page in a shape that suggests its subject).

POINT OF VIEW The perspective, or vantage point, from which a story is told is its *point of view*. If a character within the story narrates, then it is told from the *first-person point of view*. If a voice from outside the story tells it, then the story is told from the *third-person point of view*. If the knowledge of the storyteller is limited to the internal states of one character, then the storyteller has a *limited point of view*. If the storyteller's knowledge extends to the internal states of all the characters, then the storyteller has an *omniscient point of view*.

PROSE *Prose* is the ordinary form of written language and one of the three major types of literature. Most writing that is not poetry, drama, or song is considered prose. Prose occurs in two major forms: fiction and nonfiction.

PROTAGONIST The *protagonist* is the main character in a literary work. In R. K. Narayan's "An Astrologer's Day" (p. 1366), the protagonist is the astrologer.

PYRRHIC *See* Meter.

QUATRAIN *See* Stanza.

REALISM *Realism* is the presentation in art of details from actual life. During the last part of the nineteenth century and the first part of the twentieth, Realism enjoyed considerable popularity among writers in the English-speaking world. Novels often dealt with grim social realities and presented realistic portrayals of the psychological states of characters.

See also Symbolism.

REFRAIN A *refrain* is a regularly repeated line or group of lines in a poem or song.

See also Ballad.

REGIONALISM *Regionalism* is the tendency to confine one's writing to the presentation of the distinct culture of an area, including its speech, customs, and history.

RHYME *Rhyme* is the repetition of sounds at the ends of words. *End rhyme* occurs when rhyming words appear at the ends of lines. *Internal rhyme* occurs when rhyming words fall within a line. *Exact rhyme* is the use of identical rhyming sounds, as in *love* and *dove*. *Approximate*, or *slant*, *rhyme* is the use of sounds that are similar but not identical, as in *prove* and *glove*.

RHYME SCHEME *Rhyme scheme* is the regular pattern of rhyming words in a poem or stanza. To indicate a rhyme scheme, assign a different letter to each final sound in the poem or stanza. The following lines from Morris Bishop's translation of Petrarch's "Laura" (p. 675) have been marked.

She used to let her golden hair fly free	*a*
For the wind to toy and tangle and molest;	*b*
Her eyes were brighter than the radiant west.	*b*
(Seldom they shine so now.) I used to see	*a*
Pity look out of those deep eyes on me.	*a*

RHYTHM *See* Meter.

ROMANCE A *romance* is a story that presents remote or imaginative incidents rather than ordinary, realistic experience. The term *romance* was originally used to refer to medieval tales of the deeds and loves of noble knights and ladies. From the eighteenth century on, the term *romance* has been used to describe sentimental novels about love.

ROMANTICISM *Romanticism* was a literary and artistic movement of the eighteenth and nineteenth centuries. In reaction to Neoclassicism, the Romantics emphasized imagination, fancy, freedom, emotion, wildness, the beauty of the untamed natural world, the rights of the individual, the nobility of the common man, and the attractiveness of pastoral life. Important figures in the Romantic Movement include Johann Wolfgang von Goethe, Victor Hugo, and Heinrich Heine.

RUN-ON LINE A *run-on line* is a line that does not contain a pause or a stop at the end. The flow of words carries the reader to the following line. A poet may use run-on lines to avoid creating a sing-song effect, in which each line is separated from the next by a pause.

See also End-Stopped Line.

SATIRE *Satire* is writing that ridicules or holds up to contempt the faults of individuals or groups. Although a satire is often humorous, its purpose is not simply to make readers laugh but also to correct the flaws and shortcomings that it points out.

SCANSION *Scansion* is the process of analyzing the metrical pattern of a poem.

See also Meter.

SESTET *See* Stanza.

SETTING The *setting* is the time and place of the action of a literary work. A setting can provide a backdrop for the action. It can be the force that the protagonist struggles against and thus the source of the central conflict. It can also be used to create an atmosphere. In many works, the setting symbolizes a point that the author wishes to emphasize. In Albert Camus's short story "The Guest" (p. 1224), the setting is a lonely desert plateau in an Arab country occupied by France. Fearing an Arab insurrection, and unable to spare anyone for a long trip, the local French police ask a schoolteacher to take an Arab suspect to the authorities. Such a situation would only arise in an isolated colonial area. The setting also adds a grim atmosphere and conveys a theme—human freedom. In the following scene, a character must choose between two directions:

> They reached a level height made up of crumbly rocks. From there on, the plateau sloped down, eastward, toward a low plain where there were a few spindly trees and, to the south, toward outcroppings of rock that gave the landscape a chaotic look.
> Daru surveyed the two directions. There was nothing but the sky on the horizon. Not a man could be seen.

See also Mood *and* Symbol.

SHORT STORY A *short story* is a brief work of fiction. The short story resembles the longer novel, but it generally has a simpler plot and setting. In addition, a short story tends to reveal a character at a crucial moment, rather than to develop a character through many incidents.

SIMILE A *simile* is a figure of speech that compares two apparently dissimilar things using *like* or *as*. Many similes appear in the *Iliad* (p. 326), including the following:

> And swift Achilles kept on coursing Hector, nonstop as a hound in the mountains starts a fawn from its lair, hunting him down the gorges, down the narrow glens.

By comparing apparently dissimilar things, the writer of a simile surprises the reader into an appreciation of the hidden similarities of the things being compared.

See also Figurative Language.

SOLILOQUY A *soliloquy* is a long speech in a play or in a prose work made by a character who is alone and thus reveals private thoughts and feelings to the audience or reader.

See also Monologue.

SONNET A sonnet is a fourteen-line lyric poem with a single theme. Sonnets are usually written in iambic pentameter. The *Petrarchan*, or *Italian, sonnet* is divided into two parts, an eight-line octave and a six-line sestet. The octave rhymes *abba abba*, while the sestet generally rhymes *cde cde* or uses some combination of *cd* rhymes. The octave raises a question, states a problem, or presents a brief narrative, and the sestet answers the question, solves the problem, or comments on the narrative.

The *Shakespearean*, or *English, sonnet* has three four-line quatrains plus a concluding two-line couplet. The rhyme scheme of such a sonnet is usually *abab cdcd efef gg*. Each of the three quatrains usually explores a different variation of the main theme. Then, the couplet presents a summarizing or concluding statement.

See also Lyric Poem *and* Sonnet Sequence.

SONNET SEQUENCE A *sonnet sequence* is a series or group of sonnets, most often written to or about a beloved. Although each sonnet can stand alone as a separate poem, the sequence lets the poet trace the development of a relationship or examine different aspects of a single subject.

See also Sonnet.

SPEAKER The *speaker* is the imaginary voice assumed by the writer of a poem; the character who "says" the poem. This character is often not identified by name but may be identified otherwise. For instance, in the opening line of an ancient Egyptian poem (p. 37), the lovelorn speaker's desire for attention is made clear in the opening:

> I think I'll go home and lie very still,
> feigning terminal illness

Recognizing the speaker and thinking about his or her characteristics are often central to interpreting a lyric poem.

See also Persona *and* Point of View.

SPONDEE *See* Meter.

STANZA A *stanza* is a group of lines in a poem, which is seen as a unit. Many poems are divided into stanzas that are separated by spaces. Stanzas often function like paragraphs in prose. Each stanza states and develops one main idea.

Stanzas are commonly named according to the number of lines found in them, as follows:

1. *Couplet:* a two-line stanza
2. *Tercet:* a three-line stanza
3. *Quatrain:* a four-line stanza
4. *Cinquain:* a five-line stanza
5. *Sestet:* a six-line stanza
6. *Heptastich:* a seven-line stanza

7. *Octave:* an eight-line stanza

See also Sonnet.

STYLE *Style* is a writer's typical way of writing. Determinants of a writer's style include formality, use of figurative language, use of rhythm, typical grammatical patterns, typical sentence lengths, and typical methods of organization. For example, Yehuda Amichai's colloquial style in a poem such as "From the Book of Esther I Filtered the Sediment" (p. 1320), is an innovation in Hebrew literature.

See also Diction.

SURREALISM *Surrealism* is a movement in art and literature that emphasizes the irrational side of human nature. It focuses on the imaginary world of dreams and the unconscious mind. Originating in France following World War I, Surrealism was a protest against the so-called Rationalism that led the world into catastrophic war. Surrealism can be found in Latin American poems such as Octavio Paz's "Fable" (p. 1194).

SYMBOL A *symbol* is a sign, word, phrase, image, or other object that stands for or represents something else. Thus, a flag can symbolize a country, a spoken word can symbolize an object, a fine car can symbolize wealth, and so on. In literary criticism, a distinction is often made between traditional or conventional symbols—those that are part of our general cultural inheritance—and *personal symbols*—those that are created by particular authors for use in particular works.

Conventional symbolism is often based on elements of nature. For example, youth is often symbolized by greenery or springtime, middle age by summer, and old age by autumn or winter. Conventional symbols are also borrowed from religion and politics. For example, a cross may be a symbol of Christianity, or the color red may be a symbol of Marxist ideology.

SYMBOLISM *Symbolism* was a literary movement of nineteenth-century France. The Symbolist writers reacted against Realism and stressed the importance of emotional states, especially by means of symbols corresponding to these states. The Symbolists were also concerned with using sound to achieve emotional effects. Arthur Rimbaud and Paul Verlaine are among the best-known Symbolist poets. Many twentieth-century writers around the world were influenced by the Symbolist movement.

See also Realism.

SYNECDOCHE *Synecdoche* is a figure of speech in which a part of something is used to stand for the whole. For example, one might speak of "hands" to refer to the crew of a ship, "wheels" to refer to a car, or "the law" to refer to the whole criminal justice system.

See also Figurative Language.

TANKA *Tanka* is a form of Japanese poetry consisting of five lines of five, seven, five, seven, and seven syllables. Tanka is the most prevalent verse form in traditional Japanese literature. Tanka often tell a brief story or express a single feeling or thought.

TETRAMETER *See* Meter.

THEME *Theme* is the central idea, concern, or purpose in a literary work. In an essay, the theme might be directly stated in what is known as a thesis statement. In a serious literary work, the theme is usually expressed indirectly rather than directly. A light work, one written strictly for entertainment, may not have a theme.

TONE *Tone* is the writer's attitude toward the readers and toward the subject. It may be formal or informal, friendly or distant, personal or pompous. The tone of Gabriela Mistral's poem "Fear" (p. 1102) is, not surprisingly, fearful.

See also Mood.

TRADITION In literary study and practice, a *tradition* is a past body of work, developed over the course of history. A literary tradition may be unified by form (the tradition of the sonnet), by language (literature in Spanish), or by nationality (Japanese literature). A tradition develops through the acknowledgment of works, forms, and styles as classic. Writers participate in a tradition if only by following conventions about the suitable forms and subjects for literature. They make conscious use of the tradition when they use references, stories, or forms from old literature to give authority to their work.

TRAGEDY *Tragedy* is a type of drama or literature that shows the downfall or destruction of a noble or outstanding person, traditionally one who possesses a character weakness called a *tragic flaw*. The *tragic hero* is caught up in a sequence of events that inevitably results in disaster. Because the protagonist is neither a wicked villain nor an innocent victim, the audience reacts with mixed emotions—both pity and fear, according to the Greek philosopher Aristotle, who defined tragedy in the *Poetics*. The outcome of a tragedy, in which the protagonist is isolated from society, contrasts with the happy resolution of a comedy, in which the protagonist makes peace with society. Sophocles' *Oedipus the King* (p. 426) is a Greek tragedy.

See also Comedy *and* Drama.

TRIMETER *See* Meter.

TROCHEE *See* Meter.

Summary of Grammar

Nouns A **noun** names a person, place, or thing. A **common noun,** such as *country*, names any one of a class of people, places, or things. A **proper noun,** such as *Great Britain*, names a specific person, place, or thing.

Pronouns Pronouns are words that stand for nouns or for words that take the place of nouns. **Personal pronouns** refer to the person speaking; the person spoken to; or the person, place, or thing spoken about.

	Singular	Plural
First Person	I, me, my, mine	we, us, our, ours
Second Person	you, your, yours	you, your, yours
Third Person	he, him, his, she, her, hers, it, its	they, them, their, theirs

A **reflexive pronoun** ends in *-self* or *-selves* and names the person or thing receiving an action when that person or thing is the same as the one performing the action.

An **intensive pronoun** also ends in *-self* or *-selves*. It adds emphasis to a noun or pronoun.

> ". . . I should like to take breakfast with you this morning, together with my companion here, but you must not put *yourself* to any trouble." (reflexive) (Boccaccio, p. 691)

Demonstrative pronouns—such as *this*, *that*, *these*, and *those*—single out specific people, places, or things.

A **relative pronoun** begins a subordinate clause and connects it to another idea in the sentence.

> "Did you imagine I should not observe the crafty scheme *that* stole upon me. . .?" (Sophocles, p. 445)

Interrogative pronouns are used to begin questions.

> "*Who* sent you to us?" (Sophocles, p. 462)

Indefinite pronouns refer to people, places, or things, often without specifying which ones.

> *One* ate whatever one could get. (Maupassant, p. 828)

Verbs A **verb** is a word or group of words that express an action, a condition, or the fact that something exists, while indicating the time of the action, condition, or fact. An **action verb** tells what action someone or something is performing. An action verb is **transitive** if it directs action

toward someone or something named in the same sentence.

> On his airy perch among the branches Master Crow *was holding* cheese in his beak. (La Fontaine, p. 720)

An action verb is **intransitive** if it does not direct action toward something or someone named in the same sentence.

> No smoke *came* now from the chimney pot of the villa. (Calvino, p. 1253)

A **linking verb** expresses the subject's condition by connecting the subject with another word.

> She *felt* restless. . . . (Colette, p. 1049)

Helping verbs are verbs added to another verb to make a single verb phrase. They indicate the time at which an action takes place or whether it actually happens, could happen, or should happen.

> "It *can be stopped* right away." (Kafka, p. 1012)

Adjectives An **adjective** is a word used to describe what is named by a noun or pronoun or to give a noun or pronoun a more specific meaning. Adjectives answer these questions:

> What kind? *purple* hat, *happy* face
> Which one? *this* bowl, *those* cameras
> How many? *three* cars, *several* dishes
> How much? *less* attention, *enough* food

The **articles** *the*, *a*, and *an* are adjectives. *An* is used before a word beginning with a vowel sound. *This*, *that*, *these*, and *those* are used as **demonstrative adjectives** when they appear directly before a noun.

A noun may sometimes be used as an adjective:

> *language* lesson   *chemistry* book

Adverbs An **adverb** is a word that modifies a verb, an adjective, or another adverb. Adverbs answer the questions *where*, *when*, *how*, or *to what extent*.

> She will answer *soon*. (modifies verb *will answer*)
> I was *extremely* sad. (modifies adjective *sad*)
> You called *more* often than I. (modifies adverb *often*)

Prepositions A preposition is a word that relates a noun or pronoun that appears with it to another word in the sentence. It can indicate relations of time, place, causality, responsibility, and motivation. Prepositions are almost always followed by nouns or pronouns.

around the fire	*for* us
in sight	*till* sunrise

Conjunctions A conjunction is used to connect other words or groups of words.

Coordinating conjunctions connect similar kinds or groups of words:

bread *and* wine   brief *but* powerful

Correlative conjunctions are used in pairs to connect similar words or groups of words:

both Luis *and* Rosa   *neither* you *nor* I

Subordinating conjunctions indicate the connection between two ideas by placing one below the other in rank or importance:

When the man's speech returned once more, he told him of his adventure. (Marie de France, p. 602)

Interjections An **interjection** is a word or phrase that expresses feeling or emotion and functions independently of a sentence.

"*Oh*, what an awful awakening!" (Ibsen, p. 935)

Sentences A **sentence** is a group of words with a subject and predicate, expressing a complete thought. A sentence fragment is a group of words that does not express a complete thought. Sentence fragments should be avoided in writing, unless used for effect, as in realistic dialogue.

Phrases A **phrase** is a group of words without a subject and verb that functions as one part of speech. A **prepositional phrase** includes a preposition and a noun or pronoun.

before dawn   *as a result of* the rain

An **adjective phrase** is a prepositional phrase that modifies a noun or pronoun.

The likeness *of the dog* would get mixed up with that *of the cat.* (Tagore, p. 1146)

An **adverb phrase** is a prepositional phrase that modifies a verb, an adjective, or an adverb.

From every side men ran *to the succor of the dame.* (Marie de France, p. 601)

An **appositive phrase** is a noun or pronoun with modifiers, placed next to a noun or pronoun to add information and details.

And Icarus, *[Daedalus']* son, stood by and watched him, . . . (Ovid, p. 517)

A **participial phrase** is a participle that is modified by an adjective or adverb phrase or that has a complement (a group of words that completes the participle's meaning). The entire phrase acts as an adjective.

Her stepmother seemed *drained of strength.* . . . (Kawabata, p. 1385)

A **gerund** is a noun formed from the present participle of a verb (ending in *-ing*). A **gerund phrase** is a gerund with modifiers or a complement (words that complete its meaning), all acting together as a noun.

"This *getting up so early,*" he thought, "makes anyone a complete idiot." (Kafka, p. 979)

An **infinitive phrase** is an infinitive with modifiers, complements (words completing its meaning), or a subject, all acting together as a single part of speech. (In the example, the second infinitive phrase is part of the complement of the first.)

And he felt it his duty *to explain* to his traveling companions that the poor woman was *to be* pitied. . . . (Pirandello, p. 1056)

Clauses A **clause** is a group of words with its own subject and verb. An **independent clause** can stand by itself as a complete sentence. A **subordinate clause** cannot stand by itself as a complete sentence.

An **adjective clause** is a subordinate clause that modifies a noun or pronoun by telling *what kind* or *which one.*

The more stubborn among them, *who were the youngest,* still lived for a few hours with the illusion that . . . his name might be Lautaro. (García Márquez, p. 1177)

Subordinate adverb clauses modify verbs, adjectives, adverbs, or verbals by telling *where, when, in what way, to what extent, under what condition,* or *why.*

The room fell silent, and all eyes were on him, As Father Aeneas from his high couch began . . . (Virgil, p. 493)

Subordinate noun clauses act as nouns.

. . . she said, in order to remove any hesitation on his part, *that she could also send the janitor's wife to get it* . . . (Kafka, p. 996)

Summary of Capitalization and Punctuation

Capitalization

Capitalize the first word in sentences, interjections, and complete questions. Also, capitalize the first word in a quotation if the quotation is a complete sentence.

> Finally, all in one breath, he exclaimed: "The Marchesa stole a trout from me!" (Calvino, p. 1252)

Capitalize all proper nouns and adjectives.

> Trinidadian   Thames River

Capitalize titles showing family relationships when they refer to a specific person unless they are preceded by a possessive noun or pronoun.

> Uncle Oscar   Mangan's sister

Capitalize the first word and all other key words in the titles of books, periodicals, poems, stories, plays, songs, and other works of art.

> *Faust*   "Two Friends"

Punctuation

End Marks Use a **period** to end a declarative sentence, an imperative sentence, an indirect question, and most abbreviations.

> Irene never bothered anyone.
> I wonder what Irene would have done without her knitting. (Cortázar, p. 1184)

Use a **question mark** to end an interrogative sentence.

> "A knife has passed through you once?" said the astrologer.
> "Good fellow!" He bared his chest to show the scar. "What else?" (Narayan, p. 1369)

Use an **exclamation mark** after an exclamatory sentence, a forceful imperative sentence, or an interjection expressing strong emotion.

> "Oh, you and your cats!" (Calvino, p. 1252)

Commas Use a **comma** before the conjunction to separate two independent clauses in a compound sentence.

> The youth began his journey from
> the castle, and the daytime whole
> he did not meet one living soul. . . .
> (Chrétien de Troyes, p. 584)

Use commas to separate three or more words, phrases, or clauses in a series.

> . . . he opened his bag and spread out his professional equipment, which consisted of a dozen cowrie shells, a square piece of cloth with obscure mystic charts on it, a notebook, and a bundle of palmyra writing. (Narayan, p. 1366)

Use commas to separate adjectives unless they must stay in a specific order.

> Her new mother was a kind woman and they lived a quiet, happy life. (Kawabata, p. 1383)

Use a comma after an introductory word, phrase, or clause.

> As soon as Pakhom and his family reached their new abode, he applied for admission into the commune of a large village. (Tolstoy, p. 840)

Use commas to set off nonessential expressions.

> Sasha Uskov, the young man of twenty-five who was the cause of all the commotion, had arrived some time before. . . . (Chekhov, p. 851)

Use commas with places, dates, and titles.

> Cairo, Egypt
>
> September 1, 1939
>
> Reginald Farrars, M. P.

Use commas after items in addresses, after the salutation in a personal letter, after the closing in all letters, and in numbers of more than three digits.

> Paris, France
>
> Dear Randolph,
>
> Yours faithfully,
>
> 9,744

Use a comma to indicate words left out of parallel clauses, to set off a direct quotation, and to prevent a sentence from being misunderstood.

> In Rimbaud's poetry, I admire the music; in Pasternak's, the deep emotion.

> "In that case," she said, picking up her needles again, "we'll have to live on this side."
> (Cortázar, p. 1186)

Semicolons Use a **semicolon** to join independent clauses that are not already joined by a conjunction.

> She fastened it on her wrist, and shook it, throwing off blue sparks under the electric candles; a hundred tiny rainbows, blazing with color, danced on the white tablecloth. (Colette, p. 1046)

Use semicolons to avoid confusion when independent clauses or items in a series already contain commas.

> I enjoy reading ancient authors: Homer, for the action; Catullus, for his bluntness; and Plato, for his ideas.

Colons Use a **colon** before a list of items following an independent clause.

> When the greatest of French poetry is discussed, the following names are certain to be mentioned: Charles Baudelaire, Arthur Rimbaud, Paul Valéry, and Victor Hugo.

Use a colon to introduce a formal or lengthy quotation.

> Finally M. Sauvage pulled himself together: "Come on! On our way! But let's go carefully." (Maupassant, p. 831)

Use a colon to introduce an independent clause that summarizes or explains the sentence before it.

> One empty bier is decorated and carried in the procession: this is for the missing, whose bodies could not be recovered. (Thucydides, p. 386)

Quotation Marks A **direct quotation** represents a person's exact speech or thoughts and is enclosed within quotation marks.

> "We are in Japan," repeated Watanabé. (Ōgai, p. 1121)

An **indirect quotation** reports only the general meaning of what a person said or thought and does not require quotation marks.

> A woman asked me last night on the dark street how another woman was who'd already died. . . . (Amichai, p. 1320)

Always place a comma or a period inside the final quotation mark.

> Out of a great weariness I answered, "She's fine, she's fine." (Amichai, p. 1320)

Always place a question mark or an exclamation mark inside the final quotation mark if the end mark is part of the quotation; if it is not part of the quotation, place it outside the final quotation mark.

> "Why school?" I challenged my father openly. (Mahfouz, p. 1309)

Use single quotation marks for a quotation within a quotation.

> Pointing out clues about character in dialogue, the teacher told her students, "We can infer that

Margaret Atwood's mother did not approve of swearing by the fact that she substitutes 'blankety-blank' for stronger language."

Use quotation marks around the titles of short written works, episodes in a series, songs, and titles of works mentioned as parts of collections.

> "An Astrologer's Day"   "Boswell Meets Johnson"

Italics Italicize the titles of long written works, movies, television and radio shows, lengthy works of music, paintings, and sculpture. Also, italicize foreign words not yet accepted into English and words you wish to stress.

If you are writing by hand or working in some other format that does not allow you to italicize text, underline such titles and words.

> <u>Oedipus the King</u>   <u>60 Minutes</u>
>
> <u>Guernica</u>   <u>déjà vu</u>

Parentheses Use **parentheses** to set off asides and explanations only when the material is not essential or when it consists of one or more sentences.

> And to love (Thou knowest it well) is a bitter exercise. . . . (Mistral, p. 1104)

Hyphens Use a **hyphen** with certain numbers, after certain prefixes, with two or more words used as one word, with a compound modifier, and within a word when a combination of letters might otherwise be confusing.

> twenty-nine   re-create
> pre-Romantic   brother-in-law

Apostrophe Add an **apostrophe** and an *s* to show the possessive case of most singular nouns and of plural nouns that do not end in *-s* or *-es*.

> Rilke's poems   the mice's whiskers

Add an apostrophe to show the possessive case of plural nouns ending in *-s* and *-es*.

> the girls' songs   the Ortizes' car

Use an apostrophe in a contraction to indicate the position of the missing letter or letters.

> That's all I'd have to try with my boss; I'd be fired on the spot. (Kafka, p. 979)

Use an apostrophe and an *-s* to write the plurals of symbols, letters, and words used to name themselves.

> five *a*'s   no *if*'s or *but*'s

Glossary of Common Usage

among, between

Among is generally used with three or more items. *Between* is generally used with only two items.

> *Among* Ibsen's characters, my favorite has always been Nora in *A Doll House*.

> The main character is at first torn *between* social conventions and her own moral principles.

amount, number

Amount refers to quantity or a unit, whereas *number* refers to individual items that can be counted. *Amount* generally appears with a singular noun, and *number* appears with a plural noun.

> The *amount* of attention that great writers have paid to the Faust legend is remarkable.

> A considerable *number* of important writers have been fascinated by the legend of Joan of Arc.

as, because, like, as to

To avoid confusion, use *because* rather than *as* when you want to indicate cause and effect.

> *Because* he felt he had fulfilled himself as a poet, Arthur Rimbaud set down his pen and pursued a life of adventure.

Do not use the preposition *like* to introduce a clause that requires the conjunction *as*.

> *As* we might expect from the verse of Baudelaire, the tone of "Invitation to the Voyage" is sultry and musical.

The use of *as to* for *about* is awkward and should be avoided.

bad, badly

Use the predicate adjective *bad* after linking verbs such as *feel*, *look*, and *seem*. Use *badly* when an adverb is required.

> In "The Handsomest Drowned Man in the World," the men of the village feel *bad* that the women are attracted to a stranger.

> At the end of *A Doll House*, Nora chooses to leave her husband, realizing just how *badly* she'd been affected by seven years in a loveless marriage.

because of, due to

Use *due to* if it can logically replace the phrase *caused by*. In introductory phrases, however, *because of* is better usage than *due to*.

> The resurgence of interest in Ibsen's *A Doll House* in recent decades may be *due to* its feminist themes.

> *Because of* the expansion of the reading public, writers during the eighteenth century became less dependent on wealthy patrons for support.

compare, contrast

The verb *compare* can involve both similarities and differences. The verb *contrast* always involves differences. Use *to* or *with* after *compare*. Use *with* after *contrast*.

> Harvey's report *compared* the bohemian lifestyle of Baudelaire *to* that of Rimbaud, noting parallels in their writing styles as well.

> The Greeks *contrasted* inner vision *with* physical vision; thus, the legend that Homer was a blind bard indicates how highly they esteemed introspection.

continual, continuous

Continual means "occurring again and again in succession (but with pauses or breaks)," whereas *continuous* means "occurring without interruption."

> In the poem "Invitation to the Voyage," Baudelaire's *continual* use of a two-line refrain creates a feeling of the rolling ocean waves.

> Though critics assert that Pablo Neruda spent many painstaking hours shaping his verse, the exuberant voice of the speaker in "Ode to My Socks" suggests that he may have written this poem in a single *continuous* burst of inspiration.

different from, different than

The preferred usage is *different from*.

> Colette's third marriage was very *different from* her previous ones simply because it brought her great happiness and satisfaction.

farther, further

Use *farther* when you refer to distance. Use *further* when you mean "to a greater degree" or "additional."

> Discontented with his new life in Paris, the young French poet Rimbaud traveled *farther* east to quench his thirst for adventure.

> In Ibsen's *A Doll House*, Nora realizes that staying in her unhappy marriage will only bring *further* psychological abuse.

fewer, less

Use *fewer* for things that can be counted. Use *less* for amounts or quantities that cannot be counted.

> When asked to compare the two versions of the Faust legend they had read, *fewer* students preferred Christopher Marlowe's version. Most found it to be *less* dramatic than Goethe's.

just, only

Only should appear directly before the word it modifies. *Just*, used as an adverb meaning "no more than," also belongs directly before the word it modifies.

> The form of the villanelle allows a poet to use *just* two rhymes.

> Poet Arthur Rimbaud was *only* fifteen years old when he was first published.

lay, lie

Lay is a transitive verb meaning "to set or put something down." Its principal parts are *lay, laying, laid, laid*.

Lie is an intransitive verb meaning "to recline." Its principal parts are *lie, lying, lay, lain*.

> In Shakespeare's *The Tempest*, Prospero has the power to *lay* strange curses and spells on his enemies.

> According to Blaise Pascal, an individual *lies* somewhere in the midst of a paradoxical universe, unable to comprehend the extremes of nature.

plurals that do not end in *-s*

The plurals of certain nouns from Greek and Latin are formed as they were in their original language. Words such as *data, criteria, media*, and *phenomena* are plural and should be treated as such. Each has its own distinctive singular form: *datum, criterion, medium, phenomenon*.

> Are the electronic *media* of the twentieth century contributing to the death of literature?

raise, rise

Raise is a transitive verb that usually takes a direct object. *Rise* is intransitive and never takes a direct object.

> In "On an Autumn Evening in the Mountains," poet Wang Wei *raises* an allegorical question about mortality.

> As the poets in Dante's *Inferno* pass the Gates of Hell, they hear the anguished cries of the opportunists *rise* within.

that, which, who

Use the relative pronoun *that* to refer to things. Use *which* only for things and *who* only for people. Use *that* when introducing a subordinate clause that singles out a particular thing or person.

> The Ibsen play that I most enjoy is *A Doll House*.

Which is usually used to introduce a subordinate clause that is not essential to identifying the thing or person in question:

> World War II, *which* disrupted Colette's personal life, did not affect her literary output.

Who can be used to introduce either essential or non-essential subordinate clauses:

> Derek Walcott, *who* is deeply admired by many critics, won the Nobel Prize in Literature.

when, where

Do not directly follow a linking verb with *when* or *where*. Also, be careful not to use *where* when your context requires *that*.

> Evaluation is ~~when you make~~ the process of making a judgment about the quality or value of something.

> Colin read ~~where~~ that even though he was a physician, Anton Chekhov was plagued by poor health.

who, whom

Remember to use *who* only as a subject in clauses and sentences and *whom* only as an object.

> Goethe, *who* spent more than sixty years writing his masterpiece, first encountered the Faust story in a puppet show at a country fair.

> Alexander Pushkin, *whom* critics perceive as a man of plain words, wove magical tales with his simple dialogue.

Introduction to the Internet

The Internet is a series of networks that are interconnected all over the world. The Internet allows users to have almost unlimited access to information stored on the networks. Dr. Berners-Lee, a physicist, created the Internet in the 1980s by writing a small computer program that allowed pages to be linked together using key words. The Internet was mostly text-based until 1992, when a computer program called the NCSA Mosaic (National Center for Supercomputing Applications) was created at the University of Illinois. This program was the first Web browser. The development of Web browsers greatly eased the ability of the user to navigate through all the pages stored on the Web. Very soon, the appearance of the Web was altered as well. More appealing visuals were added, and sound was implemented. This change made the Web more user-friendly and more appealing to the general public.

Using the Internet for Research

Key-Word Search

Before you begin a search, you should identify your specific topic. To make searching easier, narrow your subject to a key word or a group of key words. These are your search terms, and they should be as specific as possible. For example, if you are looking for the latest concert dates for your favorite musical group, you might use the band's name as a key word. However, if you were to enter the name of the group in the query box of the search engine, you might be presented with thousands of links to information about the group that is unrelated to what you want to know. You might locate such information as band member biographies, the group's history, fan reviews of concerts, and hundreds of sites with related names containing information that is irrelevant to your search. Because you used such a broad key word, you might need to navigate through all that information before you could find a link or subheading for concert dates. In contrast, if you were to type in "Duplex Arena and [band name]," you would have a better chance of locating pages that contain this information.

How to Narrow Your Search

If you have a large group of key words and still do not know which ones to use, write out a list of all the words you are considering. Once you have completed the list, scrutinize it. Then, delete the words that are least impor-tant to your search, and highlight those that are most important.

These **key search connectors** can help you fine-tune your search:

AND: Narrows a search by retrieving documents that include both terms. For example: *baseball* AND *playoffs*

OR: Broadens a search by retrieving documents including any of the terms. For example: *playoffs* OR *championships*

NOT: Narrows a search by excluding documents containing certain words. For example: *baseball* NOT *history of*

Tips for an Effective Search

1. Remember that search engines can be case-sensitive. If your first attempt at searching fails, check your search terms for misspellings and try again.

2. If you are entering a group of key words, present them in order from the most important to the least important key word.

3. Avoid opening the link to every single page in your results list. Search engines present pages in descending order of relevancy. The most useful pages will be located at the top of the list. However, read the description of each link before you open the page.

4. Some search engines provide helpful tips for specializing your search. Take the opportunity to learn more about effective searching.

Other Ways to Search

Using Online Reference Sites How you search should be tailored to what you are hoping to find. If you are looking for data and facts, use reference sites before you jump onto a simple search engine. For example, you can find reference sites to provide definitions of words, statistics about almost any subject, biographies, maps, and concise information on many topics. Here are some useful online reference sites:

Online libraries

Online periodicals

Almanacs

Encyclopedias

You can find these sources using subject searches.

Conducting Subject Searches As you prepare to go online, consider your subject and the best way to find information to suit your needs. If you are looking for general information on a topic and you want your search results to be extensive, consider the subject search indexes on most search engines. These indexes, in the form of category and subject lists, often appear on the first page of a search engine. When you click a specific highlighted word, you will be presented with a new screen containing subcategories of the topic you chose.

Evaluating the Reliability of Internet Resources

Just as you would evaluate the quality, bias, and validity of any other research material you locate, check the source of information you find online. Compare these two sites containing information about the poet and writer Langston Hughes:

Site A is a personal Web site constructed by a college student. It contains no bibliographic information or links to sites that he used. Included on the site are several poems by Langston Hughes and a student essay about the poet's use of symbolism. It has not been updated in more than six months.

Site B is a Web site constructed and maintained by the English Department of a major university. Information on Hughes is presented in a scholarly format, with a bibliography and credits for the writer. The site includes links to other sites and indicates new features that are added weekly.

For your own research, consider the information you find on Site B to be more reliable and accurate than that on Site A. Because it is maintained by experts in their field who are held accountable for their work, the university site will be a better research tool than the student-generated one.

Tips for Evaluating Internet Sources

1. Consider who constructed and who now maintains the Web page. Determine whether this author is a reputable source. Often, the URL endings indicate a source.
   - Sites ending in *.edu* are maintained by educational institutions.
   - Sites ending in *.gov* are maintained by government agencies (federal, state, or local).
   - Sites ending in *.org* are normally maintained by nonprofit organizations and agencies.
   - Sites ending in *.com* are commercially or personally maintained.

2. Skim the official and trademarked Web pages first. It is safe to assume that the information you draw from Web pages of reputable institutions, online encyclopedias, online versions of major daily newspapers, or government-owned sites produce information as reliable as the material you would find in print. In contrast, unbranded sites or those generated by individuals tend to borrow information from other sources without providing documentation. As information travels from one source to another, it could have been muddled, misinterpreted, edited, or revised.

3. You can still find valuable information in the less "official" sites. Check for the writer's credentials, and then consider these factors:
   - Do not be misled by official-looking graphics or presentations.
   - Make sure that the information is updated enough to suit your needs. Many Web pages will indicate how recently they have been updated.
   - If the information is borrowed, notice whether you can trace it back to its original source.

Respecting Copyrighted Material

Because the Internet is a relatively new and quickly growing medium, issues of copyright and ownership arise almost daily. As laws begin to govern the use and reuse of material posted online, they may change the way that people can access or reprint material.

Text, photographs, music, and fine art printed online may not be reproduced without acknowledged permission of the copyright owner.

CITING SOURCES

In research writing, cite your sources. In the body of your paper, provide a footnote, an endnote, or an internal citation, identifying the sources of facts, opinions, or quotations. At the end of your paper, provide a bibliography or a works-cited list, a list of all the sources you cite. Follow an established format, such as Modern Library Association (MLA) Style.

Works-Cited List (MLA Style)

A works-cited list must contain accurate information sufficient to enable a reader to locate each source you cite. The basic components of an entry are as follows:

- Name of the author, editor, translator, or group responsible for the work
- Title
- Place and date of publication
- Publisher

For print materials, the information required for a citation generally appears on the copyright and title pages of a work. For the format of works-cited list entries, consult the examples at right and in the chart on page R29.

Internal Citations (MLA Style)

An internal citation briefly identifies the source from which you have taken a specific quotation, factual claim, or opinion. It refers the reader to one of the entries on your works-cited list. An internal citation has the following features:

- It appears in parentheses.
- It identifies the source by the last name of the author, editor, or translator.
- It gives a page reference, identifying the page of the source on which the information cited can be found.

Punctuation An internal citation generally falls outside a closing quotation mark but within the final punctuation of a clause or sentence. For a long quotation set off from the rest of your text, place the citation at the end of the excerpt without any punctuation following.

Special Cases

- If the author is an organization, use the organization's name, in a shortened version if necessary.
- If you cite more than one work by the same author, add the title or a shortened version of the title.

Sample Works-Cited Lists

Carwardine, Mark, Erich Hoyt, R. Ewan Fordyce, and Peter Gill. *The Nature Company Guides: Whales, Dolphins, and Porpoises.* New York: Time-Life Books, 1998.
Whales in Danger. "Discovering Whales." 18 Oct. 1999. <http://whales.magna.com.au/DISCOVER>

Neruda, Pablo. "Ode to Spring." *Odes to Opposites.* Trans. Ken Krabbenhoft. Ed. and illus. Ferris Cook. Boston: Little, Brown and Company, 1995.
The Saga of the Volsungs. Trans. Jesse L. Byock. London: Penguin Books, 1990.

List an anonymous work by title.

List both the title of the work and the title of the collection in which it is found.

Sample Internal Citations

It makes sense that baleen whales such as the blue whale, the bowhead whale, the humpback whale, and the sei whale (to name just a few) grow to immense sizes (Carwardine, Hoyt, and Fordyce 19–21). The blue whale has grooves running from under its chin to partway along the length of its underbelly. As in some other whales, these grooves expand and allow even more food and water to be taken in (Ellis 18–21).

Authors' last names

Page numbers where information can be found

MLA Style for Listing Sources

Book with one author	Pyles, Thomas. *The Origins and Development of the English Language.* 2nd ed. New York: Harcourt Brace Jovanovich, Inc., 1971.
Book with two or three authors	McCrum, Robert, William Cran, and Robert MacNeil. *The Story of English.* New York: Penguin Books, 1987.
Book with an editor	Truth, Sojourner. *Narrative of Sojourner Truth.* Ed. Margaret Washington. New York: Vintage Books, 1993.
Book with more than three authors or editors	Donald, Robert B., et al. *Writing Clear Essays.* Upper Saddle River, NJ: Prentice-Hall, Inc., 1996.
Single work from an anthology	Hawthorne, Nathaniel. "Young Goodman Brown." *Literature: An Introduction to Reading and Writing.* Ed. Edgar V. Roberts and Henry E. Jacobs. Upper Saddle River, NJ: Prentice-Hall, Inc., 1998. 376–385. [Indicate pages for the entire selection.]
Introduction in a published edition	Washington, Margaret. Introduction. *Narrative of Sojourner Truth.* By Sojourner Truth. New York: Vintage Books, 1993, pp. v–xi.
Signed article in a weekly magazine	Wallace, Charles. "A Vodacious Deal." *Time,* 14 Feb. 2000: 63.
Signed article in a monthly magazine	Gustaitis, Joseph. "The Sticky History of Chewing Gum." *American History,* Oct. 1998: 30–38.
Unsigned editorial or story	"Selective Silence." Editorial. *Wall Street Journal,* 11 Feb. 2000: A14. [If the editorial or story is signed, begin with the author's name.]
Signed pamphlet	[Treat the pamphlet as though it were a book.]
Pamphlet with no author, publisher, or date	*Are You at Risk of Heart Attack?* n.p. n.d. [n.p. n.d. indicates that there is no known publisher or date]
Filmstrips, slide programs, and videotapes	*The Diary of Anne Frank.* Dir. George Stevens. Perf. Millie Perkins, Shelley Winters, Joseph Schildkraut, Lou Jacobi, and Richard Beymer. Twentieth Century Fox, 1959.
Radio or television program transcript	"The First Immortal Generation." *Ockham's Razor.* Host Robyn Williams. Guest Damien Broderick. National Public Radio. 23 May 1999. Transcript.
Internet	*National Association of Chewing Gum Manufacturers.* 19 Dec. 1999 <http://www.nacgm.org/consumer/funfacts.html> [Indicate the date you accessed the information. Content and addresses at Web sites change frequently.]
Newspaper	Thurow, Roger. "South Africans Who Fought for Sanctions Now Scrap for Investors." *Wall Street Journal,* 11 Feb. 2000: A1+ [For a multipage article, write only the first page number on which it appears, followed by a plus sign.]
Personal interview	Smith, Jane. Personal interview. 10 Feb. 2000.
CD (with multiple publishers)	Simms, James, ed. *Romeo and Juliet.* By William Shakespeare. CD-ROM. Oxford: Attica Cybernetics Ltd.; London: BBC Education; London: HarperCollins Publishers, 1995.
Signed article from an encyclopedia	Askeland, Donald R. (1991). "Welding." *World Book Encyclopedia.* 1991 ed.

If you are applying for admission to a college, you will probably need to submit an essay as part of your application. This essay is your introduction to a college applications committee. It will help committee members get a sense of you as a person and as a student. Review the chart at right for general strategies, and then follow the guidelines below to ensure that your college application essay does the best job presenting you.

Selecting a Topic

Read the essay question on the application form with care. Mark key criteria and direction words such as *describe* and *explain*. After you have written a first draft, check to make sure you have met all of the requirements of the question. Your essay has a better chance of succeeding if it meets the requirements exactly.

General Questions About You

The essay question on a college application may be as general as "Describe a significant experience or event in your life and explain its consequences for you." To choose the right topic for such a question, think of an event or experience that truly is meaningful to you—a camping trip, a volunteer event, a family reunion. Test the subject by drafting a letter about it to a good friend or relative. If you find that your enthusiasm for the subject grows as you write, and if your discussion reveals something about your growth or your outlook on life, the topic may be the right one for your essay.

Directed Questions

The essay question on an application may be more directed than a simple "tell us about yourself." For instance, you may be asked to select three figures from history you would like to meet and to explain your choices.

In such cases, do not give an answer just because you think it will please reviewers. Instead, consult your own interests and instincts. Your most convincing writing will come from genuine interest in the subject. You might discover the best topic by jotting down a diary entry or a letter to a friend in which you discuss possible subjects.

Style

Though an essay is a chance to tell something about yourself, it is also a formal document addressed to

---

Strategies for Writing an Effective College Application Essay

- **Choose the right topic.** If you have a choice of essay topics, choose the one that interests you.
- **Organize.** Use a strong organization that carries the reader from introduction to conclusion.
- **Begin with a bang.** Open with an introduction that has a good chance of sparking the reader's interest.
- **Elaborate.** Be sure to explain why the experiences you discuss are important to you or what you learned from them.
- **Show style.** Bring life to your essay through vivid descriptions, precise word choice, and sophisticated sentence structure, such as parallelism. Consider including dialogue where appropriate.
- **Close with a clincher.** Write a conclusion that effectively sums up your ideas.
- **Do a clean job.** Proofread your essay carefully to ensure that it is error-free.

---

strangers. Use a formal to semiformal style. Avoid incomplete sentences and slang unless you are using them for clear stylistic effect. Use words with precision, selecting one or two accurate words for what you mean, rather than piling up words in the hope that one of them will hit the mark.

Format

Most applications limit the length of essays. Do not exceed the allowed space or number of words. Your college application essay should be neatly typed or printed, using adequate margins. Proofread your final draft carefully. If you submit a separate copy of the essay (rather than writing on the application form), number the pages and include your name and contact information on each page.

Reusing Your Essay

Most students apply to a number of different colleges in order to ensure their admission to a school for the next semester. Once you have written a strong essay for one application, you should consider adapting it for others.

Do not submit a single essay to several schools blindly. Always read the application essay question carefully to ensure that the essay you submit fulfills all of its requirements.

By writing **criticism**—writing that analyzes literature—readers share their responses to a written work. Criticism is also a way for a reader to deepen his or her own understanding and appreciation of the work and to help others deepen theirs.

The information in this handbook will guide you through the process of writing criticism. In addition, it will help you refine your critical perceptions to ensure that you are ready to produce work at the college level.

Understanding Criticism

There are a few different types of criticism. Each can enhance understanding and deepen appreciation of literature in a distinctive way. All types share similar functions.

The Types of Criticism

Analysis Students are frequently asked to analyze, or break into parts and examine, a passage or a work. When you write an analysis, you must support your ideas with references to the text, as in this example:

> **Conclusion:** In "Heat," the poet H.D. creates an enduring image of heat. There is no deeper meaning here; her task is to commemorate physical experience in words.

> **Support:** The poem's imagery gives heat solidity and depth. In the first stanza, the speaker asks the wind to "cut apart the heat" and, in the third stanza, to "plow through it," as if heat were a thick substance like earth.

Biographical Criticism Biographical criticism uses information about a writer's life to shed light on his or her work, as in this passage by Kenneth Silverman:

> Much of [Poe's] later writing, despite its variety of forms and styles, places and characters, is driven by the question of whether the dead remain dead. . . . [C]hildren who lose a parent at an early age, as Edgar lost Eliza Poe [his mother], invest more feeling in and magnify the parent's image. . . . The young child . . . cannot comprehend the finality of death. . . .

Historical Criticism Historical criticism traces connections between an author's work and the events, circumstances, or ideas that shaped the writer's historical era.

For example, Jean H. Hagstrum analyzes William Blake's character of Urizen by showing how the character symbolizes the Enlightenment ideas of the scientist Isaac Newton and the philosopher John Locke.

> Urizen is also an active force. Dividing, partitioning, dropping the plummet line, applying Newton's compasses to the world, he creates abstract mathematical forms. Like Locke, he shrinks the senses, narrows the perceptions, binds man to the natural fact.

The Functions of Criticism

In each of the previous examples of criticism, you can find evidence of the following critical functions:

Making Connections All criticism makes connections between two or more things. For instance, the analysis of H.D.'s poetry connects different parts of a poem (the images of heat being cut or parted by a plow).

Making Distinctions Criticism must make distinctions as well as connections. In the analysis of "Heat," the critic distinguishes between two possible purposes for poetry: first, to create an enduring image and, second, to present a deeper meaning.

Achieving Insight By making connections and distinctions, criticism achieves insight. The analysis of H.D.'s poem reaches the insight that the poem stands on its own as a work of beauty apart from any deeper meaning.

Making a Judgment Assessing the value of a work is an important function of criticism. A critic may assess a work by comparing it with other works and by using a standard such as enjoyment, insight, or beauty.

"Placing" the Work Critics guide readers not by telling them *what* to think but by giving them *terms in which to think*. In the passage quoted above, Hagstrum helps us "place" Urizen. We cannot respond to Urizen, she reminds us, as if he were an individual like Macbeth or Holden Caulfield. Instead, we respond to him best by perceiving him as a historical force—the pursuit of reason—personified. The terms on which we appreciate and understand each of these characters are different.

Writing Criticism

Like all solid writing, a work of criticism presents a thesis (a central idea) and supports it with arguments and evidence. Follow the strategies below to develop a critical thesis and gather support for it.

Formulate a Working Thesis

Once you have chosen a work or works on which to write, formulate a working thesis. First, ask yourself questions like these:

- What strikes you most about the work or the writer that your paper will address? What puzzles you most?

- In what ways is the work unlike others you have read?

- What makes the techniques used by the writer so well suited to (or so poorly chosen for) conveying the theme of the work?

Jot down notes answering your questions. Then, reread passages that illustrate your answers, jotting down notes about what each passage contributes to the work. Review your notes, and write a sentence that draws a conclusion about the work.

Gather Support

Taking Notes From the Work Once you have a working thesis, take notes on passages in the work that confirm it. To aid your search for support, consider the type of support suited to your thesis, as in the chart.

Conducting Additional Research If you are writing biographical or historical criticism, you will need to consult sources on the writer's life and era. Even if you are writing a close analysis of a poem, you should consider consulting the works of critics to benefit from their insights and understanding.

Take Notes

Consider recording notes from the works you are analyzing, as well as from any critical works you consult, on a set of note cards. A good set of note cards enables you to recall details accurately, to organize your ideas effectively, and to see connections between ideas.

If your thesis concerns . . .	look for support in the form of . . .
Character	• dialogue • character's actions • writer's descriptions of the character • other characters' reactions to the character
Theme	• fate of characters • patterns and contrasts of imagery, character, or events • mood • writer's attitude toward the action
Style	• memorable descriptions, observations • passages that "sound like" the writer • examples of rhetorical devices, such as exaggeration and irony
Historical Context	• references to historical events and personalities • evidence of social or political pressures on characters • socially significant contrasts between characters (for example, between the rich and the poor)
Literary Influences	• writer's chosen form or genre • passages that "sound like" another writer • events or situations that resemble those in other works • evidence of an outlook similar to that of another writer

One Card, One Idea If you use note cards while researching, record each key passage, theme, critical opinion, or fact on a separate note card. A good note card includes a brief quotation or summary of an idea and a record of the source, including the page number, in which you found the information. When copying a sentence from a work, use quotation marks and check to make sure you have copied it correctly.

Coding Sources Keep a working bibliography, a list of all works you consult, as you conduct research. Assign a code, such as a letter, to each work on the list. For each note you take, include the code for the source.

Coding Cards Organize your note cards by labeling each with the subtopic it concerns.

Present Support Appropriately

As you draft, consider how much support you need for each point and the form that support should take. You can provide support in the following forms:

- **Summaries** are short accounts in your own words of important elements of the work, such as events, a character's traits, or the writer's ideas. They are appropriate for background information.

- **Paraphrases** are restatements of passages from a work in your own words. They are appropriate for background and for information incidental to your main point.

- **Quotations of key passages** are direct transcriptions of the writer's words, enclosed in quotation marks or, if longer than three lines, set as indented text. If a passage is crucial to your thesis, you should quote it directly and at whatever length is necessary.

Quotations of multiple examples are required to support claims about general features of a work, such as a claim about the writer's ironic style or use of cartoonlike characters.

Revise Ideas as You Draft

When writing criticism, do not be afraid to revise your early ideas based on what you learn as you research or write further. As you draft, allow the insights—or the difficulties—that emerge to guide you back to the writer's works or other sources for clarification or support. What you discover may lead you to modify your thesis.

The chart above presents an example of the way this circular process can work.

Do's and Don'ts of Academic Writing

Avoid gender and cultural bias. Certain terms and usages reflect the bias of past generations. To eliminate bias in any academic work you do, edit with the following rules in mind:

- **Pronoun usage** When referring to an unspecified individual in a case in which his or her gender is irrelevant, use forms of the pronoun phrase *he or she*. Example: "A lawyer is trained to use <u>his or her</u> mind."

Stage of the Writing Process	The Developing Thesis Statement
Prewriting: A student rereads Sartre's story "The Wall" to find passages that support her thesis.	**First formulation:** "In his short story 'The Wall,' Sartre illustrates the belief that human life is ruled by inescapable fate."
Drafting: As the student summarizes the story's ending, she is struck by the fact that the narrator's final act has exactly the opposite effect from what he intended. She revises her thesis statement.	**Second formulation:** "In his short story 'The Wall,' Sartre demonstrates the power of fate by showing how the effects of a person's actions can completely contradict the person's intentions."
Revising: As the student rereads her first draft, she grows dissatisfied with her explanation of the story's ending. Why does the writer spend so much time showing the narrator's resignation to fate, only to have fate strike unexpectedly? She reworks her paper to support a new thesis statement.	**Final formulation:** "In his short story 'The Wall,' Sartre shows that 'fate' is a myth: However hard we try to resign ourselves to fate, we can never eliminate our responsibility for our own actions."

- **"Culture-centric" terms** Replace terms that reflect a bias toward one culture with more generally accepted synonyms. For instance, replace terms such as *primitive* (used for hunting-gathering peoples), *the Orient* (used to refer to Asia), and *Indians* (used for Native Americans), all of which suggest a view of the world centered in Western European culture.

Avoid plagiarism. Presenting someone else's ideas, research, or exact words as your own is plagiarism, the equivalent of stealing or fraud. Laws protect the rights of writers and researchers in cases of commercial plagiarism. Academic standards protect their rights in cases of academic plagiarism.

To avoid plagiarism, follow these practices:

- Read from several sources.

- Synthesize what you learn.

- Let the ideas of experts help you draw your own conclusions.

- Always credit your sources properly when using someone else's ideas to support your view.

By following these guidelines, you will also push yourself to think independently.

Forming Your Critical Vocabulary

To enhance your critical perceptions—the connections you find and the distinctions you make—improve your critical vocabulary. The following glossary shows contrasting pairs of critical terms. Some of these pairs define a spectrum along which you can place a work; others define simple opposites.

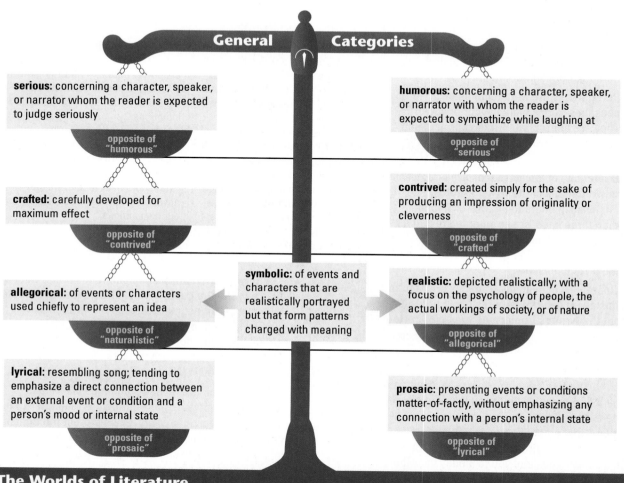

General Categories

serious: concerning a character, speaker, or narrator whom the reader is expected to judge seriously

opposite of "humorous"

humorous: concerning a character, speaker, or narrator with whom the reader is expected to sympathize while laughing at

opposite of "serious"

crafted: carefully developed for maximum effect

opposite of "contrived"

contrived: created simply for the sake of producing an impression of originality or cleverness

opposite of "crafted"

symbolic: of events and characters that are realistically portrayed but that form patterns charged with meaning

allegorical: of events or characters used chiefly to represent an idea

opposite of "naturalistic"

realistic: depicted realistically; with a focus on the psychology of people, the actual workings of society, or of nature

opposite of "allegorical"

lyrical: resembling song; tending to emphasize a direct connection between an external event or condition and a person's mood or internal state

opposite of "prosaic"

prosaic: presenting events or conditions matter-of-factly, without emphasizing any connection with a person's internal state

opposite of "lyrical"

The Worlds of Literature

In addition to categorizing elements and qualities of a work, critics categorize the imaginative world it assumes—the "rules" that govern actions and events in the work. Historically, the earliest literature projects a heroic world.

| heroic, epic, or tragic world: a stern world governed by codes of conduct and divine judgments; characters are defined by moral qualities and are capable of significant, memorable actions (deeds) | comic world: a benevolent world temporarily disordered by confusions between appearance and reality, such as mistaken identity; characters are tested by the confusion, and order is restored | naturalistic world: a world in which the actions of characters are of limited significance and the rules of reality are objective and unalterable, strictly limiting what is possible | farcical or absurd world: a world in which characters are defined by ridiculous, exaggerated qualities and reality is replaced by mechanical, meaningless situations in which characters are trapped |

Character

the people, animals, or other beings who perform or receive the action of a story

flat: marked by one dominant characteristic	**rounded:** having a complex set of characteristics
static: unchanging	**dynamic:** developing and growing
self-aware: acting with an understanding of his or her own motives and the consequences of his or her actions	**blind** or **fated:** acting with no understanding of his or her own motives or of the consequences of his or her actions

Plot

the narrated sequence of events in a work; the storyline, usually divided into an exposition (in which situation and characters are introduced), the rising action, the climax (or moment of greatest tension), the falling action, and the resolution

simple: telling of a single stream of events; each event affects the same set of characters	**complex:** telling of a number of streams of events, each involving a different set of characters (sets of characters may overlap)
dramatic: events unfold to build a maximum of tension or suspense, leading to a resolution	**episodic:** a series of loosely connected events occur, without building to a single, central climax or resolution
plot as driver: the question of "what happens next?" is intended to be the reader's primary interest in the work	**plot as vehicle:** the plot serves primarily to express a theme, display a character, or link together descriptions

Imagery

language used to suggest sensory experience, especially sensory experience linked by association to emotions and ideas

original: unique to the writer; distinctive	**conventional:** expected; patterned after previous work
sensual: devoted to re-creating sensory experience	**metaphysical:** devoted to expressing abstract ideas or complicated analogies
effusive: pouring out; piled up	**patterned:** structured; controlled

Style

the distinctive features of a writer's choice of words and imagery, sentence length and structure, rhythm, and so on

elaborate: characterized by complex detail	**direct:** simple; to the point
sincere: attempting to convey ideas without drawing attention to the style of their presentation	**parodic:** drawing attention to style in order to mock a style that other writers use seriously
straightforward: attempting to convey ideas directly	**ironic:** conveying ideas or attitudes by stating their opposites
conversational: resembling the style in which one friend might address another	**oracular:** suggesting that the writer is pronouncing deep truths without any particular concern that he or she be understood

Index of Authors and Titles
Page numbers in *italics* refer to biographical or background information.
Some works have unknown authors, so the culture and literature type are given instead (e.g., Arabic prose).

Index of Skills
(Numbers in **boldface** indicate definitions. Nonboldface numbers indicate examples.)

Index of Features

ACKNOWLEDGMENTS

Grateful acknowledgment is made to the following for copyrighted material:

The Clarendon Press, an imprint of Oxford University Press "African Proverbs: Tanzania and Kenya: The Masai: 'We begin by being foolish . . .,' 'Do not repair another man's fence . . .,' 'Nobody can say . . .,' 'It is better to be poor . . .', 'Baboons do not go far . . .', 'The hyena said . . .', 'The zebra cannot do away . . .'," from *The Masai: Their Language and Folklore* by A. C. Hollis. Published in 1905 by The Clarendon Press.

Ruth Harwood Cline and The University of Georgia Press "The Grail" by Chrétien de Troyes from *Perceval or The Story of the Grail*, translated by Ruth Harwood Cline. Copyright © 1983 by Ruth Harwood Cline. Reprinted by permission of The University of Georgia Press.

Toby Cole, Actors & Authors Agency "War" from *The Medals and Other Stories* by Luigi Pirandello. © E.P. Dutton, NY, 1932, 1967. Reprinted by permission of Toby Cole, Agent for the Pirandello Estate. All rights reserved. For performance rights in all media apply to Toby Cole, Agent for the Pirandello Estate, 295 Derby Street, #225, Berkeley, CA 94705.

Copper Canyon Press c/o The Permissions Company "Form, Shadow, Spirit" by T'ao Ch'ien, translated by David Hinton, from *Selected Poems of T'ao Ch'ien*. Copyright © 1993 by David Hinton. Reprinted with permission of Copper Canyon Press, P.O. Box 271, Port Townsend, WA 98368-0271, c/o The Permissions Company, High Bridge, New Jersey.

Darhansoff, Verrill, Feldman Literary Agents "I Am Not One of Those Who Left the Land" and "Everything Is Plundered" by Anna Akhmatova, translated by Stanley Kunitz, from *Poems of Akhmatova* by Stanley Kunitz with Max Hayward. Copyright © 1967, 1968, 1972, 1973 by Stanley Kunitz and Max Hayward. All rights reserved. Reprinted courtesy of Darhansoff Verrill Feldman Literary Agents.

Joan Daves Agency/Writer's House, Inc. c/o The Permissions Company "Fear" and "Time" by Gabriela Mistral, translated by Doris Dana, from *Selected Poems of Gabriela Mistral: A Bilingual Translation* (Baltimore: The Johns Hopkins University Press, 1971). Copyright © 1961, 1964, 1970, 1971 by Doris Dana. Reprinted with the permission of Joan Daves Agency/Writer's House, Inc., New York, on behalf of the proprietors; c/o The Permissions Company, High Bridge, New Jersey.

Dorling Kindersley Ltd. "India" from the *Ultimate Pocket Book of the World Factfile*. Copyright © 1996, 1998, 1999 by Dorling Kindersley Limited, London.

Doubleday, a division of Random House, Inc. "Marriage Is a Private Affair" from *Girls at War and Other Stories* by Chinua Achebe, copyright © 1972, 1973 by Chinua Achebe. "Half a Day" from *The Time and the Place and Other Stories* by Naguib Mahfouz, translated by Denys Johnson-Davies. Copyright © 1991 by the American University in Cairo Press. "Clouds come from time to time . . ." and "The sun's way . . ." two haikus by Matsuo Bashō from *An Introduction to Haiku* by Harold G. Henderson, copyright © 1958 by Harold G. Henderson. Used by permission of Doubleday, a division of Random House, Inc.

Dutton Signet, a division of Penguin Group (USA), Inc. "A Doll House" from *The Complete Major Prose Plays of Henrik Ibsen*, translated by Rolf Fjelde, copyright © 1965, 1970, 1978 by Rolf Fjelde. Used by permission of Dutton Signet, a division of Penguin Group (USA), Inc.

Everyman's Library "The Lay of the Werewolf" by Marie de France, translated by Eugene Mason, from *Lays of Marie de France and Other French Legends*. By permission of Everyman's Library.

Faber and Faber Limited "Folding Chairs" from *Selected Poems* by Günter Grass, translated by Michael Hamburger. Reprinted by permission of the publisher, Faber and Faber Ltd.

Farrar, Straus & Giroux, Inc. "When in early summer" from *The Seeker and Other Poems* by Nelly Sachs, translated by Ruth and Matthew Mead and Michael Hamburger. Translation copyright © 1970 by Farrar, Straus & Giroux, Inc. "Chapter XIII" from *Omeros* by Derek Walcott. Copyright © 1990 by Derek Walcott. "Freedom to Breathe" from *Stories and Prose Poems* by Alexander Solzhenitsyn, translated by Michael Glenny. Translation copyright © 1971 by Michael Glenny. "The Grownup" by Rainer Maria Rilke, translated by Randall Jarrell, from *The Complete Poems* by Randall Jarrell. Copyright © 1969, renewed 1997 by Mary von S. Jarrell. "Comrades" from *Jump and Other Stories* by Nadine Gordimer. Copyright © 1991 by Felix Licensing B.V. "A Walk to the Jetty," excerpt from *Annie John* by Jamaica Kincaid. Copyright © 1985 by Jamaica

Kincaid. Excerpt from *Nobel Lecture* by Alexander Solzhenitsyn, translated by F. D. Reeve. Translation copyright © 1972 by Farrar, Straus & Giroux. "The Bracelet" from *The Collected Stories of Colette*, edited by Robert Phelps and translated by Matthew Ward. Translation copyright © 1983 by Farrar, Straus & Giroux, Inc. "Russia 1812" from *The Expiation* by Victor Hugo, translated by Robert Lowell, from *Imitations* by Robert Lowell. Translation copyright © 1959 by Robert Lowell. Copyright renewed © 1987 by Harriet, Sheridan, and Caroline Lowell. Reprinted by permission of Farrar, Straus & Giroux, Inc.

The Estate of Angel Flores c/o The Permissions Company Paul Valery, "Palm," translated by Kate Flores, and "The Friendly Wood," translated by Vernon Watkins; Arthur Rimbaud, "Ophelia," translated by Daisy Alden, from Angel Flores, ed., *An Anthology of French Poetry from Nerval to Valery in English Translation with French Originals* (New York: Anchor Books, 1958). Copyright © 1958 and renewed 1986 by Angel Flores. Rainer Maria Rilke, "Interior of the Rose," translated by Kate Flores, from *An Anthology of German Poetry from Holderlin to Rilke in English Translation with German Originals* (New York: Anchor Books, 1960). Copyright © 1960 and renewed 1988 by Angel Flores. Reprinted with permission of the Estate of Angel Flores, c/o The Permissions Company, High Bridge, New Jersey.

Foreign Languages Press "My Old Home" by Lu Hsun, translated by Yang Hsien-Yi and Gladys Young, from *Selected Stories of Lu Hsun*. Published and copyrighted by Foreign Languages Press, Bejing, China, 1960. Reprinted by permission.

David R. Godine, Publisher, Inc. "The Albatross" from *Les Fleurs du Mal* by Charles Baudelaire, translated from the French by Richard Howard, illustrations by Michael Mazur. Copyright © 1982 by Charles Baudelaire. Reprinted by permission of David R. Godine, Publisher, Inc.

Grove/Atlantic, Inc. "I Built My House Near Where Others Dwell" by T'ao Ch'ien, translated by William Acker, from *Anthology of Chinese Literature: From early times to the fourteenth century*. Copyright © 1965 by Grove Press, Inc. "The Soul With Boundaries" by Fernando Pessoa, translated by Richard Zenith, from *Fernando Pessoa & Co.: Selected Poems*, translation copyright © 1998 by Richard Zenith. Reprinted by permission of Grove/Atlantic, Inc.

Harcourt, Inc. "Invitation to the Voyage" ("L'Invitation au Voyage") by Charles Baudelaire, from *Things of this World*, English translation, copyright © 1956 and renewed 1984 by Richard Wilbur. "The End and the Beginning" from *View with a Grain of Sand*, copyright © 1993 by Wisława Szymborska, English translation by Stanislaw Baranczak and Clare Cavanagh, copyright © 1995 by Harcourt, Inc. "The Garden of Stubborn Cats" from *Marcovaldo or the Seasons in the City* by Italo Calvino, copyright © 1963 by Giulio Einaudi editore, s.p.a., Torino, English translation by William Weaver, copyright © 1983 by Harcourt, Inc., and Martin Secker & Warburg, Ltd. Reprinted by permission of the publisher, Harcourt, Inc. This material may not be reproduced in any form or by any means without prior written permission of the publisher.

HarperCollins Publishers, Inc. "By Any Other Name" from *Gifts of Passage* by Santha Rama Rau. Copyright © 1951 by Santha Rama Rau. Copyright renewed © 1979 by Santha Rama Rau. "By Any Other Name" originally appeared in *The New Yorker*. "The Handsomest Drowned Man in the World" from *Leaf Storm and Other Stories* by Gabriel Garcia Marquez. Copyright © 1971 by Gabriel Garcia Marquez. "A Song on the End of the World" from *The Collected Poems, 1931– 1987* by Czesław Miłosz, translated by Robert Hass. Copyright © 1988 by Czesław Miłosz Royalties, Inc. Reprinted by permission of HarperCollins Publishers, Inc.

HarperCollins Publishers, Ltd. "The Manners of Kings" from *The Gulistan, or Rose Garden, of Sa'di*, translated by Edward Rehatsek.

Hill and Wang, an imprint of Farrar, Straus & Giroux, Inc. From *Night* by Elie Wiesel, translated by Stella Rodway. Copyright © 1960 by MacGibbon & Kee. Copyright renewed © 1988 by The Collins Publishing Group. Reprinted by permission of Hill and Wang, a division of Farrar, Straus & Giroux, Inc.

Hispanic Society of America "The Guitar" by Federico Garcia Lorca, from *Translations from Hispanic Poets*. Copyright © 1938 by The Hispanic Society of America. Reprinted with the permission of The Hispanic Society of America.

Barbara Hogenson Agency, Inc. "The Tiger Who Would Be King" by James Thurber, from *Further Fables for Our Time*. Copyright © 1956 by James Thurber. Copyright © renewed 1984 by Rosemary A. Thurber. Reprinted by arrangement with Rosemary A. Thurber and The Barbara Hogensen Agency, Inc.

Anselm Hollo "Food For Prophets" by Günter Grass, translated by Anselm Hollo, from *Modern European Poetry: French, German, Greek, Italian, Russian, Spanish*. Translation copyright © 1966, 2003 by Anselm Hollo. Reprinted by permission of the translator, Anselm Hollo.

Houghton Mifflin Company "Sent to Li Po as a Gift" by Tu Fu, translated by Florence Ayscough and Amy Lowell, from *Fir-Flower Tablets: Poems translated from the Chinese*. Published in 1921 by Houghton Mifflin Company, Boston, Mass. Copyright © 1921 by Florence Ayscough and Amy Lowell. Reprinted by Permission.

Ibis Editions "Twigs" by Taha Mahammad Ali, from *Never Mind: Twenty Poems and a Story*, translated by Peter Cole, Yahya Hijazi, and Gabriel Levin. Copyright © 2000 by Peter Cole, Yahya Hijazi, and Gabriel Levin. All rights reserved. Reprinted by permission of Peter Cole, Ibis Editions, P.O. Box 8074, Jerusalem, Israel, Telephone: 972-2-627-7035.

Indiana University Press "The Story of Daedalus and Icarus" by Ovid from *Ovid: Metamorphoses*, translated by Rolfe Humphries. Copyright © 1955 by Indiana University Press. Reprinted by permission of Indiana University Press.

International African Institute "African Proverbs: Liberia: The Jabo: 'The one who listens . . .', 'Children are the wisdom . . .', 'Daring talk . . .', 'One who cannot pick up an ant . . .', 'The butterfly that flies among . . .', 'A man's ways are good . . .'," from *Jabo Proverbs from Liberia: Maxims in the Life of Native Tribe*. Published for the International Institute of African Languages & Cultures by Oxford University Press, London: Humphrey Milford, 1936. By permission of the International African Institute.

The Estate of Alta Jablow "African Proverbs: Nigeria: The Yoruba: 'One does not set. . .'," from *Yes and No: The Intimate Folklore of Africa: Dilemma Tales, Proverbs and Stories of Love, and Adult Riddles* by Alta Jablow. Copyright © 1961 by Alta Jablow.

Melanie Jackson Agency, L.L.C. "Season," from *Idanre and Other Poems* by Wole Soyinka. Copyright © 1967, 1995 Wole Soyinka. All rights reserved. Reprinted by permission of Melanie Jackson Agency, L.L.C.

The Jewish Publication Society "Genesis 1–3: The Creation and the Fall," "Genesis 6–9: The Story of the Flood," "Book of Ruth" "Psalm 8," "Psalm 19," "Psalm 23," and "Psalm 137," reprinted from *Tanakh: A New Translation of the Holy Scriptures According to the Hebrew Text*. Copyright © 1985, by the Jewish Publication Society. Reprinted by permission.

John Johnson Ltd. "I have visited again" by Alexander Pushkin, translation © 1982 by D. M. Thomas, from *The Bronze Horseman: Selected Poems of Alexander Pushkin*, The Viking Press, New York, 1982. Reprinted by permission.

Alfred A. Knopf, Inc, a division of Random House, Inc. "The Guest," from *Exile and the Kingdom* by Albert Camus, translated by Justin O'Brien, copyright © 1957, 1958 by Alfred A. Knopf, Inc. a division of Random House, Inc. From *Hiroshima* by John Hersey, copyright © 1946 and renewed 1974 by John Hersey. Used by permission of Alfred A. Knopf, Inc. a division of Random House, Inc.

L. R. Lind "Laura," "The White Doe," and "Spring" from *Canzoniere* by Francesco Petrarch, translated by Morris Bishop, reprinted by permission of L.R. Lind, Editor, from *Lyric Poetry of the Italian Renaissance*, copyright 1954. Used by permission of the editor, L. R. Lind.

Marian S. MacIntyre "Caesar" by Paul Valery, translated by C. F. MacIntyre, from *War and The Poet: An Anthology of Poetry Expressing Man's Attitudes to War From Ancient Times to The Present*. Reprinted by permission.

Macmillan, Oxford, a division of Macmillan Publishers Ltd. Christopher Marlowe, *The Tragical History of Doctor Faustus*. Text of 1604, with Introduction and Notes by William Modlen (London: Macmillan & Co., repr. 1966), reproduced by permission of Macmillan, Oxford, a division of Macmillan Publishers, Ltd.

The Modern Library, an imprint of Random House, Inc. Chapter I and Chapter II from *Candide; And Philosophical Letters* by Voltaire, translated by Richard Aldington, copyright © 1928, 1956, 1984 by Random House, Inc. Used by permission of Modern Library, a division of Random House, Inc.

Jonathan Musere "African Proverbs: Uganda: The Bagada: 'A small deed out of friendship . . .,' 'Two people can keep the words a secret . . .,' 'One who loves you, warns you . . .,' 'The one who is hopeful . . .,' 'The one who has not made the journey . . .,' 'The one who travels is the one who sees

things . . .,' 'Words are easy, but friendship is difficult . . .,' and 'Where there are no dogs . . .' " from *African Proverbs and Proverbial Names* by Jonathan Musere. Copyright © 1999 by Ariko Publications. Reprinted by permission of the author, Jonathan Musere.

Museum of Science, Boston From "The Quest for Immortality" brochure. Materials courtesy of the Museum of Science, Boston.

New Directions Publishing Corporation "Jade Flower Palace" by Tu Fu, translated by Kenneth Rexroth, from *One Hundred Poems from the Chinese*, copyright © 1971 by Kenneth Rexroth. "The River-Merchant's Wife: A Letter" by Ezra Pound, from *Personae*, copyright © 1926 by Ezra Pound. "Absent Soul" (from *Lament for Ignacio Sanchez Mejias*) by Federico Garcia Lorca, translated by Stephen Spender and J.K. Gili, from *The Selected Poems of Federico Garcia Lorca*, copyright © 1955 by New Directions Publishing Corp. "Concord" by Octavio Paz, translated by Eliot Weinberger, from *Collected Poems: 1957–1987*, copyright © 1986 by Octavio Paz and Eliot Weinberger. "Fable" by Octavio Paz, translated by Muriel Rukeyser, from *Early Poems of Octavio Paz*, copyright © 1973 by Octavio Paz and Muriel Rukeyser. Reprinted by permission of New Directions Publishing Corp.

New York Times Co. "Leonardo: The Eye, the Hand, the Mind" by Holland Cotter, from *The New York Times*, January 24, 2003. Copyright © 2003 by the New York Times Co. Reprinted by permission.

North Point Press, an imprint of Farrar, Straus & Giroux, Inc. "All," "Also All," and "Assembly Line" from *A Splintered Mirror: Chinese Poetry from the Democracy Movement*, translated by Donald Finkel. Translation copyright © 1991 by Donald Finkel. Reprinted by permission of North Point Press, a division of Farrar, Straus & Giroux, Inc.

Northwestern University Press and Helen F. Pratt, Inc. Literary Agency Pasternak, Boris. "The Weeping Orchard," from *My Sister – Life*. Translated by Mark Rudman with Bohdan Boychuk. Evanston: Northwestern University Press, 1992, p.13. Copyright © 1983 by Mark Rudman. First published in 1983 by Ardis. Northwestern University Press edition 1992. All rights reserved. Reprinted by permission by Northwestern University Press.

Harold Ober Associates, Incorporated "Marriage Is a Private Affair," from *Girls at War and Other Stories* by Chinua Achebe, copyright © 1972, 1973 by Chinua Achebe. Reprinted by permission of Harold Ober Associates, Incorporated.

Oberlin College Press "She used to throw away her old crockery" and "My mother would lose herself" by Vénus Khoury-Ghata, translated by Marilyn Hacker, from *Here There Was Once a Country*, copyright © 2001 by Oberlin College. Reprinted by Oberlin College Press.

Oxford University Press, Inc., and David Higham Associates Ltd. "The First Part of the Tragedy: Night" and "Prologue in Heaven" from *Faust* by Johann Wolfgang von Goethe, translated by Louis MacNeice, copyright © 1951, 1954 by Frederick Louis MacNeice; renewed 1979 by Hedi MacNeice. Used by permission of Oxford University Press, Inc., and David Higham Associates Ltd.

Oxford University Press, UK, and Columbia University Press "The Cat Who Lived in the Palace," "Things That Arouse a Fond Memory of the Past," and "I Remember a Clear Morning" from *The Pillow Book of Sei Shōnagon* by Sei Shōnagon, translated and edited by Ivan Morris. Copyright © 1967 by Ivan Morris. Reprinted by permission.

Pantheon Books, a division of Random House, Inc. "House Taken Over" from *End of the Game and Other Stories* by Julio Cortazar, translated by Paul Blackburn, copyright © 1963, 1967 by Random House, Inc. Used by permission of Pantheon Books, a division of Random House, Inc.

Pearson Education, Inc., publishing as Pearson Prentice Hall "What Is an Insect?" from *Prentice Hall Biology* by Kenneth R. Miller, Ph.D., and Joseph Levine, Ph.D. Copyright © 2002 by Pearson Education, Inc., publishing as Pearson Prentice Hall. Used by permission.

Pearson Education Ltd. "Childhood" and "The Lion's Awakening" from *Sundiata: An Epic of Old Mali* by D. T. Niane, translated by G.D. Pickett. Copyright © 1960 by Présence Africaine (original French version: *Soundjata, ou L'Epopée Mandingue*). Copyright © 1965 by Longman Group Ltd. (English). Reprinted by permission of Pearson Education Limited.

Penguin Books Ltd., London "The Burning of Rome," from *The Annals of Imperial Rome* by Tacitus, translated by Michael Grant (Penguin Classics 1956, Sixth revised edition 1989), copyright © Michael Grant Publications Ltd., 1969. "The Fisherman and the Jinnee," from *Tales from the Thousand and One Nights*, translated by N. J. Dawood (Penguin Classics 1954, Revised edition 1973), translation copyright © N. J. Dawood, 1954, 1973. "Creation Hymn" and "Night," from *The Rig Veda, An Anthology*, translated by Wendy Doniger O'Flaherty (Penguin Classics, 1981). Copyright © Wendy Doniger O'Flaherty, 1981. "Visit" by Yevgeny Yevtushenko from *Yevtushenko: Selected Poems*, translated by Robin Milner-Gulla and Peter Levi, S.J. (Penguin Books, 1962), copyright © Robin Milner-Gulla and Peter Levi, 1962. "The Qur'an" from *The Koran*, translated by N. J. Dawood (Penguin Classics, 1956, Fifth revised edition 1990). Copyright © N. J. Dawood, 1956, 1959, 1966, 1968, 1974, 1990. "Prayer to Masks" by Léopold Sédar Senghor, translated by Gerald Moore and Ulli Beier, from *The Penguin Book of Modern African Poetry*, edited by Gerald Moore and Ulli Beier, first published as *Modern Poetry from Africa*, 1963 (Penguin Books, 1984). Copyright © Gerald Moore and Ulli Beier, 1963, 1968, 1984. "Federigo's Falcon" (originally titled "Ninth Story") from *The Decameron* by Giovanni Boccaccio, translated by G.H. McWilliam (Penguin Classics, 1972, Second Edition, 1995). Copyright © G.H. McWilliam, 1972, 1995. "Pericles' Funeral Oration" by Thucydides from *History of the Peloponnesian Wars*, translated by Rex Warner (Penguin Classics, 1954). Translation copyright © Rex Warner, 1954. "Prologue," "The Battle with Humbaba," "The Death of Enkidu," "The Story of The Flood," and "The Return," from *The Epic of Gilgamesh*, translated by N. K. Sanders (Penguin Classics 1960, Third Edition 1972). Copyright © N. K. Sanders, 1960, 1964, 1972. "I, III, IX & XLIII," from *Tao Te Ching: The Book of Meaning and Life* by Lao Tzu, translated into English by Richard Wilhelm, translated into German by H. G. Ostwald (Arkana, 1989), copyright © Eugen Diederichs Verlad GmBh & Co, Koln, 1985. English translation copyright © Routeledge & Kegan Paul, 1985. "How Siegfried Was Slain" from *The Nibelungenlied*, translated by A. T. Hatto (Penguin Classics, 1965, revised edition 1969), copyright © A. T. Hatto, 1965, 1969. Tanka: "Was it that it went to sleep . . . ," 5 lines by Ono Komachi; Tanka: "When I went to visit . . . ," 5 lines by Ki Tsurayuki; Tanka: "One cannot ask loneliness . . . ," 4 lines by Priest Jakuren; Haiku: "The cuckoo . . . ," "Seven sights were veiled . . . ," and "Summer grasses . . . ," 9 lines by Matsuo Bashō⁻; Haiku: "A World of Dew . . ." "Far-off mountain peaks . . . ," "With Bland Serenity . . . ," and "Beautiful, seen through holes . . . ," 12 lines by Yosa Buson; Haiku: "Spring Rain: Telling a tale as they go . . . ," "Soaking on the roof . . . ," "A man lives here . . . ," and "In our sedan . . . ," 12 lines by Yosa Buson, from *The Penguin Book of Japanese Verse*, translated by Geoffrey Bownas and Anthony Thwaite (Penguin Books 1964, Revised edition 1998). Translation copyright © Geoffrey Bownas and Anthony Thwaite, 1964, 1998. Reproduced by permission of Penguin Books Ltd.

The Sheep Meadow Press "Pride" by Dahlia Ravikovitch, from *A Dress of Fire*, translated by Chana Bloch, The Sheep Meadow Press, Riverdale-on-Hudson. Reprinted by permission.

Persea Books, Inc. "On Living," from *Poems of Nazim Hikmet*, translated by Randy Blasing and Mutlu Konuk. Translation copyright © 1994, 2002 by Randy Blasing and Mutlu Konuk. Reprinted by permission of Persea Books, Inc. (New York).

Peter Pauper Press, Inc. "African Proverbs: Nigeria: The Yoruba: 'A wise man who knows proverbs . . . ,' 'The day on which one starts out . . . ,' 'He who is being carried does not realize . . . ,' 'Time destroys all things.' and 'Little is better than nothing.'" "African Proverbs: Tanzania and Kenya: The Masai: 'Do not say the first thing . . . ,' and 'A man who has once been tossed by a buffalo . . .'" "African Proverbs: Ghana: The Ashanti: 'Rain beats a leopard skin . . . ,' 'If you are in hiding . . . ,' 'One falsehood . . . ,' and 'No one tests the depth of a river . . .'" from *African Proverbs*, compiled by Charlotte and Wolfe Leslau. Copyright © 1962, Peter Pauper Press. Reprinted by permission.

Princeton University Press "Ithaka" by C. P. Cavafy, from *C. P. Cavafy: Selected Poems*, translated by Edmund Keeley and Philip Sherrard. Copyright © 1972 by Edmund Keeley and Philip Sherrard. Reprinted by permission of Princeton University Press.

Random House, Inc. "Book II: How They Took the City" from *The Aeneid* by Virgil, translated by Robert Fitzgerald, copyright © 1980, 1982, 1983 by Robert Fitzgerald. Used by permission of Random House, Inc.

Rosalie Torres-Rioseco "The Glass of Milk" by Manuel Rojas, translated by Zoila Nelken, from *Short Stories of Latin America*, edited by Arturo Torres-Rioseco, translated by Zoila Nelken and Rosalie Torres-Rioseco. Copyright 1963 by Las Americas Publishing Company. Reprinted by permission of Rosalie Torres-Rioseco.

Rupert Crew Limited on behalf of Steve and Megumi Biddle "The Origins of Origami" by Steve and Megumi Biddle from *Origami: Inspired by Japanese Prints*. Copyright © 1998 by The Metropolitan Museum of Art. Introduction, instructions, diagrams and models © 1998 by Steve and Megumi Biddle. All rights reserved. Reprinted by permission.

Carl Sesar "My Woman Says There's Nobody She'd Rather Marry," "I Crossed Many Lands and a Lot of Ocean," and "I Hate Her and I Love Her" by Gaius Valerius Catullus from *Selected Poems of Catullus*, translated by Carl Sesar. Copyright © 1974, 2001 by Carl Sesar. Reprinted by permission of the translator, Carl Sesar.

Edward Seidensticker "The Jay" by Yasunari Kawabata, translated by Edward Seidensticker, from *Contemporary Japanese Literature, An Anthology of Fiction, Film, and Other Writing Since 1945*, edited by Howard Hibbett. Copyright © 1977. Reprinted by permission of the translator, Edward Seidensticker.

Simon & Schuster Adult Publishing Group "The Wooden People," reprinted with permission of Simon & Schuster Adult Publishing Group from *Popol Vuh* by Dennis Tedlock. Copyright © 1985, 1996 by Dennis Tedlock.

William Jay Smith "The Sleeper in the Valley" by Arthur Rimbaud, translated by William Jay Smith, from *Collected Translations: Italian, French, Spanish, Portuguese*, New Rivers Press, 1985, copyright © 1967 by William Jay Smith. Reprinted by permission of the translator, William Jay Smith.

Elyse Sommer "CurtainUp Guest Review: A Doll's House," copyright April 1997, Elyse Sommer, *CurtainUp*. CurtainUp.com is a 7-year-old online theater magazine: *www.curtainup.com*. Reproduced by permission of Elyse Sommer.

David Spencer "A Doll's House by Henrik Ibsen, a new version by Frank McGuinness," reviewed by David Spencer, from *www.aislesay.com*. Reprinted by permission of the author, David Spencer.

Story Line Press "Autumn Song" by Paul Verlaine, translated by Louis Simpson, from *Modern Poets of France, A Bilingual Anthology*. Copyright © 1997, 1998 by Louis Simpson. Reprinted by permission of the translator and Story Line Press.

The Swedish Academy "Imre Kertesz: Recipient of the Nobel Prize in Literature, 2002," by The Swedish Academy.

Minh Ta "Interview with Shane L. Amaya: Writer of the comic *Roland Days of Wrath*" from Comic Fan (formerly www.comicfan.com). Copyright © Minh Ta. Reproduced by permission of Minh Ta, owner of Deluge Media.

Tufts University, Perseus Project, Classics Department "from The Perseus Digital Library (*http://www.perseus.tufts.edu/Olympics/*)," reproduced by kind permission of Tufts University, Perseus Project.

Charles E. Tuttle Co, Inc. of Boston, Massachussetts and Tokyo, Japan "Zen Parables: 'A Parable,' 'The Taste of Banzo's Sword,' and 'Publishing the Sutras,'" from *Zen Flesh, Zen Bones: A Collection of Zen & Pre-Zen Writings*, compiled by Paul Reps. Reprinted by permission.

UNESCO Publishing "Under Reconstruction" by Mori Ōgai, translated by Ivan Morris, from *Modern Japanese Stories: An Anthology*, edited by Ivan Morris. Copyright © 1962 for the English translation by UNESCO Publishing. UNESCO Collection of Representative Works—Japanese Series. Reproduced by permission of UNESCO.

The University of California Press "He is More Than a Hero" and "You Know the Place: Then" by Sappho from *Sappho: A New Translation*, translated by Mary Barnard. Copyright © 1958, by The Regents of the University of California. "Lightness" and "Green" by Juan Ramon Jimenez, from *Juan Ramon Jimenez: Fifty Spanish Poems*, translated by J. B. Trend. "The Diameter of the Bomb" and "From The Book of Esther I Filtered the Sediment" by Yehuda Amichai, from *The Selected Poetry of Yehuda Amichai*, translated by Chana Boch and Stephen Mitchell. English translation copyright © 1986 by Chana Boch and Stephen Mitchell. Reprinted by permission.

The University of Chicago Press "Olympia 11" by Pindar, from *The Odes of Pindar, Second Edition*, translated by Richmond Lattimore. Copyright © 1947, 1976 by The University of Chicago Press. "He is More Than a Hero" by Sappho, from *Greek Lyrics*, translated by Richmond Lattimore. Copyright © 1949 and 1955 by Richmond Lattimore. "Numskull and the Rabbit" from *The Panchatantra*, translated by Arthur W. Ryder. Copyright © 1925 by The University of Chicago. Copyright renewed 1953 by Mary E. Ryder and Winifred Ryder. "Oedipus the King" by Sophocles, D. Grene, translator, from *The Complete Greek Tragedies: Oedipus the King, Oedipus at Colonus, Antigone,*

Volume II, D. Grene and Richmond Lattimore, editors, pp. 11–76. Copyright © 1942 by The University of Chicago Press. All rights reserved. Reprinted by permission of The University of Chicago Press.

University of Texas Press "Sonnet 49" (p. 105) and "Sonnet 71" (p. 151) from *100 Love Sonnets: Cien Sonetos de Amor*, by Pablo Neruda, translated by Stephen Tapscott. Copyright © Pablo Neruda 1959 and Fundacion Pablo Neruda, Copyright © 1986 by the University Texas Press. By permission of the University of Texas Press.

University of Texas Press "The voice of the swallow, flittering, calls to me" and "I think I'll go home and lie very still," from *Love Songs of the New Kingdom*, translated from the Ancient Egyptian by John L. Foster, illustrated with hieroglyphs drawn by John L. Foster, Copyright © 1969, 1970, 1971, 1972, 1973, 1974 by John L. Foster. By permission of the University of Texas Press.

Vedanta Society of Southern California "The Yoga of Knowledge" from *The Song of God: Bhagavad-Gita*, translated by Swami Prabhavananda and Christopher Isherwood. Copyright © 1944, 1951 by The Vedanta Society of Southern California. Reprinted by permission.

Viking Penguin, a division of Penguin Group (USA) Inc. "from Book 1: The Quarrel (originally titled "from Book 1: The Rage of Achilles")," "from Book 6: The Meeting of Hector and Andromache (originally titled "from Book 6: Hector Returns to Troy")," "from Book 24: Achilleus and Priam," "from Book 22: The Death of Hector," from *The Iliad* by Homer, translated by Robert Fagles, copyright © 1990 by Robert Fagles. "The Fox and the Crow," copyright © 1952 by Marianne Moore, renewed © 1980 by Lawrence E. Brinn and Louise Crane, Executors of the Estate, "The Oak and the Reed," from *The Fables of La Fontaine*, translated by Marianne Moore, copyright © 1952, 1953, 1954, © 1964 by Marianne Moore, renewed © 1980, 1981, 1982 by Lawrence Brinn and Louise Crane, Executors of the Estate. "On the Bottom" from *If This Is a Man (Survival in Auschwitz)* by Primo Levi, translated by Stuart Woolf, copyright © 1959 by Orion Press, Inc., © 1958 by Giulio Einaudi editore, s.p.a. "The Ingenious Gentleman Don Quixote de la Mancha" from *Don Quixote* by Miguel de Cervantes Saavedra, translated by Samuel Putnam, copyright © 1949 by The Viking Press, Inc. "Rama and Ravana in the Battle" from *The Ramayana* by R.K. Narayan, copyright © 1972 by R. K. Narayan. Used by permission of Viking Penguin, a division of Penguin Group (USA), Inc.

Visva-Bharati Publishing Department, Visva Bharati University "The Artist" by Rabindranath Tagore, from *The Housewarming and Other Selected Writings*, translated by Amiya Chakravarty, Mary Lago, and Tarun Gupta. Copyright © 1965 Amiya Chakravarty. All rights reserved. Used by permission.

W. W. Norton & Company, Inc. From *The Song of Roland*, translated by Frederick Goldin. Copyright © 1978 by W.W. Norton & Company, Inc. Cantos I, III, V, and XXXIV from the *Divine Comedy: Inferno* by Dante Alighieri, translated by John Ciardi. Copyright © 1954, 1957, 1959, 1960, 1965, 1967, 1970 by the Ciardi Family Publishing Trust. This selection may not be reproduced, stored in a retrieval system or transmitted in any form or by any means without prior written permission of the publisher. Used by permission of W.W. Norton & Company, Inc.

The Arthur Waley Estate "from *The Book of Songs*: 34" and "from *The Book of Songs*: 24," from *Translations from the Chinese*, and "from *The Analects of Confucius*," translated by Arthur Waley, George Allen & Unwin, Ltd. London. All rights reserved. Reprinted by permission of the Arthur Waley Estate.

Wallace Literary Agency, Inc. "An Astrologer's Day" by R. K. Narayan, from *The Grandmother's Tale*. Copyright © 1994 by R. K. Narayan. Ecco Press, Hopewell, NJ. Used by permission of the Wallace Literary Agency, Inc. "Sibi," from *The Mahabharata* by R. K. Narayan, from *Gods, Demons, and Others*. Copyright © 1964 by R. K. Narayan. Used by permission of the Wallace Literary Agency.

Washington Post Writers Group "A Lot of Baggage for Nora to Carry: After a History of Misinterpretation, Ibsen's Leave-Taking Heroine Finally Gets Her Due" by Lloyd Rose from *The Washington Post*, April 20, 1997. Copyright © 1997, The Washington Post. Reprinted with permission.

Gwendoline Mary Watkins "Comme on voit sur la branche . . ." ("Roses") by Pierre Ronsard, translated by Vernon Watkins. Reprinted by permission.

Witswaterarand University Press "African Proverbs: South Africa: The Zulu: 'You cannot chase two gazelles,' 'The one offended never forgets,' 'There is no river,' 'No dew ever competed,' 'It never dawns in the same way,' 'Look as you fell a tree,' 'Do not speak of rhinoceros,' 'Eyes do not see all,' 'There is no foot,' 'What has happened before,' 'Almost is not eaten,'" from *Zulu Proverbs*, edited by C. L. Sibusiso Nyembezi, M.A. Copyright 1954 Witswaterarand University Press. All rights reserved. Reprinted by permission.

The Wylie Agency, Inc. for The Estate of Italo Calvino "The Garden of Stubborn Cats" from *Marcovaldo or the Seasons in the City* by Italo Calvino, translated by William Weaver. Copyright © 1983, The Estate of Italo Calvino, reprinted by permission of the Wylie Agency, Inc.

Yale University Press "The most beautiful youth who ever happened," translated by William Kelly Simpson, from *The Literature of Ancient Egypt: An Anthology of Stories, Instructions, and Poetry*, edited, with an introduction by William Kelly Simpson, with translations by R.O. Faulkner, Edward F. Wente, Jr. and William Kelly Simpson. Copyright © 1972 by Yale University. "To Helene" by Pierre de Ronsard, from *Lyrics of the French Renaissance: Marot, Du Bellay, Ronsard*, translated by Norman R. Shapiro. Copyright © 2002 by Yale University. "The voice of the wild goose," translated by William Kelly Simpson, from *The Literature of Ancient Egypt: An Anthology of Stories, Instructions, and Poetry*, edited by William Kelly Simpson. Copyright © 1972 by Yale University. All rights reserved. This book may not be reproduced in whole or in part, in any form (except by reviewers for the public press) without written permission from the publishers. Reprinted by permission.

The Estate of Avrahm Yarmolinsky "The Drowsy Garden" by Boris Pasternak, translated by Babette Deutsch, from *Two Centuries of Russian Verse: An Anthology from Lomonosov to Voznesensky* by Avrahm Yarmolinsky. Copyright © 1949, 1962, 1965, 1966 by Avrahm Yarmolinsky. Used by permission of Tobias Yarmolinsky as Executor for the Estate of Avrahm Yarmolinsky.

Note: Every effort has been made to locate the copyright owner of material reprinted in this book. Omissions brought to our attention will be corrected in subsequent editions.

CREDITS

Cover and Title Page *Charles Bridge and the Hradcany Castle in Prague*, 1935, Oskar Kokoschka, National Gallery, Prague, Czech Republic, ©2003 Artists Rights Society (ARS), New York / Pro Litteris, Zurich; **vi–vii** *The Creation of Adam* (detail), Michelangelo, Scala/Art Resource, New York; **viii** © Matthias Kulka/CORBIS; **ix** CORBIS; **x** *Large Enso*, hanging scroll, Torei Enji, Gitter-Yelen Art Center; **xi** Araldo de Luca/CORBIS; **xii** *Achilles Deciding to Resume Fighting Upon the Death of Patroclus*, 1620, Dirck van Baburen/ Bridgeman Art Library, London/New York; **xiii (l.)** The Granger Collection, New York; **(r.)** Geoff Dann/© Dorling Kindersley; **xiv** © Dorling Kindersley; **xvi** *Three Graces* (detail), Botticelli, Giraudon/Art Resource, New York; **xviii** © Linda Bartlett/Photo Researchers, Inc.; **xxv** Bob Daemmrich/The Image Works; **xx** SuperStock; **1** *Walking Lion in Relief* (detail), 605–562 B.C., Babylonian mosaic, Mesopotamia, The Metropolitan Museum of Art, Fletcher Fund, 1931, © Copyright 1973/84 by The Metropolitan Museum of Art; **2 (t.)** Araldo de Luca/CORBIS; **(m.l.)** Head of an Acadion Ruler, Nineveh, 2300–2200 B.C., Baghdad Museum, Scala/Art Resource, New York; **(m.r.)** Boltin Picture Library; **(b.l.)** Founders Society purchase, General Membership Fund/ Bridgeman Art Library, London/New York; **(b.r.)** The Palma Collection/Getty Images; **3 (t.)** The Art Archive/Ethnic Jewelry Exhibition, Milan/Dagli Orti; **(m.)** Art Resource, New York; **(b.)** Senegalese glass painting used on *Sundiata*, from the collection of Professor Donal Cruise-O'Brien, Courtesy of Longman International Education; **4** Babylonian globe, c. 5000 B.C., The British Museum, Bridgeman/Art Resource, New York; **6** Page from the Book of the Dead, c. 1100 B.C., Egyptian, The British Museum, Photo by Michael Holford; **7** Stone/Getty Images; **8** Mary Evans/Edwin Wallace; **9** Bojan Brecelj/CORBIS; **11** *The Simurgh Brings Zal to Sam*, Leaf from *Shahnameh* by Ferdowsi, 14th century, The Metropolitan Museum of Art, Rogers Fund, 1969, © Copyright by The Metropolitan Museum of Art; **12 & 14** Photo: Herve Lewandowski. Louvre, Paris, France/Art Resource, NY; **16–17** Yann Arthus-Bertrand/CORBIS; **18** Scala/Art Resource, NY; **19** Kabul Museum, Afghanistan/Bridgeman Art Library, London/New York; **22** Front of lyre from tomb of Queen Pu-abi, Early Dynastic period, c. 2685–2290 B.C., British Museum, London; **24–25** Erich Lessing/Art Resource, NY; **26–27** Academy of Natural Sciences of Philadelphia/CORBIS; **32 & 34** Archivo Iconografico, S.A./CORBIS; **36** Peter Willi/Bridgeman Art Library, London/New York; **37** Archivo Iconografico, S.A./CORBIS; **44** *The Creation of Adam*, Michelangelo, Scala/Art Resource, New York; **46–47** *The Creation of Adam*, Michelangelo, Scala/Art Resource, New York; **48** Scala/Art Resource, NY; **50** Bettmann/CORBIS; **53** Corel Professional Photos CD-ROM™; **54** *Noah's Ark*, Aaron Douglas, Fisk University Fine Art Galleries, Nashville, Tennessee; **60** Harvey Lloyd/Getty Images; **61** Dick S. Ramsay Fund, The Brooklyn Museum; **62** Werner Forman Archive, Liverpool Museum, Liverpool/Art Resource, NY; **66** Corel Professional Photos CD-ROM™; **68** Historical Picture Archive/CORBIS; **71** The Jewish Museum, NY/Art Resource, NY; **73** *Il Buon Pastore (The Good Shepherd)*, Early Christian, 4th century, Vatican Museum, Scala/Art Resource, New York; **75** *David Composing the Psalms*, Illustrated by Paris Psalter, 10th century, Photo Bibliothèque Nationale, Paris; **81** The Granger Collection, New York; **84** CORBIS; **85** Courtesy of the Freer Gallery of Art, Smithsonian Institution, Washington, D.C.; **90** *Scheherazade and King Shahriyar* (detail), Anton Pieck. Illustration from *Stories of the Arabian Nights*. Retold by Naomi Lewis. Illus. © 1984 by B.V. Elsevier. Uitgeversmaatschappij, Amsterdam. Photo by Rex Joseph; **92** Nick Koudis/Getty Images; **95** Illustration from *Arabian Nights,* for the story "The Fisherman and the Genie," Edmund Dulac, NY, Scribner's & Sons: 1907, Photo courtesy of the New York Public Library, Astor, Lenox and Tilden Foundations; **96** Monique le Luhandre/© Dorling Kindersley; **100–101** Christie's Images/CORBIS; **106 (t.)** Bettmann/CORBIS; **(m.)** The Art Archive/Dagli Orti (A); **(b.)** New York Public Library (Rare Book Division or Print Collection. Miriam and Ira D. Wallach Division of Art, Prints and Photographs); Astor, Lenox and Tilden Foundations; **109** *Rubáiyát of Omar Khayyám*, Edmund Dulac, Photo by John Lei/Omni-Photo Communications, Inc.; **110** Photo by John Lei/Omni-Photo Communications, Inc.; **113** National Gallery Collection; By kind permission of the Trustees of the National Gallery, London/CORBIS; **115** The Art Archive/Biblioteca Nazionale Marciana Venice/Dagli Orti; **117** *Concourse of the Birds*, c. 1600, Habib Allah, The Metropolitan Museum of Art, Fletcher Fund, 1963 (63.210.11). Photograph © 1982 The Metropolitan Museum of Art; **122** Heine Schneebeli/Bridgeman Art Library, London/New York; **124** Werner Forman/Art Resource, NY; **127** Pearson Education/PH School Division; **128** Cover of Sundiata: Lion King of Mali, David Wisniewski; **131** © Michael Melford; **133** Monique le Luhandre/© Dorling Kindersley; **139** The Art Archive/Egyptian Museum, Cairo/Dagli Orti; **144** Getty Images; **150–151** *Krishna's Magic Flute*, Unknown artist, Kangra Valley, c. 18th–19th century. New York Public Library, Astor, Lenox and Tilden Foundations; **152 (t.l.)** The Granger Collection, New York; **(t.m.)** B.P.S. Walia/© Dorling Kindersley; **(t.r.)** Buddha Standing, bronze, 1st half of 7th century, The Metropolitan Museum of Art, Purchase, Bequest of Florance Waterbury, 1969, © Copyright by The Metropolitan Museum of Art; **(b.l.)** Bridgeman Art Library, London/New York; **(b.r.)** Attic Red Figure Nolan Amphora: *Hephaestus Making Armor for Achilles*, The Dutuit painter, Francis Bartlett Fund, Courtesy Museum of Fine Arts, Boston; **153 (t.l.)** Scala/Art Resource, New York; **(t.r.)** Christie's Images — All rights reserved; **(b.)** Werner Forman/Art Resource, NY; **157 (l.)** David Buffington/Getty Images; **(r.)** Art Resource, NY; **158** *Zero*, 1980–1996, Robert Indiana, Morgan Art Foundation Limited/Art Resource, NY, © Copyright ARS, NY; **159** *Rama and Lakshman Confer with the Animal Armies*, from the *Adventures of Rama*, Courtesy of the Freer Gallery of Art, Smithsonian Institution, Washington, D.C., fol. 194v, full view; **160** Dinodia/Omni-Photo Communications, Inc.; **162** Ann and Bury Peerless Picture Library/Bridgeman Art Library, London/New York; **164–165** © Matthias Kulka/CORBIS; **166** © Otto Rogge/CORBIS; **171** The Granger Collection, New York; **172** *Krishna on a Swing*, Scala/Art Resource, NY; **174** *Indra*, engraved by Marlet et Cie, The Stapleton Collection/Bridgeman Art Library, London/New York; **176** *Vishnu and Lakshmi Riding on Garuda*, Ann & Bury Peerless Picture Library/Bridgeman Art Library, London/New York; **179** *A Hawk*, Indian Mughal, 18th-century miniature, Victoria and Albert Museum, Photo by Michael Holford; **180** *King Sibi's Sacrifice to the God Indra*, Gandharan Art, c. 2nd century, Courtesy of the Trustees of the British Museum; **182** © Art Resource, New York; **184** *Arjuna and Krishna in the Chariot, Between the Two Armies*, Illustration from Bhagavad-Gita, Photo by Lynn Saville; **187** © Werner Forman/Art Resource, NY; **193** Corel Professional Photos CD-ROM™; **194** Ingo Jezierski/Getty Image; **195** *Rama and Lakshmana shooting arrows at the demon Ravana*. Gouache on paper. Dehle of Jaipur school. 19th century, © Victoria and Albert Museum, London/ Art Resource, NY; **196** Lyndsay Hebberd/CORBIS; **205** *A Lion at Rest*, The Metropolitan Museum of Art, The Alice and Nasli Heeramaneck Collection, Gift of Alice Heeramaneck, 1985 (1985.221); **207** Monique le Luhandre/© Dorling Kindersley; **212** Royalty-Free/CORBIS; **213** Bettmann/CORBIS; **216** © Dorling Kindersley; **220** David Young-Wolff/PhotoEdit; **226–227** Katsusika Hokusai (1760–1849). *The Great Wave of Kanagawa*, from *36 Views of Mount Fuji*. Private Collection. Art Resource, NY; **228 (t.l.)** Pearson Education EMG Education Management Group; **(t.r.)** Mary Evans Picture Library; **(b.)** Pawel Kumelowski/Omni-Photo Communications, Inc.; **229 (t.l.)** © Will and Deni McIntyre/Photo Researchers, Inc.; **(t.r.)** *First Landing at Kurihama, July 14, 1853*, Gessan Ogata, Courtesy of United States Naval Academy Museum; **(b.)** Reuters NewMedia Inc./CORBIS; **231** Dallas and John Heaton/CORBIS; **232** Tokyo National Museum; **233** Pearson Education Corporate Digital Archive; **234** *The Poet Li Po Admiring a Waterfall*, Hokusai, Honolulu Academy of Arts, Gift of James A. Michener; **237** Asian Art & Archaeology, Inc./CORBIS; **238 (l.)** Foto Marburg/Art Resource, NY; **(r.)** The Granger Collection, New York; **241** *Poet on a Mountain Top*, Shen Chou, The Nelson-Atkins Museum of Art, Kansas City, Missouri; **242** *Old Trees by Cold Waterfall*, 1470–1559, Wen Zhengming, The Los Angeles County Museum of Art, Ernest Larsen Blancok Memorial Fund; **248** The Granger Collection, New York; **249** *Benjamin Franklin* (detail), c. 1790, Pierre Michel Alix, National Portrait Gallery, Smithsonian Institution, Washington, D.C./Art Resource, New York; **250 (t.)** New York Public Library Picture Collection; **(b.l.)** *T'ao Ch'ien*, Collection of the National Palace Museum, Taipei, Taiwan, Republic of China; **(b.r.)** New York Public Library Picture Collection; **253** *Fishing Village in the Wind and Rain*, hanging scroll painting, 1955, Li K'e-jan, Werner Forman/Art Resource, NY; **255** *A Myriad of Trees on Strange Peaks*, Yen Wen-Kuei (Northern Sung Dynasty), The Granger Collection, New York; **257** *River and Mountains in Autumn Color*, 1120–1182, Zhao Boju, Imperial Palace Museum, Beijing, China; **259** *River Village in a Rainstorm*, Hanging scroll, ink and slight color on silk, 169.2 x 103.5 cm, Lü Wenying, Chinese, active c. 1490–1507, © The Cleveland Museum of Art, John L. Severance Fund, 70.76; **260–261** Eyewire/Getty Images; **262** Corel Professional Photos CD-ROM™; **266 (t.l.)** Kino Tsurayuki, Heibonsha/Pacific Press Service; **(m.l.)** Onono-komachi, Heibonsha/ Pacific Press Service; **(b.l.)** Jakuren Houshi, Heibonsha/Pacific Press Service; **(t.r.)** Bashō, The Granger Collection, New York; **(m.r.)** Yosa Buson, Heibonsha/Pacific Press Service; **(b.r.)** Kobayashi Issa, Heibonsha/Pacific Press Service; **268** *Snow at Senso-ji Temple in Asakusa*, Victoria and Albert Museum, London/Art Resource, NY; **270** *The Monkey Bridge in Koshu Province*, 1841, Hiroshige Hitsu, Christie's, New York; **271** *Sudden Shower on Ohashi Bridge*, Hiroshige, Art Resource, New York; **272** Artville/Getty Images; **276** Sei Shōnagon, Heibonsha/Pacific Press Service; **279** *Triptych of Snow, Moon, and Flower* (Center Panel), c. 1780's, Shunsho, Museum of Art, Tami, Japan; **281** Sei Shōnagon, Heibonsha/Pacific Press Service; **286** *The Celebrated Beauty of the Teahouse, Kagiya, at Kasamori Shrine*, Suzuki Harunobu, 18th century, The Metropolitan Museum of Art, the Henry L. Phillips Collection, Bequest of Henry L. Phillips, 1940, © Copyright by The Metropolitan Museum of Art; **288** *Large Enso*, hanging scroll, Torei Enji, Gitter-Yelen Art Center; **290** CORBIS; **291** Monique le Luhandre/© Dorling Kindersley; **297–299** Instructions, diagram and models ©1998 by Steve and Megumi Biddle. Models photograph by Les Morsillo. Photograph ©1998 The Metropolitan Museum; **304** CORBIS; **310–311** *Aeneas at Delos*, Claude Lorrain, ©National Gallery Collection; By kind permission of the Trustees of the National Gallery, London/CORBIS; **312 (t.)** Getty Images; **(m.)** Mimmo Jodice/CORBIS; **(b.l.)** Ann & Bury Peerless Picture Library/Bridgeman Art Library, London/New York; **(b.r.)** Seattle Art Museum/CORBIS; **313 (t.l.)** Roman Mosaic: Gladiator with Leopard, Galleria Borghese, Scala/Art Resource, New York; **(t.r.)** Bettmann/CORBIS; **(b.)** Michael S. Yamashita/CORBIS; **316** The Apollo Belvedere, Roman marble copy probably of Greek original of late 4th (or 1st) century B.C., Vatican Museums, Rome, Scala/Art Resource, New York; **317** Erich Lessing/Art Resource, NY; **318** Richard Quataert/Folio, Inc.; **319** *Circe Meanwhile Had Gone Her Ways . . .*, 1924, From THE ODYSSEY by Homer, William Russell Flint, Collection of the New York Public Library; Astor, Lenox and Tilden Foundations; **320** The Art Archive/Biblioteca Braidense Milan/Dagli Orti; **321** The Art Archive/Dagli Orti; **322** Bettmann/CORBIS; **325 & 326** Mimmo Jodice/CORBIS; **327** Historical Picture Archive/CORBIS; **328** Kimbell Art Museum/CORBIS; **331** Hirmer Verlag Munchen; **332** *Minerva restrains Achilles from killing Agamemnon*, Giovanni Batista Tiepolo, Scala/Art Resource, New York; **334** Liz

McAulay/© Dorling Kindersley; **336** Mimmo Jodice/CORBIS; **339** *Hector Taking Leave of Andromache*, Angelica Kauffmann, Tate Gallery, London/Art Resource, New York; **341** *Odysseus' Mission to Achilles*, Cleophrades Painter, 485–475 B.C., Staatliche Antikensammlungen und Glyptothek, Munich; **345** Mimmo Jodice/CORBIS; **348** Araldo de Luca/ CORBIS; **351** Monique le Luhandre/© Dorling Kindersley; **353** *Achilles defeating Hector*, Peter Paul Rubens, Musée des Beaux-Arts, Giraudon/Art Resource, New York; **354** *Achilles Deciding to Resume Fighting Upon the Death of Patroclus*, 1620, Dirck van Baburen/Bridgeman Art Library, London/New York **357** *Andromache and Astyanax*, 1789, Richard Cosway, Courtesy of the Trustees of Sir John Soane's Museum, London/Bridgeman Art Library, London/New York; **359 (t.)** Mimmo Jodice/CORBIS; **(b.)** "Achilles," detail from the fresco "Thetis consoling Achilles," Giovanni Battista Tiepolo, Scala/Art Resource, New York; **363** The Granger Collection, New York; **364** Nationalmuseet, Copenhagen, Denmark/Bridgeman Art Library, London/New York; **369** *Andromache Mourning Hector*, Jacques Louis David, Peter Willi/Bridgeman Art Library, London/New York; **374 (l.)** Bettmann/CORBIS; **(r.)** The Granger Collection, New York; **376** The Walters Art Museum, Baltimore; **377** Staatliche Antikensammlungen und Glyptothek, Munich. Photograph by Koppermann; **379** *Sappho and Alcaeus*, Staatliche Antikensammlungen und Glyptothek, Munich; **380** Lauros/Giraudon/Bridgeman Art Library, London/New York; **384** Bust of Thucydides, National Museum, Naples, Scala/Art Resource, New York; **389** Bildarchiv Preussischer Kulturbesitz; **391** Boltin Picture Library; **392** Monique le Luhandre/© Dorling Kindersley; **393** Antikenmuseum, Basel; **398** CORBIS; **399** Courtesy of the Library of Congress; **400** Bust of Plato, fourth century B.C., marble, Capitoline Museum, Rome, Scala/Art Resource, New York; **403** Joachim Blauel, Artothek/Neue Pinakothek, Munich; **404–405** SuperStock; **407** Alinari/Art Resource, NY: **410** Alan Schein/CORBIS; **413** Mosaic, *The School of Plato*, National Museum, Naples, Scala/Art Resource, New York; **415** *The Death of Socrates*, Jacques Louis David, The Metropolitan Museum of Art, Wolfe Fund, 1931, Catharine Lorillard Wolfe Collection, © Copyright by The Metropolitan Museum of Art; **416** Monique le Luhandre/© Dorling Kindersley; **423** The Metropolitan Museum of Art, NY, Hewitt Fund, 1911, Rogers Fund, 1921, Munsey Fund, 1936, and Anonymous Gift, 1951 (11.185); **424** Archivo Iconografico/CORBIS; **426** *Two Sphinxes Surmounted by Two Lions*, 450 B.C., Egyptian, Gable end from a relief from a tomb at Xanthos, The British Museum, London/Bridgeman/Art Resource, New York; **428–429** ImageState/Pictor Images; **429** Archivo Iconografico/CORBIS; **430** Fotopic/Omni-Photo Communications, Inc.; **433** Roman Mosaic: Theatre masks, Capitoline Museum, Rome, Scala/Art Resource, New York **437** © AFP/CORBIS Sygma; **439** Jeffrey M. Spielman/The Image Bank; **441** Archivo Iconografico, S.A./CORBIS; **442–443** Robbie Jack/CORBIS; **446** The Art Museum, Princeton University, Museum purchase, Caroline G. Mather Fund. Photographer: Bruce White; **448** Robbie Jack/CORBIS; **450** © Pizzoli Alberto/CORBIS Sygma; **453 (t.)** Bettmann/CORBIS; **(b.)** Michael Nicholson/CORBIS; **461** *Two Sphinxes Surmounted by Two Lions*, 450 B.C., Egyptian, Gable end from a relief from a tomb at Xanthos, The British Museum, London/Bridgeman/Art Resource, New York; **462** ImageState/Pictor Images; **464–465** © AFP/CORBIS Sygma; **466** © AFP/CORBIS Sygma; **468** Robbie Jack/CORBIS; **471** Monique le Luhandre/© Dorling Kindersley; **472–473** Robbie Jack/CORBIS; **478–479** Robbie Jack/CORBIS; **490** Roger Wood/CORBIS; **492** *Aeneas and Dido*, Pierre Narcisse Guérin, The Louvre, Paris, Scala/Art Resource, New York; **495** National Gallery Collection; By kind permission of the Trustees of the National Gallery, London/CORBIS; **497** © Getty Images Inc.—Hulton Archive Photos; **498** *The Wooden Horse of Troy*, Limoges Master of the Aeneid, Louvre, Paris, © Réunion des Musées Nationaux/Art Resource, NY; **500–501** Araldo de Luca/CORBIS; **506 (l.)** The Granger Collection, New York; **(r.)** Courtesy of the Library of Congress; **509** The Art Archive/Archaeological Museum Delphi/Dagli Orti; **514** Bettmann/CORBIS; **516** Réunion des Musées Nationaux/Art Resource, NY; **522** Bettmann/CORBIS; **525** Giraudon/Art Resource, NY; **526** Museo Capitolino, Rome/Bridgeman Art Library, London/New York; **527** Paolo Koch/Photo Researchers, Inc.; **528** Massimo Listri/CORBIS; **526** Omni-Photo Communications, Inc.; **542–543** Corel Professional Photos CD-ROM™; **544 (t.l.)** Courtesy of the Trustees of British Library; **(t.r.)** Werner Forman/Art Resource, NY; **(b.)** Index Stock Photography, Inc.; **545 (t.)** Mary Evans Picture Library; **(m.)** Philip Gatward/© Dorling Kindersley; **(b.)** The Granger Collection, New York; **546** Franz-Marc Frei/CORBIS; **547** Geoff Dann/© Dorling Kindersley; **548** *The Crowning of Charlemagne and Other Scenes from His Life*, V. de Beauvais, 15th century, Réunion des Musées Nationaux/Art Resource, New York, Musée Condé, Chantilly, France; **550 (t.)** Giraudon/Art Resource, NY; **(b.)** Russell Thompson/Omni-Photo Communications, Inc.; **551** Geoff Dann/© Dorling Kindersley; **552** The Art Archive/University Library Heidelberg/Dagli Orti; **553** The Granger Collection, New York; **554** *Death of Roland*, Vincent de Beauvais, Giraudon/Art Resource, NY; **556** © Dorling Kindersley; **557** Giraudon/Art Resource, NY; **559** The Granger Collection, New York; **560** © Hulton/Archive Photos; **562** Geoff Dann/© Dorling Kindersley; **563** *Death of Roland*, Vincent de Beauvais, Giraudon/Art Resource, NY; **564** Geoff Dann/© Dorling Kindersley; **566–567** The Granger Collection, New York; **568** Simone End/© Dorling Kindersley; **569** Kenneth Lilly/© Dorling Kindersley; **570** *Siegfried's Death*, Staatsbibliothek Preussischer Kulturbesitz, Berlin; Photo Bildarchiv Preussischer Kulturbesitz; **573** *The Burial of Siegfried*, Richard Jack, City of New York Art Gallery/SuperStock; **579 & 580** Shane L. Amaya, www.rolandcomic.com; **582** English Greenwich, Field and tournament armor for man, 1527, Made in the royal workshops at Greenwich, steel and gold, G. 73 in. (185.5 cm); Wt. 80 lb, 4 oz. (36.7 kg): The Metropolitan Museum of Art, Purchase, William H. Riggs Gift and Rogers Fund, 1919 (19.131.1-2). Photograph © 1987 The Metropolitan Museum of Art; **584** Courtesy of Joyce Patti/Morgan Gaynin, Inc.; **586** Martin Weigan /SuperStock; **588** Monique le Luhandre/© Dorling Kindersley; **589** Bayerische Staatsbibliothek Munchen; **590** *The Damsel of Sanct Grael*, 1857, Dante Gabriel Rossetti, Tate Gallery, London/Art Resource, NY; **593** *Perceval at Amfortas*, wall painting from the "Parsifal saga," Ferdinand Piloty, The Younger, AKG London; **595** Art Resource, NY; **596** © Dorling Kindersley; **597** *Werewolf Attacking a Man*, German woodcut, 15th century, The Granger Collection, New York; **598** Diantha York-Ripley/SuperStock; **599** Jim Stamates/Getty Images; **600** Giraudon/Art Resource, NY; **607** *Sir Galahad*, George Frederick Watts, Trustees of the National Museums & Galleries on Merseyside/Bridgeman Art Library, London/New York; **608** The Granger Collection, New York; **609** *Alfred, Lord Tennyson* (detail), c. 1840, S. Laurence, by courtesy of the National Portrait Gallery, London; **610** *Dante*, Andrea del Castagno, Firenze, Santa Apollonia, Scala/Art Resource, New York; **612** *The Forest, Inferno I*, 1862, Gustave Doré, New York Public Library Special Collections, L'Enfer de Dante Alighieri avec dessins de Gustave Doré, 1862; **614 & 615** University of Texas at Austin; **616** The Granger Collection, New York; **619** University of Texas at Austin; **623** Monique le Luhandre/© Dorling Kindersley; **624–632** The Granger Collection, New York; **635** *Paolo and Francesca*, 1855, Dante Gabriel Rossetti, Tate Gallery, London/Art Resource, NY; **638** Mary Evans Picture Library; **640** *Judecca - Lucifer, Inferno XXXIV*, 1862, Gustave Doré, New York Public Library Special Collections, L'Enfer de Dante Alighieri avec dessins de Gustave Doré, 1862; **642** Monique le Luhandre/© Dorling Kindersley; **643** *Poets emerge from Hell, Inferno XXXIV*, 139, Gustave Doré, 1862, New York Public Library Special Collections, L'Enfer de Dante Alighieri avec dessins de Gustave Doré, 1862; **648** John Heseltine/© Dorling Kindersley; **652** John Henley/CORBIS; **660–661** *The School of Athens*, Raphael, Scala/Art Resource, NY; **662 (t.)** Scala/Art Resource, NY; **(m.l.)** Bettmann/CORBIS; **(m.r.)** Boltin Picture Library; **(b.)** Philip Blenkinsop/© Dorling Kindersley; **663 (t.l.)** NASA; **(t.r.)** *Night of August 4, 1789*, or "Patriotic Delirium," Bibliothèque Nationale, Paris, Giraudon/Art Resource, New York; **(b.l.)** Réunion des Musées Nationaux/Art Resource, NY; **(b.r.)** *View of the Imperial Bank and environs*, Giraudon/Art Resource, New York; **665** *Mona Lisa*. Oil on wood (1503 and 1506) 77 x 53 cm., Leonardo da Vinci (1452–1519), Louvre, Dep. des Peintures, Paris, France. Photograph by Erich Lessing; **666** The Granger Collection, New York; **668** Florence Museo delle Scienze/AKG London; **669** *Lorenzo il Magnifico*, G. Vasari, Scala/Art Resource, New York; **670** Nicolo Orsi Battaglini/Art Resource, NY; **671** The Granger Collection, New York; **672 (l.)** *Petrarch*, Alinari/Art Resource, New York; **(r.)** *Portrait of Ronsard*, Anonymous artist, early 17th century, Giraudon/Art Resource, New York; **674 & 675** *Three Graces* (detail), Botticelli, Giraudon/Art Resource, New York; **676 (r.)** Monique le Luhandre/© Dorling Kindersley; **(l.)** D. Robert & Lorri Franz/CORBIS; **677** Corel Professional Photos CD-ROM™; **679** Cameraphoto Arte, Venice/Art Resource, NY; **680** Corel Professional Photos CD-ROM™; **685 (t.)** The Granger Collection, New York; **(b.)** *William Shakespeare* (detail), attributed to John Taylor, by courtesy of the National Portrait Gallery, London; **686** Giovanni Boccaccio, Scala/Art Resource, New York; **688** © Dorling Kindersley; **689** *Robert Cheseman*, Hans Holbein the Younger, Scala/Art Resource, New York; **690** Réunion des Musées Nationaux/Art Resource, NY; **692** The Granger Collection, New York; **693** Monique le Luhandre/© Dorling Kindersley; **698** *Miguel de Cervantes*, The Granger Collection, New York; **701** *Don Quixote*, Honoré Daumier, Scala/Art Resource, NY; **702** The Palma Collection/Getty Images; **705** *Don Quixote Preparing His Armor;* scene from the novel by Cervantes, Zacarias Velazquez Gonzalez, Caylus Anticuario, Madrid, Spain/Bridgeman Art Library, London/New York; **706** *Dulcinea del Toboso* from Cervantes, *Don Quixote*, 1839, Charles Robert Leslie, Art Resource, NY; **709** *Don Quixote and Sancho Panza Riding Clavileno*, Zacarias Velazquez Gonzalez, Caylus Anticuario, Madrid, Spain/Bridgeman Art Library, London/New York; **710** Monique le Luhandre/© Dorling Kindersley; **713** *Don Quixote and the Windmill*, Francisco J. Torrome (fl. 1890–1908), Bonhams, London/Bridgeman Art Library, London/New York; **718** *Jean de la Fontaine*, The Bettmann Archive; **721** Private Collection/Bridgeman Art Library, London/New York; **722** Alan Kearney/Getty Images; **728 (t.)** *Niccolò Machiavelli*, Florence Uffizi, Art Resource, New York; **(b.)** The Granger Collection, New York; **729 (t.)** Bettmann/CORBIS; **(b.)** The Granger Collection, New York; **730** *Voltaire in 1718*, 18th century French school after N. de Largillière, Paris, Musée Carnavalet, Giraudon, Erich Lessing/Art Resource, New York; **733** Bibliothèque Nationale, Paris, France/Bridgeman Art Library, London/New York; **735** Josef Beck/Getty Images – Taxi; **741** *A Rider on a Rearing Horse in a Profile View*, Leonardo da Vinci, Fitzwilliam Museum, University of Cambridge; **743** *Head of the Virgin in Three-Quarter View Facing to the Right*, Black and colored chalks on paper, Leonardo da Vinci, The Metropolitan Museum of Art, Harris Brisbane Dick Fund, 1951 (51.90). Photograph © 1992 The Metropolitan Museum of Art; **748** David Young-Wolff/PhotoEdit; **754–755** *Terrace at Sainte-Adresse*, Claude Oscar Monet, The Metropolitan Museum of Art, Purchased with special contributions and purchase funds given or bequeathed by friends of the Museum, 1967, © Copyright by The Metropolitan Museum of Art; **756 (t.l.)** *Napoleon Bonaparte as First Consul*, Jean Auguste Dominique Ingres, Musée des Beaux-Arts, Liège, Belgium, Scala/Art Resource, New York; **(t.m.)** Photofest; **(t.r.)** *The Stone Breakers*, Gustave Courbet/SuperStock; **(b.l.)** Joseph Sohm; *Visions of America*/CORBIS; **(b.r.)** *Fuji from Noge in Yokohama, Musashi*, Ando Hiroshige, The Newark Museum, John Cotton Dana Collection/Art Resource, NY; **757 (t.)** Private Collection/Bridgeman Art Library, London/New York; **(m.)** *A Berber of Southern Tunis*, c. 1898, Harry Hamilton Johnston, Private Collection/Bridgeman Art Library, London/New York; **(b.)** The Granger Collection, New York; **760** Erich Lessing/Art Resource, NY; **761** Burstein Collection/CORBIS; **762** *The Wanderer*

Varo de Cano, Valencia, Spain. Photo courtesy of Walter Gruen; **1187** Monique le Luhandre/© Dorling Kindersley; **1192** (t.) Thomas Victor; (m.) Eugene Richards/Magnum Photos, Inc.; (b.) Sergio Larrain/Magnum Photos, Inc.; **1195** *Kaukola Ridge at Sunset*, 1889, Albert Edelfelt, Ateneum Art Museum, Helsinki, The Central Art Archives/Matti Janas; **1196** *After Rain*, 1998, Roger Winter, Fischbach Gallery, New York; **1198** ©Getty Images, Inc. - Hulton/Archive Photos; **1199** *Barber Shop*, 1942, Cundo Bermudez, Digital Image © The Museum of Modern Art/Licensed by SCALA/Art Resource, NY; **1202** *St. Lucia—Looking at Rat Island*, Watercolor by Derek Walcott, from the collection of Michael and Judy Chastanet; **1209** Burstein Collection/CORBIS; **1210** Sigrid Estrada; **1212** *Vista II*, 1987, Hughie Lee-Smith, June Kelly Gallery; **1213** C Squared Studios/Getty Images; **1214** *San Antonio de Oriente*, Museum of Modern Art of Latin America; **1215** © Dorling Kindersley; **1217** Daniel Mackie/Digital Vision, Ltd.; **1222** © Bettmann/CORBIS; **1224–1225** *Album de voyage: Spain, Morocco, Algeria*, 1834, Eugène Delacroix. Musée Condé, Chantilly, France. Giraudon/Art Resource, NY; **1227** *Arab at the Door of His House*, Eugène Delacroix, Rijksmuseum, Amsterdam; **1228** *The Ear of Grain (L'espiga de blat)*, 1922–1923, Joan Miro, © The Museum of Modern Art/Licensed by Scala/Art Resource, NY; **1230** *Album Afrique 1835–1845. Arab of Constantine*. Auguste Raffet, Musée Condé, Chantilly, France. Giraudon/Art Resource, NY; **1233** *Seated Arab*, Eugène Delacroix, Réunion des Musées Nationaux/Art Resource, NY; **1234** Monique le Luhandre/© Dorling Kindersley; **1236–1237** © Sylvain Grandadam/Photo Researchers, Inc.; **1242** (l.) Jacques M. Chenet/CORBIS; (r.) Sovfoto/Eastfoto; **1244** *Chairs of Paris*, 1927, André Kertész, © Estate of André Kertész; **1246** Frank Siteman/Stock, Boston; **1247** Pier Giorgio Sclarandis/Black Star Publishing/PictureQuest; **1249** *Winter: Cat on a Cushion*, Théophile-Alexandre Steinlen (French, 1859–1923), color lithograph, 20 x 24 in.: The Metropolitan Museum of Art, Gift of Henry J. Plantin, 1950 (50.616.9). Photograph ©1987 The Metropolitan Museum of Art; **1251** *The Big White Cat*, Gertrude Halsband, Private Collection/Bridgeman Art Library, London/New York; **1252** Dave King/© Dorling Kindersley; **1258** (t.) Rene Burri/Magnum Photos, Inc.; (m.) © Getty Images, Inc. - Hulton Archive Photos; (b.) AP/Wide World Photos; **1260** © Getty Images Inc. - Hulton Archive Photos; **1261** CORBIS; **1262** *Concentration Camp Inmates*, February 1945, Hellmut Bachrach-Barée. Pencil and watercolor on paper, Gift of the artist. Courtesy of the Yad Vashem Art Museum, Jerusalem; **1263** *Guard with Stick*, a collage of paper cut from an office ledger, Soña Spitzova, Jewish Museum in Prague, Courtesy of the United States Holocaust Memorial Museum; **1264** *Drawing for the Transportation Bas Relief*, Dee Clements **1267** *To the Victims of Fascism*, 1946–49, Hans Grundig, Sächsische Landesbibliothek du Dresden, Abteilung Deutsche Fotothek; **1269** Bettmann/CORBIS; **1270** *1943 A.D.*, c. 1943, Ben Shahn, Courtesy of The Syracuse University Art Collection, © Estate of Ben Shahn/Licensed by VAGA, New York, NY; **1273** ©CORBIS; **1274** (t.) *Portrait of an Unknown Prisoner*, ca. 1942–43, Franciszek Jazwiecki, Auschwitz Museum; (b.) Auschwitz Museum; **1284** (l.) CORBIS-Bettmann; (r.) AP/Wide World Photos; **1286** Leslye Borden/PhotoEdit; **1289** *Aftermath*, 1945, Karl Hofer, Hamburg Kunsthalle, Hamburg, Germany/Bridgeman Art Library, London/New York; **1294** (l.) Sovfoto/Eastfoto; (r.) AP/Wide World Photos/Ron Frehm; **1298** Horace Bristol/CORBIS; **1301** Wolfgang Kaehler/CORBIS; **1306** Barry Iverson/TIMEPIX; **1308** Will and Deni McIntyre/Getty Images; **1310** *The Persistence of Memory*, 1931, Salvador Dali, oil on canvas, 9 1/2 x 13 in. © The Museum of Modern Art/Licensed by Scala/Art Resource, NY. Given anonymously. © 2002 Kingdom of Spain, Gala-Salvador Dali Foundation/Artists Rights Society (ARS), New York; **1311** Thomas Hartwell/CORBIS; **1316** (l.) Inge Morath/Magnum Photos, Inc.; (r.) Dina Gona; **1318** G. R. Roberts/Omni-Photo Communications, Inc.; **1324** FPG International Corp.; **1325** Courtesy National Archives; **1326** FPG International Corp.; **1327** AP/Wide World Photos; **1328** (t.) photography by Nina Subin; (m.) Bassouls Sophie/CORBIS Sygma; (b.) AP/Wide World Photos; **1330** *Still Life with Loaves of Bread*, Ilya Ivanovich Mashkov, State Russian Museum, St. Petersburg, Russia/Bridgeman Art Library, London/New York; **1331** Monique le Luhandre/© Dorling Kindersley; **1332 & 1333** Robert Everts/Getty Images; **1334** Owen Franken/CORBIS; **1340** (l.) Peter Jordan/Liaison Agency; (r.) Alan Mothner/AP/Wide World Photos; **1342** (t.) Charles Lenars/Explorer/Photo Researchers, Inc.; (b.) Marc and Evelyn Bernheim/Woodfin Camp & Associates; **1348** (l.) Thomas Victor; (r.) AP/Wide World Photos; **1351** Ulli Michel/CORBIS; **1352** Heini Schneebeli/Bridgeman Art Library, London/New York; **1357** *The Old African, The Medal, and the Statue*, 1988, Fodé Camara, Museum of African American Art, Collection: Abourahim Agne; **1358** Monique le Luhandre/© Dorling Kindersley; **1364** (l.) AP/Wide World Photos; (r.) Allan Grant/TIMEPIX; **1367** V. Muthuraman/SuperStock; **1368** Susan McCartney/Photo Researchers, Inc.; **1371** The Granger Collection, New York; **1372** Craig Lovell/CORBIS; **1375** © Hulton/Archive Photos; **1380** The Granger Collection, New York; **1382** SuperStock; **1384** *Yuki*, 1929, Kotondo, Courtesy Ronin Gallery, New York; **1385** Monique le Luhandre/© Dorling Kindersley; **1390** (l.), (r.) Dorothy Alexander; **1392** *Morning Rain*, 2001, Bich Nguyet, oil on canvas, Courtesy of Galeria La Vong Ltd.; **1394** *Peacefulness*, Tran Nguyen Dan, Indochina Arts Project; **1396 & 1397** Royalty-Free/CORBIS; **1404** CORBIS

Staff Credits

The people who made up the *Prentice Hall Literature World Masterpieces* team— representing design services, editorial, editorial services, manufacturing and inventory planning, market research, marketing services, education technology, planning and budgeting, product planning, production services, project office, publishing processes, and rights and permissions—are listed below. Bold type denotes the core team members.

Rosalyn Arcilla, Justin Belinski, Betsy Bostwick, Kerry Lyn Buckley, **Louise B. Capuano, Irene Ehrmann,** Philip Fried, Maggie Fritz, **Elaine Goldman,** Monduane Harris, Catherine Johnson, **Kate Krimsky,** Carol Lavis, David Liston, **Mary Luthi,** Gregory Lynch, **George Lychock,** Kerrie A. Miller, **Melissa Shustyk,** Annette Simmons, **Rita M. Sullivan, Cynthia Summers,** Elizabeth Torjussen, Doug Utigard, **Jeff Zoda**

Additional Credits

Greg Abrom, Ernest Albanese, Diane Alimena, Michele Angelucci, Penny Baker, Evonne Burgess, Rui Camarinha, John Carle, Jaime L. Cohen, Jason Cuoco, Richard Foster, Phillip Gagler, Joe Galka, Kathy Gavilanes, Michael Ginsberg, Allen Gold, Beth Hyslip, Vicki A. Kane, William McAllister, Michael McLaughlin, Art Mkrtchyan, Meg Montgomery, Kenneth J. Myett, Kim Ortell, Ray Parenteau, Dorothy Preston, Bruce Rolff, Carolyn C. Sapontzis, Mildred Schulte, Enrique Sevilla, Michele Stevens, Debi Taffet

Prentice Hall gratefully acknowledges the following teachers who provided the student models that are published in this book.

Cina Adams, Gaye Ingram, Catherine Linn, Janet Matthews, Sarah Oakes, Dr. Joy Pohl, Cathy Robbs

DATE DUE